The McGraw-Hill Reader

Issues Across the Disciplines

TWELFTH EDITION

Gilbert H. Muller

The City University of New York
LaGuardia College

D0140103

Connect
Learn
Succeed™

Connect
Learn
Succeed™

THE MCGRAW-HILL READER: ISSUES ACROSS THE DISCIPLINES, TWELFTH EDITION

Published by McGraw-Hill, a business unit of The McGraw-Hill Companies, Inc., 1221 Avenue of the Americas, New York, NY 10020. Copyright © 2014 by The McGraw-Hill Companies, Inc. All rights reserved. Printed in the United States of America. Previous editions © 2011, 2008, and 2006. No part of this publication may be reproduced or distributed in any form or by any means, or stored in a database or retrieval system, without the prior written consent of The McGraw-Hill Companies, Inc., including, but not limited to, in any network or other electronic storage or transmission, or broadcast for distance learning.

Some ancillaries, including electronic and print components, may not be available to customers outside the United States.

This book is printed on acid-free paper.

4 5 6 7 8 9 0 DOC/DOC 1 0 9 8 7 6 5

ISBN 978–0–07–340598–8
MHID 0–07–340598–1

Senior Vice President, Products & Markets: Kurt L. Strand
Vice President, General Manager, Products & Markets: Michael Ryan
Vice President, Content Production & Technology Services: Kimberly Meriwether David
Managing Director: David Patterson
Director: Susan Gouijnstook
Senior Brand Manager: Nancy Huebner
Senior Director of Development: Dawn Groundwater
Development Editor: Anne Stameshkin
Editorial Coordinator: Stephanie Lippitt

Senior Marketing Manager: Kevin Colleary
Content Project Manager: Katie Fuller
Buyer: Susan K. Culbertson
Cover Designer: Margarite Reynolds
Interior Designer: Linda Robertson
Cover Image: top, Ingram Publishing/age Fotostock; bottom, Zap Art
Content Licensing Specialist: Shawntel Schmitt
Photo Research: Emily Tietz, Editorial Image LLC
Compositor: Aptara®, Inc.
Typeface: 10/12 Century Old Style
Printer: R. R. Donnelley

All credits appearing on page or at the end of the book are considered to be an extension of the copyright page.

Library of Congress Cataloging-in-Publication Data

The McGraw-Hill Reader : Issues Across the Disciplines / [edited by] Gilbert H. Muller, the City University of New York - Laguardia. – Twelfth edition.
    pages cm
    Includes index.
    ISBN-13: 978–0–07–340598–8 — ISBN-10: 0–07–340598–1
    1. College readers. 2. Interdisciplinary approach in education—Problems, exercises, etc. 3. English language—Rhetoric–Problems, exercises, etc. 4. Academic writing—Problems, exercises, etc. I. Muller, Gilbert H., 1941
PE1417.M44 2013
808'.0427—dc23

                                                    2012039324

www.mhhe.com

About the Author

GILBERT H. MULLER is professor emeritus of English at the LaGuardia campus of the City University of New York. He has also taught at Stanford University, where he received a PhD in English and American Literature; Vassar College; and several universities overseas. Dr. Muller is the author of the award-winning *Nightmares and Visions: Flannery O'Connor and the Catholic Grotesque; Chester Himes; New Strangers in Paradise: The Immigrant Experience and Contemporary American Fiction; William Cullen Bryant: Author of America*; and other critical studies. His essays and reviews have appeared in *The New York Times, The New Republic, The Nation, The Sewanee Review, The Georgia Review,* and elsewhere. He has written and edited best-selling textbooks in English and composition, including McGraw-Hill's *The Short Prose Reader*, with Harvey Wiener, now in its thirteenth edition. Among Dr. Muller's awards are fellowships from the National Endowment for the Humanities, the Fulbright Commission, the Ford Foundation, and the Mellon Foundation.

To Parisa and Darius
My favorite readers

Brief Contents

PART 1
READING AND WRITING ACROSS THE DISCIPLINES

PART 2
ISSUES ACROSS THE DISCIPLINES

PART 3
RESEARCH WRITING FOR A NEW ERA

Contents

PART 1
READING AND WRITING ACROSS THE DISCIPLINES

PART 2
ISSUES ACROSS THE DISCIPLINES

Contents of Essays by Rhetorical Mode

NARRATION

DESCRIPTION

ILLUSTRATION

COMPARISON AND CONTRAST

ANALOGY

DEFINITION

CLASSIFICATION

PROCESS ANALYSIS

CAUSAL ANALYSIS

ARGUMENTATION AND PERSUASION

HUMOR, IRONY, AND SATIRE

Networking Assignments

CHAPTER 1

CHAPTER 2

CHAPTER 3

CHAPTER 4

CHAPTER 5

CHAPTER 6

CHAPTER 7

CHAPTER 8

CHAPTER 9

CHAPTER 10

CHAPTER 11

CHAPTER 12

CHAPTER 13

CHAPTER 14

Preface

ISSUES ACROSS DISCIPLINES, LITERACIES ACROSS MEDIA

Like its previous bestselling editions, the twelfth edition of *The McGraw-Hill Reader* continues to engage students with the finest classic and contemporary essays—works that span myriad ages, cultures, and disciplines—and prompts students to read, watch, research, listen to, interact with, and compose in multiple media.

Eudora Welty (whose work appears in this collection) speaks of reading as "a sweet devouring," and *The McGraw-Hill Reader* invites students to participate in—and enjoy— the vast and varied pleasures of responding to texts in any form; additionally, this book's approach affords opportunities to experiment with numerous contexts for academic discourse. Addressing the abiding national interest in core liberal arts programs, interdisciplinary issues, and multicultural perspectives, this edition offers students and instructors a full range of quality prose models important to writing courses, reading sequences, and key undergraduate disciplines. With the high quality of its essays, its consistent humanistic emphases, its clear organization, and its focus on the importance of digital and multimedia literacies, *The McGraw-Hill Reader* offers instructors a lively, sophisticated, and eminently flexible text for college composition programs.

Organization

Composed of three parts and 16 chapters, *The McGraw-Hill Reader* covers the major modes of writing and many of the disciplines that college students will encounter as undergraduates. In Part 1, Chapter 1 presents an overview of the ways we read and respond to texts today. Chapter 2 focuses on strategies for critical thinking, reading, and writing. Chapter 3 provides extensive coverage of argument and persuasion. In Part 2, Chapters 4 to 14 explore core liberal arts disciplines, including education, the social sciences, business and economics, the humanities, and the sciences. Each chapter asks a key question, drawn from the disciplines it represents, designed to elicit constructive class discussion and sound critical writing. Prose models encourage students to practice skills they will need throughout college—including analysis, criticism, argumentation, as well as facility with digital texts. In Part 3, Chapter 15 provides an updated tour of research, research writing, and MLA documentation. Chapter 16 uses student work to walk through the process of writing a research essay.

Highlights of the Twelfth Edition

- **Twenty-one new selections.** Fresh essays appear on topics of current and enduring interest. Topics like class and the Occupy movement, marriage equality, racism, global climate change, social networking, online dating, and the power of comics should elicit lively student response and effective writing.
- **Expanded research section now divided into two chapters:** Chapter 15: Writing a Research Project and Chapter 16: A Research Project Casebook: Working with Sources across Media.
- **Updated and new "Networking: Applying Digital and Multimedia Literacies" assignments.** Designed to foster a range of real-world literacy skills, these assignments send students online; to video, audio, or interactive sources; or away from their desks to create visual texts or conduct primary research.
- **New case study for synthesis on class and culture and three new readings for the case study on social networking.**

Proven Features

Throughout many editions, instructors and students have found the following features of *The McGraw-Hill Reader* useful:

- **A rich selection of readings.** The essays in this book have been selected carefully to embrace a rich assortment of authors, to achieve balance among constituencies, to cover major historical periods, and to provide prose models and styles for class analysis, discussion, and imitation.
- **A text that works with a wide variety of levels and approaches.** With more than one hundred selections that range from very simple essays to more abstract and complex modes of discourse, teachers and students will be able to use *The McGraw-Hill Reader* at virtually all levels of a program. This reader can be used as a writing-across-the-curricula text, as the basis for a rhetorically focused course, as a thematic reader, as a multicultural anthology, or as an in-depth reader.
- **Chapter introductions that encourage students to reflect on major issues in the discipline.** The introduction to each disciplinary chapter gives students a broad perspective on the field at hand by putting major issues and concerns in context. Each introduction ends with a previewing section that alerts students to strategies for reading, discussion, and writing.
- **Integrated and focused treatment of argument, plagiarism, summary and précis, and research.** The chapters in Parts 1 and 3 provide integrated guidelines on these topics. Additionally, argumentation is stressed throughout the text, with a writing assignment following all selections.
- **Uniform apparatus that reinforces critical reading and writing accompanies every essay.** Each selection is preceded by a brief introduction that offers biographical information about the author. The questions that follow each essay are arranged in four categories—Comprehension, Rhetoric, Writing, and Networking: Applying Digital and Multimedia Literacies—to move students from audience analysis to various modes, processes, and media of composition. The integrated design of these questions makes each essay—simple or complex, short or long, old or new—accessible to college students who possess varied reading and writing abilities.

- **Chapter 16's Research Project Casebook.** A walk through of one student's process in finding, evaluating, and working with sources to craft a research essay. The casebook examines how to choose, research, synthesize, and document sources in five widely used media: a print book, a scholarly journal article accessed through a library database, a popular magazine article accessed online, a Web site, and an image.
- **"Synthesis: Connections for Critical Thinking" sections.** The topics listed at the end of each chapter help students to gain practice in synthesis and critique, and make comparative assessments of various groups of essays.
- **Classic and Contemporary Images.** Opening each chapter, these paired images along with the accompanying "Using a Critical Perspective" questions, serve to interest students in the chapter's central topics and get them thinking and writing.

USEFUL SUPPLEMENTS

The following supplements are designed to help instructors and students derive the full benefit from *The McGraw-Hill Reader:*

- *A Guide to the McGraw-Hill Reader.* This supplement—revised by Jim Iddings, Karen Laing-Urbina, and Christian Clark (all of the College of Southern Nevada)— offers well-considered strategies for teaching individual essays, sample rhetorical analyses, answers to questions, additional thought-provoking questions, comparative essay discussion formats, and tips for prewriting and guided writing activities. There is also a bibliography of criticism and research on the teaching of composition. This guide is available for instructors at http://www.mhhe.com/mhreader12e.

ACKNOWLEDGMENTS

It is a pleasure to acknowledge the support, assistance, and guidance of numerous individuals who helped create *The McGraw-Hill Reader.* I want to thank the excellent McGraw-Hill family of assistants, editors, and executives who participated enthusiastically in the project from the outset and who encouraged me at every step. My editor, Nancy Huebner has been a loyal, enthusiastic supporter of *The McGraw-Hill Reader* for many years. Thanks, too, to others on the McGraw-Hill editorial team who have made valuable contributions to this edition: Dawn Groundwater, Zachary Norton, Katie Fuller, Arpana Kumari, Chris Greene and Leonard Behnke. Thanks to Jim Iddings, Karen Laing-Urbina, and Christian Clark (all from the College of Southern Nevada) for their excellent revisions of the *Guide to The McGraw-Hill Reader.* I also want to thank Sheryl Rose, my astute copyeditor, and Jolynn Kilburg, my superlative production editor. Above all, I offer sincere thanks to Anne Stameshkin, my development editor, who in countless ways helped make this revision fresh and exciting.

The final content and design of *The McGraw-Hill Reader,* Twelfth Edition, reflects the expertise and advice offered by college instructors across the country who gave generously of their time when asked to review the text:

Adam Cleary, Southern Illinois University-Edwardsville
Anushiya Ramaswamy, Southern Illinois University-Edwardsville

April Van Camp, Indian River State College Central
Cleatta Morris, Louisiana State University-Shreveport
Dennis Lynch, Elgin Community College
Deron Walker, California Baptist University
Dorie Larue, Louisiana State University-Shreveport
Helen Becker, Shepherd University
Heidi Hanrahan, Shepherd University
John Freeman, University of Detroit Mercy
John Hodgson, Cameron University
Patrick Quinn, College of Southern Nv
Rebecca Babcock, University of Texas Permian Basin
Rosemary Weatherston, University of Detroit Mercy
Susan Trudeau, University of Detroit Mercy
Tammy Powley, Indian River State College Central
William Carney, Cameron University

I am pleased to acknowledge support from the Mellon Foundation, the Graduate Center of The City University of New York, and the United States Department of Education (Title III and Title IV) that enabled me to develop this text.

Gilbert H. Muller

part 1

Reading and Writing across the Disciplines

chapter *1*

Reading and Responding to Texts

The McGraw-Hill Reader introduces students to the process of thinking, reading, and writing across the academic disciplines. In academic courses and the workplace, many critical reading and writing skills—the ability to analyze, critique, and synthesize information—are seemingly timeless. However, to gain a voice in this age of new media and text messaging practices, you must also master multiple literacies and technological skills and learn how to apply these skills in new and developing contexts. College assignments, work challenges, and individual lifestyles are diverse, rapidly changing, technology driven, and increasingly global. Changes in technology and society itself are transforming the way we read and respond to texts.

Today, you are composing more than ever before and in numerous environments in print and online. In all likelihood, you are texting, tweeting, and blogging (or at least reading others' blogs); maintaining Web sites of your own; creating and uploading podcasts; sharing video clips on YouTube or audio files through peer-to-peer programs; and interacting in multiple formats on social networking sites. And of course you are making electronic presentations in the classroom while still using pen and paper to fill out blue books, take at least some of your class notes, or make journal entries. In brief, your literacy environment is far more complex than in previous generations.

According to the National Council of Teachers of English, a literate person in the 21st century must be able to

- develop proficiency with the tools of technology;
- build relationships with others to pose and solve problems collaboratively and cross-culturally;
- design and share information for global communities to meet a variety of purposes;
- manage, analyze, and synthesize multiple streams of simultaneous information;
- create, critique, analyze, and evaluate multimedia texts; and
- attend to the ethical responsibilities required by these complex environments.

Clearly you need a wide range of competencies and abilities to succeed as a reader and writer in this changing and challenging world, and the way you write will often determine your academic, vocational, and personal success. In short, you need a *literate identity*—a voice attuned to the democratic sphere and global society.

Composition in all its forms—from written works to audio and visual projects—is the essence of academic life, which typically involves the reading of and responding to challenging texts. As a college student, you are swimming in an ocean of discourse; and you will need to approach texts with both focus and skills that go beyond casual reading, the type you may do for leisure or escapism. Even in courses in which a preponderance of work involves learning forms of knowledge and new technologies, such as computer science, mathematics, or biochemistry, you are sure to find a healthy amount of reading that will supplement any other work done in the classroom or laboratory. And increasingly the read-write universe that awaits you will necessitate an interactive approach fostered by Web 2.0 (and beyond) culture.

The reading and writing skills you develop during your college years will also help you in your future profession. Think of a lawyer reviewing legal history or preparing a brief, a nurse reviewing current literature on medical innovations or writing a detailed progress report on a patient's recovery, or an environmental researcher reading and writing about issues regarding pollution and global warming. All these activities require the ability to think, read, and write about complex material. Learning the tools of critical reading and writing not only teaches you the "what" of an issue but also helps you think about and respond intelligently to the relative strength of the writer's opinions, ideas, and theories. Critical thinking, reading, and writing enable you to distinguish between informed ideas and pure speculation, rational arguments and emotional ones, and organized essays and structurally deficient ones.

As you hone your critical thinking, reading, and writing skills by tackling the essays in this anthology, you should soon understand how the written word is still the primary medium with which thinkers transmit the intricacies of controversial issues involving the family, society, politics, work, gender, and class. You will encounter complex and varied texts—both in print and online, in formats you can read, see, hear, and even interact with—that require you to extract maximum meaning from them, compare your views with those of the authors you read, and respond to what you read in an informed and coherent manner. The reading selections in this textbook have been chosen specifically to assist you in developing such skills. As you tackle these texts, you will realize that sound reading habits permit you to understand the fine points of logic, reasoning, analysis, argumentation, and evaluation.

READING CRITICALLY

You can find numerous reasons to rationalize a failure to read carefully and critically. You have a headache. You're hungry. The material is boring. The writer puts you to sleep. Your roommates are talking. You have a date. In short, there are many internal and external barriers to critical reading. Fortunately, there are techniques—in a critical reading process—to guide you through this maze of distractions. Consider these five essential strategies:

1. *Develop an attitude of "critical consciousness."* In other words, do not be passive, uncritical, or alienated from the writer or the text. Instead, be active, critical, and engaged with the writer and his or her text.
2. *Read attentively.* Give your full attention to the text in order to understand it. Do not let your mind wander.
3. *Paraphrase.* Periodically restate what you read. Learn to process bits of key information. Keep a running inventory of highlights. Take mental or actual notes on the text's main points. (More information on paraphrasing and summarizing appears in this chapter and in Chapter 15.)
4. *Ask questions.* If for any reason you are uncertain about any aspect of the text, pose a question about it and try to answer it yourself. You might seek help from a friend or classmate. If you still are unable to answer your question, ask for clarification from the instructor.

5. *Control your biases.* You must both control and correct any prejudices that might interfere with the claim, information, or tone of a text. You might, for example, have misgivings about a liberal or conservative writer, or about a feminist or a creationist, but such strong emotions can erode your ability to keep an open mind and your power to think critically about a subject or issue.

These five strategies will help you begin to overcome the barriers to critical reading.

One way to view critical reading is through the concept of active reading. Active reading suggests that you, as a reader, have an obligation to yourself and the author to bring an alert, critical, and responsive perspective to your encounter with the written word. Active reading means learning to annotate (a strategy discussed later in this chapter), to reflect on what you read, and to develop personal responses in order to prepare yourself for writing assignments that your instructor will present to you during the term. This process—reading critically in order to write critically—is not merely an academic exercise. It is a skill that can enrich you as a person throughout your life and career. It will teach you to respond critically to the admonitions of politicians or to the seductions of advertisements and, if you choose, to participate intelligently in the national conversation, which can lead to a rewarding life and responsible citizenship.

When you read an essay or any other type of text, you create meaning out of the material the author has presented. If the essay is relatively simple, clear, and concise, the meaning that you construct from your reading may be very similar to what the author intended. Nevertheless, the way you interact with even the most comprehensible texts will never be identical to the way another reader interacts.

Consider an essay that you will encounter in this anthology, Langston Hughes's "Salvation" (pp. 548–551). A chapter from his autobiography, *The Big Sea* (1940), this essay tells of a childhood incident in which the young Hughes's faith was tested. The essay focuses on a church revival meeting that Hughes was taken to and the increasing pressure he sensed at the meeting to testify to the presence of Jesus in his life. At first the young Hughes holds out against the fervor of the congregation, but ultimately he pretends to be converted, or saved. That night, however, he weeps and then testifies to something entirely unexpected: the loss of faith he experienced because Jesus did not save him in a time of need.

As your class reads this essay, individuals among you may be struck by the compressed energy of the narration and the description of the event, by the swift characterization and revealing dialogue, or by the conflict and mounting tension. Moreover, the heightened personal and spiritual conflict will force class members to consider the sad irony inherent in the title "Salvation."

Even if your class arrives at a broad consensus on the intentions of the author, individual responses to the text will vary. Readers who have attended revival meetings will respond differently than those who have not. Evangelical Christians will see the text from a different perspective than will Catholics, Muslims, or Jews. Black readers (Hughes was black) may respond differently than white readers. Women may respond differently than men, and so on.

In this brief assessment of possible reader responses, we are trying to establish meaning from a shifting series of critical perspectives. Although we can establish a consensus of meaning as to what Hughes probably intended, our own interpretation and evaluation of the text will be conditioned by our personal experiences, backgrounds, attitudes, biases, and beliefs. In other words, even as the class attempts to construct a common reading, each member is also constructing a somewhat different meaning, one based on the individual's own interaction with the text.

RESPONDING TO ESSAYS

Between its print and online components, this textbook contains essays covering a variety of subjects by writers from a wealth of backgrounds and historical periods. You may be familiar with some, unfamiliar with others. All, however, have something to say and a way of saying it that others have found significant. Hence, many have stood the test of time, whether a year, a decade, or centuries. Essays are a recognized genre, or form of literature, and the finest essays have staying power. As Ezra Pound said, "Literature is news that stays news," and the best examples of the essay convey this sense of permanent value.

Sharpening your reading skills will be important because you may not be able to personally choose the essays from the text. You may find some topics and essays more interesting than others. But if you are prepared to read critically, you will be able to bring the same set of skills to any selection your instructor assigns. With this principle in mind, we present an overview of the active reading process and an example of using this process on pages 27–29 with an annotated essay titled "The Cult of Ethnicity," by Arthur M. Schlesinger Jr.

When you are given a reading assignment from the textbook, a good strategy in preparing to read is to locate the text as well as possible within its broader context. Read the biographical notes about the author. Focus on the title of the essay. What can you infer from the title? How long is the essay? Although many students delight at the thought of reading shorter texts rather than longer ones, you may find that this variable is not always the deciding one in determining how easily you "get through" the essay. Short essays can be intricate and difficult; long ones can be simpler and more transparent. A long essay on a topic in which you are interested may be more rewarding than a short essay that you find lacking in relevance.

Other basic prereading activities include noting whether there are section breaks in the essay, whether there are subheadings, whether the author has used footnotes, and if so, how extensive they are. Other preliminary questions to answer could be, What is the date of the original publication of the essay? In what medium was it originally published? Is the essay a fully contained work, or is it an excerpt from a larger text? Are there visual or mathematical aids, such as graphs, charts, diagrams, or lists? Because authors often use typographical signals to highlight things or to help organize what they have written, you might ask, Does the author use quotation marks to signal certain words? Is italic type used, and if so, what is its purpose? Are other books and authors cited in the essay? Does the author use organizational tools such as Arabic or Roman numerals? Once you have answered these questions regarding mechanics, you will be prepared to deal more substantively with the essay as a unit of meaning and communication.

Preparing to read also means understanding that you bring your own knowledge, opinions, experiences, and attitudes to the text. You are not an empty glass to be filled with the knowledge and opinions of the authors, but rather a learner who can bring to bear your own reflections on what you read even if you think your knowledge is minimal. Often we do not know just how much ability we have in thinking about a topic until we actively respond to what others confront us with in their writings. By tackling the reading assignments in the text, you will not only learn new information and confront opinions that may challenge your own but also find that reading frees up your ability to express your opinions. For this reason, most English teachers look on reading as a two-way process: an exchange between writer and reader.

Although the credentials and experience of a professional writer may seem impressive, they should not deter you from considering your own critical talents as you read. But first, you must find a way to harness those abilities.

Following is a summary for reading and responding to texts critically.

GUIDELINES FOR READING CRITICALLY

- Who is the author? What do you know about his or her life, credentials, and professional background? (*Headnotes,* or author introductions that appear at the start of the essays in this book, provide some of this information.) If there is more than one author (and 21st-century texts increasingly reflect collaborative writing processes), what is the personal or professional relationship between these writers?

- Where did the selection first appear? What do you know about this publication? Is the text an entire selection, an excerpt, or part of a chapter?

- Did the selection appear in print, online, or both? Is there something specific about its content that this format (or that multiple formats) enhances or works well with? If it is online, how interactive is the selection? What role does the reader play in its purpose and content?

- Who is the author's audience? Is this audience general, specific, or targeted even more narrowly for a highly specialized group? What assumptions does the author make about this audience's education and background and its potential interest in the subject? How does the author adjust the elements of *style*—language, sentence structure, and complexity of thought—to this audience?

- What is significant about the title? Does the title present the author's general subject in a straightforward way, hint at the topic, or create a sense of mystery, irony, or humor?

- What is the author's purpose? Normally authors write to inform, argue, persuade, entertain, express a personal idea or opinion—or a combination of these objectives. Does the author's purpose complement or seem right for the topic?

- What is the author's main point? Does the author state the main point (termed a *thesis* or *claim*) clearly and concisely in the introduction, place it elsewhere in the text, permit it to evolve slowly, or require you to infer it after reading the entire essay?

- What are the main subpoints? How do these subordinate points inform or support the main point? Are there enough subpoints? Is there sufficient information or evidence to support the main point?

- How does the author organize the essay? What constitutes the introductory section, the body or middle of the essay, and the conclusion? Are there subdivisions or numbered units, and how are they linked logically? Are there any missing links?

- How does your personal experience affect your response to the author's ideas? Do you detect any authorial biases (or your own potential biases) that influence your response?

Making Connections: Words and Images across Disciplines

The contemporary moment in composition is exciting. Many essays now combine words, images, even video or audio components. Moreover, some texts communicate with each other across time and disciplines. As you read and view the selections that follow, consider the ways in which they interact with each other and reflect national and international contexts.

Hiroshima

John Berger

__John Berger__ (b. 1926) is a prolific English writer, artist, and public intellectual. Born in London and educated at the Central School of Art and the Chelsea School of Art, Berger during a long career has carved a distinguished record as novelist, artist, essayist, playwright, screenwriter, critic, and drawing instructor. Probing the inter- section of culture and politics in much of his work, Berger operates from a Marxist perspective in analyzing the capitalist world. His credo, "seeing comes before words," underpins a critique of Western culture, which is most clearly articulated in Ways of Seeing *(1972). Berger's best-known novel,* G, *a panorama of history from the late 19th century to the outbreak of World War I, embodies his theory of perception; the novel received England's prestigious Booker Prize. In "Hiroshima," which first appeared in 1981 in the journal* New Society *and later in his essay collection* The Sense of Sight *(1985), Berger deals with the "whole incredible problem" of how we "see" or comprehend this nuclear event.*

The whole incredible problem begins with the need to reinsert those events of 6 August 1945 back into living consciousness.

I was shown a book last year at the Frankfurt Book Fair. The editor asked me some question about what I thought of its format. I glanced at it quickly and gave some reply. Three months ago I was sent a finished copy of the book. It lay on my desk unopened. Occasionally its title and cover picture caught my eye, but I did not respond. I didn't consider the book urgent, for I believed that I already knew about what I would find within it.

Did I not clearly remember the day—I was in the army in Belfast—when we first heard the news of the bomb dropped on Hiroshima? At how many meetings during the first nuclear disarmament movement had I and others not recalled the meaning of that bomb?

And then, one morning last week, I received a letter from America, accompa- nying an article written by a friend. This friend is a doctor of philosophy and a Marxist. Furthermore, she is a very generous and warm-hearted woman. The article was about the possibilities of a third world war. Vis-à-vis the Soviet Union she took, I was surprised to read, a position very close to Reagan's. She concluded by evoking the likely scale of destruction which would be caused by nuclear weapons, and then welcomed the positive possibilities that this would offer the socialist revolution in the United States.

5   It was on that morning that I opened and read the book on my desk. It is called *Unforgettable Fire.*[1]

6   The book consists of drawings and paintings made by people who were in Hiroshima on the day that the bomb was dropped, thirty-six years ago today. Often the pictures are accompanied by a verbal record of what the image represents. None of them is by a professional artist. In 1974, an old man went to the television center in Hiroshima to show to whomever was interested a picture he had painted, entitled "At about 4 pm, 6th August 1945, near Yurozuyo bridge."

7   This prompted an idea of launching a television appeal to other survivors of that day to paint or draw their memories of it. Nearly a thousand pictures were sent in, and these were made into an exhibition. The appeal was worded: "Let us leave for posterity pictures about the atomic bomb, drawn by citizens."

8   Clearly, my interest in these pictures cannot be an art-critical one. One does not musically analyze screams. But after repeatedly looking at them, what began as an impression became a certainty. These were images of hell.

9   I am not using the word as hyperbole. Between these paintings by women and men who have never painted anything else since leaving school, and who have surely, for the most part, never traveled outside Japan, between these traced memories which had to be exorcised, and the numerous representations of hell in European medieval art, there is a very close affinity.

10   This affinity is both stylistic and fundamental. And fundamentally it is to do with the situations depicted. The affinity lies in the degree of the multiplication of pain, in the lack of appeal or aid, in the pitilessness, in the equality of wretchedness, and in the disappearance of time.

> I am 78 years old. I was living at Midorimachi on the day of the A-bomb blast. Around 9 am that morning, when I looked out of my window, I saw several women coming along the street one after another towards the Hiroshima prefectural hospital. I realized for the first time, as it is sometimes said, that when people are very much frightened hair really does stand on end. The women's hair was, in fact, standing straight up and the skin of their arms was peeled off. I suppose they were around 30 years old.

11   Time and again, the sober eyewitness accounts recall the surprise and horror of Dante's verses about the Inferno. The temperature at the center of the Hiroshima fireball was 300,000 degrees centigrade. The survivors are called in Japanese *hibakuska*—"those who have seen hell."

> Suddenly, one man who was stark naked came up to me and said in a quavering voice, "Please help me!" He was burned and swollen all over from the effects of the A-bomb. Since I did not recognize him as my neighbor, I asked who he was. He answered that he was Mr. Sasaki, the son of Mr. Ennosuke Sasaki, who had a

lumber shop in Funairi town. That morning he had been doing volunteer labor service, evacuating the houses near the prefectural office in Kato town. He had been burned black all over and had started back to his home in Funairi. He looked miserable—burned and sore, and naked with only pieces of his gaiters trailing behind as he walked. Only the part of his hair covered by his soldier's hat was left, as if he was wearing a bowl. When I touched him, his burned skin slipped off. I did not know what to do, so I asked a passing driver to take him to Eba hospital.

Does not this evocation of hell make it easier to forget that these scenes be- 12 longed to life? Is there not something conveniently unreal about hell? The whole history of the twentieth century proves otherwise.

Very systematically in Europe the conditions of hells have been constructed. 13 It is not even necessary to list the sites. It is not even necessary to repeat the calculations of the organizers. We know this, and we choose to forget it.

We find it ridiculous or shocking that most of the pages concerning, for ex- 14 ample, Trotsky were torn out of official Soviet history. What has been torn out of our history are the pages concerning the experience of the two atom bombs dropped on Japan.

Of course, the facts are there in the textbooks. It may even be that school 15 children learn the dates. But what these facts mean—and originally their meaning

How survivors saw it. A painting by Kazuhiro Ishizu, aged 68.

At the Aioi bridge, by Sawami Katagiri, aged 76.

was so clear, so monstrously vivid, that every commentator in the world was shocked, and every politician was obliged to say (whilst planning differently), "Never again"—what these facts mean has now been torn out. It has been a systematic, slow and thorough process of suppression and elimination. This process has been hidden within the reality of politics.

16   Do not misunderstand me. I am not here using the word "reality" ironically, I am not politically naïve. I have the greatest respect for political reality, and I believe that the innocence of political idealists is often very dangerous. What we are considering is how in this case in the West—not in Japan for obvious reasons and not in the Soviet Union for different reasons—political and military realities have eliminated another reality.

17   The eliminated reality is both physical—

Yokogawa bridge above Tenma river, 6th August 1945, 8:30 am.
    People crying and moaning were running towards the city. I did not know why.
Steam engines were burning at Yokogawa station.
    Skin of cow tied to wire.
    Skin of girl's hip was hanging down.
    "My baby is dead, isn't she?"

and moral.

The political and military arguments have concerned such issues as deter- 18
rence, defense systems, relative strike parity, tactical nuclear weapons and—
pathetically—so-called civil defense. Any movement for nuclear disarmament
today has to contend with those considerations and dispute their false interpretation. To lose sight of them is to become as apocalyptic as the Bomb and all uto-
pias. (The construction of hells on earth was accompanied in Europe by plans for
heavens on earth.)

What has to be redeemed, reinserted, disclosed and never be allowed to be 19
forgotten, is the other reality. Most of the mass means of communication are close
to what has been suppressed.

These paintings were shown on Japanese television. Is it conceivable that the 20
BBC would show these pictures on Channel One at a peak hour? Without any
reference to "political" and "military" realities, under the straight title, *This Is How
It Was, 6th August 1945*? I challenge them to do so.

What happened on that day was, of course, neither the beginning nor the end 21
of the act. It began months, years before, with the planning of the action, and the
eventual final decision to drop two bombs on Japan. However much the world was
shocked and surprised by the bomb dropped on Hiroshima, it has to be emphasized that it was not a miscalculation, an error, or the result (as can happen in war)
of a situation deteriorating so rapidly that it gets out of hand. What happened was
consciously and precisely planned. Small scenes like this were part of the plan:

> I was walking along the Hihiyama bridge about 3 pm on 7th August. A woman,
> who looked like an expectant mother, was dead. At her side, a girl of about three
> years of age brought some water in an empty can she had found. She was trying
> to let her mother drink from it.
>
> As soon as I saw this miserable scene with the pitiful child, I embraced the girl
> close to me and cried with her, telling her that her mother was dead.

There was a preparation. And there was an aftermath. The latter included 22
long, lingering deaths, radiation sickness, many fatal illnesses which developed
later as a result of exposure to the bomb, and tragic genetical effects on generations yet to be born.

I refrain from giving the statistics: how many hundreds of thousands of dead, 23
how many injured, how many deformed children. Just as I refrain from pointing
out how comparatively "small" were the atomic bombs dropped on Japan. Such
statistics tend to distract. We consider numbers instead of pain. We calculate instead of judging. We relativize instead of refusing.

It is possible today to arouse popular indignation or anger by speaking of the 24
threat and immorality of terrorism. Indeed, this appears to be the central plank of
the rhetoric of the new American foreign policy ("Moscow is the world-base of all
terrorism") and of British policy towards Ireland. What is able to shock people
about terrorist acts is that often their targets are unselected and innocent—a
crowd in a railway station, people waiting for a bus to go home after work. The
victims are chosen indiscriminately in the hope of producing a shock effect on
political decision-making by their government.

25   The two bombs dropped on Japan were terrorist actions. The calculation was terrorist. The indiscriminacy was terrorist. The small groups of terrorists operating today are, by comparison, humane killers.

26   Another comparison needs to be made. Today terrorist groups mostly represent small nations or groupings who are disputing large powers in a position of strength. Whereas Hiroshima was perpetrated by the most powerful alliance in the world against an enemy who was already prepared to negotiate, and was admitting defeat.

27   To apply the epithet "terrorist" to the acts of bombing Hiroshima and Nagasaki is logically justifiable, and I do so because it may help to reinsert that act into living consciousness today. Yet the word changes nothing in itself.

28   The first-hand evidence of the victims, the reading of the pages which have been torn out, provokes a sense of outrage. This outrage has two natural faces. One is a sense of horror and pity at what happened; the other face is self-defensive and declares: *this should not happen again (here)*. For some the *here* is in brackets, for others it is not.

29   The face of horror, the reaction which has now been mostly suppressed, forces us to comprehend the reality of what happened. The second reaction, unfortunately, distances us from that reality. Although it begins as a straight declaration, it quickly leads into the labyrinth of defense policies, military arguments and global strategies. Finally it leads to the sordid commercial absurdity of private fall-out shelters.

30   This split of the sense of outrage into, on one hand, horror, and, on the other hand, expediency occurs because the concept of evil has been abandoned. Every culture, except our own in recent times, has had such a concept.

31   That its religious or philosophical bases vary is unimportant. The concept of evil implies a force or forces which have to be continually struggled against so that they do not triumph over life and destroy it. One of the very first written texts from Mesopotamia, 1,500 years before Homer, speaks of this struggle, which was the first condition of human life. In public thinking nowadays, the concept of evil has been reduced to a little adjective to support an opinion or hypothesis (abortions, terrorism, ayatollahs).

32   Nobody can confront the reality of 6th August 1945 without being forced to acknowledge that what happened was evil. It is not a question of opinion or interpretation, but of events.

33   The memory of these events should be continually before our eyes. This is why the thousand citizens of Hiroshima started to draw on their little scraps of paper. We need to show their drawings everywhere. These terrible images can now release an energy for opposing evil and for the lifelong struggle of that opposition.

34   And from this a very old lesson may be drawn. My friend in the United States is, in a sense, innocent. She looks beyond a nuclear holocaust without considering its reality. This reality includes not only its victims but also its planners and those who support them. Evil from time immemorial has often worn a mask of innocence. One of evil's principal modes of being is *looking beyond* (with indifference) that which is before the eyes.

August 9th: On the west embankment of a military training field was a young boy four or five years old. He was burned black, lying on his back, with his arms pointing towards heaven.

Only by looking beyond or away can one come to believe that such evil is relative, and therefore under certain conditions justifiable. In reality—the reality to which the survivors and the dead bear witness—it can never be justified.

Note

1. Edited by Japan Broadcasting Corporation, London, Wildwood House, 1981; New York, Pantheon, 1981.

COMPREHENSION

1. Summarize Berger's claim about the meaning of Hiroshima—what he terms "the whole incredible problem" (paragraph 1).
2. Underline or highlight the places where Berger refers to *images* and *words*. What is his purpose here?
3. Berger writes that "expediency occurs because the concept of evil has been abandoned" (paragraph 30). Explain what this statement means in the context of the essay.

RHETORIC

1. Why does Berger inject himself into this essay, personalizing the event that he describes and ponders? What voice and tone does he adopt in confronting "the reality of 6th August 1945"?
2. Why does Berger incorporate the paintings by Kazuhiro Ishizu and Sawami Katagiri into the essay? What is the effect?
3. How does Berger structure his argument? What is his claim? What varieties of evidence does he present to support his claim?
4. What comparative methods does Berger employ to develop his argument, and where do these strategies appear in the essay?
5. Where does Berger employ definition to advance the essay? What is his purpose in using this rhetorical strategy?

WRITING

1. Respond to Berger's "Hiroshima"—especially his comments on the nature of evil, horror, and hell—in a brief, personal essay.
2. Write an analysis of the strategies Berger uses to investigate what August 6, 1945 means to him.
3. **Writing an Argument:** Argue for or against the proposition that it was necessary to drop a nuclear bomb on Hiroshima in order to force Japan to surrender and thereby end World War II.

NETWORKING
Applying Digital and Multimedia Literacies

Collaborating in small groups, conduct a search for more online images of the aftermath of the atomic bombing of Hiroshima on August 6, 1945. Choose six images that help support your position and present them with your commentary to the class.

Synthesis: Connections for Critical Thinking

1. Both Berger and Lakoff (see next essay) investigate the importance of words and language in general when dealing with the subject of war. How does their thinking converge as they deal with Hiroshima and Iraq, respectively? What similarities and differences do you detect in their arguments and their conclusions?
2. Compare and contrast the ways in which the essays by Berger and Lakoff "talk" to each other across history and academic disciplines. What conclusions can you draw about the ways in which texts communicate with each other?
3. Examine the two classic and contemporary images at the end of this chapter. What do they contribute to the notion that essays and images have ways of talking to or influencing each other?

From Ancient Greece to Iraq, the Power of Words in Wartime

Robin Tolmach Lakoff

Robin Tolmach Lakoff *is a linguistics professor at the University of California at Berkeley and the author of* The Language War.

1 An American soldier refers to an Iraqi prisoner as "it." A general speaks not of "Iraqi fighters" but of "the enemy." A weapons manufacturer doesn't talk about people but about "targets."

2   Bullets and bombs are not the only tools of war. Words, too, play their part.

3   Human beings are social animals, genetically hard-wired to feel compassion toward others. Under normal conditions, most people find it very difficult to kill.

But in war, military recruits must be persuaded that killing other people is not 4 only acceptable but even honorable.

The language of war is intended to bring about that change, and not only for 5 soldiers in the field. In wartime, language must be created to enable combatants and noncombatants alike to see the other side as killable, to overcome the innate queasiness over the taking of human life. Soldiers, and those who remain at home, learn to call their enemies by names that make them seem not quite human— inferior, contemptible and not like "us."

The specific words change from culture to culture and war to war. The names 6 need not be obviously demeaning. Just the fact that we can name them gives us a sense of superiority and control. If, in addition, we give them nicknames, we can see them as smaller, weaker and childlike—not worth taking seriously as fully human.

The Greeks and Romans referred to everyone else as "barbarians"— 7 etymologically those who only babble, only go "bar-bar." During the American Revolution, the British called the colonists "Yankees," a term with a history that is still in dispute. While the British intended it disparagingly, the Americans, in perhaps the first historical instance of reclamation, made the word their own and gave it a positive spin, turning the derisive song "Yankee Doodle" into our first, if unofficial, national anthem.

In World War I, the British gave the Germans the nickname "Jerries," from 8 the first syllable of German. In World War II, Americans referred to the Japanese as "Japs."

The names may refer to real or imagined cultural and physical differences 9 that emphasize the ridiculous or the repugnant. So in various wars, the British called the French "Frogs." Germans have been called "Krauts," a reference to weird and smelly food. The Vietnamese were called "slopes" and "slants." The Koreans were referred to simply as "gooks."

The war in Iraq has added new examples. Some American soldiers refer to 10 the Iraqis as "hadjis," used in a derogatory way, apparently unaware that the word, which comes from the Arabic term for a pilgrimage to Mecca, is used as a term of respect for older Muslim men.

The Austrian ethnologist Konrad Lorenz suggested that the more clearly 11 we see other members of our own species as individuals, the harder we find it to kill them.

So some terms of war are collective nouns, encouraging us to see the enemy 12 as an undifferentiated mass, rather than as individuals capable of suffering. Crusaders called their enemy "the Saracen," and in World War I, the British called Germans "the Hun."

American soldiers are trained to call those they are fighting against "the 13 enemy." It is easier to kill an enemy than an Iraqi.

The word "enemy" itself provides the facelessness of a collective noun. Its 14 non-specificity also has a fear-inducing connotation; enemy means simply "those we are fighting," without reference to their identity.

The terrors and uncertainties of war make learning this kind of language especially compelling for soldiers on the front. But civilians back home also need to believe that what their country is doing is just and necessary, and that the killing they are supporting is in some way different from the killing in civilian life that is rightly punished by the criminal justice system. The use of the language developed for military purposes by civilians reassures them that war is not murder.

The linguistic habits that soldiers must absorb in order to fight make atrocities like those at Abu Ghraib virtually inevitable. The same language that creates a psychological chasm between "us" and "them" and enables American troops to kill in battle, makes enemy soldiers fit subjects for torture and humiliation. The reasoning is: They are not really human, so they will not feel the pain.

Once language draws that line, all kinds of mistreatment become imaginable, and then justifiable. To make the abuses at Abu Ghraib unthinkable, we would have to abolish war itself.

CLASSIC AND CONTEMPORARY:
READING CRITICALLY

The texts in *The McGraw-Hill Reader* cross disciplinary, linguistic, and geographic boundaries. Some are classics and some are recent pieces on timely topics. Read and respond to the two essays that follow.

As with most of the essays included in this text, these essays contain a headnote providing information about the author and are followed by questions for response and writing.

How to Mark a Book

Mortimer J. Adler

Mortimer Jerome Adler (1902–2001) was born in New York City and received his PhD from Columbia University in 1928. A staunch advocate for classical philosophy, Adler believed that there are unshakable truths—an idea rejected by most contemporary philosophers. For this reason, Adler has not been taken seriously by the academic establishment. He was a champion of knowledge, believing that philosophy should be a part of everyone's life and that the great ideas in philosophy can be of value to everyone. Many of his over 75 books attempt to edify the general reader by explaining basic philosophical concepts in everyday language. He was also chairman of the editorial board of the Encyclopaedia Britannica. *To make knowledge more accessible to everyone, he also assumed editorship of the Encyclopaedia Britannica's Great Books project, partly sponsored by the University of Chicago. This project, which has put 443 of the world's "classics" into a 54-volume set, graces the bookcases of many dens and studies in middle-class American homes. Despite his advancing years, Adler continued to work on many projects to promote his goal of universal education and enlightenment. "How to Mark a Book" is typical of his didactic, pragmatic approach to education.*

You know you have to read "between the lines" to get the most out of anything. I 1
want to persuade you to do something equally important in the course of your
reading. I want to persuade you to "write between the lines." Unless you do, you
are not likely to do the most efficient kind of reading.

I contend, quite bluntly, that marking up a book is not an act of mutilation but 2
of love.

You shouldn't mark up a book which isn't yours. Librarians (or your friends) 3
who lend you books expect you to keep them clean, and you should. If you decide
that I am right about the usefulness of marking books, you will have to buy them.
Most of the world's great books are available today, in reprint editions, at less than
a dollar.

There are two ways in which one can own a book. The first is the property 4
right you establish by paying for it, just as you pay for clothes and furniture. But
this act of purchase is only the prelude to possession. Full ownership comes only
when you have made it a part of yourself, and the best way to make yourself a part
of it is by writing in it. An illustration may make the point clear. You buy a beefsteak and transfer it from the butcher's ice-box to your own. But you do not own
the beefsteak in the most important sense until you consume it and get it into
your bloodstream. I am arguing that books, too, must be absorbed in your bloodstream to do you any good.

Confusion about what it means to own a book leads people to a false rever- 5
ence for paper, binding, and type—a respect for the physical thing—the craft of
the printer rather than the genius of the author. They forget that it is possible
for a man to acquire the idea, to possess the beauty, which a great book contains, without staking his claim by pasting his bookplate inside the cover. Having a fine library doesn't prove that its owner has a mind enriched by books; it
proves nothing more than that he, his father, or his wife, was rich enough to
buy them.

There are three kinds of book owners. The first has all the standard sets and 6
best-sellers—unread, untouched. (This deluded individual owns woodpulp and
ink, not books.) The second has a great many books—a few of them read
through, most of them dipped into, but all of them as clean and shiny as the day
they were bought. (This person would probably like to make books his own, but
is restrained by a false respect for their physical appearance.) The third has a few
books or many—every one of them dog-eared and dilapidated, shaken and loosened by continual use, marked and scribbled in from front to back. (This man
owns books.)

Is it false respect, you may ask, to preserve intact and unblemished a beauti- 7
fully printed book, an elegantly bound edition? Of course not. I'd no more scribble
all over the first edition of *Paradise Lost* than I'd give my baby a set of crayons and
an original Rembrandt! I wouldn't mark up a painting or a statue. Its soul, so to
speak, is inseparable from its body. And the beauty of a rare edition or of a richly
manufactured volume is like that of a painting or a statue.

But the soul of a book *can* be separated from its body. A book is more like the 8
score of a piece of music than it is like a painting. No great musician confuses a

symphony with the printed sheets of music. Arturo Toscanini reveres Brahms, but Toscanini's score of the C-minor Symphony is so thoroughly marked up that no one but the maestro himself can read it. The reason why a great conductor makes notations on his musical scores—marks them up again and again each time he returns to study them—is the reason why you should mark up your books. If your respect for magnificent binding or typography gets in the way, buy yourself a cheap edition and pay your respects to the author.

9   Why is marking up a book indispensable to reading it? First, it keeps you awake. (And I don't mean merely conscious; I mean wide awake.) In the second place, reading, if it is active, is thinking, and thinking tends to express itself in words, spoken or written. The marked book is usually the thought-through book. Finally, writing helps you remember the thoughts you had, or the thoughts the author expressed. Let me develop these three points.

10   If reading is to accomplish anything more than passing time, it must be active. You can't let your eyes glide across the lines of a book and come up with an understanding of what you have read. Now an ordinary piece of light fiction, like say, *Gone with the Wind,* doesn't require the most active kind of reading. The books you read for pleasure can be read in a state of relaxation, and nothing is lost. But a great book, rich in ideas and beauty, a book that raises and tries to answer great fundamental questions, demands the most active reading of which you are capable. You don't absorb the ideas of John Dewey the way you absorb the crooning of Mr. Vallee. You have to reach for them. That you cannot do while you're asleep.

11   If, when you've finished reading a book, the pages are filled with your notes, you know that you read actively. The most famous *active* reader of great books I know is President Hutchins, of the University of Chicago. He also has the hardest schedule of business activities of any man I know. He invariably reads with a pencil, and sometimes, when he picks up a book and pencil in the evening, he finds himself, instead of making intelligent notes, drawing what he calls "caviar factories" on the margins. When that happens, he puts the book down. He knows he's too tired to read, and he's just wasting time.

12   But, you may ask, why is writing necessary? Well, the physical act of writing, with your own hand, brings words and sentences more sharply before your mind and preserves them better in your memory. To set down your reaction to important words and sentences you have read, and the questions they have raised in your mind, is to preserve those reactions and sharpen those questions.

13   Even if you wrote on a scratch pad, and threw the paper away when you had finished writing, your grasp of the book would be surer. But you don't have to throw the paper away. The margins (top and bottom, as well as side), the endpapers, the very space between the lines, are all available. They aren't sacred. And, best of all, your marks and notes become an integral part of the book and stay there forever. You can pick up the book the following week or year, and there are all your points of agreement, disagreement, doubt, and inquiry. It's like resuming an interrupted conversation with the advantage of being able to pick up where you left off.

And that is exactly what reading a book should be: a conversation between you and the author. Presumably he knows more about the subject than you do; naturally, you'll have the proper humility as you approach him. But don't let anybody tell you that a reader is supposed to be solely on the receiving end. Understanding is a two-way operation; learning doesn't consist in being an empty receptacle. The learner has to question himself and question the teacher. He even has to argue with the teacher, once he understands what the teacher is saying. And marking a book is literally an expression of your differences, or agreements of opinion, with the author.

There are all kinds of devices for marking a book intelligently and fruitfully. 15
Here's the way I do it:

1. Underlining: Of major points, of important or forceful statements.
2. Vertical lines at the margin: To emphasize a statement already underlined.
3. Star, asterisk, or other doo-dad at the margin: To be used sparingly, to emphasize the ten or twenty most important statements in the book. (You may want to fold the bottom corner of each page on which you use such marks. It won't hurt the sturdy paper on which most modern books are printed, and you will be able to take the book off the shelf at any time and, by opening it at the folded-corner page, refresh your recollection of the book.)
4. Numbers in the margin: To indicate the sequence of points the author makes in developing a single argument.
5. Numbers of other pages in the margin: To indicate where else in the book the author made points relevant to the point marked; to tie up the ideas in a book, which, though they may be separated by many pages, belong together.
6. Circling of key words or phrases.
7. Writing in the margin, or at the top or bottom of the page, for the sake of: Recording questions (and perhaps answers) which a passage raised in your mind; reducing a complicated discussion to a simple statement; recording the sequence of major points right through the book. I use the end-papers at the back of the book to make a personal index of the author's points in the order of their appearance.

The front end-papers are, to me, the most important. Some people reserve 16
them for a fancy bookplate. I reserve them for fancy thinking. After I have finished reading the book and making my personal index on the back end-papers, I turn to the front and try to outline the book, not page by page, or point by point (I've already done that at the back), but as an integrated structure, with a basic unity and an order of parts. This outline is, to me, the measure of my understanding of the work.

If you're a die-hard and anti-book-marker, you may object that the margins, 17
the space between the lines, and the end-papers don't give you room enough. All right. How about using a scratch pad slightly smaller than the page-size of the book—so that the edges of the sheets won't protrude? Make your index, outlines, and even your notes on the pad, and then insert these sheets permanently inside the front and back covers of the book.

18   Or, you may say that this business of marking books is going to slow up your reading. It probably will. That's one of the reasons for doing it. Most of us have been taken in by the notion that speed of reading is a measure of our intelligence. There is no such thing as the right speed for intelligent reading. Some things should be read quickly and effortlessly, and some should be read slowly and even laboriously. The sign of intelligence in reading is the ability to read different things differently according to their worth. In the case of good books, the point is not to see how many of them you can get through, but rather how many can get through you—how many you can make your own. A few friends are better than a thousand acquaintances. If this be your aim, as it should be, you will not be impatient if it takes more time and effort to read a great book than it does a newspaper.

19   You may have one final objection to marking books. You can't lend them to your friends because nobody else can read them without being distracted by your notes. Furthermore, you won't want to lend them because a marked copy is a kind of intellectual diary, and lending it is almost like giving your mind away.

20   If your friend wishes to read your *Plutarch's Lives,* "Shakespeare," or *The Federalist Papers,* tell him gently but firmly, to buy a copy. You will lend him your car or your coat—but your books are as much a part of you as your head or your heart.

COMPREHENSION

1. Summarize what Adler means by "marking up a book."
2. In your own words, explain how you believe Adler would define the word *book.*
3. Adler mentions books throughout the essay. What particular type of book is he referring to?

RHETORIC

1. What is the tone of the essay? What can you infer from this tone about Adler's emotional relationship to books?
2. Paragraph 15 lists devices for marking a book. What is the function of enumerating them in this way? How would the tone of this section have been altered if Adler had summarized these devices in paragraph form?
3. The author makes reference to various intellectual and artistic figures and works in the essay. How does this help determine for whom the essay has been targeted?
4. Study the relationship between paragraph 9 and paragraphs 10–12. What is the rhetorical format of this section? What method of argumentation is Adler employing?
5. Adler uses the analogy that "reading a book should be: a conversation between you and the author." What other analogies can you find in the essay?
6. Adler raises objections to his argument and then refutes the objections. Where does he make use of this rhetorical device? How effective is it in advancing his argument?
7. Adler calls *Gone with the Wind* "light fiction." Is this opinion or fact? Is it a mere observation or a criticism of the book?

WRITING

1. Mark up Adler's essay in the same manner he recommends that you mark up any good piece of writing. Then write an essay using process analysis to summarize the various methods you used.
2. Compare and contrast two books: one that Adler would regard as "light reading" and one that he would regard as worthy of marking up. Indicate the primary differences between these books in terms of their diction, level of discourse, insight, purpose, and scholarship.
3. **Writing an Argument:** Argue for or against the proposition that this essay has lost its relevance owing to the introduction of new forms of educational media.

NETWORKING
Applying Digital and Multimedia Literacies

Marking a Text Electronically: Locate an online article or essay that interests you. Cut and paste the text into a new document. Then locate "Track Changes" (or a similar editing feature) in your word-processing program, and experiment with using this software to mark the article electronically. As an alternative, use a program like WebNotes (*www.webnotes.net*) or Fleck (*www.fleck.com*) to mark up the online article electronically. For you as a reader, determine whether Track Changes or a program like Fleck is as useful as the more traditional reading practices advocated by Adler. Why or why not? Which method of marking a text appeals more to you, and why? There is no single correct answer to this, but be sure that your response is backed up by specific, detailed reasons.

Does the Internet Make You Smarter or Dumber?

Nicholas Carr

Nicholas Carr writes on technology, business, and culture for numerous journals as well as on his popular blog, Rough Type. *He received a BA from Dartmouth College and an MA from Harvard University. A skeptic of the digital age, Carr shot to prominence with his provocative book,* Does IT Matter: Information Technology and the Corruption of Competitive Advantage *(2004), in which he criticizes the impact of information technology on our lives. His most recent book,* The Shallows: What the Internet Is Doing to Our Brains *(2010), was a finalist for the 2011 Pulitzer Prize in General Nonfiction. Carr lectures frequently at universities and business forums, and sits on the editorial board of advisors for* Encyclopaedia Britannica. *In this article from the June 5, 2010, edition of the* Wall Street *Journal, Carr assesses the cognitive effects of multitasking on the Net.*

1   The Roman philosopher Seneca may have put it best 2,000 years ago: "To be everywhere is to be nowhere." Today, the Internet grants us easy access to unprecedented amounts of information. But a growing body of scientific evidence suggests that the Net, with its constant distractions and interruptions, is also turning us into scattered and superficial thinkers.

2   The picture emerging from the research is deeply troubling, at least to anyone who values the depth, rather than just the velocity, of human thought. People who read text studded with links, the studies show, comprehend less than those who read traditional linear text. People who watch busy multimedia presentations remember less than those who take in information in a more sedate and focused manner. People who are continually distracted by emails, alerts and other messages understand less than those who are able to concentrate. And people who juggle many tasks are less creative and less productive than those who do one thing at a time.

3   The common thread in these disabilities is the division of attention. The richness of our thoughts, our memories and even our personalities hinges on our ability to focus the mind and sustain concentration. Only when we pay deep attention to a new piece of information are we able to associate it "meaningfully and systematically with knowledge already well established in memory," writes the Nobel Prize–winning neuroscientist Eric Kandel. Such associations are essential to mastering complex concepts.

4   When we're constantly distracted and interrupted, as we tend to be online, our brains are unable to forge the strong and expansive neural connections that give depth and distinctiveness to our thinking. We become mere signal-processing units, quickly shepherding disjointed bits of information into and then out of short-term memory.

5   In an article published in *Science* last year, Patricia Greenfield, a leading developmental psychologist, reviewed dozens of studies on how different media technologies influence our cognitive abilities. Some of the studies indicated that certain computer tasks, like playing video games, can enhance "visual literacy skills," increasing the speed at which people can shift their focus among icons and other images on screens. Other studies, however, found that such rapid shifts in focus, even if performed adeptly, result in less rigorous and "more automatic" thinking.

6   In one experiment conducted at Cornell University, for example, half a class of students was allowed to use Internet-connected laptops during a lecture, while the other had to keep their computers shut. Those who browsed the Web performed much worse on a subsequent test of how well they retained the lecture's content. While it's hardly surprising that Web surfing would distract students, it should be a note of caution to schools that are wiring their classrooms in hopes of improving learning.

7   Ms. Greenfield concluded that "every medium develops some cognitive skills at the expense of others." Our growing use of screen-based media, she said, has strengthened visual-spatial intelligence, which can improve the ability to do jobs that involve keeping track of lots of simultaneous signals, like air

traffic control. But that has been accompanied by "new weaknesses in higher-order cognitive processes," including "abstract vocabulary, mindfulness, reflection, inductive problem solving, critical thinking, and imagination." We're becoming, in a word, shallower.

In another experiment, recently conducted at Stanford University's Communication Between Humans and Interactive Media Lab, a team of researchers gave various cognitive tests to 49 people who do a lot of media multitasking and 52 people who multitask much less frequently. The heavy multitaskers performed poorly on all the tests. They were more easily distracted, had less control over their attention, and were much less able to distinguish important information from trivia. **8**

The researchers were surprised by the results. They had expected that the intensive multitaskers would have gained some unique mental advantages from all their on-screen juggling. But that wasn't the case. In fact, the heavy multitaskers weren't even good at multitasking. They were considerably less adept at switching between tasks than the more infrequent multitaskers. "Everything distracts them," observed Clifford Nass, the professor who heads the Stanford lab. **9**

It would be one thing if the ill effects went away as soon as we turned off our computers and cellphones. But they don't. The cellular structure of the human brain, scientists have discovered, adapts readily to the tools we use, including those for finding, storing and sharing information. By changing our habits of mind, each new technology strengthens certain neural pathways and weakens others. The cellular alterations continue to shape the way we think even when we're not using the technology. **10**

The pioneering neuroscientist Michael Merzenich believes our brains are being "massively remodeled" by our ever-intensifying use of the Web and related media. In the 1970s and 1980s, Mr. Merzenich, now a professor emeritus at the University of California in San Francisco, conducted a famous series of experiments on primate brains that revealed how extensively and quickly neural circuits change in response to experience. When, for example, Mr. Merzenich rearranged the nerves in a monkey's hand, the nerve cells in the animal's sensory cortex quickly reorganized themselves to create a new "mental map" of the hand. In a conversation late last year, he said that he was profoundly worried about the cognitive consequences of the constant distractions and interruptions the Internet bombards us with. The long-term effect on the quality of our intellectual lives, he said, could be "deadly." **11**

What we seem to be sacrificing in all our surfing and searching is our capacity to engage in the quieter, attentive modes of thought that underpin contemplation, reflection and introspection. The Web never encourages us to slow down. It keeps us in a state of perpetual mental locomotion. **12**

It is revealing, and distressing, to compare the cognitive effects of the Internet with those of an earlier information technology, the printed book. Whereas the Internet scatters our attention, the book focuses it. Unlike the screen, the page promotes contemplativeness. **13**

14   Reading a long sequence of pages helps us develop a rare kind of mental discipline. The innate bias of the human brain, after all, is to be distracted. Our predisposition is to be aware of as much of what's going on around us as possible. Our fast-paced, reflexive shifts in focus were once crucial to our survival. They reduced the odds that a predator would take us by surprise or that we'd overlook a nearby source of food.

15   To read a book is to practice an unnatural process of thought. It requires us to place ourselves at what T. S. Eliot, in his poem "Four Quartets," called "the still point of the turning world." We have to forge or strengthen the neural links needed to counter our instinctive distractedness, thereby gaining greater control over our attention and our mind.

16   It is this control, this mental discipline, that we are at risk of losing as we spend ever more time scanning and skimming online. If the slow progression of words across printed pages damped our craving to be inundated by mental stimulation, the Internet indulges it. It returns us to our native state of distractedness, while presenting us with far more distractions than our ancestors ever had to contend with.

COMPREHENSION

1. According to Carr, what is the relationship between cognitive development and what he terms "the division of attention" (paragraph 3)? Underline or highlight the sentences or passages that explain this relationship.
2. Why does Carr prefer traditional forms of reading to reading on the Net?
3. List the assumptions that Carr makes about multitasking on the Net. Do you agree or disagree with his assumptions? Explain your response.

RHETORIC

1. Explain the effect of the writer's allusion to Seneca in the first paragraph. How does he connect this introductory paragraph to his concluding paragraph? Do you find this strategy to be effective? Why or why not?
2. What is Carr's claim or basic argument? Does he state this claim or infer it? Justify your response.
3. What types of evidence does Carr provide to support his argument? Is this evidence sufficient or would you prefer more? Explain.
4. What is Carr's tone in this essay? What impression does he give of himself? Do you sense that he presents himself as an expert or authority on the subject? Why or why not?
5. Where does Carr employ comparison and contrast to organize and sustain his argument?

WRITING

1. Compose a personal essay on your own reading habits, comparing and contrasting reading "traditional linear text" and reading online.

2. Write an analysis of multitasking on the Net, explaining the effects you think it has on cognitive development.
3. **Writing an Argument:** Agree or disagree with Carr's claim that people "who read texts studded with links . . . comprehend less than those who read traditional linear text."

NETWORKING
Applying Digital and Multimedia Literacies

Collaborating in small groups, research at least three articles written by Carr on his blog, *Rough Type*. One of these articles should be one that has provoked a great deal of response, "The Amorality of Web 2.0" (2005). Summarize your group's response to Carr's vision of cyberspace.

Synthesis: Connections for Critical Thinking

1. How do Adler's assumptions about reading confirm some of the assertions made by Carr?
2. How do Adler and Carr establish a degree of authority over their subject matter? What authorial voice do they establish to convey this authority or expertise?
3. Compare and contrast the ways in which Adler and Carr adjust their style to their audience. What assumptions does each writer make about his audience?
4. In an essay of reflection, imagine how Adler might respond to Carr's article. Refer to both texts to amplify your response.
5. In a comparative essay, analyze the strategies that Adler and Carr employ to convince us that reading is an important cognitive activity.

ANNOTATING, NOTE TAKING, AND QUESTIONING THE TEXT

Even if some technologically advanced tools can enhance the critical reading process, Adler's essay, which focuses on traditional ways to interact with texts, reveals that you don't need anything high-tech to respond to them. Among the essential elements of close reading that have widespread appeal and application are annotating, note taking, and questioning the text.

Annotating

Annotating refers to marking your text (by hand or online) by making content notes, by using symbols such as question marks and exclamation points, and by recording personal reactions. Annotating is not mere underlining or highlighting. These latter two methods often serve little purpose in helping you comprehend a text. Most likely, when you return to passages you've marked with these simple procedures, you will have forgotten why you felt they were important. If you do underline or highlight, be sure to link your marking with a note in the margin. Simply drawing attention to someone else's words does little in the way of expanding your own thoughts on a topic. Learning is best accomplished by re-stating ideas in your own words.

Taking Notes

Many essays in your anthology will require more than simply jotting down marginal notes in order to comprehend them fully or to respond to them in depth. Just as you might take notes during a classroom lecture, you may find it useful to take notes to supplement your annotations. You may wish, for example, to type quotations so that you can see them together. Or you may wish to summarize the essay by outlining its key points, a reversal of the process you would use to develop your own essay, wherein you begin with an outline and expand it into paragraphs. By collapsing an essay into an outline, you have a handy reference of the author's thesis (main idea) and supporting points, and the methods used to develop them. Another function of note taking is to overcome the simple habit most of us have of thinking we will remember things without jotting them down or typing them, only to find out later that we cannot recall significant information from memory. You will appreciate the benefits of taking notes when you tackle lengthy essays, which may run 15 or 20 pages.

Questioning the Text

Posing key questions about a text and then answering them to the best of your ability is a helpful means of understanding an essay's substance and structure. Certain basic ques-tions, like the ones below, are salient for nearly any text you confront, and answering them for yourself can be a powerful means of enhancing your comprehension. As you read the text, such questions help you spot the significant issues that lie within most essays, regard-less of their form or length. It is a good habit to have these questions in mind as you read and then to return to them once you've thought through your responses. They serve as guideposts along the way of your reading experience and assist you in focusing on those issues that are most important to a text. When you become comfortable with them, you will probably find that your mind automatically poses them as you read, making your compre-hension of difficult texts easier.

- What is the thesis or main point of the text?
- What methods does the author use to support these points, for instance, illustration, example, description, personal experience, or history? Does he or she cite authorities or studies or statistics?
- What value position, if any, does the author present? In other words, is the author either directly or indirectly presenting her or his moral framework on an issue, or is she or he summarizing or describing an issue?
- Does the author use any special terms or expressions that need to be elucidated to understand the essay? You will find that authors, when addressing innovative or revo-lutionary ideas within the context of their times, must use vocabulary that often needs to be defined. Take, for example, the term *multiculturalism*. Exactly what might an author mean by that word?
- What is the level of discourse of the essay? Or what is the audience's level of educa-tional attainment the author presumes?
- Who is the implied audience for the essay? Is it written for a specialized profession (such as scientists or educators)? Is it written for individuals with a focus on their particular role in society, for example, as parents or consumers or citizens?

An Example   The following essay, "The Cult of Ethnicity," by the influential historian Arthur M. Schlesinger Jr., has been annotated to demonstrate how a student might respond to it. Schlesinger's essay also will be used to explain aspects of the reading and writing process as we move through this section.

The history of the world has been in great part the history of the mixing of peoples. Modern communication and transport accelerate mass migrations from one continent to another. Ethnic and racial diversity are more than ever a salient fact of the age.

But what happens when people of different origins, speaking different languages and professing different religions, inhabit the same locality and live under the same political sovereignty? Ethnic and racial conflict—far more than ideological conflict—is the explosive problem of our times.

This seems like the thesis. Where are his supports? Or is it the thesis?

On every side today ethnicity is breaking up nations. The Soviet Union, India, Yugoslavia, Ethiopia, are all in crisis. Ethnic tensions disturb and divide Sri Lanka, Burma, Indonesia, Iraq, Cyprus, Nigeria, Angola, Lebanon, Guyana, Trinidad—you name it. Even nations as stable and civilized as Britain and France, Belgium and Spain, face growing ethnic troubles. Is there any large multiethnic state that can be made to work?

Look these up. Demonstrates knowledge on the part of the author.

The answer to that question has been, until recently, the United States. "No other nation," Margaret Thatcher has said, "has so successfully combined people of different races and nations within a single culture." How have Americans succeeded in pulling off this almost unprecedented trick?

We have always been a multiethnic country. Hector St. John de Crevecoeur, who came from France in the 18th century, marveled at the astonishing diversity of the settlers—"a mixture of English, Scotch, Irish, French, Dutch, Germans and Swedes . . . this promiscuous breed." He propounded a famous question: "What then is the American, this new man?" And he gave a famous answer: "Here individuals of all nations are melted into a new race of men." *E pluribus unum.*

Historical figure— who was he?

The United States escaped the divisiveness of a multiethnic society by a brilliant solution: the creation of a brand-new national identity. The point of America was not to preserve old cultures but to *forge a new, American culture. "By an intermixture with our people," President George Washington told Vice President John Adams, immigrants will "get assimilated to our customs, measures and laws: in a word, soon become one people." This was the ideal that a century later Israel Zangwill crystallized in the title of his popular 1908 play *The Melting Pot.* And no institution was more potent in molding Crevecoeur's "promiscuous breed" into Washington's "one people" than the American public school.

*Is this a partly American phenomenon? *prevents racial and ethnic conflict*

Why?—doesn't explain Note S's use of historical process analysis Vocab.: infusion stocks zeal Eurocentric apocalyptic ferment Kleagle crucible

The new American nationality was inescapably English in language, ideas, and institutions. The pot did not melt everybody, not even all the white immigrants; deeply bred racism put black Americans, yellow Americans, red Americans and brown

Americans well outside the pale. Still, the infusion of other stocks, even of nonwhite stocks, and the experience of the New World reconfigured the British legacy and made the United States, as we all know, a very different country from Britain.

In the 20th century, new immigration laws altered the composition of the American people, and a cult of ethnicity erupted both among non-Anglo whites and among nonwhite minorities. This had many healthy consequences. The American culture at last began to give shamefully overdue recognition to the achievements of groups subordinated and spurned during the high noon of Anglo dominance, and it began to acknowledge the great swirling world beyond Europe. Americans acquired a more complex and invigorating sense of their world—and of themselves.

signals a warning—danger

But, pressed too far, the cult of ethnicity has unhealthy consequences. It gives rise, for example, to the conception of the United States as a nation composed not of individuals making their own choices but of inviolable ethnic and racial groups. It rejects the historic American goals of assimilation and integration.

Is this thesis or related to thesis?

And, in an excess of zeal, well-intentioned people seek to transform our system of education from a means of creating "one people" into a means of promoting, celebrating and perpetuating separate ethnic origins and identities. The balance is shifting from *unum* to *pluribus.*

Support against multiculturalism

That is the issue that lies behind the hullabaloo over "multiculturalism" and "political correctness," the attack on the "Eurocentric" curriculum and the rise of the notion that history and literature should be taught not as disciplines but as therapies whose function is to raise minority self-esteem. Group separatism crystallizes the differences, magnifies tensions, intensifies hostilities. Europe—the unique source of the liberating ideas of democracy, civil liberties and human rights—is portrayed as the root of all evil, and non-European cultures, their own many crimes deleted, are presented as the means of redemption.

General—where are the specific examples?

I don't want to sound apocalyptic about these developments. Education is always in ferment, and a good thing too. The situation in our universities, I am confident, will soon right itself. But the impact of separatist pressures on our public schools is more troubling. If a Kleagle of the Ku Klux Klan wanted to use the schools to disable and handicap black Americans, he would hardly come up with anything more effective than the "Afrocentric" curriculum. And if separatist tendencies go unchecked, the result can only be the fragmentation, resegregation and tribalization of American life.

Is this an exaggeration? How does he know?

I remain optimistic. My impression is that the historic forces driving toward "one people" have not lost their power. The eruption of ethnicity is, I believe, a rather superficial enthusiasm stirred by romantic ideologues on the one hand and by unscrupulous con men on the other: self-appointed spokesmen whose

Who are these people? He doesn't mention them specifically.

claim to represent their minority groups is carelessly accepted by the media. Most American-born members of minority groups, white or nonwhite, see themselves primarily as Americans rather than primarily as members of one or another ethnic group. A notable indicator today is the rate of intermarriage across ethnic lines, across religious lines, even (increasingly) across racial lines. "We Americans," said Theodore Roosevelt, "are children of the crucible."

Reality is stronger than "ideology"? Is this his "solution"?

The growing diversity of the American population makes the quest for unifying ideals and a common culture all the more urgent. In a world savagely rent by ethnic and racial antagonisms, the United States must continue as an example of how a highly differentiated society holds itself together.

A sharp conclusion→ argument? United States must be example. This is the thesis.

What has this annotating accomplished? It has allowed the reader/annotator to consider and think about what she has read, integrate her ideas with the ideas of the author, challenge those she may disagree with, raise issues for further study, find the seeds of ideas that may become the focus of an essay in response to the writing, review what she has read with more facility, and quickly and efficiently return to those parts of the essay she found the most salient.

The aforementioned strategies will assist you in responding intelligently in the classroom, remembering the main points of what you have read, and internalizing the critical reading skill so that it becomes automatic. However, such activities are not as challenging as the ultimate goal of most of your reading assignments, which will be to respond in formal writing to the works you've read. For this, you will need to enhance your study skills a bit further so that they will prepare you to write.

Formal writing assignments require you to demonstrate that you understood what you have read and are able to respond in an informed and intelligent manner to the material. They also require you to use appropriate form, organization, and exposition. Above all, regardless of what you want to express, you will have to communicate your ideas clearly and concisely. To this end, you will need to acquire skills that you can call on when it comes to writing at length about what you have read. To do so, you will find your ability to paraphrase, summarize, and quote directly from the original material particularly helpful.

When you move to this next phase, however, try to avoid a common practice among readers that causes them to waste time and effort. Many students think they have completed a reading assignment when they read the last word of an essay. They utter a sigh of relief, look inside the refrigerator for something to eat, call up friends, or browse online. However, as a critical reader, you need to spend additional time reinforcing what you have read by thinking about the author's views, considering her or his rhetorical methods, and reviewing or adding to your notes and annotations. For example, one culminating activity at this point can be to either mentally or verbally summarize what you have read. You can summarize verbally by enlisting a classmate and simply stating in your own terms the main points of your reading assignment. This oral summarizing will prevent a common problem many readers experience: the natural tendency to forget most of what they read shortly after reading.

Message-Making: An Interactive Approach

An essayist attempts to communicate a message to his or her audience. This message is the *content*. But "message making" is a process—the exchange of information through a shared system of verbal or visual symbols. Your goal in reading critically is to understand not just the informational content of a text but also how the writer shares meaning and typically tries to influence your beliefs and behavior. A good writer, to paraphrase Plato in *Phaedrus,* tries to "enchant" your mind.

From Plato to the present—including the emergence of Web 2.0 as a pathway for collaborating, sharing information, and interacting with others—theorists have stressed this interactional aspect of reading and writing. Someone constructs a message (for our purposes, a written text) and transmits it, and we have to receive it, decode it, and respond to it. Thus any "piece"of writing, whether designed to inform, persuade, or entertain, is the product of a complex process of actions and interactions by which we perceive, order, and verify (or make sense of) what we read. Whether we have the capacity to grasp the argument of a text, think logically about a thesis, or understand the cultural background of a writer and how it informs a text depends on how well we *perceive* the ways in which the writer creates meaning in the text.

Defined simply, *perception* is the process by which you create meaning for your world. As a process, it deals with the way you interpret the behavior of others as well as yourself. Thus, understanding perception helps to explain how we process information about self, others, and our world. Our senses—seeing, hearing, touching, tasting, smelling—provide us initial contact with the outside world, enabling us to establish our perceptual field of reference. However, we also perceive what we want to perceive, which we call *psychological selectivity.* There is a third form of perception known as *cultural selectivity:* from a cultural perspective, we are conditioned by our culture's code of values and modes of understanding. For example, the phenomenon of *binocular rivalry* demonstrates that people from two different cultures exposed to two pictures at the same time will remember elements compatible with their own culture. With critical reading, you can have diverging interpretations of passages or an entire text because you perceive them from different perspectives.

In addition to differences in perception, you should be mindful of how an author presents information. This can be as important as the information itself. Strategies for writing may include the overall pattern of an essay—for example, is it an argument, an explanation, a definition, an evaluation, a comparison, or a contrast? While you may not think of essays in terms of genre, as you do literature (poetry, short fiction, drama), such forms can help you to understand the motivation behind the writer's work and to seek out significant passages. For example, if the essay is argumentative, you should focus on the supporting points the author has provided, determining whether they offer adequate support for the author's point of view. In an essay arguing for the return to traditional family values, for instance, the use of one anecdote to prove a point would probably not be enough to persuade most readers.

As you read an essay, you should also consider the author's *purpose* for writing. An essay about a personal experience would probably contain physical description; at the same time, the author's purpose would probably be to communicate an element in his or her life that can provide insight into personal development in general. Among the more common purposes are the following: to inform, to persuade, to disprove, to describe, to narrate, to demonstrate, to compare and contrast, to seek a solution to a problem, to explain a process, to classify, to define, to warn, and to summarize. While most essays contain a variety of purposes, one often will stand out among the others.

All of the traditional forms of read-write culture are being transformed by new multimedia practices. We now have to make meaning from multimedia texts that incorporate such new literacy forms and representations as Amazon's Kindle (and other e-reader devices), audio editions of publications that you can listen to on a phone or MP3 player, and streaming video of authors discussing or reading from their work. Digital technologies change the ways you perceive and respond to texts. Visual representations—as a forthcoming section in this chapter reveals—are particularly significant in enhancing content while changing perceptions of the written text. In summary, new media texts alter read-write culture, presenting new opportunities for composition but also demanding new paths of perception.

PARAPHRASING, SUMMARIZING, QUOTING, AND SYNTHESIZING

As you prepare to respond to the writing of others, you need to develop skills so that your own writing will reflect the hard work that went into the reading process. To this end, you can benefit from learning some shortcuts that will assist you in garnering information about what you have read. These skills include paraphrasing, summarizing, quoting directly from, and synthesizing another author's work.

Paraphrasing

Paraphrasing means taking what you have read and putting it in your own words. Students occasionally complain about this process, using the argument that it is a waste of time to paraphrase when the author's own words are the best way to articulate his or her ideas. However, paraphrasing serves two main purposes. The more obvious one is that it prevents you from plagiarizing, even inadvertently, what you have read. In terms of learning, however, it is particularly helpful because it requires that you digest what you have read and then rewrite it. As you do so, you will develop writing patterns that over time will improve your ability to communicate. Paraphrasing forces you to truly think about what you have read and reinforces what you've read, since your mind has now been cognitively stimulated. You may find that paraphrasing often leads you to challenge the text or think more deeply about it simply because the paraphrasing process requires that you fully comprehend what you read.

It is important while paraphrasing to retain all the essential information of the original while not using any of the author's original vocabulary or style. One rule of thumb is to never use three or more words that appeared together in the original. However, you can keep words such as articles (*a, an, the*) and conjunctions (*and, for, but,* and so on).

The following are two examples of paraphrasing that demonstrate unsuccessful and successful application of the technique.

Original
But, pressed too far, the cult of ethnicity has unhealthy consequences. It gives rise, for example, to the conception of the United States as a nation composed not of individuals making their own choices but of inviolable ethnic and racial groups. It rejects the historic American goals of assimilation and integration.

Unsuccessful Paraphrase
But, pressed too far, the focus on ethnicity has dangerous consequences. It suggests that the United States is a nation made up of separate ethnic and racial groups rather than individuals. It goes against the American ideals of integration and assimilation.

There are several things wrong with paraphrase 1. Rather than change key words, the writer has merely rearranged them. The sentence structure is very similar to that of the original, as is the ordering of ideas. If the student were to incorporate this paraphrase into her or his own essay, the teacher would probably consider it a form of plagiarism. It is simply too close to the original. To truly paraphrase, you must substitute vocabulary, rearrange sentence structure, and change the length and order of sentences. These strategies are more evident in paraphrase 2.

Successful Paraphrase
Our country is made up of both individuals and groups. The recent trend to focus on the idea that one's ethnic background should have a major influence on one's perspective as a citizen goes against the moral foundations of the United States. It is the very concept of accepting American culture as one's own that has made our country strong and relatively free from cultural conflict.

Summarizing

A summary is a short, cohesive paragraph or paragraphs that are faithful to the structure and meaning of the original essay, but developed in your own words and including only the most essential elements of the original. Summaries are particularly helpful when you are planning to write lengthy assignments or assignments that require you to compare two or more sources. Because a good summary requires that you use many of the skills of active reading, it helps you to "imprint" the rhetorical features and content of what you have read in your memory, and also provides you with a means of communicating the essence of the essay to another person or group. To summarize successfully, you need to develop the ability to know what to leave out as much as what to include. As you review your source, the annotations and notes you made should help immensely. Since you want to deal with only the essentials of the original, you must delete all unimportant details and redundancies. Unlike paraphrasing, however, most summaries require that you stick to the general order of ideas as they are presented in a text. They also should not be mere retellings of what you have read, but should present the relationships among the ideas. It may be helpful to think of a summary as analogous to a news story, in which the essential details of what happened are presented in an orderly chronological fashion, because readers can best understand the gist of a story that way. It is simply the way the human mind—at least, the Western mind—operates. Another strategy in summarizing is to imagine that the audience you are summarizing for has not read the original. This places a strong responsibility on you to communicate the essentials of the text accurately.

The following six steps should help you in preparing a summary. After you've reviewed them, read the summary that follows and consider whether it seems to have fulfilled these suggestions.

1. Read the entire source at least twice and annotate it at least once before writing.
2. Write an opening sentence that states the author's thesis.
3. Explain the author's main supporting ideas, reviewing your notes to make sure you have included all of them. Be careful not to plagiarize, and use quotations only where appropriate.
4. Restate important concepts, key terms, main principles, and so on. Do not include your opinion or judge the essay in any way.
5. Present the ideas in the order in which they originally appeared. Note that in this sense summarizing is different from paraphrasing, in which staying too close to the original order of words may be detrimental to the process.

6. Review your summary once it has been completed. Consider whether someone who hasn't read the original would find your summary sufficient to understand the essence of the original work. You may also wish to have classmates or friends read the essay and furnish their verbal understanding of what you've written.

Now, review the following summary of Schlesinger's essay and determine whether it adheres to these points.

Sample Summary

Schlesinger argues that the recent surge of interest in ethnic separatism that is being touted by some whom he considers self-styled spokespersons for various ethnic groups threatens the unifying principle of our country's founders and undermines the strength of our society. This principle is that the American identity that was forged by its creators would be adopted by all peoples arriving here through a process of assimilation to our culture, values, and system of government so that cultural conflict could be avoided. Although he finds some merit in the idea that recognizing the contributions of certain groups who have been kept out of the national focus, for example, "nonwhite minorities," is a positive move, he fears that this can be taken to an extreme. The result could be the development of antagonism between ethnic groups solely on the basis of overemphasizing differences rather than recognizing similarities. He further argues that efforts to fragment American culture into subgroups can have the effect of jeopardizing their own empowerment, the opposite of the movement's intention. He gives the example of "Afrocentric" schooling, which he claims would only harm students enrolled in its curriculum. Despite this new interest in the "cult of ethnicity," the author is optimistic that it is of limited effect. He claims that most Americans still strive toward unity and identify themselves as Americans first, members of ethnic or racial groups second. He buttresses this belief by explaining that intermarriage is growing across racial, religious, and ethnic lines. This striving toward unity and identification with America among groups is particularly important today since their diversity is continuously increasing.

Quoting

Sayings and adages are extremely popular. You find them quoted in everyday speech, printed in calendars, rendered in calligraphy and framed and hung in homes, and spoken by public figures. These are, in effect, direct quotes, although the authors may be anonymous. Direct quotations often have a unique power because they capture the essence of an idea accurately and briefly. Another reason is that they are stylistically powerful. You may find in an essay a sentence or group of sentences that are worded so elegantly that you simply wish to savor them for yourself or plan to use them appropriately in a future writing assignment. Other times, you may wish to use direct quotations to demonstrate to a reader the effectiveness of an original essay or the authoritative voice of the author. And still other times, it may be necessary to quote an author because her or his vocabulary simply cannot be changed without injuring the meaning of the original. Review the following quotations taken from the Schlesinger essay, and consider how paraphrasing them would diminish their rhetorical power.

Direct Quotations That Reflect the Conciseness of the Original

"The history of the world has been in great part the history of the mixing of peoples."

"On every side today ethnicity is breaking up nations."

"And if separatist tendencies go unchecked, the result can only be the fragmentation, resegregation and tribalization of American life."

Direct Quotations That Have Particular Stylistic Strength
"The pot did not melt everybody."

"The balance is shifting from *unum* to *pluribus.*"

Direct Quotations That Establish the Writer's Authority
"The point of America was not to preserve old cultures but to forge a new, American culture. 'By an intermixture with our people,' President George Washington told Vice President John Adams, immigrants will 'get assimilated to our customs, measures and laws: in a word, soon become one people.'"

"A notable indicator today is the rate of intermarriage across ethnic lines, across religious lines, even (increasingly) across racial lines."

Direct Quotation That Demonstrates Conceptual Power
"The eruption of ethnicity, is, I believe, a rather superficial enthusiasm stirred by romantic ideologues on the one hand and by unscrupulous con men on the other."

Avoiding Plagiarism

When you employ summary, paraphrase, and quotation in an essay or a research paper, you must avoid *plagiarism*—the attempt to pass off the work of others as your own. The temptation to plagiarize is not only one of the oldest "crimes" in academe but also an unfortunate by-product of the computer revolution, for there are numerous opportunities for harried, enterprising, or—let's face it—dishonest students to download bits of information or entire texts and appropriate them without acknowledgment. At the same time, you should be aware that numerous Web sites and software programs allow your instructors to locate even the most inventive forms of plagiarism—right down to words and phrases— and that when writing research papers you may be required to attach all downloaded materials. Be warned: College teachers treat plagiarism as academic treason. If you plagiarize, you can fail a course, be suspended from college, and even be expelled.

We discuss plagiarism again in Chapters 15 and 16, which present information on writing research papers. For now, you can avoid plagiarism by following these basic rules:

- Cite (provide a reference for) all quoted, summarized, or paraphrased information in your paper, unless that information is commonly understood. (For example, you would not have to cite the information that Barack Obama won the 2008 presidential election, because it is common knowledge.)
- Cite all special phrases or unique stylistic expressions that you derive from another writer's work. You might love a phrase by one of the famous writers in this book—say, E. B. White or Virginia Woolf—but that writer invented it, and it belongs to him or her. You cannot employ it without acknowledging the source.
- Work hard to summarize and paraphrase material in your own words. Constantly check your language and sentence structure against the language and syntax in the source that you are using. If your words and sentences are too close to the original, change them.

Finally, it is perfectly legitimate to ask your instructor or a tutor in your college's writing center to look at your draft and render a verdict on any information you have summarized, paraphrased, or quoted. Whether this material has been taken intentionally or unintentionally from another source is immaterial. It is your responsibility to present honest written work.

Synthesizing: Drawing Connections from Texts

The ability to summarize, paraphrase, or quote from a single source prepares you for successful academic reading and writing. However, critical reading in college courses typically requires you to think about relationships between and among essays, newspaper articles, sections in textbooks, research findings, interviews, or other types of texts. If, for example, your instructor assigns a block of essays, you probably will need to infer relationships among these texts. We call this process of inferring relationships among various works *synthesis:* drawing connections from two or more written or nonwritten sources.

If you read online with any regularity, you are probably familiar with clicking on embedded hyperlinks or additional recommended links to materials related to the topic you are reading about. Such links encourage further synthesis by giving you access to other texts that help create a larger context for that topic. They might offer a similar, different, or now outdated perspective on a topic; definitions of certain terms; or more detailed coverage of particular organizations, people, places, theories, or anything else discussed.

You are probably already familiar with synthesis as an academic exercise. The act of reading two or more texts naturally prompts you to consider connections that link types of evidence, various ideas, or competing arguments. When you employ synthesis, you build strength in academic prose, skillfully condensing and connecting information, ideas, and arguments drawn from more than one text.

Any paper drawing on two or more sources requires you to construct relationships among materials that you quote, summarize, or paraphrase. (Remember that reading and writing are intimately connected, overlapping processes.) Suppose you paraphrase two complex passages from two texts. At the first level of critical response, you make the passages more intelligible. Then, at the next level, you convey the *essence* of the relationship between these two sources—whether it relates to the thesis or central argument, the accuracy of the data, or the structuring of materials.

In the process of synthesizing sources, you will often make judgments and arrive at conclusions about the validity of the information or arguments under consideration. In other words, you *critique* the texts—offering formalized, critical readings that express both your understanding of passages and your assessment of their content. With synthesis, what begins as an isolated moment (critically reading a single text) spirals into a series of moments (reading several texts), which demands your powers of comparative analysis and well-developed ability to evaluate relationships among sources.

The Art of Synthesis   With synthesis, you enter into a conversation with two or more writers, attempting to understand their main ideas or arguments, analyze the evidence they provide, and evaluate their conclusions. As with any academic conversation, you must present the writers' ideas with accuracy and respect—but also with an eye to the purpose or aim of your writing. The noted writer and composition specialist Peter Elbow (see his essay in Chapter 2) calls this attempt to present fairly the ideas of other writers "the believing game." In other words, you enter into the minds of other writers in order to appreciate their ideas and critical perspectives, but you do not suspend your beliefs or lose yourself entirely in the believing game. After all, you too have a specific purpose in writing: You merely want to exercise a degree of understanding and fairness as you synthesize the ideas of others.

It is relatively easy to consider two or more sources objectively when you use synthesis to explain the authors' ideas. (*Explanatory synthesis* is one of the two main types of synthesis. The other type, *argumentative synthesis,* will be treated briefly in this chapter and more fully in Chapter 3.) With explanatory synthesis, your purpose is to convey information using the tools of summary, paraphrase, and quotation to emphasize those aspects of certain texts that you find useful in constructing your essay. In a sense, you are detached and objective, an observer or conveyer of information. Your purpose in using explanatory synthesis is to inform.

To illustrate the way that explanatory synthesis interweaves information from two sources, consider the following passage, which draws on essays by Peter Elbow and Donald Murray appearing in Chapter 2:

Both Peter Elbow and Donald Murray stress the importance of process in the craft of composition, but approach the process from different perspectives. For Elbow, freewriting, or automatic writing, is the best way to improve writing. Write for ten minutes or more without stopping to edit material, Elbow declares. On the other hand, Murray states that any first draft, whether it involves freewriting or any strategy, is not the essence of composition. Instead, Murray emphasizes that a first draft is only the "start of the writing process. When a draft is completed, the job of writing can begin." For Murray, revision stands at the center of the writing process.

Here the writer hints in the first sentence that her agenda in providing this synthesis is to review at least two different theories of composition. But in synthesizing the ideas of Elbow and Murray at this point, she essentially wants to convey information objectively without necessarily agreeing or disagreeing with the writers' approaches or claims. Using paraphrase and quotation to construct her synthesis, she fairly, accurately, and objectively offers a baseline explanation of the theories of two prominent figures in the field of composition studies. The art of explanatory synthesis is to offer a balanced summary of two or more passages or complete texts without injecting too much of your own response into the materials.

With argumentative synthesis, your conversation or dialogue with other writers shifts from objective explanation to the use of source material to bolster your *claim*—a major proposition or conclusion that other readers can agree or disagree with. You still might have to explain what others have said, but now you want to give a fair hearing to their arguments over a shared issue or topic while at the same time staking out your position on the matter. To support your argument, you seek *evidence* (facts and expert opinions) from relevant sources, analyze and evaluate the merits of that evidence, and use it to support your argument.

Suppose, for an introductory social science or economics course, you plan to argue that globalization has caused the dislocation of many factory workers in the United States. Clearly, this is a complex issue that can be argued from various perspectives—not just from pro/con viewpoints but from more nuanced positions. Of course, the issue of globalization is very broad; you will need to refine the focus and limit the topic, perhaps by concentrating on just one industry or one state or region. The clearer you are about the parameters of your topic and claim, the easier it will be to locate and synthesize those sources that will provide support for your argument.

When you use argumentative synthesis, try to locate expert testimony, reliable sources, and verifiable types of evidence to reinforce your claim. Use this evidence so that it informs and strengthens your viewpoint. At the same time, you should acknowledge alternative viewpoints, for one feature of successful argument is the willingness to present and refute opposing claims. The challenge is to use any evidence that strengthens your text—but not at the risk of misrepresenting another writer's position or engaging in a biased or unfair presentation of the evidence.

Guidelines for Synthesis

1. *Consider your purpose.* Is your purpose to *explain* or to *argue*—or perhaps a combination of both? How will this purpose affect your search for sources?
2. *Select and identify your sources.* Where did the article first appear, and what might this publication tell you about the writer's perspective? Identify the author, noting his or her credentials, publications, and occupation. How does the title or subtitle reveal the writer's purpose? Does the title seem to conform to your purpose? Why or why not?
3. *Read critically and actively.* Follow the steps and procedures outlined on page 6. What is the writer's primary purpose? What is the main idea or argument? What are the minor points? How do the subpoints relate to the central point? What is the structure of the text—the introduction, middle sections, and conclusion? How does the text reinforce a key idea that you may have in mind for an essay?
4. *Take notes and summarize.* Use the techniques of print and/or electronic annotation illustrated on pages 25–27. Identify the writer's main point and rewrite it in one or two sentences.
5. *Establish connections among readings.* What relationships do you detect as you move from text to text? How do major and minor points stressed by the writers in their texts overlap or diverge? What elements of their arguments are similar and dissimilar? (Draw up a list of similar and dissimilar points for handy reference.)
6. *Write your synthesis.* First, write down your *thesis* (main point) or *claim* (argument), and develop it in an introductory paragraph. Next, draft body or middle paragraphs that offer support for the thesis or claim; write topic sentences for all paragraphs; incorporate explanatory or argumentative details drawn from the sources that you synthesize; and document your sources properly in order to avoid any charge of plagiarism. Finally, write a conclusion that grows organically from the preceding paragraphs and reinforces your main idea. And then, revise your essay. (*Note:* You can find information on the writing process and techniques of argumentation in the pages and chapters that follow in Part 1, as well as strategies for research in Part 3.)

READING AND RESPONDING TO ONLINE TEXTS

As a college student, you will be reviewing and experimenting frequently with texts that you locate online. Regardless of a text's medium, apply the same critical thinking and reading skills outlined in this chapter—along with a keen perception of the strengths and weaknesses of texts in the digital universe. For even as the Internet breaks new ground in the flow of (and access to) knowledge, the Web also contains a torrent of information—much of it unreliable. An ability to navigate these less charted waters, to interpret and judge online texts, will be crucial to your success in college and beyond.

Because online texts in all their variety—academic articles, government documents, wikis, blog postings, social networking sites, and more—constitute new models of composing, you need new ways to approach and manage them. Fortunately, college libraries across the nation are in the forefront of the attempt to harness the size, speed, and global interconnectedness of the Internet to benefit students.

For example, the UCLA Library's Web site offers "Judging Quality on the Web," a handy guide to reading online texts in an intelligent way. Here is a summary of the library's recommendations for evaluating the accuracy, usefulness, and reliability of online texts:

According to the UCLA library staff, a good Web site does all of the following:

1. Clearly states the author and/or organizational **source** of the information;
2. Clearly states the **date** the material was written and the date the site was last revised;
3. Provides **accurate** data whose parameters are clearly defined;
4. Provides **type and level** of information you need;
5. Keeps **bias** to a minimum, and clearly indicates point of view;
6. Provides live **links** to related high-quality Web sites;
7. In the case of **commercial** sites, keeps advertising separate from content, and does not let advertisers determine content; and
8. Is clearly **organized and designed** for ease of use.

Each of these guidelines might require you to consider qualifications, compare and contrast information, evaluate depth of coverage, check and review data, look elsewhere, and more. More information on online research appears in Chapters 15 and 16.

NETWORKING
Applying Digital and Multimedia Literacies

Evaluating Online Sources: Visit the UCLA Library's Web site for additional research criteria. Also, check your college library's site for guidance on evaluating online materials. What is the most useful piece of advice the site offers? Make note of it, and explore in a paragraph when this suggestion or strategy might come in handy.

READING AND ANALYZING VISUAL TEXTS

In this new era of information technology, we seem to be immersed in a visual culture requiring us to contend with and think critically about the constant flow of images we encounter. From advertising, to film, to video, to the Internet, we must respond with increasing frequency not only to written but also to visual messages—images that typically are reinforced by verbal elements. Consequently, it is important to perceive the powerful linkages that exist in today's culture between visual and verbal experience.

Frequently in courses in engineering, social science, computer science, the humanities, fine arts, and elsewhere, you have to analyze and understand visual elements that are embedded in texts. Textbooks increasingly promote visuals as frames of reference that help readers comprehend and appreciate information. Some visual elements—charts, tables, and graphs—are integral to an understanding of verbal texts. Other visuals—comic art, drawings, photographs, paintings, and advertisements—offer contexts and occasions for enjoyment and deeper understanding of the reading, writing, and thinking processes. Visual images convey messages that often are as powerful as well-composed written texts. When they appear together, image and word are like French doors, both opening to reveal a world of heightened perception and understanding.

When visual elements stand alone, as in painting and photography, they often make profound statements about the human experience and frequently reflect certain persuasive purposes that are composed as skillfully as an argumentative essay. Consider, for example, the series that the great Spanish artist Francisco Goya painted, "The Disasters of War," a powerful statement of humankind's penchant for the most grotesque and violent cruelties (p. 138). In the late 20th century, photographers of the Vietnam War, using a modern visual medium, similarly captured the pain and suffering of armed conflict, as in Eddie Adams's potent stills of the execution of a prisoner by the notorious chief of the Saigon national police, General Nguyen Ngoc Loan (p. 139). In the framed sequence, the chief of police aims his pistol at the head of the prisoner and presses the trigger, and the viewer, in that captured instant, sees the jolt of the prisoner's head and a sudden spurt of blood. Reproduced widely in the American press in February 1968, this single image did as much as any written editorial to transform the national debate over the Vietnam War.

Although paintings, photographs, advertisements, and other artistic and design forms that rely heavily on visual elements often function as instruments of persuasion, it would be simplistic to embrace uncritically the cliché "A picture is worth a thousand words." For instance, great literary artists from Homer to Norman Mailer have captured the horrors of war as vividly as artists in other media. Stephen Crane in *The Red Badge of Courage* illustrates the sordidness of America's Civil War in language as graphic as the images of the war's most noted photographer, Mathew Brady. Consider the visual impact of Crane's depiction of battlefield dead:

> The corpse was dressed in a uniform that once had been blue but was now faded to a melancholy shade of green. The eyes, staring at the youth, had changed to the dull hue to be seen on the side of a dead fish. The mouth was opened. Its red had changed to an appalling yellow. Over the grey skin of the face ran little ants. One was trundling some sort of a bundle along the upper lip.

Ultimately, the best verbal and visual texts construct meaning in vivid and memorable ways. When used in combination, verbal and visual texts can mix words and images to create uniquely powerful theses and arguments.

Just as you analyze or take apart a verbal text during the process of critical reading, you also have to think critically about visual images or elements. If you encounter charts, graphs, and tables in a text, you have to understand the information these visuals present, the implications of the numbers or statistics, the emphases and highlights that are conveyed, and the way the visual element—the picture, so to speak—shapes your understanding of the material and its relationship to the text. Sometimes the material presented in such visuals is technical, requiring you to carefully analyze, say, a bar graph: its structure, the relationship of parts to the whole, the assertions that are advanced, and the validity of the evidence conveyed. In short, critical reading of visual material is as demanding as critical reading of the printed word. Just as you often have to reread a verbal text, you also might have to return to charts, graphs, and tables, perhaps from a fresh perspective, in order to comprehend the content of the visual text.

The following questions can guide your critical analysis of such visual texts as charts, graphs, tables, photographs, maps, and Web pages:

- What is the design, format, and structure of the visual? Is it black and white, or are other colors used? How does the placement of design elements affect the message?
- Is the image abstract or realistic—or both? What is the relationship among the elements making up the image?
- Who is the intended audience? Does the image call for a specific audience response?
- What textual information do you immediately notice? What is the relationship between image and text?
- What is the purpose of the visual? What emotions or attitudes does the image convey?
- What thesis or point of view does the information in the visual suggest?
- What is the nature of the evidence, and how can it be verified?
- What emphases and relationships do you detect among the visual details?

When responding to charts, tables, and graphs, you must develop the confidence to read such visual texts accurately and critically. This means taking nothing for granted and trusting your ability to sift through the evidence and the images with a critical eye in order to understand the strategies the author or graphic artist has employed to convey a specific message.

By and large, informative visuals such as tables and graphs rarely have the striking impact of the sort of graphics found in the best commercial and political advertising or in the illustrations we encounter in slick magazines or cutting-edge comics or graphic novels. The visual elements used by advertisers, for example, take advantage of our innate capacity to be affected by symbols—from McDonald's Golden Arches to the president framed by American flags. Such visual emblems convey unspoken ideas and have enormous power to promote products, personalities, and ideas. For example, the two powerful images on pages 42–43 convey important ideas about the cultures that produced them. Visual symbols achieve even more intense effects when they are reinforced by verbal elements.

When viewing art reproductions, photographs, advertisements, and cartoons from a critical perspective, you often have to detect the explicit and implicit messages being conveyed by certain images and symbols, and the design strategies that condition your response. Because these visuals combine many different elements, you have to consider all critical details: color, light, and shadow; the number and arrangement of objects and the relationships among them; the foregrounding and backgrounding of images within the frame; the impact of typography; the impact of language if it is employed; the medium in which the visual appears; and the inferences and values that you draw from the overall composition. Learn to treat visuals in any medium as texts that need to be "read" critically. Every visual requires its own form of annotation, in which you analyze the selection and ordering of its parts and interpret the emotional effects and significant ideas and messages it presents. Throughout this text, paired "classic and contemporary" images such as the two on pages 42–43 give you opportunities to read visual texts with a critical eye.

NETWORKING
Applying Digital and Multimedia Literacies

Analyzing a Web Page: Use the questions on page 40 to analyze the Web page shown below, particularly its use of images. To see an updated version of the page, or to see it in color, visit *http://www.thenationalcampaign.org/*. Consider expanding your analysis to the larger site.

The home page of the National Campaign to Prevent Teen and Unplanned Pregnancy (*www.thenationalcampaign.org*).

Classic and Contemporary Images
HOW DO WE COMMUNICATE?

Using a Critical Perspective   Carefully examine these two illustrations. What is your overall impression of these images? What details and objects in each scene capture your attention? What similarities and differences do you detect? How does each image communicate ideas and values about the culture that has produced it? Does one appeal to you more than the other? Why or why not?

Pulitzer Prize–winning combat photographer Joe Rosenthal captured this scene of U.S. Marines raising the American flag on the Pacific Island of Iwo Jima on February 25, 1945. The campaign to capture the island from Japanese troops cost nearly 7,000 American lives. Rosenthal's photo has been reproduced widely in the media and served as the model for the Marine Corps War Memorial in Washington, D.C.

Photographer Thomas E. Franklin captured a memorable moment
in the wake of the terrorist attack on the World Trade Center in
New York City in September 2001.

Case Study: Class and Culture
Is Social Inequality Growing Worse?

No issue has greater relevance for our lives today than the growing concentration of wealth and the attendant rise of social inequality. In 1974, the top 1 percent of American families took home 9 percent of gross domestic product (GDP). In 2007, the same 1 percent accounted for 23.5 percent of GDP. Responding to this disturbing trend, the writers in the case study investigate what happens when the benefits of economic and technological change do not flow down to all classes in society. Of course, one might argue that social inequality has always existed—that we've always had poor, middle, and upper classes. But today there are far greater disparities in the distribution of national as well as global wealth. The writers in this section examine the hard facts behind the widening gap between those who benefit from the new social, financial, and technological order—and those who do not.

We Are the 99.9 Percent

Paul Krugman

Paul Krugman (b. 1953), who teaches at Princeton University, received the Nobel Prize for Economics in 2008 for his analysis of trade patterns and economic activity. Raised in the suburbs of New York City, Krugman attended Yale University for two years before transferring to Massachusetts Institute of Technology, where he received a PhD in economics in 1977. Krugman has published many highly specialized texts in economic theory, but also popular works like Peddling Prosperity *(1994), The* Accidental Theorist: And Other Dispatches from the Dismal Science *(1998), and* The Return of Depression Economics and the Crisis of 2008 *(2008). A frequent contributor to such newspapers as the* New Republic, Financial Times, *and* Mother Jones, *Krugman is currently an op-ed columnist for the* New York Times. *Known for his trenchant style and oppositional viewpoints, Krugman attempts to make complex economic trends comprehensible to a broad audience. The essay that follows appeared in the November 24, 2010, issue of the* New York Times. *(A second essay by Krugman, "The Death of Horatio Alger," starts on page 387.)*

1   "We are the 99 percent" is a great slogan. It correctly defines the issue as being the middle class versus the elite (as opposed to the middle class versus the poor). And it also gets past the common but wrong establishment notion that rising inequality is mainly about the well educated doing better than the less educated; the

big winners in this new Gilded Age have been a handful of very wealthy people, not college graduates in general.

If anything, however, the 99 percent slogan aims too low. A large fraction of   2
the top 1 percent's gains have actually gone to an even smaller group, the top 0.1 percent—the richest one-thousandth of the population.

And while Democrats, by and large, want that super-elite to make at least   3
some contribution to long-term deficit reduction, Republicans want to cut the super-elite's taxes even as they slash Social Security, Medicare and Medicaid in the name of fiscal discipline.

Before I get to those policy disputes, here are a few numbers.   4

The recent Congressional Budget Office report on inequality didn't look   5
inside the top 1 percent, but an earlier report, which only went up to 2005, did. According to that report, between 1979 and 2005 the inflation-adjusted, after-tax income of Americans in the middle of the income distribution rose 21 percent. The equivalent number for the richest 0.1 percent rose 400 percent.

For the most part, these huge gains reflected a dramatic rise in the super-   6
elite's share of pretax income. But there were also large tax cuts favoring the wealthy. In particular, taxes on capital gains are much lower than they were in 1979—and the richest one-thousandth of Americans account for half of all income from capital gains.

Given this history, why do Republicans advocate further tax cuts for the very   7
rich even as they warn about deficits and demand drastic cuts in social insurance programs?

Well, aside from shouts of "class warfare!" whenever such questions are   8
raised, the usual answer is that the super-elite are "job creators"—that is, that they make a special contribution to the economy. So what you need to know is that this is bad economics. In fact, it would be bad economics even if America had the idealized, perfect market economy of conservative fantasies.

After all, in an idealized market economy each worker would be paid exactly   9
what he or she contributes to the economy by choosing to work, no more and no less. And this would be equally true for workers making $30,000 a year and executives making $30 million a year. There would be no reason to consider the contributions of the $30 million folks as deserving of special treatment.

But, you say, the rich pay taxes! Indeed, they do. And they could—and should,   10
from the point of view of the 99.9 percent—be paying substantially more in taxes, not offered even more tax breaks, despite the alleged budget crisis, because of the wonderful things they supposedly do.

Still, don't some of the very rich get that way by producing innovations that are   11
worth far more to the world than the income they receive? Sure, but if you look at who really makes up the 0.1 percent, it's hard to avoid the conclusion that, by and large, the members of the super-elite are overpaid, not underpaid, for what they do.

For who are the 0.1 percent? Very few of them are Steve Jobs–type innova-   12
tors; most of them are corporate bigwigs and financial wheeler-dealers. One recent analysis found that 43 percent of the super-elite are executives at nonfinancial companies, 18 percent are in finance and another 12 percent are lawyers or in real

estate. And these are not, to put it mildly, professions in which there is a clear relationship between someone's income and his economic contribution.

13   Executive pay, which has skyrocketed over the past generation, is famously set by boards of directors appointed by the very people whose pay they determine; poorly performing C.E.O.'s still get lavish paychecks, and even failed and fired executives often receive millions as they go out the door.

14   Meanwhile, the economic crisis showed that much of the apparent value created by modern finance was a mirage. As the Bank of England's director for financial stability recently put it, seemingly high returns before the crisis simply reflected increased risk-taking—risk that was mostly borne not by the wheeler-dealers themselves but either by naïve investors or by taxpayers, who ended up holding the bag when it all went wrong. And as he waspishly noted, "If risk-making were a value-adding activity, Russian roulette players would contribute disproportionately to global welfare."

15   So should the 99.9 percent hate the 0.1 percent? No, not at all. But they should ignore all the propaganda about "job creators" and demand that the super-elite pay substantially more in taxes.

COMPREHENSION

1. Summarize Krugman's views on the "super-elite." Does he control his biases in discussing this social and economic class? Justify your response by citing specific words, usages, and sentences.
2. According to Krugman, why should the super-elite pay more in taxes?
3. Krugman writes as an economist, explaining class from the perspective of wealth. How does his expertise shape his writing?

RHETORIC

1. Krugman wrote this essay as an op-ed piece for the *New York Times*. How does the article reflect newspaper style? Point to specific details to support your analysis.
2. How does Krugman's title capture the broad subject of his essay? Do you find the title to be effective? Why or why not?
3. In his introduction, Krugman alludes to "this new Gilded Age." What is he referring to? Why is this allusion relevant to his topic?
4. What is Krugman's claim or central argument, and where does he state it?
5. What forms of evidence does Krugman provide to support his argument?

WRITING

1. Write an essay in which you present your own personal views about the rich or super-rich.
2. Read Krugman's "The Death of Horatio Alger." Then write a comparative essay pointing out the similarities and differences in the two selections.
3. **Writing an Argument:** Argue for or against the proposition that the "99 percent slogan" runs the danger of precipitating class warfare.

NETWORKING
Applying Digital and Multimedia Literacies

Collaborating in small groups, go online and locate at least five articles on the controversy over the widening disparities in wealth in the United States. Summarize your findings in a class discussion.

Forty Acres and a Gap in Wealth

Henry Louis Gates Jr.

Henry Louis Gates Jr. (b. 1950) is an educator, writer, editor, and documentary filmmaker. He was born in West Virginia and educated at Yale University and Clare College, Cambridge, where he received a PhD in 1979. He is a distinguished professor at Harvard University. Gates has written and edited numerous books addressing the issues of race, identity, and African American history and culture, and has contributed essays to dozens of periodicals including Critical Inquiry, Black World, *the* Yale Review, *and the* Antioch Review. *His work applies contemporary literary theories to African and African American literature so that readers can develop a deep understanding of the structure, significance, methods, and meanings of this body of work. Many of his theoretical insights are summarized in* The Signifying Monkey: Towards a Theory of Afro-American Literary Criticism *(1988). Among his many awards is the prestigious MacArthur Prize. Gates has also popularized the African American experience in film, including the widely viewed program* In Search of Our Roots *created for PBS. In the following essay, published in the* New York Times *in 2007, Gates analyzes the widening class divide separating black families. (A second essay by Gates, "Delusions of Grandeur," begins on page 381.)*

1   Last week, the Pew Research Center published the astonishing finding that 37 percent of African-Americans polled felt that "blacks today can no longer be thought of as a single race" because of a widening class divide. From Frederick Douglass to the Rev. Dr. Martin Luther King Jr., perhaps the most fundamental assumption in the history of the black community has been that Americans of African descent, the descendants of the slaves, either because of shared culture or shared oppression, constitute "a mighty race," as Marcus Garvey often put it.

2   "By a ratio of 2 to 1," the report says, "blacks say that the values of poor and middle-class blacks have grown more dissimilar over the past decade. In contrast, most blacks say that the values of blacks and whites have grown more alike."

3   The message here is that it is time to examine the differences between black families on either side of the divide for clues about how to address an increasingly entrenched inequality. We can't afford to wait any longer to address the causes of persistent poverty among most black families.

4   This class divide was predicted long ago, and nobody wanted to listen. At a conference marking the 40th anniversary of Daniel Patrick Moynihan's infamous report on the problems of the black family, I asked the conservative scholar James Q. Wilson and the liberal scholar William Julius Wilson if ours was the generation presiding over an irreversible, self-perpetuating class divide within the African-American community.

5   "I have to believe that this is not the case," the liberal Wilson responded with willed optimism. "Why go on with this work otherwise?" The conservative Wilson nodded. Yet, no one could imagine how to close the gap.

6   In 1965, when Moynihan published his report, suggesting that the out-of-wedlock birthrate and the number of families headed by single mothers, both about 24 percent, pointed to dissolution of the social fabric of the black community, black scholars and liberals dismissed it. They attacked its author as a right-wing bigot. Now we'd give just about anything to have those statistics back. Today,

69 percent of black babies are born out of wedlock, while 45 percent of black households with children are headed by women.

How did this happen? As many theories flourish as pundits—from slavery 7 and segregation to the decline of factory jobs, crack cocaine, draconian drug laws and outsourcing. But nobody knows for sure.

I have been studying the family trees of 20 successful African-Americans, peo- 8 ple in fields ranging from entertainment and sports (Oprah Winfrey, the track star Jackie Joyner-Kersee) to space travel and medicine (the astronaut Mae Jemison and Ben Carson, a pediatric neurosurgeon). And I've seen an astonishing pattern: 15 of the 20 descend from at least one line of former slaves who managed to obtain property by 1920—a time when only 25 percent of all African-American families owned property.

Ten years after slavery ended, Constantine Winfrey, Oprah's great-grandfather, 9 bartered eight bales of cleaned cotton (4,000 pounds) that he picked on his own time for 80 acres of prime bottomland in Mississippi. (He also learned to read and write while picking all that cotton.)

Sometimes the government helped: Whoopi Goldberg's great-great- 10 grandparents received their land through the Southern Homestead Act. "So my family got its 40 acres and a mule," she exclaimed when I showed her the deed, referring to the rumor that freed slaves would receive land that had been owned by their masters.

Well, perhaps not the mule, but 104 acres in Florida. If there is a meaningful 11 correlation between the success of accomplished African-Americans today and their ancestors' property ownership, we can only imagine how different black-white relations would be had "40 acres and a mule" really been official government policy in the Reconstruction South.

The historical basis for the gap between the black middle class and under- 12 class shows that ending discrimination, by itself, would not eradicate black poverty and dysfunction. We also need intervention to promulgate a middle-class ethic of success among the poor, while expanding opportunities for economic betterment.

Perhaps Margaret Thatcher, of all people, suggested a program that 13 might help. In the 1980s, she turned 1.5 million residents of public housing projects in Britain into homeowners. It was certainly the most liberal thing Mrs. Thatcher did, and perhaps progressives should borrow a leaf from her playbook.

The telltale fact is that the biggest gap in black prosperity isn't in income, 14 but in wealth. According to a study by the economist Edward N. Wolff, the median net worth of non-Hispanic black households in 2004 was only $11,800—less than 10 percent that of non-Hispanic white households, $118,300. Perhaps a bold and innovative approach to the problem of black poverty—one floated during the Civil War but never fully put into practice—would be to look at ways to turn tenants into homeowners. Sadly, in the wake of the subprime mortgage debacle, an enormous number of houses are being repossessed. But for the black poor, real progress may come only once they have an ownership stake in American society.

15   People who own property feel a sense of ownership in their future and their society. They study, save, work, strive and vote. And people trapped in a culture of tenancy do not.

16   The sad truth is that the civil rights movement cannot be reborn until we identify the causes of black suffering, some of them self-inflicted. Why can't black leaders organize rallies around responsible sexuality, birth within marriage, parents reading to their children and students staying in school and doing homework? Imagine Al Sharpton and Jesse Jackson distributing free copies of Virginia Hamilton's collection of folktales "The People Could Fly" or Dr. Seuss, and demanding that black parents sign pledges to read to their children. What would it take to make inner-city schools havens of learning?

17   John Kenneth Galbraith once told me that the first step in reversing the economic inequalities that blacks face is greater voter participation, and I think he was right. Politicians will not put forth programs aimed at the problems of poor blacks while their turnout remains so low.

18   If the correlation between land ownership and success of African-Americans argues that the chasm between classes in the black community is partly the result of social forces set in motion by the dismal failure of 40 acres and a mule, then we must act decisively. If we do not, ours will be remembered as the generation that presided over a permanent class divide, a slow but inevitable process that began with the failure to give property to the people who had once been defined as property.

COMPREHENSION

1. Why does Gates open his essay by summarizing a report from the Pew Research Center? Exactly what is the Pew Research Center, and how reliable are its data?
2. What is the significance of Gates's title? Highlight, underline, or circle key references to "forty acres and a mule" that appear in the essay.
3. How does Gates's point of view about the black middle class relate to his broader theory about class in African American society?

RHETORIC

1. What is Gates's purpose in this essay: to report a problem, argue a point, present information objectively, or what? Justify your response with reference to the text.
2. Gates refers to several historical and public figures. Identify these allusions and explain what each contributes to the essay.
3. How does Gates's selection of evidence support his position on class divisions within African American society?
4. Analyze the problem-solution strategy that Gates employs to organize the essay.
5. What purpose does comparative analysis serve in the development of the essay?

WRITING

1. Keeping in mind Gates's comments about the black community, write a problem-solution essay that presents your own position on the issue.
2. Write an essay in which you analyze the problem of "entrenched inequality" within a specific ethnic group or within American society in general.
3. **Writing an Argument:** Gates writes, "We can't afford to wait any longer to address the causes of persistent poverty among most black families." Agree or disagree with this statement in an argumentative essay that takes into account the fact that poverty in the United States has increased in general—not just within the black community.

NETWORKING
Applying Digital and Multimedia Literacies

As a class project, help to arrange a viewing of the PBS episode in which Gates interviews Oprah Winfrey and shares genealogical information about her roots.

The Rich Are Different from You and Me

Chrystia Freeland

Chrystia Freeland (b. 1968) is the editor of Thomson Reuters Digital and formerly managing editor of the Financial Times. *Born in Alberta, Canada, Freeland received her undergraduate degree from Harvard University; subsequently she attended St. Anthony's College, Oxford, as a Rhodes scholar. Freeland has been an overseas correspondent for various newspapers and has contributed articles to the* Washington Post *and Toronto's* Globe and Mail. *She is the author of* Sale of the Century *(2000), a study of Russia's transition from communism to capitalism. In this selection from the July/August 2011 issue of the* Atlantic *magazine, Freeland discusses the differences between the very rich and the rest of the global population.*

The rich are always with us, as we learned from the Bette Davis film of that name, 1 released in the teeth of the Great Depression. The most memorable part of that movie was its title—but that terrific phrase turns out not to be entirely true. In every society, some people are richer than others, but across time and geography, the gap between the rich and the rest has varied widely.

The reality today is that the rich—especially the very, very rich—are vaulting 2 ahead of everyone else. Between 2002 and 2007, 65 percent of all income growth in the U.S. went to the richest 1 percent of the population. That lopsided distribution means that today, half of the national income goes to the richest 10 percent. In 2007, the top 1 percent controlled 34.6 percent of the wealth—significantly more than the bottom 90 percent, who controlled just 26.9 percent.

3   That is a huge shift from the post-war decades, whose golden glow may have arisen largely from the era's relative income equality. During the Second World War, and in the four decades that followed, the top 10 percent took home just a third of the national income. The last time the gap between the people on top and everyone else was as large as it is today was during the Roaring '20s.

4   The rise of today's super-rich is a global phenomenon. It is particularly marked in the United States, but it is also happening in other developed economies like the United Kingdom and Canada. Income inequality is also increasing in most of the go-go emerging-market economies, and is now as high in Communist China as it is in the U.S.

5   These global super-rich work and play together. They jet between the Four Seasons in Shanghai and the Four Seasons in New York to do business; descend on Davos, Switzerland, to network; and travel to St. Bart's to vacation. Many are global nomads with a fistful of passports and several far-flung homes. They have more in common with one another than with the folks in the hinterland back home, and increasingly, they are forming a nation unto themselves.

6   This international plutocracy is emerging at a moment when globalization and the technology revolution are hollowing out the middle class in most Western industrialized nations. Many of today's super-rich started out in the middle and make most of their money through work, not inheritance. Ninety-five years ago, the richest 1 percent of Americans received only 20 percent of their income from paid work; in 2004, that income proportion had tripled, to 60 percent.

7   These meritocrats are the winners in a winner-take-all world. Among the big political questions of our age are whether they will notice that everyone else is falling behind, and whether they will decide it is in their interests to do something about that.

COMPREHENSION

1. How would you describe Freeland's opinion of the super-rich in this piece? Does she control for biases or not? Explain.
2. Highlight, underline, or score the details that Freeland provides in her effort to define the super-rich and distinguish them from the rest of the population.
3. According to Freeland, why have the super-rich become a global phenomenon? What are the global super-rich like?

RHETORIC

1. Freeland's title contains an allusion, and the first paragraph has another. Identify these two references and explain how they inform the writer's subject.

2. What is Freeland's purpose in this essay? Does she present a simple thesis or main idea in support of her topic, or does she have an opinion that suggests an argument in the making? Justify your response.
3. List the ways in which Freeland uses comparative elements and also cause-and-effect analysis in this essay.
4. How does Freeland incorporate definition into the substance and organization of the essay?
5. What is Freeland's tone or voice in the concluding paragraph?

WRITING

1. In an essay of analysis, present your own understanding of the super-rich as both a national and a global phenomenon.
2. Select a well-known figure from the world of the super-rich—for example, Bill Gates or Oprah Winfrey—and create a case study of this individual. Conduct research if necessary.
3. **Writing an Argument:** Freeland's title makes a very broad claim. Defend or attack her statement. Is it generally true that the rich are different from the majority of people who are not?

NETWORKING *Applying Digital and Multimedia Literacies*	
In small groups, prepare for a class debate on Freeland's assertion that "globalization and the technology revolution are hollowing out the middle class in most Western industrialized nations." Locate online at least three articles that provide useful evidence to support your position.	

The Broken Contract:

Inequality and American Decline

George Packer

George Packer (b. 1960) comes from a distinguished academic family at Stanford University. His mother, Nancy Packer, is a fiction writer; and his father, Herbert Packer, a professor of law. Packer's sister, Ann Packer, is a well-known novelist. Packer himself is a journalist, novelist, and playwright. He graduated from Yale University in 1982 and served in the Peace Corps in Togo. Among his books are Blood of the Liberals *(2000) and* The Assassins' Gate: America in Iraq *(2005). Packer has been a staff writer at the* New Yorker *since 2003. He has also written for the* New York Times, Harper's, The Nation, *and other publications. In the essay that follows, which appeared in* Foreign Affairs *in 2011, Packer analyzes the institutional forces in politics, business, and the media that seem to be pulling America apart.*

1 Iraq was one of those wars where people actually put on pounds. A few years ago, I was eating lunch with another reporter at an American-style greasy spoon in Baghdad's Green Zone. At a nearby table, a couple of American contractors were finishing off their burgers and fries. They were wearing the contractor's uniform: khakis, polo shirts, baseball caps, and Department of Defense identity badges in plastic pouches hanging from nylon lanyards around their necks. The man who had served their food might have been the only Iraqi they spoke with all day. The Green Zone was set up to make you feel that Iraq was a hallucination and you were actually in Normal, Illinois. This narcotizing effect seeped into the consciousness of every American who hunkered down and worked and partied behind its blast walls—the soldier and the civilian, the diplomat and the journalist, the important and the obscure. Hardly anyone stayed longer than a year; almost everyone went home with a collection of exaggerated war stories, making an effort to forget that they were leaving behind shoddy, unfinished projects and a country spiraling downward into civil war. As the two contractors got up and ambled out of the restaurant, my friend looked at me and said, "We're just not that good anymore."

2   The Iraq war was a kind of stress test applied to the American body politic. And every major system and organ failed the test: the executive and legislative branches, the military, the intelligence world, the forprofits, the nonprofits, the media. It turned out that we were not in good shape at all—without even realizing it. Americans just hadn't tried anything this hard in around half a century. It is easy, and completely justified, to blame certain individuals for the Iraq tragedy. But over the years, I've become more concerned with failures that went beyond individuals, and beyond Iraq—concerned with the growing arteriosclerosis of American institutions. Iraq was not an exceptional case. It was a vivid symptom of a long-term trend, one that worsens year by year. The same ailments that led to the disastrous occupation were on full display in Washington this past summer, during the debt-ceiling debacle: ideological rigidity bordering on fanaticism, an indifference to facts, an inability to think beyond the short term, the dissolution of national interest into partisan advantage.

3   Was it ever any different? Is it really true that we're just not that good anymore? As a thought experiment, compare your life today with that of someone like you in 1978. Think of an educated, reasonably comfortable couple perched somewhere within the vast American middle class of that year. And think how much less pleasant their lives are than yours. The man is wearing a brown and gold polyester print shirt with a flared collar and oversize tortoiseshell glasses; she's got on a high-waisted, V-neck rayon dress and platform clogs. Their morning coffee is Maxwell House filter drip. They drive an AMC Pacer hatchback, with a nonfunctioning air conditioner and a tape deck that keeps eating their eight-tracks. When she wants to make something a little daring for dinner, she puts together a pasta primavera.

They type their letters on an IBM Selectric, the new model with the corrective ribbon. There is only antenna television, and the biggest thing on is *Laverne and Shirley.* Long-distance phone calls cost a dollar a minute on weekends; air travel is prohibitively expensive. The city they live near is no longer a place where they spend much time: trash on the sidewalks, junkies on the corner, vandalized pay phones, half-deserted subway cars covered in graffiti.

By contemporary standards, life in 1978 was inconvenient, constrained, and 4 ugly. Things were badly made and didn't work very well. Highly regulated industries, such as telecommunications and airlines, were costly and offered few choices. The industrial landscape was decaying, but the sleek information revolution had not yet emerged to take its place. Life before the Android, the Apple Store, FedEx, HBO, Twitter feeds, Whole Foods, Lipitor, air bags, the Emerging Markets Index Fund, and the Pre-K Gifted and Talented Program prep course is not a world to which many of us would willingly return.

The surface of life has greatly improved, at least for educated, reasonably 5 comfortable people—say, the top 20 percent, socioeconomically. Yet the deeper structures, the institutions that underpin a healthy democratic society, have fallen into a state of decadence. We have all the information in the universe at our fingertips, while our most basic problems go unsolved year after year: climate change, income inequality, wage stagnation, national debt, immigration, falling educational achievement, deteriorating infrastructure, declining news standards. All around, we see dazzling technological change, but no progress. Last year, a Wall Street company that few people have ever heard of dug an 800-mile trench under farms, rivers, and mountains between Chicago and New York and laid fiber-optic cable connecting the Chicago Mercantile Exchange and the New York Stock Exchange. This feat of infrastructure building, which cost $300 million, shaves three milliseconds off high-speed, high-volume automated trades—a big competitive advantage. But passenger trains between Chicago and New York run barely faster than they did in 1950, and the country no longer seems capable, at least politically, of building faster ones. Just ask people in Florida, Ohio, and Wisconsin, whose governors recently refused federal money for high-speed rail projects.

We can upgrade our iPhones, but we can't fix our roads and bridges. We in- 6 vented broadband, but we can't extend it to 35 percent of the public. We can get 300 television channels on the iPad, but in the past decade 20 newspapers closed down all their foreign bureaus. We have touch-screen voting machines, but last year just 40 percent of registered voters turned out, and our political system is more polarized, more choked with its own bile, than at any time since the Civil War. There is nothing today like the personal destruction of the McCarthy era or the street fights of the 1960s. But in those periods, institutional forces still existed in politics, business, and the media that could hold the center together. It used to be called the establishment, and it no longer exists. Solving fundamental problems with a can-do practicality—the very thing the world used to associate with America, and that redeemed us from our vulgarity and arrogance—now seems beyond our reach.

The Unwritten Contract

7 Why and how did this happen? Those are hard questions. A roundabout way of answering them is to first ask, when did this start to happen? Any time frame has an element of arbitrariness, and also contains the beginning of a theory. Mine goes back to that shabby, forgettable year of 1978. It is surprising to say that in or around 1978, American life changed—and changed dramatically. It was, like this moment, a time of widespread pessimism—high inflation, high unemployment, high gas prices. And the country reacted to its sense of decline by moving away from the social arrangement that had been in place since the 1930s and 1940s.

8   What was that arrangement? It is sometimes called "the mixed economy"; the term I prefer is "middle-class democracy." It was an unwritten social contract among labor, business, and government—between the elites and the masses. It guaranteed that the benefits of the economic growth following World War II were distributed more widely, and with more shared prosperity, than at any time in human history. In the 1970s, corporate executives earned 40 times as much as their lowest-paid employees. (By 2007, the ratio was over 400 to 1.) Labor law and government policy kept the balance of power between workers and owners on an even keel, leading to a virtuous circle of higher wages and more economic stimulus. The tax code restricted the amount of wealth that could be accumulated in private hands and passed on from one generation to the next, thereby preventing the formation of an inherited plutocracy. The regulatory agencies were strong enough to prevent the kind of speculative bubbles that now occur every five years or so: between the Great Depression and the Reagan era there was not a single systemwide financial crisis, which is why recessions during those decades were far milder than they have since become. Commercial banking was a stable, boring business. (In movies from the 1940s and 1950s, bankers are dull, solid pillars of the community.) Investment banking, cordoned off by the iron wall of the Glass-Steagall Act, was a closed world of private partnerships in which rich men carefully weighed their risks because they were playing with their own money. Partly as a result of this shared prosperity, political participation reached an all-time high during the postwar years (with the exception of those, such as black Americans in the South, who were still denied access to the ballot box).

9   At the same time, the country's elites were playing a role that today is almost unrecognizable. They actually saw themselves as custodians of national institutions and interests. The heads of banks, corporations, universities, law firms, foundations, and media companies were neither more nor less venal, meretricious, and greedy than their counterparts today. But they rose to the top in a culture that put a brake on these traits and certainly did not glorify them. Organizations such as the Council on Foreign Relations, the Committee for Economic Development, and the Ford Foundation did not act on behalf of a single, highly privileged point of view—that of the rich. Rather, they rose above the country's conflicting interests and tried to unite them into an overarching idea of the national interest. Business leaders who had fought the New Deal as vehemently as the U.S. Chamber of Commerce is now fighting

health-care and financial reform later came to accept Social Security and labor unions, did not stand in the way of Medicare, and supported other pieces of Lyndon Johnson's Great Society. They saw this legislation as contributing to the social peace that ensured a productive economy. In 1964, Johnson created the National Commission on Technology, Automation, and Economic Progress to study the effects of these coming changes on the work force. The commission included two labor leaders, two corporate leaders, the civil rights activist Whitney Young, and the sociologist Daniel Bell. Two years later, they came out with their recommendations: a guaranteed annual income and a massive job-training program. This is how elites once behaved: as if they had actual responsibilities.

Of course, the consensus of the postwar years contained plenty of injustice. 10 If you were black or female, it made very little room for you. It could be stifling and conformist, authoritarian and intrusive. Yet those years also offered the means of redressing the very wrongs they contained: for example, strong government, enlightened business, and activist labor were important bulwarks of the civil rights movement. Nostalgia is a useless emotion. Like any era, the postwar years had their costs. But from where we stand in 2011, they look pretty good.

The Rise of Organized Money

Two things happened to this social arrangement. The first was the 1960s. The 11 story is familiar: youth rebellion and revolution, a ferocious backlash now known as the culture wars, and a permanent change in American manners and morals. Far more than political utopia, the legacy of the 1960s was personal liberation. Some conservatives argue that the social revolution of the 1960s and 1970s prepared the way for the economic revolution of the 1980s, that Abbie Hoffman and Ronald Reagan were both about freedom. But Woodstock was not enough to blow apart the middle-class democracy that had benefited tens of millions of Americans. The Nixon and Ford presidencies actually extended it. In his 2001 book, *The Paradox of American Democracy,* John Judis notes that in the three decades between 1933 and 1966, the federal government created 11 regulatory agencies to protect consumers, workers, and investors. In the five years between 1970 and 1975, it established another 12, including the Environmental Protection Agency, the Occupational Safety and Health Administration, and the Consumer Product Safety Commission. Richard Nixon was a closet liberal, and today he would be to the left of Senator Olympia Snowe, the moderate Republican.

The second thing that happened was the economic slowdown of the 1970s, 12 brought on by "stagflation" and the oil shock. It eroded Americans' paychecks and what was left of their confidence in the federal government after Vietnam, Watergate, and the disorder of the 1960s. It also alarmed the country's business leaders, and they turned their alarm into action. They became convinced that capitalism itself was under attack by the likes of Rachel Carson and Ralph Nader, and they organized themselves into lobbying groups and think tanks that quickly became familiar and powerful players in U.S. politics: the Business Roundtable, the Heritage Foundation, and others. Their budgets and influence soon rivaled those of the older, consensus-minded groups, such as the Brookings Institution. By the mid-1970s, chief executives had stopped believing that they had an obligation to act as disinterested stewards of the national economy. They became a special interest; the interest they represented was their own. The neoconservative writer Irving Kristol played a key role in focusing executives' minds on this narrower and more urgent agenda. He told them, "Corporate philanthropy should not be, and cannot be, disinterested."

13   Among the non-disinterested spending that corporations began to engage in, none was more interested than lobbying. Lobbying has existed since the beginning of the republic, but it was a sleepy, bourbon-and-cigars practice until the mid- to late 1970s. In 1971, there were only 145 businesses represented by registered lobbyists in Washington; by 1982, there were 2,445. In 1974, there were just over 600 registered political action committees, which raised $12.5 million that year; in 1982, there were 3,371, which raised $83 million. In 1974, a total of $77 million was spent on the midterm elections; in 1982, it was $343 million. Not all this lobbying and campaign spending was done by corporations, but they did more and did it better than anyone else. And they got results.

14   These changes were wrought not only by conservative thinkers and their allies in the business class. Among those responsible were the high-minded liberals, the McGovernites and Watergate reformers, who created the open primary, clean election laws, and "outsider" political campaigns that relied heavily on television advertising. In theory, those reforms opened up the political system to previously disenfranchised voters by getting rid of the smoke-filled room, the party caucus, and the urban boss—exchanging Richard Daley for Jesse Jackson. In practice, what replaced the old politics was not a more egalitarian new politics. Instead, as the parties lost their coherence and authority, they were overtaken by grass-roots politics of a new type, driven by direct mail, beholden to special interest groups, and funded by lobbyists. The electorate was transformed from coalitions of different blocs—labor, small business, the farm vote—to an atomized nation of television watchers. Politicians began to focus their energies on big dollars for big ad buys. As things turned out, this did not set them free to do the people's work: as Senator Tom Harkin, the Iowa Democrat, once told me, he and his colleagues spend half their free time raising money.

15   This is a story about the perverse effects of democratization. Getting rid of elites, or watching them surrender their moral authority, did not necessarily empower ordinary people. Once Walter Reuther of the United Auto Workers and Walter Wriston of Citicorp stopped sitting together on Commissions to Make the World a Better Place and started paying lobbyists to fight for their separate interests in Congress, the balance of power tilted heavily toward business. Thirty years later, who has done better by the government—the United Auto Workers or Citicorp?

In 1978, all these trends came to a head. That year, three reform bills were 16 brought up for a vote in Congress. One of the bills was to establish a new office of consumer representation, giving the public a consumer advocate in the federal bureaucracy. A second bill proposed modestly increasing the capital gains tax and getting rid of the three-martini-lunch deduction. A third sought to make it harder for employers to circumvent labor laws and block union organizing. These bills had bipartisan backing in Congress; they were introduced at the very end of the era when bipartisanship was routine, when necessary and important legislation had support from both parties. The Democrats controlled the White House and both houses of Congress, and the bills were popular with the public. And yet, one by one, each bill went down in defeat. (Eventually, the tax bill passed, but only after it was changed; instead of raising the capital gains tax rate, the final bill cut it nearly in half.)

How and why this happened are explored in Jacob Hacker and Paul Pierson's 17 recent book, *Winner-Take-All Politics*. Their explanation, in two words, is organized money. Business groups launched a lobbying assault the likes of which Washington had never seen, and when it was all over, the next era in American life had begun. At the end of the year, the midterm elections saw the Republicans gain 15 seats in the House and three in the Senate. The numbers were less impressive than the character of the new members who came to Washington. They were not politicians looking to get along with colleagues and solve problems by passing legislation. Rather, they were movement conservatives who were hostile to the very idea of government. Among them was a history professor from Georgia named Newt Gingrich. The Reagan revolution began in 1978.

Organized money did not foist these far-reaching changes on an unsuspect- 18 ing public. In the late 1970s, popular anger at government was running high, and President Jimmy Carter was a perfect target. This was not a case of false consciousness; it was a case of a fed-up public. Two years later, Reagan came to power in a landslide. The public wanted him.

But that archetypal 1978 couple with the AMC Pacer was not voting to see 19 its share of the economic pie drastically reduced over the next 30 years. They were not fed up with how little of the national income went to the top one percent or how unfairly progressive the tax code was. They did not want to dismantle government programs such as Social Security and Medicare, which had brought economic security to the middle class. They were not voting to weaken government itself, as long as it defended their interests. But for the next three decades, the dominant political faction pursued these goals as though they were what most Americans wanted. Organized money and the conservative movement seized that moment back in 1978 to begin a massive, generation-long transfer of wealth to the richest Americans. The transfer continued in good economic times and bad, under Democratic presidents and Republican, when Democrats controlled Congress and when Republicans did. For the Democrats, too, went begging to Wall Street and corporate America, because that's where the money was. They accepted the perfectly legal bribes just as eagerly as Republicans, and when the moment came, some of them voted almost as obediently. In 2007, when Congress was considering closing a loophole in the law that allowed hedge fund managers to pay a tax rate of 15 percent on most of their earnings—considerably less than their secretaries—it was New York's Democratic senator Charles Schumer who rushed to their defense and made sure it did not happen. As Bob Dole, then a Republican senator, said back in 1982, "Poor people don't make campaign contributions."

Mocking the American Promise

20 This inequality is the ill that underlies all the others. Like an odorless gas, it pervades every corner of the United States and saps the strength of the country's democracy. But it seems impossible to find the source and shut it off. For years, certain politicians and pundits denied that it even existed. But the evidence became overwhelming. Between 1979 and 2006, middle-class Americans saw their annual incomes after taxes increase by 21 percent (adjusted for inflation). The poorest Americans saw their incomes rise by only 11 percent. The top one percent, meanwhile, saw their incomes increase by 256 percent. This almost tripled their share of the national income, up to 23 percent, the highest level since 1928. The graph that shows their share over time looks almost flat under Kennedy, Johnson, Nixon, Ford, and Carter, followed by continual spikes under Reagan, the elder Bush, Clinton, and the younger Bush.

21 Some argue that this inequality was an unavoidable result of deeper shifts: global competition, cheap goods made in China, technological changes. Although those factors played a part, they have not been decisive. In Europe, where the same changes took place, inequality has remained much lower than in the United States. The decisive factor has been politics and public policy: tax rates, spending choices, labor laws, regulations, campaign finance rules. Book after book by economists and other scholars over the past few years has presented an airtight case: over the past three decades, the government has consistently favored the rich. This is the source of the problem: our leaders, our institutions.

22 But even more fundamental than public policy is the long-term transformation of the manners and morals of American elites—what they became willing to do that they would not have done, or even thought about doing, before. Political changes precipitated, and in turn were aided by, deeper changes in norms of responsibility and self-restraint. In 1978, it might have been economically feasible and perfectly legal for an executive to award himself a multimillion-dollar bonus while shedding 40 percent of his work force and requiring the survivors to take annual furloughs without pay. But no executive would have wanted the shame and outrage that would have followed—any more than an executive today would want to be quoted using a racial slur or photographed with a paid escort. These days, it is hard to open a newspaper without reading stories about grotesque overcompensation at the top and widespread hardship below. Getting rid of a taboo is easier than establishing one, and once a prohibition erodes, it can never be restored in quite the same way. As Leo Tolstoy wrote, "There are no conditions of life to

which a man cannot get accustomed, especially if he sees them accepted by everyone around him."

The persistence of this trend toward greater inequality over the past 30 years 23 suggests a kind of feedback loop that cannot be broken by the usual political means. The more wealth accumulates in a few hands at the top, the more influence and favor the well-connected rich acquire, which makes it easier for them and their political allies to cast off restraint without paying a social price. That, in turn, frees them up to amass more money, until cause and effect become impossible to distinguish. Nothing seems to slow this process down—not wars, not technology, not a recession, not a historic election. Perhaps, out of a well-founded fear that the country is coming apart at the seams, the wealthy and their political allies will finally have to rein themselves in, and, for example, start thinking about their taxes less like Stephen Schwarzman and more like Warren Buffett.

In the meantime, inequality will continue to mock the American promise of 24 opportunity for all. Inequality creates a lopsided economy, which leaves the rich with so much money that they can binge on speculation, and leaves the middle class without enough money to buy the things they think they deserve, which leads them to borrow and go into debt. These were among the long-term causes of the financial crisis and the Great Recession. Inequality hardens society into a class system, imprisoning people in the circumstances of their birth—a rebuke to the very idea of the American dream. Inequality divides us from one another in schools, in neighborhoods, at work, on airplanes, in hospitals, in what we eat, in the condition of our bodies, in what we think, in our children's futures, in how we die. Inequality makes it harder to imagine the lives of others—which is one reason why the fate of over 14 million more or less permanently unemployed Americans leaves so little impression in the country's political and media capitals. Inequality corrodes trust among fellow citizens, making it seem as if the game is rigged. Inequality provokes a generalized anger that finds targets where it can—immigrants, foreign countries, American elites, government in all forms—and it rewards demagogues while discrediting reformers. Inequality saps the will to conceive of ambitious solutions to large collective problems, because those problems no longer seem very collective. Inequality undermines democracy.

COMPREHENSION

1. Summarize Packer's main argument in this essay. According to Packer, how does the current condition in the United States differ from the situation in earlier periods?
2. What distinctions does Packer draw between the "unbroken contract" and the "broken contract"? What conclusions about this divergence does the writer draw? Would you agree or disagree with his conclusions? Explain.
3. According to Packer, what are the reasons for inequality in American life? List all these reasons and causes.

RHETORIC

1. What is Packer's claim or argument? Does he state this claim or imply it? Explain. What types of evidence does he present to support his claim?
2. Describe the tone of this essay—the writer's point of view. What words and phrases capture this tone or personal voice? What expectations does Packer have for the audience he is addressing? How does he establish his authority and ethical stance in writing for this audience?
3. Why does Packer subdivide this essay, using subtitles to indicate movement from one section to the next? What relationships do you see between and among these sections? How does the writer maintain coherence as he makes transitions from one section to the next?
4. Why does Packer begin his essay by offering an overview of the Iraq war in paragraphs 1–2? Does he return to the war in this essay? Why or why not?
5. Identify and explain Packer's use of comparison and contrast, cause-and-effect analysis, and process analysis in the essay.

WRITING

1. Using Packer's essay as a point of reference, write an essay entitled "The Unwritten Contract."
2. Compose a comparative essay in which you write about your parents' childhood and your own. Use this comparative strategy to make a comment about inequality in America across two generations.
3. **Writing an Argument:** Agree or disagree with the following proposition that appears in Packer's essay: "Inequality will continue to mock the American promise of opportunity for all."

NETWORKING
Applying Digital and Multimedia Literacies

Explore online digital resources that focus on a single topic mentioned by Packer in his essay—for example, the Green Zone in Baghdad, *Laverne and Shirley*, the McCarthy era. Compose an essay based on your findings.

Synthesis: Connections for Critical Writing

1. Annotate each of the four essays in this casebook. Then write one-paragraph summaries for each selection.
2. The writers in this casebook have a great deal to say about inequality. What key elements figure in this debate? Offer your own critique of the problem, integrating the main ideas of this debate into your paper.
3. Which writer in this section is most sympathetic to your own views? Respond to this question in an evaluative essay.
4. How do you think Henry Louis Gates Jr. would respond to the essay by George Packer? Would he agree or disagree with Packer's commentary? Respond in a comparative essay.
5. Where do you think the writers in this unit would stand on the question of raising taxes on the wealthy? Compose a speculative essay on this subject.

chapter 2

Critical Writing: Process and Communication

New methods of communication—notably, various digital technologies and the emergence of Web 2.0 interactions and collaborations—might characterize 21st-century literacies, but regardless of the new media at your disposal, you still have to know how to write. Whether you have been provided an assignment by your instructor or developed your own topic, the various tools for critical reading and analysis covered in the first chapter should equip you with the foundation for embarking on college writing assignments. You might use the Internet to gather information, to chat about the assignment, or to e-mail the instructor with a pressing question about an essay you have read; however, the Web only facilitates or partially informs the many challenges of composition.

Even if your instructor encourages you to put your essay in a digital format, remember that composing an essay in any medium is a dynamic, recursive process. It is especially dynamic today when you can share your writing with other students around the world, submit assignments electronically for review by others, have conversations about drafts and assignments in chat rooms and on message boards, and so forth.

Whether you write for a local or global audience, you usually compose an essay in a three-part process: invention (also called prewriting), drafting, and revising and editing. Of course, in actual practice these stages should not be treated as strictly linear or clear-cut "steps." (Revision, for example, typically occurs at every stage of the writing process, especially when using the many word-processing tools at your disposal.) As your word-processing talents and mastery of other digital options suggest, you often move back and forth within the overall writing process as you generate the raw materials of composition and gradually refine them.

We therefore should acknowledge at the outset that everyone approaches the writing process somewhat differently. Your needs and skills likely differ from the student sitting next to you, as do your specific cultural practices and your possible knowledge of other languages. To illuminate this varied and supple writing process, we will examine strategies employed by several student and professional writers, including one student, Jamie Taylor, as she read and responded to the essay by Schlesinger presented in the first chapter. But first we require an overview of the writing process, starting with the origin and development of a writer's ideas.

Annie Dillard, one of the many celebrated essayists appearing in this book (see her "An American Childhood" on pages 241–247), stresses the primacy of the creative imagination in the writing process. Dillard uses the extended metaphor of building a house to describe the three stages in the writing process: prewriting ("The line of words is a miner's pick, a woodcarver's gouge, a surgeon's probe. You wield it, and it digs a path you follow"), drafting ("You lay down the words carefully, watching all the angles"), and revising ("The part you must jettison is not only the best-written part; it is also, oddly, the part which was to have been the very point").

Think of the process of writing as a craft involving the planning, transcribing, polishing, and production of a text for an audience. In Old English, the word *craft* signifies strength and power. By treating writing as a craft, you empower yourself to make the most complex compositional tasks manageable. By thinking of the writing process as a habit of mind involving prewriting, writing, and revision, you can create effective essays and documents. (And remember that in the world of 21st-century literacy, typified by blogs, social networking sites, reader lists, and more, you might be interacting with other students and communities—and writing collaboratively.)

INVENTION

Invention, or prewriting, which you encountered as you negotiated the reading-writing connection in Chapter 1, is the discovery, exploration, and planning stage of the composing process. It is the stage in which you discover a reason to write, select and narrow a subject, consider audience and purpose, perhaps determine the tone or personal voice you wish to employ, and engage in preliminary writing activities designed to generate textual material.

During invention, you are free to let ideas incubate, to let thoughts and writing strategies ripen. You are also free to get in the mood to write. Ernest Hemingway used to sharpen all his pencils as preparation for a day's writing; the French philosopher Voltaire soaked his feet in cold water to get the creative juices flowing. As a digital native, you might want to chat with a classmate via texts or IM, bounce ideas around with others in an online discussion forum, do searches for and read articles about your topic, consult a relevant e-book, or even adopt a virtual identity for yourself (Annie Dillard? Ernest Hemingway?) in a blog, or on Second Life. Professional writers understand the importance of prewriting activities in the composing process, but college writers often undervalue or ignore them completely.

Considering Purpose and Audience

Any writing situation requires you to make choices and decisions about purpose, audience, planning, writing, revision, and transmission of your text. Determining your purpose or goal—the reason you are writing—at the outset of the composing process is one of the first steps. It prevents you from expending useless energy on thinking that is ultimately unimportant, misdirected, or unrelated to the problem because it forces you to ask, What do I hope to obtain from this text? With a specific purpose in mind, you start to anticipate the type of composing task ahead of you and to identify the problems that might be inherent in this task.

Traditionally, the main forms of writing—narration, description, exposition, and argumentation—help to guide or mold your purpose.

Classic and Contemporary Images

HOW DO WE COMPOSE?

Using a Critical Perspective   Consider these two illustrations of authors engaged in the writing process. What is the dominant impression in each photo? What similarities and differences do you see? Which setting seems more conducive to your writing process, and why?

The American novelist Edith Wharton (1862–1937), sitting at her desk, writing.

Children's book authors Jennifer Jacobson and Jane Kurtz
writing together at a coffee shop.

Form	Purpose	Example
Narration	To relate a sequence of events	To tell about an accident
Description	To provide a picture or produce an impression	To describe a moth
Exposition	To explain, inform, or analyze	To compare two teachers
Argumentation	To convince or persuade	To oppose abortion

Most writing actually combines more than one of these rhetorical modes or forms, but these basic categories help shape your text to a specific purpose.

Even as you determine your purpose, you must also create common ground between yourself and your audience. In fact, to define your audience is to define part of your purpose. Think of your audience as the readers of your text. What do they know about the topic? How do they perceive you—your status, expertise, and credibility? In turn, what do you know about their opinions and backgrounds? Are they likely to agree or disagree with you? (This last question is especially important in argumentative writing, which will be discussed in Chapter 3.) By defining your audience carefully, you can begin to tailor your text. Only by analyzing your readership will you be able to appeal to an audience.

Moreover, you need to know that in the real-world environment of the 21st century, especially the world of work, you often need to identify multiple audiences for a variety of purposes. Even in an academic setting, your primary audience might be your professor, but secondary readers might be classmates you share your work with or a college publication that might be interested in reprinting your essay.

Choosing an Appropriate Tone

Tone is the attitude that you plan to take with your audience. It is the *voice* that your readers will hear when they read your essay. Part of the task of invention is to select a voice that is appropriate to the writing task, the situation, and the audience you address. The intimate or even profane voice that you use when texting a close friend would not be the appropriate tone for an essay you compose for your philosophy professor.

As you think critically about your writing task, it should be clear that your audience has expectations that go beyond the form and content of your essay. Most important, this audience will be listening for the voice that you project. Perhaps, if you are reporting an event factually, you will want to project a balanced, objective, largely dispassionate tone. On the other hand, if you are writing a narrative essay on the death of a family member, your tone might be one of controlled emotion or poignant in effect. Likewise, the tone of an argumentative essay might be logical, insistent, compelling (if you have a persuasive goal), even satirical. Different writing situations demand different tones.

Consider tone as integral to the interactive and social dimension of the writing process. It requires a degree of self-awareness, for tone at all times should inspire trust: you should sound reasonable, well informed about your subject, and fair. Above all, you do not want to sound abrupt, long-winded, sarcastic, or just plain confused. Effective writers know how to move easily among various ranges of tone as they plan their writing task.

Generating Ideas: Freewriting and Brainstorming

When you start a writing project, you need to generate ideas as you search for something to say. Some writers doodle, others create cluster trees of ideas, and still others prefer extensive lists. Two especially useful methods of getting in touch with what you already know or believe are freewriting and brainstorming.

Freewriting is quite simple. Merely select a predetermined amount of time, say, from 5 to 15 minutes, and write or type everything that you can think of regarding the subject at hand. Don't worry about punctuation or grammar. This activity is mainly to get your cognitive wheels rolling. Brainstorming is a variant of freewriting in which you jot down or type ideas and questions, often in numbered form. If you find freewriting and brainstorming helpful, you will probably find the length of time that suits you best. When you have finished, review what you have written. A well-known composition expert, Peter Elbow, explains the value of freewriting in the selection starting on page 105. The freewriting that Elbow describes can help any writer generate ideas, but freewriting and brainstorming can also help writers respond to others' ideas. For example, examine the following freewriting and brainstorming exercises by a student, James Moore, which he wrote after reading an excerpt from Schlesinger's "The Cult of Ethnicity."

Freewriting Sample

This essay shows that the author really knows his history because he cites so many historical figures, places, and can quote word for word authorities that back up his argument. He makes a great argument that America's strength is in its diversity and at the same time its unity. I never thought of these two things as being able to complement one another. I always thought of them as being separate. It opens my mind to a whole new way of thinking. One thing that would have strengthened his argument, though, is the fact that although he criticizes people who want to separate themselves into subgroups, he doesn't really mention them by name. He's great when it comes to advancing his own argument but he seems to be a bit too general when he comes to attacking the opposition. I would have liked it if he had mentioned by name people who are undermining America's strengths and listen in their own words.

Brainstorming Sample

1. The author says that ideological conflict isn't such a big problem, but what about the gap between rich and poor? Maybe if there were less of a gap, people wouldn't look for "false idols."
2. Schlesinger seems to be part of the white mainstream. Does this mean he is destined not to understand fully the reasons why people on the margins of society get so tempted to join "cults"?
3. He uses supporting points very well but doesn't exactly explain why "multiculturalism" and "political correctness" are happening now in our society. What is it about today that has opened the door to these ideas?
4. There are so many references to places with ethnic tensions around the world. It would be great to study one of them and see if they have any similarities to the ones that exist in the United States.
5. He seems to be writing for a very educated audience. I wonder really if he can reach the "common person" with this kind of sophisticated writing. I don't know about most of the places he mentions.
6. What's the solution? That could be the start of a topic for my paper. I don't think the author offers any.

Let's consider the benefits these processes can have. First, you can comment on the subject matter of the essay without censoring your thoughts. This prepares you for the second reading by marshaling a more coherent idea of your perspective. Freewriting and brainstorming can be tools that help you understand how you can have something to contribute in the writer-reader "conversation" or help you see a topic in a new way. For example, in the freewriting example, Moore discovered for himself the idea that the strength of American society is a combination of commonality and diversity. Second, during the brainstorming process, you might come up with a potential idea for a response essay, as Moore did in the example.

Now let us return to the prewriting process that Jamie Taylor followed.

Brainstorming Notes

1. Schlesinger seems to be saying that multiculturalism poses a danger because it threatens to create ethnic divisiveness rather than healthy identification.
2. This not only undermines us now, but threatens the very democratic principles upon which the United States was founded.
3. He says America must set an example for the rest of the world, which is torn with racial and ethnic strife.
4. He believes that there is a small group of individuals with a "hidden agenda" who are trying to create this divisiveness. These individuals are self-centered and have their own interests at heart, not the interests of the people they represent.
5. One flaw in the essay was that it seemed vague. He didn't mention any names or give specific examples. Only generalities.
6. He suggests the "battle" will be won by ordinary citizens; for example, he cites the many inter-marriages occurring today.
7. Although he sees danger, he is optimistic because he thinks democracy is a strong institution.
8. He writes from a position of authority. He cites many historical figures and seems very well read.
9. The major problem I see in his essay is that he seems to lump everyone together in the same boat. He doesn't give enough credit to the average person to see through the hollowness of false idols. You don't need a Ph.D. to see the silliness of so many ideas floating around out there.
10. So many things to consider, how should I focus my essay??? What should be my theme??
11. Hmmm. Idea!!! Since I agree with his basic points, but find he doesn't provide specifics, and doesn't give the average person enough credit to see through the emptiness of cult rhetoric, why not use my personal observations to write a response paper in which I show just how reasonable we are in distinguishing mere rhetoric from substance?

Outlining

In addition to this brainstorming, Taylor developed a scratch outline—yet another prewriting strategy—to guide her into the drafting stage of the composing process.

Outline

I. Introduction: Summarize essay and thesis; provide counterthesis.
II. University life as a demonstration of "ethnic" democracies.
III. The emptiness and false promises of self-styled ethnic leaders.
IV. The rejection of "home-grown" cults.
V. Conclusion.

Many word-processing programs offer outlining software that you might want to use in lieu of pen and paper. And there are a number of free online outlining (or mind-mapping) programs; some of these, such as SproutLiner (*http://sproutliner.com/*) and InfoQube (*http://www.infoqube.biz*), offer the convenience of being able to bookmark relevant links within your outline to external sites, or to pages of your own Web-based project. Others, such as FreeMind (*http://freemind.sourceforge.net*), offer the chance to draw connections among complex information groups.

Although Taylor employed brainstorming and a scratch outline to organize her thoughts prior to writing her essay, not everyone uses these prewriting activities. Some students need to go through a series of prewriting activities, while others can dive into a first draft. Nevertheless, the process of discovering the materials and form for an essay includes a search for ideas, a willingness to discard ideas and strategies that don't work, an ability to look at old ideas in a fresh way, and a talent for moving back and forth across a range of composing activities. Rarely does that flash of insight or first draft produce the ideal flow of words resulting in a well-written and well-ordered essay.

DRAFTING

Everyone approaches the composing process differently. There are, however, certain basic principles for this stage; these are discussed in the following section.

Developing the Thesis

Every essay requires a main idea or thesis that holds all your information together. What you seek is not just any idea relevant to the bulk of your topic, but the underlying idea that best expresses your purpose in writing the essay. Your thesis is the controlling idea for the entire essay.

The thesis requires you to take a stand on your topic. It is your reason for wanting to inform or persuade an audience. The noted teacher and scholar Sheridan Baker has expressed nicely this need to take a stand or assume an angle of interpretation: "When you have something to say about *cats,* you have found your underlying idea. You have something to fight about: not just 'Cats,' but 'The cat is really man's best friend.'" Not all thesis statements involve arguments or fights. Nevertheless, you cannot have a thesis unless you have something to demonstrate or prove.

The thesis statement, which normally appears as a single sentence near the beginning of your essay, serves several important functions:

- It introduces the topic to the reader.
- It limits the topic to a single idea.
- It expresses your approach to the topic—the opinion, attitude, or outlook that creates your special angle of interpretation for the topic.
- It may provide the reader with hints about the way the essay will develop.
- It should arouse the reader's interest by revealing your originality and your honest commitment to the topic.

Here is a sample thesis statement by a student:

The automobile—America's metallic monster—takes up important public space, pollutes the environment, and makes people lazy, rude, and overweight.

In this thesis, the writer has staked out a position, limited the topic, and given the reader some idea of how the essay will develop.

Your thesis cannot always be captured in a single sentence. Indeed, professional writers often offer an implied or unstated thesis or articulate a thesis statement that permeates an entire paragraph. Always ask if a thesis hooks you. Do you find it provocative? Do you know where the author is coming from? Does the author offer a map for the entire essay? These are some of the issues to consider as you compose your own thesis sentences.

Writing Introductory Paragraphs

A good introduction should be like a door that entices readers into the world of your essay, arousing their curiosity about the topic and thesis with carefully chosen material and through a variety of techniques. The introduction, normally a single paragraph composed of a few sentences, serves several important functions:

- It introduces the topic.
- It states the writer's attitude toward the subject, normally in the form of a thesis statement.
- It offers readers a guide to the essay.
- It draws readers into the topic through a variety of techniques.

A solid introduction informs, orients, interests, and engages the audience. "Beginnings," wrote the English novelist George Eliot, "are always troublesome." Getting the introduction just right takes effort, considerable powers of invention, and often several revisions. Fortunately, there are special strategies that make effective introductions possible:

- Use a subject-clarification-thesis format. Present the essay's general subject, clarify and explain the topic briefly, and then present your attitude toward the topic in a thesis statement.
- Offer a brief story or incident that sets the stage for your topic and frames your thesis.
- Start with a shocking, controversial, or intriguing opinion.
- Begin with a comparison or contrast.
- Use a quotation or reference to clarify and illustrate your topic and thesis.
- Ask a question or series of questions directed toward establishing your thesis.
- Offer several relevant examples to support your thesis.
- Begin with a vivid description that supports your main idea.
- Cite a statistic or provide data.
- Correct a false assumption.

All these strategies should introduce your topic and state your thesis. They should be relatively brief and should direct the reader into the body of the essay. Finally, they should reveal your perspective and your tone or voice. In each introductory paragraph, the reader—your audience—should sense that you are prepared to address your topic in an honest and revealing manner.

Writing Body Paragraphs

The body is the middle of the essay. Usually, the body consists of a series of paragraphs whose purpose is to satisfy your readers' expectations about the topic and thesis you

presented in the introduction. The body of an essay gives substance, stability, and balance to your thesis. It offers facts, details, explanations, and claims supporting your
main idea.

Body paragraphs reflect your ability to think critically, logically, and carefully about
your topic. They are self-conscious units of expression whose indentations signal a new
main point (or topic sentence) or unified and coherent unit of thought. The contour created
by the series of body paragraphs that you design grows organically from the rhetorical or
composing strategies that you select. As the English critic Herbert Read states in *English
Prose Style,* "As thought takes shape in the mind, it takes *a* shape. . . . There is about good
writing a visual actuality. It exactly reproduces what we should metaphorically call the contour of our thought. . . . The paragraph is the perception of this contour or shape." In other
words, we see in the shape of an essay the shape of our thoughts. The contour created by
the series of body paragraphs proceeds naturally from the material you include and the
main point you use to frame this material in each paragraph.

Effective paragraph development depends on your ability to create a unit of thought
that is *unified* and *coherent,* and that presents ideas that flesh out the topic sentence or
controlling idea for the paragraph, thereby informing or convincing the reader. To achieve
a sense of completeness as you develop body paragraphs, be sure to have enough topic
sentences and sufficient examples or evidence for each key idea. College writers often
have problems writing complete essays with adequately developed body paragraphs.
Remember that topic sentences are relatively general ideas. Your primary task is to make
readers understand what those ideas mean or why they are important. Your secondary
task is to keep readers interested in those central thoughts. The only way to accomplish
these two related goals is by explaining the central ideas through various kinds of evidence
or support.

Choosing Strategies for Development   Different topics and paragraphs lend themselves to
different types of development. These types of rhetorical approaches are essentially special
writing and reasoning strategies designed to support your critical evaluation of a topic or
hypothesis. Among the major rhetorical approaches are description, narration, illustration,
process analysis, comparison and contrast, causal analysis, definition, classification, and
argumentation. Each strategy might very well serve as your dominant approach to a topic.
Alternatively, your essay might reflect a variety of methods. Remember, however, that any
blending of rhetorical strategies should not be a random sampling of approaches but should
contribute to your overall point.

Description   Good descriptive writing is often your best tool for explaining your observations about objects, people, scenes, and events. Simply, description is the creation of a
picture using words. It is the translation of what the writer sees into what the writer wants
the reader to imagine. Description has many applications in academic courses. For example,
for a psychology course, you might need to describe the behavior of an autistic child. At an
archaeological dig or site, you might need to indicate accurately how a section of the exca-
vated area looks. In a botany course, you might need to describe in detail a particular plant.

Effective description depends on several characteristics:

- It conveys ideas through images that appeal to our various senses: sight, hearing,
  touch, smell, and taste.
- It selects and organizes details carefully in a clearly identifiable spatial ordering—left
  to right, top to bottom, near to far, and so forth.

- It creates a dominant impression, a special mood or feeling.
- It is objective or subjective depending on the writer's purpose, the demands of an assignment, or the expectations of an audience.

In the following paragraph from her book *Spanish Harlem,* Patricia Cayo Sexton captures the sights, sounds, and rhythms of life in New York's East Harlem:

> Later, when the children return from school, the sidewalks and streets will jump with activity. Clusters of men, sitting on orange crates on the sidewalks, will play checkers or cards. The women will sit on the stoop, arms folded, and watch the young at play; and the young men, flexing their muscles, will look for some adventure. Vendors, ringing their bells, will hawk hot dogs, orange drinks, ice cream; and the caressing but often jarring noise of honking horns, music, children's games, and casual quarrels, whistles, singing, will go on late into the night. When you are in it you don't notice the noise, but when you stand away and listen to a taped conversation, the sound suddenly appears as a background roar. This loud stimulation of the senses may produce some of the emotionalism of the poor.

Narration   Telling stories—or narration—is a basic pattern of organizing your thoughts. You employ narration on a daily basis—to tell what happened at work, in the cafeteria, or on Saturday night. Narration is also essential to many forms of academic writing, ranging from history, to sociology, to science. When planning and writing narration, keep in mind the following guidelines:

1. Present the events of your narration in a logical and coherent order. Make certain that you link events through the use of appropriate transitional words.
2. Select the narrative details carefully in order to suit the purpose of the essay. Narrate only those aspects of the event that serve to illustrate and support your thesis.
3. Choose a point of view and perspective suitable for your topic and audience. Narrative point of view may be either first or third person. A first-person narrative (*I, we*) is suitable for stories about yourself. A third-person narrative (*he, she, it, they*) conveys stories about others. The narrative perspective you use depends on your audience and purpose. Obviously, you would use a different perspective and tone in narrating a laboratory experiment than you would narrating a soccer match you participated in.
4. Use dialogue, if appropriate to your topic, to add realism and interest to your narrative.
5. Limit the scope of the event you are narrating, and bring it to a suitable conclusion or climax.

When narration is used for informational or expository purposes, the story makes a point, illustrates a principle, or explains something. In other words, in expository narration, the event tends to serve as evidence in support of your thesis.

Here is a sample student paragraph based on narration:

Like most little girls I thought it would be very grown up to get my hair done in a beauty parlor instead of by my mother or older sister. For more than a month I cried and badgered my family. Finally, after hearing enough of my whining, my mother gave in and made an appointment for me. At the beauty parlor, I sat with my mother and a few older women, naively waiting for my transformation into another Shirley Temple.

Finally the hairdresser placed me in a chair and began to chop a mass of hair onto the floor and then subject me to a burning sensation as rollers wound my remaining hair tight. The result was a classic example of the overworked permanent. At home later that day, I tried washing and rewashing my hair to remove the tangled mess. It took a week until I would see anyone without a scarf or hat over my head and a month before I could look at someone without feeling that they were making fun of me the minute I turned my back. In a way I feel that such a fruitless journey to the hairdresser actually helped me along the road to adulthood since it was a perfect example of a disappointment that only time and patience, rather than tantrums and senseless worrying, can overcome.

Narration answers the question, What happened? It can be used to tell real or fictional stories, to relate historical events, to present personal experience, or to support an analysis of events. It has broad utility in college as a critical writing skill.

Illustration   To make your paragraph or essay complete—without padding, repetition, or digression—be sure to have sufficient examples or illustrations to support key ideas. Different topics lend themselves to different types of examples or supporting evidence. Here are some types of illustration that will help you write well-developed paragraphs and essays:

- *Fact:* The Supreme Court ordered the desegregation of public schools in 1964.
- *Statistic:* A majority of schools in San Diego that were once 90 percent black are now almost 45 percent white.
- *Example:* One example of the success of San Diego's integration effort is its magnet schools.
- *Personal experience:* I attended the new computer science magnet school from 1996 to 1998. . . .
- *Quotation:* According to the *Phi Delta Kappan,* "On the first day of Los Angeles's mandatory desegregation program, 17,700 out of the total of 40,000 were not on the bus."
- *Process:* With the magnet concept, a school first creates a special theme and emphasis for its curriculum. Then it . . . .
- *Comparison and contrast:* In contrast, when Los Angeles announced its forced busing plan, an estimated 15.1 percent of the white population moved out of the system into private schools.
- *Case study:* Jamie, an eighth-grader, had seen very few black students at the Math-Science Center prior to the implementation of San Diego's desegregation plan. . . .

Illustrations develop your paragraph beyond the topic sentence. Such illustrations or examples may be short or extended. However, to make sure that your paragraphs are complete and properly developed, watch out for weak or poorly presented illustrations. For every main idea or topic sentence in a paragraph, use specific supporting evidence that sufficiently proves or amplifies your point. If you do not have the right evidence in the proper amount, your paragraph and essay will be underdeveloped, as in the following case:

The concept of choice does seem to appeal to students. On the first day of San Diego's new plan, the only people who were absent from the programs who had volunteered were those who were sick.

This two-sentence paragraph has promise but does not follow through with the main idea adequately. The concept at the heart of the topic sentence is clearer and more complete in the revised version:

The concept of choice does seem to appeal to San Diego's parents and students. On the first day of San Diego's new plan, the only people who were absent from the program who had volunteered were those who were sick. In contrast, on the first day of Los Angeles's mandatory desegregation program, 17,700 out of the total of 40,000 were not on the bus, according to the *Phi Delta Kappan*. Moreover, when Los Angeles announced its busing plan, an estimated 15.1 percent of the white population moved out of the district or into a private school. In San Diego, there was virtually no "white flight."

In the revision, the student chose to use contrasting evidence, highly specific in nature, to provide adequate support for the topic sentence. Other details and illustrative strategies might have been selected. In selecting illustrative material, you should always ask, Are there other examples that are more lively, specific, concrete, revealing, or interesting? It is not enough to just present examples. Illustration should be as effective as possible.

    Process Analysis   When you describe how something works, how something is assembled, how something is done, or how something happens, you are explaining or analyzing a process. The complexity of your explanation will depend on how complex the process itself is, how detailed you want your explanation to be, and what you want your audience to be able to do or understand as a result of reading your explanation. Are you providing relatively simple how-to-do-it instructions for a relatively simple task, or are you attempting to explain a complicated laboratory experiment or computer program? The explanation of a process can make demands on your analytical and problem-solving abilities because you have to break down operations into component parts and actions. Process analysis always involves the systematic presentation of step-by-step or stage-by-stage procedures. You must show *how* the steps or parts in a process lead to its completion or resolution.

    The explanation of processes is relevant to many college courses. Such topics as the stages of economic growth, Hobbes's view of the evolution of the state, the origins of the city, the development of the English lyric, the phenomenon of photosynthesis, and the history of abstract art could benefit from process analysis. Often process analysis can be combined with other writing strategies or even be subordinated to a more dominant writing strategy like narration, to which it bears a certain resemblance.

    As with all other forms of mature and effective writing, you must assess your audience when writing process papers. You must decide whether you primarily want to inform or to give directions. When you give directions, you normally can assume that your audience wants to learn to do what you tell them about. If your primary purpose is to inform, you must assess the degree of interest of general readers and approach your subject from an objective perspective. Remember that there are natural, physical, mechanical, technical, mental, and historical types of processes. Certain topics might cut across these types, yet in each instance, your purpose is to direct the reader in how to do something or to inform the reader about the nature of the process.

    Your analysis of a process can occur at the paragraph level, or it can control the development of an entire essay. Note how Laurence J. Peter, author of the book *The Peter Prescription,* uses process to structure the following paragraph:

If you are inexperienced in relaxation techniques, begin by sitting in a comfortable chair with your feet on the floor and your hands resting easily in your lap.

Close your eyes and breathe evenly, deeply, and gently. As you exhale each breath let your body become more relaxed. Starting with one hand direct your attention to one part of your body at a time. Close your fist and tighten the muscles of your forearm. Feel the sensation of tension in your muscles. Relax your hand and let your forearm and hand become completely limp. Direct all your attention to the sensation of relaxation as you continue to let all tension leave your hand and arm. Continue this practice once or several times each day, relaxing your other hand and arm, your legs, back, abdomen, chest, neck, face, and scalp. When you have this mastered and can relax completely, turn your thoughts to scenes of natural tranquility from your past. Stay with your inner self as long as you wish, whether thinking of nothing or visualizing only the loveliest of images. Often you will become completely unaware of your surroundings. When you open your eyes you will find yourself refreshed in mind and body.

Peter establishes his relationship and his purpose with his audience in the very first sentence, and then offers step-by-step procedures that move readers toward a full understanding of the process. Remember that you are the expert when writing about a process and that you have to think carefully about the degree of knowledge that your audience shares.

To develop a process paper, follow these guidelines:

1. Select an appropriate topic.
2. Decide whether your primary purpose is to direct or explain.
3. Determine the knowledge gap between you and your audience.
4. Explain necessary equipment or define special terms.
5. Organize paragraphs in a complete sequence of steps.
6. Explain each step clearly and completely.
7. State results or outcomes.

Numerous subjects lend themselves to process analysis. You must decide, especially for a particular course, which topic is most appropriate and which topic you know or want to learn about the most.

Comparison and Contrast   Comparison and contrast is an analytical method organizing thought to show similarities and differences between two persons, places, things, or ideas. Comparing and contrasting comes naturally to us. If, for example, you must decide on which candidate to vote for, you might compare the party affiliations, records, and positions on issues of both candidates to find the one who best meets your expectations. Comparison and contrast serves three useful purposes in writing:

- To evaluate the relative worth or performance of two things by comparing them point for point
- To increase understanding of two familiar things by exploring them for significant similarities and differences
- To explain something unfamiliar by comparing it with something familiar

The organization of comparison-and-contrast paragraphs and essays is fairly specialized and somewhat more prescribed than other methods of writing. The following are some basic guidelines for preparing comparison-and-contrast papers.

Most important, limit your comparison to only two subjects (from here on we'll refer to them as A and B). If you attempt to work with more, you may find that your writing becomes confused. In addition, subjects A and B should be from the same category of things. You would do better, for example, to compare two jazz pianists than to compare a jazz pianist and Dixieland jazz as a whole. Moreover, there needs to be a *purpose* for your comparison. Unless you explain your purpose, the comparison, which might otherwise be structurally sound, will ultimately seem meaningless.

The organization of comparison-and-contrast papers generally follows two basic patterns, or methods: the *block method* and the *alternating method*. The block method presents all material on subject A and then all material on subject B. With the block method, each subtopic must be the same for both subjects. The alternating method presents all the material on each subtopic together, analyzing these subtopics in an AB, AB, AB pattern. Although there is no hard-and-fast rule, the alternating method is probably the best choice for most essays in order to avoid the standard pitfalls of the block method. Unless you are an experienced writer, using the block method can lead to an insufficiently developed paper, with some subtopics receiving more attention than others. It can also lead to a paper that seems like two separate essays, with a big chunk about subject A followed by a disconnected chunk about subject B. Whether you are using the block or the alternating method, follow through in an orderly manner, stating clearly the main thesis or reason for establishing the comparison, and providing clear transitions as you move from idea to idea.

Consider the following paragraph, written by a student, John Shin:

The story of Noah and the Great Flood is probably the best known story of a deluge in the Mesopotamian Valley. However, there are several other accounts of a large flood in the valley. Of these, the Akkadian story of Utnapishtim, as told by Gilgamesh, is the most interesting due to its similarities to the biblical story of Noah. Utnapishtim is a king who is forewarned of the coming of a great flood. He is advised to build an ark and does so. After many days the waters recede and Utnapishtim exits the ark and is turned into a god. The stories of Noah and Utnapishtim bear a striking resemblance in several parts: a god or gods cause a flood to punish men and women; arks, of certain dimensions, are built; animals are taken on board; birds are released to find land; and the arks come to rest on mountains. These parallels are so striking that many think the two to be the same tale.

Given the design of this paragraph, we can assume that Shin could develop body paragraphs that deal in detail with each of the key resemblances in the order they are mentioned: the coming of the flood, the building of the ark, the animals taken on board, the release of the birds, and the lodging of both arks on mountains. By employing the alternating method, he constructs a well-organized comparative framework for his analysis of the story of Noah and the story of Utnapishtim.

Causal Analysis   Frequently in college writing, you must explain the causes or effects of some event, situation, or phenomenon. This type of investigation is termed *causal analysis*. When you analyze something, you divide it into its logical parts or processes for the purpose of close examination. Thus phenomena as diverse as divorce in America, the Civil War, carcinogens in asbestos, the death of Martin Luther King Jr., or the 2010 earthquake in Haiti can be analyzed in terms of their causes and effects.

Cause-and-effect relationships are part of everyday thinking and living. Why did you select the college you now attend? Why did you stop dating Freddy or Barbara, and what effect has this decision had on your life? Why did the football team lose five straight games? You need causal analysis to explain why something occurred, to predict what will occur, and to make informed choices based on your perceptions. With causal analysis, you cannot simply tell a story, summarize an event, or describe an object or phenomenon. Instead, you must explain the *why* and *what* of a topic. The analysis of causes seeks to explain why a particular condition occurred. The analysis of effects seeks to explain what the consequences or results were, are, or will be.

Causal reasoning is common to writing in many disciplines: history, economics, politics, sociology, literature, science, education, and business, to list a few. Some essays and reports focus on causes, others on effects, and still others on both causes and effects. Sometimes even the simplest sort of causal reasoning based on personal experience does not admit to the complete separation of causes and effects but depends instead on the recognition that causes and effects are interdependent. For example, the following paragraph from a student's sociology paper focuses on a cause-and-effect relationship:

My parents came to New York with the dream of saving enough money to return to Puerto Rico and buy a home with some land and fruit trees. Many Puerto Ricans, troubled by the problem of life on the island, find no relief in migration to New York City. They remain poor, stay in the barrio, are unable to cope with American society and way of life, and experience the destruction of their traditionally close family life. My parents were fortunate. After spending most of their lives working hard, they saved enough to return to the island. Today they tend their orange, lemon, banana, and plantain trees in an area of Puerto Rico called "El Paraíso." It took them most of a lifetime to find their paradise—in their own backyard.

Here the writer blends personal experience with a more objective analysis of causes and effects, presenting the main cause-effect relationship in the first sentence, analyzing typical effects, providing an exception to this conventional effect, and describing the result.

Sometimes you will want to focus exclusively on causes or on effects. For example, in a history course, the topic might be to analyze why World War II occurred, as this student sought to do:

It is popularly accepted that Hitler was the major cause of World War II, but the ultimate causes go much deeper than one personality. There were long-standing German grievances against reparations levied on the nation following its defeat in World War I. Moreover, there were severe economic strains that caused resentment among the German people. Compounding these problems was the French and English reluctance to work out a sound disarmament policy and American noninvolvement in the matter. Finally, there was the European fear that Communism was a much greater danger than National Socialism. All these factors contributed to the outbreak of World War II.

Note that in his attempt to explain fully the causes of an event, the writer goes beyond *immediate* causes, that is, the most evident causes that trigger the event being analyzed. He tries to identify the *ultimate* causes, the deep-rooted reasons that completely explain the problem. In order to present a sound analysis of a problem, you need to be able to trace events logically to their underlying origins. Similarly, you have to engage in strategic thinking about immediate and ultimate effects in order to explain fully an event's results.

Writing about cause-and-effect relationships demands sound critical thinking skills with attention to logic and thorough preparation for the demands of the assignment. To write effective and logical essays of causal analysis, follow these guidelines:

1. Be honest, objective, and reasonable when establishing your thesis. As a critical thinker, you have to avoid prejudices and logical fallacies, including unsupportable claims, broad generalizations and overstatements, and false relationships. (For a discussion of logical fallacies, see pages 158–160.)

2. Distinguish between causes and effects, and decide whether you plan to focus on causes, effects, or both. As a prewriting strategy, draw up a list of causes and a corresponding list of effects. You can then organize your paper around the central causes and effects.
3. Distinguish clearly between immediate and ultimate causes and effects. Explore those causes and effects that best serve the purpose of your paper and your audience's expectations.
4. Provide evidence. Do not rely on simple assertions. Statistics and testimony from reliable authorities are especially effective types of evidence to support your analysis.
5. Try to establish links between causes or effects. Seek a logical sequence of related elements, a chain of causality that helps readers understand the totality of your topic.

Ultimately, there are many ways to write about causes and effects, depending on whether you are looking for explanations, reasons, consequences, connections, results, or any combination of these elements.

Definition   Concepts or general ideas often require careful definition if readers are to make sense of them or make intelligent decisions. Could you discuss supply and demand in economic theory without knowing the concept of the invisible hand? And isn't it best to know what a politician actually believes in before casting your vote? Concepts form the core of any discipline, line of inquiry, or problem. Because concepts are abstract, they may mean different things to different readers. In order to make ourselves understood, we must be able to specify their meaning in a particular context.

There are three types of definition. The simple *lexical* definition, or dictionary definition, is useful when briefly identifying concrete, commonplace, or uncontroversial terms for the reader. Many places, persons, and things can be defined in this manner. The *extended* definition is an explanation that might involve a paragraph or an entire essay. It is frequently used for abstract, complex, or controversial terms. In the *stipulative* definition, you offer a special definition of a term or set limitations on your use of the term. A solid definition, whether it is lexical, extended, or stipulative, involves describing the essential nature and characteristics of a concept that distinguish it from related ideas.

Consider the following paragraph by a student, Geeta Berrera:

The degree of loneliness that we feel can range from the mild or temporary case to a severe state which may eventually lead to depression or other psychological disorders. Being able to recognize the signs and signals of loneliness may help you to avoid it in the future. Do you find yourself unable to communicate with others? If so, you might be lonely. Do you find it difficult to put your faith in other human beings? If so, then you are setting up a situation that may be conducive to loneliness because you are preventing yourself from becoming too close to another person. Do you find yourself spending great amounts of time alone on a regular basis? Do you find that you are never invited to parties or other social events? Are you unable to love or care for another human being because you are afraid of permanent responsibilities and commitments? These are all signs and signals of either loneliness or situations that may eventually lead to loneliness. Loneliness is the feeling of sadness or grief experienced by a person at the realization that he or she lacks the companionship of other people.

Notice how Berrera introduces and emphasizes the central concept—loneliness—that is defined in this paragraph. She adds to the definition through a series of questions and answers—a strategy that permits her to analyze the qualities or manifestations of the concept. These symptoms serve as examples that reveal what is distinctive or representative about the condition of loneliness.

Definition can be used for several purposes. It may explain a difficult concept like phenomenology or a lesser-known activity like cricket. Definition can be used to identify and illustrate the special nature of a person, object, or abstract idea.

Classification Classification is a mode of critical thinking and writing based on the division of a concept into groups and subgroups, and the examination of important elements within these groups. We have generalized ideas of classes of objects that help us organize and thereby understand the world. Many of these concepts lend themselves to classification. You think and talk frequently about types of college teachers, types of cars, types of boyfriends or girlfriends, and types of movies or music. When registering for courses, you know that English is in the humanities, psychology in the social sciences, and geology in the physical sciences; you select these courses on the basis of consistent classification principles, perhaps distribution requirements or the demands of your major. What you are doing is thinking about concepts within a class, sorting out and organizing information, and often evaluating possible alternatives. Classification, in short, is a basic mode of critical thought.

As a pattern of writing, classification enables you to make sense of large and potentially complex concepts. You divide a concept into groups and subgroups, and you classify elements within categories. Assume, for instance, that your politics professor asks for an analysis of the branches of the U.S. federal government. You divide the federal government into the executive, legislative, and judicial branches, and, depending on your purpose, you subdivide even further into departments, agencies, and so forth. Then, according to some consistent principle or thesis—say, a critical look at the erosion of the division of powers—you develop information for each category reflecting common characteristics. Essentially, if you classify in a rigorous and logical way, you sort out for analysis the parts and ideas within a scheme, progressing from general to specific in your treatment of the topic.

In developing a classification essay, you also have to determine the *system* of classification that works best for the demands of the assignment. The system you select would depend to an extent on your reader's expectations and the nature of the subject. Imagine that you have been asked to write an essay on sports by a physiology teacher, a psychology teacher, or a sociology teacher. Your system might be types of sports injuries for the physiology professor, behavior patterns of tennis players for your psychology professor, or levels of violence and aggression in team sports for your sociology professor. For a broad concept like sports, there are many possible classificatory systems depending on the purpose of your paper.

Although several classification and division strategies might be appropriate for any given concept, the following guidelines should be reviewed and applied for any classification essay:

1. Think about the controlling principle for your classification. *Why* are you classifying the concept? *What* is the significance? Create a thesis statement that gives your reader a clear perspective on your classification scheme.
2. Divide the subject into major categories and subdivide categories consistently. Make certain that you isolate all important categories and that these categories do not overlap excessively.

3. Arrange the classification scheme in an effective, emphatic order—as a chronology, in spatial terms, in order of importance, or from simple to complex.
4. Present and analyze each category in a clear sequence, proceeding through the categories until the classification scheme is complete.
5. Define or explain any difficult concepts within each category, providing relevant details and evidence.
6. Combine classification with other appropriate writing strategies—comparison and contrast, process analysis, definition, and so forth.

Examine the following student paragraph:

To many people, fishing is finding a "fishy-looking" spot, tossing a hooked worm into the water, and hoping that a hungry fish just happens to be nearby. Anyone who has used this haphazard method can attest to the fact that failures usually outnumber successes. The problem with the "bait and wait" method is that it is very limited. The bait has less chance of encountering a fish than it would if it were presented in different areas of water. A more intelligent approach to fishing is to use the knowledge that at any given moment fish can be in three parts of a lake. Assuming that a lake has fish, anglers will find them on the surface, in the middle, or on the bottom of the lake. Fishing each of these areas involves the use of a separate technique. By fishing the surface, fishing the middle, or fishing the bottom, you greatly increase the chances of catching a fish.

This example is the student's introductory paragraph to a classification essay that blends description, process analysis, comparison and contrast, and the use of evidence to excellent effect. From the outset, however, the reader knows that this will be a classification essay.

Argumentation   Argumentation is a form of critical thinking in which you try to convince an audience to accept your position on a topic or persuade members of this audience to act in a certain way. In a sense, everything is an argument, for much of what you read and write, see and hear, is designed to elicit a desired response. Whether reading texts, viewing various media forms, or listening to the spoken word (especially of politicians), you know that just about anything is potentially debatable.

Argumentation in writing, however, goes beyond ordinary disagreements. With an argumentative essay, your purpose is to convince or persuade readers in a logical, reasonable, and appealing way. In other words, with formal argumentation, you must distinguish mere personal opinion from opinions based on reasons derived from solid evidence. An argumentative essay has special features and even step-by-step processes that will be treated in greater detail in Chapter 3. For now, it is worth noting that solid argumentative writing can combine many of the forms and purposes that have been discussed in this chapter. Your understanding of such forms and purposes of discourse as narration, illustration, analysis, and comparison and contrast, and the ways these strategies can combine in powerful ways, will help you compose solid argumentative essays.

Above all, with argumentation, you must develop what Virginia Woolf called "some fierce attachment to an idea." Once you commit yourself to a viewpoint on a topic or issue, you will find it easy to bring an argumentative edge to your writing. Consider the following excerpt from a well-known essay by Caroline Bird that begins with the provocative title "College Is a Waste of Time and Money":

A great majority of our 9 million college students are in school not because they want to be or because they want to learn. They are there because it has become the thing to do or because college is a pleasant place to be; because it's the only way they can get parents or taxpayers to support them without working at a job they don't like; because Mother wanted them to go, or some other reason entirely irrelevant to the course of studies for which college is supposedly organized.

Clearly, Bird's claim has that argumentative edge you encounter in essays designed to convince readers of a particular viewpoint or position on an issue. Do you agree or disagree with Bird's claim? How would you respond to her assertions? What evidence would you provide to support your claim?

Argumentation is a powerful way to tap into the aspirations, values, and conduct of your audience. It makes demands on readers and writers to do something, believe something, or even become somebody different—say, a more tolerant person or a more active citizen. True, argument can provoke conflict, but it can also resolve it. In fact, many experts today emphasize the value of argument in solving problems and defusing or managing conflicts.

At the outset of any argument process, you must recognize that you have a problem to solve and decisions to make. Problem solving often is at the heart of argumentation; it is a process in which situations, issues, and questions are analyzed and debated, and decisions arrived at. The basic steps to problem solving in argumentation are these:

1. Define and analyze the problem. Examine all available information to identify the problem precisely.
2. Interpret the facts and review alternative approaches.
3. Make a claim or a decision—that is, assert the best course of action.
4. Implement the decision in order to persuade or convince your audience that the problem has been addressed and solved.
5. Evaluate the outcome in follow-up documents.

At times, it will be hard to diagnose a problem and find solutions for it. At other times, there is no ideal solution to a problem. Argumentation is not a simple academic exercise but rather an indispensable tool in personal and professional situations. It is indispensable in addressing increasingly complex political, economic, social, and technological trends on both a domestic and a global scale. Moreover, argument can produce ethically constructive and socially responsible results. Argument makes special demands on a writer that will be treated comprehensively in Chapter 3.

Writing End Paragraphs

If an essay does not have a strong, appropriate ending, it may leave the reader feeling confused or dissatisfied, with the sense that the intention and promises built up in earlier parts of the essay have not been fulfilled. In contrast, an effective closing paragraph leaves the reader with the impression that the essay is complete and satisfying.

The techniques that follow permit you to end your essay emphatically and with grace:

- Use a full-circle pattern by echoing or repeating a phrase, idea, or detail that you presented in your introductory paragraph.
- State your conclusions, proofs, or theories based on the facts and supporting ideas of the essay. This strategy works especially well in papers for social science, science, and philosophy courses.
- Show the outcome or effects of the facts and ideas of the essay.

- Suggest a solution as a way to clarify your position on the problem you have discussed.
- Ask a question that sums up the main point of the essay.
- Offer an anecdote, allusion, or lighthearted point that sums up your thesis.
- Use a quotation that supports your main point or illuminates an aspect of the topic.

Other basic ways to end an essay include restating your thesis and main points, calling for action, providing a final summary evaluation, and looking at future consequences based on the essay's analysis or argument. A closing, like your introduction, should be brief. It is your one last attempt at clarity, your one last chance to illuminate your topic.

Student Essay

Here is the essay that Jamie Taylor wrote in response to Schlesinger's "The Cult of Ethnicity." Consider the strategies that she used to make her composing process a success.

Jamie Taylor
Humanities 101, sec. 008
Professor Fred Segal
4 November 2012

Cultist Behavior or Doltish Behavior?

The introductory paragraph presents Schlesinger's main argument, amplifies Schlesinger's inferred claims, and then presents the writer's counterargument.

In Schlesinger's "The Cult of Ethnicity," the author warns that there are forces at work within our nation that undermine our principles of democracy. These forces come in the guise of individuals and groups who claim that they know what's right for the people whom they represent. Although he doesn't mention them all specifically, one can infer he means that certain leaders from the African American community, the Latino community, the Native American community, the Asian community, and so forth are advocating strong identification within groups to keep their identities alive since they claim Eurocentric culture has had a history of stealing and suppressing their own historic roots. But Schlesinger seems to fear that only divisiveness can result. In this regard, he does not give the individual enough credit. Rather than have a paternalistic attitude about what he fears these groups are doing, he should give more credit to the members of these groups to be able to discern which messages regarding ethnicity to accept as being benign and which to reject as being downright silly.

Take, for example, the many clubs in the average college or university. Nearly every ethnic group is represented by one of these organizations. For example, my university has many groups that represent African Americans, Latinos, Asians, Native Americans, even subgroups like the Korean Society, the Chinese Student Association, and so on. Belonging to these groups gives students a healthy place to socialize, discuss common areas of interest and concern, and assist with community outreach. For example, many of these clubs sponsor programs to give demonstrations of cultural traditions such as cooking,

FIGURE 2.1 During the Puerto Rican Parade, participants
share some cultural traditions and fashions with the community.

dance, clothing, and so on to civic and business groups. They
also assist the needy in gaining access to social services, particularly for shut-ins and the elderly who may not speak English.
Also, there is strength in numbers, and the fact that these clubs
are popular attests to the fact that they tolerate a range of ideas
so that no one "ideology" is promoted over another. Besides, if
that were to happen, it is the right of the organization to vote a
person out of office or membership. To say that these clubs promote divisiveness would be like saying that the Newman Society
for Catholic students or Hillel House for Jewish students promotes religious intolerance.

Second, self-styled leaders of various racial and ethnic
groups—in their efforts to be divisive—actually help people to
see through their rhetoric, or at least, to apply only that which is
reasonable and reject that which is intolerable. Because of today's media, such leaders cannot "hide" their views and thus
can become their own worst enemies when presenting them in
front of a national audience. For example, Louis Farrakhan has

The first body
paragraph presents
Taylor's first point
supported with
evidence and
examples.

FIGURE 2.2 On June 9, 2009, a security guard at the
Holocaust museum in Washington, D.C. was shot and killed
by a white supremacist and known Holocaust denier who
entered the museum wielding a rifle and began shooting.

The second point offers a unique slant on divisive ethnic and racial leaders and the ability of Americans to reject their claims. Again, specific examples and evidence buttress Taylor's argument.

not only alienated Jewish individuals owing to his open anti-Semitism, and many among the gay population for his antigay sentiments, but many African Americans as well, particularly women, who often condemn him for his patriarchal views regarding the family and society. A simple proof of his lack of power is the fact that he has been presenting these antidemocratic ideals for decades now, and there is little evidence that anyone is listening to them. Another example is the late Rabbi Meyer Kahane, who advocated the expulsion of all Arabs from Israel. An open opponent of democracy, he was condemned by Jewish leaders in the United States to the point where he was shunned from any discussion regarding religious issues.

The writer's third and final point encompasses a variety of "antidemocratic" groups and rejects their "postures."

Finally, one can feel confident that even within the margins of mainstream white America, cultist groups are their own worst enemy. Take, for example, the various groups of survivalists (primarily white Americans), white extremists and separatists, antigay groups, and radical anti-abortionists. The philosophy and tactics of these organizations are condemned by the vast majority of Americans owing to their antidemocratic postures, not to mention their often violent, even murderous activities. They may capture the headlines for a while, but they will never capture the hearts of Americans so long as we stay true to the "measures and laws" that Washington spoke of in his discussion with John Adams.

In conclusion, the open democratic society we have created is just too strong a force to be weakened or undermined by "romantic ideologies" or "unscrupulous con men" as Schlesinger puts it. Mr. Schlesinger has little to worry about. Just look around your school or university cafeteria. There's no white section or Latino section or Asian section: Nowadays, it's just one big American section.

The conclusion returns to Schlesinger, while recapitulating Taylor's main points.

REVISING

Revising—the rethinking and rewriting of material—takes place during every stage of the composing process. It is integral to the quest for clarity and meaning. "Writing and rewriting are a constant search for what one's saying," declares celebrated American author John Updike. Similarly, the famous essayist E. B. White admits, "I rework a lot to make it clear." If these two great prose stylists revise material in order to seek clarity for their ideas, then you too should adopt the professional attitude that you can improve what you first say or think and what you first put down on paper. In fact, one trait that distinguishes experienced from inexperienced writers is that the experienced writers understand fully the need to revise.

Revision is an art. It is the only way to make your writing match the vision of what you want to accomplish. Whether at word, sentence, paragraph, or essay level, you should develop a repertoire of choices that will permit you to solve writing problems and sharpen your ideas. You might also share your draft with another reader who can let you know what is or is not working and give you suggestions for improvement. To make the process of revision worthwhile, you should ask yourself the following questions during your prewriting and drafting activities (you can also give these questions to your reader):

- Is the essay long enough (or too long) to meet the demands of the assignment?
- Is the topic suitable for the assignment?
- Do you have a clear thesis statement?
- Does your writing make sense? Are you communicating with your reader instead of just with yourself?
- Have you included everything that is important to the development of your thesis or argument?
- Is there anything you should discard?
- Do you offer enough examples or evidence to support your key ideas?
- Have you ordered and developed paragraphs logically?
- Do you have a clear beginning, middle, and end?

Once you have answered these questions, you will be able to judge the extent to which you have to revise your first draft.

Proofreading

Proofreading is part of the revision process. You do not have a final copy until you have carefully checked your essay for mistakes and inconsistencies. Proofreading differs from the sort of revision that moves you from an initial draft to subsequent versions of an essay in that it does not offer the opportunity to make major changes in content or organization. It does give you a last chance to correct typos and other minor errors that arise from carelessness, haste, or inaccuracy during the writing process.

When you proofread, do so word by word and line by line. Concentrate on spelling, punctuation, grammar, mechanics, and paragraph form. Read each sentence aloud—from the computer screen or a printed hard copy. If something sounds or looks wrong to you, consult a handbook, dictionary, or other reference work. Then make corrections accordingly.

Here are some basic guidelines for proofreading your essay:

1. Check the title. Are words capitalized properly?
2. Check all words in the essay that should be capitalized.
3. Check the spelling of any word you are uncertain about.
4. Check the meaning of any word you think you might have misused.
5. Check to see if you have unintentionally omitted or repeated any words.
6. Check paragraph form. Have you indented each paragraph?
7. Check to make certain you have smooth, grammatically correct sentences. This is your last chance to eliminate awkward and grammatically incorrect sentences.
8. Check to make sure your paper follows your professor's formatting guidelines, such as appropriate margins, font size, and documentation style (see Chapters 15 and 16 for more on documentation).

Responding to Editorial Comments

Even when you submit what you *think* is the final version of your essay, your teacher might not agree that the essay has reached its best possible form. Teachers are experienced in detecting essays' strengths and weaknesses, pinpointing mistakes, and suggesting how material can be improved. Their comments are not attacks; they do want you to pay attention to them, to recognize and correct errors, and possibly to revise your essay once again—most likely for a higher grade. If you receive editorial comment in an objective manner and respond to it constructively, you will become a more effective writer.

When reading your essays, your instructor will use standard correction symbols that appear in English handbooks. He or she will make additional comments in the margins and compose an overall assessment of the paper at the end. Any worthwhile comment on your paper will blend supportive observations with constructive criticism. Often your instructor will offer concrete suggestions for revision. When you receive a graded paper, you typically are expected to make the necessary revisions and either add it to your portfolio or resubmit the essay.

Ultimately, refinement is integral to the entire writing process. From reading materials that you confront at the outset and respond to in various ways, you move through many composing stages to create a finished product. In *The Field of Vision,* the American novelist and critic Wright Morris refers to the important task of refinement that confronts the writer: "By raw material, I mean that comparatively crude ore that has not yet been processed by the imagination—what we refer to as *life,* or as experience, in contrast to art. By technique I mean the way the artist smelts this material down for human consumption."

Your best writing is the result of this smelting process, which involves the many strategies covered in this introduction that are designed to help you acquire greater control over the art of critical reading and writing. Donald M. Murray's essay "The Maker's Eye," starting on page 109, offers one writer's summation of the stages of the revision process.

A Portfolio on Writing and Communication

Leave Your Name at the Border

Manuel Muñoz

Manuel Muñoz (b. 1972) grew up in Dinuba, California, a small town close to Fresno. Muñoz attended Harvard University (1990–1993) and received an MFA in creative writing from Cornell University. Subsequently he worked for the publisher Houghton Mifflin in Boston and for Grand Central Publishing in New York City. He has written two award-winning collections of short stories, Zigzagger *(2003) and* The Faith Healer of Olive Avenue *(2007). Muñoz currently teaches creative writing at the University of Arizona in Tucson. In the following essay, published in the* New York Times *on August 1, 2007, Muñoz interrogates the meanings of names—in English and Spanish.*

At the Fresno airport, as I made my way to the gate, I heard a name over the   1
intercom. The way the name was pronounced by the gate agent made me want to see what she looked like. That is, I wanted to see whether she was Mexican. Around Fresno, identity politics rarely deepen into exacting terms, so to say "Mexican" means, essentially, "not white." The slivered self-identifications Chicano, Hispanic, Mexican-American and Latino are not part of everyday life in the Valley. You're either Mexican or you're not. If someone wants to know if

you were born in Mexico, they'll ask. Then you're From Over There—de alla. And leave it at that.

2   The gate agent, it turned out, was Mexican. Well-coiffed, in her 30s, she wore foundation that was several shades lighter than the rest of her skin. It was the kind of makeup job I've learned to silently identify at the mall when I'm with my mother, who will say nothing about it until we're back in the car. Then she'll point to the darkness of her own skin, wondering aloud why women try to camouflage who they are.

3   I watched the Mexican gate agent busy herself at the counter, professional and studied. Once again, she picked up the microphone and, with authority, announced the name of the missing customer: "Eugenio Reyes, please come to the front desk."

4   You can probably guess how she said it. Her Anglicized pronunciation wouldn't be unusual in a place like California's Central Valley. I didn't have a Mexican name there either: I was an instruction guide.

5   When people ask me where I'm from, I say Fresno because I don't expect them to know little Dinuba. Fresno is a booming city of nearly 500,000 these days, with a diversity—white, Mexican, African-American, Armenian, Hmong and Middle Eastern people are all well represented—that shouldn't surprise anyone. It's in the small towns like Dinuba that surround Fresno that the awareness of cultural difference is stripped down to the interactions between the only two groups that tend to live there: whites and Mexicans. When you hear a Mexican name spoken in these towns, regardless of the speaker's background, it's no wonder that there's an "English way of pronouncing it."

6   I was born in 1972, part of a generation that learned both English and Spanish. Many of my cousins and siblings are bilingual, serving as translators for those in the family whose English is barely functional. Others have no way of following the Spanish banter at family gatherings. You can tell who falls into which group: Estella, Eric, Delia, Dubina, Melanie.

7   It's intriguing to watch "American" names begin to dominate among my nieces and nephews and second cousins, as well as with the children of my hometown friends. I am not surprised to meet 5-year-old Brandon or Kaitlyn. Hardly anyone questions the incongruity of matching these names with last names like Trujillo or Zepeda. The English-only way of life partly explains the quiet erasure of cultural difference that assimilation has attempted to accomplish. A name like Kaitlyn Zepeda doesn't completely obscure her ethnicity, but the half-step of her name, as a gesture, is almost understandable.

8   Spanish was and still is viewed with suspicion: Always the language of the vilified illegal immigrant, it segregated schoolchildren into English-only and bilingual programs; it defined you, above all else, as part of a lower class. Learning English, though, brought its own complications. It was simultaneously the language of the white population and a path toward the richer, expansive identity of "American." But it took getting out of the Valley for me to understand that "white" and "American" were two very different things.

Something as simple as saying our names "in English" was our unwittingly 9
complicit gesture of trying to blend in. Pronouncing Mexican names correctly
was never encouraged. Names like Daniel, Olivia and Marco slipped right into the
mutability of the English language.

I remember a school ceremony at which the mathematics teacher, a white 10
man, announced the names of Mexican students correctly and caused some
confusion, if not embarrassment. Years later we recognized that he spoke in
deference to our Spanish-speaking parents in the audience, caring teacher
that he was.

These were difficult names for a non-Spanish speaker: Araceli, Nadira, Luis (a 11
beautiful name when you glide the u and the i as you're supposed to). We had
been accustomed to having our birth names altered for convenience. Concepcion
was Connie. Ramon was Raymond. My cousin Esperanza was Hope—but her
name was pronounced "Hopie" because any Spanish speaker would automatically
pronounce the e at the end.

Ours, then, were names that stood as barriers to a complete embrace of an 12
American identity, simply because their pronunciations required a slip into
Spanish, the otherness that assimilation was supposed to erase. What to do
with names like Amado, Lucio or Elida? There are no English "equivalents,"
no answer when white teachers asked, "What does your name mean?" when
what they really wanted to know was "What's the English one?" So what you
heard was a name butchered beyond recognition, a pronunciation that pointed
the finger at the Spanish language as the source of clunky sound and ugly
rhythm.

My stepfather, from Ojos de Agua, Mexico, jokes when I ask him about the 13
names of Mexicans born here. He deliberately stumbles over pronunciations,
imitating our elders who have difficulty with Bradley and Madelyn. "Ashley
Sanchez. Tu crees?" He wonders aloud what has happened to the "nombres del
rancho"—traditional Mexican names that are hardly given anymore to children
born in the States: Heraclio, Madaleno, Otilia, Dominga.

My stepfather's experience with the Anglicization of his name—Antonio 14
to Tony—ties into something bigger than learning English. For him, the erasure of his name was about deference and subservience. Becoming Tony
gave him a measure of access as he struggled to learn English and get more
fieldwork.

This isn't to say that my stepfather welcomed the change, only that he 15
could not put up much resistance. Not changing put him at risk of being
passed over for work. English was a world of power and decisions, of smooth,
uninterrupted negotiation. Clear communication meant you could go unsu-
pervised. Every gesture made toward convincing an employer that English
was on its way to being mastered had the potential to make a season of fieldwork profitable.

It's curious that many of us growing up in Dinuba adhered to the same 16
rules. Although as children of farm workers we worked in the fields at an early
age, we'd also had the opportunity to stay in one town long enough to finish

school. Most of us had learned English early and splintered off into a dual existence of English at school, Spanish at home. But instead of recognizing the need
for fluency in both languages, we turned it into a peculiar kind of battle. English
was for public display. Spanish was for privacy—and privacy quickly turned to
shame.

17   The corrosive effect of assimilation is the displacement of one culture over
another, the inability to sustain more than one way of being. It isn't a code word
for racial and ethnic acculturation only. It applies to needing to belong, of seeing
from the outside and wondering how to get in and then, once inside, realizing
there are always those still on the fringe.

18   When I went to college on the East Coast, I was confronted for the first time
by people who said my name correctly without prompting; if they stumbled,
there was a quick apology and an honest plea to help with the pronunciation. But
introducing myself was painful: already shy, I avoided meeting people because I
didn't want to say my name, felt burdened by my own history. I knew that my
small-town upbringing and its limitations on Spanish would not have been toler-
ated by any of the students of color who had grown up in large cities, in places
where the sheer force of their native languages made them dominant in their
neighborhoods.

19   It didn't take long for me to assert the power of code-switching in public, the
transferring of words from one language to another, regardless of who might be
listening. I was learning that the English language composed new meanings when
its constrictions were ignored, crossed over or crossed out. Language is all about
manipulation, or not listening to the rules.

20   When I come back to Dinuba, I have a hard time hearing my name said
incorrectly, but I have an even harder time beginning a conversation with others
about why the pronunciation of our names matters. Leaving a small town
requires an embrace of a larger point of view, but a town like Dinuba remains
forever embedded in an either/or way of life. My stepfather still answers to
Tony and, as the United States–born children grow older, their Anglicized
names begin to signify who does and who does not "belong"—who was born
here and who is de alla.

21   My name is Manuel. To this day, most people cannot say it correctly, the way
it was intended to be said. But I can live with that because I love the alliteration of
my full name. It wasn't the name my mother, Esmeralda, was going to give me. At
the last minute, my father named me after an uncle I would never meet. My name
was to have been Ricardo. Growing up in Dinuba, I'm certain I would have become
Ricky or even Richard, and the journey toward the discovery of the English
language's extraordinary power in even the most ordinary of circumstances
would probably have gone unlearned.

22   I count on a collective sense of cultural loss to once again swing the names
back to our native language. The Mexican gate agent announced Eugenio Reyes,
but I never got a chance to see who appeared. I pictured an older man, cowboy hat

in hand, but I made the assumption on his name alone, the clash of privileges I imagined between someone de alla and a Mexican woman with a good job in the United States. Would she speak to him in Spanish? Or would she raise her voice to him as if he were hard of hearing?

But who was I to imagine this man being from anywhere, based on his 23 name alone? At a place of arrivals and departures, it sank into me that the currency of our names is a stroke of luck: because mine was not an easy name, it forced me to consider how language would rule me if I allowed it. Yet I discovered that only by leaving. My stepfather must live in the Valley, a place that does not allow that choice, every day. And Eugenio Reyes—I do not know if he was coming or going.

COMPREHENSION

1. In the context of the overall essay, what does Muñoz mean when he writes, "The slivered self-identifications Chicano, Hispanic, Mexican-American and Latino are not part of everyday life in the Valley" (paragraph 1)?
2. According to Muñoz, what is the relationship of names to American identity?
3. Explain what Muñoz means by the "corrosive effect of assimilation" (paragraph 17).

RHETORIC

1. Where does Muñoz integrate words in Spanish into his essay? What is his purpose?
2. Why does Muñoz start his essay with a vignette of his encounter with an airline gate agent? Where does he return to this episode, and what is the effect?
3. Is Muñoz simply stating a thesis or arguing a point? Justify your response.
4. Why does Muñoz introduce so many names in this essay? What is his point, and what is the effect?
5. Explain the ways in which Muñoz uses comparison and contrast to structure large parts of his essay. What other rhetorical strategies can you detect?

WRITING

1. In an essay, explain the ways in which people respond to your first or last name. Use these responses to investigate the cultural importance of names in the United States today.
2. Muñoz speaks of the "collective sense of cultural loss" (paragraph 22) that comes from assimilation. Write an essay in which you analyze this phenomenon in relation to language usage.
3. **Writing an Argument:** Argue for or against the proposition that the "English way of pronouncing" (paragraph 5) should be a standard expectation and requirement in school and work.

NETWORKING
Applying Digital and Multimedia Literacies

How Many of Me? Expand on question 1 above under Writing by researching the cultural significance of your name (first and/or last), or a friend's name, online. What resources did you use, and which source was most helpful, given your specific purpose? Why? You can see how many people share your first or last name—or both—at the Web site *How Many of Me* (*http://howmanyofme.com/*). Why might there be so many or so few people who share your first and/or last name?

Turning the Page on Disaster

Edwidge Danticat

Edwidge Danticat (b. 1969) was born in Port-au-Prince, Haiti. Her father immigrated to New York when she was two years old, and her mother left two years later, leaving Danticat to be raised by an aunt and uncle in a household speaking French and Creole. At the age of twelve, Danticat joined her parents in Brooklyn's large Haitian community. While attending Clara Barton High School, she published her first short story. She was fourteen. "Writing had given me a voice. My silence was destroyed completely." Danticat received a BA in French literature from Barnard College and an MFA in creative writing from Brown University. She is a prolific writer in several genres. Among her better known works are the short story collection Krik? Krak! *(1996); the novel* Farming of Bones *(1998), which received a National Book Award; and a memoir,* Brother, I'm Dying *(2007). Danticat is a vocal advocate for Haitian issues. In the following essay, which appeared in the January 2011 issue of* Good Housekeeping, *Danticat recounts her experiences reading to children in post-earthquake Haiti.*

1   One year ago this month, the world turned upside down for Haiti. An estimated 300,000 people died and 1.5 million became homeless after a 7.0-magnitude earthquake struck the island nation. Thousands of displaced men, women, and children gathered in makeshift camps—tent cities—which over the long, hot months following the quake became more and more of a permanent fixture of the landscape.

2   I am a writer who was born in Haiti 41 years ago. I lived in one of the capital's poorest urban neighborhoods, Bel Air, until I was 12. But I am also a reader whose first memories include being given a copy of Ludwig Bemelmans' *Madeline* by my beloved uncle Joseph when I was 4. That book, with its spunky and industrious

heroine, changed my life. That, and being told traditional Haitian folktales by my aunts and grandmothers, sparked my imagination. My maternal grandmother Grace's approach to catastrophe also marked me strongly as a child. "If there's anything you can do in a bad situation," she used to say, "you should at least try to do it, even if it makes sense to no one else."

I thought of this often while at home in Miami in the days following the earthquake. I flew to Port-au-Prince three weeks later. My cousin Maxo and his 10-year-old son Nozial had died, and three of Maxo's other children had been buried in the rubble of our family house before being rescued. Amid the ruins was a primary school that Maxo's father, my uncle Joseph, had started.   3

On earlier visits to my uncle's school, I had read to the youngest children a few mornings during recess. I read to them in part because I loved reading and loved watching their faces light up as they became enthralled in a good story. But I also read to them because although Haiti has a strong and rich oral storytelling tradition, poor children are not used to being read to. Books are expensive, and many destitute parents have not attended school themselves.   4

In many cases, Haitian children get too much of a different kind of story. During politically volatile periods, it is not unusual for a child to walk past corpses on the street. One Christmas season, schools had to close early due to a kidnapping wave.   5

Enter now an earthquake that Haitians onomatopoetically call goudougoudou because of the way the earth roared when the ground shook. Enter the thousands of children who watched parents, friends, and siblings die, many of whom barely escaped themselves only to lose one or two limbs to agonizing amputations.   6

How, once the immediate needs of food and water and medicine and tents are momentarily met, can these children be comforted?   7

Enter reading. I first heard about Li, Li, Li!—"Read, Read, Read!" in Creole— from Michelle Karshan, an American in Port-au-Prince who, along with her U.S.-based daughters Riva and Caitlin, started the read-aloud program less than a month after the earthquake.   8

Karshan was born in New York City, where she founded a library in an immigration detention center. For the past 15 years, however, she has been living in Haiti, running a prison health program and a project to help deportees from the United States reintegrate into Haitian life.   9

Karshan had once invited me to read at a benefit for the criminal-deportees program, and I had organized a book drive for the program's library. So I was not surprised when she told me that she wanted to start a read-aloud program for kids displaced by the earthquake.   10

With public education nearly nonexistent (only 45 percent of Haiti's children had been enrolled in school before the quake), most parents had to send their children to mediocre private schools that were often expensive. Post-quake, there are even fewer of those schools and fewer families who can afford them.   11

Li, Li, Li!'s readers are Haitians—artists, teachers, students—who travel in pairs and read to 3,000 children a month at 25 displacement camps in Port-au-Prince and other areas, including Croix-des-Bouquets and Léogâne (which was at   12 the quake's epicenter and lost over 80 percent of its buildings). When the readers arrive at a camp, they are mobbed and greeted by the children as if they were rock stars or circus performers.

13   At a camp in Delmas, a suburb of Port-au-Prince, a blue tarp covers a school-yard shaded by a massive almond tree. The boys wear bright yellow tops and maroon pants, and the girls are in plaid jumpers. Given that most of these kids live in small, scorching tents and wash up in public places, they look exceptionally neat, their uniforms creased to perfection with charcoal-fueled irons. The children, ranging in age from 5 to 17, cram into rows of narrow school benches.

14   "Bonjour, Mademoiselle," they shout, greeting 32-year-old Natacha Micourt, one of Li, Li, Li!'s readers. Natacha is a painter who was also working as a freelance typist when the earthquake hit. She was in an upstairs bedroom at her family's con-crete house and was babysitting her 2-year-old niece when the house collapsed on top of them. They ended up in a narrow crevice with half of Natacha's body lodged on top of the child's.

15   Natacha's niece cried through several terrifying aftershocks, then fell asleep, at which point Natacha was convinced that the little girl was dead. "I was sure we were both going to die," Natacha says. "I thought no one would ever find us. There were many aftershocks, and it felt like each one was burying us deeper, pushing us further beneath the ground."

16   In the meantime, her older brother Reginald, a French teacher who also reads for Li, Li, Li!, gathered some neighbors together and began to dig for them. Each time a piece of the rubble was moved, the debris shifted, creating new po tential dangers. After two and a half days under the rubble, Natacha and her niece were freed. Apart from some injuries, they were both all right. After being treated at a mobile clinic, they camped at the houses of other relatives and finally moved in with a family friend whose house had been spared.

17   When Michelle started Li, Li, Li!, the siblings immediately came to mind because Reginald had tutored one of Michelle's daughters in French, and Natacha was interested in engaging children in the arts. The two soon joined a group of six others who'd been picked after some initial training. They were each given a modest, donation-funded salary of $250 U.S. a month (now it is $300) and pic-ture books that had been translated into Creole for the readings. Natacha, who paints dreamlike landscapes and portraits in the bright and colorful Haitian naïf style, loves to read from *The Adventures of Clifford the Big Red Dog*, a book and television character that she is familiar with in part because of her niece. In Natacha's and the children's world, Clifford speaks Haitian Creole, just like they do.

18   At the camp, Natacha reads with a lilting voice and often stops to question the children to see if they are paying attention. Call-and-response is an essential part of Haitian storytelling, and the children delight in it.

19   Natacha's goal is primarily to make the children laugh. "Kids who are now laughing were crying so much after the earthquake," she says. "Many are always reliving the whole thing in their heads, but when I read them a story, all of that disappears for a moment. They become children again."

I am itching to tell a story after Natacha, and end up reading one written by my 20
husband, Fedo, whose company publishes children's books in Creole. *Konpe Chat
ak Konpé Chen: Ala Mize Dous* ("Brother Cat and Brother Dog, What Sweet
Misery!") is based on a Haitian folktale in which a cat learns the true definition of
misery. There is also humor in the story, since the cat, after hearing a disappointed
honey seller declare that she is miserable over a broken bottle of honey, mistakenly
thinks that "misery" might be a bottle of honey. For children who are just learning
new ways to define misery for themselves, the story is especially poignant. "What
does 'misery' mean to you?" I ask a little boy with a contagious laugh.

"Life," he says.   21

There are no tents in the camp we visit in Pernier 37, a hamlet outside Port- 22
au-Prince, just bedsheets of various colors spread over wooden sticks. When it
rains, the bare ground becomes soaked and the adults must stand in knee-deep
mud holding the children in their arms. Because of their rather remote location,
the 400 or so displaced residents have not seen much in terms of local or international aid and do not have many outside contacts. An Israeli-sponsored water
truck occasionally stops by (after our visit, a donation of tents will replace the
sheets), but the rest of the time they are on their own.

As 40 or so children in the camp gather to listen to the Li, Li, Li! readers, 23
many look listless and tired. Some have swollen bellies and reddened hair, telltale
signs of malnutrition. Sitting on pieces of tarp and cardboard, some while cradling
the heads of younger siblings in their laps, the children are joined by elderly
women and breastfeeding mothers, all looking for a momentary reprieve from a
sweltering and monotonous day.

Of the many places I visit with the Li, Li, Li! readers, the children seem happiest 24
at the Fontamara neighborhood center. Not far from the epicenter of the earthquake, the walled compound and raised courtyard somehow survived intact. Many
of the 50 or so children who show up for the reading early Saturday morning are
still living in temporary shelters—some alone, others with their parents or surviving relatives. These children are fed two meals a day and participate in cultural
enrichment programs organized by CHEDEVE—a Haitian acronym for Circle for
Self-Fulfillment and Educational Development that also sounds like the Creole
word for "masterpiece."

Roosevelt Hyppolite, a 34-year-old former waiter, started CHEDEVE before 25
the earthquake (in partnership with the U.S. organization Kledèv) to keep kids
from the neighborhood out of gangs. With the help of a local athletic coach and
schoolteacher, he organizes soccer matches, dance classes, and reading programs
for children and teenagers, which makes him a perfect collaborator for Li, Li, Li!

"All the kids here and their families have extreme financial hardships," he 26
says as the kids cheerfully belt out a welcoming song for the Li, Li, Li! readers.
"Some lost their parents and have no one to take care of them." After reading
the frightening tale of a mean school bus driver to the Fontamara kids, Makenton
Louis, a towering 36-year-old father of five, inspires another song: Children
are treasures, they sing. Respect them. Educate them. Don't hit them. Take
care of them.

27   When I return to Port-au-Prince a few months later, I learn that Hyppolite was forced to ask the Li, Li, Li! readers to stay away from the neighborhood after a violent incident attributed to a prisoner who'd escaped from the national penitentiary during the quake. The children were confined to the relative security of their or their friends' houses for several weeks. Now Li, Li, Li! readers have been invited back, but the incident is emblematic of post-earthquake existence for the children of Haiti, whose daily lives are constrained by terrible events beyond their control.

28   Yet when I revisit some of the Li, Li, Li! readers, I see that they have become more comfortable interacting with the kids and more at ease with themselves. Natacha Micourt and her brother Reginald have moved into a more structurally sound house since the earthquake, and Natacha has started painting again, which she had thought impossible after the earthquake. University student Isabelle Castille—who lost 20 family members in the quake—has moved back to her old house, though as a safety precaution she sleeps at night in a tent in front of its cracked walls. In her off hours she often reads to the neighborhood kids.

29   "Everyone lost something," she told me on my first visit, "and because of that we became one."

30   In the fall, a cholera epidemic had Li, Li, Li!'s staff briefing children and adults on how to avoid contracting or spreading the disease and where to obtain medical care. Perhaps storybooks cannot solve all their problems. But many of the tent cities now have child-friendly spaces, sponsored by the International Rescue Committee or other local or international nongovernmental organizations—havens and oases where children can draw and sing and play and, yes, read and be read to before returning to the harsh and uncertain reality of their daily lives.

COMPREHENSION

1. How does Danticat characterize the role and value of reading for children after the disastrous earthquake in Haiti in 2010?
2. Highlight and list the children and adults mentioned by Danticat in her article. Explain how they interact.
3. Summarize the importance of reading in Danticat's life. What does reading tell her about Haitians in the aftermath of the earthquake that she might not have fully known before?

RHETORIC

1. Danticat writes from the perspective of a Haitian American. How does her voice shape the content of the essay? What does she reveal about herself and her environment? Explain the effect of her "I" or first-person point of view.
2. How would you characterize Danticat's use of description? What is the dominant effect?

3. Danticat wrote this essay for a popular magazine whose audience is composed largely of women. How does she tailor her style for this primary audience? What elements of the essay might appeal to a broader, more diverse audience?

4. What refrain or repeated phrase serves to unify this essay? How effective do you find it, and why?

5. What is Danticat's main purpose in this essay? Does she merely want to inform, provide a slice of life, perhaps persuade? Respond with specific reference to elements in the text.

WRITING

1. If you volunteered to read poems or stories to a group of children, what would they be? Discuss five works that you would share with this group, explaining what you would want to accomplish.

2. Write an essay of reflection on what reading meant to you as a child.

3. **Writing an Argument:** Argue for or against the proposition that reading to children in the aftermath of a tragedy is a useful way to invest time and money.

NETWORKING
Applying Digital and Multimedia Literacies

Search online for information on the graphic artist Matt Bors. Locate his collaborative work with Haitian graphic artists and watch the video "Spotlight on Haiti." Why and how might conveying stories of the situation in Haiti through images, or *graphic reporting,* be a particularly effective way to, as the Cartoon Movement says, "give Haiti a voice"? Download or print relevant images and use them to begin a discussion with classmates.

Mother Tongue

Amy Tan

Amy Tan *(b. 1952) was born in California, several years after her parents immigrated to San Francisco from China. She attended San Jose State University and the University of California, Berkeley. Before devoting herself full-time to the writing of fiction, Tan worked as a reporter and technical writer. Her fiction, deeply autobiographical, focuses on the lives of Chinese-American women trying to reconcile their traditional heritage with contemporary American culture. Tan's first novel,* The Joy Luck Club *(1989), catapulted her to fame. Her other books include* The Kitchen God's Wife *(1991),* The Hundred Secret Senses *(1996),* The Bonesetter's Daughter *(2001), and* Saving the Fish from Drowning *(2005). Tan's reflections* *on her career as a writer appear in* The Opposite of Fate *(2003). In "Mother Tongue," which first appeared in* The Threepenny Review *in 1990 and which has since become a contemporary classic, Tan considers the various languages or forms of communication she has used since childhood when conversing with her mother.*

1   I am not a scholar of English or literature. I cannot give you much more than personal opinions on the English language and its variations in this country or others.

2   I am a writer. And by that definition, I am someone who has always loved language. I am fascinated by language in daily life. I spend a great deal of my time thinking about the power of language—the way it can evoke an emotion, a visual image, a complex idea, or a simple truth. Language is the tool of my trade. And I use them all—all the Englishes I grew up with.

3   Recently, I was made keenly aware of the different Englishes I do use. I was giving a talk to a large group of people, the same talk I had already given to half a dozen other groups. The nature of the talk was about my writing, my life, and my book, *The Joy Luck Club.* The talk was going along well enough, until I remembered one major difference that made the whole talk sound wrong. My mother was in the room. And it was perhaps the first time she had heard me give a lengthy speech, using the kind of English I have never used with her. I was saying things like, "The intersection of memory upon imagination" and "There is an aspect of my fiction that relates to thus-and-thus"—a speech filled with carefully wrought grammatical phrases, burdened, it suddenly seemed to me, with nominalized forms, past perfect tenses, conditional phrases, all the forms of standard English that I had learned in school and through books, the forms of English I did not use at home with my mother.

4   Just last week, I was walking down the street with my mother, and I again found myself conscious of the English I was using, the English I do use with her. We were talking about the price of new and used furniture and I heard myself saying this: "Not waste money that way." My husband was with us as well, and he didn't notice any switch in my English. And then I realized why. It's because over the twenty years we've been together I've often used the same kind of English with him, and sometimes he even uses it with me. It has become our language of intimacy, a different sort of English that relates to family talk, the language I grew up with.

5   So you'll have some idea of what this family talk I heard sounds like, I'll quote what my mother said during a recent conversation which I videotaped and then transcribed. During this conversation, my mother was talking about a political gangster in Shanghai who had the same last name as her family's, Du, and how the gangster in his early years wanted to be adopted by her family, which was rich by comparison. Later, the gangster became more powerful, far richer than my mother's family, and one day showed up at my mother's wedding to pay his respects. Here's what she said in part:

6   "Du Yusong having business like fruit stand. Like off the street kind. He is Du like Du Zong—but not Tsung-ming Island people. The local people call putong, the river east side, he belong to that side local people. That man want to ask

Du Zong father take him in like become own family. Du Zong father wasn't look down on him, but didn't take seriously, until that man big like become a mafia. Now important person, very hard to inviting him. Chinese way, came only to show respect, don't stay for dinner. Respect for making big celebration, he shows up. Mean gives lots of respect. Chinese custom. Chinese social life that way. If too important won't have to stay too long. He come to my wedding. I didn't see, I heard it. I gone to boy's side, they have YMCA dinner. Chinese age I was nineteen."

You should know that my mother's expressive command of English belies 7 how much she actually understands. She reads the *Forbes* report, listens to *Wall Street Week,* converses daily with her stockbroker, reads all of Shirley MacLaine's books with ease—all kinds of things I can't begin to understand. Yet some of my friends tell me they understand 50 percent of what my mother says. Some say they understand 80 to 90 percent. Some say they understand none of it, as if she were speaking pure Chinese. But to me, my mother's English is perfectly clear, perfectly natural. It's my mother tongue. Her language, as I hear it, is vivid, direct, full of observation and imagery. That was the language that helped shape the way I saw things, expressed things, made sense of the world.

Lately, I've been giving more thought to the kind of English my mother 8 speaks. Like others, I have described it to people as "broken" or "fractured" English. But I wince when I say that. It has always bothered me that I can think of no way to describe it other than "broken," as if it were damaged and needed to be fixed, as if it lacked a certain wholeness and soundness. I've heard other terms used, "limited English," for example. But they seem just as bad, as if everything is limited, including people's perceptions of the limited English speaker.

I know this for a fact, because when I was growing up, my mother's "limited" 9 English limited *my* perception of her. I was ashamed of her English. I believed that her English reflected the quality of what she had to say. That is, because she expressed them imperfectly her thoughts were imperfect. And I had plenty of empirical evidence to support me: the fact that people in department stores, at banks, and at restaurants did not take her seriously, did not give her good service, pretended not to understand her, or even acted as if they did not hear her.

My mother has long realized the limitations of her English as well. When I 10 was fifteen, she used to have me call people on the phone to pretend I was she. In this guise, I was forced to ask for information or even to complain and yell at people who had been rude to her. One time it was a call to her stockbroker in New York. She had cashed out her small portfolio and it just so happened we were going to go to New York the next week, our very first trip outside California. I had to get on the phone and say in an adolescent voice that was not very convincing, "This is Mrs. Tan."

And my mother was standing in the back whispering loudly, "Why he don't 11 send me check, already two weeks late. So mad he lie to me, losing me money."

And then I said in perfect English, "Yes, I'm getting rather concerned. You 12 had agreed to send the check two weeks ago, but it hasn't arrived."

13   Then she began to talk more loudly. "What he want, I come to New York tell him front of his boss, you cheating me?" And I was trying to calm her down, make her be quiet, while telling the stockbroker, "I can't tolerate any more excuses. If I don't receive the check immediately, I am going to have to speak to your manager when I'm in New York next week." And sure enough, the following week there we were in front of this astonished stockbroker, and I was sitting there red-faced and quiet, and my mother, the real Mrs. Tan, was shouting at his boss in her impeccable broken English.

14   We used a similar routine just five days ago, for a situation that was far less humorous. My mother had gone to the hospital for an appointment, to find out about a benign brain tumor a CAT scan had revealed a month ago. She said she had spoken very good English, her best English, no mistakes. Still, she said, the hospital did not apologize when they said they had lost the CAT scan and she had come for nothing. She said they did not seem to have any sympathy when she told them she was anxious to know the exact diagnosis, since her husband and son had both died of brain tumors. She said they would not give her any more information until the next time and she would have to make another appointment for that. So she said she would not leave until the doctor called her daughter. She wouldn't budge. And when the doctor finally called her daughter, me, who spoke in perfect English—lo and behold—we had assurances the CAT scan would be found, promises that a conference call on Monday would be held, and apologies for any suffering my mother had gone through for a most regrettable mistake.

15   I think my mother's English almost had an effect on limiting my possibilities in life as well. Sociologists and linguists probably will tell you that a person's developing language skills are more influenced by peers. But I do think that the language spoken in the family, especially in immigrant families which are more insular, plays a large role in shaping the language of the child. And I believe that it affected my results on achievement tests, IQ tests, and the SAT. While my English skills were never judged as poor, compared to math, English could not be considered my strong suit. In grade school I did moderately well, getting perhaps B's, sometimes B-pluses, in English and scoring perhaps in the sixtieth or seventieth percentile on achievement tests. But those scores were not good enough to override the opinion that my true abilities lay in math and science, because in those areas I achieved A's and scored in the ninetieth percentile or higher.

16   This was understandable. Math is precise; there is only one correct answer. Whereas, for me at least, the answers on English tests were always a judgment call, a matter of opinion and personal experience. Those tests were constructed around items like fill-in-the-blank sentence completion, such as, "Even though Tom was _____, Mary thought he was _____." And the correct answer always seemed to be the most bland combinations of thoughts, for example, "Even though Tom was shy, Mary thought he was charming," with the grammatical structure "even though" limiting the correct answer to some sort of semantic opposites, so you wouldn't get answers like, "Even though Tom was foolish, Mary thought he was ridiculous." Well, according to my mother, there were very few

limitations as to what Tom could have been and what Mary might have thought of him. So I never did well on tests like that.

The same was true with word analogies, pairs of words in which you were 17 supposed to find some sort of logical, semantic relationship—for example, "*Sunset* is to *nightfall* as _____ is to _____." And here you would be presented with a list of four possible pairs, one of which showed the same kind of relationship: *red* is to *stoplight, bus* is to *arrival, chills* is to *fever, yawn* is to *boring*. Well, I could never think that way. I knew what the tests were asking, but I could not block out of my mind the images already created by the first pair, "*sunset* is to *nightfall*"— and I would see a burst of colors against a darkening sky, the moon rising, the lowering of a curtain of stars. And all the other pairs of words—red, bus, stop-light, boring—just threw up a mass of confusing images, making it impossible for me to sort out something as logical as saying: "A sunset precedes nightfall" is the same as "a chill precedes a fever." The only way I would have gotten that answer right would have been to imagine an associative situation, for example, my being disobedient and staying out past sunset, catching a chill at night, which turns into feverish pneumonia as punishment, which indeed did happen to me.

I have been thinking about all this lately, about my mother's English, about 18 achievement tests. Because lately I've been asked, as a writer, why there are not more Asian Americans represented in American literature. Why are there few Asian Americans enrolled in creative writing programs? Why do so many Chinese students go into engineering? Well, these are broad sociological questions I can't begin to answer. But I have noticed in surveys—in fact, just last week—that Asian students, as a whole, always do significantly better on math achievement tests than in English. And this makes me think that there are other Asian-American students whose English spoken in the home might also be described as "broken" or "limited." And perhaps they also have teachers who are steering them away from writing and into math and science, which is what happened to me.

Fortunately, I happen to be rebellious in nature and enjoy the challenge of 19 disproving assumptions made about me. I became an English major my first year in college, after being enrolled as pre-med. I started writing nonfiction as a free-lancer the week after I was told by my former boss that writing was my worst skill and I should hone my talents toward account management.

But it wasn't until 1985 that I finally began to write fiction. And at first I wrote 20 using what I thought to be wittily crafted sentences, sentences that would finally prove I had mastery over the English language. Here's an example from the first draft of a story that later made its way into *The Joy Luck Club,* but without this line: "That was my mental quandary in its nascent state." A terrible line, which I can barely pronounce.

Fortunately, for reasons I won't get into today, I later decided I should envision 21 a reader for the stories I would write. And the reader I decided upon was my mother, because these were stories about mothers. So with this reader in mind—and in fact she did read my early drafts—I began to write stories using all the Englishes I grew up with: the English I spoke to my mother, which for lack of a better term might be described as "simple"; the English she used with me, which for lack of a better term might be described as "broken"; my translation of her Chinese, which could certainly be described as "watered down"; and what I imagined to be her translation of her Chinese if she could speak in perfect English, her internal language, and for that I sought to preserve the essence, but neither an English nor a Chinese structure. I wanted to capture what language ability tests can never reveal: her intent, her passion, her imagery, the rhythms of her speech and the nature of her thoughts.

22   Apart from what any critic had to say about my writing, I knew I had succeeded where it counted when my mother finished reading my book and gave me her verdict: "So easy to read."

COMPREHENSION

1. Explain the pun in the title of Tan's essay. How does this pun echo throughout the essay?
2. Tan refers to "all the Englishes I grew up with" (paragraph 2). How many "Englishes" does she discuss, and how does she distinguish among them? According to the writer, what are the ways in which language can work?
3. What observations does Tan make about Asian Americans and standard test scores? Why does she introduce this topic into an essay that, after all, focuses on her mother?

RHETORIC

1. Why does Tan begin her essay by confessing that she is "not a scholar of English or literature" (paragraph 1)? Does this disclaimer undermine her authority to speak about language? Why or why not?
2. Explain Tan's use of classification and division to organize her essay. Into what two main categories does she divide the languages she employs?
3. Identify places in the essay where Tan uses definition. What is her purpose in providing such basic definitions?
4. What is Tan's purpose in telling stories involving the use of language? How do these narrative moments affect the tone of the essay?
5. Do you detect an argument in this essay? If so, where does Tan present her claim, and how does she support it? If not, what is the thesis of the piece?
6. Analyze the conclusion. Why does Tan end with an image of her mother responding to her daughter's first novel? Do you think that her mother is Tan's intended audience? Why or why not?

WRITING

1. Write an essay that classifies the "different Englishes" that people use in everyday life—at home, work, school, and elsewhere.
2. In an analytical paper, identify and evaluate the various rhetorical strategies that Tan employs to compose her essay.
3. **Writing an Argument:** Take a position on the proposition that the United States should be an "English-only" nation.

NETWORKING *Applying Digital and Multimedia Literacies*	

Listening and Synthesizing: Conduct an online search to locate and listen to the podcast of student newspaper *InsideVandy*'s interview with Chancellor Nicholas Zeppos of Vanderbilt University. Expanding on assignment 3 under "Writing," synthesize his positions into your argument, providing solid reasons why you agree, agree with qualifications, or disagree with his position on an "English-Only" referendum in Davidson County, Tennessee.

Freewriting

Peter Elbow

Peter Elbow *(b. 1935) was born in New York and received degrees from Williams College, Exeter College, Oxford, and Brandeis University. He has taught at the University of Massachusetts at Amherst, the State University of New York at Stony Brook, the Massachusetts Institute of Technology, Franconia College, and Evergreen State College. He is considered by some writing teachers to have revolutionized the teaching of writing through his popularization of the concept and practice called "freewriting." He is the author or editor of more than 15 books on writing, including* Writing without Teachers, Writing with Power, Embracing Contraries, What Is English? *and, most recently,* Everyone Can Write: Essays toward a Hopeful Theory of Writing and Teaching Writing *(2000). In "Freewriting," taken from* Writing without Teachers, *Elbow explains an exercise for writing students that he helped popularize in American colleges, universities, and writing workshops.*

The most effective way I know to improve your writing is to do freewriting exercises 1 regularly. At least three times a week. They are sometimes called "automatic writing," "babbling," or "jabbering" exercises. The idea is simply to write for ten minutes (later on, perhaps fifteen or twenty). Don't stop for anything. Go quickly without rushing. Never stop to look back, to cross something out, to wonder how to spell something, to wonder what word or thought to use, or to think about what you are doing. If you can't think of a word or a spelling, just use a squiggle or else write, "I can't think of it." Just put down something. The easiest thing is just to put down whatever is in your mind. If you get stuck it's fine to write "I can't think what to say, I can't think what to say" as many times as you want; or repeat the last word you wrote over and over again; or anything else. The only requirement is that you *never* stop.

2   What happens to a freewriting exercise is important. It must be a piece of writing which, even if someone reads it, doesn't send any ripples back to you. It is like writing something and putting it in a bottle in the sea. The teacherless class helps your writing by providing maximum feedback. Freewritings help you by providing no feedback at all. When I assign one, I invite the writer to let me read it. But also tell him to keep it if he prefers. I read it quickly and make no comments at all and I do not speak with him about it. The main thing is that a freewriting must never be evaluated in any way; in fact there must be no discussion or comment at all.

3   Here is an example of a fairly coherent exercise (sometimes they are very incoherent, which is fine):

> I think I'll write what's on my mind, but the only thing on my mind right now is what to write for ten minutes. I've never done this before and I'm not prepared in any way—the sky is cloudy today, how's that? now I'm afraid I won't be able to think of what to write when I get to the end of the sentence—well, here I am at the end of the sentence—here I am again, again, again, again, at least I'm still writing—Now I ask is there some reason to be happy that I'm still writing—ah yes! Here comes the question again—What am I getting out of this? What point is there in it? It's almost obscene to always ask it but I seem to question everything that way and I was gonna say something else pertaining to that but I got so busy writing down the first part that I forgot what I was leading into. This is kind of fun oh don't stop writing—cars and trucks speeding by somewhere out the window, pens clittering across people's papers. The sky is cloudy—is it symbolic that I should be mentioning it? Huh? I dunno. Maybe I should try colors, blue, red, dirty words—wait a minute—no can't do that, orange, yellow, arm tired, green pink violet magenta lavender red brown black green—now that I can't think of any more colors—just about done—relief? maybe.

Freewriting may seem crazy but actually it makes simple sense. Think of the difference between speaking and writing. Writing has the advantage of permitting more editing. But that's its downfall too. Almost everybody interposes a massive and complicated series of editings between the time words start to be born into consciousness and when they finally come off the end of the pencil or typewriter onto the page. This is partly because schooling makes us obsessed with the "mistakes" we make in writing. Many people are constantly thinking about spelling and grammar as they try to write. I am always thinking about the awkwardness, wordiness, and general mushiness of my natural verbal product as I try to write down words.

4   But it's not just "mistakes" or "bad writing" we edit as we write. We also edit unacceptable thoughts and feelings, as we do in speaking. In writing there is more time to do it so the editing is heavier: when speaking, there's someone right there waiting for a reply and he'll get bored or think we're crazy if we don't come out with *something*. Most of the time in speaking, we settle for the catch-as-catch-can way in which the words tumble out. In writing, however, there's a chance to try to get them right. But the opportunity to get them right is a terrible burden: you can work for two hours trying to get a paragraph "right" and discover it's not right at all. And then give up.

Editing, *in itself,* is not the problem. Editing is usually necessary if we want to 5
end up with something satisfactory. The problem is that editing goes on *at the
same time* as producing. The editor is, as it were, constantly looking over the
shoulder of the producer and constantly fiddling with what he's doing while he's
in the middle of trying to do it. No wonder the producer gets nervous, jumpy,
inhibited, and finally can't be coherent. It's an unnecessary burden to try to think
of words and also worry at the same time whether they're the right words.

The main thing about freewriting is that it is *nonediting.* It is an exercise in 6
bringing together the process of producing words and putting them down on the
page. Practiced regularly, it undoes the ingrained habit of editing at the same time
you are trying to produce. It will make writing less blocked because words will
come more easily. You will use up more paper, but chew up fewer pencils.

Next time you write, notice how often you stop yourself from writing down 7
something you were going to write down. Or else cross it out after it's written.
"Naturally," you say, "it wasn't any good." But think for a moment about the occasions when you spoke well. Seldom was it because you first got the beginning just
right. Usually it was a matter of a halting or even garbled beginning, but you kept
going and your speech finally became coherent and even powerful. There is a
lesson here for writing: trying to get the beginning just right is a formula for
failure—and probably a secret tactic to make yourself give up writing. Make some
words, whatever they are, and then grab hold of that line and reel in as hard as
you can. Afterwards you can throw away lousy beginnings and make new ones.
This is the quickest way to get into good writing.

The habit of compulsive, premature editing doesn't just make writing hard. It 8
also makes writing dead. Your voice is damped out by all the interruptions,
changes, and hesitations between the consciousness and the page. In your natural
way of producing words there is a sound, a texture, a rhythm—a voice—which is
the main source of power in your writing. I don't know how it works, but this voice
is the force that will make a reader listen to you, the energy that drives the meanings through his thick skull. Maybe you don't *like* your voice; maybe people have
made fun of it. But it's the only voice you've got. It's your only source of power.
You better get back into it, no matter what you think of it. If you keep writing in it,
it may change into something you like better. But if you abandon it, you'll likely
never have a voice and never be heard.

Freewritings are vacuums. Gradually you will begin to carry over into your 9
regular writing some of the voice, force, and connectedness that creep into those
vacuums.

COMPREHENSION

1. What is the thesis of the essay? Is it implied or stated directly in the text?
2. In paragraph 5, Elbow refers to the "producer" and the "editor." Who are they? Where
    are they located? How did they develop?
3. In paragraph 8, the author makes a connection between one's personal "voice" and the
    idea of "power." Why does Elbow focus so strongly on this connection?

RHETORIC

1. Elbow frequently uses the "imperative" (or command) sentence form in the opening paragraph. Why? What would have been the effect had he used the simple declarative form?
2. Writers often use examples to help illustrate their point. Does the example of a freewriting exercise Elbow provides in paragraph 3 help you to understand the method? Why or why not?
3. The author uses colloquial terms such as "squiggle" (paragraph 1), "crazy" and "mushiness" (paragraph 3), and "lousy" (paragraph 7). How does his use of such words affect the tone of the essay?
4. Are there any elements in Elbow's own style that suggest his essay may have started as a freewriting exercise? Consider the reasons he provides for the importance of freewriting—for example, generating ideas, discovering one's own voice, or expressing oneself succinctly and naturally.
5. Elbow is himself a college writing teacher. Based on your assessment of the tone of the essay, whom do you think is his intended audience? Is it broad or narrow? Specialized or general? Or could he have in mind more than one type of audience? Explain your answer.
6. Note the number of times Elbow begins his sentences with coordinating conjunctions ("but," "and," "or"). For example, in paragraph 4, he does it three times. Many writing teachers frown on this method of structuring sentences. Why does Elbow employ it?
7. Compare the essay's introduction to its conclusion. Note how the introduction is rather long and the conclusion is quite short (two sentences, in fact). How do these two elements contribute to the overall "pace" of the essay?

WRITING

1. During one week, complete three freewriting exercises. Wait one week, and then review what you have written. Explore any insights your freewriting gives you into your writer's "voice"— your concerns, interests, style, and "power."
2. Write an expository paper explaining the difficulties you have when writing an essay homework assignment or writing an essay-length response during an exam.
3. Write a comparison and contrast essay wherein you examine the similarities and differences of speaking and writing.
4. **Writing an Argument:** Write an essay in which you support or discourage the act of freewriting.

NETWORKING
Applying Digital and Multimedia Literacies

Paper vs. Screen: When freewriting, do you prefer to do so on paper or on your computer? In a paragraph, discuss what you see as two or three key advantages to your preferred way of freewriting, acknowledging (and rebutting) at least one anticipated counterargument.

The Maker's Eye: Revising Your Own Manuscripts

Donald M. Murray

Donald M. Murray *(1917–2006) has combined a career as teacher, journalist, fiction writer, poet, and author of several important textbooks on writing. He has worked as a teacher, journalist, and editor for* Time *magazine. His books include* A Writer Teaches Writing, Write to Learn, Read to Write, *and more recently* Shoptalk: Learning to Write with Writers *(1991),* Crafting a Life in Essay, Story, Poem *(1996), and* The Craft of Revision *(1997). In this essay, originally published in the magazine* The Writer, *Murray argues for the absolute importance of the revision process to the writer. As he presents the stages of the revision process, Murray illustrates their usefulness to any writer—whether beginner or experienced—and offers his personal views and those of other authors.*

When students complete a first draft, they consider the job of writing done—and 1 their teachers too often agree. When professional writers complete a first draft, they usually feel that they are at the start of the writing process. When a draft is completed, the job of writing can begin.

That difference in attitude is the difference between amateur and professional, 2 inexperience and experience, journeyman and craftsman. Peter F. Drucker, the prolific business writer, calls his first draft "the zero draft"—after that he can start counting. Most writers share the feeling that the first draft, and all of those which follow, are opportunities to discover what they have to say and how best they can say it.

To produce a progression of drafts, each of which says more and says it more 3 clearly, the writer has to develop a special kind of reading skill. In school we are taught to decode what appears on the page as finished writing. Writers, however, face a different category of possibility and responsibility when they read their own drafts. To them the words on the page are never finished. Each can be changed and rearranged, can set off a chain reaction of confusion or clarified meaning. This is a different kind of reading, which is possibly more difficult and certainly more exciting.

Writers must learn to be their own best enemy. They must accept the criti- 4 cism of others and be suspicious of it; they must accept the praise of others and be even more suspicious of it. Writers cannot depend on others. They must detach themselves from their own pages so that they can apply both their caring and their craft to their own work.

Such detachment is not easy. Science fiction writer Ray Bradbury suppos- 5 edly puts each manuscript away for a year to the day and then rereads it as a stranger. Not many writers have the discipline or the time to do this. We must read when our judgment may be at its worst, when we are close to the euphoric moment of creation.

6   Then the writer, counsels novelist Nancy Hale, "should be critical of everything that seems to him most delightful in his style. He should excise what he most admires, because he wouldn't thus admire it if he weren't . . . in a sense protecting it from criticism." John Ciardi, the poet, adds, "The last act of the writing must be to become one's own reader. It is, I suppose, a schizophrenic process, to begin passionately and to end critically, to begin hot and to end cold; and, more important, to be passion-hot and critic-cold at the same time."

7   Most people think that the principal problem is that writers are too proud of what they have written. Actually, a greater problem for most professional writers is one shared by the majority of students. They are overly critical, think everything is dreadful, tear up page after page, never complete a draft, see the task as hopeless.

8   The writer must learn to read critically but constructively, to cut what is bad, to reveal what is good. Eleanor Estes, the children's book author, explains: "The writer must survey his work critically, coolly, as though he were a stranger to it. He must be willing to prune, expertly and hard-heartedly. At the end of each revision, a manuscript may look . . . worked over, torn apart, pinned together, added to, deleted from, words changed and words changed back. Yet the book must maintain its original freshness and spontaneity."

9   Most readers underestimate the amount of rewriting it usually takes to produce spontaneous reading. This is a great disadvantage to the student writer, who sees only a finished product and never watches the craftsman who takes the necessary step back, studies the work carefully, returns to the task, steps back, returns, steps back, again and again. Anthony Burgess, one of the most prolific writers in the English-speaking world, admits, "I might revise a page twenty times." Roald Dahl, the popular children's writer, states, "By the time I'm nearing the end of a story, the first part will have been reread and altered and corrected at least 150 times. . . . Good writing is essentially rewriting. I am positive of this."

10   Rewriting isn't virtuous. It isn't something that ought to be done. It is simply something that most writers find they have to do to discover what they have to say and how to say it. It is a condition of the writer's life.

11   There are, however, a few writers who do little formal rewriting, primarily because they have the capacity and experience to create and review a large number of invisible drafts in their minds before they approach the page. And some writers slowly produce finished pages, performing all the tasks of revision simultaneously, page by page, rather than draft by draft. But it is still possible to see the sequence followed by most writers most of the time in rereading their own work.

12   Most writers scan their drafts first, reading as quickly as possible to catch the larger problems of subject and form, then move in closer and closer as they read and write, reread and rewrite.

13   The first thing writers look for in their drafts is *information*. They know that a good piece of writing is built from specific, accurate, and interesting information.

The writer must have an abundance of information from which to construct a readable piece of writing.

Next writers look for *meaning* in the information. The specifics must build a 14 pattern of significance. Each piece of specific information must carry the reader toward meaning.

Writers reading their own drafts are aware of *audience.* They put themselves 15 in the reader's situation and make sure that they deliver information which a reader wants to know or needs to know in a manner which is easily digested. Writers try to be sure that they anticipate and answer the questions a critical reader will ask when reading the piece of writing.

Writers make sure that the *form* is appropriate to the subject and the audience. 16 Form, or genre, is the vehicle which carries meaning to the reader, but form cannot be selected until the writer has adequate information to discover its significance and an audience which needs or wants that meaning.

Once writers are sure the form is appropriate, they must then look at the 17 *structure,* the order of what they have written. Good writing is built on a solid framework of logic, argument, narrative, or motivation which runs through the entire piece of writing and holds it together. This is the time when many writers find it most effective to outline as a way of visualizing the hidden spine by which the piece of writing is supported.

The element on which writers may spend a majority of their time is *develop-* 18 *ment.* Each section of a piece of writing must be adequately developed. It must give readers enough information so that they are satisfied. How much information is enough? That's as difficult as asking how much garlic belongs in a salad. It must be done to taste, but most beginning writers underdevelop, underestimating the reader's hunger for information.

As writers solve development problems, they often have to consider ques- 19 tions of *dimension.* There must be a pleasing and effective proportion among all the parts of the piece of writing. There is a continual process of subtracting and adding to keep the piece of writing in balance.

Finally, writers have to listen to their own voices. *Voice* is the force which drives 20 a piece of writing forward. It is an expression of the writer's authority and concern. It is what is between the words on the page, what glues the piece of writing together. A good piece of writing is always marked by a consistent, individual voice.

As writers read and reread, write and rewrite, they move closer and closer to 21 the page until they are doing line-by-line editing. Writers read their own pages with infinite care. Each sentence, each line, each clause, each phrase, each word, each mark of punctuation, each section of white space between the type has to contribute to the clarification of meaning.

Slowly the writer moves from word to word, looking through language to see 22 the subject. As a word is changed, cut, or added, as a construction is rearranged, all the words used before that moment and all those that follow that moment must be considered and reconsidered.

Writers often read aloud at this stage of the editing process, muttering or 23 whispering to themselves, calling on the ear's experience with language. Does this sound right—or that? Writers edit, shifting back and forth from eye to page to ear to page. I find I must do this careful editing in short runs, no more than fifteen or twenty minutes at a stretch, or I become too kind with myself. I begin to see what I hope is on the page, not what actually is on the page.

24   This sounds tedious if you haven't done it, but actually it is fun. Making something right is immensely satisfying, for writers begin to learn what they are writing about by writing. Language leads them to meaning, and there is the joy of discovery, of understanding, of making meaning clear as the writer employs the technical skills of language.

25   Words have double meanings, even triple and quadruple meanings. Each word has its own potential for connotation and denotation. And when writers rub one word against the other, they are often rewarded with a sudden insight, an unexpected clarification.

26   The maker's eye moves back and forth from word to phrase to sentence to paragraph to sentence to phrase to word. The maker's eye sees the need for variety and balance, for a firmer structure, for a more appropriate form. It peers into the interior of the paragraph, looking for coherence, unity, and emphasis, which make meaning clear.

27   I learned something about this process when my first bifocals were prescribed. I had ordered a larger section of the reading portion of the glass because of my work, but even so, I could not contain my eyes within this new limit of vision. And I still find myself taking off my glasses and bending my nose towards the page, for my eyes unconsciously flick back and forth across the page, back to another page, forward to still another, as I try to see each evolving line in relation to every other line.

28   When does this process end? Most writers agree with the great Russian writer Tolstoy, who said, "I scarcely ever reread my published writings, if by chance I come across a page, it always strikes me: all this must be rewritten; this is how I should have written it."

29   The maker's eye is never satisfied, for each word has the potential to ignite new meaning. This article has been twice written all the way through the writing process, and it was published four years ago. Now it is to be republished in a book. The editors make a few small suggestions, and then I read it with my maker's eye. Now it has been re-edited, re-revised, re-read, re-re-edited, for each piece of writing to the writer is full of potential and alternatives.

30   A piece of writing is never finished. It is delivered to a deadline, torn out of the typewriter on demand, sent off with a sense of accomplishment and shame and pride and frustration. If only there were a couple more days, time for just another run at it, perhaps then . . .

COMPREHENSION

1. In paragraph 1, what does Murray mean by the statement "When a draft is completed, the job of writing can begin"? Isn't a draft a form of writing?

2. According to Murray, what are the major differences between student and professional writers? Why do the differences help make the "professional" more accomplished at his or her work?

3. What are the differences between the reading styles of novice and experienced writers? How do the differences affect their own writings?

RHETORIC

1. Compare the introduction of this essay to that of Elbow's "Freewriting." How do they differ in tone and structure?

2. Murray begins to classify various aspects of the writer's concern in paragraph 13. Why does he wait so long to begin this analysis? Why are certain key words in paragraphs 13–20 italicized?

3. Murray uses analogy, comparing one thing with another, very different thing, to make the writing process concrete and familiar. Identify some of these analogies. Why are they models of clarity?

4. Murray refers to a writer as "the maker" several times in the essay. What does he imply by this usage? What other professions might be included in this category?

5. What is the purpose of the essay? Is it to inform? To persuade? To serve as a model? Anything else? Explain your response.

6. Murray ends the essay with an ellipsis. Why?

7. Notice the sentence in paragraph 29 that has four consecutive words with the prefix "re-." What is the purpose and effect of this rhetorical device?

WRITING

1. Murray focuses on the process, craft, and purpose of the writer, but he does not define "writer." Write an extended definition explaining what he means by this occupation or profession.

2. Write an essay explaining your own writing process. Do not be intimidated if it is not like the one described by Murray. Compare and contrast your method with that of one or more of your classmates.

3. **Writing an Argument:** Murray suggests that revision is actually "fun" (paragraph 24). Do you agree or disagree? Write an essay defending your position.

NETWORKING
Applying Digital and Multimedia Literacies

Redefining *Writer:* After completing question 1 under Writing, write a new definition for *writer* that takes into account the changing technologies and mediums we work in today. Compare and contrast this definition with the one Murray's essay suggests.

Writing Is Easy

Steve Martin

Steve Martin *(b. 1945), the self-styled "wild and crazy guy," is a star of stand-up comedy and film. He is also a prolific author of humorous essays, plays and screen-plays, and novellas. Martin recounts his colorful life and rise to fame in* Born Standing Up: A Comic's Life *(2007). Born in Waco, Texas, but growing up in southern California, Martin lived close to Disneyland, where one of his earliest part-time jobs was selling guidebooks and magic tricks while observing comedy acts. After eight years at the Magic Kingdom, Martin found work at Knott's Berry Farm, where he acted in a melodrama and experimented with comedic and magic acts. Martin took time to attend California State University at Long Beach, majoring in philosophy, before transferring to UCLA to major in theater. He landed a job as a writer for the* Smothers Brothers Comedy Hour *and achieved his first film success when he starred in* The Jerk *(1979). Martin's popular films include* All of Me *(1984),* Dirty Rotten Scoundrels *(1988),* Bowfinger *(1999),* Cheaper by the Dozen *(2003), and* The Pink Panther 2 *(2009). Among his several books are* Pure Drivel *(1998),* WASP and Other Plays *(1998),* Shopgirl *(2000), and* The Pleasure of My Company *(2003). In the following essay, which first appeared in the June 24, 1996, issue of the* New Yorker, *Martin muses that there's no trick to being a writer in sunny California.*

1   Writing is the most easy, pain-free, and happy way to pass the time of all the arts. As I write this, for example, I am sitting comfortably in my rose garden and typing on my new computer. Each rose represents a story, so I'm never at a loss for what to type. I just look deep into the heart of the rose, read its story, and then write it down. I could be typing kjfiu joew.mv jiw and enjoy it as much as typing words that actually make sense, because I simply relish the movements of my fingers on the keys. It is true that sometimes agony visits the head of a writer. At those moments, I stop writing and relax with a coffee at my favorite restaurant, knowing that words can be changed, rethought, fiddled with, and ultimately de-nied. Painters don't have that luxury. If they go to a coffee shop, their paint dries into a hard mass.

Location, Location, Location

2   I would like to recommend that all writers live in California, because here, in between those moments when one is looking into the heart of a rose, one can look up at the calming blue sky. I feel sorry for writers—and there are some pretty famous ones—who live in places like South America and Czechoslovakia, where I imagine it gets pretty dank. These writers are easy to spot. Their books are often filled with disease and negativity. If you're going to write about disease, I would

say California is the place to do it. Dwarfism is never funny, but look at what happened when it was dealt with in California. Seven happy dwarfs. Can you imagine seven dwarfs in Czechoslovakia? You would get seven melancholic dwarfs at best—seven melancholic dwarfs and no handicap-parking spaces.

Love in the Time of Cholera: Why It's a Bad Title

I admit that "Love in the Time of . . ." is a great title, up to a point. You're reading 3 along, you're happy, it's about love. I like the way the word Time comes in—a nice, nice feeling. Then the morbid Cholera appears. I was happy till then. Why not "Love in the Time of the Blue, Blue, Bluebirds"? "Love in the Time of Oozing Sores and Pustules" is probably an earlier title the author used as he was writing in a rat-infested tree house on an old Smith Corona. The writer, whoever he is, could have used a couple of weeks in Pacific Daylight Time.

A Little Experiment

I took the following passage, which was no doubt written in some depressing 4 place, and attempted to rewrite it under the sunny influence of California:

> Most people deceive themselves with a pair of faiths: they believe in eternal memory (of people, things, deeds, nations) and in redressibility (of deeds, mistakes, sins, wrongs). Both are false faiths. In reality the opposite is true; everything will be forgotten and nothing will be redressed.
>
> —Milan Kundera

Sitting in my garden, watching the bees glide from flower to flower, I let the above 5 paragraph filter through my mind. The following New Paragraph emerged:

> I feel pretty.
> Oh, so pretty.
> I feel pretty, and witty, and bright.

Kundera was just too wordy. Sometimes the delete key is your best friend.

Writer's Block: A Myth

Writer's block is a fancy term made up by whiners so they can have an excuse to 6 drink alcohol. Sure, a writer can get stuck for a while, but when that happens to a real author—say a Socrates or a Rodman—he goes out and gets an "as told to." The alternative is to hire yourself out as an "as heard from," thus taking all the credit. The other trick I use when I have a momentary stoppage is virtually foolproof, and I'm happy to pass it along. Go to an already-published novel and find a sentence that you absolutely adore. Copy it down in your manuscript. Usually, that sentence will lead you to another sentence, and pretty soon your own ideas will start to flow. If they don't, copy down the next sentence in the novel. You can safely use up to three sentences of someone else's work—unless you're friends, then two. The odds of being found out are very slim, and even if you are, there's usually no jail time.

A Demonstration of Actual Writing

7   It's easy to talk about writing, and even easier to do it. Watch:

> Call me Ishmael. It was cold, very cold here in the mountain of Kilimanjaroville. I could hear a bell. It was tolling. I know exactly for who it was tolling, too. It was tolling for me, Ishmael Twist. [Author's note: I am now stuck. I walk over to a rose and look into its heart.] That's right, Ishmael Twist.

This is an example of what I call "pure" Writing, which occurs when there is no possibility of its becoming a screenplay. Pure writing is the most rewarding of all, because it is constantly accompanied by a voice that repeats, "Why am I writing this?" Then, and only then, can the writer hope for his finest achievement: the voice of a reader uttering its complement, "Why am I reading this?"

COMPREHENSION

1. What do you think Martin's purpose is in writing this essay? Why does he declare that every writer should live in California? What does Martin say about those writers who live in regions like Eastern Europe and South America?
2. According to Martin, what are some of the benefits of writing on a computer? How does he take advantage of 21st-century, computer-generated writing? How does he abuse this medium—and toward what purpose?
3. What preconceptions about writing—and contemporary literacy in general—does Martin satirize in this essay?

RHETORIC

1. What does Martin's title lead you to expect of his essay? At what point do you realize that he takes a comic approach to his subject? What elements and forms of comedy do you detect?
2. How does Martin's personal voice (and also what you might know about him as a celebrity) contribute to your appreciation of the writer's purpose and to the essay itself?
3. Martin aims his essay at a general audience—but also an audience that is sufficiently well read to appreciate his allusions to other writers. Who are these writers and their works?
4. Martin's essay begins with a paragraph that jumps from one association to another. Why is this introductory strategy effective, given Martin's purpose and audience?
5. Why does Martin use subheadings? Do you sense any progression from unit to unit? Why or why not?
6. What rhetorical strategies (pp. 73–83) do you detect? How do they serve to develop and organize the essay?

WRITING

1. Imitating Martin, write a comic essay on your approach to writing essays.
2. Martin speaks of "writer's block." Write an essay on this topic, using either a personal or objective tone of voice.

3. **Writing an Argument:** Argue for or against the proposition that one must find the ideal place ("Location, Location, Location," as Martin calls it) in order to write effectively.

NETWORKING
Applying Digital and Multimedia Literacies

Engaging with the Author behind a Text: Do some informal online research to find out more about Martin's career. Go beyond merely written sources, seeking out some video, audio, and/or visual texts. Where did you begin your search, and why? List at least four sites that you visited and at least two different textual formats you explored, and share your findings. Did learning more about Martin add something to your reading of this essay? Why or why not? Discuss.

Sex, Lies and Conversation: Why Is It So Hard for Men and Women to Talk to Each Other?

Deborah Tannen

Deborah Tannen (b. 1945), born in Brooklyn, New York, holds a PhD in linguistics from the University of California at Berkeley. She is University Professor and Professor of Linguistics at Georgetown University. Tannen published numerous specialized articles and books on language and linguistics before becoming nationally known as a best-selling author. She publishes regularly in such magazines as Vogue *and* New York, *and her book* That's Not What I Meant: How Conversational Style Makes or Breaks Your Relations with Others *(1986) drew national attention to her work on interpersonal communication. Her other popular books on communication include* You Just Don't Understand: Women and Men in Conversation *(1990),* Talking from 9 to 5: How Women's and Men's Conversational Styles Affect Who Gets Heard, Who Gets Credit, and What Gets Done at Work *(1994), and* I Only Say This Because I Love You: How the Way We Talk Can Make or Break Family Relationships Throughout Our Lives *(2001). The following essay was published in the* Washington Post *in 1990.*

I was addressing a small gathering in a suburban Virginia living room—a women's ₁ group that had invited men to join them. Throughout the evening, one man had been particularly talkative, frequently offering ideas and anecdotes, while his wife sat silently beside him on the couch. Toward the end of the evening, I commented that women frequently complain that their husbands don't talk to them. This man quickly concurred. He gestured toward his wife and said, "She's the talker in our family." The room burst into laughter; the man looked puzzled and hurt. "It's true," he explained. "When I come home from work I have nothing to say. If she didn't keep the conversation going, we'd spend the whole evening in silence."

2   This episode crystallizes the irony that although American men tend to talk more than women in public situations, they often talk less at home. And this pattern is wreaking havoc with marriage.

3   The pattern was observed by political scientist Andrew Hacker in the late '70s. Sociologist Catherine Kohler Riessman reports in her new book *Divorce Talk* that most of the women she interviewed—but only a few of the men—gave lack of communication as the reason for their divorces. Given the current divorce rate of nearly 50 percent, that amounts to millions of cases in the United States every year—a virtual epidemic of failed conversation.

4   In my own research, complaints from women about their husbands most often focused not on tangible inequities such as having given up the chance for a career to accompany a husband to his, or doing far more than their share of daily life-support work like cleaning, cooking, social arrangements and errands. Instead, they focused on communication: "He doesn't listen to me," "He doesn't talk to me." I found, as Hacker observed years before, that most wives want their husbands to be, first and foremost, conversational partners, but few husbands share this expectation of their wives.

5   In short, the image that best represents the current crisis is the stereotypical cartoon scene of a man sitting at the breakfast table with a newspaper held up in front of his face, while a woman glares at the back of it, wanting to talk.

Linguistic Battle of the Sexes

6 How can women and men have such different impressions of communication in marriage? Why the widespread imbalance in their interests and expectations?

7   In the April [1990] issue of *American Psychologist,* Stanford University's Eleanor Maccoby reports the results of her own and others' research showing that children's development is most influenced by the social structure of peer interactions. Boys and girls tend to play with children of their own gender, and their sex-separate groups have different organizational structures and interactive norms.

8   I believe these systematic differences in childhood socialization make talk between women and men like cross-cultural communication, heir to all the attraction and pitfalls of that enticing but difficult enterprise. My research on men's and women's conversations uncovered patterns similar to those described for children's groups.

9   For women, as for girls, intimacy is the fabric of relationships, and talk is the thread from which it is woven. Little girls create and maintain friendships by exchanging secrets; similarly, women regard conversation as the cornerstone of friendship. So a woman expects her husband to be a new and improved version of a best friend. What is important is not the individual subjects that are discussed

but the sense of closeness, of a life shared, that emerges when people tell their thoughts, feelings, and impressions.

Bonds between boys can be as intense as girls', but they are based less on 10 talking, more on doing things together. Since they don't assume talk is the cement that binds a relationship, men don't know what kind of talk women want, and they don't miss it when it isn't there.

Boys' groups are larger, more inclusive, and more hierarchical, so boys must 11 struggle to avoid the subordinate position in the group. This may play a role in women's complaints that men don't listen to them. Some men really don't like to listen, because being the listener makes them feel one-down, like a child listening to adults or an employee to a boss.

But often when women tell men, "You aren't listening," and the men protest, 12 "I am," the men are right. The impression of not listening results from misalignments in the mechanics of conversation. The misalignment begins as soon as a man and a woman take physical positions. This became clear when I studied videotapes made by psychologist Bruce Dorval of children and adults talking to their same-sex best friends. I found that at every age, the girls and women faced each other directly, their eyes anchored on each other's faces. At every age, the boys and men sat at angles to each other and looked elsewhere in the room, periodically glancing at each other. They were obviously attuned to each other, often mirroring each other's movements. But the tendency of men to face away can give women the impression they aren't listening even when they are. A young woman in college was frustrated: Whenever she told her boyfriend she wanted to talk to him, he would lie down on the floor, close his eyes, and put his arm over his face. This signaled to her, "He's taking a nap." But he insisted he was listening extra hard. Normally, he looks around the room, so he is easily distracted. Lying down and covering his eyes helped him concentrate on what she was saying.

Analogous to the physical alignment that women and men take in conversation 13 is their topical alignment. The girls in my study tended to talk at length about one topic, but the boys tended to jump from topic to topic. The second-grade girls exchanged stories about people they knew. The second-grade boys teased, told jokes, noticed things in the room and talked about finding games to play. The sixth-grade girls talked about problems with a mutual friend. The sixth-grade boys talked about 55 different topics, none of which extended over more than a few turns.

Listening to Body Language

Switching topics is another habit that gives women the impression men aren't 14 listening, especially if they switch to a topic about themselves. But the evidence of the 10th-grade boys in my study indicates otherwise. The 10th-grade boys sprawled across their chairs with bodies parallel and eyes straight ahead, rarely looking at each other. They looked as if they were riding in a car, staring out the windshield. But they were talking about their feelings. One boy was upset because a girl had told him he had a drinking problem, and the other was feeling alienated from all his friends.

15   Now, when a girl told a friend about a problem, the friend responded by asking probing questions and expressing agreement and understanding. But the
boys dismissed each other's problems. Todd assured Richard that his drinking
was "no big problem" because "sometimes you're funny when you're off your
butt." And when Todd said he felt left out, Richard responded, "Why should you?
You know more people than me."

16   Women perceived such responses as belittling and unsupportive. But the
boys seemed satisfied with them. Whereas women reassure each other by implying, "You shouldn't feel bad because I've had similar experiences," men do so by
implying, "You shouldn't feel bad because your problems aren't so bad."

17   There are even simpler reasons for women's impression that men don't listen.
Linguist Lynette Hirschman found that women make more listener-noise, such as
"mhm," "uhuh," and "yeah," to show "I'm with you." Men, she found, more often
give silent attention. Women who expect a stream of listener-noise interpret silent
attention as no attention at all.

18   Women's conversational habits are as frustrating to men as men's are to
women. Men who expect silent attention interpret a stream of listener-noise as over-
reaction or impatience. Also, when women talk to each other in a close, comfortable
setting, they often overlap, finish each other's sentences and anticipate what the
other is about to say. This practice, which I call "participatory listenership," is often
perceived by men as interruption, intrusion and lack of attention.

19   A parallel difference caused a man to complain about his wife, "She just wants
to talk about her own point of view. If I show her another view, she gets mad at
me." When most women talk to each other, they assume a conversationalist's job
is to express agreement and support. But many men see their conversational duty
as pointing out the other side of an argument. This is heard as disloyalty by
women, and refusal to offer the requisite support. It is not that women don't want
to see other points of view, but that they prefer them phrased as suggestions and
inquiries rather than as direct challenges.

20   In his book *Fighting for Life,* Walter Ong points out that men use "agonistic" or
warlike, oppositional formats to do almost anything; thus discussion becomes debate, and conversation a competitive sport. In contrast, women see conversation as
a ritual means of establishing rapport. If Jane tells a problem and June says she has
a similar one, they walk away feeling closer to each other. But this attempt at establishing rapport can backfire when used with men. Men take too literally women's
ritual "troubles talk," just as women mistake men's ritual challenges for real attack.

The Sounds of Silence

21 These differences begin to clarify why women and men have such different expectations about communication in marriage. For women, talk creates intimacy.
Marriage is an orgy of closeness: you can tell your feelings and thoughts, and still
be loved. Their greatest fear is being pushed away. But men live in a hierarchical
world, where talk maintains independence and status. They are on guard to protect themselves from being put down and pushed around.

This explains the paradox of the talkative man who said of his silent wife, "She's 22 the talker." In the public setting of a guest lecture, he felt challenged to show his intelligence and display his understanding of the lecture. But at home, where he has nothing to prove and no one to defend against, he is free to remain silent. For his wife, being home means she is free from the worry that something she says might offend someone, or spark disagreement, or appear to be showing off; at home she is free to talk.

The communication problems that endanger marriage can't be fixed by me- 23 chanical engineering. They require a new conceptual framework about the role of talk in human relationships. Many of the psychological explanations that have become second nature may not be helpful, because they tend to blame either women (for not being assertive enough) or men (for not being in touch with their feelings). A sociolinguistic approach by which male-female conversation is seen as cross-cultural communication allows us to understand the problem and forge solutions without blaming either party.

Once the problem is understood, improvement comes naturally, as it did to 24 the young woman and her boyfriend who seemed to go to sleep when she wanted to talk. Previously, she had accused him of not listening, and he had refused to change his behavior, since that would be admitting fault. But then she learned about and explained to him the differences in women's and men's habitual ways of aligning themselves in conversation. The next time she told him she wanted to talk, he began, as usual, by lying down and covering his eyes. When the familiar negative reaction bubbled up, she reassured herself that he really was listening. But then he sat up and looked at her. Thrilled she asked why. He said, "You like me to look at you when we talk, so I'll try to do it." Once he saw their differences as cross-cultural rather than right and wrong, he independently altered his behavior.

Women who feel abandoned and deprived when their husbands won't listen 25 to or report daily news may be happy to discover their husbands trying to adapt once they understand the place of small talk in women's relationships. But if their husbands don't adapt, the women may still be comforted that for men, this is not a failure of intimacy. Accepting the difference, the wives may look to their friends or family for that kind of talk. And husbands who can't provide it shouldn't feel their wives have made unreasonable demands. Some couples will still decide to divorce, but at least their decisions will be based on realistic expectations.

In these times of resurgent ethnic conflicts, the world desperately needs 26 cross-cultural understanding. Like charity, successful cross-cultural communication should begin at home.

COMPREHENSION

1. What is the thesis or claim of this essay? Where does Tannen most clearly articulate it?
2. To advance her argument, the author cites political scientists and sociologists, while she herself is a linguist. What exactly is the nature of these three professions? What do professionals in the first two fields do? Why does Tannen use their observations in developing her argument?

3. Why does the author employ a question in her title? What other device does she employ in her title to capture the reader's attention? (*Hint:* It is a reference to the title of a movie.)

RHETORIC

1. Tannen begins her essay with an anecdote. Is this an effective way of opening this particular essay? Why or why not?
2. Besides anecdotes, the author uses statistics, social science research, appeals to authority, and definition in advancing her argument. Find at least one example of each device. Explain the effectiveness or lack thereof.
3. Where and how does the author imply that she is an authority on the subject? How does this contribute to or detract from her ability to win the reader's confidence?
4. Tannen divides her essay into four sections: one untitled and three with headings. How does each section relate to the others structurally and thematically?
5. The author dramatically states that "given the current divorce rate of nearly 50 percent" the United States has a "virtual epidemic of failed conversation" (paragraph 3). Is this fact or opinion? Does it serve to heighten or weaken the import of her thesis?
6. Concerning the lack of proper communication between men and women, Tannen states, "Once the problem is understood, improvement comes naturally" (paragraph 24). Is this statement substantiated or backed up with evidence? Explain.
7. Explain the analogy the author employs in the final paragraph. Is it a good or poor analogy? Explain.

WRITING

1. Another linguist has written an essay titled "The Communication Panacea," which argues that much of what is blamed on lack of communication actually has economic and political causes. Argue for or against this proposition in the light of the ideas advanced in Tannen's essay.
2. Using some of the observational methods described in the essay, conduct your own ethnographic research by observing a couple communicating. Write a report discussing your findings.
3. **Writing an Argument:** Tannen states, "Once the problem is understood, improvement comes naturally." Argue for or against this proposition.

NETWORKING
Applying Digital and Multimedia Literacies

Exploring Gender and Online Communication: Search online to locate and then read the overview of "How Women and Men Use the Internet," a report by Deborah Fallows for the Pew Internet and American Life Project. How might the issues raised in Tannen's article inform the different ways men and women use the Web and communicate online?

Politics and the English Language

George Orwell

George Orwell (1903–1950) was the pseudonym of Eric Arthur Blair, an English novelist, essayist, and journalist. Orwell served with the Indian Imperial Police from 1922 to 1927 in Burma, fought in the Spanish Civil War, and acquired from his experience a disdain of totalitarian and imperialistic systems. This attitude is reflected in the satiric fable Animal Farm *(1945) and in the bleak, futuristic novel* 1984 *(1949). This essay, one of the more famous of the twentieth century, relates sloppy thinking and writing with political oppression.*

1   Most people who bother with the matter at all would admit that the English language is in a bad way, but it is generally assumed that we cannot by conscious action do anything about it. Our civilization is decadent, and our language—so the argument runs—must inevitably share in the general collapse. It follows that any struggle against the abuse of language is a sentimental archaism, like preferring candles to electric light or hansom cabs to airplanes. Underneath this lies the half-conscious belief that language is a natural growth and not an instrument which we shape for our own purposes.

2   Now, it is clear that the decline of a language must ultimately have political and economic causes: It is not due simply to the bad influence of this or that individual writer. But an effect can become a cause, reinforcing the original cause and producing the same effect in an intensified form, and so on indefinitely. A man may take to drink because he feels himself to be a failure, and then fail all the more completely because he drinks. It is rather the same thing that is happening to the English language. It becomes ugly and inaccurate because our thoughts are foolish, but the slovenliness of our language makes it easier for us to have foolish thoughts. The point is that the process is reversible. Modern English, especially written English, is full of bad habits which spread by imitation and which can be avoided if one is willing to take the necessary trouble. If one gets rid of these habits one can think more clearly, and to think clearly is a necessary first step towards political regeneration: so that the fight against bad English is not frivolous and is not the exclusive concern of professional writers. I will come back to this presently, and I hope that by that time the meaning of what I have said here will have become clearer. Meanwhile, here are five specimens of the English language as it is now habitually written.

3   These five passages have not been picked out because they are especially bad—I could have quoted far worse if I had chosen—but because they illustrate various of the mental vices from which we now suffer. They are a little below the average, but are fairly representative samples. I number them so that I can refer back to them when necessary:

1. I am not, indeed, sure whether it is not true to say the Milton who once seemed not unlike a seventeenth-century Shelley had not become, out of an experience even more bitter in each year, more alien (sic) to the founder of that Jesuit sect which nothing could induce him to tolerate.
   —Professor Harold Laski (essay in *Freedom of Expression*)

2. Above all, we cannot play ducks and drakes with a native battery of idioms which prescribes such egregious collocations of vocables as the basic *put up with* for *tolerate* or *put at a loss* for *bewilder.*
   —Professor Lancelot Hogben (*Interglossa*)

3. On the one side we have the free personality: by definition it is not neurotic, for it has neither conflict nor dream. Its desires, such as they are, are transparent, for they are just what institutional approval keeps in the forefront of consciousness; another institutional pattern would alter their number and intensity; there is little in them that is natural, irreducible, or culturally dangerous. But on the other side, the social bond itself is nothing but the mutual reflection of these self-secure integrities. Recall the definition of love. Is not this the very picture of a small academic? Where is there a place in this hall of mirrors for either personality or fraternity?
   —Essay on psychology in *Politics* (New York)

4. All the "best people" from the gentlemen's clubs, and all the frantic Fascist captains, united in common hatred of Socialism and bestial horror of the rising tide of the mass revolutionary movement, have turned to acts of provocation, to foul incendiarism, to medieval legends of poisoned wells, to legalize their own destruction to proletarian organizations, and rouse the agitated petty-bourgeoisie to chauvinistic fervor on behalf of the fight against the revolutionary way out of the crisis.

   —Communist pamphlet

5. If a new spirit is to be infused into this old country, there is one thorny and contentious reform which must be tackled, and that is the humanization and galvanization of the BBC. Timidity here will bespeak canker and atrophy for the soul. The heart of Britain may be sound and of strong beat, for instance, but the British lion's roar at present is like that of Bottom in Shakespeare's *Midsummer Night's Dream*—as gentle as any sucking dove. A virile new Britain cannot continue indefinitely to be traduced in the eyes, or rather ears, of the world by the effete languors of Langham Place, brazenly masquerading as "standard English." When the Voice of Britain is heard at nine o'clock, better far and infinitely less ludicrous to hear aitches honestly dropped than the present priggish, inflated, inhibited, schoolma'amish braying of blameless bashful mewing maidens!
   —Letter in *Tribune*

4   Each of these passages has faults of its own, but, quite apart from avoidable ugliness, two qualities are common to all of them. The first is staleness of imagery; the other is lack of precision. The writer either has a meaning and cannot express it, or he inadvertently says something else, or he is almost indifferent as to

whether his words mean anything or not. This mixture of vagueness and sheer incompetence is the most marked characteristic of modern English prose, and especially of any kind of political writing. As soon as certain topics are raised, the concrete melts into the abstract and no one seems able to think of turns of speech that are not hackneyed: prose consists less and less of *words* chosen for the sake of their meaning, and more of *phrases* tacked together like the sections of a prefabricated henhouse. I list below, with notes and examples, various of the tricks by means of which the work of prose construction is habitually dodged:

Dying Metaphors

A newly invented metaphor assists thought by evoking a visual image, while on the other hand a metaphor which is technically "dead" (e.g., *iron resolution*) has in effect reverted to being an ordinary word and can generally be used without loss of vividness. But in between these two classes there is a huge dump of wornout metaphors which have lost all evocative power and are merely used because they save people the trouble of inventing phrases for themselves. Examples are: *Ring the changes on, take up the cudgels for, toe the line, ride roughshod over, stand shoulder to shoulder with, play into the hands of, no axe to grind, grist to the mill, fishing in troubled waters, rift within the lute, on the order of the day, Achilles' heel, swan song, hotbed.* Many of these are used without knowledge of their meaning (what is a "rift," for instance?), and incompatible metaphors are frequently mixed, a sure sign that the writer is not interested in what he is saying. Some metaphors now current have been twisted out of their original meaning without those who use them even being aware of the fact. For example, *toe the line* is sometimes written *tow the line.* Another example is *the hammer and the anvil,* now always used with the implication that the anvil gets the worst of it. In real life it is always the anvil that breaks the hammer, never the other way about: A writer who stopped to think what he was saying would be aware of this, and would avoid perverting the original phrase.

Operators, or Verbal False Limbs

These save the trouble of picking out appropriate verbs and nouns, and at the same time pad each sentence with extra syllables which give it an appearance of symmetry. Characteristic phrases are: *render inoperative, militate against, prove unacceptable, make contact with, be subjected to, give rise to, give grounds for, have the effect of, play a leading part (role) in, make itself felt, take effect, exhibit a tendency to, serve the purpose of,* etc. etc. The keynote is the elimination of simple verbs. Instead of being a single word, such as *break, stop, spoil, mend, kill,* a verb becomes a *phrase,* made up of a noun or adjective tacked on to some general-purposes verb such as *prove, serve, form, play, render.* In addition, the passive voice is wherever possible used in preference to the active, and noun constructions are used instead of gerunds (*by examination of* instead of *by examining*). The range of verbs is further cut down by means of the *-ize* and *de-* formations, and banal statements are given an appearance of profundity by means of the *not un-* formation. Simple conjunctions and prepositions are replaced by such phrases as *with respect to, having regard to, the fact that, by dint of, in view of, in the interests of, on the hypothesis that;* and the ends of sentences are saved from anti-climax by such resounding commonplaces as *greatly to be desired, cannot be left out of account, a development to be expected in the near future, deserving of serious consideration, brought to a satisfactory conclusion,* and so on and so forth.

Pretentious Diction

7 Words like *phenomenon, element, individual* (as noun), *objective, categorical, effective, virtual, basic, primary, promote, constitute, exhibit, exploit, utilize, eliminate, liquidate,* are used to dress up simple statements and give an air of scientific impartiality to biased judgments. Adjectives like *epoch-making, epic, historic, unforgettable, triumphant, age-old, inevitable, inexorable, veritable,* are used to dignify the sordid processes of international politics, while writing that aims at glorifying war usually takes on an archaic color, its characteristic words being: *realm, throne, chariot, mailed fist, trident, sword, shield, buckler, banner, jackboot, clarion.* Foreign words and expressions such as *cul de sac, ancien régime, deus ex machina, mutatis mutandis, status quo, Gleichschaltung, Weltanschauung,* are used to give an air of culture and elegance. Except for the useful abbreviations *i.e., e.g.,* and *etc.,* there is no real need for any of the hundreds of foreign phrases now current in English. Bad writers, and especially scientific, political and sociological writers, are nearly always haunted by the notion that Latin or Greek words are grander than Saxon ones, and unnecessary words like *expedite, ameliorate, predict, extraneous, deracinated, clandestine, subaqueous* and hundreds of others constantly gain ground from their Anglo-Saxon opposite numbers.[1] The jargon peculiar to Marxist writing (*hyena, hangman, cannibal, petty bourgeois, these gentry, lacquey, flunkey, mad dog, White Guard,* etc.) consists largely of words and phrases translated from Russian, German or French; but the normal way of coining a new word is to use a Latin or Greek root with the appropriate affix and, where necessary, the *-ize* formation. It is often easier to make up words of this kind (*deregionalize, impermissible, extramarital, non-fragmentatory* and so forth) than to think up the English words that will cover one's meaning. The result, in general, is an increase in slovenliness and vagueness.

---

[1]An interesting illustration of this is the way in which the English flower names which were in use till very recently are being ousted by Greek ones, *snapdragon* becoming *antirrhinum, forget-me-not* becoming *myosotis,* etc. It is hard to see any practical reason for this change of fashion: it is probably due to an instinctive turning-away from the more homely word and a vague feeling that the Greek word is scientific.

Meaningless Words

In certain kinds of writing, particularly in art criticism and literary criticism, it 8
is normal to come across long passages which are almost completely lacking in
meaning.[2] Words like *romantic, plastic, values, human, dead, sentimental,
natural, vitality,* as used in art criticism, are strictly meaningless, in the sense
that they not only do not point to any discoverable object, but are hardly even
expected to do so by the reader. When one critic writes, "The outstanding feature of Mr. X's work is its living quality," while another writes, "The immediately striking thing about Mr. X's work is its peculiar deadness," the reader
accepts this as a simple difference of opinion. If words like *black* and *white*
were involved, instead of the jargon words *dead* and *living,* he would see at
once that language was being used in an improper way. Many political words
are similarly abused. The word *Fascism* has now no meaning except in so far as
it signifies "something not desirable." The words *democracy, socialism, freedom,
patriotic, realistic, justice,* have each of them several different meanings which
cannot be reconciled with one another. In the case of a word like *democracy,* not
only is there no agreed definition, but the attempt to make one is resisted from
all sides. It is almost universally felt that when we call a country democratic we
are praising it: Consequently the defenders of every kind of régime claim that
it is a democracy, and fear that they might have to stop using the word if it were
tied down to any one meaning. Words of this kind are often used in a consciously dishonest way. That is, the person who uses them has his own private
definition, but allows his hearer to think he means something quite different.
Statements like *Marshal Pétain was a true patriot, The Soviet press is the freest
in the world, The Catholic Church is opposed to persecution,* are almost always
made with intent to deceive. Other words used in variable meanings, in most
cases more or less dishonestly, are: *class, totalitarian, science, progressive, reactionary, bourgeois, equality.*

Now that I have made this catalogue of swindles and perversions, let me 9
give another example of the kind of writing that they lead to. This time it must
of its nature be an imaginary one. I am going to translate a passage of good
English into modern English of the worst sort. Here is a well-known verse from
Ecclesiastes:

> I returned, and saw under the sun, that the race is not to the swift, nor the
> battle to the strong, neither yet bread to the wise, nor yet riches to men of
> understanding, nor yet favor to men of skill; but time and chance happeneth to
> them all.

---

[2]*Example:* "Comfort's catholicity of perception and image, strangely Whitmanesque in range, almost
the exact opposite in aesthetic compulsion, continues to evoke that trembling atmospheric accumulative
hinting at a cruel, an inexorably serene timelessness. . . . Wrey Gardiner scores by aiming at simple
bullseyes with precision. Only they are not so simple, and through this contented sadness runs more
than the surface bittersweet of resignation." (*Poetry Quarterly*)

10   Here it is in modern English:

> Objective consideration of contemporary phenomena compels the conclusion that
> success or failure in competitive activities exhibits no tendency to be commensurate
> with innate capacity, but that a considerable element of the unpredictable must
> invariably be taken into account.

11   This is a parody, but not a very gross one. Exhibit (3) above, for instance,
contains several patches of the same kind of English. It will be seen that I have
not made a full translation. The beginning and ending of the sentence follow the
original meaning fairly closely, but in the middle the concrete illustrations—
race, battle, bread—dissolve into the vague phrase "success or failure in competitive activities." This had to be so, because no modern writer of the kind I am
discussing—no one capable of using phrases like "objective consideration of
contemporary phenomena"—would ever tabulate his thoughts in that precise
and detailed way. The whole tendency of modern prose is away from concreteness. Now analyze these two sentences a little more closely. The first contains
49 words but only 60 syllables, and all its words are those of everyday life. The
second contains 38 words of 90 syllables: 18 of its words are from Latin roots,
and one from Greek. The first sentence contains six vivid images, and only one
phrase ("time and chance") that could be called vague. The second contains not
a single fresh, arresting phrase, and in spite of its 90 syllables it gives only a
shortened version of the meaning contained in the first. Yet without a doubt it is
the second kind of sentence that is gaining ground in modern English. I do not
want to exaggerate. This kind of writing is not yet universal, and outcrops of
simplicity will occur here and there in the worst-written page. Still, if you or I
were told to write a few lines on the uncertainty of human fortunes, we should
probably come much nearer to my imaginary sentence than to the one from
Ecclesiastes.

12   As I have tried to show, modern writing at its worst does not consist in picking out words for the sake of their meaning and inventing images in order to
make the meaning clearer. It consists in gumming together long strips of words
which have already been set in order by someone else, and making the results
presentable by sheer humbug. The attraction of this way of writing is that it is
easy. It is easier—even quicker, once you have the habit—to say *In my opinion it
is a not unjustifiable assumption that* than to say *I think.* If you use ready-made
phrases, you not only don't have to hunt about for words; you also don't have to
bother with the rhythms of your sentences, since these phrases are generally so
arranged as to be more or less euphonious. When you are composing in a hurry—
when you are dictating to a stenographer, for instance, or making a public
speech—it is natural to fall into a pretentious, latinized style. Tags like *a consideration which we should do well to bear in mind* or *a conclusion to which all of us
would readily assent* will save many a sentence from coming down with a bump.
By using stale metaphors, similes and idioms, you save much mental effort, at the
cost of leaving your meaning vague, not only for your reader but for yourself. This
is the significance of mixed metaphors. The sole aim of a metaphor is to call up a

visual image. When these images clash—as in *The Fascist octopus has sung its swan song, the jackboot is thrown into the melting-pot*—it can be taken as certain that the writer is not seeing a mental image of the objects he is naming; in other words he is not really thinking. Look again at the examples I gave at the beginning of this essay. Professor Laski (1) uses five negatives in 53 words. One of these is superfluous, making nonsense of the whole passage, and in addition there is the slip *alien* for akin, making further nonsense, and several avoidable pieces of clumsiness which increase the general vagueness. Professor Hogben (2) plays ducks and drakes with a battery which is able to write prescriptions, and, while disapproving of the everyday phrase *put up with,* is unwilling to look *egregious* up in the dictionary and see what it means. In (3), if one takes an uncharitable attitude towards it, [it] is simply meaningless: probably one could work out its intended meaning by reading the whole of the article in which it occurs. In (4) the writer knows more or less what he wants to say, but an accumulation of stale phrases chokes him like tea leaves blocking a sink. In (5) words and meaning have almost parted company. People who write in this manner usually have a general emotional meaning—they dislike one thing and want to express solidarity with another—but they are not interested in the detail of what they are saying. A scrupulous writer, in every sentence that he writes, will ask himself at least four questions, thus: What am I trying to say? What words will express it? What image or idiom will make it clearer? Is this image fresh enough to have an effect? And he will probably ask himself two more: Could I put it more shortly? Have I said anything that is avoidably ugly? But you are not obliged to go to all this trouble. You can shirk it by simply throwing your mind open and letting the ready-made phrases come crowding in. They will construct your sentences for you—even think your thoughts for you, to a certain extent—and at need they will perform the important service of partially concealing your meaning even from yourself. It is at this point that the special connection between politics and the debasement of language becomes clear.

In our time it is broadly true that political writing is bad writing. Where it is 13 not true, it will generally be found that the writer is some kind of rebel, expressing his private opinions, and not a "party line." Orthodoxy, of whatever color, seems to demand a lifeless, imitative style. The political dialects to be found in pamphlets, leading articles, manifestos, White Papers and the speeches of Under-Secretaries do, of course, vary from party to party, but they are all alike in that one almost never finds in them a fresh, vivid, home-made turn of speech. When one watches some tired hack on the platform mechanically repeating the familiar phrases—*bestial atrocities, iron heel, blood-stained tyranny, free peoples of the world, stand shoulder to shoulder*—one often has a curious feeling that one is not watching a live human being but some kind of dummy: a feeling which suddenly becomes stronger at moments when the light catches the speaker's spectacles and turns them into blank discs which seem to have no eyes behind them. And this is not altogether fanciful. A speaker who uses that kind of phraseology has gone some distance towards turning himself into a machine. The appropriate noises are coming out of his larynx, but his brain is not involved as it would be if he were choosing his words for himself. If the speech he is making is one that he is accustomed to make over and over again, he may be almost unconscious of what he is saying, as one is when one utters the responses in church. And this reduced state of consciousness, if not indispensable, is at any rate favorable to political conformity.

14   In our time, political speech and writing are largely the defense of the indefensible. Things like the continuance of British rule in India, the Russian purges and deportations, the dropping of the atom bombs on Japan, can indeed be defended, but only by arguments which are too brutal for most people to face, and which do not square with the professed aims of political parties. Thus political language has to consist largely of euphemism, question-begging and sheer cloudy vagueness. Defenseless villages are bombarded from the air, the inhabitants driven out into the countryside, the cattle machine-gunned, the huts set on fire with incendiary bullets: This is called *pacification.* Millions of peasants are robbed of their farms and sent trudging along the roads with no more than they can carry: This is called *transfer of population or rectification of frontiers.* People are imprisoned for years without trial, or shot in the back of the neck or sent to die of scurvy in Arctic lumber camps: This is called *elimination of unreliable elements.* Such phraseology is needed if one wants to name things without calling up mental pictures of them. Consider for instance some comfortable English professor defending Russian totalitarianism. He cannot say outright, "I believe in killing off your opponents when you can get good results by doing so." Probably, therefore, he will say something like this:

> While freely conceding that the Soviet régime exhibits certain features which the humanitarian may be inclined to deplore, we must, I think, agree that a certain curtailment of the right to political opposition is an unavoidable concomitant of transitional periods, and that the rigors which the Russian people have been called upon to undergo have been amply justified in the sphere of concrete achievement.

15   The inflated style is itself a kind of euphemism. A mass of Latin words falls upon the facts like soft snow, blurring the outlines and covering up all the details. The great enemy of clear language is insincerity. When there is a gap between one's real and one's declared aims, one turns as it were instinctively to long words and exhausted idioms, like a cuttlefish squirting out ink. In our age there is no such thing as "keeping out of politics." All issues are political issues, and politics itself is a mass of lies, evasions, folly, hatred and schizophrenia. When the general atmosphere is bad, language must suffer. I should expect to find—this is a guess which I have not sufficient knowledge to verify—that the German, Russian and Italian languages have all deteriorated in the last ten or fifteen years, as a result of dictatorship.

16   But if thought corrupts language, language can also corrupt thought. A bad usage can spread by tradition and imitation, even among people who should and do know better. The debased language that I have been discussing is in some ways very convenient. Phrases like *a not unjustifiable assumption, leaves much to*

be desired, would serve no good purpose, a consideration which we should do well to bear in mind, are a continuous temptation, a packet of aspirins always at one's elbow. Look back through this essay, and for certain you will find that I have again and again committed the very faults I am protesting against. By this morning's post I have received a pamphlet dealing with conditions in Germany. The author tells me that he "felt impelled" to write it. I open it at random, and here is almost the first sentence that I see: "(The Allies) have an opportunity not only of achieving a radical transformation of Germany's social and political structure in such a way as to avoid a nationalistic reaction in Germany itself, but at the same time of laying the foundations of a cooperative and unified Europe." You see, he "feels impelled" to write—feels, presumably, that he has something new to say—and yet his words, like cavalry horses answering the bugle, group themselves automatically into the familiar dreary pattern. This invasion of one's mind by ready-made phrases *(lay the foundations, achieve a radical transformation)* can only be prevented if one is constantly on guard against them, and every such phrase anaesthetizes a portion of one's brain.

I said earlier that the decadence of our language is probably curable. Those 17 who deny this would argue, if they produced an argument at all, that language merely reflects existing social conditions, and that we cannot influence its development by any direct tinkering with words and constructions. So far as the general tone or spirit of a language goes, this may be true, but it is not true in detail. Silly words and expressions have often disappeared, not through any evolutionary process but owing to the conscious action of a minority. Two recent examples were *explore every avenue* and *leave no stone unturned,* which were killed by the jeers of a few journalists. There is a long list of fly-blown metaphors which could similarly be got rid of if enough people would interest themselves in the job; and it should also be possible to laugh the *not un-* formation out of existence,[3] to reduce the amount of Latin and Greek in the average sentence, to drive out foreign phrases and strayed scientific words, and, in general, to make pretentiousness unfashionable. But all these are minor points. The defense of the English language implies more than this, and perhaps it is best to start by saying what it does *not* imply.

To begin with, it has nothing to do with archaism, with the salvaging of 18 obsolete words and turns of speech, or with the setting up of a "standard English" which must never be departed from. On the contrary, it is especially concerned with the scrapping of every word or idiom which has outworn its usefulness. It has nothing to do with correct grammar and syntax, which are of no importance so long as one makes one's meaning clear, or with the avoidance of Americanisms, or with having what is called a "good prose style." On the other hand it is not concerned with fake simplicity and the attempt to make written English colloquial. Nor does it even imply in every case preferring the Saxon word to the Latin one, though it does imply using the fewest and shortest

---

[3]One can cure oneself of the *not un-* formation by memorizing this sentence: *A not unblack dog was chasing a not unsmall rabbit across a not ungreen field.*

words that will cover one's meaning. What is above all needed is to let the meaning choose the word, and not the other way about. In prose, the worst thing one can do with words is to surrender to them. When you think of a concrete object, you think wordlessly, and then, if you want to describe the thing you have been visualizing, you probably hunt about till you find the exact words that seem to fit it. When you think of something abstract you are more inclined to use words from the start, and unless you make a conscious effort to prevent it, the existing dialect will come rushing in and do the job for you, at the expense of blurring or even changing your meaning. Probably it is better to put off using words as long as possible and get one's meaning as clear as one can through pictures or sensations. Afterwards one can choose—not simply *accept*—the phrases that will best cover the meaning, and then switch around and decide what impression one's words are likely to make on another person. This last effort of the mind cuts out all stale or mixed images, all prefabricated phrases, needless repetitions, and humbug and vagueness generally. But one can often be in doubt about the effect of a word or a phrase, and one needs rules that one can rely on when instinct fails. I think the following rules will cover most cases:

 i.   Never use a metaphor, simile or other figure of speech which you are used to seeing in print.
 ii. Never use a long word where a short one will do.
 iii. If it is possible to cut a word out, always cut it out.
 iv. Never use the passive where you can use the active.
 v.   Never use a foreign phrase, a scientific word or a jargon word if you can think of an everyday English equivalent.
 vi. Break any of these rules sooner than say anything outright barbarous.

19   These rules sound elementary, and so they are, but they demand a deep change of attitude in anyone who has grown used to writing in the style now fashionable. One could keep all of them and still write bad English, but one could not write the kind of stuff that I quoted in those five specimens at the beginning of this article.

20   I have not here been considering the literary use of language, but merely language as an instrument for expressing and not for concealing or preventing thought. Stuart Chase and others have come near to claiming that all abstract words are meaningless, and have used this as a pretext for advocating a kind of political quietism. Since you don't know what Fascism is, how can you struggle against Fascism? One need not swallow such absurdities as this, but one ought to recognize that the present political chaos is connected with the decay of language, and that one can probably bring about some improvement by starting at the verbal end. If you simplify your English, you are freed from the worst follies of orthodoxy. You cannot speak any of the necessary dialects, and when you make a stupid remark its stupidity will be obvious, even to yourself. Political language—and with variations this is true of all political parties,

from Conservatives to Anarchists—is designed to make lies sound truthful and murder respectable, and to give an appearance of solidity to pure wind. One cannot change this all in a moment, but one can at least change one's own habits, and from time to time one can even, if one jeers loudly enough, send some worn-out and useless phrase—some *jackboot, Achilles' heel, hotbed, melting pot, acid test, veritable inferno* or other lump of verbal refuse—into the dustbin where it belongs.

COMPREHENSION

1. What is Orwell's purpose? For what type of audience is he writing? Where does he summarize his concerns for readers?
2. According to Orwell, "thought corrupts language" and "language can also corrupt thought" (paragraph 16). Give examples of these assertions in the essay.
3. In what ways does Orwell believe that politics and language are related?

RHETORIC

1. Orwell himself uses similes and metaphors. Locate five of them, and explain their relationship to the author's analysis.
2. Orwell claims that concrete language is superior to abstract language. Give examples of Orwell's attempt to write concretely.
3. One of the most crucial rhetorical devices in this essay is definition. What important concepts does Orwell define? What methods of definition does he tend to use?
4. Identify an example of hypothetical reasoning in the essay. How does it contribute to the thesis of the essay?
5. After having given five examples of bad English, why does Orwell, in paragraph 10, give another example? How does this example differ from the others? What does it add to the essay?
6. Explain the use of extended analogy in paragraph 14.

WRITING

1. In an analytical essay, assess the state of language in politics today. Cite examples from newspapers and television reports.
2. Prepare an essay analyzing the use and abuse of any word that sparks controversy today—for example, *abortion, AIDS,* or *greed.*
3. **Writing an Argument:** Orwell claims that "the decline of a language must ultimately have political and economic causes" (paragraph 2). Is this claim true? Answer this question in an argumentative essay.

NETWORKING
Applying Digital and Multimedia Literacies

1. **Analyzing and Synthesizing a Graphic:** The graphic below is from the *New York Times'* 2008 online election coverage. Read the description, note the words used, and discuss, in small groups or as a class, why some words or phrases were used extensively by both parties and others were used much more by one or the other. What might Orwell think about the words these politicians used—and this graphic display of them?

2. **Choosing a Graphic Medium:** Why might this particular content lend itself better to graphic, rather than written, form?

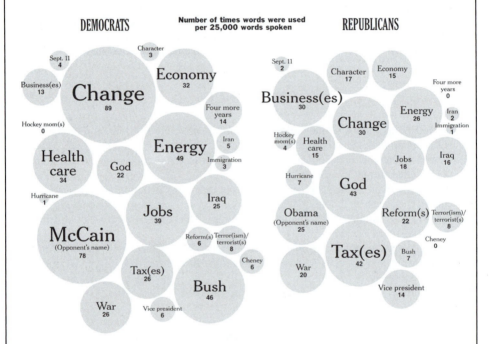

DEMOCRATS   **Number of times words were used per 25,000 words spoken**   REPUBLICANS

THE WORDS THEY USED

The words that speakers used at the two political conventions show the themes that the parties have highlighted. Republican speakers have talked about reform and character far more frequently than the Democrats. And Republicans were more likely to talk about businesses and taxes, while Democrats were more likely to mention jobs or the economy. *The New York Times,* September 4, 2008. Copyright © 2008 The New York Times Co. Reprinted with permission.

Synthesis: Connections
for Critical Thinking

1. Examine the "how-to" aspect of the essays by Elbow and Murray. What general strategies do they use to develop a comprehensive process analysis of an elusive subject—for example, reading or writing? Write an essay in which you compare the tactics these writers employ to demonstrate their processes.
2. Study the tone of Schlesinger's essay "The Cult of Ethnicity" (in Chapter 1). How does he remain "civil" while arguing against a contemporary view he seems to abhor? Next, study Amy Tan's "Mother Tongue" and Manuel Muñoz's "Leave Your Name at the Border" and examine how they use narration in addressing the complex subject of language(s). Make some general observations about how the stylistic elements of an essay contribute to the ability of the author to communicate difficult subjects in a manner that is appealing to the reader.
3. Synthesize the ideas in Elbow's "Freewriting" and those in Murray's "The Maker's Eye" so that you can write a coherent essay on writing that takes into account the transition from inspiration to craft.
4. Compare and contrast Martin's satiric take on how to write with Elbow's or Murray's approach. How might Martin's piece be helpful to writers? Consider his use of humor in your response.
5. Tannen, Muñoz, and Tan write personal essays about the impact of language on their lives. Write a comparative essay in which you analyze the similarities and differences in their approach to the topic.
6. How do Orwell and Tannen treat the communication process? How are their topics similar and dissimilar? Write a comparative essay on this topic.

chapter 3

Reading and Writing Effective Arguments

You encounter various forms of argumentation in everyday situations, in Internet-based discourse and online communities, and of course in many college courses where debate is the essence of class discussion. People argue for many reasons, but one of the most compelling is to sift through opposing or competing viewpoints in order to achieve a mutually satisfying consensus that everyone can live with. In our increasingly globalized world, where diverse peoples and belief systems can converge in a nanosecond, we must find ways to learn more about and consider positions different from our own, and to communicate our beliefs in ways that are thoughtful, considerate, and interesting. You will be better prepared to address consequential issues in a personal, academic, professional, or civic context—whether you are convincing someone to share your position or to take action, and whether you are making a point or refuting one—if you learn more about argumentation as a mode of thinking, reading, and writing.

As a common form of academic writing, *argumentation* seeks to explore differences of opinion and attempts to promote agreement. As such, argument is useful not only in classroom situations but also in the realm of civic life and discourse, for it provides reasons for people to agree with a particular point of view or at least come to an understanding of an individual's or a group's perspective on an issue. Aristotle, who wrote the first major work on argument, thought that the best and most effective argumentative writing blends rational, emotional, and ethical appeals in order to move an audience—whether one person or an entire nation—to some desired action. Aristotle's threefold approach to argument might serve you especially well as you navigate and evaluate the many Web sites, wikis, blogs, social networking sites, and other online publications and venues that offer resources (but also pitfalls) for writers today.

When you engage in argumentation, you offer reasons to support a position, belief, or conclusion. A typical argumentative essay presents a debatable thesis and defends it in logical fashion. Closely allied with argumentation is *persuasion,* in which the writer appeals to readers' intelligence, emotions, and beliefs in order to influence them to adopt a position or act in a certain way. Logic and persuasive appeal often combine when a writer tries to convince an audience that his or her position is valid and that other perspectives, while understandable perhaps, require reconsideration.

It is important to distinguish between oral arguments and written ones. Admittedly, both spoken and written arguments have a common purpose in their attempt to convince someone to agree with a particular position, make a certain decision, or take a specific action. In both your oral and written arguments, you will usually invoke reasons and attempt to manipulate language skillfully. However, with an oral argument, you rarely have access to the types of specific evidence needed to support your reasons, nor do you have the time or ability to marshal reasons and evidence in well-organized and coherent ways. Oral arguments, as you well know, tend to involve excessive emotion; after all, oral arguments often erupt spontaneously and are rarely thoughtfully constructed and presented.

Unlike most oral arguments, effective written arguments are carefully and logically planned, organized, researched, and revised. The writer analyzes the audience and anticipates objections to the assertions being made. As she or he develops the argument, the writer considers and selects various rhetorical strategies—for example, analysis, definition, or comparison and contrast—to shape the presentation. Moreover, the writer has time to choose the appropriate language and style for the argument, exploring the use of striking diction, figurative language, rhythmic sentence patterns, and various tonalities and shades of meaning during the prewriting, drafting, and revision stages. Finally, especially when composing arguments for college courses, writers must attend to logic and the techniques of valid persuasive appeal.

LEARNING THE LANGUAGE OF ARGUMENT

Writers of argument often employ various modes of exposition like definition, comparison and contrast, illustration, and analysis, but they incorporate these modes of critical thinking as the means of justifying, or supporting, a logical position. The study of the special language, logic, and structure of argumentation fills volumes. For college writing, there is a core group of critical terms that you should know before you design an argumentative paper:

- A *claim* is a statement to be justified or upheld. It is the main idea or position that you plan to present in an argument.
- *Thesis, proposition, assertion,* and *premise* are all similar to a claim in that each is a positive statement or declaration to be supported with reasons and evidence. *Premise,* however, should be distinguished from the other terms: It is a statement or assumption that is established before an argument is begun and is important to an understanding of logic and various errors or fallacies in reasoning.
- *Grounds* are the reasons, support, and evidence presented to support your claim.
- A *warrant* is a stated or unstated belief, rule, or principle that underlies an argument. A *backing* is an even broader principle that serves as the foundation for a warrant.
- The *major proposition* is the main point of an argument, which is supported by the minor propositions.
- The *minor propositions* are the reasons you offer in support of the major proposition.
- *Evidence* is that part of the argument that supports the minor propositions. In argumentation, effective evidence is based either on facts, examples, statistics, and other forms of evidence or on accepted opinions. Without adequate evidence, the audience will not accept your major and minor propositions. Evidence in argument must be accurate and true.
- A *fact* is a verifiable statement. A valid *opinion* is a judgment based on the facts and careful deductive or inductive reasoning. *Induction* is a process of reasoning by which you develop evidence in order to reach a useful generalization. *Deduction* is a process of reasoning that proceeds from the general to the particular.
- A valid *conclusion* of an argument derives logically from the major and minor propositions. The logical conclusion is termed the *inference,* in which you arrive at a decision by reasoning from the previous evidence.

Classic and Contemporary Images
WHAT IS AN ARGUMENT?

Using a Critical Perspective   What images and strategies do the Spanish artist Francisco de Goya and the American photographer Eddie Adams employ to construct an argument about war? What exactly is their argument? Comment on the nature and effectiveness of the details they use to illustrate their position. Which work do you find more powerful or engaging? Explain.

Horrified by the excesses of the Napoleonic invasion of his homeland and
the Spanish war for independence, the Spanish artist Francisco de Goya
(1746–1828) painted *The Third of May, 1808,* a vivid rendition
of an execution during wartime.

Another wartime execution, this time captured on film by Eddie Adams
in an image that won the Pulitzer Prize for spot news photography
in 1969, brought home to Americans the horrors and
ambiguities of the war in Vietnam.

- A *fallacy* is a line of incorrect reasoning from premises.
- *Refutation* is the acknowledgment and handling of opposing viewpoints. You must anticipate opposing viewpoints and counter them effectively (what we term *rebuttal*) in order to convince or persuade readers.

Constructing an effective argument depends on the careful arrangement of major and minor propositions, evidence, and refutation. Like a lawyer, you build a position and subject your opponent's position to dissection in an effort to win the case.

USING THE TEST OF JUSTIFICATION

Whatever its components, whether a writer can construct an argument or not essentially hinges on the concept of *justification*—the recognition that a subject lends itself to legitimate difference of opinion. Justification also involves proving or demonstrating that a claim is in accordance with the reasons and evidence offered to support it.

Not all statements require justification. A statement that is a verifiable fact or a commonly accepted assumption or belief—what we term a *warrant*—generally does not need justification. To test the concept of justification, consider the following four statements.

1. President John F. Kennedy was assassinated on November 22, 1963.
2. Children shouldn't smoke.
3. Abortion is the destruction of a human life.
4. African Americans should receive reparations for the damages caused by slavery.

Which of these statements require justification? The first statement about President Kennedy is a verifiable fact, and the second statement strikes any reasonable audience as common sense. Thus, the first two statements do not require justification and consequently could not be the subject of a useful argument, although the second statement could serve as the warrant for a more specific claim about smoking by children. In contrast, the third statement, concerning abortion, makes a critical assumption that would elicit either agreement or disagreement but in either case would demand substantiation. Similarly, the fourth statement, about reparations for slavery, is an issue that is debatable from a variety of positions. Therefore, statements 3 and 4 require justification: They are open to argumentation.

READING AND ANALYZING ARGUMENTS

From the time of Aristotle to the present, numerous critical approaches to the study of argument have been devised. One of the most useful recent approaches to argument appears in *An Introduction to Reasoning* and *The Uses of Argument* by British logician and philosopher Stephen Toulmin. In his studies, Toulmin observes that any argument involves a *claim* supported by *reasons* and *evidence*. Whether writing a memo to your instructor contesting a certain grade, or a letter to the editor of your campus newspaper advocating a change in the cafeteria vendor because the food is terrible, or a petition to provide more parking spaces for commuting students, the argumentative method is the same. Essentially, you make a general assertion—a claim—and then offer the smaller propositions or supporting reasons along with the relevant facts, examples, statistics, and expert testimony to justify all claims. And underlying the nature of claims and evidence is recognition of the importance of *warrants,* those unstated beliefs that lead from evidence to claim.

Here is the way Toulmin presents his model:

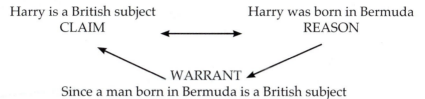

Harry is a British subject
CLAIM

Harry was born in Bermuda
REASON

WARRANT
Since a man born in Bermuda is a British subject

In truth, Toulmin's example is basic and perhaps too simplistic. The claims that you deal with when reading or writing arguments typically are more complex and controversial than Toulmin's diagram suggests, and the need for extensive evidence more demanding. Nevertheless, Toulmin's model offers a useful way to understand the nature of argumentative reasoning.

Understanding Claims and Warrants

When you argue in writing, you make a specific claim, which is an assertion that you plan to prove. You present this claim or proposition as being true, and you support the claim with a series of logically related statements that are true. Think of the claim as the thesis or the main point of the argument that holds all other logically related statements together. The claim is the main idea that you set out to prove, and in a well-reasoned argument, everything makes the claim seem inevitable. Any paper you write that fails to state a claim—your position in an argument—will leave readers shaking their heads and wondering if you actually have an argument to present.

Think of a claim as an arguable point, one that you can build a carefully reasoned paper around. By applying the test of justification, you can exclude numerous opinions, nonarguable propositions, and statements of taste and fact that might be common in everyday situations but not legitimate subjects for papers. To say "Turn down that rap music" to your roommate is the sort of command (containing perhaps an implied opinion) that doesn't in itself qualify as a claim but could get you involved in a heated conversation. To transform this command into a legitimate claim or an arguable point, you would have to state a proposition that expresses your main idea about rap.

Suppose, for example, that you want to write an argumentative paper on hip-hop or rap music. What claim would you actually make about rap music and the culture that supports it? What reasons or grounds would you produce in support of your claim?

A complex, extended argument in essay form often reveals several types of claims that the writer advances. A *claim about meaning* (What is rap music?) is a proposition that defines or interprets a subject as it establishes an arguable point. A *claim about value* (Rap music is good or bad) advances an ideally open-minded view of the subject based on a coherent framework of aesthetic or ethical values. A *claim about policy* (Music stations should be forced to regulate the most offensive forms of rap music) advances propositions concerning laws, regulations, and initiatives designed to produce specific outcomes. Finally, *claims about consequences* (Children who listen to rap musicians begin to mimic their vulgar behavior) are rooted in propositions involving various forms of cause-and-effect relationships. Constructing an argument around one or more of these types of claims is essential to gaining an audience's assent.

Many claims, of course, cannot be presented as absolute propositions—certainly not as absolute as Aristotle's major premise in his famous syllogism (see page 145) that "all human beings are mortal." Writers must seek common ground with readers and foster a degree of trust by anticipating that some members of any audience will disagree with their claim, treat it with skepticism, and perhaps even respond with hostility. For this reason, it is important to qualify or clarify the nature of your claim. A *qualifier* restricts the absoluteness of a claim by using such cue words and phrases as *sometimes, probably, usually,* and *in most cases.*

Qualifiers can also explain certain circumstances or conditions under which the claim might not be true. The use of qualifiers enables the writer to anticipate certain audience reactions and handle them in an effective and subtle way.

Even more important than the possible need to qualify a claim is the need to justify it in a new way: by linking the claim with reasons and evidence in such a way that the audience sees the train of thinking that leads from the data to the claim. If you look again at the model that Toulmin provides, you see that the datum "Harry was born in Bermuda" does not completely support the claim "Harry is a British subject." What is required is what Toulmin calls a *warrant,* a form of justification—a general belief, principle, or rule—that links the claim and the data or support. Thus the warrant "Since a man born in Bermuda is a British subject" explains *why* the claim follows from the datum.

Another way of understanding this admittedly challenging concept of warrant is to treat it as the process of thinking that leads writers to hold the opinions they present. Thought of from this perspective, we can see that a weak or unclear warrant will undermine an argument and render it invalid. For example, the claim "Sara graduated from an excellent high school and consequently should do well in college" is based on the warrant or unstated (and untested) belief that all students who graduate from good high schools perform well at the college level. Obviously, this warrant is not satisfactory: To state that college success is based solely on the quality of one's high school education is to base the argument on a warrant that few readers would find acceptable. If, on the other hand, a writer claims that "Sara graduated from an excellent high school with a 3.97 cumulative average, the third highest in her class, and consequently should do well in college," we see that the warrant establishing the link between claim and conclusion becomes more acceptable. In fact, there is a consensus, or general belief, among experts that a person's grade point average in high school is a sound predictor—perhaps sounder than SAT scores—of his or her potential for success in college.

If you disagree with a writer's assumptions, you basically are questioning the warrants underlying the argument. An effective argument should rest on an acceptable warrant and also on the *backing*—some explanation or support—for it. Remember that even if a warrant, stated or unstated, is clear, understood, and backed with support, readers might still disagree with it. For example, one could argue that Sara might have obtained her lofty GPA in high school by taking easy courses and that consequently we cannot readily predict her success in college. Not everyone will accept even the most reasonable of warrants.

Reasoning from Evidence

Evidence is the data, or *grounds,* used to make claims or general assertions clear, concrete, and convincing. In argumentation, the presentation of evidence must be examined from the perspective of logic or sound reasoning. Central to logic is the relationship of evidence to a *generalization,* a statement or conclusion that what is applicable in one situation also applies to similar situations. You cannot think and write clearly unless you test evidence to see that it supports your claims, assumptions, or general statements. Evidence in an argumentative essay creates a common ground of understanding that you and your reader can share.

You know that one of the keenest pleasures in reading mystery fiction or viewing whodunits on television or film is the quest for evidence. The great writers of crime and mystery fiction—Edgar Allan Poe, Sir Arthur Conan Doyle, Agatha Christie—were adept at creating a chain of clues, or evidence, leading with the inevitability of logic to the solution to the crime. Whether it is a letter lying on a desk in Poe's "The Purloined Letter" or a misplaced chair in Christie's *The Murder of Roger Ackroyd,* it is evidence that we seek in order to solve the crime.

In argumentative writing, evidence is used more to prove a point than to solve a mystery. College writers must know what constitutes evidence—examples, facts, statistics, quotations and information from authoritative sources, personal experience, careful reasoning—and how to use it to support certain claims. They must also determine if the evidence and assumptions surrounding the evidence are valid.

Here are some basic questions about evidence to consider when reading and writing argumentative essays:

- *Is the evidence typical and representative?* Examples must fairly represent the condition or situation if your claim is to be valid. If evidence is distorted or unrepresentative, a claim will not be logical or convincing.
- *Is the evidence relevant?* The evidence should speak directly to the claim. It should not utilize peripheral or irrelevant data.
- *Is the evidence specific and detailed?* In reading and writing arguments, do not trust broad, catchall statements presented as "evidence." Valid evidence should involve accurate quotations, paraphrases, and presentations of data from authoritative sources.
- *Is the evidence accurate and reliable?* A claim is only as valid as the data supporting it. Facts should come from reliable sources. (See page 75 and Chapter 15 for help with evaluating sources.) Current rather than outdated evidence should predominate in a current argument. Sources should be cited accurately for the convenience of the reader. Although personal observation and personal experience are admissible as types of evidence, such testimony rarely serves as conclusive proof for a claim.
- *Is the evidence sufficient?* There must be enough evidence to support claims and reasons. One extended piece of evidence, no matter how carefully selected, rarely is sufficient to win an argument.

Any argumentative essay should provide a clear, logical link between the writer's claim, assertion, generalization, or conclusion and the evidence. If an argumentative essay reveals false or illogical reasoning—that is, if the step from the evidence to the generalization is wrong, confusing, or deceptive—readers will not accept the truth of the claim or the validity of the evidence.

THINKING CRITICALLY ABOUT ARGUMENTS

Whether you are reading another writer's argument or starting to plan one of your own, you need to consider the purposes of the argument. When you are reading an argument, you should also look for the appeals to reason, emotion, and ethics the writer is using and decide whether those appeals are effective for you, the writer's audience. In your own arguments, you will need to decide the types of appeals that will carry the most weight with *your* audience.

The Purpose of Argumentation

As a college writer, your general aim is to communicate or convey messages in essay form to a literate and knowledgeable audience of teachers and scholars. When thinking about the subject for an essay, you also have to consider a more specialized *purpose*—the special nature or aim—behind your composition. You might have to report the result of an experiment in animal behavior, analyze a poem, compare and contrast Mario Puzo's novel *The Godfather* with its film adaptation, or assert the need for capital punishment. In each instance, your essay requires a key rhetorical strategy or set of strategies. These strategies reflect your purpose—your intention—in developing the essay.

An argumentative essay may serve one or more purposes:

- To present a position, belief, or conclusion in a rational and effective way
- To defend a position against critics or detractors
- To persuade people to agree with a position or take a certain action
- To attack a position without necessarily presenting an alternative or opposing viewpoint

An effective argumentative essay often combines a variety of forms and purposes. For example, an argumentative essay on legalizing marijuana might explain effects, analyze laws, or evaluate experiments, among a broad range of options. When you take time to consider your purpose before you even begin to write, the decisions you make will help you to think more clearly about both the design and intention of your essay.

Appeals to Reason, Emotion, and Ethics

As the definitions of special terms and the discussion of justification presented earlier in the chapter suggest, argumentation places a premium on rational discourse. In fact, the *appeal to reason* is the fundamental purpose of argumentation. However, classical rhetorical theory acknowledges that the *appeal to emotion* and the *appeal to ethics* are also important elements in the construction of argument and the effort to persuade. A mere presentation of reasons is usually not an effective argument. For your argument to be effective, you need to pay attention to the value of strategic emotional and ethical appeals.

Appeals to Reason   The *appeal to reason* or logic is the primary instrument of effective argument. The most common way of developing an argument according to the principles of sound reasoning is *deduction,* which is most readily understood as an ordering of ideas from the general to the particular. With deduction, you move from a general assertion through reasons and support focused on the main assertion. Consider the following student paragraph, which uses the deductive method:

Anti-marijuana laws make people contemptuous of the legal system. This contempt is based in part on the key fact that there are too many contradictions and inconsistencies in criminal penalties for marijuana use. Laws vary radically from state to state. In Texas, you can be sentenced to life imprisonment for first-time use of marijuana. In contrast, in the District of Columbia, the same "crime" would most likely result in a suspended sentence.

Deduction is a convincing way of arranging ideas and information logically. By stating the proposition or generalization first, you present the most important idea. Then, as in the paragraph above, you move to more specific ideas and details. Examined more rigorously, deductive reasoning involves a process of critical thinking known as *syllogism,* in which you move from a major statement or premise, through another minor premise, to a third statement or conclusion. Aristotle's famous syllogism captures this mental process:

Major premise: All human beings are mortal.

Minor premise: Socrates is a human being.

Conclusion: Socrates is mortal.

The soundness of any deductive argument rests on the *truth* of the premises and the *validity* of the syllogism itself. In other words, if you grant the truth of the premises, you must also grant the conclusion. The deductive method can be used effectively in many forms of expository as well as argumentative essays.

Inductive reasoning reverses the process of deduction by moving from particular ideas to general ones. In the paragraph that follows, from an essay by F. M. Esfandiary, "The Mystical West Puzzles the Practical East," the writer presents various ideas and evidence that lead to a major proposition at the end:

Twenty-five hundred years ago, Buddha, like other Eastern philosophers before him, said: "He who sits still, wins." Asia, then immobilized in primitive torpor, had no difficulty responding. It sat still. What it won for sitting still was the perpetuation of famines and terrorizing superstitions, oppression of children, subjugation of women, emasculation of men, fratricidal wars, persecutions, mass killings. The history of Asia, like the history of all mankind, is a horrendous account of human suffering.

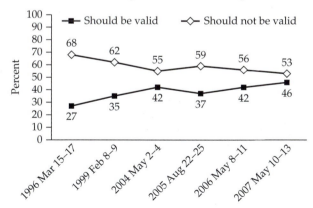

Do you think marriages between same-sex couples should or should not be recognized by the law as valid, with the same rights as traditional marriages?

Logical Appeal. This graph uses polling data to show the growth of popular support for marriage equality between 1996 and 2007. Quantifiable data usually add solid support to an argument, and such data can have a powerful (and instant) impact when expressed visually in a graph or chart.
Source: Gallup.com.

By presenting his supporting—and provocative—ideas first, the author is able to interest us before we reach the climactic argument at the end of the paragraph. Of course, whether we accept Esfandiary's argument—his statement of truth—or are prepared to debate his claim depends on the strength of the reasons and evidence he offers.

Many of the argumentative essays you read and much of the argumentative writing you undertake will reflect the mental processes of deduction and induction. The novelist Robert M. Pirsig offers his version of these critical thinking strategies in his cult classic, *Zen and the Art of Motorcycle Maintenance:*

> If the cycle goes over a bump and the engine misfires, and then goes over another bump and the engine misfires, and then goes over another bump and the engine misfires, and then goes over a long smooth stretch of road and there is no misfiring, and then goes over a fourth bump and the engine misfires again, one can logically conclude that the misfiring is caused by the bumps. That is induction: reasoning from particular experiences to general truths.
>
> Deductive inferences do the reverse. They start with general knowledge and predict a specific observation. For example if, from reading the hierarchy of facts about the machine the mechanic knows the horn of the cycle is powered exclusively by electricity from the battery, then he can logically infer that if the battery is dead the horn will not work. That is deduction.

Constructing an argument through the use of logical reasoning is a powerful way to convince or persuade a particular audience about the validity of your claims.

Appeals to Emotion   In addition to developing your argument logically using the appeal to reason, you should consider the value of incorporating *appeals to emotion* into an argumentative paper. A letter home asking for more money would in all likelihood require a certain carefully modulated emotional appeal. Martin Luther King Jr.'s famous "I Have a Dream" speech at the 1963 March on Washington, which begins on page 330, is one of the finest contemporary examples of emotional appeal. King's speech ends with this invocation:

> When we let freedom ring, when we let it ring from every village and every hamlet, from every state and every city, we will be able to speed up that day when all of God's children, black men and white men, Jews and Gentiles, Protestants and Catholics, will be able to join hands and sing in the words of the old Negro spiritual, "Free at last! Free at last! Thank God almighty, we are free at last!"

King's skillful application of balanced biblical cadences and connotative and figurative language, and a strong, almost prophetic tone demonstrates the value of carefully crafted emotional appeal in the hands of an accomplished writer of argument.

Of course, in constructing an argument, you should avoid the sort of cynical manipulation of emotion that is common in the world of spoken discourse and the media in general. (For a list of unfair emotional appeals, see page 158.) But honest emotional appeal provides a human context for the rational ideas and evidence you present in an argumentative essay—ideas that might otherwise be uninteresting to your audience. Assuredly, if you want to persuade your audience to undertake a particular course of action, you must draw members of this audience closer to you as a person, and perhaps even inspire them by your feelings about the subject or issue. In truth, you *must* establish rapport with your reader in

Emotional appeal. In the context of an argument for marriage equality, this photograph of two brides on their wedding day would appeal to readers' feelings: This is a happy couple. Their dresses might remind people of their own weddings, creating a sense of shared experience and interests. Photographs can make powerful emotional appeals, but in academic arguments, pathos needs to be supported by logos and ethos.

an argumentative essay. If you fail to engage the reader's feelings, the best-constructed rational appeal could fall flat.

Appeals to Ethics   For an emotional appeal to achieve maximum effectiveness, it must reinforce not only the rational strength of your argument but also the ethical basis of your ideas. When you use *ethical appeal,* you present yourself as a well-informed, fair-minded, honest person. Aristotle acknowledged the importance of *ethos,* or the character of the writer, in the construction of argument, for if you create a sense that you are trustworthy, your readers or listeners will be inspired or persuaded. The "sound" or "voice" of your essay, which you convey to the reader through your style and tone, and which can only be perfected through the process of careful drafting and revision, will help in convincing the audience to share your opinion.

In an appeal to ethics, you try to convince the reader that you are a person of sound character—that you possess good judgment and values. As a person of goodwill and good sense, you also demonstrate an ability to empathize with your audience, to understand their viewpoints and perspectives. The psychologist Carl Rogers suggests that a willingness to embrace a potentially adversarial audience, to treat this audience more like an ally in an ethical cause, is a highly effective way to establish goodwill and the credibility of your beliefs. In Rogerian argument, your willingness to understand an opposing viewpoint and actually rephrase it reflectively for mutual understanding enables you to further establish your ethical and personal qualities. As the world grows more and more interconnected,

Ethical appeal. In this photograph, President Obama signs the Matthew Shepard bill into law on October 28, 2009, recognizing crimes motivated by a victim's sexual orientation as hate crimes. A claim could be made that this mobilization of support from the federal government demonstrates a step toward (and argument for) equal rights for the GLBT community. In an essay, you would need to support such an appeal with logic, too.

and the pace of globalization accelerates, Rogerian argument might offer a form of cross-cultural discourse that bridges divides among people.

You can appreciate the powerful combination of rational, emotional, and ethical appeals in Abraham Lincoln's Gettysburg Address, which follows for analysis and discussion.

The Gettysburg Address

Abraham Lincoln

Abraham Lincoln (1809–1865) was born the son of a pioneer in 1809 in Hodgesville, Kentucky, and moved to Illinois in 1831. After brief experiences as a clerk, postmaster, and county surveyor, he studied law and was elected to the state legislature in 1834. A prominent member of the newly formed Republican Party, Lincoln became president on the eve of the Civil War. In 1862, after the Union victory at Antietam, Lincoln issued the Emancipation Proclamation freeing the slaves—the crowning achievement of an illustrious presidency. Although he was an outstanding orator and debater throughout his political career, the Gettysburg Address is one of his greatest speeches—and certainly his most famous one. It was delivered at the dedication of the Gettysburg National Cemetery in 1863. Its form and content reflect the philosophical and moral views of the time as well as the rhetorical skill of its speaker. Lincoln was assassinated by John Wilkes Booth in 1865, shortly after Robert E. Lee's surrender and the end of the Civil War.

Four score and seven years ago our fathers brought forth on this continent, a new 1
nation, conceived in Liberty, and dedicated to the proposition that all men are created equal.

Now we are engaged in a great civil war, testing whether that nation, or any 2
nation so conceived and so dedicated, can long endure. We are met on a great battlefield of that war. We have come to dedicate a portion of that field as a final resting-place for those who here gave their lives that that nation might live. It is altogether fitting and proper that we should do this.

But, in a larger sense, we cannot dedicate—we cannot consecrate—we cannot 3
hallow—this ground. The brave men, living and dead, who struggled here have consecrated it, far above our poor power to add or detract. The world will little note, nor long remember, what we say here, but it can never forget what they did here. It is for us the living, rather, to be dedicated here to the unfinished work which they who fought here have thus far so nobly advanced. It is rather for us to be here dedicated to the great task remaining before us—that from these honored dead we take increased devotion to that cause for which they gave the last full measure of devotion; that we here highly resolve that these dead shall not have died in vain; that this nation, under God, shall have a new birth of freedom; and that government of the people, by the people, for the people, shall not perish from the earth.

COMPREHENSION

1. Although this speech was supposed to be a "dedication," Lincoln states that "we cannot dedicate." What does he mean by this?
2. Lincoln uses abstract words such as "liberty," "freedom," and "nation." What does he mean specifically by each of these terms?
3. What exactly happened "four score and seven years ago" in the context of the speech? Why is this reference so significant to the purpose of Lincoln's address?

RHETORIC

1. Note the progression of imagery from that of "death" to that of "birth." How does this structure contribute to the claim and coherence of the speech?
2. How do the syntax, punctuation, and choice of the first-person plural form of address contribute to our understanding that this message was intended to be spoken rather than written?
3. Note how Lincoln refers to the combatants as "brave" and "honored." How does he suggest that their struggle was distinguished from that of "us the living"? How does this comparison and contrast create clear similarities and differences between those who fought and those who are present to carry on the work of the soldiers?

4. The American Civil War was a battle between the North and the South as were the opponents at the Battle of Gettysburg. However, Lincoln does not mention this. What is the reason behind this omission? How does it make the speech focus on more comprehensive issues?

5. Besides being president, Lincoln was by definition a politician. In what ways can we determine that this is a political speech as well as a dedication?

6. Speeches are intended to be heard. What are some elements—for example, vocabulary, syntax, length or brevity of the sentences, and juxtaposition of sentences—that appeal to the sense of sound?

7. Does this speech appeal primarily to the intellect or the emotions, or equally to the two? What are two or three sentences that demonstrate one or both of these appeals? What was the rationale behind your selections? Does Lincoln include any ethical appeals?

WRITING

1. Research the actual historical events that occurred during the Battle of Gettysburg. Write an argumentative essay in which you discuss the significance of this particular speech at this point in the Civil War. Use a minimum of three secondary source materials.

2. Read the speech three times. Then write a paraphrase of it. Examine your paraphrase to discover what elements you recalled. Then reread the speech and write an expository essay focusing on how the structure of the speech contributed to helping you recall the information you did remember.

NETWORKING
Applying Digital and Multimedia Literacies

Using Search Phrases: Do an online search for the literary influences on the language and style of Abraham Lincoln. Try a search phrase such as "Lincoln AND reading." Select three authoritative hits and write a research paper titled "Literary Influences on Abraham Lincoln." (See Chapter 15 for information about citing your sources correctly.)

WRITING POWERFUL ARGUMENTS

One of the most common writing assignments in college courses, especially courses in the humanities and social sciences, is the argumentative essay. Unlike narrative and descriptive essays and the major forms of expository writing—comparison and contrast, definition, classification, process, and causal analysis—the argumentative paper requires the writer to take a stand and to support a position as effectively as possible. As mentioned earlier, the rhetorical strategies underlying expository or informative writing often appear in argumentative papers. However, given the purpose of the argumentative essay, you must present your ideas as powerfully as possible in order to advance your point of view and convince your readers to accept your position or take a specific course of action. For this reason, you must construct your argumentative paper carefully and effectively.

Argument, as stated in Chapter 2, is not a mere academic enterprise but rather an integral part of our personal, social, and professional lives. Whether you consider the 2012 presidential debates, recent decisions of the Supreme Court, actions taken by the United States in the Middle East, or tax provisions enacted by Congress—argument determines in many ways the nature of life in the United States. More personally, argument—whether in the form of reviews or commercials—influences the films we watch, the music we listen to, the clothes we wear, and the food we eat. And argument—the way you sell yourself in an interview—can get you a job or lose it.

In many other ways, argument impacts your professional life. It is most clearly in evidence in newspaper and television journalism and communications, where argument and persuasion express an institution's deepest convictions. Consider the role of editorials and the op-ed page of any newspaper (including your college newspaper) in the nation. Editorial writing offers carefully crafted debates and informed opinions on a variety of topics and issues. Many newspapers also develop guidelines to promote convincing but open-minded positions on the issues of the day.

A deputy editorial page director for the *Chicago Tribune* offers a series of questions for essays that, with slight modification, provide an excellent guide for writing an argument:

- *To whom are you writing?* Are you writing to authorities? Power elites? Professors? Average readers? Yourself?
- *What is your attitude?* Are you angry? Pleased? Perplexed? What tone will you project?
- *What, exactly, are you trying to accomplish?* An official response? A public change of attitude? An explanation? Entertainment?
- *What are you contributing to the debate?* What's the added value here? Just your opinion? New facts? New arguments, contexts, or dimensions to consider?
- *Do you have something new to say?* Are you advancing the conversation or just rehashing old facts, opinions, and wisdom? Aside from an opinion, do you have a solution?
- *Have you fiercely attacked your own premise?* Will your position survive scrutiny? How would your opponents answer your most compelling arguments? Are you correct or simply wrong?
- *Are you stirring up a "three-bowler"?* This borrowed phrase refers to the reader who is so bored with your writing that her face falls in the cereal bowl not once or twice but three times. You must compose your argument in such a way that the reader is hooked by your writing and persuaded by the force of your argument.

The process for writing powerful arguments that appears in this section is useful, but it is not a formula. Ultimately, you can construct powerful arguments in numerous ways, but you always must consider the relationship between your ideas, your purpose, and your audience. And you should be aware that argument has increasingly broad implications: How you present yourself in argument—your voice or ethical bearing—might have consequences in the public sphere, both on- and offline.

Identify an Issue

Not every subject lends itself to useful or necessary argument. The notion that "*everything is an argument*" probably contains a grain of truth, but in reality some things make for more powerful arguments than others. Certain subjects—for example, stamp collecting—might appeal to you personally and powerfully, but are they worth arguing about? Consequently, your first step in writing an effective argumentative essay is to identify a subject that contains an issue—in other words, a subject that will elicit two or more differing opinions.

Clearly, there are certain subjects that touch on current problems and inspire strong opinions. President Lincoln's Gettysburg Address dealt with a monumental issue central to the very survival of the nation; for virtually everyone in the United States at that time, the issues raised by Lincoln were debatable. Similarly, the issue of the right to bear arms can produce two diametrically opposed and seemingly irreconcilable viewpoints. Whether or not we should have embarked on a war of choice rather than necessity in Iraq continues to influence current discourse. Social and political issues tend to be ripe subjects for debate, fostering pro and con viewpoints. But remember that there are often more than two sides to a complex issue. Such issues, by their very nature, often raise powerful and conflicting systems of belief that place heavy burdens on the writer to provide convincing reasons and evidence to support a claim.

Not all issues in argumentative papers have to be of national or global concern. In fact, issues like capital punishment, gay marriage, or global climate change might not be of special interest to you. However, if an instructor requires an argumentative essay on one of these broad hot-button topics, you will need to prepare to write the paper by first establishing an argumentative perspective on it—in other words, by choosing your side on the issue. Fortunately, you often have opportunities to select issues of more immediate, personal, or local concern: Should fast-food franchises be permitted in the student cafeteria? Should there be a campus policy on hate language? Should sophomores be required to pass standardized tests in reading, writing, and mathematics before advancing to their junior year? Many powerfully constructed arguments can deal with issues close to home and with subjects that are of considerable personal interest. Whether dealing with an issue mandated by the instructor or selecting your own issue for an argumentative paper, ask yourself at the outset of this critical process what your position on the issue is and how it can be developed through logic and evidence.

Take a Stand and Clarify Your Claim

Once you have identified an issue that lends itself to argumentation—an issue that people might reasonably disagree about—you must take a clear stand on this issue. In other words, your claim will advance your viewpoint over all other viewpoints. The aim is not to defeat an opponent but to persuade readers—your audience—to accept your opinion. Consequently, the first step at this stage is to establish as clearly as possible what your claim is going to be. You might want to experiment with one or more of the following strategies:

- Gather and explore information on the issue from debates on radio, television, or the Internet. (For help with critically evaluating online and electronic sources, see Chapter 15.)
- Brainstorm or write informally about the issue, writing up your immediate response to it—how it makes you feel or what you think about it. If the issue provokes an emotional response, what are the causes? What are your more thoughtful or intellectual responses to the issue?
- List some preliminary reasons you respond to the issue in the way you do. By listing reasons, as well as the types of evidence you will need to support those reasons, you will be able to determine at an early stage whether you have enough material for a solid argumentative paper and what forms of research you will have to conduct.
- Keep notes of examples, facts, and ideas that might support your claim.
- Begin to think about possible objections to your position, and list these opposing viewpoints.

There are numerous strategies to think and write critically as you approach an issue during the prewriting stage. Essentially, you want to begin to articulate and pinpoint your claim, and thereby start to limit, control, and clarify the scope of your argument.

Once you have developed a preliminary approach to an issue, you should be prepared to state your claim in the form of a thesis sentence. From your reading of the information on the thesis statement in the second chapter of this textbook (see page 71), you know that you must limit the scope and purpose of your thesis or claim. Too broad a claim will be hard to cover in convincing fashion in a standard argumentative paper. One useful way to limit and clarify your claim is to consider the purpose of your argument. Do you want to argue a position on a particular issue? Do you want to argue that a certain activity, belief, or situation is good or bad, harmful or beneficial, effective or ineffective? Do you want to persuade readers to undertake or avoid a particular course of action? Do you want readers to simply consider an issue in a new light? Do you want readers to endorse your interpretation or evaluation of an artistic or literary work? By sifting through the primary purposes of argument, which involve value judgments, policies, and interpretations, you will arrive at the main point of your argument—your claim.

Analyze Your Audience

All writing can be considered a process of communication, a conversation with an audience of readers. In argumentative writing, it is especially important to establish a common ground of belief with your readers if you expect them to accept your claim or undertake a certain course of action. Of course, you cannot change your ideas and approaches to an issue merely to please a particular audience. However, you do not construct an argumentative paper in order to be misunderstood, disbelieved, or rejected. Within the limits set by who you are, what you believe, and what your purpose is, you can match your argumentative style and approach to audience expectations.

To establish common ground with your audience, it is important to know them well so that you can dispose them favorably to your claim and the reasons and evidence supporting it. Your audience might be a professor, a prospective employer, an admissions or financial aid officer, an editor, or a member of your family. If you determine the nature of your audience *before* you compose the first draft of your argumentative paper, you will be able to tailor style, content, and tone to a specific person or group.

Try to imagine and anticipate audience expectations by asking basic questions about your readers:

- What are the age, gender, professional background, educational level, and political orientation of most of the members of the audience?
- How much does the audience know about the issue? Is it an audience of experts or a general audience with only limited knowledge of the issue?
- What does the audience expect from you in terms of the purpose behind your claim? Does the audience expect you to prove your claim or persuade them to accept it, or both?
- Will the audience be friendly, hostile, or neutral toward your argument? What political, cultural, ethical, or religious factors contribute to the audience's probable position on this issue?
- What else do you know about the audience's opinions, attitudes, and values? How might these factors shape your approach to the argument?

Suppose you are planning to write an argumentative essay on pollution. What common expectations would an English professor, a sociology professor, and a chemistry professor have concerning your argument? What differences in approach and content would be dictated by your decision to write for one of these instructors? Or consider these different audiences for a paper on the topic of pollution: a group of grade school children in your hometown, or the Environmental Protection Agency, or the manager of a landfill operation, or a relative in Missouri whose town has been experiencing chemical pollution. In each instance, the type and nature of the audience will influence your approach to the issue and even your purpose. Remember that through your *purpose* you find the proper context for your argument. Any writer who wants to communicate effectively with his or her audience will adjust the content and tone of an argument so as not to lose, confuse, or mislead the reader.

Establish Your Tone

You recall from Chapter 2 that by *tone* we mean the attitude you take toward your subject. Tone is the personal *voice* that a reader "hears" in your writing. This voice may vary, depending on the situation, your purpose, and your audience. It may be personal or impersonal and range across a spectrum of attitudes: serious or humorous, subjective or objective, straightforward or ironic, formal or casual, and so forth. You adjust your tone to match your purpose in writing.

In argumentation an effective tone will be a true and trustworthy reflection of the writing situation. After all, you are writing an argumentative essay in order to convince and persuade, and consequently, you need to sound like a reasonable, well-organized, and rational individual. When writing for college instructors, that "community of scholars," you must be especially careful to maintain a reasonable and principled tone and attend to ethical responsibilities, including the need to document sources with integrity. You do not have to sound scholarly, legalistic, or overly technical in presenting your argument, but you do have to employ a personal voice that is appropriate to the writing occasion and audience expectations.

To achieve an appropriate tone in argumentative writing, you will often need to be forceful in presenting your ideas. Remember that you are staking out a position, perhaps on a controversial issue, and you must seem willing to defend it. Try to maintain a consistent voice of authority, but do not be overbearing: Do not move from the lecture hall to the locker room, mixing voices in a way that will confuse or alienate your audience. A tone or voice that exceeds the limits of good taste and commonly accepted norms of argumentative style is likely to be ineffectual. A voice that is too emotional, overblown, or irrational will in all likelihood alienate the reader and erode your claim.

Your tone—your voice—is a revelation of yourself. It derives from your claims and supporting ideas, your language and sentence structure. Even if your audience is one person—typically, your professor—you certainly must present yourself to that audience as convincingly as possible. When your tone is adjusted to the issue, the claim, and the supporting evidence, and also to the nature of the opposition, you stand a good chance of writing an effective argumentative essay.

Develop and Organize the Grounds for Your Claim

You establish the validity of your claim by setting out the reasons and evidence—the *grounds*—that support your main point. Whereas the claim presents your general proposition or point of view, as you develop your grounds you organize the argument into minor propositions, evidence, and refutation. By establishing the grounds for your claim, you explain the particular perspective or point of view you take on an issue. The grounds for your claim permit the reader to "see" the strength of your position.

There are numerous ways to state the primary reasons or grounds for holding your position. Think of these primary reasons as minor propositions underlying the basis of your claim—reasons that readers would find it difficult to rebut or reject. Three possible models for organizing claims and grounds in an essay can now be considered:

Model 1
Introduction: statement and clarification of claim

First minor proposition and evidence

Second minor proposition and evidence

Third minor proposition and evidence

Refutation of opposing viewpoints for minor propositions

Conclusion

Model 2
Introduction: statement and clarification of claim

First minor proposition and evidence; refutation

Second minor proposition and evidence; refutation

Third minor proposition and evidence; refutation

Conclusion

Model 3
Statement and clarification of claim

Summary of opposing viewpoints and refutation

First minor proposition and evidence

Second minor proposition and evidence

Third minor proposition and evidence

Conclusion

In practice, arguments rarely adhere slavishly to these models. In fact, you can arrange your argument in numerous ways. However, the models can serve a useful purpose, especially in exams that require argumentative responses to a question, for they provide a handy template for your answer. In argument, to support your claim, you will need substantial reasons, sometimes more than the three minor propositions illustrated in these models. Remember that one reason generally will not provide sufficient grounds to prove an argument. Moreover, you should keep in mind the need to distinguish between your *opinions,* which in the broadest sense are beliefs that you cannot verify logically, and reasons, which are based on logic, evidence, and direct proof.

Gather and Evaluate Your Evidence

Once you have established your claim and your reasons, you can turn your attention to developing evidence for your claim, a subject introduced in the first chapter. Collecting evidence is a bit like the strategies for successful fishing presented by the student in his classification paragraph in the second chapter (see page 82): You want to fish the top, the middle, and the bottom of your subject. Phrased somewhat differently, you want to cast a wide net as you seek evidence designed to support your claim and reasons.

At the outset, a carefully designed online search can yield ample evidence, permitting you to establish links to sites and listservs where you can download or print full or abstracted texts from periodicals, books, documents, and reports. Remember, however, that searching online can be like navigating a minefield: Useless "facts," misinformation, hoaxes, and informational marketing ploys mix with serious research, honest reporting, and critical analysis. To guard against the pitfalls involved in relying exclusively on browser-based searching, you should also make a trip to the college library. Research librarians can help you to evaluate Web sites and direct you to the best sources—both traditional and electronic—for the types of evidence you are seeking. (For more on library and online research, see Chapter 15.) Depending on your subject, you might consider interviewing individuals who can provide expert testimony designed to support your claim and reasons. Finally, your personal experience and the experiences of your friends and acquaintances might provide useful evidence, although such kinds of anecdotal or first-hand support should be treated judiciously and not serve as the entire basis for your paper. For instance, you and your friends might claim that a current horror movie is great, but such personal evidence must be tempered by a willingness to consult established critics for additional support.

If you cast a wide net and fish the whole lake, you will almost always catch more than you require. Yet the very process of searching comprehensively for evidence can produce exciting, unintended consequences. You might, for example, discover that certain evidence suggests a need to revise or qualify your claim. Evidence can also help you to articulate or confirm the warrants that are the foundation of your argument, for experts writing on an issue often state the assumptions, principles, or beliefs that offer connections between a claim and its grounds. The insights gained by considering other evidence might cause you to develop a new reason for your claim that you had not considered initially. You might also discover evidence that helps you to refute the ideas of your anticipated opposition. Having a wealth of evidence at your disposal is an embarrassment of riches that you can exploit skillfully.

After you have collected adequate evidence to bolster your claim and the key reasons supporting that claim, the next necessary step is to evaluate and select the best evidence available to you. Writers who carefully evaluate and select their evidence produce effective arguments. At the outset, the nature of the writing situation—an exam, a term paper, a letter to the editor—will dictate to an extent the type of evidence you need to evaluate. In most instances, however, your evidence should be *credible, comprehensive,* and *current.* Your evidence is credible when your sources are reliable and the evidence itself is representative. Your evidence is comprehensive when you provide a broad range of facts, information, and data designed to cover all aspects of your argument. In presenting evidence comprehensively, you also make certain that there is sufficient support for each of your reasons—not too much evidence for one and too little for another, but an even balance between and among the minor propositions. Finally, always try to locate the most current evidence available to support your claim. Data and statistics often do not age well and tend to lose their relevance. However, in some arguments, older evidence can be compared with newer information. For example, a paper arguing that immigration to the United States is out of control could make skillful use of data from the 1960 Census *and* the 2010 Census.

Evidence is the heart of any argument. Without evidence, readers will not be interested in your claim and supporting reasons. Make certain that the evidence—the facts, examples, and details—you present is accurate and skillfully presented so that readers become interested in your more abstract propositions, identify with your position, and come away convinced of the validity of your argument.

Consider Your Warrants

Even as you clarify your claim and assemble your reasons and evidence, you must also consider the assumptions underlying your argument. Think of the assumption or warrant as the link between a claim and the supporting evidence—the underlying set of beliefs or principles governing your essential perception of the world and the human condition. Warrants answer the question of *how* the data are connected to the claim. Sometimes these warrants are stated, but often they remain unstated. In either instance, they are not necessarily self-evident or universally accepted. They are significant nevertheless, for as generalizations that are far broader than claims and evidence, warrants serve as the bedrock of an argument.

Warrants help to guarantee that a reader will accept your argument, and consequently, it is important to consider them. When you are writing for a friendly or supportive audience, you can usually assume that your readers will accept the warrants supporting your claim, and so you might not even need to state them. For example, if you claim in a report for your biology professor that creationism should not be taught in high school science classrooms, your argument is based on several assumptions or warrants: that the Constitution, for example, requires the separation of church and state, or that there is no scientific basis for creationism. In fact, when making your claim about creationism before a scientist, you also are relying on certain *backings,* which are the principles underlying the warrants themselves—for instance, the idea that a scientist is concerned with scientific objectivity rather than literal interpretations of the Bible, or that scientists deal with the empirical reality and not matters of faith. But what if you were to make your claim in a letter to a local school board, several of whose members want to revise the ninth-grade earth science curriculum to emphasize creationism and evolution equally? In this instance, you would be presenting your argument to a potentially skeptical or hostile audience, so you would have to state your warrants clearly, bolster them with adequate support, and establish solid causal links between your warrants and your backing.

Whether you are writing an argumentative paper or reading an argumentative essay critically, you need to develop the habit of looking for and evaluating the warrants and the backing behind the argument. If you are reading an argumentative essay, and the warrants are stated, it will make this task easier. If the warrants are unstated, you will have to detect and evaluate them. If you are writing an argumentative essay, you should consider whether your audience will probably understand and consent to the warrants that serve as the foundation of your paper. If you have any doubt, then you should include them.

Deal with Opposing Viewpoints

To make your argument as effectively as possible, you need to acknowledge and deal with opposing viewpoints. Any controversial issue is going to have more than one viewpoint, and you must recognize contending claims and handle them fairly. As suggested in the section on audience analysis, you can enhance your credibility by describing these opposing viewpoints fully and accurately, with a respectful rather than hostile tone, even as you demonstrate that your position is the most reasonable and valid.

As a prewriting strategy for refutation, you might try dividing a sheet of paper or your computer screen into three columns, labeling them, from left to right, "Supporting Viewpoints," "Opposing Viewpoints," and "Refutation." Then list the main supporting points for your claim, thinking of possible opposing responses and writing them down as you go. Imagining how the opposition will respond to your supporting reasons will help you to develop refutations, or counterarguments. You can use the resulting chart as a guide to organize sections of your argumentative paper.

The listing technique for refutation forces you to acknowledge opposing viewpoints and also to refute them in a systematic way. It is perfectly appropriate—and even necessary—to demonstrate the weakness or insufficiency of opposing arguments, for refutation strengthens your position. Any complex argument that you present will not be complete unless you skillfully refute all predictable opposing viewpoints, using one of the following techniques:

- Question the opposition's claim: Is it too flimsy or broad, overstated, or improperly grounded in minor propositions?
- Question the evidence: Is it insufficient, outdated, or inaccurate?
- Question the warrants and backing of an opposing argument—those assumptions and beliefs that underpin the opposition's claim.
- Concede some part of the opposition's viewpoint, a subtle but extremely attractive strategy that shows that you are a courteous and unbiased thinker and writer, and that therefore constitutes an appeal to ethics.

Avoid Unfair Emotional Appeals and Errors in Reasoning

When you write and revise an argumentative essay, you need to avoid certain temptations and dangers that are unique to this form of discourse. You always have to make certain that your argumentative strategies are fair and appropriate and that you have avoided oversimplifying your argument. You also need to resist the temptation to include persuasive appeals that distort critical reasoning and to avoid errors in logical reasoning.

Emotional appeals are effective when used appropriately in argumentation, but used unfairly they can distort your logical reasoning. Such loaded arguments are filled with appeals to the reader's emotions, fears, and prejudices. Here are three of the most common fallacies of emotional distortion to avoid:

1. *Transfer* is the association of a proposition with a famous person. Transfer can be either positive ("In the spirit of President Franklin Delano Roosevelt, we should create a jobs program for the nation's unemployed") or negative ("President George W. Bush was the symbol of unbridled capitalism"). Another term for negative transfer is *name calling*. In both the positive and negative types of transfer, however, there is no logical basis for the connection.
2. *Argumentum ad hominem* (to the man) is a strategy that discredits a person in an effort to discredit his or her argument. It attacks the person rather than the position: "Richards is a homosexual and consequently cannot understand the sanctity of heterosexual marriage." In this instance, the individual becomes a false issue.
3. *Argumentum ad populum* (to the people) deliberately arouses an audience's emotions about certain institutions and ideas. Certain words have strong positive or negative connotations. Such words as *patriotism* and *motherhood* are *virtue* words that often

prompt the creation of *glittering generalities*. Suggestive words can be used to distort meaning by illogical association and to manipulate an audience to take a stand for or against a proposition: "USC should not take the *totalitarian* step of requiring athletes to maintain a full course load." A related strategy is the *bandwagon* approach, in which the writer generalizes falsely that the crowd or majority is always right: "Everyone is voting for Erikson and you should too."

These unfair emotional appeals are often found in political speech writing, advertising, and propaganda. When you write argumentative essays, you should use persuasive appeal to reinforce rather than distort the logical presentation of your ideas, blending reasonable claims and valid emotional and ethical appeals to convince rather than trick your audience into agreeing with you.

Equally important is the need to avoid errors in reasoning in the construction of an argument. Here are seven types of errors in reasoning, or *logical fallacies,* that are common in argumentative writing:

1. *Hasty generalizations.* A hasty generalization is a conclusion based on insufficient, unrepresentative, or untrue evidence: "The president of the college successfully raised 100 million dollars, so other college presidents should be able to do the same." When you indulge in hasty generalizations, you jump to false conclusions. Hasty generalizations are also at the heart of stereotyping—the uncritical application of an oversimplified generalization to a group or to individual members of the group. Make certain that you have adequate and accurate evidence to support any claim or conclusion.

2. *Broad generalizations.* A broad generalization typically employs words like *all, never,* and *always* to state something absolutely or categorically. It is actually a form of overstatement, as in the sentence "Freud always treated sexuality as the basis of human behavior." Usually, readers can easily find exceptions to such sweeping statements, so it is best to qualify them.

3. *Oversimplification.* Oversimplification reduces alternatives. Several forms of oversimplification can be distinguished:

   a. *Either/or.* Don't assume that there are only two sides to an issue, only two possibilities, only yes or no, only right or wrong: "Either we make English a one-year requirement or college students will not be able to write well."

   b. *No choice.* Don't assume that there is only one possibility: "The United States has no other alternative than to build the Star Wars missile defense system." Parents and politicians are prone to no-other-choice propositions.

   c. *No harm or cost.* Don't assume that a potential benefit will not have significant harms, consequences, or costs: "We should sell North Korea as much wheat as it needs." No-harm generalizations or arguments may overlook dangerous implications. Always consider alternative evidence.

   d. *One solution.* Don't assume that a complicated issue has only one solution: "Embryonic stem cells should not be used for research, for using them in this way will lead to the destruction of human life." Always consider evidence for other solutions or alternative approaches to issues and problems.

4. *Begging the question.* Do not assume in your premises or in your evidence what is to be proved in the conclusion. For example, if you argue that vandalism by teenagers is unavoidable because teenagers are young and irresponsible, you are begging the question because you are not proving your premise. Another form of begging the question is to take a conclusion for granted before it is proved.

5. *False cause-and-effect relationships.* Perhaps the most common error in trying to establish causal relationships is known as the *post hoc, ergo propter hoc* fallacy (after this, therefore because of this). The fact that one event *follows* another is not proof that the first *caused* the second. If you maintain, for instance, that there is an increase in the crime rate every time there is a full moon, you are falsely identifying an unrelated event as a cause. Many superstitions—popular, political, and otherwise—illogically assume that one event somehow causes another.

6. *Disconnected ideas.* Termed *non sequitur* (it does not follow), this fault in reasoning arises when there is no logical connection between two or more ideas. Put differently, an argument's conclusion is not related to its premises: "Barack Obama makes a good president because he works out every morning." Sometimes you think that a connection exists but you fail to state it in writing. For example, you may think that presidents need to stay in shape for several reasons. In other words, *you* may see the logical connection between your ideas, but if you don't make it explicit, readers may think there is a non sequitur.

7. *Weak or false analogies.* An *analogy* is a type of comparison that explains a subject by comparing it to the features of another essentially dissimilar subject: "Unless we learn to think critically about the Niagara of information that washes over us every day, we will be lost in a flood of rumors and gossip." Analogies can be used to illustrate a point, although they should always be used carefully and with discretion. More significantly, an analogy can *never* function as evidence or logical proof of a position.

The hallmark of argumentation is sound critical thinking. If you present your claims, grounds, and evidence carefully; are willing to assemble the best and most objective data; treat the opposition with respect; and are flexible in responding to new ideas, you will be well on your way to constructing a solid argumentative essay. A successful argumentative paper reveals a writer who possesses an inquiring mind—who is able to judge opinions on the basis of evidence, reason well, and back up ideas and beliefs in a convincing and valid way.

Argumentative Synthesis

Synthesis, as discussed in Chapter 1, is the process we use to combine information from two or more sources and infer relationships among them. Whereas the primary aim of explanatory synthesis is to convey information, the aim of argumentative synthesis is to convince readers that a claim is correct or valid. Whether we evaluate the relative quality of the readings (in other words, provide a *critique* of the texts) or draw material from readings to support a claim of our own, argumentative synthesis requires us to take a position on the materials at hand.

With explanatory synthesis, as we have seen, we try to accurately identify the key ideas and purposes of various writers, but we do not argue for or against a certain viewpoint. For example, here is the student's thesis based on the readings by Elbow and Murray from Chapter 2:

Both Peter Elbow and Donald Murray stress the importance of process in the craft of composition, but approach the process from different perspectives.

In this instance, the student makes a modest but useful attempt to convey information accurately through explanatory synthesis.

Consider the shift from explanation to argument as the writer now takes sides in presenting the ideas of Elbow and Murray:

Although Peter Elbow's theory of freewriting might be useful to certain students with basic writing problems, Donald Murray in his stress on revision offers far more useful advice for mainstream college students who want to improve their writing.

Observe how the writer moves from explanatory to argumentative synthesis as she critiques the two readings and their authors. She takes sides. She presents a claim (which she will have to support with convincing grounds or evidence). She wants us to agree with her interpretation and assessment.

Critiquing As you prepare for argumentative synthesis, rely on the strategies for critical reading and writing that were outlined in Chapters 1 and 2 as well as the guidelines for argumentative synthesis presented in this chapter. At the outset, it would also be wise to focus your critical response on *critiquing*—the evaluation of each text's quality or worth based on a clearly defined set of guidelines. With critiquing, you cannot rely on a personal opinion or preference. Critiquing demands clear criteria and objective assessment of the text. It is a necessary aspect of successful argumentative synthesis.

When critiquing texts, you follow either *general academic standards* of evaluation (criteria that apply to many disciplines) or *discipline-specific standards* (for instance, criteria used by scholars in cognitive psychology or specialists in international law). In most cases, you will be working with general standards when critiquing sources in college composition courses. You will consider issues like the style, organization, importance of subject, effectiveness of a writer's claim, and quality of evidence as the evaluative criteria for your critique. Stated differently, you will agree, disagree, or (in certain cases) agree *and* disagree to varying degrees with a writer and his or her text—but do so from the vantage point of informed judgment.

The formal demands of critiquing are neither mysterious, intimidating, or overwhelming. In everyday situations, we engage in critiquing: arguing over the merits of two recent films, evaluating the skills of various sports stars, praising our favorite musicians, supporting one candidate for political office over all others, or logging into a Web site to check and perhaps comment on the best (or worst) professors on campus. Writing a formal critique is perhaps more of a challenge than situations from everyday life, but if you follow basic steps the process of critiquing becomes manageable.

1. *Carefully read and evaluate each text.* Annotate the selection: Cite the source of the article and the author's intended audience, look for the thesis or claim, identify the author's purpose (to inform, argue, or entertain), highlight the primary and secondary evidence, and consider the style and organization of the piece.
2. *Summarize your findings,* focusing on the author's main points.
3. *Evaluate the reading.* Consider the overall validity of the author's presentation: Has the writer achieved his or her purpose? What is the quality of the supporting evidence? Is the information or evidence convincing and representative? Has the author interpreted material correctly and argued logically?
4. *Write your response.* Establish your claim, focusing on specific aspects of the text that best illuminate your thesis or argument. Explain to what extent you agree or disagree with the author and what standards you are applying. Offer examples to explain your judgments and support your interpretation.
5. *Revise the draft.* Clarify your position in relation to the author's text. Check the accuracy of your information about the text. Make certain that your assessment or interpretation is based on clear criteria. Refine and thoroughly develop your assertions, correcting any fallacies in reasoning and argumentation.

Guidelines for Argumentative Synthesis As you read and respond to texts using argumentative synthesis, you might find certain essays easy to understand. However, you should be prepared to contend with challenging subjects—for instance, essays about genetic engineering or the Constitutional implications of electronic surveillance. In each instance, you will have to make complex topics intelligible for your primary and secondary audiences. Sometimes your instructor will offer clear guidelines for determining the relative strengths and weaknesses of the texts. Or your instructor might ask you to formulate your own argument based on several assigned texts and/or your own research on the subject. Whether the instructor assigns the texts or you locate sources on your own, you must decide on how best to treat these texts fairly and accurately while at the same time positing a claim, organizing evidence and documenting sources (see Chapter 15), and presenting findings in a coherent way.

As you start to formulate a strategy, realize that there is no single solution to effective argumentative synthesis. In reality, argumentative synthesis, like any form of writing, is a recursive, or back-and-forth, process in which the strategies you employ can be drawn from a vast repertoire of rhetorical possibilities. For example, you could use the block method explained in the section in Chapter 2 on comparison and contrast (see page 78) to organize a paper in which you critique essays A and B, which present opposing viewpoints on a recent film. For a different assignment requiring you to defend a position on Wal-Mart, you might have to synthesize material from several sources, relying on the introduction to writing research papers that appears in Chapter 15. Even with the many strategies available to you, it is possible to establish a set of useful guidelines for argumentative synthesis:

1. *Analyze the assignment.* Determine whether your primary purpose will be to critique texts or to argue your position based on several readings. (While it is easy to separate these goals, it should be evident that critiquing sources is relevant to both.)
2. *Select and carefully review the readings.* Perhaps your instructor will assign the readings—which should make your task easier. But if you have to find the readings, whether your purpose is to critique the texts or generate your own argument, you will have to highlight the key claims, warrants, and support in those texts that suit your essential aim.
3. *Take notes and formulate a claim or major proposition.* Critically read and reread passages, identifying key claims and presentation of ideas. Label and define terms that the author introduces. Write brief summaries, preferably in single sentences, of all texts. Formulate your claim, checking it against the texts you are critiquing to make certain it is accurate and conclusive. Decide on an organizational plan: Will you, for instance, rely on comparison and contrast, classification, or some other strategy to structure your claim?
4. *Write the first draft.* Establish your claim at the outset. Introduce the authors, texts, or passages that you will critique. Present the key definition, principle, or standard of evaluation you will apply to analyze and assess these texts. Evaluate the validity of each text, pointing to such elements as logic, evidence, weight or importance of the subject, and overall presentation. Agree or disagree with a text's assumptions and viewpoints. Document your sources. (See Chapters 15 and 16.)
5. *Revise your synthesis.* Refine the introduction so that your claim is clearly defined. Improve the organization of the main parts of your synthesis, making certain that support is well ordered, critical observations are compelling, transitions are strong, and information about the texts under consideration is presented in a fair and balanced way. Strengthen the conclusion by stating convincingly the importance of your insights and findings and the validity of your argument.

Argumentative synthesis, like all types of argumentative writing, presents a claim about which reasonable people might agree or disagree. The challenge is to formulate your synthesis in such a way that it convinces or persuades your audience to agree with your assessment and basic viewpoint.

Case Study for Synthesis
SOCIAL NETWORKING: FRIEND OR FOE?

Following is a collection of essays dealing with the impact of online communities on relationships. All of these essays take positions or debatable viewpoints on social networking, and all of the authors offer provocative analyses and arguments. As you read, consider how each author establishes a perspective on the topic, makes a claim, and organizes support for that claim. Test your talent for engaging in argumentative synthesis by responding to the activities at the end of this case study.

Do I *Really* Have To Join Twitter?

What to do if you're just not that into microblogging but don't want to be left behind.

Farhad Manjoo

Farhad Manjoo *(b. 1978) is* Slate's *technology columnist and the author of* True Enough: Learning to Live in a Post-Fact Society. *This essay was posted on* Slate *on April 10, 2009.*

Twitter is growing so fast it's sometimes easy to forget that to a lot of people, the concept is completely bizarre. According to comScore, the microblogging site received about 10 million visitors in February—a 700 percent increase over last year. To the initiated, the surge seems justified. Committed Twitterers argue that the 140-character-or-less tweet represents the next great mode of human communication. To vast swaths of the population, though, Twitter is inscrutable: *Wait a minute—you want me to keep a perpetual log of my boring life for all the world to see? What if I just spend my free time watching* Golden Girls? 1

In other words, it's hard for many to shake the feeling that Twitter is a waste of time. It's not only Luddites who feel this way; in the last few months, a surprising 2 number of people in the tech industry—people who fancy themselves the earliest of early adopters—have mentioned to me that they have a hard time wrapping their heads around the service. Many float the idea that Twitter is little more than an overhyped, media-driven sensation.

3   Is Twitter a fad? It's certainly received more than 140 characters of love from the press recently; everywhere you look, someone in the news is tweeting. But the people on TV rarely seem to address something very basic: What's the point of tweeting? And should you do it? I get variations on this question often from readers. Let's say you're a moderately tech-savvy person who takes well to new forms of gabbing—you've got an easy facility with blogs, you log in to Facebook when you need it, you text, you IM, and perhaps you even talk to your friends through Skype. Is it time for you to jump into microblogging, too? Would you be missing out on some important cultural touchstone if you sat out this round of techno-innovation? The short answer: Eh, go ahead and give it a try if you like, but there's nothing lame about waiting to see whether Twitter pans out.

4   Much of what we do online has obvious analogues in the past: E-mail and IM replace letters and face-to-face chatting. Blogging is personal pamphleteering. Skype is the new landline. Social networks let us map our real-life connections to the Web. It's not surprising, then, that these new tools deliver obvious social utility—Facebook is the best way to get in touch with old friends, and instant messaging is the quickest way to collaborate with your colleagues across the country. Twitter is different. It's not a faster or easier way of doing something you did in the past, unless you were one of those people who wrote short "quips" on bathroom stalls. It's a totally alien form of communication. Microblogging mixes up features of e-mail, IM, blogs, and social networks to create something not just novel but also confusing, and doing it well takes time and patience. That's not to say it isn't useful; to some people in some situations, Twitter is irreplaceable. But it is not—or, at least, not yet—a necessary way to stay socially relevant in the information age.

5   As a practical matter, Twitter is a cinch to get into: You sign up, pick a few people to follow, then start typing out your thoughts, making sure to keep each post below the 140-character limit. . . . But Twitter, unlike Facebook, favors one-way connections—you can follow my posts, but I don't have to follow yours. As a result, novice Twitterers are met with instant discouragement—you start out with nobody reading your posts, and because the people you follow don't have to follow you, there's no guarantee that you'll ever convince great numbers of people to listen to what you have to say. Twitter is not a meritocracy; you may be the cleverest quipper in your circle, but celebrities and people in the media inevitably win the most followers. There is no justice in the fact that a banal Twitterer like Sen. Claire McCaskill has attracted an audience of more than 19,000. (A typically riveting McCaskill tweet: "Leaving for KC soon. Meeting about American car manufacturing. Then on to Springfield. Press avail there.") But that's how Twitter goes; if you join, be prepared to deal with a lot of people who are undeservedly more popular than yourself.

Take the Data out of Dating

Alexis Madrigal

Alexis Madrigal graduated from Harvard University magna cum laude. He is a senior editor and the lead technology writer for theatlantic.com. *Formerly a staff writer in science at* Wired.com, *Madrigal is the author of* Powering the Dream: The History and Promise of Green Technology. *The essay that follows appeared in* theatlantic.com *in its December 2010 edition.*

The air in Santa Cruz was warm and still as I sat among perfect roses in the back- 1 yard of the bride's parents. At the key moment of this nontraditional Jewish wedding, the friend presiding over the ceremony took a moment to explain the Hebrew word *kadosh*. It's translated as "holy," or "the holy one," but it also connotes the act of setting apart or elevating one thing above all other things of a type. Marriage is holy because each partner says, "You are the one person I choose out of all the people in the world."

If only you could Google your way to The One. The search engine, in its own 2 profane way, is a *kadosh* generator. Its primary goal is to find the perfect Web page for you out of all the Web pages in the world, to elevate it to No. 1.

The Santa Cruz couple had met in a time-honored way—through a friend— 3 but the number of such encounters is decreasing. One reputable estimate suggests that 74 percent of singles looking for a mate now turn to dating sites like eHarmony, Match.com, and OkCupid, which use algorithms to pair people up based on answers to sets of questions.

But even e-yentas find prognosticating love difficult. Date-mining software 4 needs lots of tuning to create good matches, so the services track everything would-be lovebirds do. Their romantic-data trails become grist for matchmaking improvements.

OkCupid, which according to *The Boston Globe* aspires to be the Google of 5 online dating, has been particularly aggressive about tracking users. The company's goal is to stimulate "three-ways"—a double entendre that, to someone at OkCupid, means a person sent a note, received a reply, and fired off a follow-up.

"Imagine if you had a video camera at every bar in the country," Sam Yagan, 6 a co-founder of OkCupid, told me. "You'd have all these data that reveal things about society and predict them. This isn't a survey. It isn't a lab experiment. These are millions of people going about their lives. We just happen to be able to track and quantify everything about it."

The company can quantify things you could guess but might rather not prove. 7 For instance, all races of women respond better to white men than they should based on the men's looks. Black women, as a group, are the least likely to have their missives returned, but they are the most likely to respond to messages.

8   I asked Yagan whether OkCupid might try tailoring its algorithm to surface more statistically successful racial combinations. Such a measure wasn't out of the question, he said. "Imagine we did a lot of research, and we found that there were certain demographic or psychographic attributes that were predictors of three-ways. Hispanic men and Indian women, say," Yagan suggested. "If we thought that drove success, we could tweak it so those matches showed up more often. Not because of a social mission, but because if it's working, there needs to be more of it."

9   Imagine the reverse, though, in the past or future. What if the dating sites had existed in the 1950s? How would they have dealt with interracial matches? Given the female response to white men in 2010, should white men show up more often? "We could do some really screwed-up things," Yagan admits. Imagine war broke out with China, causing Chinese users' ratings to plummet: would dating Web sites start reducing the number of Chinese people showing up in other groups' searches?

10   Algorithms are made to restrict the amount of information the user sees— that's their raison d'être. By drawing on data about the world we live in, they end up reinforcing whatever societal values happen to be dominant, without our even noticing. They are normativity made into code—albeit a code that we barely understand, even as it shapes our lives.

11   We're not going to stop using algorithms. They're too useful. But we need to be more aware of the algorithmic perversity that's creeping into our lives. The short-term fit of a dating match or a Web page doesn't measure the long-term value it may hold. *Statistically likely* does not mean correct, or just, or fair. Google-generated *kadosh* is meretricious, offering a desiccated kind of choice. It's when people deviate from what we predict they'll do that they prove they are individuals, set apart from all others of the human type.

Tweet Like an Egyptian

Kevin Clarke

Kevin Clarke *writes about technology for a variety of publications. The following essay appeared in* uscatholic.org *in the April 2011 edition. Clarke also has a blog at this site.*

1   In the early days of the World Wide Web, HTML wizards maintained the googly-eyed optimism of people who thought they were changing the world. Here was a civically electrifying form of communication that would obliterate time and space and the distance between people. Agonizing over our 2,400 baud TCP connections, and sharing strategies over regional bulletin board systems, there was a brief shining moment of giddy joy in the very new and unironic enthusiasm for the very bold.

Then the retailers and the marketers and the pornographers arrived. In the 2 space of just a few months the Internet transformed from the electronic marketplace of new ideas and experiences into, well, just the same old marketplace of crud nobody really needed.

But since January in the Arab world that early promise of revolution and real 3 change that drove the first Internet reasserted itself. It was not just that the protesters for human freedom, civil rights, economic justice, and the end of soul-crushing oligarchy in Egypt and elsewhere used the latest social networking technologies of the Internet to organize themselves and outmaneuver the entrenched authority in their respective societies. It was not just that they used the Internet to get their message out to the rest of the world and to inspire like-minded protests in other nations.

The young people who took to the streets in Egypt and Tunisia were not 4 demanding a freedom they could only imagine, they were demanding the freedom they had already experienced in their virtual lives, a freedom they wanted to translate into their actual daily lives. On the Internet they had already learned what it looked and felt like to inhabit a society where opinions were welcome and thoughts could be freely expressed, an alternative reality that encouraged the limitlessness of imagination and the life-affirming energy of human freedom.

But the Internet did even more. It empowered them with the information they 5 needed to question and challenge authority in their nonvirtual societies.

Wikileaks has endured white-hot criticism for its purported irresponsibility in 6 releasing U.S. classified documents and diplomatic cables that capture what U.S. officials really think about conditions and political characters around the world. The data dump orchestrated by Wikileaks, a new kind of communication outlet that could only have been brought to life via the infrastructure, capability, and spirit of the Internet, has been condemned as a threat to the lives of confidential sources and to diplomacy as we know it. So far, however, what it has mostly proved to be is a regime-shattering tool of information sharing.

Most people in Tunisia endured a begrudging awareness of the larcenous 7 leadership of the Ben Ali regime. But something about seeing the depth of that larceny and civic indifference spelled out in a U.S. State Department cable was the electronic straw that broke the camel's back and propelled people into the streets.

No one knows where this new era of Internet-generated people power may 8 ultimately lead. In chaos there is both opportunity and danger. It's still possible that the energy for change and thirst for freedom on the Arab streets today could be subverted. Revolutions have been co-opted before. But it is at least as likely that the Internet will continue to be a viaduct of energy and information that empowers and enlightens rather than degrades and distracts. It maintains its potential to be a force that makes real the spiritual connectedness of all people.

Maybe it will be a force strong enough to rouse the democratic impulses of 9 the people in a nation which, though materially better off than many other states, maintains levels of income and resource inequity and poverty that rival any demoralized society in the developing world. If you're wondering what state I'm talking about, get online and explore a little bit.

I'm So Totally, Digitally, Close to You

Clive Thompson

Clive Thompson is a Canadian journalist, blogger, and science and technology writer who has contributed articles to the New York Times Magazine, *the* Washington Post, Wired, *and other publications. He maintains a popular blog,* Collision Detection. *This essay appeared in the* New York Times Magazine *on September 7, 2008.*

1   On Sept. 5, 2006, Mark Zuckerberg changed the way that Facebook worked, and in the process he inspired a revolt. Zuckerberg, a doe-eyed 24-year-old C.E.O., founded Facebook in his dorm room at Harvard two years earlier, and the site quickly amassed nine million users. By 2006, students were posting heaps of personal details onto their Facebook pages, including lists of their favorite TV shows, whether they were dating (and whom), what music they had in rotation and the various ad hoc "groups" they had joined (like "Sex and the City" Lovers). All day long, they'd post "status" notes explaining their moods—"hating Monday," "skipping class b/c i'm hung over." After each party, they'd stagger home to the dorm and upload pictures of the soused revelry, and spend the morning after commenting on how wasted everybody looked. Facebook became the de facto public commons—the way students found out what everyone around them was like and what he or she was doing.

2   But Zuckerberg knew Facebook had one major problem: It required a lot of active surfing on the part of its users. Sure, every day your Facebook friends would update their profiles with some new tidbits; it might even be something particularly juicy, like changing their relationship status to "single" when they got dumped. But unless you visited each friend's page every day, it might be days or weeks before you noticed the news, or you might miss it entirely. Browsing Facebook was like constantly poking your head into someone's room to see how she was doing. It took work and forethought. In a sense, this gave Facebook an inherent, built-in level of privacy, simply because if you had 200 friends on the site—a fairly typical number—there weren't enough hours in the day to keep tabs on every friend all the time.

3   "It was very primitive," Zuckerberg told me when I asked him about it last month. And so he decided to modernize. He developed something he called News Feed, a built-in service that would actively broadcast changes in a user's page to every one of his or her friends. Students would no longer need to spend their time zipping around to examine each friend's page, checking to see if there was any new information. Instead, they would just log into Facebook, and News Feed would appear: a single page that—like a social gazette from the 18th century—delivered a long list of up-to-the-minute gossip about their friends, around the clock, all in one place. "A stream of everything that's going on in their lives," as Zuckerberg put it.

When students woke up that September morning and saw News Feed, the 4 first reaction, generally, was one of panic. Just about every little thing you changed on your page was now instantly blasted out to hundreds of friends, including potentially mortifying bits of news—*Tim and Lisa broke up; Persaud is no longer friends with Matthew*—and drunken photos someone snapped, then uploaded and tagged with names. Facebook had lost its vestigial bit of privacy. For students, it was now like being at a giant, open party filled with everyone you know, able to eavesdrop on what everyone else was saying, all the time.

"Everyone was freaking out," Ben Parr, then a junior at Northwestern University, 5 told me recently. What particularly enraged Parr was that there wasn't any way to opt out of News Feed, to "go private" and have all your information kept quiet. He created a Facebook group demanding Zuckerberg either scrap News Feed or provide privacy options. "Facebook users really think Facebook is becoming the Big Brother of the Internet, recording every single move," a California student told The Star-Ledger of Newark. Another chimed in, "Frankly, I don't need to know or care that Billy broke up with Sally, and Ted has become friends with Steve." By lunchtime of the first day, 10,000 people had joined Parr's group, and by the next day it had 284,000.

Zuckerberg, surprised by the outcry, quickly made two decisions. The first 6 was to add a privacy feature to News Feed, letting users decide what kind of information went out. But the second decision was to leave News Feed otherwise intact. He suspected that once people tried it and got over their shock, they'd like it.

He was right. Within days, the tide reversed. Students began e-mailing 7 Zuckerberg to say that via News Feed they'd learned things they would never have otherwise discovered through random surfing around Facebook. The bits of trivia that News Feed delivered gave them more things to talk about—*Why do you hate Kiefer Sutherland?*—when they met friends face to face in class or at a party. Trends spread more quickly. When one student joined a group—proclaiming her love of Coldplay or a desire to volunteer for Greenpeace—all her friends instantly knew, and many would sign up themselves. Users' worries about their privacy seemed to vanish within days, boiled away by their excitement at being so much more connected to their friends. (Very few people stopped using Facebook, and most people kept on publishing most of their information through News Feed.) Pundits predicted that News Feed would kill Facebook, but the opposite happened. It catalyzed a massive boom in the site's growth. A few weeks after the News Feed imbroglio, Zuckerberg opened the site to the general public (previously, only students could join), and it grew quickly; today, it has 100 million users.

When I spoke to him, Zuckerberg argued that News Feed is central to Face- 8 book's success. "Facebook has always tried to push the envelope," he said. "And at times that means stretching people and getting them to be comfortable with things they aren't yet comfortable with. A lot of this is just social norms catching up with what technology is capable of."

9   In essence, Facebook users didn't *think* they wanted constant, up-to-the-minute updates on what other people are doing. Yet when they experienced this sort of omnipresent knowledge, they found it intriguing and addictive. Why?

10   Social scientists have a name for this sort of incessant online contact. They call it "ambient awareness." It is, they say, very much like being physically near someone and picking up on his mood through the little things he does—body language, sighs, stray comments—out of the corner of your eye. Facebook is no longer alone in offering this sort of interaction online. In the last year, there has been a boom in tools for "microblogging": posting frequent tiny updates on what you're doing. The phenomenon is quite different from what we normally think of as blogging, because a blog post is usually a written piece, sometimes quite long: a statement of opinion, a story, an analysis. But these new updates are something different. They're far shorter, far more frequent and less carefully considered. One of the most popular new tools is Twitter, a Web site and messaging service that allows its two-million-plus users to broadcast to their friends haiku-length updates—limited to 140 characters, as brief as a mobile-phone text message—on what they're doing. There are other services for reporting where you're traveling (Dopplr) or for quickly tossing online a stream of the pictures, videos or Web sites you're looking at (Tumblr). And there are even tools that give your location. When the new iPhone, with built-in tracking, was introduced in July, one million people began using Loopt, a piece of software that automatically tells all your friends exactly where you are.

11   For many people—particularly anyone over the age of 30—the idea of describing your blow-by-blow activities in such detail is absurd. Why would you subject your friends to your daily minutiae? And conversely, how much of their trivia can you absorb? The growth of ambient intimacy can seem like modern narcissism taken to a new, supermetabolic extreme—the ultimate expression of a generation of celebrity-addled youths who believe their every utterance is fascinating and ought to be shared with the world. Twitter, in particular, has been the subject of nearly relentless scorn since it went online. "Who really cares what I am doing, every hour of the day?" wondered Alex Beam, a *Boston Globe* columnist, in an essay about Twitter last month. "Even I don't care."

12   Indeed, many of the people I interviewed, who are among the most avid users of these "awareness" tools, admit that at first they couldn't figure out why anybody would want to do this. Ben Haley, a 39-year-old documentation specialist for a software firm who lives in Seattle, told me that when he first heard about Twitter last year from an early-adopter friend who used it, his first reaction was that it seemed silly. But a few of his friends decided to give it a try, and they urged him to sign up, too.

13   Each day, Haley logged on to his account, and his friends' updates would appear as a long page of one- or two-line notes. He would check and recheck the account several times a day, or even several times an hour. The updates were indeed pretty banal. One friend would post about starting to feel sick; one posted random thoughts like "I really hate it when people clip their nails on the bus"; another Twittered whenever she made a sandwich—and she

made a sandwich every day. Each so-called tweet was so brief as to be virtually meaningless.

But as the days went by, something changed. Haley discovered that he was 14
beginning to sense the rhythms of his friends' lives in a way he never had before. When one friend got sick with a virulent fever, he could tell by her Twitter updates when she was getting worse and the instant she finally turned the corner. He could see when friends were heading into hellish days at work or when they'd scored a big success. Even the daily catalog of sandwiches became oddly mesmerizing, a sort of metronomic *click* that he grew accustomed to seeing pop up in the middle of each day.

This is the paradox of ambient awareness. Each little update—each individual 15
bit of social information—is insignificant on its own, even supremely mundane. But taken together, over time, the little snippets coalesce into a surprisingly sophisticated portrait of your friends' and family members' lives, like thousands of dots making a pointillist painting. This was never before possible, because in the real world, no friend would *bother* to call you up and detail the sandwiches she was eating. The ambient information becomes like "a type of E.S.P.," as Haley described it to me, an invisible dimension floating over everyday life.

"It's like I can distantly read everyone's mind," Haley went on to say. "I love 16
that. I feel like I'm getting to something raw about my friends. It's like I've got this heads-up display for them." It can also lead to more real-life contact, because when one member of Haley's group decides to go out to a bar or see a band and Twitters about his plans, the others see it, and some decide to drop by—ad hoc, self-organizing socializing. And when they do socialize face to face, it feels oddly as if they've never actually been apart. They don't need to ask, "So, what have you been up to?" because they already know. Instead, they'll begin discussing something that one of the friends Twittered that afternoon, as if picking up a conversation in the middle.

Facebook and Twitter may have pushed things into overdrive, but the idea 17
of using communication tools as a form of "co-presence" has been around for a while. The Japanese sociologist Mizuko Ito first noticed it with mobile phones: lovers who were working in different cities would send text messages back and forth all night—tiny updates like "enjoying a glass of wine now" or "watching TV while lying on the couch." They were doing it partly because talking for hours on mobile phones isn't very comfortable (or affordable). But they also discovered that the little Ping-Ponging messages felt even more intimate than a phone call.

"It's an aggregate phenomenon," Marc Davis, a chief scientist at Yahoo and 18
former professor of information science at the University of California at Berkeley, told me. "No message is the single-most-important message. It's sort of like when you're sitting with someone and you look over and they smile at you. You're sitting here reading the paper, and you're doing your side-by-side thing, and you just sort of let people know you're aware of them." Yet it is also why it can be extremely hard to understand the phenomenon until you've experienced it. Merely looking at a stranger's Twitter or Facebook feed isn't interesting, because it seems like

blather. Follow it for a day, though, and it begins to feel like a short story; follow it for a month, and it's a novel.

19   You could also regard the growing popularity of online awareness as a reaction to social isolation, the modern American disconnectedness that Robert Putnam explored in his book *Bowling Alone.* The mobile workforce requires people to travel more frequently for work, leaving friends and family behind, and members of the growing army of the self-employed often spend their days in solitude. Ambient intimacy becomes a way to "feel less alone," as more than one Facebook and Twitter user told me.

20   When I decided to try out Twitter last year, at first I didn't have anyone to follow. None of my friends were yet using the service. But while doing some Googling one day I stumbled upon the blog of Shannon Seery, a 32-year-old recruiting consultant in Florida, and I noticed that she Twittered. Her Twitter updates were pretty charming—she would often post links to camera-phone pictures of her two children or videos of herself cooking Mexican food, or broadcast her agonized cries when a flight was delayed on a business trip. So on a whim I started "following" her—as easy on Twitter as a click of the mouse—and never took her off my account. (A Twitter account can be "private," so that only invited friends can read one's tweets, or it can be public, so anyone can; Seery's was public.) When I checked in last month, I noticed that she had built up a huge number of online connections: She was now following 677 people on Twitter and another 442 on Facebook. How in God's name, I wondered, could she follow so many people? Who precisely are they? I called Seery to find out.

21   "I have a rule," she told me. "I either have to know who you are, or I have to know *of* you." That means she monitors the lives of friends, family, anyone she works with, and she'll also follow interesting people she discovers via her friends' online lives. Like many people who live online, she has wound up following a few strangers—though after a few months they no longer feel like strangers, despite the fact that she has never physically met them.

22   I asked Seery how she finds the time to follow so many people online. The math seemed daunting. After all, if her 1,000 online contacts each post just a couple of notes each a day, that's several thousand little social pings to sift through daily. What would it be like to get thousands of e-mail messages a day? But Seery made a point I heard from many others: awareness tools aren't as cognitively demanding as an e-mail message. E-mail is something you have to stop to open and assess. It's personal; someone is asking for 100 percent of your attention. In contrast, ambient updates are all visible on one single page in a big row, and they're not really directed at you. This makes them skimmable, like newspaper headlines; maybe you'll read them all, maybe you'll skip some. Seery estimated that she needs to spend only a small part of each hour actively reading her Twitter stream.

23   Yet she has, she said, become far more gregarious online. "What's really funny is that before this 'social media' stuff, I always said that I'm not the type of person who had a ton of friends," she told me. "It's so hard to make plans and

have an active social life, having the type of job I have where I travel all the time and have two small kids. But it's easy to tweet all the time, to post pictures of what I'm doing, to keep social relations up." She paused for a second, before continuing: "Things like Twitter have actually given me a much bigger social circle. I know more about more people than ever before."

I realized that this is becoming true of me, too. After following Seery's Twitter 24 stream for a year, I'm more knowledgeable about the details of her life than the lives of my two sisters in Canada, whom I talk to only once every month or so. When I called Seery, I knew that she had been struggling with a three-day migraine headache; I began the conversation by asking her how she was feeling.

Online awareness inevitably leads to a curious question: What sort of relation- 25 ships are these? What does it mean to have hundreds of "friends" on Facebook? What kind of friends are they, anyway?

In 1998, the anthropologist Robin Dunbar argued that each human has a 26 hard-wired upper limit on the number of people he or she can personally know at one time. Dunbar noticed that humans and apes both develop social bonds by engaging in some sort of grooming; apes do it by picking at and smoothing one another's fur, and humans do it with conversation. He theorized that ape and human brains could manage only a finite number of grooming relationships: unless we spend enough time doing social grooming—chitchatting, trading gossip or, for apes, picking lice—we won't really feel that we "know" someone well enough to call him a friend. Dunbar noticed that ape groups tended to top out at 55 members. Since human brains were proportionally bigger, Dunbar figured that our maximum number of social connections would be similarly larger: about 150 on average. Sure enough, psychological studies have confirmed that human groupings naturally tail off at around 150 people: the "Dunbar number," as it is known. Are people who use Facebook and Twitter increasing their Dunbar number, because they can so easily keep track of so many more people?

As I interviewed some of the most aggressively social people online— 27 people who follow hundreds or even thousands of others—it became clear that the picture was a little more complex than this question would suggest. Many maintained that their circle of true intimates, their very close friends and family, had not become bigger. Constant online contact had made those ties immeasurably richer, but it hadn't actually increased the number of them; deep relationships are still predicated on face time, and there are only so many hours in the day for that.

But where their sociality had truly exploded was in their "weak ties"— 28 loose acquaintances, people they knew less well. It might be someone they met at a conference, or someone from high school who recently "friended" them on Facebook, or somebody from last year's holiday party. In their pre-Internet lives, these sorts of acquaintances would have quickly faded from their attention. But when one of these far-flung people suddenly posts a personal note to your feed, it is essentially a reminder that they exist. I have noticed this effect myself. In the last few months, dozens of old work colleagues I knew from

10 years ago in Toronto have friended me on Facebook, such that I'm now suddenly reading their stray comments and updates and falling into oblique, funny conversations with them. My overall Dunbar number is thus 301: Facebook (254) + Twitter (47), double what it would be without technology. Yet only 20 are family or people I'd consider close friends. The rest are weak ties—maintained via technology.

29   This rapid growth of weak ties can be a very good thing. Sociologists have long found that "weak ties" greatly expand your ability to solve problems. For example, if you're looking for a job and ask your friends, they won't be much help; they're too similar to you, and thus probably won't have any leads that you don't already have yourself. Remote acquaintances will be much more useful, because they're farther afield, yet still socially intimate enough to want to help you out. Many avid Twitter users—the ones who fire off witty posts hourly and wind up with thousands of intrigued followers—explicitly milk this dynamic for all it's worth, using their large online followings as a way to quickly answer almost any question. Laura Fitton, a social-media consultant who has become a minor celebrity on Twitter—she has more than 5,300 followers—recently discovered to her horror that her accountant had made an error in filing last year's taxes. She went to Twitter, wrote a tiny note explaining her problem, and within 10 minutes her online audience had provided leads to lawyers and better accountants. Fritton joked to me that she no longer buys anything worth more than $50 without quickly checking it with her Twitter network.

30   "I outsource my entire life," she said. "I can solve any problem on Twitter in six minutes." (She also keeps a secondary Twitter account that is private and only for a much smaller circle of close friends and family—"My little secret," she said. It is a strategy many people told me they used: one account for their weak ties, one for their deeper relationships.)

31   It is also possible, though, that this profusion of weak ties can become a problem. If you're reading daily updates from hundreds of people about whom they're dating and whether they're happy, it might, some critics worry, spread your emotional energy too thin, leaving less for true intimate relationships. Psychologists have long known that people can engage in "parasocial" relationships with fictional characters, like those on TV shows or in books, or with remote celebrities we read about in magazines. Parasocial relationships can use up some of the emotional space in our Dunbar number, crowding out real-life people. Danah Boyd, a fellow at Harvard's Berkman Center for Internet and Society who has studied social media for 10 years, published a paper this spring arguing that awareness tools like News Feed might be creating a whole new class of relationships that are nearly parasocial—peripheral people in our network whose intimate details we follow closely online, even while they, like Angelina Jolie, are basically unaware we exist.

32   "The information we subscribe to on a feed is not the same as in a deep social relationship," Boyd told me. She has seen this herself; she has many virtual admirers that have, in essence, a parasocial relationship with her. "I've been very, very sick, lately and I write about it on Twitter and my blog, and I get

all these people who are writing to me telling me ways to work around the health-care system, or they're writing saying, 'Hey, I broke my neck!' And I'm like, 'You're being very nice and trying to help me, but though you feel like you know me, you don't.'" Boyd sighed. "They can *observe* you, but it's not the same as *knowing* you."

When I spoke to Caterina Fake, a founder of Flickr (a popular photo-sharing 33 site), she suggested an even more subtle danger: that the sheer ease of following her friends' updates online has made her occasionally lazy about actually taking the time to visit them in person. "At one point I realized I had a friend whose child I had seen, via photos on Flickr, grow from birth to 1 year old," she said. "I thought, I really should go meet her in person. But it was weird; I also felt that Flickr had satisfied that getting-to-know you satisfaction, so I didn't feel the urgency. But then I was like, Oh, that's not sufficient! I *should* go in person!" She has about 400 people she follows online but suspects many of those relationships are tissue-fragile. "These technologies allow you to be much more broadly friendly, but you just spread yourself much more thinly over many more people."

What is it like to never lose touch with anyone? One morning this summer at 34 my local cafe, I overheard a young woman complaining to her friend about a recent Facebook drama. Her name is Andrea Ahan, a 27-year-old restaurant entrepreneur, and she told me that she had discovered that high-school friends were uploading old photos of her to Facebook and tagging them with her name, so they automatically appeared in searches for her.

She was aghast. "I'm like, my God, these pictures are completely hideous!" 35 Ahan complained, while her friend looked on sympathetically and sipped her coffee. "I'm wearing all these totally awful '90s clothes. I look like crap. And I'm like, Why are you people in my life, anyway? I haven't seen you in 10 years. I don't *know* you anymore!" She began furiously detagging the pictures—removing her name, so they wouldn't show up in a search anymore.

Worse, Ahan was also confronting a common plague of Facebook: the re- 36 cent ex. She had broken up with her boyfriend not long ago, but she hadn't "unfriended" him, because that felt too extreme. But soon he paired up with another young woman, and the new couple began having public conversations on Ahan's ex-boyfriend's page. One day, she noticed with alarm that the new girlfriend was quoting material Ahan had e-mailed privately to her boyfriend; she suspected he had been sharing the e-mail with his new girlfriend. It is the sort of weirdly subtle mind game that becomes possible via Facebook, and it drove Ahan nuts.

"Sometimes I think this stuff is just crazy, and everybody has got to get a life 37 and stop obsessing over everyone's trivia and gossiping," she said.

Yet Ahan knows that she cannot simply walk away from her online life, be- 38 cause the people she knows online won't stop talking about her, or posting unflattering photos. She needs to stay on Facebook just to monitor what's being said about her. This is a common complaint I heard, particularly from people in their 20s who were in college when Facebook appeared and have never lived as adults without online awareness. For them, participation isn't optional. If you don't dive in, other people will define who you are. So you constantly stream your pictures, your thoughts, your relationship status and what you're doing—right now!—if only to ensure the virtual version of you is accurate, or at least the one you want to present to the world.

39   This is the ultimate effect of the new awareness: It brings back the dynamics of small-town life, where everybody knows your business. Young people at college are the ones to experience this most viscerally, because, with more than 90 percent of their peers using Facebook, it is especially difficult for them to opt out. Zeynep Tufekci, a sociologist at the University of Maryland, Baltimore County, who has closely studied how college-age users are reacting to the world of awareness, told me that athletes used to sneak off to parties illicitly, breaking the no-drinking rule for team members. But then camera phones and Facebook came along, with students posting photos of the drunken carousing during the party; savvy coaches could see which athletes were breaking the rules. First the athletes tried to fight back by waking up early the morning after the party in a hungover daze to detag photos of themselves so they wouldn't be searchable. But that didn't work, because the coaches sometimes viewed the pictures live, as they went online at 2 A.M. So parties simply began banning all camera phones in a last-ditch attempt to preserve privacy.

40   "It's just like living in a village, where it's actually hard to lie because everybody knows the truth already," Tufekci said. "The current generation is never unconnected. They're never losing touch with their friends. So we're going back to a more normal place, historically. If you look at human history, the idea that you would drift through life, going from new relation to new relation, that's very new. It's just the 20th century."

41   Psychologists and sociologists spent years wondering how humanity would adjust to the anonymity of life in the city, the wrenching upheavals of mobile immigrant labor—a world of lonely people ripped from their social ties. We now have precisely the opposite problem. Indeed, our modern awareness tools reverse the original conceit of the Internet. When cyberspace came along in the early '90s, it was celebrated as a place where you could reinvent your identity—become someone new.

42   "If anything, it's identity-constraining now," Tufekci told me. "You can't play with your identity if your audience is always checking up on you. I had a student who posted that she was downloading some Pearl Jam, and someone wrote on her wall, 'Oh, *right*, ha-ha—I know you, and you're not into *that*.'" She laughed. "You know that old cartoon? 'On the Internet, nobody knows you're a dog'? On the Internet today, *everybody* knows you're a dog! If you don't want people to know you're a dog, you'd better stay away from a keyboard."

Or, as Leisa Reichelt, a consultant in London who writes regularly about   43
ambient tools, put it to me: "Can you imagine a Facebook for children in kindergarten, and they never lose touch with those kids for the rest of their lives? What's that
going to do to them?" Young people today are already developing an attitude toward their privacy that is simultaneously vigilant and laissez-faire. They curate
their online personas as carefully as possible, knowing that everyone is watching—
but they have also learned to shrug and accept the limits of what they can control.

It is easy to become unsettled by privacy-eroding aspects of awareness tools.   44
But there is another—quite different—result of all this incessant updating: a
culture of people who know much more about themselves. Many of the avid
Twitterers, Flickrers and Facebook users I interviewed described an unexpected
side-effect of constant self-disclosure. The act of stopping several times a day to
observe what you're feeling or thinking can become, after weeks and weeks, a
sort of philosophical act. It's like the Greek dictum to "know thyself," or the thera-
peutic concept of mindfulness. (Indeed, the question that floats eternally at the top
of Twitter's Web site—"What are you doing?"—can come to seem existentially
freighted. What *are* you doing?) Having an audience can make the self-reflection
even more acute, since, as my interviewees noted, they're trying to describe their
activities in a way that is not only accurate but also interesting to others: the status
update as a literary form.

Laura Fitton, the social-media consultant, argues that her constant status   45
updating has made her "a happier person, a calmer person" because the process
of, say, describing a horrid morning at work forces her to look at it objectively. "It
drags you out of your own head," she added. In an age of awareness, perhaps the
person you see most clearly is yourself.

Synthesis: Connections for Argumentation

1. Annotate all four essays and then write brief, one-paragraph summaries of each.
2. Discuss with classmates the fascination that young people have with online social networking sites. Explore the various reasons that the writers in this case study give to
   explain this trend and their claims and viewpoints on the subject.
3. In an essay of argumentative synthesis, evaluate the relative effectiveness of each
   writer's claim. Using objective criteria, identify those authors who are most successful
   and those who are least effective in presenting their claims.
4. In an essay that uses Rogerian argument, explain that the overall impact of social networking is not wholly positive or negative but rather a combination of effects that
   might be potentially good or bad. Incorporate relevant data and information from the
   essays in this case study that would be useful in making your case.

NETWORKING
Applying Digital and Multimedia Literacies

1. Go to at least three of the social networking sites mentioned by the writers in this case study, or to other sites that you know about. Compose an argumentative essay in which you assess the nature and content of these sites.
2. With one or two other class members, go online and investigate one of the following topics: cyberbullying; freedom on the Internet; sexual exploitation on the Web; online gaming. Locate at least three articles on the selected issue. Report your findings to the class. Compose your own essay, based on these sources, in which you state your viewpoint on the issue.
3. Argue for or against the proposition that trying to find love on the Internet is a futile endeavor. Research at least two sites to support your position on online romance. In addition, locate two or more articles on the subject, and incorporate the authors' viewpoints into your essay of argumentative synthesis.

part 2

Issues across the Disciplines

chapter 4

Education and Society
How, What, and Why Do We Learn?

In "Learning to Read and Write," a chapter from his autobiography, Frederick Douglass offers a spirited affirmation of the rights we all should have to pursue an education. For Douglass, who was born into slavery, knowledge began not only with experience but also with the need to articulate that experience through literacy. The ability to read and write should be the possession of all human beings, and Douglass was willing to risk punishment—even death—to gain that ability. Today, all over the globe, as ethnic and political conflicts arise, men and women face the same challenge of expressing themselves. For even with a tool like the Internet, if one does not have the tools to express oneself or if the expression of thought is suppressed, the vehicle for conveying ideas, no matter how powerful, is rendered useless.

Perhaps the struggle for an education always involves a certain amount of effort and risk, but the struggle also conveys excitement and the deep, abiding satisfaction that derives from achieving knowledge of oneself and of the world. Time and again in the essays in this chapter, we discover that there is always a price to be paid for acquiring knowledge, developing intellectual skills, and attaining wisdom. However, numerous task forces and national commissions tell us that students today are not willing to pay this price and that, as a consequence, we have become academically mediocre. Is it true that we no longer delight in educating ourselves through reading, as Richard Rodriguez recounts in "The Lonely, Good Company of Books"? Is it true that we take libraries for granted—we expect them to be available but never visit them? A democratic society requires an educated citizenry, people who refuse to commit intellectual suicide or self-neglect. The writers in this chapter, who take many pathways to understanding, remind us that we cannot afford to be passive or compliant when our right to an education is challenged.

Today we are in an era of dynamic change in attitudes toward education. Such issues as sex education, multiculturalism, racism, sexism, and immigration suggest the liveliness of the educational debate on campus. Any debate over contemporary education touches on the themes of politics, economics, religion, or the social agenda, forcing us to recognize that configurations of power are at the heart of virtually all educational issues in society today.

Without education, many of our ideas and opinions can be stereotyped or prejudiced, bearing no relationship to the truth. It is easy to understand how such views can arise if we are merely passive vessels for others' uninformed opinions rather than active learners who seek true knowledge. If we judge the tenor of the essayists in this section, we discover that many of them are subversives, waging war against both ignorance *and* received dogma.

180

These writers treat education as the key to upsetting the status quo and effecting change. Operating from diverse backgrounds, they challenge many assumptions about our educational system and invite us to think critically about its purpose.

PREVIEWING THE CHAPTER

As you read the essays in this chapter and respond to them in discussion and writing, consider the following questions:

- What is the main educational issue that the author deals with?
- What tone does the author establish in treating the subject? Does the author take a positive or a negative position?
- Does the author define *education?* If so, how? If not, does the author suggest what he or she means by it?
- What is the impact of society at large on how education is perceived?
- What forms of evidence do the authors use to support their views on education?
- How do the rhetorical features of the essays that focus on personal experience differ from those of the essays that examine education from a more global perspective?
- What have you learned about the value of education from reading these selections?
- Which essays persuaded you the most? Which the least? Why?

Classic and Contemporary Images

DOES EDUCATION CHANGE OVER TIME?

Using a Critical Perspective   Consider these two photographs of students in science laboratories, the first from the 19th century and the second from the present. What is the setting of each laboratory like? Who are the people? What does each photographer frame and leave out of the scene? Which educational setting seems more conducive to scientific or educational inquiry? Why?

Founded in 1833, Oberlin College in Ohio was the first U.S. college
to grant undergraduate degrees to women. The photograph reprinted
here shows both male and female students in a zoology lab
at Oberlin sometime during the 1890s.

At the beginning of the 21st century, most colleges and universities in the United States are coeducational, and it is no longer unusual to see both male and female students in a laboratory setting, as shown in this contemporary photo of a biology lab at the University of Maine.

Classic and Contemporary Essays
WHAT IS THE VALUE OF EDUCATION?

A famous adage proclaims that "the pen is mightier than the sword." In Frederick Douglass's narrative and the excerpt from the work of Richard Rodriguez, we get two portraits that demonstrate the truth of the adage. Douglass's efforts at becoming fully literate freed him from what would have been a life of slavery. No weapon could have done that for him. It is obvious that Douglass learned his lesson well, for his prose is stately, clear, direct, and precise. His story speaks of a determined youth and man who had a powerful motivation in learning to read and write. Would he have done so without this motivation? Perhaps, because he seems to be a very self-directed individual, as is evident from the anecdotes he relates. Rodriguez, too, has a strong motivation to master, and even to excel at, reading and writing. Writing nearly 150 years after Douglass, and at a time when he needn't fear slavery looming over him, Rodriguez nevertheless perceived that by emulating his teachers, who promoted book reading, his own reading would make him a better person. He, like Douglass, sensed that there was something about acquiring knowledge and about expanding one's view of the world by learning how others viewed it that would provide him with a certain amount of independence. As you read the following two essays, you may wish to consider whether the quiet, modest tone each author projects may have something to do with the subject matter. For reading, although active and mind-opening, is still a private and "lonely" activity.

Learning to Read and Write

Frederick Douglass

Frederick Douglass *(1817–1895) was an American abolitionist, orator, and journalist. Born of the union between a slave and a white man, Douglass later escaped to Massachusetts. An impassioned antislavery speech brought him recognition as a powerful orator; thereafter he was much in demand for speaking engagements. He described his experience as a black man in America in* Narrative of the Life of Frederick Douglass *(1845). After managing to buy his freedom, Douglass founded the* North Star, *a newspaper he published for the next 17 years. In the following excerpt from his stirring autobiography, Douglass recounts the tremendous obstacles he overcame in his efforts to become literate.*

1   I lived in Master Hugh's family about seven years. During this time, I succeeded in learning to read and write. In accomplishing this, I was compelled to resort to various stratagems. I had no regular teacher. My mistress, who had kindly commenced

to instruct me, had, in compliance with the advice and direction of her husband, not only ceased to instruct, but had set her face against my being instructed by any one else. It is due, however, to my mistress to say of her, that she did not adopt this course of treatment immediately. She at first lacked the depravity indispensable to shutting me up in mental darkness. It was at least necessary for her to have some training in the exercise of irresponsible power, to make her equal to the task of treating me as though I were a brute.

My mistress was, as I have said, a kind and tender-hearted woman; and in the 2 simplicity of her soul she commenced, when I first went to live with her, to treat me as she supposed one human being ought to treat another. In entering upon the duties of a slaveholder, she did not seem to perceive that I sustained to her the relation of a mere chattel, and that for her to treat me as a human being was not only wrong, but dangerously so. Slavery proved as injurious to her as it did to me. When I went there, she was a pious, warm, and tender-hearted woman. There was no sorrow or suffering for which she had not a tear. She had bread for the hungry, clothes for the naked, and comfort for every mourner that came within her reach. Slavery soon proved its ability to divest her of these heavenly qualities. Under its influence, the tender heart became stone, and the lamb-like disposition gave way to one of tiger-like fierceness. The first step in her downward course was in her ceasing to instruct me. She now commenced to practise her husband's precepts. She finally became even more violent in her opposition than her husband himself. She was not satisfied with simply doing as well as he had commanded; she seemed anxious to do better. Nothing seemed to make her more angry than to see me with a newspaper. She seemed to think that here lay the danger. I have had her rush at me with a face made all up of fury, and snatch from me a newspaper, in a manner that fully revealed her apprehension. She was an apt woman; and a little experience soon demonstrated, to her satisfaction, that education and slavery were incompatible with each other.

From this time I was most narrowly watched. If I was in a separate room any 3 considerable length of time, I was sure to be suspected of having a book, and was at once called to give an account of myself. All this, however, was too late. The first step had been taken. Mistress, in teaching me the alphabet, had given me the *inch,* and no precaution could prevent me from taking the *ell.*

The plan which I adopted, and the one by which I was most successful, was 4 that of making friends of all the little white boys whom I met in the street. As many of these as I could, I converted into teachers. With their kindly aid, obtained at different times and in different places, I finally succeeded in learning to read. When I was sent on errands, I always took my book with me, and by doing one part of my errand quickly, I found time to get a lesson before my return. I used also to carry bread with me, enough of which was always in the house, and to which I was always welcome; for I was much better off in this regard than many of the poor white children in our neighborhood. This bread I used to bestow upon the hungry little urchins, who, in return, would give me that more valuable bread of knowledge. I am strongly tempted to give the names of two or three of those little boys, a testimonial of the gratitude and affection I bear them; but prudence forbids—not that it would injure me, but it might embarrass them; for it is almost an unpardonable offence to teach slaves to read in this Christian country. It is enough to say of the dear little fellows, that they lived on Philpot Street, very near Durgin and Bailey's ship-yard. I used to talk this matter of slavery over with them. I would sometimes say to them, I wished I could be as free as they would be when they got to be men. "You will be free as soon as you are twenty-one, *but I am a slave for life!* Have not I as good a right to be free as you have?" These words used to trouble them; they would express for me the liveliest sympathy, and console me with the hope that something would occur by which I might be free.

5   I was now about twelve years old, and the thought of being a *slave for life* began to bear heavily upon my heart. Just about this time, I got hold of a book entitled "The Colombian Orator." Every opportunity I got, I used to read this book. Among much of other interesting matter, I found in it a dialogue between a master and his slave. The slave was represented as having run away from his master three times. The dialogue represented the conversation which took place between them, when the slave was retaken the third time. In this dialogue, the whole argument in behalf of slavery was brought forward by the master, all of which was disposed of by the slave. The slave was made to say some very smart as well as impressive things in reply to his master—things which had the desired though unexpected effect; for the conversation resulted in the voluntary emancipation of the slave on the part of the master.

6   In the same book, I met with one of Sheridan's mighty speeches on and in behalf of Catholic emancipation. These were choice documents to me. I read them over and over again with unabated interest. They gave tongue to interesting thoughts of my own soul, which had frequently flashed through my mind, and died away for want of utterance. The moral which I gained from the dialogue was the power of truth over the conscience of even a slaveholder. What I got from Sheridan was a bold denunciation of slavery, and a powerful vindication of human rights. The reading of these documents enabled me to utter my thoughts, and to meet the arguments brought forward to sustain slavery; but while they relieved me of one difficulty, they brought on another even more painful than the one of which I was relieved. The more I read, the more I was led to abhor and detest my enslavers. I could regard them in no other light than a band of successful robbers, who had left their homes, and gone to Africa, and stolen us from our homes, and in a strange land reduced us to slavery. I loathed them as being the meanest as well as the most wicked of men. As I read and contemplated the subject, behold! that very discontentment which Master Hugh had predicted would follow my learning to read had already come, to torment and sting my soul to unutterable anguish. As I writhed under it, I would at times feel that learning to read had been a curse rather than a blessing. It had given me a view of my wretched condition, without the remedy. It opened my eyes to the horrible pit, but to no ladder upon which to get out. In moments of agony, I envied my fellow-slaves for their stupidity. I have often wished myself a beast. I preferred the condition of the meanest reptile to my own. Any thing, no matter what, to get rid of thinking! It was this everlasting thinking of my condition that tormented me. There was no getting rid of it. It was pressed upon me by every object within sight or hearing, animate or

inanimate. The silver trump of freedom had roused my soul to eternal wakeful-
ness. Freedom now appeared, to disappear no more forever. It was heard in every
sound, and seen in every thing. It was ever present to torment me with a sense of
my wretched condition. I saw nothing without seeing it, I heard nothing without
hearing it, and felt nothing without feeling it. It looked from every star, it smiled in
every calm, breathed in every wind, and moved in every storm.

I often found myself regretting my own existence, and wishing myself dead; 7
and but for the hope of being free, I have no doubt but that I should have killed myself, or done something for which I should have been killed. While in this state of
mind, I was eager to hear anyone speak of slavery. I was a ready listener. Every little
while, I could hear something about the abolitionists. It was some time before I
found what the word meant. It was always used in such connections as to make it an
interesting word to me. If a slave ran away and succeeded in getting clear, or if a
slave killed his master, set fire to a barn, or did any thing very wrong in the mind of
a slaveholder, it was spoken of as the fruit of *abolition.* Hearing the word in this connection very often, I set about learning what it meant. The dictionary afforded me
little or no help. I found it was "the act of abolishing"; but then I did not know what
was to be abolished. Here I was perplexed. I did not dare to ask any one about its
meaning, for I was satisfied that it was something they wanted me to know very little about. After a patient waiting, I got one of our city papers, containing an account
of the number of petitions from the north, praying for the abolition of slavery in the
District of Columbia, and of the slave trade between the States. From this time I
understood the words *abolition* and *abolitionist,* and always drew near when that
word was spoken, expecting to hear something of importance to myself and fellow-
slaves. The light broke in upon me by degrees. I went one day down on the wharf of
Mr. Waters; and seeing two Irishmen unloading a scow of stone, I went, unasked,
and helped them. When we had finished, one of them came to me and asked me if I
were a slave. I told him I was. He asked, "Are ye a slave for life?" I told him that I
was. The good Irishman seemed to be deeply affected by the statement. He said to
the other that it was a pity so fine a little fellow as myself should be a slave for life.
He said it was a shame to hold me. They both advised me to run away to the north;
that I should find friends there, and that I should be free. I pretended not to be interested in what they said, and treated them as if I did not understand them; for I
feared they might be treacherous. White men have been known to encourage slaves
to escape, and then, to get the reward, catch them and return them to their masters.
I was afraid that these seemingly good men might use me so; but I nevertheless
remembered their advice, and from that time I resolved to run away. I looked forward to a time at which it would be safe for me to escape. I was too young to think
of doing so immediately; besides, I wished to learn how to write, as I might have
occasion to write my own pass. I consoled myself with the hope that I should one
day find a good chance. Meanwhile, I would learn to write.

The idea as to how I might learn to write was suggested to me by being in 8
Durgin and Bailey's ship-yard, and frequently seeing the ship carpenters, after hew-
ing, and getting a piece of timber ready for use, write on the timber the name of that
part of the ship for which it was intended. When a piece of timber was intended for

the larboard side, it would be marked thus—"L." When a piece was for the starboard side, it would be marked thus—"S." A piece for the larboard side forward, would be marked thus—"L. F." When a piece was for starboard side forward, it would be marked thus—"S. F." For larboard aft, it would be marked thus—"L. A." For starboard aft, it would be marked thus—"S. A." I soon learned the names of these letters, and for what they were intended when placed upon a piece of timber in the ship-yard. I immediately commenced copying them, and in a short time was able to make the four letters named. After that, when I met with any boy who I knew could write, I would tell him I could write as well as he. The next word would be, "I don't believe you. Let me see you try it." I would then make the letters which I had been so fortunate as to learn, and ask him to beat that. In this way I got a good many lessons in writing, which it is quite possible I should never have gotten in any other way. During this time, my copy-book was the board fence, brick wall, and pavement; my pen and ink was a lump of chalk. With these, I learned mainly how to write. I then commenced and continued copying the Italics in Webster's Spelling Book, until I could make them all without looking on the book. By this time, my little Master Thomas had gone to school, and learned how to write, and had written over a number of copy-books. These had been brought home, and shown to some of our near neighbors, and then laid aside. My mistress used to go to class meeting at the Wilk Street meetinghouse every Monday afternoon, and leave me to take care of the house. When left thus, I used to spend the time in writing in the spaces left in Master Thomas's copy-book, copying what he had written. I continued to do this until I could write a hand very similar to that of Master Thomas. Thus, after a long, tedious effort for years, I finally succeeded in learning how to write.

COMPREHENSION

1. What strategies does Douglass use to continue his education after his mistress's abandonment?
2. Why did the author's mistress find his reading newspapers particularly threatening?
3. Why does Douglass call learning to read "a curse rather than a blessing" (paragraph 6)?

RHETORIC

1. What is the thesis of Douglass's narration? How well is it supported and developed by the body paragraphs? Explain.
2. The first couple of sentences in the story, though simple, are very powerful. How do they serve to set up the mood of the piece and the reader's expectations?
3. Cite examples of Douglass's use of metaphors, and discuss why they work in those paragraphs.
4. How would you describe Douglass's writing style and level of language? Does it reveal anything about his character? Justify your response.
5. Explain the way in which the author uses comparison and contrast.
6. What is Douglass's definition of *abolition*, and how does he help the reader define it? How does this method contribute to the reader's understanding of the learning process?

WRITING

1. What does Douglass mean when he writes that "education and slavery were incompatible with each other" (paragraph 2)? Write an essay in which you consider the relationship between the two.
2. Both Douglass and his mistress were in inferior positions to Master Hugh. Write an essay in which you compare and contrast their positions in society at the time.
3. Illiteracy is still a major problem in the United States. Write an account of what your day-to-day life would be like if you couldn't write or read. What impact would this deficiency have on your life? Use concrete examples to illustrate your narrative.
4. **Writing an Argument:** Write an essay in which you argue for or against the proposition that American education continues to discriminate against minority groups.

NETWORKING
Applying Digital and Multimedia Literacies

Analyzing a News Report on 21st-Century Illiteracy: Go to *http://www.cbsnews.com/video/watch/?id=4711567n* and watch this 2009 CBS report on adult illiteracy in the United States. What challenges has John Jones faced because of his illiteracy? Why do you think the report chose to focus not only on larger statistics, such as results from the Board of Education's report, but also on illiteracy's effects on an individual? How does John Jones's story contribute to the report's purpose and argument? How does the report make use of its medium (television) to convey its message?

The Lonely, Good Company of Books

Richard Rodriguez

Richard Rodriguez (b. 1944) was born in San Francisco and received degrees from Stanford University and Columbia University. He also did graduate study at the University of California, Berkeley, and at the Warburg Institute, London. Rodriguez became a nationally known writer with the publication of his autobiography, Hunger of Memory: The Education of Richard Rodriguez *(1982). In it, he describes the struggles of growing up biculturally—feeling alienated from his Spanish-speaking parents yet not wholly comfortable in the dominant culture of the United States. He opposes bilingualism and affirmative action as they are now practiced in the United States, and his stance has caused much controversy in educational and intellectual circles. Rodriguez continues to write about social issues such as acculturation, education, and language in* Days of Obligation: An Argument with My Mexican Father *(1992) and* Brown: The Last Discovery of America *(2002). In the following essay, Rodriguez records his childhood passion for reading.*

1   From an early age I knew that my mother and father could read and write both Spanish and English. I had observed my father making his way through what, I now suppose, must have been income tax forms. On other occasions I waited apprehensively while my mother read onion-paper letters air-mailed from Mexico with news of a relative's illness or death. For both my parents, however, reading was something done out of necessity and as quickly as possible. Never did I see either of them read an entire book. Nor did I see them read for pleasure. Their reading consisted of work manuals, prayer books, newspapers, recipes. . . .

2   In our house each school year would begin with my mother's careful instruction: "Don't write in your books so we can sell them at the end of the year." The remark was echoed in public by my teachers, but only in part: "Boys and girls, don't write in your books. You must learn to treat them with great care and respect."

3   OPEN THE DOORS OF YOUR MIND WITH BOOKS, read the red and white poster over the nun's desk in early September. It soon was apparent to me that reading was the classroom's central activity. Each course had its own book. And the information gathered from a book was unquestioned. READ TO LEARN, the sign on the wall advised in December. I privately wondered: What was the connection between reading and learning? Did one learn something only by reading it? Was an idea only an idea if it could be written down? In June, CONSIDER BOOKS YOUR BEST FRIENDS. Friends? Reading was, at best, only a chore. I needed to look up whole paragraphs of words in a dictionary. Lines of type were dizzying, the eye having to move slowly across the page, then down, and across. . . . The sentences of the first books I read were coolly impersonal. Toned hard. What most bothered me, however, was the isolation reading required. To console myself for the loneliness I'd feel when I read, I tried reading in a very soft voice. Until: "Who is doing all that talking to his neighbor?" Shortly after, remedial reading classes were arranged for me with a very old nun.

4   At the end of each school day, for nearly six months, I would meet with her in the tiny room that served as the school's library but was actually only a storeroom for used textbooks and a vast collection of *National Geographics*. Everything about our sessions pleased me: the smallness of the room; the noise of the janitor's broom hitting the edge of the long hallway outside the door; the green of the sun, lighting the wall; and the old woman's face blurred white with a beard. Most of the time we took turns. I began with my elementary text. Sentences of astonishing simplicity seemed to me lifeless and drab: "The boys ran from the rain. . . . She wanted to sing. . . . The kite rose in the blue." Then the old nun would read from her favorite books, usually biographies of early American presidents. Playfully she ran through complex sentences, calling the words alive with her voice, making it seem that the author somehow was speaking directly to me. I smiled just to listen to her. I sat there and sensed for the very first time some possibility of fellowship between a reader and a writer, a communication, never *intimate* like that I heard spoken words at home convey, but one nonetheless *personal*.

5   One day the nun concluded a session by asking me why I was so reluctant to read by myself. I tried to explain; said something about the way written words made me feel all alone—almost, I wanted to add but didn't, as when I spoke to

myself in a room just emptied of furniture. She studied my face as I spoke; she seemed to be watching more than listening. In an uneventful voice she replied that I had nothing to fear. Didn't I realize that reading would open up whole new worlds? A book could open doors for me. It could introduce me to people and show me places I never imagined existed. She gestured toward the bookshelves. (Bare-breasted African women danced, and the shiny hubcaps of automobiles on the back covers of the *Geographic* gleamed in my mind.) I listened with respect. But her words were not very influential. I was thinking then of another consequence of literacy, one I was too shy to admit but nonetheless trusted. Books were going to make me "educated." *That* confidence enabled me, several months later, to overcome my fear of the silence.

In fourth grade I embarked upon a grandiose reading program. "Give me the 6 names of important books," I would say to startled teachers. They soon found out that I had in mind "adult books." I ignored their suggestion of anything I suspected was written for children. (Not until I was in college, as a result, did I read *Huckleberry Finn* or *Alice's Adventures in Wonderland.*) Instead, I read *The Scarlet Letter* and Franklin's *Autobiography.* And whatever I read I read for extra credit. Each time I finished a book, I reported the achievement to a teacher and basked in the praise my effort earned. Despite my best efforts, however, there seemed to be more and more books I needed to read. At the library I would literally tremble as I came upon whole shelves of books I hadn't read. So I read and I read and I read: *Great Expectations;* all the short stories of Kipling; *The Babe Ruth Story;* the entire first volume of the *Encyclopaedia Britannica* (A–ANSTEY); the *Iliad; Moby Dick; Gone with the Wind; The Good Earth; Ramona; Forever Amber; The Lives of the Saints; Crime and Punishment; The Pearl.* . . . Librarians who initially frowned when I checked out the maximum ten books at a time started saving books they thought I might like. Teachers would say to the rest of the class, "I only wish the rest of you took reading as seriously as Richard obviously does."

But at home I would hear my mother wondering, "What do you see in your 7 books?" (Was reading a hobby like her knitting? Was so much reading even healthy for a boy? Was it the sign of "brains"? Or was it just a convenient excuse for not helping around the house on Saturday mornings?) Always, "What do you see . . . ?"

What *did* I see in my books? I had the idea that they were crucial for my 8 academic success, though I couldn't have said exactly how or why. In the sixth grade I simply concluded that what gave a book its value was some major idea or theme it contained. If that core essence could be mined and memorized, I would become learned like my teachers. I decided to record in a notebook the themes of the books that I read. After reading *Robinson Crusoe,* I wrote that its theme was "the value of learning to live by oneself." When I completed *Wuthering Heights,* I noted the danger of "letting emotions get out of control." Rereading these brief moralistic appraisals usually left me disheartened. I couldn't believe that they were really the source of reading's value. But for many years, they constituted the only means I had of describing to myself the educational value of books.

9   In spite of my earnestness, I found reading a pleasurable activity. I came to enjoy the lonely, good company of books. Early on weekday mornings, I'd read in my bed. I'd feel a mysterious comfort then, reading in the dawn quiet—the blue-gray silence interrupted by the occasional churning of the refrigerator motor a few rooms away or the more distant sounds of a city bus beginning its run. On weekends I'd go to the public library to read, surrounded by old men and women. Or, if the weather was fine, I would take my books to the park and read in the shade of a tree. Neighbors would leave for vacation and I would water their lawns. I would sit through the twilight on the front porches or in backyards, reading to the cool, whirling sounds of the sprinklers.

10   I also had favorite writers. But often those writers I enjoyed most I was least able to value. When I read William Saroyan's *The Human Comedy,* I was immediately pleased by the narrator's warmth and the charm of his story. But as quickly I became suspicious. A book so enjoyable to read couldn't be very "important." Another summer I determined to read all the novels of Dickens. Reading his fat novels, I loved the feeling I got—after the first hundred pages—of being at home in a fictional world where I knew the names of the characters and cared about what was going to happen to them. And it bothered me that I was forced away at the conclusion, when the fiction closed tight, like a fortune-teller's fist—the futures of all the major characters neatly resolved. I never knew how to take such feelings seriously, however. Nor did I suspect that these experiences could be part of a novel's meaning. Still, there were pleasures to sustain me after I'd finish my books. Carrying a volume back to the library, I would be pleased by its weight. I'd run my fingers along the edge of the pages and marvel at the breadth of my achievement. Around my room, growing stacks of paperback books reinforced my assurance.

11   I entered high school having read hundreds of books. My habit of reading made me a confident speaker and writer of English. Reading also enabled me to sense something of the shape, the major concerns, of Western thought. (I was able to say something about Dante and Descartes and Engels and James Baldwin in my high school term papers.) In these various ways, books brought me academic success as I hoped that they would. But I was not a good reader. Merely bookish, I lacked a point of view when I read. Rather, I read in order to acquire a point of view. I vacuumed books for epigrams, scraps of information, ideas, themes—anything to fill the hollow within me and make me feel educated. When one of my teachers suggested to his drowsy tenth-grade English class that a person could not have a "complicated idea" until he had read at least two thousand books, I heard the remark without detecting either its irony or its very complicated truth. I merely determined to compile a list of all the books I had ever read. Harsh with myself, I included only once a title I might have read several times. (How, after all, could one read a book more than once?) And I included only those books over a hundred pages in length. (Could anything shorter be a book?)

12   There was yet another high school list I compiled. One day I came across a newspaper article about the retirement of an English professor at a nearby state college. The article was accompanied by a list of the "hundred most important books of Western Civilization." "More than anything else in my life," the professor

told the reporter with finality, "these books have made me all that I am." That was the kind of remark I couldn't ignore. I clipped out the list and kept it for the several months it took me to read all of the titles. Most books, of course, I barely understood. While reading Plato's *Republic,* for instance, I needed to keep looking at the book jacket comments to remind myself what the text was about. Nevertheless, with the special patience and superstition of a scholarship boy, I looked at every word of the text. And by the time I reached the last word, relieved, I convinced myself that I had read *The Republic.* In a ceremony of great pride, I solemnly crossed Plato off my list.

COMPREHENSION

1. What was Rodriguez's parents' attitude toward reading? Did it influence his attitude? Cite examples from the essay that support your opinion.
2. What does Rodriguez mean by the "fellowship between a reader and a writer" (paragraph 4)? Why does he differentiate between "intimate" and "personal" forms of communication?
3. Rodriguez hoped that reading would fill "the hollow" inside him. What was the cause of his emptiness? Did he succeed in filling the void? Why did he find reading a lonely experience? Did reading fulfill any of his expectations?

RHETORIC

1. What is the thesis of Rodriguez's essay? Is it stated or implied? Explain.
2. How does the author's use of narrative advance his views on reading and education?
3. What is the writer's tone? How effective is it in conveying his point of view?
4. Rodriguez uses uppercase letters (small capitals) when referring to signs advocating reading. Why does he use this device? How does it support his point of view?
5. The essay ends with an ironic anecdote. Why did Rodriguez choose to conclude this way? Does it satisfactorily illustrate his attitude?
6. What words or phrases imply that there is an ethnic component in Rodriguez's conflict? Is the subtlety effective? Justify your response.

WRITING

1. Rodriguez's parents had a pragmatic attitude toward reading. What was the attitude in your home as you were growing up? Did your parents encourage your interest in reading? Did they read themselves? What is the first book you remember reading by yourself? Write an essay in which you describe your reading history.
2. Is reading still a significant source of information and entertainment, or has it been usurped by television? Is it important (or necessary) to be a reader today?
3. **Writing an Argument:** Rodriguez believed reading would make him "educated." Do you agree or disagree? Is reading vital to a person's education? How do you define *education?* Can it be acquired only through reading, or are there other contributing factors? Write an argumentative essay on this topic.

NETWORKING
Applying Digital and Multimedia Literacies

Considering the Impact of e-Books: Locate online and read "How the e-Book Will Change the Way We Read and Write" from the *Wall Street Journal*. If Richard Rodriguez had embarked on reading in a world like the one Johnson describes, how might his experience with books have been different? In what ways do you think it would have been less, or more, rewarding? What do you see as some advantages of reading offline, alone, and what are some advantages of reading online, in a network?

Synthesis: Classic and Contemporary Questions for Comparison

1. Both Rodriguez and Douglass were motivated to educate themselves in a society inimical to this achievement. Compare and contrast their struggles and attitudes in their quests for knowledge.
2. Pretend you are Rodriguez, and write a letter to Douglass addressing the issues of minorities and education in present-day America. What would Rodriguez say about the progress of minorities in our society?
3. Although Rodriguez and Douglass treat a similar theme, they communicate their messages differently. Which narration do you consider more powerful, and why?
4. Rodriguez explores the theme of isolation in his story. Is there any evidence that this feeling was shared by Douglass in his efforts to learn how to read? Use proof from both narratives to support your view.
5. Slavery was an obvious obstacle to Douglass's attempt to educate himself. What impeded Rodriguez's progress? Were similar forces at work? Cite examples from Rodriguez's narrative to prove your point.

What College Can Mean to the Other America

Mike Rose

Mike Rose (b. 1944) is a nationally recognized writer, educator, and specialist in composition. He was born in Altoona, Pennsylvania to Italian immigrants, and moved with his parents to a working-class neighborhood in south Los Angeles when he was seven years old. Rose recounts his early years and education in a bestselling book, Lives on the Boundary *(1989). Based on his own experience of having been tracked into a vocational slot in high school, Rose advocates a reevaluation of remedial*

writers in such books as Writer's Block *(1984),* When a Writer Can't Write *(1985),*
and other texts. He also is a prominent spokesperson for the value of public education
in a democracy, a position articulated in his collection of essays, Why School?
Reclaiming Education for All of Us *(2009), and elsewhere. Rose received a PhD in*
education from UCLA, and he has taught there for nearly forty years. In this essay
that he wrote for The Chronicle of Higher Education *in 2011, Rose argues for*
educational policy initiatives that will benefit the poor.

The stakes go beyond the economic to the basic civic question: What kind of society   1
do we want to become?

It has been nearly 50 years since Michael Harrington wrote *The Other America*,   2
pulling the curtain back on invisible poverty within the United States. If he were
writing today, Harrington would find the same populations he described then:
young, marginally educated people who drift in and out of low-pay, dead-end jobs,
and older displaced workers, unable to find work as industries transform and
shops close. But he would find more of them, especially the young, their situation
worsened by further economic restructuring and globalization. And while the
poor he wrote about were invisible in a time of abundance, ours are visible in a
terrible recession, although invisible in most public policy. In fact, the poor are
drifting further into the dark underbelly of American capitalism.

One of the Obama administration's mantras is that we need to "out-innovate,   3
out-educate, and out-build" our competition in order to achieve fuller prosperity.
The solution to our social and economic woes lies in new technologies, in the cutting
edge. This is our "Sputnik moment," a very American way to frame our problems.
However, the editors of *The Economist* wrote a few months back that this explanation
of our economic situation is "mostly nonsense."

Instead, the business-friendly, neoliberal magazine offered a sobering—at   4
times almost neo-Marxist—assessment of what it considers the real danger in our
economy, something at the core of Harrington's analysis: chronic, ingrained
joblessness that is related to our social and economic structure. We are looking
toward the horizon of innovation when we should be looking straight in front of us
at the tens of millions of chronically unemployed Americans and providing comprehensive occupational, educational, and social services. Otherwise, to cite an
earlier issue of *The Economist* that also dealt with American inequality, we risk
"calcifying into a European-style class-based society." For people without school
or work, we already have.

There are a few current policy initiatives that are aimed at helping the disadvan-   5
taged gain economic mobility, mostly through some form of postsecondary education. Sadly, the most ambitious of these—the federal American Graduation
Initiative—was sacrificed during the health-care negotiations, although some
smaller projects remained in the stimulus package and the Department of Education. Private foundations, notably Gates and Lumina, have been sponsoring such
efforts as well. These efforts reach a small percentage of poor and low-income
Americans and, on average, are aimed at the more academically skilled among
them—although many still require remedial English and mathematics. A certificate

or degree alone will not automatically lift them out of hard times—there is a bit of magic-bullet thinking in these college initiatives—but getting a decent basic education could make a significant difference in their lives. At the least, these efforts are among the few antipoverty measures that have some degree of bipartisan support.

6   For the last year and a half, I have been spending time at an inner-city community college that serves this population, and I have seen firsthand the effects of poverty and long-term joblessness. Although some students attend the college with the goal of transfer, the majority come for its well-regarded occupational programs. More than 90 percent must take one or more basic-skills courses; 60 percent are on financial aid. A fair number have been through the criminal-justice system.

7   As I have gotten to know these students, the numbers have come alive. Many had chaotic childhoods, went to underperforming schools, and never finished high school. With low-level skills, they have had an awful time in the labor market. Short-term jobs, long stretches of unemployment, no health care. Many, the young ones included, have health problems that are inadequately treated if treated at all. I remember during my first few days on the campus noticing the number of people who walked with a limp or irregular gait.

8   What really strikes me, though, is students' level of engagement, particularly in the occupational programs. There are a few people who seem to be marking time, but most listen intently as an instructor explains the air-supply system in a diesel engine or the way to sew supports into an evening dress. And they do and redo an assignment until they get it right. Hope and desire are brimming. Many of the students say this is the first time school has meant anything to them. More than a few talk about turning their lives around. It doesn't take long to imagine the kind of society we would have if more people had this opportunity.

9   But right at the point when opportunity is offered, it is being threatened by severe budget cuts in education and social services. For several years, the college—like so many in the United States—has been able to offer only a small number of summer classes, and classes are being cut during the year. Enrollment in existing classes is growing. Student-support services are scaled back. And all the while, more people are trying to enroll at the college; some will have to be turned away, and those who are admitted will tax an already burdened system.

10   Given the toll the recession has taken on state and local governments, policy makers face "unprecedented challenges" and say they "have no other choice" but to make cuts in education. Secretary of Education Arne Duncan, borrowing a now-ubiquitous phrase, has called the necessity to do more with less "the new normal."

11   I don't dispute the difficulty of budgeting in the recession, nor the fact that education spending includes waste that should be cut. But we need to resist the framing of our situation as inevitable and normal. This framing makes the recession a catastrophe without culpability, neutralizing the civic and moral dimensions of both the causes of the recession and the way policy makers respond to it.

12   The civic and moral dimensions also are diminished by the powerful market-based orientation to economic and social problems. Antigovernment, anti-welfare-state, antitax—this ideology undercuts broad-scale public responses to inequality.

13   If the editors of *The Economist* are right, the deep cuts in education—especially to programs and institutions that help poor people connect to school or work—will

have disastrous long-term economic consequences that far outweigh immediate budgetary gains. And rereading *The Other America* reminds us that the stakes go beyond the economic to the basic civic question: What kind of society do we want to become? Will there be another Michael Harrington 50 years from now writing about an America that has a higher rate of poverty and even wider social divides?

COMPREHENSION

1. Circle, underline, highlight, or flag all references that Rose makes to Michael Harrington and his book, *The Other America*. Explain the importance that Rose gives to Harrington's study and its relevance to his topic.
2. Summarize Rose's perception of the current state of educational policy for the poor in the United States.
3. Why does Rose venture to a community college to investigate his subject? What does he learn there?

RHETORIC

1. Examine Rose's introductory paragraph. How does he structure this opening unit? Where does he state his thesis or claim, and how effective do you find this placement?
2. Rose writes for an academic audience in this essay—and specifically for college administrators. How does he tailor his message for this audience? What secondary audiences would be interested in his argument and analysis?
3. Explain Rose's tone and voice in this essay. Where does he personalize his argument, and what is the effect?
4. How does Rose use a problem-solution pattern of organization in developing his argument? Point to specific passages where this pattern becomes apparent.
5. What is the relationship of Rose's concluding paragraph to his claim and to the evidence that he offers in the body of his essay?

WRITING

1. Compose a position paper in which you outline your own plan for addressing the educational needs of the poor in American society.
2. In a personal essay, explore your own place in American society—or in the nation where you were born and raised—and how this molded your educational experience.
3. **Writing an Argument:** Argue for or against the proposition that the two major political parties in the United States are not seriously interested in providing a solid education for the poor.

NETWORKING
Applying Digital and Multimedia Literacies

Collaborating in small groups, go online to find out more about Michael Harrington's seminal study, *The Other America*. Based on your findings and discussion, present your response to the work of both Harrington and Rose.

Sex Ed

Anna Quindlen

Anna Quindlen (b. 1953) was born in Philadelphia and educated at Barnard College (BA, 1974). A journalist and novelist, she began her writing career as a reporter for the New York Post *and later moved on to the* New York Times, *where she was a syndicated columnist. Quindlen has written a number of books, including* Living Out Loud *(1986),* Object Lessons *(1991),* One True Thing *(1994),* Blessings *(2002),* Being Perfect *(2005), and* Rise and Shine *(2006). Quindlen received the Pulitzer Prize for Commentary in 1992. In this essay, Quindlen focuses on the problem of teenage pregnancy and suggests that children be given more than textbook information to help them cope with their sexuality.*

1   Several years ago I spent the day at a family planning clinic in one of New York City's poorest neighborhoods. I sat around a Formica table with a half-dozen sixteen-year-old girls and listened with some amazement as they showed off their knowledge of human sexuality.

2   They knew how long sperm lived inside the body, how many women out of a hundred using a diaphragm were statistically likely to get pregnant and the medical term for the mouth of the cervix. One girl pointed out all the parts of the female reproductive system on a placard; another recited the stages of the ovulation cycle from day one to twenty-eight. There was just one problem with this performance: Although the results of their laboratory tests would not be available for fifteen more minutes, every last one of them was pregnant.

3   I always think of that day when someone suggests that sex education at school is a big part of the answer to the problem of teenage pregnancy. I happen to be a proponent of such programs; I think human sexuality is a subject for dispassionate study, like civics and ethics and dozens of other topics that have a moral component. I'd like my sons to know as much as possible about how someone gets pregnant, how pregnancy can be avoided, and what it means when avoidance techniques have failed.

4   I remember adolescence about as vividly as I remember anything, however, and I am not in the least convinced that that information alone will significantly alter the rate of teenage pregnancy. It seemed to me that day in the clinic, and on days I spent at schools and on street corners, that teenage pregnancy has a lot more to do with what it means to be a teenager than with how someone gets pregnant. When I was in high school, at the tail end of the sixties, there was a straightforward line on sex among my friends. Boys could have it; girls couldn't. A girl who was not a virgin pretended she was. A girl who was sleeping with her boyfriend, no matter how long-playing the relationship, pretended she was not.

5   It is the nature of adolescence that there is no past and no future, only the present, burning as fierce, bright, and merciless as a bare light bulb. Girls

had sex with boys because nothing seemed to matter except right now, not pregnancy, not parental disapprobation, nothing but those minutes, this dance, that face, those words. Most of them knew that pregnancy could result, but they assured themselves that they would be the lucky ones who would not get caught. Naturally, some of them were wrong, and in my experience they did one of three things: They went to Puerto Rico for a mysterious weekend trip; visited an aunt in some faraway state for three months and came back with empty eyes and a vague reputation; or got married, quickly, in Empire-waist dresses.

What seems to have changed most since then is that there is little philosophical 6 counterpoint, hypocritical or not, to the raging hormones of adolescence, and that so many of the once-hidden pregnancies are hidden no more.

Not long after the day at the family planning clinic, I went to a public high 7 school in the suburbs. In the girl's room was this graffito: Jennifer Is a Virgin. I asked the kids about it and they said it was shorthand for geek, nerd, weirdo, somebody who was so incredibly out of it that they were in high school and still hadn't had sex. If you were a virgin, they told me, you just lied about it so that no one would think you were that immature. The girls in the family planning clinic told me much the same thing—that everyone did it, that the boys wanted it, that not doing it made them seem out of it. The only difference, really, was that the girls in the clinic were poor and would have their babies, and the girls in the high school were well-to-do and would have abortions. Pleasure didn't seem to have very much to do with sex for either group. After she learned she was pregnant, one of the girls at the clinic said, without a trace of irony, that she hoped child-birth didn't hurt as much as sex had. Birth control was easily disposed of in both cases. The pill, the youngsters said, could give you a stroke; the IUD could make you sterile. A diaphragm was disgusting.

One girl told me the funniest thing her boyfriend—a real original thinker— 8 had told her: They couldn't use condoms because it was like taking a shower with a raincoat on. She was a smart girl and pretty, and I wanted to tell her that it sounded as if she was sleeping with a jerk who didn't deserve her. But that is the kind of basic fact of life that must be taught not in the classroom, not by a stranger, but at home by the family. It is this that, finally, I will try to teach my sons about sex, after I've explained fertile periods and birth control and all the other mechanics that are important to understand but never really go to the heart of the matter: I believe I will say that when you sleep with someone you take off a lot more than your clothes.

COMPREHENSION

1. Does Quindlen approve of sex education? Explain.
2. How does the writer characterize the attitude of adolescents regarding sex and pregnancy?
3. What advice or information about sex will the writer give her sons? Why?

RHETORIC

1. Why did Quindlen choose "Sex Ed" as a title? What is its significance in relation to the thesis?
2. What is Quindlen's thesis? Where is it contained in the essay? Is it directly stated or implied?
3. Is Quindlen's writing an argumentative essay? Support your position with citations from the text.
4. What point is the writer making through use of accumulated details in paragraph 2?
5. What does Quindlen mean by the term "moral component" in paragraph 3? Where else in the essay does she allude to it? How does she employ definition in this essay?
6. What does Quindlen mean by her final statement that "when you sleep with someone you take off a lot more than your clothes"? How does this ending serve to underscore the thesis of the essay?

WRITING

1. Write a paper analyzing the most common forms of birth control available and listing the advantages and disadvantages of each.
2. In an essay, consider possible solutions to the problem of teenage pregnancy. What role do you think sex education has in ameliorating the problem? Use support from the Quindlen essay if applicable.
3. **Writing an Argument:** Quindlen claims that sex education is like "civics" and "ethics" and should be taught in schools. Do you agree or disagree? Write an essay defending your position.

NETWORKING
Applying Digital and Multimedia Literacies

Interpreting Advocacy Group Web Sites: Explore each of the following Web sites, each of which is published by an advocacy group dedicated to preventing teen pregnancy. For each, sum up (in 1–2 sentences) its position on educating teens about sex. How does the site's various features, as well as its design; organization; and use of images, video, and links, contribute to its message?

- U.S. Department of Health and Human Services: http://www.policyalmanac.org/health/archive/hhs_teenage_pregnancy.shtml
- Stayteen.org: http://www.stayteen.org/teen-pregnancy
- The National Campaign to Prevent Teen and Unplanned Pregnancy: http://www.thenationalcampaign.org
- The Candie's Foundation, including videos featuring Bristol Palin: http://www.candiesfoundation.org/videos.html

The Next Kind of Integration

Emily Bazelon

Emily Bazelon *(b. 1971) is an American essayist and journalist as well as senior editor for the online magazine* Slate. *She was born in Philadelphia and graduated from Yale University in 1993 and Yale Law School in 2000. After law school, Bazelon served as a law clerk on the United States Court of Appeals for the First Circuit. Prior to joining the staff at* Slate, *she was a writer and senior editor at* Legal Affairs *magazine. Bazelon's writing focuses on law, family affairs, and women's issues, especially abortion rights; she is considered a prominent pro-choice advocate. Her writing has appeared in the* Atlantic, *the* Washington Post, *the* New Republic, *and elsewhere. This essay, which appeared in the* New York Times Magazine *in 2008, examines (as the title suggests) a fresh approach to affirmative action.*

In June of last year, a conservative majority of the Supreme Court, in a 5-to-4   1
decision, declared the racial-integration efforts of two school districts unconstitutional. Seattle and Louisville, Ky., could no longer assign students to
schools based on their race, Chief Justice John Roberts wrote in his lead opinion in *Meredith v. Jefferson County School Board* (and its companion case, *Parents
Involved in Community Schools v. Seattle School District No. 1*). Justice Stephen
Breyer sounded a sad and grim note of dissent. Pointing out that the court was
rejecting student-assignment plans that the districts had designed to stave off
de facto resegregation, Breyer wrote that "to invalidate the plans under review
is to threaten the promise of *Brown.*" By invoking *Brown v. Board of Education*, the court's landmark 1954 civil rights ruling, Breyer accused the majority
of abandoning a touchstone in the country's efforts to overcome racial
division. "This is a decision that the court and the nation will come to regret,"
he concluded.

Breyer's warning, along with even more dire predictions from civil rights   2
groups, helped place the court's ruling at the center of the liberal indictment of
the Roberts court. In Louisville, too, the court's verdict met with resentment. Last
fall, I asked Pat Todd, the assignment director for the school district of Jefferson
County, which encompasses Louisville and its suburbs, whether any good could
come of the ruling. She shook her head so hard that strands of blond hair loosened from her bun. "No," she said with uncharacteristic exasperation, "we're
already doing what we should be."

Todd was referring to Louisville's success in distributing black and white stu-   3
dents, which it does more evenly than any district in the country with a comparable
black student population; almost every school is between 15 and 50 percent
African-American. The district's combination of school choice, busing and magnet
programs has brought general, if not uniform, acceptance—rather than white

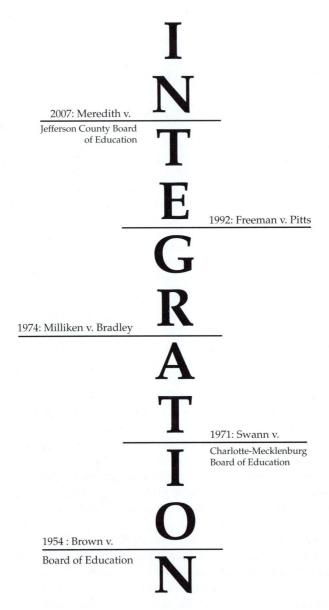

flight and disaffection, the legacy of desegregation in cities like Boston and Kansas City, Mo. The student population, which now numbers nearly 100,000, has held steady at about 35 percent black and 55 percent white, along with a small and growing number of Hispanics and Asians.

4   With its decision in *Meredith*, the court was forcing Louisville to rethink the way it would assign elementary-school students and, in the process, to confront some tricky questions. Is the purpose of integration simply to mix students of different colors for the sake of equity or to foster greater familiarity and comfort

among the races? Should integration necessarily translate into concrete gains like greater achievement for all students? If so, is mixing students by race the most effective mechanism for attaining it?

In Louisville, the achievement gap between whites and blacks is 20 percent- 5 age points at many grade levels. For Todd and her team, whatever their reservations about the decision in *Meredith,* coming up with an alternative assignment plan was an opportunity to think about a new kind of integration and what it might accomplish. In Louisville, integration would no longer focus solely on race but also on the barriers of class, of advantage and disadvantage. Other cities have been thinking along these lines. In the wake of the Supreme Court's decision, four other districts—Des Moines, Burlington, Vt., Omaha and Beaumont, Tex.— announced a switch to class-based integration. Seattle, too, is discussing setting aside 5 to 15 percent of the spots (a relatively small percentage) in desired high schools for low-income students. Some of the plans go into effect this fall; others, including Louisville's, begin a year from September.

The chief justice didn't address the idea of class-based integration in his opinion. 6 But Justice Anthony Kennedy did, in a separate concurrence. And because Kennedy cast the fifth vote for the majority, his view controls the law. Though he agreed with Roberts that public school districts should not make school assignments based on the race of individual students, he added that the court's ruling "should not prevent school districts from continuing the important work of bringing together students of different racial, ethnic and economic backgrounds."

How were schools to do this? Around the country, school-district lawyers 7 studied Kennedy's opinion and came to a rough consensus. In its amicus brief before the court, the Bush administration cited socioeconomic integration as a "race neutral" alternative to race-based assignment plans. Kennedy picked up on this, and no other justice wrote to contradict him. As a result, the school-district lawyers concluded that districts could assign an individual child to a school based on any kind of socioeconomic measure they chose—income, assets, parental education attainment. Districts could also be "race conscious," according to Kennedy, when they drew school boundaries, chose sites for new schools and directed money to particular programs. But in these situations, they would usually be limited to taking into account the racial composition of a neighborhood rather than the race of an individual student.

In terms of the court's jurisprudence, this is a major change. Race has been 8 the organizing principle of integration since *Brown v. Board of Education.* At the time of the court's ruling in *Meredith,* hundreds of districts were pursuing some sort of racial integration, with or without a court order, while only a few dozen at most were trying any form of socioeconomic integration. Over the years, racial integration has proved to have tangible benefits. Amy Stuart Wells, an education professor at Columbia Teachers College, has found that going to school with substantial numbers of white students helped black students to form cross-racial friendships and, by giving them access to white social networks, eventually to find work in jobs higher up the economic ladder.

9   However important these gains are, they are long-term and cannot be easily or quickly assessed. And increasingly, schools are held to a standard of immediately measurable outcomes. The No Child Left Behind Act, signed into law in 2002, demands student test scores that climb ever upward, with a mandate for all students to be proficient in reading and math by 2014. Test scores may not be the best way to assess the quality of a teacher or a school, but the pressure to improve scores, whatever its shortcomings, is itself on the rise. And if high test scores are the goal, it turns out, class-based integration may be the more effective tool.

10   Researchers have been demonstrating this result since 1966, when Congress asked James S. Coleman, a Johns Hopkins sociologist, to deliver a report on why the achievement of black students lagged far behind that of white ones. The expected answer was that more than a decade after *Brown,* black kids were still often going to inferior schools with small budgets. But Coleman found that the varying amount of money spent on schools didn't account for the achievement gap. Instead, the greater poverty of black families did. When high concentrations of poor kids went to school together, Coleman reported, all the students at the school tended to learn less.

11   How much less was later quantified. The Harvard sociologist Christopher Jencks reanalyzed Coleman's data in the 1970s and concluded that poor black sixth-graders in majority middle-class schools were 20 months ahead of poor black sixth-graders in majority low-income schools. The statistics for poor white students were similar. In the last 40 years, Coleman's findings, known informally as the Coleman Report, have been confirmed again and again. Most recently, in a 2006 study, Douglas Harris, an economist at the University of Wisconsin, found that when more than half the students were low-income, only 1.1 percent of schools consistently performed at a "high" level (defined as two years of scores in the top third of the U.S. Department of Education's national achievement database in two grades and in two subjects: English and math). By contrast, 24.2 percent of schools that are majority middle-class met Harris's standard.

12   There are, of course, determined urban educators who have proved that select schools filled with poor and minority students can thrive—in the right circumstances, with the right teachers and programs. But consistently good education at schools with such student bodies remains the rare exception. The powerful effect of the socioeconomic makeup of a student body on academic achievement has become "one of the most consistent findings in research on education," Gary Orfield, a U.C.L.A. education professor, and Susan Eaton, a research director at Harvard Law, wrote in their 1996 book, *Dismantling Desegregation.*

13   Most researchers think that this result is brought about by the advantages that middle-class students bring with them. Richard Kahlenberg of the Century Foundation lays them out in his 2001 book, *All Together Now*: more high-level classes, more parent volunteers and peers who on average have twice the vocabulary and half the behavioral problems of poor students. And, especially,

more good teachers. Harris, the economist, says that poor minority students still don't have comparable access to effective teachers, measured by preparation and experience. The question, then, is whether a plan that integrates a district by class as well as by race will help win for all its schools the kind of teaching that tends to be linked to achievement. "The evidence indicates that it would," Harris says.

Ronald Ferguson, an economist at the Kennedy School of Government at 14 Harvard, is less persuaded. His research highlights the nagging persistence of a racial achievement gap in well-off suburbs. "What happens with the achievement gap in a place like Louisville," he says, "will depend on how vigilant their leaders are to make sure high-quality instruction is delivered across the board." Such teaching is more likely in a school with a critical mass of middle-class parents, he concedes. But he stresses that to reap the benefits, poor kids have to be evenly distributed among classrooms and not just grouped together in the lowest tracks. "To the degree a district takes the kids who struggle the most academically and spreads them across different classrooms, they're making teachers' work more doable," he says. "And that may be the biggest effect."

Once they started looking for them, Todd and her colleagues saw the effects of class 15 division and poverty in the Jefferson County schools. Thorough racial desegregation had not, it seemed, led to thorough class desegregation. At 40 of 90 elementary schools in the district, 75 percent or more of the students came from low-income homes. And the effects of these high concentrations of poverty were striking: poor students in Louisville, black and white, fared worse when they attended schools filled with other poor kids. In elementary school, 61 percent of poor students at mostly low-income schools scored proficient in reading, compared with 71 percent of poor students at majority-middle-class schools. For math, the comparative proficiency rates were 52 percent to 63 percent. Because black students were disproportionately poor, they were more likely to attend high-poverty schools, and this was contributing to the district's pronounced black-white achievement gap.

Todd and her planners wanted to tackle the problem, she says, but they were 16 mindful of going too far in their efforts and losing the support of parents. In other districts—including Cincinnati, Evanston, Ill., Bibb County, Ga., and Madison, Wis.—the reaction to the Supreme Court's ruling had been to move to dismantle racial-integration programs. Todd and other school officials didn't want integration redefined to turn into no integration all. To get a handle on a new plan, Todd, turned to an heir of James Coleman: the researcher John Powell.

In the 1960s, Powell was one of the only African-American students in his ad- 17 vanced high-school classes in Detroit; when he became the class valedictorian, a teacher told him he wasn't the smartest student. He now directs the Kirwan Institute for the Study of Race and Ethnicity at Ohio State University, and he says he still thinks that race is a category with singular power. But he also appreciates the stark effects of segregating poor kids. "Ever since the Coleman Report, we've seen that there's a high correlation between good schools and schools that are integrated socioeconomically as well as racially," he says. "I think everyone agrees that what we need are more good schools."

18   In Louisville, Powell lent his expertise to Todd and her team. They came up with a computer-generated map that shows what Powell defines as the district's areas of "low opportunity." Todd, who is 61 and taught every grade in the Louisville schools before becoming an administrator, went over the map with me one day last December. The map used two different measures of class to identify Jefferson County's areas of disadvantage: income level and the educational attainment of adults. (To gauge disadvantage, districts embarking on class-based integration often use who among their students receives free or reduced lunch; Powell, however, contends that this is a relatively crude measure.) Using census data, Todd's team identified the zones in the district in which households fall below the average income and education levels, with fewer adults who have finished high school or gone to college or beyond. Finally, the team added one more factor: a higher-than-average number of minorities, almost all of them African-Americans or Hispanics.

19   The map's class-plus-race formula revealed a major partition. One region, which Todd's team called Geographic Area A, is a mermaid-shaped swath of blue, with its head in Louisville's West End, just south of the Ohio River, and its tail to the south. The region encompasses the parts of the district with a higher-than-average minority population, lower-than-average median income and lower-than-average adult educational attainment. In Geographic Area A live about 30 percent of Jefferson County's students. The rest of the county, colored yellow, included everyone else—the better off, better educated and whiter Geographic Area B.

20   What if the district were to use this map as a guide for school integration? Instead of maintaining each school as no less than 15 percent and no more than 50 percent black, Todd's team could propose that each school have no less than 15 percent and no more than 50 percent of students from Geographic Area A. By distributing students from the district's residential zones of disadvantage, the new plan would integrate the schools by class. There would no longer be 40 elementary schools with heavily poor-student populations. There could potentially be no such schools.

21   Given the presumed boost to test scores resulting from distributing poor students more widely, you might wonder why Todd's team retained race as an admissions factor at all. To answer this, it's worth considering the country's existing examples of purely class-based integration. The best known is in Wake County, N.C. With 134,000 students, the Wake County school district ranks 19 among the country's 20 largest, spanning 800 square miles that include bleak tracts in the city of Raleigh, mansion-filled suburban cul-de-sacs and rural roads ending in the fresh earth of a new subdivision. The student population is about half white, one-quarter African-American and one-quarter Hispanic, Asian and multiracial. The district voluntarily pursued race-based integration in the 1980s and '90s. In 2000, after the U.S. Court of Appeals for the Fourth Circuit began to frown on the use of race in student assignment—a harbinger of the Supreme Court's stance last year—the district began assigning kids to schools based on the income level of the geographic zone they lived in. The aim was to balance the schools so that no more than 40 percent of the students at each one come from a low-income area. (This year, the district added another goal: to have no more than 25 percent of students at any one school for whom English is a second language.)

Wake County adopted class-based integration with the hard-nosed goal of 22 raising test scores. The strategy was simple: no poor schools, no bad schools. And indeed, the district has posted striking improvements in the test scores of black and low-income students: in 1995, only 40 percent of the black students in Wake County in the third through eighth grades scored at grade level in state reading tests; by last year, the rate had almost doubled, to 82.5 percent. Statewide scores for black students also got better over the same time period, but not by as much. Wake County's numbers improve as students get older: 92 percent of all eighth graders read at or above grade level, including about 85 percent of black students and about 80 percent of low-income students. (Math scores are lower, following a statewide trend that reflects a change in the grading scale.) The district has achieved these results even as the share of low-income students over all has increased from about 30 percent a decade ago to about 40 percent today.

But the lessons of Wake County, Powell and Todd argue, don't apply every- 23 where. "In different districts, you have different geographic patterns," Powell says. "So you need different integration models to shop around." To begin with, Louisville is less affluent—more than 60 percent of its elementary school students receive free or reduced lunches, compared with Wake County's 40 percent. In Wake County, the vast majority of the poor students are black and Hispanic, and so mixing kids by class tightly correlates to mixing them by race. But in Jefferson County, more than a third of the kids who receive free or reduced lunches are white. As a result, redistributing students by class alone might still isolate them by race.

This is a limitation of class-based integration that holds true elsewhere. The city 24 of San Francisco, for instance, has undergone substantial racial resegregation since retooling its diversity plan to emphasize socioeconomic factors. Even in Wake County, the fraction of students in racially segregated schools has climbed a bit over the last decade, from 25 percent to 32 percent. A 2006 paper by the education researchers Sean Reardon, John T. Yun and Michal Kurlaender crunched census data across the country and concluded that "given the extent of residential racial segregation in the United States, it is unlikely that race-neutral income-integration policies will significantly reduce school racial segregation, although there is reason to believe that such policies are likely to have other beneficial effects on schooling."

Many big cities have a different problem. Simple demographics dictate that they 25 can't really integrate their schools at all, by either race or class. Consider the numbers for Detroit (74 percent low-income students; 91 percent black), Los Angeles (77 percent low-income; 85 percent black and Hispanic), New York City (74 percent; 63 percent), Washington (64 percent; 93 percent), Philadelphia (71 percent; 79 percent), Chicago (74 percent; 88 percent) and Boston (71 percent; 76 percent). In theory, big cities can diversify their schools by class and race by persuading many more middle-class and white parents to choose public school over private school or by combining forces with the well-heeled suburbs that surround them. But short of those developments, big cities are stuck. "The options have shrunk," says Tom Payzant, a former superintendent of schools in Boston.

Notably, there are a good many districts that have evaded this predicament. 26 They are particularly found in the South, in part because of a historical accident.

Because it was predominantly rural for longer, the South has more countywide school districts than the North. An unintended consequence was to ease the way to integration. Instead of city schools filled with poor black and Hispanic kids separated from a burgeoning ring of suburban districts stocked with affluent whites (and in some places, Asians), *one* district controls student assignment for the region.

27   Even in school districts with a mix of students of different races and income levels, however, there is no one-size-fits-all approach to socioeconomic integration, as underscored by the differences between Wake County and Jefferson County. Wake County's demographics entail that mixing kids by class, on its own, produces a fair degree of racial integration. Jefferson County's demographics don't necessarily work this way. And so civil rights lawyers suggest that districts configured like Jefferson County should continue to pursue racial diversity directly. They point to cities like Berkeley, Calif., which has an assignment plan that primarily relies on socioeconomics, but like Geography Area A also factors in the racial composition of a neighborhood to guard against resegregation along racial lines. "It's not either-or," says Anurima Bhargava, an education lawyer at the NAACP Legal Defense Fund.

28   In addition, there's a tacit liberal constitutional agenda at work in hybrid class-race approaches to integration: better to test Kennedy's opinion, with its support for the drawing of "race conscious" school boundaries, than to retreat further than is in fact required. "For Kennedy, there are ways of taking race into account," John Powell says. "It's just the method that's in question. How do you do it? We need to find out what's still permitted." He also points out that African-Americans are more likely than whites to be poor over generations—a bigger hurdle than a short stint in a low-income bracket.

29   The continuing attention to race aligns with the internal politics of Louisville and its suburbs. Many of today's parents grew up there and tend to remember and care about overcoming their county's Jim Crow legacy. In 1975, when a federal judge first ordered the city and its suburbs to desegregate, the Ku Klux Klan demonstrated, and the next day about 150 white protestors attacked eight school buses filled with black students. "We had tough times here when the buses burned," says Ann El-more, a black member of the Jefferson County School Board. "We can still include race as a factor in our plan, and let me say I think it's important that we do."

30 Elsewhere in the United States, it is too soon to tell how the politics of class-based integration (Wake County) or class-plus-race (Jefferson County) will play out. Rich-ard Kahlenberg makes the case for shifting integration policies primarily or solely to being class-based over the next decade or two. What's fair, he asks, about giving a spot in a coveted magnet program to the son of a South Asian college professor or an African-American politician over the daughter of a white waitress? Over time, such injustices threaten to sour white parents on the whole diversity enterprise, whereas giving poor kids a boost, whatever their color, is far less controversial. Polls at the time of the Supreme Court's 2003 decision in *Grutter v. Bollinger*, which con-cerned affirmative action at public universities, showed public support running 2 to 1 for giving poorer kids a leg up in going to college, as opposed to 2 to 1 against race-based preferences. In her majority opinion in the case, Justice Sandra Day

O'Connor famously said she thought that racial preferences would continue only for another 25 years. Barack Obama has said, looking ahead to his daughters' college applications, that they don't deserve an admissions break—an acknowledgment that the mix of race, affirmative action and privilege is a complicated one.

To catch on nationwide, however, class-based integration would have to gen- 31 erate momentum that it has so far lacked. In his State of the Union address in January, President Bush urged action "to help liberate poor children trapped in failing public schools." And yet a provision in the No Child Left Behind Act that theoretically allows students to transfer depends on the availability of open spaces elsewhere and has barely been utilized. The administration may have advocated class-based integration to the Supreme Court, but Bush officials haven't used their signature education law to make it happen.

If Congress were to revise No Child Left Behind to encourage more transfers 32 of poor students to middle-class schools, would poor students drag down their better-off peers? In the end, the prospects of class-based integration will probably rise or fall on the answer to this question. Socioeconomic integration may be good for the have-nots, but if the haves think their kids are paying too great a price, they will kill it off at the polls. Richard Kahlenberg argues that the key is to ensure there is a solidly middle-class majority at as many schools as possible. That majority will then set the tone, he argues. Kahlenberg says that more research is needed to pin down the percentage of middle-class kids that a school needs to have to serve all its students well. Maybe a school can go as high as 50 percent low-income without losing ground. Or maybe it's telling that in Wake County, a proposal to increase the ceiling for low-income students from 40 percent to 50 percent died a swift death last fall after concerted protest.

Whatever the exact answer, there is some support for the view that schools can 33 handle a substantial fraction of poor students without sacrificing performance. In Wake County, test scores of middle-class students have risen since instituting income-based integration. Additionally, Kahlenberg points out that middle-class students are generally less influenced by a school's environment because they tend to learn more at home, and that the achievement of white students has not declined in specific schools that experienced racial (and thus some class) desegregation.

Would schools need to track students by ability to protect middle-class stu- 34 dents, who are more often higher-achieving than their low-income peers? Perhaps not. In a 2006 longitudinal study of an accelerated middle-school math program in Nassau County, N.Y., which grouped students heterogeneously, the authors found that students at all achievement levels, as well as minority and low-income students, were more likely than the students in tracked classes to take advanced math in high school. In addition, the kids who came into the program as math whizzes performed as well as other top-achievers in homogenous classes.

This study underscores Ronald Ferguson's point about the value of seating stu- 35 dents of different backgrounds and abilities in class together, as opposed to tracking them. Still, it's worth noting that less than 15 percent of the students studied in Nassau County were low-income. So the math study doesn't tell us what happens to the high-achieving middle-class kids when close to half of their classmates aren't as well off.

36 At the end of February, Todd started showing the map of mermaid-shaped Geographic Area A, which she hoped to use to implement the new assignment system, to the parents of Jefferson County. Todd would start her presentation with quotes from Justice Kennedy and from Justice Breyer's dissent; she especially wanted to remind her audiences of the sentiment Breyer expressed by quoting former Justice Thurgood Marshall: "Unless our children begin to learn together, there is little hope that our people will ever learn to live together."

37 Todd's first stop was at a forum sponsored jointly by the Urban League and the NAACP groups associated with Louisville's black establishment. Most of their members supported the school district, but some clergy members who worked with the city's black youth spoke against it. The Rev. John Carter, associate minister at Green Street Baptist Church, pointed to the district's black-white achievement gap and called for a return to neighborhood schools and an earlier era of black self-reliance.

38 As more forums followed in high-school auditoriums across the county, white parents asked a different question: How would the new assignment plan affect their kids? Would they be forced to switch schools in second, third or fourth grade? "We like the diversity," a white parent named Niki Noe told me the next morning at her son's elementary school, St. Matthews. "But if we have to go to Chenoweth"—a school with lower test scores—"we'll pull out and go to private school."

39 That's a serious threat to the district's well-being, but one that Todd anticipated. She designed a grandfather clause for kids like Noe's, so that the new assignments would apply almost entirely to new students. Meanwhile, at every meeting, Todd polled parents on whether they cared about maintaining diverse schools. The University of Kentucky also conducted a telephone survey with 654 parents of elementary schoolers. In April, Todd called me, elated and relieved, with the results: 88 percent of parents supported enrollment guidelines "to ensure that students learn with students from different races and backgrounds." Todd said she had dropped Breyer's dissent in *Meredith* from her presentation; she was no longer feeling frustrated with the court. "It's been a personal emotional trek, but I think we've come out better for it," she said in May.

40 Carter, the proponent of black-self reliance, was feeling more at ease, too. He had come to see the virtue of mixing kids by income level. "Once I did the research, I was pretty impressed by the economic part of it," he said. Carter had taken note of the district's data showing that a switch to neighborhood schools, as he had first advocated, would mean that median household income would range from a high of more than $100,000 at the wealthiest school to about $8,300 at the poorest. A split between rich students and poor schools, he agreed, was the wrong path.

41 It is, of course, the path taken by most of the country. And yet at the end of May, the Jefferson County School Board voted unanimously to make Geographic Area A the basis for integrating elementary schools for the 2009 school year, a new chapter in the district's history. As the schools shift to the new class-plus-race formula, the district will closely watch the test scores of black students and poor students, hoping for an upsurge, and those of middle-class students, hoping

to see achievement hold steady. And if they do, maybe the court's decision in *Meredith* will come to seem less like a cause for regret and more like an unexpected opportunity.

COMPREHENSION

1. According to Bazelon, what are the positive and negative aspects of class-based integration?
2. Summarize the challenges confronting the Louisville, Kentucky school system in light of the Supreme Court decision in the case of *Meredith v. Jefferson County School Board*.
3. List the many school systems and districts mentioned by Bazelon. What do they share in common? How do they differ?

RHETORIC

1. What is the purpose of Bazelon's opening paragraph? Does she avoid a negative or critical tone? How does she avoid taking sides in the debate over affirmative action? Or do you think that she does reflect a bias? Explain.
2. Does Bazelon provide a thesis statement? Why or why not? How might her essay embody or imply a thesis?
3. Bazelon divides her essay into sections. How many are there? What is unique about each section? How do all sections relate to the writer's main subject?
4. Where do definition, comparison and contrast, and causal analysis appear as rhetorical strategies in this essay?
5. Consider the relationship of the introductory paragraph to the conclusion. Why do these beginning and end units provide an effective frame for the essay? Does Bazelon's voice or tone change? Explain.

WRITING

1. Compose a demographic case study of your high school or more generalized school district. Analyze your school experience based on the racial and socioeconomic composition of the school body. Draw conclusions about each group's academic performance.
2. Write your own response to the Supreme Court's decision in the Louisville school case. Conduct additional research if necessary.
3. **Writing an Argument:** Argue for or against the proposition that class-based integration is the solution to educational inequality in America.

NETWORKING
Applying Digital and Multimedia Literacies

Collaborating with one other class member, visit the blog that Bazelon maintains at *Slate* (*XXFactor* or *DoubleX*). Locate here and elsewhere Bazelon's writing on school bullying and cyber-bullying. Also find responses to Bazelon, especially to the writer's three-part series on the death of a fifteen-year-old girl in Hadley, Massachusetts who was the victim of bullying. Share your findings in a class discussion.

Unplugged: The Myth of Computers in the Classroom

David Gelernter

David Gelernter (b. 1955) is a professor of computer science at Yale University. He is a leading figure in the field of human cognition and a seminal thinker in the field known as parallel computing. Gelernter, who was injured by a package sent by the Unabomber in 1993, is the author of Mirror Worlds *(1991),* The Muse in the Machine *(1994),* 1939: The Lost World of the Fair *(1995), and* Machine Beauty *(1998). In the following essay, published in the* New Republic *in 1994, Gelernter offers a cogent analysis of the limits of technology in the classroom.*

1 Over the last decade an estimated $2 billion has been spent on more than 2 million computers for America's classrooms. That's not surprising. We constantly hear from Washington that the schools are in trouble and that computers are a godsend. Within the education establishment, in poor as well as rich schools, the machines are awaited with nearly religious awe. An inner-city principal bragged to a teacher friend of mine recently that his school "has a computer in every classroom . . . despite being in a bad neighborhood!"

2 Computers should be in the schools. They have the potential to accomplish great things. With the right software, they could help make science tangible or teach neglected topics like art and music. They help students form a concrete idea of society by displaying onscreen a version of the city in which they live—a picture that tracks real life moment by moment.

3 In practice, however, computers make our worst educational nightmares come true. While we bemoan the decline of literacy, computers discount words in favor of pictures and pictures in favor of video. While we fret about the decreasing cogency of public debate, computers dismiss linear argument and promote fast, shallow romps across the information landscape. While we worry about basic skills, we allow into the classroom software that will do a student's arithmetic or correct his spelling.

4 Take multimedia. The idea of multimedia is to combine text, sound and pictures in a single package that you browse on screen. You don't just *read* Shakespeare; you watch actors performing, listen to songs, view Elizabethan buildings. What's wrong with that? By offering children candy-coated books, multimedia is guaranteed to sour them on unsweetened reading. It makes the printed page look even more boring than it used to look. Sure, books will be available in the classroom, too—but they'll have all the appeal of a dusty piano to a teen who has a Walkman handy.

5 So what if the little nippers don't read? If they're watching Olivier instead, what do they lose? The text, the written word along with all of its attendant pleasures.

Besides, a book is more portable than a computer, has a higher-resolution display, can be written on and dog-eared and is comparatively dirt cheap.

Hypermedia, multimedia's comrade in the struggle for a brave new class- 6
room, is just as troubling. It's a way of presenting documents on screen without imposing a linear start-to-finish order. Disembodied paragraphs are linked by theme; after reading one about the First World War, for example, you might be able to choose another about the technology of battleships, or the life of Woodrow Wilson, or hemlines in the '20s. This is another cute idea that is good in minor ways and terrible in major ones. Teaching children to understand the orderly un-folding of a plot or a logical argument is a crucial part of education. Authors don't merely agglomerate paragraphs; they work hard to make the narrative read a certain way, prove a particular point. To turn a book or a document into hypertext is to invite readers to ignore exactly what counts—the story.

The real problem, again, is the accentuation of already bad habits. Dynamit- 7
ing documents into disjointed paragraphs is one more expression of the sorry fact that sustained argument is not our style. If you're a newspaper or magazine editor and your readership is dwindling, what's the solution? Shorter pieces. If you're a politician and you want to get elected, what do you need? Tasty sound bites. Logi-cal presentation be damned.

Another software species, "allow me" programs, is not much better. These 8
programs correct spelling and, by applying canned grammatical and stylistic rules, fix prose. In terms of promoting basic skills, though, they have all the vir-tues of a pocket calculator.

In Kentucky, as *The Wall Street Journal* recently reported, students in grades 9
K–3 are mixed together regardless of age in a relaxed environment. It works great, the *Journal* says. Yes, scores on computation tests have dropped 10 percent at one school, but not to worry: "Drilling addition and subtraction in an age of calculators is a waste of time," the principal reassures us. Meanwhile, a Japanese educator in-forms University of Wisconsin mathematician Richard Akey that in his country, "calculators are not used in elementary or junior high school because the primary emphasis is on helping students develop their mental abilities." No wonder Japanese kids blow the pants off American kids in math. Do we really think "drilling addition and subtraction in an age of calculators is a waste of time"? If we do, then "drilling reading in an age of multimedia is a waste of time" can't be far behind.

Prose-correcting programs are also a little ghoulish, like asking a computer for 10
tips on improving your personality. On the other hand, I ran this article through a spell-checker, so how can I ban the use of such programs in schools? Because to misspell is human; to have no idea of correct spelling is to be semiliterate.

There's no denying that computers have the potential to perform inspiring feats in 11
the classroom. If we are ever to see that potential realized, however, we ought to agree on three conditions. First, there should be a completely new crop of chil-dren's software. Most of today's offerings show no imagination. There are hun-dreds of similar reading and geography and arithmetic programs, but almost nothing on electricity or physics or architecture. Also, they abuse the technical

capacities of new media to glitz up old forms instead of creating new ones. Why not build a time-travel program that gives kids a feel for how history is structured by zooming you backward? A spectrum program that lets users twirl a frequency knob to see what happens?

12   Second, computers should be used only during recess or relaxation periods. Treat them as fillips, not as surrogate teachers. When I was in school in the '60s, we all loved educational films. When we saw a movie in class, everybody won: Teachers didn't have to teach, and pupils didn't have to learn. I suspect that classroom computers are popular today for the same reasons.

13   Most important, educators should learn what parents and most teachers already know: You cannot teach a child anything unless you look him in the face. We should not forget what computers are. Like books—better in some ways, worse in others—they are devices that help children mobilize their own resources and learn for themselves. The computer's potential to do good is modestly greater than a book's in some areas. Its potential to do harm is vastly greater, across the board.

COMPREHENSION

1. State Gelernter's thesis or claim in one sentence.
2. In the final paragraph, Gelernter defines what he believes to be the most important shortcoming of the computer as a teaching tool. Explain the reason why this weakness is so significant.
3. In your own words, explain the author's dislike of hypermedia as a pedagogic tool (as expressed in paragraph 6) and why the orderly arrangement of paragraphs in a book is superior to this newer technological capability.

RHETORIC

1. The introductory paragraph goes from a general fact to a specific quotation. What is the effect of this method of paragraph patterning?
2. Much of Gelernter's argument hinges on providing evidence that one medium is superior to another. Explain terms such as *linear argument* (paragraph 3), *agglomerate paragraphs* (paragraph 6), and *"allow me" programs* (paragraph 8). How do these terms help Gelernter prove his point?
3. The essay has a three-part structure, each section divided by space. How would you characterize the purpose of each section? How does the author use transitions to move from one section to the next?
4. Gelernter states that the overuse of computers in the classroom can hinder the development of clear thinking and reasoned argument. How clearly written is *his* essay? How reasoned is his argument? Gather evidence for your answer by reviewing the essay and determining whether each sentence seems to flow logically to the next and whether each paragraph seems to move reasonably to the next.
5. The author uses metaphors, similes, and other rhetorical devices. Explain the effectiveness of expressions such as "have all the appeal of a dusty piano to a teen who has a Walkman handy" (paragraph 4), "dynamiting documents" (paragraph 7), and "software species" (paragraph 8). Locate other unconventional descriptions.

6. Who is the intended audience for this essay? Educators? Parents? Students? Politicians? What evidence can you cite to back up your view?
7. What rhetorical device is Gelernter using in his title? What is the implicit meaning of the title?

WRITING

1. Visit the writing or reading computer lab in your school. As an objective observer, study the interaction of student and computer. Write a descriptive essay focusing on the demeanor and behavior of the student and the atmosphere of the classroom. If you wish, compare it to a traditional classroom.
2. Copy a paragraph from the essay, and enter it into a word-processing program that has a grammar-check function. Record any comments that the program makes in response to its evaluation of the writing. Do the computer's responses to the author's sentence structure make sense?

NETWORKING
Applying Digital and Multimedia Literacies

WRITING AN ARGUMENT   Weighing the Potential of Smart Classrooms: Select one of the teaching capabilities of modern computers—multimedia, hypertext, or spell- and grammar-check programs. Argue for the benefits of one of these features, noting how it could be used effectively in a smart classroom. Consider at least one counterargument to your position, and describe how you would rebut it.

When Bright Girls Decide That Math Is "a Waste of Time"

Susan Jacoby

Susan Jacoby *(b. 1945) has worked as an educator and as a reporter for the* Washington Post *and a columnist for the* New York Times. *As a freelance journalist in the former Soviet Union (from 1969 to 1971), she produced two books about her experiences. Jacoby now contributes to the* Nation *and* McCall's; *her books include* The Possible She *(1979), a collection of autobiographical essays;* Wild Justice: The Evolution of Revenge *(1983);* Half-Jew: A Daughter's Search for Her Buried Past *(2000); and* The Age of American Unreason *(2008). In this essay from the* New York Times, *Jacoby examines the reasons girls are often deficient in math and science.*

1   Susannah, a 16-year-old who has always been an A student in every subject from algebra to English, recently informed her parents that she intended to drop physics and calculus in her senior year of high school and replace them with a drama seminar and a work-study program. She expects a major in art or history in college, she explained, and "any more science or math will just be a waste of my time."

2   Her parents were neither concerned by nor opposed to her decision. "Fine, dear," they said. Their daughter is, after all, an outstanding student. What does it matter if, at age 16, she has taken a step that may limit her understanding of both machines and the natural world for the rest of her life?

3   This kind of decision, in which girls turn away from studies that would give them a sure footing in the world of science and technology, is a self-inflicted female disability that is, regrettably, almost as common today as it was when I was in high school. If Susannah had announced that she had decided to stop taking English in her senior year, her mother and father would have been horrified. I also think they would have been a good deal less sanguine about her decision if she were a boy.

4   In saying that scientific and mathematical ignorance is a self-inflicted female wound, I do not, obviously, mean that cultural expectations play no role in the process. But the world does not conspire to deprive modern women of access to science as it did in the 1930s, when Rosalyn S. Yalow, the Nobel Prize–winning physicist, graduated from Hunter College and was advised to go to work as a secretary because no graduate school would admit her to its physics department. The current generation of adolescent girls—and their parents, bred on old expectations about women's interests—are active conspirators in limiting their own intellectual development.

5   It is true that the proportion of young women in science-related graduate and professional schools, most notably medical schools, has increased significantly in the past decade. It is also true that so few women were studying advanced science and mathematics before the early 1970s that the percentage increase in female enrollment does not yet translate into large numbers of women actually working in science.

6   The real problem is that so many girls eliminate themselves from any serious possibility of studying science as a result of decisions made during the vulnerable period of midadolescence, when they are most likely to be influenced—on both conscious and subconscious levels—by the traditional belief that math and science are "masculine" subjects.

7   During the teen-age years the well-documented phenomenon of "math anxiety" strikes girls who never had any problem handling numbers during earlier schooling. Some men, too, experience this syndrome—a form of panic, akin to a phobia, at any task involving numbers—but women constitute the overwhelming majority of sufferers. The onset of acute math anxiety during the teen-age years is, as Stalin was fond of saying, "not by accident."

8   In adolescence girls begin to fear that they will be unattractive to boys if they are typed as "brains." Science and math epitomize unfeminine braininess in a way

that, say, foreign languages do not. High-school girls who pursue an advanced interest in science and math (unless they are students at special institutions like the Bronx High School of Science where everyone is a brain) usually find that they are greatly outnumbered by boys in their classes. They are, therefore, intruding on male turf at a time when their sexual confidence, as well as that of the boys, is most fragile.

A 1981 assessment of female achievement in mathematics, based on research conducted under a National Institute for Education grant, found significant differences in the mathematical achievements of 9th and 12th graders. At age 13 girls were equal to or slightly better than boys in tests involving algebra, problem solving and spatial ability; four years later the boys had outstripped the girls.   9

It is not mysterious that some very bright high-school girls suddenly decide that math is "too hard" and "a waste of time." In my experience, self-sabotage of mathematical and scientific ability is often a conscious process. I remember deliberately pretending to be puzzled by geometry problems in my sophomore year in high school. A male teacher called me in after class and said, in a baffled tone, "I don't see how you can be having so much trouble when you got straight A's last year in my algebra class."   10

The decision to avoid advanced biology, chemistry, physics and calculus in high school automatically restricts academic and professional choices that ought to be wide open to anyone beginning college. At all coeducational universities women are overwhelmingly concentrated in the fine arts, social sciences and traditionally female departments like education. Courses leading to degrees in science- and technology-related fields are filled mainly by men.   11

In my generation, the practical consequences of mathematical and scientific illiteracy are visible in the large number of special programs to help professional women overcome the anxiety they feel when they are promoted into jobs that require them to handle statistics.   12

The consequences of this syndrome should not, however, be viewed in narrowly professional terms. Competence in science and math does not mean one is going to become a scientist or mathematician any more than competence in writing English means one is going to become a professional writer. Scientific and mathematical illiteracy—which has been cited in several recent critiques by panels studying American education from kindergarten through college— produces an incalculably impoverished vision of human experience.   13

Scientific illiteracy is not, of course, the exclusive province of women. In certain intellectual circles it has become fashionable to proclaim a willed, aggressive ignorance about science and technology. Some female writers specialize in ominous, uninformed diatribes against genetic research as a plot to remove control of childbearing from women, while some well-known men of letters proudly announce that they understand absolutely nothing about computers, or, for that matter, about electricity. This lack of understanding is nothing in which women or men ought to take pride.   14

15   Failure to comprehend either computers or chromosomes leads to a terrible sense of helplessness, because the profound impact of science on everyday life is evident even to those who insist they don't, won't, can't understand why the changes are taking place. At this stage of history women are more prone to such feelings of helplessness than men because the culture judges their ignorance less harshly and because women themselves acquiesce in that indulgence.

16   Since there is ample evidence of such feelings in adolescence, it is up to parents to see that their daughters do not accede to the old stereotypes about "masculine" and "feminine" knowledge. Unless we want our daughters to share our intellectual handicaps, we had better tell them no, they can't stop taking mathematics and science at the ripe old age of 16.

COMPREHENSION

1. What reasons does Jacoby give for girls' deficiency in math and science?
2. Why does Jacoby call it a "self-inflicted female disability" (paragraph 3)?
3. What are the consequences of being math- and science-illiterate?

RHETORIC

1. Explain the main idea of Jacoby's essay in your own words.
2. Does the writer use abstract or concrete language in her essay? Cite examples to support your response.
3. What technique does Jacoby use in paragraphs 1 and 2? How does it aid in setting up her argument?
4. What rhetorical strategies does the writer use in her essay?
5. How does the use of dialogue aid in developing paragraph 10? What effect does the general use of dialogue have on Jacoby's point?
6. How is Jacoby's conclusion consistent in tone with the rest of the essay? Does it supply a sense of unity? Why or why not?

WRITING

1. Write an essay describing a school-related phobia you once had or continue to have (for example, in math, writing, physical education, or biology). Explain where you think that fear came from, how it affected your performance in school, and what you did (or are doing) to cope with the problem.
2. Write an essay about the need for math and science literacy in today's world. Use support from Jacoby's essay.
3. **Writing an Argument:** Write an argumentation essay proposing that math and science phobia is not "self-inflicted" but is caused primarily by the continued presence of sexism in society.

| **NETWORKING** |
| *Applying Digital and Multimedia Literacies* |

Analyzing How Design Informs a Web Site's Purpose: Find *BrainCake,* the Web site of the Girls' Math and Science Partnership. Watch the whole opening video, and then explore the site itself. How might an organization like this one address the issues Susan Jacoby raises in her essay? How does this Web site aim to make science and math (and the Carnegie Science Center's programs) seem appealing and important to girls ages 11–17—and to their parents? What questions might Jacoby have for its organizers?

Two Cheers for *Brown v. Board of Education*

Clayborne Carson

Clayborne Carson *(b. 1944) is professor of history and director of the Martin Luther King Jr. Papers Project at Stanford University. He was born in Buffalo, New York, and educated at the University of California at Los Angeles, where he received his BA (1967), MA (1968), and PhD (1977). A specialist in African-American and civil rights history, Carson has written and edited numerous books, including* In Struggle: SNCC and the Black Awakening of the 1960s *(1981, rev. ed. 1995), which received the Frederick Jackson Turner Award;* Eyes on the Prize: America's Civil Rights Years *(1987); and* The Malcolm X File *(1991). Asked by Coretta Scott King to handle her late husband's literary estate, Carson is the lead editor of* The Papers of Martin Luther King Jr. *(University of California Press). "It was a job you couldn't say no to," Carson said. In this essay, published in the* Journal of American History *in 2004, Carson offers an evaluation of the impact of a major Supreme Court decision on school segregation.*

My gratuitous opinion of *Brown v. Board of Education* (1954) is somewhat 1
ambivalent and certainly arrives too late to alter the racial policies of the past fifty years. But for those of us who practice history, hindsight offers a far more reliable kind of wisdom than does foresight. We see clearly now that while the *Brown* decision informed the attitudes that have shaped contemporary American race relations, it did not resolve persistent disputes about the nation's civil rights policies. The Supreme Court's unanimous opinion in *Brown* broke decisively with the racist interpretations of traditional American values set forth in

Scott v. Sandford (1857) and *Plessy v. Ferguson* (1896), offering instead the optimistic "American Creed" that Gunnar Myrdal saw as the solution to "the Negro problem."[1] Like the two earlier landmark decisions, *Brown* overestimated the extent of ideological consensus among Americans and soon exacerbated racial and regional conflicts instead of resolving them. The Court's ruling against school segregation encouraged African Americans to believe that the entire structure of white supremacy was illegitimate and legally vulnerable. But the civil rights struggles *Brown* inspired sought broader goals than the decision could deliver, and that gap fostered frustration and resentment among many black Americans. In short, the decision's virtues and limitations reflect both the achievements and the failures of the efforts made in the last half century to solve America's racial dilemma and to realize the nation's egalitarian ideals.

2   That the *Brown* decision spurred subsequent civil rights progress seems apparent, but its impact and its significance as a source of inspiration are difficult to measure.[2] Although the Court's initial unwillingness to set firm timetables for school desegregation undercut *Brown*'s immediate impact, African Americans expanded the limited scope of the decision by individual and collective challenges to the Jim Crow system. Small-scale protests escalated during the decade after 1954, becoming a sustained mass movement against all facets of segregation and discrimination in the North as well as the South. Civil rights protests and litigation prompted Congress to pass the Civil Rights Act of 1964 and the Voting Rights Act of 1965, both of which extended the *Brown* decision's egalitarian principles well beyond education. The historic mass struggle that followed *Brown* ultimately destroyed the legal foundations of the Jim Crow system, and their destruction prepared the way for a still more far-reaching expansion of prevailing American conceptions of civil rights and of the role of government in protecting those rights. During the past forty years, women and many minority groups, including immigrants and people with disabilities, have gained new legal protections modeled on the civil rights gains of African Americans.[3]

---

[1]*Scott v. Sandford,* 19 How. 393 (1857); *Plessy v. Ferguson,* 163 U.S. 537 (1896); *Brown v. Board of Education,* 347 U.S. 483 (1954); Gunnar Myrdal, *An American Dilemma: The Negro Problem and Modern Democracy* (2 vols., New York, 1944).

[2]On *Brown*'s direct and indirect consequences, see, for example, Michael J. Klarman, "How *Brown* Changed Race Relations: The Backlash Thesis," *Journal of American History,* 81 (June 1994), 81–118. Klarman correctly points out that *Brown* had limited impact on school desegregation, especially in the Deep South, and stimulated southerm white resistance to racial reform. He concludes that the contributions of *Brown* to the broader civil rights struggle were mostly indirect.

[3]Cf. Hugh Davis Graham, *The Civil Rights Era: Origins and Development of National Policy, 1960–1972* (New York, 1990); Hugh Davis Graham, *Collision Course: The Strange Convergence of Affirmative Action and Immigration Policy in America* (New York, 2002); and John D. Skrentny, *The Minority Rights Revolution* (Cambridge, Mass., 2002).

But the *Brown* decision also created racial aspirations that remain unreal- 3
ized. Although the decision may have been predicated on the notion of a shared
American creed, most white Americans were unwilling to risk their own racial
privileges to bring about racial equality. The decision was neither universally
accepted nor consistently enforced. "Instead, it provoked overwhelming resistance
in the South and only tepid interest in the North," the historian John Higham
insisted. "In the South the decision released a tidal wave of racial hysteria that
swept moderates out of office or turned them into demagogues. State and local
officials declined to obstruct a revival of the Ku Klux Klan. Instead, they
employed every conceivable device to maintain segregation, including harassment and dissolution of NAACP chapters."[4] By the 1970s, resistance to school
desegregation had become national. Northern whites in Boston and elsewhere
demonstrated their unwillingness to send their children to predominantly black
schools or to allow large-scale desegregation that would drastically alter the
racial composition of "their" schools in "their" neighborhoods. Voters in the
states of Washington and California passed initiatives to restrict the right of
school boards (Washington) and state courts (California) to order busing to
achieve school desegregation (the Supreme Court later held the Washington
initiative unconstitutional). Nationwide, white racial resentments encouraged an
enduring shift of white voters from the Democratic to the Republican party. The
1964 election would be the last presidential contest in which the majority of
black voters and of white voters backed the same candidate. Since 1974, when
the Supreme Court's *Milliken v. Bradley* decision set limits on busing, the legal
meaning of desegregation has been scaled back to conform to American racial
and political realities.[5]

African Americans generally applauded the *Brown* decision when it was 4
announced, but the Court's failure to realize *Brown*'s bold affirmation of egalitarian ideals fueled subsequent black discontent and disillusionment. *Brown*
cited studies that demonstrated the harmful psychological impact of enforced
segregation on black students, reporting, "To separate them from others of
similar age and qualifications solely because of their race generates a feeling of
inferiority as to their status in the community that may affect their hearts and
minds in a way unlikely ever to be undone." Yet the Court did not offer an effective means to correct the problem it had identified. During the decades after

[4]John Higham, "Introduction: A Historical Perspective," in *Civil Rights and Civil Wrongs: Black-White Relations since World War II,* ed. John Higham (University Park, 1997), 4. See also Klarman, "How *Brown* Changed Race Relations"; Numan V. Bartley, *The Rise of Massive Resistance: Race and Politics in the South in the 1950s* (Baton Rouge, 1969); and Neil McMillen, *The Citizens' Council: Organized Resistance to the Second Reconstruction, 1954–1964* (Urbana, 1971).

[5]See Ronald P. Formisano, *Boston against Busing: Race, Class, and Ethnicity in the 1960s and 1970s* (Chapel Hill, 1991); and J. Anthony Lukas, *Common Ground: A Turbulent Decade in the Lives of Three American Families* (New York, 1985). *Washington v. Seattle School District,* 458 U.S. 457 (1982); *Crawford v. Los Angeles Board of Education,* 458 U.S. 527 (1982); *Milliken v. Bradley,* 418 U.S. 717 (1974). See Gary Orfield and Susan E. Eaton, *Dismantling Desegregation: The Quiet Reversal of* Brown v. Board of Education (New York, 1996).

Brown, most southern black children continued to suffer the psychological consequences of segregation, while a small minority assumed the often considerable psychological and physical risks of attending newly integrated public schools. Rather than bringing large numbers of black and white students together in public schools, the *Brown* decision—and the subsequent years of litigation and social conflict—enabled a minority of black students to attend predominantly white schools. Ten years after the *Brown* decision, according to data compiled by the U.S. Department of Education, almost 98 percent of southern black students still attended predominantly black schools. Now, at the beginning of the twenty-first century, the Court's ideal of educational opportunity as "a right which must be made available to all on equal terms" is still far from being realized. American schools, both public and private, are still highly segregated. According to a recent study, the typical Latino or black student in the United States still attends a school where members of minority groups are predominant.[6]

5   Certainly, the *Brown* decision's most significant deficiency is its failure to address the concerns of the majority of African American students who have been unable or unwilling to seek better educational opportunities by leaving predominantly black schools for predominantly white ones. While it opened the door for the Little Rock Nine, who desegregated Central High School in 1957, the *Brown* decision offered little solace to the hundreds of students who remained at Little Rock's all-black Horace Mann High School. When Arkansas officials reacted to desegregation by closing all of Little Rock's high schools, those students were denied even segregated educational opportunities.[7] With the encouragement of the lawyers for the National Association for the Advancement of Colored People's (NAACP) Legal Defense and Education Fund, the Supreme Court largely abandoned previous efforts to enforce the separate but equal mandate in order to adopt a narrowly conceived strategy for achieving equal educational opportunity through desegregation. The pre-*Brown* equalization effort had encouraged social scientists to develop increasingly sophisticated ways of measuring differences in the quality of schools. But during the 1950s, pro–civil rights scholars shifted their focus from the educational environment of black students in black schools to the psychological state of black students experiencing desegregation. The NAACP's initial strategy of forcing southern states to equalize facilities at all-black schools had resulted in tangible improvements, whereas the removal of racial barriers in public schools was advertised as offering intangible psychological gains.

---

[6]*Brown v. Board of Education,* 347 U.S. at 494, 493; Gary Orfield and Chungmei Lee, "*Brown* at Fifty: King's Dream or Plessy's Nightmare?" Jan. 17, 2004, *The Civil Rights Project, Harvard University.* <http://www.civilrightsproject.harvard.edu/research/reseg04/resegregation04.php> (April 4, 2004). In every region of the nation, at least 30% of black students still attend schools with less than 10% white enrollment. *Ibid.*

[7]Cf. Melba Beals, *Warriors Don't Cry: A Searing Memoir of the Battle to Integrate Little Rock's Central High* (New York, 1995); and Melba Beals, *White Is a State of Mind: A Memoir* (New York, 1995).

For Thurgood Marshall, who headed the NAACP legal staff, the equalization 6
effort had always been a means of achieving the ultimate goal of desegregation.
After the Supreme Court decided in *Sweatt v. Painter* (1950) that a makeshift segregated law school at a black college could not provide educational opportunities
equal to those offered by the University of Texas Law School, Marshall exulted,
"The complete destruction of *all* enforced segregation is now in sight." Despite
having attended predominantly black schools at every stage of his academic career, he saw segregation as a racial stigma that could not be removed by increased
state appropriations for Jim Crow schools. In the early 1950s he noted that social
scientists were "almost in universal agreement that segregated education produces inequality." He therefore concluded "that segregated schools, perhaps
more than any other single factor, are of major concern to the individual of public
school age and contribute greatly to the unwholesomeness and unhappy development of the personality of Negroes which the color caste system in the United
States has produced."[8]

Few African Americans would wish to return to the pre-*Brown* world of 7
legally enforced segregation, but in the half century since 1954, only a minority
of Americans has experienced the promised land of truly integrated public education. By the mid-1960s, with dual school systems still in place in many areas of
the Deep South, and with de facto segregation a recognized reality in urban areas,
the limitations of *Brown* had become evident to many of those who had spear-
headed previous civil rights struggles. The ideological gulf that appeared in
African American politics during the period was largely the result of efforts to
draw attention to the predominantly black institutions neglected in the drive for
racial integration. The black power movement arose in part as an effort by
African Americans to control and improve such institutions. Some black power
proponents exaggerated the benefits of racial separatism, but their extremism
can be best understood as a reaction against the unbalanced post-*Brown* strategy
of seeking racial advancement solely through integration. Although James S.
Coleman's landmark 1966 study of equality of educational opportunity found
that black children attending integrated schools did better than students attending predominantly black schools, it was by no means clear that the gap was the
result of interracial interactions rather than of differences in the socioeconomic
backgrounds of the students involved. By the late 1960s, growing numbers of
black leaders had concluded that improvement of black schools should take
priority over school desegregation. In 1967, shortly before the National
Advisory Commission on Civil Disorders warned that the United States was
"moving toward two societies, one white, one black—separate and unequal,"
Martin Luther King Jr. acknowledged the need to refocus attention, at least in
the short run, on "schools in ghetto areas." He also insisted that "the drive for

[8]*Sweatt v. Painter,* 339 U.S. 629 (1950); *Baltimore Afro-American,* June 17, 1950, quoted in Juan
Williams, *Thurgood Marshall: American Revolutionary* (New York, 1998), 195; Thurgood Marshall,
"An Evaluation of Recent Efforts to Achieve Racial Integration in Education through Resort to the
Courts," *Journal of Negro Education,* 21 (Summer 1952), 316–27, esp. 322.

immediate improvements in segregated schools should not retard progress toward integrated education later." Even veterans of the NAACP's legal campaign
had second thoughts. "*Brown* has little practical relevance to central city
blacks," Constance Baker Motley commented in 1974. "Its psychological and
legal relevance has already had its effect."[9]

8   Black power advocates sometimes sought to replace the narrow strategy of
achieving racial advancement through integration with the equally narrow strategy
of achieving it through racial separatism. In both instances, claims of psychological gains often substituted for measurable racial advancements, but the continued
popularity of Afrocentric educational experiments indicates that many African
Americans now see voluntary segregation as psychologically uplifting. Having
personally experienced the burden of desegregating numerous classrooms and
having watched my son move with great success from a predominantly black
college to a predominantly white law school, I am skeptical of sweeping claims
about the impact of racial environment on learning. While believing that debates
among African Americans during the last half century about their destiny have
been useful, I regret that those debates have often exacerbated ideological conflict
rather than encouraging us toward collective action. Rather than having to choose
between overcoming racial barriers and improving black community institutions,
we should be able to choose both.

9   In hindsight, the nation would have been better served if the *Brown* decision
had evinced a more realistic understanding of the deep historical roots of America's
racial problems—perhaps a little more familiarity with the writings of W. E. B.
DuBois and Carter C. Woodson as well as those of Myrdal and his colleagues.
Rather than blandly advising that desegregation of public schools be achieved with
"all deliberate speed," the Supreme Court—and the NAACP lawyers who argued
before it—should have launched a two-pronged attack, not only against racial segregation but also against inferior schools, whatever their racial composition. Such an
attack would have heeded the admonition that DuBois offered in 1935, soon after
his forced resignation as editor of the NAACP's journal, the *Crisis:*

> Theoretically, the Negro needs neither segregated schools nor mixed schools.
> What he needs is Education. . . . Other things being equal, the mixed school is the
> broader, more natural basis for the education of all youth. It gives wider contacts;
> it inspires great self-confidence; and suppresses the inferiority complex. But other
> things seldom are equal, and in that case, Sympathy, Knowledge, and the Truth,
> outweigh all that the mixed school can offer.[10]

---

[9]J. S. Coleman et al., *Equality of Educational Opportunity* (Washington, 1966), *passim; Report
of the National Advisory Commission on Civil Disorders* (New York, 1968), 1; Martin Luther
King Jr., *Where Do We Go from Here: Chaos or Community?* (New York, 1967), 228. For
Constance Baker Motley's statement (quoted from the *New York Times,* May 13, 1974), see
James T. Patterson, Brown v. Board of Education: *A Civil Rights Milestone and Its Troubled
Legacy* (New York, 2001), 168.

[10]*Brown v. Board of Education,* 349 U.S. 294 (1955); W. E. B. DuBois, "Does the Negro Need Separate
Schools?" *Journal of Negro Education,* 4 (July 1935), in *The Oxford W. E. B. DuBois Reader,* ed. Eric J.
Sundquist (New York, 1996), 431.

Because the *Brown* decision was a decisive departure from *Plessy*'s separate 10
but equal principle, it was an important turning point in African American history.
Nevertheless, fifty years later the Court's assumptions about the psychological
consequences of legally enforced segregation seem dated. The Jim Crow system
no longer exists, but most black American schoolchildren still attend predominantly black public schools that offer fewer opportunities for advancement than
typical predominantly white public schools. Moreover, there is no contemporary
civil rights movement able to alter that fact. Yet, if *Brown* represents a failed attempt to achieve comprehensive racial advancement, the opinion nonetheless
still challenges us by affirming egalitarian ideals that remain relevant: "In these
days, it is doubtful that any child may reasonably be expected to succeed in life if
he is denied the opportunity of an education. Such an opportunity, where the
state has undertaken to provide it, is a right which must be made available to all
on equal terms."[11]

COMPREHENSION

1. According to Carson, what are the benefits and shortcomings of the *Brown v. Board of
   Education* decision? Why does he give two cheers (instead of the traditional three
   cheers) for the Supreme Court's 1954 verdict?
2. What are the psychological effects of both segregation and desegregation on black
   students?
3. Why does Carson say that the impact of the *Brown* decision is difficult to measure?
   What evidence does he provide to support this assessment?

RHETORIC

1. Who is Carson's audience for this essay? How does he fit his style to the expectations
   he holds for this specific audience? Provide examples of vocabulary, syntax, and
   abstract language to support your response. Why would the article also be of interest
   to a more general audience?
2. Carson lays out a well-informed argument. What is his claim or major proposition?
   What are his warrants? What is his support? How does he deal with opposing
   viewpoints? What conclusions does he draw to convince the reader of his position?
3. Analyze the pattern of cause and effect that Carson presents in this essay.
4. Carson has very strong topic sentences at the start of virtually every paragraph. List
   these topic sentences, and then show how they control the flow of his thoughts within
   paragraphs while at the same time advancing his argument.
5. Examine the writer's footnotes. What are his sources? What range and variety of
   evidence do these notes suggest?

[11] *"Brown v. Board of Education of Topeka:* Opinion on Segregation Laws," in *Civil Rights and African
Americans: A Documentary History,* ed. Albert P. Blaustein and Robert I. Zangrando (Evanston,
1991), 436.

WRITING

1. Using Carson's article as a reference point, write an essay describing the ethnic and racial composition of your former high school or the college you now attend. How does this demographic profile support some of Carson's key insights into *Brown v. Board of Education?*
2. Write an essay in which you offer your own analysis of the ways in which varieties of discrimination you encounter in education can have psychological consequences. Feel free to offer personal experience to support your analysis.
3. **Writing an Argument:** Unlike Carson, who argues both sides of the *Brown* decision in terms of the historical aftermath, write an argumentative essay in which you defend or criticize the results of *Brown* since 1954. Conduct research and collaborate with class members if you wish.

NETWORKING
Applying Digital and Multimedia Literacies

Supporting an Argument with Visuals: Enhance your response to the Writing an Argument assignment above by incorporating three images from the electronic exhibit *In Pursuit of Freedom & Equality: Kansas and the African American Public School Experience, 1855–1955* (find this by doing a Google search). Be sure to credit your sources and not to misuse the images; that said, you can certainly debate what they *mean* in this argument and either draw on or argue with the way they are portrayed in the exhibit.

Synthesis: Connections for Critical Thinking

1. Compare and contrast the rhetoric of the personal essay as it is represented in Rodriguez's "The Lonely, Good Company of Books" with the rhetoric of such expository and argumentative essays as Quindlen's "Sex Ed" or Carson's "Two Cheers for *Brown v. Board of Education.*"
2. Analyze an event in your education when you had a disagreement with a teacher or administrator. Explain and explore whether the differences in viewpoint were based on emotional perspective, intellectual perspective, or both.
3. Select the essay in this chapter you find most pertinent to your life as a student. Explain why you selected the essay, and explore your intellectual and emotional responses to it.
4. Does your college seem to support Jacoby's views regarding the educational lives of women? Explain why or why not.
5. Argue for or against the view that the publicized sexual activity of politicians and other celebrities makes the decision whether to keep sex education out of the schools entirely moot.
6. It is 2050. Write an essay in which you explore the demographics of a typical college classroom. Refer to the ideas contained in the Bazelon, Jacoby, and Carson essays.

7. Write an essay that classifies at least three educational issues that the authors in this chapter examine. Establish a clear thesis to unify the categories you establish.
8. Analyze the patterns and techniques used by Rose, Gelernter, and Jacoby to advance their claims about education today.

NETWORKING
Applying Digital and Multimedia Literacies

---

1. Do an online search for *sex education* and *France* (or another country of your choice). Write an essay describing the policies of your chosen country on the topic.
2. Argue for or against the proposition that despite Gelernter's warnings about the purported shortcomings of computers in the classroom, in the future many students will prefer to obtain a degree completely via computer and the Internet. To support your viewpoint, research and report on at least three online sites that offer college degrees.

chapter 5

Family Life and Gender Roles

How Do We Become Who We Are?

Every culture has its own ideas about what identity is, how it is formed, and where it comes from. What is the influence of family, of environment, of gender, and, as we saw in Chapter 4, of education on the creation of identity? Although it is challenging to reconcile these various cross-cultural ideas, the writers in this chapter attempt to make sense of identity from the perspectives of family and gender, and they invite readers to liberate themselves from the tyranny of stereotyping.

Families nourish us during childhood, and the values our families seek to maintain usually affect our identities in powerful ways, whether we adopt them wholly, modify them, or reject them outright. Writers have always been aware of the importance of the family in human development and behavior, and have written about it from various perspectives, using narration, sociological and psychological analysis, and cultural criticism, among other approaches. Tolstoy wrote that "happy families are all alike; every unhappy family is unhappy in its own way." But we shall discover that Tolstoy had a limited view of family life and its values—probably circumscribed by the mores of the time he lived in. Some of our finest essayists and observers of social life today demonstrate in this chapter that what constitutes the definition of a family is up for grabs as we begin the new millennium.

The family is one of the few institutions that we find in every society throughout the world, at least every thriving society. Anthropologists, sociologists, and psychologists tell us that family patterns are exceedingly diverse even in the same societies. In the past and even more so today, children grow up in many ways: in nuclear and in nontraditional households; in single-parent and in dual-parent arrangements; in extended families and in blended families; and in patriarchal and matriarchal, heterosexual and homosexual, monogamous and polygamous situations. And the dynamics of family life assume added dimension as we move across cultures, studying European families, African American families, Hispanic families, Asian families, and so forth. Even within these groups, we find variables that affect family life and values, such as economic class, social class, and educational levels.

Unlike in previous periods in our history, Americans today seem to be groping for a definition of what constitutes the happy family. With the influences of the media and of peer pressure on children, the rise in the number of latchkey children, and the fact that there is a growing diversity of cultures in America owing to the new wave of immigration, the family appears to be less of a traditional haven than it was even a generation ago. This chapter contains vivid accounts of the long-standing bonds within the family that have been treasured

228

for their capacity to build values of love and sharing. It also contains essays that demonstrate how family life is filled with emotional complexities and conflicts that the child must negotiate as she or he finds meaning and attempts to construct an identity. Each writer, whether writing narration, exposition, or argumentation, shows how significant the family is for the development of our values, personalities, and lifestyles.

As much as our identities are shaped by powerful institutional forces like the family, what we are might be even more powerfully determined by the forces of sexuality and gender. Freud asserted that human behavior is rooted in sexuality, that gender (rather than family or school or any social institution) is destiny. Clearly, notions of what it means to be a man or a woman have an impact on the construction of our identities.

The identity issues discussed in this chapter might prove to be controversial, but they will encourage you to confront your sense of identity. These essays are like a mirror in which you can see and evaluate what you really are.

PREVIEWING THE CHAPTER

As you read the essays in this chapter and respond to them in discussion and writing, consider the following questions:

- What form of rhetoric is the author using: narration, exposition, or argumentation? Why is this form appropriate for the author's purpose?
- What perspective does the writer take on the subject of identity formation? Is the writer optimistic, pessimistic, or something else?
- What are the cultural, social, and economic issues addressed in the essay?
- How do you regard the authority of the author? Does she or he seem to be speaking from experience and knowledge? In essays that explain or argue, does the evidence appear substantial or questionable? Explain.
- What stylistic devices does the author employ to re-create a memory, explain a function, or argue a stance regarding an issue of identity?
- Which essays appear alike in purpose and method, and why?
- What have you learned or discovered about your own identity from reading these essays?
- Do you prefer one rhetorical form over another—for example, personal narration over argumentation? If so, why?

Classic and Contemporary Images

HOW DO WE RESPOND TO MARRIAGE?

Using a Critical Perspective What was your first impression of Brueghel's *Rustic Wedding* and Elise Amendola's *Gay Marriage?* What details do you see? What senses do the artist and the photographer draw on to convey the atmosphere of the wedding? What does each want to say about the institution of marriage? How do you know?

The Flemish artist Pieter Brueghel the Elder (1525–1569) was one of the greatest painters of the 16th century and was renowned for his exuberant depictions of peasant life. His son Pieter Brueghel the Younger (1564–1638) copied many of his father's works and also painted religious subjects. He was responsible for *Rustic Wedding*, shown here.

Hillary, left, and Julie Goodridge, lead plaintiffs in the landmark Massachusetts
gay marriage lawsuit, receive their wedding rings from their daughter, Annie, 8,
as Unitarian Reverend William Sinkford presides over their marriage
ceremony in Boston during the first day of state-sanctioned gay marriage
in the United States on May 17, 2004.

Classic and Contemporary Essays
HOW DOES CHILDHOOD SHAPE US?

E. B. White and Ann Hood represent two generations, but each writer was raised with enduring values regarding the function, structure, and role of the family. Both authors are superb stylists. White writes in clear, elegiac prose that marches in a quiet, even rhythm. Tradition is to be treasured; continuity is to be celebrated. For White, it seems, pleasure derives from connectivity and permanence—in nature as well as family life. Like E. B. White, the contemporary novelist and essayist Ann Hood recaptures a sense of the past and family life through a style that is purposefully fast-paced. Hood's site of memory is not a lake in Maine as it is in White's essay, but rather a road that she travels time and again. The route that she takes is as familiar to her as the lake is to White. And both lake and road are symbolic of the creative effort by these two writers to recapture the past—a tapestry of childhood and family life that can be recreated through the very act of writing.

Once More to the Lake

E. B. White

E(lwyn) B(rooks) White (1899–1985), perhaps the finest American essayist of the 20th century, was at his most distinctive in his treatments of people and nature. A recipient of the National Medal for Literature, and associated for years with the New Yorker, *White is the author of* One Man's Meat *(1942),* Here Is New York *(1949), and* The Second Tree from the Corner *(1954), among numerous other works. He was also one of the most talented writers of literature for children, the author of* Stuart Little *(1945),* Charlotte's Web *(1952), and* The Trumpet of the Swan *(1970). In this essay, White combines narration and description to make a poignant and vivid statement about past and present, youth and age, life and death.*

1   One summer, along about 1904, my father rented a camp on a lake in Maine and took us all there for the month of August. We all got ringworm from some kittens and had to rub Pond's Extract on our arms and legs night and morning, and my father rolled over in a canoe with all his clothes on; but outside of that the vacation was a success and from then on none of us ever thought there was any place in the world like that lake in Maine. We returned summer after summer—always on August 1st for one month. I have since become a saltwater man, but sometimes in summer there are days when the restlessness of the tides and the fearful cold of the sea water and the incessant wind which blows across the afternoon and into

the evening make me wish for the placidity of a lake in the woods. A few weeks ago this feeling got so strong I bought myself a couple of bass hooks and a spinner and returned to the lake where we used to go, for a week's fishing and to revisit old haunts.

I took along my son, who had never had any fresh water up his nose and who had seen lily pads only from train windows. On the journey over to the lake I began to wonder what it would be like. I wondered how time would have marred this unique, this holy spot—the coves and streams, the hills that the sun set behind, the camps and the paths behind the camps. I was sure the tarred road would have found it out and I wondered in what other ways it would be desolated. It is strange how much you can remember about places like that once you allow your mind to return into the grooves which lead back. You remember one thing, and that suddenly reminds you of another thing. I guess I remembered clearest of all the early mornings, when the lake was cool and motionless, remembered how the bedroom smelled of the lumber it was made of and of the wet woods whose scent entered through the screen. The partitions in the camp were thin and did not extend clear to the top of the rooms, and as I was always the first up I would dress softly so as not to wake the others, and sneak out into the sweet outdoors and start out in the canoe, keeping close along the shore in the long shadows of the pines. I remembered being very careful never to rub my paddle against the gunwale for fear of disturbing the stillness of the cathedral.

The lake had never been what you would call a wild lake. There were cottages sprinkled around the shores, and it was in farming country although the shores of the lake were quite heavily wooded. Some of the cottages were owned by nearby farmers, and you would live at the shore and eat your meals at the farmhouse. That's what our family did. But although it wasn't wild, it was a fairly large and undisturbed lake and there were places in it which, to a child at least, seemed infinitely remote and primeval.

I was right about the tar: It led to within half a mile of the shore. But when I got back there, with my boy, and we settled into a camp near a farmhouse and into the kind of summertime I had known, I could tell that it was going to be pretty much the same as it had been before—I knew it, lying in bed the first morning, smelling the bedroom, and hearing the boy sneak quietly out and go off along the shore in a boat. I began to sustain the illusion that he was I, and therefore, by simple transposition, that I was my father. This sensation persisted, kept cropping up all the time we were there. It was not an entirely new feeling, but in this setting it grew much stronger. I seemed to be living a dual existence. I would be in the middle of some simple act, I would be picking up a bait box or laying down a table fork, or I would be saying something, and suddenly it would be not I but my father who was saying the words or making the gesture. It gave me a creepy sensation.

We went fishing the first morning. I felt the same damp moss covering the worms in the bait can, and saw the dragonfly alight on the tip of my rod as it hovered a few inches from the surface of the water. It was the arrival of this fly that convinced me beyond any doubt that everything was as it always had been, that the years were a mirage and there had been no years. The small waves were the same, chucking the rowboat under the chin as we fished at anchor, and the boat was the same boat, the same color green and the ribs broken in the same place, and under the floor-boards the same fresh-water leavings and débris—the dead hellgrammite, the wisps of moss, the rusty discarded fishhook, the dried blood from yesterday's catch. We stared silently at the tips of our rods, at the dragonflies that came and went. I lowered the tip of mine into the water, tentatively, pensively dislodging the fly, which darted two feet away, poised, darted two feet back, and came to rest again a little farther up the rod. There had been no years between the ducking of this dragonfly and the other one—the one that was part of memory. I looked at the boy, who was silently watching his fly, and it was my hands that held his rod, my eyes watching. I felt dizzy and didn't know which rod I was at the end of.

6   We caught two bass, hauling them in briskly as though they were mackerel, pulling them over the side of the boat in a businesslike manner without any landing net, and stunning them with a blow on the back of the head. When we got back for a swim before lunch, the lake was exactly where we had left it, the same number of inches from the dock, and there was only the merest suggestion of a breeze. This seemed an utterly enchanted sea, this lake you could leave to its own devices for a few hours and come back to, and find that it had not stirred, this constant and trustworthy body of water. In the shallows, the dark, water-soaked sticks and twigs, smooth and old, were undulating in clusters on the bottom against the clean ribbed sand, and the track of the mussel was plain. A school of minnows swam by, each minnow with its small individual shadow, doubling the attendance, so clear and sharp in the sunlight. Some of the other campers were in swimming, along the shore, one of them with a cake of soap, and the water felt thin and clear and unsubstantial. Over the years there had been this person with the cake of soap, this cultist, and here he was. There had been no years.

7   Up to the farmhouse to dinner through the teeming, dusty field, the road under our sneakers was only a two-track road. The middle track was missing, the one with the marks of the hooves and the splotches of dried, flaky manure. There had always been three tracks to choose from in choosing which track to walk in; now the choice was narrowed down to two. For a moment I missed terribly the middle alternative. But the way led past the tennis court, and something about the way it lay there in the sun reassured me; the tape had loosened along the back-line, the alleys were green with plantains and other weeds, and the net (installed in June and removed in September) sagged in the dry noon, and the whole place steamed with midday heat and hunger and emptiness. There was a choice of pie for dessert, and one was blueberry and one was apple, and the waitresses were the same country girls, there having been no passage of time, only the illusion of it as in a dropped curtain—the waitresses were still fifteen; their hair had been washed, that was the only difference—they had been to the movies and seen the pretty girls with the clean hair.

8   Summertime, oh summertime, pattern of life indelible, the fade-proof lake, the woods unshatterable, the pasture with the sweetfern and the juniper forever and ever, summer without end; this was the background, and the life along the

shore was the design, the cottagers with their innocent and tranquil design, their tiny docks with the flagpole and the American flag floating against the white clouds in the blue sky, the little paths over the roots of the trees leading from camp to camp and the paths leading back to the outhouses and the can of lime for sprinkling, and at the souvenir counters at the store the miniature birch-bark canoes and the post cards that showed things looking a little better than they looked. This was the American family at play, escaping the city heat, wondering whether the newcomers in the camp at the head of the cove were "common" or "nice," wondering whether it was true that the people who drove up for Sunday dinner at the farmhouse were turned away because there wasn't enough chicken.

It seemed to me, as I kept remembering all this, that those times and those   9 summers had been infinitely precious and worth saving. There had been jollity and peace and goodness. The arriving (at the beginning of August) had been so big a business in itself, at the railway station the farm wagon drawn up, the first smell of the pine-laden air, the first glimpse of the smiling farmer, and the great importance of the trunks and your father's enormous authority in such matters, and the feel of the wagon under you for the long ten-mile haul, and at the top of the last long hill catching the first view of the lake after eleven months of not seeing this cherished body of water. The shouts and cries of the other campers when they saw you, and the trunks to be unpacked, to give up their rich burden. (Arriving was less exciting nowadays, when you sneaked up in your car and parked it under a tree near the camp and took out the bags and in five minutes it was all over, no fuss, no loud wonderful fuss about trunks.)

Peace and goodness and jollity. The only thing that was wrong now, really, 10 was the sound of the place, an unfamiliar nervous sound of the outboard motors. This was the note that jarred, the one thing that would sometimes break the illusion and set the years moving. In those other summertimes all motors were inboard; and when they were at a little distance, the noise they made was a sedative, an ingredient of summer sleep. They were one-cylinder and two-cylinder engines, and some were make-and-break and some were jump-spark, but they all made a sleepy sound across the lake. The one-lungers throbbed and fluttered, and the twin-cylinder ones purred and purred, and that was a quiet sound too. But now the campers all had outboards. In the daytime, in the hot mornings, these motors made a petulant, irritable sound; at night, in the still evening when the afterglow lit the water, they whined about one's ears like mosquitoes. My boy loved our rented outboard, and his great desire was to achieve singlehanded mastery over it, and authority, and he soon learned the trick of choking it a little (but not too much), and the adjustment of the needle valve. Watching him I would remember the things you could do with the old one-cylinder engine with the heavy flywheel, how you could have it eating out of your hand if you got really close to it spiritually. Motor boats in those days didn't have clutches, and you would make a landing by shutting off the motor at the proper time and coasting in with a dead rudder. But there was a way of reversing them, if you learned the trick, by cutting the switch and putting it on again exactly on the final dying revolution of the flywheel, so that it would kick back against compression and begin reversing.

Approaching a dock in a strong following breeze, it was difficult to slow up sufficiently by the ordinary coasting method, and if a boy felt he had complete mastery over his motor, he was tempted to keep it running beyond its time and then
reverse it a few feet from the dock. It took a cool nerve, because if you threw the
switch a twentieth of a second too soon you would catch the flywheel when it still
had speed enough to go up past center, and the boat would leap ahead, charging
bull-fashion at the dock.

11   We had a good week at the camp. The bass were biting well and the sun
shone endlessly, day after day. We would be tired at night and lie down in the
accumulated heat of the little bedrooms after the long hot day and the breeze
would stir almost imperceptibly outside and the smell of the swamp drift in
through the rusty screens. Sleep would come easily and in the morning the red
squirrel would be on the roof, tapping out his gay routine. I kept remembering
everything, lying in bed in the mornings—the small steamboat that had a long
rounded stern like the lip of a Ubangi, and how quietly she ran on the moonlight
sails, when the older boys played their mandolins and the girls sang and we ate
doughnuts dipped in sugar, and how sweet the music was on the water in the
shining night, and what it had felt like to think about girls then. After breakfast
we would go up to the store and the things were in the same place—minnows in
a bottle, the plugs and spinners disarranged and pawed over by the youngsters
from the boys' camp, the fig newtons and the Beeman's gum. Outside, the road
was tarred and cars stood in front of the store. Inside, all was just as it had always
been, except there was more Coca-Cola and not so much Moxie and root beer
and birch beer and sarsaparilla. We would walk out with a bottle of pop apiece
and sometimes the pop would backfire up our noses and hurt. We explored the
streams, quietly, where the turtles slid off the sunny logs and dug their way into
the soft bottom, and we lay on the town wharf and fed worms to the tame bass.
Everywhere we went I had trouble making out which was I, the one walking at
my side, the one walking in my pants.

12   One afternoon while we were there at that lake a thunderstorm came up. It
was like the revival of an old melodrama that I had seen long ago with childish
awe. The second-act climax of the drama of the electrical disturbance over a lake
in America had not changed in any important respect. This was the big scene, still
the big scene. The whole thing was so familiar, the first feeling of oppression and
heat and a general air around camp of not wanting to go very far away. In midafter-
noon (it was all the same) a curious darkening of the sky, and a lull in everything that had made life tick; and then the way the boats suddenly swung the
other way at their moorings with the coming of a breeze out of the new quarter,
and the premonitory rumble. Then the kettle drum, then the snare, then the bass
drum and cymbals, then crackling light against the dark, and the gods grinning
and licking their chops in the hills. Afterward the calm, the rain steadily rustling
in the calm lake, the return of light and hope and spirits, and the campers running
out in joy and relief to go swimming in the rain, their bright cries perpetuating the
deathless joke about how they were getting simply drenched, and the children
screaming with delight at the new sensation of bathing in the rain, and the joke

about getting drenched linking the generations in a strong indestructible chain. And the comedian who waded in carrying an umbrella.

When the others went swimming my son said he was going in too. He pulled 13 his dripping trunks from the line where they had hung all through the shower, and wrung them out. Languidly, and with no thought of going in, I watched him, his hard little body, skinny and bare, saw him wince slightly as he pulled up around his vitals the small, soggy, icy garment. As he buckled the swollen belt suddenly my groin felt the chill of death.

COMPREHENSION

1. At what point in the essay do you begin to sense White's main purpose? What is his purpose? What type of reader might his purpose appeal to?
2. What motivates White to return to the lake in Maine? Explain the "simple transposition" that he mentions in paragraph 4. List the illustrations that he gives of this phenomenon. What change does he detect in the lake?
3. Explain the significance of White's last sentence. Where are there foreshadowings of this statement?

RHETORIC

1. Describe White's use of figurative language in paragraphs 2, 10, and 12.
2. Identify those words and phrases that White invokes to establish the sense of mystery about the lake. Why are these words and their connotations important to the nature of the illusion that he describes?
3. Explain the organization of the essay in terms of the following paragraph units: 1–4, 5–7, 8–10, and 11–13. Explain the function of paragraphs 8 and 12.
4. There are many vivid and unusual descriptive details in this essay—for example, the dragonfly in paragraph 5 and the two-track road in paragraph 7. How does White create symbolic overtones for these descriptive details and others? Why is the lake itself a complex symbol? Explain with reference to paragraph 6.
5. Describe the persona that White creates for himself in the essay. How does this persona function?
6. What is the relation between the introductory and concluding paragraphs, specifically in terms of irony of statement?

WRITING

1. Explore in an essay the theme of nostalgia in "Once More to the Lake." What are the beauties and the dangers of nostalgia? Can the past ever be recaptured or relived? Justify your answer.
2. Referring to revisiting a site on the lake that he had visited years before with his father, White remarks in paragraph 4, "I could tell that it was going to be pretty much the same as it had been before." How does this observation reflect the general sentiment White has about the role and function of the family? Respond to the question in an analytical essay.

3. **Writing an Argument:** Argue for or against the proposition that nostalgia can obscure the true nature of family relationships and even suppress painful memories that
should be confronted.

NETWORKING
Applying Digital and Multimedia Literacies

Alluding to Print on the Web: Do a Google Images search for *once more to the
lake*. Explore how various people around the world used this caption or description
with their own photographs, blog entries, or professional articles. Choose three or
four examples and discuss how they use this allusion to the E. B. White essay. Do
they mention the piece itself, or only its title? What power of nostalgia might this essay possess in and of itself, for readers who have known it for years? What books,
poems, stories, or songs make you nostalgic—for family, friends, a particular time in
your life? How does thinking about these specific examples influence your response
to question 3 under Writing?

Street Scenes

Ann Hood

*Ann Hood (b. 1956) is a prize-winning novelist and essayist. She was born and raised
in West Warwick, Rhode Island, and received a BA from the University of Rhode Island
in 1978. Subsequently she was a flight attendant for Trans World Airlines until 1986.
"As a flight attendant," she recalls, "I carried a notebook with me and wrote on the
subway to the airport, on the plane, and in hotels on layovers. In fact that's where I
wrote* Somewhere Off the Coast of Maine" *(Hood's first novel, published in 1987).
Hood has published a dozen novels, most recently* Little Lion *(2011). She has also
written two memoirs and a short story collection,* An Ornithologist's Guide to Life
(2004). Her essays and fiction have appeared in such diverse publications as McCall's,
the Paris Review, *the* New York Times, *and* Cosmopolitan. *In this piece from the
Spring 2011 issue of* American Scholar, *Hood finds herself driving on a road that for
her links past, present, and future.*

1   Yesterday, I did it again. Driving from my house in Providence to my mother's house
in West Warwick, 12 miles down Route 95 South, I took Exit 12, the same exit I've
taken to go home since I got my driver's license in 1972. Off the exit, I come up by
the Toys R Us on my right and the junior college on my left. At the light sits Rhode
Island's first mall, built in October of 1967, when I was 10 years old. I got my first pair
of bell-bottoms there, and a Nehru jacket, and more 45s than I can remember. At
some point, while I lived out of state, they changed its name from Midland Mall to the

Rhode Island Mall. But I still call it Midland Mall. At the next light, I find myself looking at the Dunkin' Donuts where my mother would take me at three in the morning
for coffee and a plain cruller when I was in high school and suffered insomnia.

That's when I realized I'd done it again. I'd followed the route that is as familiar 2
to me as my mother's Chloe perfume–cigarette smoke smell, as familiar as the
pattern of freckles on my chest. Ahead of me sits River Street, the street that should
lead me on a meandering series of curves and turns until I reach the hill on top of
which my mother's house sits. But during the flooding here in Rhode Island last
spring, the Pawtuxet River rose higher than it had in a hundred years. The shopping
mall, Route 95, and River Street were under water. River Street is closed indefinitely.
What I see from the driver's seat of my VW are orange cones keeping me out.

For most of my childhood, River Street connected me to the rest of the world. 3
It was not a broad or beautiful street. It had potholes. Lots of them. Tired mill
houses painted off-shades of green and yellow lined half of it. The other half had
some commercial buildings: a barber shop, an Italian deli, a gun store. The roller
rink sat in a lot farther back, long-abandoned railroad tracks cut the street in half,
and a small bridge on one end stretched over the Pawtuxet River, which was
brown and frothy back in the '60s. But at the other end there was a Dunkin' Donuts, and beyond that pink square building was the world: two shopping malls,
two fancy restaurants (The Golden Lantern and The Duncan Fyffe), and the on-
ramp to Route 95. Route 95 could take me to Maine or all the way to Florida.
When it first opened, I imagined that all I had to do was get on that highway and
magically I would be under palm trees eating oranges.

Those railroad tracks led to a big empty lot that remained deserted except for 4
litter most of the year. But every August a carnival came to town and set up its
flashy rides and impossible-to-win games there. I lost my first tooth at that carnival, biting into a candy apple. The highlight of the carnival was the Little Miss
Natick Beauty Pageant, and the summer I was six, my mother entered me in it.
My Auntie Julia, a seamstress, sewed me a leopard bikini. My Great Aunt Nuneen
set my hair in rags to make perfect banana curls. Because I had no talent to speak
of, my mother taught me a poem to recite for the talent competition:

> I have 10 little fingers and 10 little toes,
> Long blonde hair and a turned up nose,
> A great big smile and a cute little figure,
> Stay away boys! Till I get bigger!

She choreographed it, too, showing me when to hold up my fingers and how 5
to sashay my hips. For the last two lines, I marched right up to the judges' table
and wagged my fingers at them. With that, I won Little Miss Natick 1963. I got a
giant trophy, my picture in the paper, and a ride in a parade perched on top of my
Uncle Eddie's white Cadillac convertible. The mother of one of the other contestants stole my leopard bikini, cut it into shreds, and threw it in a swimming pool
because her daughter lost. It was that kind of town. And River Street, with its
shabby beauty, epitomized it.

6   I pull into the Dunkin' Donuts parking lot. I have a choice. I can backtrack, head north again on Route 5 and take the shortcut, past the sewage treatment plant. Or I can continue south, down Route 2, which is now clogged with strip malls and big-box stores. Neither option feels right. For 38 years, River Street has taken me where I want to go. It took me to get those bell-bottoms. It took me to college, to the airport and train station. It took me to meet lovers and friends in far-flung places. It is the street I traveled on a hot summer day in 1982 when I learned that my brother Skip had died and I needed to get home. It is the street that led to the hospital where I was born and where my father died. For 38 years, River Street has taken me back home.

7   I get out of my car and the smell of doughnuts surrounds me like a hug. Growing up, I wanted nothing more than to go as far away as I could, way beyond that shiny Dunkin' Donuts. Now, a middle-aged woman, I want to drive down this street and feel the bumps of its untended road, let my body lean into the wide curve near where my cousin Anthony had a deli, see the little girl I once was, alone and friendless in my elementary school playground playing jacks, and the sassy teenager I became, storming out of Sacred Heart Church because I disagreed with the priest. Is it possible to love a street lined with years of disappointment and the echoes of carnival laughter? With a gun shop and a roller rink and mill houses? Standing there, yearning to travel it again, I realize I do love that street. River Street, which used to point to my future, now holds the connection to my past, to my long-ago childhood dreams and hopes, in its waterlogged arms. From that Dunkin' Donuts parking lot, I stand at its edge, to catch a glimpse of them.

COMPREHENSION

1. Hood speaks of a compulsive activity. What is it, and why is this compulsion revealing? What is her purpose in sharing this behavior with readers?
2. According to Hood, what was her childhood like? Who were the principal people in her life?
3. What ultimately is Hood's perception of childhood? How does childhood relate to her present circumstance and to future prospects?

RHETORIC

1. Hood is best known as a novelist. What elements of fiction do you detect in the essay? (For example, how does Hood create a certain mood or atmosphere?) Identify specific sentences and passages to support your response.
2. What is Hood's thesis? Where does this main idea appear or must we infer it? Explain.
3. Hood moves between present and past tenses in constructing her narrative. What is her purpose and what is the effect?
4. How might the repeated reference to Dunkin' Donuts function as a symbol in this essay?
5. How does Hood link her introductory and concluding paragraphs? In what ways do these two units frame her intended meaning?

WRITING

1. Write a narrative and descriptive essay about a place or route that is important to you and that you frequently return to.
2. Analyze three or more events in your childhood that are sources of influence for you today.
3. **Writing an Argument:** Hood implies that childhood shapes adult life and behavior. How do you feel about this idea? Are we inevitably molded by childhood or can we escape it if desired? Compose an argumentative essay in response to these questions.

NETWORKING
Applying Digital and Multimedia Literacies

Do a keyword search in your library's online databases for popular and scholarly articles about *family values*. Write an extended analysis about the result of this initial search. Which databases did you search? What kinds of sources did they (and these keywords) lead you to? If the term *family values* is defined in any of the abstracts you encountered, compile a few of these definitions and apply them to the essays by White and Hood.

Synthesis: Classic and Contemporary Questions for Comparison

1. Compare and contrast the tone of each writer. How does tone affect purpose? How does it affect mood? Select at least three passages from White and three from Hood that demonstrate how their tones differ. Do they offer any hints as to the "voice" or personality of the writers? Why or why not?
2. Consider that White was born in 1899 and Hood in 1956. What are their respective world views? What variables help us distinguish their concerns and outlooks—for example, gender, class, and environment?
3. What central values does each author have regarding the family? How are they similar? How do they differ? How do their values reflect their times?

An American Childhood

Annie Dillard

Annie Dillard *(b. 1945 in Pittsburgh) received her BA and MA degrees from Hollins College. Her first book,* Pilgrim at Tinker Creek *(1975), won the Pulitzer Prize for general nonfiction. Her other published works of nonfiction include* Teaching a Stone to Talk *(1982) and* An American Childhood *(1987). Dillard expanded her range of writing with the publication of her first novel,* The Living *(1992), and her latest novel,*

The Maytrees (2007). She has received awards from the National Endowment for the Arts and the Guggenheim Foundation as well as many other sources. As an essayist, poet, memoirist, and literary critic, she focuses her themes on the relationships among the self, nature, religion, and faith. Her writing is recognizable by its observations of the minutiae of life and its search for meaning in unlikely places, such as a stone or an insect. In this passage from An American Childhood, *the author gives us a portrait of her mother by focusing on her small idiosyncrasies of speech, gesture, and attitude.*

1   One Sunday afternoon Mother wandered through our kitchen, where Father was making a sandwich and listening to the ball game. The Pirates were playing the New York Giants at Forbes Field. In those days, the Giants had a utility infielder named Wayne Terwilliger. Just as Mother passed through, the radio announcer cried—with undue drama—"Terwilliger bunts one!"

2   "Terwilliger bunts one?" Mother cried back, stopped short. She turned. "Is that English?"

3   "The player's name is Terwilliger," Father said. "He bunted."

4   "That's marvelous," Mother said. "'Terwilliger bunts one.' No wonder you listen to baseball. 'Terwilliger bunts one.'"

5   For the next seven or eight years, Mother made this surprising string of syllables her own. Testing a microphone, she repeated, "Terwilliger bunts one"; testing a pen or a typewriter, she wrote it. If, as happened surprisingly often in the course of various improvised gags, she pretended to whisper something else in my ear, she actually whispered, "Terwilliger bunts one." Whenever someone used a French phrase, or a Latin one, she answered solemnly, "Terwilliger bunts one." If Mother had had, like Andrew Carnegie, the opportunity to cook up a motto for a coat of arms, hers would have read simply and tellingly, "Terwilliger bunts one." (Carnegie's was "Death to Privilege.")

6   She served us with other words and phrases. On a Florida trip, she repeated tremulously, "That . . . is a royal poinciana." I don't remember the tree; I remember the thrill in her voice. She pronounced it carefully, and spelled it. She also liked to say "portulaca."

7   The drama of the words "Tamiami Trail" stirred her, we learned on the same Florida trip. People built Tampa on one coast, and they built Miami on another. Then—the height of visionary ambition and folly—they piled a slow, tremendous road through the terrible Everglades to connect them. To build the road, men stood sunk in muck to their armpits. They fought off cottonmouth moccasins and six-foot alligators. They slept in boats, wet. They blasted muck with dynamite, cut jungle with machetes; they laid logs, dragged drilling machines, hauled dredges, heaped limestone. The road took fourteen years to build up by the shovelful, a Panama Canal in reverse, and cost hundreds of lives from tropical, mosquito-carried diseases. Then, capping it all, some genius thought of the word Tamiami: they called the road from Tampa to Miami, this very road under our spinning wheels, the Tamiami Trail. Some called it Alligator Alley. Anyone could drive over this road without a thought.

8   Hearing this, moved, I thought all the suffering of road building was worth it (it wasn't my suffering), now that we had this new thing to hang these new words on—Alligator Alley for those who liked things cute, and, for connoisseurs

like Mother, for lovers of the human drama in all its boldness and terror, the Tamiami Trail.

Back home, Mother cut clips from reels of talk, as it were, and played them 9 back at leisure. She noticed that many Pittsburghers confuse "leave" and "let." One kind relative brightened our morning by mentioning why she'd brought her son to visit: "He wanted to come with me, so I left him." Mother filled in Amy and me on locutions we missed. "I can't do it on Friday," her pretty sister told a crowded dinner party, "because Friday's the day I lay in the stores."

(All unconsciously, though, we ourselves used some pure Pittsburghisms. We 10 said "tele pole," pronounced "telly pole," for that splintery sidewalk post I loved to climb. We said "slippy"—the sidewalks are "slippy." We said, "That's all the farther I could go." And we said, as Pittsburghers do say, "This glass needs washed," or "The dog needs walked"—a usage our father eschewed; he knew it was not standard English, nor even comprehensible English, but he never let on.)

"Spell 'poinsettia,'" Mother would throw out at me, smiling with pleasure. 11 "Spell 'sherbet.'" The idea was not to make us whizzes, but, quite the contrary, to remind us—and I, especially, needed reminding—that we didn't know it all just yet.

"There's a deer standing in the front hall," she told me one quiet evening in 12 the country.

"Really?"   13

"No. I just wanted to tell you something once without your saying, 'I know.'"   14

Supermarkets in the middle 1950s began luring, or bothering, customers by 15 giving out Top Value Stamps or Green Stamps. When, shopping with Mother, we got to the head of the checkout line, the checker, always a young man, asked, "Save stamps?"

"No," Mother replied genially, week after week, "I build model airplanes." I 16 believe she originated this line. It took me years to determine where the joke lay.

Anyone who met her verbal challenges she adored. She had surgery on one of 17 her eyes. On the operating table, just before she conked out, she appealed feelingly to the surgeon, saying, as she had been planning to say for weeks, "Will I be able to play the piano?" "Not on me," the surgeon said. "You won't pull that old one on me."

It was, indeed, an old one. The surgeon was supposed to answer, "Yes, my 18 dear, brave woman, you will be able to play the piano after this operation," to which Mother intended to reply, "Oh, good, I've always wanted to play the piano." This pat scenario bored her; she loved having it interrupted. It must have galled her that usually her acquaintances were so predictably unalert; it must have galled her that, for the length of her life, she could surprise everyone so continually, so easily, when she had been the same all along. At any rate, she loved anyone who, as she put it, saw it coming, and called her on it.

She regarded the instructions on bureaucratic forms as straight lines. "Do you 19 advocate the overthrow of the United States government by force or violence?" After some thought she wrote, "Force." She regarded children, even babies, as straight men. When Molly learned to crawl, Mother delighted in buying her gowns with drawstrings at the bottom, like Swee'pea's, because, as she explained energetically, you could easily step on the drawstring without the baby's noticing, so that she crawled and crawled and crawled and never got anywhere except into a small ball at the gown's top.

20 When we children were young, she mothered us tenderly and dependably; as we got older, she resumed her career of anarchism. She collared us into her gags. If she answered the phone on a wrong number, she told the caller, "Just a minute," and dragged the receiver to Amy or me, saying, "Here, take this, your name is Cecile," or, worse, just, "It's for you." You had to think on your feet. But did you want to perform well as Cecile, or did you want to take pity on the wretched caller?

21   During a family trip to the Highland Park Zoo, Mother and I were alone for a minute. She approached a young couple holding hands on a bench by the seals, and addressed the young man in dripping tones: "Where have you been? Still got those baby-blue eyes; always did slay me. And this"—a swift nod at the dumbstruck young woman, who had removed her hand from the man's—"must be the one you were telling me about. She's not so bad, really, as you used to make out. But listen, you know how I miss you, you know where to reach me, same old place. And there's Ann over there—see how she's grown? See the blue eyes?"

22   And off she sashayed, taking me firmly by the hand, and leading us around briskly past the monkey house and away. She cocked an ear back, and both of us heard the desperate man begin, in a high-pitched wail, "I swear, I never saw her before in my life . . ."

23 On a long, sloping beach by the ocean, she lay stretched out sunning with Father and friends, until the conversation gradually grew tedious, when without forethought she gave a little push with her heel and rolled away. People were stunned. She rolled deadpan and apparently effortlessly, arms and legs extended and tidy, down the beach to the distant water's edge, where she lay at ease just as she had been, but half in the surf, and well out of earshot.

24   She dearly loved to fluster people by throwing out a game's rules at a whim— when she was getting bored, losing in a dull sort of way, and when everybody else was taking it too seriously. If you turned your back, she moved the checkers around on the board. When you got them all straightened out, she denied she'd touched them; the next time you turned your back, she lined them up on the rug or hid them under your chair. In a betting rummy game called Michigan, she routinely played out of turn, or called out a card she didn't hold, or counted backward, simply to amuse herself by causing an uproar and watching the rest of us do double-takes and have fits. (Much later, when serious suitors came to call, Mother subjected them to this fast card game as a trial by ordeal; she used it as an intelligence test and a measure of spirit. If the poor man could stay a round without breaking down or running out, he got to marry one of us, if he still wanted to.)

25   She excelled at bridge, playing fast and boldly, but when the stakes were low and the hands dull, she bid slams for the devilment of it, or raised her opponents' suit to bug them, or showed her hand, or tossed her cards in a handful behind her back in a characteristic swift motion accompanied by a vibrantly innocent look. It drove our stolid father crazy. The hand was over before it began, and the guests were appalled. How do you score it, who deals now, what do you do with a crazy person who is having so much fun? Or they were down seven, and the guests were appalled. "Pam!" "Dammit, Pam!" He groaned. What ails such people? What on earth possesses them? He rubbed his face.

She was an unstoppable force; she never let go. When we moved across town, 26 she persuaded the U.S. Post Office to let her keep her old address—forever— because she'd had stationery printed. I don't know how she did it. Every new post office worker, over decades, needed to learn that although the Doaks' mail is addressed to here, it is delivered to there.

Mother's energy and intelligence suited her for a greater role in a larger 27 arena—mayor of New York, say—than the one she had. She followed American politics closely; she had been known to vote for Democrats. She saw how things should be run, but she had nothing to run but our household. Even there, small minds bugged her; she was smarter than the people who designed the things she had to use all day for the length of her life.

"Look," she said. "Whoever designed this corkscrew never used one. Why 28 would anyone sell it without trying it out?" So she invented a better one. She showed me a drawing of it. The spirit of American enterprise never faded in Mother. If capitalizing and tooling up had been as interesting as theorizing and thinking up, she would have fired up a new factory every week, and chaired several hundred corporations.

"It grieves me," she would say, "it grieves my heart," that the company that made 29 one superior product packaged it poorly, or took the wrong tack in its advertising. She knew, as she held the thing mournfully in her two hands, that she'd never find another. She was right. We children wholly sympathized, and so did Father; what could she do, what could anyone do, about it? She was Samson in chains. She paced.

She didn't like the taste of stamps so she didn't lick stamps; she licked the 30 corner of the envelope instead. She glued sandpaper to the sides of kitchen drawers, and under kitchen cabinets, so she always had a handy place to strike a match. She designed, and hounded workmen to build against all norms, doubly wide kitchen counters and elevated bathroom sinks. To splint a finger, she stuck it in a lightweight cigar tube. Conversely, to protect a pack of cigarettes, she carried it in a Band-Aid box. She drew plans for an over-the-finger toothbrush for babies, an oven rack that slid up and down, and—the family favorite—Lendalarm. Lendalarm was a beeper you attached to books (or tools) you loaned friends. After ten days, the beeper sounded. Only the rightful owner could silence it.

She repeatedly reminded us of P. T. Barnum's dictum: You could sell anything 31 to anybody if you marketed it right. The adman who thought of making Americans believe they needed underarm deodorant was a visionary. So, too, was the hero who made a success of a new product, Ivory soap. The executives were horrified, Mother told me, that a cake of this stuff floated. Soap wasn't supposed to float. Anyone would be able to tell it was mostly whipped-up air. Then some inspired adman made a leap: Advertise that it floats. Flaunt it. The rest is history.

She respected the rare few who broke through to new ways. "Look," she'd 32 say, "here's an intelligent apron." She called upon us to admire intelligent control knobs and intelligent pan handles, intelligent andirons and picture frames and knife sharpeners. She questioned everything, every pair of scissors, every knitting needle, gardening glove, tape dispenser. Hers was a restless mental vigor that just about ignited the dumb household objects with its force.

33   Torpid conformity was a kind of sin; it was stupidity itself, the mighty stream
against which Mother would never cease to struggle. If you held no minority opinions, or if you failed to risk total ostracism for them daily, the world would be a
better place without you.

34   Always I heard Mother's emotional voice asking Amy and me the same few
questions: "Is that your own idea? Or somebody else's?" "*Giant* is a good movie," I
pronounced to the family at dinner. "Oh, really?" Mother warmed to these occasions. She all but rolled up her sleeves. She knew I hadn't seen it. "Is that your
considered opinion?"

35   She herself held many unpopular, even fantastic, positions. She was scathingly
sarcastic about the McCarthy hearings while they took place, right on our livingroom television; she frantically opposed Father's wait-and-see calm. "We don't know
enough about it," he said. "I do," she said. "I know all I need to know."

36   She asserted, against all opposition, that people who lived in trailer parks were
not bad but simply poor, and had as much right to settle on beautiful land, such as rural
Ligonier, Pennsylvania, as did the oldest of families in the finest of hidden houses.
Therefore, the people who owned trailer parks, and sought zoning changes to permit
trailer parks, needed our help. Her profound belief that the country-club pool sweeper
was a person, and that the department-store saleslady, the bus driver, telephone
operator, and house-painter were people, and even in groups the steelworkers who
carried pickets and the Christmas shoppers who clogged intersections were people—
this was a conviction common enough in democratic Pittsburgh, but not altogether
common among our friends' parents, or even, perhaps, among our parents' friends.

37   Opposition emboldened Mother, and she would take on anybody on any issue—
the chairman of the board, at a cocktail party, on the current strike; she would fly
at him in a flurry of passion, as a songbird selflessly attacks a big hawk.

38   "Eisenhower's going to win," I announced after school. She lowered her magazine and looked me in the eyes: "How do you know?" I was doomed. It was fatal
to say, "Everyone says so." We all knew well what happened. "Do you consult this
Everyone before you make your decisions? What if Everyone decided to round up
all the Jews?" Mother knew there was no danger of cowing me. She simply tried
to keep us all awake. And in fact it was always clear to Amy and me, and to Molly
when she grew old enough to listen, that if our classmates came to cruelty, just as
much as if the neighborhood or the nation came to madness, we were expected to
take, and would be each separately capable of taking, a stand.

COMPREHENSION

1. Dillard creates a picture of her mother's personality through a number of anecdotes
    and explanations. How would you sum up the mother's personality?
2. Dillard's mother appears to have a special appreciation for words and language. To
    what purpose does she apply this appreciation? What effect does it have on her family
    and acquaintances?
3. What values does the mother hold? What behaviors and attitudes does she abhor and
    discourage?

RHETORIC

1. In paragraph 7, Dillard explains that the highway from Tampa to Miami is referred to either as "Tamiami Trail" or "Alligator Alley." What is the connotation of each of these terms? Why does her mother prefer to call it "Tamiami Trail"?
2. The author herself seems to have inherited a special fascination for language. Study her use of dashes and semicolons in paragraphs 26 and 27. How do they help contribute to energetic writing?
3. What are the functions of the spaces between paragraphs 19 and 20, 22 and 23, and 32 and 33? How do these divisions contribute to the structure of the essay as a whole?
4. How does Dillard use her writing talents to create paragraph 8 out of one long sentence? What other examples can you provide of long sentences in the essay? How do they contribute to the overall style of the writing?
5. What is the overall emotional "tone" of the writer toward her subject—admiring, or loving, or cautionary? What adjectives does she use in describing her mother that provide the reader with clues to the tone?
6. Dillard quotes her mother directly on several occasions. Can we assume that she is quoting precisely, given that the essay was written years after the incidents described? Does it matter?
7. The final paragraph not only provides closure to the essay but transmits a lesson the mother wants her family to learn. How do the style and structure of this paragraph contribute to the ultimate message of the essay? In other words, how does the form help convey the meaning?

WRITING

1. Write a descriptive essay about someone you know very well, using at least five anecdotes from that person's life, so that by the end of the essay, we have a mental picture of your subject's personality, values, and attitudes. This could be someone in your biological family, or someone else you are or were very close to.
2. Describe an incident in your life when the unexpected taught you an important lesson.
3. **Writing an Argument:** Argue for or against the proposition that an effective parent should have—at least—a touch of unconventionality.

NETWORKING
Applying Digital and Multimedia Literacies

Creating a Playlist Narrative: Enhance your response to question 1 under Writing by creating a playlist of five songs that contribute to your description of that person you are or were close to. For each song, write a short paragraph about what it says about either this person or your relationship with him or her. The specific song might have a story behind it—if so, tell it—or it might describe (literally or figuratively) some aspect or quality of that person's character, appearance, beliefs, experiences, interests, location, talents, regrets, or hopes. What is the music capable of describing about this person that words couldn't?

In Sable and Dark Glasses

Joan Didion

Joan Didion *(b. 1934) is a celebrated American essayist, nonfiction writer, novelist, and screenwriter. Born in Sacramento, California, Didion grew up as a self-described "shy, bookish child" who felt most at home in libraries as her family moved from place to place. Didion graduated from the University of California, Berkeley in 1956. In her senior year, she won first place in an essay contest sponsored by* Vogue, *with the prize an entry-level position at the magazine. During her two years at* Vogue, *Didion rose to associate feature editor; wrote her first novel,* Run, River *(1963); and met her future husband, the writer John Gregory Dunne. In 1964, Didion and Dunne married and moved to Los Angeles, which would be their home until Dunne died in 2004. Among Didion's best known works are the novel* A Book of Common Prayer *(1977); the nonfiction books* Slouching Toward Bethlehem *(1968),* The White Album *(1979),* Miami *(1987), and* The Year of Magical Thinking *(2006); and the screenplay for the film* A Star is Born *(1974). In this essay, published in* Vogue *in 2011, Didion recounts vivid scenes from her childhood.*

1   I never had much interest in being a child. As a way of being it seemed flat, failed to engage. When I was in fact a child, six and seven and eight years old, I was utterly baffled by the enthusiasm with which my cousin Brenda, a year and a half younger, accepted her mother's definition of her as someone who needed to go to bed at six-thirty and finish every bite of three vegetables, one of them yellow, with every meal. Brenda was also encouraged to make a perfect white sauce, and to keep a chart showing a gold star for every time she brushed her teeth. I, meanwhile, was trying to improve the dinner hour by offering what I called "lettuce cocktails" (a single leaf of iceberg lettuce and crushed ice in a stemmed glass), and inventing elaborate scenarios featuring myself as an adult, specifically an adult 24 years old, an age on which I settled because my mother had assured me that 24 was the best, her favorite year. Over those years during which I was determined to bypass childhood, she and I discussed this question of age at a length she must have found tedious, but perhaps she did not: We are talking here about a woman, my mother, who tied what she construed to be her first gray hair in a bow and mailed it to her sister Gloria, she of the yellow-vegetable dictum. I once asked her what made 24 so memorable. It seemed that she had been married when she was 24. It seemed that I had been born when she was 24. It seemed that 24 was (I can hardly believe our discussions of age deteriorated to this, but possibly the lettuce cocktails had edged us both into a casino mode) her "lucky number."

2   My own fantasies of what life would be like at 24 tended to the more spectacular. In these dramas of my own devise I was sometimes wearing a sable coat, although I had never seen one. I was wearing this sable coat in an urban setting that looks in retrospect not unlike Shubert Alley. I was at other times walking on a moor, although

I had not yet read those English novels in which moors figured heavily. But here is how I most often preferred to visualize myself: not on a moor, not in Shubert Alley, but standing on the steps of a public building somewhere in South America (Argentina comes first to mind, although Argentina was like the sable coat, never actually seen, more concept than reality), wearing dark glasses and avoiding paparazzi. If you were to have asked me why I was standing on the steps of this public building in Argentina, I would have had a ready answer: I was standing on the steps of this public building in Argentina because I was getting a divorce. Hence the dark glasses, hence the paparazzi. I would let other six-year-olds (Brenda, say) imagine their wedding days, their princess dresses, their Juliet caps and seed pearls and clouds of white tulle: I had moved briskly on to the day of my (Buenos Aires) divorce, and the black silk mantilla the occasion would clearly require.

As a matter of fact I already had a black silk mantilla, dredged by me from one 3 of the many mysterious boxes in which my mother kept the clues to being 24. In another of those boxes I found the Jean Patou cape, red velvet with a white fur collar, that she reported having worn when she left her wedding reception. I also found the ankle-length red lace dress she wore when she "gave teas," a form of entertainment more popular than anyone might imagine it to have been in the part of rural California in which we then lived. My mother "gave teas" the way other mothers breathed. Her own mother "gave teas." All of their friends "gave teas," each involving butter cookies extruded from a metal press and pastel bonbons ordered from See's. "Giving a tea" was a process that entailed, as I had observed it, arranging translucent slices of lemon on white Wedgwood plates and spreading little pinwheel sandwiches with cream cheese and watercress, per the same Boston Cooking School Cookbook from which Brenda was being taught to make the perfect white sauce. And then, the most important step of all, the key to the eventual effect, the very point of giving a tea: taking that red lace dress from its box and dropping it over its own slip of ivory chiffon.

There were eventually other clues to adult life to be found in my mother's 4 boxes. There was the white silk shirt strewn with star-shaped silver sequins that she wore when my father was stationed at Peterson Field in Colorado Springs and she took me ice-skating at the Broadmoor Hotel. There was her petit-point evening bag. There was the plaid seersucker suit in which she crossed the country by train when, en route to meet my father in North Carolina in 1942, we traveled from Los Angeles to New Orleans on the Southern Pacific's Sunset Limited, a transcontinental train so crowded in those early days of World War II that my mother and small brother and I spent much of the trip standing in the couplings between the cars. I remember the rancid smell of the grease in the couplings. I remember a sailor on the train, a survivor of the USS *Wasp*, who once at a siding somewhere in the Southwest got off the train and came back with a Coca-Cola for my mother and a present for me, a silver-and-turquoise Navajo bracelet. I still today have the bracelet, too small now for my wrist. I also still today have snapshots taken on that trip. In these snapshots, which mainly show my mother and brother and me at moments when we have just missed or are just about to miss one or another key connection, for example looking forlorn between trains in Union Station in Los Angeles or for another example looking somewhat less forlorn between trains on the veranda of the St. Charles Hotel in New Orleans, my mother is wearing the plaid seersucker suit, spectator pumps, and, pinned at her temples, white silk gardenias.

5   From the snapshot evidence of the period, which shows me in pleated skirts and handknit cardigans and what appears to have been a Brownie uniform, she would have been less than entirely on board for the sable coat and the Buenos Aires divorce. The sable coat and the Buenos Aires divorce would have been more my grandmother's territory. It was my grandmother who knit the cardigans, yet it was also my grandmother who presented a more evolved idea of how I should appear to the world. She gave me Stroock vicuna coats, Lilly Daché hats, and flasks of Elizabeth Arden On Dit sealed with translucent paper and gold thread. The Lilly Daché hats were meant to encourage me to go to church. The Elizabeth Arden On Dit was meant to encourage me to get over the mumps. Brenda, as the next oldest granddaughter, was also the beneficiary of this method of child-rearing. When our grandmother took us for the day to San Francisco she ordered us Dungeness Crab Louis at El Prado and bought us dewy bunches of violets at the flower stand across Union Square. Both my mother and her sister Gloria seemed to feel a pro forma obligation to register disapproval of these tactics. "What will they have to look forward to?" I remember Gloria asking my grandmother.

6   "Let that be the greatest of your worries," I remember my grandmother answering.

7   Meanwhile I made up games to play with Brenda. In one game we were getting on an elevator at I. Magnin in San Francisco when we heard the operator speak. This is what the operator always said: "There is only room for one more." The operator had a spectral white face and spoke in an eerie voice. The spectral white face and eerie voice should (always) have warned us but we (always) missed the signals: This I. Magnin elevator was of course about to plunge, with Brenda and me on board, to the bottom of its shaft. I recognize this now as one more version of the hoary tale in which some stranger with a spectral face (an elevator operator, a nurse, a hotel clerk, a taxi driver, or, better still, a hearse driver) either does or does not save the life of the protagonist, by delivering the line about "only room for one more." The best version of this takes place not in an elevator but in a hospital, where the (inevitable) young woman discovers (too late) that the corridor she is about to enter—the corridor, of course, where there is "only room for one more"—leads to the hospital morgue.

8   This was Brenda's favorite game. I am ashamed to say that I could scare her witless with it, and often did. "Do only room for one more again," she would plead, and I would. My own favorite among our games, and this may or may not say something about the difference between growing up on yellow vegetables and growing up on lettuce cocktails, involved going page by page through an issue of *Vogue* and choosing what to "buy." Brenda could buy whatever she wanted from the left-hand pages; I was limited to the right. The point was to see which of us could assemble, given the options only as they turned up, the most desirable wardrobe. The rules, which I invented even as we turned the glossy pages, were quite strict. Either editorial or advertising pages qualified, but every page had to be considered. Dismissal of a page required a "reason," provided by me.

I am mortified to remember that I prevailed on Brenda to play this mindless 9
game for hours. I am also mortified to remember that 20 years later, when I was
no longer in danger of being mistaken for a child and Brenda herself was getting
married, I was still trying to run the game, make the rules, have it my way. There
would be at Brenda's wedding, I promised her, nothing banal, nothing ordinary.
She could forget the princess dress. She could forget the Juliet cap. She could
forget the seed pearls, the clouds of white tulle. I had decreed: There would instead be checked gingham and wreaths of daisies. I was the older cousin. We
would therefore do it my way. I myself would make the wreaths.

When the day of the wedding arrived I did make the wreaths, cutting tiny slits 10
in each stem and threading the daisies into one another. Cutting the slits and
threading the daisies took longer than I had planned. I was in fact still making the
wreaths as the guests were being seated. The bridesmaids waited in their checked
gingham dresses. Brenda waited in her own checked gingham dress. Her wedding, she later pointed out, turned out to be one more of my lettuce-cocktail
moments. That she might have preferred a yellow-vegetable moment never, not
ever, not once, not when I was pressing the gingham dresses and not when I was
threading the daisy wreaths, crossed my mind.

COMPREHENSION

1. In recalling her childhood, what does Didion reveal about her behavior, orientation, and beliefs?
2. Underline, highlight, or circle Didion's numerous references to clothing. What is her purpose here? How does the title capture this emphasis on dress, and from what perspective? According to Didion, what is the function of dress and other domestic rituals?
3. How does Didion distinguish herself from her cousin Brenda? What does Didion conclude about this relationship?

RHETORIC

1. Didion published this memoir in a magazine that is read largely by women. How does she tailor the piece for this specific audience? Might the essay appeal to a broader audience? Why or why not?
2. What tone or personal voice does Didion create to describe her childhood? What bearing does this self-description have on her thesis or claim?
3. Compare the introductory and concluding paragraphs. How do they serve to establish the boundaries of the essay?
4. What elements of style do you find especially effective in this essay? For example, what allusions can you detect? What is the rhetorical effect of Didion's repeated use of semicolons? Why are many of her sentences so complex in design?
5. Didion is a novelist who uses the techniques of fiction in her nonfiction. How do you see these strategies operating in this essay?

WRITING

1. Write a narrative essay in which you tell of a period in childhood when you wished you were older or played adult games.
2. Didion has been credited with popularizing the *new journalism*. Find out more about this literary movement, and then write an analytical essay applying the concept to Didion's article.
3. **Writing an Argument:** Do you agree or disagree with Didion's implicit suggestion that at some point in their lives, children or young people develop a distaste for childhood or yearn to be grown-ups? Respond to this issue in an argumentative essay.

NETWORKING
Applying Digital and Multimedia Literacies

In small groups, find at least three Web sites about Joan Didion's life and work. Focus on two events in her life: the death of her husband and that of her daughter. Examine how she has responded to these episodes in her writing, interviews, and work for the theater. Share your findings in a class discussion.

Why Gay Marriage Is Good for Straight America

Andrew Sullivan

Andrew Sullivan (b. 1963) is a prolific and provocative writer, editor, and blogger. Born and raised in England, he was educated at Magdalen College, Oxford before moving to the United States to earn advanced degrees in public administration and politics at Harvard University. Identifying himself as Catholic, conservative, and gay, Sullivan was editor of the New Republic *from 1991 to 1996. He began his influential blog,* The Daily Dish, *in 2000, taking it initially to the* Atlantic Monthly *magazine's Web site. Sullivan left* Atlantic Monthly *in 2011 to begin blogging at the* Daily Beast. *Among his notable books are* Virtually Normal: An Argument about Homosexuality *(1995) and* The Conservative Soul: How We Lost It, How to Get It Back *(2006). In this essay from the July 25, 2011, issue of* Newsweek, *Sullivan offers a highly personal defense of marriage equality.*

1 As a child, when I thought of the future, all I could see was black. I wasn't miserable or depressed. I was a cheerful boy, as happy playing with my posse of male friends in elementary school as I was when I would occasionally take a day by

myself in the woodlands that surrounded the small town I grew up in. But when I thought of the distant future, of what I would do and be as a grown-up, there was a blank. I simply didn't know how I would live, where I would live, who I could live with. I knew one thing only: I couldn't be like my dad. For some reason, I knew somewhere deep down that I couldn't have a marriage like my parents.

It's hard to convey what that feeling does to a child. In retrospect, it was a 2 sharp, displacing wound to the psyche. At the very moment you become aware of sex and emotion, you simultaneously know that for you, there is no future coupling, no future family, no future home. In the future, I would be suddenly exiled from what I knew: my family, my friends, every household on television, every end to every romantic movie I'd ever seen. My grandmother crystallized it in classic and slightly cruel English fashion: "You're not the marrying kind," she said. It was one of those things that struck a chord of such pain, my pride forced me to embrace it. "No, I'm not," I replied. "I like my freedom."

This wasn't a lie. But it was a dodge, and I knew it. And when puberty struck 3 and I realized I might be "one of them," I turned inward. It was a strange feeling— both the exhilaration of sexual desire and the simultaneous, soul-splintering panic that I was going to have to live alone my whole life, lying or euphemizing, concocting some public veneer to hide a private shame. It was like getting into an elevator you were expecting to go up, the doors closing, and then suddenly realizing you were headed down a few stories. And this was when the future went black for me, when suicide very occasionally entered my mind, when my only legitimate passion was getting A grades, because at that point it was all I knew how to do. I stayed away from parties; I didn't learn to drive; I lost contact with those friends whose interest suddenly became girls; and somewhere in me, something began to die.

They call it the happiest day of your life for a reason. Getting married is often the 4 hinge on which every family generation swings open. In my small-town life, it was far more important than money or a career or fame. And I could see my grandmother's point: the very lack of any dating or interest in it, the absence of any intimate relationships, or of any normal teenage behavior, did indeed make me seem just a classic loner. But I wasn't. Because nobody is. "In everyone there sleeps/A sense of life lived according to love," as the poet Philip Larkin put it, as well as the fear of never being loved. That, as Larkin added, nothing cures. And I felt, for a time, incurable.

You can have as many debates about gay marriage as you want, and over the last 5 22 years of campaigning for it, I've had my share. You can debate theology, and the divide between church and state, the issue of procreation, the red herring of polygamy, and on and on. But what it all really comes down to is the primary institution of love. The small percentage of people who are gay or lesbian were born, as all humans are, with the capacity to love and the need to be loved. These things, above everything, are what make life worth living. And unlike every other minority, almost all of us grew up among and part of the majority, in families where the highest form of that love was between our parents in marriage. To feel you will never know that, never feel that, is to experience a deep psychic wound that takes years to recover from. It is to become psychologically homeless. Which is why, I think, the concept of "coming out" is not quite right. It should really be called "coming home."

6   In the end, I had to abandon my home in order to find it again and know the place for the first time. I left England just after my 21st birthday for America and its simple foundational promise: the pursuit of happiness. And I gave myself permission to pursue it. I will never forget the moment I first kissed another man; it was as if a black-and-white movie suddenly turned into color. I will never forget the first time I slept next to another man—or rather tried to sleep. Never for a moment did I actually feel or truly believe any of this was wrong, let alone an "intrinsic evil," as my strict Catholicism told me that it was. It was so natural, so spontaneous, so joyous, it could no more be wrong than breathing. And as I experienced intimacy and love for the first time as an adult, all that brittleness of the gay adolescent, all that white-knuckled embarrassment, all those ruses and excuses and dark, deep depressions lifted. Yes, this was happiness. And America for me will always represent it.

7   And that is why marriage equality is, to my mind, the distillation of America. If you're a heterosexual reading this, have you ever considered for a millisecond that your right to pursue happiness did not include your right to marry the person you love? And that is why, over the centuries, the U.S. Supreme Court has upheld the right to marry for everyone, citizen or even traveler, as a core, inalienable right, bestowed by the Declaration of Independence itself. The court has ruled that the right to marry precedes the Bill of Rights; it has decided that prisoners on death row have a right to marry, even if they can never consummate it. It has ruled that no limitations may be put on it for anyone—deadbeat dads, multiple divorcees, felons, noncitizens. Hannah Arendt wrote in 1959 that "the right to marry whoever one wishes is an elementary human right. . . . Even political rights, like the right to vote, and nearly all other rights enumerated in the Constitution, are secondary to the inalienable human rights to 'life, liberty and the pursuit of happiness' proclaimed in the Declaration of Independence; and to this category the right to home and marriage unquestionably belongs." And, of course, after a long struggle, interracial marriage was finally declared a constitutional right, in perhaps the most sweeping ruling ever, with the court declaring that civil marriage was one of the "basic civil rights of man, fundamental to our very existence and survival." Barack Obama is a historic American figure not because he is black, but because he is the son of a black father and a white mother. He is the living embodiment of the pursuit of happiness that marriage represented.

8   I still didn't think it would ever happen to me. I thought I was too emotionally damaged, my emotions and sexuality severed by all those years of loneliness and arrested emotional development. I thought my heart had too much scar tissue, and I could live my life well enough with just friendship and occasional sexual encounters or dates. But when I first set eyes on my husband, I knew I had lucked out. Some things you simply know. And when we finally got married, a few years later, and our mothers walked us down the makeshift garden aisle, and my sister gave the reading through tears, and one of our beagles howled through the vows, and my father put his arms around me and hugged, I did not hear civilization crumble. I felt a wound being healed. It is a rare privilege to spend your adult life fighting for a right that was first dismissed as a joke, only finally to achieve it in six states and Washington, D.C. But how much rarer to actually stumble upon someone

who could make it a reality. And to have it happen to me in my own lifetime! This joy is compounded, deepened, solidified by the knowledge that somewhere, someone just like I was as a kid will be able to look to the future now and not see darkness—but the possibility of love and home. That, I realized, was really what I had been fighting for two decades: to heal the child I had once been—and the countless children in the present and future whose future deserved, needed, begged for a model of commitment and responsibility and love.

And that is why it has been such a tragedy that conservatives decided this   9
was a battle they were determined to fight against, an advance they were dedicated to reversing. It made no sense to me. Here was a minority asking for responsibility and commitment and integration. And conservatives were determined to keep them in isolation, stigmatized and kept on an embarrassing, unmentionable margin, where gays could be used to buttress the primacy of heterosexuality. We were for them merely a drop shadow for heterosexuality. What they could not see was that the conservative tradition of reform and inclusion, of social change through existing institutions, of the family and personal responsibility, all led inexorably toward civil marriage for gays.

Yes, the main stumbling block was religion. But we were not talking of reli-   10
gious marriage and were more than eager to insist, as in New York state, on the inviolable religious freedom of churches, mosques, and synagogues to retain their bans on gay marriage. We were talking about civil marriage—and in that respect, religious tradition had long since ceased to apply. Civil divorce changed marriage far more drastically for far more people than allowing the small percentage who were excluded to be included. And no one doubted an atheist's right to marry, outside of any church or any religion, just as no one doubted the marriages of childless couples, or infertile ones. In fact, every single argument against marriage equality for gays collapsed upon inspection. And when the data showed that in the era of gay marriage, straight marriage had actually strengthened somewhat, divorce rates had declined, and marriages lasted longer, even those who worried about unintended consequences conceded that the argument was essentially over. And that is why it remains so appropriate that George W. Bush's solicitor general, Ted Olson, would lead the legal fight against Proposition 8 in California; that a Reagan-appointed judge, Anthony Kennedy, would be the foremost Supreme Court justice affirming gay and lesbian equality; and that in Albany, in the end, the winning votes came from Republicans who voted their conscience.

Of course this is new and not so new. For a long time, gays and lesbians   11
braver than I was were effectively married and lived together, risking violence and opprobrium and isolation. For decades these bonds existed, and we knew of them even if we never spoke of them. I saw them up close as a young man in the darkest years of the AIDS plague. I saw spouses holding their dying husbands, cradling them at the hour of their death, inserting catheters, cleaning broken bodies, tending to terrified souls. This proved beyond any doubt for me that gay couples were as capable of as much love and tenacity and tenderness and fidelity as heterosexual couples. And when I heard their bonds denigrated or demonized, dismissed or belittled, the sadness became a kind of spur. For so long, so much

pain. For so many, so much grief compounded by stigma. But we did not just survive the plague. We used it to forge a new future. And in the years of struggle, as more and more heterosexuals joined us, we all began finally to see that this was not really about being gay. It was about being human.

12   Just like being gay is no longer necessarily about being an outsider. It is about being an American.

COMPREHENSION

1. Briefly summarize Sullivan's childhood. How especially did he envision his future?
2. According to Sullivan, why did he immigrate to the United States after his 21st birthday? What did he find in America?
3. Explain what Sullivan means by his statement, "marriage equality is . . . the distillation of America" (paragraph 7).

RHETORIC

1. What voice does Sullivan create in this essay? What appeals to emotion, reason, and ethics does he make? How do these appeals contribute to his argument?
2. How does Sullivan use the rhetorical strategies of comparison and contrast, definition, and classification to organize this essay?
3. Sullivan employs analogy, allusion, and figurative language as stylistic elements in this essay. Identify these strategies and evaluate their contribution to Sullivan's argument.
4. Where does Sullivan acknowledge various forces of opposition to his argument? How does he refute those who oppose his position? In your mind, is his argument persuasive? Why or why not?
5. Sullivan's conclusion is very brief. Do you find it successful or not? Explain.

WRITING

1. Write a personal essay that explains your own sexual orientation, linking it to American values and the American experience.
2. Read Lisa Miller's "Our Mutual Joy: The Religious Case for Gay Marriage," which begins on page 569. Then write a comparative essay that analyzes the approaches of Sullivan and Miller to their subject.
3. **Writing an Argument:** Respond to Sullivan's claim that marriage equality is "the distillation of America."

NETWORKING
Applying Digital and Multimedia Literacies

Collaborating in small groups, conduct research on Sullivan's blog. Each member should read and summarize one or two of Sullivan's postings. Then discuss how Sullivan manages to be a Catholic, conservative, and homosexual. Share your insights with the class.

Family Values

Richard Rodriguez

Richard Rodriguez *(b. 1944) received degrees from Stanford University and Columbia University. He also did graduate study at the University of California, Berkeley, and at the Warburg Institute in London. He is a writer and editor for* Pacifica News Service *and a contributing editor and writer for many major American magazines and journals including* Harper's *and the* Los Angeles Times. *His books include* Hunger of Memory: The Education of Richard Rodriguez *(1982) and* Days of Obligation: An Argument with My Mexican Father *(1992). Both books have been profoundly influential in the public discussion on race, bilingualism, affirmative action, and biculturalism. He has also made many appearances as a commentator on the* PBS NewsHour. *In the following essay, originally published in the Sunday "Opinion" section of the* Los Angeles Times *in 1992, he addresses the concept of "family values" and focuses on the controversial thesis that homosexuality—rather than being a threat to family values—is actually a buttress against their dissolution.*

I am sitting alone in my car, in front of my parents' house—a middle-aged man 1 with a boy's secret to tell. What words will I use to tell them? I hate the word *gay,* find its little affirming sparkle more pathetic than assertive. I am happier with the less polite *queer.* But to my parents I would say *homosexual,* avoiding the Mexican slang *joto* (I had always heard it said in our house with hints of condescension), though *joto* is less mocking than the sissy-boy *maricon.*

The buzz on everyone's lips now: Family values. The other night on TV, the 2 vice president of the United States, his arm around his wife, smiled into the camera and described homosexuality as "mostly a choice." But how would he know? Homosexuality never felt like a choice to me.

A few minutes ago Rush Limbaugh, the radio guy with a voice that reminds 3 me, for some reason, of a butcher's arms, was banging his console and booming a near-reasonable polemic about family values. Limbaugh was not very clear about which values exactly he considers to be family values. A divorced man who lives alone in New York?

My parents live on a gray, treeless street in San Francisco not far from the 4 ocean. Probably more than half of the neighborhood is immigrant. India lives next door to Greece, who lives next door to Russia. I wonder what the Chinese lady next door to my parents makes of the politicians' phrase *family values.*

What immigrants know, what my parents certainly know, is that when you 5 come to this country, you risk losing your children. The assurance of family—continuity, inevitability—is precisely what America encourages its children to overturn. *Become your own man.* We who are native to this country know this too, of course, though we are likely to deny it. Only a society so guilty about its betrayal of family would tolerate the pieties of politicians regarding family values.

6   On the same summer day that Republicans were swarming in Houston (buzzing about family values), a friend of mine who escaped family values awhile back and who now wears earrings resembling intrauterine devices was complaining to me over coffee about the Chinese. The Chinese will never take over San Francisco, my friend said, because the Chinese do not want to take over San Francisco. The Chinese do not even see San Francisco! All they care about is their damn families. All they care about is double-parking smack in front of the restaurant on Clement Street and pulling granny out of the car—and damn anyone who happens to be in the car behind them or the next or the next.

7   Politicians would be horrified by such an American opinion, of course. But then, what do politicians, Republicans or Democrats, really know of our family life? Or what are they willing to admit? Even in that area where they could reasonably be expected to have something to say—regarding the relationship of family life to our economic system—the politicians say nothing. Republicans celebrate American economic freedom, but Republicans don't seem to connect that economic freedom to the social breakdown they find appalling. Democrats, on the other hand, if more tolerant of the drift from familial tradition, are suspicious of the very capitalism that creates social freedom.

8   How you become free in America: Consider the immigrant. He gets a job. Soon he is earning more money than his father ever made (his father's authority is thereby subtly undermined). The immigrant begins living a life his father never knew. The immigrant moves from one job to another, changes houses. His economic choices determine his home address—not the other way around. The immigrant is on his way to becoming his own man.

9   When I was broke a few years ago and trying to finish a book, I lived with my parents. What a thing to do! A major theme of America is leaving home. We trust the child who forsakes family connections to make it on his own. We call that the making of a man.

10   Let's talk about this man stuff for a minute. America's ethos is anti-domestic. We may be intrigued by blood that runs through wealth—the Kennedys or the Rockefellers—but they seem European to us. Which is to say, they are movies. They are Corleones. Our real pledge of allegiance: We say in America that nothing about your family—your class, your race, your pedigree—should be as important as what you yourself achieve. We end up in 1992 introducing ourselves by first names.

11   What authority can Papa have in a country that formed its identity in an act of Oedipal rebellion against a mad British king? Papa is a joke in America, a stock sitcom figure—Archie Bunker or Homer Simpson. But my Mexican father went to work every morning, and he stood in a white smock, making false teeth, oblivious of the shelves of grinning false teeth mocking his devotion.

12   The nuns in grammar school—my wonderful Irish nuns—used to push Mark Twain on me. I distrusted Huck Finn, he seemed like a gringo kid I would steer clear of in the schoolyard. (He was too confident.) I realize now, of course, that Huck is the closest we have to a national hero. We trust the story of a boy who has no home and is restless for the river. (Huck's Pap is drunk.) Americans are more forgiving of Huck's wildness than of the sweetness of the Chinese boy who walks

to school with his mama or grandma. (There is no worse thing in America than to be a mama's boy, nothing better than to be a real boy—all boy—like Huck, who eludes Aunt Sally, and is eager for the world of men.)

There's a bent old woman coming up the street. She glances nervously as she 13 passes my car. What would you tell us, old lady, of family values in America?

America is an immigrant country, we say. Motherhood—parenthood—is less 14 our point than adoption. If I had to assign gender to America, I would note the consensus of the rest of the world. When America is burned in effigy, a male is burned. Americans themselves speak of Uncle Sam.

Like the Goddess of Liberty, Uncle Sam has no children of his own. He steals 15 children to make men of them, mocks all reticence, all modesty, all memory. Uncle Sam is a hectoring Yankee, a skinflint uncle, gaunt, uncouth, unloved. He is the American Savonarola—hater of moonshine, destroyer of stills, burner of cocaine. Sam has no patience with mamas' boys.

You betray Uncle Sam by favoring private over public life, by seeking to ex- 16 empt yourself, by cheating on your income taxes, by avoiding jury duty, by trying to keep your boy on the farm.

Mothers are traditionally the guardians of the family against America— 17 though even Mom may side with America against queers and deserters, at least when the Old Man is around. Premature gray hair. Arthritis in her shoulders. Bowlegged with time, red hands. In their fiercely flowered housedresses, mothers are always smarter than fathers in America. But in reality they are betrayed by their children who leave. In a thousand ways. They end up alone.

We kind of like the daughter who was a tomboy. Remember her? It was always 18 easier to be a tomboy in America than a sissy. Americans admired Annie Oakley more than they admired Liberace (who, nevertheless, always remembered his mother). But today we do not admire Annie Oakley when we see Mom becoming Annie Oakley.

The American household now needs two incomes, everyone says. Meaning: 19 Mom is *forced* to leave home out of economic necessity. But lots of us know lots of moms who are sick and tired of being mom, or only mom. It's like the nuns getting fed up, teaching kids for all those years and having those kids grow up telling stories of how awful Catholic school was! Not every woman in America wants her life's work to be forgiveness. Today there are moms who don't want their husbands' names. And the most disturbing possibility: What happens when Mom doesn't want to be Mom at all? Refuses pregnancy?

Mom is only becoming an American like the rest of us. Certainly, people all 20 over the world are going to describe the influence of feminism on women (all over the world) as their "Americanization." And rightly so.

Nothing of this, of course, will the politician's wife tell you. The politician's wife 21 is careful to follow her husband's sentimental reassurances that nothing has changed about America except perhaps for the sinister influence of deviants. Like myself.

I contain within myself an anomaly at least as interesting as the Republican 22 Party's version of family values. I am a homosexual Catholic, a communicant in a tradition that rejects even as it upholds me.

23   I do not count myself among those Christians who proclaim themselves protectors of family values. They regard me as no less an enemy of the family than the "radical feminists." But the joke about families that all homosexuals know is that we are the ones who stick around and make families possible. Call on us. I can think of 20 or 30 examples. A gay son or daughter is the only one who is "free" (married brothers and sisters are too busy). And, indeed, because we have admitted the inadmissible about ourselves (that we are queer)—we are adepts at imagination—we can even imagine those who refuse to imagine us. We can imagine Mom's loneliness, for example. If Mom needs to be taken to church or to the doctor or ferried between Christmas dinners, depend on the gay son or lesbian daughter.

24   I won't deny that the so-called gay liberation movement, along with feminism, undermined the heterosexual household, if that's what politicians mean when they say family values. Against churchly reminders that sex was for procreation, the gay bar as much as the birth-control pill taught Americans not to fear sexual pleasure. In the past two decades—and, not coincidentally, parallel to the feminist movement—the gay liberation movement moved a generation of Americans toward the idea of a childless adulthood. If the women's movement was ultimately more concerned about getting out of the house and into the workplace, the gay movement was in its way more subversive to puritan America because it stressed the importance of play.

25   Several months ago, the society editor of the morning paper in San Francisco suggested (on a list of "must haves") that every society dame must have at least one gay male friend. A ballet companion. A lunch date. The remark was glib and incorrect enough to beg complaints from homosexual readers, but there was a truth about it as well. Homosexual men have provided women with an alternate model of masculinity. And the truth: The Old Man, God bless him, is a bore. Thus are we seen as preserving marriages? Even Republican marriages?

26   For myself, homosexuality is a deep brotherhood but does not involve domestic life. Which is why, my married sisters will tell you, I can afford the time to be a writer. And why are so many homosexuals such wonderful teachers and priests and favorite aunts, if not because we are freed from the house? On the other hand, I know lots of homosexual couples (male and female) who model their lives on the traditional heterosexual version of domesticity and marriage. Republican politicians mock the notion of a homosexual marriage, but ironically such marriages honor the heterosexual marriage by imitating it.

27   "The only loving couples I know," a friend of mine recently remarked, "are all gay couples."

28   This woman was not saying that she does not love her children or that she is planning a divorce. But she was saying something about the sadness of American domestic life: the fact that there is so little joy in family intimacy. Which is perhaps why gossip (public intrusion into the private) has become a national industry. All day long, in forlorn houses, the television lights up a freakish parade of husbands and mothers-in-law and children upon the stage of Sally or Oprah or Phil. They tell on each other. The audience ooohhhs. Then a psychiatrist-shaman appears at the end to dispense prescriptions—the importance of family members granting one another more "space."

29   The question I desperately need to ask you is whether we Americans have ever truly valued the family. We are famous, or our immigrant ancestors were

famous, for the willingness to leave home. And it is ironic that a crusade under the banner of family values has been taken up by those who would otherwise pass themselves off as patriots. For they seem not to understand America, nor do I think they love the freedoms America grants. Do they understand why, in a country that prizes individuality and is suspicious of authority, children are disinclined to submit to their parents? You cannot celebrate American values in the public realm without expecting them to touch our private lives. As Barbara Bush remarked recently, family values are also neighborhood values. It may be harmless enough for Barbara Bush to recall a sweeter America—Midland, Texas, in the 1950s. But the question left begging is why we chose to leave Midland, Texas. Americans like to say that we can't go home again. The truth is that we don't want to go home again, don't want to be known, recognized. Don't want to respond in the same old ways. (And you know you will if you go back there.)

Little 10-year-old girls know that there are reasons for getting away from the 30 family. They learn to keep their secrets—under lock and key—addressed to Dear Diary. Growing up queer, you learn to keep secrets as well. In no place are those secrets more firmly held than within the family house. You learn to live in closets. I know a Chinese man who arrived in America about 10 years ago. He got a job and made some money. And during that time he came to confront his homosexuality. And then his family arrived. I do not yet know the end of this story.

The genius of America is that it permits children to leave home, it permits us 31 to become different from our parents. But the sadness, the loneliness of America, is clear too.

Listen to the way Americans talk about immigrants. If, on the one hand, there 32 is impatience when today's immigrants do not seem to give up their family, there is also a fascination with this reluctance. In Los Angeles, Hispanics are considered people of family. Hispanic women are hired to be at the center of the American family—to babysit and diaper, to cook and to clean and to ease the dying. Hispanic attachment to family is seen by many Americans, I think, as the reason why Hispanics don't get ahead. But if Asians privately annoy us for being so family oriented, they are also stereotypically celebrated as the new "whiz kids" in school. Don't Asians go to college, after all, to honor their parents?

More important still is the technological and economic ascendancy of Asia, 33 particularly Japan, on the American imagination. Americans are starting to wonder whether perhaps the family values of Asia put the United States at a disadvantage. The old platitude had it that ours is a vibrant, robust society for being a society of individuals. Now we look to Asia and see team effort paying off.

In this time of national homesickness, of nostalgia, for how we imagine America 34 used to be, there are obvious dangers. We are going to start blaming each other for the loss. Since we are inclined, as Americans, to think of ourselves individually, we are disinclined to think of ourselves as creating one another or influencing one another.

But it is not the politician or any political debate about family values that has 35 brought me here on a gray morning to my parents' house. It is some payment I owe to my youth and to my parents' youth. I imagine us sitting in the living room, amid my mother's sentimental doilies and the family photographs, trying to take the measure of the people we have turned out to be in America.

36   A San Francisco poet, when he was in the hospital and dying, called a priest to his bedside. The old poet wanted to make his peace with Mother Church. He wanted baptism. The priest asked why. "Because the Catholic Church has to accept me," said the poet. "Because I am a sinner."

37   Isn't willy-nilly inclusiveness the point, the only possible point to be derived from the concept of family? Curiously, both President Bush and Vice President Quayle got in trouble with their constituents recently for expressing a real family value. Both men said that they would try to dissuade a daughter or granddaughter from having an abortion. But, finally, they said they would support her decision, continue to love her, never abandon her.

38   There are families that do not accept. There are children who are forced to leave home because of abortions or homosexuality. There are family secrets that Papa never hears. Which is to say there are families that never learn the point of families.

39   But there she is at the window. My mother has seen me and she waves me in. Her face asks: Why am I sitting outside? (Have they, after all, known my secret for years and kept it, out of embarrassment, not knowing what to say?) Families accept, often by silence. My father opens the door to welcome me in.

COMPREHENSION

1. The title of this essay is "Family Values." What does Rodriguez mean by *family values?* According to the author, do Americans respect family values as they claim? Why or why not?
2. According to Rodriguez, do immigrants newly arrived to the United States possess a traditional allegiance to family values? Explain your answer.
3. In the conclusion, the author reflects—regarding his homosexuality—that "families accept, often in silence." Is this an aspect of traditional family values? Why or why not?
4. Why does Rodriguez think that gay men and women are often the primary upholders of family values within their families?
5. What is the thesis of the essay? Is it implicit or explicit? Explain.

RHETORIC

1. Although much of this essay is expository, Rodriguez begins and ends with an event—that is, visiting his family to announce his homosexuality. Why has he shaped his essay in this way? What is problematic about his relationship to the gay community? Why does he feel uncomfortable with the term *gay* to denote homosexual?
2. Rodriguez employs considerable irony in his essay. For example, in paragraph 15, he notes that two icons of American democracy, the Goddess of Liberty and Uncle Sam, are childless. Select two other ironic statements he makes in order to point out the contradiction between the idea of family values in America and the actual state of family values.
3. In paragraph 20, Rodriguez uses the term "Americanization." What does he mean by this term? How is it central to his thesis?
4. Does Rodriguez suggest that much of what is said in public regarding "family values" in America is hypocritical? If so, what group or groups does he focus on? How does he support his argument?

5. Explain the meaning of the following stylistic flourishes: "the word *gay* . . . [is a] little affirming sparkle more pathetic than assertive" (paragraph 1), "America's ethos is anti-domestic" (paragraph 10), "Oedipal rebellion" (paragraph 11), "American Savonarola" (paragraph 15), "psychiatrist-shaman" (paragraph 28), "national homesickness" (paragraph 34), and "willy-nilly inclusiveness" (paragraph 37).

6. In paragraph 10, Rodriguez states that the Kennedys and Rockefellers "are movies." What does he mean?

7. Describe the emotional tone of this essay, considering that it is written by a man who is openly gay and understands that he is considered suspect and outside the mainstream of the American "value" system. Is it angry? Thoughtful? Defiant? Sympathetic? Select three or four passages that led you to your conclusion regarding tone.

WRITING

1. Interview a member of your grandparents' generation, a member of your parents' generation, and a member of your own generation regarding their views on family values. Write an essay summarizing the similarities and differences among the three views.

2. Interview a counselor at your college or university. Ask the counselor to explain the various issues surrounding family conflict he or she comes across in the course of his or her job. Write an essay exploring your interview findings. Be sure to obtain permission from your interviewee and follow appropriate guidelines for protecting his or her anonymity.

3. **Writing an Argument:** Argue for or against the proposition that American society today is more tolerant of homosexuals than when Rodriguez published this essay in 1992.

NETWORKING
Applying Digital and Multimedia Literacies

Synthesizing Blog Entries: Locate and read some recent entries from author/blogger Andrew Sullivan's *The Daily Dish* and Sullivan's 1987 essay "Here Comes the Groom" (from the *New Republic* and available on Sullivan's blog). From these sources, what do you make of Sullivan's relationship with the gay community? With the right? With the left? How do these relationships influence his take on family values?

The Estrangement

Jamaica Kincaid

Jamaica Kincaid (b. 1949) was born Elaine Potter Richardson in St. John's, Antigua. She came to the United States at age 16 and attended the New School for Social Research and Franconia College. In time she became a staff writer for the New

Yorker *and started to publish her fiction in* Rolling Stone, *the* Paris Review, *and elsewhere. She has taught at several colleges, including Harvard University and currently Claremont-McKenna College, while compiling a distinguished body of fiction and nonfiction. Among her notable works are* Annie John *(1985),* A Small Place *(1988),* Lucy *(1991),* The Autobiography of My Mother *(1996), and* Among Flowers: A Walk in the Himalaya *(2005). In "The Estrangement," which appeared originally in a 2008 issue of* AARP Magazine, *Kincaid offers an account of the complicated relationship with her mother.*

1 Three years before my mother died, I decided not to speak to her again. And why? During a conversation over the telephone, she had once again let me know that my accomplishments—becoming a responsible and independent woman—did not amount to very much, that the life I lived was nothing more than a silly show, that she truly wished me dead. I didn't disagree. I didn't tell her that it would be just about the best thing in the world not to hear this from her.

2 And so, after that conversation, I never spoke to her, said a word to her of any kind, and then she died, and her death was a shock to me, not because I would miss her presence and long for it but because I could not believe that such a presence could ever be stilled.

3 For many years and many a time, her children, of which I was the only female, wondered what would happen to her, as we wondered what would happen to us; because she seemed to us not a mother at all but a God, not a Goddess but a God.

4 How to explain in this brief space what I mean? When we were children and in need of a mother's love and care, there was no better mother to provide such an ideal entity. When we were adolescents, and embracing with adolescent certainty our various incarnations, she could see through the thinness of our efforts, she could see through the emptiness of our aspirations; when we fell apart, there she was, bringing us dinner in jail or in a hospital ward, cold compresses for our temples, or just standing above us as we lay flat on our backs in bed. That sort of mother is God.

5 I am the oldest, by nine, eleven, and thirteen years, of four children. My three brothers and I share only our mother; they have the same father, I have a different one. I knew their father very well, better than they did, but I did not know my own. (When I was seven months in her womb, my mother quarreled with the man with whom she had conceived me and then ran away with the money he had been saving up to establish a little business for himself. He never forgave her.) I didn't mind not knowing my real father because in the place I am from, Antigua, when people love you, your blood relationship to them is not necessarily the most important component. My mother's husband, the father of my brothers, loved me, and his love took on the shape of a father's love: He told me about himself when he was a boy and the things he loved to do and the ways in which his life changed for better and worse, giving me some idea about how he came to be himself, my father, the father of my brothers, the person married to my mother.

6 She was a very nice person, apparently; that is what everybody said about her at her funeral. There were descriptions of her good and selfless deeds, kindnesses,

generosity, testaments of her love expressed in humor. We, her children, looked at one another in wonder then, for such a person as described was not at all known to us. The person we knew, our Mother, said horrible things to us more often than not.

The youngest of my three brothers died of AIDS when he was thirty-three years of age. In the years he spent actively dying, our mother tended to him with the greatest tenderness, a tenderness that was absent all the time before he was dying. Before he got sick, before he became afflicted with that disease, his mother, my mother too, quarreled with him and disparaged him. This was enabled by the fact that he did not know how to go off somewhere and make a home of any kind for himself. Yes, he had been unable to move out into the world, away from this woman, his mother, and become the sole possessor of his own destiny, with all the loss and gain that this implies. 7

The two remaining brothers and I buried her right next to him, and we were not sure we should have done that: For we didn't know then, and still don't know even now, if he wanted to spend eternity lying beside her, since we were sure we would rather be dead than spend eternity lying next to her. 8

Is this clear? It is to me right now as I write it: I would rather be dead than spend eternity with our mother! And do I really mean that when I say it? Yes, I really mean just that: After being my mother's daughter, I would rather be dead than spend eternity with her. 9

By the time my mother died, I was not only one of her four children, I had become the mother of two children: a girl and then a boy. This was bliss, my two children in love with me, and I with them. Nothing has gone wrong, as far as I can see, but tears have been shed over my not being completely enthusiastic about going to a final basketball game in a snowstorm, or my saying something I should have kept in my mind's mouth. A particularly unforgivable act in my children's eyes is a book's dedication I made to them; it read: "With blind, instinctive, and confused love to Annie and Harold, who from time to time are furiously certain that the only thing standing between them and a perfect union with their mother is the garden, and from time to time, they are correct." 10

I wrote this with a feeling of overbrimming love for them, my children. I was not thinking of my own mother directly, not thinking of her at all consciously at that exact time, but then again, I am always thinking of my mother; I believe every action of a certain kind that I make is completely influenced by her, completely infused with her realness, her existence in my life. 11

I am now middle-aged (fifty-nine years of age); I not only hope to live for a very long time after this, I will be angry in eternity if this turns out not to be the case. And so in eternity will my children want to be with me? And in eternity will I, their mother, want to be with them? 12

In regard to my children, eternity is right now, and I always want to be with them. In regard to my mother, my progenitor, eternity is beyond now, and is that not forever? I will not speak to her again in person, of that I am certain, but I am not sure that I will never speak to her again. For in eternity is she in me, and are even my children speaking to her? I do not know, I do not know. 13

COMPREHENSION

1. How does Kincaid describe her mother? Do you think she is fair-minded or biased in her perceptions? Explain.
2. In what ways does Kincaid resemble her mother? In what ways is she unlike this "God"? Is she aware of the complexities in this mother-daughter relationship? Why or why not? How does her mother's death alter her perception of this relationship?
3. Kincaid offers a brief, concentrated portrait of her family. Who are its members? Do you find this family to be traditional or atypical? Justify your response.

RHETORIC

1. What is the significance of Kincaid's title? What are its possible meanings? Does the title capture the complete meaning of the essay? Why or why not?
2. Does this essay have a thesis or claim? Justify your response by careful reference to the text.
3. Locate the details of her mother's life that Kincaid presents, and explain why the writer has selected these details. What tone emerges from these details?
4. This essay has three parts. What is the relationship among them?
5. Why does Kincaid pose a series of questions in the last two paragraphs? What is the final effect?

WRITING

1. Compose an honest and revealing appraisal of your relationship with your mother or another family member.
2. Write an essay in which you consider the roles that mothers play in various cultures. Base this essay on your own background and personal knowledge.
3. **Writing an Argument:** Can we ever escape or distance ourselves from the influence of our parents in our lives? Is such an escape even necessary or desirable? Write an argumentative essay in response to these questions.

NETWORKING
Applying Digital and Multimedia Literacies

Negotiating Parents, Privacy, and Technology: How do relatively recent innovations, like the wide use of personal cell phones and of social networking sites, influence your relationship with parents or guardians? Is your mother your Facebook friend? Is it harder to become independent and distance yourself from family when you can reach each other anywhere, anytime? In an essay, explore how parents or guardians and their adult children can create boundaries while staying connected in a 21st-century family.

Digital Scheherazades
in the Arab World

Fatema Mernissi

Fatema Mernissi *(b. 1940), a contemporary sociologist, university professor, and feminist scholar, was born in Fez, Morocco. She received a degree in political science at Mohammad V University and a degree in sociology at the Sorbonne in Paris. In 1973, she earned a PhD in sociology at Brandeis University. At present, she is a research scholar at the University Institute for Scientific Research in Rabat. Mernissi's work focuses on the intersection of gender and religion in Muslim society. Among her numerous publications are* The Veil and the Male Elite *(1975),* Islam and Democracy *(1992), and* Scheherazade Goes West *(2001). Two memoirs,* Dreams of Trespass *(1994) and* Harem Days *(1999), recount her life growing up as Muslim, Moroccan, and female. In this essay, published in* Current History *in 2006, Mernissi assesses the changing roles of women in the Arab Gulf as technology influences the thinking of a previously all-male elite.*

In May 2005, I listened attentively to the questions of the 30 journalists my Spanish 1
publisher had scheduled to meet with me in Madrid to promote the translation of my book, *Les Sindbads marocains: Voyage dans le Maroc civique (Moroccan Sinbads: Travels through Civic Morocco)*. From their questions, which all dealt with the veil and terrorism, it was clear that they had no clue about the strategic issue mobilizing the Arab world: *alfitna raqmiya* (digital chaos), the destruction of space frontiers by information technology.

The key problem that makes everyone anxious today in the Arab world—elites 2
and masses, heads of state and street vendors, men and women—is the digital chaos induced by information technologies such as the Internet. These new technologies have destroyed the *hudud,* the frontier that divided the universe into a sheltered private arena, where women and children were supposed to be protected, and a public one where adult males exercised their presumed problem-solving authority.

Now, according to a best-selling book, *The Internet and Love (Al Internet Wa* 3
I-Hub), by Imam Qaradawi, a star host on the Arab television network Al Jazeera, the satellite and the Internet have spawned apocalyptic chaos in Arab civilization by destroying that division of spheres. The imam's book, which is advertised on the popular IslamOnline website, is alerting crowds to the fact that Arab women and youth now navigate freely on the web and communicate intimately with strangers, escaping religious and parental censorship.

"Since the World Wide Web invaded our lives," explains Qaradawi, "we have 4
been going through nonstop transformations. . . . The faraway has become nearer with a simple push on the keyboard. This has deeply affected our societies, which

have suffered from a lack of communication and the lack of educational quality enter-tainment. . . . Suddenly, the new technologies have provided opportunities to commu-nicate and entertain oneself, and this without the supervision of a censoring authority or a controller to whom you are accountable. . . . This leaves individual responsibility as the sole controlling agency. And unfortunately, we have never cared to develop an educational system which focused on developing individual responsibility."

5   But what is also new is that even imams suggest we stop thinking about static solutions like strengthening authority and reinforcing hudud and focus instead on inventing strategies that nurture a civilization of ethical nomadism, where indi-vidual responsibility creates order. The Arab world is a besieged place, but in many quarters the response to chaos is quietly shifting from crying to action. This shift helps explain the emergence of what I call "digital Scheherazades," after the fictional storyteller of *1,001 Nights.* Her successors are Arab women who take advantage of new communication strategies as the only initiatives likely to liberate both themselves and their countries.

Digital Chaos

6   Imagine the anxiety of a parent reading "The Electronic Disfiguration of Our Chil-dren," an article by an Egyptian psychoanalyst, Dr. Khalil Fadel, that appeared in the Kuwait-based *Al Arabi,* one of the most widely circulated cultural magazines in the region. Fadel identifies the child as the most vulnerable victim of the West-ern-made electronic war games that invade "our children's rooms and are avail-able in the cyber-cafés which now exist on every street corner." According to Fadel, these war games are responsible for inciting violent behavior among Arab youth because they glorify "solitude, narcissism, and hatred of the other," all of which reflect the cultural choices of the Westerners who produce these games.

7   But if electronic war games are bad enough, sex is worse, according to an article—"Electronic Sex Attack on the Arab World"—by Ahmed Mohamed Ali in the Saudi-based magazine *Al Majalla.* Ali, who believes this attack was first launched in 1999, describes "the unimaginable profit made from selling virtual prostitution or electronic sex on the Internet" to Arabs. Parents, he says, quoting Al-Hami Abdelaziz, an Egyptian psychology professor, are totally at a loss about what to do: "They know that the future of their children depends on their mastering such technologies, but they are afraid they will slip into these pornographic web-sites. The fact is that the parents are totally unarmed and ill-equipped to protect their children from such dangers."

8   Add to this the booming Arab satellite industry of erotic video-clips targeting youth. These clips constitute a terrifying challenge to the Islamic vision of the world, where sex belongs exclusively to the private sphere (which explains why no straightforward pornographic films are to be found on Arab satellite stations such as Arabsat and Nilesat). The video-clip is a tricky phenomenon, since its official objective is entertainment through music and songs. For Arabs, music and songs, just like poetry, have been regarded, even before Islam and since, as important sources of licit pleasure. Now they must confront the digital chaos induced by

music video-clips that slip into explicit sex between unmarried people surrounding the singer. As Patricia Kabala has written, the video-clip "has without doubt become a symbol of access via satellite television stations and the Internet to the previously inaccessible sexually explicit material that state-controlled television channels in the Middle East censored and continue to censor."

Yet what is interesting once again is that instead of wasting time in complaints 9 as Arabs usually do, a new attitude has appeared, the desire to invent solutions. Some ethically minded operators are trying to exploit that very video-clip technology to spread Islamic values among the youth. To counteract the sexual flood, investing in video-clips to promote young attractive religious singers as role models—such as Sami Yusuf Yusu, a British-born Muslim of Azeri origin—is one of the emerging positive responses to the previously frightening new information technologies. The lesson one gets from reading about the video-clip debate is that either you transform yourself into an agile digital surfer or you fade away.

It is this kind of immense civilizational shift in the Arab world, where men are 10 finally embarking on becoming skilled digital nomads instead of decrying the frontier's collapse and dreaming of harems for their wives, that I tried to share with the Spanish journalists obsessed by the veil and terrorism during my Madrid encounter in May 2005. Although the Spanish city of Gibraltar is just 13 kilometers from the Moroccan port of Tangiers, I realized that Spaniards had no idea about the revolution that information technologies have produced in our part of the world. And one reason for this is the fact that in Madrid's plush hotel, which advertised itself as satellite-connected, I could not connect to my favorite, Al Jazeera, or to any one of the two hundred pan-Arab satellite channels beaming now in the Mediterranean.

At one point, I tried to illustrate this change by sharing with them the extraor- 11 dinary emergence of women I saw in the Arab Gulf during a visit to Bahrain in March 2005. I tried to describe to them Mai al-Khalifa, a historian who in less than a decade has created modern spaces such as museums and cultural centers that encourage dialogue between the sexes and the generations. I tried to explain that this unexpected emergence of women in the oil-rich Arab Gulf is more significant than the question of the veil in the Muslim migrant community, but the Spanish journalists were trapped in their own veils and terror.

I left Madrid feeling guilty and helpless, an intellectual unable to carry out 12 her job of facilitating dialogue. The journalists continued to haunt me after my return to Morocco, and when I saw al-Khalifa on a pan-Arab satellite television one day, I caught myself wishing they could share that experience with me.

The Historian on TV

The café near University Mohamed V in Rabat was full of young students and teach- 13 ers when al-Khalifa appeared on Al Arabia, a new rival of Al Jazeera that is financed by the Saudis. The manager of the café automatically turned up the television's volume because he was a fan of Turki al-Dakhil, the show's anchor, an electrifying young man who appears on the screen dressed in the Gulf region's traditional white robes just to surprise you by his insolent remarks toward all kinds of authorities.

14   At this moment, I noticed a striking change in the café: Conversations came to a halt even though al-Khalifa was dressed like a professional woman in a white suit and looked very much on guard, unlike belly dancers who blink their eyes and sway hands and buttocks. The dynamics of what occurred in my Rabat café were as important for me as what was happening on the television screen. (When I was a child, the only women one could see in my hometown, Fez, in movies or on television when it made its appearance in Morocco in the 1960s, were belly dancers and singers; intellectual women were not part of the fare.)

15   It was by chance that I was in the café, because I am a rather homebound creature. I was invited there by Kamal, one of my favorite colleagues, who is a *1,001 Nights* expert. He was intrigued by what I had told him about my March 2005 Bahrain trip because there is very little cultural exchange between North Africa and the Gulf. The gender ratio in the café was typical of Morocco: 10 women among 40 or so customers. Moroccan women, starting with myself, are so exhausted by their daily chores that they rarely think about going out in the evening.

16   One of al-Khalifa's best-known books deals with the Qarmatians, a controversial group of Shiites who rebelled in the tenth century against the Sunni Abbasid caliphs, described as terrorists by some historians and as the founders of the first republic in Islam by others. I thought this would be the topic al-Dakhil, the Al Arabia host, would start with. To my great surprise, he opted for a very personal angle instead: Why was al-Khalifa so controversial in her own country? One has to realize that the title of the show is *Idaat,* which literally means "Flashes." The host is supposed to help the viewer discover some secret corner of those he invites to his show.

17   Why, wondered al-Dakhil, was al-Khalifa generating so much debate in Bahrain concerning the projects she promoted as one of the first women to hold an official position? (Al-Khalifa was the first woman to be appointed in Bahrain as assistant undersecretary for culture and national heritage.) Was it because she was a woman, or because she was incompetent, coming from an academic background and being thus unfit for practical work? Some people at the Ministry of Information, al-Dakhil argued, were saying that academics are too isolated in their ivory towers to be effective cultural operators.

18   "That intellectuals are unable to invent effective cultural strategies is a totally wrong assumption," al-Khalifa responded brusquely, brushing her black hair away from her face. Such statements, she added, are typical of bureaucrats who are in fact totally unfit to design the dynamic cultural strategies the Arab world needs to face the challenges posed by new technologies, and this for the simple reason that they lack vision. "I am an intellectual who has both a clear vision (*ruya*) of the future and the capacity to go ahead and act by undertaking successful innovative projects." Only intellectuals, she stressed, have *ruya,* a precious gift amid today's global chaos.

19   The reaction to al-Khalifa's response in the café was amazing. The crowd laughed merrily. One of the students stood up to declaim the Palestinian Mahmoud Darwish's poem about his compatriot Edward Said, in which he celebrates a

strong vision rooted in one's reading of the past as the key allowing the Palestinian diaspora to survive and thrive: "If your past is a tough experience, make your future meaningful by developing a vision. . . . My dream directs my steps. And my vision places my dream in my lap like a friendly cat."

The Vision Thing

The absence of a clear vision of the future has been identified by Arab intellectuals 20 as a contributor to the dangerous political disengagement of Arab youth and their confusion, which makes them vulnerable to the violence spread on the Internet. The new voices of the Arab diaspora include the Palestinian Khaled Hroub, who lives in London but is extremely influential among young Arabs because he hosts a show on Al Jazeera. He argues in his recent book on Hamas that the generational gap is particularly explosive in Arab society.

Indeed, one of the causes of terrorism is the demographic split between the 21 aging minority of decision makers and the youthful majority they are supposed to represent. In a burlesque article published in the very academic journal of the Arab League, Hroub notices that being "decadently old" (*chaykhoukha*) does not help Arab leaders design pertinent strategies for the majority of the population, which is young. The tiny minority that monopolizes political decisions, he says, "operates on a set of concepts and reasoning frameworks that have very little relevancy to the youth's own problems." It is this politico-demographic divide, he concludes, that explains "the disastrous scorn of our younger generations for politics." And this brings us to the enigma of why the café youth reacted so strongly when the word *ruya* came up on the television show.

To stop terrorism, Arab leaders have to provide Arab youth with a vision of a fu- 22 ture in which they have a role to play as defenders of an ethical planet, explains Nabil Abdel-Fattah of the Al Ahram Center for Political and Strategic Studies in Egypt. The frustration of Arab youth results from the elite's failure to articulate a clear ethical view of a future in which every individual has a mission and a purpose. It is this emergence of the *ruya* as the antidote to terrorism that explains the café crowd's response to al-Khalifa's defiant answer to her television host. She was reminding him that her *ruya* is the likely reason why some Bahrain government bureaucrats were angered by her audacious cultural projects such as museums and cultural centers that teach children to understand that diversity is the root of their identity.

Because Arabs in general and youth in particular are fed up with fanaticism 23 and censorship, neighborhood cafés are turning, thanks to the new culture-focus satellite television outlets such as Al Jazeera and Al Arabia, to debates over *ruya,* visions of the future as the key to empowerment.

Many men in the café followed the rough exchange between al-Dakhil and his 24 guest with beaming smiles, including my colleague Kamal. I asked him why he was smiling and he said because al-Khalifa's quick response to al-Dakhil was so spontaneous: "I think Arab intellectuals should create a fund to support this lady," he said, "because she is creating fantastic publicity for us. If she continues appearing on television shows making such statements, we, the poor marginalized intellectuals, will soon be receiving well-paid job offers to replace our vision-blind bureaucrats in all the 22 Arab states!"

25   Kamal was right, because very few Arab male intellectuals would have dared to declare with so much self-confidence, as al-Khalifa did on television, that they are visionaries and that only far-sighted thinkers can invent futuristic strategies for an Arab world doubly assaulted by both new information technologies and the powerful American military. Yet one of the positive changes initiated by these assaults is that people have stopped complaining and are going one step further toward identifying concrete solutions: first defeat the bureaucrats who have monopolized power for decades.

26   It is a daring message that increasingly bold women, making use of the new information technologies, are proclaiming to fellow Arabs. In the Arab Gulf, the amazing thing about this new breed of women is that growing numbers of them, like al-Khalifa, do not limit themselves to writing but manage to jump into action as well. "She, like Sheikha Hussa Al-Sabah from Kuwait, builds museums and cultural centers like other women turn out couscous tagines!" remarked my colleague, who always condemned my decision not to get involved in politics. For Kamal, who, unlike me, became involved in politics and paid for it by having trouble with the Moroccan police, it is clear that now only intellectuals can help rulers to engineer power and engage the future.

27   The challenge for the intellectuals is to help rulers equip the youth to navigate responsibly on the Internet. In particular, these solutions must help young people navigate not only in space but also in time. In a globalized planet where meeting strangers daily is the only way to make a living, mastering time is the secret of graceful navigation. To travel in the past, that is, to navigate in time, is the best way to teach oneself tolerance and respect for diversity.

28   Mobility is the name of the game, be they men or women, local or exiled, Sunni or Shiite, upper-class or from modest backgrounds. We are seeing a sudden shift from complaining about the West and its technological superiority to deciding to begin using the new information technologies to protect ourselves by participating in building a more just and humanist planet. Oil wealth, which makes it easy for visionaries to step quickly from vision to realization, has helped fuel this shift in the Arab Gulf. But so has the emergence of women in a region supposedly condemned to archaic conservatism.

Women Can Play Too

29 Is it because the threats of destabilization and terrorism are so great in the oil-rich Arab Gulf that emirs and sheikhs are keen on promoting e-government and women as information technology and financial allies? Or is it because the new information technologies are perceived by them as a fantastic opportunity to get rid of American domination and empower themselves to become global cyber-surfers? What is certain is that electronic surfing has become a favorite sport of the Gulf rulers, and they are discovering a secret rule of this game: that it is essential for women to join in.

Al-Khalifa's emergence in Bahrain is impossible to understand if you do not 30 realize that Bahrain is one of the first Arab countries to invest in e-government. The first step was the creation of an electronic visa system—an e-visa service— that went into operation in mid-2004. The second was reported on the front page of the *Bahrain Tribune* on March 9, 2005: "King Stresses Larger Role for Women." The story explained that "His Majesty the King, Hamad bin Isa al-Khalifa, yester- day requested all government and civil administrations and organizations to help implement the National Strategy for the Advancement of Bahraini Women."

To make sure that his routine-inclined bureaucrats grasped what he meant, 31 the king provided a detailed description: "The implementation of the National Strategy, the first of its type in the country, will help us achieve our objective, which is to see women assume their roles fully as dependable partners to men and fully capable of contributing to building the family, the society, and the state, and eventually, to be involved in making decisions in modern Bahrain."

It is important to note, in this context, that the number of women employed in 32 Bahrain has risen from just over 5 percent in 1971 to more than 40 percent today. Now how can you explain this strange coincidence between the onset of e-government and women's invasion of the labor force and their promotion as public actors if not by a cataclysmic shift in the region's ideological references? Is there not a repu- diation of fanatic conservatism to embark on new horizons where power implies feminization of decision making?

In a humorous 2004 article entitled "The 50 Most Powerful Arab Women," 33 which appeared in the Dubai-based Arabic version of *Forbes* magazine, the editor, Rasha Owais, and her team undertook a survey to answer that question. They came to the conclusion that, beyond the traditional profile of the wives and daughters of heads of state, a new breed of digitally literate and financially skilled women has emerged on the Arab scene.

Some of them do fit the profile of wives of leaders, but—unlike, say, Egypt's 34 Suzan Mubarak or Queen Rania of Jordan—the new Digital Scheherazades are themselves communication wizards. For example, Sheikha Muza, the wife of

A woman in charge: Sheikha Lubna al-Qasimi, minister of economy and planning for the UAE, speaks during a meeting in Abu Dhabi.

the emir of Qatar, the man who financed Al Jazeera, launched in September 2005 the first Arab children's channel. The ambitious objective, financed by a foundation she controls, is to snatch Arab kids from the foreign television influence by providing them with a new ethical content where education and entertainment mix.

35   Being from a royal family helps, of course, but not automatically: I know many wives of powerful, rich men who spend their time swallowing antidepression pills. Self-confidence and ability seem to be key characteristics of the new Digital Scheherazades.

36   When you start looking for them instead of focusing on the veiled women, as many Europeans do, you are amazed by their rapidly growing number. The minister of economy and planning for the United Arab Emirates, for example, is a woman: Lubna al-Qasimi. Before assuming this post, al-Qasimi, who has a computer science degree from the University of California, was a senior manager of the Information Systems department of the Dubai Port Authority and participated in the launch of her country as a planetary digital hub.

Investing in Female Brains

37 Did al-Qasimi owe her success to her being the niece of Sheikh Sultan bin Mohammed al-Qasimi, the ruler of Sharjah, one of the United Arab Emirate kingdoms? There are numerous nieces of powerful emirs and sheikhs in the Gulf who never manage to emerge as top players in the power game. One of her favorite slogans is "I have earned my desk."

38   Indeed, those who still identify the region with veiling women and traditional archaism miss the essential point: the Arab Gulf's previously all-male ruling elite is investing in female brains as the winning card for information-fueled power. "We have a system for our children whereby we encourage them to gain experience outside the group first," says Muhamed al-Sayer, the billionaire chairman of a Kuwait-based group of companies. "For example, my daughter Lulwa spent eight years with Gulf Bank and is its head of Treasury. Male and female family members are offered the same opportunities."

39   It is this fascinating paradox that explains the emergence of Digital Scheherazades. Because men in the Arab Gulf have chosen to invest in communication as a power base, we can understand why one of the most important modern museum initiatives in Kuwait was that of Hussa al-Sabah, who forced Saddam Hussein to give back the cultural heritage pieces stolen from Kuwait after Iraq's invasion, and whose main supporter was her husband. Kuwait is also home to the very young Maha al-Ghunaim, the vice chairwoman and managing director of Global Investment House, which had net profits of $73 million in 2004.

40   In Qatar, where the clever emir propelled his tiny capital of Doha into a global player by financing Al Jazeera, one would expect to find Digital Scheherazades taking advantage of the kingdom's new information technologies. Such is the case with Hanadi Nasser, a businesswoman who has become a key player as the managing director of Amwal, a well-funded Qatari investment company.

The Caliph's Partner

According to my friend Kamal, Caliph Harun al-Rashid, who took power in Baghdad   41
in 786 AD, is the key to elucidating the enigma of the Digital Scheherazades. The
caliph's wife, Zubaida, made herself famous by digging wells along the Baghdad-
Mecca road she had built to transform Muslims' yearly hajj into a comfortable and
engaging trip.

Both Harun and Zubaida were heroes of the *1,001 Nights,* invented by eighth-   42
and ninth-century Baghdad male street-storytellers who mirrored in their tales
the fascination of Muslim elites and crowds with strangers as a source of magic
diversity. And the primary fascinating strangers for men are indeed women. So,
although Scheherazade, the storyteller of the *1,001 Nights,* was supposed to be
Persian, it was Arab women like Princess Zubaida—who managed to seduce the
Caliph Harun while digging wells and building walls to provide creature comforts
during the hajj—who inspired our Baghdad storytellers.

These male storytellers forbade in their fiction the imaginary Scheherazade   43
to speak during the day and condemned her to limit her activity to the night only,
but modern historians are discovering that Zubaida exercised her power 24
hours a day.

Limiting women's power to the night while forbidding them from exercising   44
authority during daylight—the monopoly of males—is a deep-seated reflex that
goes back far into history. It is well condensed in the slogan-like sentence that
ends mechanically each of the 1,001 stories: "When dawn overtook Scheherazade,
she lapsed into silence." But limiting women's power to the private sphere has always been a male fiction. And the defensive fear of the feminine has always gone
together with the fear of strangers. When the leaders of a nation embark on communication as their way to glory, welcoming the different other as a partner is the
magic shift that explains their success.

To understand why modern Arab Gulf emirs are suddenly investing in in-   45
formation technology as their power base and promoting women as their partners, we must go back to Harun, who did the same when he decided to invest
in the paper industry to launch Islam as a communication-powered civilization
whose main weapon was the Arabic language. Just as today, Arabs were scientifically backward in the eighth century, but their switch to communication
enabled them to catch up with other nations by using language to navigate and
conduct dialogue. Arabic, the language of illiterate pagans, was transformed
into a medium of religion, the law, and sciences, promoting the Arabs to global
prominence.

Are we witnessing once again the emergence of women as brainy allies when   46
men opt for communication as their power base? Just to make sure you do not
take me to be blindly optimistic, let me tell you that Western television companies
such as the BBC and CBC are worried about competition in the United States
from Al Jazeera, which has decided to launch an English language channel. As a
woman, I will be more than thrilled if the competition between East and West
switches from bombs and armies to communication strategies.

COMPREHENSION

1. Who is Scheherazade? (If necessary, check Google or another site for information.) Where does she (or the connotations she evokes) appear in the essay?
2. What does Mernissi mean by "digital chaos"? What examples does she provide to illuminate this idea?
3. Explain the connections between digital chaos and the changing roles of women in Muslim society.

RHETORIC

1. Is Mernissi's purpose to inform or to argue—or perhaps both? Justify your response by citing specific sentences and passages.
2. Mernissi's essay appeared in the journal *Current History*. What assumptions does she make about her primary audience? How does she establish her authority for this audience? How might the article appeal to a broader audience?
3. What is the effect of Mernissi's dividing the essay into sections? How does she manage transitions?
4. Analyze the ways in which Scheherazade serves as both symbol and organizing strategy in the essay.
5. Mernissi uses several forms of evidence to support her key ideas. Identify these various strategies of exemplification, and cite specific passages reflecting them.
6. The author is a noted feminist scholar. How do her feminist assumptions affect the tone of the essay? Where does she inject personal opinion? Where, if anywhere, does she make ethical and emotional appeals?

WRITING

1. Although Mernissi writes about a part of the world that might not be familiar, she raises issues that have not just regional but global implications. Write an analytical essay in which you examine the ways in which "digital chaos" is changing gender relationships in the United States or elsewhere.
2. Write a comparative essay linking the articles by Andrew Sullivan and Fatema Mernissi appearing in this chapter.

NETWORKING
Applying Digital and Multimedia Literacies

WRITING AN ARGUMENT   Exploring the Effectiveness of New Communication Strategies: Do you believe that "new communication strategies," as Mernissi terms it, can actually liberate women and reform society? Argue for or against this proposition.

Synthesis: Connections for Critical Thinking

1. Annie Dillard's "An American Childhood" and E. B. White's "Once More to the Lake" explore the experience of childhood from a different perspective. Do they share a common voice or mood? What is distinctive about each essay? Which essay do you prefer, and why? Consider the style and emotional impact of the writing.
2. Both Andrew Sullivan's "Why Gay Marriage Is Good for America" and Richard Rodriguez's "Family Values" attempt to alter stereotypes commonly held about contemporary families. What type of family does each author address? How do the authors differ in their rhetorical strategies and their use of supporting points to buttress their arguments? Who is the implied audience for each of the essays? How did you reach your conclusion?
3. Argue for or against the claim that Kincaid's portrayal of her mother and Mernissi's analysis of Arab men are biased.
4. Argue for or against the idea that descriptions of the relatively new types of family relationships described by Mernissi's "Digital Scheherazades in the Arab World" or in Rodriguez's "Family Values" are presented in a biased, romanticized manner.
5. Argue for or against the view that changes in society and its norms—specifically, increased geographical mobility, an evolving workplace, ideas about economic class, individual liberties, and sexual preference—have resulted in new forms of identity. Use examples from the work of Hood, Mernissi, and Rodriguez.
6. Select the two more substantially argued essays in this chapter, Mernissi's "Digital Scheherazades in the Arab World" and Rodriguez's "Family Values." Compare and contrast their methods of argumentation.
7. Establish your own definition of what it means to be a male or a female. Refer to the essays of Didion, Kincaid, Mernissi, and Rodriguez.

NETWORKING
Applying Digital and Multimedia Literacies

1. Join several newsgroups or chat rooms that focus on online dating. Compare and contrast the ideological focus of the conversations among members.
2. Create your own blog, and post a selected quote regarding the family taken from one of your essays. Enable comments so fellow students can respond regarding the quotation. At the end of the semester, write a report and summary of the responses you received. You may ask students to include their country of origin or their ethnicity to help you find possible connections between these factors and the responses.

chapter 6

History, Culture, and Civilization

Are We Citizens of the World?

In the 21st century, the paroxysms caused by conflicts among peoples, nations, ethnic groups, and cultures continue to shake continents. The United States might have emerged from the cold war as the dominant superpower, but numerous local and global challenges remain. We seem to be at a crossroads in history, culture, and civilization, but does the future hold great promise or equally great danger—or both?

The future assuredly holds significant peril as well as promise. History tells us that while there has never been complete absence of barbarism and nonrational behavior in human affairs, there have been societies, cultures, and nations committed to harmonious, or civil, conduct within various social realms. While it is clear that we have not attained an ideal state of cultural or world development, at the same time, we have advanced beyond the point in primitive civilization at which someone chipped at a stone in order to make a better tool.

As we consider the course of contemporary civilization, we must contend with our own personal histories and cultures as well as with the interplay of contradictory global forces. We have become increasingly concerned with finding a purpose beyond the parameters of our very limiting personal and nationalistic identities, something that the Czech writer and statesman Václav Havel calls the "divine revolution." Indeed, we have entered an era of renewed ethnic strife, in which a preoccupation with cultural difference seems stronger than the desire for universal civilization. The writers assembled here grapple with these contradictions; they search for those constituents of history and culture that might hasten the advent of a civilized world.

The idea of civilization suggests a pluralistic ethos whereby people of diverse histories and backgrounds can maintain cultural identities but also coexist with other cultural representatives in a spirit of tolerance and mutual respect. The wars, upheavals, and catastrophes of the 20th century were spawned by a narrow consciousness. Hopefully, in the new century, all of us can advance the goal of a universal civilization based on the best that we have been able to create for humankind.

PREVIEWING THE CHAPTER

As you read the essays in this chapter and respond to them in discussion and writing, consider the following questions:

- How does the author define *culture, history,* or *civilization?* Is this definition stated or implied? Is it broad or narrow? Explain.
- Is the writer hopeful or pessimistic about the state of culture and history?
- What values does the author seem to think are necessary to advance the idea of history and culture?
- Is the author's tone objective or subjective? What is his or her purpose? Does the author have a personal motive in addressing the topic in the way he or she does?
- Which areas of knowledge—for example, history, philosophy, and political science—does the author bring to bear on the subject?
- Do you agree or disagree with the author's view of the contemporary state of civilization?
- What cultural problems and historical conflicts are raised by the author in his or her treatment of the subject?
- Does the author have a narrow or a broad focus on the relationship of history and culture to the larger society?
- How does the medium the author writes in contribute to his or her perspective on culture, history, or civilization?
- Which authors altered your perspective on a topic, and why?
- Based on your reading of these essays, how would you define *civilization?* Are you hopeful about the current state of civilization?

Classic and Contemporary Images
How Do We Become Americans?

Using a Critical Perspective   Compare the scene of early-20th-century immigrants at New York City's Ellis Island with the March 1999 X-ray photo taken by Mexican authorities of human forms and cargo in a truck. What mood is conveyed by each representation? Does each photograph have a thesis or argument? Explain. Which photo do you find more engaging and provocative, and why?

From the time of the first European settlers, the North American continent has experienced wave after wave of immigration from every part of the world. One period of heavy immigration occurred in the late 19th and early 20th centuries, when millions of people from eastern and southern Europe entered the United States through Ellis Island in New York City, as shown in this classic photograph.

More recently, immigrants continue to come from all over the world,
often entering the country illegally. The X-ray photo shows
a wide shot and a close-up image of people being smuggled
across Mexico's border with Guatemala.

Classic and Contemporary Essays
ARE WE MOVING TOWARD A WORLD CULTURE?

Both of these essays address the issues of national and global identification. As you read them, consider not only the differing styles and strategies of discourse of their authors, but also their common themes and claims. In addition, consider that J. B. Priestley writes from a classically British experience of the nation-state, while Ishmael Reed is writing as a representative of a racial and (to his mind) cultural minority. Both, however, write within the context of the modern democratic state. And both are forthright and direct in their arguments, offering cultural analysis, appeals to authority, and historical evidence. As keen observers of the modern political scene, Priestley and Reed examine the very contours of civilization. But Priestley, a more traditional or classical writer than Reed, operates from a uniquely English perspective rooted in a clear sense of region. On the other hand, Reed, whose style is more informal, operates from an African American perspective rooted in an understanding that much of Western civilization draws its roots from a multiplicity of sources, not just European. We might be examining the reflections of two different personalities, but consider also the ways in which their agendas overlap.

Wrong Ism

J. B. Priestley

John Boynton Priestley (1894–1984), best-selling English novelist and popular dramatist, was also a prolific writer of essays, many of them involving social and political criticism. His work includes The English Novel *(1927),* The Good Companions *(1929),* Time and the Conways *(1937),* An Inspector Calls *(1946), and* The English *(1973). This selection from* Essays of Five Decades *(1968) offers an astute analysis of contemporary political habits.*

1 There are three isms that we ought to consider very carefully—regionalism, nationalism, internationalism. Of these three the one there is most fuss about, the one that starts men shouting and marching and shooting, the one that seems to have all the depth and thrust and fire, is of course nationalism. Nine people out of ten, I fancy, would say that of this trio it is the one that really counts, the big boss. Regionalism and internationalism, they would add, are comparatively small, shadowy, rather cranky. And I believe all this to be quite wrong. Like many another big boss, nationalism is largely bogus. It is like a bunch of flowers made of plastics.

The real flowers belong to regionalism. The mass of people everywhere may 2
never have used the term. They are probably regionalists without knowing it.
Because they have been brought up in a certain part of the world, they have
formed perhaps quite unconsciously a deep attachment to its landscape and
speech, its traditional customs, its food and drink, its songs and jokes. (There are
of course always the rebels, often intellectuals and writers, but they are not the
mass of people.) They are rooted in their region. Indeed, without this attachment
a man can have no roots.

So much of people's lives, from earliest childhood onwards, is deeply inter- 3
twined with the common life of the region, they cannot help feeling strongly about
it. A threat to it is a knife pointing at the heart. How can life ever be the same if
bullying strangers come to change everything? The form and colour, the very
taste and smell of dear familiar things will be different, alien, life-destroying. It
would be better to die fighting. And it is precisely this, the nourishing life of the
region, for which common men have so often fought and died.

This attachment to the region exists on a level far deeper than that of any 4
political hocus-pocus. When a man says "my country" with real feeling, he is
thinking about his region, all that has made up his life, and not about that political
entity, the nation. There can be some confusion here simply because some countries are so small—and ours is one of them—and so old, again like ours, that
much of what is national is also regional. Down the centuries, the nation, itself, so
comparatively small, has been able to attach to itself the feeling really created by
the region. (Even so there is something left over, as most people in Yorkshire or
Devon, for example, would tell you.) This probably explains the fervent patriotism
developed early in small countries. The English were announcing that they were
English in the Middle Ages, before nationalism had arrived elsewhere.

If we deduct from nationalism all that it has borrowed or stolen from regional- 5
ism, what remains is mostly rubbish. The nation, as distinct from the region, is
largely the creation of power-men and political manipulators. Almost all nationalist
movements are led by ambitious frustrated men determined to hold office. I am
not blaming them. I would do the same if I were in their place and wanted power
so badly. But nearly always they make use of the rich warm regional feeling, the
emotional dynamo of the movement, while being almost untouched by it themselves. This is because they are not as a rule deeply loyal to any region themselves. Ambition and a love of power can eat like acid into the tissues of regional
loyalty. It is hard, if not impossible, to retain a natural piety and yet be forever
playing both ends against the middle.

Being itself a power structure, devised by men of power, the nation tends to 6
think and act in terms of power. What would benefit the real life of the region,
where men, women and children actually live, is soon sacrificed for the power and
prestige of the nation. (And the personal vanity of presidents and ministers themselves, which historians too often disregard.) Among the new nations of our time
innumerable peasants and labourers must have found themselves being cut down
from five square meals a week to three in order to provide unnecessary airlines,
military forces that can only be used against them and nobody else, great conference

halls and official yachts and the rest. The last traces of imperialism and colonialism may have to be removed from Asia and Africa, where men can no longer endure being condemned to a permanent inferiority by the colour of their skins; but even so, the modern world, the real world of our time, does not want and would be far better without more and more nations, busy creating for themselves the very paraphernalia that western Europe is now trying to abolish. You are compelled to answer more questions when trying to spend half a day in Cambodia than you are now travelling from the Hook of Holland to Syracuse.

7   This brings me to internationalism. I dislike this term, which I used only to complete the isms. It suggests financiers and dubious promoters living nowhere but in luxury hotels; a shallow world of entrepreneurs and impresarios. (Was it Sacha Guitry who said that impresarios were men who spoke many languages but all with a foreign accent?) The internationalism I have in mind here is best described as world civilisation. It is life considered on a global scale. Most of our communications and transport already exist on this high wide level. So do many other things from medicine to meteorology. Our astronomers and physicists (except where they have allowed themselves to be hush-hushed) work here. The UN special agencies, about which we hear far too little, have contributed more and more to this world civilisation. All the arts, when they are arts and not chunks of nationalist propaganda, naturally take their place in it. And it grows, widens, deepens, in spite of the fact that for every dollar, ruble, pound or franc spent in explaining and praising it, a thousand are spent by the nations explaining and praising themselves.

8   This world civilisation and regionalism can get along together, especially if we keep ourselves sharply aware of their quite different but equally important values and rewards. A man can make his contribution to world civilisation and yet remain strongly regional in feeling: I know several men of this sort. There is of course the danger—it is with us now—of the global style flattening out the regional, taking local form, colour, flavour, away for ever, disinheriting future generations, threatening them with sensuous poverty and a huge boredom. But to understand and appreciate regionalism is to be on guard against this danger. And we must therefore make a clear distinction between regionalism and nationalism.

9   It is nationalism that tries to check the growth of world civilisation. And nationalism, when taken on a global scale, is more aggressive and demanding now than it has ever been before. This in the giant powers is largely disguised by the endless fuss in public about rival ideologies, now a largely unreal quarrel. What is intensely real is the glaring nationalism. Even the desire to police the world is nationalistic in origin. (Only the world can police the world.) Moreover, the nation-states of today are for the most part far narrower in their outlook, far more inclined to allow prejudice against the foreigner to impoverish their own style of living, than the old imperial states were. It should be part of world civilisation that men with particular skills, perhaps the product of the very regionalism they are rebelling against, should be able to move easily from country to country, to exercise those skills, in anything from teaching the violin to running a new type of factory to managing an old hotel. But nationalism, especially of the newer sort, would rather see

everything done badly than allow a few non-nationals to get to work. And people face a barrage of passports, visas, immigration controls, labour permits; and in this respect are worse off than they were in 1900. But even so, in spite of all that nationalism can do—so long as it keeps its nuclear bombs to itself—the internationalism I have in mind, slowly creating a world civilisation, cannot be checked.

Nevertheless, we are still backing the wrong ism. Almost all our money goes 10 on the middle one, nationalism, the rotten meat between the two healthy slices of bread. We need regionalism to give us roots and that very depth of feeling which nationalism unjustly and greedily claims for itself. We need internationalism to save the world and to broaden and heighten our civilisation. While regional man enriches the lives that international man is already working to keep secure and healthy, national man, drunk with power, demands our loyalty, money and applause, and poisons the very air with his dangerous nonsense.

COMPREHENSION

1. What thesis does Priestley present? State the thesis in your own words.
2. Define *regionalism, nationalism,* and *internationalism* as Priestley presents these terms.
3. Explain Priestley's objections to nationalism. Where does he state these objections in the essay? What alternative does he propose?

RHETORIC

1. What striking metaphor does the author develop to capture the essence of nationalism? What is its sensory impact? Analyze another example of metaphorical language in the essay.
2. How does the suffix *-ism* function stylistically in the essay?
3. What is Priestley's principle of classification in this essay? How does he maintain proportion in the presentation of categories?
4. Analyze the relationship between definition and classification in the essay.
5. Examine Priestley's use of comparison and contrast.
6. Explain the connection between the introductory and concluding paragraphs.

WRITING

1. Priestley makes many assumptions about regionalism, nationalism, and internationalism. Which assumptions do you accept? Which assumptions do you reject? Explain in an essay.
2. Write a classification essay on at least three related isms: capitalism, socialism, and communism; Protestantism, Catholicism, and Judaism; or regionalism, nationalism, and internationalism.
3. **Writing an Argument:** Take issue with Priestley's assertion that the "real flowers belong to regionalism," and argue that regionalism today is a destructive force in world affairs.

NETWORKING
Applying Digital and Multimedia Literacies

Considering the Isms of Online Communities: Write an essay arguing that a particular online community—such as a social networking site (Facebook, Twitter, Google+, Meetup, Craigslist), a virtual community like Second Life, a gaming site or subscription (such as X-Box Live), or similar—contributes primarily to a sense of internationalism, nationalism, regionalism, and/or isolationism. Use specific evidence to support your argument.

America: The Multinational Society

Ishmael Reed

Ishmael Reed (b. 1938), an American novelist, poet, and essayist, is the founder and editor (along with Al Young) of Quilt *magazine, begun in 1981. In his writing, Reed uses a combination of standard English, black dialect, and slang to interrogate American society. He believes that African Americans must move away from identification with Europe in order to rediscover their African qualities. Reed's books include* Flight to Canada *(1976),* The Terrible Twos *(1982),* The Terrible Threes *(1989),* Japanese by Spring *(1993), and* The Reed Reader *(2000). In addition, he has written volumes of verse, including* A Secretary to the Spirits *(1975), and has published collections of his essays, including* Airing Dirty Laundry *(1993). In the following essay from* Writin' Is Fightin' *(1990), Reed seeks to debunk the myth of the European ideal and argues for a universal definition of culture.*

At the annual Lower East Side Jewish Festival yesterday, a Chinese woman ate a pizza slice in front of Ty Thuan Duc's Vietnamese grocery store. Beside her a Spanish-speaking family patronized a cart with two signs: "Italian Ices" and "Kosher by Rabbi Alper." And after the pastrami ran out, everybody ate knishes.

—New York Times, *June 23, 1983*

1   On the day before Memorial Day, 1983, a poet called me to describe a city he had just visited. He said that one section included mosques, built by the Islamic people who dwelled there. Attending his reading, he said, were large numbers of Hispanic people, forty thousand of whom lived in the same city. He was not talking about a fabled city located in some mysterious region of the world. The city he'd visited was Detroit.

2   A few months before, as I was leaving Houston, Texas, I heard it announced on the radio that Texas's largest minority was Mexican American, and though a

foundation recently issued a report critical of bilingual education, the taped voice used to guide the passengers on the air trams connecting terminals in Dallas Airport is in both Spanish and English. If the trend continues, a day will come when it will be difficult to travel through some sections of the country without hearing commands in both English and Spanish; after all, for some western states, Spanish was the first written language and the Spanish style lives on in the western way of life.

Shortly after my Texas trip, I sat in an auditorium located on the campus of 3 the University of Wisconsin at Milwaukee as a Yale professor—whose original work on the influence of African cultures upon those of the Americas has led to his ostracism from some monocultural intellectual circles—walked up and down the aisle, like an old-time southern evangelist, dancing and drumming the top of the lectern, illustrating his points before some serious Afro-American intellectuals and artists who cheered and applauded his performance and his mastery of information. The professor was "white." After his lecture, he joined a group of Milwaukeeans in a conversation. All of the participants spoke Yoruban, though only the professor had ever traveled to Africa.

One of the artists told me that his paintings, which included African and 4 Afro-American mythological symbols and imagery, were hanging in the local McDonald's restaurant. The next day I went to McDonald's and snapped pictures of smiling youngsters eating hamburgers below paintings that could grace the walls of any of the country's leading museums. The manager of the local McDonald's said, "I don't know what you boys are doing, but I like it," as he commissioned the local painters to exhibit in his restaurant.

Such blurring of cultural styles occurs in everyday life in the United States to 5 a greater extent than anyone can imagine and is probably more prevalent than the sensational conflict between people of different backgrounds that is played up and often encouraged by the media. The result is what the Yale professor, Robert Thompson, referred to as a cultural bouillabaisse, yet members of the nation's present educational and cultural Elect still cling to the notion that the United States belongs to some vaguely defined entity they refer to as "Western civilization," by which they mean, presumably, a civilization created by the people of Europe, as if Europe can be viewed in monolithic terms. Is Beethoven's Ninth Symphony, which includes Turkish marches, a part of Western civilization, or the late nineteenth- and twentieth-century French paintings, whose creators were influenced by Japanese art? And what of the cubists, through whom the influence of African art changed modern painting, or the surrealists, who were so impressed with the art of the Pacific Northwest Indians that, in their map of North America, Alaska dwarfs the lower forty-eight in size?

Are the Russians, who are often criticized for their adoption of "Western" 6 ways by Tsarist dissidents in exile, members of Western civilization? And what of the millions of Europeans who have black African and Asian ancestry, black Africans having occupied several countries for hundreds of years? Are these "Europeans" members of Western civilization, or the Hungarians, who originated across the Urals in a place called Greater Hungary, or the Irish, who came from the Iberian Peninsula?

7   Even the notion that North America is part of Western civilization because our "system of government" is derived from Europe is being challenged by Native American historians who say that the founding fathers, Benjamin Franklin especially, were actually influenced by the system of government that had been adopted by the Iroquois hundreds of years prior to the arrival of large numbers of Europeans.

8   Western civilization, then, becomes another confusing category like Third World, or Judeo-Christian culture, as man attempts to impose his small-screen view of political and cultural reality upon a complex world. Our most publicized novelist recently said that Western civilization was the greatest achievement of mankind, an attitude that flourishes on the street level as scribbles in public restrooms: "White Power," "Niggers and Spics Suck," or "Hitler was a prophet," the latter being the most telling, for wasn't Adolph [sic] Hitler the archetypal monoculturalist who, in his pigheaded arrogance, believed that one way and one blood was so pure that it had to be protected from alien strains at all costs? Where did such an attitude, which has caused so much misery and depression in our national life, which has tainted even our noblest achievements, begin? An attitude that caused the incarceration of Japanese-American citizens during World War II, the persecution of Chicanos and Chinese Americans, the near-extermination of the Indians, and the murder and lynchings of thousands of Afro-Americans.

9   Virtuous, hardworking, pious, even though they occasionally would wander off after some fancy clothes, or rendezvous in the woods with the town prostitute, the Puritans are idealized in our schoolbooks as "a hardy band" of no-nonsense patriarchs whose discipline razed the forest and brought order to the New World (a term that annoys Native American historians). Industrious, responsible, it was their "Yankee ingenuity" and practicality that created the work ethic. They were simple folk who produced a number of good poets, and they set the tone for the American writing style, of lean and spare lines, long before Hemingway. They worshiped in churches whose colors blended in with the New England snow, churches with simple structures and ornate lecterns.

10   The Puritans were a daring lot, but they had a mean streak. They hated the theater and banned Christmas. They punished people in a cruel and inhuman manner. They killed children who disobeyed their parents. When they came in contact with those whom they considered heathens or aliens, they behaved in such a bizarre and irrational manner that this chapter in the American history comes down to us as a late-movie horror film. They exterminated the Indians, who taught them how to survive in a world unknown to them, and their encounter with the calypso culture of Barbados resulted in what the tourist guide in Salem's Witches' House refers to as the Witchcraft Hysteria.

11   The Puritan legacy of hard work and meticulous accounting led to the establishment of a great industrial society; it is no wonder that the American industrial revolution began in Lowell, Massachusetts, but there was the other side, the strange and paranoid attitudes toward those different from the Elect.

The cultural attitudes of that early Elect continue to be voiced in everyday 12
life in the United States: the president of a distinguished university, writing a letter to the *Times*, belittling the study of African civilizations; the television network
that promoted its show on the Vatican art with the boast that this art represented
"the finest achievements of the human spirit." A modern up-tempo state of complex rhythms that depends upon contacts with an international community can
no longer behave as if it dwelled in a "Zion Wilderness" surrounded by beasts
and pagans.

When I heard a schoolteacher warn the other night about the invasion of the 13
American educational system by foreign curriculums, I wanted to yell at the television set, "Lady, they're already here." It has already begun because the
world is here. The world has been arriving at these shores for at least ten thousand years from Europe, Africa, and Asia. In the late nineteenth and early
twentieth centuries, large numbers of Europeans arrived, adding their cultures to those of the European, African, and Asian settlers who were already
here, and recently millions have been entering the country from South America
and the Caribbean, making Yale Professor Bob Thompson's bouillabaisse
richer and thicker.

One of our most visionary politicians said that he envisioned a time when the 14
United States could become the brain of the world, by which he meant the reposi-
tory of all of the latest advanced information systems. I thought of that remark
when an enterprising poet friend of mine called to say that he had just sold a poem
to a computer magazine and that the editors were delighted to get it because they
didn't carry fiction or poetry. Is that the kind of world we desire? A humdrum
homogeneous world of all brains but no heart, no fiction, no poetry; a world of
robots with human attendants bereft of imagination, of culture? Or does North
America deserve a more exciting destiny? To become a place where the cultures
of the world crisscross. This is possible because the United States is unique in the
world: The world is here.

COMPREHENSION

1. Why does Reed believe that the conventional notion of Western or European civilization is misleading when applied to the American experience?
2. According to Reed, what are the origins of our monoculturalist view?
3. What are the dangers of such a narrow view? What historical examples does Reed
   allude to?

RHETORIC

1. How do paragraphs 1–4 help set the stage for Reed's discourse? Does this section
   contain his thesis?
2. Does the computer analogy in Reed's conclusion work? Do his rhetorical questions
   underscore the thesis?

3. Comment on the author's extensive use of details and examples. How do they serve to support his point? Which examples are especially illuminating, and why?
4. What kind of humor does Reed use in his essay? Does its use contribute to the force of his essay? Why or why not?
5. Is Reed's reasoning inductive or deductive? Justify your answer.
6. How does Reed employ definitions to structure his essay?

WRITING

1. How does America's insistence that it "belongs to . . . 'Western Civilization'" affect its dealings with other nations? How does it influence the way it treats its own citizens? Explore these questions in a causal-analysis essay, using support from Reed.
2. Write an essay in which you consider how a multinational United States affects you on a day-to-day basis. How does it enrich your life or the life of the country? Use specific examples and details to support your opinion.
3. **Writing an Argument:** Write an essay arguing that a multinational society is often riddled with complex problems. What are some of the drawbacks or disadvantages of such a society? What causes these conflicts? Explore these issues in your writing.

NETWORKING
Applying Digital and Multimedia Literacies

Comparing Style across Media: Go to Thirteen.org and find the video for "An Evening with Ishmael Reed and Al Young." Watch Ishmael Reed discuss the concept of being an "ethnic gate-crasher," an advocate of transnationalism. How does this brief video influence your reading of "America: The Multinational Society"? What does Reed convey through his physical presence and voice? Discuss the advantages and disadvantages of this conversational style of conveying ideas, as opposed to the formal, text-only presentation of an essay.

Synthesis: Classic and Contemporary Questions for Comparison

1. How do the respective tones of Priestley's and Reed's essays differ? What clues are contained in the texts that make this difference evident? Use examples from both.
2. In his essay, Priestley argues against nationalism and professes to be a proponent of regionalism and internationalism. Compare Priestley's view with Reed's argument that to be an "American" means to accept the variety of influences that have converged into a "multinational society." How do these arguments differ? How are they similar?
3. Discuss both Priestley's and Reed's essays in terms of formality of voice. Does one author speak with more authority than the other? Or are they equally authoritative, but employing the stylistic modes of their times? Use examples from both essays.

America's "Oh Sh*t" Moment

Niall Ferguson

Niall Ferguson *(b. 1964), who was born in Glasgow, Scotland, is a British historian and media personality. With degrees from Magdalen College, Oxford, including a Doctor of Philosophy, Ferguson is an influential public intellectual whose work focuses on the economic forces shaping history, society, and civilization. His books include* The Assault of Money *(2008) and* Civilization: The West and the Rest *(2011). Ferguson also has presented five well-received television series. He writes a weekly column for* Newsweek, *where the essay that follows, dealing with the prospects for American decline, appeared in 2011.*

Don't call me a "declinist." I really don't believe the United States—or Western ₁ civilization, more generally—is in some kind of gradual, inexorable decline.

But that's not because I am one of those incorrigible optimists who agree ₂ with Winston Churchill that the United States will always do the right thing, albeit when all other possibilities have been exhausted.

In my view, civilizations don't rise, fall, and then gently decline, as inevitably ₃ and predictably as the four seasons or the seven ages of man. History isn't one smooth, parabolic curve after another. Its shape is more like an exponentially steepening slope that quite suddenly drops off like a cliff.

If you don't know what I mean, pay a visit to Machu Picchu, the lost city of the ₄ Incas. In 1530 the Incas were the masters of all they surveyed from the heights of the Peruvian Andes. Within less than a decade, foreign invaders with horses, gunpowder, and lethal diseases had smashed their empire to smithereens. Today tourists gawp at the ruins that remain.

The notion that civilizations don't decline but collapse inspired the anthropologist ₅ Jared Diamond's 2005 book, *Collapse.* But Diamond focused, fashionably, on manmade environmental disasters as the causes of collapse. As a historian, I take a broader view. My point is that when you look back on the history of past civilizations, a striking feature is the speed with which most of them collapsed, regardless of the cause.

The Roman Empire didn't decline and fall sedately, as historians used to ₆ claim. It collapsed within a few decades in the early fifth century, tipped over the edge of chaos by barbarian invaders and internal divisions. In the space of a generation, the vast imperial metropolis of Rome fell into disrepair, the aqueducts broken, the splendid marketplaces deserted.

The Ming dynasty's rule in China also fell apart with extraordinary speed in ₇ the mid-17th century, succumbing to internal strife and external invasion. Again, the transition from equipoise to anarchy took little more than a decade.

A more recent and familiar example of precipitous decline is, of course, the ₈ collapse of the Soviet Union. And, if you still doubt that collapse comes suddenly, just think of how the postcolonial dictatorships of North Africa and the Middle East imploded this year. Twelve months ago, Messrs. Ben Ali, Mubarak, and Gaddafi seemed secure in their gaudy palaces. Here yesterday, gone today.

9   What all these collapsed powers have in common is that the complex social systems that underpinned them suddenly ceased to function. One minute rulers had legitimacy in the eyes of their people; the next they didn't.

10   This process is a familiar one to students of financial markets. Even as I write, it is far from clear that the European Monetary Union can be salvaged from the dramatic collapse of confidence in the fiscal policies of its peripheral member states. In the realm of power, as in the domain of the bond vigilantes, you're fine until you're not fine—and when you're not fine, you're suddenly in a terrifying death spiral.

11   Remember that poster that used to hang in every college dorm, of a runaway steam train that has crashed through the wall of a rail station and hit the street below, nose first? The caption was: "Oh sh*t!" I believe it's time to ask how close the United States is to the "Oh sh*t!" moment—the moment we suddenly crash downward like that train.

12   The West first surged ahead of the Rest after about 1500 thanks to a series of institutional innovations that I call the "killer applications":

1. *Competition.* Europe was politically fragmented into multiple monarchies and republics, which were in turn internally divided into competing corporate entities, among them the ancestors of modern business corporations.
2. *The Scientific Revolution.* All the major 17th-century breakthroughs in mathematics, astronomy, physics, chemistry, and biology happened in Western Europe.
3. *The Rule of Law and Representative Government.* An optimal system of social and political order emerged in the English-speaking world, based on private-property rights and the representation of property owners in elected legislatures.
4. *Modern Medicine.* Nearly all the major 19th- and 20th-century breakthroughs in health care were made by Western Europeans and North Americans.

5. *The Consumer Society.* The Industrial Revolution took place where there was both a supply of productivity-enhancing technologies and a demand for more, better, and cheaper goods, beginning with cotton garments.

6. *The Work Ethic.* Westerners were the first people in the world to combine more extensive and intensive labor with higher savings rates, permitting sustained capital accumulation.

For hundreds of years, these killer apps were essentially monopolized by 13 Europeans and their cousins who settled in North America and Australasia. They are the best explanation for what economic historians call "the great divergence": the astonishing gap that arose between Western standards of living and those in the rest of the world.

In 1500 the average Chinese was richer than the average North American. 14 By the late 1970s the American was more than 20 times richer than the Chinese. Westerners not only grew richer than "Resterners." They grew taller, healthier, and longer-lived. They also grew more powerful. By the early 20th century, just a dozen Western empires—including the United States—controlled 58 percent of the world's land surface and population, and a staggering 74 percent of the global economy.

Beginning with Japan, however, one non-Western society after another 15 has worked out that these apps can be downloaded and installed in non-Western operating systems. That explains about half the catching up that we have witnessed in our lifetimes, especially since the onset of economic reforms in China in 1978.

Now, I am not one of those people filled with angst at the thought of a world 16 in which the average American is no longer vastly richer than the average Chinese. Indeed, I welcome the escape of hundreds of millions of Asians from poverty, not to mention the improvements we are seeing in South America and parts of Africa. But there is a second, more insidious cause of the "great reconvergence," which I do deplore—and that is the tendency of Western societies to delete their own killer apps.

Ask yourself: who's got the work ethic now? The average South Korean works 17 about 39 percent more hours per week than the average American. The school year in South Korea is 220 days long, compared with 180 days here. And you don't have to spend too long at any major U.S. university to know which students really drive themselves: the Asians and Asian-Americans.

18   The consumer society? Did you know that 26 of the 30 biggest shopping malls in the world are now in emerging markets, mostly in Asia? Only three are in the United States. And, boy, do they look forlorn these days, as maxed-out Americans struggle to pay down their debts.

19   Modern medicine? Well, we certainly outspend everyone else. As a share of gross domestic product, the United States spends twice what Japan spends on health care and more than three times what China spends. Yet life expectancy in the U.S. has risen from 70 to 78 in the past 50 years, compared with leaps from 68 to 83 in Japan and from 43 to 73 in China.

20   The rule of law? For a real eye-opener, take a look at the latest World Economic Forum (WEF) Executive Opinion Survey. On no fewer than 15 of 16 different issues relating to property rights and governance, the United States fares worse than Hong Kong. Indeed, the U.S. makes the global top 20 in only one area: investor protection. On every other count, its reputation is shockingly bad. The U.S. ranks 86th in the world for the costs imposed on business by organized crime, 50th for public trust in the ethics of politicians, 42nd for various forms of bribery and 40th for standards of auditing and financial reporting.

21   What about science? It's certainly true that U.S.-based scientists continue to walk off with plenty of Nobel Prizes each year. But Nobel winners are old men. The future belongs not to them but to today's teenagers. Here's another striking statistic. Every three years the Organization of Economic Cooperation and Development's Program for International Student Assessment tests the educational attainment of 15-year-olds around the world. The latest data on "mathematical literacy" reveal that the gap between the world leaders—the students of Shanghai and Singapore—and their American counterparts is now as big as the gap between U.S. kids and teenagers in Albania and Tunisia.

22   The late, lamented Steve Jobs convinced Americans that the future would be "Designed by Apple in California. Assembled in China." Yet statistics from the World Intellectual Property Organization show that already more patents originate in Japan than in the U.S., that South Korea overtook Germany to take third place in 2005, and that China is poised to overtake Germany too.

23   Finally, there's competition, the original killer app that sent the fragmented West down a completely different path from monolithic imperial China. Well, the WEF has conducted a comprehensive Global Competitiveness survey every year since 1979. Since the current methodology was adopted in 2004, the United States' average competitiveness score has fallen from 5.82 to 5.43, one of the steepest declines among developed economies. China's score, meanwhile, has leapt up from 4.29 to 4.90.

24   And it's not only that we're becoming less competitive abroad. Perhaps more disturbing is the decline of meaningful competition at home, as the social mobility of the postwar era has given way to an extraordinary social polarization. You don't have to be an Occupy Wall Street leftist to believe that the American super-rich

elite—the 1 percent that collects 20 percent of the income—has become danger-ously divorced from the rest of society, especially from the underclass at the bottom of the income distribution.

But if we are headed toward collapse, what would an American "Oh sh*t!" 25 moment look like? An upsurge in civil unrest and crime, as happened in the 1970s? A loss of faith on the part of investors and a sudden Greek-style leap in government borrowing costs? How about a spike of violence in the Middle East, from Iraq to Afghanistan, as insurgents capitalize on our troop withdrawals? Or a paralyzing cyberattack from the rising Asian superpower we complacently underrate?

Is there anything we can do to prevent such disasters? Social scientist 26 Charles Murray calls for a "civic great awakening"—a return to the original values of the American republic. He's got a point. Far more than in Europe, most Americans remain instinctively loyal to the killer applications of Western ascen-dancy, from competition all the way through to the work ethic. They know the country has the right software. They just can't understand why it's running so damn slowly.

What we need to do is to delete the viruses that have crept into our system: 27 the anticompetitive quasi monopolies that blight everything from banking to public education; the politically correct pseudosciences and soft subjects that deflect good students away from hard science; the lobbyists who subvert the rule of law for the sake of the special interests they represent—to say nothing of our crazily dysfunctional system of health care, our overleveraged personal finances and our newfound unemployment ethic.

Then we need to download the updates that are running more successfully in 28 other countries, from Finland to New Zealand, from Denmark to Hong Kong, from Singapore to Sweden.

And finally we need to reboot our whole system. 29

I refuse to accept that Western civilization is like some hopeless old version of 30 Microsoft DOS, doomed to freeze, then crash. I still cling to the hope that the United States is the Mac to Europe's PC, and that if one part of the West can successfully update and reboot itself, it's America.

But the lesson of history is clear. Voters and politicians alike dare not post- 31 pone the big reboot. Decline is not so gradual that our biggest problems can simply be left to the next administration, or the one after that.

If what we are risking is not decline but downright collapse, then the time 32 frame maybe even tighter than one election cycle.

COMPREHENSION

1. What does Ferguson mean when he states, "History isn't one smooth, parabolic curve after another" (paragraph 3)? What evidence does he provide to support this comment?
2. List and summarize the "killer applications" that the writer presents.
3. According to Ferguson, is the United States destined to face an "Oh Sh*t" moment? Why or why not?

RHETORIC

1. What is the effect of Ferguson's title? Are you shocked by it? Why or why not? What is his intention in presenting this shocking title, and how does it influence the tone of the essay?
2. How does the introductory section (paragraphs 1–3) help to establish Ferguson's claim? What is his claim, and where does he state it?
3. Explain the grounds and types of support that Ferguson provides to reinforce his claim.
4. How does Ferguson use classification and process analysis to advance his claim and organize parts of the essay?
5. Why does Ferguson use analogies drawn from computer science and digital sources? Where do these analogies appear? What is the effect?

WRITING

1. Compose your own essay entitled "America's 'Oh Sh*t' Moment." Base your essay in part on a careful rereading of Ferguson's text.
2. Ferguson refers to Jared Diamond's book *Collapse* to support his analysis of the decline of civilizations. An essay by Diamond begins on page 684. After reading Diamond's essay, write a comparative analysis of the two texts.
3. **Writing an Argument:** Do you agree or disagree with Ferguson's assertion, "What we need to do is to delete the viruses that have crept into our system"? Respond to this statement in an argumentative essay.

NETWORKING
Applying Digital and Multimedia Literacies

Composing a Hyperlinked Essay: To support your argument in question 3 under Writing, research one of the civilizations mentioned by Ferguson—the Roman Empire, the Ming Dynasty, or the Soviet Union—and write an analysis of the causes contributing to this civilization's decline. Format your essay as an electronic or online text, using hyperlinks to enhance your content and take readers to relevant sites that support your analysis of the civilization you've chosen to focus on or the related argument you are making about our own. Use at least six carefully chosen hyperlinks in your essay.

1776 and All That: America after September 11

Edward Hoagland

Edward Hoagland (b. 1932) is an acknowledged American master of both fiction and nonfiction; he is especially adept in the art of nature writing. Hoagland had published his first award-winning novel, Cat Man *(1956), before he graduated from*

Harvard University, and in the following decades he wrote 16 additional books, including Walking the Dead Diamond River *(1973),* African Calliope *(1976),* Tigers and Ice *(1999), and a memoir,* Compass Points *(2001). Among his honors are a Guggenheim Fellowship, an O. Henry Award, and an award from the American Academy of Arts and Letters. Hoagland, a world traveler constantly in search of raw personal experience set against natural backdrops and ecological crises, taught at Bennington College for two decades before retiring in 2005. In the essay that follows, which appeared in the* Nation *shortly after the events of 9/11, Hoagland warns us about the dangers awaiting a nation forgetful of its revolutionary origins.*

The country is riven and ailing, with a guns-plus-butter nuttiness in some of its 1
governing echelons and the sort of lapsed logic implicit in the collapse of trust in money-center capitalism, which has been an undergirding theory of a good deal of the work that many people do. The tallest buildings, real profit centers, fall, as "wogs" and "ragheads" defy us, perhaps comparably to how the "gooks" in Vietnam did (from whose example Osama bin Laden may have learned that we could be defeated). But that was on foreign soil, and we believed that we had pulled our punches and beaten ourselves, and so remained triumphalist for the remainder of the twentieth century, as we had been practically since Reconstruction.

Now we're not so sure. For the first time since the War of 1812 we have been 2
damaged in continental America by foreigners, having made other people hate us, though we had never needed to pay attention to such matters before. Proxies could fight the malcontents for us in places like Central America, and the Japanese and Germans, would-be conquerors, had not felt much real animus, becoming close, amicable allies after the war. Our first World War II hero, Colin Kelly, three days after Pearl Harbor, flew his B-17 bomber (as media myth had it) in kamikaze fashion to hit a Japanese cruiser, before the Japanese made a practice of it. To give your life for your country, like Nathan Hale, is an ideal that's since evaporated.

Obese individually and as a nation, and trying to stall the aging process, we 3
talk instead of cars and taxes, sports and movies, cancer and entitlements, but with a half-unmentioned inkling too of what more ominously may be in store—a premonition that our righteous confidence might have served us just a bit too well. We never agonized a lot about killing off the Indians, or our slaving history either, once that was over, or being the only nuclear power ever to incinerate multitudes of people. We've hardly seemed to notice when free enterprise segues into simple greed, because our religious beginnings countenanced rapacity, as long as you tithed. Settling the seaboard in official belts of piety, whether Puritan, Anglican, Quaker or Dutch Reformed (only the frontier tended to be atheistic), we seized land and water with abandon, joined by Catholics, Lutherans, Methodists and what have you, westward ho. Each group encouraged its rich men to creep like a camel through the eye of the needle, and political freedoms were gradually canted away from the pure ballot box toward influence-buying.

We swallowed all of that because the New World dream envisioned every- 4
body working hard and getting fairly rich, except when undertows of doubt pervaded our prosperity, as in the 1930s and 1960s; or now when, feeling gridlocked,

we wonder if we haven't gone too far and used the whole place up. We seem to need some kind of condom invented just for greed—a latex sac where spasms of that particular vice can be ejaculated, captured and contained. Like lust, it's not going to go away. Nor will Monopoly games do the trick, any more than porno-graphic videos erase impulses that might result in harm. The old phrase patrons of prostitutes used to use—"getting your ashes hauled"—said it pretty well, and if we could persuade people to think of greed, as well, that way and expel its de-structiveness perhaps into a computer screen, trapping the piggishness in cyber-space might save a bit of Earth. The greediest guys would not be satisfied, but greed might be looked on as slightly outre.

5   Some vertigo or "near death" experience of global warming may be re-quired to trip the necessary degree of alarm. The droughts and water wars, a polar meltdown and pelagic crisis—too much saltwater and insufficient fresh. In the meantime, dried-up high plains agriculture and Sunbelt golf greens in the Republicans' heartlands will help because African famines are never enough. We need a surge of altruism, artesian decency. The oddity of greed nowadays is that it is so often solo—in the service of one ego—not ducal or kingly, as the apparatus of an unjust state. Overweening possession, such as McMansions and so on, will be loony in the century we are entering upon—ecologically, econom-ically, morally, commonsensically. But how will we realize this, short of disas-trous procrastination? Hurricanes and centrifugal violence on the home front, not to mention angry Arabs flying into the World Trade Center? That astounded us: both the anger and the technological savvy. These camel-herding primitives whom we had manipulated, fleeced, romanticized and patronized for genera-tions, while pumping out their oil and bottling them up in monarchies and emir-ates that we cultivated and maintained, while jeering at them with casual racism in the meantime, when we thought of it, for not having democracies like ours. To discover that satellite TV, the Internet and some subversive preaching should suddenly provide them access to divergent opinions disconcerts if it doesn't frighten us, as does their willingness to counterpose rudimentary suicide mis-sions to the helicopter gunships and F-16s we provide the Israelis. "Don't they value life?"

6   They won't be the last. The Vietcong were as culturally different from the Palestinians as we are and yet succeeded in winning a country for themselves, at a tremendous but bearable cost, which the Palestinians will also undoubtedly do. Self-sacrifice can be a match for weaponry, not because the Americans or Israelis value Asian or Arab life—at key junctures and for essentially racist reasons they have not—but because of the value they place on their own citizenry. As many as fifty Vietnamese lives were lost for every American's, but that was not a high enough ratio for us, even though, unlike some Israelis, we don't ascribe to ourselves a biblical imprimatur. So we let them have their land, and the domino calamities that had been famously predicted did not result.

7   To equate our own revolution with anybody else's is quite offensive to us. Mostly, in fact, we prefer to forget that we had a revolutionary past and kicked thousands of wealthy Tories into Canada, seizing their property. We were slow to

condemn apartheid in South Africa, having scarcely finished abolishing our own at the time, and have been slow in general to support self-governance in the warmer climates or to acknowledge suffering among people whose skins are beiger than ours. And if our income per capita is sixty or eighty times theirs, that doesn't strike us as strange. We are a bootstrap country, after all. They should pay us heed. And the whole United Nations is "a cesspool," according to a recent New York City mayor.

But primitive notions like those of Ed Koch invite a primitive response. 8 And box-cutters in the hands of Taliban fundamentalists are not our main problem. We have gratuitously destroyed so much of nature that the Taliban's smashing up of Buddhist statues, as comparative vandalism, will someday seem quite minuscule. We have also denatured our own nominal religions: that is, taken the bite of authenticity out of Christianity, for instance. Our real problem, I think, is a centrifugal disorientation and disbelief. There is a cost to cynicism (as in our previous activities in Afghanistan), and the systematic demonizing of communitarianism during the cold war made it harder afterward for us to reject as perverse the double-talking profiteering implicit in phenomena like Enron, when we had thought that anything was better than collective regulation and planning.

But ceasing to believe in revolutionary democracy—whether of the secular 9 or Christian (or Emersonian) variety—has proven costly. A decent regard for the welfare of other people, in international as well as local life, is going to be more than just a matter of private virtue. In a shrinking world it may be a survival tool. Fanaticism doesn't carry as far unless catastrophic economic conditions lurk in the background, as we learned in the case of Germany between the two world wars but then, when non-Caucasians were involved, forgot. Our foreign aid budget, once the cold war ended, collapsed into spectacular stinginess, and our sole response to September 11 has been police work. This can probably erase Al Qaeda—which became after its instant victory that one morning quite superfluous anyway—but not the knowledge of our vulnerability to any handful of smart and angry plotters in this technological age. We might see an explosion of those.

Our national self-absorption (in which the focus seems more on trying to stay 10 young than helping the young) may give capitalism a bad name. Simple hedonism and materialism was not the point of crossing the ocean. Our revolution was better than that. It was to paint the world anew.

COMPREHENSION

1. According to Hoagland, what are the main reasons that America "is riven and ailing" (paragraph 1)? How has the 9/11 disaster served to highlight this national malaise?
2. What does Hoagland mean by "obesity," and how does this term illuminate certain national problems?
3. Explain Hoagland's assessment of America's role in world affairs. Do you agree or disagree with his critique, and why?

RHETORIC

1. What is Hoagland's claim, and where does he state his main proposition most clearly? What are his minor propositions, and what forms of evidence does he provide to support his admittedly complex argument?
2. What assumptions does Hoagland make about the audience for this essay? How do you know?
3. Explain the tone of this essay. Point to specific aspects of style that reinforce this tone. For example, what is the effect of the extended metaphor, "We seem to need some kind of condom invented just for greed . . ." (paragraph 4)? What other types of figurative language does Hoagland employ?
4. What allusions to American history does Hoagland make, and what is his purpose?
5. How do comparison and contrast, causal analysis, and definition serve to structure this essay?

WRITING

1. Write an essay of causal analysis in which you explain why international terrorists would want to inflict harm on America.
2. Take one of Hoagland's assertions (for example, that we are "[o]bese individually and as a nation"), and write your own analysis of this idea.
3. **Writing an Argument:** Argue for or against Hoagland's claim that Americans have forgotten their revolutionary origins and no longer have a "decent regard for the welfare of other people, in international as well as local life" (paragraph 9).

NETWORKING
Applying Digital and Multimedia Literacies

Using Visuals in Argument: In your argument paper for question 3 under Writing, find and integrate two or three images to support and enhance your position. Be sure to correctly document and provide captions for the visuals you use (see Chapters 15 and 16).

Just Walk on By: Black Men and Public Space

Brent Staples

Brent Staples *(b. 1951) is an author, journalist, and member of the editorial board for the* New York Times. *The oldest of nine children, Staples was born in the industrial city of Chester, Pennsylvania; he received a BA from Widener University (1973) and a PhD from the University of Chicago (1982). His books include the award-winning*

Parallel Time: Growing Up in Black and White *(1995)*. *"Being black," Staples observes, "enriches my experience; it doesn't define me. . . . I'm writing about universal themes—family and leaving home and developing your own identity—which all Americans can enjoy and understand." Staples typically writes about controversial social and educational issues. In this essay from* Literary Cavalcade, *Staples ponders the impact and consequences of racial stereotyping.*

My first victim was a woman—white, well-dressed, probably in her early twen- 1 ties. I came upon her late one evening on a deserted street in Hyde Park, a relatively affluent neighborhood in an otherwise mean, impoverished section of Chicago. As I swung onto the avenue behind her, there seemed to be a discreet, uninflammatory distance between us. Not so. She cast back a worried glance. To her, the youngish black man—a broad six feet two inches with a beard and billowing hair, both hands shoved into the pockets of a bulky military jacket—seemed menacingly close. After a few more quick glimpses, she picked up her pace and was soon running in earnest. Within seconds she disappeared into a cross street.

That was more than a decade ago. I was twenty-two years old, a graduate stu- 2 dent newly arrived at the University of Chicago. It was in the echo of that terrified woman's footfalls that I first began to know the unwieldy inheritance I'd come into—the ability to alter public space in ugly ways. It was clear that she thought herself the quarry of a mugger, a rapist, or worse. Suffering a bout of insomnia, however, I was stalking sleep, not defenseless wayfarers. As a softy who is scarcely able to take a knife to a raw chicken—let alone hold it to a person's throat—I was surprised, embarrassed, and dismayed all at once. Her flight made me feel like an accomplice in tyranny. It also made it clear that I was indistinguishable from the muggers who occasionally seeped into the area from the surrounding ghetto. That first encounter, and those that followed, signified that a vast, unnerving gulf lay between nighttime pedestrians—particularly women—and me. And I soon gathered that being perceived as dangerous is a hazard in itself. I only needed to turn a corner into a dicey situation, or crowd some frightened, armed person in a foyer somewhere, or make an errant move after being pulled over by a policeman. Where fear and weapons meet—and they often do in urban America—there is always the possibility of death.

In that first year, my first away from my hometown, I was to become thor- 3 oughly familiar with the language of fear. At dark, shadowy intersections in Chicago, I could cross in front of a car stopped at a traffic light and elicit the thunk, thunk, thunk, thunk of the driver—black, white, male, or female—hammering down the door locks. On less traveled streets after dark, I grew accustomed to but never comfortable with people who crossed to the other side of the street rather than pass me. Then there were the standard unpleasantries with police, doormen, bouncers, cabdrivers, and others whose business is to screen out troublesome individuals before there is any nastiness.

I moved to New York two years ago and I have remained an avid night walker. 4 In central Manhattan, the near-constant crowd cover minimizes tense, one-on-one street encounters. Elsewhere—visiting friends in SoHo, where sidewalks are narrow and tightly spaced buildings shut out the sky—things can get very taut indeed.

5   Black men have a firm place in New York mugging literature. Norman Podhoretz in his famed (or infamous) 1963 essay, "My Negro Problem—And Ours," recalls growing up in terror of black males; they "were tougher than we were, more ruthless," he writes—and as an adult on the Upper West Side of Manhattan, he continues, he cannot constrain his nervousness when he meets black men on certain streets. Similarly, a decade later, the essayist and novelist Edward Hoagland extols a New York where once "Negro bitterness bore down mainly on other Negroes." Where some see mere panhandlers, Hoagland sees a "mugger who is clearly screwing up his nerve to do more than just ask for money." But Hoagland has "the New Yorker's quick-hunch posture for broken-field maneuvering," and the bad guy swerves away.

6   I often witness that "hunch posture" from women after dark on the warren-like streets of Brooklyn where I live. They seem to set their faces on neutral and, with their purse straps strung across their chests bandolier style, they forge ahead as though bracing themselves against being tackled. I understand, of course, that the danger they perceive is not a hallucination. Women are particularly vulnerable to street violence, and young black males are drastically overrepresented among the perpetrators of the violence. Yet these truths are no solace against the kind of alienation that comes of being ever the suspect, against being set apart, a fearsome entity with whom pedestrians avoid making eye contact.

7   It is not altogether clear to me how I reached the ripe old age of twenty-two without being conscious of the lethality nighttime pedestrians attributed to me. Perhaps it was because in Chester, Pennsylvania, the small, angry industrial town where I came of age in the 1960s, I was scarcely noticeable against a backdrop of gang warfare, street knifings, and murders. I grew up one of the good boys, had perhaps a half-dozen fistfights. In retrospect, my shyness of combat has clear sources.

8   Many things go into the making of a young thug. One of those things is the consummation of the male romance with the power to intimidate. An infant discovers that random flailings send the baby bottle flying out of the crib and crashing to the floor. Delighted, the joyful babe repeats those motions again and again, seeking to duplicate the feat. Just so, I recall the points at which some of my boyhood friends were finally seduced by the perception of themselves as tough guys. When a mark cowered and surrendered his money without resistance, myth and reality merged—and paid off. It is, after all, only manly to embrace the power to frighten and intimidate. We, as men, are not supposed to give an inch of our lane on the highway; we are to seize the fighter's edge in work and in play and even in love; we are to be valiant in the face of hostile forces.

9   Unfortunately, poor and powerless young men seem to take all this nonsense literally. As a boy, I saw countless tough guys locked away; I have since buried several, too. They were babies, really—a teenage cousin, a brother of twenty-two, a childhood friend in his mid-twenties—all gone down in episodes

of bravado played out in the streets. I came to doubt the virtues of intimidation early on. I chose, perhaps even unconsciously, to remain a shadow—timid, but a survivor.

The fearsomeness mistakenly attributed to me in public places often has a 10 perilous flavor. The most frightening of these confusions occurred in the late 1970s and early 1980s when I worked as a journalist in Chicago. One day, rushing into the office of a magazine I was writing for with a deadline story in hand, I was mistaken for a burglar. The office manager called security and, with an ad hoc posse, pursued me through the labyrinthine halls, nearly to my editor's door. I had no way of proving who I was. I could only move briskly toward the company of someone who knew me.

Another time I was on assignment for a local paper and killing time before an 11 interview. I entered a jewelry store on the city's affluent Near North Side. The proprietor excused herself and returned with an enormous red Doberman pinscher straining at the end of a leash. She stood, the dog extended toward me, silent to my questions, her eyes bulging nearly out of her head. I took a cursory look around, nodded, and bade her good night. Relatively speaking, however, I never fared as badly as another black male journalist. He went to nearby Waukegan, Illinois, a couple of summers ago to work on a story about a murderer who was born there. Mistaking the reporter for the killer, police hauled him from his car at gunpoint and but for his press credentials would probably have tried to book him. Such episodes are not uncommon. Black men trade tales like this all the time.

In "My Negro Problem—And Ours," Podhoretz writes that the hatred he 12 feels for blacks makes itself known to him through a variety of avenues—one being his discomfort with that "special brand of paranoid touchiness" to which he says blacks are prone. No doubt he is speaking here of black men. In time, I learned to smother the rage I felt at so often being taken for a criminal. Not to do so would surely have led to madness—via that special "paranoid touchiness" that so annoyed Podhoretz at the time he wrote the essay.

I began to take precautions to make myself less threatening. I move about 13 with care, particularly late in the evening. I give a wide berth to nervous people on subway platforms during the wee hours, particularly when I have exchanged business clothes for jeans. If I happen to be entering a building behind some people who appear skittish, I may walk by, letting them clear the lobby before I return, so as not to seem to be following them. I have been calm and congenial on those rare occasions when I've been pulled over by the police.

And on late-evening constitutionals along streets less traveled by, I employ 14 what has proved to be an excellent tension-reducing measure: I whistle melodies from Beethoven and Vivaldi and the more popular classical composers. Even steely New Yorkers hunching toward nighttime destinations seem to relax, and occasionally they even join in the tune. Virtually everybody seems to sense that a mugger wouldn't be warbling bright, sunny selections from Vivaldi's *Four Seasons*. It is my equivalent of the cowbell that hikers wear when they are in bear country.

COMPREHENSION

1. What does Staples mean by the "power to alter public space"? What examples does he provide to explain this concept?
2. Summarize your impression of the writer. What aspects of his personality do you find prominent? What social and cultural forces have molded his sense of self?
3. According to Staples, what ultimately are the dangers in racial stereotyping? Do you agree or disagree with his assessment, and why?

RHETORIC

1. How do the title and introductory paragraph provoke the reader's interest? What mood do these opening elements create?
2. How does Staples use narration and description to illustrate his thesis? What is his main point?
3. This essay offers an extended definition of racial stereotyping. What strategies does Staples employ to flesh out this definition?
4. Locate examples of the writer's stylistic effort to convey the emotions of fear, anger, anxiety, and potential violence. How does such language affect his thesis?
5. How does the final sentence capture the tone and mood of the essay?

WRITING

1. Write an essay in which you tell about an occasion when you were either a victim or perpetrator of stereotyping.
2. Compose an extended definition of stereotyping, analyzing the causes and effects of this phenomenon.
3. **Writing an Argument:** Can stereotyping ever be beneficial? Argue for or against this question in a persuasive essay.

NETWORKING
Applying Digital and Multimedia Literacies

Creating a Poster Series: Design a series of posters that explore how stereotypes affect or influence interactions among people on a college campus (or within another type of community)—and that, collectively, make a point about these effects. Observe people as they interact in social contexts and in formal ones and listen closely to what people say in conversations; take notes, and also either take photographs, create illustrations or creative figures (such as graphs), or use images from an existing source to depict what you've observed. Use these images as a prominent component of your posters and use minimal, effective text (a tagline, a series of parallel words or phrases) to clarify or cleverly suggest your purpose or point. (*Note:* If you take your own photos, whether they are staged shots or cameos, be sure to ask your subjects for written permission to feature them in your poster series.)

The Myth of the Latin Woman:
I Just Met a Girl Named María

Judith Ortiz Cofer

Judith Ortiz Cofer *(b. 1952) was born in Puerto Rico and immigrated to the United States in 1956. Once a bilingual teacher in Florida public schools, Cofer has written several books of poetry; plays; a novel,* The Line of the Sun *(1989); an award-winning collection of essays and poems,* Silent Dancing: A Partial Remembrance of a Puerto Rican Childhood *(1990); and a collection of short stories,* An Island Like You: Stories of the Barrio *(1995). Her more recent books include* Woman in Front of the Sun: On Becoming a Writer *(2000),* The Meaning of Consuelo *(2003), and* A Love Story Beginning in Spanish *(2005). She is a professor of English and creative writing at the University of Georgia. In the following essay, she offers both personal insight and philosophical reflection on the theme of ethnic stereotyping.*

On a bus trip to London from Oxford University where I was earning some graduate   1
credits one summer, a young man, obviously fresh from a pub, spotted me and as if struck by inspiration went down on his knees in the aisle. With both hands over his heart he broke into an Irish tenor's rendition of "María" from *West Side Story.* My politely amused fellow passengers gave his lovely voice the round of gentle applause it deserved. Though I was not quite as amused, I managed my version of an English smile: no show of teeth, no extreme contortions of the facial muscles— I was at this time of my life practicing reserve and cool. Oh, that British control, how I coveted it. But "María" had followed me to London, reminding me of a prime fact of my life: You can leave the island, master the English language, and travel as far as you can, but if you are a Latina, especially one like me who so obviously belongs to Rita Moreno's gene pool, the island travels with you.

This is sometimes a very good thing. It may win you that extra minute of   2
someone's attention. But with some people, the same things can make *you* an island—not a tropical paradise but an Alcatraz, a place nobody wants to visit. As a Puerto Rican girl living in the United States and wanting like most children to "belong," I resented the stereotype that my Hispanic appearance called forth from many people I met.

Growing up in a large urban center in New Jersey during the 1960s, I suffered   3
from what I think of as "cultural schizophrenia." Our life was designed by my parents as a microcosm of their *casas* on the island. We spoke in Spanish, ate Puerto Rican food bought at the *bodega,* and practiced strict Catholicism at a

church that allotted us a one-hour slot each week for mass, performed in Spanish by a Chinese priest trained as a missionary for Latin America.

4   As a girl I was kept under strict surveillance by my parents, since my virtue and modesty were, by their cultural equation, the same as their honor. As a teenager I was lectured constantly on how to behave as a proper *senorita*. But it was a conflicting message I received, since the Puerto Rican mothers also encouraged their daughters to look and act like women and to dress in clothes our Anglo friends and their mothers found too "mature" and flashy. The difference was, and is, cultural; yet I often felt humiliated when I appeared at an American friend's party wearing a dress more suitable to a semiformal than to a playroom birthday celebration. At Puerto Rican festivities, neither the music nor the colors we wore could be too loud.

5   I remember Career Day in our high school, when teachers told us to come dressed as if for a job interview. It quickly became obvious that to the Puerto Rican girls "dressing up" meant wearing their mother's ornate jewelry and clothing, more appropriate (by mainstream standards) for the company Christmas party than as daily office attire. That morning I had agonized in front of my closet, trying to figure out what a "career girl" would wear. I knew how to dress for school (at the Catholic school I attended, we all wore uniforms), I knew how to dress for Sunday mass, and I knew what dresses to wear for parties at my relatives' homes. Though I do not recall the precise details of my Career Day outfit, it must have been a composite of these choices. But I remember a comment my friend (an Italian American) made in later years that coalesced my impressions of that day. She said that at the business school she was attending, the Puerto Rican girls always stood out for wearing "everything at once." She meant, of course, too much jewelry, too many accessories. On that day at school we were simply made the negative models by the nuns, who were themselves not credible fashion experts to any of us. But it was painfully obvious to me that to the others, in their tailored skirts and silk blouses, we must have seemed "hopeless" and "vulgar." Though I now know that most adolescents feel out of step much of the time, I also know that for the Puerto Rican girls of my generation that sense was intensified. The way our teachers and classmates looked at us that day in school was just a taste of the cultural clash that awaited us in the real world, where prospective employers and men on the street would often misinterpret our tight skirts and jingling bracelets as a "come-on."

6   Mixed cultural signals have perpetuated certain stereotypes—for example, that of the Hispanic woman as the "hot tamale" or sexual firebrand. It is a one-dimensional view that the media have found easy to promote. In their special vocabulary, advertisers have designated "sizzling" and "smoldering" as the adjectives of choice for describing not only the foods but also the women of Latin America. From conversations in my house I recall hearing about the harassment that Puerto Rican women endured in factories where the "boss-men" talked to them as if sexual innuendo was all they understood, and worse, often gave them the choice of submitting to their advances or being fired.

It is custom, however, not chromosomes, that leads us to choose scarlet over   7
pale pink. As young girls it was our mothers who influenced our decisions about
clothes and colors—mothers who had grown up on a tropical island where the
natural environment was a riot of primary colors, where showing your skin was
one way to keep cool as well as to look sexy. Most important of all, on the island,
women perhaps felt freer to dress and move more provocatively since, in most
cases, they were protected by the traditions, mores, and laws of a Spanish/Catholic
system of morality and machismo whose main rule was: *You may look at my sister,*
but if you touch her I will kill you. The extended family and church structure could
provide a young woman with a circle of safety in her small pueblo on the island; if
a man "wronged" a girl, everyone would close in to save her family honor.

My mother has told me about dressing in her best party clothes on Saturday   8
nights and going to the town's plaza to promenade with her girlfriends in front of
the boys they liked. The males were thus given an opportunity to admire the
women and to express their admiration in the form of *piropos:* erotically charged
street poems they composed on the spot. (I have myself been subjected to a few
piropos while visiting the island, and they can be outrageous, although custom
dictates that they must never cross into obscenity.) This ritual, as I understand it,
also entails a show of studied indifference on the woman's part; if she is "decent,"
she must not acknowledge the man's impassioned words. So I do understand how
things can be lost in translation. When a Puerto Rican girl dressed in her idea of
what is attractive meets a man from the mainstream culture who has been trained
to react to certain types of clothing as a sexual signal, a clash is likely to take
place. I remember the boy who took me to my first formal dance leaning over to
plant a sloppy, overeager kiss painfully on my mouth; when I didn't respond with
sufficient passion, he remarked resentfully: "I thought you Latin girls were supposed to mature early," as if I were expected to *ripen* like a fruit or vegetable, not
just grow into womanhood like other girls.

It is surprising to my professional friends that even today some people, in-   9
cluding those who should know better, still put others "in their place." It happened to me most recently during a stay at a classy metropolitan hotel favored by
young professional couples for weddings. Late one evening after the theater, as I
walked toward my room with a colleague (a woman with whom I was coordinating
an arts program), a middle-aged man in a tuxedo, with a young girl in satin and
lace on his arm, stepped directly into our path. With his champagne glass
extended toward me, he exclaimed "Evita!"

Our way blocked, my companion and I listened as the man half-recited, half-   10
bellowed "Don't Cry for Me, Argentina." When he finished, the young girl said:
"How about a round of applause for my daddy?" We complied, hoping this would
bring the silly spectacle to a close. I was becoming aware that our little group was
attracting the attention of the other guests. "Daddy" must have perceived this too,
and he once more barred the way as we tried to walk past him. He began to shout-
sing a ditty to the tune of "La Bamba"—except the lyrics were about a girl named
María whose exploits rhymed with her name and gonorrhea. The girl kept saying
"Oh, Daddy" and looking at me with pleading eyes. She wanted me to laugh along

with the others. My companion and I stood silently waiting for the man to end his offensive song. When he finished, I looked not at him but at his daughter. I advised her calmly never to ask her father what he had done in the army. Then I walked between them and to my room. My friend complimented me on my cool handling of the situation, but I confessed that I had really wanted to push the jerk into the swimming pool. This same man—probably a corporate executive, well-educated, even worldly by most standards—would not have been likely to regale an Anglo woman with a dirty song in public. He might have checked his impulse by assuming that she could be somebody's wife or mother, or at least *somebody* who might take offense. But, to him, I was just an Evita or a María: merely a character in his cartoon-populated universe.

11   Another facet of the myth of the Latin woman in the United States is the menial, the domestic—María the housemaid or countergirl. It's true that work as domestics, as waitresses, and in factories is all that's available to women with little English and few skills. But the myth of the Hispanic menial—the funny maid, mispronouncing words and cooking up a spicy storm in a shiny California kitchen—has been perpetuated by the media in the same way that "Mammy" from *Gone with the Wind* became America's idea of the black woman for generations. Since I do not wear my diplomas around my neck for all to see, I have on occasion been sent to that "kitchen" where some think I obviously belong.

12   One incident has stayed with me, though I recognize it as a minor offense. My first public poetry reading took place in Miami, at a restaurant where a luncheon was being held before the event. I was nervous and excited as I walked in with notebook in hand. An older woman motioned me to her table, and thinking (foolish me) that she wanted me to autograph a copy of my newly published slender volume of verse, I went over. She ordered a cup of coffee from me, assuming that I was the waitress. (Easy enough to mistake my poems for menus, I suppose.) I know it wasn't an intentional act of cruelty. Yet of all the good things that happened later, I remember that scene most clearly, because it reminded me of what I had to overcome before anyone would take me seriously. In retrospect I understand that my anger gave my reading fire. In fact, I have almost always taken any doubt in my abilities as a challenge, the result most often being the satisfaction of winning a convert, of seeing the cold, appraising eyes warm to my words, the body language change, the smile that indicates I have opened some avenue for communication. So that day as I read, I looked directly at that woman. Her lowered eyes told me she was embarrassed at her faux pas, and when I willed her to look up at me, she graciously allowed me to punish her with my full attention. We shook hands at the end of the reading and I never saw her again. She has probably forgotten the entire incident, but maybe not.

13   Yet I am one of the lucky ones. There are thousands of Latinas without the privilege of an education or the entrees into society that I have. For them life is a constant struggle against the misconceptions perpetuated by the myth of the Latina. My goal is to try to replace the old stereotypes with a much more interesting

set of realities. Every time I give a reading, I hope the stories I tell, the dreams and fears I examine in my work, can achieve some universal truth that will get my audience past the particulars of my skin color, my accent, or my clothes.

I once wrote a poem in which I called all Latinas "God's brown daughters." 14 This poem is really a prayer of sorts, offered upward, but also, through the human-to-human channel of art, outward. It is a prayer for communication and for respect. In it, Latin women pray "in Spanish to an Anglo God/with a Jewish heritage," and they are "fervently hoping/that if not omnipotent,/at least He be bilingual."

COMPREHENSION

1. What is the thesis of the essay?
2. What does Cofer mean by the expression "cultural schizophrenia" (paragraph 3)?
3. Define the following words: *coveted* (paragraph 1), *Anglo* (paragraph 4), *coalesced* (paragraph 5), *machismo* (paragraph 7), and *entrees* (paragraph 13).

RHETORIC

1. Cofer uses many anecdotes in her discussion of stereotyping. How does this affect the tone of the essay?
2. Who is the implied audience for this essay? What aspects of the writing led you to your conclusion?
3. This essay is written in the first person, which tends to reveal a lot about the writer's personality. What adjectives come to mind when you think of the writer's singular voice?
4. Although this essay has a sociological theme, Cofer demonstrates that she has a poet's sensitivity toward language. What in the following sentence from paragraph 7 demonstrates this poetic style: "It is custom, however, not chromosomes, that leads us to choose scarlet over pale pink"? Select two other sentences from the essay that demonstrate Cofer's stylistic talent, and explain why they, too, are poetic.
5. In paragraph 8, Cofer contrasts cultural perceptions related to Hispanic and Anglo behavior. How is the paragraph structured so that this difference is demonstrated dramatically?
6. Cofer uses quotation marks to emphasize the connotation of certain words. Explain the significance of the following words: *mature* (paragraph 4), *hopeless* (paragraph 5), *hot tamale* (paragraph 6), *wronged* (paragraph 7), and *decent* (paragraph 8).

WRITING

1. Write a problem-solution essay in which you discuss the reasons behind cultural stereotyping and provide suggestions on how to overcome stereotyped thinking.
2. **Writing an Argument:** In an essay, argue for or against the proposition that stereotyping is excusable because it often is based on learned assumptions about which an individual cannot be expected to have knowledge.

NETWORKING
Applying Digital and Multimedia Literacies

Examining Stereotypes in Television Shows and Commercials: Select an ethnic, racial, or cultural group, and explain how group members undergo stereotyping through their depiction in the media, particularly television shows or commercials. Use specific examples from specific programs or commercials to support your claims.

Yellow Woman and a Beauty of the Spirit

Leslie Marmon Silko

Leslie Marmon Silko (b. 1948) was born in Albuquerque, New Mexico, and grew up on the Laguna Pueblo Reservation on the Rio Grande plateau. Of mixed Laguna, Mexican, and European American ancestry, Silko attended the University of New Mexico (BA, 1969) and briefly enrolled in law school before deciding to pursue a career as a writer. Associated with the Native American Renaissance, Silko has written stories, novels, essays, and poetry exploring Native American myths and traditions as well as the relationship of the tribes to contemporary culture. Silko has taught at the University of New Mexico and the University of Arizona, and has received numerous awards, including a prestigious five-year MacArthur Foundation grant. Her best-known work includes the novels Ceremony *(1977) and* Gardens in the Dunes *(1999); a collection of poetry,* Laguna Woman *(1974); a collection of short stories,* Storyteller *(1981); and an autobiography,* Sacred Water *(1993). Silko has also published a collection of essays,* Yellow Woman and a Beauty of the Spirit *(1996); in the title essay from this collection, Silko examines her mixed ancestry and explains traditional Pueblo culture.*

1   From the time I was a small child, I was aware that I was different. I looked different from my playmates. My two sisters looked different too. We didn't look quite like the other Laguna Pueblo children, but we didn't look quite white either. In the 1880s, my great-grandfather had followed his older brother west from Ohio to the New Mexico Territory to survey the land for the U.S. government. The two Marmon brothers came to the Laguna Pueblo reservation because they had an Ohio cousin who already lived there. The Ohio cousin was involved in

sending Indian children thousands of miles away from their families to the War Department's big Indian boarding school in Carlisle, Pennsylvania. Both brothers married full-blood Laguna Pueblo women. My great-grandfather had first married my great-grandmother's older sister, but she died in childbirth and left two small children. My great-grandmother was fifteen or twenty years younger than my great-grandfather. She had attended Carlisle Indian School and spoke and wrote English beautifully.

I called her Grandma A'mooh because that's what I heard her say whenever 2 she saw me. *A'mooh* means "granddaughter" in the Laguna language. I remember this word because her love and her acceptance of me as a small child were so important. I had sensed immediately that something about my appearance was not acceptable to some people, white and Indian. But I did not see any signs of that strain or anxiety in the face of my beloved Grandma A'mooh.

Younger people, people my parents' age, seemed to look at the world in a 3 more modern way. The modern way included racism. My physical appearance seemed not to matter to the old-time people. They looked at the world very differently; a person's appearance and possessions did not matter nearly as much as a person's behavior. For them, a person's value lies in how that person interacts with other people, how that person behaves toward the animals and the earth. That is what matters most to the old-time people. The Pueblo people believed this long before the Puritans arrived with their notions of sin and damnation, and racism. The old-time beliefs persist today; thus I will refer to the old-time people in the present tense as well as the past. Many worlds may coexist here.

I spent a great deal of time with my great-grandmother. Her house was next 4 to our house, and I used to wake up at dawn, hours before my parents or younger sisters, and I'd go wait on the porch swing or on the back steps by her kitchen door. She got up at dawn, but she was more than eighty years old, so she needed a little while to get dressed and to get the fire going in the cookstove. I had been carefully instructed by my parents not to bother her and to behave, and to try to help her any way I could. I always loved the early mornings when the air was so cool with a hint of rain smell in the breeze. In the dry New Mexico air, the least hint of dampness smells sweet.

My great-grandmother's yard was planted with lilac bushes and iris; there 5 were four o'clocks, cosmos, morning glories, and hollyhocks, and old-fashioned rosebushes that I helped her water. If the garden hose got stuck on one of the big rocks that lined the path in the yard, I ran and pulled it free. That's what I came to do early every morning: to help Grandma water the plants before the heat of the day arrived.

Grandma A'mooh would tell about the old days, family stories about relatives 6 who had been killed by Apache raiders who stole the sheep our relatives had been herding near Swahnee. Sometimes she read Bible stories that we kids liked because of the illustrations of Jonah in the mouth of a whale and Daniel surrounded by lions. Grandma A'mooh would send me home when she took her nap, but when the sun got low and the afternoon began to cool off, I would be back on the porch swing, waiting for her to come out to water the plants and to haul in firewood for the evening. When Grandma was eighty-five, she still chopped her own kindling. She used to let me carry in the coal bucket for her, but she would not allow me to use the ax. I carried armloads of kindling too, and I learned to be proud of my strength.

7   I was allowed to listen quietly when Aunt Susie or Aunt Alice came to visit Grandma. When I got old enough to cross the road alone, I went and visited them almost daily. They were vigorous women who valued books and writing. They were usually busy chopping wood or cooking but never hesitated to take time to answer my questions. Best of all they told me the *hummah-hah* stories, about an earlier time when animals and humans shared a common language. In the old days, the Pueblo people had educated their children in this manner; adults took time out to talk to and teach young people. Everyone was a teacher, and every activity had the potential to teach the child.

8   But as soon as I started kindergarten at the Bureau of Indian Affairs day school, I began to learn more about the differences between the Laguna Pueblo world and the outside world. It was at school that I learned just how different I looked from my classmates. Sometimes tourists driving past on Route 66 would stop by Laguna Day School at recess time to take photographs of us kids. One day, when I was in the first grade, we all crowded around the smiling white tourists, who peered at our faces. We all wanted to be in the picture because afterward the tourists sometimes gave us each a penny. Just as we were all posed and ready to have our picture taken, the tourist man looked at me. "Not you," he said and motioned for me to step away from my classmates. I felt so embarrassed that I wanted to disappear. My classmates were puzzled by the tourists' behavior, but I knew the tourists didn't want me in their snapshot because I looked different, because I was part white.

9   In the view of the old-time people, we are all sisters and brothers because the Mother Creator made all of us—all colors and all sizes. We are sisters and brothers, clanspeople of all the living beings around us. The plants, the birds, fish, clouds, water, even the clay—they are all related to us. The old-time people believe that all things, even rocks and water, have spirit and being. They understood that all things want only to continue being as they are; they need only to be left as they are. Thus the old folks used to tell us kids not to disturb the earth unnecessarily. All things as they were created exist already in harmony with one another as long as we do not disturb them.

10   As the old story tells us, Tse'itsi'nako, Thought Woman, the Spider, thought of her three sisters, and as she thought of them, they came into being. Together with Thought Woman, they thought of the sun and the stars and the moon. The Mother Creators imagined the earth and the oceans, the animals and the people, and the *ka'tsina* spirits that reside in the mountains. The Mother Creators imagined all the plants that flower and the trees that bear fruit. As Thought Woman and her sisters thought of it, the whole universe came into being. In this universe, there is no absolute good or absolute bad; they are only balances and harmonies that ebb and flow. Some years the desert receives abundant rain, other years

there is too little rain, and sometimes there is so much rain that floods cause destruction. But rain itself is neither innocent nor guilty. The rain is simply itself.

My great-grandmother was dark and handsome. Her expression in photo- 11 graphs is one of confidence and strength. I do not know if white people then or now would consider her beautiful. I do not know if the old-time Laguna Pueblo people considered her beautiful or if the old-time people even thought in those terms. To the Pueblo way of thinking, the act of comparing one living being with another was silly, because each being or thing is unique and therefore incompara- bly valuable because it is the only one of its kind. The old-time people thought it was crazy to attach such importance to a person's appearance. I understood very early that there were two distinct ways of interpreting the world. There was the white people's way and there was the Laguna way. In the Laguna way, it was bad manners to make comparisons that might hurt another person's feelings.

In everyday Pueblo life, not much attention was paid to one's physical appear- 12 ance or clothing. Ceremonial clothing was quite elaborate but was used only for the sacred dances. The traditional Pueblo societies were communal and strictly egalitarian, which means that no matter how well or how poorly one might have dressed, there was no social ladder to fall from. All food and other resources were strictly shared so that no one person or group had more than another. I mention social status because it seems to me that most of the definitions of beauty in con- temporary Western culture are really codes for determining social status. People no longer hide their face-lifts and they discuss their liposuctions because the point of the procedures isn't just cosmetic, it is social. It says to the world, "I have enough spare cash that I can afford surgery for cosmetic purposes."

In the old-time Pueblo world, beauty was manifested in behavior and in 13 one's relationships with other living beings. Beauty was as much a feeling of harmony as it was a visual, aural, or sensual effect. The whole person had to be beautiful, not just the face or the body; faces and bodies could not be separated from hearts and souls. Health was foremost in achieving this sense of well- being and harmony; in the old-time Pueblo world, a person who did not look healthy inspired feelings of worry and anxiety, not feelings of well-being. A healthy person, of course, is in harmony with the world around her; she is at peace with herself too. Thus an unhappy person or spiteful person would not be considered beautiful.

In the old days, strong, sturdy women were most admired. One of my most 14 vivid preschool memories is of the crew of Laguna women, in their forties and fifties, who came to cover our house with adobe plaster. They handled the ladders with great ease, and while two women ground the adobe mud on stones and added straw, another woman loaded the hod with mud and passed it up to the two women on ladders, who were smoothing the plaster on the wall with their hands. Since women owned the houses, they did the plastering. At Laguna, men did the basket making and the weaving of fine textiles; men helped a great deal with the child care too. Because the Creator is female, there is no stigma on being female; gender is not used to control behavior. No job was a man's job or a woman's job; the most able person did the work.

15   My Grandma Lily had been a Ford Model A mechanic when she was a teen-ager. I remember when I was young, she was always fixing broken lamps and appliances. She was small and wiry, but she could lift her weight in rolled roofing or boxes of nails. When she was seventy-five, she was still repairing washing machines in my uncle's coin-operated laundry.

16   The old-time people paid no attention to birthdays. When a person was ready to do something, she did it. When she no longer was able, she stopped. Thus the traditional Pueblo people did not worry about aging or about looking old because there were no social boundaries drawn by the passage of years. It was not remark-able for young men to marry women as old as their mothers. I never heard any-one talk about "women's work" until after I left Laguna for college. Work was there to be done by any able-bodied person who wanted to do it. At the same time, in the old-time Pueblo world, identity was acknowledged to be always in a flux; in the old stories, one minute Spider Woman is a little spider under a yucca plant, and the next instant she is a sprightly grandmother walking down the road.

17   When I was growing up, there was a young man from a nearby village who wore nail polish and women's blouses and permed his hair. People paid little attention to his appearance; he was always part of a group of other young men from his village. No one ever made fun of him. Pueblo communities were and still are very independent, but they also have to be tolerant of individual eccentricities because survival of the group means everyone has to cooperate.

18   In the old Pueblo world, differences were celebrated as signs of the Mother Creator's grace. Persons born with exceptional physical or sexual differences were highly respected and honored because their physical differences gave them special positions as mediators between this world and the spirit world. The great Navajo medicine man of the 1920s, the Crawler, had a hunchback and could not walk upright, but he was able to heal even the most difficult cases.

19   Before the arrival of Christian missionaries, a man could dress as a woman and work with the women and even marry a man without any fanfare. Likewise, a woman was free to dress like a man, to hunt and go to war with the men, and to marry a woman. In the old Pueblo worldview, we are all a mixture of male and female, and this sexual identity is changing constantly. Sexual inhibition did not begin until the Christian missionaries arrived. For the old-time people, marriage was about teamwork and social relationships, not about sexual excitement. In the days before the Puritans came, marriage did not mean an end to sex with people other than your spouse. Women were just as likely as men to have a *si'ash,* or lover.

20   New life was so precious that pregnancy was always appropriate, and preg-nancy before marriage was celebrated as a good sign. Since the children belonged to the mother and her clan, and women owned and bequeathed the houses and farmland, the exact determination of paternity wasn't critical. Although fertility was prized, infertility was no problem because mothers with unplanned pregnancies gave their babies to childless couples within the clan in open adoption arrangements. Children called their mother's sisters "mother" as well, and a child became attached to a number of parent figures.

In the sacred kiva ceremonies, men mask and dress as women to pay homage 21 and to be possessed by the female energies of the spirit beings. Because differences in physical appearance were so highly valued, surgery to change one's face and body to resemble a model's face and body would be unimaginable. To be different, to be unique was blessed and was best of all.

The traditional clothing of Pueblo women emphasized a woman's sturdiness. 22 Buckskin leggings wrapped around the legs protected her from scratches and injuries while she worked. The more layers of buckskin, the better. All those layers gave her legs the appearance of strength, like sturdy tree trunks. To demonstrate sisterhood and brotherhood with the plants and animals, the old-time people make masks and costumes that transform the human figures of the dancers into the animal beings they portray. Dancers paint their exposed skin; their postures and motions are adapted from their observations. But the motions are stylized. The observer sees not an actual eagle or actual deer dancing, but witnesses a human being, a dancer, gradually changing into a woman/buffalo or a man/deer. Every impulse is to reaffirm the urgent relationships that human beings have with the plant and animal world.

In the high desert plateau country, all vegetation, even weeds and thorns, 23 becomes special, and all life is precious and beautiful because without the plants, the insects, and the animals, human beings living here cannot survive. Perhaps human beings long ago noticed the devastating impact human activity can have on the plants and animals; maybe this is why tribal cultures devised the stories about humans and animals intermarrying, and the clans that bind humans to animals and plants through a whole complex of duties.

We children were always warned not to harm frogs or toads, the beloved 24 children of the rain clouds, because terrible floods would occur. I remember in the summer the old folks used to stick bog bolls of cotton on the outside of their screen doors as bait to keep the flies from going in the house when the door was opened. The old folks staunchly resisted the killing of flies because once, long, long ago, when human beings were in a great deal of trouble, a Green Bottle Fly carried the desperate messages of human beings to the Mother Creator in the Fourth World, below this one. Human beings had outraged the Mother Creator by neglecting the Mother Corn altar while they dabbled with sorcery and magic. The Mother Creator disappeared, and with her disappeared the rain clouds, and the plants and the animals too. The people began to starve, and they had no way of reaching the Mother Creator down below. Green Bottle Fly took the message to the Mother Creator, and the people were saved. To show their gratitude, the old folks refused to kill any flies.

The old stories demonstrate the interrelationships that the Pueblo people have 25 maintained with their plant and animal clanspeople. Kochininako, Yellow Woman, represents all women in the old stories. Her deeds span the spectrum of human behavior and are mostly heroic acts, though in at least one story, she chooses to join the secret Destroyer Clan, which worships destruction and death. Because Laguna Pueblo cosmology features a female Creator, the status of women is equal with the status of men, and women appear as often as men in the old stories as hero figures. Yellow Woman is my favorite because she dares to cross traditional boundaries of ordinary behavior during times of crisis in order to save the Pueblo; her power lies in her courage and in her uninhibited sexuality, which the old-time Pueblo stories celebrate again and again because fertility was so highly valued.

26   The old stories always say that Yellow Woman was beautiful, but remember that the old-time people were not so much thinking about physical appearances. In each story, the beauty that Yellow Woman possesses is the beauty of her passion, her daring, and her sheer strength to act when catastrophe is imminent.

27   In one story, the people are suffering during a great drought and accompanying famine. Each day, Kochininako has to walk farther and farther from the village to find fresh water for her husband and children. One day she travels far, far to the east, to the plains, and she finally locates a freshwater spring. But when she reaches the pool, the water is churning violently as if something large had just gotten out of the pool, Kochininako does not want to see what huge creature had been at the pool, but just as she fills her water jar and turns to hurry away, a strong, sexy man in buffalo skin leggings appears by the pool. Little drops of water glisten on his chest. She cannot help but look at him because he is so strong and so good to look at. Able to transform himself from human to buffalo in the wink of an eye, Buffalo Man gallops away with her on his back. Kochininako falls in love with Buffalo Man, and because of this liaison, the Buffalo People agree to give their bodies to the hunters to feed the starving Pueblo. Thus Kochininako's fearless sensuality results in the salvation of the people of her village, who are saved by the meat the Buffalo People "give" to them.

28   My father taught me and my sisters to shoot .22 rifles when we were seven; I went hunting with my father when I was eight, and I killed my first mule deer buck when I was thirteen. The Kochininako stories were always my favorite because Yellow Woman had so many adventures. In one story, as she hunts rabbits to feed her family, a giant monster pursues her, but she has the courage and presence of mind to outwit it.

29   In another story, Kochininako has a fling with Whirlwind Man and returns to her husband ten months later with twin baby boys. The twin boys grow up to be great heroes of the people. Once again, Kochininako's vibrant sexuality benefits her people.

30   The stories about Kochininako made me aware that sometimes an individual must act despite disapproval, or concern for appearances or what others may say. From Yellow Woman's adventures, I learned to be comfortable with my differences. I even imagined that Yellow Woman had yellow skin, brown hair, and green eyes like mine, although her name does not refer to her color, but rather to the ritual color of the east.

31   There have been many other moments like the one with the camera-toting tourist in the schoolyard. But the old-time people always say, remember the stories, the stories will help you be strong. So all these years I have depended on Kochininako and the stories of her adventures.

Kochininako is beautiful because she has the courage to act in times of great 32 peril, and her triumph is achieved by her sensuality, not through violence and destruction. For these qualities of the spirit, Yellow Woman and all women are beautiful.

COMPREHENSION

1. Silko devotes part of this essay to recollections of her great-grandmother, Grandma A'mooh. What is her great-grandmother like? What does the writer learn from Grandma A'mooh? Why is the essay more about Pueblo women than men?
2. Explain what you learned about traditional Pueblo culture from this essay. What values does the writer associate with this "old-time" culture? According to Silko, how does this culture contrast both explicitly and implicitly with modern Anglo culture? How did this traditional culture sustain her as a young girl?
3. Silko summarizes several Pueblo stories. What are the main ones? Why does she especially like the story of Kochininako, or Yellow Woman?

RHETORIC

1. What is Silko's thesis? Does this thesis appear in a single sentence? If so, what is it? If not, what is the implied thesis?
2. What strategy does the writer use to both start and conclude this essay? Is this strategy effective? Justify your response.
3. Silko provides an extended definition of Pueblo culture in this selection. Explain how she uses description, narration, comparison and contrast, and analysis to develop this definition.
4. While Silko's primary purpose is to define or explain Pueblo culture, she also provides several supporting definitions. Identify them, and explain how they contribute to the broader definition.
5. Is the diction in this essay concrete or abstract? Specific or general? Identify several passages to support your answer.
6. Consider the essay as an argument. What is the claim? What is the supporting evidence? What warrants underpin the argument? How effective is the argument, and why?

WRITING

1. Working in a group, create a list of all the features of traditional Pueblo culture that Silko discusses. Choose two or three and write brief summaries of each.
2. Using Silko's essay as a frame of reference, write a comparative essay in which you discuss contemporary American cultural values in relationship to "old-time" Pueblo values and traditions.
3. **Writing an Argument:** Argue for or against the proposition that traditional Pueblo culture is superior to contemporary American culture. Use at least three topics drawn from Silko's essay—for example, approach to diversity and difference, treatment of women, or respect for the environment—to develop your argumentative essay.

NETWORKING
Applying Digital and Multimedia Literacies

Vetting Online Sources (a Public Domain e-Book): Do an online search to find a compilation of Pueblo stories that was written in 1910 by Charles Lummis. Click on the link to the book's introduction, titled "The Brown Story-Tellers," and consider how Lummis's purpose for sharing these stories differs from Silko's. Would you use Lummis's retellings as sources in a paper? Why, why not, and if so, in what context?

A World Not Neatly Divided

Amartya Sen

Amartya Sen *(b. 1933), born in Santiniketan, India, was awarded the Nobel Prize in Economics in 1988 for his groundbreaking work on welfare economics. Educated at Presidency College in Calcutta and Cambridge University (PhD, 1959), Sen has taught at Harvard University, the London School of Economics, and Oxford University; currently, he is a professor at Trinity College, Cambridge University. His major works, all of which investigate the role of poverty and inequality in the world, include* Collective Choice and Social Welfare *(1970),* On Economic Inequality *(1973),* Poverty and Famines: An Essay on Entitlement and Deprivation *(1981),* Commodities and Capabilities *(1985),* Development as Freedom *(1999), and* Identity and Violence: The Illusion of Destiny *(2006). In the following essay, which appeared in the* New York Times *in 2001, Sen suggests that generalizations about "civilization" tend to blur the realities of complex cultures.*

1   When people talk about clashing civilizations, as so many politicians and academics do now, they can sometimes miss the central issue. The inadequacy of this thesis begins well before we get to the question of whether civilizations must clash. The basic weakness of the theory lies in its program of categorizing people of the world according to a unique, allegedly commanding system of classification. This is problematic because civilizational categories are crude and inconsistent and also because there are other ways of seeing people (linked to politics, language, literature, class, occupation, or other affiliations).

2   The befuddling influence of a singular classification also traps those who dispute the thesis of a clash: To talk about "the Islamic world" or "the Western world" is already to adopt an impoverished vision of humanity as unalterably divided. In fact, civilizations are hard to partition in this way, given the diversities within each society as well as the linkages among different countries and cultures. For example, describing India as a "Hindu civilization" misses the fact that India has more Muslims than any other country except Indonesia and possibly Pakistan. It is futile

to try to understand Indian art, literature, music, food, or politics without seeing the extensive interactions across barriers of religious communities. These include Hindus and Muslims, Buddhists, Jains, Sikhs, Parsees, Christians (who have been in India since at least the fourth century, well before England's conversion to Christianity), Jews (present since the fall of Jerusalem), and even atheists and agnostics. Sanskrit has a larger atheistic literature than exists in any other classical language. Speaking of India as a Hindu civilization may be comforting to the Hindu fundamentalist, but it is an odd reading of India.

A similar coarseness can be seen in the other categories invoked, like "the 3 Islamic world." Consider Akbar and Aurangzeb, two Muslim emperors of the Mogul dynasty in India. Aurangzeb tried hard to convert Hindus into Muslims and instituted various policies in that direction, of which taxing the non-Muslims was only one example. In contrast, Akbar reveled in his multiethnic court and pluralist laws, and issued official proclamations insisting that no one "should be interfered with on account of religion" and that "anyone is to be allowed to go over to a religion that pleases him."

If a homogeneous view of Islam were to be taken, then only one of these 4 emperors could count as a true Muslim. The Islamic fundamentalist would have no time for Akbar; Prime Minister Tony Blair, given his insistence that tolerance is a defining characteristic of Islam, would have to consider excommunicating Aurangzeb. I expect both Akbar and Aurangzeb would protest, and so would I. A similar crudity is present in the characterization of what is called "Western civilization." Tolerance and individual freedom have certainly been present in European history. But there is no dearth of diversity here, either. When Akbar was making his pronouncements on religious tolerance in Agra, in the 1590s, the Inquisitions were still going on; in 1600, Giordano Bruno was burned at the stake, for heresy, in Campo dei Fiori in Rome.

Dividing the world into discrete civilizations is not just crude. It propels us 5 into the absurd belief that this partitioning is natural and necessary and must overwhelm all other ways of identifying people. That imperious view goes not only against the sentiment that "we human beings are all much the same," but also against the more plausible understanding that we are diversely different. For example, Bangladesh's split from Pakistan was not connected with religion, but with language and politics.

Each of us has many features in our self-conception. Our religion, important as 6 it may be, cannot be an all-engulfing identity. Even a shared poverty can be a source of solidarity across the borders. The kind of division highlighted by, say, the so-called "antiglobalization" protesters—whose movement is, incidentally, one of the most globalized in the world—tries to unite the underdogs of the world economy and goes firmly against religious, national, or "civilizational" lines of division.

The main hope of harmony lies not in any imagined uniformity, but in the 7 plurality of our identities, which cut across each other and work against sharp divisions into impenetrable civilizational camps. Political leaders who think and act in terms of sectioning off humanity into various "worlds" stand to make the world more flammable—even when their intentions are very different. They also end up, in the case of civilizations defined by religion, lending authority to religious leaders seen as spokesmen for their "worlds." In the process, other voices are muffled and other concerns silenced. The robbing of our plural identities not only reduces us; it impoverishes the world.

COMPREHENSION

1. According to Sen, what is the "basic weakness" underlying the idea that the world is composed of "clashing civilizations" (paragraph 1)?
2. What does the writer mean by "singular classification" (paragraph 2)? Why is classifying people in terms of their civilization "crude and inconsistent"? Why is applying singular classification to religions and other features of society wrong?
3. What, according to Sen, is "the main hope of harmony" (paragraph 7) in the world?

RHETORIC

1. What argumentative strategy does Sen employ in the introductory paragraph? What point of view is he arguing against?
2. While arguing against a certain type of classification, Sen actually uses classification as a rhetorical strategy. How, precisely, does he employ classification to organize his argument?
3. What examples does Sen use to support his argument? Why does he use them? Why does he decide not to provide illustrations near the end of the selection?
4. What transitional devices serve to unify the essay?
5. How effective is Sen's concluding paragraph? Does it serve to confirm his claim? Why or why not?

WRITING

1. Write an essay about the problems you see in your community or on campus. Explain how singular classification might explain some of these problems.
2. In an analytical essay, explain how singular classification might help explain the events of September 11, 2001.
3. **Writing an Argument:** Write an essay in which you demonstrate that singular classification actually can be helpful in framing public discourse about groups, nations, or civilizations.

NETWORKING
Applying Digital and Multimedia Literacies

Scripting a Presentation: Use PowerPoint or a similar storyboarding program to create an oral presentation responding to question 1 under Writing. Use animation, images, and text together to effectively illustrate your point about singular classification's role in a specific problem or problems on your campus.

Synthesis: Connections for Critical Thinking

1. Cofer writes about Latino culture and Silko about Native American culture in their respective essays. What connections do they make between their subjects and cultural affiliation and alienation? How do they present their ideas? How are their tones similar? How are they different?
2. Write an essay exploring the topic of culture and civilization in the essays by Ferguson, Sen, and Silko.
3. Consider the current position of women in our culture. Refer to at least two essays in this chapter to support your main observations.
4. How does one's experience of being an outsider or stranger to a culture affect one's understanding of that culture? Use essays from this chapter to support your key points.
5. Write an essay exploring the shape of contemporary civilization as it is reflected in the essays in this chapter. Cite specific support from at least three of the selections you have read.
6. How does a nation maintain a strong sense of self and still remain open to outside influences? Is a national identity crucial to a nation's survival? Use the opinions of representative authors in this chapter to address the question.
7. Is there such a thing as ethnic character, something that distinguishes Native Americans from African Americans, or Latinos from Asian Americans? What factors contribute to identification with culture and with nation? Cite at least three essays in this chapter.
8. Argue for or against the proposition that Americans are ignorant of both the contributions and the values of non-Western cultures in our country. Refer specifically to Reed, Staples, Silko, and Hoagland.

NETWORKING
Applying Digital and Multimedia Literacies

1. Set up and save a chat (on G-chat or another IM platform) with three to five class members, and discuss the differences in cultural perspectives among the writers in this chapter. If conversation wanes or you want to engage with expert opinions, drive the discussion to additional sources by linking to articles, blog posts, or videos on the topic.
2. Conduct an online search for reliable information on Judith Ortiz Cofer and Ishmael Reed. Keeping track of your sources, and using sources from at least three different media, write a brief research paper on these writers' perceptions of ethnicity and the American experience.

chapter 7

Government, Politics, and Social Justice

How Do We Decide What Is Fair?

Recent studies indicate that American students have an extremely limited understanding of government and politics. In fact, one-third of all high school juniors cannot identify the main purpose of the Declaration of Independence or say in which century it was signed. This document is one of the selections in this chapter. If we are ignorant of such a basic instrument in the making of our history and society, what might that say about our concepts of citizenship? Do we now see ourselves purely as economic units—that is, in terms of our ability or potential to make money—or as consumers—that is, in terms of the roles we play in spending it? Other notable essays on government, politics, and social justice in this chapter will help us understand our cultural legacies and what has traditionally been thought of as the impetus in developing America as a country.

Skilled writers can bring politics and issues of social justice to life, enabling us to develop a sense of the various processes that have influenced the development of cultures over time. By studying the course of history and politics, we develop causal notions of how events are interrelated and how traditions have evolved. The study of history and politics can be an antidote to the continuous "present tense" of the media, which often have the power to make us believe we live from moment to moment, discouraging reflection on serious issues such as why we live the way we do and how we came to be the people we are. Essays, speeches, documents, biographies, narratives, and many other literary forms capture events and illuminate the past while holding up a mirror to the present. On the one hand, our political story can be brought to life out of the plain but painfully eloquent artifacts of oral culture. On the other, Thomas Jefferson employs classical rhetorical structures—notably argumentation—in outlining democratic vistas in the Declaration of Independence.

Even the briefest reflection will remind us of how important political processes and institutions are. Put simply, a knowledge of government and politics, and of our quest for social justice, validates our memory, a remembrance of how important the past is to our current existence. When, for example, Martin Luther King Jr. approaches the subject of oppression from a theological perspective, we are reminded of how important the concept of freedom is to our heritage and the various ways it can be addressed. Indeed, had we been more familiar with chapters in human history, we might have avoided some of the commensurate responses to the crises in our own era. The essays in this chapter help remind us—as the philosopher Santayana warned—that "those who forget the lessons of history are doomed to repeat them."

322

Only with a knowledge of government and politics can we make informed choices. Through a study of government and politics, we learn about challenges and opportunities, conflicts and their resolutions, and the use and abuse of power across time in numerous cultures and civilizations. It is through the study of historical processes and political institutions that we seek to define ourselves and to learn how we have evolved.

PREVIEWING THE CHAPTER

As you read the selections in this chapter and respond to them in discussion and writing, consider the following questions:

- On what specific events does the author concentrate? What is the time frame?
- What larger historical and political issues concern the author?
- From what perspective does the author treat the subject—from that of participant, observer, commentator, or some other role?
- What is the author's purpose in treating events and personalities—to explain, to instruct, to amuse, to criticize, or to celebrate?
- What does the author learn about history and politics from his or her inquiry into events?
- What sorts of conflicts—historical, political, economic, social, religious—emerge in the essay?
- Are there any correspondences among the essays? What analogies do the authors themselves draw?
- What is the relationship of people and personalities to the events under consideration?
- Which biases and ideological positions do you detect in the authors' works?
- How has your understanding of history and politics been challenged by the essays in this chapter?

Classic and Contemporary Images

HAVE WE MADE ADVANCES IN CIVIL RIGHTS?

Using a Critical Perspective   Are you optimistic or skeptical about the lofty words in the Declaration of Independence announcing that everyone is created equal? How do these two visual texts, one advertising a slave auction and the other presenting a campaign poster for President Barack Obama, affect your response? What aspects of these visual texts stand out? What is your emotional and ethical response to the images? What do the two illustrations tell us about the evolution of equal rights and justice in the United States?

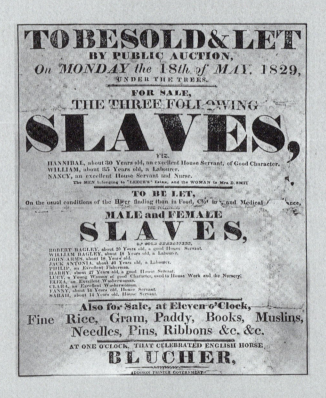

Advertisement of slaves for sale by the company Hewlett & Bright,
May 13, 1835.

Hope, by Shepard Fairey. Street artist and illustrator Shepard Fairey created this iconic poster, based on an Associated Press photograph, for the 2008 Obama presidential campaign.

Classic and Contemporary Essays
WHAT IS THE AMERICAN DREAM?

Both Thomas Jefferson and Martin Luther King Jr. are now safely ensconced within the pantheon of American historical figures. The following two writing samples help indicate why. Both are concerned with perhaps the most significant issue that concerns contemporary humankind: freedom. Jefferson creates a doctrine that is powerful owing to his use of concise and powerful language, which he employs both to enumerate British offenses and to call on his fellow Americans to revolt if need be. While his list of grievances may seem unquestionably correct to the contemporary mind, one must consider that Jefferson was a product of the Enlightenment, when philosophers had finally turned their attention to the primacy of individual rights after millennia of living under monarchic rule. King also provides us with the powerful theme of freedom in his famous speech; while his reflections address the peculiarly American racial divide, his style contains many biblical references, and his rhetoric is that of the sermon. You should consider why these two documents, regardless of their historical context, seem to be milestones in our nation's history.

The Declaration of Independence
In Congress, July 4, 1776

Thomas Jefferson

Thomas Jefferson (1743–1826) was governor of Virginia during the American Revolution, America's first secretary of state, and the third president of the United States. He had a varied and monumental career as politician, public servant, scientist, architect, educator (he founded the University of Virginia), and man of letters. Jefferson attended the Continental Congress in 1775, where he wrote the rough draft of the Declaration of Independence. Other hands made contributions to the document that was signed on July 4, 1776, but the wording, style, structure, and spirit of the final version are distinctly Jefferson's. Like Thomas Paine, Benjamin Franklin, James Madison, and other major figures of the Revolutionary era, Jefferson was notable for his use of prose as an instrument for social and political change. In the Declaration of Independence, we see the direct, precise, logical, and persuasive statement of revolutionary principles that makes the document one of the best-known and best-written texts in world history. Jefferson died in his home at Monticello on July 4, 50 years to the day from the signing of the Declaration of Independence.

When in the Course of human events it becomes necessary for one people to dis- 1
solve the political bands which have connected them with another, and to assume
among the powers of the earth, the separate and equal station to which the Laws
of Nature and of Nature's God entitle them, a decent respect to the opinions of
mankind requires that they should declare the causes which impel them to the
separation.

We hold these truths to be self-evident, that all men are created equal, that 2
they are endowed by their Creator with certain unalienable Rights, that among
these are Life, Liberty and the pursuit of Happiness.—That to secure these
rights, Governments are instituted among Men, deriving their just powers
from the consent of the governed.—That whenever any Form of Government
becomes destructive of these ends, it is the Right of the People to alter or to
abolish it, and to institute new Government, laying its foundation on such principles and organizing its powers in such form, as to them shall seem most
likely to effect their Safety and Happiness. Prudence, indeed, will dictate that
Governments long established should not be changed for light and transient
causes; and accordingly all experience hath shewn that mankind are more
disposed to suffer, while evils are sufferable, than to right themselves by abolishing the forms to which they are accustomed. But when a long train of abuses
and usurpations, pursuing invariably the same Object evinces a design to
reduce them under absolute Despotism, it is their right, it is their duty, to
throw off such Government, and to provide new Guards for their future security.—Such has been the patient sufferance of these Colonies; and such is now
the necessity which constrains them to alter their former Systems of Government. The history of the present King of Great Britain is a history of repeated
injuries and usurpations, all having in direct object the establishment of an
absolute Tyranny over these States. To prove this, let Facts be submitted to a
candid world.

He has refused his Assent to Laws, the most wholesome and necessary for 3
the public good.

He has forbidden his Governors to pass Laws of immediate and pressing 4
importance, unless suspended in their operation till his Assent should be obtained;
and when so suspended, he has utterly neglected to attend to them.

He has refused to pass other Laws for the accommodation of large districts of 5
people, unless those people would relinquish the right of Representation in the
Legislature, a right inestimable to them and formidable to tyrants only.

He has called together legislative bodies at places unusual, uncomfortable, 6
and distant from the depository of their public Records, for the sole purpose of
fatiguing them into compliance with his measures.

He has dissolved Representative Houses repeatedly, for opposing with manly 7
firmness his invasions on the rights of the people.

He has refused for a long time, after such dissolutions, to cause others to be 8
elected; whereby the Legislative powers, incapable of Annihilation, have returned
to the People at large for their exercise; the State remaining in the mean time
exposed to all the dangers of invasion from without, and convulsions within.

9   He has endeavored to prevent the population of these States; for that purpose obstructing the Laws for Naturalization of Foreigners; refusing to pass others to encourage their migrations hither, and raising the conditions of new Appropriations of Lands.

10   He has obstructed the Administration of Justice, by refusing his Assent to Laws for establishing Judiciary powers.

11   He has made Judges dependent on his Will alone, for the tenure of their offices, and the amount and payment of their salaries.

12   He has erected a multitude of New Offices, and sent hither swarms of Officers to harass our people, and eat out their substance.

13   He has kept among us, in times of peace, Standing Armies without the Consent of our legislatures.

14   He has affected to render the Military independent of and superior to the Civil power.

15   He has combined with others to subject us to a jurisdiction foreign to our constitution, and unacknowledged by our laws; giving his Assent to their Acts of pretended Legislation:

> For quartering large bodies of armed troops among us:

> For protecting them, by a mock Trial, from punishment for any Murders which they should commit on the Inhabitants of these States:

> For cutting off our Trade with all parts of the world:

> For imposing Taxes on us without our Consent:

> For depriving us in many cases, of the benefits of Trial by jury:

> For transporting us beyond Seas to be tried for pretended offences:

> For abolishing the free System of English Laws in a neighboring Province, establishing therein an Arbitrary government, and enlarging its Boundaries so as to render it at once an example and fit instrument for introducing the same absolute rule into these Colonies:

> For taking away our Charters, abolishing our most valuable Laws and altering fundamentally the Forms of our Governments:

> For suspending our own Legislatures, and declaring themselves invested with power to legislate for us in all cases whatsoever.

16   He has abdicated Government here, by declaring us out of his Protection and waging War against us.

17   He has plundered our seas, ravaged our Coasts, burnt our towns, and destroyed the lives of our people.

18   He is at this time transporting large Armies of foreign Mercenaries to complete the works of death, desolation and tyranny, already begun with circumstances of Cruelty & Perfidy scarcely paralleled in the most barbarous ages, and totally unworthy the Head of a civilized nation.

19   He has constrained our fellow Citizens taken Captive on the high Seas to bear Arms against their Country, to become the executioners of their friends and Brethren, or to fall themselves by their Hands.

He has excited domestic insurrections amongst us, and has endeavored to bring 20 on the inhabitants of our frontiers, the merciless Indian Savages, whose known rule of warfare, is an undistinguished destruction of all ages, sexes and conditions.

In every stage of these Oppressions We have Petitioned for Redress in the 21 most humble terms: Our repeated Petitions have been answered only by repeated injury. A Prince, whose character is thus marked by every act which may define a Tyrant, is unfit to be the ruler of a free people.

Nor have We been wanting in attentions to our British brethren. We have 22 warned them from time to time of attempts by their legislature to extend an unwarrantable jurisdiction over us. We have reminded them of the circumstances of our emigration and settlement here. We have appealed to their native justice and magnanimity, and we have conjured them by the ties of our common kindred to disavow these usurpations, which would inevitably interrupt our connections and correspondence. They too have been deaf to the voice of justice and of consanguinity. We must, therefore, acquiesce in the necessity, which denounces our Separation, and hold them, as we hold the rest of mankind, Enemies in War, in Peace Friends.

We, therefore, the Representatives of the United States of America, in General 23 Congress, Assembled, appealing to the Supreme Judge of the world for the rectitude of our intentions, do, in the Name, and by Authority of the good People of these Colonies, solemnly publish and declare, That these United Colonies are, and of Right ought to be Free and Independent States; that they are Absolved from all Allegiance to the British Crown, and that all political connection between them and the State of Great Britain, is and ought to be totally dissolved; and that as Free and Independent States, they have full Power to levy War, conclude Peace, contract Alliances, establish Commerce, and to do all other Acts and Things which Independent States may of right do. And for the support of this Declaration, with a firm reliance on the protection of divine Providence, we mutually pledge to each other our Lives, our Fortunes and our sacred Honor.

COMPREHENSION

1. Explain Jefferson's main and subordinate purposes in this document.
2. What is Jefferson's key assertion or argument? Mention several reasons that he gives to support his argument.
3. Summarize Jefferson's definition of human nature and government.

RHETORIC

1. There are many striking words and phrases in the Declaration of Independence, notably in the beginning. Locate three such examples, and explain their connotative power and effectiveness.
2. Jefferson and his colleagues had to draft a document designed for several audiences. What audiences did they have in mind? How do their language and style reflect their awareness of multiple audiences?

3. The Declaration of Independence is a classic model of syllogistic reasoning and deductive argument (see the Glossary). What is its major premise, and where is this premise stated? The minor premise? The conclusion?
4. What sort of inductive evidence does Jefferson offer?
5. Why is the middle portion, or body, of the Declaration of Independence considerably longer than the introduction or conclusion? What holds the body together?
6. Explain the function and effect of parallel structure in this document.

WRITING

1. Discuss the relevance of the Declaration of Independence to politics today.
2. Explain in an essay why the Declaration of Independence is a model of effective prose.
3. Write your own declaration of independence—from family, employer, required courses, or the like. Develop this declaration as an op-ed piece for a newspaper.
4. **Writing an Argument:** Do you believe that "all men are created equal"? Justify your answer in an argumentative essay.

NETWORKING
Applying Digital and Multimedia Literacies

Reading and Responding to a Web Site: Locate and explore *ushistory.org*'s Web site about the Declaration of Independence. In the menu on the left, choose several sections to explore: under "Document," you can see images of actual drafts of the text and read transcripts of it in several incarnations, including final. The "Related Information" page links to information about people, events, and other laws that influenced the document. Among other resources are two timelines (one chronicling the events of the Revolutionary War) and Jefferson's personal account of writing the Declaration of Independence. After spending some time with the site, write a reader response essay arguing that its contextual information either enhances or distracts from the content of the document itself. Support your position with specific examples.

I Have a Dream

Martin Luther King Jr.

Martin Luther King Jr. (1929–1968) was born in Atlanta, Georgia, and received degrees from Morehouse College, Crozer Theological Seminary, Boston University, and Chicago Theological Seminary. As Baptist clergyman, civil rights leader, founder and president of the Southern Christian Leadership Conference, and 1964 Nobel Peace Prize winner, King was a celebrated advocate of nonviolent resistance to

*achieve equality and racial integration in the world. King was a gifted orator and a
highly persuasive writer. His books include* Stride toward Freedom *(1958),* Letter
from Birmingham City Jail *(1963),* Strength to Love *(1963),* Why We Can't Wait
(1964), and Where Do We Go from Here: Chaos or Community? *(1967), a book
published shortly before he was assassinated on April 4, 1968, in Memphis, Tennessee.
This selection, a milestone of American oratory, was the keynote address at the
March on Washington, August 28, 1963.*

I am happy to join with you today in what will go down in history as the greatest 1
demonstration for freedom in the history of our nation.

Fivescore years ago, a great American, in whose symbolic shadow we stand 2
today, signed the Emancipation Proclamation. This momentous decree came as a
great beacon light of hope to millions of Negro slaves who had been seared in the
flames of withering injustice. It came as a joyous daybreak to end the long night of
their captivity.

But one hundred years later, the Negro still is not free; one hundred years 3
later, the life of the Negro is still sadly crippled by the manacles of segregation
and the chains of discrimination; one hundred years later, the Negro lives on a
lonely island of poverty in the midst of a vast ocean of material prosperity; one
hundred years later, the Negro is still languishing in the corners of American
society and finds himself in exile in his own land.

So we've come here today to dramatize a shameful condition. In a sense 4
we've come to our nation's capital to cash a check. When the architects of our
republic wrote the magnificent words of the Constitution and the Declaration of
Independence, they were signing a promissory note to which every American
was to fall heir. This note was the promise that all men, yes, black men as well as
white men, would be guaranteed the unalienable rights of life, liberty, and the
pursuit of happiness.

It is obvious today that America has defaulted on this promissory note in so 5
far as her citizens of color are concerned. Instead of honoring this sacred obligation,
America has given the Negro people a bad check; a check which has come back
marked "insufficient funds." We refuse to believe that there are insufficient funds
in the great vaults of opportunity of this nation. And so we've come to cash this
check, a check that will give us upon demand the riches of freedom and the
security of justice.

We have also come to this hallowed spot to remind America of the fierce 6
urgency of now. This is no time to engage in the luxury of cooling off or to take
the tranquilizing drug of gradualism. Now is the time to make real the promises
of democracy; now is the time to rise from the dark and desolate valley of segregation to the sunlit path of racial justice; now is the time to lift our nation from the
quicksands of racial injustice to the solid rock of brotherhood; now is the time to
make justice a reality for all God's children. It would be fatal for the nation to
overlook the urgency of the moment. This sweltering summer of the Negro's
legitimate discontent will not pass until there is an invigorating autumn of freedom and equality.

7   Nineteen sixty-three is not an end, but a beginning. And those who hope that the Negro needed to blow off steam and will now be content, will have a rude awakening if the nation returns to business as usual.

8   There will be neither rest nor tranquility in America until the Negro is granted his citizenship rights. The whirlwinds of revolt will continue to shake the foundations of our nation until the bright day of justice emerges.

9   But there is something that I must say to my people who stand on the warm threshold which leads into the palace of justice. In the process of gaining our rightful place we must not be guilty of wrongful deeds.

10   Let us not seek to satisfy our thirst for freedom by drinking from the cup of bitterness and hatred. We must forever conduct our struggle on the high plane of dignity and discipline. We must not allow our creative protest to degenerate into physical violence. Again and again we must rise to the majestic heights of meeting physical force with soul force.

11   The marvelous new militancy which has engulfed the Negro community must not lead us to a distrust of all white people, for many of our white brothers, as evidenced by their presence here today, have come to realize that their destiny is tied up with our destiny and they have come to realize that their freedom is inextricably bound to our freedom. This offense we share mounted to storm the battlements of injustice must be carried forth by a biracial army. We cannot walk alone.

12   And as we walk, we must make the pledge that we shall always march ahead. We cannot turn back. There are those who are asking the devotees of civil rights, "When will you be satisfied?" We can never be satisfied as long as the Negro is the victim of the unspeakable horrors of police brutality.

13   We can never be satisfied as long as our bodies, heavy with fatigue of travel, cannot gain lodging in the motels of the highways and the hotels of the cities. We cannot be satisfied as long as the Negro's basic mobility is from a smaller ghetto to a larger one.

14   We can never be satisfied as long as our children are stripped of their selfhood and robbed of their dignity by signs stating "for whites only." We cannot be satisfied as long as a Negro in Mississippi cannot vote and a Negro in New York believes he has nothing for which to vote. No, we are not satisfied, and we will not be satisfied until justice rolls down like waters and righteousness like a mighty stream.

15   I am not unmindful that some of you have come here out of excessive trials and tribulation. Some of you have come fresh from narrow jail cells. Some of you have come from areas where your quest for freedom left you battered by the storms of persecution and staggered by the winds of police brutality. You have been the veterans of creative suffering. Continue to work with the faith that unearned suffering is redemptive.

16   Go back to Mississippi; go back to Alabama; go back to South Carolina; go back to Georgia; go back to Louisiana; go back to the slums and ghettos of the northern cities, knowing that somehow this situation can, and will be changed. Let us not wallow in the valley of despair.

17   So I say to you, my friends, that even though we must face the difficulties of today and tomorrow, I still have a dream. It is a dream deeply rooted in the American

dream that one day this nation will rise up and live out the true meaning of its creed—we hold these truths to be self-evident, that all men are created equal.

I have a dream that one day on the red hills of Georgia, sons of former slaves 18 and sons of former slave-owners will be able to sit down together at the table of brotherhood.

I have a dream that one day, even the state of Mississippi, a state sweltering 19 with the heat of injustice, sweltering with the heat of oppression, will be transformed into an oasis of freedom and justice.

I have a dream that my four little children will one day live in a nation where 20 they will not be judged by the color of their skin but by the content of their character. I have a dream today!

I have a dream that one day, down in Alabama, with its vicious racists, with its 21 governor having his lips dripping with the words of interposition and nullification, that one day, right there in Alabama, little black boys and black girls will be able to join hands with little white boys and white girls as sisters and brothers. I have a dream today!

I have a dream that one day every valley shall be exalted, every hill and 22 mountain shall be made low, the rough places shall be made plain, and the crooked places shall be made straight and the glory of the Lord will be revealed and all flesh shall see it together.

This is our hope. This is the faith that I go back to the South with.   23

With this faith we will be able to hew out of the mountain of despair a stone of 24 hope. With this faith we will be able to transform the jangling discords of our nation into a beautiful symphony of brotherhood.

With this faith we will be able to work together, to pray together, to struggle to- 25 gether, to go to jail together, to stand up for freedom together, knowing that we will be free one day. This will be the day when all of God's children will be able to sing with new meaning—"my country 'tis of thee; sweet land of liberty; of thee I sing; land where my fathers died, land of the pilgrims' pride; from every mountain side, let freedom ring"—and if America is to be a great nation, this must become true.

So let freedom ring from the prodigious hilltops of New Hampshire.   26

Let freedom ring from the mighty mountains of New York.   27

Let freedom ring from the heightening Alleghenies of Pennsylvania.   28

Let freedom ring from the snow-capped Rockies of Colorado.   29

Let freedom ring from the curvaceous slopes of California.   30

But not only that.   31

Let freedom ring from Stone Mountain of Georgia.   32

Let freedom ring from Lookout Mountain of Tennessee.   33

Let freedom ring from every hill and molehill of Mississippi, from every 34 mountainside, let freedom ring.

And when we allow freedom to ring, when we let it ring from every village 35 and hamlet, from every state and city, we will be able to speed up that day when all of God's children—black men and white men, Jews and Gentiles, Catholics and Protestants—will be able to join hands and to sing in the words of the old Negro spiritual, "Free at last, free at last; thank God Almighty, we are free at last."

COMPREHENSION

1. What is the main purpose of this speech? Where does King state this purpose most clearly?
2. Why does King make use of "fivescore years ago" (paragraph 2)? How is this more appropriate than simply saying "a hundred years ago"?
3. Who is King's audience? Where does he acknowledge the special historical circumstances influencing his speech?

RHETORIC

1. From what sources does King adapt phrases to give his work allusive richness?
2. What do the terms *interposition* and *nullification* (paragraph 21) mean? What is their historical significance?
3. Why does King make use of repetition? Does this technique work well in print? Explain.
4. What is the purpose of the extended metaphor in paragraphs 4 and 5? Which point in paragraph 3 does it refer to?
5. In which paragraphs does King address the problems of African Americans?
6. Why is this selection titled "I Have a Dream"? How do dreams serve as a motif for this speech?

WRITING

1. "I Have a Dream" is considered by many people to be among the greatest speeches delivered by an American. Do you think it deserves to be? Explain in an essay.
2. Write a comparative essay analyzing King's assessment of black Americans' condition in 1963 and their condition today. What do you think King would say if he knew of contemporary conditions?
3. Write your own "I Have a Dream" essay, basing it on your vision of America or of a special people.
4. **Writing an Argument:** Prepare a newspaper editorial advocating a solution to one aspect of racial, ethnic, or sexual injustice.

NETWORKING
Applying Digital and Multimedia Literacies

Seeing vs. Reading the Text of a Speech: On YouTube or Vimeo, locate a video of Martin Luther King giving his famous "I Have a Dream" speech. How is the experience of watching and listening to this speech different from reading it? Compare and contrast these two types of experiencing a text, using "I Have a Dream" as an example. Consider what, beyond the words themselves, is *happening* in this video.

Synthesis: Classic and Contemporary Questions for Comparison

1. Compare the Declaration of Independence with King's speech in terms of language, style, and content. Are they equally powerful and resonant? Cite specific passages from the essays to illustrate your response.
2. Rewrite the Declaration of Independence in modern English as you believe Dr. King might have written it, reflecting his concerns about the African American and other minorities in this country. Include a list of grievances similar to the ones concerning British rule.
3. Write a research paper about the lives and times of King and Jefferson. Compare and contrast any significant events or pertinent biographical data in their backgrounds.

The Right Road to America?

Amy Chua

Amy Chua (b. 1962) is a lawyer, educator, and writer whose work focuses on relationships between law and economic development, ethnic conflict, and globalization. She was born into an immigrant family in Champaign, Illinois; her father, a famous computer scientist who received an appointment at the University of California, Berkeley, moved the family to the West Coast when Chua was eight years old. Chua graduated from Harvard College in 1984 with a degree in economics; she received a JD from Harvard Law School in 1987. Chua worked in corporate law before beginning her teaching career at Duke Law School. In 2007, she joined the faculty at Yale Law School. Chua's first two books, World on Fire *(2003) and* Day of Empire *(2007), are studies of ethnic conflict and what the author terms "hyperpower" decline. Her third book, the memoir* Battle Hymn of the Tiger Mother *(2011), ignited a storm over parenting styles when Chua claimed that Chinese mothers are superior to their American counterparts. In this essay, which appeared in the December 16, 2007, issue of the* Washington Post, *Chua turns personal history into a nuanced examination of the immigration debate.*

If you don't speak Spanish, Miami really can feel like a foreign country. In any 1 restaurant, the conversation at the next table is more likely to be Spanish than English. And Miami's population is only 65 percent Hispanic. El Paso is 76 percent Latino. Flushing, N.Y., is 60 percent immigrant, mainly Chinese.

Chinatowns and Little Italys have long been part of America's urban 2 landscape, but would it be all right to have entire U.S. cities where most people spoke and did business in Chinese, Spanish or even Arabic? Are too many Third World, non-English-speaking immigrants destroying our national identity?

3   For some Americans, even asking such questions is racist. At the other end of the spectrum, the conservative talk show host Bill O'Reilly fulminates against floods of immigrants who threaten to change America's "complexion" and replace what he calls the "white Christian male power structure."

4   But for the large majority in between, Democrats and Republicans alike, these questions are painful, with no easy answers. At some level, most of us cherish our legacy as a nation of immigrants. But are all immigrants really equally likely to make good Americans? Are we, as the Harvard political scientist Samuel Huntington warns, in danger of losing our core values and devolving "into a loose confederation of ethnic, racial, cultural, and political groups, with little or nothing in common apart from their location in the territory of what had been the United States of America"?

5   My parents arrived in the United States in 1961, so poor that they couldn't afford heat their first winter. I grew up speaking only Chinese at home (for every English word accidentally uttered, my sister and I got one whack of the chopsticks). Today, my father is a professor at Berkeley, and I'm a professor at Yale Law School. As the daughter of immigrants, a grateful beneficiary of America's tolerance and opportunity, I could not be more pro-immigrant.

6   Nevertheless, I think Huntington has a point.

7   Around the world today, nations face violence and instability as a result of their increasing pluralism and diversity. Across Europe, immigration has resulted in unassimilated, largely Muslim enclaves that are hotbeds of unrest and even terrorism. The riots in France last month were just the latest manifestation. With Muslims poised to become a majority in Amsterdam and elsewhere within a decade, major West European cities could undergo a profound transformation. Not surprisingly, virulent anti-immigration parties are on the rise.

8   Not long ago, Czechoslovakia, Yugoslavia and the Soviet Union disintegrated when their national identities proved too weak to bind together diverse peoples. Iraq is the latest example of how crucial national identity is. So far, it has found no overarching identity strong enough to unite its Kurds, Shiites and Sunnis.

9   The United States is in no danger of imminent disintegration. But this is because it has been so successful, at least since the Civil War, in forging a national identity strong enough to hold together its widely divergent communities. We should not take this unifying identity for granted.

10   The greatest empire in history, ancient Rome, collapsed when its cultural and political glue dissolved, and peoples who had long thought of themselves as Romans turned against the empire. In part, this fragmentation occurred because of a massive influx of immigrants from a very different culture. The "barbarians" who sacked Rome were Germanic immigrants who never fully assimilated.

11   Does this mean that it's time for the United States to shut its borders and reassert its "white, Christian" identity and what Huntington calls its Anglo-Saxon, Protestant "core values"?

12   No. The anti-immigration camp makes at least two critical mistakes.

First, it neglects the indispensable role that immigrants have played in 13
building American wealth and power. In the 19th century, the United States
would never have become an industrial and agricultural powerhouse without
the millions of poor Irish, Polish, Italian and other newcomers who mined coal,
laid rail and milled steel. European immigrants led to the United States' winning the race for the atomic bomb. Today, American leadership in the Digital
Revolution—so central to our military and economic preeminence—owes an
enormous debt to immigrant contributions. Andrew Grove (cofounder of Intel),
Vinod Khosla (Sun Microsystems) and Sergey Brin (Google) are immigrants.
Between 1995 and 2005, 52 percent of Silicon Valley start-ups had one key
immigrant founder. And Vikram S. Pundit's appointment to the helm of CitiGroup
last Tuesday means that 14 chief executives of Fortune 100 companies are
foreign-born.

The United States is in a fierce global competition to attract the world's best 14
high-tech scientists and engineers—most of whom are not white Christians. Just this
past summer, Microsoft opened a large new software development center in Canada,
in part because of the difficulty of obtaining U.S. visas for foreign engineers.

Second, anti-immigration talking heads forget that their own scapegoating 15
vitriol will, if anything, drive immigrants farther from the U.S. mainstream. One
reason we don't have Europe's enclaves is our unique success in forging an ethnically and religiously neutral national identity, uniting individuals of all backgrounds. This is America's glue, and people like Huntington and O'Reilly
unwittingly imperil it.

Nevertheless, immigration naysayers also have a point. 16

America's glue can be subverted by too much tolerance. Immigration advo- 17
cates are too often guilty of an uncritical political correctness that avoids hard
questions about national identity and imposes no obligations on immigrants. For
these well-meaning idealists, there is no such thing as too much diversity.

The right thing for the United States to do—and the best way to keep 18
Americans in favor of immigration—is to take national identity seriously while
maintaining our heritage as a land of opportunity. U.S. immigration policy should
be tolerant but also tough. Here are five suggestions:

Overhaul admission priorities. Since 1965, the chief admission criterion has 19
been family reunification. This was a welcome replacement for the ethnically
discriminatory quota system that preceded it. But once the brothers and sisters of
a current U.S. resident get in, they can sponsor their own extended families. In
2006, more than 800,000 immigrants were admitted on this basis. By contrast,
only about 70,000 immigrants were admitted on the basis of employment skills,
with an additional 65,000 temporary visas granted to highly skilled workers.

This is backwards. Apart from nuclear families (spouse, minor children, pos- 20
sibly parents), the special preference for family members should be drastically
reduced. As soon as my father got citizenship, his relatives in the Philippines
asked him to sponsor them. Soon, his mother, brother, sister and sister-in-law
were also U.S. citizens or permanent residents. This was nice for my family, but
frankly there was nothing especially fair about it. Instead, the immigration system

should reward ability and be keyed to the country's labor needs—skilled or unskilled, technological or agricultural. In particular, we should significantly increase the number of visas for highly skilled workers, putting them on a fast track for citizenship.

21   Make English the official national language. A common language is critical to cohesion and national identity in an ethnically diverse society. Americans of all backgrounds should be encouraged to speak more languages—I've forced my own daughters to learn Mandarin (minus the threat of chopsticks)—but offering Spanish-language public education to Spanish-speaking children is the wrong kind of indulgence. "Native language education" should be overhauled, and more stringent English proficiency requirements for citizenship should be set up.

22   Immigrants must embrace the nation's civic virtues. It took my parents years to see the importance of participating in the larger community. When I was in third grade, my mother signed me up for Girl Scouts. I think she liked the uniforms and merit badges, but when I told her that I was picking up trash and visiting soup kitchens, she was horrified.

23   For many immigrants, only family matters. Even when immigrants get involved in politics, they tend to focus on protecting their own and protesting discrimination. That they can do so is one of the great virtues of U.S. democracy. But a mindset based solely on taking care of your own factionalizes our society.

24   Like all Americans, immigrants have a responsibility to contribute to the social fabric. It's up to each immigrant community to fight off an enclave mentality and give back to their new country. It's not healthy for Chinese to hire only Chinese, or Koreans only Koreans. By contrast, the free health clinic set up by Muslim Americans in Los Angeles—serving the entire poor community—is a model to emulate. Immigrants are integrated at the moment when they realize that their success is inextricably intertwined with everyone else's.

25   Enforce the law. Illegal immigration, along with terrorism, is the chief cause of today's anti-immigration backlash. It is also inconsistent with the rule of law, which, as any immigrant from a developing country will tell you, is a critical aspect of U.S. national identity. But if we're serious about this problem, we need to enforce the law against not only illegal aliens, but also those who hire them. It's the worst of all worlds to allow U.S. employers who hire illegal aliens—thus keeping the flow of illegal workers coming—to break the law while demonizing the aliens as lawbreakers. An Arizona law set to take effect on Jan. 1 will tighten the screws on employers who hire undocumented workers, but this issue can't be left up to a single state.

26   Make the United States an equal-opportunity immigration magnet. That the 11 million to 20 million illegal immigrants are 80 percent Mexican and Central American is itself a problem. This is emphatically not for the reason Huntington gives—that Hispanics supposedly don't share America's core values. But if the U.S. immigration system is to reflect and further our ethnically neutral identity, it must itself be ethnically neutral, offering equal opportunity to Sudanese, Estonians, Burmese and so on. The starkly disproportionate ratio of Latinos—

reflecting geographical fortuity and a large measure of law-breaking—is inconsistent with this principle.

Immigrants who turn their backs on American values don't deserve to be 27 here. But those of us who turn our backs on immigrants misunderstand the secret of America's success and what it means to be American.

COMPREHENSION

1. What issues and questions does Chua raise concerning immigration in the United States and other nations?
2. According to Chua, what is the rationale for immigration reform?
3. How does Chua characterize Samuel Huntington's views on immigration?

RHETORIC

1. Why does Chua pose a question in the title and also in subsequent paragraphs? What is the effect?
2. How does Chua establish her authority or credibility in this essay? In what ways does she present herself as an objective lawyer presenting both sides of a case?
3. What is Chua's basic argument? What is her purpose in presenting counterarguments?
4. Where does Chua employ a listing of recommendations? How effective do you find this strategy, and why?
5. Why does Chua personalize the debate over immigration by referring to her family?

WRITING

1. Using Chua's essay as a reference point, write an essay in which you propose changes in current American immigration policy.
2. Compare and contrast immigration policy in the United States and one other nation. Conduct research if necessary.
3. **Writing an Argument:** Argue for or against the proposition that undocumented aliens deserve a pathway to citizenship.

NETWORKING
Applying Digital and Multimedia Literacies

Analyzing Critiques Across Media: Collaborating with another class member, use online news archives and search engines to find at least three articles or reviews and at least two video stories or podcast/radio pieces about Chua's provocative memoir, *Battle Hymn of the Tiger Mother*. How would you characterize your sampling of its critical reception—and/or how readers responded to it? Share your insights with the class.

Is Texas America?

Molly Ivins

Molly Ivins *(1944–2007), a humorous and typically irreverent newspaper commentator whose syndicated column appeared in about 350 newspapers, was born in California but grew up in Texas. The Lone Star State—and especially the Bush family—animated Ivins's writing and prompted her satirical assessment of Texas; its people, politics, and culture. She called Texas the Great State, "reactionary, cantankerous, and hilarious." Growing up in an affluent family, she learned to confront her conservative Republican father, arguing with him over civil rights and the Vietnam War. Ivins attended Smith College and the Institute for Political Science in Paris before earning a master's degree at the Columbia Graduate School of Journalism. She worked for several newspapers, including the* New York Times *and the monthly* Texas Observer, *and published six books, among them* Molly Ivins Can't Say That, Can She? *(1991) and two books on George Bush,* Shrub: The Short but Happy Life of George Bush *(2000) and* Bushwacked *(2003). "There are two kinds of humor," Ivins once observed; one "makes us chuckle about our foibles and shared humanity. The other kind holds people up to public contempt and ridicule. That's what I do." In fact, the following essay, published in the* Nation *in 2003, indicates that Ivins is adept at both kinds of humor.*

1 Well, sheesh. I don't know whether to warn you that because George Dubya Bush is president the whole damn country is about to be turned into Texas (a singularly horrible fate: as the country song has it: "Lubbock on Everythang") or if I should try to stand up for us and convince the rest of the country we're not all that insane.

2   Truth is, I've spent much of my life trying, unsuccessfully, to explode the myths about Texas. One attempts to explain—with all good will, historical evidence, nasty statistics and just a bow of recognition to our racism—that Texas is not *The Alamo* starring John Wayne. We're not *Giant,* we ain't a John Ford western. The first real Texan I ever saw on TV was *King of the Hill*'s Boomhauer, the guy who's always drinking beer and you can't understand a word he says.

3   So, how come trying to explode myths about Texas always winds up reinforcing them? After all these years, I do not think it is my fault. The fact is, it's a damned peculiar place. Given all the horseshit, there's bound to be a pony in here somewhere. Just by trying to be honest about it, one accidentally underlines its sheer strangeness.

4   Here's the deal on Texas. It's big. So big there's about five distinct and different places here, separated from one another geologically, topographically, botanically, ethnically, culturally and climatically. Hence our boring habit of specifying East, West and South Texas, plus the Panhandle and the Hill Country. The majority of the state's blacks live in East Texas, making it more like the Old South than the Old South is anymore. West Texas is, more or less, like *Giant,* except, like every

Copyright © 2002 by Karen Caldicott.

place else in the state, it has an incurable tendency toward the tacky and all the cowboys are brown. South Texas is 80 percent Hispanic and a weird amalgam of cultures. You get names now like Shannon Rodriguez, Hannah Gonzalez and Tiffany Ruiz. Even the Anglos speak English with a Spanish accent. The Panhandle, which sticks up to damn near Kansas, is High Plains, like one of those square states, Nebraska or the Dakotas, except more brown folks. The Hill Country, smack dab in the middle, resembles nothing else in the state.

Plus, plopped on top of all this, we have three huge cities, all among the ten 5 largest in the country. Houston is Los Angeles with the climate of Calcutta, Dallas is Dutch (clean, orderly and conformist), while San Antonio is Monterrey North. Many years ago I wrote of this state: "The reason the sky is bigger here is because there aren't any trees. The reason folks here eat grits is because they ain't got no taste. Cowboys mostly stink and it's hot, oh God, is it hot. . . . Texas is a mosaic of cultures, which overlap in several parts of the state, with the darker layers on the bottom. The cultures are black, Chicano, Southern, freak, suburban and shitkicker. (Shitkicker is dominant.) They are all rotten for women." All that's changed in thirty years is that suburban is now dominant, shitkicker isn't so ugly as it once was and the freaks are now Goths or something. So it could be argued we're becoming more civilized.

In fact, it was always easy to argue that: Texas has symphony orchestras and 6 great universities and perfect jewels of art museums (mostly in Fort Worth, of all places). It has lots of people who birdwatch, write PhD theses on esoteric subjects and speak French, for chrissake. But what still makes Texas Texas is that it's ignorant, cantankerous and ridiculously friendly. Texas is still resistant to Howard Johnsons, interstate highways and some forms of phoniness. It is the place least likely to become a replica of everyplace else. It's authentically awful, comic and weirdly charming, all at the same time.

7   Culturally, Texans rather resemble both Alaskans (hunt, fish, hate government) and Australians (drink beer, hate snobs). The food is quite good—Mexican, barbecue, chili, shrimp and chicken-fried steak, an acquired taste. The music is country, blues, folk, mariachi, rockabilly and everything else you can think of. Mexican music—norteño, ranchero—is poised to cross over, as black music did in the 1950s.

8   If you want to understand George W. Bush—unlike his daddy, an unfortunate example of a truly Texas-identified citizen—you have to stretch your imagination around a weird Texas amalgam: religion, anti-intellectualism and machismo. All big, deep strains here, but still an odd combination. Then add that Bush is just another li'l upper-class white boy out trying to prove he's tough.

9   The politics are probably the weirdest thing about Texas. The state has gone from one-party Democrat to one-party Republican in thirty years. Lyndon said when he signed the Civil Rights Act in 1964 that it would take two generations and cost the Democrats the South. Right on both counts. We like to think we're "past race" in Texas, but of course East Texas remains an ugly, glaring exception. After James Byrd Jr. was dragged to death near Jasper, only one prominent white politician attended his funeral—US Senator Kay Bailey Hutchison. Dubya, then governor, put the kibosh on the anti–hate crimes bill named in Byrd's memory. (The deal-breaker for Bush was including gays and lesbians. At a meeting last year of the Texas Civil Liberties Union board, vicious hate crimes against gays in both Dallas and Houston were discussed. I asked the board member from Midland if they'd been having any trouble with gay-bashing out there. "Hell, honey," she said, with that disastrous frankness one can grow so fond of, "there's not a gay in Midland would come out of the closet for fear people would think they're a Democrat.")

10   Among the various strains of Texas right-wingism (it is factually incorrect to call it conservatism) is some leftover loony John Birchism, now morphed into militias; country-club economic conservatism, à la George Bush *père;* and the usual batty antigovernment strain. Of course Texas grew on the tender mercies of the federal government—rural electrification, dams, generations of master pork-barrel politicians and vast subsidies to the oil and gas industry. But that has never interfered with Texans' touching but entirely erroneous belief that this is the Frontier, and that in the Old West every man pulled his own weight and depended on no one else. The myth of rugged individualism continues to afflict a generation raised entirely in suburbs with names like "Flowering Forest Hills of Lubbock."

11   The Populist movement was born in the Texas Hill Country, as genuinely democratic an uprising as this country has ever known. It produced legendary politicians for generations, including Ralph Yarborough, Sam Rayburn, Lyndon and even into the 1990s, with Agriculture Commissioner Jim Hightower. I think it is not gone, but only sleeping.

12 Texans retain an exaggerated sense of state identification, routinely identifying themselves when abroad as Texans, rather than Americans or from the United States. That aggravated provincialism has three sources. First, the state is so big (though not so big as Alaska, as they are sure to remind us) that it can take a

couple of days hard travel just to get out of it. Second, we reinforce the sense of difference by requiring kids to study Texas history, including roughly ten years as an independent country. In state colleges, the course in Texas government is mandatory. Third, even national advertising campaigns pitch brands with a Texas accent here and certain products, like the pickup truck, are almost invariably sold with a Texas pitch. (Makes sense: Texas leads the nation with more than four million registered pickups.)

The founding myth is the Alamo. I was raised on the Revised Standard 13 Version, which holds that while it was stupid of Travis and the gang to be there at all (Sam Houston told them to get the hell out), it was still an amazing last stand. Stephen Harrigan in *The Gates of the Alamo* is closer to reality, but even he admits in the end there was something romantic and even noble about the episode, like having served in the Abraham Lincoln Brigade during the Spanish Civil War.

According to the demographers at Texas A&M (itself a source of much Texas 14 lore), Texas will become "majority minority" in 2008. Unfortunately, we won't see it in the voting patterns for at least a generation, and by then the Republicans will have the state so tied up by redistricting (recently the subject of a massive stand-off, now over, in the legislature), it's unlikely to shift for another generation beyond that. The Christian right is heavily dominant in the Texas Republican Party. It was the genius of Karl Rove/George W. Bush to straddle the divide between the Christian right and the country club conservatives, which is actually a significant class split. The politics of resentment plays a large role on the Christian right: Fundamentalists are perfectly aware that they are held in contempt by "the intellectuals." (William Brann of Waco once observed, "The trouble with our Texas Baptists is that we do not hold them under water long enough." He was shot to death by an irate Baptist.) In Texas, "intellectual" is often used as a synonym for "snob." George W. Bush perfectly exemplifies that attitude.

Here in the National Laboratory for Bad Government, we have an antiquated and 15 regressive tax structure—high property, high sales, no income tax. We consistently rank near the bottom by every measure of social service, education and quality of life (leading to one of our state mottoes, "Thank God for Mississippi"). Yet the state is incredibly rich in more than natural resources. The economy is now fully diversified, so plunges in the oil market can no longer throw the state into the bust cycle.

It is widely believed in Texas that the highest purpose of government is to 16 create "a healthy bidness climate." The legislature is so dominated by special interests that the gallery where the lobbyists sit is called "the owners' box." The consequences of unregulated capitalism, of special interests being able to buy government through campaign contributions, are more evident here because Texas is "first and worst" in this area. That Enron was a Texas company is no accident: Texas was also Ground Zero in the savings-and-loan scandals, is continually the site of major ripoffs by the insurance industry and has a rich history of gigantic chicanery going way back. Leland Beatty, an agricultural consultant, calls Enron "Billie Sol Estes Goes to College." Economists call it "control fraud" when a corporation is rotten from the head down. I sometimes think Texas government is a case of control fraud too.

17   We are currently saddled with a right-wing ideologue sugar daddy, James Leininger out of San Antonio, who gives immense campaign contributions and wants school vouchers, abstinence education and the like in return. The result is a crew of breathtakingly right-wing legislators. This session, Representative Debbie Riddle of Houston said during a hearing, "Where did this idea come from that everybody deserves free education, free medical care, free whatever? It comes from Moscow, from Russia. It comes straight out of the pit of hell."

18   Texans for Lawsuit Reform, *aka* the bidness lobby, is a major player and has effectively eviscerated the judiciary with a two-pronged attack. While round after round of "tort reform" was shoved through the legislature, closing off access to the courts and protecting corporations from liability for their misdeeds, Karl Rove was busy electing all nine state Supreme Court justices. So even if you should somehow manage to get into court, you are faced with a bench noted for its canine fidelity to corporate special interests.

19   Here's how we make progress in Texas. Two summers ago, Governor Goodhair Perry (the man has a head of hair every Texan can be proud of, regardless of party) appointed an Enron executive to the Public Utilities Commission. The next day, Governor Goodhair got a $25,000 check from Ken Lay. Some thought there might be a connection. The guv was forced to hold a press conference, at which he explained that the whole thing was "totally coincidental." So that was a big relief.

20   We don't have a sunshine law in Texas; it's more like a partly cloudy law. But even here a major state appointee has to fill out a bunch of forms that are then public record. When the governor's office put out the forms on the Enron guy, members of the press, that alert guardian watchdog of democracy, noticed that the question about any unfortunate involvement with law enforcement looked funny. The governor's office had whited out the answers. A sophisticated cover-up. The alert guardian watchdogs were on the trail. We soon uncovered a couple of minor traffic violations and the following item: While out hunting a few years earlier, the Enron guy accidentally shot a whooping crane. As a result he had to pay a $15,000 fine under what is known in Texas as the In Danger Species Act. We print this. A state full of sympathetic hunters reacted with, "Hell, anybody could accidentally shoot a whooper." But the press stayed on the story and was able to report that the guy shot the whooper while on a goose hunt. Now the whooper is a large bird—runs up to five feet tall. The goose—short. Now we have a state full of hunters saying, "Hell, if this boy is too dumb to tell a whooper from a goose, maybe he shouldn't be regulatin' public utilities." He was forced to resign.

21   As Willie Nelson sings, if we couldn't laugh, we would all go insane. This is our redeeming social value and perhaps our one gift to progressives outside our borders. We do laugh. We have no choice. We have to have fun while trying to stave off the forces of darkness because we hardly ever win, so it's the only fun we get to have. We find beer and imagination helpful. The Billion Bubba March, the Spam-o-rama, the time we mooned the Klan, being embedded with the troops at the Holiday Inn in Ardmore, Oklahoma, singing "I'm Just an Asshole from El Paso" with Kinky Friedman and the Texas Jewboys, and "Up Against the Wall, Redneck Mother" with

Ray Wylie Hubbard laughing at the loonies in the lege—does it get better than this? The late Bill Kugle of Athens is buried in the Texas State Cemetery. On the front of his stone are listed his service in the Marines in World War II, his years in the legislature, other titles and honors. On the back of the stone is, "He never voted for a Republican and never had much to do with them either."

We have lost some great freedom fighters in Texas during the past year. Billie 22 Carr, the great Houston political organizer (you'd've loved her: She got invited to the White House during the middle of the Monica mess, sashayed through the receiving line, looked Bill Clinton in the eye and said, "You dumb son of a bitch"), always said she wanted her funeral to be like her whole life in politics: It should start half an hour late, she wanted a balanced delegation of pallbearers—one black, one brown, two women—and she wanted an open casket and a name tag stuck over her left tit that said, "Hi there! My name is Billie Carr." We did it all for her.

At the funeral of Malcolm McGregor, the beloved legislator and bibliophile 23 from El Paso, we heard "The Eyes of Texas" and the Aggie War Hymn played on the bagpipes. At the service for Maury Maverick Jr. of San Antonio, and at his request, J. Frank Dobie's poem "The Mustangs" was read by the poet Naomi Shihab Nye. The last stanza is:

> So sometimes yet, in the realities of silence and solitude,
> For a few people unhampered a while by things,
> The mustangs walk out with dawn, stand high, then
> Sweep away, wild with sheer life, and free, free, free—
> Free of all confines of time and flesh.

COMPREHENSION

1. How does Ivins answer the question posed by her title? In other words, what does Texas have that the United States in general possesses? What, according to Ivins, is unique about Texas?
2. In paragraph 9, Ivins writes, "The politics are probably the weirdest thing about Texas." What examples does she give to support her statement?
3. Ivins seems to warn us about the excesses of Texas life and politics, but clearly she is also fascinated by her home state. Does she reconcile these conflicting perspectives? Why or why not?

RHETORIC

1. What is Ivins's claim or main proposition? What are her minor propositions? Do you think that her argument is sound or valid? Justify your response.
2. How does Ivins establish herself as an authority on Texas? Would you accuse her of bias? Why or why not? Why might her opinions be congenial to an audience reading the *Nation*?
3. Ivins uses phrases like "Well, sheesh" (paragraph 1), "plopped on top"(paragraph 5), and "for crissake" (paragraph 6) in the essay. What is the effect of this colloquial style and tone? What is her purpose?
4. Locate varieties of humor in the essay. Do you think that Ivins employs humor effectively to advance her argument? Explain your response.

5. The essay contains four main sections. What is the core topic of each section? How do these topics overlap? What transitions serve to link the parts?
6. Throughout the essay, Ivins alludes to many aspects of Texas life, culture, people, and politics that we might not be familiar with. Do these allusions detract from the essay or make it too topical? Why, for instance, would Ivins want to end her essay with reference to the deaths of two Texans and an allusion to a poem by J. Frank Dobie?

WRITING

1. Write a humorous essay on the state in which you grew up. Decide in advance what varieties of humor and what tone you want to use.
2. Go online or to a library and find out more about a Texan (for instance, George W. Bush), a Texas trait (like *machismo*), or a Texas institution (for example, the state legislature), and then write an essay that seeks to either confirm or refute Ivins's presentation of the subject.
3. **Writing an Argument:** In an essay, argue for or against the proposition that Ivins is too biased and cruel in her exposé of Texas. Defend or refute her argument on a point-by-point basis.

NETWORKING
Applying Digital and Multimedia Literacies

Reading a Visual in Context: In a two- or three-page response, summarize, analyze, and interpret the illustration that accompanies this essay (see p. 341). In your response, consider how it works with this piece and what each text lends to the other.

Cyberspace: If You Don't Love It, Leave It

Esther Dyson

Esther Dyson (b. 1951) was born in Zurich, Switzerland; grew up in Princeton, New Jersey; and received a BA in economics from Harvard University. She is the daughter of Freeman Dyson, a physicist prominent in arms control. She is the editor and publisher of the widely respected computer newsletter Release 1.0, *which is circulated to many computer industry leaders. She is also chairperson of the Electronic Frontier Foundation and on the boards of the Santa Fe Institute, the Global Business Network, and the Institute for East/West Studies. She served as a reporter for* Forbes *magazine for four years. The following essay appeared in the* New York Times Magazine *in July 1995. In it, Dyson defends the free-market approach to cyberspace content, arguing that regulation of the Internet is simply impossible and counterproductive.*

Something in the American psyche loves new frontiers. We hanker after wide- 1
open spaces; we like to explore; we like to make rules instead of follow them. But
in this age of political correctness and other intrusions on our national cult of independence, it's hard to find a place where you can go and be yourself without
worrying about the neighbors.

There is such a place: cyberspace. Lost in the furor over porn on the Net is the 2
exhilarating sense of freedom that this new frontier once promised—and still does
in some quarters. Formerly a playground for computer nerds and techies, cyberspace now embraces every conceivable constituency: schoolchildren, flirtatious
singles, Hungarian-Americans, accountants—along with pederasts and porn fans.
Can they all get along? Or will our fear of kids surfing for cyberporn behind their
bedroom doors provoke a crackdown?

The first order of business is to grasp what cyberspace *is*. It might help to 3
leave behind metaphors of highways and frontiers and to think instead of real
estate. Real estate, remember, is an intellectual, legal, artificial environment constructed *on top of* land. Real estate recognizes the difference between parkland
and shopping mall, between red-light zone and school district, between church,
state and drugstore.

In the same way, you could think of cyberspace as a giant and unbounded 4
world of virtual real estate. Some property is privately owned and rented out;
other property is common land; some places are suitable for children, and others
are best avoided by all but the kinkiest citizens. Unfortunately, it's those places
that are now capturing the popular imagination: places that offer bomb-making
instructions, pornography, advice on how to procure stolen credit cards. They
make cyberspace sound like a nasty place. Good citizens jump to a conclusion:
Better regulate it.

The most recent manifestation of this impulse is the Exon-Coats Amendment, 5
a well-meaning but misguided bill drafted by Senators Jim Exon, Democrat of
Nebraska, and Daniel R. Coats, Republican of Indiana, to make cyberspace "safer"
for children. Part of the telecommunications reform bill passed by the Senate and
awaiting consideration by the House, the amendment would outlaw making "inde-
cent communication" available to anyone under 18.[1] Then there's the Amateur
Action bulletin board case, in which the owners of a porn service in Milpitas,
Calif., were convicted in a Tennessee court of violating "community standards"
after a local postal inspector requested that the material be transmitted to him.

Regardless of how many laws or lawsuits are launched, regulation won't work. 6

Aside from being unconstitutional, using censorship to counter indecency 7
and other troubling "speech" fundamentally misinterprets the nature of cyberspace. Cyberspace isn't a frontier where wicked people can grab unsuspecting
children, nor is it a giant television system that can beam offensive messages at
unwilling viewers. In this kind of real estate, users have to *choose* where they visit,
what they see, what they do. It's optional, and it's much easier to bypass a place on

---

[1]The Communication Decency Act (CDA) was passed by Congress, but the Supreme Court ruled
that it was unconstitutional in 1996.

the Net than it is to avoid walking past an unsavory block of stores on the way to your local 7-Eleven.

8   Put plainly, cyberspace is a voluntary destination—in reality, many destinations. You don't just get "onto the Net"; you have to go someplace in particular. That means that people can choose where to go and what to see. Yes, community standards should be enforced, but those standards should be set by cyberspace communities themselves, not by the courts or by politicians in Washington. What we need isn't government control over all these electronic communities: We need self-rule.

9 What makes cyberspace so alluring is precisely the way in which it's *different* from shopping malls, television, highways and other terrestrial jurisdictions. But let's define the territory:

10   First, there are private e-mail conversations, akin to the conversations you have over the telephone or voice mail. These are private and consensual and require no regulation at all.

11   Second, there are information and entertainment services, where people can download anything from legal texts and lists of "great new restaurants" to game software or dirty pictures. These places are like bookstores, malls and movie houses—places where you go to buy something. The customer needs to request an item or sign up for a subscription; stuff (especially pornography) is not sent out to people who don't ask for it. Some of these services are free or included as part of a broader service like Compuserve or America Online; others charge and may bill their customers directly.

12   Third, there are "real" communities—groups of people who communicate among themselves. In real-estate terms, they're like bars or restaurants or bathhouses. Each active participant contributes to a general conversation, generally through posted messages. Other participants may simply listen or watch. Some are supervised by a moderator; others are more like bulletin boards—anyone is free to post anything. Many of these services started out unmoderated but are now imposing rules to keep out unwanted advertising, extraneous discussions or increasingly rude participants. Without a moderator, the decibel level often gets too high.

13   Ultimately, it's the rules that determine the success of such places. Some of the rules are determined by the supplier of content; some of the rules concern prices and membership fees. The rules may be simple: "Only high-quality content about oil-industry liability and pollution legislation: $120 an hour." Or: "This forum is unmoderated, and restricted to information about copyright issues. People who insist on posting advertising or unrelated material will be asked to desist (and may eventually be barred)." Or: "Only children 8 to 12, on school-related topics and only clean words. The moderator will decide what's acceptable."

14   Cyberspace communities evolve just the way terrestrial communities do: People with like-minded interests band together. Every cyberspace community has its own character. Overall, the communities on Compuserve tend to be more techy or professional; those on America Online, affluent young singles; Prodigy, family oriented. Then there are independents like Echo, a hip, downtown New York

service, or Women's Wire, targeted to women who want to avoid the male culture prevalent elsewhere on the Net. There's SurfWatch, a new program allowing access only to locations deemed suitable for children. On the Internet itself, there are lots of passionate noncommercial discussion groups on topics ranging from Hungarian politics (Hungary-Online) to copyright law.

And yes, there are also porn-oriented services, where people share dirty 15 pictures and communicate with one another about all kinds of practices, often anonymously. Whether these services encourage the fantasies they depict is subject to debate—the same debate that has raged about pornography in other media. But the point is that no one is forcing this stuff on anybody.

What's unique about cyberspace is that it liberates us from the tyranny of 16 government, where everyone lives by the rule of the majority. In a democracy, minority groups and minority preferences tend to get squeezed out, whether they are minorities of race and culture or minorities of individual taste. Cyberspace allows communities of any size and kind to flourish; in cyberspace, communities are chosen by the users, not forced on them by accidents of geography. This freedom gives the rules that preside in cyberspace a moral authority that rules in terrestrial environments don't have. Most people are stuck in the country of their birth, but if you don't like the rules of a cyberspace community, you can just sign off. Love it or leave it. Likewise, if parents don't like the rules of a given cyberspace community, they can restrict their children's access to it.

What's likely to happen in cyberspace is the formation of new communities, 17 free of the constraints that cause conflict on earth. Instead of a global village, which is a nice dream but impossible to manage, we'll have invented another world of self-contained communities that cater to their own members' inclinations without interfering with anyone else's. The possibility of a real market-style evolution of governance is at hand. In cyberspace, we'll be able to test and evolve rules governing what needs to be governed—intellectual property, content and access control, rules about privacy and free speech. Some communities will allow anyone in; others will restrict access to members who qualify on one basis or another. Those communities that prove self-sustaining will prosper (and perhaps grow and split into subsets with ever-more-particular interests and identities). Those that can't survive—either because people lose interest or get scared off—will simply wither away.

In the near future, explorers in cyberspace will need to get better at defining 18 and identifying their communities. They will need to put in place—and accept— their own local governments, just as the owners of expensive real estate often prefer to have their own security guards rather than call in the police. But they will rarely need help from any terrestrial government.

Of course, terrestrial governments may not agree. What to do, for instance, 19 about pornography? The answer is labeling—not banning—questionable material. In order to avoid censorship and lower the political temperature, it makes sense for cyberspace participants themselves to agree on a scheme for questionable items, so that people or automatic filters can avoid them. In other words, posting pornography in "alt.sex.bestiality" would be OK; it's easy enough for software manufacturers to build an automatic filter that would prevent you—or your child—from ever seeing that item on a menu. (It's as if all the items were wrapped with labels on the wrapper.) Someone who posted the same material under the title "Kid-Fun" could be sued for mislabeling.

20   Without a lot of fanfare, private enterprises and local groups are already producing a variety of labeling and ranking services, along with kid-oriented sites like Kidlink, EdWeb and Kids' Space. People differ in their tastes and values and can find services or reviewers on the Net that suit them in the same way they select books and magazines. Or they can wander freely if they prefer, making up their own itinerary.

21   In the end, our society needs to grow up. Growing up means understanding that there are no perfect answers, no all-purpose solutions, no government-sanctioned safe havens. We haven't created a perfect society on earth and we won't have one in cyberspace either. But at least we can have individual choice—and individual responsibility.

COMPREHENSION

1. The title of the essay is a variation of a phrase popularized in the 1960s. What is the original expression, and what was its significance? What is its relevance to this essay?
2. What is Dyson's thesis? Is it stated explicitly? If so, where in the essay does it occur? If it is merely suggested, how is it suggested, and where?
3. There are many forms of new media that are not considered communities. Why does Dyson refer to cyberspace as a community?
4. According to Dyson, what distinguishes cyberspace from physical space?
5. What does Dyson mean when she states that cyberspace needs "self-rule" (paragraph 8)?

RHETORIC

1. How does Dyson use her introduction to foreshadow her main concerns about censorship in cyberspace?
2. How does Dyson use metaphor in paragraphs 10–12 to help us understand the structure of cyberspace? Why is metaphor a particularly useful literary device when explaining a new concept?
3. Key to Dyson's views on cyberspace is that it is a "voluntary destination" (paragraph 8). What evidence does Dyson present that it is voluntary? What argument can be made that it is not always "voluntary"?
4. Who is the implied audience for this essay? What level of education does one need to have and how sophisticated about the world of cyberspace does one need to be in order to comprehend and process the author's views? Explain your answer.
5. Dyson refers to laws, rules, and regulations as strategies that various interest groups may use to determine access to content in cyberspace. How does Dyson distinguish these three related tactics? What significance does differentiating these methods have in her presentation of her argument?
6. Dyson concludes her essay with an analogy between human society and cyberspace culture. Why does she save this final support for last? How does it extend her argument rather than merely restate it?

WRITING

1. In paragraph 17, Dyson refers to the "global village," a term coined by the media critic Marshall McLuhan. For a research project, study McLuhan's views on the nature of the global village, and compare and contrast them to Dyson's views of the nature of cyberspace.
2. **Writing an Argument:** Dyson argues that technology can create filters, labeling and ranking services to prevent children from viewing inappropriate material. In an essay, argue for or against the proposition that there can be a nontechnological solution to this issue—for example, instilling values in children or developing a society that does not create a mystique about taboo subject matter.

NETWORKING
Applying Digital and Multimedia Literacies

Exploring Virtual Communities: In a comparison-and-contrast essay, select three cyberspace communities and describe each one's character (refer to Dyson's reference to cyberspace characters in paragraph 14).

Grant and Lee:
A Study in Contrasts

Bruce Catton

Bruce Catton (1899–1978) was born in Petosky, Michigan. After serving in the Navy during World War I, he attended Oberlin College but left in his junior year to pursue a career in journalism. From 1942 to 1952, Catton served in the government, first on the War Production Board and later in the departments of Commerce and the Interior. He left government to devote himself to literary work as a columnist for the Nation *and a historian of the Civil War. His many works include* A Stillness at Appomattox *(1953), which won the 1954 Pulitzer Prize;* Mr. Lincoln's Army *(1951);* The Centennial History of the Civil War *(1961–1965); and* Prefaces to History *(1970). In the following selection, Catton presents vivid portraits of two well-known but little understood figures from American history.*

When Ulysses S. Grant and Robert E. Lee met in the parlor of a modest house at Appomattox Court House, Virginia, on April 9, 1865, to work out the terms for the surrender of Lee's Army of Northern Virginia, a great chapter in American life came to a close, and a great new chapter began. 1

2   These men were bringing the Civil War to its virtual finish. To be sure, other armies had yet to surrender, and for a few days the fugitive Confederate government would struggle desperately and vainly, trying to find some way to go on living now that its chief support was gone. But in effect it was all over when Grant and Lee signed the papers. And the little room where they wrote out the terms was the scene of one of the poignant, dramatic contrasts in American history.

3   They were two strong men, these oddly different generals, and they represented the strengths of two conflicting currents that, through them, had come into final collision.

4   Back of Robert E. Lee was the notion that the old aristocratic concept might somehow survive and be dominant in American life.

5   Lee was tidewater Virginia, and in his background were family, culture, and tradition . . . the age of chivalry transplanted to a New World which was making its own legends and its own myths. He embodied a way of life that had come down through the age of knighthood and the English country squire. America was a land that was beginning all over again, dedicated to nothing much more complicated than the rather hazy belief that all men had equal rights and should have an equal chance in the world. In such a land Lee stood for the feeling that it was somehow of advantage to human society to have a pronounced inequality in the social structure. There should be a leisure class, backed by ownership of land; in turn, society itself should be keyed to the land as the chief source of wealth and influence. It would bring forth (according to this ideal) a class of men with a strong sense of obligation to the community; men who lived not to gain advantage for themselves, but to meet the solemn obligations which had been laid on them by the very fact that they were privileged. From them the country would get its leadership; to them it could look for the higher values—of thought, of conduct, of personal deportment—to give it strength and virtue.

6   Lee embodied the noblest elements of this aristocratic ideal. Through him, the landed nobility justified itself. For four years, the Southern states had fought a desperate war to uphold the ideals for which Lee stood. In the end, it almost seemed as if the Confederacy fought for Lee; as if he himself was the Confederacy . . . the best thing that the way of life for which the Confederacy stood could ever have to offer. He had passed into legend before Appomattox. Thousands of tired, underfed, poorly clothed Confederate soldiers, long since past the simple enthusiasm of the early days of the struggle, somehow considered Lee the symbol of everything for which they had been willing to die. But they could not quite put this feeling into words. If the Lost Cause, sanctified by so much heroism and so many deaths, had a living justification, its justification was General Lee.

7   Grant, the son of a tanner on the Western frontier, was everything Lee was not. He had come up the hard way and embodied nothing in particular except the eternal toughness and sinewy fiber of the men who grew up beyond the mountains. He was one of a body of men who owed reverence and obeisance to no one, who were self-reliant to a fault, who cared hardly anything for the past but who had a sharp eye for the future.

These frontier men were the precise opposites of the tidewater aristocrats. 8
Back of them, in the great surge that had taken people over the Alleghenies and
into the opening Western country, there was a deep, implicit dissatisfaction with a
past that had settled into grooves. They stood for democracy, not from any
reasoned conclusion about the proper ordering of human society, but simply because they had grown up in the middle of democracy and knew how it worked.
Their society might have privileges, but they would be privileges each man had
won for himself. Forms and patterns meant nothing. No man was born to anything,
except perhaps to a chance to show how far he could rise. Life was competition.

Yet along with this feeling had come a deep sense of belonging to a national 9
community. The Westerner who developed a farm, opened a shop, or set up in
business as a trader, could hope to prosper only as his own community prospered—
and his community ran from the Atlantic to the Pacific and from Canada down to
Mexico. If the land was settled, with towns and highways and accessible markets,
he could better himself. He saw his fate in terms of the nation's own destiny. As its
horizons expanded, so did his. He had, in other words, an acute dollars-and-cents
stake in the continued growth and development of his country.

And that, perhaps, is where the contrast between Grant and Lee becomes 10
most striking. The Virginia aristocrat, inevitably, saw himself in relation to his own
region. He lived in a static society which could endure almost anything except
change. Instinctively, his first loyalty would go to the locality in which that society
existed. He would fight to the limit of endurance to defend it, because in defending
it he was defending everything that gave his own life its deepest meaning.

The Westerner, on the other hand, would fight with an equal tenacity for the 11
broader concept of society. He fought so because everything he lived by was tied
to growth, expansion, and a constantly widening horizon. What he lived by would
survive or fall with the nation itself. He could not possibly stand by unmoved in
the face of an attempt to destroy the Union. He would combat it with everything
he had, because he could only see it as an effort to cut the ground out from
under his feet.

So Grant and Lee were in complete contrast, representing two diametrically 12
opposed elements in American life. Grant was the modern man emerging; beyond
him, ready to come on the stage, was the great age of steel and machinery, of
crowded cities and a restless burgeoning vitality. Lee might have ridden down
from the old age of chivalry, lance in hand, silken banner fluttering over his head.
Each man was the perfect champion of his cause, drawing both his strengths and
his weaknesses from the people he led.

Yet it was not all contrast, after all. Different as they were—in background, in 13
personality, in underlying aspiration—these two great soldiers had much in common. Under everything else, they were marvelous fighters. Furthermore, their
fighting qualities were really very much alike.

Each man had, to begin with, the great virtue of utter tenacity and fidelity. 14
Grant fought his way down the Mississippi Valley in spite of acute personal
discouragement and profound military handicaps. Lee hung on in the trenches at
Petersburg after hope itself had died. In each man there was an indomitable

quality . . . the born fighter's refusal to give up as long as he can still remain on his feet and lift his two fists.

15   Daring and resourcefulness they had, too; the ability to think faster and move faster than the enemy. These were the qualities which gave Lee the dazzling campaigns of Second Manassas and Chancellorsville and won Vicksburg for Grant.

16   Lastly, and perhaps greatest of all, there was the ability, at the end, to turn quickly from war to peace once the fighting was over. Out of the way these two men behaved at Appomattox came the possibility of a peace of reconciliation. It was a possibility not wholly realized, in the years to come, but which did, in the end, help the two sections to become one nation again . . . after a war whose bitterness might have seemed to make such a reunion wholly impossible. No part of either man's life became him more than the part he played in their brief meeting in the McLean house at Appomattox. Their behavior there put all succeeding generations of Americans in their debt. Two great Americans, Grant and Lee—very different, yet under everything very much alike. Their encounter at Appomattox was one of the great moments of American history.

COMPREHENSION

1. What is the central purpose of Catton's study? Cite evidence to support your view. Who is his audience?
2. What is the primary appeal to readers of describing history through the study of individuals rather than through the recording of events? How does Catton's essay reflect this appeal?
3. According to Catton, what special qualities did Grant and Lee share, and what qualities set them apart?

RHETORIC

1. What role does the opening paragraph play in setting the tone for the essay? Is the tone typical of what you would expect of an essay describing military generals? Explain your view. How does the conclusion echo the introductory paragraph?
2. Note that the sentence "Two great Americans, Grant and Lee—very different, yet under everything very much alike" (paragraph 16) has no verb. What does this indicate about Catton's style? What other sentences contain atypical syntax? What is their contribution to the unique quality of the writing?
3. Although this essay is about a historical era, there is a notable lack of specific facts—dates, statistics, and events. What has Catton focused on instead?
4. What is the function of the one-sentence paragraph 3?
5. Paragraphs 9, 10, 12, and 13 begin with coordinating conjunctions. How do these transitional words give the paragraphs their special coherence? How would more typical introductory expressions, such as *in addition, furthermore,* or *moreover,* have altered this coherence?
6. What strategy does Catton use in comparing and contrasting the two generals? Study paragraphs 5–16. Which are devoted to describing each man separately, and which include aspects of both men? What is the overall effectiveness of the comparisons?

WRITING

1. Does Lee's vision of society exist in the United States today? If not, why not? If so, where do you find this vision? Write a brief essay on this topic.
2. Select two well-known individuals in the same profession—for example, politics, entertainment, or sports. Make a list for each, enumerating the different aspects of their character, behavior, beliefs, and background. Using this as an outline, devise an essay comparing and contrasting the two.
3. **Writing an Argument:** Apply, in an argumentative essay, Catton's observation about "two diametrically opposed elements in American life" (paragraph 12) to the current national scene.

NETWORKING
Applying Digital and Multimedia Literacies

Creating a Hyperlinked Essay: Approach question 2 under Writing as an electronic essay that links readers to relevant Web sites to enhance their reading experience. Link to at least six locations.

American Dreamer

Bharati Mukherjee

Bharati Mukherjee (b. 1940) was born in Calcutta, India, and learned to read and write by age three. In 1947, she moved to Britain with her family. After receiving her BA from the University of Calcutta and her MA in English and ancient Indian culture from the University of Boroda, she came to the United States, where she received an MFA in creative writing and a PhD in English and comparative literature at the University of Iowa. Mukherjee is the author of Jasmine *(1989) and* The Middleman and Other Stories, *which won the 1988 National Book Critic's Circle Award for Fiction. Her more recent work includes the novels* Desirable Daughters *(2002) and* The Tree Bride *(2004). She is currently a professor at the University of California, Berkeley. Mukherjee is often interested in and writing about issues of cultural identity. In the following essay, which first appeared in the magazine* Mother Jones *in 1997, she examines why "hyphenated Americans" always seem to be members of nonwhite groups.*

The United States exists as a sovereign nation. "America," in contrast, exists as a 1
myth of democracy and equal opportunity to live by, or as an ideal goal to reach.

I am a naturalized U.S. citizen, which means that, unlike native-born citizens, 2
I had to prove to the U.S. government that I merited citizenship. What I didn't

have to disclose was that I desired "America," which to me is the stage for the drama of self-transformation.

3   I was born in Calcutta and first came to the United States—to Iowa City, to be precise—on a summer evening in 1961. I flew into a small airport surrounded by cornfields and pastures, ready to carry out the two commands my father had written out for me the night before I left Calcutta: Spend two years studying creative writing at the Iowa Writers' Workshop, then come back home and marry the bridegroom he selected for me from our caste and class.

4   In traditional Hindu families like ours, men provided and women were provided for. My father was a patriarch and I a pliant daughter. The neighborhood I'd grown up in was homogeneously Hindu, Bengali-speaking, and middle-class. I didn't expect myself to ever disobey or disappoint my father by setting my own goals and taking charge of my future.

5   When I landed in Iowa 35 years ago, I found myself in a society in which almost everyone was Christian, white, and moderately well-off. In the women's dormitory I lived in my first year, apart from six international graduate students (all of us were from Asia and considered "exotic"), the only non-Christian was Jewish, and the only nonwhite an African-American from Georgia. I didn't anticipate then, that over the next 35 years, the Iowa population would become so diverse that it would have 6,931 children from non-English-speaking homes registered as students in its schools, nor that Iowans would be in the grip of a cultural crisis in which resentment against immigrants, particularly refugees from Vietnam, Sudan, and Bosnia, as well as unskilled Spanish-speaking workers, would become politicized enough to cause the Immigration and Naturalization Service to open an "enforcement" office in Cedar Rapids in October for the tracking and deporting of undocumented aliens.

6   In Calcutta in the '50s, I heard no talk of "identity crisis"—communal or individual. The concept itself—a person not knowing who he or she is—was unimaginable in our hierarchical, classification-obsessed society. One's identity was fixed, derived from religion, caste, patrimony, and mother tongue. A Hindu Indian's last name announced his or her forefathers' caste and place of origin. A Mukherjee could only be a Brahmin from Bengal. Hindu tradition forbade inter-caste, interlanguage, interethnic marriages. Bengali tradition even discouraged emigration: To remove oneself from Bengal was to dilute true culture.

7   Until the age of 8, I lived in a house crowded with 40 or 50 relatives. My identity was viscerally connected with ancestral soil and genealogy. I was who I was because I was Dr. Sudhir Lal Mukherjee's daughter, because I was a Hindu Brahmin, because I was Bengali-speaking, and because my *desh*—the Bengali word for homeland—was an East Bengal village called Faridpur.

8 The University of Iowa classroom was my first experience of coeducation. And after not too long, I fell in love with a fellow student named Clark Blaise, an American of Canadian origin, and impulsively married him during a lunch break in a lawyer's office above a coffee shop.

9   That act cut me off forever from the rules and ways of upper-middle-class life in Bengal, and hurled me into a New World life of scary improvisations and heady

explorations. Until my lunch-break wedding, I had seen myself as an Indian foreign student who intended to return to India to live. The five-minute ceremony in the lawyer's office suddenly changed me into a transient with conflicting loyalties to two very different cultures.

The first 10 years into marriage, years spent mostly in my husband's native 10 Canada, I thought of myself as an expatriate Bengali permanently stranded in North America because of destiny or desire. My first novel, *The Tiger's Daughter,* embodies the loneliness I felt but could not acknowledge, even to myself, as I negotiated the no man's land between the country of my past and the continent of my present. Shaped by memory, textured with nostalgia for a class and culture I had abandoned, this novel quite naturally became an expression of the expatriate consciousness.

It took me a decade of painful introspection to put nostalgia in perspective and 11 to make the transition from expatriate to immigrant. After a 14-year stay in Canada, I forced my husband and our two sons to relocate to the United States. But the transition from foreign student to U.S. citizen, from detached onlooker to committed immigrant, has not been easy.

The years in Canada were particularly harsh. Canada is a country that 12 officially, and proudly, resists cultural fusion. For all its rhetoric about a cultural "mosaic," Canada refuses to renovate its national self-image to include its changing complexion. It is a New World country with Old World concepts of a fixed, exclusivist national identity. Canadian official rhetoric designated me as one of the "visible minority" who, even though I spoke the Canadian languages of English and French, was straining "the absorptive capacity" of Canada. Canadians of color were routinely treated as "not real" Canadians. One example: In 1985 a terrorist bomb, planted in an Air-India jet on Canadian soil, blew up after leaving Montreal, killing 329 passengers, most of whom were Canadians of Indian origin. The prime minister of Canada at the time, Brian Mulroney, phoned the prime minister of India to offer Canada's condolences for India's loss.

Those years of race-related harassments in Canada politicized me and deep- 13 ened my love of the ideals embedded in the American Bill of Rights. I don't forget that the architects of the Constitution and the Bill of Rights were white males and slaveholders. But through their declaration, they provided us with the enthusiasm for human rights, and the initial framework from which other empowerments could be conceived and enfranchised communities expanded.

I am a naturalized U.S. citizen and I take my American citizenship very seriously. 14 I am not an economic refugee, nor am I a seeker of political asylum. I am a voluntary immigrant. I became a citizen by choice, not by simple accident of birth.

Yet these days, questions such as who is an American and what is American 15 culture are being posed with belligerence, and being answered with violence. Scapegoating of immigrants has once again become the politicians' easy remedy for all that ails the nation. Hate speeches fill auditoriums for demagogues willing to profit from stirring up racial animosity. An April [1996] Gallup poll indicated that half of Americans would like to bar almost all legal immigration for the next five years.

16   The United States, like every sovereign nation, has a right to formulate its immigration policies. But in this decade of continual, large-scale diasporas, it is imperative that we come to some agreement about who "we" are, and what our goals are for the nation, now that our community includes people of many races, ethnicities, languages, and religions.

17   The debate about American culture and American identity has to date been monopolized largely by Eurocentrists and ethnocentrists whose rhetoric has been flamboyantly divisive, pitting a phantom "us" against a demonized "them."

18 All countries view themselves by their ideals. Indians idealize the cultural continuum, the inherent value system of India, and are properly incensed when foreigners see nothing but poverty, intolerance, strife, and injustice. Americans see themselves as the embodiments of liberty, openness, and individualism, even as the world judges them for drugs, crime, violence, bigotry, militarism, and homelessness. I was in Singapore in 1994 when the American teenager Michael Fay was sentenced to caning for having spraypainted some cars. While I saw Fay's actions as those of an individual, and his sentence as too harsh, the overwhelming local sentiment was that vandalism was an "American" crime, and that flogging Fay would deter Singapore youths from becoming "Americanized."

19   Conversely, in 1994, in Tavares, Florida, the Lake County School Board announced its policy (since overturned) requiring middle school teachers to instruct their students that American culture, by which the board meant European-American culture, is inherently "superior to other foreign or historic cultures." The policy's misguided implication was that culture in the United States has not been affected by the American Indian, African-American, Latin-American, and Asian-American segments of the population. The sinister implication was that our national identity is so fragile that it can absorb diverse and immigrant cultures only by recontextualizing them as deficient.

20   Our nation is unique in human history in that the founding idea of "America" was in opposition to the tenet that a nation is a collection of like-looking, like-speaking, like-worshipping people. The primary criterion for nationhood in Europe is homogeneity of culture, race, and religion—which has contributed to blood-soaked balkanization in the former Yugoslavia and the former Soviet Union.

21   America's pioneering European ancestors gave up the easy homogeneity of their native countries for a new version of Utopia. Now, in the 1990s, we have the exciting chance to follow that tradition and assist in the making of a new American culture that differs from both the enforced assimilation of a "melting pot" and the Canadian model of a multicultural "mosaic."

22   The multicultural mosaic implies a contiguity of fixed, self-sufficient, utterly distinct cultures. Multiculturalism, as it has been practiced in the United States in the past 10 years, implies the existence of a central culture, ringed by peripheral cultures. The fallout of official multiculturalism is the establishment of one culture as the norm and the rest as aberrations. At the same time, the multiculturalist emphasis on race- and ethnicity-based group identity leads to a lack of respect for individual differences within each group, and to vilification of those individuals

who place the good of the nation above the interests of their particular racial or ethnic communities.

We must be alert to the dangers of an "us" vs. "them" mentality. In California, this 23 mentality is manifesting itself as increased violence between minority, ethnic communities. The attack on Korean-American merchants in South Central Los Angeles in the wake of the Rodney King beating trial is only one recent example of the tragic side effects of this mentality. On the national level, the politicization of ethnic identities has encouraged the scapegoating of legal immigrants, who are blamed for economic and social problems brought about by flawed domestic and foreign policies.

We need to discourage the retention of cultural memory if the aim of that 24 retention is cultural balkanization. We must think of American culture and nation-hood as a constantly reforming, transmogrifying "we."

In this age of diasporas, one's biological identity may not be one's only 25 identity. Erosions and accretions come with the act of emigration. The experience of cutting myself off from a biological homeland and settling in an adopted homeland that is not always welcoming to its dark-complexioned citizens has tested me as a person, and made me the writer I am today.

I choose to describe myself on my own terms, as an American, rather than as an 26 Asian-American. Why is it that hyphenation is imposed only on nonwhite Americans? Rejecting hyphenation is my refusal to categorize the cultural landscape into a center and its peripheries; it is to demand that the American nation deliver the promises of its dream and its Constitution to all its citizens equally.

My rejection of hyphenation has been misrepresented as race treachery by 27 some India-born academics on U.S. campuses who have appointed themselves guardians of the "purity" of ethnic cultures. Many of them, though they reside permanently in the United States and participate in its economy, consistently denounce American ideals and institutions. They direct their rage at me because, by becoming a U.S. citizen and exercising my voting rights, I have invested in the present and not the past; because I have committed myself to help shape the future of my adopted homeland; and because I celebrate racial and cultural mongrelization.

What excites me is that as a nation we have not only the chance to retain 28 those values we treasure from our original cultures but also the chance to acknowledge that the outer forms of those values are likely to change. Among Indian immigrants, I see a great deal of guilt about the inability to hang on to what they commonly term "pure culture." Parents express rage or despair at their U.S.-born children's forgetting of, or indifference to, some aspects of Indian culture. Of those parents I would ask: What is it we have lost if our children are acculturating into the culture in which we are living? Is it so terrible that our children are discovering or are inventing homelands for themselves?

Some first-generation Indo-Americans, embittered by racism and by unofficial 29 "glass ceilings," construct a phantom identity, more-Indian-than-Indians-in-India, as a defense against marginalization. I ask: Why don't you get actively involved in fighting discrimination? Make your voice heard. Choose the forum most appropriate for you. If you are a citizen, let your vote count. Reinvest your energy and resources into revitalizing your city's disadvantaged residents and neighborhoods. Know your constitutional rights, and when they are violated, use the agencies of redress the Constitution makes available to you. Expect change, and when it comes, deal with it!

30   As a writer, my literary agenda begins by acknowledging that America has transformed me. It does not end until I show that I (along with the hundreds of thousands of immigrants like me) am minute by minute transforming America. The transformation is a two-way process: It affects both the individual and the national-cultural identity.

31   Others who write stories of migration often talk of arrival at a new place as a loss, the loss of communal memory and the erosion of an original culture. I want to talk of arrival as a gain.

COMPREHENSION

1. What is the significance of the title? In what way is Mukherjee a "dreamer"? In what way does the United States inspire "dreaming"?
2. In paragraph 6, Mukherjee states that in India she had a strong sense of identity. Why was it difficult for her to feel at ease with her American identity?
3. A country is a geographical area with national boundaries as well as an underlying concept and ideal. Does Mukherjee focus on these aspects of the United States and Canada equally, or does she emphasize one more than the other? Explain.

RHETORIC

1. The essay is divided into four parts. Why did the author adopt this structure? What is the focus of each? How does each section function rhetorically in relation to the other three?
2. Mukherjee introduces her essay with her own explanations of the terms "America" and "the United States." What is her purpose, considering that this is an autobiographical essay?
3. Mukherjee explores her transition from "expatriate" to "immigrant" to "U.S. citizen" in paragraphs 10 and 11. Explain the significance of each term in general and each term's particular role in the author's cultural metamorphosis.
4. Mukherjee rejects and condemns the belligerence toward and scapegoating of immigrants. How would you characterize the effect of these attacks on Mukherjee, an immigrant herself? Note, in particular, her statements in paragraphs 13 and 26.
5. How does Mukherjee employ irony in paragraph 12 to demonstrate the double standard imposed on individuals who do not fit the stereotypical mold of what it means to be a "citizen"?
6. In paragraph 14, the author states, "I take my American citizenship very seriously." Is the tone of the essay serious? Explain your view.
7. As you define the following words, identify the intended audience for this essay: *exclusivist* (paragraph 12), *demagogues* (paragraph 15), *diasporas* (paragraph 16), *ethnocentrists* and *demonized* (paragraph 17), and *balkanization* (paragraph 24).

WRITING

1. In a personal essay, write about a time in your life when your allegiance, honesty, or integrity was unfairly questioned. Be sure to use specifics such as the circumstances of who, what, where, when, and why. Also describe your feelings at the time and the emotional outcome.
2. Write an essay based on personal experience or observation, explaining whether Mukherjee is correct in stating that "hyphenation is imposed only on nonwhite Americans" (paragraph 26). A variation on this theme might be an exploration why "hyphenated" terms used to describe certain white American groups have a different tone and purpose than terms used for nonwhites.
3. **Writing an Argument:** In her conclusion, Mukherjee criticizes "guardians of the 'purity' of ethnic cultures." Is there such a thing as a "pure" ethnic culture? Write an essay arguing your viewpoint.

NETWORKING
Applying Digital and Multimedia Literacies

Making an Oral Argument: Write a speech, arguing for or against the proposition that a course on cultural diversity should be taught at your college or university. Consider whether other ways of approaching the subject would be more profitable, or whether the subject needs to be addressed at all. Use logical, ethical, and emotional appeals.

Stranger in the Village

James Baldwin

James Baldwin (1924–1988), a major American essayist, novelist, short-story writer, and playwright, was born and grew up in Harlem. He won a Eugene Saxon Fellowship and lived in Europe from 1948 to 1956. Always an activist in civil rights causes, Baldwin focused in his essays and fiction on the black search for identity in modern America and on the myth of white superiority. Among his principal works are Go Tell It on the Mountain *(1953),* Notes of a Native Son *(1955),* Giovanni's Room *(1956),* Nobody Knows My Name *(1961),* Another Country *(1962), and* If Beale Street Could Talk *(1974). One of the finest contemporary essayists, Baldwin had a rare talent for portraying the deepest concerns about civilization in an intensely personal style, as the following essay indicates.*

From all available evidence no black man had ever set foot in this tiny Swiss 1
village before I came. I was told before arriving that I would probably be a "sight"

for the village; I took this to mean that people of my complexion were rarely seen in Switzerland, and also that city people are always something of a "sight" outside of the city. It did not occur to me—possibly because I am an American—that there could be people anywhere who had never seen a Negro.

2   It is a fact that cannot be explained on the basis of the inaccessibility of the village. The village is very high, but it is only four hours from Milan and three hours from Lausanne. It is true that it is virtually unknown. Few people making plans for a holiday would elect to come here. On the other hand, the villagers are able, presumably, to come and go as they please—which they do: to another town at the foot of the mountain, with a population of approximately five thousand, the nearest place to see a movie or go to the bank. In the village there is no movie house, no bank, no library, no theater; very few radios, one jeep, one station wagon; and, at the moment, one typewriter, mine, an invention which the woman next door to me here had never seen. There are about six hundred people living here, all Catholic—I conclude this from the fact that the Catholic church is open all year round, whereas the Protestant chapel, set off on a hill a little removed from the village, is open only in the summertime when the tourists arrive. There are four or five hotels, all closed now, and four or five *bistros,* of which, however, only two do any business during the winter. These two do not do a great deal, for life in the village seems to end around nine or ten o'clock. There are a few stores, butcher, baker, *épicerie,* a hardware store, and a money-changer—who cannot change travelers' checks, but must send them down to the bank, an operation which takes two or three days. There is something called the *Ballet Haus,* closed in the winter and used for God knows what, certainly not ballet, during the summer. There seems to be only one schoolhouse in the village, and this for the quite young children; I suppose this to mean that their older brothers and sisters at some point descend from these mountains in order to complete their education— possibly, again, to the town just below. The landscape is absolutely forbidding, mountains towering on all four sides, ice and snow as far as the eye can reach. In this white wilderness, men and women and children move all day, carrying wash- ing, wood, buckets of milk or water, sometimes skiing on Sunday afternoons. All week long boys and young men are to be seen shoveling snow off the rooftops, or dragging wood down from the forest in sleds.

3   The village's only real attraction, which explains the tourist season, is the hot spring water. A disquietingly high proportion of these tourists are cripples, or semi-cripples, who come year after year—from other parts of Switzerland, usually—to take the waters. This lends the village, at the height of the season, a rather terrifying air of sanctity, as though it were a lesser Lourdes. There is often something beautiful, there is always something awful, in the spectacle of a person who has lost one of his faculties, a faculty he never questioned until it was gone, and who struggles to recover it. Yet people remain people, on crutches or indeed on deathbeds; and wherever I passed, the first summer I was here, among the native villagers or among the lame, a wind passed with me—of astonishment, curiosity, amusement, and outrage. The first summer I stayed two weeks and never intended to return. But I did return in the winter, to work; the village offers,

obviously, no distractions whatever and has the further advantage of being extremely cheap. Now it is winter again, a year later, and I am here again. Everyone in the village knows my name, though they scarcely ever use it, knows that I come from America—though this, apparently, they will never really believe: black men come from Africa—and everyone knows that I am the friend of the son of a woman who was born here, and that I am staying in their chalet. But I remain as much a stranger today as I was the first day I arrived, and the children shout *Neger! Neger!* as I walk along the streets.

It must be admitted that in the beginning I was far too shocked to have any 4 real reaction. In so far as I reacted at all, I reacted by trying to be pleasant—it being a great part of the American Negro's education (long before he goes to school) that he must make people "like" him. This smile-and-the-world-smiles-with-you routine worked about as well in this situation as it had in the situation for which it was designed, which is to say that it did not work at all. No one, after all, can be liked whose human weight and complexity cannot be, or has not been, admitted. My smile was simply another unheard-of phenomenon which allowed them to see my teeth—they did not, really, see my smile and I began to think that, should I take to snarling, no one would notice any difference. All of the physical characteristics of the Negro which had caused me, in America, a very different and almost forgotten pain were nothing less than miraculous—or infernal—in the eyes of the village people. Some thought my hair was the color of tar, that it had the texture of wire, or the texture of cotton. It was jocularly suggested that I might let it all grow long and make myself a winter coat. If I sat in the sun for more than five minutes some daring creature was certain to come along and gingerly put his fingers on my hair, as though he were afraid of an electric shock, or put his hand on my hand, astonished that the color did not rub off. In all of this, in which it must be conceded there was the charm of genuine wonder and in which there was certainly no element of intentional unkindness, there was yet no suggestion that I was human: I was simply a living wonder.

I knew that they did not mean to be unkind, and I know it now; it is necessary, 5 nevertheless, for me to repeat this to myself each time I walk out of the chalet. The children who shout *Neger!* have no way of knowing the echoes this sound raises in me. They are brimming with good humor and the more daring swell with pride when I stop to speak with them. Just the same, there are days when I cannot pause and smile, when I have no heart to play with them; when, indeed, I mutter sourly to myself, exactly as I muttered on the streets of a city these children have never seen, when I was no bigger than these children are now: *Your* mother *was a nigger.* Joyce is right about history being a nightmare—but it may be the nightmare from which no one can awaken. People are trapped in history and history is trapped in them.

There is a custom in the village—I am told it is repeated in many villages—of 6 "buying" African natives for the purpose of converting them to Christianity. There stands in the church all year round a small box with a slot for money, decorated with a black figurine, and into this box the villagers drop their francs. During the *carnaval* which precedes Lent, two village children have their faces blackened—

out of which bloodless darkness their blue eyes shine like ice—and fantastic horsehair wigs are placed on their blond heads; thus disguised, they solicit among the villagers for money for the missionaries in Africa. Between the box in the church and the blackened children, the village "bought" last year six or eight African natives. This was reported to me with pride by the wife of one of the *bistro* owners and I was careful to express astonishment and pleasure at the solicitude shown by the village for the souls of black folk. The *bistro* owner's wife beamed with a pleasure far more genuine than my own and seemed to feel that I might now breathe more easily concerning the souls of at least six of my kinsmen.

7   I tried not to think of these so lately baptized kinsmen, of the price paid for them, or the peculiar price they themselves would pay, and said nothing about my father, who having taken his own conversion too literally never, at bottom, forgave the white world (which he described as heathen) for having saddled him with a Christ in whom, to judge at least from their treatment of him, they themselves no longer believed. I thought of white men arriving for the first time in an African village, strangers there, as I am a stranger here, and tried to imagine the astounded populace touching their hair and marveling at the color of their skin. But there is a great difference between being the first white man to be seen by Africans and being the first black man to be seen by whites. The white man takes the astonishment as tribute, for he arrives to conquer and to convert the natives, whose inferiority in relation to himself is not even to be questioned; whereas I, without a thought of conquest, find myself among a people whose culture controls me, has even, in a sense, created me, people who have cost me more in anguish and rage than they will ever know, who yet do not even know of my existence. The astonishment with which I might have greeted them, should they have stumbled into my African village a few hundred years ago, might have rejoiced their hearts. But the astonishment with which they greet me today can only poison mine.

8   And this is so despite everything I may do to feel differently, despite my friendly conversations with the *bistro* owner's wife, despite their three-year-old son who has at last become my friend, despite the *saluts* and *bonsoirs* which I exchange with people as I walk, despite the fact that I know that no individual can be taken to task for what history is doing, or has done. I say that the culture of these people controls me—but they can scarcely be held responsible for European culture. America comes out of Europe, but these people have never seen America nor have most of them seen more of Europe than the hamlet at the foot of their mountain. Yet they move with an authority which I shall never have; and they regard me, quite rightly, not only as a stranger in their village but as a suspect latecomer, bearing no credentials, to everything they have—however unconsciously—inherited.

9   For this village, even were it incomparably more remote and incredibly more primitive, is the West, the West onto which I have been so strangely grafted. These people cannot be, from the point of view of power, strangers anywhere in the world; they have made the modern world, in effect, even if they do not know it. The most illiterate among them is related, in a way that I am not, to Dante, Shakespeare, Michelangelo, Aeschylus, da Vinci, Rembrandt, and Racine; the

cathedral at Chartres says something to them which it cannot say to me, as indeed would New York's Empire State Building, should anyone here ever see it. Out of their hymns and dances come Beethoven and Bach. Go back a few centuries and they are in their full glory—but I am in Africa, watching the conquerors arrive.

The rage of the disesteemed is personally fruitless, but it is also absolutely 10 inevitable; this rage, so generally discounted, so little understood even among the people whose daily bread it is, is one of the things that makes history. Rage can only with difficulty, and never entirely, be brought under the domination of the intelligence and is therefore not susceptible to any arguments whatever. This is a fact which ordinary representatives of the *Herrenvolk,* having never felt this rage and being unable to imagine it, quite fail to understand. Also, rage cannot be hidden, it can only be dissembled. This dissembling deludes the thoughtless, and strengthens rage and adds, to rage, contempt. There are, no doubt, as many ways of coping with the resulting complex of tensions as there are black men in the world, but no black man can hope ever to be entirely liberated from this internal warfare—rage, dissembling, and contempt having inevitably accompanied his first realization of the power of white men. What is crucial here is that, since white men represent in the black man's world so heavy a weight, white men have for black men a reality which is far from being reciprocal; and hence all black men have toward all white men an attitude which is designed, really, either to rob the white man of the jewel of his naïveté, or else to make it cost him dear.

The black man insists, by whatever means he finds at his disposal, that the 11 white man cease to regard him as an exotic rarity and recognize him as a human being. This is a very charged and difficult moment, for there is a great deal of will power involved in the white man's naïveté. Most people are not naturally reflective any more than they are naturally malicious, and the white man prefers to keep the black man at a certain human remove because it is easier for him thus to preserve his simplicity and avoid being called to account for crimes committed by his forefathers, or his neighbors. He is inescapably aware, nevertheless, that he is in a better position in the world than black men are, nor can he quite put to death the suspicion that he is hated by black men therefore. He does not wish to be hated, neither does he wish to change places, and at this point in his uneasiness he can scarcely avoid having recourse to those legends which white men have created about black men, the most usual effect of which is that the white man finds himself enmeshed, so to speak, in his own language which describes hell, as well as the attributes which lead one to hell, as being as black as night.

Every legend, moreover, contains its residuum of truth, and the root function 12 of language is to control the universe by describing it. It is of quite considerable significance that black men remain, in the imagination, and in overwhelming numbers in fact, beyond the disciplines of salvation; and this despite the fact the West has been "buying" African natives for centuries. There is, I should hazard, an instantaneous necessity to be divorced from this so visibly unsaved stranger, in whose heart, moreover, one cannot guess what dreams of vengeance are being nourished; and, at the same time, there are few things on earth more attractive than the idea of the unspeakable liberty which is allowed the unredeemed. When, beneath the black mask, a human being begins to make himself felt one cannot escape a certain awful wonder as to what kind of human being it is. What one's imagination makes of other people is dictated, of course, by the laws of one's own personality and it is one of the ironies of black-white relations that, by means of what the white man imagines the black man to be, the black man is enabled to know who the white man is.

13   I have said, for example, that I am as much a stranger in this village today as I was the first summer I arrived, but this is not quite true. The villagers wonder less about the texture of my hair than they did then, and wonder rather more about me. And the fact that their wonder now exists on another level is reflected in their attitudes and in their eyes. There are the children who make those delightful, hilarious, sometimes astonishingly grave overtures of friendship in the unpredictable fashion of children; other children, having been taught that the devil is a black man, scream in genuine anguish as I approach. Some of the older women never pass without a friendly greeting, never pass, indeed, if it seems that they will be able to engage me in conversation; other women look down or look away or rather contemptuously smirk. Some of the men drink with me and suggest that I learn how to ski—partly, I gather, because they cannot imagine what I would look like on skis—and want to know if I am married, and ask questions about my *métier.* But some of the men have accused *le sale négre*—behind my back—of stealing wood and there is already in the eyes of some of them that peculiar, intent, paranoiac malevolence which one sometimes surprises in the eyes of American white men when, out walking with their Sunday girl, they see a Negro male approach.

14   There is a dreadful abyss between the streets of this village and the streets of the city in which I was born, between the children who shout *Neger!* today and those who shouted *Nigger!* yesterday—the abyss is experience, the American experience. The syllable hurled behind me today expresses, above all, wonder: I am a stranger here. But I am not a stranger in America and the same syllable riding on the American air expresses the war my presence has occasioned in the American soul.

15   For this village brings home to me this fact: that there was a day, and not really a very distant day, when Americans were scarcely Americans at all but discontented Europeans, facing a great unconquered continent and strolling, say, into a marketplace and seeing black men for the first time. The shock this spectacle afforded is suggested, surely, by the promptness with which they decided that these black men were not really men but cattle. It is true that the necessity on the part of the settlers of the New World of reconciling their moral assumptions with the fact—and the necessity—of slavery enhanced immensely the charm of this idea, and it is also true that this idea expresses, with a truly American bluntness, the attitude which to varying extents all masters have had toward all slaves.

16   But between all former slaves and slave owners and the drama which begins for Americans over three hundred years ago at Jamestown, there are at least two differences to be observed. The American Negro slave could not suppose, for one thing, as slaves in past epochs had supposed and often done, that he would ever be able to wrest the power from his master's hands. This was a supposition which

the modern era, which was to bring about such vast changes in the aims and dimensions of power, put to death; it only begins, in unprecedented fashion, and with dreadful implications, to be resurrected today. But even had this supposition persisted with undiminished force, the American Negro slave could not have used it to lend his condition dignity, for the reason that this supposition rests on another: that the slave in exile yet remains related to his past, has some means—if only in memory—of revering and sustaining the forms of his former life, is able, in short, to maintain his identity.

This was not the case with the American Negro slave. He is unique among 17 the black men of the world in that his past was taken from him, almost literally, at one blow. One wonders what on earth the first slave found to say to the first dark child he bore. I am told that there are Haitians able to trace their ancestry back to African kings, but any American Negro wishing to go back so far will find his journey through time abruptly arrested by the signature on the bill of sale which served as the entrance paper for his ancestor. At the time—to say nothing of the circumstances— of the enslavement of the captive black man who was to become the American Negro, there was not the remotest possibility that he would ever take power from his master's hands. There was no reason to suppose that his situation would ever change, nor was there, shortly, anything to indicate that his situation had ever been different. It was his necessity, in the words of E. Franklin Frazier, to find a "motive for living under American culture or die." The identity of the American Negro comes out of this extreme situation, and the evolution of this identity was a source of the most intolerable anxiety in the minds and the lives of his masters.

For the history of the American Negro is unique also in this: that the question 18 of his humanity, and of his rights therefore as a human being, became a burning one for several generations of Americans, so burning a question that it ultimately became one of those used to divide the nation. It is out of this argument that the venom of the epithet *Nigger!* is derived. It is an argument which Europe has never had, and hence Europe quite sincerely fails to understand how or why the argu- ment arose in the first place, why its effects are so frequently disastrous and always so unpredictable, why it refuses until today to be entirely settled. Europe's black possessions remained—and do remain—in Europe's colonies, at which remove they represented no threat whatever to European identity. If they posed any problem at all for the European conscience, it was a problem which remained comfortingly abstract: in effect, the black man, *as a man,* did not exist for Europe. But in America, even as a slave, he was an inescapable part of the general social fabric and no American could escape having an attitude toward him. Americans attempt until today to make an abstraction of the Negro, but the very nature of these abstractions reveals the tremendous effects the presence of the Negro has had on the American character.

When one considers the history of the Negro in America it is of the greatest 19 importance to recognize that the moral beliefs of a person, or a people, are never really as tenuous as life—which is not moral—very often causes them to appear; these create for them a frame of reference and a necessary hope, the hope being that when life has done its worst they will be enabled to rise above themselves and to triumph over life. Life would scarcely be bearable if this hope did not exist. Again, even when the worst has been said, to betray a belief is not by any means to have put oneself beyond its power; the betrayal of a belief is not the same thing as ceasing to believe. If this were not so there would be no moral standards in the world at all. Yet one must also recognize that morality is based on ideas and that all ideas are dangerous—dangerous because ideas can only lead to action and where the action leads no man can say. And dangerous in this respect: that confronted with the impossibility of becoming free of them, one can be driven to the most inhuman excesses. The ideas on which American beliefs are based are not, though Americans often seem to think so, ideas which originated in America. They came out of Europe. And the establishment of democracy on the American continent was scarcely as radical a break with the past as was the necessity, which Americans faced, of broadening this concept to include black men.

20   This was, literally, a hard necessity. It was impossible, for one thing, for Americans to abandon their beliefs, not only because these beliefs alone seemed able to justify the sacrifices they had endured and the blood that they had spilled, but also because these beliefs afforded them their only bulwark against a moral chaos as absolute as the physical chaos of the continent it was their destiny to conquer. But in the situation in which Americans found themselves, these beliefs threatened an idea which, whether or not one likes to think so, is the very warp and woof of the heritage of the West, the idea of white supremacy.

21   Americans have made themselves notorious by the shrillness and the brutality with which they have insisted on this idea, but they did not invent it; and it has escaped the world's notice that those very excesses of which Americans have been guilty imply a certain, unprecedented uneasiness over the idea's life and power, if not, indeed, the idea's validity. The idea of white supremacy rests simply on the fact that white men are the creators of civilization (the present civilization, which is the only one that matters; all previous civilizations are simply "contributions" to our own) and are therefore civilization's guardians and defenders. Thus it was impossible for Americans to accept the black man as one of themselves, for to do so was to jeopardize their status as white men. But not so to accept him was to deny his human reality, his human weight and complexity, and the strain of denying the overwhelmingly undeniable forced Americans into rationalizations so fantastic that they approached the pathological.

22   At the root of the American Negro problem is the necessity of the American white man to find a way of living with the Negro in order to be able to live with himself. And the history of this problem can be reduced to the means used by Americans—lynch law and law, segregation and legal acceptance, terrorization and concession—either to come to terms with this necessity, or to find a way around it, or (most usually) to find a way of doing both these things at once. The resulting spectacle, at once foolish and dreadful, led someone to make the quite accurate observation that "the Negro-in-America is a form of insanity which overtakes white men."

23   In this long battle, a battle by no means finished, the unforeseeable effects of which will be felt by many future generations, the white man's motive was the

protection of his identity; the black man was motivated by the need to establish an identity. And despite the terrorization which the Negro in America endured and endures sporadically until today, despite the cruel and totally inescapable ambivalence of his status in his country, the battle for his identity has long ago been won. He is not a visitor to the West, but a citizen there, an American; as American as the Americans who despise him, the Americans who fear him, the Americans who love him—the Americans who became less than themselves, or rose to be greater than themselves by virtue of the fact that the challenge he represented was inescapable. He is perhaps the only black man in the world whose relationship to white men is more terrible, more subtle, and more meaningful than the relationship of bitter possessed to uncertain possessor. His survival depended, and his development depends, on his ability to turn his peculiar status in the Western world to his own advantage and, it may be, to the very great advantage of that world. It remains for him to fashion out of his experience that which will give him sustenance, and a voice.

The cathedral at Chartres, I have said, says something to the people of this 24 village which it cannot say to me; but it is important to understand that this cathedral says something to me which it cannot say to them. Perhaps they are struck by the power of the spires, the glory of the windows; but they have known God, after all, longer than I have known him, and in a different way, and I am terrified by the slippery bottomless well to be found in the crypt, down which heretics were hurled to death, and by the obscene, inescapable gargoyles jutting out of the stone and seeming to say that God and the devil can never be divorced. I doubt that the villagers think of the devil when they face a cathedral because they have never been identified with the devil. But I must accept the status which myth, if nothing else, gives me in the West before I can hope to change the myth.

Yet, if the American Negro has arrived at his identity by virtue of the abso- 25 luteness of his estrangement from his past, American white men still nourish the illusion that there is some means of recovering the European innocence, of returning to a state in which black men do not exist. This is one of the greatest errors Americans can make. The identity they fought so hard to protect has, by virtue of that battle, undergone a change: Americans are as unlike any other white people in the world as it is possible to be. I do not think, for example, that it is too much to suggest that the American vision of the world—which allows so little reality, generally speaking, for any of the darker forces in human life, which tends until today to paint moral issues in glaring black and white—owes a great deal to the battle waged by Americans to maintain between themselves and black men a human separation which could not be bridged. It is only now beginning to be borne in on us—very faintly, it must be admitted, very slowly, and very much against our will—that this vision of the world is dangerously inaccurate, and perfectly useless. For it protects our moral high-mindedness at the terrible expense of weakening our grasp of reality. People who shut their eyes to reality simply invite their own destruction, and anyone who insists on remaining in a state of innocence long after that innocence is dead turns himself into a monster.

The time has come to realize that the interracial drama acted out on the 26 American continent has not only created a new black man, it has created a new white man, too. No road whatever will lead Americans back to the simplicity of this European village where white men still have the luxury of looking on me as a stranger. I am not, really, a stranger any longer for any American alive. One of the things that distinguishes Americans from other people is that no other people has ever been so deeply involved in the lives of black men, and vice versa. This fact faced, with all its implications, it can be seen that the history of the American Negro problem is not merely shameful, it is also something of an achievement. For even when the worst has been said, it must also be added that the perpetual challenge posed by this problem was always, somehow, perpetually met. It is precisely this black-white experience which may prove of indispensable value to us in the world we face today. This world is white no longer, and it will never be white again.

COMPREHENSION

1. According to Baldwin, what distinguishes Americans from other people? What is his purpose in highlighting these differences?
2. What connections between Europe, Africa, and America emerge from this essay? What is the relevance of the Swiss village to this frame of reference?
3. In the context of the essay, explain what Baldwin means by his statement "People are trapped in history and history is trapped in them" (paragraph 5).

RHETORIC

1. Analyze the effect of Baldwin's repetition of "there is" and "there are" constructions in paragraph 2. What does the parallelism at the start of paragraph 8 accomplish? Locate other examples of parallelism in the essay.
2. Analyze the image of winter in paragraph 2 and its relation to the rest of the essay.
3. Where in the essay is Baldwin's complex thesis condensed for the reader? What does this placement of thesis reveal about the logical method of development in the essay?
4. How does Baldwin create his introduction? What is the focus? What key motifs does he present that will inform the rest of the essay? What is the relationship of paragraph 5 to paragraph 6?
5. What paragraphs constitute the second section of the essay? What example serves to unify this section? What major shift in emphasis occurs in the third part of the essay? Explain the cathedral of Chartres as a controlling motif between these two sections.
6. What comparisons and contrasts help structure and unify the essay?

WRITING

1. Examine the paradox implicit in Baldwin's statement in the final paragraph that the history of the American Negro problem is "something of an achievement."
2. Describe a time when you felt yourself a "stranger" in a certain culture.
3. **Writing an Argument:** Write an argumentative essay on civilization based on the last sentence in Baldwin's essay: "This world is white no longer, and it will never be white again."

NETWORKING
Applying Digital and Multimedia Literacies

Analyzing a Debate: Search online to find the video of a Cambridge University debate between James Baldwin and William F. Buckley Jr. What is the central disagreement between these two men? How are the issues raised in "Stranger in the Village" also addressed in this argument? Who do you see as "winning" this debate, and why?

Synthesis: Connections for Critical Thinking

1. Discuss the views that Mukherjee and Baldwin have in common regarding the refusal of American culture to accept the "otherness" of those it perceives as not behaving like or looking like the conventional "American." Expand your discussion to present your own views about the similarities and differences in the ways "white" America views immigrants and "black" Americans.
2. Compare and contrast the diction, level of discourse, style, and vocabulary of Ivins and Chua.
3. Both Thomas Jefferson and Martin Luther King Jr. made powerful appeals to the government in power on behalf of their people. Write a comparison-and-contrast essay that examines the language, style, and content of both essays.
4. Select the three essays you find the most and the least appealing or compelling in this chapter. Discuss why you selected them, and explore the way you developed your viewpoint.
5. Analyze the comparative methods of Catton and Chua.
6. Compare and contrast the difficulties Baldwin had in attempting to "fit in" to an alien European culture with the experiences Mukherjee describes of a nonwhite American trying to assimilate into the dominant culture.
7. Interview five parents and ask them if and how they control the online content their children view. Report your findings to your class.

NETWORKING
Applying Digital and Multimedia Literacies

1. On Facebook or in a Google+ Hangout, discuss with classmates Dyson's views on cyberspace regulation. Write a summary of your discussion.
2. Conduct online research on Ivins, Mukherjee, and Baldwin. Write an analysis of how their senses of place influence their ideas.

chapter 8

Business and Economics
How Do We Earn Our Keep?

Work is central to the human experience; in fact, it is work and its economic and social outcomes that provide us with the keys to an understanding of culture and civilization. Work tells us much about scarcity and abundance, poverty and affluence, the haves and have-nots in any society, as well as a nation's economic imperatives. Whether it is the rise and fall of cities, the conduct of business and corporations, or the economic policies of government, we see in the culture of work an attempt to impose order on nature. Work is our handprint on the world.

The work we perform and the careers we pursue also define us in very personal ways. "I'm a professor at Harvard" or "I work for Google" serve as identity badges. (Robert Reich, a contributor to this chapter, once worked at Harvard.) For what we do explains, at least in part, what and who we are. The very act of looking for work illuminates one's status in society, one's background, one's aspirations. Jonathan Swift, in his classic essay "A Modest Proposal," written in 1729, demonstrates how labor reveals economic and political configurations of power. Over 250 years later, Reich tells us the same thing in his analysis of the changing nature of work and the way these changes create an even broader gap between rich and poor.

Work is not merely an important human activity but an essential one for social and psychological health. You might like your work, or you might loathe it; be employed or unemployed; enjoy the reputation of a workaholic or a person who lives for leisure time; view work as a curse or as a duty. Regardless, it is work that occupies a central position in your relationship to society. In fact, Sigmund Freud spoke of work as the basis of one's social reality.

Regardless of your perspective on the issue, it is important to understand the multiple dimensions of work. In both traditional and modern societies, work prepares us for economic and social roles. It affects families, school curricula, and public policy. Ultimately, as many authors here suggest, it determines our self-esteem. Through work we come to terms with ourselves and our environment. The nature and purpose of the work we do provide us with a powerful measure of our worth.

PREVIEWING THE CHAPTER

As you read the essays in this chapter and respond to them in discussion and writing, consider the following questions:

- What are the significant forms of support the author uses in viewing the world of work: observation, statistics, personal experience, history, and so on?
- What assumptions does the author make about the value of work?
- Does the author discuss work in general or focus on one particular aspect of work?
- How does the writer define *work?* In what ways, if any, does she or he expand on the simple definition of work as "paid employment"?
- What issues of race, class, and gender does the author raise?
- What is the relationship of work to the changing social, political, and economic systems depicted in the author's essay?
- What tone does the writer take in his or her presentation of the work experience?
- What psychological insights does the author offer into the culture of work?
- What does the writer's style reveal about her or his attitude toward work?

Classic and Contemporary Images
WILL WORKERS BE DISPLACED BY MACHINES?

Using a Critical Perspective   Diego Rivera's mural and the photograph of an automobile assembly line present industrial scenes that reveal the impact of technology on workers. What details are emphasized in each illustration? How are these two images similar and dissimilar? What, for example, is the relation of human beings to the machines that are the centerpiece of each photograph? Are the artist and photographer objective or subjective in the presentation of each scene? Explain.

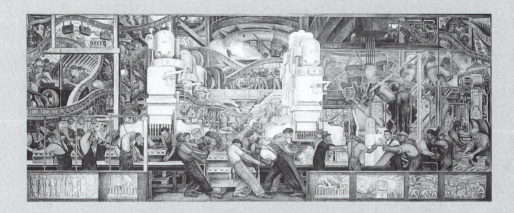

In the era known as the "Machine Age," 1918–1941, many artists, industrial designers, and architects in the United States and Europe evoked the mechanisms and images of industry in their works. During this time, the Mexican painter Diego Rivera (1886–1957) created a mural for the Detroit Institute of Arts (1932–33), a portion of which is reprinted here.

Today, computers are used to help
control assembly lines, as shown in
this photo of an automobile assembly line.

Classic and Contemporary Essays
DOES EQUAL OPPORTUNITY EXIST?

Virginia Woolf's "Professions for Women" is ironic from the start as she readily admits she can speak expertly of only one profession, her own, which is writing. But her message is clear regarding the effect of living in a male-dominated society. Simply put, it is very difficult to break the shackles of conditioning that one acquires from being told over and over again by one's culture that gender is destiny, regardless of what one aspires to. The author—through personal experience—demonstrates how this discrimination has a profound effect on the ability to see with one's own eyes and to think with one's own mind. Henry Louis Gates Jr. presents an interesting variation on this theme. Although the outcome is the same, the premise is reversed. He demonstrates how correlating supposedly positive attributes to a group—that is, superior athletic performance and race—results in the same deadening of the sense of personal ambition and a limiting of the scope of what one can aspire to. The thoughtful reader should be able to learn valuable lessons from comparing and contrasting these essays—one of which is that misguided perception all too often can be a self-fulfilling prophecy.

Professions for Women

Virginia Woolf

Virginia Woolf (1882–1941), novelist and essayist, was the daughter of Sir Leslie Stephen, a famous critic and writer on economics. An experimental novelist, Woolf attempted to portray consciousness through a poetic, symbolic, and concrete style. Her novels include Jacob's Room *(1922),* Mrs. Dalloway *(1925),* To the Lighthouse *(1927), and* The Waves *(1931). She was also a perceptive reader and critic; her criticism appears in* The Common Reader *(1925) and* The Second Common Reader *(1933). In the following essay, which was delivered originally as a speech to the Women's Service League in 1931, Woolf argues that women must overcome several "angels," or phantoms, in order to succeed in professional careers.*

1   When your secretary invited me to come here, she told me that your Society is concerned with the employment of women and she suggested that I might tell you something about my own professional experiences. It is true I am a woman; it is true I am employed; but what professional experiences have I had? It is difficult to say. My profession is literature; and in that profession there are fewer experiences

for women than in any other, with the exception of the stage—fewer, I mean, that are peculiar to women. For the road was cut many years ago—by Fanny Burney, by Aphra Behn, by Harriet Martineau, by Jane Austen, by George Eliot—many famous women, and many more unknown and forgotten, have been before me, making the path smooth, and regulating my steps. Thus, when I came to write, there were very few material obstacles in my way. Writing was a reputable and harmless occupation. The family peace was not broken by the scratching of a pen. No demand was made upon the family purse. For ten and sixpence one can buy paper enough to write all the plays of Shakespeare—if one has a mind that way. Pianos and models, Paris, Vienna and Berlin, masters and mistresses, are not needed by a writer. The cheapness of writing paper is, of course, the reason why women have succeeded as writers before they have succeeded in the other professions.

But to tell you my story—it is a simple one. You have only got to figure to 2 yourselves a girl in a bedroom with a pen in her hand. She had only to move that pen from left to right—from ten o'clock to one. Then it occurred to her to do what is simple and cheap enough after all—to slip a few of those pages into an envelope, fix a penny stamp in the corner, and drop the envelope into the red box at the corner. It was thus that I became a journalist; and my effort was rewarded on the first day of the following month—a very glorious day it was for me—by a letter from an editor containing a check for one pound ten shillings and sixpence. But to show you how little I deserve to be called a professional woman, how little I know of the struggles and difficulties of such lives, I have to admit that instead of spending that sum upon bread and butter, rent, shoes and stockings, or butcher's bills, I went out and bought a cat—a beautiful cat, a Persian cat, which very soon involved me in bitter disputes with my neighbors.

What could be easier than to write articles and to buy Persian cats with the 3 profits? But wait a moment. Articles have to be about something. Mine, I seem to remember, was about a novel by a famous man. And while I was writing this review, I discovered that if I were going to review books I should need to do battle with a certain phantom. And the phantom was a woman, and when I came to know her better I called her after the heroine of a famous poem, "The Angel in the House." It was she who used to come between me and my paper when I was writing reviews. It was she who bothered me and wasted my time and so tormented me that at last I killed her. You who come of a younger and happier generation may not have heard of her—you may not know what I mean by the Angel in the House. I will describe her as shortly as I can. She was intensely sympathetic. She was immensely charming. She was utterly unselfish. She excelled in the difficult arts of family life. She sacrificed herself daily. If there was a chicken, she took the leg; if there was a draught she sat in it—in short she was so constituted that she never had a mind or a wish of her own, but preferred to sympathize always with the minds and wishes of others. Above all—I need not say it—she was pure. Her purity was supposed to be her chief beauty—her blushes, her great grace. In those days—the last of Queen Victoria—every house had its Angel. And when I came to write I encountered her with the very first words. The shadow of her wings fell on my page; I heard the rustling of her skirts in the room.

Directly, that is to say, I took my pen in hand to review that novel by a famous man, she slipped behind me and whispered: "My dear, you are a young woman. You are writing about a book that has been written by a man. Be sympathetic; be tender; flatter; deceive; use all the arts and wiles of our sex. Never let anybody guess that you have a mind of your own. Above all, be pure." And she made as if to guide my pen. I now record the one act for which I take some credit to myself, though the credit rightly belongs to some excellent ancestors of mine who left me a certain sum of money—shall we say five hundred pounds a year—so that it was not necessary for me to depend solely on charm for my living. I turned upon her and caught her by the throat. I did my best to kill her. My excuse, if I were to be had up in a court of law, would be that I acted in self-defense. Had I not killed her she would have killed me. She would have plucked the heart out of my writing. For, as I found, directly I put pen to paper, you cannot review even a novel without having a mind of your own, without expressing what you think to be the truth about human relations, morality, sex. And all these questions, according to the Angel in the House, cannot be dealt with freely and openly by women; they must charm, they must conciliate, they must—to put it bluntly—tell lies if they are to succeed. Thus, whenever I felt the shadow of her wing or the radiance of her halo upon my page, I took up the inkpot and flung it at her. She died hard. Her fictitious nature was of great assistance to her. It is far harder to kill a phantom than a reality. She was always creeping back when I thought I had dispatched her. Though I flatter myself that I killed her in the end, the struggle was severe; it took much time that had better have been spent upon learning Greek grammar; or in roaming the world in search of adventures. But it was a real experience; it was an experience that was bound to befall all women writers at that time. Killing the Angel in the House was part of the occupation of a woman writer.

4   But to continue my story. The Angel was dead; what then remained? You may say that what remained was a simple and common object—a young woman in a bedroom with an inkpot. In other words, now that she had rid herself of falsehood, that young woman had only to be herself. Ah, but what is "herself"? I mean, what is a woman? I assure you, I do not know. I do not believe that you know. I do not believe that anybody can know until she has expressed herself in all the arts and professions open to human skill. That indeed is one of the reasons why I have come here—out of respect for you, who are in process of showing us by your experiments what a woman is, who are in process of providing us, by your failures and successes, with that extremely important piece of information.

5   But to continue the story of my professional experiences. I made one pound ten and six by my first review; and I bought a Persian cat with the proceeds. Then I grew ambitious. A Persian cat is all very well, I said; but a Persian cat is not enough. I must have a motor car. And it was thus that I became a novelist—for it is a very strange thing that people will give you a motor car if you will tell them a story. It is a still stranger thing that there is nothing so delightful in the world as telling stories. It is far pleasanter than writing reviews of famous novels. And yet, if I am to obey your secretary and tell you my professional experiences as a novelist, I must tell you about a very strange experience that befell me as a

novelist. And to understand it you must try first to imagine a novelist's state of mind. I hope I am not giving away professional secrets if I say that a novelist's chief desire is to be as unconscious as possible. He has to induce in himself a state of perpetual lethargy. He wants life to proceed with the utmost quiet and regularity. He wants to see the same faces, to read the same books, to do the same things day after day, month after month, while he is writing, so that nothing may break the illusion in which he is living—so that nothing may disturb or disquiet the mysterious nosings about, feelings round, darts, dashes and sudden discoveries of that very shy and illusive spirit, the imagination. I suspect that this state is the same both for men and women. Be that as it may, I want you to imagine me writing a novel in a state of trance. I want you to figure to yourselves a girl sitting with a pen in her hand, which for minutes, and indeed for hours, she never dips into the inkpot. The image that comes to my mind when I think of this girl is the image of a fisherman lying sunk in dreams on the verge of a deep lake with a rod held out over the water. She was letting her imagination sweep unchecked round every rock and cranny of the world that lies submerged in the depths of our unconscious being. Now came the experience, the experience that I believe to be far commoner with women writers than with men. The line raced through the girl's fingers. Her imagination had rushed away. It had sought the pools, the depths, the dark places where the largest fish slumber. And then there was a smash. There was an explosion. There was foam and confusion. The imagination had dashed itself against something hard. The girl was roused from her dream. She was indeed in a state of the most acute and difficult distress. To speak without figure she had thought of something, something about the body, about the passions which it was unfitting for her as a woman to say. Men, her reason told her, would be shocked. The consciousness of what men will say of a woman who speaks the truth about her passions had roused her from her artist's state of unconsciousness. She could write no more. The trance was over. Her imagination could work no longer. This I believe to be a very common experience with women writers—they are impeded by the extreme conventionality of the other sex. For though men sensibly allow themselves great freedom in these respects, I doubt that they realize or can control the extreme severity with which they condemn such freedom in women.

These then were two very genuine experiences of my own. These were two of 6 the adventures of my professional life. The first—killing the Angel in the House— I think I solved. She died. But the second, telling the truth about my own experiences as a body, I do not think I solved. I doubt that any woman has solved it yet. The obstacles against her are still immensely powerful—and yet they are very difficult to define. Outwardly, what is simpler than to write books? Outwardly, what obstacles are there for a woman rather than for a man? Inwardly, I think, the case is very different; she has still many ghosts to fight, many prejudices to overcome. Indeed it will be a long time still, I think, before a woman can sit down to write a book without finding a phantom to be slain, a rock to be dashed against. And if this is so in literature, the freest of all professions for women, how is it in the new professions which you are now for the first time entering?

7   Those are the questions that I should like, had I time, to ask you. And indeed, if I have laid stress upon these professional experiences of mine, it is because I believe that they are, though in different forms, yours also. Even when the path is nominally open—when there is nothing to prevent a woman from being a doctor, a lawyer, a civil servant—there are many phantoms and obstacles, as I believe, looming in her way. To discuss and define them is I think of great value and importance; for thus only can the labor be shared, the difficulties be solved. But besides this, it is necessary also to discuss the ends and the aims for which we are fighting, for which we are doing battle with these formidable obstacles. Those aims cannot be taken for granted; they must be perpetually questioned and examined. The whole position, as I see it—here in this hall surrounded by women practicing for the first time in history I know not how many different professions— is one of extraordinary interest and importance. You have won rooms of your own in the house hitherto exclusively owned by men. You are able, though not without great labor and effort, to pay the rent. You are earning your five hundred pounds a year. But this freedom is only a beginning; the room is your own, but it is still bare. It has to be furnished; it has to be decorated; it has to be shared. How are you going to furnish it, how are you going to decorate it? With whom are you going to share it, and upon what terms? These, I think, are questions of the utmost importance and interest. For the first time in history you are able to ask them; for the first time you are able to decide for yourselves what the answers should be. Willingly would I stay and discuss those questions and answers—but not tonight. My time is up; and I must cease.

COMPREHENSION

1. This essay was presented originally as a speech. What internal evidence indicates that it was intended as a talk? How do you respond to it today as a reader?
2. Who or what is the "angel" that Woolf describes in this essay? Why must she kill it? What other obstacles does a professional woman encounter?
3. Paraphrase the last two paragraphs of this essay. What is the essence of Woolf's argument?

RHETORIC

1. There is a significant amount of figurative language in the essay. Locate and explain examples. What does the figurative language contribute to the tone of the essay?
2. How do we know that Woolf is addressing an audience of women? Why does she pose so many questions, and what does this strategy contribute to the rapport she wants to establish? Explain the effect of the last two sentences.
3. How does Woolf use analogy to structure part of her argument?
4. Why does Woolf rely on personal narration? How does it affect the logic of her argument?
5. Evaluate Woolf's use of contrast to advance her argument.
6. Where does Woolf place her main proposition? How emphatic is it, and why?

WRITING

1. How effectively does Woolf use her own example as a professional writer to advance a broader proposition concerning all women entering professional life? Answer this question in a brief essay.
2. Discuss the problems and obstacles that you anticipate when you enter your chosen career.
3. **Writing an Argument:** Argue for or against the proposition that Woolf's essay has little relevance for women planning careers today.

NETWORKING
Applying Digital and Multimedia Literacies

Repurposing Text for a New Genre: Condense and rewrite Woolf's speech/essay as a blog entry. Preserve and do not distort her central message, but do not use more than 500 words. What else, besides length, will you modify to fit this new form?

Delusions of Grandeur

Henry Louis Gates Jr.

Henry Louis Gates Jr. (b. 1950) is an educator, writer, and editor. He was born in West Virginia and educated at Yale and at Clare College in Cambridge. Gates has had a varied career, working as a general anesthetist in Tanzania and as a staff correspondent for Time *magazine in London. His essays have appeared in such diverse publications as* Black American Literature Forum, Yale Review, New York Times Book Review, *and* Sports Illustrated. *He is also the author of* Figures in Black: Words, Signs and the Racial Self *(1987) and* The Signifying Monkey: A Theory of Afro-American Literary Criticism *(1988) and is the editor, with Nellie Y. McKey, of* The Norton Anthology of African American Literature *(1996), and, with Hollis Robbins,* The Annotated Uncle Tom's Cabin *(2007). In this article from* Sports Illustrated, *Gates turns his attention to the limited career choices presented as viable to African American youth and to public misconceptions about blacks in sports.*

Standing at the bar of an all-black VFW post in my hometown of Piedmont, W.Va., I 1 offered five dollars to anyone who could tell me how many African-American professional athletes were at work today. There are 35 million African-Americans, I said.

"Ten million!" yelled one intrepid soul, too far into his cups. 2

"No way . . . more like 500,000," said another. 3

"You mean *all* professional sports," someone interjected, "including golf and 4 tennis, but not counting the brothers from Puerto Rico?" Everyone laughed.

5   "Fifty thousand, minimum," was another guess.

6   Here are the facts:

There are 1,200 black professional athletes in the U.S.

There are 12 times more black lawyers than black athletes.

There are 2½ times more black dentists than black athletes.

There are 15 times more black doctors than black athletes.

7   Nobody in my local VFW believed these statistics; in fact, few people would believe them if they weren't reading them in the pages of *Sports Illustrated*. In spite of these statistics, too many African-American youngsters still believe that they have a much better chance of becoming another Magic Johnson or Michael Jordan than they do of matching the achievements of Baltimore Mayor Kurt Schmoke or neurosurgeon Dr. Benjamin Carson, both of whom, like Johnson and Jordan, are black.

8   In reality, an African-American youngster has about as much chance of becoming a professional athlete as he or she does of winning the lottery. The tragedy for our people, however, is that few of us accept that truth.

9   Let me confess that I love sports. Like most black people of my generation— I'm 40—I was raised to revere the great black athletic heroes, and I never tired of listening to the stories of triumph and defeat that, for blacks, amount to a collective epic much like those of the ancient Greeks: Joe Louis's demolition of Max Schmeling; Satchel Paige's dazzling repertoire of pitches; Jesse Owens's in-your-face performance in Hitler's 1936 Olympics; Willie Mays's over-the-shoulder basket catch; Jackie Robinson's quiet strength when assaulted by racist taunts; and a thousand other grand tales.

10   Nevertheless, the blind pursuit of attainment in sports is having a devastating effect on our people. Imbued with a belief that our principal avenue to fame and profit is through sport, and seduced by a win-at-any-cost system that corrupts even elementary school students, far too many black kids treat basketball courts and football fields as if they were classrooms in an alternative school system. "O.K., I flunked English," a young athlete will say. "But I got an A plus in slamdunking."

11   The failure of our public schools to educate athletes is part and parcel of the schools' failure to educate almost everyone. A recent survey of the Philadelphia school system, for example, stated that "more than half of all students in the third, fifth and eighth grades cannot perform minimum math and language tasks." One in four middle school students in that city fails to pass to the next grade each year. It is a sad truth that such statistics are repeated in cities throughout the nation. Young athletes—particularly young black athletes—are especially ill-served. Many of them are functionally illiterate, yet they are passed along from year to year for the greater glory of good old Hometown High. We should not be surprised to learn, then, that only 26.6 percent of black athletes at the collegiate level earn their degrees. For every successful educated black professional athlete,

there are thousands of dead and wounded. Yet young blacks continue to aspire to careers as athletes, and it's no wonder why; when the University of North Carolina recently commissioned a sculptor to create archetypes of its student body, guess which ethnic group was selected to represent athletes?

Those relatively few black athletes who do make it in the professional ranks 12 must be prevailed upon to play a significant role in the education of all of our young people, athlete and nonathlete alike. While some have done so, many others have shirked their social obligations: to earmark small percentages of their incomes for the United Negro College Fund; to appear on television for educational purposes rather than merely to sell sneakers; to let children know the message that becoming a lawyer, a teacher or a doctor does more good for our people than winning the Super Bowl; and to form productive liaisons with educators to help forge solutions to the many ills that beset the black community. These are merely a few modest proposals.

A similar burden falls upon successful blacks in all walks of life. Each of us 13 must strive to make our young people understand the realities. Tell them to cheer Bo Jackson but to emulate novelist Toni Morrison or businessman Reginald Lewis or historian John Hope Franklin or Spelman College president Johnetta Cole— the list is long.

Of course, society as a whole bears responsibility as well. Until colleges 14 stop using young blacks as cannon fodder in the big-business wars of so-called nonprofessional sports, until training a young black's mind becomes as important as training his or her body, we will continue to perpetuate a system akin to that of the Roman gladiators, sacrificing a class of people for the entertainment of the mob.

COMPREHENSION

1. What does Gates suggest is the general assumption made about blacks in sports?
2. Why do American schools continue to perpetuate the myth that Gates is writing about?
3. According to Gates, what should successful black athletes do to help guide the career choices of young blacks?

RHETORIC

1. What is Gates's thesis? Where does it appear?
2. How does the introductory paragraph work to set up the writer's focus?
3. State Gates's purpose in using statistics in his essay.
4. What is the tone of Gates's essay? Cite specific sections where this tone seems strongest.
5. Examine the accumulation of facts in paragraph 11. How does this technique underscore Gates's point?
6. Explain Gates's allusion to Roman gladiators in his conclusion. How does it aid in emphasizing his main point?

WRITING

1. Write a brief essay in which you analyze your personal reaction to Gates's statistics. Were you surprised by them? What assumptions did you have about the number of black professional athletes? Why do you think most Americans share these assumptions?
2. Write a biographical research paper on the life and career of a black athlete.
3. **Writing an Argument:** Pretend you are addressing a group of young African Americans at an elementary school. Argue that sports and entertainment should (or should not) be their career choices.

NETWORKING
Applying Digital and Multimedia Literacies

Creating a Graphic from Data: Use selected statistics from this essay to create an effective graph, table, or chart.

Synthesis: Classic and Contemporary Questions for Comparison

1. Examine the argumentative styles of Woolf and Gates. What are their main propositions? Their minor propositions? What evidence do they provide?
2. Woolf first presented her paper as a speech before an audience of women. Gates wrote his essay as an opinion piece for *Sports Illustrated*. Write a comparative audience analysis of the two selections. Analyze the purpose, tone, style, and any other relevant aspects of these essays.
3. Argue for or against the proposition that white women and black men face the same barriers to employment in today's professions. Refer to the essays by Woolf and Gates to support your position.

The Money: Starting Out

Junot Diaz

Junot Diaz (b. 1968) is an award-winning Dominican American writer and creative writing professor at Massachusetts Institute of Technology. He was born in Santo Domingo, the third child in a family of five. His family moved to New Jersey when Diaz was six. The family lived less than a mile from what Diaz recalls as "one of the largest landfills in New Jersey." Despite hardships that include his father's abandonment of the family, Diaz completed a BA at Rutgers University in

1992 and an MFA at Cornell University in 1995. While at Cornell, Diaz wrote most of the stories that appear in his first collection, Drown *(1966). In 2008, Diaz received the Pulitzer Prize for his novel,* The Brief Wondrous Life of Oscar Wao *(2007), an immigrant family saga drawing on the author's own experience. In 2010, Diaz was selected to sit on the Pulitzer Prize board of jurors, the first Latino appointed to the twenty-member panel. The essay that follows, which reflects Diaz's focus in his writing on the immigrant experience, appeared in the June 13–20, 2011 issue of the* New Yorker.

All the Dominicans I knew in those days sent money home. My mother didn't 1 have a regular job besides caring for us five kids, so she scrimped the loot together from whatever came her way. My father was always losing his forklift jobs, so it wasn't like she ever had a steady flow. But my grandparents were alone in Santo Domingo, and those remittances, beyond material support, were a way, I suspect, for Mami to negotiate the absence, the distance, caused by our diaspora. She chipped dollars off the cash Papi gave her for our daily expenses, forced our already broke family to live even broker. That was how she built the nut—two, maybe three hundred dollars—that she sent home every six months or so.

We kids knew where the money was hidden, but we also knew that to touch it 2 would have meant a violent punishment approaching death. I, who could take the change out of my mother's purse without thinking, couldn't have brought myself even to look at that forbidden stash.

So what happened? Exactly what you'd think. The summer I was twelve, my 3 family went away on a "vacation"—one of my father's half-baked get-to-know-our-country-better-by-sleeping-in-the-van extravaganzas—and when we returned to Jersey, exhausted, battered, we found our front door unlocked. My parents' room, which was where the thieves had concentrated their search, looked as if it had been tornado-tossed. The thieves had kept it simple; they'd snatched a portable radio, some of my *Dungeons & Dragons* hardcovers, and, of course, Mami's remittances.

It's not as if the robbery came as a huge surprise. In our neighborhood, cars 4 and apartments were always getting jacked, and the kid stupid enough to leave a bike unattended for more than a tenth of a second was the kid who was never going to see that bike again. Everybody got hit; no matter who you were, eventually it would be your turn.

And that summer it was ours.   5

Still, we took the burglary pretty hard. When you're a recent immigrant, it's 6 easy to feel targeted. Like it wasn't just a couple of assholes that had it in for you but the whole neighborhood—hell, maybe the whole country.

No one took the robbery as hard as my mom, though. She cursed the neigh- 7 borhood, she cursed the country, she cursed my father, and of course she cursed us kids, swore that we had run our gums to our idiot friends and they had done it.

And this is where the tale should end, right? Wasn't as if there was going to be 8 any "C.S.I."-style investigation or anything. Except that a couple of days later I was moaning about the robbery to these guys I was hanging with at that time and they were cursing sympathetically, and out of nowhere it struck me. You know when you get one of those moments of mental clarity? When the nictitating membrane obscuring the world suddenly lifts? That's what happened. I realized that these two dopes I called my friends had done it. They were shaking their heads, mouthing all the right words, but I could see the way they looked at each other, the Raskolnikov glances. I knew.

9   Now, it wasn't like I could publicly denounce these dolts or go to the police. That would have been about as useless as crying. Here's what I did: I asked the main dope to let me use his bathroom (we were in front of his apartment) and while I pretended to piss I unlatched the window. Then we all headed to the park as usual, but I pretended that I'd forgotten something back home. Ran to the dope's apartment, slid open the bathroom window, and in broad daylight wriggled my skinny ass in.

10   Where the hell did I get these ideas? I have not a clue. I guess I was reading way too much *Encyclopedia Brown and the Three Investigators* in those days. And if mine had been a normal neighborhood this is when the cops would have been called and my ass would have been caught burglarizing.

11   The dolt and his family had been in the U.S. all their lives and they had a ton of stuff, a TV in every room, but I didn't have to do much searching. I popped up the dolt's mattress and underneath I found my D. & D. books and most of my mother's money. He had thoughtfully kept it in the same envelope.

12   And that was how I solved the Case of the Stupid Morons. My one and only case.

13   The next day at the park, the dolt announced that someone had broken into his apartment and stolen all his savings. This place is full of thieves, he complained bitterly, and I was, like, No kidding.

14   It took me two days to return the money to my mother. The truth was I was seriously considering keeping it. But in the end the guilt got to me. I guess I was expecting my mother to run around with joy, to crown me her favorite son, to cook me my favorite meal. Nada. I'd wanted a party or at least to see her happy, but there was nothing. Just two hundred and some dollars and fifteen hundred or so miles—that's all there was.

COMPREHENSION

1. What point is Diaz making about his childhood and family life?
2. According to Diaz, what is the role of money in Dominican immigrant life? What function does money serve for his mother?
3. How does Diaz's fascination with fiction and film influence his behavior?

RHETORIC

1. How does Diaz's title reflect the content of the essay?
2. How would you describe Diaz's audience for this essay? How successful is the writer in tailoring his style to this audience? Justify your response.

3. What is Diaz's thesis? Does he state or imply his main idea? Explain.
4. Trace the sequence of narrative events in this essay. What fictive techniques does Diaz rely on to advance the action?
5. Comment on Diaz's use of colloquial language. Point to specific examples. How does this language contribute to the tone of the essay?

WRITING

1. In a narrative essay, describe a time or episode in childhood when the notion of money became apparent to you.
2. Write an essay in which you consider the role of money in your family's life. What values and opinions concerning money did family members instill in you?
3. **Writing an Argument:** Argue for or against the proposition that children have an innate sense of right and wrong. Relate your argument to Diaz's essay.

NETWORKING
Applying Digital and Multimedia Literacies

Comparing Narrative, Argument, and Fiction: Working alone or with another class member, locate (online) the 1999 op-ed article that Diaz, with Edwidge Danticat (see her essay on page 94), published in the *New York Times* concerning the deportation of Haitians and Haitian Dominicans by the Dominican government. How does Diaz's writing—its content, form, structure, and voice—differ when he is telling a story (in "The Money") from when he is making a case (in "The Dominican Republic's War . . .")? How do these modes overlap? For instance, how do Diaz and Danticat use narrative to help drive their op-ed piece? Now locate a Junot Diaz short story either online (text, audio, or video) or at the library. What are some similarities and differences between his fiction and an essay like "The Money"? Share your insights in a brief essay.

The Death of Horatio Alger

Paul Krugman

Paul Krugman (b. 1953), who teaches at Princeton University, received the Nobel Prize for Economics in 2008 for his analysis of trade patterns and economic activity. Raised in the suburbs of New York City, Krugman attended Yale University for two years before transferring to Massachusetts Institute of Technology, where he received his PhD in economics in 1977. Krugman has published many highly specialized texts in economic theory, but also more popular works like Peddling Prosperity *(1994),* The Accidental Theorist: And Other Dispatches from the Dismal Science *(1998), and* The Return of Depression Economics and the Crisis of 2008 *(2008). A frequent contributor to such newspapers and magazines as the* New Republic, Financial Times, *and* Mother Jones, *Krugman currently is an op-ed columnist for the* New York Times. *Known for his trenchant style and oppositional viewpoints, Krugman attempts to make complex economic trends comprehensible to a broad audience. In this essay from the* Nation, *published in 2004, Krugman looks into the causes of economic inequality.*

1   The other day I found myself reading a leftist rag that made outrageous claims about America. It said that we are becoming a society in which the poor tend to stay poor, no matter how hard they work; in which sons are much more likely to inherit the socioeconomic status of their father than they were a generation ago.

2   The name of the leftist rag? *BusinessWeek,* which published an article titled "Waking Up from the American Dream." The article summarizes recent research showing that social mobility in the United States (which was never as high as legend had it) has declined considerably over the past few decades. If you put that research together with other research that shows a drastic increase in income and wealth inequality, you reach an uncomfortable conclusion: America looks more and more like a class-ridden society.

3   And guess what? Our political leaders are doing everything they can to fortify class inequality, while denouncing anyone who complains—or even points out what is happening—as a practitioner of "class warfare."

4   Let's talk first about the facts on income distribution. Thirty years ago we were a relatively middle-class nation. It had not always been thus: Gilded Age America was a highly unequal society, and it stayed that way through the 1920s. During the 1930s and '40s, however, America experienced what the economic historians Claudia Goldin and Robert Margo have dubbed the Great Compression: a drastic narrowing of income gaps, probably as a result of New Deal policies. And the new economic order persisted for more than a generation: Strong unions; taxes on inherited wealth, corporate profits and high incomes; close public scrutiny of corporate management—all helped to keep income gaps relatively small. The economy was hardly egalitarian, but a generation ago the gross inequalities of the 1920s seemed very distant.

5   Now they're back. According to estimates by the economists Thomas Piketty and Emmanuel Saez—confirmed by data from the Congressional Budget Office—between 1973 and 2000 the average real income of the bottom 90 percent of American taxpayers actually fell by 7 percent. Meanwhile, the income of the top 1 percent rose by 148 percent, the income of the top 0.1 percent rose by 343 percent and the income of the top 0.01 percent rose 599 percent. (Those numbers exclude capital gains, so they're not an artifact of the stock-market bubble.) The distribution of income in the United States has gone right back to Gilded Age levels of inequality.

6   Never mind, say the apologists, who churn out papers with titles like that of a 2001 Heritage Foundation piece, "Income Mobility and the Fallacy of Class-Warfare Arguments." America, they say, isn't a caste society—people with high

incomes this year may have low incomes next year and vice versa, and the rou̇.
to wealth is open to all. That's where those commies at *BusinessWeek* come in:
As they point out (and as economists and sociologists have been pointing out for
some time), America actually is more of a caste society than we like to think.
And the caste lines have lately become a lot more rigid.

  ❡ The myth of income mobility has always exceeded the reality: As a general   7
rule, once they've reached their 30s, people don't move up and down the income
ladder very much. Conservatives often cite studies like a 1992 report by Glenn
Hubbard, a Treasury official under the elder Bush who later became chief
economic adviser to the younger Bush, that purport to show large numbers of
Americans moving from low-wage to high-wage jobs during their working lives.
But what these studies measure, as the economist Kevin Murphy put it, is mainly
"the guy who works in the college bookstore and has a real job by his early 30s."
Serious studies that exclude this sort of pseudo-mobility show that inequality in
average incomes over long periods isn't much smaller than inequality in annual
incomes.

  It is true, however, that America was once a place of substantial intergenera-   8
tional mobility: Sons often did much better than their fathers. A classic 1978 survey found that among adult men whose fathers were in the bottom 25 percent of
the population as ranked by social and economic status, 23 percent had made it
into the top 25 percent. In other words, during the first thirty years or so after
World War II, the American dream of upward mobility was a real experience for
many people.

  Now for the shocker: The *BusinessWeek* piece cites a new survey of today's   9
adult men, which finds that this number has dropped to only 10 percent. That is,
over the past generation upward mobility has fallen drastically. Very few children
of the lower class are making their way to even moderate affluence. This goes
along with other studies indicating that rags-to-riches stories have become vanish-
ingly rare, and that the correlation between fathers' and sons' incomes has risen
in recent decades. In modern America, it seems, you're quite likely to stay in the
social and economic class into which you were born.

  BusinessWeek attributes this to the "Wal-Martization" of the economy, the pro-   10
liferation of dead-end, low-wage jobs and the disappearance of jobs that provide
entry to the middle class. That's surely part of the explanation. But public policy
plays a role—and will, if present trends continue, play an even bigger role in the
future.

  Put it this way: Suppose that you actually liked a caste society, and you were   11
seeking ways to use your control of the government to further entrench the
advantages of the haves against the have-nots. What would you do?

  One thing you would definitely do is get rid of the estate tax, so that large   12
fortunes can be passed on to the next generation. More broadly, you would seek
to reduce tax rates both on corporate profits and on unearned income such as
dividends and capital gains, so that those with large accumulated or inherited
wealth could more easily accumulate even more. You'd also try to create tax shelters mainly useful for the rich. And more broadly still, you'd try to reduce tax

390 Chapter 8   Business and Economics

rates on people with high incomes, shifting the burden to the payroll tax and other revenue sources that bear most heavily on people with lower incomes.

13   Meanwhile, on the spending side, you'd cut back on healthcare for the poor, on the quality of public education and on state aid for higher education. This would make it more difficult for people with low incomes to climb out of their difficulties and acquire the education essential to upward mobility in the modern economy.

14   And just to close off as many routes to upward mobility as possible, you'd do everything possible to break the power of unions, and you'd privatize government functions so that well-paid civil servants could be replaced with poorly paid private employees.

15   It all sounds sort of familiar, doesn't it?

16   Where is this taking us? Thomas Piketty, whose work with Saez has transformed our understanding of income distribution, warns that current policies will eventually create "a class of rentiers in the U.S., whereby a small group of wealthy but untalented children controls vast segments of the U.S. economy and penniless, talented children simply can't compete." If he's right—and I fear that he is—we will end up suffering not only from injustice, but from a vast waste of human potential.

17   Goodbye, Horatio Alger. And goodbye, American Dream.

COMPREHENSION

1. What reasons does Krugman give for the creation of a caste society in the United States?
2. Who is Horatio Alger? Why doesn't Krugman explain who he is in his essay?
3. Krugman alludes to the "leftist rag" *BusinessWeek*. What can you infer about the contents and political opinions of this publication?

RHETORIC

1. What is Krugman's claim, and where does he state it most clearly?
2. Comment on the types of evidence that Krugman uses to support his argument. Do you find this evidence to be sufficient and convincing? Why or why not?
3. Krugman's style is quite impersonal. Locate examples of this style, and explain the overall effect.
4. Much of this essay involves comparative analysis. What subjects and ideas does Krugman compare and contrast?
5. Krugman's conclusion is very brief. Do you find it effective? Explain.

WRITING

1. Do you think that your life will be better economically than that of your parents? Write a personal essay in response to this question.

2. Write your own analysis of class inequality in the United States or in another nation that you are familiar with.
3. **Writing an Argument:** Write a rebuttal to Krugman, arguing that the American Dream is still alive and well.

NETWORKING
Applying Digital and Multimedia Literacies

Making a Brochure: Create a brochure titled either "The American Dream Is Alive and Well" or "The Myth of Upward Mobility." Avoiding propaganda or other fallacious forms of argument, make a solid, convincing case. Consider creating or finding visuals to use in this project.

Globalization: The Super-Story

Thomas L. Friedman

Thomas L. Friedman (b. 1953) was born in Minneapolis, Minnesota. He majored in Mediterranean studies at Brandeis University (BA 1975) and received an MA in modern Middle Eastern studies from Oxford University in 1978. As journalist, author, television commentator, and op-ed contributor to the New York Times, *Friedman tries to provide unbiased viewpoints on cultural, political, and economic issues. From 1979 to 1984 he was the* Times *correspondent in Beirut, Lebanon, and subsequently until 1988 served as bureau chief in Jerusalem. His book recounting his 10 years in the Middle East,* From Beirut to Jerusalem *(1983), received the National Book Award for nonfiction. Friedman also has published* The Lexus and the Olive Tree: Understanding Globalization *(2000),* The World Is Flat: A Brief History of the Twenty-First Century *(2005),* Hot, Flat, and Crowded: Why We Need a Green Revolution—And How It Can Renew America *(2008), and a collection of essays,* Longitudes and Attitudes: Explaining the World after September 11 *(2002), which contains the following selection.*

I am a big believer in the idea of the super-story, the notion that we all carry 1 around with us a big lens, a big framework, through which we look at the world, order events, and decide what is important and what is not. The events of 9/11 did not happen in a vacuum. They happened in the context of a new international system—a system that cannot explain everything but *can* explain and connect more things in more places on more days than anything else. That new international system is called globalization. It came together in the late 1980s and replaced the previous international system, the cold war system, which had reigned since the end of World War II. This new system is the lens, the super-story, through which I viewed the events of 9/11.

2   I define globalization as the inexorable integration of markets, transportation systems, and communication systems to a degree never witnessed before—in a way that is enabling corporations, countries, and individuals to reach around the world farther, faster, deeper, and cheaper than ever before, and in a way that is enabling the world to reach into corporations, countries, and individuals farther, faster, deeper, and cheaper than ever before.

3   Several important features of this globalization system differ from those of the cold war system in ways that are quite relevant for understanding the events of 9/11. I examined them in detail in my previous book, *The Lexus and the Olive Tree,* and want to simply highlight them here.

4   The cold war system was characterized by one overarching feature—and that was *division.* That world was a divided-up, chopped-up place, and whether you were a country or a company, your threats and opportunities in the cold war system tended to grow out of who you were divided from. Appropriately, this cold war system was symbolized by a single word—*wall,* the Berlin Wall.

5   The globalization system is different. It also has one overarching feature— and that is *integration.* The world has become an increasingly interwoven place, and today, whether you are a company or a country, your threats and opportunities increasingly derive from who you are connected to. This globalization system is also characterized by a single word—*web,* the World Wide Web. So in the broadest sense we have gone from an international system built around division and walls to a system increasingly built around integration and webs. In the cold war we reached for the hotline, which was a symbol that we were divided but at least two people were in charge—the leaders of the United States and the Soviet Union. In the globalization system we reach for the Internet, which is a symbol that we are all connected and nobody is quite in charge.

6   Everyone in the world is directly or indirectly affected by this new system, but not everyone benefits from it, not by a long shot, which is why the more it becomes diffused, the more it also produces a backlash by people who feel overwhelmed by it, homogenized by it, or unable to keep pace with its demands.

7   The other key difference between the cold war system and the globalization system is how power is structured within them. The cold war system was built primarily around nation-states. You acted on the world in that system through your state. The cold war was a drama of states confronting states, balancing states, and aligning with states. And, as a system, the cold war was balanced at the center by two superstates, two superpowers: the United States and the Soviet Union.

8   The globalization system, by contrast, is built around three balances, which overlap and affect one another. The first is the traditional balance of power between nation-states. In the globalization system, the United States is now the sole and dominant superpower and all other nations are subordinate to it to one degree or another. The shifting balance of power between the United States and other states, or simply between other states, still very much matters for the stability of this system. And it can still explain a lot of the news you read on the front page of the paper, whether it is the news of China balancing Russia, Iran balancing Iraq, or India confronting Pakistan.

The second important power balance in the globalization system is between 9 nation-states and global markets. These global markets are made up of millions of investors moving money around the world with the click of a mouse. I call them the Electronic Herd, and this herd gathers in key global financial centers—such as Wall Street, Hong Kong, London, and Frankfurt—which I call the Supermarkets. The attitudes and actions of the Electronic Herd and the Supermarkets can have a huge impact on nation-states today, even to the point of triggering the downfall of governments. Who ousted Suharto in Indonesia in 1998? It wasn't another state, it was the Supermarkets, by withdrawing their support for, and confidence in, the Indonesian economy. You also will not understand the front page of the newspaper today unless you bring the Supermarkets into your analysis. Because the United States can destroy you by dropping bombs, but the Supermarkets can destroy you by downgrading your bonds. In other words, the United States is the dominant player in maintaining the globalization game board, but it is hardly alone in influencing the moves on that game board.

The third balance that you have to pay attention to—the one that is really the 10 newest of all and the most relevant to the events of 9/11—is the balance between individuals and nation-states. Because globalization has brought down many of the walls that limited the movement and reach of people, and because it has simultaneously wired the world into networks, it gives more power to *individuals* to influence both markets and nation-states than at any other time in history. Whether by enabling people to use the Internet to communicate instantly at almost no cost over vast distances, or by enabling them to use the Web to transfer money or obtain weapons designs that normally would have been controlled by states, or by enabling them to go into a hardware store now and buy a five-hundred-dollar global positioning device, connected to a satellite, that can direct a hijacked airplane—globalization can be an incredible force-multiplier for individuals. Individuals can increasingly act on the world stage directly, unmediated by a state.

So you have today not only a superpower, not only Supermarkets, but also 11 what I call "super-empowered individuals." Some of these super-empowered individuals are quite angry, some of them quite wonderful—but all of them are now able to act much more directly and much more powerfully on the world stage.

Osama bin Laden declared war on the United States in the late 1990s. After he 12 organized the bombing of two American embassies in Africa, the U.S. Air Force retaliated with a cruise missile attack on his bases in Afghanistan as though he were another nation-state. Think about that: on one day in 1998, the United States fired 75 cruise missiles at bin Laden. The United States fired 75 cruise missiles, at $1 million apiece, at a person! That was the first battle in history between a superpower and a super-empowered angry man. September 11 was just the second such battle.

Jody Williams won the Nobel Peace Prize in 1997 for helping to build an inter- 13 national coalition to bring about a treaty outlawing land mines. Although nearly 120 governments endorsed the treaty, it was opposed by Russia, China, and the United States. When Jody Williams was asked, "How did you do that? How did you organize one thousand different citizens' groups and nongovernmental organizations on five continents to forge a treaty that was opposed by the major powers?" she had a very brief answer: "E-mail." Jody Williams used e-mail and the networked world to super-empower herself.

14   Nation-states, and the American superpower in particular, are still hugely important today, but so too now are Supermarkets and super-empowered individuals. You will never understand the globalization system, or the front page of the morning paper—or 9/11—unless you see each as a complex interaction between all three of these actors: states bumping up against states, states bumping up against Supermarkets, and Supermarkets and states bumping up against super-empowered individuals—many of whom, unfortunately, are super-empowered angry men.

COMPREHENSION

1. What is Friedman's "super-story"? How does he define it?
2. What are the main features of globalization? How does globalization differ from the system characterized by the cold war? Explain the "three balances" (paragraphs 8–10) that Friedman writes about.
3. What does Friedman mean by "super-empowered" individuals (paragraph 11)?

RHETORIC

1. What is Friedman's thesis or claim in this essay? Where does it appear?
2. How and why does Friedman create a personal voice as well as a colloquial style in this selection? What is the effect?
3. What definitions does Friedman establish? Are the definitions too abstract, or does he provide sufficient explanations and evidence? Explain.
4. Locate instances of classification and of comparison and contrast. Why does Friedman use these rhetorical strategies? How do the two methods complement each other?
5. Friedman uses several metaphors in this essay. What are they, and how do they function to enhance meaning?
6. Why does the writer discuss 9/11 in the final three paragraphs? What is the effect on the overall message and purpose of the essay?

WRITING

1. In groups of three or four, use Friedman's essay to brainstorm about globalization. Construct a list of ideas and attributes. Using this list, write a definition essay exploring the subject of globalization. Include comparison and contrast or classification, or both, to help organize the essay.
2. Write a personal essay on how you think globalization is affecting your life.
3. **Writing an Argument:** Write a letter to Friedman, either agreeing or disagreeing with his opinions concerning globalization, supporting or refuting his ideas, or offering alternative views.

NETWORKING
Applying Digital and Multimedia Literacies

Crafting a Comment: Like letters to the editors of newspapers, comments on on-line articles and blog posts offer readers a chance to question or otherwise engage with published texts. Approach question 3 under Writing from a more concise angle: Imagine as you craft your response that it will be a comment posted after the article, a comment visible, potentially, to anyone from around the world. Include one or two link(s) to credible articles, data, or Web sites that support your response.

Nickel and Dimed

Barbara Ehrenreich

Barbara Ehrenreich (b. 1941) was born in Butte, Montana. The daughter of working-class parents, she attended Reed College (BA 1963) and Rockefeller University, where she received a PhD in biology in 1968. After deciding not to pursue a career in science, Ehrenreich turned to political causes, using her scientific training to investigate a broad range of social issues. A prolific writer, Ehrenreich has contributed to Time, *the* New Republic, *the* Progressive, *and other magazines. She also has written several books, including* The American Health Empire *(1970),* Complaints and Disorders: The Sexual Politics of Sickness *(1978),* Nickel and Dimed: On (Not) Getting By in America *(2001),* Dancing in the Streets *(2007), and a collection of essays,* This Land Is Their Land: Reports from a Divided Nation *(2008). In the following excerpt from* Nickel and Dimed, *Ehrenreich recounts her experience working for a large cleaning agency.*

I am rested and ready for anything when I arrive at The Maids' office suite Mon- 1 day at 7:30 A.M. I know nothing about cleaning services like this one, which, according to the brochure I am given, has over three hundred franchises nationwide, and most of what I know about domestics in general comes from nineteenth-century British novels and *Upstairs, Downstairs.* Prophetically enough, I caught a re-run of that very show on PBS over the weekend and was struck by how terribly correct the servants looked in their black-and-white uniforms and how much wiser they were than their callow, egotistical masters. We too have uniforms, though they are more oafish than dignified—ill-fitting and in an overloud combination of kelly-green pants and a blinding sunflower-yellow polo shirt. And, as is explained in writing and over the next day and a half of training, we too have a special code of decorum. No smoking anywhere, or at least not within fifteen minutes of arrival at a house. No drinking, eating, or gum chewing in a house. No cursing in a house, even if the owner is not present, and—perhaps to keep us in practice—no obscenities even in the office. So this is Downstairs, is my chirpy first thought. But I have no idea, of course, just how far down these stairs will take me.

2   Forty minutes go by before anyone acknowledges my presence with more than a harried nod. During this time the other employees arrive, about twenty of them, already glowing in their uniforms, and breakfast on the free coffee, bagels, and doughnuts The Maids kindly provides for us. All but one of the others are female, with an average age I would guess in the late twenties, though the range seems to go from prom-fresh to well into the Medicare years. There is a pleasant sort of bustle as people get their breakfasts and fill plastic buckets with rags and bottles of cleaning fluids, but surprisingly little conversation outside of a few references to what people ate (pizza) and drank (Jell-O shots are mentioned) over the weekend. Since the room in which we gather contains only two folding chairs, both of them occupied, the other new girl and I sit cross-legged on the floor, silent and alert, while the regulars get sorted into teams of three or four and dispatched to the day's list of houses. One of the women explains to me that teams do not necessarily return to the same houses week after week, nor do you have any guarantee of being on the same team from one day to the next. This, I suppose, is one of the advantages of a corporate cleaning service to its customers: There are no sticky and possibly guilt-ridden relationships involved, because the customers communicate almost entirely with Tammy, the office manager, or with Ted, the franchise owner and our boss. The advantage to the cleaning person is harder to determine, since the pay compares so poorly to what an independent cleaner is likely to earn—up to $15 an hour, I've heard. While I wait in the inner room, where the phone is and Tammy has her desk, to be issued a uniform, I hear her tell a potential customer on the phone that The Maids charges $25 per person-hour. The company gets $25 and we get $6.65 for each hour we work? I think I must have misheard, but a few minutes later I hear her say the same thing to another inquirer. So the only advantage of working here as opposed to freelancing is that you don't need a clientele or even a car. You can arrive straight from welfare or, in my case, the bus station—fresh off the boat.

3   At last, after all the other employees have sped off in the company's eye-catching green-and-yellow cars, I am led into a tiny closet-sized room off the inner office to learn my trade via videotape. The manager at another maid service where I'd applied had told me she didn't like to hire people who had done cleaning before because they were resistant to learning the company's system, so I prepare to empty my mind of all prior house-cleaning experience. There are four tapes—dusting, bathrooms, kitchen, and vacuuming—each starring an attractive, possibly Hispanic young woman who moves about serenely in obedience to the male voiceover: For vacuuming, begin in the master bedroom; when dusting, begin with the room directly off the kitchen. When you enter a room, mentally divide it into sections no wider than your reach. Begin in the section to your left and, within each section, move from left to right and top to bottom. This way nothing is ever overlooked.

4   I like *Dusting* best, for its undeniable logic and a certain kind of austere beauty. When you enter a house, you spray a white rag with Windex and place it

in the left pocket of your green apron. Another rag, sprayed with disinfectant, goes in the middle pocket, and a yellow rag bearing wood polish in the right-hand pocket. A dry rag, for buffing surfaces, occupies the right-hand pocket of your slacks. Shiny surfaces get Windexed, wood gets wood polish, and everything else is wiped dust-free with disinfectant. Every now and then Ted pops in to watch with me, pausing the video to underscore a particularly dramatic moment: "See how she's working around the vase? That's an accident waiting to happen." If Ted himself were in a video, it would have to be a cartoon, because the only features sketched onto his pudgy face are brown buttonlike eyes and a tiny pug nose; his belly, encased in a polo shirt, overhangs the waistline of his shorts. "You know, all this was figured out with a stopwatch," he tells me with something like pride. When the video warns against oversoaking our rags with cleaning fluids, he pauses it to tell me there's a danger in undersoaking too, especially if it's going to slow me down. "Cleaning fluids are less expensive than your time." It's good to know that *something* is cheaper than my time, or that in the hierarchy of the company's values I rank above Windex.

Vacuuming is the most disturbing video, actually a double feature beginning 5 with an introduction to the special backpack vacuum we are to use. Yes, the vacuum cleaner actually straps onto your back, a chubby fellow who introduces himself as its inventor explains. He suits up, pulling the straps tight across and under his chest and then says proudly into the camera: "See, I *am* the vacuum cleaner." It weighs only ten pounds, he claims, although, as I soon find out, with the attachments dangling from the strap around your waist, the total is probably more like fourteen. What about my petulant and much-pampered lower back? The inventor returns to the theme of human/machine merger: When properly strapped in, we too will be vacuum cleaners, constrained only by the cord that attaches us to an electrical outlet, and vacuum cleaners don't have backaches. Somehow all this information exhausts me, and I watch the second video, which explains the actual procedures for vacuuming, with the detached interest of a cineast. Could the model maid be an actual maid and the model home someone's actual dwelling? And who are these people whose idea of decorating is matched pictures of mallard ducks in flight and whose house is perfectly characterless and pristine even before the model maid sets to work?

At first I find the videos on kitchens and bathrooms baffling, and it takes me 6 several minutes to realize why: There is no *water,* or almost no water, involved. I was taught to clean by my mother, a compulsive housekeeper who employed water so hot you needed rubber gloves to get into it and in such Niagara-like quantities that most microbes were probably crushed by the force of it before the soap suds had a chance to rupture their cell walls. But germs are never mentioned in the videos provided by The Maids. Our antagonists exist entirely in the visible world—soap scum, dust, counter crud, dog hair, stains, and smears—and are to be attacked by damp rag or, in hard-core cases, by Dobie (the brand of plastic scouring pad we use). We scrub only to remove impurities that might be detectable to a customer by hand or by eye; otherwise our only job is to wipe. Nothing is said about the possibility of transporting bacteria, by rag or by hand, from bathroom to kitchen or even from one house to the next. It is the "cosmetic touches" that the videos emphasize and that Ted, when he wanders back into the room, continually directs my eye to. Fluff up all throw pillows and arrange them symmetrically. Brighten up stainless steel sinks with baby oil. Leave all spice jars, shampoos, etc., with their labels facing outward. Comb out the fringes of Persian carpets with a pick. Use the vacuum cleaner to create a special, fernlike pattern in the carpets. The loose ends of toilet paper and paper towel rolls have to be given a special fold (the same one you'll find in hotel bathrooms). "Messes" of loose paper, clothing, or toys are to be stacked into "neat messes." Finally, the house is to be sprayed with the cleaning service's signature floral-scented air freshener, which will signal to the owners, the moment they return home, that, yes, their house has been "cleaned."

7   After a day's training, I am judged fit to go out with a team, where I soon discover that life is nothing like the movies, at least not if the movie is *Dusting*. For one thing, compared with our actual pace, the training videos were all in slow motion. We do not walk to the cars with our buckets full of cleaning fluids and utensils in the morning, we run, and when we pull up to a house, we run with our buckets to the door. Liza, a good-natured woman in her thirties who is my first team leader, explains that we are given only so many minutes per house, ranging from under sixty for a 1½-bathroom apartment to two hundred or more for a multibathroom "first timer." I'd like to know why anybody worries about Ted's time limits if we're being paid by the hour but hesitate to display anything that might be interpreted as attitude. As we get to each house, Liza assigns our tasks, and I cross my fingers to ward off bathrooms and vacuuming. Even dusting, though, gets aerobic under pressure, and after about an hour of it—reaching to get door tops, crawling along floors to wipe baseboards, standing on my bucket to attack the higher shelves—I wouldn't mind sitting down with a tall glass of water. But as soon as you complete your assigned task, you report to the team leader to be assigned to help someone else. Once or twice, when the normal process of evaporation is deemed too slow, I am assigned to dry a scrubbed floor by putting rags under my feet and skating around on it. Usually, by the time I get out to the car and am dumping the dirty water used on floors and wringing out rags, the rest of the team is already in the car with the motor running. Liza assures me that they've never left anyone behind at a house, not even, presumably, a very new person whom nobody knows.

8   In my interview, I had been promised a thirty-minute lunch break, but this turns out to be a five-minute pit stop at a convenience store, if that. I bring my own sandwich—the same turkey breast and cheese every day—as do a couple of the others; the rest eat convenience store fare, a bagel or doughnut salvaged from our free breakfast, or nothing at all. The two older married women I'm teamed up with eat best—sandwiches and fruit. Among the younger women, lunch consists of a slice of pizza, a "pizza pocket" (a roll of dough surrounding some pizza sauce), or a small bag of chips. Bear in mind we are not office workers, sitting around idling at the basal metabolic rate. A poster on the wall in the office cheerily displays the number of calories burned per minute at our various tasks, ranging from

about 3.5 for dusting to 7 for vacuuming. If you assume an average of 5 calories per minute in a seven-hour day (eight hours minus time for travel between houses), you need to be taking in 2,100 calories in addition to the resting minimum of, say, 900 or so. I get pushy with Rosalie, who is new like me and fresh from high school in a rural northern part of the state, about the meagerness of her lunches, which consist solely of Doritos—a half-bag from the day before or a freshly purchased small-sized bag. She just didn't have anything in the house, she says (though she lives with her boyfriend and his mother), and she certainly doesn't have any money to buy lunch, as I find out when I offer to fetch her a soda from a Quik Mart and she has to admit she doesn't have eighty-nine cents. I treat her to the soda, wishing I could force her, mommylike, to take milk instead. So how does she hold up for an eight- or even nine-hour day? "Well," she concedes, "I get dizzy sometimes."

How poor are they, my coworkers? The fact that anyone is working this job at all can be taken as prima facie evidence of some kind of desperation or at least a history of mistakes and disappointments, but it's not for me to ask. In the prison movies that provide me with a mental guide to comportment, the new guy doesn't go around shaking hands and asking, "Hi there, what are you in for?" So I listen, in the cars and when we're assembled in the office, and learn, first, that no one seems to be homeless. Almost everyone is embedded in extended families or families artificially extended with housemates. People talk about visiting grandparents in the hospital or sending birthday cards to a niece's husband; single mothers live with their own mothers or share apartments with a coworker or boyfriend. Pauline, the oldest of us, owns her own home, but she sleeps on the living room sofa, while her four grown children and three grandchildren fill up the bedrooms. 9

But although no one, apparently, is sleeping in a car, there are signs, even at the beginning, of real difficulty if not actual misery. Half-smoked cigarettes are returned to the pack. There are discussions about who will come up with fifty cents for a toll and whether Ted can be counted on for prompt reimbursement. One of my teammates gets frantic about a painfully impacted wisdom tooth and keeps making calls from our houses to try to locate a source of free dental care. When my—or, I should say, Liza's—team discovers there is not a single Dobie in our buckets, I suggest that we stop at a convenience store and buy one rather than drive all the way back to the office. But it turns out I haven't brought any money with me and we cannot put together $2 between the four of us. 10

The Friday of my first week at The Maids is unnaturally hot for Maine in early September—95 degrees, according to the digital time-and-temperature displays offered by banks that we pass. I'm teamed up with the sad-faced Rosalie and our leader, Maddy, whose sullenness, under the circumstances, is almost a relief after Liza's relentless good cheer. Liza, I've learned, is the highest-ranking cleaner, a sort of supervisor really, and said to be something of a snitch, but Maddy, a single mom of maybe twenty-seven or so, has worked for only three months and broods about her child care problems. Her boyfriend's sister, she tells me on the drive to our first house, watches her eighteen-month-old for $50 a week, which is a stretch 11 on The Maids' pay, plus she doesn't entirely trust the sister, but a real day care center could be as much as $90 a week. After polishing off the first house, no problem, we grab "lunch"—Doritos for Rosalie and a bag of Pepperidge Farm Goldfish for Maddy—and head out into the exurbs for what our instruction sheet warns is a five-bathroom spread and a first-timer to boot. Still, the size of the place makes us pause for a moment, buckets in hand, before searching out an appropriately humble entrance. It sits there like a beached ocean liner, the prow cutting through swells of green turf, windows without number. "Well, well," Maddy says, reading the owner's name from our instruction sheet. "Mrs. W. and her big-ass house. I hope she's going to give us lunch."

12   Mrs. W. is not in fact happy to see us, grimacing with exasperation when the black nanny ushers us into the family room or sunroom or den or whatever kind of specialized space she is sitting in. After all, she already has the nanny, a cook-like person, and a crew of men doing some sort of finishing touches on the construction to supervise. No, she doesn't want to take us around the house, because she already explained everything to the office on the phone, but Maddy stands there, with Rosalie and me behind her, until she relents. We are to move everything on all surfaces, she instructs during the tour, and get underneath and be sure to do every bit of the several miles, I calculate, of baseboards. And be mindful of the baby, who's napping and can't have cleaning fluids of any kind near her.

13   Then I am let loose to dust. In a situation like this, where I don't even know how to name the various kinds of rooms, The Maids' special system turns out to be a lifesaver. All I have to do is keep moving from left to right, within rooms and between rooms, trying to identify landmarks so I don't accidentally do a room or a hallway twice. Dusters get the most complete biographical overview, due to the necessity of lifting each object and tchotchke individually, and I learn that Mrs. W. is an alumna of an important women's college, now occupying herself by monitoring her investments and the baby's bowel movements. I find special charts for this latter purpose, with spaces for time of day, most recent fluid intake, consistency, and color. In the master bedroom, I dust a whole shelf of books on pregnancy, breastfeeding, the first six months, the first year, the first two years—and I wonder what the child care–deprived Maddy makes of all this. Maybe there's been some secret division of the world's women into breeders and drones, and those at the maid level are no longer supposed to be reproducing at all. Maybe this is why our office manager, Tammy, who was once a maid herself, wears inch-long fake nails and tarty little outfits—to show she's advanced to the breeder caste and can't be sent out to clean anymore.

14   It is hotter inside than out, un-air-conditioned for the benefit of the baby, I suppose, but I do all right until I encounter the banks of glass doors that line the side and back of the ground floor. Each one has to be Windexed, wiped, and buffed—inside and out, top to bottom, left to right, until it's as streakless and invisible as a material substance can be. Outside, I can see the construction guys knocking back Gatorade, but the rule is that no fluid or food item can touch a maid's lips when she's inside a house. Now, sweat, even in unseemly quantities, is nothing new to me. I live in a subtropical area where even the inactive can expect to be

moist nine months out of the year. I work out, too, in my normal life and take a certain macho pride in the *V*s of sweat that form on my T-shirt after ten minutes or more on the StairMaster. But in normal life fluids lost are immediately replaced. Everyone in yuppie-land—airports, for example—looks like a nursing baby these days, inseparable from their plastic bottles of water. Here, however, I sweat without replacement or pause, not in individual drops but in continuous sheets of fluid soaking through my polo shirt, pouring down the backs of my legs. The eyeliner I put on in the morning—vain twit that I am—has long since streaked down onto my cheeks, and I could wring my braid out if I wanted to. Working my way through the living room(s), I wonder if Mrs. W. will ever have occasion to realize that every single doodad and *objet* through which she expresses her unique, individual self is, from another vantage point, only an obstacle between some thirsty person and a glass of water.

When I can find no more surfaces to wipe and have finally exhausted the sup- 15 ply of rooms, Maddy assigns me to do the kitchen floor. OK, except that Mrs. W. is *in* the kitchen, so I have to go down on my hands and knees practically at her feet. No, we don't have sponge mops like the one I use in my own house; the hands-and-knees approach is a definite selling point for corporate cleaning services like The Maids. "We clean floors the old-fashioned way—*on our hands and knees*" (emphasis added), the brochure for a competing firm boasts. In fact, whatever advantages there may be to the hands-and-knees approach—you're closer to your work, of course, and less likely to miss a grimy patch—are undermined by the artificial drought imposed by The Maids' cleaning system. We are instructed to use less than half a small bucket of lukewarm water for a kitchen and all adjacent scrubbable floors (breakfast nooks and other dining areas), meaning that within a few minutes we are doing nothing more than redistributing the dirt evenly around the floor. There are occasional customer complaints about the cleanliness of our floors—for example, from a man who wiped up a spill on his freshly "cleaned" floor only to find the paper towel he employed for this purpose had turned gray. A mop and a full bucket of hot soapy water would not only get a floor cleaner but would be a lot more dignified for the person who does the cleaning. But it is this primal posture of submission—and of what is ultimately anal accessibility—that seems to gratify the consumers of maid services.

I don't know, but Mrs. W.'s floor is hard—stone, I think, or at least a stonelike 16 substance—and we have no knee pads with us today. I had thought in my middle-class innocence that knee pads were one of Monica Lewinsky's prurient fantasies, but no, they actually exist, and they're usually a standard part of our equipment. So here I am on my knees, working my way around the room like some fanatical penitent crawling through the stations of the cross, when I realize that Mrs. W. is staring at me fixedly—so fixedly that I am gripped for a moment by the wild possibility that I may have once given a lecture at her alma mater and she's trying to figure out where she's seen me before. If I were recognized, would I be fired? Would she at least be inspired to offer me a drink of water? Because I have decided that if water is actually offered, I'm taking it, rules or no rules, and if word of this infraction gets back to Ted, I'll just say I thought it would be rude to refuse.

Not to worry, though. She's just watching that I don't leave out some stray square inch, and when I rise painfully to my feet again, blinking through the sweat, she says, "Could you just scrub the floor in the entryway while you're at it?"

17   I rush home to the Blue Haven at the end of the day, pull down the blinds for privacy, strip off my uniform in the kitchen—the bathroom being too small for both a person and her discarded clothes—and stand in the shower for a good ten minutes, thinking all this water is *mine.* I have paid for it, in fact, I have earned it. I have gotten through a week at The Maids without mishap, injury, or insurrection. My back feels fine, meaning I'm not feeling it at all; even my wrists, damaged by carpal tunnel syndrome years ago, are issuing no complaints. Coworkers warned me that the first time they donned the backpack vacuum they felt faint, but not me. I am strong and I am, more than that, good. Did I toss my bucket of filthy water onto Mrs. W.'s casual white summer outfit? No. Did I take the wand of my vacuum cleaner and smash someone's Chinese porcelain statues or Hummel figurines? Not once. I was at all times cheerful, energetic, helpful, and as competent as a new hire can be expected to be. If I can do one week, I can do another, and might as well, since there's never been a moment for job-hunting. The 3:30 quitting time turns out to be a myth; often we don't return to the office until 4:30 or 5:00. And what did I think? That I was going to go out to interviews in my soaked and stinky postwork condition? I decide to reward myself with a sunset walk on Old Orchard Beach.

18   On account of the heat, there are still a few actual bathers on the beach, but I am content to sit in shorts and T-shirt and watch the ocean pummel the sand. When the sun goes down I walk back into the town to find my car and am amazed to hear a sound I associate with cities like New York and Berlin. There's a couple of Peruvian musicians playing in the little grassy island in the street near the pier, and maybe fifty people—locals and vacationers—have gathered around, offering their bland end-of-summer faces to the sound. I edge my way through the crowd and find a seat where I can see the musicians up close—the beautiful young guitarist and the taller man playing the flute. What are they doing in this rinky-dink blue-collar resort, and what does the audience make of this surprise visit from the dark-skinned South? The melody the flute lays out over the percussion is both utterly strange and completely familiar, as if it had been imprinted in the minds of my own peasant ancestors centuries ago and forgotten until this very moment. Everyone else seems to be as transfixed as I am. The musicians wink and smile at each other as they play, and I see then that they are the secret emissaries of a worldwide lower-class conspiracy to snatch joy out of degradation and filth. When the song ends, I give them a dollar, the equivalent of about ten minutes of sweat.

COMPREHENSION

1. Why do women work for The Maids when they could earn more money as independent cleaners? How does Ehrenreich distinguish her cleaning practices from her coworkers'? Why do the maids emphasize "cosmetic touches" (paragraph 6)?

2. Describe the plight of Ehrenreich's coworkers. What "signs . . . of real difficulty if not actual misery" (paragraph 10) does she detect? What, if anything, does she do to help them?
3. Who is Mrs. W.? What is her lifestyle like, and what does she expect of the maids? How does she treat Ehrenreich?

RHETORIC

1. How does Ehrenreich structure her narrative? How much time elapses? What elements of conflict develop? What transitional devices does she employ to unify the action?
2. Where does the writer employ description, and for what purpose? What descriptive details seem most striking to you? How, for example, does Ehrenreich bring her co-workers and Mrs. W. to life?
3. Identify those instances where the writer uses process analysis and comparison and contrast to organize her essay. Why does she select these strategies?
4. Explain the tone of this selection. What elements of irony and sarcasm do you detect?
5. Do you think this essay provides a straightforward account of Ehrenreich's experience working for The Maids, or does she have an argumentative point? Justify your response.
6. How does the writer conclude this selection? What elements in the last paragraph capture the main purpose behind her account?

WRITING

1. Write a narrative and descriptive essay of a job you have held that involved menial labor. Establish a time frame. Describe any colleagues who worked with you. Have a thesis or an argument that you either state explicitly or permit to emerge from the account.
2. Compare and contrast a bad job that you have held and a job that provided you with a degree of satisfaction.
3. **Writing an Argument:** In *Nickel and Dimed,* Ehrenreich set out to find minimum-wage jobs in several parts of the United States, including a Wal-Mart in Minnesota and a restaurant in Florida. However, she knew at the outset that these jobs were temporary and that she had the luxury of going back to her comfortable life and her career as a writer and activist. Argue for or against the proposition that Ehrenreich was being unethical and exploitative in her behavior. Refer to this selection to support your position.

NETWORKING
Applying Digital and Multimedia Literacies

Examining Comments on a Blog: Find Barbara Ehrenreich's blog and locate the 2009 entry "Rich Get Poorer, Poor Disappear." After reading the entry itself at least twice, go through the comments. How many, and which commenters, make valuable contributions to the conversation? How many, and which do not? Based on your findings, what makes a good blog comment? Do you think blog comments should be moderated by the blog's author? Why or why not?

Why the Rich Are Getting Richer
and the Poor, Poorer

Robert Reich

Robert Reich (b. 1946) is a professor of Public Policy at the University of California at Berkeley. He served as secretary of labor in the first Clinton administration and, before that, as a professor of economics at Harvard University. He has written numerous books on economics and has been a prominent lecturer for a dozen years. His books include The Next American Frontier *(1983) and* The Work of Nations *(1991), which takes its title from Adam Smith's classic work on economics* The Wealth of Nations, *written in 1776. Reich is known for his ability to "think outside the box," in other words, to see things from a unique and original perspective. Here he warns of what exists—perhaps in front of our very noses—but that we are too caught up in the moment to consider.*

The division of labor is limited by the extent of the market.
        —*Adam Smith,* An Inquiry into the Nature and Causes
                    of the Wealth of Nations *(1776)*

1   Regardless of how your job is officially classified (manufacturing, service, managerial, technical, secretarial, and so on), or the industry in which you work (automotive, steel, computer, advertising, finance, food processing), your real competitive position in the world economy is coming to depend on the function you perform in it. Herein lies the basic reason why incomes are diverging. The fortunes of routine producers are declining. In-person servers are also becoming poorer, although their fates are less clear-cut. But symbolic analysts—who solve, identify, and broker new problems—are, by and large, succeeding in the world economy.

2   All Americans used to be in roughly the same economic boat. Most rose or fell together as the corporations in which they were employed, the industries comprising such corporations, and the national economy as a whole became more productive—or languished. But national borders no longer define our economic fates. We are now in different boats, one sinking rapidly, one sinking more slowly, and the third rising steadily.

3   The boat containing routine producers is sinking rapidly. Recall that by mid-century routine production workers in the United States were paid relatively well. The giant pyramidlike organizations at the core of each major industry coordinated their prices and investments—avoiding the harsh winds of competition and thus maintaining healthy earnings. Some of these earnings, in turn, were reinvested in new plants and equipment (yielding ever-larger-scale economies); another portion went

to top managers and investors. But a large and increasing portion went to middle managers and production workers. Work stoppages posed such a threat to high-volume production that organized labor was able to exact an ever-larger premium for its cooperation. And the pattern of wages established within the core corporations influenced the pattern throughout the national economy. Thus the growth of a relatively affluent middle class, able to purchase all the wondrous things produced in high volume by the core corporations.

But, as has been observed, the core is rapidly breaking down into global webs 4 which earn their largest profits from clever problem-solving, -identifying, and brokering. As the costs of transporting standard things and of communicating information about them continue to drop, profit margins on high-volume, standardized production are thinning, because there are few barriers to entry. Modern factories and state-of-the-art machinery can be installed almost anywhere on the globe. Routine producers in the United States, then, are in direct competition with millions of routine producers in other nations. Twelve thousand people are added to the world's population every hour, most of whom, eventually, will happily work for a small fraction of the wages of routine producers in America.[1]

The consequence is clearest in older, heavy industries, where high-volume, 5 standardized production continues its ineluctable move to where labor is cheapest and most accessible around the world. Thus, for example, the Maquiladora factories clustered along the Mexican side of the U.S. border in the sprawling shanty towns of Tijuana, Mexicali, Nogales, Agua Prieta, and Ciudad Juárez—factories owned mostly by Americans, but increasingly by Japanese—in which more than a half million routine producers assemble parts into finished goods to be shipped into the United States.

The same story is unfolding worldwide. Until the late 1970s, AT&T had de- 6 pended on routine producers in Shreveport, Louisiana, to assemble standard telephones. It then discovered that routine producers in Singapore would perform the same tasks at a far lower cost. Facing intense competition from other global webs, AT&T's strategic brokers felt compelled to switch. So in the early 1980s they stopped hiring routine producers in Shreveport and began hiring cheaper routine producers in Singapore. But under this kind of pressure for ever lower high-volume production costs, today's Singaporean can easily end up as yesterday's Louisianan. By the late 1980s, AT&T's strategic brokers found that routine producers in Thailand were eager to assemble telephones for a small fraction of the wages of routine producers in Singapore. Thus, in 1989, AT&T stopped hiring Singaporeans to make telephones and began hiring even cheaper routine producers in Thailand.

---

[1]The reader should note, of course, that lower wages in other areas of the world are of no particular attraction to global capital unless workers there are sufficiently productive to make the labor cost of producing *each unit* lower there than in higher-wage regions. Productivity in many low-wage areas of the world has improved due to the ease with which state-of-the-art factories and equipment can be installed there.

7   The search for ever lower wages has not been confined to heavy industry. Routine data processing is equally footloose. Keypunch operators located anywhere around the world can enter data into computers, linked by satellite or transoceanic fiber-optic cable, and take it out again. As the rates charged by satellite networks continue to drop, and as more satellites and fiber-optic cables become available (reducing communication costs still further), routine data processors in the United States find themselves in ever more direct competition with their counterparts abroad, who are often eager to work for far less.

8   By 1990, keypunch operators in the United States were earning, at most, $6.50 per hour. But keypunch operators throughout the rest of the world were willing to work for a fraction of this. Thus, many potential American data-processing jobs were disappearing, and the wages and benefits of the remaining ones were in decline. Typical was Saztec International, a $20-million-a-year data-processing firm headquartered in Kansas City, whose American strategic brokers contracted with routine data processors in Manila and with American-owned firms that needed such data-processing services. Compared with the average Philippine income of $1,700 per year, data-entry operators working for Saztec earn the princely sum of $2,650. The remainder of Saztec's employees were American problem-solvers and -identifiers, searching for ways to improve the worldwide system and find new uses to which it could be put.[2]

9   By 1990, American Airlines was employing over 1,000 data processors in Barbados and the Dominican Republic to enter names and flight numbers from used airline tickets (flown daily to Barbados from airports around the United States) into a giant computer bank located in Dallas. Chicago publisher R. R. Donnelley was sending entire manuscripts to Barbados for entry into computers in preparation for printing. The New York Life Insurance Company was dispatching insurance claims to Castleisland, Ireland, where routine producers, guided by simple directions, entered the claims and determined the amounts due, then instantly transmitted the computations back to the United States. (When the firm advertised in Ireland for twenty-five data-processing jobs, it received six hundred applications.) And McGraw-Hill was processing subscription renewal and marketing information for its magazines in nearby Galway. Indeed, literally millions of routine workers around the world were receiving information, converting it into computer-readable form, and then sending it back—at the speed of electronic impulses—whence it came.

10   The simple coding of computer software has also entered into world commerce. India, with a large English-speaking population of technicians happy to do routine programming cheaply, is proving to be particularly attractive to global webs in need of this service. By 1990, Texas Instruments maintained a software development facility in Bangalore, linking fifty Indian programmers by satellite to TI's Dallas headquarters. Spurred by this and similar ventures, the

[2]John Maxwell Hamilton, "A Bit Player Buys into the Computer Age," *New York Times Business World,* December 3, 1989, p. 14.

Indian government was building a teleport in Poona, intended to make it easier and less expensive for many other firms to send their routine software design specifications for coding.[3]

This shift of routine production jobs from advanced to developing nations is a great boon to many workers in such nations who otherwise would be jobless or working for much lower wages. These workers, in turn, now have more money with which to purchase symbolic-analytic services from advanced nations (often embedded within all sorts of complex products). The trend is also beneficial to everyone around the world who can now obtain high-volume, standardized products (including information and software) more cheaply than before. 11

But these benefits do not come without certain costs. In particular the burden is borne by those who no longer have good-paying routine production jobs within advanced economies like the United States. Many of these people used to belong to unions or at least benefited from prevailing wage rates established in collective bargaining agreements. But as the old corporate bureaucracies have flattened into global webs, bargaining leverage has been lost. Indeed, the tacit national bargain is no more. 12

Despite the growth in the number of new jobs in the United States, union membership has withered. In 1960, 35 percent of all nonagricultural workers in America belonged to a union. But by 1980 that portion had fallen to just under a quarter, and by 1989 to about 17 percent. Excluding government employees, union membership was down to 13.4 percent.[4] This was a smaller proportion even than in the early 1930s, before the National Labor Relations Act created a legally protected right to labor representation. The drop in membership has been accompanied by a growing number of collective bargaining agreements to freeze wages at current levels, reduce wage levels of entering workers, or reduce wages overall. This is an important reason why the long economic recovery that began in 1982 produced a smaller rise in unit labor costs than any of the eight recoveries since World War II—the low rate of unemployment during its course notwithstanding. 13

Routine production jobs have vanished fastest in traditional unionized industries (autos, steel, and rubber, for example), where average wages have kept up with inflation. This is because the jobs of older workers in such industries are protected by seniority; the youngest workers are the first to be laid off. Faced with a choice of cutting wages or cutting the number of jobs, a majority of union members (secure in the knowledge that there are many who are junior to them who will be laid off first) often have voted for the latter. 14

Thus the decline in union membership has been most striking among young men entering the work force without a college education. In the early 1950s, more 15

[3]Udayan Gupta, "U.S.-Indian Satellite Link Stands to Cut Software Costs," *Wall Street Journal,* March 6, 1989, p. B2.
[4]*Statistical Abstract of the United States* (Washington, D.C.: U.S. Government Printing Office, 1989), p. 416, table 684.

than 40 percent of this group joined unions; by the late 1980s, less than 20 percent (if public employees are excluded, less than 10 percent).[5] In steelmaking, for example, although many older workers remained employed, almost half of all routine steelmaking jobs in America vanished between 1974 and 1988 (from 480,000 to 260,000). Similarly with automobiles: During the 1980s, the United Auto Workers lost 500,000 members—one-third of their total at the start of the decade. General Motors alone cut 150,000 American production jobs during the 1980s (even as it added employment abroad). Another consequence of the same phenomenon: The gap between the average wages of unionized and nonunionized workers widened dramatically—from 14.6 percent in 1973 to 20.4 percent by the end of the 1980s.[6] The lesson is clear. If you drop out of high school or have no more than a high school diploma, do not expect a good routine production job to be awaiting you.

16   Also vanishing are lower- and middle-level management jobs involving routine production. Between 1981 and 1986, more than 780,000 foremen, supervisors, and section chiefs lost their jobs through plant closings and layoffs.[7] Large numbers of assistant division heads, assistant directors, assistant managers, and vice presidents also found themselves jobless. GM shed more than 40,000 white-collar employees and planned to eliminate another 25,000 by the mid-1990s.[8] As America's core pyramids metamorphosed into global webs, many middle-level routine producers were as obsolete as routine workers on the line.

17   As has been noted, foreign-owned webs are hiring some Americans to do routine production in the United States. Philips, Sony, and Toyota factories are popping up all over—to the self-congratulatory applause of the nation's governors and mayors, who have lured them with promises of tax abatements and new sewers, among other amenities. But as these ebullient politicians will soon discover, the foreign-owned factories are highly automated and will become far more so in years to come. Routine production jobs account for a small fraction of the cost of producing most items in the United States and other advanced nations, and this fraction will continue to decline sharply as computer-integrated robots take over. In 1977, it took routine producers thirty-five hours to assemble an automobile in the United States; it is estimated that by the mid-1990s, Japanese-owned factories in America will be producing finished automobiles using only eight hours of a routine producer's time.[9]

18   The productivity and resulting wages of American workers who run such robotic machinery may be relatively high, but there may not be many such jobs to

[5]Calculations from Current Population Surveys by L. Katz and A. Revenga, "Changes in the Structure of Wages: U.S. and Japan," National Bureau of Economic Research, September 1989.

[6]U.S. Department of Commerce, Bureau of Labor Statistics, "Wages of Unionized and Nonunionized Workers," various issues.

[7]U.S. Department of Labor, Bureau of Labor Statistics, "Reemployment Increases among Displaced Workers," *BLS News,* USDL 86-414, October 14, 1986, table 6.

[8]*Wall Street Journal,* February 16, 1990, p. A5.

[9]Figures from the International Motor Vehicles Program, Massachusetts Institute of Technology, 1989.

go around. A case in point: In the late 1980s, Nippon Steel joined with America's ailing Inland Steel to build a new $400 million cold-rolling mill fifty miles west of Gary, Indiana. The mill was celebrated for its state-of-the-art technology, which cut the time to produce a coil of steel from twelve days to about one hour. In fact, the entire plant could be run by a small team of technicians, which became clear when Inland subsequently closed two of its old cold-rolling mills, laying off hundreds of routine workers. Governors and mayors take note: Your much-ballyhooed foreign factories may end up employing distressingly few of your constituents.

Overall, the decline in routine jobs has hurt men more than women. This is [19] because the routine production jobs held by men in high-volume metal bending manufacturing industries had paid higher wages than the routine production jobs held by women in textiles and data processing. As both sets of jobs have been lost, American women in routine production have gained more equal footing with American men—equally poor footing, that is. This is a major reason why the gender gap between male and female wages began to close during the 1980s.

The second of the three boats, carrying in-person servers, is sinking as well, but [20] somewhat more slowly and unevenly. Most in-person servers are paid at or just slightly above the minimum wage and many work only part-time, with the result that their take-home pay is modest, to say the least. Nor do they typically receive all the benefits (health care, life insurance, disability, and so forth) garnered by routine producers in large manufacturing corporations or by symbolic analysts affiliated with the more affluent threads of global webs.[10] In-person servers are sheltered from the direct effects of global competition and, like everyone else, benefit from access to lower-cost products from around the world. But they are not immune to its indirect effects.

For one thing, in-person servers increasingly compete with former routine [21] production workers, who, no longer able to find well-paying routine production jobs, have few alternatives but to seek in-person service jobs. The Bureau of Labor Statistics estimates that of the 2.8 million manufacturing workers who lost their jobs during the early 1980s, fully one-third were rehired in service jobs paying at least 20 percent less.[11] In-person servers must also compete with high school graduates and dropouts who years before had moved easily into routine production jobs but no longer can. And if demographic predictions about the American work force in the first decades of the twenty-first century are correct (and they are likely to be, since most of the people who will comprise the work force are already identifiable), most new entrants into the job market will be black or Hispanic men, or women—groups that in years past have possessed relatively weak technical skills. This will result in an even larger number of people crowding

[10]The growing portion of the American labor force engaged in in-person services, relative to routine production, thus helps explain why the number of Americans lacking health insurance increased by at least 6 million during the 1980s.
[11]U.S. Department of Labor, Bureau of Labor Statistics, "Reemployment Increases among Disabled Workers," October 14, 1986.

into in-person services. Finally, in-person servers will be competing with growing numbers of immigrants, both legal and illegal, for whom in-person services will comprise the most accessible jobs. (It is estimated that between the mid-1980s and the end of the century, about a quarter of all workers entering the American labor force will be immigrants.[12])

22   Perhaps the fiercest competition that in-person servers face comes from labor-saving machinery (much of it invented, designed, fabricated, or assembled in other nations, of course). Automated tellers, computerized cashiers, automatic car washes, robotized vending machines, self-service gasoline pumps, and all similar gadgets substitute for the human beings that customers once encountered. Even telephone operators are fast disappearing, as electronic sensors and voice simulators become capable of carrying on conversations that are reasonably intelligent and always polite. Retail sales workers—among the largest groups of in-person servers—are similarly imperiled. Through personal computers linked to television screens, tomorrow's consumers will be able to buy furniture, appliances, and all sorts of electronic toys from their living rooms—examining the merchandise from all angles, selecting whatever color, size, special features, and price seem most appealing, and then transmitting the order instantly to warehouses from which the selections will be shipped directly to their homes. So, too, with financial transactions, airline and hotel reservations, rental car agreements, and similar contracts, which will be executed between consumers in their homes and computer banks somewhere else on the globe.[13]

23   Advanced economies like the United States will continue to generate sizable numbers of new in-person service jobs, of course, the automation of older ones notwithstanding. For every bank teller who loses her job to an automated teller, three new jobs open for aerobics instructors. Human beings, it seems, have an almost insatiable desire for personal attention. But the intense competition nevertheless ensures that the wages of in-person servers will remain relatively low. In-person servers—working on their own, or else dispersed widely amid many small establishments, filling all sorts of personal-care niches—cannot readily organize themselves into labor unions or create powerful lobbies to limit the impact of such competition.

24   In two respects, demographics will work in favor of in-person servers, buoying their collective boat slightly. First, as has been noted, the rate of growth of the American work force is slowing. In particular, the number of young workers is shrinking. Between 1985 and 1995, the number of the eighteen- to twenty-four-year-olds will have declined by 17.5 percent. Thus, employers will have more incentive to hire and train in-person servers whom they might previously have avoided. But this demographic relief from the competitive pressures will be only temporary. The cumulative procreative energies of the postwar baby-boomers

[12]Federal Immigration and Naturalization Service, *Statistical Yearbook* (Washington, D.C.: U.S. Government Printing Office, 1986, 1987).
[13]See Claudia H. Deutsch, "The Powerful Push for Self-Service," *New York Times,* April 9, 1989, section 3, p. 1.

(born between 1946 and 1964) will result in a new surge of workers by 2010 or thereabouts.[14] And immigration—both legal and illegal—shows every sign of increasing in years to come.

Next, by the second decade of the twenty-first century, the number of Ameri- 25 cans aged sixty-five and over will be rising precipitously, as the babyboomers reach retirement age and live longer. Their life expectancies will lengthen not just because fewer of them will have smoked their way to their graves and more will have eaten better than their parents, but also because they will receive all sorts of expensive drugs and therapies designed to keep them alive—barely. By 2035, twice as many Americans will be elderly as in 1988, and the number of octogenarians is expected to triple. As these decaying baby-boomers ingest all the chemicals and receive all the treatments, they will need a great deal of personal attention. Millions of deteriorating bodies will require nurses, nursing-home operators, hospital administrators, orderlies, home-care providers, hospice aides, and technicians to operate and maintain all the expensive machinery that will monitor and temporarily stave off final disintegration. There might even be a booming market for euthanasia specialists. In-person servers catering to the old and ailing will be in strong demand.[15]

One small problem: the decaying baby-boomers will not have enough money 26 to pay for these services. They will have used up their personal savings years before. Their Social Security payments will, of course, have been used by the government to pay for the previous generation's retirement and to finance much of the budget deficits of the 1980s. Moreover, with relatively fewer young Americans in the population, the supply of housing will likely exceed the demand, with the result that the boomers' major investments—their homes—will be worth less (in inflation-adjusted dollars) when they retire than they planned for. In consequence, the huge cost of caring for the graying boomers will fall on many of the same people who will be paid to care for them. It will be like a great sump pump: In-person servers of the twenty-first century will have an abundance of health-care jobs, but a large portion of their earnings will be devoted to Social Security payments and income taxes, which will in turn be used to pay their salaries. The net result: No real improvement in their standard of living.

The standard of living of in-person servers also depends, indirectly, on the stan- 27 dard of living of the Americans they serve who are engaged in world commerce. To the extent that *these* Americans are richly rewarded by the rest of the world for what they contribute, they will have more money to lavish upon in-person services. Here we find the only form of "trickle-down" economics that has a basis in reality. A waitress in a town whose major factory has just been closed is unlikely to earn a high wage or enjoy much job security; in a swank resort populated by film producers and

---

[14]U.S. Bureau of the Census, Current Population Reports, Series P-23, no. 138, tables 2-1, 4-6. See W. Johnson, A. Packer, et al., *Workforce 2000: Work and Workers for the 21st Century* (Indianapolis: Hudson Institute, 1987).

[15]The Census Bureau estimates that by the year 2000, at least 12 million Americans will work in health services—well over 6 percent of the total work force.

banking moguls, she is apt to do reasonably well. So, too, with nations. In-person servers in Bangladesh may spend their days performing roughly the same tasks as in-person servers in the United States, but have a far lower standard of living for their efforts. The difference comes in the value that their customers add to the world economy.

28   Unlike the boats of routine producers and in-person servers, however, the vessel containing America's symbolic analysts is rising. Worldwide demand for their insights is growing as the ease and speed of communicating them steadily increases. Not every symbolic analyst is rising as quickly or as dramatically as every other, of course; symbolic analysts at the low end are barely holding their own in the world economy. But symbolic analysts at the top are in such great demand worldwide that they have difficulty keeping track of all their earnings. Never before in history has opulence on such a scale been gained by people who have earned it, and done so legally.

29   Among symbolic analysts in the middle range are American scientists and researchers who are busily selling their discoveries to global enterprise webs. They are not limited to American customers. If the strategic brokers in General Motors' headquarters refuse to pay a high price for a new means of making high-strength ceramic engines dreamed up by a team of engineers affiliated with Carnegie Mellon University in Pittsburgh, the strategic brokers of Honda or Mercedes-Benz are likely to be more than willing.

30   So, too, with the insights of America's ubiquitous management consultants, which are being sold for large sums to eager entrepreneurs in Europe and Latin America. Also, the insights of America's energy consultants, sold for even larger sums to Arab sheikhs. American design engineers are providing insights to Olivetti, Mazda, Siemens, and other global webs; American marketers, techniques for learning what worldwide consumers will buy; American advertisers, ploys for ensuring that they actually do. American architects are issuing designs and blueprints for opera houses, art galleries, museums, luxury hotels, and residential complexes in the world's major cities; American commercial property developers, marketing these properties to worldwide investors and purchasers.

31   Americans who specialize in the gentle art of public relations are in demand by corporations, governments, and politicians in virtually every nation. So, too, are American political consultants, some of whom, at this writing, are advising the Hungarian Socialist Party, the remnant of Hungary's ruling Communists, on how to salvage a few parliamentary seats in the nation's first free election in more than forty years. Also at this writing, a team of American agricultural consultants is advising the managers of a Soviet farm collective employing 1,700 Russians eighty miles outside Moscow. As noted, American investment bankers and lawyers specializing in financial circumnavigations are selling their insights to Asians and Europeans who are eager to discover how to make large amounts of money by moving large amounts of money.

32   Developing nations, meanwhile, are hiring American civil engineers to advise on building roads and dams. The present thaw in the Cold War will no doubt expand these opportunities. American engineers from Bechtel (a global firm notable

for having employed both Caspar Weinberger and George Shultz for much larger sums than either earned in the Reagan administration) have begun helping the Soviets design and install a new generation of nuclear reactors. Nations also are hiring American bankers and lawyers to help them renegotiate the terms of their loans with global banks, and Washington lobbyists to help them with Congress, the Treasury, the World Bank, the IMF, and other politically sensitive institutions. In fits of obvious desperation, several nations emerging from communism have even hired American economists to teach them about capitalism.

Almost everyone around the world is buying the skills and insights of Americans 33 who manipulate oral and visual symbols—musicians, sound engineers, film producers, makeup artists, directors, cinematographers, actors and actresses, boxers, scriptwriters, songwriters, and set designers. Among the wealthiest of symbolic analysts are Steven Spielberg, Bill Cosby, Charles Schulz, Eddie Murphy, Sylvester Stallone, Madonna, and other star directors and performers—who are almost as well known on the streets of Dresden and Tokyo as in the Back Bay of Boston. Less well rewarded but no less renowned are the unctuous anchors on Turner Broadcasting's Cable News, who appear daily, via satellite, in places ranging from Vietnam to Nigeria. Vanna White is the world's most-watched game-show hostess. Behind each of these familiar faces is a collection of American problem-solvers, -identifiers, and brokers who train, coach, advise, promote, amplify, direct, groom, represent, and otherwise add value to their talents.[16]

There are also the insights of senior American executives who occupy the 34 world headquarters of global "American" corporations and the national or regional headquarters of global "foreign" corporations. Their insights are duly exported to the rest of the world through the webs of global enterprise. IBM does not export many machines from the United States, for example. Big Blue makes machines all over the globe and services them on the spot. Its prime American exports are symbolic and analytic. From IBM's world headquarters in Armonk, New York, emanate strategic brokerage and related management services bound for the rest of the world. In return, IBM's top executives are generously rewarded.

The most important reason for this expanding world market and increasing global 35 demand for the symbolic and analytic insights of Americans has been the dramatic improvement in worldwide communication and transportation technologies. Designs, instructions, advice, and visual and audio symbols can be communicated more and more rapidly around the globe, with ever greater precision and at ever-lower cost. Madonna's voice can be transported to billions of listeners, with perfect clarity, on digital compact discs. A new invention emanating from engineers in Battelle's laboratory in Columbus, Ohio, can be sent almost anywhere via modem, in a form that will allow others to examine it in three dimensions through enhanced computer graphics. When face-to-face meetings are still

---

[16]In 1989, the entertainment business summoned to the United States $5.5 billion in foreign earnings— making it among the nation's largest export industries, just behind aerospace. U.S. Department of Commerce, International Trade Commission, "Composition of U.S. Exports," various issues.

required—and videoconferencing will not suffice—it is relatively easy for designers, consultants, advisers, artists, and executives to board supersonic jets and, in
a matter of hours, meet directly with their worldwide clients, customers, audiences, and employees.

36   With rising demand comes rising compensation. Whether in the form of licensing fees, fees for service, salaries, or shares in final profits, the economic result is much the same. There are also nonpecuniary rewards. One of the best-kept
secrets among symbolic analysts is that so many of them enjoy their work. In fact,
much of it does not count as work at all, in the traditional sense. The work of routine producers and in-person servers is typically monotonous; it causes muscles
to tire or weaken and involves little independence or discretion. The "work" of
symbolic analysts, by contrast, often involves puzzles, experiments, games, a significant amount of chatter, and substantial discretion over what to do next. Few
routine producers or in-person servers would "work" if they did not need to earn
the money. Many symbolic analysts would "work" even if money were no object.

37 At mid-century, when America was a national market dominated by core pyramid-
shaped corporations, there were constraints on the earnings of people at the highest rungs. First and most obviously, the market for their services was largely limited
to the borders of the nation. In addition, whatever conceptual value they might contribute was small relative to the value gleaned from large scale—and it was dependent on large scale for whatever income it was to summon. Most of the problems to
be identified and solved had to do with enhancing the efficiency of production and
improving the flow of materials, parts, assembly, and distribution. Inventors
searched for the rare breakthrough revealing an entirely new product to be made in
high volume; management consultants, executives, and engineers thereafter tried
to speed and synchronize its manufacture, to better achieve scale efficiencies; advertisers and marketers sought then to whet the public's appetite for the standard
item that emerged. Since white-collar earnings increased with larger scale, there
was considerable incentive to expand the firm; indeed, many of America's core corporations grew far larger than scale economies would appear to have justified.

38   By the 1990s, in contrast, the earnings of symbolic analysts were limited neither by the size of the national market nor by the volume of production of the
firms with which they were affiliated. The marketplace was worldwide, and conceptual value was high relative to value added from scale efficiencies.

39   There had been another constraint on high earnings, which also gave
way by the 1990s. At mid-century, the compensation awarded to top executives and advisers of the largest of America's core corporations could not be
grossly out of proportion to that of low-level production workers. It would be
unseemly for executives who engaged in highly visible rounds of bargaining
with labor unions, and who routinely responded to government requests to
moderate prices, to take home wages and benefits wildly in excess of what
other Americans earned. Unless white-collar executives restrained themselves, moreover, blue-collar production workers could not be expected to
restrain their own demands for higher wages. Unless both groups exercised

restraint, the government could not be expected to forbear from imposing direct controls and regulations.

At the same time, the wages of production workers could not be allowed to 40 sink too low, lest there be insufficient purchasing power in the economy. After all, who would buy all the goods flowing out of American factories if not American workers? This, too, was part of the tacit bargain struck between American managers and their workers.

Recall the oft-repeated corporate platitude of the era about the chief executive's 41 responsibility to carefully weigh and balance the interests of the corporation's disparate stakeholders. Under the stewardship of the corporate statesman, no set of stakeholders—least of all white-collar executives—was to gain a disproportionately large share of the benefits of corporate activity; nor was any stakeholder— especially the average worker—to be left with a share that was disproportionately small. Banal though it was, this idea helped to maintain the legitimacy of the core American corporation in the eyes of most Americans, and to ensure continued economic growth.

But by the 1990s, these informal norms were evaporating, just as (and largely 42 because) the core American corporation was vanishing. The links between top executives and the American production worker were fading: An ever-increasing number of subordinates and contractees were foreign, and a steadily growing number of American routine producers were working for foreign-owned firms. An entire cohort of middle-level managers, who had once been deemed "white collar," had disappeared; and, increasingly, American executives were exporting their insights to global enterprise webs.

As the American corporation itself became a global web almost indistinguish- 43 able from any other, its stakeholders were turning into a large and diffuse group, spread over the world. Such global stakeholders were less visible, and far less noisy, than national stakeholders. And as the American corporation sold its goods and services all over the world, the purchasing power of American workers became far less relevant to its economic survival.

Thus have the inhibitions been removed. The salaries and benefits of America's 44 top executives, and many of their advisers and consultants, have soared to what years before would have been unimaginable heights, even as those of other Americans have declined.

COMPREHENSION

1. To what does the title allude? Why is this allusion significant to the meaning of the title?
2. To whom does Reich refer when he mentions "symbolic analysts"? Regardless of their occupation, what do all symbolic analysts have in common regarding the nature of their work?
3. What has traditionally been the image of and the nature of work among the white-collar workers to whom Reich alludes? Why are they now one of the groups in danger of losing employment opportunities?

RHETORIC

1. Reich uses the central metaphor of the "boat" in describing the state of economics and employment. Why? What connotations are associated with this image in regard to financial security?
2. How does Reich's introduction prepare you for the major themes he addresses in the body of his essay?
3. Examine the section breaks at the start of paragraphs 3, 11, 20, 35, and 37. How does each section relate to the theme of the essay as a whole? What transitional devices does Reich use to bridge one section to the next?
4. Paragraphs 5, 6, 9, and 16 cite specific and detailed examples of the effects of the changing global economy. How does this contribute to conveying Reich's authority regarding the subject he is discussing?
5. Reich describes a dire situation for the American worker. How would you characterize the tone of this description? Is it angry, resigned, impartial, or accusatory? You may use these or any other adjectives as long as you explain your view.
6. Why does Reich open his essay with an epigraph from Adam Smith? What is the relationship of the quotation to the overall theme of the essay? How does the tone of the epigraph contrast with the tone of the title?
7. What is the author's purpose? Is it to inform, to explain, to warn, to enlighten, to offer solutions, or a combination of any of these? Explain your view.

WRITING

1. In a classification essay, describe three areas of academic concentration at your college or university that can help prepare one for a job as a symbolic analyst.
2. In an expository essay, explain whether you believe the discrepancy between high-wage and low-wage workers will increase, decrease, or remain the same. Reference at least one essay from Chapter 1's casebook on class.
3. **Writing an Argument:** In an essay, argue for or against the proposition that as long as one knows which careers command the highest salaries, it is up to the individual to decide whether he or she should pursue a job in those fields.

NETWORKING
Applying Digital and Multimedia Literacies

Participating in a Newsgroup: Join a newsgroup with a special interest in the global economy. Post a general question to its members, asking whether they agree with Reich's analysis of the changing job market. Collect and synthesize the responses.

A Modest Proposal Preventing the Children of Poor People in Ireland from Being a Burden to Their Parents or Country, and for Making Them Beneficial to the Public

Jonathan Swift

Jonathan Swift (1667–1745) is best known as the author of three satires: A Tale of a Tub *(1704),* Gulliver's Travels *(1726), and* A Modest Proposal *(1729). In these satires, Swift pricks the balloon of many of his contemporaries' and our own most cherished prejudices, pomposities, and delusions. He was also a famous churchman, an eloquent spokesman for Irish rights, and a political journalist. The following selection, perhaps the most famous satiric essay in the English language, offers modest advice to a nation suffering from poverty, overpopulation, and political injustice.*

It is a melancholy object to those who walk through this great town or travel in 1 the country, when they see the streets, the roads, and cabin doors, crowded with beggars of the female-sex, followed by three, four, or six children, all in rags and importuning every passenger for an alms. These mothers, instead of being able to work for their honest livelihood, are forced to employ all their time in strolling to beg sustenance for their helpless infants, who, as they grow up, either turn thieves for want of work, or leave their dear native country to fight for the Pretender in Spain, or sell themselves to the Barbadoes.

I think it is agreed by all parties that this prodigious number of children in 2 the arms, or on the backs, or at the heels of their mothers, and frequently of their fathers, is in the present deplorable state of the kingdom a very great additional grievance; and therefore whoever could find out a fair, cheap, and easy method of making these children sound, useful members of the commonwealth would deserve so well of the public as to have his statue set up for a preserver of the nation.

But my intention is very far from being confined to provide only for the children 3 of professed beggars; it is of a much greater extent, and shall take in the whole number of infants at a certain age who are born of parents in effect as little able to support them as those who demand our charity in the streets.

As to my own part, having turned my thoughts for many years upon this 4 important subject, and maturely weighted the several schemes of other projectors, I have always found them grossly mistaken in their computation. It is true, a child just dropped from its dam may be supported by her milk for a solar year, with little other nourishment; at most not above the value of two shillings, which the mother may certainly get, or the value in scraps, by her lawful occupation of begging; and it is exactly at one year old that I propose to provide for them in such a manner as instead of being a charge upon their parents or the parish, or wanting food and raiment for the rest of their lives, they shall on the contrary contribute to the feeding, and partly to the clothing, of many thousands.

5   There is likewise another great advantage in my scheme, that it will prevent those voluntary abortions, and that horrid practice of women murdering their bastard children, alas, too frequent among us, sacrificing the poor innocent babes, I doubt, more to avoid the expense than the shame, which would move tears and pity in the most savage and inhuman breast.

6   The number of souls in this kingdom being usually reckoned one million and a half, of these I calculate there may be about two hundred thousand couples whose wives are breeders; from which number I subtract thirty thousand couples who are able to maintain their own children, although I apprehend there cannot be so many under the present distresses of the kingdom; but this being granted, there will remain an hundred and seventy thousand breeders. I again subtract fifty thousand for those women who miscarry, or whose children die by accident or disease within the year. There only remain an hundred and twenty thousand children of poor parents annually born. The question therefore is, how this number shall be reared and provided for, which, as I have already said, under the present situation of affairs, is utterly impossible by all the methods hitherto proposed. For we can neither employ them in handicraft or agriculture; we neither build houses (I mean in the country) nor cultivate land. They can very seldom pick up a livelihood by stealing till they arrive at six years old, except where they are of towardly parts; although I confess they learn the rudiments much earlier, during which time they can however be looked upon only as probationers, as I have been informed by a principal gentleman in the county of Cavan, who protested to me that he never knew above one or two instances under the age of six, even in a part of the kingdom so renowned for the quickest proficiency in that art.

7   I am assured by our merchants that a boy or girl before twelve years old is no salable commodity; and even when they come to this age they will not yield above three pounds, or three pounds and half a crown at most on the Exchange; which cannot turn to account either to the parents or the kingdom, the charge of nutriment and rags having been at least four times that value.

8   I shall now therefore humbly propose my own thoughts, which I hope will not be liable to the least objection.

9   I have been assured by a very knowing American of my acquaintance in London, that a young healthy child well nursed is at a year old a most delicious, nourishing, and wholesome food, whether stewed, roasted, baked or boiled; and I make no doubt that it will equally serve in a fricassee or a ragout.

I do therefore humbly offer it to public consideration that of the hundred and 10 twenty thousand children, already computed, twenty thousand may be reserved for breed, whereof only one fourth part to be males, which is more than we allow to sheep, black cattle, or swine; and my reason is that these children are seldom the fruits of marriage, a circumstance not much regarded by our savages, therefore one male will be sufficient to serve four females. That the remaining hundred thousand may at a year old be offered in sale to the persons of quality and fortune through the kingdom, always advising the mother to let them suck plentifully in the last month, so as to render them plump and fat for a good table. A child will make two dishes at an entertainment for friends; and when the family dines alone, the fore or hind quarter will make a reasonable dish, and seasoned with a little pepper or salt will be very good boiled on the fourth day, especially in winter.

I have reckoned upon a medium that a child just born will weigh twelve 11 pounds, and in a solar year if tolerably nursed increaseth to twenty-eight pounds.

I grant this food will be somewhat dear, and therefore very proper for land- 12 lords, who, as they have already devoured most of the parents, seem to have the best title to the children.

Infant's flesh will be in season throughout the year, but more plentiful in 13 March, and a little before and after. For we are told by a grave author, an eminent French physician, that fish being a prolific diet, there are more children born in Roman Catholic countries about nine months after Lent than at any other season: therefore, reckoning a year after Lent, the markets will be more glutted than usual, because the number of popish infants is at least three to one in this kingdom; and therefore it will have one other collateral advantage, by lessening the number of Papists among us.

I have already computed the charge of nursing a beggar's child (in which 14 list I reckon all cottagers, laborers, and four fifths of the farmers) to be about two shillings per annum, rags included: and I believe no gentleman would repine to give ten shillings for the carcass of a good fat child, which, as I have said, will make four dishes of excellent nutritive meat, when he hath only some particular friend or his own family to dine with him. Thus the squire will learn to be a good landlord, and grow popular among the tenants; the mother will have eight shillings net profit, and be fit for work till she produces another child.

Those who are more thrifty (as I must confess the times require) may flay 15 the carcass; the skin of which artificially dressed will make admirable gloves for ladies, and summer boots for fine gentlemen.

As to our city of Dublin, shambles may be appointed for this purpose in the 16 most convenient parts of it, and butchers we may be assured will not be wanting; although I rather recommend buying the children alive, and dressing them hot from the knife as we do roasting pigs.

A very worthy person, a true lover of his country, and whose virtues I highly 17 esteem, was lately pleased in discoursing on this matter to offer a refinement upon my scheme. He said that many gentlemen of this kingdom, having of late destroyed their deer, he conceived that the want of venison might be well supplied by the bodies of young lads and maidens, not exceeding fourteen years of age nor under twelve, so great a number of both sexes in every county being now ready to starve for want of work and service; and these to be disposed of by their parents, if alive, or otherwise by their nearest relations. But with due deference to so excellent a friend and so deserving a patriot, I cannot be altogether in his sentiments; for as to the males, my American acquaintance assured me from frequent experience that their flesh was generally tough and lean, like that of our schoolboys, by continual exercise, and their taste disagreeable; and to fatten them would not answer the charge. Then as to the females, it would, I think with humble submission, be a loss to the public, because they soon would become breeders themselves: and besides, it is not improbable that some scrupulous people might be apt to censure such a practice (although indeed very unjustly) as a little bordering upon cruelty; which, I confess, hath always been with me the strongest objection against any project, how well so ever intended.

18   But in order to justify my friend, he confessed that this expedient was put into his head by the famous Psalmanazar, a native of the island Formosa, who came from thence to London above twenty years ago, and in conversation told my friend that in his country when any young person happened to be put to death, the executioner sold the carcass to persons of quality as a prime dainty; and that in his time the body of a plump girl of fifteen, who was crucified for an attempt to poison the emperor, was sold to his Imperial Majesty's prime minister of state, and other great mandarins of the court, in joints from the gibbet, at four hundred crowns. Neither indeed can I deny that if the same use were made of several plump young girls in this town, who without one single groat to their fortunes cannot stir abroad without a chair, and appear at the playhouse and assemblies in foreign fineries which they never will pay for, the kingdom would not be the worse.

19   Some persons of a desponding spirit are in great concern about that vast number of poor people who are aged, diseased, or maimed, and I have been desired to employ my thoughts what course may be taken to ease the nation of so grievous an encumbrance. But I am not in the least pain upon that matter, because it is very well known that they are every day dying and rotting by cold and famine, and filth and vermin, as fast as can be reasonably expected. And as to the younger laborers, they are now in almost as hopeful a condition. They cannot get work, and consequently pine away for want of nourishment to a degree that if at any time they are accidentally hired to common labor, they have not strength to perform it; and thus the country and themselves are happily delivered from the evils to come.

20   I have too long digressed, and therefore shall return to my subject. I think the advantages by the proposal which I have made are obvious and many, as well as of the highest importance.

For first, as I have already observed, it would greatly lessen the number of 21 Papists, with whom we are yearly overrun, being the principal breeders of the nation as well as our most dangerous enemies; and who stay at home on purpose to deliver the kingdom to the Pretender, hoping to take their advantage by the absence of so many good Protestants, who have chosen rather to leave their country than to stay at home and pay tithes against their conscience to an Episcopal curate.

Secondly, the poorer tenants will have something valuable of their own, which 22 by law may be made liable to distress, and help to pay their landlord's rent, their corn and cattle being already seized and money a thing unknown.

Thirdly, whereas the maintenance of an hundred thousand children, from 23 two years old and upwards, cannot be computed at less than ten shillings a piece per annum, the nation's stock will be thereby increased fifty thousand pounds per annum, besides the profit of a new dish introduced to the tables of all gentlemen of fortune in the kingdom who have any refinement in taste. And the money will circulate among ourselves, the goods being entirely of our own growth and manufacture.

Fourthly, the constant breeders, besides the gain of eight shillings sterling 24 per annum by the sale of their children, will be rid of the charge of maintaining them after the first year.

Fifthly, this food would likewise bring great custom to taverns, where the 25 vintners will certainly be so prudent as to procure the best receipts for dressing it to perfection, and consequently have their houses frequented by all the fine gentlemen, who justly value themselves upon their knowledge in good eating; and a skillful cook, who understands how to oblige his guests, will contrive to make it as expensive as they please.

Sixthly, this would be a great inducement to marriage, which all wise nations 26 have either encouraged by rewards or enforced by laws and penalties. It would increase the care and tenderness of mothers toward their children, when they were sure of a settlement for life to the poor babes, provided in some sort by the public, to their annual profit instead of expense. We should see an honest emulation among the married women, which of them could bring the fattest child to the market. Men would become as fond of their wives during the time of their pregnancy as they are now of their mares in foal, their cows in calf, or sows when they are ready to farrow; nor offer to beat or kick them (as is too frequent a practice) for fear of a miscarriage.

Many other advantages might be enumerated. For instance, the addition of 27 some thousand carcasses in our exportation of barreled beef, the propagation of swine's flesh, and improvement in the art of making good bacon, so much wanted among us by the great destruction of pigs, too frequent at our tables, which are no way comparable in taste or magnificence to a well-grown, fat yearling child, which roasted whole will make a considerable figure at a lord mayor's feast or any other public entertainment. But this and many others I omit, being studious of brevity.

28   Supposing that one thousand families in this city would be constant customers for infants' flesh, besides others who might have it at merry meetings,
particularly weddings and christenings, I compute that Dublin would take off
annually about twenty thousand carcasses, and the rest of the kingdom
(where probably they will be sold somewhat cheaper) the remaining eighty
thousand.

29   I can think of no one objection that will possibly be raised against this proposal, unless it should be urged that the number of people will be thereby
much lessened in the kingdom. This I freely own, and it was indeed one principal design in offering it to the world. I desire the reader will observe, that I
calculate my remedy for this one individual kingdom of Ireland and for no
other that ever was, is, or I think ever can be upon earth. Therefore let no man
talk to me of other expedients: of taxing our absentees at five shillings a pound:
of using neither clothes nor household furniture except what is of our own
growth and manufacture: of utterly rejecting the materials and instruments
that promote foreign luxury: of curing the expensiveness of pride, vanity, idle-
ness, and gaming in our women: of introducing a vein of parsimony, prudence,
and temperance: of learning to love our country, in the want of which we differ
even from Laplanders and the inhabitants of Topinamboo: of quitting our ani-
mosities and factions, nor acting any longer like the Jews, who were murdering
one another at the very moment their city was taken: of being a little cautious
not to sell our country and conscience for nothing: of teaching landlords to
have at least one degree of mercy toward their tenants: lastly, of putting a spirit
of honesty, industry, and skill into our shopkeepers; who, if a resolution could
be now taken to buy only our native goods, would immediately unite to cheat
and exact upon us in the price, the measure and the goodness, nor could ever
yet be brought to make one fair proposal of just dealing, though often and ear-
nestly invited to it.

30   Therefore I repeat, let no man talk to me of these and the like expedients, till
he hath at least some glimpse of hope that there will ever be some hearty and
sincere attempt to put them in practice.

31   But as to myself, having been wearied out for many years with offering vain,
idle, visionary thoughts, and at length utterly despairing of success, I fortunately
fell upon this proposal, which, as it is wholly new, so it hath something solid and
real, of no expense and little trouble, full in our own power, and whereby we can
incur no danger in disobliging England. For this kind of commodity will not bear
exportation, the flesh being of too tender a consistence to admit a long continuance in salt, although perhaps I could name a country which would be glad to eat
up our whole nation without it.

32   After all, I am not so violently bent upon my own opinion as to reject any offer
proposed by wise men, which shall be found equally innocent, cheap, easy, and
effectual. But before something of that kind shall be advanced in contradiction
to my scheme, and offering a better, I desire the author or authors will be
pleased maturely to consider two points. First, as things now stand, how they
will be able to find food and raiment for an hundred thousand useless mouths

and backs. And secondly, there being a round million of creatures in human figure throughout this kingdom, whose sole subsistence put into a common stock would leave them in debt two millions of pounds sterling, adding those who are beggars by profession to the bulk of farmers, cottagers, and laborers, with their wives and children who are beggars in effect; I desire those politicians who dislike my overture, and may perhaps be so bold to attempt an answer, that they will first ask the parents of these mortals whether they would not at this day think it a great happiness to have been sold for food at a year old in the manner I prescribe, and thereby have avoided such a perpetual scene of misfortunes as they have since gone through by the oppression of landlords, the impossibility of paying rent without money or trade, the want of common sustenance, with neither house nor clothes to cover them from the inclemencies of the weather, and the most inevitable prospect of entailing the like or greater miseries upon their breed forever.

I profess, in the sincerity of my heart, that I have not the least personal interest in endeavoring to promote this necessary work, having no other motive than the public good of my country, by advancing our trade, providing for infants, relieving the poor, and giving some pleasure to the rich. I have no children by which I can propose to get a single penny; the youngest being nine years old, and my wife past childbearing. 33

COMPREHENSION

1. Who is Swift's audience for this essay? Defend your answer.
2. Describe the persona in this essay. How is the unusual narrative personality (as distinguished from Swift's personality) revealed by the author in degrees? How can we tell that the speaker's opinions are not shared by Swift?
3. What are the major propositions behind Swift's modest proposal? What are the minor propositions?

RHETORIC

1. Explain the importance of the word *modest* in the title. What stylistic devices does this "modesty" contrast with?
2. What is the effect of Swift's persistent reference to people as "breeders," "dams," "carcass," and the like? Why does he define *children* in economic terms? Find other words that contribute to this motif.
3. Analyze the purpose of the relatively long introduction, consisting of paragraphs 1–7. How does Swift establish his ironic-satiric tone in this initial section?
4. What contrasts and discrepancies are at the heart of Swift's ironic statement in paragraphs 9 and 10? Explain both the subtlety and savagery of the satire in paragraph 12.
5. Paragraphs 13–20 develop six advantages of Swift's proposal, while paragraphs 21–26 list them in enumerative manner. Analyze the progression of these propositions. What is the effect of the listing? Why is Swift parodying argumentative techniques?

6. How does the author both sustain and suspend the irony in paragraph 29? How is the strategy repeated in paragraph 32? How does the concluding paragraph cap his satiric commentary on human nature?

WRITING

1. Discuss Swift's social, political, religious, and economic views as they are revealed in the essay.
2. Write a comprehensive critique of America's failure to address the needs of its poor.
3. **Writing an Argument:** Write a modest proposal—on, for example, how to end the drug problem—advancing an absurd proposition through various argumentative techniques.

NETWORKING
Applying Digital and Multimedia Literacies

Navigating Online Criticism: Go online to locate various critical responses to Swift's famous essay. Review at least five entries from online journals, magazines, or blogs that you would determine *credible sources*, analyzing the basic thesis or claim by each writer. Synthesize your findings in a brief essay.

Synthesis: Connections for Critical Thinking

1. Using the essays of Ehrenreich and Reich, compare the effects of work on human relationships.
2. Write a definition essay titled "What Is Work?" Refer to any of the selections in this chapter to substantiate your opinions.
3. Describe the potential effect of the global marketplace as described by Reich and Friedman.
4. Compare the writings of Swift, Ehrenreich, Krugman, and Reich in terms of the options of those on the lowest rungs of the economic system in Western society.
5. Woolf and Swift are considered to be "classic" writers. What makes their essays "classics"?
6. Monitor and record three business news television shows that focus on analysis and commentary. Analyze the discourse of the moderators, hosts, and guests. As an alternative method, review selected business news Web sites, and subject them to the same analysis.

7. To what extent is American society guided by a business ethic? For example, have Americans historically been so preoccupied with wealth that the quest for money has actually become a distinguishing mark of the national character? Or does the merging of business and religion (what social scientists term the Protestant work ethic) reflect a uniquely American trait? Discuss these issues in an analytical and argumentative essay.

8. Compare and contrast the use of irony and satire in the essays by Diaz and Swift.

NETWORKING
Applying Digital and Multimedia Literacies

---

1. Examine your own college's or university's Web site, and review its philosophy regarding the relationship of college studies to the world of work.
2. Locate several Web sites for job seekers—for example, Monster.com, Idealist.org, and Craigslist. Enter the job classification you are interested in, and compare and contrast the number and types of jobs advertised for three cities. Do a similar search and comparison for federal and state government jobs advertised online.

chapter 9

Media and Popular Culture
What Is the Message?

We are surrounded today as never before by images, sounds, and texts—by what Todd Gitlin, who has an essay in this chapter, terms a "media torrent." Radio and television programs, newspapers and Internet sites, MTV and video games, iPods and cell phone gadgetry increasingly mold our place in culture and society. Indeed, the power of media in our waking and subliminal lives might very well condition our understanding (or misunderstanding) of reality. Today, we can download "reality."

Today's media universe, fueled by new technology, is transforming our sense of the world. Consider the ways in which computers permit us to enter the media stream, making us willing, even compulsive, participants in and consumers of popular culture. Video games, streaming advertisements, wraparound music, newsgroups, chat rooms, and more—all provide data and sensation at warp computer speed. Some slow down the torrent: Bloggers (a word that didn't exist until recently) interrogate their lives and the "facts," even holding newspapers and television news channels accountable for information. But if, as Marshall McLuhan declared, the medium is the message, then any medium, whether old or new, has the power to reflect or construct versions of reality.

Perhaps Americans have moved from a print-based culture to an aural/visual one, preferring electronic media for information, distraction, and entertainment. For centuries books were the molders of popular taste and culture. Tocqueville in *Democracy in America* was amazed by the fact that in the rudest pioneer's hut there was a copy of Shakespeare—and probably, we might add, a copy of the best seller of all time, the Bible. Today's typical household might have more media for iPads, MP3 players, and gaming consoles than books in a library. Of course, print media—say, a book on the ways in which major political parties manipulate the media—offer us the opportunity to scrutinize facts and sources in ways that shock jocks on radio, or talk show hosts on television, or participants in chat rooms cannot. The *medium* or *source* from which we receive sounds, images, and text—the place from which we enter the media torrent—determines the version of reality we carry with us. We can even drown in this torrent, as people who have been captured in virtual reality can attest.

The writers in this chapter invite us to enter the media deluge from a variety of places. They ask broad cultural questions about how we conduct our everyday lives and what choices we make. These questions have both local and worldwide implications, because media and their technological helpmates have created a global village permitting the instant transmission of ideas and images, as well as a subtle transfer of culture—typically American—to the remotest parts of the planet. Whether we navigate the torrent intelligently or succumb passively to the images and sounds washing over us, it is clear that the media in this century will have an increasingly significant impact on human experience.

PREVIEWING THE CHAPTER

As you read the essays in this chapter and respond to them in discussion and writing, consider the following questions:

- What is the main media form and issue on which the author focuses?
- What tone or attitude does the author take toward the subject?
- How does the author fit his or her analysis into the context of popular culture? What social, economic, psychological, or political problems or controversies are treated?
- Which areas of expertise does the author bring to bear on the subject?
- What form of rhetoric—narration and description, exposition, argument—does the writer use? If argument, what is the author's claim? What evidence does she or he provide to support this claim?
- Which essays are similar in subject, thesis, style, purpose, or method, and why?
- What have you learned about the media and popular culture from reading these essays?
- Which essays did you find the most compelling or persuasive? The least? Why?

Classic and Contemporary Images
WHAT DO GANGSTER FILMS REVEAL ABOUT US?

Using a Critical Perspective The best gangster films—like *Little Caesar, The God-father,* and the *Sopranos* series—challenge viewers to form ethical opinions about and interpretations of the tale of crime that unfolds. Even if you haven't seen either the film or TV show depicted here, what do you think is happening in each frame? What details do you focus on? Do the two characters capture the essence of the gangster life, and why? What aspects of film art—framing, the use of close-up or distance shots, the handling of light, shadow, and color—convey an ethical statement? More broadly, in what ways can film art serve as a commentary on American life?

During the 1930s, the first decade of sound films, actors such as Edward G. Robinson, James Cagney, and Paul Muni created the classic portrait of the gangster as a tough-talking, violent outlaw in films such as *Little Caesar* (1930), *The Public Enemy* (1931), and *Scarface* (1932).

HBO's award-winning series *The Sopranos* provided a more nuanced portrait of the gangster as a member of a corrupt, and corrupting, organization with shifting loyalties. For example, Tony Soprano, the character played by James Gandolfini, is a family man beset by so many problems that he must seek psychiatric help.

Classic and Contemporary Essays
WHY ARE WE FASCINATED BY BAD MEN
IN POPULAR CULTURE?

Both Robert Warshow and Lauren Goodlad examine the portrayal of "bad" men in popular culture, and specifically our fascination with this type in television and film. Warshow in his highly allusive essay argues that the gangster in American film is a type of urban tragic hero. On the other hand, Goodlad, whose essay is also filled with references to other works, argues from a feminist perspective that Don Draper, the protagonist in the wildly popular AMC series *Mad Men,* is an "icon of masculinity-in-crisis." Essentially, both writers suggest that bad, mad men—gangsters, rogues, outlaws, even some businessmen—exert a powerful hold on our imagination because they represent a flawed mythology of American success. These bad men are ill-fated from the start because they are compelled to operate in an unforgiving cultural and economic universe. They are doomed to anxiety and failure because their key point of cultural reference—the American Dream—is intrinsically corrupt. Ultimately both writers urge us to go beyond our fascination with media types of tragic men to examine the ethical dimensions of the world they inhabit.

The Gangster as Tragic Hero

Robert Warshow

Robert Warshow *(1917–1955) attended the University of Michigan and worked for the U.S. Army Security Agency from 1942 to 1946. After the war, he served as an editor of* Commentary, *writing film criticism for this magazine and also for* Partisan Review. *Before his untimely death from a heart attack, Warshow had written several brilliant essays on film and on popular culture. Writing of Warshow, Lionel Trilling observed, "I believe that certain of his pieces establish themselves in the line of Hazlitt, a tradition in which I would place only one other writer of our time, George Orwell." One of these brilliant essays, focusing on the interrelation of film and society, is "The Gangster as Tragic Hero," which appeared in* The Immediate Experience: Movies, Games, Theatre and Other Aspects of Popular Culture *(1962).*

1   America, as a social and political organization, is committed to a cheerful view of life. It could not be otherwise. The sense of tragedy is a luxury of aristocratic societies, where the fate of the individual is not conceived of as having a direct and legitimate political importance, being determined by a fixed and supra-political—that is,

non-controversial—moral order or fate. Modern equalitarian societies, how-ever, whether democratic or authoritarian in their political forms, always base themselves on the claim that they are making life happier; the avowed function of the modern state, at least in its ultimate terms, is not only to regulate social relations, but also to determine the quality and possibilities of human life in general. Happiness thus becomes the chief political issue—in a sense, the only political issue—and for that reason it can never be treated as an issue at all. If an American or a Russian is unhappy, it implies a certain reprobation of his so-ciety, and therefore, by a logic of which we can all recognize the necessity, it becomes an obligation of citizenship to be cheerful; if the authorities find it necessary, the citizen may even be compelled to make a public display of his cheerfulness on important occasions, just as he may be conscripted into the army in time of war.

Naturally, this civic responsibility rests most strongly upon the organs of 2 mass culture. The individual citizen may still be permitted his private unhappi-ness so long as it does not take on political significance, the extent of this toler-ance being determined by how large an area of private life the society can accommodate. But every production of mass culture is a public act and must conform with accepted notions of the public good. Nobody seriously questions the principle that it is the function of mass culture to maintain public morale, and certainly nobody in the mass audience objects to having his morale main-tained.[1] At a time when the normal condition of the citizen is a state of anxiety, euphoria spreads over our culture like the broad smile of an idiot. In terms of attitudes towards life, there is very little difference between a "happy" movie like *Good News,* which ignores death and suffering, and a "sad" movie like *A Tree Grows in Brooklyn,* which uses death and suffering as incidents in the ser-vice of a higher optimism.

But, whatever its effectiveness as a source of consolation and a means of pres- 3 sure for maintaining "positive" social attitudes, this optimism is fundamentally satisfying to no one, not even to those who would be most disoriented without its support. Even within the area of mass culture, there always exists a current of op-position, seeking to express by whatever means are available to it that sense of desperation and inevitable failure which optimism itself helps to create. Most of-ten, this opposition is confined to rudimentary or semi-literate forms: in mob poli-tics and journalism, for example, or in certain kinds of religious enthusiasm. When it does enter the field of art, it is likely to be disguised or attenuated: in an unspecific form of expression like jazz, in the basically harmless nihilism of the Marx Brothers, in the continually reasserted strain of hopelessness that often seems to be the real meaning of the soap opera. The gangster film is remarkable

---

[1]In her testimony before the House Committee on Un-American Activities, Mrs. Leila Rogers said that the movie *None But the Lonely Heart* was un-American because it was gloomy. Like so much else that was said during the unhappy investigation of Hollywood, this statement was at once stupid and illuminating. One knew immediately what Mrs. Rogers was talking about; she had simply been insensitive enough to carry her philistinism to its conclusion.

in that it fills the need for disguise (though not sufficiently to avoid arousing uneasiness) without requiring any serious distortion. From its beginnings, it has
been a consistent and astonishingly complete presentation of the modern sense
of tragedy.[2]

4   In its initial character, the gangster film is simply one example of the movies'
constant tendency to create fixed dramatic patterns that can be repeated indefinitely with a reasonable expectation of profit. One gangster film follows another
as one musical or one Western follows another. But this rigidity is not necessarily
opposed to the requirements of art. There have been very successful types of art
in the past which developed such specific and detailed conventions as almost to
make individual examples of the type interchangeable. This is true, for example,
of Elizabethan revenge tragedy and Restoration comedy.

5   For such a type to be successful means that its conventions have imposed
themselves upon the general consciousness and become the accepted vehicles of
a particular set of attitudes and a particular aesthetic effect. One goes to any individual example of the type with very definite expectations, and originality is to be
welcomed only in the degree that it intensifies the expected experience without
fundamentally altering it. Moreover, the relationship between the conventions
which go to make up such a type and the real experience of its audience or the
real facts of whatever situation it pretends to describe is of only secondary importance and does not determine its aesthetic force. It is only in an ultimate sense
that the type appeals to its audience's experience of reality; much more immediately, it appeals to previous experience of the type itself: It creates its own field of
reference.

6   Thus the importance of the gangster film, and the nature and intensity of its
emotional and aesthetic impact, cannot be measured in terms of the place of the
gangster himself or the importance of the problem of crime in American life.
Those European moviegoers who think there is a gangster on every corner in
New York are certainly deceived, but defenders of the "positive" side of American
culture are equally deceived if they think it relevant to point out that most Americans
have never seen a gangster. What matters is that the experience of the gangster
as an experience of art is universal to Americans. There is almost nothing we understand better or react to more readily or with quicker intelligence. The Western
film, though it seems never to diminish in popularity, is for most of us no more
than the folklore of the past, familiar and understandable only because it has been
repeated so often. The gangster film comes much closer. In ways that we do not
easily or willingly define, the gangster speaks for us, expressing that part of the
American psyche which rejects the qualities and the demands of modern life,
which rejects "Americanism" itself.

---

[2]Efforts have been made from time to time to bring the gangster film into line with the prevailing
optimism and social constructiveness of our culture; *Kiss of Death* is a recent example. These efforts
are usually unsuccessful; the reasons for their lack of success are interesting in themselves, but I
shall not be able to discuss them here.

The gangster is the man of the city, with the city's language and knowledge, 7 with its queer and dishonest skills and its terrible daring, carrying his life in his hands like a placard, like a club. For everyone else, there is at least the theoretical possibility of another world—in that happier American culture which the gangster denies, the city does not really exist; it is only a more crowded and more brightly lit country—but for the gangster there is only the city; he must inhabit it in order to personify it: not the real city, but that dangerous and sad city of the imagination which is so much more important, which is the modern world. And the gangster—though there are real gangsters—is also, and primarily, a creature of the imagination. The real city, one might say, produces only criminals; the imaginary city produces the gangster: He is what we want to be and what we are afraid we may become.

Thrown into the crowd without background or advantages, with only those 8 ambiguous skills which the rest of us—the real people of the real city—can only pretend to have, the gangster is required to make his way, to make his life and impose it on others. Usually, when we come upon him, he has already made his choice or the choice has already been made for him, it doesn't matter which: We are not permitted to ask whether at some point he could have chosen to be something else than what he is.

The gangster's activity is actually a form of rational enterprise, involving fairly 9 definite goals and various techniques for achieving them. But this rationality is usually no more than a vague background; we know, perhaps, that the gangster sells liquor or that he operates a numbers racket; often we are not given even that much information. So his activity becomes a kind of pure criminality: He hurts people. Certainly our response to the gangster film is most consistently and most universally a response to sadism; we gain the double satisfaction of participating vicariously in the gangster's sadism and then seeing it turned against the gangster himself.

But on another level the quality of irrational brutality and the quality of 10 rational enterprise become one. Since we do not see the rational and routine aspects of the gangster's behavior, the practice of brutality—the quality of unmixed criminality—becomes the totality of his career. At the same time, we are always conscious that the whole meaning of this career is a drive for success: the typical gangster film presents a steady upward progress followed by a very precipitate fall. Thus brutality itself becomes at once the means to success and the content of success—a success that is defined in its most general terms, not as accomplishment or specific gain, but simply as the unlimited possibility of aggression. (In the same way, film presentations of businessmen tend to make it appear that they achieve their success by talking on the telephone and holding conferences and that success *is* talking on the telephone and holding conferences.)

From this point of view, the initial contact between the film and its audi- 11 ence is an agreed conception of human life: that man is a being with the possibilities of success or failure. This principle, too, belongs to the city; one must emerge from the crowd or else one is nothing. On that basis the necessity of the action is established, and it progresses, by inalterable paths to the point where the gangster lies dead and the principle has been modified: There is really only one possibility—failure. The final meaning of the city is anonymity and death.

12   In the opening scene of *Scarface,* we are shown a successful man; we know he is successful because he has just given a party of opulent proportions and because he is called Big Louie. Through some monstrous lack of caution, he permits himself to be alone for a few moments. We understand from this immediately that he is about to be killed. No convention of the gangster film is more strongly established than this: It is dangerous to be alone. And yet the very conditions of success make it impossible not to be alone, for success is always the establishment of an *individual* pre-eminence that must be imposed on others, in whom it automatically arouses hatred; the successful man is an outlaw. The gangster's whole life is an effort to assert himself as an individual, to draw himself out of the crowd, and he always dies *because* he is an individual; the final bullet thrusts him back, makes him, after all, a failure. "Mother of God," says the dying Little Caesar, "is this the end of Rico?"—speaking of himself thus in the third person because what has been brought low is not the undifferentiated *man,* but the individual with a name, the gangster, the success; even to himself he is a creature of the imagination. (T. S. Eliot has pointed out that a number of Shakespeare's tragic heroes have this trick of looking at themselves dramatically; their true identity, the thing that is destroyed when they die, is something outside themselves—not a man, but a style of life, a kind of meaning.)

13   At bottom, the gangster is doomed because he is under the obligation to succeed, not because the means he employs are unlawful. In the deeper layers of the modern consciousness, *all* means are unlawful, every attempt to succeed is an act of aggression, leaving one alone and guilty and defenseless among enemies: One is *punished* for success. This is our intolerable dilemma: that failure is a kind of death and success is evil and dangerous, is—ultimately—impossible. The effect of the gangster film is to embody this dilemma in the person of the gangster and resolve it by his death. The dilemma is resolved because it is *his* death, not ours. We are safe; for the moment, we can acquiesce in our failure, we can choose to fail.

COMPREHENSION

1. What are the "organs of mass culture" (paragraph 2)? What properties do they all have in common?
2. Define the term *tragic hero* as Warshow uses it in his title.
3. Compare and contrast Warshow's concepts of the "real city" with those of the "imaginary city" as they relate to modern life and mass culture.

RHETORIC

1. Although the ultimate focus of the essay is on the "gangster," the subject is not referred to until paragraph 4. Why does Warshow need so much exposition before focusing on his main topic?
2. What do terms such as *supra-political* (paragraph 1), *harmless nihilism* (paragraph 3), and *general consciousness* (paragraph 5) suggest about the tone of the essay? What do they imply concerning the target audience for the essay?
3. Study the topic sentence of each paragraph. Are the topic sentences successful in setting up the material that follows? How does this strategy enhance or detract from the coherence of the author's argument?
4. Essayists usually provide their thesis at the beginning of their essays. Where does Warshow provide the thesis in his essay? What is the purpose and effect of placing it where he does?
5. The author explains the nature of the gangster film genre—its function, characters, themes, plots, meanings, and so on—*before* he cites specific films. Is this a rhetorical weakness in the essay, or does it give the essay particular potency? Explain.
6. Does the conclusion summarize the main points of the essay, bolster them, or provide new insights into them? Or does it do a combination of these things? Explain.
7. Study the introductory paragraph and the conclusion. What themes are reiterated or complemented? How do these two paragraphs serve to provide both thematic and structural coherence?

WRITING

1. Select a genre of television show or movie. Analyze its conventions and the degree to which these conventions transgress the implicit values of our society.
2. **Writing an Argument:** Argue for or against the proposition that genre movies are a form of escapism that distorts the individual's concept of the actual society he or she lives in and its citizens.

NETWORKING
Applying Digital and Multimedia Literacies

Analyzing a Film: Select a contemporary gangster movie. Using Warshow's criteria, demonstrate—via reference to its characters, plot, and theme—how your selection reinforces the author's thesis.

Why We Love "Mad Men"

Lauren M. E. Goodlad

Lauren M. E. Goodlad *has degrees from Cornell University (BS), New York University (MA), and Columbia University (PhD). She is an associate professor of English at the University of Illinois at Urbana-Champaign, where she teaches Victorian literature and directs the Unit for Criticism and Interpretative Theory. Goodlad has published* Victorian Literature and the Victorian State *(2003) and most recently is a co-editor of* Goth: Undead Subculture *(2007). She worked in the 1980s as a cosmetics and fragrance copywriter in New York City. In the following essay, which was published in the* Chronicle of Higher Education *in 2009, Goodlad combines her personal response to* Mad Men *with unique feminist critical inquiry.*

1   Like most women who call themselves feminists, I've spent my life avoiding men like Don Draper, the incorrigible ladies' man at the center of *Mad Men,* a show about a Madison Avenue advertising agency in the early 1960s. I took a pass on the show during its first season, catching up with it on DVD when the mounting enthusiasm of friends and co-workers piqued my curiosity.

2   By the time the season-three premier was promoted this month, my friends (men and women in their 30s and 40s) had taken to posting Madmenized avatars of themselves on their Facebook pages. And I was one of them, styling myself on madmenyourself.com in a chic red dress, gloves, and cat's-eye glasses. What had happened to make these politically progressive adults in the last days of their youth identify with characters from their parents' generation?

3   I have been intrigued by the mysteries of culture before. In the 1990s, I was writing on gothic subculture and the phenomenon of "men who feel and cry"— men like Anne Rice's vampires, Tim Burton's Edward Scissorhands, and Nine Inch Nails' Trent Reznor, all of whom beckoned young men to dramatize emotion in ways that previous generations had scorned as unmasculine. Alongside those men in black were harsher specimens of masculinity in crisis: men like Tyler Durden, the split personality who launches an underground subculture called Fight Club.

4   While superficially different, both kinds of men were desperate to feel, through catharsis or brutal violence. Yet most of these tales focused on men's relationships with one another, like Tyler's two halves, or Lestat and Louis in Rice's *Interview with the Vampire.* They were men searching for their feelings in the company of other men.

5   And now comes Don Draper, icon of masculinity-in-crisis for the 21st century. Don is in pain, yes, and hurting himself, too (for all his spectacular emotional reserve). But he is also different. No tears or blood on that impeccably pressed

Jon Hamm as Don Draper in the AMC series *Mad Men*.

suit. No close ties to other men. What is it that makes this odd blend of Jay Gatsby, American Gigolo, and the Man in the Gray Flannel Suit so captivating a figure for today?

When I asked a sample of folks close to hand what they thought of the show, strangely enough, the first three said virtually the same thing—all references to Don: *"The guy is hot."* (OK, my mother, a veteran of the *Mad Men* era, said "very handsome," not "hot.") To be sure, the show need not be experienced as the story of a "hot" guy in crisis. A close female colleague, indifferent to Don's eros, tunes in mostly for the Peggy Olson narrative. And there is my husband, who enjoys the show for its complexity and period detail, but hates Don Draper for his selfishness and lies. Like Don, my husband is a hard-working professional father of two in his late 30s. Unlike Don . . . well, you could call him the anti-Don.

Although Don Draper is the show's center of gravity, a constellation of intriguing personalities surrounds him. Several of those characters suggest series that might have been: *Mad Women,* in which Joan Holloway and Peggy Olson take different paths in the struggle for integrity in a man's world; *Mad Closet,* the story of Salvatore Romano's slow-motion sexual awakening; *Bad Men,* a close study of Pete Campbell's toxic cocktail of ambition and insecurity; *Race Men,* in which Paul Kinsey strives to be a hero in the civil-rights movement without exposing himself as an insufferable honkie; *Sad Men,* a nighttime soap in which Roger Sterling deludes himself about his impending mortality; and of course *Mod Men,* a show about style.

8   And then there is Don's beautiful wife, Betty, who, though clearly his better half, is not his patsy. A kind of Donna Reed on steroids, she is much, much more than the first woman on television to have a passionate affair with a household appliance. Her vigorous horsemanship, her facility with a shotgun: These are the signs that though raised to follow the grooves, Betty cannot be underestimated. Witness the end of the first season when, opening the phone bill, she learns that Don has been checking up on her with her psychoanalyst. We think she is in the dark about Don's infidelity; but then, as she lies on the couch, we learn that she has known all along. Betty's decision to tell the good doctor wasn't Freud's talking cure but a savvy move on the chess board that is the Draper marriage. She knows that the shrink will tell Don, so that Don will learn, with a minimum of confrontation, that his fooling around isn't fooling anyone.

9   Conventional wisdom says that women are irresistibly attracted to power. And yet, professionally speaking, Don's position is precarious. Less Gordon Gekko in *Wall Street* than Montgomery Clift's character in *A Place in the Sun,* he is vulnerable to corporate management, professional rivals, and the whims of clients. With no family connections to buttress him, Don has nothing to sell but himself. If he is powerful, it's because the particular commodity he has to offer is selling itself: the trick of making selling seem magical in a consumer society. That is why Don's "hotness" is not the garden-variety sort—not the televised equivalent of an Abercrombie & Fitch ad—but the aspect of his character that connects his existential crisis to ours.

10   Don's sexual tensions bespeak his brilliance as an ad man. His genius for spinning fantasies works in boardroom and bedroom alike. Though superficially a "man's man," he does not long for intimacy with other men. Women are his métier; their desire is the complement to the seductive powers his clients pay him to wield. This is not to say that "sex sells"—a crude logic that Don despises. It is to say that in a consumer society, the fine art of selling is a lot like sex.

11   While his milieu is fundamentally misogynistic, Don himself is far less so. At home he is a possessive, philandering husband, but at work he is the least sexist of the lot, respecting the feelings of middle-age women and promoting his talented secretary.

12   If Betty is stuck playing Don's Madonna—the angelic mother he never had—the other women in his life are more like female variations on Don. There is Midge, the independent bohemian who doesn't make breakfast; Bobbie Barrett, the shrewd businesswoman whose frank sexual hunger ignites Don's kinky side; and Rachel, also a businesswoman, but memorable as the one who got away. Her Jewishness stands for a kind of depth that might cut through Don's mad world if only his desire to connect could trump his need to seduce. In one of many grace

notes, Don, in need of a pseudonym, calls himself Tilden Katz—the man Rachel marries after she ends their affair. It is Don imagining himself as an anti-Don.

In the title poem of *Meditations in an Emergency,* a collection by Frank O'Hara 13 that Don reads, the speaker writes, "no one trusts me" because "I am always looking away." As we eventually learn, Don sends this book to the widow of the man whose identity he stole. But Don's past is really window dressing for a more systemic crisis. There are lots of men with Don's issues who aren't orphans and didn't change their names. If there is anyone who trusts Don it is Peggy, a woman whose loyalty he values too much to throw away—perhaps because he knows that she is like him: Her talent for selling will take her places.

For some viewers, the secret of *Mad Men*'s success is the pleasure of watch- 14 ing characters who don't know, as we do, that "change is gonna come." If that's true, we have more reason to be anxious voyeurs than smug ones. We may know more than Don, Roger, and Betty about the dangers of booze and cigarettes—but we still die as they do (and die increasingly of cancer). And while we have made real gains in sexual and racial equality, the price we have paid is the reactionary anger that haunts every aspect of our social being.

The open secret of our time is that we are less secure than were our precursors 15 in the *Mad Men* era. If we know them to be in the grips of a cold war that finally came to an end, we know ourselves to be losing wars of our own making—a boundless "war on terror" and the destruction of our own environment. We do not watch *Mad Men* because we imagine ourselves as free of vice and illusions; we watch it because we know that our lives, too, are one long meditation in an emergency.

In the dwindling prosperity that is capitalism in the 21st century, every one of 16 us knows that we must sell ourselves, make our pitch, compete for our place in the sun. Though Don has a nice house and car, like most of us, he will never join the big leagues. Among us today, he would not be a Wall Street banker or CEO, for he is not cut from that cloth. His golden parachute is the dream of another life in a California that, if it ever existed, exists no more.

"The guy is hot." If we feast our eyes on Don, wanting him and wanting to be 17 like him, it is perhaps because we, too, want to make it look that good. As Frank O'Hara wrote, "It is easy to be beautiful; it is difficult to appear so." Don gratifies the illusion that a life lived as a commodity can somehow be meaningful; that if we close our eyes, the art of selling will be like the best sex we ever had.

COMPREHENSION

1. Why does Goodlad identify herself as a feminist and why would a self-styled feminist defend a character like Don Draper? How does this defense of Don work in Goodlad's feminist interpretation of *Mad Men?* Provide examples from the essay to support your response.
2. According to Goodlad, the main character in *Mad Men*, Don Draper, is an "icon of masculinity-in-crisis" (paragraph 5). What does she mean by this phrase? Where in the essay does she explore this idea?
3. What observations does Goodlad make about American culture in this essay?

RHETORIC

1. Goodlad summarizes various plotlines and introduces primary characters in *Mad Men*. Why does she devote so much space to this overview? What assumptions is she making about her primary audience, who typically would be college teachers and administrators? (Recall that this essay appeared in the *Chronicle of Higher Education.*) What information does she convey that the average viewer might not know or find interesting?
2. What is Goodlad's thesis? Does she state or imply her main idea? Explain.
3. Identify the allusions that Goodlad uses in this essay. What is her purpose in referring to other characters and works, ranging from Anne Rice's vampires to Frank O'Hara? (Who *was* Frank O'Hara?)
4. Goodlad makes a number of assertions regarding the cultural significance of *Mad Men*. What are they, and do they effectively support her thesis? Are these assertions facts or opinions? Explain your viewpoint.
5. Which paragraphs constitute what we might consider to be Goodlad's conclusion? Is this conclusion effective? Why or why not?

WRITING

1. Watch one episode of *Mad Men*, and then write your own critical response to it.
2. **Writing an Argument:** It could be argued that television series like *Mad Men*, *Boardwalk Empire,* and *Breaking Bad* engage in negative stereotyping. Which side of the debate do you take? Write an argumentative essay on this topic. State your claim, offer evidence, and structure the argument carefully in a series of key reasons in support of your claim.

NETWORKING
Applying Digital and Multimedia Literacies

Critically Interpreting a Television Series: Write a feminist interpretation of a television series that you watch regularly or are familiar with.

Synthesis: Classic and Contemporary Questions for Comparison

1. Warshow critiques the function and role of the gangster in popular media, whereas Goodlad focuses on an analysis of one television series in which the life of an ad man is articulated. How do these different focuses determine the thesis of each essay? What are the positive and negative consequences of addressing a broad issue in "The Gangster as Tragic Hero" without using one extended example, as opposed to the detailed analysis of one TV series in "Why We Love 'Mad Men'"?
2. Goodlad writes an admittedly feminist critique of *Mad Men*. How would you categorize Warshow's critical approach? Is he interested in theory? Why or why not?

An Album of Advertisements:
Images of Culture

The advertisements that appear in this album reflect various ideas in the popular culture—what we value and what we desire. Advertising clearly is a powerful force in molding popular culture and taste. Consider what the advertisements in this album say about popular culture and how they embody forms of argument and persuasion that promote a product, person, or idea.

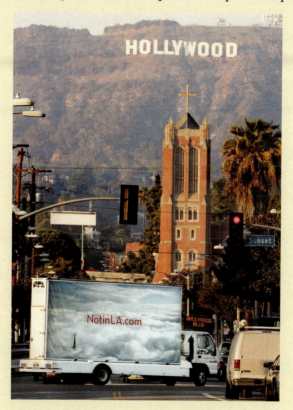

Mobile Outdoor Advertising: NotinLA.com

CONSIDERING THE ADVERTISEMENT

1. What seems to be the purpose behind this mobile ad? What evidence can you cite to support your response? Why would it be helpful to go to the Web site to decipher the ad's message?
2. In an argumentative essay, explain why you think this NotinLA.com ad is or is not successful.

Classic Advertisement: An early 1960s magazine advertisement for a refrigerator, featuring an attractive model in a stylish dress.

CONSIDERING THE ADVERTISEMENTS

1. Analyze the use of fashion, fantasy, and story to "sell" products—from a refrigerator (in the magazine ad) to a television show and clothing (in the window display). Who is the intended audience for each ad, and what techniques are being used to appeal to that audience? What cultural assumptions and ideals does each ad build on? Using these classic and contemporary ads as a reference point, write an essay arguing for or against the proposition that the methods and goals of advertising have not changed or improved over time, even though the culture may have changed.

Contemporary Advertisement: A cross-promotional Banana Republic/*Mad Men* window display (top); a scene from *Mad Men*, featuring the ad men's stylish suits (bottom)

2. Imagine that you work for either Banana Republic or *Mad Men*'s network, AMC. Write a proposal for a cross-promotional ad campaign exactly like, or similar to, the one featured in this window display. Describe what the ads would look like, what forms they would take, where they would be featured, and who their target audience would be. Throughout, provide persuasive reasons for why this venture would be beneficial to both the store and the show. As part of your research, watch at least two episodes of *Mad Men* and visit a Banana Republic store (on foot or online). As an alternative, propose a similar ad campaign for another television show and store.

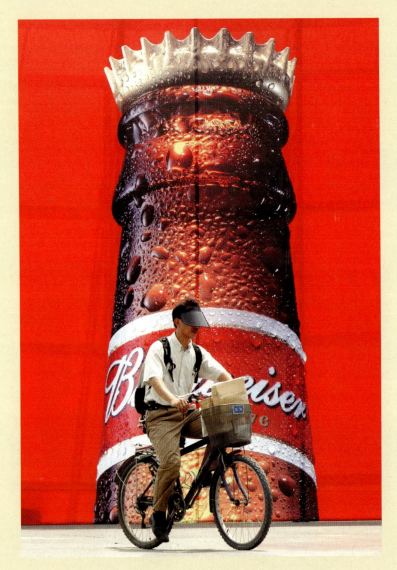

International Advertising: Budweiser in China

CONSIDERING THE ADVERTISEMENT

1. Explain the way in which these photographs capture the power of advertising to promote an American product overseas. What details hold your attention? Why is the poster advertising Budweiser so large?

2. In an essay, argue for or against the idea that advertising American products like Budweiser, Starbucks, or McDonald's overseas is a form of "cultural imperialism" that harms the societies of other countries.

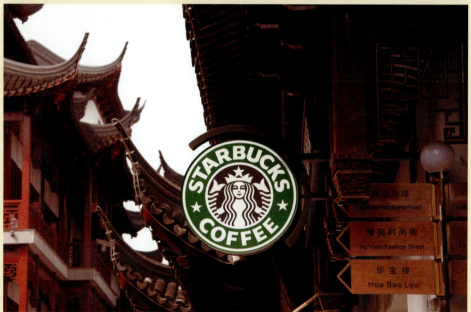

International Branding: Starbucks in the Near East and China

Issue Advertising: Healthcare Reform Videos (MoveOn.org)

CONSIDERING THE ADVERTISEMENTS

1. Via the Chapter 10 Networking page (at *www.mhhe.com/mhreader11e*), watch "Protect Insurance Companies PSA" and "We Can't Afford to Wait" (both sponsored by MoveOn.org). Compare the videos' central claims, as well as their purposes, audiences, contents, and tones. How does each video make logical, ethical, and/or emotional appeals?

2. "Protect Insurance Companies" parodies a commercial sponsored by a group opposing healthcare reform. Make an argument for or against the effectiveness of parody as argument, using an analysis of this video as support for your point.

Issue Advertising: Healthcare Reform Flyer (USCCB.org)

3. Explain the various details and visual elements that create the "message" in this flyer from USCCB.org, a Web site advocating universal healthcare—with stipulations. Then, via the Chapter 10 Networking page, explore the USCCB Web site. In an essay, analyze the argumentative techniques underlying the verbal and nonverbal elements on the site's home page and other relevant pages. Link to or integrate images you discuss into your essay. Alternately, apply this assignment to another Web site and issue of your choosing.

4. Explore what advantages a short video or Web site has over print, audio, or static visual texts as a medium for persuasion. What opportunities might an online location afford? What are some limitations of this genre or location?

Anti-Advertising: God billboard.

CONSIDERING THE ADVERTISEMENT

1. What is your response to this billboard ad? Are you surprised, shocked, or amused, and why? Who might have paid for the billboard ad? What is the ad's purpose? Why might some viewers find the ad controversial? Why might the ad be considered a humorous form of anti-advertising?
2. Write an essay in which you contend that various expressions of faith should or should not be used in advertising, or that God should or should not be used to promote a product, person, or idea.

3. Compare and contrast Warshow's and Goodlad's observations about American culture in their respective essays. In which of these essays do you find these cultural insights to be most convincing, and why?

A Nation of Vidiots

Jeffrey Sachs

Jeffrey Sachs *(b. 1954) is an internationally renowned economics advisor, the director of Earth Institute, and joint professor of sustainable development and health policy and management at Columbia University. Sachs was born in Detroit, Michigan. He received his BA (1976), MA (1978), and PhD (1980) from Harvard University, and subsequently taught there for twenty years before moving to Columbia. As an advisor to the World Bank, World Health Organization, United Nations, and other international organizations, Sachs is in the forefront of efforts to promote sustainable development, disease control, and environmental protection. He is the author of hundreds of popular and scholarly articles and many books, including* The End of Poverty *(2005),* Common Wealth *(2008), and* The Price of Civilization *(2011). The essay that follows appeared in the online magazine* Project Syndicate *in 2011.*

The past half-century has been the age of electronic mass media. Television has 1 reshaped society in every corner of the world. Now an explosion of new media devices is joining the TV set: DVDs, computers, game boxes, smart phones, and more. A growing body of evidence suggests that this media proliferation has countless ill effects.

The United States led the world into the television age, and the implications 2 can be seen most directly in America's long love affair with what Harlan Ellison memorably called "the glass teat." In 1950, fewer than 8% of American households owned a TV; by 1960, 90% had one. That level of penetration took decades longer to achieve elsewhere, and the poorest countries are still not there.

True to form, Americans became the greatest TV watchers, which is probably 3 still true today, even though the data are somewhat sketchy and incomplete. The best evidence suggests that Americans watch more than five hours per day of television on average—a staggering amount, given that several hours more are spent in front of other video-streaming devices. Other countries log far fewer viewing hours. In Scandinavia, for example, time spent watching TV is roughly half the US average.

The consequences for American society are profound, troubling, and a 4 warning to the world—though it probably comes far too late to be heeded. First, heavy TV viewing brings little pleasure. Many surveys show that it is almost like an addiction, with a short-term benefit leading to long-term unhappiness and remorse. Such viewers say that they would prefer to watch less than they do.

5   Moreover, heavy TV viewing has contributed to social fragmentation. Time that used to be spent together in the community is now spent alone in front of the screen. Robert Putnam, the leading scholar of America's declining sense of community, has found that TV viewing is the central explanation of the decline of "social capital," the trust that binds communities together. Americans simply trust each other less than they did a generation ago. Of course, many other factors are at work, but television-driven social atomization should not be understated.

6   Certainly, heavy TV viewing is bad for one's physical and mental health. Americans lead the world in obesity, with roughly two-thirds of the US population now overweight. Again, many factors underlie this, including a diet of cheap, unhealthy fried foods, but the sedentary time spent in front of the TV is an important influence as well.

7   At the same time, what happens mentally is as important as what happens physically. Television and related media have been the greatest purveyors and conveyors of corporate and political propaganda in society.

8   America's TV ownership is almost entirely in private hands, and owners make much of their money through relentless advertising. Effective advertising campaigns, appealing to unconscious urges—typically related to food, sex, and status—create cravings for products and purchases that have little real value for consumers or society.

9   The same, of course, has happened to politics. American politicians are now brand names, packaged like breakfast cereal. Anybody—and any idea—can be sold with a bright ribbon and a catchy jingle.

10   All roads to power in America lead through TV, and all access to TV depends on big money. This simple logic has put American politics in the hands of the rich as never before.

11   Even war can be rolled out as a new product. The Bush administration promoted the premises of the Iraq war—Saddam Hussein's non-existent weapons of mass destruction—in the familiar colorful, fast-paced, and graphics-heavy style of television advertising. Then the war itself began with the so-called "shock and awe" bombing of Baghdad—a made-for-TV live spectacle aimed at ensuring high ratings for the US-led invasion.

12   Many neuroscientists believe that the mental-health effects of TV viewing might run even deeper than addiction, consumerism, loss of social trust, and political propaganda. Perhaps TV is rewiring heavy viewers' brains and impairing their cognitive capacities. The American Academy of Pediatrics recently warned that TV viewing by young children is dangerous for their brain development, and called on parents to keep children under two away from the TV and similar media.

13   A recent survey in the US by the organization Common Sense Media reveals a paradox, but one that is perfectly understandable. Children in poor American households today not only watch more TV than children in wealthy households, but are also more likely to have a television in their room. When a commodity's consumption falls as income rises, economists call it an "inferior" good.

To be sure, the mass media can be useful as a provider of information, educa- 14
tion, entertainment, and even political awareness. But too much of it is confronting us with dangers that we need to avoid.

At the very least, we can minimize those dangers. Successful approaches 15
around the world include limits on TV advertising, especially to young children;
noncommercial, publicly owned TV networks like the BBC; and free (but limited)
TV time for political campaigns.

Of course, the best defense is our own self-control. We can all leave the TV off 16
more hours per day and spend that time reading, talking with each other, and re-
building the bases of personal health and social trust.

COMPREHENSION

1. Do you find Sachs's article too harsh or extreme? Justify your response with reference
   to the text.
2. List, highlight, or circle the objections Sachs has to television viewing.
3. Does Sachs find any useful value in watching television? Why or why not?

RHETORIC

1. Which paragraphs constitute Sachs's introduction? How does this introduction relate
   to the body of the essay?
2. Where does Sachs present his claim? Why does he place it here?
3. How does Sachs develop his argument? What forms of support does he provide?
4. How does the author's use of colloquial language, starting with his coinage "vidiots,"
   affect the tone of his argument?
5. Where does Sachs incorporate emotional and ethical appeals into his argument? What
   is the effect?

WRITING

1. Analyze in depth one of the many issues raised by Sachs in his essay—for example,
   television viewing and obesity, or cognitive development, or poverty.
2. Write a personal essay on your own television viewing habits.
3. **Writing an Argument:** Agree or disagree with Sachs's assertion that we have become "a nation of vidiots."

NETWORKING
Applying Digital and Multimedia Literacies

Researching an Organization: Sachs is president and co-founder of the *Millennium
Promise Alliance*. Conduct online research on this organization (see Chapters 15
and 16) and evaluate it. Share your findings—including a list of your sources—
and insights in a brief report, written or oral.

My Creature from the Black Lagoon

Stephen King

Stephen King (b. 1947) was born in Portland, Maine. Raised by his mother, he spent parts of his childhood in Indiana, Connecticut, Massachusetts, and Maine. He graduated from the University of Maine at Orono in 1970 with a degree in English. During his early writing career, he sold several stories to mass market men's magazines and taught English in Hampden, Maine. In 1973, his novel Carrie *sold enough copies that he could devote his energies to writing full-time. He is the author of about 100 books, most focusing on horror and the occult. A number have been adapted for film and television, including* Carrie, The Dead Zone, The Shining, Christine, Pet Sematary, Stand by Me, *and* The Green Mile. *Besides writing, he belongs to an all-writers rock-and-roll band (with Dave Barry and Amy Tan) and is a major contributor to local and national charities. In the following selection, taken from* Danse Macabre *(1981), King compares and contrasts the responses of adults and children to horror movies.*

1   The first movie I can remember seeing as a kid was *Creature from the Black Lagoon.* It was at the drive-in, and unless it was a second-run job I must have been about seven, because the film, which starred Richard Carlson and Richard Denning, was released in 1954. It was also originally released in 3-D, but I cannot remember wearing the glasses, so perhaps I did see a rerelease.

2   I remember only one scene clearly from the movie, but it left a lasting impression. The hero (Carlson) and the heroine (Julia Adams, who looked absolutely spectacular in a one-piece white bathing suit) are on an expedition somewhere in the Amazon basin. They make their way up a swampy, narrow waterway and into a wide pond that seems an idyllic South American version of the Garden of Eden.

3   But the Creature is lurking—naturally. It's a scaly, batrachian monster that is remarkably like Lovecraft's half-breed, degenerate aberrations—the crazed and blasphemous results of liaisons between gods and human women (it's difficult to get away from Lovecraft). This monster is slowly and patiently barricading the mouth of the stream with sticks and branches, irrevocably sealing the party of anthropologists in.

4   I was barely old enough to read at that time, the discovery of my father's box of weird fiction still years away. I have a vague memory of boyfriends in my mom's life during that period—from 1952 until 1958 or so; enough of a memory to be sure she had a social life, not enough to even guess if she had a sex life. There was Norville, who smoked Luckies and kept three fans going in his two-room apartment during the summer; and there was Milt, who drove a Buick and wore gigantic blue shorts in the summertime; and another fellow, very small, who was, I believe, a cook in a French restaurant. So far as I know, my mother came close to marrying none of them. She'd gone that route once. Also, that was a time when

a woman, once married, became a shadow figure in the process of decision-making and bread-winning. I think my mom, who could be stubborn, intractable, grimly persevering and nearly impossible to discourage, had gotten a taste for captaining her own life. And so she went out with guys, but none of them became permanent fixtures.

It was Milt we were out with that night, he of the Buick and the large blue 5 shorts. He seemed to genuinely like my brother and me, and to genuinely not mind having us along in the back seat from time to time (it may be that when you have reached the calmer waters of your early forties, the idea of necking at the drive-in no longer appeals so strongly . . . even if you have a Buick as large as a cabin cruiser to do it in). By the time the Creature made his appearance, my brother had slithered down onto the floor of the back and had fallen asleep. My mother and Milt were talking, perhaps passing a Kool back and forth. They don't matter, at least not in this context; nothing matters except the big black-and-white images up on the screen, where the unspeakable Thing is walling the handsome hero and the sexy heroine into . . . into . . . the Black Lagoon!

I knew, watching, that the Creature had become *my* Creature; I had bought it. 6 Even to a seven-year-old, it was not a terribly convincing Creature. I did not know then it was good old Ricou Browning, the famed underwater stuntman, in a molded latex suit, but I surely knew it was some guy in some kind of a monster suit . . . just as I knew that, later on that night, he would visit me in the black lagoon of my dreams, looking much more realistic. He might be waiting in the closet when we got back; he might be standing slumped in the blackness of the bathroom at the end of the hall, stinking of algae and swamp rot, all ready for a post-midnight snack of small boy. Seven isn't old, but it is old enough to know that you get what you pay for. You own it, you bought it, it's yours. It is old enough to feel the dowser suddenly come alive, grow heavy, and roll over in your hands, pointing at hidden water.

My reaction to the Creature on that night was perhaps the perfect reaction, 7 the one every writer of horror fiction or director who has worked in the field hopes for when he or she uncaps a pen or a lens: total emotional involvement, pretty much undiluted by any real thinking process—and you understand, don't you, that when it comes to horror movies, the only thought process really necessary to break the mood is for a friend to lean over and whisper, "See the zipper running down his back?"

I think that only people who have worked in the field for some time truly un- 8 derstand how fragile this stuff really is, and what an amazing commitment it imposes on the reader or viewer of intellect and maturity. When Coleridge spoke of "the suspension of disbelief" in his essay on imaginative poetry, I believe he knew that disbelief is not like a balloon, which may be suspended in air with a minimum of effort; it is like a lead weight, which has to be hoisted with a clean and a jerk and held up by main force. Disbelief isn't light; it's heavy. The difference in sales between Arthur Hailey and H. P. Lovecraft may exist because everyone believes in cars, and banks, but it takes a sophisticated and muscular intellectual act to believe, even for a little while, in Nyarlathotep, the Blind Faceless One, the Howler in the Night. And whenever I run into someone who expresses a feeling along the lines of, "I don't read fantasy or go to any of those movies; none of it's real," I feel a kind of sympathy. They simply can't lift the weight of fantasy. The muscles of the imagination have grown too weak.

9   In this sense, kids are the perfect audience for horror. The paradox is this: Children, who are physically quite weak, lift the weight of unbelief with ease. They are the jugglers of the invisible world—a perfectly understandable phenomenon when you consider the perspective they must view things from. Children deftly manipulate the logistics of Santa Claus's entry on Christmas Eve (he can get down small chimneys by making himself small, and if there's no chimney there's the letter slot, and if there's no letter slot there's always the crack under the door), the Easter Bunny, God (big guy, sorta old, white beard, throne), Jesus ("How do you think he turned the water into wine?" I asked my son Joe when he—Joe, not Jesus—was five; Joe's idea was that he had something "kinda like magic Kool-Aid, you get what I mean?"), the devil (big guy, red skin, horse feet, tail with an arrow on the end of it, Snidely Whiplash moustache), Ronald McDonald, the Burger King, the Keebler Elves, Dorothy and Toto, the Lone Ranger and Tonto, a thousand more.

10   Most parents think they understand this openness better than, in many cases, they actually do, and try to keep their children away from anything that smacks too much of horror and terror—"Rated PG (or G in the case of *The Andromeda Strain*), but may be too intense for younger children," the ads for *Jaws* read—believing, I suppose, that to allow their kids to go to a real horror movie would be tantamount to rolling a live hand grenade into a nursery school.

11   But one of the odd Döppler effects that seems to occur during the selective forgetting that is so much a part of "growing up" is the fact that almost *everything* has a scare potential for the child under eight. Children are literally afraid of their own shadows at the right time and place. There is the story of the four-year-old who refused to go to bed at night without a light on in his closet. His parents at last discovered he was frightened of a creature he had heard his father speak of often; this creature, which had grown large and dreadful in the child's imagination, was the "twi-night double-header."

12   Seen in this light, even Disney movies are minefields of terror, and the animated cartoons, which will apparently be released and rereleased even unto the end of the world,[1] are usually the worst offenders. There are adults today, who, when questioned, will tell you that the most frightening thing they saw at the movies as children was Bambi's father shot by the hunter, or Bambi and his mother

---

[1]In one of my favorite Arthur C. Clarke stories, this actually happens. In this vignette, aliens from space land on earth after the Big One has finally gone down. As the story closes, the best brains of this alien culture are trying to figure out the meaning of a film they have found and learned how to play back. The film ends with the words *A Walt Disney Production.* I have moments when I really believe that there would be no better epitaph for the human race, or for a world where the only sentient being absolutely guaranteed of immortality is not Hitler, Charlemagne, Albert Schweitzer, or even Jesus Christ—but is, instead, Richard M. Nixon, whose name is engraved on a plaque placed on the airless surface of the moon.

running before the forest fire. Other Disney memories which are right up there with the batrachian horror inhabiting the Black Lagoon include the marching brooms that have gone totally out of control in *Fantasia* (and for the small child, the real horror inherent in the situation is probably buried in the implied father-son relationship between Mickey Mouse and the old sorcerer; those brooms are making a terrible mess, and when the sorcerer/father gets home, there may be PUNISHMENT. . . . This sequence might well send the child of strict parents into an ecstasy of terror); the night on Bald Mountain from the same film; the witches in *Snow White* and *Sleeping Beauty,* one with her enticingly red poisoned apple (and what small child is not taught early to fear the idea of POISON?), the other with her deadly spinning wheel; this holds all the way up to the relatively innocuous *One Hundred and One Dalmatians* which features the logical granddaughter of those Disney witches from the thirties and forties—the evil Cruella DeVille, with her scrawny, nasty face, her loud voice (grownups sometimes forget how terrified young children are of loud voices, which come from the giants of their world, the adults), and her plan to kill all the dalmatian puppies (read "children," if you're a little person) and turn them into dogskin coats.

Yet it is the parents, of course, who continue to underwrite the Disney pro- 13 cedure of release and rerelease, often discovering goosebumps on their own arms as they rediscover what terrified them as children . . . because what the good horror film (or horror sequence in what may be billed a "comedy" or an "animated cartoon") does above all else is to knock the adult props out from under us and tumble us back down the slide into childhood. And there our own shadow may once again become that of a mean dog, a gaping mouth, or a beckoning dark figure.

Perhaps the supreme realization of this return to childhood comes in David 14 Cronenberg's marvelous horror film *The Brood,* where a disturbed woman is literally producing "children of rage" who go out and murder the members of her family, one by one. About halfway through the film, her father sits dispiritedly on the bed in an upstairs room, drinking and mourning his wife, who has been the first to feel the wrath of the brood. We cut to the bed itself . . . and clawed hands suddenly reach out from beneath it and dig into the carpeting near the doomed father's shoes. And so Cronenberg pushes us down the slide; we are four again, and all of our worst surmises about what might be lurking under the bed have turned out to be true.

The irony of all this is that children are better able to deal with fantasy and 15 terror *on its own terms* than their elders are. You'll note I've italicized the phrase "on its own terms." An adult is able to deal with the cataclysmic terror of something like *The Texas Chainsaw Massacre* because he or she understands that it is all make-believe, and that when the take is done the dead people will simply get up and wash off the stage blood. The child is not so able to make this distinction, and *Chainsaw Massacre* is quite rightly rated R. Little kids do not need this scene, any more than they need the one at the end of *The Fury* where John Cassavetes quite literally blows apart. But the point is, if you put a little kid of six in the front row at a screening of *The Texas Chainsaw Massacre* along with an adult who was temporarily unable to distinguish between make-believe and "real things" (as Danny Torrance, the little boy in *The Shining* puts it)—if, for instance, you had given the adult a hit of Yellow Sunshine LSD about two hours before the movie started—my guess is that the kid would have maybe a week's worth of bad dreams. The adult might spend a year or so in a rubber room, writing home with Crayolas.

16   A certain amount of fantasy and horror in a child's life seems to me a perfectly okay, useful sort of thing. Because of the size of their imaginative capacity, children are able to handle it, and because of their unique position in life, they are able to put such feelings to work. They understand their position very well, too. Even in such a relatively ordered society as our own, they understand that their survival is a matter almost totally out of their hands. Children are "dependents" up until the age of eight or so in every sense of the word; dependent on mother and father (or some reasonable facsimile thereof) not only for food, clothing, and shelter, but dependent on them not to crash the car into a bridge abutment, to meet the school bus on time, to walk them home from Cub Scouts or Brownies, to buy medicines with childproof caps, dependent on them to make sure they don't electrocute themselves while screwing around with the toaster or while trying to play with Barbie's Beauty Salon in the bathtub.

17   Running directly counter to this necessary dependence is the survival directive built into all of us. The child realizes his or her essential lack of control, and I suspect it is this very realization which makes the child uneasy. It is the same sort of free-floating anxiety that many air travelers feel. They are not afraid because they believe air travel to be unsafe; they are afraid because they have surrendered control, and if something goes wrong all they can do is sit there clutching airsick bags or the in-flight magazine. To surrender control runs counter to the survival directive. Conversely, while a thinking, informed person may understand intellectually that travel by car is much more dangerous than flying, he or she is still apt to feel much more comfortable behind the wheel, because she/he has control . . . or at least an illusion of it.

18   This hidden hostility and anxiety toward the airline pilots of their lives may be one explanation why, like the Disney pictures which are released during school vacations in perpetuity, the old fairy tales also seem to go on forever. A parent who would raise his or her hands in horror at the thought of taking his/her child to see *Dracula* or *The Changeling* (with its pervasive imagery of the drowning child) would be unlikely to object to the baby sitter reading "Hansel and Gretel" to the child before bedtime. But consider: The tale of Hansel and Gretel begins with deliberate abandonment (oh yes, the stepmother masterminds that one, but she is the symbolic mother all the same, and the father is a spaghetti-brained nurd who goes along with everything she suggests even though he knows it's wrong—thus we can see her as amoral, him as actively evil in the Biblical and Miltonian sense), it progresses to kidnapping (the witch in the candy house), enslavement, illegal detention, and finally justifiable homicide and cremation. Most mothers and fathers would never take their children to see *Survive,* that quickie Mexican exploitation flick about the rugby players who survived the aftermath of a plane

crash in the Andes by eating their dead teammates, but these same parents find little to object to in "Hansel and Gretel," where the witch is fattening the children up so she can eat them. We give this stuff to the kids almost instinctively, understanding on a deeper level, perhaps, that such fairy stories are the perfect points of crystallization for those fears and hostilities.

Even anxiety-ridden air travelers have their own fairy tales—all those *Airport* 19 movies, which, like "Hansel and Gretel" and all those Disney cartoons, show every sign of going on forever . . . but which should only be viewed on Thanksgivings, since all of them feature a large cast of turkeys.

My gut reaction to *Creature from the Black Lagoon* on that long-ago night was 20 a kind of terrible, waking swoon. The nightmare was happening right in front of me; every hideous possibility that human flesh is heir to was being played out on that drive-in screen.

Approximately twenty-two years later, I had a chance to see *Creature from the* 21 *Black Lagoon* again—not on TV, with any kind of dramatic build and mood broken up by adverts for used cars, K-Tel disco anthologies, and Underalls pantyhose, thank God, but intact, uncut . . . and even in 3-D. Guys like me who wear glasses have a hell of a time with 3-D, you know; ask anyone who wears specs how they like those nifty little cardboard glasses they give you when you walk in the door. If 3-D ever comes back in a big way, I'm going to take myself down to the local Pearle Vision Center and invest seventy bucks in a special pair of prescription lenses: one red, one blue. Annoying glasses aside, I should add that I took my son Joe with me—he was then five, about the age I had been myself, that night at the drive-in (and imagine my surprise—my *rueful* surprise—to discover that the movie which had so terrified me on that long-ago night had been rated G by the MPAA . . . just like the Disney pictures).

As a result, I had a chance to experience that weird doubling back in time that 22 I believe most parents only experience at the Disney films with their children, or when reading them the Pooh books or perhaps taking them to the Shrine or the Barnum & Bailey circus. A popular record is apt to create a particular "set" in a listener's mind, precisely because of its brief life of six weeks to three months, and "golden oldies" continue to be played because they are the emotional equivalent of freeze-dried coffee. When the Beach Boys come on the radio singing "Help Me, Rhonda," there is always that wonderful second or two when I can re-experience the wonderful, guilty joy of copping my first feel (and if you do the mental subtraction from my present age of thirty-three, you'll see that I was a little backward in that respect). Movies and books do the same thing, although I would argue that the mental set, its depth and texture, tends to be a little richer, a little more complex, when re-experiencing films and a lot more complex when dealing with books.

With Joe that day I experienced *Creature from the Black Lagoon* from the 23 other end of the telescope, but this particular theory of set identification still applied; in fact, it prevailed. Time and age and experience have all left their marks on me, just as they have on you; time is not a river, as Einstein theorized—it's a big . . . buffalo herd that runs us down and eventually mashes us into the ground, dead and bleeding, with a hearing-aid plugged into one ear and a colostomy bag instead of a .44 clapped on one leg. Twenty-two years later I knew that the Creature was really good old Ricou Browning, the famed underwater stuntman, in a molded latex suit, and the suspension of disbelief, that mental clean-and-jerk, had become a lot harder to accomplish. But I did it, which may mean nothing, or which may mean (I hope!) that the buffalo haven't got me yet. But when that weight of disbelief was finally up there, the old feelings came flooding in, as they flooded in some five years ago when I took Joe and my daughter Naomi to their first movie, a reissue of *Snow White and the Seven Dwarfs*. There is a scene in that film where, after Snow White has taken a bite from the poisoned apple, the dwarfs take her into the forest, weeping copiously. Half the audience of little kids was also in tears; the lower lips of the other half were trembling. The set identification in that case was strong enough so that I was also surprised into tears. I hated myself for being so blatantly manipulated, but manipulated I was, and there I sat, blubbering into my beard over a bunch of cartoon characters. But it wasn't Disney that manipulated me; I did it myself. It was the kid inside who wept, surprised out of dormancy and into schmaltzy tears . . . but at least awake for awhile.

24   During the final two reels of *Creature from the Black Lagoon,* the weight of disbelief is nicely balanced somewhere above my head, and once again director Jack Arnold places the symbols in front of me and produces the old equation of the fairy tales, each symbol as big and as easy to handle as a child's alphabet block. Watching, the child awakes again and knows that this is what dying is like. Dying is when the Creature from the Black Lagoon dams up the exit. Dying is when the monster gets you.

25   In the end, of course, the hero and heroine, very much alive, not only survive but triumph—as Hansel and Gretel do. As the drive-in floodlights over the screen came on and the projector flashed its GOOD NIGHT, DRIVE SAFELY slide on that big white space (along with the virtuous suggestion that you ATTEND THE CHURCH OF YOUR CHOICE), there was a brief feeling of relief, almost of resurrection. But the feeling that stuck longest was the swooning sensation that good old Richard Carlson and Julia Adams were surely going down for the third time, and the image that remains forever after is of the creature slowly and patiently walling its victims into the Black Lagoon; even now I can see it peering over that growing wall of mud and sticks.

26   Its eyes. Its ancient eyes.

COMPREHENSION

1. Why does King claim that it is harder for an author to successfully bring a horror tale to life than a standard "realistic" one? What special skills does the horror writer need?
2. Why are children the "perfect audience for horror" (paragraph 9)? What exists in the structure of most horror films that makes them suitable for children?
3. King titles his essay "My Creature from the Black Lagoon" rather than using the original title *The Creature from the Black Lagoon*. Why?

4. Why does King think it is ironic that many Disney movies are G-rated while "horror" movies often contain warnings about content for children?
5. In paragraph 23, King remarks that he is pleased that he is still able to get a thrill from watching a horror movie even though he is an adult and understands the artifice behind the monster. Why does he feel this is a positive response? Why does he believe it would be beneficial for most adults to react this way?

RHETORIC

1. In paragraph 9, King attempts to reproduce the sense of what it is like to think like a child. How does he achieve this effect? What is his purpose?
2. How does King structure paragraph 18 to compare and contrast horror movies with "fairy tales"? What is his rhetorical intent?
3. What vocabulary choices does King use in his introduction to set up his conversational style of writing? What relationship does King intend to create between the writer and reader by employing this type of discourse?
4. In paragraphs 4 and 5, King recounts a childhood anecdote. What is the purpose of describing the outing to the drive-in theater with his mother's boyfriend, Milt? How does King structure these two paragraphs so that they culminate rhetorically in a device similar to that employed in horror movies?
5. Although much of King's writing is informal, he does use references to popular culture, literature, and science in his writing. What is the significance and meaning of the following terms and phrases: *batrachian* (paragraph 3), *suspension of disbelief* (paragraph 8), *Döppler effects* (paragraph 11), *twi-night double-header* (paragraph 11), *possibility that human flesh is heir to* (paragraph 20), and *golden oldies* (paragraph 22)?
6. The conclusion is only five words: two sentence fragments. Why did King choose to end his essay this way?
7. King uses irony in his essay for comic effect; for example, in paragraph 25, what is the irony in the "sign-off" at the drive-in movie theater that reads: ATTEND THE CHURCH OF YOUR CHOICE?

WRITING

1. Compare and contrast the benefits or drawbacks, or both, of an adult reading a story to a child versus taking a child to the movies.
2. **Writing an Argument:** In an essay, argue for or against the proposition that horror movies are scarier when viewed at the movie theater than on home video.

NETWORKING
Applying Digital and Multimedia Literacies

Comparing Print and Film: Select a horror or science fiction book you've read that has been adapted for the screen. Compare and contrast the effects of each version. Which was more captivating? More engaging? More horrifying? More believable? Explain your view.

Red, White, and Beer

Dave Barry

Dave Barry (b. 1947) was born in Armonk, New York. He graduated from Haverford College in 1969 and was a reporter and editor at the Daily Local News *from 1971 to 1975 and subsequently a columnist for the* Miami Herald. *Besides writing his columns, Barry has written numerous books, all with his unique, amusing point of view. His books include* Stay Fit and Healthy until You're Dead *(1985),* Dave Barry's Greatest Hits *(1988),* Dave Barry Turns 40 *(1990),* Dave Barry's Only Travel Guide You'll Ever Need *(1991), and* Dave Barry's History of the Millennium (So Far) *(2007). Barry won the 1988 Pulitzer Prize for commentary. In the following piece, he comments on the relation between television commercials and patriotism.*

1   Lately I've been feeling very patriotic, especially during commercials. Like, when I see those strongly pro-American Chrysler commercials, the ones where the winner of the Bruce Springsteen Sound-Alike Contest sings about how The Pride Is Back, the ones where Lee Iacocca himself comes striding out and practically challenges the president of Toyota to a knife fight, I get this warm, proud feeling inside, the same kind of feeling I get whenever we hold routine naval maneuvers off the coast of Libya.

2   But if you want to talk about *real* patriotism, of course, you have to talk about beer commercials. I would have to say that Miller is the most patriotic brand of beer. I grant you it tastes like rat saliva, but we are not talking about taste here. What we are talking about, according to the commercials, is that Miller is by God an *American* beer, "born and brewed in the U.S.A.," and the men who drink it are American men, the kind of men who aren't afraid to perspire freely and shake a man's hand. That's mainly what happens in Miller commercials: Burly American men go around, drenched in perspiration, shaking each other's hands in a violent and patriotic fashion.

3   You never find out exactly why these men spend so much time shaking hands. Maybe shaking hands is just their simple straightforward burly masculine American patriotic way of saying to each other: "Floyd, I am truly sorry I drank all that Miller beer last night and went to the bathroom in your glove compartment." Another possible explanation is that, since there are never any women in the part of America where beer commercials are made, the burly men have become lonesome and desperate for any form of physical contact. I have noticed that sometimes, in addition to shaking hands, they hug each other. Maybe very late at night, after the David Letterman show, there are Miller commercials in which the burly men engage in slow dancing. I don't know.

I do know that in one beer commercial, I think this is for Miller—although it 4
could be for Budweiser, which is also a very patriotic beer—the burly men build a
house. You see them all getting together and pushing up a brand-new wall. Me, I
worry some about a house built by men drinking beer. In my experience, you run
into trouble when you ask a group of beer-drinking men to perform any task more
complex than remembering not to light the filter ends of cigarettes.

For example, in my younger days, whenever anybody in my circle of friends 5
wanted to move, he'd get the rest of us to help, and, as an inducement, he'd buy
a couple of cases of beer. This almost always produced unfortunate results, such
as the time we were trying to move Dick "The Wretch" Curry from a horrible
fourth-floor walk-up apartment in Manhattan's Lower East Side to another horrible fourth-floor walk-up apartment in Manhattan's Lower East Side, and we hit
upon the labor-saving concept of, instead of carrying The Wretch's possessions
manually down the stairs, simply dropping them out the window, down onto the
street, where The Wretch was racing around, gathering up the broken pieces of
his life and shrieking at us to stop helping him move, his emotions reaching a
fever pitch when his bed, which had been swinging wildly from a rope, entered
the apartment two floors below his through what had until seconds earlier been
a window.

This is the kind of thinking you get, with beer. So I figure what happens, in 6
the beer commercial where the burly men are building the house, is they push
the wall up so it's vertical, and then, after the camera stops filming them, they just
keep pushing, and the wall crashes down on the other side, possibly onto somebody's pickup truck. And then they all shake hands.

But other than that, I'm in favor of the upsurge in retail patriotism, which is 7
lucky for me because the airwaves are saturated with pro-American commercials.
Especially popular are commercials in which the newly restored Statue of Liberty—
and by the way, I say Lee Iacocca should get some kind of medal for that, or at
least be elected president—appears to be endorsing various products, as if she
were Mary Lou Retton or somebody. I saw one commercial strongly suggesting
that the Statue of Liberty uses Sure brand underarm deodorant.

I have yet to see a patriotic laxative commercial, but I imagine it's only a mat- 8
ter of time. They'll show some actors dressed up as hard-working country folk,
maybe at a church picnic, smiling at each other and eating pieces of pie. At least
one of them will be a black person. The Statue of Liberty will appear in the background. Then you'll hear a country-style singer singing:

> Folks 'round here they love this land;
> They stand by their beliefs;
> An' when they git themselves stopped up;
> They want some quick relief.

Well, what do you think? Pretty good commercial concept, huh? 9
Nah, you're right. They'd never try to pull something like that. They'd put the 10
statue in the *foreground*.

COMPREHENSION

1. What does Barry mean by "retail patriotism" (paragraph 7)? How does the essay's title illustrate this concept?
2. According to Barry, what makes beer commercials, especially those for Miller, patriotic?
3. In Barry's opinion, what do sexism, patriotism, and beer have in common?

RHETORIC

1. Barry doesn't explicitly state his thesis anywhere in the essay. In your own words, what is his implied thesis? Use evidence from the essay to support your view.
2. Barry uses irony and humor very effectively in this piece. Cite some examples of his humor, and analyze how he achieves the desired effect.
3. The writer uses specific brand names in his essay. How does this device help strengthen his argument? Would eliminating them make the essay less persuasive? Why or why not?
4. Barry seems to digress from his point in paragraphs 4–6. Why does he do this? How does this digression serve the purpose of the piece?
5. Does the anecdote Barry uses in paragraph 5 ring true? Why or why not? What purpose does it serve in the essay? Does its plausibility affect the strength of Barry's argument?
6. How does paragraph 10 function as a conclusion? Is it in keeping with the essay's tone and style? Is it an effective device? Justify your response.

WRITING

1. Write an essay titled "Patriotism," using both denotative and connotative definitions of the word.
2. **Writing an Argument:** In an essay, argue for or against the claim that television advertising has had a harmful impact on American and global consumers.

NETWORKING
Applying Digital and Multimedia Literacies

Analyzing TV Commercials: Barry's essay examines how television sells patriotism. Write an essay analyzing how television sells other abstract ideas, such as success, love, freedom, or democracy. Pattern your essay after Barry's, using humor. Also, use specific television commercials you have seen as examples.

Wonder Woman

Gloria Steinem

Gloria Steinem *(b. 1934) was born and raised in Toledo, Ohio; she attended Smith College, receiving a BA in government in 1956. A noted feminist and political activist, Steinem in 1968 helped to found* New York *magazine; in 1971 she cofounded* Ms. *magazine and served as its editor. Whether campaigning for Robert Kennedy, defending raising money for the United Farm Workers, or championing women's reproductive rights, Steinem has been on the cutting edge of American politics and social activism for almost five decades. Her books include* The Thousand Indias *(1957),* Outrageous Acts and Everyday Rebellions *(1983),* Marilyn: Norma Jean *(1986),* Revolution from Within *(1992),* Moving beyond Words *(1994), and* Doing Sixty and Seventy *(2006). In the following essay, Steinem explains why the comic book heroine Wonder Woman (who was on the first cover of* Ms.*) was such a formative influence during her childhood.*

Wonder Woman is the only female super-hero to be published continuously since 1
comic books began—indeed, she is one of the few to have existed at all or to be
anything other than part of a male super-hero group—but this may strike many
readers as a difference without much distinction. After all, haven't comic books
always been a little disreputable? Something that would never have been assigned
in school? The answer to those questions is yes, which is exactly why they are
important. Comic books have power—including over the child who still lives
within each of us—because they are *not* part of the "serious" grown-up world.

I remember hundreds of nights reading comic books under the covers with a 2
flashlight; dozens of car trips while my parents told me I was ruining my eyes and
perhaps my mind ("brain-deadeners" was what my mother called them); and
countless hours spent hiding in a tree or some other inaccessible spot where I
could pore over their pages in sweet freedom. Because my family's traveling
meant I didn't go to school regularly until I was about twelve, comic books joined
cereal boxes and ketchup labels as the primers that taught me how to read. They
were even cheap enough to be the first things I bought on my own—a customer
who couldn't see over the countertop but whose dignity was greatly enhanced by
making a choice, counting out carefully hoarded coins, and completing a grown-
up exchange.

I've always wondered if this seemingly innate drive toward independence in 3
children isn't more than just "a movement toward mastery," as psychologists
say. After all, each of us is the result of millennia of environment and heredity, a
unique combination that could never happen before—or again. Like a seed that
contains a plant, a child is already a unique person; an ancient spirit born into a

body too small to express itself, or even cope with the world. I remember feeling the greatest love for my parents whenever they allowed me to express my own will, whether that meant wearing an inappropriate hat for days on end, or eating dessert before I had finished dinner.

4   Perhaps it's our memories of past competence and dreams for the future that create the need for super-heroes in the first place. Leaping skyscrapers in a single bound, seeing through walls, and forcing people to tell the truth by encircling them in a magic lasso—all would be satisfying fantasies at any age, but they may be psychological necessities when we have trouble tying our shoes, escaping a worldview composed mainly of belts and knees, and getting grown-ups to *pay attention.*

5   The problem is that the super-heroes who perform magical feats—indeed, even mortal heroes who are merely competent—are almost always men. A female child is left to believe that, even when her body is as big as her spirit, she will still be helping with minor tasks, appreciating the accomplishments of others, and waiting to be rescued. Of course, pleasure is to be found in all these experiences of helping, appreciating, and being rescued; pleasure that should be open to boys, too. Even in comic books, heroes sometimes work in groups or are called upon to protect their own kind, not just helpless females. But the truth is that a male super-hero is more likely to be vulnerable, if only to create suspense, than a female character is to be powerful or independent. For little girls, the only alternative is suppressing a crucial part of ourselves by transplanting our consciousness into a male character—which usually means a white one, thus penalizing girls of color doubly, and boys of color, too. Otherwise, choices remain limited: in the case of girls, to an "ideal" life of sitting around like a Technicolor clotheshorse, getting into jams with villains, and saying things like, "Oh, Superman! I'll always be grateful to you"; in the case of boys of color, to identifying with villains who may be the only ethnic characters with any power; and in the case of girls of color, to making an impossible choice between parts of their identity. It hardly seems worth learning to tie our shoes.

6   I'm happy to say that I was rescued from this dependent fate at the age of seven or so; rescued (Great Hera!) by a woman. Not only did she have the wisdom of Athena and Aphrodite's power to inspire love, she was also faster than Mercury and stronger than Hercules. In her all-woman home on Paradise Island, a refuge of ancient Amazon culture protected from nosy travelers by magnetic thought-fields that created an area known to the world as the Bermuda Triangle, she had come to her many and amazing powers naturally. Together with her Amazon sisters, she had been trained in them from infancy and perfected them in Greek-style contests of dexterity, strength, and speed. The lesson was that each of us might have unknown powers within us, if we only believed and practiced them. (To me, it always seemed boring that Superman had bullet-proof skin, X-ray vision, and the ability to fly. Where was the contest?) Though definitely white, as were all her Amazon sisters, she was tall and strong, with dark hair and eyes—a relief from the weak, bosomy, blonde heroines of the 1940s.

Of course, this Amazon did need a few fantastic gadgets to help her once she 7
entered a modern world governed by Ares, God of War, not Aphrodite, Goddess
of Love: a magic golden lasso that compelled all within its coils to obey her
command, silver bracelets that repelled bullets, and an invisible plane that carried
her through time as well as space. But she still had to learn how to throw the lasso
with accuracy, be agile enough to deflect bullets from her silver-encased wrists,
and navigate an invisible plane.

Charles Moulton, whose name appeared on each episode as Wonder Woman's 8
writer and creator, had seen straight into my heart and understood the fears of
violence and humiliation hidden there. No longer did I have to pretend to like
the "POW!" and "SPLAT!" of boys' comic books, from Captain Marvel to the Green
Hornet. No longer did I have nightmares after looking at ghoulish images of torture
and murder, bloody scenes made all the more realistic by steel-booted Nazis and
fang-toothed Japanese who were caricatures of World War II enemies then marching in every newsreel. (Eventually, the sadism of boys' comic books was so
extreme that it inspired Congressional hearings, and publishers were asked to limit
the number of severed heads and dripping entrails—a reminder that television
wasn't the first popular medium selling sadism to boys.) Best of all, I could stop
pretending to enjoy the ridicule, bossing-around, and constant endangering of
female characters. In these Amazon adventures, only the villains bought the idea
that "masculine" meant aggression and "feminine" meant submission. Only the
occasional female accomplice said things like "Girls want superior men to boss
them around," and even they were usually converted to the joys of self-respect by
the story's end.

This was an Amazon super-hero who never killed her enemies. Instead, she 9
converted them to a belief in equality and peace, to self-reliance, and respect for
the rights of others. If villains destroyed themselves, it was through their own actions or some unbloody accident. Otherwise, they might be conquered by force,
but it was a force tempered by love and justice.

In short, she was wise, beautiful, brave, and explicitly out to change "a world 10
torn by the hatreds and wars of men."

She was Wonder Woman. 11

Only much later, when I was in my thirties and modern feminism had begun 12
to explain the political roots of women's status—instead of accepting some
"natural" inferiority decreed by biology, God, or Freud—did I realize how hard
Charles Moulton had tried to get an egalitarian worldview into comic book form.
From Wonder Woman's birth myth as Princess Diana of Paradise Island, "that
enlightened land," to her adventures in America disguised as Diana Prince, a
be-spectacled army nurse and intelligence officer (a clear steal from Superman's
Clark Kent), this female super-hero was devoted to democracy, peace, justice, and
"liberty and freedom for all womankind."

One typical story centers on Prudence, a young pioneer in the days of the 13
American frontier, where Wonder Woman has been transported by the invisible
plane that doubles as a time machine. After being rescued from a Perils of Pauline
life, Prudence finally realizes her own worth, and also the worth of all women.

"From now on," she says proudly to Wonder Woman, "I'll rely on myself, not on a man." Another story ends with Wonder Woman explaining her own long-running romance with Captain Steve Trevor, the American pilot whose crash-landing on Paradise Island was Aphrodite's signal that the strongest and wisest of all the Amazons must answer the call of a war-torn world. As Wonder Woman says of this colleague whom she so often rescues: "I can never love a dominant man."

14   The most consistent villain is Ares, God of War, a kind of metavillain who considers women "the natural spoils of war" and insists they stay home as the slaves of men. Otherwise, he fears women will spread their antiwar sentiments, create democracy in the world, and leave him dishonored and unemployed. That's why he keeps trying to trick Queen Hippolyte, Princess Diana's mother, into giving up her powers as Queen of the Amazons, thus allowing him to conquer Paradise Island and destroy the last refuge of ancient feminism. It is in memory of a past time when the Amazons did give in to the soldiers of Ares, and were enslaved by them, that Aphrodite requires each Amazon to wear a pair of cufflike bracelets. If captured and bound by them (as Wonder Woman sometimes is in particularly harrowing episodes), an Amazon loses all her power. Wearing them is a reminder of the fragility of female freedom.

15   In America, however, villains are marked not only by their violence, but by their prejudice and lust for money. Thomas Tighe, woman-hating industrialist, is typical. After being rescued by Wonder Woman from accidental imprisonment in his own bank vault, he refuses to give her the promised reward of a million dollars. Though the money is needed to support Holliday College, the home of the band of college girls who aid Wonder Woman, Tighe insists that its students must first complete impossible tests of strength and daring. Only after Wonder Woman's powers allow them to meet every challenge does Tighe finally admit: "You win, Wonder Woman! . . . I am no longer a woman hater." She replies: "Then you're the real winner, Mr. Tighe! Because when one ceases to hate, he becomes stronger!"

16   Other villains are not so easily converted. Chief among them is Dr. Psycho, perhaps a parody of Sigmund Freud. An "evil genius" who "abhors women," the mad doctor's intentions are summed up in this scene-setting preface to an episode called "Battle for Womanhood": "With weird cunning and dark, forbidden knowledge of the occult, Dr. Psycho prepares to change the independent status of modern American women back to the days of the sultans and slave markets, clanking chains and abject captivity. But sly and subtle Psycho reckons without Wonder Woman!"

17   When I looked into the origins of my proto-feminist super-hero, I discovered that her pseudonymous creator had been a very non-Freudian psychologist named William Moulton Marston. Also a lawyer, businessman, prison reformer, and inventor of the lie-detector test (no doubt the inspiration for Wonder Woman's magic lasso), he had invented Wonder Woman as a heroine for little girls, and also as a conscious alternative to the violence of comic books for boys. In fact, Wonder Woman did attract some boys as readers, but the integrated world of comic book trading revealed her true status: at least three Wonder Woman comic books were

necessary to trade for one of Superman. Among the many male super-heroes, only Superman and Batman were to be as long-lived as Wonder Woman, yet she was still a second-class citizen.

Of course, it's also true that Marston's message wasn't as feminist as it might 18 have been. Instead of portraying the goal of full humanity for women and men, which is what feminism has in mind, he often got stuck in the subject/object, winner/loser paradigm of "masculine" versus "feminine," and came up with female superiority instead. As he wrote: "Women represent love; men represent force. Man's use of force without love brings evil and unhappiness. Wonder Woman proves that women are superior to men because they have love in addition to force." No wonder I was inspired but confused by the isolationism of Paradise Island: Did women have to live separately in order to be happy and courageous? No wonder even boys who could accept equality might have felt less than good about themselves in some of these stories: Were there *any* men who could escape the cultural instruction to be violent?

Wonder Woman herself sometimes got trapped in this either/or choice. As 19 she muses to herself: "Some girls love to have a man stronger than they are to make them do things. Do I like it? I don't know, it's sort of thrilling. But isn't it more fun to make a man obey?" Even female villains weren't capable of being evil on their own. Instead, they were hyperfeminine followers of men's commands. Consider Priscilla Rich, the upper-class antagonist who metamorphoses into the Cheetah, a dangerous she-animal. "Women have been submissive to men," wrote Marston, "and taken men's psychology [force without love] as their own."

In those wartime years, stories could verge on a jingoistic, even racist patrio- 20 tism. Wonder Woman sometimes forgot her initial shock at America's unjust patriarchal system and confined herself to defeating a sinister foreign threat by proving that women could be just as loyal and brave as men in service of their country. Her costume was a version of the Stars and Stripes. Some of her adversaries were suspiciously short, ugly, fat, or ethnic as a symbol of "un-American" status. In spite of her preaching against violence and for democracy, the good guys were often in uniform, and no country but the United States was seen as a bastion of freedom.

But Marston didn't succumb to stereotypes as often as most comic book writ- 21 ers of the 1940s. Though Prudence, his frontier heroine, is threatened by monosyllabic Indians, Prudence's father turns out to be the true villain, who has been cheating the Indians. And the irrepressible Etta Candy, one of Wonder Woman's band of college girls, is surely one of the few fat-girl heroines in comics.

There are other unusual rewards. Queen Hippolyte, for instance, is a rare 22 example of a mother who is good, powerful, and a mentor to her daughter. She founds nations, fights to protect Paradise Island, and is a source of strength to Wonder Woman as she battles the forces of evil and inequality. Mother and daughter stay in touch through a sort of telepathic TV set, and the result is a team of equals who are separated only by experience. In the flashback episode in which Queen Hippolyte succumbs to Hercules, she is even seen as a sexual being. How many girl children grew to adulthood with no such example of a strong, sensual mother—except for these slender stories? How many mothers preferred sons, or believed the patriarchal myth that competition is "natural" between mothers and daughters, or tamed their daughters instead of encouraging their wildness and strength? We are just beginning to realize the sense of anger and loss in girls whose mothers had no power to protect them, or forced them to conform out of fear for their safety, or left them to identify only with their fathers if they had any ambition at all.

23   Finally, there is Wonder Woman's ability to unleash the power of self-respect within the women around her; to help them work together and support each other. This may not seem revolutionary to male readers accustomed to stories that depict men working together, but for females who are usually seen as competing for the favors of men—especially little girls who may just be getting to the age when girlfriends betray each other for the approval of boys—this discovery of sisterhood can be exhilarating indeed. Women get a rare message of independence, of depending on themselves, not even on Wonder Woman. "You saved yourselves," as she says in one of her inevitable morals at story's end. "I only showed you that you could."

24   Whatever the shortcomings of William Marston, his virtues became clear after his death in 1947. Looking back at the post-Marston stories I had missed the first time around—for at twelve or thirteen, I thought I had outgrown Wonder Woman and had abandoned her—I could see how little her later writers understood her spirit. She became sexier-looking and more submissive, violent episodes increased, more of her adversaries were female, and Wonder Woman herself required more help from men in order to triumph. Like so many of her real-life sisters in the postwar era of conservatism and "togetherness" of the 1950s, she had fallen on very hard times.

25   By the 1960s, Wonder Woman had given up her magic lasso, her bullet-deflecting bracelets, her invisible plane, and all her Amazonian powers. Though she still had adventures and even practiced karate, any attractive man could disarm her. She had become a kind of female James Bond, though much more boring because she was denied his sexual freedom. She was Diana Prince, a mortal who walked about in boutique, car-hop clothes and took the advice of a male mastermind named "I Ching."

26   It was in this sad state that I first rediscovered my Amazon super-hero in 1972. *Ms.* magazine had just begun, and we were looking for a cover story for its first regular issue to appear in July. Since Joanne Edgar and other of its founding editors had also been rescued by Wonder Woman in their childhoods, we decided to rescue Wonder Woman in return. Though it wasn't easy to persuade her publishers to let us put her original image on the cover of a new and unknown feminist magazine, or to reprint her 1940s Golden Age episodes inside, we finally succeeded. Wonder Woman appeared on newsstands again in all her original glory, striding through city streets like a colossus, stopping planes and bombs with one hand and rescuing buildings with the other.

27   Clearly, there were many nostalgic grown-ups and heroine-starved readers of all ages. The consensus of response seemed to be that if we had all read more about Wonder Woman and less about Dick and Jane, we might have been a lot better off.

As for her publishers, they, too, were impressed. Under the direction of Dorothy Woolfolk, the first woman editor of Wonder Woman in all her long history, she was returned to her original Amazon status—golden lasso, bracelets, and all.

One day some months after her rebirth, I got a phone call from one of Wonder Woman's tougher male writers. "Okay," he said, "she's got all her Amazon powers back. She talks to the Amazons on Paradise Island. She even has a Black Amazon sister named Nubia. Now will you leave me alone?" 28

I said we would. 29

In the 1970s, Wonder Woman became the star of a television series. As played by Lynda Carter, she was a little blue of eye and large of breast, but she still retained her Amazon powers, her ability to convert instead of kill, and her appeal for many young female viewers. There were some who refused to leave their TV sets on Wonder Woman night. A few young boys even began to dress up as Wonder Woman on Halloween—a true revolution. 30

In the 1980s, Wonder Woman's story line was revamped by DC Comics, which reinvented its male super-heroes Superman and Batman at about the same time. Steve Trevor became a veteran of Vietnam; he remained a friend, but was romantically involved with Etta Candy. Wonder Woman acquired a Katharine Hepburn–Spencer Tracy relationship with a street-smart Boston detective named Ed Indelicato, whose tough-guy attitude played off Wonder Woman's idealism. She also gained a friend and surrogate mother in Julia Kapatelis, a leading archaeologist and professor of Greek culture at Harvard University who can understand the ancient Greek that is Wonder Woman's native tongue, and be a model of a smart, caring, single mother for girl readers. Julia's teenage daughter, Vanessa, is the age of many readers and goes through all of their uncertainties, trials, and tribulations, but has the joy of having a powerful older sister in Wonder Woman. There is even Myndi Mayer, a slick Hollywood public relations agent who turns Wonder Woman into America's hero, and is also in constant danger of betraying Diana's idealistic spirit. In other words, there are many of the currents of society today, from single mothers to the worries of teenage daughters and a commercial culture, instead of the simpler plots of America's dangers in World War II. 31

You will see whether Wonder Woman carries her true Amazon spirit into the present. If not, let her publishers know. She belongs to you. 32

Since Wonder Woman's beginnings more than a half century ago, however, a strange thing has happened: The Amazon myth has been rethought as archaeological relics have come to light. Though Amazons had been considered figments of the imagination, perhaps the mythological evidence of man's fear of woman, there is a tentative but growing body of evidence to support the theory that some Amazon-like societies did exist. In Europe, graves once thought to contain male skeletons—because they were buried with weapons or were killed by battle wounds—have turned out to hold skeletons of females after all. In the jungles of Brazil, scientists have found caves of what appears to have been an all-female society. The caves are strikingly devoid of the usual phallic design and theme; 33

they feature, instead, the triangular female symbol, and the only cave that does bear male designs is believed to have been the copulatorium, where Amazons mated with males from surrounding tribes, kept only the female children, and returned male infants to the tribe. Such archaeological finds have turned up not only along the Amazon River in Brazil, but at the foot of the Atlas Mountains in northwestern Africa, and on the European and Asiatic sides of the Black Sea.

34   There is still far more controversy than agreement, but a shared supposition of these myths is this: Imposing patriarchy on the gynocracy of pre-history took many centuries and great cruelty. Rather than give up freedom and worship only male gods, some bands of women resisted. They formed all-woman cultures that survived by capturing men from local tribes, mating with them, and raising their girl children to have great skills of body and mind. These bands became warriors and healers who were sometimes employed for their skills by patriarchal cultures around them. As a backlash culture, they were doomed, but they may also have lasted for centuries.

35   Perhaps that's the appeal of Wonder Woman, Paradise Island, and this comic book message. It's not only a child's need for a lost independence, but an adult's need for a lost balance between women and men, between humans and nature. As the new Wonder Woman says to Vanessa, "Remember your *power,* little sister."

36   However simplified, that is Wonder Woman's message: Remember Our Power.

COMPREHENSION

1. According to Steinem, why are children drawn to comic books and superheroes?
2. Why did Wonder Woman appeal especially to Steinem? What distinctions does she draw between the ways boys and girls view action heroes?
3. The writer traces the development of Wonder Woman from her inception during the 1940s to the 1980s. How did Wonder Woman change over the years? How did she remain true to her creator's (William Marston) conception of her? What does Steinem think about these changes?

RHETORIC

1. What is this essay's persuasive thesis?
2. At whom is this essay aimed—lovers of comic books, or women, or a general audience? On what do you base your conclusion?
3. In part, this is a personal essay. How does Steinem create her persona or self-image? Does the personal element enhance or detract from the analysis? Explain your response.
4. Sort out the complex cause-and-effect relationships in this essay. How does the comparative method reinforce the writer's analysis?
5. What types of evidence does the writer provide? Is it sufficient to convince readers? Where, if anywhere, would more detail be helpful?
6. Steinem divides the essay into five sections. What is her purpose? How successful is she in maintaining the essay's unity by employing this method?
7. What paragraphs form the writer's conclusion? How do they recapitulate and add to the substance of the overall essay?

WRITING

1. Compare and contrast the ways in which females and males approach action heroes. Refer to specific icons like Batman, Spiderman, Ellen Ripley, or Buffy the Vampire Slayer to support your assessment.
2. **Writing an Argument:** Think about the numerous action or superheroes that young children and adolescents encounter today in various media forms. Write an essay in which you contend that exposure to such superheroes either does or does not encourage violent behavior in young people.

NETWORKING
Applying Digital and Multimedia Literacies

Reading Action Heroes in Different Media: Write a personal essay about your favorite action hero or heroine—drawn from comics, television shows, or computer games. Explain why this figure appeals to you and what this appeal reveals about the broader culture. In your exploration, include a discussion of how this particular medium/genre was ideal for this character.

Supersaturation, or, The Media Torrent and Disposable Feeling

Todd Gitlin

__Todd Gitlin__ (b. 1943) was born and grew up in New York City. He received a PhD in sociology from the University of California at Berkeley and was president of Students for a Democratic Society (SDS) in the 1960s. Gitlin is professor of culture, journalism, and sociology at New York University and has held the chair in American civilization at the École des hautes études en sciences sociales in Paris. Gitlin also lectures at home and abroad on contemporary culture and history. He is the North American editor of the Web site openDemocracy.net. Among his notable books are Inside Prime Time *(1983),* The Twilight of Common Dreams: Why America Is Wracked by Culture Wars *(1995),* Media Unlimited: How the Torrent of Images and Sounds Overwhelms Our Lives *(2001), and* The Bulldozer and the Big Tent: Blind Republicans *(2008). In the selection from* Media Unlimited *that follows, Gitlin offers an overview of the ways in which the media influence our contemporary lives.*

On my bedroom wall hangs a print of Vermeer's *The Concert,* painted around 1660. A young woman is playing a spinet. A second woman, probably her maid, holds a letter. A cavalier stands between them, his back to us. A landscape is painted on the raised lid of the spinet, and on the wall hang two paintings, a land-scape and *The Procuress,* a work by Baburen, another Dutch artist, depicting a man and two women in a brothel. As in many seventeenth-century Dutch paint-ings, the domestic space is decorated by paintings. In wealthy Holland, many homes, and not only bourgeois ones, featured such renderings of the outer world. These pictures were pleasing, but more: They were proofs of taste and prosperity, amusements and news at once.

2   Vermeer froze instants, but instants that spoke of the relative constancy of the world in which his subjects lived. If he had painted the same room in the same house an hour, a day, or a month later, the letter in the maid's hand would have been different, and the woman might have been playing a different selection, but the paintings on the far wall would likely have been the same. There might have been other paintings, etchings, and prints elsewhere in the house, but they would not have changed much from month to month, year to year.

3   In what was then the richest country in the world, "everyone strives to embel-lish his house with precious pieces, especially the room toward the street," as one English visitor to Amsterdam wrote in 1640, noting that he had observed paint-ings in bakeries, butcher's shops, and the workshops of blacksmiths and cob-blers.[1] Of course, the number of paintings, etchings, and prints in homes varied considerably. One tailor owned five paintings, for example, while at the high end, a 1665 inventory of a lavish patrician's house in Amsterdam held two maps and thirteen paintings in one grand room, twelve paintings in his widow's bedroom, and seven in the maid's room. Still, compared with today's domestic imagery, the grandest Dutch inventories of that prosperous era were tiny.[2] Even in the better-off households depicted by Vermeer, the visual field inhabited by his figures was relatively scanty and fixed.[3]

4   Today, Vermeer's equivalent, if he were painting domestic scenes, or shooting a spread for *Vanity Fair,* or directing commercials or movies, would also display his figures against a background of images; and if his work appeared on-screen, there is a good chance that he would mix in a soundtrack as well. Most of the im-ages would be portraits of individuals who have never walked in the door—not in the flesh—and yet are recognized and welcomed, though not like actual persons. They would rapidly segue into others—either because they had been edited into a video montage, or because they appear on pages meant to be leafed through. Today's Vermeer would discover that the private space of the home offers up

[1]Peter Mundy, quoted by Geert Mak, *Amsterdam,* trans. Philipp Blom (Cambridge, Mass.: Harvard University Press, 2000), p. 109.

[2]Simon Schama, *The Embarrassment of Riches: An Interpretation of Dutch Culture in the Golden Age* (New York: Knopf, 1987), pp. 313–19. Schama notes that research in the relevant archives is "still in its early days" (p. 315).

[3]Many bourgeois Dutch houses also featured a camera lucida, a mounted magnifying lens trained on objects in the vicinity. Because the lens was movable, motion could be simulated—distant objects being brought nearer and sent farther away. But because the apparatus was mounted in a fixed location, the range of objects in motion was limited to those actually visible from the window. (Svetlana Alpers, personal communication, October 8, 1999.)

vastly more impressions of the larger world than was possible in 1660. In seventeenth-century Delft, painters did not knock on the door day and night offering fresh images for sale. Today, though living space has been set apart from working space, as would have been the case only for the wealthier burghers of Vermeer's time, the outside world has entered the home with a vengeance—in the profusion of media.

The flow of images and sounds through the households of the rich world, and the richer parts of the poor world, seems unremarkable today. Only a visitor from an earlier century or an impoverished country could be startled by the fact that life is now played out against a shimmering multitude of images and sounds, emanating from television, videotapes, videodiscs, video games, VCRs, computer screens, digital displays of all sorts, always in flux, chosen partly at will, partly by whim, supplemented by words, numbers, symbols, phrases, fragments, all passing through screens that in a single minute can display more pictures than a prosperous seventeenth-century Dutch household contained over several lifetimes, portraying in one day more individuals than the Dutch burgher would have beheld in the course of years, and in one week more bits of what we have come to call "information" than all the books in all the households in Vermeer's Delft. And this is not yet to speak of our sonic surroundings: the music, voices, and sound effects from radios, CD players, and turntables. Nor is it to speak of newspapers, magazines, newsletters, and books. Most of the faces we shall ever behold, we shall behold in the form of images.

Because they arrive with sound, at home, in the car, the elevator, or the waiting room, today's images are capable of attracting our attention during much of the day. We may ignore most of them most of the time, take issue with them or shrug them off (or think we are shrugging them off), but we must do the work of dispelling them—and even then, we know we can usher them into our presence whenever we like. Iconic plenitude is the contemporary condition, and it is taken for granted. To grow up in this culture is to grow into an expectation that images and sounds will be there for us on command, and that the stories they compose will be succeeded by still other stories, all bidding for our attention, all striving to make sense, all, in some sense, *ours*. Raymond Williams, the first analyst to pay attention to the fact that television is not just pictures but flow, and not just flow but drama upon drama, pointed out more than a quarter century ago, long before hundred-channel cable TV and VCRs, that

> we have never as a society acted so much or watched so many others acting. . . .
> [W]hat is really new . . . is that drama . . . is built into the rhythms of everyday life.
> In earlier periods drama was important at a festival, in a season, or as a conscious
> journey to a theater; from honouring Dionysus or Christ to taking in a show.
> What we have now is drama as habitual experience: more in a week, in many
> cases, than most human beings would previously have seen in a lifetime.[4]

[4]"Drama in a Dramatised Society," in Alan O'Connor, ed., *Raymond Williams on Television* (Toronto: Between the Lines, 1989 [1974]), pp. 3–5. *Flow* comes up in Williams's *Television: Technology and Cultural Form* (New York: Schocken, 1975), p. 86 ff.

7   Around the time Vermeer painted *The Concert,* Blaise Pascal, who worried about the seductive power of distraction among the French royalty, wrote that "near the persons of kings there never fail to be a great number of people who see to it that amusement follows business, and who watch all the time of their leisure to supply them with delights and games, so that there is no blank in it."[5] In this one respect, today almost everyone—even the poor—in the rich countries resembles a king, attended by the courtiers of the media offering a divine right of choice.

Measures of Magnitude

8 Statistics begin—but barely—to convey the sheer magnitude of this in-touchness, access, exposure, plenitude, glut, however we want to think of it.

9   In 1999, a television set was on in the average American household more than seven hours a day, a figure that has remained fairly steady since 1983. According to the measurements of the A. C. Nielsen Company, the standard used by advertisers and the television business itself, the average individual watched television about four hours a day, not counting the time when the set was on but the individual in question was not watching. When Americans were asked to keep diaries of how they spend their time, the time spent actually watching dropped to a still striking three hours a day—probably an undercount. In 1995, of those who watched, the percentage who watched "whatever's on," as opposed to any specific program, was 43 percent, up from 29 percent in 1979.[6] Though cross-national comparisons are elusive because of differences in measurement systems, the numbers in other industrialized nations seem to be comparable—France, for example, averaging three and a half hours per person.[7] One survey of forty-three nations showed the United States ranking third in viewing hours, after Japan and Mexico. None of this counts time spent discussing programs, reading about their stars, or thinking about either.[8]

10   Overall, wrote one major researcher in 1990, "watching TV is the dominant leisure activity of Americans, consuming 40 percent of the average person's free time as a primary activity [when people give television their undivided attention]. Television takes up more than half of our free time if you count . . . watching TV while doing something else like eating or reading . . . [or] when you have the set on but you aren't paying attention to it."[9] Sex, race, income, age, and marital status

---

[5]*Pensées,* trans. W. F. Trotter (www.eserver.org/philosophy/pascal-pensees.txt), sec. 2, par. 142.
[6]Robert D. Putnam, *Bowling Alone: The Collapse and Revival of American Community* (New York: Simon and Schuster, 2000), p. 222, citing John P. Robinson and Geoffrey Godbey, *Time for Life: The Surprising Ways Americans Use Their Time,* 2nd ed. (University Park: Pennsylvania State University Press, 1999), pp. 136–53, 340–41, 222.
[7]This April 2001 figure for individuals fifteen and older comes from Mediamat (Mediametrie www.mediametria.fr/television/mediamat_mensuel/2001/avril.html).
[8]Putnam, *Bowling Alone,* p. 480, citing Eurodata TV (*One Television Year in the World: Audience Report,* April 1999).
[9]John P. Robinson, "I Love My TV," *American Demographics,* September 1990, p. 24.

make surprisingly little difference in time spent.[10] Neither, at this writing, has the Internet diminished total media use, even if you don't count the Web as part of the media. While Internet users do watch 28 percent less television, they spend more time than nonusers playing video games and listening to the radio and recorded music—obviously a younger crowd. Long-term users (four or more years) say they go on-line for more than two hours a day, and boys and girls alike spend the bulk of their Internet time entertaining themselves with games, hobbies, and the like.[11] In other words, the Internet redistributes the flow of unlimited media but does not dry it up. When one considers the overlapping and additional hours of exposure to radio, magazines, newspapers, compact discs, movies (available via a range of technologies as well as in theaters), and comic books, as well as the accompanying articles, books, and chats about what's on or was on or is coming up via all these means, it is clear that the media flow into the home—not to mention outside—has swelled into a torrent of immense force and constancy, an accompaniment to life that has become a central experience *of* life.

The place of media in the lives of children is worth special attention—not simply because children are uniquely impressionable but because their experience shapes everyone's future; if we today take a media-soaked environment for granted, surely one reason is that we grew up in it and can no longer see how remarkable it is. Here are some findings from a national survey of media conditions among American children aged two through eighteen. The average American child lives in a household with 2.9 televisions, 1.8 VCRs, 3.1 radios, 2.6 tape players, 2.1 CD players, 1.4 video game players, and 1 computer. Ninety-nine percent of these children live in homes with one or more TVs, 97 percent with a VCR, 97 percent with a radio, 94 percent with a tape player, 90 percent with a CD player, 70 percent with a video game player, 69 percent with a computer. Eighty-eight percent live in homes with two or more TVs, 60 percent in homes with three or more. Of the 99 percent with a TV, 74 percent have cable or satellite service.[12] And so on, and on, and on.

The uniformity of this picture is no less astounding. A great deal about the lives of children depends on their race, sex, and social class, but access to major media does not. For TV, VCR, and radio ownership, rates do not vary significantly among white, black, and Hispanic children, or between girls and boys.

---

[10]Robert Kubey and Mihaly Csikszentmihalyi, *Television and the Quality of Life: How Viewing Shapes Everyday Experience* (Hillsdale, N.J.: Lawrence Erlbaum Associates, 1990), pp. 71–73.
[11]UCLA Center for Communication Policy, *The UCLA Internet Report: Surveying the Digital Future,* November 2000, pp. 10, 17, 18, 14 (www.ccp.ucla.edu).
[12]Donald F. Roberts, *Kids and Media @ the New Millennium* (Menlo Park, Calif.: Henry J. Kaiser Family Foundation, 1999), p. 9, table 1. There were 3,155 children in the sample, including over-samples of black and Hispanic children, to ensure that results in these minority populations would also be statistically significant. As best as a reader can discern, this was a reliable study, with a margin of error of no more than plus-or-minus five percentage points. Since the results for younger children, ages two to seven, come from parents' reports, they may well be conservative, since parents may be uninformed of the extent of their children's viewing or may be underplaying it in order not to feel ashamed before interviewers.

For television and radio, rates do not vary significantly according to the income of the community.[13]

13   How accessible, then, is the media cavalcade at home? Of children eight to eighteen, 65 percent have a TV in their bedrooms, 86 percent a radio, 81 percent a tape player, 75 percent a CD player. Boys and girls are not significantly different in possessing this bounty, though the relative usages do vary by medium. Researchers also asked children whether the television was "on in their homes even if no one is watching 'most of the time,' 'some of the time,' 'a little of the time,' or 'never.'" Homes in which television is on "most of the time" are termed *constant television households.* By this measure, 42 percent of all American households with children are constant television households. Blacks are more likely than whites or Hispanics to experience TV in their lives: 56 percent of black children live in constant television households (and 69 percent have a TV in their bedrooms, compared to 48 percent of whites). The lower the family education and the median income of the community, the greater the chance that a household is a constant television household.[14]

14   As for time, the average child spent six hours and thirty-two minutes per day exposed to media of all kinds, of which the time spent reading books and magazines—not counting schoolwork—averaged about forty-five minutes. For ages two to seven, the average for total media was four hours and seventeen minutes; for ages eight to thirteen, eight hours and eight minutes, falling to seven hours and thirty-five minutes for ages fourteen to eighteen.[15] Here, race and social class do count. Black children are most exposed, followed by Hispanics, then whites. At all age levels, the amount of exposure to all media varies inversely with class, from six hours and fifty-nine minutes a day for children in households where the median income for the zip code is under $25,000 to six hours and two minutes for children whose zip code median income is over $40,000. The discrepancy for TV exposure is especially pronounced, ranging from three hours and six minutes a day for children whose zip code incomes are under $25,000 to two hours and twenty-nine minutes for children whose zip code incomes are over $40,000.[16] Still,

---

[13]Ibid., p. 11, tables 3-A, 3-B, 3-C.

[14]Ibid., pp. 13–15, tables 4, 5-A, 5-B, 6. In general, fewer western European or Israeli children than Americans have TVs in their bedrooms, but 70 percent in Great Britain do. Next highest in Europe is 64 percent in Denmark. The lows are 31 percent in Holland and 24 percent in Switzerland. Leen d'Haenens, "Old and New Media: Access and Ownership in the Home," in Sonia Livingstone and Moira Bovill, eds., *Children and Their Changing Media Environment: A European Comparative Study* (London: Lawrence Erlbaum Associates, 2001), p. 57.

[15]Roberts, *Kids and Media,* pp. 21–23, tables 8-C, 8-D.

[16]The same point applies to differences in media use throughout the prosperous world. As the economist Adair Turner writes: "European Internet penetration lags the US by 18 to 24 months. When cars or television sets were first introduced, the lag was more like 15 years. . . . The shortness of the lag also suggests that social concern about a 'digital divide,' whether within or between nations, is largely misplaced. . . . Time lags between different income groups in the penetration of personal computers, Internet connections or mobile phones are much shorter, once again because all these products are cheap. . . . At the global level the same scepticism about a digital divide should prevail. Africa may lag 15 years or so behind US levels of PC and Internet penetration, but it lags more like a century behind in basic literacy and health care." Adair Turner, "Not the e-economy," *Prospect* (London), April 2001 (www.prospect-magazine.co.uk/highlights/essay_turner_april01).

these differences are not vast. Given everything that divides the rich from the poor, the professional from the working class—differences in physical and mental health, infant mortality, longevity, safety, vulnerability to crime, prospects for stable employment, and so on—the class differences in media access and use are surprisingly slender. So are the differences between American and western European children, the latter averaging six hours a day total, though in Europe only two and a quarter of those hours are spent with TV.[17]

All such statistics are crude, of course. Most of them register the time   15 that people *say* they spend. They are—thankfully—not checked by total surveillance. Moreover, the meaning of *exposure* is hard to assess, since the concept encompasses rapt attention, vague awareness, oblivious coexistence, and all possible shadings in between. As the images glide by and the voices come and go, how can we assess what goes on in people's heads? Still, the figures do convey some sense of the media saturation with which we live— and so far we have counted only what can be counted at home. These numbers don't take into account the billboards, the TVs at bars and on planes, the Muzak in restaurants and shops, the magazines in the doctor's waiting room, the digital displays at the gas pump and over the urinal, the ads, insignias, and logos whizzing by on the sides of buses and taxis, climbing the walls of buildings, making announcements from caps, bags, T-shirts, and sneakers. To vary our experience, we can pay to watch stories about individuals unfold across larger-than-life-size movie screens, or visit theme parks and troop from image to image, display to display. Whenever we like, on foot or in vehicles, we can convert ourselves into movable nodes of communication, thanks to car radios, tape, CD, and game players, cell phones, beepers, Walkmen, and the latest in "personal communication systems"— and even if we ourselves refrain, we find ourselves drawn willy-nilly into the soundscape that others broadcast around us.

Crucially, who we are is how we live our time—or *spend* it, to use the term   16 that registers its intrinsic scarcity. What we believe, or say we believe, is less important. We vote for a way of life with our time. And increasingly, when we are not at work or asleep, we are in the media torrent. (Sometimes at work, we are also there, listening to the radio or checking out sports scores, pin-ups, or headlines on the Internet.) Steadily more inhabitants of the wealthy part of the world have the means, incentives, and opportunities to seek private electronic companionship. The more money we have to spend, the more personal space each household member gets. With personal space comes solitude, but this solitude is instantly crowded with images and soundtracks. To a degree that was unthinkable in the seventeenth century, life experience has become an experience in the presence of media.

---

[17]Johannes W. J. Beentjes et al., "Children's Use of Different Media: For How Long and Why?" in Livingstone and Bovill, eds., *Children and Their Changing Media Environment,* p. 96.

COMPREHENSION

1. What does Gitlin's title mean? How are the concepts of "supersaturation" and "disposable feeling" reflected in the essay?
2. Summarize Gitlin's treatment of Vermeer. Who was Vermeer? How, according to the writer, would Vermeer's art be produced today?
3. List some of the facts and statistics that the writer presents to support his idea that we are caught in a "media torrent."

RHETORIC

1. What is Gitlin's argument? Where does he state his claim most clearly? What appeals to logic, ethics, and emotion does he make? Does he rely on his own opinions? Justify your answer.
2. How does the writer maintain unity between the two parts of this essay? Why, for example, does he open his essay with the story of Vermeer? How does Vermeer serve as a unifying element? What other unifying motifs can you find?
3. What varieties of evidence does the writer provide to bolster his argument? Does he rely on anecdotal or actual evidence? How do you know?
4. The writer employs a range of rhetorical strategies in this essay. Point to places where he uses description, comparison and contrast, classification, definition, and causal analysis.
5. Is the author's style personal, informal, or formal? How does this style explain Gitlin's relationship to his audience and the expectations he holds of his readers?
6. What strategy does the writer use in his conclusion? Is this strategy effective? Why or why not?
7. What do Gitlin's footnotes add to the essay? Why are they important?

WRITING

1. Write an essay in which you explain how one medium—television or the Internet, for example—has affected or changed your life. Make sure that you provide adequate detail or evidence.
2. **Writing an Argument:** Write an essay in which you either agree or disagree with Gitlin's claim that increasingly "we are in a media torrent." Use appeals to logic, ethics, and emotion to advance your claim. Make certain that you have adequate evidence to support your major and minor propositions.

NETWORKING
Applying Digital and Multimedia Literacies

Comparing New and Old Media: Write a comparative essay in which you analyze the similarities and differences between an "old" and a "new" component of the media—actual books and e-books or audio books, or telephones and cell phones, for example. Use visuals to enhance and support your comparisons.

Escape from Wonderland: Disney and the Female Imagination

Deborah Ross

Deborah Ross is professor of English at Hawai'i Pacific University, where she teaches writing, literature, and humanities. She specializes in popular culture, especially from the perspective of gender. In the following research paper, published in a 2004 issue of Marvels & Tales: Journal of Fairy-Tale Studies, *Ross analyzes a series of Disney films, all based on children's books and fairy tales; she evaluates the Disney ideology as it affects the imaginative and actual lives of girls.*

In 1989, Disney's little mermaid first asked the musical question, "When's it my 1 turn?" She asked it again in 1996, when her movie was re-released in theaters, and she continues to ask it, frequently, in many of our living rooms. Never has a protagonist had so many turns to demand a turn: Yet, seemingly, she remains unsatisfied. If even the heroine in a Disney "girls' movie" does not enjoy being a girl, how must the girls watching her feel about it?

Behind this gender question lurks a larger political one. If Ariel's feminist 2 rhetoric is undercut by more conservative elements in her movie, so is the environmentalism of *The Lion King,* the multiculturalism of *Pocahontas,* the valuing of difference in *The Hunchback of Notre Dame*—in short, all the quasi-liberal sentiments that focus groups have no doubt caused to grace the surface of the last decade's Disney features. Ideology in Disney is a much vexed question, and I will not attempt here to untangle a knot which began forming for critics when Walt first denied having any politics back in the thirties, and which has only grown in mass and complexity since his death, as his corporation's management style has evolved to cope with a burgeoning staff of artists and technicians, changing public tastes, and changing perceptions of those tastes.

One generalization I do suggest, however, is that Disney the man and the 3 corporation are known for a belief in control. The top-down management style Disney epitomizes—Auschwitz (Giroux 55), or Mouschwitz (Lewis 88), is a frequent analogy—thrives on homogeneity and rigid adherence to rules. These are features often decried in Disney production and product, both by critics of capitalism, such as Benjamin and Adorno,[1] and by far less radical proponents of individualism and open debate, from early Disney biographer Richard Schickel to educator Henry Giroux. Yet imagination, the company's major commodity, does

---

[1]Miriam Hansen discusses Benjamin's and Adorno's objections to Disney in some detail. Jack Zipes's critique of Disney also occurs within a larger argument about the "freezing" of fairy tales into myths to perpetuate bourgeois, patriarchal values (see his Introduction and Chapter 3).

not easily lend itself to a program of control. To encourage imagination in artists, and arouse it in viewers, is to invite unique self-expression rather than homogeneity, and spontaneity rather than predictability. Link imagination to the animated cartoon, an art form with roots in dada, surrealism, and radical politics, and matters could well get out of hand.[2]

4   I believe that this conflict between control and imaginative freedom is visible in the animated features that have come out of the Disney studios, from *Snow White and the Seven Dwarfs* to *Lilo and Stitch*. Of course, ambiguity is rarely viewed now as either a moral or an aesthetic flaw, and the presence of elements that contradict each other may well be preferable to consistent, monologic disapproval of imagination. Neither, however, do conflict and contradiction in themselves necessarily create a space for viewers to question values and exercise judgment. Much depends on how the elements relate to each other, or how an audience is likely to relate them. An audience even partially looking for guides to behavior along with entertainment will have to resolve apparent ambiguities into one suggested course of action. Giroux's attack on Disney rests on the contention that for children, these movies, however apparently bland, do have a didactic effect (18). For them, ambiguity at its best ultimately resolves into a connected but complex world view that embraces difference and spontaneity; at its worst, it can produce confusion and anxiety.

5   I wish to explore the overall impressions these films may give children about the value of their own imaginations, and thus about their own value as unique individuals able to envision, and eventually to enact, change. In particular, to get back to Ariel, I am concerned about what girls may learn about this potentially explosive aspect of their characters that could so easily burst the bounds of traditional femininity. To help answer this question, I have chosen to examine the way various elements of image, story, and dialogue interact to influence the valuation of imagination in three of Disney's girls' movies: *Alice in Wonderland* (1951), *The Little Mermaid* (1989), and *Beauty and the Beast* (1991, re-released 2001).

6   I have chosen these three because, although one might be called "prefeminist" and the other two "post-," all specifically concern young women who fantasize about a life more vivid and exciting than their reality. I will suggest that some of these films' discomfort with female imagination has roots far back in didactic narrative for girls by looking at Charlotte Lennox's 1759 novel, *The Female Quixote,* which concerns the fortunes of a young woman who might be considered the great-grandmother, or prototype, of the Disney heroine. Then, comparing the three Disney movies with their written fairy-tale sources, I will show how much more confusing a many-tongued message can become when it is told in pictures as well as words.

---

[2]Janet Wasko notes that Disney deliberately avoided the more "anarchistic and inventive" styles of animation employed at other studios (115). My own belief, on which my approach to Disney is based, is that where there is animation, anarchy can never be wholly suppressed. For discussion of the roots of animation in surrealism and dada, see Inez Hedges.

Girls have been learning from stories where to draw the line between fantasy and 7
reality probably since the first story was told, but one sees this didactic purpose especially clearly beginning in the seventeenth century, when romances and literary
fairy tales were first written specifically for, about, and even by women. Samuel
Johnson was greatly concerned about the effects of fiction on "the young, the ignorant, and the idle," and Paul Hunter has shown that there was indeed a class of new
readers early in the eighteenth century who were socially displaced and looking to
novels for moral and social guidance as well as entertainment (Hunter 271–72).
From that time till the present, conservative authors have used romances and
novels to teach girls that their dreams are dangerous and of little relevance to their
daily lives. Progressive or feminist authors, on the other hand, have encouraged
young women readers' belief in fantasy to help them visualize what they want,
perhaps as a first step toward going after it. For example, it can be argued (as I have
done elsewhere) that European women's experience with romantic fiction gradually
gained them the right, first, to refuse to cooperate in arranged marriages, and eventually, to choose husbands for themselves.[3]

Charlotte Lennox's *The Female Quixote* illustrates both these conservative 8
and progressive plot patterns, for it both draws upon and criticizes earlier romances, which themselves often both celebrated and punished female imagination and expressiveness.[4] Therefore, like Disney's movies today, which also use
material from the romance and fairy-tale tradition, Lennox's novel can be more
muddling than enlightening to young people seeking instruction on the conduct
of real life. As the title suggests, the premise is that a young girl is at least as likely
to have her head turned by reading romances as Cervantes's knight-errant had
been over a century before. Appropriately, the romances devoured by this quixote,
Arabella, are the largely female-centered French romances of d'Urfé and Scudéry,
which focus more on love than on questing, and in which males are present
mainly either to carry off or rescue heroines. A reader who takes too literally
stories in which women wield such power, albeit of a limited kind, will not adjust
well to woman's lot: being ignored, submitting always to others' convenience, like
Jane Austen in her letters, perpetually waiting to be "fetched" by a male relative
(Austen 9–10). Thus Arabella's reading sets her up to make many ridiculous
mistakes, and ultimately to be humbled, or humiliated, when she learns her own
real unimportance.

The novel shows its author's ambivalence about Arabella's fantasy in several 9
ways. Overtly, she presents it as an adolescent error the heroine must grow out of
in order to find happiness. Yet her very frank satire of the world to which Arabella's
cure forces her to conform leaves readers wondering, along with the heroine,

---

[3]I develop this argument in *The Excellence of Falsehood.* Marina Warner (169, 277–78) and Jack
Zipes (21–23, 28) discuss the seventeenth-century *précieuses'* preoccupation with the issue of
forced marriage.

[4]Warner discusses ambivalence about the old woman or "Mother Goose" figure who narrates fairy
tales throughout the first half of *From the Beast to the Blonde,* and more specifically the power of the
female voice in her discussion of "The Little Mermaid" (394).

whether the world of romance might not be preferable. Romances also receive implicit support from the central "real" narrative's resemblance to romance: beautiful heroine, beloved by the perfect man, whom after trials and separations she marries, presumably to live happily ever after. If the novel presents a romantic story under the guise of realism, then perhaps Arabella is not so quixotic after all.

10   *The Female Quixote* thus presents contradictory impressions about the worthiness of the heroine's desires, the degree to which those desires are ultimately fulfilled or frustrated, and the amount of satisfaction with the outcome the tone directs the reader to feel. Critics of our own time naturally enjoy this ambivalence (the novel has had a comeback of sorts in the last decades and is available in paperback), which particularly lends itself to feminist approaches of the *Madwoman in the Attic,* conformist text–radical subtext variety. Yet the fact that this novel might well make a madwoman out of any young female reader looking for a framework for understanding life should also be part of our critical awareness. Critics may find it a useful model for highlighting similar constellations of ideological paradox in other stories about women's imagination, stories which also leave their audiences struggling to integrate contradictory messages.

11   Disney's female quixotes are at least as sorely beset by ambiguity as Arabella. The heroines' fantasies reveal desires for many things, including novelty, excitement, power, sex, and knowledge. Some of these desires are ridiculed, others respected; some are fulfilled, others surrendered. And the paradoxes in the plots are further complicated by words and images that seem at times to be telling stories of their own.

12   The presence of conservative elements in Disney's *Alice in Wonderland* is not surprising, considering that it was released in 1951, when "Hollywood's dark prince" was still very much alive, fighting unions, castigating the League of Women Voters, and exerting strong control over the studio's output.[5] One would perhaps not expect, though, to find an American movie of the mid-twentieth century so much more stereotypically Victorian than its nineteenth-century British source.

13   Of course, Lewis Carroll's *Alice's Adventures in Wonderland* and *Through the Looking Glass* are not typical of Victorian children's literature. In particular, most girls' stories of this era promoted humility, devotion, punctuality, and tidiness, implying that adventure (as a countess once told Lennox's Arabella) is something a nice girl would be wise to avoid (Lennox 365). The Alice stories, on the other hand, present adventure as positive: Whether wondrous or frightening, it leads the heroine in the direction of personal growth and control over her surroundings. Alice learns how to manage her size, how to talk back to a queen, and, finally, how to wear the crown of adulthood. Carroll celebrates childhood as a brief, fleeting time in which even girls may follow talking rabbits before being overtaken by the "dull reality" (115) of womanhood.

---

[5]I refer here to the title of Marc Eliot's Disney biography. Holly Allen and Michael Denning discuss politics at the Disney studio during the 1940s. For a full discussion of Disney's rather complex politics, see Steven Watts.

The Disney movie begins with the same positive message about girls' fanta- 14
sies. In her opening conversation, Disney's Alice, like Carroll's, expresses the
usual quixotic desires: to escape boredom (with lessons), to satisfy curiosity
(about the white rabbit), and above all, to exert power. Things would be different
"in my world," she notes, though her sister ridicules her ambition. Books, for one
thing, would all have pictures—a remark given to Alice by Carroll in a way that
almost invites someone to make an Alice movie. The first few minutes of the
movie do seem to deliver what Alice wants by introducing such pictorial wonders
as singing flowers and surrealistic insects.

Soon, however, the plot darkens, signaled by small but significant cuts and 15
alterations in the original dialogue. Speaking with the Cheshire Cat, who tells her
everyone in the neighborhood is mad, Alice speaks Carroll's line, "But I don't
want to go among mad people" (63). The cat responds that everyone in Wonderland
is mad, but he does not go on to say that Alice too is mad, so that already Disney's
Alice is presented as out of her element, the lone sane and rational creature
among lunatics.

After the mad tea party, in a section of plot invented for the movie, Disney's 16
Alice has had enough craziness and wants to go home. Overjoyed to find what
looks like a path—symbolic of her now acknowledged need for order and direction—she is reduced to helpless tears when it is erased by a fanciful broom creature. She then passively sits down to wait to be rescued, all the while lecturing
herself about the importance of reason and patience, and berating herself for the
curiosity that once again has led her into trouble. The movie takes a line from
early in the story, "She generally gave herself very good advice (though she very
seldom followed it)" (23), puts it in the first person, and makes it the center of a
self-lacerating musical lament in which Alice abandons for good her fantasy of
excitement and power to dwindle into a tiny, forlorn figure in the center of a large,
dark frame. In the end of the movie, the defiance and assertiveness of the line,
"You're only a pack of cards," are lost, as she utters it while fleeing for her life
from the menacing gang of wonders she has created. She is saved, not by facing
them down with dawning maturity and confidence, like the "real" Alice, but by
waking up.[6]

British reviewers at the time of the movie's release, when the militantly in- 17
nocuous Enid Blyton held sway over English children's imaginations, objected to
Disney's "anarchic" alteration of what they saw as a serene and placid children's
tale (Allan 137). But Carroll's story is in fact far more tolerant of anarchy, in the
sense of irrationality, than the Disney version. The images used to tell the story
further support this rationalist message. Despite Disney artist Claude Coats's
comment that the staff had "let [them]selves go with some wild designs" (Allan 138),
the visuals in fact are rather staid and restrained, mainly literal, representational
renderings of the story done in the highly finished, realistic style for which the

---

[6]Donald Britton comments that in the Disney cartoon universe, "children don't become adults;
rather, adults kill children" (120).

studio was famous. The fall down the rabbit hole, for example, which marks Alice's entry into the dream state, might have lent itself to surrealistic treatment like that of *Dumbo*'s "Pink Elephants on Parade" sequence, but instead it is simply a serial listing in images of the objects Carroll mentions that Alice sees on her way down.

18   Surrealism does appear, briefly, in the visual puns formed by the caterpillar's smoke (as he asks "why [k]not"), and in the wild proliferation of crockery at the tea party, the cups and saucers truly "animated" and seeming to breed like, well, rabbits. Yet the story-line ensures that just as this style reaches its climax, Alice is reaching the limits of her fear of imagination. What might have been delightful Daliesque creatures—telephone-ducks, drum-frogs—function rather to frighten the heroine at a point in the plot when she has rejected all this "nonsense" and is anxious to get home to write a book about it.[7] Writing a story, she has decided, is much safer than living one.

19   Thus all elements combine to entrap the unwary viewer: to entice her to fantasize—even to pay money for the privilege—and then to make her feel, like Alice, guilty and ashamed.

20 Contrasting Alice's defeated whining with Ariel's anthem of independence in *The Little Mermaid,* one is apt to feel girls have come a long way. Here, as Laura Sells and Marina Warner observe, the tale on which the movie is based is ostensibly more conservative than Disney's retelling (Sells 176, 177, 181; Warner 397, 403).[8] Hans Christian Andersen's story is a tragic celebration of feminine self-sacrifice. His mermaid fantasizes about becoming human partly because, like Alice, she is curious about a world she has only glimpsed (here, from below rather than from above). But that world interests her mainly because in it dwells a man who resembles a handsome statue she already adores. Her love is partly sexual, of course, since she needs to be human from the waist down to win the hero. But her ultimate desire is spiritual, for only by marrying a human can a mermaid, who normally lives three hundred years and then turns into sea-foam, gain a soul and eternal life.

21   In pursuit of this desire Andersen's mermaid is willing to spend all she has: her voice, her health, and eventually her life. She buys her new legs, from which blood oozes with every agonizing step, by letting the sea witch cut out her tongue. The permanent loss of her voice means playing dumb in more ways than one, as she can only listen demurely as the prince lectures her about her own world, the sea (166).[9] Failing to bring the prince to a proposal, she could save her own life by killing him, but she chooses instead to die. Her many acts of self-torture earn her a slight reprieve as she is turned into a spirit of the air, instead of sea-foam,

[7]Dali had been at the studio in 1946, and Robin Allan believes his influence was still apparent in Alice (137).

[8]See also Wasko 134.

[9]See Warner's discussion on the significance of this silence, and of the blood which in Andersen's tale connects pain with the dawning of female sexuality (387–408).

and given a chance to gain a soul by performing more selfless deeds. Andersen gives her this reward, not for having a dream, but for desiring martyrdom. No real authorial punishment is needed for a female quixote so intent on punishing herself.

Naturally in the Disney version the mutilation and blood would have to go. 22 But much more would have to be altered to make this tragic story look and sound so convincingly like a triumph of adolescent self-will and entitlement, as befit the close of the "me decade." (Warner comments on how often, while she can speak, Ariel utters the verb "want" [403].) For example, instead of making the mermaid love the human world because she loves a human, the movie has Ariel love a human mainly because she is already curious enough about his world to have collected a cave full of human souvenirs (in Andersen's story this collection belongs to a mermaid sister). Like Alice before her initiation, Ariel imagines this other world as in a sense more her own than her actual world. She believes it to be a utopia of free movement: She dreams of legs first for "jumping" and "dancing" and "strolling," and only secondarily for marrying.

There is nothing masochistic about this mermaid's fantasy; nor is she willing 23 to sacrifice herself to fulfill it, though she is willing to gamble. Her voice, for example, is not permanently lost but poured into a shell, ready to be returned to her if she succeeds, and she has every intention of succeeding. Eighties heroine that she is, she means to have it all: voice, soul, legs, and husband.

For the most part, the movie seems to present this female quixote's fantasy 24 positively and reward her with her desire, as the older generation, in the person of her father, learns to abandon prejudice and let teenagers live their own lives. But there are undercurrents here, so to speak, that work against the theme of imaginative freedom. The odd thing about Ariel's quixotism—what makes the audience recognize it *as* quixotism—is that the exotic world of her fantasy is, to us, boring and commonplace. Even a two-year-old viewer knows, as the heroine does not, that forks are not used to comb hair, and that human fathers do indeed "reprimand their daughters," just like old King Triton. Thus we laugh at Ariel's naïve reveries, as Andersen's listeners must have laughed at his mermaid's amazed reaction to birds (150). In the end, it seems ludicrous that Ariel should put so much rebellious energy into becoming the girl next door.

The visual style of the movie makes Andersen's painful story seem oddly 25 encouraging by comparison. Andersen shifts points of view back and forth between the mermaids, who see our world as exotic, and his own audience, who glamorize the unknown world below. He provides lavish descriptions of the shore as well as the sea in order to reawaken his listeners' sense of wonder at their own city lights, sunsets, forests, and hills (151–52). An outsider's desire to live here thus becomes quite understandable. The movie contains no such balance, for beauty and splendor are mainly found "Under the Sea," the title of the dizzying production number in which Sebastian the crab tries to convince Ariel that there's no place like home. Here creatures and objects are surrealistically combined and transformed into an underwater orchestra. Here in abundance are the magical bubbles that have signaled fun with physics in Disney movies from *Snow White* to

Dumbo to *Cinderella*. The world of humans, in contrast, though picturesque, is static and finite. When Ariel takes a bath at Eric's palace, while mundane, gossiping laundresses wash her clothes, one is forced to notice that bubbles here just don't *do* anything. Similarly, Grimsby's pipe, which Ariel mistakes for a musical instrument, produces more soot than smoke—nothing approaching the punning puffs from the caterpillar's hookah in *Alice,* or even the smoky ink that billows about in the sea witch's cave. Clearly, Sebastian is right: It is "better down where it's wetter."

26   The images the movie uses to tell the story thus give its trendy feminism a reverse spin. Whatever Ariel might *say,* or sing, what we see her *do* is flee a world of infinite possibility to settle in the land of the banal. Her fantasy is a sort of anti-fantasy. Yes, she gets her legs, she makes her stand, she marches—but only down the aisle, to marry some guy named Eric.

27   Many fairy tales, and many more movies, end with a wedding, and for this reason they often draw censure from critics, such as Janet Wasko (116) and Elizabeth Bell (114, 155), who would like to see our daughters presented with other options. Without question there ought to be more than one girls' story out there, relentlessly repeated with minor variations. I would also argue, however, that just as in life there are marriages and marriages, so in fiction living happily ever after is not always a euphemism for dying. When the marriage seems to grant the heroine true personal fulfillment and possibilities for further growth, the ending may actually seem like the beginning of a new life. Such is the case with *Beauty and the Beast,* a tale endowed by ancient archetypes with a feminine power that resists the attempts of individual authors, such as Madame Leprince de Beaumont in 1757, to tie its heroine down to mediocrity. With *The Little Mermaid* behind us, we might expect Disney's version to dole out a similarly dull and didactic message, clothed in mock-progressive nineties clichés of gender equality. But in Disney's *Beauty and the Beast,* thanks in part to the screenplay by Linda Woolverton (the first woman writer of a Disney animated feature), imagination flows freely in the words and the images, allowing the tale to work its magic.[10]

28   One problem with the plot that ends in marriage, of course, is its reduction of the heroine to an object of desire, and therefore a heroine actually named Beauty would not, on the face of it, seem like a good role model. In this tale, however, with its roots penetrating beyond the Cupid and Psyche tale from Apuleius's *The Golden Ass* to very old stories about beast bridegrooms (Warner 275; Zipes 24–25), the heroine is more subject than object because her quest for a desirable mate drives the plot. (Apuleius intensifies the female point of view by having the tale narrated by an old woman [Warner 275].) Of course, the whole question of the story's sexual politics hinges on whether the heroine's desire can be consciously controlled, by herself or by others; whether, as is often said in Christian wedding ceremonies, love is an act of will rather than a feeling; whether, therefore, she can make herself love the one she "ought." Conservative versions of

[10]See Bell 114; Murphy 133–34; Warner 313.

Beauty and the Beast do tend to assume such schooling of the will is possible, as Jack Zipes emphasizes (29–40). Nevertheless, an important feature even in such versions is that the beast, though he may be dutifully or even cheerfully endured, cannot become a handsome prince until the heroine actively wants him, truly chooses him for reasons of her own. The young female audience is thus reassured that sex in conjunction with love is pleasant rather than frightening (Bettelheim 306; Warner 312–13); in other words, the beast of one's choice is not a beast at all.

At about the same time Charlotte Lennox was composing *The Female Quixote,* 29 Madame Leprince de Beaumont, with similar concerns about young women's imaginations, was dressing this ancient tale in anti-romance, turning to her own purpose a Scudérian vocabulary of love that, to her readers, would be all too familiar. Beauty feels "esteem" for the Beast because of his "great service" to her, and eventually she comes to feel "tenderness" for him as she wants to care for him and ease his distress (Beaumont 37). Out of this tenderness comes a desire to marry him—including, one supposes, some sexual feeling. The romance code word for active sexual desire—"inclination"—never appears.[11] By telling her young readers that esteem and tenderness are the best basis for marriage, Beaumont warns them not to wait for the handsome, witty lover of their fantasies; in the closing words of the rewarding fairy: "You have preferred virtue before either wit or beauty, and you deserve to find one in whom all these are united" (47). In this way, the author joins the tradition of conservative writers who urge girls to face reality and, to the very limited extent they will be permitted to choose, to choose wisely.[12] Still, while schooling the reader in what she ought to desire, Beaumont cannot avoid conveying the importance of the heroine's will, for until Beauty desires the Beast, a beast he will remain.

The Disney movie reaches past Beaumont to draw upon older strains of the 30 story. For example, here, as in some older versions, including that of Beaumont's immediate predecessor, Madame de Villeneuve (Warner 290–91), it is the Beast rather than Beauty who is supposed to learn self-control. The heroine is therefore permitted—even encouraged—to fantasize to her heart's content. Where Beaumont only noted that Beauty liked to read, Disney enlarges on Belle's taste in books, which turns out to be just like Arabella's: fairy tales and romances about swordfights, magic, a prince in disguise, and above all, a "she" at the center of the action. Nor is she content just to read about "adventure in the great wide somewhere." Given the chance to tour the Beast's library—ordinarily for Belle the greatest of temptations—she chooses instead to explore the forbidden west wing of his castle, as if somehow aware that she will find there the escape from "provincial life" she has been longing and singing for. For all her quixotism, however, Belle, unlike Arabella, is seen as "rather odd" only by her neighbors, not by her audience.

[11]See the Map of Tender in Scudéry's *Clelia* (1:42).
[12]See Warner 292–94.

31   Certainly, as several commentators observe, the movie has its share of politically correct modern touches to underscore the heroine's self-determination (Warner 316–17; Zipes 46). Interestingly, however, each apparent innovation in fact draws on the French romance tradition that Belle and Arabella revere. Most notably, the movie makes contemporary-sounding statements about gender stereotypes by introducing a new character as foil to the Beast, the hypermasculine Gaston, who boasts in a Sigmund Romberg-ish aria, "I'm especially good at expectorating," "I use antlers in all of my decorating," and "every last inch of me's covered with hair." He is the real beast, of course, an animal who sneers at the Beast for being so openly in touch with his feminine side, "the Male Chauvinist Pig [. . .] that would turn the women of any primetime talkshow audience into beasts themselves" (Jeffords 170). But Gaston is not really new. He dates back, beyond the Cocteau movie often cited as his source, to the French romance villain who loves the heroine selfishly, determined to possess her by force: by winning her in a duel, carrying her off, or scheming to get her parents to give her to him. Gaston arranges to have Belle's eccentric father locked in a madhouse unless she agrees to marry him. Then he nearly kills the Beast under the illusion that the winner gets Belle as prize. The Beast, in contrast, is the romance hero who fights the villain to win the heroine's freedom, not her hand, which he will accept only as her gift. In fact, he would rather die than oppress her. By choosing the Beast over Gaston, Belle helps this ancient story confirm the value of a woman's equal right to a will of her own.

32   Gaston also helps this movie make another observation mistakenly thought of as modern: that men and women aren't nearly as different as some men would like them to be. This idea is found in women's romantic writing from the seventeenth century on,[13] and it reverberates in Belle's opening song as she wishes for someone who understands her and shares her interests. Naturally she chooses to marry the gentleman who gives her the key to his extensive library, not the "positively primeval" clod who throws her book in the mud with a warning about what happens to society when women are taught to read. And in the end, when the spell is broken and the Beast resumes his original shape, he markedly resembles Belle, unruly bangs and all. By marrying a man who can help her get what she wants, and who wants the same things, symbolically she is marrying an aspect of herself.[14]

33   The Beast's oddly familiar new face is not the only image in the movie that makes one feel the heroine's fantasy is a worthy one. Much creativity was lavished on the look of the castle that provides the atmosphere of old romance. Although for most of the movie it resembles a Gothic ruin, and Belle comes here at first as a prisoner, it is really a house of magic in which every object is alive, or "animated"—most famously the dinnerware that dances and sings "Be Our Guest." And the enchantment does not quite end with the breaking of the spell,

[13]See for example the pastoral lyrics of Aphra Behn.
[14]See Clarissa Pinkola Estes for an interpretation of the Beast as an aspect of the heroine's own personality (272–73). Warner also discusses how the beast in modern versions of the tale, including Disney's, functions to help the heroine get in touch with her own inner beast, or sexuality (307–13).

but is rather replaced with a different kind of magic as the castle comes into its original baroque splendor with a seeming infinity of detail, something new around every corner, and always a new corner, for the eye to explore. As Belle waltzes with her Prince around that gorgeous marble hall, the title tune welling up around them, one may see as well as feel that she's getting not just a husband, but more books than she can read in a lifetime, and a home as big and beautiful as her imagination.

Neither age, divorce, nor parenthood has yet made me cynical enough to see the ending of this movie without a sob of satisfaction. But then Disney did begin training me to react in just that way from a very early age (the first movie I ever saw, at the age of five, was *Sleeping Beauty*). Critics have been warning the public for decades about the Disney program to bring about the complete "invasion and control of children's imaginations" (Schickel 18), as well as the silencing of fairy tales' originally female voice (Warner 416–17); no doubt I am a cipher in the company's success. How much more complete the Disney conquest will become for our children and grandchildren, with the constant replay made possible by video and DVD, is definitely cause for concern. 34

The market forces that drive Disney today are dangerous, to be sure, as is the ideology of the marketplace the movies promote, as Giroux and others warn. Fortunately, however, because the overriding goal is self-promotion—because Disney will absorb and use whatever works, or whatever sells the product—the movies lack the philosophical consistency of propaganda.[15] Thus films like *Beauty and the Beast,* which pays more than lip-service to the liberating potential of fantasy, can sometimes appear. 35

Nevertheless, the fact that many Disney movies implant seeds of guilt and fear to spring up along with children's developing imaginations is a serious problem. The mixed messages noticeable in *Alice* are present in earlier movies such as *Dumbo* and "The Sorcerer's Apprentice" in *Fantasia.* They continue in more recent examples such as *Hercules* and *The Hunchback of Notre Dame,* in which only evil and terrifying characters wield the transformative power that is, in essence, the animator's art; thus these movies almost identify themselves as products of black magic.[16] Some recent films seem almost to reject the notion of animation altogether, striking the eye most forcibly with stills such as the battlefield in *Mulan,* or the cathedral of Notre Dame—breathtaking, to be sure, but unlike the Beast's castle, completely static. Clearly the reluctance to embrace imagination with both arms is still present among the many and shifting ideas that make up the Disney ethos. 36

The inconsistencies found in these movies do not lighten either the parent's burden of guiding the young in their adventures with the media, or the critic's task 37

---

[15]Giroux notes inconsistent values among elements in the films (5, 91). Wasko emphasizes consistent elements that make "classic Disney" a recognizable "brand" (3, 152), but does not explore tensions among the elements she lists as consistent, such as "work ethic" vs. "escape fantasy" (114).

[16]A notable exception is *The Emperor's New Groove,* in which magic transformative potions intended as evil by the villain turn positive and bring about both the narrative and visual climax of the movie.

of understanding the various manifestations of culture. On the contrary, they oblige us to do more than count the number of profane words or violent acts or exposed body parts; and also to do more than catalogue plots, count the numbers of males and females, and quantify relative levels of aggression. Instead, we must watch carefully the interplay of elements within the films and notice how many stories are going on at one time. Watching the faces of our children as they watch, we will often find that imagination, in these movies, is like Alice's garden—just beyond a little locked door, the key to which is tantalizingly, frustratingly out of reach.

WORKS CITED*

Alice in Wonderland. Dir. Clyde Geronimi, Hamilton Luske, and Wilfred Jackson. Walt Disney Company, 1951.

Allan, Robin. "Alice in Disneyland." *Sight and Sound* 54 (Spring 1985): 136–38.

Allen, Holly, and Michael Denning. "The Cartoonists' Front." *South Atlantic Quarterly* 92.1 (1993): 89–117.

Andersen, Hans Christian. "The Little Mermaid." *Hans Christian Andersen: His Classic Fairy Tales.* Trans. Erik Haugaard. Garden City, NY: Doubleday, 1978. 149–70.

Apuleius. *Transformations of Lucius Otherwise Known as the Golden Ass.* Trans. Robert Graves. New York: Noonday, 1998.

Austen, Jane. *Selected Letters.* Oxford: Oxford UP, 1985.

Beaumont, Madame Leprince de. *Beauty and the Beast.* Trans. P. H. Muir. New York: Knopf, 1968.

Beauty and the Beast. Dir. Gary Trousdale and Kirk Wise. Walt Disney Company, 1991.

Behn, Aphra. *The Works of Aphra Behn: Poetry.* Ed. Janet Todd. Columbus: Ohio UP, 1992.

Bell, Elizabeth. "Somatexts at the Disney Shop." Bell, Haas, and Sells 107–24.

Bell, Elizabeth, Lynda Haas, and Laura Sells, eds. *From Mouse to Mermaid: The Politics of Film, Gender, and Culture.* Bloomington: Indiana UP, 1995.

Bettelheim, Bruno. *The Uses of Enchantment.* New York: Vintage, 1977.

Britton, Donald. "The Dark Side of Disneyland." *Mythomania: Fantasies, Fables, and Sheer Lies in Contemporary American Popular Art.* By Bernard Welt. Los Angeles: Art Issues, 1996. 113–26.

Carroll, Lewis. *Alice's Adventures in Wonderland and Through the Looking-Glass.* New York: New American Library, 1960.

Cinderella. Dir. Hamilton Luske and Wilfred Jackson. Walt Disney Company, 1950.

Dumbo. Dir. Ben Sharpsteen. Walt Disney Company, 1941.

Eliot, Marc. *Walt Disney: Hollywood's Dark Prince.* New York: Birch Lane, 1993.

The Emperor's New Groove. Dir. Mark Dindal. Walt Disney Company, 2000.

Estes, Clarissa Pinkola. *Women Who Run with the Wolves.* New York: Ballantine, 1992.

*As noted in the Networking question that follows, this Works Cited section does not follow the latest MLA style. The spacing has also been condensed.

Fantasia. Dir. Ford Beebe and Bill Roberts. Walt Disney Company, 1942.

Gilbert, Sandra, and Susan Gubar. *The Madwoman in the Attic.* New Haven: Yale UP, 1979.

Giroux, Henry. *The Mouse That Roared: Disney and the End of Innocence.* Lanham, MD: Rowman, 1999.

Hansen, Miriam. "Of Mice and Ducks: Benjamin and Adorno on Disney." *South Atlantic Quarterly* 92.1 (1993): 27–61.

Hedges, Inez. *Languages of Revolt: Dada and Surrealist Literature and Film.* Durham: Duke UP, 1983.

Hercules. Dir. Ron Clements and John Musker. Walt Disney Company, 1997.

The Hunchback of Notre Dame. Dir. Gary Trousdale and Kirk Wise. Walt Disney Company, 1996.

Hunter, J. Paul. "'The Young, the Ignorant, and the Idle': Some Notes on Readers and the Beginnings of the English Novel." *Anticipations of the Enlightenment in England, France, and Germany.* Ed. Alan Charles Kors and Paul J. Korshin. Philadelphia: U of Pennsylvania P, 1987. 259–82.

Jeffords, Susan. "The Curse of Masculinity." Bell, Haas, and Sells 161–72.

Johnson, Samuel. *The Rambler.* Ed. W. J. Bate and Albrecht B. Strauss. New Haven: Yale UP, 1969.

Lennox, Charlotte. *The Female Quixote,* 1759. Boston: Pandora, 1986.

Lewis, Jon. "Disney after Disney." *Disney Discourse: Producing the Magic Kingdom.* Ed. Eric Smoodin. New York: Routledge, 1994.

Lilo and Stitch. Dir. Dean DeBlois and Chris Sanders (III). Walt Disney Company, 2002.

The Lion King. Dir. Rob Minkoff and Roger Allers. Walt Disney Company, 1994.

The Little Mermaid. Dir. John Musker and Ron Clements. Walt Disney Company, 1989.

Mulan. Dir. Tony Bancroft and Barry Cook. Walt Disney Company, 1998.

Murphy, Patrick D. "'The Whole Wide World Was Scrubbed Clean': The Androcentric Animation of Denatured Disney." Bell, Haas, and Sells 125–36.

Pocahontas. Dir. Mike Gabriel and Eric Goldberg. Walt Disney Company, 1995.

Ross, Deborah. *The Excellence of Falsehood.* Lexington: UP of Kentucky, 1991.

Schickel, Richard. *The Disney Version.* New York: Simon, 1968.

Scudéry, Madeleine de. *Clelia.* Trans. John Davies. London: Herringman, 1678.

Sells, Laura. "'Where Do the Mermaids Stand?' Voice and Body in *The Little Mermaid.*" Bell, Haas, and Sells 175–92.

The Sleeping Beauty. Dir. Clyde Geronimi. Walt Disney Company, 1959.

Snow White and the Seven Dwarfs. Dir. David Hand. Walt Disney Company, 1938.

Warner, Marina. *From the Beast to the Blonde: On Fairy Tales and Their Tellers.* New York: Noonday, 1994.

Wasko, Janet. *Understanding Disney.* Cambridge, UK: Polity, 2001.

Watts, Steven. "Walt Disney: Art and Politics in the American Century." *Journal of American History* 82.1 (June 1995): 84–110.

Zipes, Jack. *Fairy Tale as Myth/Myth as Fairy Tale.* Lexington: UP of Kentucky, 1994.

COMPREHENSION

1. How does Ross define the ideology inherent in Disney's films for girls?
2. Summarize the content of the three films that Ross discusses. What similarities and differences does Ross see among them?
3. According to the writer, what is a "female quixote"? Where does she treat this concept directly and indirectly?

RHETORIC

1. This essay appeared in a specialized scholarly journal. What "scholarly" elements appear in the paper? How does Ross adjust her style to this specialized audience? What strategies does she use to make the essay accessible to a wider audience?
2. Where does Ross state her claim most clearly? Analyze the varieties of evidence that she uses to support her claim and the minor propositions.
3. How does the writer organize her essay? What are the main divisions, and how do they cohere?
4. Why does Ross cite other scholars and writers? How does this strategy affect the power of her argument?
5. Ross elaborates a definition of the Disney "program" or ideology. What rhetorical strategies does she use to create this extended definition?
6. How effective do you find the concluding paragraph? Justify your response.

WRITING

1. Select one Disney movie and write an analysis of its "program"—its ethical message or ideology.
2. In an expository essay, explain why children's stories or fairy tales have such a hold on young people's imaginations.
3. **Writing an Argument:** Write a persuasive essay on the benefits of children's literature and film—even the films that Walt Disney produced. Present at least three extended examples to support your claim.

NETWORKING
Applying Digital and Multimedia Literacies

Updating Citations to Reflect Current MLA Style: Since this essay was published, the MLA has made some changes to their guidelines for documenting sources; one change includes noting the medium of each source. Refer to Chapter 15 to help update Ross's Works Cited page; beyond this book's coverage, consult the MLA's Web site, or the seventh edition of the *MLA Handbook,* published in 2009.

Synthesis: Connections for Critical Thinking

1. Examine the role of the media in society and the responsibilities or duties to humanity of individuals associated with the media. Use at least three essays from this chapter to illustrate or support your thesis.
2. Define *popular culture,* using the essays of Barry, Sachs, Ross, and Steinem as reference points, along with any additional essays that you consider relevant.
3. Use the essays of Warshow, Goodlad, Ross, and Gitlin to explore the connections of media representations to American cultural experience. What strategies do these writers use? Are their goals similar?
4. Use the essays of Sachs and Barry to explore the importance of both the causes and effects of the media promoting particular lifestyles to the public.
5. Goodlad explores the cultural significance of *Mad Men*, and Barry presents beer commercials as communicating the traditional "patriotic symbols" of America. Do these authors have similar or differing points of view regarding the issues they address? Refer specifically to selections in each essay to support your view.
6. After reading the essays of Warshow, Sachs, and King, research the issue of the difference between popular entertainment and art. On the basis of your research, discuss whether there are legitimate criteria that distinguish the two forms. Apply these criteria to gangster films, rap music, and horror films.

NETWORKING
Applying Digital and Multimedia Literacies

Select several images of real "gangsters" or other "bad" men from magazines, or print out online images of them. Compare and contrast them with advertisements depicting gangsters from contemporary crime movies such as *The Departed* or *Pulp Fiction*. What are the similarities and differences in the subjects' dress, demeanor, facial expression, and so on? What can you conclude from your comparisons?

chapter *10*

Literature and the Arts
Why Do They Matter?

Imagine a world without fiction, poetry, or drama, without music, art, or other fine arts. We are so accustomed to taking the arts in their totality for granted that it is hard for us to conceive of contemporary culture without them. Our fondness for stories or paintings or any other creative form might help us understand our culture or might even move us to action. Yet the value of various artistic forms doesn't derive exclusively from their ability to tell us something about life. The arts can also take us into an imaginative realm offering perhaps more intense experiences than anything we encounter in the "real" world.

Think of literature and the arts as an exercise in imaginative freedom. You are free to select the books you read, the music that appeals to you, the exhibitions and concerts you attend, and the entertainment software with which you interact. Some of your decisions might be serious and consequential to your education. Other decisions, perhaps to watch a few soap operas on a rainy afternoon or to buy the latest potboiler, are less important. The way you view the arts—whether as a way to learn something about the temper of civilization or as a temporary escape from conventional reality—is entirely a matter of taste. Regardless of your purpose or intent, you approach literature and the arts initially for the sheer exhilaration and pleasure they provide. Art, as Plato observed, is a dream for awakened minds.

The arts awaken you to the power and intensity of the creative spirit. At the same time, you make judgments and evaluations of the nature of your creative encounter. When you assert that you like this painting or dislike that poem, you are assessing the work and the value of the artistic experience. Clearly, you develop taste and become more equipped to discern the more subtle elements of art the more you are exposed to it. Perhaps you prefer to keep your experience of literature and the other arts a pleasurable pastime or an escape from reality. Or you may wish to participate in them as a creative writer, musician, painter, or photographer. Ultimately, you may come to view literature and the arts as a transformational experience, a voyage of discovery in which you encounter diverse peoples and cultures, learn to see the world in creative terms, and begin to perceive your own creative potential in a new light.

PREVIEWING THE CHAPTER

As you read the essays in this chapter and respond to them in discussion and writing, consider the following questions:

- According to the author, what is the value of the art or literary form under discussion?
- What function does literature or art serve?
- Is the writer's perspective subjective or objective, and why?
- How does the author define his or her subject—whether it is poetry, fiction, art, or photography?
- Is the writer's experience of literature or art similar to or different from your own?
- In what ways do gender and race influence the writer's perspective on the subject?
- What is the main idea that the author wants to present about literature or the arts? Do you agree or disagree with this key concept?
- What have you learned about the importance of literature and the arts from reading these essays?

Classic and Contemporary Images
HOW DO WE EVALUATE A WORK OF ART?

Using a Critical Perspective   Although "greatness" in art and literature might be in the mind of the beholder, it could be argued that you need certain standards of excellence or judgment to determine the quality of any work. The artist's or writer's control of the medium, the projection of a unique vision, the evidence of a superlative style—all enter into the evaluation process. As you consider these sculptures by Auguste Rodin and Jeff Koons, try to evaluate their relative worth. Which work reflects greater artistic control? What makes the sculpture appealing, and why? Which work strikes you as "new" or original, or modern? Explain your response and criteria for evaluation.

Auguste Rodin (1840–1917), a French sculptor famous for his bronze and marble figures, is thought by some critics to be one of the greatest portraitists in the history of sculpture. Yet he was also criticized in his time for the excessive realism and sensuousness of his figures. *Walking Man* hints at some of the objections contemporary critics lodged against Rodin's work.

Jeff Koons (b. 1955) is an American artist who, like Rodin, has had his admirers and detractors. Koons studied at the Art Institute of Chicago and elsewhere before becoming a commodities trader in New York City, which helped fund the materials for his art. *Rabbit* reflects Koons's fondness for popular culture and the way in which he takes consumer goods and repositions them as art objects.

Classic and Contemporary Essays
WHAT IS THE VALUE OF LITERATURE?

Although Eudora Welty was born at the beginning of the 20th century in a small Mississippi town and Sherman Alexie half a century later on a tribal reservation in the state of Washington, half a continent away, these writers share a reverence for the importance of literature in their childhood. Of course, there are understandable differences in the types of literature that formed their young minds. Welty, you will discover, grew up in a loving, middle-class household where virtually every room contained books—a treasury of English and European novels, classic fairy tales, and famous works of literature in the Western tradition. Alexie, on the other hand, from a family that was "middle-class by reservation standards" but in actuality poor, had a father who was addicted to alcohol but also to pulp fiction—westerns, detective stories, spy thrillers, comic books featuring action heroes. And despite their disparate backgrounds, lives, and reading tastes, Welty and Alexie grew up to be writers. They might represent different regional, ethnic, and cultural backgrounds, and they speak as a woman and man of different forms of knowledge and experience, but both attest to the value of literature. As they recount their childhood, Welty and Alexie struggle to establish an identity that will last a lifetime. They succeed in convincing us that whether one child reads Dickens and the other Superman comic books, their ideas and insights into the world derive from the active reading of texts.

One Writer's Beginnings

Eudora Welty

Eudora Welty (1909–2001), a celebrated American writer, was born and died in Jackson, Mississippi. Raised in a close-knit bookish family, Welty attended the Mississippi State College for Women for two years and then the University of Wisconsin (BA, 1929). In the 1930s she returned to Mississippi and worked for the Works Progress Administration as a reporter and photographer, traveling the state and recording the lives of its citizens during the Depression years. She also began a career as a short-story writer and novelist. Welty's superb short fiction collections include A Curtain of Green *(1941),* The Wide Net *(1943), and* Collected Stories *(1980), which received an American Book Award. She received the Pulitzer Prize for her novel* The Optimist's Daughter *(1972). The recipient of the President's Medal of Freedom and numerous other major awards, Welty spent virtually her entire life writing about the South but in ways that transcend her region, radiating outward to embrace universal truths. In the selection that follows, one of three lectures delivered at Harvard University in 1983 and published in her memoir* One Writer's Beginnings *(1984), Welty speaks of the value of literature and the arts in her life.*

I learned from the age of two or three that any room in our house, at any time of 1
day, was there to read in, or to be read to. My mother read to me. She'd read to me in the big bedroom in the mornings, when we were in her rocker together, which ticked in rhythm as we rocked, as though we had a cricket accompanying the story. She'd read to me in the diningroom on winter afternoons in front of the coal fire, with our cuckoo clock ending the story with "Cuckoo," and at night when I'd got in my own bed. I must have given her no peace. Sometimes she read to me in the kitchen while she sat churning, and the churning sobbed along with *any* story. It was my ambition to have her read to me while *I* churned; once she granted my wish, but she read off my story before I brought her butter. She was an expressive reader. When she was reading "Puss in Boots," for instance, it was impossible not to know that she distrusted *all* cats.

It had been startling and disappointing to me to find out that story books had 2
been written by *people,* that books were not natural wonders, coming up of themselves like grass. Yet regardless of where they came from, I cannot remember a time when I was not in love with them—with the books themselves, cover and binding and the paper they were printed on, with their smell and their weight and with their possession in my arms, captured and carried off to myself. Still illiterate, I was ready for them, committed to all the reading I could give them.

Neither of my parents had come from homes that could afford to buy many 3
books, but though it must have been something of a strain on his salary, as the youngest officer in a young insurance company, my father was all the while carefully selecting and ordering away for what he and Mother thought we children should grow up with. They bought first for the future.

Besides the bookcase in the livingroom, which was always called "the library," 4
there were the encyclopedia tables and dictionary stand under windows in our diningroom. Here to help us grow up arguing around the diningroom table were the Unabridged Webster, the Columbia Encyclopedia, Compton's Pictured Encyclopedia, the Lincoln Library of Information, and later the Book of Knowledge. And the year we moved into our new house, there was room to celebrate it with the new 1925 edition of the Britannica, which my father, his face always deliberately turned toward the future, was of course disposed to think better than any previous edition.

In "the library," inside the mission-style bookcase with its three diamond-latticed 5
glass doors, with my father's Morris chair and the glass-shaded lamp on its table beside it, were books I could soon begin on—and I did, reading them all alike and as they came, straight down their rows, top shelf to bottom. There was the set of Stoddard's Lectures, in all its late nineteenth-century vocabulary and vignettes of peasant life and quaint beliefs and customs, with matching halftone illustrations: Vesuvius erupting, Venice by moonlight, gypsies glimpsed by their campfires. I didn't know then the clue they were to my father's longing to see the rest of the world. I read straight through his other love-from-afar: the Victrola Book of the

Opera, with opera after opera in synopsis, with portraits in costume of Melba, Caruso, Galli-Curci, and Geraldine Farrar, some of whose voices we could listen to on our Red Seal records.

6   My mother read secondarily for information; she sank as a hedonist into novels. She read Dickens in the spirit in which she would have eloped with him. The novels of her girlhood that had stayed on in her imagination, besides those of Dickens and Scott and Robert Louis Stevenson, were *Jane Eyre, Trilby, The Woman in White, Green Mansions, King Solomon's Mines.* Marie Corelli's name would crop up but I understood she had gone out of favor with my mother, who had only kept *Ardath* out of loyalty. In time she absorbed herself in Galsworthy, Edith Wharton, above all in Thomas Mann of the *Joseph* volumes.

7   *St. Elmo* was not in our house; I saw it often in other houses. This wildly popular Southern novel is where all the Edna Earles in our population started coming from. They're all named for the heroine, who succeeded in bringing a dissolute, sinning roué and atheist of a lover (St. Elmo) to his knees. My mother was able to forgo it. But she remembered the classic advice given to rose growers on how to water their bushes long enough: "Take a chair and *St. Elmo.*"

8   To both my parents I owe my early acquaintance with a beloved Mark Twain. There was a full set of Mark Twain and a short set of Ring Lardner in our bookcase, and those were the volumes that in time united us all, parents and children.

9   Reading everything that stood before me was how I came upon a worn old book without a back that had belonged to my father as a child. It was called *Sanford and Merton.* Is there anyone left who recognizes it, I wonder? It is the famous moral tale written by Thomas Day in the 1780s, but of him no mention is made on the title page of *this* book; here it is *Sanford and Merton in Words of One Syllable* by Mary Godolphin. Here are the rich boy and the poor boy and Mr. Barlow, their teacher and interlocutor, in long discourses alternating with dramatic scenes— danger and rescue allotted to the rich and the poor respectively. It may have only words of one syllable, but one of them is "quoth." It ends with not one but two morals, both engraved on rings: "Do what you ought, come what may," and "If we would be great, we must first learn to be good."

10   This book was lacking its front cover, the back held on by strips of pasted paper, now turned golden, in several layers, and the pages stained, flecked, and tattered around the edges; its garish illustrations had come unattached but were preserved, laid in. I had the feeling even in my heedless childhood that this was the only book my father as a little boy had of his own. He had held onto it, and might have gone to sleep on its coverless face: He had lost his mother when he was seven. My father had never made any mention to his own children of the book, but he had brought it along with him from Ohio to our house and shelved it in our bookcase.

11   My mother had brought from West Virginia that set of Dickens; those books looked sad, too—they had been through fire and water before I was born, she told me, and there they were, lined up—as I later realized, waiting for *me.*

12   I was presented, from as early as I can remember, with books of my own, which appeared on my birthday and Christmas morning. Indeed, my parents could not give me books enough. They must have sacrificed to give me on my sixth or

seventh birthday—it was after I became a reader for myself—the ten-volume set of Our Wonder World. These were beautifully made, heavy books I would lie down with on the floor in front of the diningroom hearth, and more often than the rest volume 5, *Every Child's Story Book,* was under my eyes. There were the fairy tales—Grimm, Andersen, the English, the French, "Ali Baba and the Forty Thieves"; and there was Aesop and Reynard the Fox; there were the myths and legends, Robin Hood, King Arthur, and St. George and the Dragon, even the history of Joan of Arc; a whack of *Pilgrim's Progress* and a long piece of *Gulliver.* They all carried their classic illustrations. I located myself in these pages and could go straight to the stories and pictures I loved; very often "The Yellow Dwarf" was first choice, with Walter Crane's Yellow Dwarf in full color making his terrifying appearance flanked by turkeys. Now that volume is as worn and backless and hanging apart as my father's poor *Sanford and Merton.* The precious page with Edward Lear's "Jumblies" on it has been in danger of slipping out for all these years. One measure of my love for Our Wonder World was that for a long time I wondered if I would go through fire and water for it as my mother had done for Charles Dickens; and the only comfort was to think I could ask my mother to do it for me.

I believe I'm the only child I know of who grew up with this treasure in the 13 house. I used to ask others, "Did you have Our Wonder World?" I'd have to tell them The Book of Knowledge could not hold a candle to it.

I live in gratitude to my parents for initiating me—and as early as I begged for 14 it, without keeping me waiting—into knowledge of the word, into reading and spelling, by way of the alphabet. They taught it to me at home in time for me to begin to read before starting to school. I believe the alphabet is no longer considered an essential piece of equipment for traveling through life. In my day it was the keystone to knowledge. You learned the alphabet as you learned to count to ten, as you learned "Now I lay me" and the Lord's Prayer and your father's and mother's name and address and telephone number, all in case you were lost.

My love for the alphabet, which endures, grew out of reciting it but, before that, 15 out of seeing the letters on the page. In my own story books, before I could read them for myself, I fell in love with various winding, enchanting-looking initials drawn by Walter Crane at the heads of fairy tales. In "Once upon a time," an "O" had a rabbit running it as a treadmill, his feet upon flowers. When the day came, years later, for me to see the Book of Kells, all the wizardry of letter, initial, and word swept over me a thousand times over, and the illumination, the gold, seemed a part of the word's beauty and holiness that had been there from the start.

. . .

Learning stamps you with its moments. Childhood's learning is made up of mo- 16 ments. It isn't steady. It's a pulse.

In a children's art class, we sat in a ring on kindergarten chairs and drew 17 three daffodils that had just been picked out of the yard; and while I was drawing, my sharpened pencil and the cup of the yellow daffodil gave off whiffs just alike. That the pencil doing the drawing should give off the same smell as the flower it drew seemed a part of the art lesson—as shouldn't it be? Children, like animals, use all their senses to discover the world. Then artists come along and discover it the same way, all over again. Here and there, it's the same world. Or now and then we'll hear from an artist who's never lost it.

18   In my sensory education I include my physical awareness of the *word*. Of a certain word, that is; the connection it has with what it stands for. At around age six, perhaps, I was standing by myself in our front yard waiting for supper, just at that hour in a late summer day when the sun is already below the horizon and the risen full moon in the visible sky stops being chalky and begins to take on light. There comes the moment, and I saw it then, when the moon goes from flat to round. For the first time it met my eyes as a globe. The word "moon" came into my mouth as though fed to me out of a silver spoon. Held in my mouth the moon became a word. It had the roundness of a Concord grape Grandpa took off his vine and gave me to suck out of its skin and swallow whole, in Ohio.

19   This love did not prevent me from living for years in foolish error about the moon. The new moon just appearing in the west was the rising moon to me. The new should be rising. And in early childhood the sun and moon, those opposite reigning powers, I just as easily assumed rose in east and west respectively in their opposite sides of the sky, and like partners in a reel they advanced, sun from the east, moon from the west, crossed over (when I wasn't looking) and went down on the other side. My father couldn't have known I believed that when, bending behind me and guiding my shoulder, he positioned me at our telescope in the front yard and, with careful adjustment of the focus, brought the moon close to me.

20   The night sky over my childhood Jackson was velvety black. I could see the full constellations in it and call their names; when I could read, I knew their myths. Though I was always waked for eclipses, and indeed carried to the window as an infant in arms and shown Halley's Comet in my sleep, and though I'd been taught at our diningroom table about the solar system and knew the earth revolved around the sun, and our moon around us, I never found out the moon didn't come up in the west until I was a writer and Herschel Brickell, the literary critic, told me after I misplaced it in a story. He said valuable words to me about my new profession: "Always be sure you get your moon in the right part of the sky."

                                    . . .

21 My mother always sang to her children. Her voice came out just a little bit in the minor key. "Wee Willie Winkie's" song was wonderfully sad when she sang the lullabies.

22   "Oh, but now there's a record. She could have her own record to listen to," my father would have said. For there came a Victrola record of "Bobby Shafftoe" and "Rock-a-Bye Baby," all of Mother's lullabies, which could be played to take her place. Soon I was able to play her my own lullabies all day long.

23   Our Victrola stood in the diningroom. I was allowed to climb onto the seat of a diningroom chair to wind it, start the record turning, and set the needle playing. In a second I'd jumped to the floor, to spin or march around the table as the music called for—now there were all the other records I could play too. I skinned back onto the chair just in time to lift the needle at the end, stop the record and turn it over, then change the needle. That brass receptacle with a hole in the lid gave off a metallic smell like human sweat, from all the hot needles that were fed it. Winding

up, dancing, being cocked to start and stop the record, was of course all in one the act of *listening*—to "Overture to *Daughter of the Regiment*," "Selections from *The Fortune Teller*," "Kiss Me Again," "Gypsy Dance from *Carmen*," "Stars and Stripes Forever," "When the Midnight Choo-Choo Leaves for Alabam," or whatever came next. Movement must be at the very heart of listening.

Ever since I was first read to, then started reading to myself, there has never 24 been a line read that I didn't *hear.* As my eyes followed the sentence, a voice was saying it silently to me. It isn't my mother's voice, or the voice of any person I can identify, certainly not my own. It is human, but inward, and it is inwardly that I listen to it. It is to me the voice of the story or the poem itself. The cadence, whatever it is that asks you to believe, the feeling that resides in the printed word, reaches me through the reader-voice. I have supposed, but never found out, that this is the case with all readers—to read as listeners—and with all writers, to write as listeners. It may be part of the desire to write. The sound of what falls on the page begins the process of testing it for truth, for me. Whether I am right to trust so far I don't know. By now I don't know whether I could do either one, reading or writing, without the other.

My own words, when I am at work on a story, I hear too as they go, in the same 25 voice that I hear when I read in books. When I write and the sound of it comes back to my ears, then I act to make my changes. I have always trusted this voice.

COMPREHENSION

1. What is the significance of the essay's title? Does Welty write about one continuous "beginning" or a series of beginnings? Explain.
2. What does Welty mean when she says that her mother was a "hedonist" (paragraph 6)? Does Welty also become a hedonist? Why or why not?
3. Explain the nature of Welty's "sensory" education.

RHETORIC

1. Welty alludes to dozens of works of literature. What does she assume about her audience's knowledge of these works? Can you appreciate the essay even if you are not familiar with most of this literature? Justify your response.
2. What is Welty's thesis, and how does she develop it?
3. What determines the order in which Welty organizes her essay, which she divides into three parts?
4. Welty includes several descriptive passages in this essay. Where are these passages, and what do they contribute to the overall meaning of the selection?
5. How do the last two paragraphs of the essay echo the first two paragraphs?

WRITING

1. Write a description of a scene or series of events from your childhood in which you were reading (or being read to), engaged in an art project, or listening to music. In your essay, explain the impact of this memory or activity on your current life.

2. Write an essay explaining the importance of providing children with sensory stimuli involving reading, artwork, and music.

3. **Writing an Argument:** Argue for or against the proposition that children today read less than those of previous generations—and suffer the consequences.

NETWORKING
Applying Digital and Multimedia Literacies

Can e-Readers Save Reading? It's looking likely that children will soon be reading most texts—from textbooks to novels to comics—electronically. How might an electronic format make reading *more* engaging for today's kids? How might this new form enhance, rather than detract from, reading as a sensory experience?

Superman and Me

Sherman Alexie

Sherman Alexie *(b. 1966) grew up and still lives on the Spokane Indian Reservation in Wellpinit, Washington. A Spokane/Coeur d'Alene tribal member, Alexie contended with a life-threatening illness when he was young, but managed to attend Gonzaga University before transferring to Washington State University (BA, 1991). Alexie writes and creates in many modes, and is also a performer. As many of the titles of his works suggest, the Native American experience informs his short stories, novels, poetry, songs, and films. Alexie's fiction includes* Reservation Blues *(1995),* Ten Little Indians: Stories *(2003), and* Flight, A Novel *(2007); his poetry has been collected in* First Indian on the Moon *(1993),* The Man Who Loves Salmon *(1998), and other volumes. In the following essay, Alexie attests to the importance of literature—all kinds of literature—in his life.*

1   I learned to read with a Superman comic book. Simple enough, I suppose. I cannot recall which particular Superman comic book I read, nor can I remember which villain he fought in that issue. I cannot remember the plot, nor the means by which I obtained the comic book. What I can remember is this: I was 3 years old, a Spokane Indian boy living with his family on the Spokane Indian Reservation in eastern Washington state. We were poor by most standards, but one of my parents usually managed to find some minimum-wage job or another, which made us middle-class by reservation standards. I had a brother and three sisters. We lived on a combination of irregular paychecks, hope, fear, and government surplus food.

2   My father, who is one of the few Indians who went to Catholic school on purpose, was an avid reader of westerns, spy thrillers, murder mysteries, gangster epics, basketball player biographies, and anything else he could find. He bought

his books by the pound at Dutch's Pawn Shop, Goodwill, Salvation Army, and Value Village. When he had extra money, he bought new novels at supermarkets, convenience stores, and hospital gift shops. Our house was filled with books. They were stacked in crazy piles in the bathroom, bedrooms, and living room. In a fit of unemployment-inspired creative energy, my father built a set of bookshelves and soon filled them with a random assortment of books about the Kennedy assassination, Watergate, the Vietnam War, and the entire 23-book series of the Apache westerns. My father loved books, and since I loved my father with an aching devotion, I decided to love books as well.

I can remember picking up my father's books before I could read. The words 3 themselves were mostly foreign, but I still remember the exact moment when I first understood, with a sudden clarity, the purpose of a paragraph. I didn't have the vocabulary to say "paragraph," but I realized that a paragraph was a fence that held words. The words inside a paragraph worked together for a common purpose. They had some specific reason for being inside the same fence. This knowledge delighted me. I began to think of everything in terms of paragraphs. Our reservation was a small paragraph within the United States. My family's house was a paragraph, distinct from the other paragraphs of the LeBrets to the north, the Fords to our south, and the Tribal School to the west. Inside our house, each family member existed as a separate paragraph but still had genetics and common experiences to link us. Now, using this logic, I can see my changed family as an essay of seven paragraphs: mother, father, older brother, the deceased sister, my younger twin sisters, and our adopted little brother.

At the same time I was seeing the world in paragraphs, I also picked up that 4 Superman comic book. Each panel, complete with picture, dialogue, and narrative was a three-dimensional paragraph. In one panel, Superman breaks through a door. His suit is red, blue, and yellow. The brown door shatters into many pieces. I look at the narrative above the picture. I cannot read the words, but I assume it tells me that "Superman is breaking down the door." Aloud, I pretend to read the words and say, "Superman is breaking down the door." Words, dialogue, also float out of Superman's mouth. Because he is breaking down the door, I assume he says, "I am breaking down the door." Once again, I pretend to read the words and say aloud, "I am breaking down the door." In this way, I learned to read.

This might be an interesting story all by itself. A little Indian boy teaches 5 himself to read at an early age and advances quickly. He reads "Grapes of Wrath" in kindergarten when other children are struggling through "Dick and Jane." If he'd been anything but an Indian boy living on the reservation, he might have been called a prodigy. But he is an Indian boy living on the reservation and is simply an oddity. He grows into a man who often speaks of his childhood in the third person, as if it will somehow dull the pain and make him sound more modest about his talents.

A smart Indian is a dangerous person, widely feared and ridiculed by Indians and 6 non-Indians alike. I fought with my classmates on a daily basis. They wanted me to stay quiet when the non-Indian teacher asked for answers, for volunteers, for help. We were Indian children who were expected to be stupid. Most lived up to those expectations inside the classroom but subverted them on the outside. They struggled with basic reading in school but could remember how to sing a few dozen powwow songs. They were monosyllabic in front of their non-Indian teachers but could tell complicated stories and jokes at the dinner table. They submissively ducked their heads when confronted by a non-Indian adult but would slug it out with the Indian bully who was 10 years older. As Indian children, we were expected to fail in the non-Indian world. Those who failed were ceremonially accepted by other Indians and appropriately pitied by non-Indians.

7   I refused to fail. I was smart. I was arrogant. I was lucky. I read books late into the night, until I could barely keep my eyes open. I read books at recess, then during lunch, and in the few minutes left after I had finished my classroom assignments. I read books in the car when my family traveled to powwows or basketball games. In shopping malls, I ran to the bookstores and read bits and pieces of as many books as I could. I read the books my father brought home from the pawnshops and secondhand. I read the books I borrowed from the library. I read the backs of cereal boxes. I read the newspaper. I read the bulletins posted on the walls of the school, the clinic, the tribal offices, the post office. I read junk mail. I read auto-repair manuals. I read magazines. I read anything that had words and paragraphs. I read with equal parts joy and desperation. I loved those books, but I also knew that love had only one purpose. I was trying to save my life.

8   Despite all the books I read, I am still surprised I became a writer. I was going to be a pediatrician. These days, I write novels, short stories, and poems. I visit schools and teach creative writing to Indian kids. In all my years in the reservation school system, I was never taught how to write poetry, short stories, or novels. I was certainly never taught that Indians wrote poetry, short stories, and novels. Writing was something beyond Indians. I cannot recall a single time that a guest teacher visited the reservation. There must have been visiting teachers. Who were they? Where are they now? Do they exist? I visit the schools as often as possible. The Indian kids crowd the classroom. Many are writing their own poems, short stories, and novels. They have read my books. They have read many other books. They look at me with bright eyes and arrogant wonder. They are trying to save their lives. Then there are the sullen and already defeated Indian kids who sit in the back rows and ignore me with theatrical precision. The pages of their notebooks are empty. They carry neither pencil nor pen. They stare out the window. They refuse and resist. "Books," I say to them. "Books," I say. I throw my weight against their locked doors. The door holds. I am smart. I am arrogant. I am lucky. I am trying to save our lives.

COMPREHENSION

1. Do you find it paradoxical that Alexie learned to read with a Superman comic book? Why or why not? What does Alexie learn from reading the Superman comic?
2. What connections do you see between Alexie and his father?
3. What does Alexie mean when he writes, "A smart Indian is a dangerous person . . . " (paragraph 6)?

RHETORIC

1. Does Alexie state or imply his thesis? State his thesis in your own words.
2. What is Alexie's purpose in writing this essay?
3. Why does Alexie divide his essay into two parts? Do you find this organizational scheme effective? Why or why not?
4. Explain the importance of comparison and contrast in this essay.
5. Alexie's concluding paragraph is quite long. Does it serve as an effective ending? Why or why not?

WRITING

1. Write a personal essay about the types of popular literature that you liked to read as a child.
2. **Writing an Argument:** Do you agree or disagree with Alexie's claim that a literate person—especially a member of any group that has experienced discrimination—is necessarily a dangerous individual? Write an argumentative essay in response to this question.

NETWORKING
Applying Digital and Multimedia Literacies

Comparing Reading and Viewing Habits: Write a comparative essay in which you discuss the reading and viewing habits of your parents and your own tastes. Which media do each of you prefer for popular entertainment, and which do you prefer to get the news? Do you tend to *learn* more from watching a program, reading a print text, or reading an online hyperlinked text? Explore why.

Synthesis: Classic and Contemporary Essays for Comparison

1. Summarize and critique these two writers' agendas, explaining where their ideas overlap and where they diverge.
2. According to both writers, reading in childhood is important. How do Welty and Alexie support this claim? What types of evidence do they present?
3. Compare and contrast the style of each essay. Which essay seems more accessible to you, and why?
4. Imagine what Alexie might say about Welty's essay. What would he see in it that might inform his own writing?

NETWORKING
Applying Digital and Multimedia Literacies

Go online and find out more about these two writers. Focus on Welty's life in Jackson, Mississippi, and Alexie's life on the Spokane Indian Reservation. Then write a brief essay summarizing the importance of place in their writing.

Moving Along

John Updike

John Updike (1932–2009), a major American novelist, short-story writer, poet, and critic, was born in Shillington, Pennsylvania. He graduated from Harvard University (AB, 1954) and attended the Ruskin School of Drawing and Fine Art at Oxford University. Associated for decades with the New Yorker, *where his short fiction, poetry, reviews, and criticism frequently appeared, Updike carved for himself a rare reputation as a master of several literary genres. He published more than 40 books during his career. Focusing in his fiction on suburban middle-class life, Updike received two Pulitzer prizes and many other major awards, including a National Book Award for his novel* The Centaur *(1963). His fiction includes the much-admired "Rabbit" quintet, five novels that track one central character, first introduced in* Rabbit, Run *(1960), through the passages in his life. Updike's poetry collections include* The Carpentered Hen and Other Tame Creatures *(1958) and* Americana: And Other Poems *(2001). Updike included the following essay in* Just Looking *(1981), a collection of his art criticism.*

1   In dreams, one is frequently travelling, and the more hallucinatory moments of our waking life, many of them, are spent in cars, trains, and airplanes. For millennia, Man has walked or run to where he wanted to go; the first naked ape who had the mad idea of mounting a horse (or was it a *Camelops?*) launched a series of subtle internal dislocations of which jet lag is a vivid modern form. When men come to fly through space at near the speed of light, they will return to earth a century later but only a few years older. Now, driving (say) from Boston to Pittsburgh in a day, we arrive feeling greatly aged by the engine's innumerable explosive heartbeats, by the monotony of the highway surface and the constant windy press of unnatural speed. Beside the highway, a clamorous parasitic life signals for attention and halt; localities where generations have lived, bred, labored, and died are flung through the windshield and out through the rearview mirror. Men on the move brutalize themselves and render the world they arrow through phantasmal.

2   Our two artists, separated by two centuries, capture well the eeriness of travel. In the Punjab Hills painting, Baz Bahadur, prince of Malwa, has eloped with the lovely Rupmati; in order to keep him faithful to her, the legend goes, she takes him riding by moonlight. The moon appears to exist not only in the sky but behind a grove of trees. Deer almost blend into the mauve-gray hills. A little citadel basks in starlight on a hilltop. In this soft night, nothing is brighter than the scarlet pasterns of the horses. Baz Bahadur's steed bears on his hide a paler version of the starry sky, and in his violet genitals carries a hint of this nocturnal ride's sexual undercurrent. To judge from the delicacy of their gestures and glances, the riders are being borne along as smoothly as on a merry-go-round. Though these lovers and their panoply are formalized to static perfection, if we cover them, a surprising depth appears in the top third of the painting, and carries the eye away.

Artist unknown, *Baz Bahadur and Rupmati Riding by Moonlight,* c. 1780. Pahari miniature in Kangra style, 8¾ × 6¼". The British Museum, Department of Oriental Antiquities, London.

The riders in Roy de Forest's contemporary painting move through a forest as 3 crowded, garish, and menacing as the neon-lit main drag of a city. A throng of sinister bystanders, one built of brick and another with eyes that are paste gems, witness the passage of this *Canoe of Fate,* which with the coarseness of its stitching and the bulk of its passengers would make slow headway even on a less crowded canvas. Beyond the mountains, heavenly medallions and balloons of stippled color pre-empt space. Only the gesture of the black brave, echoing that of George Washington in another fabulous American crossing, gives a sense of direction and promises to open a path. Two exotic birds, a slavering wolf, and what may be a fair captive (gazing backward toward settlements where other red-haired bluefaces mourn her) freight the canoe with a suggestion of allegory, of myths to which we have lost the key. The personnel of the aboriginal New World, at any rate, are here deep-dyed but not extinguished by the glitter and jazz of an urban-feeling wilderness.

In both representations, the movement is from right to left, like that of writing 4 in the Semitic languages, like the motion of a mother when she instinctively shifts

Roy de Forest, *Canoe of Fate,* 1974. Polymer on canvas, 66¾ × 90¼". Philadelphia Museum of Art, The Adele Haas Turner and Beatrice Pastorius Turner Fund.

her baby to her left arm, to hold it closer to her heart. It feels natural, this direction, and slightly uphill. We gaze at these dreamlike tapestries of travel confident that no progress will be made—we will awaken in our beds.

COMPREHENSION

1. According to Updike, why does the idea of travel have such a hold on the collective imagination? What is the relationship of the travel motif to art?
2. Describe the two paintings that Updike analyzes in this essay. What other famous painting does he allude to in paragraph 3?
3. Why does Updike emphasize the "eeriness" of the two paintings? What is he saying about the human psyche?

RHETORIC

1. How does Updike design his introductory paragraph? What is his purpose?
2. What is Updike's thesis? Does he state or imply it? Explain.
3. Identify specific passages that highlight Updike's descriptive style. What types of figurative language does he employ?

4. Explain Updike's comparative method. What do the reproductions of the two paintings contribute to the overall comparative effect? Would this brief essay be as effective without these images? Why or why not?

5. Why is Updike's concluding paragraph relatively brief when compared with the preceding paragraphs? Is this end paragraph effective? Justify your response.

WRITING

1. Consider the two paintings that Updike reproduces, and write your own comparative essay based on them.

2. **Writing an Argument:** Argue for or against the proposition that when viewing a work of art, it is not necessary to relate it—as Updike does—to human behavior.

NETWORKING
Applying Digital and Multimedia Literacies

Analyzing Themes in Fine Art: Select two paintings that reflect what you consider to be a common theme, and write a comparative essay about them. Provide images of these paintings in your essay. Recommended sites for viewing paintings include the Metropolitan Museum of Art, the Art Institute of Chicago, the Louvre, the New Mexico Museum of Art, the Tate, and Online Museum Resources on Asian Art.

Understanding Comics

Scott McCloud

Scott McCloud (b. 1960) is an award-winning cartoonist and leading theorist on comic art. He was born in Boston, Massachusetts and raised in the nearby town of Lexington. McCloud decided in his junior year in high school that he wanted to be a comic artist; he received a Bachelor of Fine Arts from Syracuse University (1982), majoring in illustration. He created the science fiction superhero series Zot! *in 1984, a comics odyssey tracing the adventures of two teenagers existing in parallel worlds. McCloud also composes for mainstream comics including DC Comics'* Superman *series. He is equally well known as a theorist of the genre, the "Aristotle of comics." In* Understanding Comics *(1993),* Reinventing Comics *(2000), and* Making Comics *(2006), McCloud offers a far-ranging account of the history, vocabulary, and methods of the medium. On his Web site McCloud is an active promoter of new comics technology, the rights of comic artists to royalties, and the importance of comics in popular culture. In this excerpt from* Understanding Comics, *McCloud establishes the uniqueness of comics as an art form.*

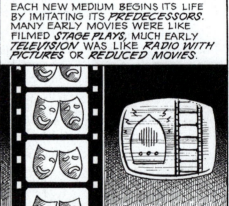

WORDS AND PICTURES IN COMBINATION MAY NOT BE MY *DEFINITION* OF COMICS, BUT THE COMBINATION HAS HAD *TREMENDOUS INFLUENCE* ON ITS *GROWTH*.

com·ics (kom'iks)n. pl... form, used with a singular... Juxtaposed pictoria... her images in deliberate... ence, intended to conve... and/or to prod... response in the... **2:**Superheroes... costumes, fight... villains who want...

A HUGE RANGE OF HUMAN EXPERIENCES CAN BE *PORTRAYED* IN COMICS THROUGH EITHER WORDS OR PICTURES.

AS A RESULT--AND DESPITE ITS MANY *OTHER* POTENTIAL USES -- COMICS HAVE BECOME *FIRMLY IDENTIFIED* WITH THE ART OF *STORYTELLING*.

AND *INDEED*, WORDS AND PICTURES HAVE *GREAT* POWERS TO TELL STORIES WHEN CREATORS FULLY EXPLOIT THEM *BOTH*.

DADA
BIOGRAPHY HORROR
ROMANCE SURREALISM
BLANK VERSE HISTORICAL FICTION
EPIC POETRY FOLK TALES
SOCIAL ALLEGORY EROTICA
SEQUENTIAL ART MYSTERY
ADAPTATIONS RELIGIOUS TOPICS
STREAM OF CONSCIOUSNESS
SATIRE

AND SO FAR, WE'VE ONLY SEEN THE *TIP OF THE ICEBERG!*

AS CHILDREN, WE "SHOW AND TELL" *INTERCHANGEABLY*, WORDS AND IMAGES COMBINING TO TRANSMIT A *CONNECTED SERIES OF IDEAS*.

IT'S GOT ONE OF *THESE* THINGS.

THE DIFFERENT WAYS IN WHICH WORDS AND PICTURES CAN *COMBINE* IN COMICS IS VIRTUALLY *UNLIMITED*.

BUT LET'S TRY TO BREAK IT DOWN INTO SOME DISTINCT *CATEGORIES*.

PERHAPS THE MOST *COMMON* TYPE OF WORD/PICTURE COMBINATION IS THE *INTER-DEPENDENT,* WHERE WORDS AND PICTURES GO *HAND IN HAND* TO CONVEY AN IDEA THAT NEITHER COULD CONVEY *ALONE.*

MEANWHILE...

DID ANYONE *SEE* YOU?

THIS IS ALL I NEED TO *STOP* HIM!

I ASK YOU, DOES THIS GUY LOOK LIKE A *C.E.O.* TO *YOU?*?

"AND JUST *GUESS* WHO DROVE UP IN BOB'S TRUCK AN HOUR LATER!"

HEY, MARGE!

OH, MY GOD!

HE'S LYING. UH-HUH.

"AFTER COLLEGE, I PURSUED A CAREER IN *HIGH FINANCE.*"

HURRY UP, WILLYA?!

INTERDEPENDENT COMBINATIONS AREN'T ALWAYS AN *EQUAL BALANCE* THOUGH AND MAY FALL *ANYWHERE* ON A SCALE BETWEEN TYPES ONE AND TWO.

GENERALLY SPEAKING, THE MORE IS SAID WITH *WORDS,* THE MORE THE PICTURES CAN BE FREED TO GO EXPLORING AND *VICE VERSA.*

COMPREHENSION

1. What does McCloud mean by "the curse of being judged by the standards of the old"? What new standards does he propose?
2. Underline, circle, or highlight the "categories" that McCloud presents.
3. How does McCloud explain the world of comics as an art form?

RHETORIC

1. Explain the sequence of words and images that McCloud creates in order to establish a definition of comic art.
2. How does the author create an argument about comics? What is his claim?
3. Identify the forms of support presented by McCloud to sustain his argument.
4. How does McCloud use classification as a method to organize his sequence of words and images?
5. How does the author create a narrative voice or persona? Do you find this personal voice to be engaging? Why or why not?

WRITING

1. Write an essay entitled "Comics and Culture."
2. Select a comic or graphic novel and analyze the ways in which it conforms to the prescriptions laid down by McCloud.
3. **Writing an Argument:** Argue for or against the proposition that comics are a legitimate form of art.

NETWORKING
Applying Digital and Multimedia Literacies

Purpose, Audience, and Design in a Professional Web Site: Go to the artist's official Web site *(http://www.ScottMcCloud.com)*. Review the contents, sample the links, find out more about the artist, and in discussion or writing, consider how the design and layout of the site serves its contents' purpose. In your response, be sure to address what this purpose is and who McCloud would probably identify as the site's intended audience.

Finding Neverland

David Gates

David Gates (b. 1947) is an American journalist and fiction writer. Gates attended Bard College and the University of Connecticut in the mid-1960s, subsequently working as a cab driver and in other capacities while refining his literary craft. His first novel, Jernigan *(1991), was nominated for a Pulitzer Prize. Both his second novel,* Preston Falls *(1998), and the collection* The Wonders of the Invisible World: Stories *(1999), were finalists for the National Book Critics Circle Award. Gates is a senior editor and writer at* Newsweek, *covering books, music, and the arts. He also teaches in the graduate writing programs at Bennington College and New School University. In this essay from the July 13, 2009, issue of* Newsweek, *Gates surveys the life, death, and career of music legend Michael Jackson.*

True, for a while he was the king of pop—a term apparently originated by his friend Elizabeth Taylor—and he's the last we're ever likely to have. Before Michael Jackson came Frank Sinatra, Elvis Presley, and the Beatles; after him has come absolutely no one, however brilliant or however popular, who couldn't be ignored by vast segments of an ever-more-fragmented audience. Not Kurt Cobain, not Puffy, not Mariah Carey, not Céline Dion, not Beyoncé, not Radiohead—not even Madonna, his closest competitor. When the news of his death broke, the traffic on Twitter caused the site to crash, even though he hadn't had a hit song for years. But starting long before and continuing long after he lorded over the world of entertainment in the 1980s—his 1982 *Thriller* remains the bestselling album of all time—Jackson was the Prince of Artifice. As the prepubescent frontboy of the Jackson 5, he sang in a cherubic mezzo-soprano of sexual longing he could not yet have fully felt. As a young man, however accomplished and even impassioned his singing was, he never had the sexual credibility of a James Brown or a Wilson Pickett, in part because of his still-high-pitched voice, in part because he seemed never to fully inhabit himself—whoever that self was. In middle age, he consciously took on the role of Peter Pan, with his Neverland Ranch and its amusement-park rides, with his lost-boy "friends" and with what he seemed to believe was an ageless, androgynous physical appearance—let's hope he believed it—thanks to straightened hair and plastic surgery. (No one—least of all Jackson himself—would have wanted to see the Dorian Gray portrait in his attic.) He did his best to construct an alternate reality on top of what must have been an initially miserable life: Imagine *Gypsy* with—as Jackson claimed in interviews—a physically abusive

father in place of Mama Rose, set among Jehovah's Witnesses. Which was the more imaginative creation: his music or his persona?

2   In retrospect, so much of what Jackson achieved seems baldly symbolic. This was the black kid from Gary, Ind., who ended up marrying Elvis's daughter, setting up Neverland in place of Graceland, and buying the Beatles' song catalog—bold acts of appropriation and mastery, if not outright aggression. (Of course, Elvis and the Beatles had come out of obscurity, too, but that was a long, long time ago, in a galaxy far away.) He made trademarks of the very emblems of his remoteness: his moonwalk dance and his jeweled glove—*noli me tangere,* and vice versa. He morphed relentlessly from the most adorable of kiddie performers (his 1972 movie-soundtrack hit, "Ben," was a love song to a pet rat) to the most sinister of superstars: not by adopting a campy persona, like those of his older contemporaries Alice Cooper or Ozzy Osbourne, but in real life, dodging accusations of child molestation, one of which led to a trial and acquittal in 2005. (One shrink concluded at the time that he was not a pedophile, but merely a case of arrested development.) The 2002 episode in which he briefly dangled his son Prince Michael II (a.k.a. Blanket) over a balcony in Berlin, above horrified, fascinated

fans, seemed like a ritualized attempt to dispose of his own younger self. And eventually his several facial surgeries, a skin ailment, serious weight loss, and God knows what else made him look like both a vampire and a mummy—Peter Pan's undead evil twins. That is, like the skeletal, pale-faced zombies he danced with in Jon Landis's 14-minute "Thriller" video. When you watch it today, it appears to be a whole stage full of Michael Jacksons, the real one now the least familiar-looking, the most unreal of all.

But whatever strictly personal traumas Jackson may have reenacted and 3 transcended—and then re-reenacted—he performed his dance of death as a central figure in America's long racial horror show. He was, quintessentially, one of those "pure products of America," who, as William Carlos Williams wrote in 1923, "go crazy." To take the uplifting view, enunciated after his death by the likes of the Rev. Al Sharpton, he was a transracial icon, a black person whom white Americans took to their hearts and whose blackness came to seem incidental. In this he resembles such figures as Nat (King) Cole, Sammy Davis Jr., Sidney Poitier, Harry Belafonte, Sam Cooke, Jimi Hendrix, Arthur Ashe, Michael Jordan, Oprah Winfrey, Tiger Woods, and, inevitably, Barack Obama. As a singer-dancer, he clearly belongs not just in the tradition of Jackie Wilson, James Brown, and the Temptations—who seem to have been among his immediate inspirations—but also in the tradition of such dancing entertainers as Fred Astaire and Gene Kelly, who, in turn, drew from such black performers as Bill (Bojangles) Robinson. In the 1978 film version of *The Wiz,* Jackson even seemed to appropriate and reinvent Ray Bolger's role as the Scarecrow in *The Wizard of Oz.* And as a messianic global superstar, he resembles no one so much as his father-in-law, Elvis Presley (who died long before Jackson married his daughter), a transracial figure from the other side of the color line. When Presley's first records were played on the radio in Memphis, DJs made a point of noting that he graduated from the city's all-white Humes High School, lest listeners mistake him for black. Given the ubiquity of television, nobody mistook the wispy-voiced young Michael Jackson for white, but it seemed, superficially, not to matter.

Yet Jackson, always the artificer, surely knew that part of his own appeal to 4 white audiences—who contributed substantially to the $50 million to $75 million a year he earned in his prime—lay initially in his precocious cuteness, and when he was a grown man, in his apparent lack of adult sexuality. He was energetic, charismatic, and supremely gifted, but sexually unassertive—unlike swaggeringly heterosexual black male performers from Big Joe Turner ("Shake, Rattle, and Roll") to Jay-Z ("Big Pimpin'"). He neutered himself racially, too: his hair went from kinky to straight, his lips from full to thin, his nose from broad to pinched, his skin from dark to a ghastly pallor. You can't miss the connection between these forms of neutering if you know the history of white America's atavistic dread of black male sexuality; the 1955 murder of 14-year-old Emmett Till, for supposedly flirting with a white woman, is just one *locus classicus.* That happened only three years before Jackson was born; when he was 13, he was singing "Ben." No wonder Jackson chose—with whatever degree of calculation—to remake himself as an American Dream of innocence and belovedness.

5   No wonder, either, that the artifice eventually turned scary, and the face of
the icon came to look more and more corpselike. Readers of Toni Morrison's latest novel, *A Mercy,* might recall the passage in which an African woman tells
about her first sight of white slavers: "There we see men we believe are ill or
dead. We soon learn they are neither. Their skin is confusing." That's the middle-
aged Michael Jackson to a T. Jackson arguably looked his "blackest" on the original cover of 1979's *Off the Wall;* by *Thriller,* the transformation had begun. *Off
the Wall* was his declaration of manhood: It came out the year he turned 21, and
you could make the case that it was his greatest purely musical moment. Why
did he feel so deeply uncomfortable with himself? The hopeless task of sculpting
and bleaching yourself into a simulacrum of a white man suggests a profound
loathing of blackness. If Michael Jackson couldn't be denounced as a race traitor,
who could? Somehow, though, black America overlooked it, and continued to
buy his records, perhaps because some African-Americans, with their hair relax-
ers and skin-lightening creams, understood why Jackson was remaking himself,
even if they couldn't condone it.

6   As with Ernest Hemingway—another case of deeply confused identity and
(who knew?) androgynous sexuality—we need to look past the deliberate creation of an image and a persona to appreciate the artistry. A more masterly enter-
tainer never took the stage. In 1988, the *New York Times* dance critic Anna
Kisselgoff called him "a virtuoso . . . who uses movement for its own sake. Yes,
Michael Jackson is an avant-garde dancer, and his dances could be called abstract.
Like Merce Cunningham, he shows us that movement has a value of its own." Bet-
ter yet, Astaire himself once called Jackson to offer his compliments. As a singer,
Jackson was too much of a chameleon—from the tenderness of "I'll Be There" to
the rawness of "The Way You Make Me Feel" to the silken sorrow of "She's Out of
My Life"—to stamp every song with his distinct personality, as Sinatra did, or Ray
Charles, or Hank Williams. But these are demigods—Jackson was merely a giant.
(And how'd you like *their* dancing?) As a musical conceptualizer, probably only
James Brown has had a comparable influence: Jackson and his visionary pro-
ducer, Quincy Jones, fused disco, soul, and pop in a manner that can still be heard
every hour of every day on every top-40 radio station—only not as well. Tommy
Mottola, former head of Sony Music, called Jackson "the corner-stone to the en-
tire music business." The best recordings by Jackson and Jones—"Don't Stop 'Til
You Get Enough," "Billie Jean"—belong identifiably to their time, as do Sinatra's
1950s recordings with the arranger Nelson Riddle. Yet like Sinatra's "I've Got the
World on a String" or "In the Wee Small Hours of the Morning," they're so perfect
of their kind that they'll never sound dated.

7   The night before he died, Jackson was rehearsing at the Staples Center in Los
Angeles for an epic comeback—a series of 50 concerts, beginning in July, at
London's O2 Arena. If that sounds impossibly grandiose, consider that all 50
shows had already sold out. People around him had been wondering if he was really up to it, and the opening had already been put off by a week. He was 50 years
old, after all: long in the tooth for a *puer aeternus*—eight years older than Elvis
when he left the building, and a quarter century past his peak. Jackson had had

health problems for years. Drug problems, too, apparently: In 2007, according to the Associated Press, an L.A. pharmacy sued him, claiming he owed $100,000 for two years' worth of prescription meds. And money problems: In 2008, the ranch nearly went into foreclosure—he defaulted on a $24.5 million debt—and even the $50 million he stood to realize from his potentially grueling London concerts might not have helped that much. And of course, just problems: His very existence—as a son, as a black man—was problematic. In his last days, did the prospect of a comeback, of remythologizing himself one more time, excite him as much as it excited his fans? Did his magical moments in performance have an incandescent density that outweighed what must often have been burdensome hours and days? Ask him sometime, if you see him. Whatever his life felt like from inside, from outside it was manifestly a work of genius, whether you want to call it a triumph or a freak show—those are just words. We'd never seen anyone like this before, either in his artistic inventiveness or his equally artistic self-invention, and we won't forget him—until the big Neverland swallows us all.

COMPREHENSION

1. Summarize Gates's perception of Michael Jackson. How do you interpret the title? Why does Gates call Jackson an "artificer"? What does Gates mean by Jackson's "androgynous sexuality"?
2. Gates alludes to many stars from the world of music, dance, literature, and the arts. Which celebrities can you identify? What is Gates's purpose in listing so many of them?
3. What, in Gates's opinion, is Michael Jackson's legacy?

RHETORIC

1. Does this essay have an explicitly stated thesis? If so, where is it? If the thesis is implied, paraphrase it.
2. The first paragraph of this essay is quite long. What is Gates's strategy and purpose here? Does this lengthy opening paragraph weaken or strengthen the body of the essay? Explain.
3. Identify and comment on Gates's use of figurative language in this essay. How does figurative language—and Gates's overall style—influence the essay's tone?
4. What comparative points does Gates make about Jackson and other artists? How does the comparative method serve to organize the essay?
5. Explain the effect of the last paragraph, which resembles the introductory paragraph in length. Do you think this resemblance was intentional? Why or why not?

WRITING

1. Write your own evaluation of Michael Jackson or another celebrity musician who died within the last 10 years (such as Amy Winehouse or Whitney Houston), explaining why you think this artist's achievement is important.

2. Write a comparative essay in which you discuss two artists from the world of music, film, or television.
3. **Writing an Argument:** Argue for or against the proposition that the media make too much of the deaths of prominent celebrities.

NETWORKING
Applying Digital and Multimedia Literacies

Creating a Photo Biography: Strengthen your position in question 1 under Writing by adding a photo biography of Michael Jackson (or another musician-celebrity whose career you've chosen to evaluate). This biography should consist of 12 to 15 images that help tell the story of the celebrity's career; use succinct but compelling captions to supply narration that informs your evaluation.

The Dark Art of Description

Patricia Hampl

Patricia Hampl (b. 1946) is an American writer, poet, memoirist, and educator. Hampl was born in St. Paul, Minnesota. She earned a BA from the University of Minnesota in 1968 and an MFA at the University of Iowa in 1970. After stints as an editor and freelance writer between 1973 and 1978, Hampl joined the faculty at the University of Minnesota in Minneapolis where she is currently the English Regents Professor. A recipient of prestigious Guggenheim and MacArthur fellowships, Hampl is best known as a superb memoirist. Her first autobiography, A Romantic Education *(1981), is an introspective account of Hampl's Czech heritage. A second memoir,* Virgin Time: In Search of the Contemplative Life *(1992), explores her Roman Catholic upbringing. Hampl's critically acclaimed* The Florist's Daughter *(2007) is an emotionally charged account of her mother's death. Hampl lectures widely and is on the permanent faculty at the Prague Summer Program. This essay was originally the keynote address at the Bedell NonfictioNow conference on November 1, 2007.*

1   I was coming down the last lap of my most recent book, a memoir about my mother and father, and I was painfully aware of just how specific every bit of writing is, full of choices and chances, not theoretical at all, not the business of sweeping statements or smart ideas about "form" or "genre" or anything remotely theoretical. Just subject-verb-object and the hope of meaning.

2   Two nights away from the finish of my book, I was working late. I looked away from the computer screen for a moment and there was my dog staring at me intently. She was on the verge of speech. I could see it. *Come to bed.* Her eyes said

this clearly. It was almost 2 a.m. and for the past four hours I'd been changing commas to dashes and then back again to commas with the obsessive focus only a fanatic can sustain.

You've become a crazy person again, I said right out loud. The dog padded away. 3

The great short story writer J.F. Powers was once stopped by a colleague in the corridor at their university. The man asked him how things were going. Powers allowed that it had been a tough day—"I spent the morning trying to decide whether to have my character call his friend *pal* or *chum*," he said. 4

That's where I often find myself—thinking how important the choice of *pal* or *chum* is, how whatever truth writing lays claim to resides in a passion for just such quite mad distinctions. This monomania is what a friend of mine calls the 600-pound gorilla of a book. Once the 600-pound gorilla gets hold of you, you're his (or hers). "Those last weeks of finishing a book are a world in themselves," she said. "I think that gorilla is the reason most of us write—it's a real high, but it's also a subconscious agreement not to be available or even normal for as long as it takes." 5

But as soon as you—or I, anyway—break away from the gorilla's embrace of a particular book, those big, rangy theoretical questions begin to make their approach again. Maybe this is especially true of memoir, the odd enterprise of "writing a life" that has captivated our literary life for the last two decades or so. We tend to think of the novel as the classic narrative form—ever evolving, but familiar, its stately provenance long the preserve of academic interest and the center of trade publishing. Whereas the memoir seems new or somehow "modern," a rather suspect literary upstart. And therefore a form that invites interrogation. 6

But strictly speaking, autobiography is a genre far older than the novel and is hard-wired into Western literary history. Perhaps from that first injunction of the oracle at Delphi—*Know thyself*—Western culture has been devoted to the exploration of individual consciousness and the unspooling of individual life. 7

That commandment to *know thyself* was central to antiquity. Plato uttered a version of it; Cicero used it in a tract on the development of social concord. It was such a pillar of cultural, even spiritual value that in the early Christian period Clement of Alexandria felt compelled to claim that the saying had been borrowed by the Greeks from scripture, thus binding the two developing spiritualities—pagan and monotheistic—together in a seamless endeavor. 8

Closer to modernity, Goethe is supposed to have said with a shudder, "Know thyself? If I knew myself, I'd run away." And Andre Gide probably expressed this revulsion best: "Know thyself! A maxim as pernicious as it is ugly. Whoever observes himself arrests his own development. A caterpillar who wanted to know itself well would never become a butterfly." 9

But the strongest indictment of the form I have ever encountered came from a student in Indiana who had been conscripted by his Freshman Comp teacher to attend a reading I gave some years ago. He sprawled in his chair with his baseball cap on backwards, his eloquent body language making it clear he was far, far away. Can't win them all, I decided, and carried on, my eye straying back to him like a tongue drawn to the absence of a just-pulled tooth. 10

11   During the Q&A I fielded the decorous questions the students posed. And then, suddenly, apparently in response to something I'd said, my anti-hero sat bolt-upright and was waving his hand urgently, his face alight with interest. Ah—a convert. I called on him, smiling.

12   "I get it," he said. "Nothin's ever happened to you—and you write books about it."

13   He was right, of course. And in pronouncing this acute literary critical remark, he touched on the most peculiar aspect of the rise of the memoir in our times— namely, that fundamentally it isn't about having a more interesting life than someone else. True, there is a strand of autobiographical writing that relies on the documentation of extraordinary circumstances, lives lived in extremity, often at great peril. But such memoirs have always been part of literary history. What characterizes the rise of memoir in recent times is precisely the opposite condition—not a gripping "narrative arc," but the quality of voice, the story of perception rather than action.

14   The self is not the subject of memoir, in this kind of book, but its instrument. And the work of the self is not to "narrate" but to describe. There is something fundamentally photographic about memoir, photographic rather than cinematic. Not a story, but a series of tableaus we are given to consider. No memoirist is surprised by the absences and blanks in action, for another unavoidable quality of autobiography as I am thinking of it—as lyrical quest literature—is that it is as much about reticence as it is about revelation.

15   It is often remarked that the advent of the movies and the ever faster pace of modern life have conspired to make description a less essential part of prose narrative in our own times. We don't need to be told what things look like—we are inundated with images, pictures, moving or static. In this view, we need the opposite of the photographic quality so beloved of nineteenth-century descriptive writing in which the landscape is rolled out, sentence after sentence, the interior of a room and the interior of the character's mind meticulously presented.

16   We require writing, instead, that subsumes description, leaps right over it to frame episode and to create the much sought-after "narrative arc." The motto— even the mantra—of this narrative model is of course the commandment of introductory fiction writing workshops: *Show, don't tell.*

17   But as recent memoir writing shows, descriptive writing abounds. And it proves, finally, not to be about the object described. Or not only. Description in memoir is where the consciousness of the writer and the material of the story are established in harmony, where the self is lost in the material, in a sense. In fiction of the show-don't-tell variety narrative scenes that "show" and dutifully do not "tell" are advanced by volleys of dialogue in which the author's presence is successfully obscured by the dramatic action of the dialogue of his characters. But in description we hear and feel the absorption of the author in the material. We sense the presence of the creator of the scene.

18   This personal absorption is what we mean by "style." It is strange that we would choose so oddly surfacey a word—style—for this most soulful aspect of writing. We could, perhaps more exactly, call this relation between consciousness and its subject "integrity." What else is the articulation of perception?

Style is a word usually claimed by fashion and the most passing aesthetic 19
values. But maybe that's as it should be because style in writing is terribly
perishable. It can rot—that is what we mean when we recognize writing to be
"precious," for example. But at its best and most essential, style is the register
between a writer's consciousness and the material he is committed to wrestling to
the page. It is the real authority of a writer, more substantial than plot, less
ego-dependent than voice.

In 1951, Alfred Kazin published his memoir of his boyhood in Brooklyn, *A* 20
Walker in the City, the book that establishes modern American memoir. The critic
Leslie Fiedler admired the book but was also frustrated by it. It "perversely
refuses to be a novel," he said with some annoyance, as if Kazin's book, deeply
dependent on descriptive writing, were refusing to behave. And it was. It was
refusing to obey the commandment to "Show, Don't Tell."

When you read "The Block and Beyond," a much-anthologized chapter from 21
Kazin's memoir, it is impossible to discuss the main characters and certainly not its
plot or even its narrative structure. It is a rhapsodic evocation of a place and time.
And once read, it is impossible to forget, as indelible and inevitable as a poem.

What Kazin was able to do—what every memoirist can attempt—in liberating 22
himself from the demands of show-don't-tell narrative was to enter into reflection,
into speculation, into interpretation, and to use the fragment, the image, the
vignette, rather than narratively linked scenes to form his world and his book. He
was able to show *and* tell. To write a story and write an essay—all in the same tale,
braided and twined together. The root of this double power lies in description.

I was one of those enthralled teenage readers of long nineteenth-century Eng- 23
lish novels. I toiled my way through dense descriptions of gloomy heaths and
bogs to get to the airy volleys of dialogue that lofted back and forth down the page
to give me what I wanted—would Jane and Mr. Rochester . . . or would they not?
Would Dorothea Brooke awaken—would Mr. Lydgate? I didn't relish the descriptive passages. I endured them. Just as Jane and Dorothea endured their parched
lives, as if these endless descriptive passages were the desert to be crossed before the paradise of dialogue and the love story could be entered.

Yet all this description was, after all, the *world* of the book—not simply be- 24
cause it gave the book "a sense of place" as the old literary cliche puts it. It wasn't
a "sense of place" I cared about in these passages, but the meeting place of perception with story—the place where someone *claimed* the story, where I could
glimpse the individual consciousness, the creator of the scene. The person pulling
the wires and making Jane and Dorothea move. I was looking, I suppose, for a
sign of intimacy with the invisible author. That "dear reader" moment so familiar
in nineteenth-century novels—think of Thackeray pausing to have a chat with the
reader—with you!—about how to live on nothing a year. Think of George Eliot
breaking off to describe the furnishings of Dorothea's ardent mind.

Henry James is probably the crown prince of nineteenth-century describers, a 25
flâneur of the sentence, a lounge lizard of the paragraph, taking his own sweet time
to unfurl an observation, smoking the cheroot of his thought in the contemplative

after-dinner puffery of a man who knows how to draw out the pleasure of his rare tobacco. Or—because James himself never hesitates to pile up opposing figures of speech until he has sliced his thought to the refracted transparency he adores—maybe I'll just switch metaphors and say that James sits mildly at his torture apparatus, turning the crank in meticulously calibrated movements as the reader lies helplessly strained upon the rack of his ever-expanding sentences, the exquisite pain of the lengthening description almost breaking the bones of attention. In short (as James often says after gassing on for a nice fat paragraph or two on the quality of a Venetian sunset or the knowing lift of a European eyebrow glimpsed across a table by an artless American ingénue), in short, he loves to carry on.

26   Carrying on, I was discovering, is what it is to describe. A lot. At length. To trust description above plot, past character development, and even theme. To understand that to describe is both humbler and more essential than to think of compositional imponderables such as "voice" or to strain toward superstructures like "narrative arc." To trust that the act of description will *find* voice and out of its streaming attention will take hold of narration.

27   By the time I was considering all of this, I had passed from being a reader and had become that more desperate literary type—a writer trying to figure out how to do it myself. I had no idea how to "sustain a narrative" and didn't even understand at the time (the late 1970s) that I was writing something called "a memoir." Yet when I read *Speak, Memory* by Vladimir Nabokov and later read his command—*Caress the detail, the divine detail*—I knew I had found the motto I could live by, the one that prevailed over "Show, Don't Tell."

28   Perhaps only someone as thoroughly divested of his paradise as Nabokov had been of his boyhood Russia and his family, his native language and all his beloved associations and privileged expectations, could enshrine the detail, the fragment, as the divinity of his literary religion, could trust the truths to be found in the DNA of detail, attentively rendered in ardent description. The dutiful observation that is the yeoman's work of description finally ascended, Nabokov demonstrated, to the transcendent reality of literature, to metaphor itself.

29   Nabokov was asked in an interview if his characters ever "took over." He replied icily that *his* characters were his galley slaves.

30   Yet when it was a matter of locating the godhead of literary endeavor, even a writer as unabashedly imperious as Nabokov did not point to himself and his intentions but to the lowly detail. *Caress the detail, the divine detail.* Next to grand conceptions like plot, which is the legitimate government of most stories, or character, which is the crowned sovereign, the detail looks like a ragged peasant with a half-baked idea of revolution and a crazy, sure glint in its eye. But here, according to Nabokov, resides divinity.

31   Henry James put his faith in something at least as insubstantial. "If one was to undertake to . . . report with truth on the human scene," he wrote, "it could but be because notes had been from the cradle the ineluctable consequence of one's greatest inward energy . . . to take them was as natural as to look, to think, to feel, to recognize, to remember." He considered his habit the basis of literature and called it "the rich principle of the Note."

Such "notes" are of course details, observations. Description. In attending 32 to these details, in the act of description, the more dynamic aspects of narrative have a chance to reveal themselves—not as "action" or "conflict" or any of the theoretical and technical terms we persist in thinking of as the sources of form. Rather, description gives the authorial mind a place to be in relation with the reality of the world.

It was surely this desire for the world—that is for the world's memoir, which 33 is history—that drew me to memoir, that seemingly personal form. And it was to description I tended, not to narrative, not to story. Maybe the root of the desire to write is always lost—properly lost—in the non-literary earth of our real lives. And craft, as we think of it, is just the jargon we give to that darker, earthier medium.

I know it was my mother who was the storyteller in our house. I was her audi- 34 ence. Her dear reader, in a way. I dimly—and sometimes bitterly—understood that nothing much was happening in our modest Midwestern lives, yet I clung to the drama with which she infused every vignette, every encounter at the grocery store.

And when I sought to make sense of the world that kept slipping away to the 35 past, to loss and forgetfulness, when I protested inwardly at that disappearance, it was to description I instinctively turned. Coming from a background in poetry and therefore being a literalist, it didn't occur to me to copy other prose writers. If I wanted to learn to write descriptively, I needed—what else?—pictures.

I took myself off to the Minneapolis Institute of Arts and plunked myself 36 down in front of a Bonnard. I wrote the painting. Described it. I went home and looked at a teacup on my table—I wrote that too. Still life descriptions that ran on for several pages. I wrote and wrote, describing my way through art galleries and the inadvertent still lives of my house and my memory, my grandmother's garden, her Sunday dinners.

To my growing astonishment, these long descriptive passages, sometimes 37 running two, three pages or longer, had a way of sheering off into narrative after all. The teacup I was describing had been given to me by my mother. And once I thought of the fact that she had bought these cups, made in Czechoslovakia, as a bride just before the Second World War, I was writing about that war, about my mother and her later disappointments which somehow were—and were not—part of this fragile cup. Description—which had seemed like background in novels, static and inert as a butterfly pinned to the page of my notebook, proved to be a dynamic engine that stoked voice and even more propelled the occasional narrative arc. Description, written from the personal voice of my own perception, proved even to be the link with the world's story, with history itself. Here was my mother's teacup, made in Czechoslovakia before the War, and here, therefore, was not only my mother's heartbreak but Europe's. The detail was surely divine, offering up miracle after miracle of connections out of the faithful consideration of the fragments before me.

We sense this historical power at the heart of autobiographical writing in the 38 testaments from the Holocaust, from the Gulag, from every marginal and abused life that has found the courage to speak its truth which is often its horror, to preserve its demonic details—and in so doing has seen them become divine. Nadezhda Mandelstam, Anne Frank, Primo Levi—to name only a very few. In time we will, surely, see such documents from Guantanamo and the unknown places of extreme rendition.

39　　The history of whole countries, of an entire era and even lost populations depends sometimes on a little girl faithfully keeping her diary. The great contract of literature consists in this: you tell me your story and somehow I get my story. If we are looking for another reason to explain the strangely powerful grip of the first-person voice on contemporary writing perhaps we need look no farther than the power of Anne Frank's equation—that to write one's life enables the world to preserve its history.

40　　But what of lives lived in the flyover? Lives that don't have that powerful, if terrible, historical resonance of radical suffering. Ordinary lives, in a word. Alfred Kazin's life—or yours. And certainly mine in middling Minnesota in the middle of the twentieth century. Why bother to describe it? Because of course, all details are divine, not just Nabokov's. In fact, perhaps the poorer the supposed value, the more the detail requires description to assure its divinity.

41　　Which brings me to—if not a story, at least a fragment, a vignette. Early in my teaching life, I went (foolishly) through a killer snowstorm in Minneapolis to get to my University office because I had student conferences scheduled. By the time I arrived, the University had closed and the campus was empty, whipped by white shrouds of blizzard snow, the wind whistling down the Mall. I sat in my office in the empty building, cursing my ruinous work ethic, wondering if the buses would keep running so I could get home.

42　　Then a rap on my office door. I opened it and there, like an extra out of *Doctor Zhivago,* stood my 11 a.m. appointment, a quiet sophomore named Tommy.

43　　He looked anxious. He was really glad I was there, he said, because he had a big problem with the assignment. I had asked the students to write short autobiographies. "I just can't write anything about my life," he said miserably, his head down, his overshoes puddling on the floor.

44　　I waited for the disclosure. What would it be—child abuse, incest, what murder or mayhem could this boy not divulge? What had brought him trooping through the blizzard to get help with his life story? How would I get him to Student Counseling?

45　　"See, I come from Fridley," he said, naming one of the nowhere-suburbs sprawling drearily beyond the freeway north of Minneapolis.

46　　I stared at him. I didn't, for a moment, comprehend that this was the dark disclosure, this the occasion of his misery: being from Fridley meant, surely, that he had nothing worth writing about.

47　　There it was again—nothin' had ever happened to him and I was asking him to write about it.

48　　"I have good news for you, Tommy," I said. "The field's wide open—nobody has told what it's like to grow up in Fridley yet. It's all yours."

49　　All he needed to do was sit down and describe. And because the detail is divine, if you caress it into life, you find the world you have lost or ignored, the world ruined or devalued. The world you alone can bring into being, bit by broken bit. And so you create your own integrity, which is to say your voice, your style.

COMPREHENSION

1. Summarize what the author means by "the dark art of description." Highlight key passages that illuminate her definition.
2. According to Hampl, what is the uniqueness and value of memoir?
3. What distinctions does Hampl draw between the novel and memoir? Which writers does she use most prominently to establish this comparison?

RHETORIC

1. What rhetorical function does Hampl's opening anecdote serve in the overall context of the essay? How does her concluding anecdote reinforce her meaning?
2. What is Hampl's purpose in alluding to so many writers? Do you find this catalogue of writers to be useful in framing her thesis? Justify your response by referring to passages in the text.
3. Hampl wrote this piece as a keynote address at a literary conference. What assumptions does she make about the values and interests of her audience? How does she demonstrate special authority in dealing with her subject?
4. How does Hampl employ definition and the comparative method as rhetorical strategies?
5. What types of figurative language appear in the essay? How do similes, metaphors, and other varieties affect the tone of the piece?

WRITING

1. Compose a brief memoir about a place where you grew up. Use the "dark art of description" to evoke this place.
2. Select one writer's quotation from Hampl's text and respond to it in an essay of reflection.
3. **Writing an Argument:** Hampl asserts that "ordinary lives" are worthy of memoir. Agree or disagree with her claim in an argumentative essay.

NETWORKING
Applying Digital and Multimedia Literacies

Memoirs across Media: Hampl alludes to the Holocaust, the Gulag, Guantanamo, and "the historical power at the heart of autobiographical writing" (paragraph 38). Conduct online research into the writers she mentions in the context of this paragraph. Then expand your research to include examples of video autobiographies or documentaries. Consider what hearing or seeing a person's story contributes to its historical power. Conversely, what are some advantages of using only written words? Prepare a research paper using these examples to explain the power of memoir to capture the horrors of contemporary history.

Regarding the Torture of Others

Susan Sontag

Susan Sontag (1933–2004), one of the most influential critics of her generation, was born in New York City and grew up in Tucson, Arizona, and Los Angeles. After graduating from high school at the age of 15, she started studies at the University of California at Berkeley; subsequently, she received degrees from the University of Chicago and Harvard University. As an art critic as well as a political and cultural commentator, Sontag brought intellectual rigor to her subjects. The main body of her work in prose consists of two collections of essays, Against Interpretation *(1966) and* Where the Stress Falls *(2001), as well as* Trip to Hanoi *(1968),* Illness as Metaphor *(1978), and* AIDS and Its Metaphors *(1988). In addition, Sontag wrote fiction, including* Volcano Lover *(1992) and* In America: A Novel *(2001), and several films and plays. In this essay, published in the* New York Times Magazine *in 2004, Sontag offers a meditation on the photographs of torture taken by American troops at Abu Ghraib prison in Baghdad.*

I.

1   For a long time—at least six decades—photographs have laid down the tracks of how important conflicts are judged and remembered. The Western memory museum is now mostly a visual one. Photographs have an insuperable power to determine what we recall of events, and it now seems probable that the defining association of people everywhere with the war that the United States launched pre-emptively in Iraq last year will be photographs of the torture of Iraqi prisoners by Americans in the most infamous of Saddam Hussein's prisons, Abu Ghraib.

An Iraqi detainee at Abu Ghraib: The horror of what is shown in the photographs cannot be separated from the horror that the photographs were taken.

The Bush administration and its defenders have chiefly sought to limit a public- 2 relations disaster—the dissemination of the photographs—rather than deal with the complex crimes of leadership and of policy revealed by the pictures. There was, first of all, the displacement of the reality onto the photographs themselves. The administration's initial response was to say that the president was shocked and disgusted by the photographs—as if the fault or horror lay in the images, not in what they depict. There was also the avoidance of the word "torture." The prisoners had possibly been the objects of "abuse," eventually of "humiliation"—that was the most to be admitted. "My impression is that what has been charged thus far is abuse, which I believe technically is different from torture," Secretary of Defense Donald Rumsfeld said at a press conference. "And therefore I'm not going to address the 'torture' word."

Words alter, words add, words subtract. It was the strenuous avoidance of the 3 word "genocide" while some 800,000 Tutsis in Rwanda were being slaughtered, over a few weeks' time, by their Hutu neighbors 10 years ago that indicated the American government had no intention of doing anything. To refuse to call what took place in Abu Ghraib—and what has taken place elsewhere in Iraq and in Afghanistan and at Guantánamo Bay—by its true name, torture, is as outrageous as the refusal to call the Rwandan genocide a genocide. Here is one of the definitions of torture contained in a convention to which the United States is a signatory: *"any act by which severe pain or suffering, whether physical or mental, is intentionally inflicted on a person for such purposes as obtaining from him or a third person information or a confession."* (The definition comes from the 1984 Convention Against Torture and Other Cruel, Inhuman or Degrading Treatment or Punishment. Similar definitions have existed for some time in customary law and in treaties, starting with Article 3—common to the four Geneva conventions of 1949—and many recent human rights conventions.) The 1984 convention declares, *"No exceptional circumstances whatsoever, whether a state of war or a threat of war, internal political instability or any other public emergency may be invoked as a justification of torture."* And all covenants on torture specify that it includes treatment intended to humiliate the victim, like leaving prisoners naked in cells and corridors.

Whatever actions this administration undertakes to limit the damage of the 4 widening revelations of the torture of prisoners in Abu Ghraib and elsewhere— trials, courts-martial, dishonorable discharges, resignation of senior military figures and responsible administration officials and substantial compensation to the victims—it is probable that the "torture" word will continue to be banned. To acknowledge that Americans torture their prisoners would contradict everything this administration has invited the public to believe about the virtue of American intentions and America's right, flowing from that virtue, to undertake unilateral action on the world stage.

Even when the president was finally compelled, as the damage to America's 5 reputation everywhere in the world widened and deepened, to use the "sorry" word, the focus of regret still seemed the damage to America's claim to moral superiority. Yes, President Bush said in Washington on May 6, standing alongside

King Abdullah II of Jordan, he was "sorry for the humiliation suffered by the Iraqi prisoners and the humiliation suffered by their families." But, he went on, he was "equally sorry that people seeing these pictures didn't understand the true nature and heart of America."

6   To have the American effort in Iraq summed up by these images must seem, to those who saw some justification in a war that did overthrow one of the monster tyrants of modern times, "unfair." A war, an occupation, is inevitably a huge tapestry of actions. What makes some actions representative and others not? The issue is not whether the torture was done by individuals (i.e., "not by everybody")—but whether it was systematic. Authorized. Condoned. All acts are done by individuals. The issue is not whether a majority or a minority of Americans performs such acts but whether the nature of the policies prosecuted by this administration and the hierarchies deployed to carry them out makes such acts likely.

II.

7 Considered in this light, the photographs are us. That is, they are representative of the fundamental corruptions of any foreign occupation together with the Bush adminstration's distinctive policies. The Belgians in the Congo, the French in Algeria, practiced torture and sexual humiliation on despised recalcitrant natives. Add to this generic corruption the mystifying, near-total unpreparedness of the American rulers of Iraq to deal with the complex realities of the country after its "liberation." And add to that the overarching, distinctive doctrines of the Bush administration, namely that the United States has embarked on an endless war and that those detained in this war are, if the president so decides, "unlawful combatants"—a policy enunciated by Donald Rumsfeld for Taliban and Qaeda prisoners as early as January 2002—and thus, as Rumsfeld said, "technically" they "do not have any rights under the Geneva Convention," and you have a perfect recipe for the cruelties and crimes committed against the thousands incarcerated without charges or access to lawyers in American-run prisons that have been set up since the attacks of Sept. 11, 2001.

8   So, then, is the real issue not the photographs themselves but what the photographs reveal to have happened to "suspects" in American custody? No: the horror of what is shown in the photographs cannot be separated from the horror that the photographs were taken—with the perpetrators posing, gloating, over their helpless captives. German soldiers in the Second World War took photographs of the atrocities they were committing in Poland and Russia, but snapshots in which the executioners placed themselves among their victims are exceedingly rare, as may be seen in a book just published, "Photographing the Holocaust," by Janina Struk. If there is something comparable to what these pictures show it would be some of the photographs of black victims of lynching taken between the 1880's and 1930's, which show Americans grinning beneath the naked mutilated body of a black man or woman hanging behind them from a tree. The lynching photographs were souvenirs of a collective action whose participants felt perfectly justified in what they had done. So are the pictures from Abu Ghraib.

The lynching pictures were in the nature of photographs as trophies—taken 9
by a photographer in order to be collected, stored in albums, displayed. The pictures taken by American soldiers in Abu Ghraib, however, reflect a shift in the use
made of pictures—less objects to be saved than messages to be disseminated,
circulated. A digital camera is a common possession among soldiers. Where once
photographing war was the province of photojournalists, now the soldiers themselves are all photographers—recording their war, their fun, their observations of
what they find picturesque, their atrocities—and swapping images among themselves and e-mailing them around the globe.

There is more and more recording of what people do, by themselves. At least 10
or especially in America, Andy Warhol's ideal of filming real events in real time—
life isn't edited, why should its record be edited?—has become a norm for countless Webcasts, in which people record their day, each in his or her own reality
show. Here I am—waking and yawning and stretching, brushing my teeth, making breakfast, getting the kids off to school. People record all aspects of their
lives, store them in computer files and send the files around. Family life goes with
the recording of family life—even when, or especially when, the family is in the
throes of crisis and disgrace. Surely the dedicated, incessant home-videoing of
one another, in conversation and monologue, over many years was the most astonishing material in "Capturing the Friedmans," the recent documentary by
Andrew Jarecki about a Long Island family embroiled in pedophilia charges.

An erotic life is, for more and more people, that which can be captured in 11
digital photographs and on video. And perhaps the torture is more attractive, as
something to record, when it has a sexual component. It is surely revealing, as
more Abu Ghraib photographs enter public view, that torture photographs are
interleaved with pornographic images of American soldiers having sex with one

Most of the pictures,
like this one of a young
woman with a naked
man on a leash, seem to
depict part of a larger
confluence of torture and
pornography.

another. In fact, most of the torture photographs have a sexual theme, as in those showing the coercing of prisoners to perform, or simulate, sexual acts among themselves. One exception, already canonical, is the photograph of the man made to stand on a box, hooded and sprouting wires, reportedly told he would be electrocuted if he fell off. Yet pictures of prisoners bound in painful positions, or made to stand with outstretched arms, are infrequent. That they count as torture cannot be doubted. You have only to look at the terror on the victim's face, although such "stress" fell within the Pentagon's limits of the acceptable. But most of the pictures seem part of a larger confluence of torture and pornography: A young woman leading a naked man around on a leash is classic dominatrix imagery. And you wonder how much of the sexual tortures inflicted on the inmates of Abu Ghraib was inspired by the vast repertory of pornographic imagery available on the Internet—and which ordinary people, by sending out Webcasts of themselves, try to emulate.

III.

12 To live is to be photographed, to have a record of one's life, and therefore to go on with one's life oblivious, or claiming to be oblivious, to the camera's nonstop attentions. But to live is also to pose. To act is to share in the community of actions recorded as images. The expression of satisfaction at the acts of torture being inflicted on helpless, trussed, naked victims is only part of the story. There is the deep satisfaction of being photographed, to which one is now more inclined to respond not with a stiff, direct gaze (as in former times) but with glee. The events are in part designed to be photographed. The grin is a grin for the camera. There would be something missing if, after stacking the naked men, you couldn't take a picture of them.

13   Looking at these photographs, you ask yourself, How can someone grin at the sufferings and humiliation of another human being? Set guard dogs at the genitals and legs of cowering naked prisoners? Force shackled, hooded prisoners to masturbate or simulate oral sex with one another? And you feel naïve for asking, since the answer is, self-evidently, People do these things to other people. Rape and pain inflicted on the genitals are among the most common forms of torture. Not just in Nazi concentration camps and in Abu Ghraib when it was run by Saddam Hussein. Americans, too, have done and do them when they are told, or made to feel, that those over whom they have absolute power deserve to be humiliated, tormented. They do them when they are led to believe that the people they are torturing belong to an inferior race or religion. For the meaning of these pictures is not just that these acts were performed, but that their perpetrators apparently had no sense that there was anything wrong in what the pictures show.

14   Even more appalling, since the pictures were meant to be circulated and seen by many people: it was all fun. And this idea of fun is, alas, more and more—contrary to what President Bush is telling the world—part of "the true nature and heart of America." It is hard to measure the increasing acceptance of brutality in American life, but its evidence is everywhere, starting with the video games of killing that

are a principal entertainment of boys—can the video game "Interrogating the Terrorists" really be far behind?—and on to the violence that has become endemic in the group rites of youth on an exuberant kick. Violent crime is down, yet the easy delight taken in violence seems to have grown. From the harsh torments inflicted on incoming students in many American suburban high schools—depicted in Richard Linklater's 1993 film, "Dazed and Confused"—to the hazing rituals of physical brutality and sexual humiliation in college fraternities and on sports teams, America has become a country in which the fantasies and the practice of violence are seen as good entertainment, fun.

What formerly was segregated as pornography, as the exercise of extreme 15 sadomasochistic longings—as in Pier Paolo Pasolini's last, near-unwatchable film, "Salò" (1975), depicting orgies of torture in the Fascist redoubt in northern Italy at the end of the Mussolini era—is now being normalized, by some, as high-spirited play or venting. To "stack naked men" is like a college fraternity prank, said a caller to Rush Limbaugh and the many millions of Americans who listen to his radio show. Had the caller, one wonders, seen the photographs? No matter. The observation—or is it the fantasy?—was on the mark. What may still be capable of shocking some Americans was Limbaugh's response: "Exactly!" he exclaimed. "Exactly my point. This is no different than what happens at the Skull and Bones initiation, and we're going to ruin people's lives over it, and we're going to hamper our military effort, and then we are going to really hammer them because they had a good time." "They" are the American soldiers, the torturers. And Limbaugh went on: "You know, these people are being fired at every day. I'm talking about people having a good time, these people. You ever heard of emotional release?"

Shock and awe were what our military promised the Iraqis. And shock and 16 the awful are what these photographs announce to the world that the Americans have delivered: a pattern of criminal behavior in open contempt of international

What formerly was segregated as pornography, as the exercise of extreme sadomasochistic longings, is being normalized, by some, as high-spirited play or venting.

humanitarian conventions. Soldiers now pose, thumbs up, before the atrocities they commit, and send off the pictures to their buddies. Secrets of private life that, formerly, you would have given nearly anything to conceal, you now clamor to be invited on a television show to reveal. What is illustrated by these photographs is as much the culture of shamelessness as the reigning admiration for unapologetic brutality.

IV.

17 The notion that apologies or professions of "disgust" by the president and the secretary of defense are a sufficient response is an insult to one's historical and moral sense. The torture of prisoners is not an aberration. It is a direct consequence of the with-us-or-against-us doctrines of world struggle with which the Bush administration has sought to change, change radically, the international stance of the United States and to recast many domestic institutions and prerogatives. The Bush administration has committed the country to a pseudo-religious doctrine of war, endless war—for "the war on terror" is nothing less than that. Endless war is taken to justify endless incarcerations. Those held in the extralegal American penal empire are "detainees"; "prisoners," a newly obsolete word, might suggest that they have the rights accorded by international law and the laws of all civilized countries. This endless "global war on terrorism"—into which both the quite justified invasion of Afghanistan and the unwinnable folly in Iraq have been folded by Pentagon decree—inevitably leads to the demonizing and dehumanizing of anyone declared by the Bush administration to be a possible terrorist: a definition that is not up for debate and is, in fact, usually made in secret.

18   The charges against most of the people detained in the prisons in Iraq and Afghanistan being nonexistent—the Red Cross reports that 70 to 90 percent of those being held seem to have committed no crime other than simply being in the wrong place at the wrong time, caught up in some sweep of "suspects"—the principal justification for holding them is "interrogation." Interrogation about what? About anything. Whatever the detainee might know. If interrogation is the point of detaining prisoners indefinitely, then physical coercion, humiliation and torture become inevitable.

19   Remember: We are not talking about that rarest of cases, the "ticking time bomb" situation, which is sometimes used as a limiting case that justifies torture of prisoners who have knowledge of an imminent attack. This is general or nonspecific information-gathering, authorized by American military and civilian administrators to learn more of a shadowy empire of evildoers about whom Americans know virtually nothing, in countries about which they are singularly ignorant: In principle, any information at all might be useful. An interrogation that produced no information (whatever information might consist of) would count as a failure. All the more justification for preparing prisoners to talk. Softening them up, stressing them out—these are the euphemisms for the bestial practices in American prisons where suspected

terrorists are being held. Unfortunately, as Staff Sgt. Ivan (Chip) Frederick noted in his diary, a prisoner can get too stressed out and die. The picture of a man in a body bag with ice on his chest may well be of the man Frederick was describing.

The pictures will not go away. That is the nature of the digital world in which 20 we live. Indeed, it seems they were necessary to get our leaders to acknowledge that they had a problem on their hands. After all, the conclusions of reports compiled by the International Committee of the Red Cross, and other reports by journalists and protests by humanitarian organizations about the atrocious punishments inflicted on "detainees" and "suspected terrorists" in prisons run by the American military, first in Afghanistan and later in Iraq, have been circulating for more than a year. It seems doubtful that such reports were read by President Bush or Vice President Dick Cheney or Condoleezza Rice or Rumsfeld. Apparently it took the photographs to get their attention, when it became clear they could not be suppressed; it was the photographs that made all this "real" to Bush and his associates. Up to then, there had been only words, which are easier to cover up in our age of infinite digital self-reproduction and self-dissemination, and so much easier to forget.

So now the pictures will continue to "assault" us—as many Americans are 21 bound to feel. Will people get used to them? Some Americans are already saying they have seen enough. Not, however, the rest of the world. Endless war: endless stream of photographs. Will editors now debate whether showing more of them, or showing them uncropped (which, with some of the best-known images, like that of a hooded man on a box, gives a different and in some instances more appalling view), would be in "bad taste" or too implicitly political? By "political," read: critical of the Bush administration's imperial project. For there can be no doubt that the photographs damage, as Rumsfeld testified, "the reputation of the honorable men and women of the armed forces who are courageously and responsibly and professionally defending our freedom across the globe." This damage—to our reputation, our image, our success as the lone superpower—is what the Bush administration principally deplores. How the protection of "our freedom"—the freedom of 5 percent of humanity—came to require having American soldiers "across the globe" is hardly debated by our elected officials.

Already the backlash has begun. Americans are being warned against indulg- 22 ing in an orgy of self-condemnation. The continuing publication of the pictures is being taken by many Americans as suggesting that we do not have the right to defend ourselves: After all, they (the terrorists) started it. They—Osama bin Laden? Saddam Hussein? what's the difference?—attacked us first. Senator James Inhofe of Oklahoma, a Republican member of the Senate Armed Services Committee, before which Secretary Rumsfeld testified, avowed that he was sure he was not the only member of the committee "more outraged by the outrage" over the photographs than by what the photographs show. "These prisoners," Senator Inhofe explained, "you know they're not there for traffic violations. If they're in Cellblock 1-A or 1-B, these prisoners, they're murderers, they're terrorists,

In this photograph, Specialist Charles Graner Jr., who identified men in another Abu Ghraib photo, poses over handcuffed detainees lying on the floor.

they're insurgents. Many of them probably have American blood on their hands, and here we're so concerned about the treatment of those individuals." It's the fault of "the media" which are provoking, and will continue to provoke, further violence against Americans around the world. More Americans will die. Because of these photos.

23   There is an answer to this charge, of course. Americans are dying not because of the photographs but because of what the photographs reveal to be happening, happening with the complicity of a chain of command—so Maj. Gen. Antonio Taguba implied, and Pfc. Lynndie England said, and (among others) Senator Lindsey Graham of South Carolina, a Republican, suggested, after he saw the Pentagon's full range of images on May 12. "Some of it has an elaborate nature to it that makes me very suspicious of whether or not others were directing or encouraging," Senator Graham said. Senator Bill Nelson, a Florida Democrat, said that viewing an uncropped version of one photo showing a stack of naked men in a hallway—a version that revealed how many other soldiers were at the scene, some not even paying attention—contradicted the Pentagon's assertion that only rogue soldiers were involved. "Somewhere along the line," Senator Nelson said of the torturers, "they were either told or winked at." An attorney for Specialist Charles Graner Jr., who is in the picture, has had his client identify the men in the uncropped version; according to the *Wall Street Journal,* Graner said that four of the men were military intelligence and one a civilian contractor working with military intelligence.

V.

24 But the distinction between photograph and reality—as between spin and policy—can easily evaporate. And that is what the administration wishes to happen. "There are a lot more photographs and videos that exist," Rumsfeld

acknowledged in his testimony. "If these are released to the public, obviously, it's going to make matters worse." Worse for the administration and its programs, presumably, not for those who are the actual—and potential?—victims of torture.

The media may self-censor but, as Rumsfeld acknowledged, it's hard to 25 censor soldiers overseas, who don't write letters home, as in the old days, that can be opened by military censors who ink out unacceptable lines. Today's soldiers instead function like tourists, as Rumsfeld put it, "running around with digital cameras and taking these unbelievable photographs and then passing them off, against the law, to the media, to our surprise." The administration's effort to withhold pictures is proceeding along several fronts. Currently, the argument is taking a legalistic turn: now the photographs are classified as evidence in future criminal cases, whose outcome may be prejudiced if they are made public. The Republican chairman of the Senate Armed Services Committee, John Warner of Virginia, after the May 12 slide show of image after image of sexual humiliation and violence against Iraqi prisoners, said he felt "very strongly" that the newer photos "should not be made public. I feel that it could possibly endanger the men and women of the armed forces as they are serving and at great risk."

But the real push to limit the accessibility of the photographs will come 26 from the continuing effort to protect the administration and cover up our misrule in Iraq—to identify "outrage" over the photographs with a campaign to undermine American military might and the purposes it currently serves. Just as it was regarded by many as an implicit criticism of the war to show on television photographs of American soldiers who have been killed in the course of the invasion and occupation of Iraq, it will increasingly be thought unpatriotic to disseminate the new photographs and further tarnish the image of America.

After all, we're at war. Endless war. And war is hell, more so than any of the 27 people who got us into this rotten war seem to have expected. In our digital hall of mirrors, the pictures aren't going to go away. Yes, it seems that one picture is worth a thousand words. And even if our leaders choose not to look at them, there will be thousands more snapshots and videos. Unstoppable.

COMPREHENSION

1. Summarize Sontag's harsh condemnation of the Bush administration's prosecution of the Iraq war.
2. Sontag writes that the photographs coming out of Abu Ghraib "are us" (paragraph 7). What does she mean? Would you agree or disagree with the implications of her statement? Why?
3. Explain what Sontag finds to be uniquely powerful about photography as an art form.

RHETORIC

1. Sontag structures her essay around the dual subjects of photography and the American involvement in Iraq. Explain what her purpose is and how she links these two subjects.
2. What is Sontag's claim and in what place(s) does she state it? Where does she make logical, ethical, and emotional appeals? Are you persuaded by her argument? Why or why not?
3. Sontag includes six illustrations in the essay similar to the four we have included here. What is her objective? Does she mention additional photographs? How do the photographs enhance the message?
4. Sontag divides her essay into five numbered sections. How does each section serve to advance her argument?
5. How does Sontag's use of connotation and definition—of *torture, enemy combatants, the erotic life,* and so forth—serve her purpose?
6. What conclusions does Sontag draw "regarding the torture of others"?

WRITING

1. Sontag alludes to the popular radio commentator Rush Limbaugh. Find out more about this personality, and in an expository essay explain why Limbaugh would disagree with Sontag's argument.
2. **Writing an Argument:** Conduct your own research on Abu Ghraib, and then stake out an argumentative position on it. Develop logical, ethical, and emotional appeals to support your position.

NETWORKING
Applying Digital and Multimedia Literacies

Using Visuals and Hyperlinks to Enhance a Definition Essay: Write your own extended definition of torture, linking it to a specific situation like Abu Ghraib. Add visuals and hyperlinks to support your definition.

Saving the Life That Is Your Own:
The Importance of Models
in the Artist's Life

Alice Walker

Alice Walker (b. 1941) was born in Eatonton, Georgia, and now lives in San Francisco and Mendocino County, California. She attended Spelman College and graduated from Sarah Lawrence College. A celebrated and prolific novelist, short-story writer, poet, and essayist, she has also been active in the civil rights movement. Walker often draws on both her personal experience and historical records to reflect on the African American experience. Her books include The Color Purple *(1976), which won the American Book Award and the Pulitzer prize;* You Can't Keep a Good Woman Down *(1981);* Living in the World: Selected Essays, 1973–1987 *(1987);* The Temple of My Familiar *(1989);* By the Light of My Father's Smile *(1999);* The Way Forward Is with a Broken Heart *(2001) and* Devil's My Enemy *(2008). The following essay, from* In Search of Our Mothers' Gardens *(1983), offers a highly personalized and perceptive analysis of the importance of influence on both art and life.*

There is a letter Vincent van Gogh wrote to Emile Bernard that is very meaning- 1
ful to me. A year before he wrote the letter, van Gogh had had a fight with his
domineering friend Gauguin, left his company, and cut off, in desperation and
anguish, his own ear. The letter was written in Saint-Remy, in the South of
France, from a mental institution to which van Gogh had voluntarily committed
himself.

I imagine van Gogh sitting at a rough desk too small for him, looking out 2
at the lovely Southern light, and occasionally glancing critically next to him at
his own paintings of the landscape he loved so much. The date of the letter is
December 1889. Van Gogh wrote:

> However hateful painting may be, and however cumbersome in the times we are
> living in, if anyone who has chosen this handicraft pursues it zealously, he is a
> man of duty, sound and faithful.
>
> Society makes our existence wretchedly difficult at times, hence our impo-
> tence and the imperfection of our work.
>
> . . . I myself am suffering under an absolute lack of models.
>
> But on the other hand, there are beautiful spots here. I have just done five size
> 30 canvasses, olive trees. And the reason I am staying on here is that my health is
> improving a great deal.
>
> What I am doing is hard, dry, but that is because I am trying to gather new
> strength by doing some rough work, and I'm afraid abstractions would make me soft.

3   Six months later, van Gogh—whose health was "improving a great deal"—committed suicide. He had sold one painting during his lifetime. Three times was his work noticed in the press. But these are just details.

4   The real Vincent van Gogh is the man who has "just done five size 30 canvasses, olive trees." To me, in context, one of the most moving and revealing descriptions of how a real artist thinks. And the knowledge that when he spoke of "suffering under an absolute lack of models" he spoke of that lack in terms of both the intensity of his commitment and the quality and singularity of his work, which was frequently ridiculed in his day.

5   The absence of models, in literature as in life, to say nothing of painting, is an occupational hazard for the artist, simply because models in art, in behavior, in growth of spirit and intellects—even if rejected—enrich and enlarge one's view of existence. Deadlier still, to the artist who lacks models, is the curse of ridicule, the bringing to bear on an artist's best work, especially his or her most original, most strikingly deviant, only a fund of ignorance and the presumption that, as an artist's critic, one's judgment is free of the restrictions imposed by prejudice, and is well informed, indeed, about all the art in the world that really matters.

6   What is always needed in the appreciation of art, or life, is the larger perspective. Connections made, or at least attempted, where none existed before, the straining to encompass in one's glance at the varied world the common thread, the unifying theme through immense diversity, a fearlessness of growth, of search, of looking, that enlarges the private and the public world. And yet, in our particular society, it is the narrowed and narrowing view of life that often wins.

7   Recently, I read at a college and was asked by one of the audience what I considered the major difference between the literature written by black and by white Americans. I had not spent a lot of time considering this question, since it is not the difference between them that interests me, but, rather, the way black writers and white writers seem to me to be writing one immense story—the same story, for the most part—with different parts of this immense story coming from a multitude of different perspectives. Until this is generally recognized, literature will always be broken into bits, black and white, and there will always be questions, wanting neat answers, such as this.

8   Still, I answered that I thought, for the most part, white American writers tended to end their books and their characters' lives as if there were no better existence for which to struggle. The gloom of defeat is thick.

9   By comparison, black writers seem always involved in a moral and/or physical struggle, the result of which is expected to be some kind of larger freedom. Perhaps this is because our literary tradition is based on the slave narratives, where escape for the body and freedom for the soul went together, or perhaps this is because black people have never felt themselves guilty of global, cosmic sins.

10   This comparison does not hold up in every case, of course, and perhaps does not really hold up at all. I am not a gatherer of statistics, only a curious reader, and this has been my impression from reading many books by black and white writers.

There are, however, two books by American women that illustrate what I am 11
talking about: *The Awakening,* by Kate Chopin, and *Their Eyes Were Watching God,*
by Zora Neale Hurston.

The plight of Mme Pontellier is quite similar to that of Janie Crawford. 12
Each woman is married to a dull, society-conscious husband and living in a
dull, propriety-conscious community. Each woman desires a life of her own and
a man who loves her and makes her feel alive. Each woman finds such a man.

Mme Pontellier, overcome by the strictures of society and the existence of 13
her children (along with the cowardice of her lover), kills herself rather than
defy the one and abandon the other. Janie Crawford, on the other hand, refuses
to allow society to dictate behavior to her, enjoys the love of a much younger,
freedom-loving man, and lives to tell others of her experience.

When I mentioned these two books to my audience, I was not surprised to 14
learn that only one person, a young black poet in the first row, had ever heard of
Their Eyes Were Watching God (*The Awakening* they had fortunately read in their
"Women in Literature" class), primarily because it was written by a black woman,
whose experience—in love and life—was apparently assumed to be unimportant
to the students (and the teachers) of a predominantly white school.

Certainly, as a student, I was not directed toward this book, which would have 15
urge me more toward freedom and experience than toward comfort and security, but was directed instead toward a plethora of books by mainly white male
writers who thought most women worthless if they didn't enjoy bullfighting or
hadn't volunteered for the trenches in World War I.

Loving both these books, knowing each to be indispensable to my own 16
growth, my own life, I choose the model, the example, of Janie Crawford. And yet
this book, as necessary to me and to other women as air and water, is again out of
print. But I have distilled as much as I could of its wisdom in this poem about its
heroine, Janie Crawford:

> I love the way Janie Crawford
> left her husbands
> the one who wanted to change her
> into a mule
> and the other who tried to interest her
> in being a queen.
> A woman, unless she submits,
> is neither a mule
> nor a queen
> though like a mule she may suffer
> and like a queen pace the floor.

It has been said that someone asked Toni Morrison why she writes the kind 17
of books she writes, and that she replied: Because they are the kind of books I
want to read.

This remains my favorite reply to that kind of question. As if anyone reading 18
the magnificent, mysterious *Sula* or the grim, poetic *The Bluest Eye* would require more of a reason for their existence than for the brooding, haunting

Wuthering Heights, for example, or the melancholy, triumphant *Jane Eyre.* (I am not speaking here of the most famous short line of that book, "Reader, I married him," as the triumph, but, rather, of the triumph of Jane Eyre's control over her own sense of morality and her own stout will, which are but reflections of her creator's, Charlotte Brontë, who no doubt wished to write the sort of books *she* wished to read.)

19   Flannery O'Connor has written that more and more the serious novelist will write, not what other people want, and certainly not what other people expect, but whatever interests her or him. And that the direction taken, therefore, will be away from sociology, away from the "writing of explanation," of statistics, and further into mystery, into poetry, and into prophecy. I believe this is true, *fortunately true;* especially for "Third World Writers"; Morrison, Marquez, Ahmadi, Camara Laye make good examples. And not only do I believe it is true for serious writers in general, but I believe, as firmly as did O'Connor, that this is our only hope—in a culture so in love with flash, with trendiness, with superficiality, as ours—of acquiring a sense of essence, of timelessness, and of vision. Therefore, to write the books one wants to read is both to point in the direction of vision and, at the same time, to follow it.

20   When Toni Morrison said she writes the kind of books she wants to read, she was acknowledging the fact that in a society in which "accepted literature" is so often sexist and racist and otherwise irrelevant or offensive to so many lives, she must do the work of two. She must be her own model as well as the artist attending, creating, learning from, realizing the model, which is to say, herself.

21   (It should be remembered that, as a black person, one cannot completely identify with a Jane Eyre, or with her creator, no matter how much one admires them. And certainly, if one allows history to impinge on one's reading pleasure, one must cringe at the thought of how Heathcliff, in the New World far from Wuthering Heights, amassed his Cathy-dazzling fortune.) I have often been asked why, in my own life and work, I have felt such a desperate need to know and assimilate the experiences of earlier black women writers, most of them unheard of by you and by me, until quite recently; why I felt a need to study them and to teach them.

22   I don't recall the exact moment I set out to explore the works of black women, mainly those in the past, and certainly, in the beginning, I had no desire to teach them. Teaching being for me, at that time, less rewarding than stargazing on a frigid night. My discovery of them—most of them out of print, abandoned, discredited, maligned, nearly lost—came about, as many things of value do, almost by accident. As it turned out—and this should not have surprised me—I found I was in need of something that only one of them could provide.

23   Mindful that throughout my four years at a prestigious black and then a prestigious white college I had heard not one word about early black women writers, one of my first tasks was simply to determine whether they had existed. After this, I could breathe easier, with more assurance about the profession I myself had chosen.

But the incident that started my search began several years ago: I sat down at 24
my desk one day, in a room of my own, with key and lock, and began preparations
for a story about voodoo, a subject that had always fascinated me. Many of the
elements of this story I had gathered from a story my mother several times told
me. She had gone, during the Depression, into town to apply for some government surplus food at the local commissary, and had been turned down, in a particularly humiliating way, by the white woman in charge.

My mother always told this story with a most curious expression on her face. 25
She automatically raised her head higher than ever—it was always high—and
there was a look of righteousness, a kind of holy *heat* coming from her eyes. She
said she had lived to see this same white woman grow old and senile and so badly
crippled she had to get about on *two* sticks.

To her, this was clearly the working of God, who, as in the old spiritual, ". . . may 26
not come when you want him, but he's right on time!" To me, hearing the story for
about the fiftieth time, something else was discernible: the possibilities of the story,
for fiction.

What, I asked myself, would have happened if, after the crippled old lady died, 27
it was discovered that someone, my mother perhaps (who would have been mortified at the thought, Christian that she is), had voodooed her?

Then, my thoughts sweeping me away into the world of hexes and conjurings 28
of centuries past, I wondered how a larger story could be created out of my mother's
story; one that would be true to the magnitude of her humiliation and grief, and to
the white woman's lack of sensitivity and compassion.

My third quandary was: How could I find out all I needed to know in order to 29
write a story that used *authentic* black witchcraft?

Which brings me back, almost, to the day I became really interested in black 30
women writers. I say "almost" because one other thing, from my childhood, made
the choice of black magic a logical and irresistible one for my story. Aside from
my mother's several stories about root doctors she had heard of or known, there
was the story I had often heard about my "crazy" Walker aunt.

Many years ago, when my aunt was a meek and obedient girl growing up in a 31
strict, conventionally religious house in the rural South, she had suddenly thrown
off her meekness and had run away from home, escorted by a rogue of a man
permanently attached elsewhere.

When she was returned home by her father, she was declared quite mad. In the 32
backwoods South at the turn of the century, "madness" of this sort was cured not by
psychiatry but by powders and by spells. (One can see Scott Joplin's *Treemonisha* to
understand the role voodoo played among black people of that period.) My aunt's
madness was treated by the community conjurer, who promised, and delivered, the
desired results. His treatment was a bag of white powder, bought for fifty cents, and
sprinkled on the ground around her house, with some of it sewed, I believe, into the
bodice of her nightgown.

So when I sat down to write my story about voodoo, my crazy Walker aunt 33
was definitely on my mind.

34   But she had experienced her temporary craziness so long ago that her story had all the excitement of a might-have-been. I needed, instead of family memories, some hard facts about the *craft* of voodoo, as practiced by Southern blacks in the nineteenth century. (It never once, fortunately, occurred to me that voodoo was not worthy of the interest I had in it, or was too ridiculous to study seriously.)

35   I began reading all I could find on the subject of "The Negro and His Folkways and Superstitions." There were Botkin and Puckett and others, all white, most racist. How was I to believe anything they wrote, since at least one of them, Puckett, was capable of wondering, in his book, if "The Negro" had a large enough brain?

36   Well, I thought, where are the *black* collectors of folklore? Where is the *black* anthropologist? Where is the *black* person who took the time to travel the back roads of the South and collect the information I need: how to cure heat trouble, treat dropsy, hex somebody to death, lock bowels, cause joints to swell, eyes to fall out, and so on. Where was this black person?

37   And that is when I first saw, in a *footnote* to the white voices of authority, the name Zora Neale Hurston.

38   Folklorist, novelist, anthropologist, serious student of voodoo, also all-around black woman, with guts enough to take a slide rule and measure random black heads in Harlem; not to prove their inferiority, but to prove that whatever their size, shape, or present condition of servitude, those heads contained all the intelligence anyone could use to get through this world.

39   Zora Hurston, who went to Barnard to learn how to study what she really wanted to learn: the ways of her own people, and what ancient rituals, customs, and beliefs had made them unique.

40   Zora, of the sandy-colored hair and the daredevil eyes, a girl who escaped poverty and parental neglect by hard work and a sharp eye for the main chance.

41   Zora, who left the South only to return to look at it again. Who went to root doctors from Florida to Louisiana and said, "Here I am. I want to learn your trade."

42   Zora, who had collected all the black folklore I could ever use.

43   *That Zora.*

44   And having found *that Zora* (like a golden key to a storehouse of varied treasure), I was hooked.

45   What I had discovered, of course, was a model. A model, who, as it happened, provided more than voodoo for my story, more than one of the greatest novels America had produced—though, being America, it did not realize this. She had provided, as if she knew someday I would come along wandering in the wilderness, a nearly complete record of her life. And though her life sprouted an occasional wart, I am eternally grateful for that life, warts and all.

46   It is not irrelevant, nor is it bragging (except perhaps to gloat a little on the happy relatedness of Zora, my mother and me), to mention here that the story I

wrote, called "The Revenge of Hannah Kemhuff," based on my mother's experiences during the Depression, and on Zora Hurston's folklore collection of the 1920s, and on my own response to both out of a contemporary existence, was immediately published and was later selected, by a reputable collector of short stories, as one of the *Best Short Stories of 1974.*

47   I mention it because this story might never have been written, because the very bases of its structure, authentic black folklore, viewed from a black perspective, might have been lost.

48   Had it been lost, my mother's story would have had no historical underpinning, none I could trust, anyway. I would not have written the story, which I enjoyed writing as much as I've enjoyed writing anything in my life, had I not known that Zora had already done a thorough job of preparing the ground over which I was then moving.

49   In that story I gathered up the historical and psychological threads of the life my ancestors lived, and in the writing of it I felt joy and strength and my own continuity. I had that wonderful feeling writers get sometimes, not very often, of being *with* a great many people, ancient spirits, all very happy to see me consulting and acknowledging them, and eager to let me know, through the joy of their presence, that, indeed, I am not alone.

50   To take Toni Morrison's statement further, if that is possible, in my own work I write not only what I want to read—understanding fully and indelibly that if I don't do it no one else is so vitally interested, or capable of doing it to my satisfaction—I write all the things *I should have been able to read.* Consulting, as belatedly discovered models, those writers—most of whom, not surprisingly, are women—who understood that their experience as ordinary human beings was also valuable, and in danger of being misrepresented, distorted, or lost:

Zora Hurston—novelist, essayist, anthropologist, autobiographer;

Jean Toomer—novelist, poet, philosopher, visionary, a man who cared what women felt;

Colette—whose crinkly hair enhances her French, part-black face; novelist, playwright, dancer, essayist, newspaperwoman, lover of women, men, small dogs; fortunate not to have been born in America;

Anaïs Nin—recorder of everything, no matter how minute;

Tillie Olson—a writer of such generosity and honesty, she literally saves lives;

Virginia Woolf—who has saved so many of us.

51   It is, in the end, the saving of lives that we writers are about. Whether we are "minority" writers or "majority." It is simply in our power to do this.

52   We do it because we care. We care that Vincent van Gogh mutilated his ear. We care that behind a pile of manure in the yard he destroyed his life. We care that Scott Joplin's music *lives!* We care because we know this: *The life we save is our own.*

COMPREHENSION

1. Explain the significance of Walker's title. How does it serve her purpose and guide readers to her thesis? What is her thesis?
2. According to the author, what is the importance of models in art? What is the relationship of models to life? List the models in Walker's life. Which of them stand out?
3. Paraphrase Walker's remarks on the relationship between black American and white American writing.

RHETORIC

1. Walker uses many allusions in this essay. Identify as many as you can. What is the allusion in the title? Comment on the general effectiveness of her allusions.
2. Is the author's style and choice of diction suitable to her subject matter and to her audience? Why or why not?
3. Why does the author personalize her treatment of the topic? What does she gain? Is there anything lost?
4. Walker employs several unique structuring devices in this essay. Cite at least three, and analyze their utility.
5. Explain Walker's use of examples to reinforce her generalizations and to organize the essay.
6. Which paragraphs constitute Walker's conclusion? What is their effect?

WRITING

1. Write an essay expanding the meaning of Walker's remark "What is always needed in the appreciation of art, or life, is the larger perspective" (paragraph 6).
2. If you were planning on a career as a writer, artist, actor, or musician, who would your models be, and why?
3. **Writing an Argument:** Argue for or against Walker's proposition that the absence of models in art and life is an "occupational hazard" (paragraph 5).

NETWORKING
Applying Digital and Multimedia Literacies

Keeping an "Importance of Models" Blog: Consider the importance of models in your life as a student (and as whatever else you are becoming or hope to become: a dancer, a basketball player, a social worker, a business executive, a nurse). Start and maintain a blog where you devote entries to individuals whom you've either studied from afar or studied with, who inform and influence your intellectual, artistic, athletic, professional, and/or personal growth. In each entry, describe this person and explain, with examples, what he or she has done or said that inspires you; record what you've learned and are continuing to learn from this person.

Synthesis: Connections for Critical Thinking

1. Write an essay comparing and contrasting literature and any other art form. What merits does each form have? Are there any limitations in either form? Which do you find more satisfying? Which form is more accessible? Use at least three essays in this chapter to illustrate or support your thesis.
2. Write an essay exploring the importance of role models in art and literature. Refer to the essays by Walker, Welty, Hampl, and McCloud to address the issue.
3. Analyze the illustrations that appear in the essays by Updike, McCloud, and Sontag. What is the purpose of these illustrations? What do the images contribute to the text?
4. Welty, Alexie, Walker, and other writers in this chapter provide extended examples of art and artists. How do they develop these examples? What strategies do they use? Are their goals similar or not? Explain your response.
5. Use the essays by Welty, Updike, and Hampl to explore the question of excellence in the arts. Answer this question: How do you know the work of art is good?
6. Examine the role of the artist in society and the artist's purpose in or duty to society. How would the writers in this chapter address this issue?

NETWORKING
Applying Digital and Multimedia Literacies

After visiting several news Web sites, write an essay in which you explain the importance of photography and photojournalism. Connect your findings to the ideas presented by Sontag in her essay.

chapter *11*

Philosophy, Ethics, and Religion

What Do We Believe?

You do not have to be an academician in an ivory tower to think about religion and the destiny of humankind or about questions of right and wrong. All of us possess beliefs about human nature and conduct, about "rival conceptions of God" (to use C. S. Lewis's phrase), about standards of behavior and moral duty. In fact, as Robert Coles argues in an essay appearing in this chapter, even children make ethical choices every day and are attuned to the "moral currents and issues in the large society."

Most of us have a system of ethical and religious beliefs, a philosophy of sorts, although it may not be a fully logical and systematic philosophy, and we may not be conscious that it determines what we do in everyday life. This system of beliefs and values is transmitted to us by family members, friends, educators, religious figures, and representatives of social groups. Such a philosophical system is not unyielding or unchanging, because our typical conflicts and dilemmas often force us to test our ethical assumptions and our values. For example, you may believe in nonviolence, but what would you do if someone threatened physical harm to you or a loved one? Or you may oppose the death penalty but encounter an essay that causes you to reassess your position. Our beliefs about nonviolence, capital punishment, abortion, cheating, equality, and so on are often paradoxical and place us in a universe of ethical dilemmas.

Your ability to resolve such dilemmas and make complex ethical decisions depends on your storehouse of knowledge and experience and on how well formulated your philosophy or system of beliefs is. When you know what is truly important in your life, you can make choices and decisions carefully and responsibly. Growing up in a world with competing views on morality often makes these choices that much harder, for constellations of cultures, beliefs, and influences contribute to our own personal development. As Plato observes in his classic "The Allegory of the Cave," the idea of what is truly good and correct never appears without wisdom and effort.

In this context, religion is also intrinsically connected to our sense of morality and ethics. Our personal code of ethics often has a religious grounding. Our religion often determines the way in which we apply our ethics—for instance, it may determine our attitudes toward contraception, equality of the races or the sexes, and evolution. In all instances, competing religious and secular values may force us to make hard decisions about our positions on significant cultural issues. All authors in this chapter seek the essence of the values and ideas that we develop during our brief time on this planet and that lend meaning and vitality to our lives.

PREVIEWING THE CHAPTER

As you read the essays in this chapter and respond to them in discussion and writing, consider the following questions:

- On what ethical or religious problem or conflict does the author focus?
- Is the author's view of life optimistic or pessimistic? Why?
- Do you agree or disagree with the philosophical or religious perspective that the author adopts?
- Is there a clear solution to the issue the author investigates?
- Does the author present rational arguments or engage in emotional appeals and weak reasoning?
- Does the author approach ethical, theological, and philosophical issues in an objective or in a subjective way?
- How significant is the ethical or philosophical subject addressed by the author?
- What social, political, or racial issues are raised by the author?
- Are there religious dimensions to the essay? If so, how does religion reinforce the author's philosophical inquiry?
- How do these essays encourage you to examine your attitudes and values? In reading them, what do you discover about your system of beliefs and the beliefs of society at large?

Classic and Contemporary Images

DO WE BELIEVE IN GOOD AND EVIL?

Using a Critical Perspective Comment on the composition of each of these works of art. How does each artist present the supernatural beings depicted? What do you notice about the organization of the images? From what angle does the artist approach the depiction? What do the artists have in common? Is the overall impression or effect of each illustration the same or different? Explain.

Angels, supernatural beings who serve as messengers from God, are found in the literature and imagery of Judaism, Christianity, and Islam from ancient times to the present, as in the Islamic painting from India shown here.

In more recent times, the sculptor Jacob Epstein (1880–1959) created a bronze
statue of St. Michael for Coventry Cathedral in England. The ancient
cathedral at Coventry was destroyed by German bombs in 1940.
During the 1950s, a new cathedral was built near the ruins of the old one.
With his spear in hand and his wings outstretched, St. Michael
stands in triumph over the prone, chained figure of the devil.

Classic and Contemporary Essays
HOW STRONG IS YOUR FAITH?

Most of us identify with the religion of our family and ancestors. Our profession of faith thus is not innate but conditioned by this allegiance to family, society, and culture. We come to religious belief through others, and then personally embrace, test, or reject this faith as adults. By large margins, we tend to stay within the religious tradition we have inherited whether it be Christian, Muslim, Jewish, Hindu, Buddhist, or some other belief system. Some of us might experience crises of faith—that dark night of the soul that has tested even great religious figures. Some of us—8 percent of Americans—might reject religion entirely. The two writers who open this section—Langston Hughes and Marjane Satrapi—do not take their religious upbringing uncritically. Admittedly they reflect different nations, cultures, religions, and races. (They also create or compose their texts in different media forms.) Nevertheless, both writers interrogate the varieties of religious experience that conditioned their childhood. Composing their narratives as adults, they test their faith and reach surprising conclusions. As you read "Salvation" by Langston Hughes and "The Veil" by Marjane Satrapi, consider the ways in which these writers, recalling childhood moments, arrive at fundamental truths about their mortal souls.

Salvation

Langston Hughes

James Langston Hughes (1902–1967), poet, playwright, fiction writer, biographer, and essayist, was for more than 50 years one of the most productive and significant American authors. In The Weary Blues *(1926),* Simple Speaks His Mind *(1950),* The Ways of White Folks *(1940),* Selected Poems *(1959), and dozens of other books, he strove, in his own words, "to explain the Negro condition in America." This essay, from his 1940 autobiography* The Big Sea, *reflects the sharp, humorous, often bittersweet insights contained in Hughes's examination of human behavior.*

1   I was saved from sin when I was going on thirteen. But not really saved. It happened like this. There was a big revival at my Auntie Reed's church. Every night for weeks there had been much preaching, singing, praying, and shouting, and some very hardened sinners had been brought to Christ, and the membership of the church had grown by leaps and bounds. Then just before the revival ended, they held a special meeting for children, "to bring the young lambs to the fold."

My aunt spoke of it for days ahead. That night I was escorted to the front row and placed on the mourners' bench with all the other young sinners, who had not yet been brought to Jesus.

My aunt told me that when you were saved you saw a light, and something happened to you inside! And Jesus came into your life! And God was with you from then on! She said you could see and hear and feel Jesus in your soul. I believed her. I had heard a great many old people say the same thing and it seemed to me they ought to know. So I sat there calmly in the hot, crowded church, waiting for Jesus to come to me. 2

The preacher preached a wonderful rhythmical sermon, all moans and shouts and lonely cries and dire pictures of hell, and then he sang a song about the ninety and nine safe in the fold, but one little lamb was left out in the cold. Then he said: "Won't you come? Won't you come to Jesus? Young lambs, won't you come?" And he held out his arms to all us young sinners there on the mourners' bench. And the little girls cried. And some of them jumped up and went to Jesus right away. But most of us just sat there. 3

A great many old people came and knelt around us and prayed, old women with jet-black faces and braided hair, old men with work-gnarled hands. And the church sang a song about the lower lights are burning, some poor sinners to be saved. And the whole building rocked with prayer and song. 4

Still I kept waiting to *see* Jesus. 5

Finally all the young people had gone to the altar and were saved, but one boy and me. He was a rounder's son named Westley. Westley and I were surrounded by sisters and deacons praying. It was very hot in the church, and getting late now. Finally Westley said to me in a whisper: "God damn! I'm tired o' sitting here. Let's get up and be saved." So he got up and was saved. 6

Then I was left all alone on the mourners' bench. My aunt came and knelt at my knees and cried, while prayers and song swirled all around me in the little church. The whole congregation prayed for me alone, in a mighty wail of moans and voices. And I kept waiting serenely for Jesus, waiting, waiting—but he didn't come. I wanted to see him, but nothing happened to me. Nothing! I wanted something to happen to me, but nothing happened. 7

I heard the songs and the minister saying: "Why don't you come? My dear child, why don't you come to Jesus? Jesus is waiting for you. He wants you. Why don't you come? Sister Reed, what is this child's name?" 8

"Langston," my aunt sobbed. 9

"Langston, why don't you come? Why don't you come and be saved? Oh, Lamb of God! Why don't you come?" 10

Now it was really getting late. I began to be ashamed of myself, holding everything up so long. I began to wonder what God thought about Westley, who certainly hadn't seen Jesus either, but who was now sitting proudly on the platform, swinging his knickerbockered legs and grinning down at me, surrounded by deacons and old women on their knees praying. God had not struck Westley dead for taking his name in vain or for lying in the temple. So I decided that maybe to save further trouble, I'd better lie, too, and say that Jesus had come, and get up and be saved. 11

12   So I got up.

13   Suddenly the whole room broke into a sea of shouting, as they saw me rise. Waves of rejoicing swept the place. Women leaped in the air. My aunt threw her arms around me. The minister took me by the hand and led me to the platform.

14   When things quieted down, in a hushed silence, punctuated by a few ecstatic "Amens," all the new young lambs were blessed in the name of God. Then joyous singing filled the room.

15   That night, for the last time in my life but one—for I was a big boy twelve years old—I cried. I cried, in bed alone, and couldn't stop. I buried my head under the quilts, but my aunt heard me. She woke up and told my uncle I was crying because the Holy Ghost had come into my life, and because I had seen Jesus. But I was really crying because I couldn't bear to tell her that I had lied, that I had deceived everybody in the church, that I hadn't seen Jesus, and that now I didn't believe there was a Jesus any more, since he didn't come to help me.

COMPREHENSION

1. What does the title tell you about the subject of this essay? How would you state, in your own words, the thesis that emerges from the title and the essay?
2. How does Hughes recount the revival meeting he attended? What is the dominant impression?
3. Explain Hughes's shifting attitude toward salvation in this essay. Why is he disappointed in the religious answers provided by his church? What does he say about salvation in the last paragraph?

RHETORIC

1. Key words and phrases in this essay relate to the religious experience. Locate five of these words and expressions, and explain their connotations.
2. Identify the level of language in the essay. How does Hughes employ language effectively?
3. Where is the thesis statement in the essay? Consider the following: the use of dialogue, the use of phrases familiar to you (idioms), and the sentence structure. Cite examples of these elements.
4. How much time elapses, and why is this important to the effect? How does the author achieve narrative coherence?
5. Locate details and examples in the essay that are especially vivid and interesting. Compare your list with what others have listed. What are the similarities? The differences?
6. What is the tone of the essay? What is the relationship between tone and point of view?

WRITING

1. Describe a time in your life when you suppressed your feelings about religion because you thought friends or adults would misunderstand.
2. Write a narrative account of the most intense religious experience in your life.
3. **Writing an Argument:** In an argumentative essay, explain why you think or do not think that politicians today often profess their religious beliefs simply to satisfy voters and not because of firmly held religious sentiments.

NETWORKING
Applying Digital and Multimedia Literacies

Using Multiple Media as Support: Support your response to question 3 under Writing with citations from books and articles, but also with sources like TV news broadcasts, Webcasts, documentaries, photographs, maps, graphs, and/or podcasts. Incorporate sources from at least three different types of media—of which at least one of them is digital and one, print. Alternatively, respond to question 2 under Writing and incorporate, reference, or link to at least two different types of media to augment your narrative.

The Veil

Marjane Satrapi

Marjane Satrapi (b.1967) is an Iranian-born French graphic novelist, animated film director, and children's book author. She was born in Rasht, Iran and grew up in Tehran in a progressive family. In 1983, she was sent to Vienna, Austria to escape the Islamic regime, which was looking into her family members' radical background. After high school, Satrapi returned to Tehran and eventually received an MA from Azad University. Following a failed marriage, she moved to Strasbourg, France, where she embarked on a career as a graphic novelist. Her two graphic nonfiction narratives, Persepolis *(2003) and* Persepolis 2 *(2004), brought her international acclaim. The animated film based on these works was nominated for an Academy Award in 2008. Today, Satrapi lives in Paris with her second husband. "The Veil" constitutes the opening chapter of* Persepolis.

EVERYWHERE IN THE STREETS THERE WERE DEMONSTRATIONS FOR AND AGAINST THE VEIL.

AT ONE OF THE DEMONSTRATIONS, A GERMAN JOURNALIST TOOK A PHOTO OF MY MOTHER.

I WAS REALLY PROUD OF HER. HER PHOTO WAS PUBLISHED IN ALL THE EUROPEAN NEWSPAPERS.

AND EVEN IN ONE MAGAZINE IN IRAN. MY MOTHER WAS REALLY SCARED.

HAVE YOU SEEN THIS?

DON'T WORRY DARLING.

SHE DYED HER HAIR,

AND WORE DARK GLASSES FOR A LONG TIME.

I REALLY DIDN'T KNOW WHAT TO THINK ABOUT THE VEIL. DEEP DOWN I WAS VERY RELIGIOUS BUT AS A FAMILY WE WERE VERY MODERN AND AVANT-GARDE.

I WAS BORN WITH RELIGION.

AT THE AGE OF SIX I WAS ALREADY SURE I WAS THE LAST PROPHET. THIS WAS A FEW YEARS BEFORE THE REVOLUTION.

O' Celestial light!

BEFORE ME THERE HAD BEEN A FEW OTHERS.

I AM THE LAST PROPHET.

A WOMAN?

I WANTED TO BE A PROPHET...

BECAUSE OUR MAID DID NOT EAT WITH US.

BECAUSE MY FATHER HAD A CADILLAC.

AND, ABOVE ALL, BECAUSE MY GRANDMOTHER'S KNEES ALWAYS ACHED.

COME HERE MARJI!! HELP ME TO STAND UP.

DON'T WORRY, SOON YOU WON'T HAVE ANY MORE PAIN. YOU'LL SEE.

COMPREHENSION

1. What can you infer about Satrapi's attitude toward the Iranian Revolution, the Islamic Republic, wearing the veil, and religion in general?
2. What is Satrapi's family like? What are their political values?
3. Why does the young Marjane want to be a prophet? What type of prophet would she want to be?

RHETORIC

1. How does Satrapi integrate words and images to convey her thesis?
2. Why does Satrapi's visual style rely exclusively on black and white? What is her purpose?
3. What comic elements can you locate in this visual text?
4. How does Satrapi achieve narrative unity as the reader moves from panel to panel?
5. Explain Satrapi's strategy for conveying varieties of emotion in this graphic narrative. Do you think that graphic nonfiction can produce stronger emotions than texts composed exclusively in words? Why or why not?

WRITING

1. In an essay of analysis, explain the strategies used by Satrapi to convey her experience of childhood, society, and religion.
2. Compare and contrast the graphic nonfiction methods of Scott McCloud (see page 503) and Marjane Satrapi.
3. **Writing an Argument:** Some critics contend that Satrapi's graphic art is too simplistic. Do you agree or disagree with this evaluation? Respond to the controversy in an argumentative essay.

NETWORKING
Applying Digital and Multimedia Literacies

Adaptations in Other Media: Arrange a class viewing of the animated film version of *Persepolis*. Afterward, discuss the similarities and differences between the nonfiction novel and the film.

Synthesis: Classic and Contemporary Essays for Comparison

1. Hughes entitles his text "Salvation" and Satrapi "The Veil." What elements and levels of irony do you find in these titles and the writers' narrative strategies? Are both texts ironic in the same way? Explain.

2. Both Hughes and Satrapi interrogate religion from the perspective of childhood experience. Why is childhood in particular a time in life when religious questions are especially relevant? Ultimately, how does each writer come to terms with his or her faith?

3. In your opinion, which writer is more successful in conveying the theme of religious conflict through textual method and style, considering that Hughes relies on words and paragraphs and Satrapi on words and images in panels? Might they be equally successful in their respective genres?

I Listen to My Parents and I Wonder What They Believe

Robert Coles

Robert Coles (b. 1929), author and psychologist, won the Pulitzer Prize in general nonfiction for volumes 1 and 2 of Children of Crisis, *in which he examines with compassion and intelligence the effects of the controversy over integration on children in the South. Walker Percy praised Coles because he "spends his time listening to people and trying to understand them." In its final form,* Children of Crisis *has five volumes, and Coles has widened its focus to include the children of the wealthy and the poor, the exploited and the exploiters. In collaboration with Jane Coles, he completed* Women in Crisis II *(1980). He has also written* The Secular Mind *(1999),* Lives of Moral Leadership *(2000), and* Bruce Springsteen's America *(2003). Below, Coles demonstrates his capacity to listen to and to understand children.*

1   Not so long ago children were looked upon in a sentimental fashion as "angels," or as "innocents." Today, thanks to Freud and his followers, boys and girls are understood to have complicated inner lives; to feel love, hate, envy and rivalry in various and subtle mixtures; to be eager participants in the sexual and emotional politics of the home, neighborhood and school. Yet some of us parents still cling to the notion of childhood innocence in another way. We do not see that our children also make ethical decisions every day in their own lives, or realize how attuned they may be to moral currents and issues in the larger society.

2   In Appalachia I heard a girl of eight whose father owns coal fields (and gas stations, a department store and much timberland) wonder about "life" one day: "I'll be walking to the school bus, and I'll ask myself why there's some who are poor and their daddies can't find a job, and there's some who are lucky like me. Last month there was an explosion in a mine my daddy owns, and everyone became upset. Two miners got killed. My daddy said it was their own fault, because they'll be working and they get careless. When my mother asked if there was anything wrong with the safety down in the mine, he told her no and she shouldn't

ask questions like that. Then the Government people came and they said it was the owner's fault—Daddy's. But he has a lawyer and the lawyer is fighting the Government and the union. In school, kids ask me what I think, and I sure do feel sorry for the two miners and so does my mother—I know that. She told me it's just not a fair world and you have to remember that. Of course, there's no one who can be sure there won't be trouble; like my daddy says, the rain falls on the just and the unjust. My brother is only six and he asked Daddy awhile back who are the 'just' and the 'unjust,' and Daddy said there are people who work hard and they live good lives, and there are lazy people and they're always trying to sponge off others. But I guess you have to feel sorry for anyone who has a lot of trouble, because it's poured-down, heavy rain."

Listening, one begins to realize that an elementary-school child is no stranger 3 to moral reflection—and to ethical conflict. This girl was torn between her loyalty to her particular background, its values and assumptions, and to a larger affiliation— her membership in the nation, the world. As a human being whose parents were kind and decent to her, she was inclined to be thoughtful and sensitive with respect to others, no matter what their work or position in society. But her father was among other things a mineowner, and she had already learned to shape her concerns to suit that fact of life. The result: a moral oscillation of sorts, first toward nameless others all over the world and then toward her own family. As the girl put it later, when she was a year older: "You should try to have 'good thoughts' about everyone, the minister says, and our teacher says that too. But you should honor your father and mother most of all; that's why you should find out what they think and then sort of copy them. But sometimes you're not sure if you're on the right track."

Sort of copy them. There could be worse descriptions of how children acquire 4 moral values. In fact, the girl understood how girls and boys all over the world "sort of" develop attitudes of what is right and wrong, ideas of who the just and the unjust are. And they also struggle hard and long, and not always with success, to find out where the "right track" starts and ends. Children need encouragement or assistance as they wage that struggle.

In home after home that I have visited, and in many classrooms, I have met 5 children who not only are growing emotionally and intellectually but also are trying to make sense of the world morally. That is to say, they are asking themselves and others about issues of fair play, justice, liberty, equality. Those last words are abstractions, of course—the stuff of college term papers. And there are, one has to repeat, those in psychology and psychiatry who would deny elementary-school children access to that "higher level" of moral reflection. But any parent who has listened closely to his or her child knows that girls and boys are capable of wondering about matters of morality, and knows too that often it is their grown-up protectors (parents, relatives, teachers, neighbors) who are made uncomfortable by the so-called "innocent" nature of the questions children may ask or the statements they may make. Often enough the issue is not the moral capacity of children but the default of us parents who fail to respond to inquiries put to us by our daughters and sons—and fail to set moral standards for both ourselves and our children.

6   Do's and don't's are, of course, pressed upon many of our girls and boys. But a moral education is something more than a series of rules handed down, and in our time one cannot assume that every parent feels able—sure enough of her own or his own actual beliefs and values—to make even an initial explanatory and disciplinary effect toward a moral education. Furthermore, for many of us parents these days it is a child's emotional life that preoccupies us.

7   In 1963, when I was studying school desegregation in the South, I had extended conversations with Black and white elementary-school children caught up in a dramatic moment of historical change. For longer than I care to remember, I concentrated on possible psychiatric troubles, on how a given child was managing under circumstances of extreme stress, on how I could be of help—with "support," with reassurance, with a helpful psychological observation or interpretation. In many instances I was off the mark. These children weren't "patients"; they weren't even complaining. They were worried, all right, and often enough they had things to say that were substantive—that had to do not so much with troubled emotions as with questions of right and wrong in the real-life dramas taking place in their worlds.

8   Here is a nine-year-old white boy, the son of ardent segregationists, telling me about his sense of what desegregation meant to Louisiana in the 1960s: "They told us it wouldn't happen—never. My daddy said none of us white people would go into schools with the colored. But then it did happen, and when I went to school the first day I didn't know what would go on. Would the school stay open or would it close up? We didn't know what to do; the teacher kept telling us that we should be good and obey the law, but my daddy said the law was wrong. Then my mother said she wanted me in school even if there were some colored kids there. She said if we all stayed home she'd be a 'nervous wreck.' So I went.

9   "After a while I saw that the colored weren't so bad. I saw that there are different kinds of colored people, just like with us whites. There was one of the colored who was nice, a boy who smiled, and he played real good. There was another one, a boy, who wouldn't talk with anyone. I don't know if it's right that we all be in the same school. Maybe it isn't right. My sister is starting school next year, and she says she doesn't care if there's 'mixing of the races.' She says they told her in Sunday school that everyone is a child of God, and then a kid asked if that goes for the colored too and the teacher said yes, she thought so. My daddy said that it's true, God made everyone—but that doesn't mean we all have to be living together under the same roof in the home or the school. But my mother said we'll never know what God wants of us but we have to try to read His mind, and that's why we pray. So when I say my prayers I ask God to tell me what's the right thing to do. In school I try to say hello to the colored, because they're kids, and you can't be mean or you'll be 'doing wrong,' like my grandmother says."

10   Children aren't usually long-winded in the moral discussions they have with one another or with adults, and in quoting this boy I have pulled together comments he made to me in the course of several days. But everything he said was of interest to me. I was interested in the boy's changing racial attitudes. It was clear he was trying to find a coherent, sensible moral position too. It was also borne in on me that if one spends days, weeks in a given home, it is hard to escape a particular moral climate just as significant as the psychological one.

In many homes parents establish moral assumptions, mandates, priorities. 11
They teach children what to believe in, what not to believe in. They teach children
what is permissible or not permissible—and why. They may summon up the
Bible, the flag, history, novels, aphorisms, philosophical or political sayings, personal memories—all in an effort to teach children how to behave, what and whom
to respect and for which reasons. Or they may neglect to do so, and in so doing
teach their children *that*—a moral abdication, of sorts—and in this way fail their
children. Children need and long for words of moral advice, instruction, warning, as
much as they need words of affirmation or criticism from their parents about other
matters. They must learn how to dress and what to wear, how to eat and what to eat;
and they must also learn how to behave under X or Y or Z conditions, and why.

All the time, in 20 years of working with poor children and rich children, Black 12
children and white children, children from rural areas and urban areas and in every
region of this country, I have heard questions—thoroughly intelligent and discern-
ing questions—about social and historical matters, about personal behavior, and so
on. But most striking is the fact that almost all those questions, in one way or another, are moral in nature: Why did the Pilgrims leave England? Why didn't they
just stay and agree to do what the king wanted them to do? . . . Should you try to
share all you've got or should you save a lot for yourself? . . . What do you do when
you see others fighting—do you try to break up the fight, do you stand by and
watch or do you leave as fast as you can? . . . Is it right that some people haven't got
enough to eat? . . . I see other kids cheating and I wish I could copy the answers too;
but I won't cheat, though sometimes I feel I'd like to and I get all mixed up. I go
home and talk with my parents, and I ask them what should you do if you see kids
cheating—pay no attention, or report the kids or do the same thing they are doing?

Those are examples of children's concerns—and surely millions of American 13
parents have heard versions of them. Have the various "experts" on childhood stressed
strongly enough the importance of such questions—and the importance of the hunger
we all have, no matter what our age or background, to examine what we believe in, are
willing to stand up for, and what we are determined to ask, likewise, of our children?

Children not only need our understanding of their complicated emotional 14
lives; they also need a constant regard for the moral issues that come their way as
soon as they are old enough to play with others and take part in the politics of the
nursery, the back yard and the schoolroom. They need to be told what they must
do and what they must not do. They need control over themselves and a sense of
what others are entitled to from them—cooperation, thoughtfulness, an attentive
ear and eye. They need discipline not only to tame their excesses of emotion but
discipline also connected to stated and clarified moral values. They need, in other
words, something to believe in that is larger than their own appetites and urges
and, yes, bigger than their "psychological drives." They need a larger view of the
world, a moral context, as it were—a faith that addresses itself to the meaning of
this life we all live and, soon enough, let go of.

Yes, it is time for us parents to begin to look more closely at what ideas 15
our children have about the world; and it would be well to do so before they
become teenagers and young adults and begin to remind us, as often happens,

of how little attention we did pay to their moral development. Perhaps a nine-year-old girl from a well-off suburban home in Texas put it better than anyone else I've met:

> I listen to my parents, and I wonder what they believe in more than anything else. I asked my mom and my daddy once: What's the thing that means most to you? They said they didn't know but I shouldn't worry my head too hard with questions like that. So I asked my best friend, and she said she wonders if there's a God and how do you know Him and what does He want you to do—I mean, when you're in school or out playing with your friends. They talk about God in church, but is it only in church that He's there and keeping an eye on you? I saw a kid steal in a store, and I know her father has a lot of money—because I hear my daddy talk. But stealing's wrong. My mother said she's a "sick girl," but it's still wrong what she did. Don't you think?

16   There was more—much more—in the course of the months I came to know that child and her parents and their neighbors. But those observations and questions—a "mere child's"—reminded me unforgettably of the aching hunger for firm ethical principles that so many of us feel. Ought we not begin thinking about this need? Ought we not all be asking ourselves more intently what standards we live by—and how we can satisfy our children's hunger for moral values?

COMPREHENSION

1. How does Coles's title capture the substance of his essay? What is his thesis?
2. According to Coles, why do parents have difficulty explaining ethics to their children? On what aspects of their children's development do they tend to concentrate? Why?
3. There is an implied contrast between mothers' and fathers' attitudes toward morality in Coles's essay. Explain this contrast, and cite examples for your explanation.

RHETORIC

1. What point of view does Coles use here? How does that viewpoint affect the tone of the essay?
2. Compare Coles's sentence structure with the sentence structure of the children he quotes. How do they differ?
3. Does this essay present an inductive or a deductive argument? Give evidence for your answer.
4. How does paragraph 13 differ from paragraphs 3, 10, and 16? How do all four paragraphs contribute to the development of the essay?
5. Explain the line of reasoning in the first paragraph. Why does Coles allude to Freud? How is that allusion related to the final sentence of the paragraph?
6. What paragraphs constitute the conclusion of the essay? Why? How do they summarize Coles's argument?

WRITING

1. Write an essay describing conflict between your parents' ethical views and your own.
2. **Writing an Argument:** Coles asserts the need for clear ethical values. How have your parents provided such values? What kind of values will you give your children? Answer these questions in a brief argumentative essay.

NETWORKING
Applying Digital and Multimedia Literacies

Conducting and Using Audio Interviews: Gather evidence, from conversations with friends and relatives, about an ethical issue such as poverty, world starvation, abortion, or capital punishment. With permission from all interviewees, record your conversations using your computer or another recording device. If your essay is an electronic/online document, include links to audio excerpts or even full interviews with some of your subjects.

What's God Got to Do with It?

Karen Armstrong

Karen Armstrong (b. 1945), who was educated in an English convent and subsequently earned a doctorate from St. Anne's College, Oxford, is a renowned historian, public lecturer, and radio and television broadcaster. A former nun, Armstrong is the author of more than a dozen books on religion, among them The Gospel according to Woman *(1987),* A History of God *(1993), and* Muhammad: A Prophet for Our Time *(2006). She also has written two autobiographies tracing her own spiritual journey:* Through the Narrow Gate *(1981) and* Beginning the World *(1983). Much of Armstrong's work, as the next essay indicates, explores the world's religions from ethical and cross-cultural perspectives.*

The activity that we call religion is complex. Religious and non-religious people 1
alike often share the same misperceptions. Today in the West, it is often assumed that religion is all about the supernatural and that it is inseparable from belief in an external, personalised deity. Critics claim that religion encourages escapist fantasies that cannot be verified. The explosion of terrorism (which is often given a religious justification) has convinced many people that religion is incurably violent. I have lost count of the number of times a taxi driver has informed me that religion has been the cause of all the wars in history.

2   Yet we find something very different when we look back to the period that the
German philosopher Karl Jaspers called the "Axial Age" (c. 900 to 200 BCE) because it proved to be pivotal to the spiritual development of humanity. In this era, in
four distinct regions of the world, the traditions that have continued to nourish
humanity either came into being or put down roots. Hinduism, Buddhism and
Jainism emerged in India; Confucianism and Taoism in China; monotheism was
born in Israel; and philosophical rationalism developed in Greece. It was a period of astonishing creativity; we have never really succeeded in going beyond the
insights of such sages as the Buddha, the mystics of the Upanishads, Confucius,
Lao-tzu, and the great Hebrew prophets. Rabbinic Judaism, Christianity and Islam,
for example, can be seen as a later flowering of the religion that had developed in
Israel during the Axial Age.

3   Despite interesting and revealing differences in emphasis, these traditions all
reached remarkably similar solutions. They can, perhaps, tell us something important about the structure of our humanity. The God of Israel was an important
symbol of transcendence, but in the other Axial faiths the gods were not very important. Confucius discouraged speculation about spirits and the afterlife: How
could you talk about other-worldly phenomena, when there was so much that you
did not understand about earthly matters?

4   During the Indian Axial Age, the ancient Vedic deities retreated from the
religious imagination. They were seen as unsatisfactory expressions of the sacred,
and were either demoted to human status or seen as aspects of the psyche. Many
of the Axial sages were reaching beyond the gods to a more impersonal
transcendence—to Brahman, Nirvana or the Tao—that was also inseparable
from humanity. Yogins and Taoists did not believe that their ecstatic trances
represented an encounter with the supernatural, but regarded them as entirely
natural to humanity. Later, the more sophisticated theologians in all three of the
monotheistic religions would make similar claims about the experience of the
reality that they called God.

5   None of these sages was interested in dogma or metaphysics. A person's
theological opinions were a matter of total indifference to a teacher like the Buddha.
He insisted that nobody should ever take any religious teaching, from however
august a source, on faith or at second hand. One of the Buddha's disciples pes-
tered him continuously about metaphysics: Was there a God? Who created the
world? He was so preoccupied with these matters that he neglected his yoga and
ethical practice. The Buddha told him that he was like a man who had been shot
with a poisoned arrow but refused to have any medical treatment until he discovered the name of his assailant and what village he came from: He would die before
he got this perfectly useless information.

6   The Taoists were also wary of dogmatic conformity; they believed that the
kind of certainty that many seek in religion was unrealistic and a sign of immatu-
rity. Eventually, the Chinese preferred to synthesise the schools which had developed during their Axial Age, because no single tradition could have the monopoly
of truth. In all four regions, when a sage started to insist upon strict orthodoxy,
this was usually a sign that the Axial Age was drawing to a close.

The prophets of Israel were more like political commentators than theologians; 7
they found the divine in analysis of current events rather than metaphysics. Jesus, as
far as we know, spent no time discussing the trinity or original sin, which would later
become so important to Christians; and the Koran dismisses theological dogmatism
as *zannah,* self-indulgent guesswork that makes people stupidly quarrelsome and
sectarian.

Religion was not about believing credal propositions, but about behaving in a 8
way that changed you at a profound level. Human beings have always sought what
the Greeks called *ekstasis,* a "stepping out" of the mundane, in moments when we
feel deeply touched within and lifted momentarily beyond ourselves. The Axial
sages all believed that if we stepped outside of our egotism and greed, we would
transcend ourselves and achieve an enhanced humanity. Yoga, for instance, one of
the great spiritual technologies of the Axial Age, was a formidable assault on the
ego, designed to take the "I" out of the practitioner's thinking.

But the safest way to achieve this *ekstasis* was by the practice of compassion. 9
Compassion—the ability to feel with another—was not simply the litmus test of
any true religiosity, but the chief way of encountering the ineffable reality of
Nirvana, Brahman, God and Tao. For the Buddha, compassion brought about
ceto-vimutti, the "release of the mind" that was a synonym for the supreme
enlightenment of Nirvana, a sacred realm of peace in the core of one's being.

All the Axial religions, in different ways, regarded what has been called the 10
Golden Rule as the essence of religion: "Do not do to others what you would not
like them to do to you." Confucius was the first to formulate this maxim. It was, he
said, the thread that pulled all his teachings together and should be practised all
day and every day. Five hundred years later, Rabbi Hillel was asked to sum up the
whole of Jewish teaching while he stood on one leg. He replied: "That which is
hateful to you, do not do to your neighbour. That is the Torah. The rest is commentary. Go and study it."

The Chinese sage Mo-tzu (c. 480–390) insisted that we had to have *jian ai,* 11
"concern for everybody." The priestly authors of Leviticus urged the Israelites to
love and honour the stranger; the Buddha taught layfolk and monks alike a
method of meditation called "the Immeasurables," in which they systematically
extended benevolent thoughts to the four corners of the world. Jesus told his
disciples to love their enemies. This impartial sympathy would break down the
barricades of egotism, because it was offered with little hope of any return.

If a ruler practised *jian ai,* Mo-tzu taught, war would be impossible. The Axial 12
religions all developed in regions that were convulsed by violence on an unprecedented scale. Iron weaponry meant that warfare had become more deadly; states
had become more coercive; in the market place, merchants preyed on each other
aggressively. In every case, throughout the Axial Age, the catalyst for religious
change was always a disciplined revulsion towards this violence.

In the 9th century, the ritualists of India systematically extracted all the 13
violence from the sacrificial ritual, and in seeking the cause of aggression in the
psyche, discovered the inner self. Renouncers, Buddhists and Jains all insisted

that *ahimsa,* "harmlessness," was an indispensable prerequisite to enlightenment. In the Tao Te Ching, Lao-tzu pointed out that violence could only elicit more violence. The sage-ruler must always seek to bring a military campaign to a speedy end: "Bring it to a conclusion, but do not intimidate." Some of the gospels present Jesus as a man of *ahimsa* who taught his followers to turn the other cheek.

14   Socrates, one of the greatest figures of the Axial Age, also condemned retaliation as evil. In general, however, the Greeks did not eschew violence. Ultimately, they did not have a religious Axial Age. Their great transformation was philosophical, scientific and mathematical, and pagan religion continued to flourish in Greece until it was forcibly replaced by Christianity in the 5th century CE.

15   Compassion is an unpopular virtue. All too often, religious people have preferred to be right rather than compassionate. They have shielded themselves from the demands of empathy by making secondary and peripheral goals—such as theological correctness or sexual orthodoxy—central to their faith. As the Chinese sages pointed out, vehement professions of belief were essentially egotistic, a pompous trumpeting of self, and, therefore, they impeded enlightenment. Denominational chauvinism, like nationalism, should also be seen as a form of collective egotism or, in monotheistic terms, idolatry.

16   Nevertheless, in our torn, conflicted world, we need to revive the Axial ethos. This does not require orthodox belief and need not involve the supernatural. In the Axial Age, individualism was beginning to supersede the older tribal or communal expressions of identity. The sages were trying to moderate the clash of competing egos and they were all concerned about the plight of society. We are still rampant, chronic individualists, but our technology has created a global village, which is interconnected electronically, militarily, politically and economically. If we want to survive, it makes practical sense to cultivate *jian ai.* We need to apply the Golden Rule politically, and learn that other nations, however remote from our own, are as important as ours.

COMPREHENSION

1. How does Armstrong answer the question posed by her title?
2. Identify the main religions mentioned by Armstrong. How are they alike and unlike? What idea or principle serves to unify them?
3. Armstrong writes of the Axial Age. Describe this period as she presents it. Why, according to Armstrong, is it important?

RHETORIC

1. What is Armstrong's claim? What is her persuasive purpose, and what techniques of argumentation does she employ to convince the reader? How convinced are you?
2. How do the first two paragraphs serve as an introduction to the essay?
3. Explain the writer's use of definition, classification and division, and comparison and contrast to organize her essay.
4. Does this essay reflect inductive or deductive reasoning? Justify your answer.

5. Why does the writer divide the essay into two sections? What relationships do you detect between the parts? What transitions does she use?
6. Armstrong's conclusion suggests a certain causality linking periods of history. How persuasive do you find her presentation of these historic interconnections, and how effective do you find the conclusion?

WRITING

1. Select a religion other than your own that Armstrong discusses, and write an explanatory essay in which you suggest ways in which this system of belief is relevant to some of today's most pressing global problems.
2. **Writing an Argument:** Answer the question posed by Armstrong in her title, relying on logical and ethical appeals.

NETWORKING
Applying Digital and Multimedia Literacies

Using Your Library's Online Databases: Conduct research on the Axial Age using a subscription database, and write an extended definition of this period.

Our Mutual Joy: The Religious Case for Gay Marriage

Lisa Miller

Lisa Miller is a senior writer and religion editor at Newsweek. *She writes the magazine's Belief Watch column and also prepares longer articles on spirituality and belief. After graduating from Oberlin College (BA, 1984), Miller began her career at the* Harvard Business Review; *she also held positions at the* New Yorker *and the* Wall Street Journal *before joining* Newsweek *as the magazine's society editor in 2000. Miller's essay on gay marriage and Scripture, which appeared in* Newsweek's *December 15, 2008, issue, provoked thousands of responses, some supportive but others taking issue with her argument.*

1 Let's try for a minute to take the religious conservatives at their word and define marriage as the Bible does. Shall we look to Abraham, the great patriarch, who slept with his servant when he discovered his beloved wife Sarah was infertile? Or to Jacob, who fathered children with four different women (two sisters and their servants)? Abraham, Jacob, David, Solomon and the kings of Judah and Israel—all these fathers and heroes were polygamists. The New Testament model of marriage is hardly better. Jesus himself was single and preached an indifference to earthly attachments—especially family. The apostle Paul (also single) regarded marriage as an act of last resort for those unable to contain their animal lust. "It is better to marry than to burn with passion," says the apostle, in one of the most lukewarm endorsements of a treasured institution ever uttered. Would any contemporary heterosexual married couple—who likely woke up on their wedding day harboring some optimistic and newfangled ideas about gender equality and romantic love—turn to the Bible as a how-to script?

2 Of course not, yet the religious opponents of gay marriage would have it be so.

3 The battle over gay marriage has been waged for more than a decade, but within the last six months—since California legalized gay marriage and then, with a ballot initiative in November, amended its Constitution to prohibit it—the debate has grown into a full-scale war, with religious-rhetoric slinging to match. Not since 1860, when the country's pulpits were full of preachers pronouncing on slavery, pro and con, has one of our basic social (and economic) institutions been so subject to biblical scrutiny. But whereas in the Civil War the traditionalists had their James Henley Thornwell—and the advocates for change, their Henry Ward Beecher—this time the sides are unevenly matched. All the religious rhetoric, it seems, has been on the side of the gay-marriage opponents, who use Scripture as the foundation for their objections.

4 The argument goes something like this statement, which the Rev. Richard A. Hunter, a United Methodist minister, gave to the Atlanta *Journal-Constitution* in June: "The Bible and Jesus define marriage as between one man and one woman. The church cannot condone or bless same-sex marriages because this stands in opposition to Scripture and our tradition."

5 To which there are two obvious responses: First, while the Bible and Jesus say many important things about love and family, neither explicitly defines marriage as between one man and one woman. And second, as the examples above illustrate, no sensible modern person wants marriage—theirs or anyone else's—to look in its particulars anything like what the Bible describes. "Marriage" in America refers to two separate things, a religious institution and a civil one, though it is most often enacted as a messy conflation of the two. As a civil institution, marriage offers practical benefits to both partners: contractual rights having to do with taxes; insurance; the care and custody of children; visitation rights; and inheritance. As a religious institution; marriage offers something else: a commitment of both partners before God to love, honor and cherish each other—in sickness and in health, for richer and poorer—in accordance with God's will. In a religious marriage, two people promise to take care of each other, profoundly, the way they believe God cares for them. Biblical literalists will disagree, but the

Bible is a living document, powerful for more than 2,000 years because its truths speak to us even as we change through history. In that light, Scripture gives us no good reason why gays and lesbians should not be (civilly and religiously) married—and a number of excellent reasons why they should.

In the Old Testament, the concept of family is fundamental, but examples of 6 what social conservatives would call "the traditional family" are scarcely to be found. Marriage was critical to the passing along of tradition and history, as well as to maintaining the Jews' precious and fragile monotheism. But as the Barnard University Bible scholar Alan Segal puts it, the arrangement was between "one man and as many women as he could pay for." Social conservatives point to Adam and Eve as evidence for their one man, one woman argument—in particular, this verse from Genesis: "Therefore shall a man leave his mother and father, and shall cleave unto his wife, and they shall be one flesh." But as Segal says, if you believe that the Bible was written by men and not handed down in its leather bindings by God, then that verse was written by people for whom polygamy was the way of the world. (The fact that homosexual couples cannot procreate has also been raised as a biblical objection, for didn't God say, "Be fruitful and multiply"? But the Bible authors could never have imagined the brave new world of international adoption and assisted reproductive technology—and besides, heterosexuals who are infertile or past the age of reproducing get married all the time.)

Ozzie and Harriet are nowhere in the New Testament either. The biblical Jesus 7 was—in spite of recent efforts of novelists to paint him otherwise—emphatically unmarried. He preached a radical kind of family, a caring community of believers, whose bond in God superseded all blood ties. Leave your families and follow me, Jesus says in the gospels. There will be no marriage in heaven, he says in Matthew. Jesus never mentions homosexuality, but he roundly condemns divorce (leaving a loophole in some cases for the husbands of unfaithful women).

8   The apostle Paul echoed the Christian Lord's lack of interest in matters of the flesh. For him, celibacy was the Christian ideal, but family stability was the best alternative. Marry if you must, he told his audiences, but do not get divorced. "To the married I give this command (not I, but the Lord); a wife must not separate from her husband." It probably goes without saying that the phrase "gay marriage" does not appear in the Bible at all.

9 If the Bible doesn't give abundant examples of traditional marriage, then what are the gay-marriage opponents really exercised about? Well, homosexuality, of course—specifically sex between men. Sex between women has never, even in biblical times, raised as much ire. In its entry on "Homosexual Practices," the Anchor Bible Dictionary notes that nowhere in the Bible do its authors refer to sex between women, "possibly because it did not result in true physical 'union' (by male entry)." The Bible does condemn gay male sex in a handful of passages. Twice Leviticus refers to sex between men as "an abomination" (King James version), but these are throwaway lines in a peculiar text given over to codes for living in the ancient Jewish world, a text that devotes verse after verse to treatments for leprosy, cleanliness rituals for menstruating women and the correct way to sacrifice a goat—or a lamb or a turtle dove. Most of us no longer heed Leviticus on haircuts or blood sacrifices; our modern understanding of the world has surpassed its prescriptions. Why would we regard its condemnation of homosexuality with more seriousness than we regard its advice, which is far lengthier, on the best price to pay for a slave?

10   Paul was tough on homosexuality, though recently progressive scholars have argued that his condemnation of men who "were inflamed with lust for one another" (which he calls "a perversion") is really a critique of the worst kind of wickedness: self-delusion, violence, promiscuity and debauchery. In his book "The Arrogance of Nations," the scholar Neil Elliott argues that Paul is referring in this famous passage to the depravity of the Roman emperors, the craven habits of Nero and Caligula, a reference his audience would have grasped instantly. "Paul is not talking about what we call homosexuality at all," Elliott says. "He's talking about a certain group of people who have done everything in this list. We're not dealing with anything like gay love or gay marriage. We're talking about really, really violent people who meet their end and are judged by God." In any case, one might add, Paul argued more strenuously against divorce—and at least half of the Christians in America disregard that teaching.

11   Religious objections to gay marriage are rooted not in the Bible at all, then, but in custom and tradition (and, to talk turkey for a minute, a personal discomfort with gay sex that transcends theological argument). Common prayers and rituals reflect our common practice: The Episcopal Book of Common Prayer

describes the participants in a marriage as "the man and the woman." But common practice changes—and for the better; as the Rev. Martin Luther King Jr. said, "The arc of history is long, but it bends toward justice." The Bible endorses slavery, a practice that Americans now universally consider shameful and barbaric. It recommends the death penalty for adulterers (and in Leviticus, for men who have sex with men, for that matter). It provides conceptual shelter for anti-Semites. A mature view of scriptural authority requires us, as we have in the past, to move beyond literalism. The Bible was written for a world so unlike our own, it's impossible to apply its rules, at face value, to ours.

Marriage, specifically, has evolved so as to be unrecognizable to the wives of 12 Abraham and Jacob. Monogamy became the norm in the Christian world in the sixth century; husbands' frequent enjoyment of mistresses and prostitutes became taboo by the beginning of the 20th. (In the *Newsweek* Poll, 55 percent of respondents said that married heterosexuals who have sex with someone other than their spouses are more morally objectionable than a gay couple in a committed sexual relationship.) By the mid-19th century, U.S. courts were siding with wives who were the victims of domestic violence, and by the 1970s most states had gotten rid of their "head and master" laws, which gave husbands the right to decide where a family would live and whether a wife would be able to take a job. Today's vision of marriage as a union of equal partners, joined in a relationship both romantic and pragmatic, is, by very recent standards, radical, says Stephanie Coontz, author of "Marriage, a History."

Religious wedding ceremonies have already changed to reflect new con- 13 ceptions of marriage. Remember when we used to say "man and wife" instead of "husband and wife"? Remember when we stopped using the word "obey"? Even Miss Manners, the voice of tradition and reason, approved in 1997 of that change. "It seems," she wrote, "that dropping 'obey' was a sensible editing of a service that made assumptions about marriage that the society no longer holds."

14   We cannot look to the Bible as a marriage manual, but we can read it for universal truths as we struggle toward a more just future. The Bible offers inspiration and warning on the subjects of love, marriage, family and community. It speaks eloquently of the crucial role of families in a fair society and the risks we incur to ourselves and our children should we cease trying to bind ourselves together in loving pairs. Gay men like to point to the story of passionate King David and his friend Jonathan, with whom he was "one spirit" and whom he "loved as he loved himself." Conservatives say this is a story about a platonic friendship, but it is also a story about two men who stand up for each other in turbulent times, through violent war and the disapproval of a powerful parent. David rends his clothes at Jonathan's death and, in grieving, writes a song:

> I grieve for you, Jonathan my brother;
> You were very dear to me.
> Your love for me was wonderful,
> More wonderful than that of women.

15   Here, the Bible praises enduring love between men. What Jonathan and David did or did not do in privacy is perhaps best left to history and our own imaginations.

16   In addition to its praise of friendship and its condemnation of divorce, the Bible gives many examples of marriages that defy convention yet benefit the greater community. The Torah discouraged the ancient Hebrews from marrying outside the tribe, yet Moses himself is married to a foreigner, Zipporah. Queen Esther is married to a non-Jew and, according to legend, saves the Jewish people. Rabbi Arthur Waskow, of the Shalom Center in Philadelphia, believes that Judaism thrives through diversity and inclusion. "I don't think Judaism should or ought to want to leave any portion of the human population outside the religious process," he says. "We should not want to leave [homosexuals] outside the sacred tent." The marriage of Joseph and Mary is also unorthodox (to say the least), a case of an unconventional arrangement accepted by society for the common good. The boy needed two human parents, after all.

17   In the Christian story, the message of acceptance for all is codified. Jesus reaches out to everyone, especially those on the margins, and brings the whole Christian community into his embrace. The Rev. James Martin, a Jesuit priest and author, cites the story of Jesus revealing himself to the woman at the well—no matter that she had five former husbands and a current boyfriend—as evidence of Christ's all-encompassing love. The great Bible scholar Walter Brueggemann, emeritus professor at Columbia Theological Seminary, quotes the apostle Paul

when he looks for biblical support of gay marriage: "There is neither Greek nor Jew, slave nor free, male nor female, for you are all one in Jesus Christ." The religious argument for gay marriage, he adds, "is not generally made with reference to particular texts, but with the general conviction that the Bible is bent toward inclusiveness."

The practice of inclusion, even in defiance of social convention, the reaching out 18 to outcasts, the emphasis on togetherness and community over and against chaos, depravity, indifference—all these biblical values argue for gay marriage. If one is for racial equality and the common nature of humanity, then the values of stability, monogamy and family necessarily follow. Terry Davis is the pastor of First Presbyterian Church in Hartford, Conn., and has been presiding over "holy unions" since 1992. "I'm against promiscuity—love ought to be expressed in committed relationships, not through casual sex, and I think the church should recognize the validity of committed same-sex relationships," he says.

Still, very few Jewish or Christian denominations do officially endorse gay 19 marriage, even in the states where it is legal. The practice varies by region, by church or synagogue, even by cleric. More progressive denominations—the United Church of Christ, for example—have agreed to support gay marriage. Other denominations and dioceses will do "holy union" or "blessing" ceremonies, but shy away from the word "marriage" because it is politically explosive. So the frustrating, semantic question remains: Should gay people be married in the same, sacramental sense that straight people are? I would argue that they should. If we are all God's children, made in his likeness and image, then to deny access to any sacrament based on sexuality is exactly the same thing as denying it based on skin color—and no serious (or even semiserious) person would argue that. People get married "for their mutual joy," explains the Rev. Chloe Breyer, executive director of the Interfaith Center in New York, quoting the Episcopal marriage ceremony. That's what religious people do: care for each other in spite of difficulty, she adds. In marriage, couples grow closer to God: "Being with one another in community is how you love God. That's what marriage is about."

More basic than theology, though, is human need. We want, as Abraham 20 did, to grow old surrounded by friends and family and to be buried at last peacefully among them. We want, as Jesus taught, to love one another for our own good—and, not to be too grandiose about it, for the good of the world. We want our children to grow up in stable homes. What happens in the bedroom, really, has nothing to do with any of this. My friend the priest James Martin says his favorite Scripture relating to the question of homosexuality is Psalm 139, a song that praises the beauty and imperfection in all of us and that glorifies God's knowledge of our most secret selves: "I praise you because I am fearfully and wonderfully made." And then he adds that in his heart he believes that if Jesus were alive today, he would reach out especially to the gays and lesbians among us, for "Jesus does not want people to be lonely and sad." Let the priest's prayer be our own.

COMPREHENSION

1. What is important about the main title of Miller's essay, "Our Mutual Joy"? According to Miller, what does the Bible say about the traditional family, heterosexual love, and gay marriage?
2. What does Miller mean when she writes, "Ozzie and Harriet are nowhere in the New Testament . . ." (paragraph 7)?
3. What is Miller's purpose in relating the story of King David and his friend Jonathan? What other biblical tales does she recount, and why?

RHETORIC

1. How would you describe Miller's voice in paragraph 1? Does she sustain this voice and tone throughout the essay? Is her writing style subjective or objective? Justify your response.
2. What is Miller's claim, and where does she state it most clearly? What constitutes her primary and secondary support? What types of evidence does she present? How does she contend with opposing viewpoints?
3. What connections do you perceive among the three major parts of this essay? How do the beginning and ending paragraphs relate to each other? How does Miller's organizational strategy support the essay's content?
4. In what way might this essay be considered an extended comparative analysis? What is being compared or contrasted, and how is the comparison structured?
5. Miller is fond of recurring motifs. Identify some of these motifs, and explain how these repeated references help to support her claim.

WRITING

1. Write an essay in which you elaborate on Miller's statement, "Religious wedding ceremonies have already changed to reflect new conceptions of marriage."
2. Write a comparative essay explaining the two diverging ways in which the Bible—or another religious text with which you are familiar—can be used to support or reject gay marriage.
3. **Writing an Argument:** Using your own religious background as a foundation, argue for or against marriage equality.

NETWORKING
Applying Digital and Multimedia Literacies

Using Visuals as Appeals: How do the photographs support Miller's position? What type of appeal do they make, how effective are they in doing so, and why?

The Pleasures of Imagination

Paul Bloom

Paul Bloom *(b. 1963) is a professor of psychology and cognitive science at Yale University. He was born in Montreal, Quebec, Canada. Bloom earned a BA from McGill University in 1985 and a PhD in cognitive psychology at Massachusetts Institute of Technology in 1990. While teaching at the University of Arizona from 1990 to 1999, and later at Yale, Bloom conducted award-winning interdisciplinary work on the moral capacities of babies and young children. In 2006, he was made a Fellow of the American Psychological Society in recognition of his "sustained out-standing contributions to the science of psychology." Bloom has published three groundbreaking books:* How Children Learn the Meaning of Words *(2000),* Descartes' Baby: How the Science of Child Development Explains What Makes Us Human *(2004), and* How Pleasure Works: The New Science of Why We Like What We Like *(2010). Bloom writes frequently for major scholarly and popular print outlets. In this essay from* The Chronicle of Higher Education, *Bloom explores the allure of the imagination and its power to transform our experience of reality.*

How do Americans spend their leisure time? The answer might surprise you. The most common voluntary activity is not eating, drinking alcohol, or taking drugs. It is not socializing with friends, participating in sports, or relaxing with the family. While people sometimes describe sex as their most pleasurable act, time-management studies find that the average American adult devotes just four minutes per day to sex.

Our main leisure activity is, by a long shot, participating in experiences that we know are not real. When we are free to do whatever we want, we retreat to the imagination—to worlds created by others, as with books, movies, video games, and television (over four hours a day for the average American), or to worlds we ourselves create, as when daydreaming and fantasizing. While citizens of other countries might watch less television, studies in England and the rest of Europe find a similar obsession with the unreal.

This is a strange way for an animal to spend its days. Surely we would be better off pursuing more adaptive activities—eating and drinking and fornicating, establishing relationships, building shelter, and teaching our children. Instead, 2-year-olds pretend to be lions, graduate students stay up all night playing video games, young parents hide from their offspring to read novels, and many men spend more time viewing Internet pornography than interacting with real women. One psychologist gets the puzzle exactly right when she states on her Web site: "I am interested in when and why individuals might choose to watch the television show *Friends* rather than spending time with actual friends."

One solution to this puzzle is that the pleasures of the imagination exist because they hijack mental systems that have evolved for real-world pleasure.

We enjoy imaginative experiences because at some level we don't distinguish them from real ones. This is a powerful idea, one that I think is basically—though not entirely—right. (Certain phenomena, including horror movies and masochistic daydreams, require a different type of explanation.)

5   The capacity for imaginative pleasure is universal, and it emerges early in development. All normal children, everywhere, enjoy playing and pretending. There are cultural differences in the type and frequency of play. A child in New York might pretend to be an airplane; a hunter-gatherer child will not. In the 1950s, American children played Cowboys and Indians; not so much anymore. In some cultures, play is encouraged; in others, children have to sneak off to do it. But it is always there. Failure to play and pretend is a sign of a neurological problem, one of the early symptoms of autism.

6   Developmental psychologists have long been interested in children's appreciation of the distinction between pretense and reality. We know that children who have reached their fourth birthday tend to have a relatively sophisticated understanding, because when we ask them straight out about what is real and what is pretend, they tend to get it right. What about younger children? Two-year-olds pretend to be animals and airplanes, and they can understand when other people do the same thing. A child sees her father roaring and prowling like a lion, and might run away, but she doesn't act as though she thinks her father is actually a lion. If she believed that, she would be terrified. The pleasure children get from such activities would be impossible to explain if they didn't have a reasonably sophisticated understanding that the pretend is not real.

7   It is an open question how early this understanding emerges, and there is some intriguing experimental work exploring this. My own hunch is that even babies have some limited grasp of pretense, and you can see this from casual interaction. A useful way to spend time with a 1-year-old is to put your face up close and wait for the baby to grab at your glasses or nose or hair. Once there is contact, pull your head back and roar in mock rage. The first time you get a bit of surprise, maybe concern, a dash of fear, but then you put your head back and wait for the baby to try again. She will, and then you give the pretend-startled response. Many babies come to find this hilarious. (If the baby is an eye-poker, you can wrestle over keys instead.) For this to work, though, the baby has to know that you are not even a little bit angry; the baby must know that you are pretending.

8   Why do we get pleasure from the imagination? Isn't it odd that toddlers enjoy pretense, and that children and adults are moved by stories, that we have feelings about characters and events that we know do not exist? As the title of a classic philosophy article put it, how can we be moved by the fate of Anna Karenina?

9   The emotions triggered by fiction are very real. When Charles Dickens wrote about the death of Little Nell in the 1840s, people wept—and I'm sure that the death of characters in J.K. Rowling's *Harry Potter* series led to similar tears. (After her final book was published, Rowling appeared in interviews and told about the letters she got, not all of them from children, begging her to spare the lives of beloved characters such as Hagrid, Hermione, Ron, and, of course, Harry Potter

himself.) A friend of mine told me that he can't remember hating anyone the way he hated one of the characters in the movie *Trainspotting*, and there are many people who can't bear to experience certain fictions because the emotions are too intense. I have my own difficulty with movies in which the suffering of the characters is too real, and many find it difficult to watch comedies that rely too heavily on embarrassment; the vicarious reaction to this is too unpleasant. These emotional responses are typically muted compared with the real thing. Watching a movie in which someone is eaten by a shark is less intense than watching someone really being eaten by a shark. But at every level—physiological, neurological, psychological—the emotions are real, not pretend.

Does this suggest that people believe, at some level, that the events are real? 10 Do we sometimes think that fictional characters actually exist and fictional events actually occur? Of course, people get fooled, as when parents tell their children about Santa Claus, the Tooth Fairy, and the Easter Bunny, or when an adult mistakes a story for a documentary, or vice versa. But the idea here is more interesting than that—it is that even once we consciously know something is fictional, there is a part of us that believes it's real.

There is something to this: It can be devilishly hard to pull apart fiction from 11 reality. There are several studies showing that reading a fact in a story—and knowing that it is fiction—increases the likelihood that you believe the fact to be true. And this makes sense, because stories are mostly true. If you were to read a novel that takes place in London toward the end of the 1980s, you would learn a lot about how people in that time and place talked to one another, what they ate, how they swore, and so on, because any decent storyteller has to include these truths as a backdrop for the story. The average person's knowledge of law firms, emergency rooms, police departments, prisons, submarines, and mob hits is not rooted in real experience or nonfictional reports. It is based on stories. Someone who watched cop shows on television would absorb many truths about contemporary police work ("You have the right to remain silent . . ."), and a viewer of a realistic movie such as *Zodiac* would learn more. Indeed, many people seek out certain types of fiction (historical novels, for example) because they want a painless way of learning about reality.

We go too far sometimes. Fantasy can be confounded with reality. For example, the publication of *The Da Vinci Code* led to a booming tourism industry in 12 Scotland, by people accepting the novel's claims about the location of the Holy Grail. Then there is the special problem of confusing actors with the characters they play. Leonard Nimoy, an actor born in Boston to Yiddish-speaking Russian immigrants, was frequently confused with his best-known role, Mr. Spock, from the planet Vulcan. This was sufficiently frustrating that he published a book called *I Am Not Spock* (and then, 20 years later, published *I Am Spock*). Or consider the actor Robert Young, star of one of the first medical programs, *Marcus Welby, M.D.*, who reported getting thousands of letters asking for medical advice. He later exploited this confusion by appearing in his doctor persona (wearing a white lab coat) on television commercials for aspirin and decaffeinated coffee. There is, then, an occasional blurring between fact and reality.

13   In the end, though, those brought to tears by Anna Karenina are perfectly aware that she is a character in a novel; those people who wailed when J.K. Rowling killed off Dobby the House Elf knew full well that he doesn't exist. And even young children appreciate the distinction between reality and fiction; when you ask them, "Is such-and-so real or make-believe?," they get it right.

14   Why, then, are we so moved by stories?

15   David Hume tells the story of a man who is hung out of a high tower in a cage of iron. He knows himself to be perfectly secure, but, still, he "cannot forebear trembling." Montaigne gives a similar example, saying that if you put a sage on the edge of a precipice, "he must shudder like a child." My colleague, the philosopher Tamar Gendler, describes the Grand Canyon Skywalk, a glass walkway that extends 70 feet from the canyon's rim. It is supposedly a thrilling experience. So thrilling that some people drive several miles over a dirt road to get there and then discover that they are too afraid to step onto the walkway. In all of these cases, people know they are perfectly safe, but they are nonetheless frightened.

16   In an important pair of papers, Gendler introduces a novel term to describe the mental state that underlies these reactions: She calls it "alief." Beliefs are attitudes that we hold in response to how things are. Aliefs are more primitive. They are responses to how things seem. In the above example, people have beliefs that tell them they are safe, but they have aliefs that tell them they are in danger. Or consider the findings of Paul Rozin, a professor of psychology at the University of Pennsylvania, that people often refuse to drink soup from a brand-new bedpan, eat fudge shaped like feces, or put an empty gun to their head and pull the trigger. Gendler notes that the belief here is: The bedpan is clean, the fudge is fudge, the gun is empty. But the alief is stupid, screaming, "Filthy object! Dangerous object! Stay away!"

17   The point of alief is to capture the fact that our minds are partially indifferent to the contrast between events that we believe to be real versus those that seem to be real, or that are imagined to be real. This extends naturally to the pleasures of the imagination. Those who get pleasure voyeuristically watching real people have sex will enjoy watching actors having sex in a movie. Those who like observing clever people interact in the real world will get the same pleasure observing actors pretend to be such people on television. Imagination is Reality Lite—a useful substitute when the real pleasure is inaccessible, too risky, or too much work.

18   Often we experience ourselves as the agent, the main character, of an imaginary event. To use a term favored by psychologists who work in this area, we get transported. This is how daydreams and fantasies typically work; you imagine winning the prize, not watching yourself winning the prize. Certain video games work this way as well: They establish the illusion of running around shooting aliens, or doing tricks on a skateboard, through visual stimulation that fools a part of you into thinking—or alieving—that you, yourself, are moving through space.

19   For stories, though, you have access to information that the character lacks. The philosopher Noël Carroll gives the example of the opening scene in *Jaws*. You can't be merely taking the teenager's perspective as she swims in the dark, because she is cheerful, and you are terrified. You know things that she doesn't. You

hear the famous, ominous music; she doesn't. You know that she is in a movie in which sharks eat people; she thinks that she is living a normal life.

This is how empathy works in real life. You would feel the same way seeing 20 someone happily swim while a shark approaches her. In both fiction and reality, then, you simultaneously make sense of the situation from both the character's perspective and from your own.

Samuel Johnson, writing about Shakespeare, said: "The delight of tragedy 21 proceeds from our consciousness of fiction; if we thought murders and treasons real, they would please no more." Johnson was a brilliant writer, but plainly he had never heard of O.J. Simpson. If he had, he'd realize that we get plenty of pleasure from real tragedy. Indeed, Shakespeare's tragedies depict precisely the sorts of events that we most enjoy witnessing in the real world—complex and tense social interactions revolving around sex, love, family, wealth, and status.

I have argued that our emotions are partially insensitive to the contrast be- 22 tween real versus imaginary, but it is not as if we don't care—real events are typi- cally more moving than their fictional counterparts. This is in part because real events can affect us in the real world, and in part because we tend to ruminate about the implications of real-world acts. When the movie is finished or the show is canceled, the characters are over and done with. It would be odd to worry about how Hamlet's friends are coping with his death because these friends don't exist; to think about them would involve creating a novel fiction. But every real event has a past and a future, and this can move us. It is easy enough to think about the families of those people whom O.J. Simpson was accused of murdering.

But there are also certain compelling features of the imagination. Just as artificial 23 sweeteners can be sweeter than sugar, unreal events can be more moving than real ones. There are three reasons for this. First, fictional people tend to be wittier and more clever than friends and family, and their adventures are usually much more in- teresting. I have contact with the lives of people around me, but this is a small slice of humanity, and perhaps not the most interesting slice. My real world doesn't include an emotionally wounded cop tracking down a serial killer, a hooker with a heart of gold, or a wisecracking vampire. As best I know, none of my friends has killed his father and married his mother. But I can meet all of those people in imaginary worlds.

Second, life just creeps along, with long spans where nothing much happens. 24 The O.J. Simpson trial lasted months, and much of it was deadly dull. Stories solve this problem—as the critic Clive James once put it, "Fiction is life with the dull bits left out." This is one reason why *Friends* is more interesting than your friends.

Finally, the technologies of the imagination provide stimulation of a sort that 25 is impossible to get in the real world. A novel can span birth to death and can show you how the person behaves in situations that you could never otherwise observe. In reality you can never truly know what a person is thinking; in a story, the writer can tell you.

So while reality has its special allure, the imaginative techniques of books, 26 plays, movies, and television have their own power. The good thing is that we do not have to choose. We can get the best of both worlds by taking an event that people know is real and using the techniques of the imagination to transform it into an experience that is more interesting and powerful than the normal perception of reality could ever be. The best example of this is an art form that has been invented in my lifetime, one that is addictively powerful, as shown by the success of shows such as *The Real World, Survivor, The Amazing Race*, and *Fear Factor*.

27   What could be better than reality television?

COMPREHENSION

1. According to Bloom, what is the relationship between fantasy and reality? Does the author think the "pleasure of imagination," which begins in infancy and extends throughout our lives, is without risks or interruptions? Explain.
2. Bloom's essay cuts across a number of academic disciplines. What are the main areas that his research draws upon, and how does he link these disciplines?
3. Bloom discusses the work of the philosopher Tamar Gendler. What is significant about her research, and how does Bloom link her theories to his own explanation of the connections between our imagined worlds, our emotions, and the real world?

RHETORIC

1. Which paragraphs constitute Bloom's introduction? How does he organize these introductory paragraphs? What transition does he make to the body of the essay?
2. Would you say that Bloom presents an argument in this essay, or is he merely analyzing the "pleasure of the imagination"? Justify your answer with specific citations from the text.
3. How does Bloom employ the comparative method to organize his essay? What are his main points of comparison?
4. Where does Bloom insert questions as a rhetorical device? What is his purpose?
5. What forms of evidence does Bloom present? What assumptions does Bloom make about his audience in presenting such a variety of evidence?

WRITING

1. **Writing an Argument:** Argue for or against the proposition that the imaginary life is a positive force in helping us to make sense of the world.
2. Compare and contrast the essay by Bloom with the essay in this chapter by Coles.
3. Compose a personal essay on the nature of your fantasies or imaginary life, and how this life impinges on your sense of reality.

NETWORKING
Applying Digital and Multimedia Literacies

Retype the essay in a Word document and create an interactive, hyperlinked version. Give careful thought to where you will link to and why. As you work, consider and maintain the delicate balance between providing readers with new, supplemental information or exciting tangents and distracting them from the main text.

The Allegory of the Cave

Plato

Plato *(427–347 BCE), pupil and friend of Socrates, was one of the greatest philosophers of the ancient world. Plato's surviving works are all dialogues and epistles, many of the dialogues purporting to be conversations of Socrates and his disciples. Two key aspects of his philosophy are the dialectical method—represented by the questioning and probing of the particular event to reveal the general truth—and the existence of Forms. Plato's best-known works include the* Phaedo, Symposium, Phaedrus, *and* Timaeus. *The following selection, from the* Republic, *is an early description of the nature of Forms.*

And now, I said, let me show in a figure how far our nature is enlightened or unen- 1
lightened: Behold! human beings living in an underground den, which has a mouth open towards the light and reaching all along the den; here they have been from their childhood, and have their legs and necks chained so that they cannot move, and can only see before them, being prevented by the chains from turning round their heads. Above and behind them a fire is blazing at a distance, and between the fire and the prisoners there is a raised way; and you will see, if you look, a low wall built along the way, like the screen which marionette players have in front of them, over which they show the puppets.

I see. 2

And do you see, I said, men passing along the wall carrying all sorts of 3
vessels, and statues and figures of animals made of wood and stone and various materials, which appear over the wall? Some of them are talking, others silent.

You have shown me a strange image, and they are strange prisoners. 4

Like ourselves, I replied; and they see only their own shadows, or the shadows 5
of one another, which the fire throws on the opposite wall of the cave?

True, he said; how could they see anything but the shadows if they were 6
never allowed to move their heads?

And of the objects which are being carried in like manner they would only see 7
the shadows?

Yes, he said. 8

And if they were able to converse with one another, would they not suppose 9
that they were naming what was actually before them?

Very true. 10

And suppose further that the prison had an echo which came from the other 11
side, would they not be sure to fancy when one of the passersby spoke that the voice which they heard came from the passing shadow?

No question, he replied. 12

13   To them, I said, the truth would be literally nothing but the shadows of the images.

14   That is certain.

15   And now look again, and see what will naturally follow if the prisoners are released and disabused of their error. At first, when any of them is liberated and compelled suddenly to stand up and turn his neck round and walk and look towards the light, he will suffer sharp pains; the glare will distress him and he will be unable to see the realities of which in his former state he had seen the shadows; and then conceive some one saying to him, that what he saw before was an illusion, but that now, when he is approaching nearer to being and his eye is turned towards more real existence, he has a clearer vision—what will be his reply? And you may further imagine that his instructor is pointing to the objects as they pass and requiring him to name them—will he not be perplexed? Will he not fancy that the shadows which he formerly saw are truer than the objects which are now shown to him?

16   Far truer.

17   And if he is compelled to look straight at the light, will he not have a pain in his eyes which will make him turn away to take refuge in the objects of vision which he can see, and which he will conceive to be in reality clearer than the things which are now being shown to him?

18   True, he said.

19   And suppose once more, that he is reluctantly dragged up a steep and rugged ascent, and held fast until he is forced into the presence of the sun himself, is he not likely to be pained and irritated? When he approaches the light his eyes will be dazzled and he will not be able to see anything at all of what are now called realities.

20   Not all in a moment, he said.

21   He will require to grow accustomed to the sight of the upper world. And first he will see the shadows best, next the reflections of men and other objects in the water, and then the objects themselves; then he will gaze upon the light of the moon and the stars and the spangled heaven; and he will see the sky and the stars by night better than the sun or the light of the sun by day?

22   Certainly.

23   Last of all he will be able to see the sun, and not mere reflections of him in the water, but he will see him in his own proper place, and not in another; and he will contemplate him as he is.

24   Certainly.

25   He will then proceed to argue that this is he who gives the season and the years, and is the guardian of all that is in the visible world, and in a certain way the cause of all things which he and his fellows have been accustomed to behold?

26   Clearly, he said, he would first see the sun and then reason about him.

27   And when he remembered his old habitation, and the wisdom of the den and his fellow-prisoners, do you not suppose that he would felicitate himself on the change, and pity them?

Certainly, he would.   28

And if they were in the habit of conferring honors among themselves on   29
those who were quickest to observe the passing shadows and to remark which
of them went before, and which followed after, and which were together; and
who were therefore best able to draw conclusions as to the future, do you
think that he would care for such honors and glories, or envy the possessors of
them? Would he not say with Homer, Better to be the poor servant of a poor
master, and to endure anything, rather than think as they do and live after
their manner?

Yes, he said, I think that he would rather suffer anything than entertain these   30
false notions and live in this miserable manner.

Imagine once more, I said, such an one coming suddenly out of the sun to   31
be replaced in his old situation; would he not be certain to have his eyes full of
darkness?

To be sure, he said.   32

And if there were a contest, and he had to compete in measuring the shadows   33
with the prisoners who had never moved out of the den, while his sight was still
weak, and before his eyes had become steady (and the time which would be
needed to acquire this new habit of sight might be very considerable) would he
not be ridiculous? Men would say of him that up he went and down he came without his eyes; and that it was better not even to think of ascending; and if any one
tried to loose another and lead him up to the light, let them only catch the of-
fender, and they would put him to death.

No question, he said.   34

This entire allegory, I said, you may now append, dear Glaucon, to the previ-   35
ous argument; the prison-house is the world of sight, the light of fire is the sun,
and you will not misapprehend me if you interpret the journey upwards to be the
ascent of the soul into the intellectual world according to my poor belief, which, at
your desire, I have expressed—whether rightly or wrongly God knows. But,
whether true or false, my opinion is that in the world of knowledge the idea of
good appears last of all, and is seen only with an effort; and, when seen, is also
inferred to be the universal author of all things beautiful and right, parent of light
and of the lord of light in this visible world, and the immediate source of reason
and truth in the intellectual; and that this is the power upon which he who would
act rationally either in public or private life must have his eye fixed.

I agree, he said, as far as I am able to understand you.   36

Moreover, I said, you must not wonder that those who attain to this beautiful   37
vision are unwilling to descend to human affairs; for their souls are ever hastening
into the upper world where they desire to dwell; which desire of theirs is very
natural, if our allegory may be trusted.

Yes, very natural.   38

And is there anything surprising in one who passes from divine contempla-   39
tions to the evil state of man, misbehaving himself in a ridiculous manner; if, while
his eyes are blinking and before he has become accustomed to the surrounding
darkness, he is compelled to fight in courts of law, or in other places, about the

images or the shadows of images of justice, and is endeavoring to meet the conceptions of those who have never yet seen absolute justice?

40   Anything but surprising, he replied.

41   Any one who has common sense will remember that the bewilderments of the eyes are of two kinds, and arise from two causes, either from coming out of the light or from going into the light, which is true of the mind's eye, quite as much as of the bodily eye; and he who remembers this when he sees any one whose vision is perplexed and weak, will not be too ready to laugh; he will first ask whether that soul of man has come out of the brighter light, and is unable to see because unaccustomed to the dark, or having turned from darkness to the day is dazzled by excess of light. And he will count the one happy in his condition and state of being, and he will pity the other; or, if he have a mind to laugh at the soul which comes from below into the light, there will be more reason in this than in the laugh which greets him who returns from above out of the light into the den.

42   That, he said, is a very just distinction.

COMPREHENSION

1. What does Plato hope to convey to readers of his allegory?
2. According to Plato, do human beings typically perceive reality? To what does he compare the world?
3. According to Plato, what often happens to people who develop a true idea of reality? How well do they compete with others? Who is usually considered superior? Why?

RHETORIC

1. Is the conversation portrayed here realistic? How effective is this conversational style at conveying information?
2. How do you interpret such details of this allegory as the chains, the cave, and the fire? What connotations do such symbols have?
3. How does Plato use conversation to develop his argument? What is Glaucon's role in the conversation?
4. Note examples of transition words that mark contrasts between the real and the shadow world. How does Plato use contrast to develop his idea of the true real world?
5. Plato uses syllogistic reasoning to derive human behavior from his allegory. Trace his line of reasoning, noting transitional devices and the development of ideas in paragraphs 5–14. Find and describe a similar line of reasoning.
6. In what paragraph does Plato explain his allegory? Why do you think he locates his explanation where he does?

WRITING

1. Are Plato's ideas still influencing contemporary society? How do his ideas affect our evaluation of materialism, sensuality, sex, and love?
2. Write an allegory based on a sport, business, or space flight to explain how we act in the world.

NETWORKING
Applying Digital and Multimedia Literacies

Adapting from the Page to the Screen: In an extended essay, try to convince your audience that *The Matrix* films are based on Plato's essay.

Not about Islam?

Salman Rushdie

Salman Rushdie (b. 1947), a well-known novelist, essayist, and critic, was born in Bombay, India, into a middle-class Muslim family that relocated to Pakistan following the bloody Partition. He attended public school in Pakistan and England and graduated from Kings College at Cambridge University. Rushdie first received critical acclaim for Midnight's Children *(1981) and* Shame *(1983). With the publication of his controversial novel* Satanic Verses *(1989) and the subsequent* fatwa, *or religious edict, issued by Ayatollah Khomeini ordering his death for blasphemy against Islam and his depiction of Muhammad, Rushdie went into hiding for several years. In 1998, the Islamic Republic of Iran announced that it would not carry out Rushdie's death sentence, but the* fatwa *remains in force. Rushdie's work includes* Imaginary Homelands: Essays and Criticism *(1991),* The Moor's Last Sigh *(1995),* Fury *(2001),* Shalimar the Clown *(2005), and the* Enchantress of Florence *(2009). In the selection that follows, published in the* New York Times *in 2001, shortly after the 9/11 attacks, Rushdie confronts the issue of Islamic terrorism.*

"This isn't about Islam." The world's leaders have been repeating this mantra 1 for weeks, partly in the virtuous hope of deterring reprisal attacks on innocent Muslims living in the West, partly because if the United States is to maintain its coalition against terror it can't afford to allege that Islam and terrorism are in any way related.

The trouble with this necessary disclaimer is that it isn't true. If this isn't 2 about Islam, why the worldwide Muslim demonstrations in support of Osama bin Laden and Al-Qaida? Why did those ten thousand men armed with swords and axes mass on the Pakistan-Afghanistan frontier, answering some mullah's call to jihad? Why are the war's first British casualties three Muslim men who died fighting on the Taliban side?

Why the routine anti-Semitism of the much-repeated Islamic slander that 3 "the Jews" arranged the hits on the World Trade Center and Pentagon, with the oddly self-deprecating explanation offered by the Taliban leadership among others; that Muslims could not have the technological know-how or organizational sophistication to pull off such a feat? Why does Imran Khan, the Pakistani ex–sports star turned politician, demand to be shown the evidence of Al-Qaida's guilt while apparently turning a deaf ear to the self-incriminating statements of Al-Qaida's own spokesmen (there will be a rain of aircraft from the skies, Muslims in the West are warned not to live or work in tall buildings, et cetera)? Why all the talk about U.S. military infidels desecrating the sacred soil of Saudi Arabia, if some sort of definition of what is sacred is not at the heart of the present discontents?

4   Let's start calling a spade a spade. Of course this is "about Islam." The question is, what exactly does that mean? After all, most religious belief isn't very theological. Most Muslims are not profound Quranic analysts. For a vast number of "believing" Muslim men, "Islam" stands, in a jumbled, half-examined way, not only for the fear of God—the fear more than the love, one suspects—but also for a cluster of customs, opinions, and prejudices that include their dietary practices; the sequestration or near-sequestration of "their" women; the sermons delivered by their mullah of choice; a loathing of modern society in general, riddled as it is with music, godlessness, and sex; and a more particularized loathing (and fear) of the prospect that their own immediate surroundings could be taken over—"Westoxicated"—by the liberal Western-style way of life.

5   Highly motivated organizations of Muslim men (oh, for the voices of Muslim women to be heard) have been engaged, over the last thirty years or so, on growing radical political movements out of this mulch of "belief." These Islamists—we must get used to this word, "Islamists," meaning those who are engaged upon such political projects, and learn to distinguish it from the more general and politically neutral "Muslim"—include the Muslim Brotherhood in Egypt, the blood-soaked combatants of the FIS and GIA in Algeria, the Shia revolutionaries of Iran, and the Taliban. Poverty is their great helper, and the fruit of their efforts is paranoia. This paranoid Islam, which blames outsiders, "infidels," for all the ills of Muslim societies, and whose proposed remedy is the closing of those societies to the rival project of modernity, is presently the fastest-growing version of Islam in the world.

6   This is not really to go along with Samuel Huntington's thesis about the "clash of civilizations," for the simple reason that the Islamists' project is turned not only against the West and "the Jews" but also against their fellow Islamists. Whatever the public rhetoric, there's little love lost between the Taliban and Iranian regimes. Dissensions between Muslim nations run at least as deep as, if not deeper than, those nations' resentment of the West. Nevertheless, it would be absurd to deny that this self-exculpatory, paranoiac Islam is an ideology with widespread appeal.

7   Twenty years ago, when I was writing a novel about power struggles in a fictionalized Pakistan, it was already de rigueur in the Muslim world to blame all its troubles on the West and, in particular, the United States. Then as now, some of these criticisms were well-founded; no room here to rehearse the geopolitics of the Cold

War, and America's frequently damaging foreign policy "tilts," to use the Kissinger term, toward (or away from) this or that temporarily useful (or disapproved-of) nation-state, or America's role in the installation and deposition of sundry unsavory leaders and regimes. But I wanted then to ask a question which is no less important now: Suppose we say that the ills of our societies are not primarily America's fault— that we are to blame for our own failings? How would we understand them then? Might we not, by accepting our own responsibility for our problems, begin to learn to solve them for ourselves?

It is interesting that many Muslims, as well as secularist analysts with roots in 8 the Muslim world, are beginning to ask such questions now. In recent weeks Muslim voices have everywhere been raised against the obscurantist "hijack" of their religion. Yesterday's hotheads (among them Yusuf Islam, a.k.a. Cat Stevens) are improbably repackaging themselves as today's pussycats. An Iraqi writer quotes an earlier Iraqi satirist: "The disease that is in us, is from us." A British Muslim writes that "Islam has become its own enemy." A Lebanese writer friend, returning from Beirut, tells me that, in the aftermath of September 11, public criticism of Islamism has become much more outspoken. Many commentators have spoken of the need for a Reformation in the Muslim world. I'm reminded of the way non-communist socialists used to distance themselves from the tyrannous "actually existing" socialism of the Soviets; nevertheless, the first stirrings of this counterproject are of great significance. If Islam is to be reconciled with modernity, these voices must be encouraged until they swell into a roar.

Many of them speak of another Islam, their personal, private faith, and the 9 restoration of religion to the sphere of the personal, its de-politicization, is the nettle that all Muslim societies must grasp in order to become modern. The only aspect of modernity in which the terrorists are interested is technology, which they see as a weapon that can be turned against its makers. If terrorism is to be defeated, the world of Islam must take on board the secularist-humanist principles on which the modern is based, and without which their countries' freedom will remain a distant dream.

COMPREHENSION

1. What is Rushdie's response to statements that 9/11 was not "about Islam"?
2. What distinction does Rushdie draw between "Muslims" and "Islamists"? What, according to the writer, is the proper role of religion in the contemporary world?
3. Explain Rushdie's solution to some of the problems confronting Islamic nations today.

RHETORIC

1. How would you describe Rushdie's tone? Identify words, phrases, and sentences that capture his attitude toward his subject. How does the fact that he writes in the immediate aftermath of the events of September 11, 2001, affect the tone? How do his personal difficulties bear on his approach to the subject?

2. What is the key claim that the writer makes in this essay? Is it stated or implied?
3. Where does Rushdie engage in rebuttal of his opponents' points? Does he refute these points clearly and adequately? Why or why not?
4. What reasons and evidence does the writer offer to support his contention that if Muslim nations accepted responsibility for their internal conditions rather than blaming the West, they could solve their own problems?
5. Where does the writer apply the comparative method to advance his argument?
6. How does Rushdie support his premise that Islamic societies want to become modernized and can do so if their religion returns to "the sphere of the personal" (paragraph 9)?

WRITING

1. Write a personal essay in which you explain what you think the proper role of religion should be in the post–September 11 world.
2. Write a comparative essay in which you distinguish between "Islam" and "Islamists." Conduct research if necessary.
3. **Writing an Argument:** Take issue with Rushdie's claim that September 11, 2001, is "about Islam." Rebut his reasons, offering ideas and support for your alternative explanation.

NETWORKING
Applying Digital and Multimedia Literacies

Creating an Interactive Argument: Condense your argument in question 3 under Writing into a 500-word blog post, complete with hyperlinks to sites that bolster support for your position. Encourage readers to post comments, which you should then respond to. Remember to keep the conversation civil and respectful, and the argument both rational and well supported; if comments get personal, rude, or worse, delete and do not respond to them.

Synthesis: Connections for Critical Thinking

1. Explore the connection between Plato, the philosopher, and Coles, the psychiatrist. How do their essays complement each other? How does Coles's attitude toward existence reflect Plato's philosophy of the cave?
2. What distinguishes a "true" religious belief from a superstition? What are their various functions? Is one more valid than the other? Explain your answer with reference to Satrapi, Hughes, and Armstrong.
3. Coles argues that the moral education of children is essential to a well-functioning society. What function does superstition serve in the lives of children that a pure moral education may fail to provide?

4. Based on your reading of Armstrong, explain whether you think she would agree or disagree with Rushdie's observations about Islam.
5. What is the difference between philosophy and religion? Is it merely a matter of belief? Address this question in an essay, using support from writers in this chapter.
6. Write an essay titled "The Purpose of Life." Using examples and evidence from their works, choose three writers in this chapter to develop this theme.

NETWORKING
Applying Digital and Multimedia Literacies

1. Working with classmates, create your own interactive blog or Web site displaying an excerpt from Miller's essay. Ask for personal responses from all its visitors, and report your findings.
2. Research online the role of cults in American society, particularly among young people. Focus on finding specific practices they have that can inflict self-harm or harm on others.

chapter *12*

Health and Medicine
What Are the Challenges?

Today, medicine and the health sciences are recasting our lives and the world we know. From stem-cell research, to the abortion debate, to the AIDS epidemic, we are dealing with enormous medical challenges and controversies. At the same time, commonplace conditions ranging from starvation to the common cold continue to defy solutions. There are surely medical breakthroughs—new drugs, therapies, technologies, and delivery systems—that offer some cause for optimism. However, we must acknowledge the ongoing reality of illness, both physical and psychological, and the serious imbalance in individuals' access to health care.

It could be argued that medical science presents an unequal playing field to Americans and people worldwide, for health care clearly is a privilege rather than a right. For millions of people in the United States and billions around the world, health care is rudimentary or nonexistent. College students, of course, are among the privileged. They typically enjoy health insurance, access to campus clinics or affiliated hospitals, counseling and psychiatric intervention, and an entire network of other health care support systems. Health care at an American college or university is a model that we would wish for any culture, society, or nation.

Medicine and health care are also subjects for civic discourse, cultural argument, and political debate. Disputes over medicine—abortion, cloning, drug addiction, and more—are also part of everyday life. The subject was an integral part of the most recent U.S. presidential election and assuredly will resurface in future election cycles. And, of course, the media (as we discussed in an earlier chapter) exploit our fascination with health and medicine. Television shows feature extreme surgical makeovers and contests among oversized people competing to lose the most weight. Magazines and television promote potentially dangerous body images. On the Internet, people suffering from anorexia and other dietary disorders can find solace and support.

The writers in this chapter contend with some of the most pressing issues confronting medical science today. Some of the writers are physicians. Some authors personalize their subject; others offer objective analysis or compelling arguments. All raise moral and ethical issues as they deal with ways in which medicine is shaping our personalities and our lives.

PREVIEWING THE CHAPTER

As you read the essays in this chapter and respond to them in discussion and writing, consider the following questions:

- What is the writer's subject? What perspective on medicine or health does she or he take?
- What is the writer's purpose: to explain, narrate, argue, or persuade?
- Do you find the writer's tone to be subjective or objective? Does the author have a personal motive in addressing the topic in the way he or she does?
- What moral, ethical, or religious issues does the writer raise in connection with medicine or health science?
- What logical, emotional, and ethical appeals does the author make to his or her audience?
- Which level of specialized knowledge—history, science, medicine, or some other area—does the author bring to bear on the subject? What level of authority does she or he bring to the topic?
- What cultural, economic, or political problems does the author connect to the medical topic under consideration?
- Do you agree or disagree with the author's thesis or claim, and why?
- Which essays appear similar in subject, thesis, or perspective?
- Which essays did you find most compelling or convincing, and why?
- Which ones changed your opinion or altered your thinking on the subject?

Classic and Contemporary Images
WHAT DOES MEDICAL RESEARCH TELL US?

Using a Critical Perspective   The medical universe has changed radically since 1632, when Rembrandt painted *The Anatomy Lesson of Professor Nicolaes Tulp*. Flash forward to 2004 and move from Holland to New York City, where photographer Gary Bramnick captured the release of conjoined twins after successful surgery. As you consider these visual texts, answer these questions: What is the main purpose of the artist or the photographer? What elements in each image contribute to the overall effect? How is the human subject portrayed, and which scene evokes the strongest emotional reaction? How does the much earlier scene relate to the contemporary one?

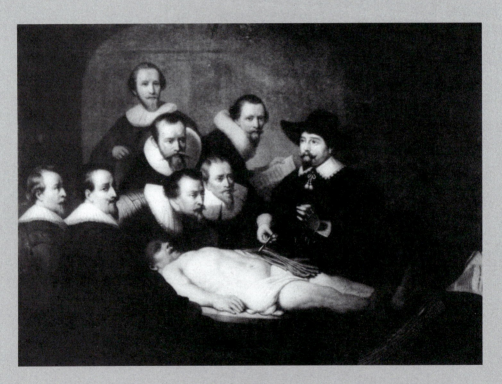

Rembrandt van Rijn (1606–1669) was the most gifted painter, draftsman, and etcher of Holland's Golden Age. *The Anatomy Lesson* (1632) is a group portrait of the Amsterdam surgeon's guild, whose members, led by Dr. Nicolaes Tulp, were unsurpassed in the surgical techniques of the period.

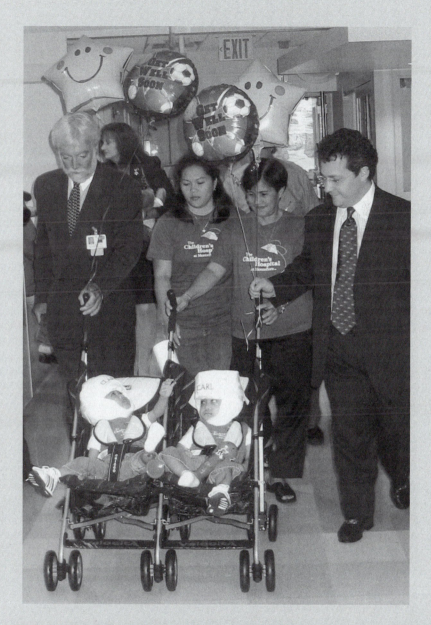

Clarence and Carl Aguirre, formerly conjoined twins who were separated by surgery, are followed by their mother Arlene Aguirre, center left, and grandmother Evelyn, center right, as they leave Children's Hospital at Montefiore in New York, flanked by the doctors who performed the surgery, Dr. James T. Goodrich, left, and Dr. David A. Staffenberg. Nurses loaded the boys into separate ambulances, which took off with a police escort for Blythedale Children's Hospital in Valhalla, where they and their mother lived between operations at Montefiore.

Classic and Contemporary Essays
CAN WE AVOID EPIDEMICS?

We would like to think that the 21st century will avoid a plague like the one that swept through Asia and Europe during the 14th century. Yet the AIDS epidemic proves to be intractable and growing in sub-Saharan Africa, Asia, Russia, and the Indian subcontinent, while outbreaks of new potential epidemics like Ebola and SARS pose serious challenges for medical researchers and dangers for humankind. Plagues seem to be as old and persistent as civilization itself. Looking back to the 14th century, the noted historian Barbara Tuchman tells the story of the Black Death—the bubonic plague—that devastated Europe, resulting in the extinction of perhaps one-third of the population. With a historian's eye for narrative and detail, she describes the symptoms associated with plague, the process by which it spread inexorably from one nation to the next, and the religious, political, and cultural impact of the disease on the continent. Like Tuchman, Jill Lepore is a historian with wide-ranging research interests in American culture and civilization. However, Lepore in her essay deals with the 20th century while implying that we are facing new epidemics or plague years. Both writers trace the origins of emerging plagues and their consequences. Lepore also makes a pointed argument about the failure of the American health care system and the media to deal rationally with diseases that might or might not be of epidemic proportions. As you read these two essays, consider the rhetorical strategies that Tuchman and Lepore employ to render their respective vision of epidemics in vivid and compelling ways.

"This Is the End of the World": The Black Death

Barbara Tuchman

Barbara Tuchman *(1912–1989) was born in New York City and graduated from Radcliffe College. A self-taught historian, she worked as a writer for the* Nation *magazine and during World War II served as an editor at the U.S. Office of War Information. Her book* The Guns of August *(1960), a narrative history of the outbreak of World War I, won the Pulitzer prize. She won it again for her book* Stilwell and the American Experience in China: 1911–45 *(1971). Her other books include such best-sellers as* A Distant Mirror: The Calamitous 14th Century *(1978) and* The First Salute *(1989). In her later years, she was a lecturer at Harvard University and at the U.S. Naval War College. In this selection, excerpted from* A Distant Mirror, *Tuchman explains in her vivid narrative style the effects of the bubonic plague on Western Europe.*

In October 1347, two months after the fall of Calais, Genoese trading ships put 1
into the harbor of Messina in Sicily with dead and dying men at the oars. The
ships had come from the Black Sea port of Caffa (now Feodosiya) in the Crimea,
where the Genoese maintained a trading post. The diseased sailors showed
strange black swellings about the size of an egg or an apple in the armpits and
groin. The swellings oozed blood and pus and were followed by spreading boils
and black blotches on the skin from internal bleeding. The sick suffered severe
pain and died quickly within five days of the first symptoms. As the disease
spread, other symptoms of continuous fever and spitting of blood appeared instead of the swellings or buboes. These victims coughed and sweated heavily and
died even more quickly, within three days or less, sometimes in 24 hours. In both
types everything that issued from the body—breath, sweat, blood from the buboes and lungs, bloody urine, and blood-blackened excrement—smelled foul. Depression and despair accompanied the physical symptoms, and before the end
"death is seen seated on the face."

The disease was bubonic plague, present in two forms: one that infected the 2
bloodstream, causing the buboes and internal bleeding, and was spread by contact; and a second, more virulent pneumonic type that infected the lungs and was
spread by respiratory infection. The presence of both at once caused the high
mortality and speed of contagion. So lethal was the disease that cases were known
of persons going to bed well and dying before they woke, of doctors catching the
illness at a bedside and dying before the patient. So rapidly did it spread from one
to another that to a French physician, Simon de Covino, it seemed as if one sick
person "could infect the whole world." The malignity of the pestilence appeared
more terrible because its victims knew no prevention and no remedy.

The physical suffering of the disease and its aspect of evil mystery were ex- 3
pressed in a strange Welsh lament which saw "death coming into our midst like
black smoke, a plague which cuts off the young, a rootless phantom which has no
mercy for fair countenance. Woe is me of the shilling in the armpit! It is seething,
terrible . . . a head that gives pain and causes a loud cry . . . a painful angry knob. . . .
Great is its seething like a burning cinder . . . a grievous thing of ashy color." Its eruption is ugly like the "seeds of black peas, broken fragments of brittle sea-coal . . . the
early ornaments of black death, cinders of the peelings of the cockle weed, a mixed
multitude, a black plague like halfpence, like berries. . . . "

Rumors of a terrible plague supposedly arising in China and spreading 4
through Tartary (Central Asia) to India and Persia, Mesopotamia, Syria, Egypt,
and all of Asia Minor had reached Europe in 1346. They told of a death toll so
devastating that all of India was said to be depopulated, whole territories covered
by dead bodies, other areas with no one left alive. As added up by Pope Clement
VI at Avignon, the total of reported dead reached 23,840,000. In the absence of a
concept of contagion, no serious alarm was felt in Europe until the trading ships
brought their black burden of pestilence into Messina while other infected ships
from the Levant carried it to Genoa and Venice.

By January 1348 it penetrated France via Marseille, and North Africa via Tunis. 5
Shipborne along coasts and navigable rivers, it spread westward from Marseille

through the ports of Languedoc to Spain and northward up the Rhône to Avignon, where it arrived in March. It reached Narbonne, Montpellier, Carcassonne, and Toulouse between February and May, and at the same time in Italy spread to Rome and Florence and their hinterlands. Between June and August it reached Bordeaux, Lyon, and Paris, spread to Burgundy and Normandy, and crossed the Channel from Normandy into southern England. From Italy during the same summer it crossed the Alps into Switzerland and reached eastward to Hungary.

6   In a given area the plague accomplished its kill within four to six months and then faded, except in the larger cities, where, rooting into the close-quartered population, it abated during the winter, only to reappear in spring and rage for another six months.

7   In 1349 it resumed in Paris, spread to Picardy, Flanders, and the Low Countries, and from England to Scotland and Ireland as well as to Norway, where a ghost ship with a cargo of wool and a dead crew drifted offshore until it ran aground near Bergen. From there the plague passed into Sweden, Denmark, Prussia, Iceland, and as far as Greenland. Leaving a strange pocket of immunity in Bohemia, and Russia unattacked until 1351, it had passed from most of Europe by mid-1350. Although the mortality rate was erratic, ranging from one fifth in some places to nine tenths or almost total elimination in others, the overall estimate of modern demographers has settled—for the area extending from India to Iceland—around the same figure expressed in Froissart's casual words: "a third of the world died." His estimate, the common one at the time, was not an inspired guess but a borrowing of St. John's figure for mortality from plague in Revelation, the favorite guide to human affairs of the Middle Ages.

8   A third of Europe would have meant about 20 million deaths. No one knows in truth how many died. Contemporary reports were an awed impression, not an accurate count. In crowded Avignon, it was said, 400 died daily; 7,000 houses emptied by death were shut up; a single graveyard received 11,000 corpses in six weeks; half the city's inhabitants reportedly died, including 9 cardinals or one third of the total, and 70 lesser prelates. Watching the endlessly passing death carts, chroniclers let normal exaggeration take wings and put the Avignon death toll at 62,000 and even at 120,000, although the city's total population was probably less than 50,000.

9   When graveyards filled up, bodies at Avignon were thrown into the Rhône until mass burial pits were dug for dumping the corpses. In London in such pits corpses piled up in layers until they overflowed. Everywhere reports speak of the sick dying too fast for the living to bury. Corpses were dragged out of homes and left in front of doorways. Morning light revealed new piles of bodies. In Florence the dead were gathered up by the Compagnia della Misericordia—founded in 1244 to care for the sick—whose members wore red robes and hoods masking the face except for the eyes. When their efforts failed, the dead lay putrid in the streets for days at a time. When no coffins were to be had, the bodies were laid on boards, two or three at once, to be carried to graveyards or common pits. Families dumped their own relatives into the pits, or buried them so hastily and thinly "that dogs dragged them forth and devoured their bodies."

Burial of the plague victims. From Annales de Gilles de Muisit.

Amid accumulating death and fear of contagion, people died without last rites 10
and were buried without prayers, a prospect that terrified the last hours of the
stricken. A bishop in England gave permission to laymen to make confession to
each other as was done by the Apostles, "or if no man is present then even to a
woman," and if no priest could be found to administer extreme unction, "then faith
must suffice." Clement VI found it necessary to grant remissions of sin to all who
died of the plague because so many were unattended by priests. "And no bells
tolled," wrote a chronicler of Siena, "and nobody wept no matter what his loss
because almost everyone expected death. . . . And people said and believed, 'This
is the end of the world.'"

In Paris, where the plague lasted through 1349, the reported death rate was 11
800 a day, in Pisa 500, in Vienna 500 to 600. The total dead in Paris numbered
50,000 or half the population. Florence, weakened by the famine of 1347, lost
three to four fifths of its citizens, Venice two thirds, Hamburg and Bremen, though
smaller in size, about the same proportion. Cities, as centers of transportation,
were more likely to be affected than villages, although once a village was infected,
its death rate was equally high. At Givry, a prosperous village in Burgundy of
1,200 to 1,500 people, the parish register records 615 deaths in the space of fourteen weeks, compared to an average of thirty deaths a year in the previous decade. In three villages of Cambridgeshire, manorial records show a death rate of
47 percent, 57 percent, and in one case 70 percent. When the last survivors, too
few to carry on, moved away, a deserted village sank back into the wilderness and
disappeared from the map altogether, leaving only a grass-covered ghostly outline
to show where mortals once had lived.

12   In enclosed places such as monasteries and prisons, the infection of one person usually meant that of all, as happened in the Franciscan convents of Carcassonne and Marseille, where every inmate without exception died. Of the 140 Dominicans at Montpellier only seven survived. Petrarch's brother Gherardo, member of a Carthusian monastery, buried the prior and 34 fellow monks one by one, sometimes three a day, until he was left alone with his dog and fled to look for a place that would take him in. Watching every comrade die, men in such places could not but wonder whether the strange peril that filled the air had not been sent to exterminate the human race. In Kilkenny, Ireland, Brother John Clyn of the Friars Minor, another monk left alone among dead men, kept a record of what had happened lest "things which should be remembered perish with time and vanish from the memory of those who come after us." Sensing "the whole world, as it were, placed within the grasp of the Evil One," and waiting for death to visit him too, he wrote, "I leave parchment to continue this work, if perchance any man survive and any of the race of Adam escape this pestilence and carry on the work which I have begun." Brother John, as noted by another hand, died of the pestilence, but he foiled oblivion.

13   The largest cities of Europe, with populations of about 100,000, were Paris and Florence, Venice and Genoa. At the next level, more than 50,000 were Ghent and Bruges in Flanders, Milan, Bologna, Rome, Naples, and Palermo, and Cologne. London hovered below 50,000, the only city in England except York with more than 10,000. At the level of 20,000 to 50,000 were Bordeaux, Toulouse, Montpellier, Marseille, and Lyon in France, Barcelona, Seville, and Toledo in Spain, Siena, Pisa, and other secondary cities in Italy, and the Hanseatic trading cities of the Empire. The plague raged through them all, killing anywhere from one third to two thirds of their inhabitants. Italy, with a total population of 10 to 11 million, probably suffered the heaviest toll. Following the Florentine bankruptcies, the crop failures and workers' riots of 1346–47, the revolt of Cola di Rienzi that plunged Rome into anarchy, the plague came as the peak of successive calamities. As if the world were indeed in the grasp of the Evil One, its first appearance on the European mainland in January 1348 coincided with a fearsome earthquake that carved a path of wreckage from Naples up to Venice. Houses collapsed, church towers toppled, villages were crushed, and the destruction reached as far as Germany and Greece. Emotional response, dulled by horrors, underwent a kind of atrophy epitomized by the chronicler who wrote, "And in these days was burying without sorrowe and wedding without friendschippe."

14   In Siena, where more than half the inhabitants died of the plague, work was abandoned on the great cathedral, planned to be the largest in the world, and never resumed, owing to loss of workers and master masons and "the melancholy and grief" of the survivors. The cathedral's truncated transept still stands in permanent witness to the sweep of death's scythe. Angolo di Tura, a chronicler of Siena, recorded the fear of contagion that froze every other instinct. "Father abandoned child, wife husband, one brother another," he wrote, "for this plague seemed to strike through the breath and sight. And so they died. And no one

could be found to bury the dead for money or friendship. . . . And I, Angolo di Tura, called the Fat, buried my five children with my own hands, and so did many others likewise."

There were many to echo his account of inhumanity and few to balance it, for the plague was not the kind of calamity that inspired mutual help. Its loathsomeness and deadliness did not herd people together in mutual distress, but only prompted their desire to escape each other. "Magistrates and notaries refused to come and make the wills of the dying," reported a Franciscan friar of Piazza in Sicily; what was worse, "even the priests did not come to hear their confessions." A clerk of the Archbishop of Canterbury reported the same of English priests who "turned away from the care of their benefices from fear of death." Cases of parents deserting children and children their parents were reported across Europe from Scotland to Russia. The calamity chilled the hearts of men, wrote Boccaccio in his famous account of the plague in Florence that serves as introduction to the *Decameron*. "One man shunned another . . . kinsfolk held aloof, brother was forsaken by brother, oftentimes husband by wife; nay, what is more, and scarcely to be believed, fathers and mothers were found to abandon their own children to their fate, untended, unvisited as if they had been strangers." Exaggeration and literary pessimism were common in the 14th century, but the Pope's physician, Guy de Chauliac, was a sober, careful observer who reported the same phenomenon: "A father did not visit his son, nor the son his father. Charity was dead."

Yet not entirely. In Paris, according to the chronicler Jean de Venette, the nuns of the Hôtel Dieu or municipal hospital, "having no fear of death, tended the sick with all sweetness and humility." New nuns repeatedly took the places of those who died, until the majority "many times renewed by death now rest in peace with Christ as we may piously believe."

When the plague entered northern France in July 1348, it settled first in Normandy and, checked by winter, gave Picardy a deceptive interim until the next summer. Either in mourning or warning, black flags were flown from church towers of the worst-stricken villages of Normandy. "And in that time," wrote a monk of the abbey of Fourcarment, "the mortality was so great among the people of Normandy that those of Picardy mocked them." The same unneighborly reaction was reported of the Scots, separated by a winter's immunity from the English. Delighted to hear of the disease that was scourging the "southrons," they gathered forces for an invasion, "laughing at their enemies." Before they could move, the savage mortality fell upon them too, scattering some in death and the rest in panic to spread the infection as they fled.

In Picardy in the summer of 1349 the pestilence penetrated the castle of Coucy to kill Enguerrand's mother, Catherine, and her new husband. Whether her nine-year-old son escaped by chance or was perhaps living elsewhere with one of his guardians is unrecorded. In nearby Amiens, tannery workers, responding quickly to losses in the labor force, combined to bargain for higher wages. In another place villagers were seen dancing to drums and trumpets, and on being asked the reason, answered that, seeing their neighbors die day by day while their village remained immune, they believed they could keep the plague from entering "by the jollity that is in us. That is why we dance." Further north in Tournai on the border of Flanders, Gilles de Muisit, Abbot of St. Martin's, kept one of the epidemic's most vivid accounts. The passing bells rang all day and all night, he recorded, because sextons were anxious to obtain their fees while they could. Filled with the sound of mourning, the city became oppressed by fear, so that the authorities forbade the tolling of bells and the wearing of black and restricted funeral services to two mourners. The silencing of funeral bells and of criers' announcements of deaths was ordained by most cities. Siena imposed a fine on the wearing of mourning clothes by all except widows.

19   Flight was the chief recourse of those who could afford it or arrange it. The rich fled to their country places like Boccaccio's young patricians of Florence, who settled in a pastoral palace "removed on every side from the roads" with "wells of cool water and vaults of rare wines." The urban poor died in their burrows, "and only the stench of their bodies informed neighbors of their death." That the poor were more heavily afflicted than the rich was clearly remarked at the time, in the north as in the south. A Scottish chronicler, John of Fordun, stated flatly that the pest "attacked especially the meaner sort and common people— seldom the magnates." Simon de Covino of Montpellier made the same observation. He ascribed it to the misery and want and hard lives that made the poor more susceptible, which was half the truth. Close contact and lack of sanitation was the unrecognized other half. It was noticed too that the young died in greater proportion than the old. Simon de Covino compared the disappearance of youth to the withering of flowers in the fields.

20   In the countryside peasants dropped dead on the roads, in the fields, in their houses. Survivors in growing helplessness fell into apathy, leaving ripe wheat uncut and livestock untended. Oxen and asses, sheep and goats, pigs and chickens ran wild and they too, according to local reports, succumbed to the pest. English sheep, bearers of the precious wool, died throughout the country. The chronicler Henry Knighton, canon of Leicester Abbey, reported 5,000 dead in one field alone, "their bodies so corrupted by the plague that neither beast nor bird would touch them," and spreading an appalling stench. In the Austrian Alps wolves came down to prey upon sheep and then, "as if alarmed by some invisible warning, turned and fled back into the wilderness." In remote Dalmatia bolder wolves descended upon a plague-stricken city and attacked human survivors. For want of herdsmen, cattle strayed from place to place and died in hedgerows and ditches. Dogs and cats fell like the rest.

21   The dearth of labor held a fearful prospect because the 14th century lived close to the annual harvest both for food and for next year's seed. "So few servants and laborers were left," wrote Knighton, "that no one knew where to turn for help." The sense of a vanishing future created a kind of dementia of despair. A Bavarian chronicler of Neuberg on the Danube recorded that "Men and women . . . wandered around as if mad" and let their cattle stray "because no one had any inclination to concern themselves about the future." Fields went uncultivated, spring seed unsown. Second growth with nature's awful energy

crept back over cleared land, dikes crumbled, salt water reinvaded and soured the lowlands. With so few hands remaining to restore the work of centuries, people felt, in Walsingham's words, that "the world could never again regain its former prosperity."

Though the death rate was higher among the anonymous poor, the known 22 and the great died too. King Alfonso XI of Castile was the only reigning monarch killed by the pest, but his neighbor King Pedro of Aragon lost his wife, Queen Leonora, his daughter Marie, and a niece in the space of six months. John Cantacuzene, Emperor of Byzantium, lost his son. In France the lame Queen Jeanne and her daughter-in-law Bonne de Luxemburg, wife of the Dauphin, both died in 1349 in the same phase that took the life of Enguerrand's mother. Jeanne, Queen of Navarre, daughter of Louis X, was another victim. Edward III's second daughter, Joanna, who was on her way to marry Pedro, the heir of Castile, died in Bordeaux. Women appear to have been more vulnerable than men, perhaps because, being more housebound, they were more exposed to fleas. Boccaccio's mistress Fiammetta, illegitimate daughter of the King of Naples, died, as did Laura, the beloved—whether real or fictional—of Petrarch. Reaching out to us in the future, Petrarch cried, "Oh happy posterity who will not experience such abysmal woe and will look upon our testimony as a fable."

In Florence Giovanni Villani, the great historian of his time, died at 68 in 23 the midst of an unfinished sentence: ". . . *e dure questo pistolenza fino a* . . . (in the midst of this pestilence there came to an end . . .)." Siena's master painters, the brothers Ambrogio and Pietro Lorenzetti, whose names never appear after 1348, presumably perished in the plague, as did Andrea Pisano, architect and sculptor of Florence. William of Ockham and the English mystic Richard Rolle of Hampole both disappear from mention after 1349. Francisco Datini, merchant of Prato, lost both his parents and two siblings. Curious sweeps of mortality afflicted certain bodies of merchants in London. All eight wardens of the Company of Cutters, all six wardens of the Hatters, and four wardens of the Goldsmiths died before July 1350. Sir John Pulteney, master draper and four times Mayor of London, was a victim, likewise Sir John Montgomery, Governor of Calais.

Among the clergy and doctors the mortality was naturally high because of the 24 nature of their professions. Out of 24 physicians in Venice, 20 were said to have lost their lives in the plague, although according to another account, some were believed to have fled or to have shut themselves up in their houses. At Montpellier, site of the leading medieval medical school, the physician Simon de Covino reported that, despite the great number of doctors, "hardly one of them escaped." In Avignon, Guy de Chauliac confessed that he performed his medical visits only because he dared not stay away for fear of infamy, but "I was in continual fear." He claimed to have contracted the disease but to have cured himself by his own treatment; if so, he was one of the few who recovered.

Clerical mortality varied with rank. Although the one-third toll of cardinals 25 reflects the same proportion as the whole, this was probably due to their concentration in Avignon. In England, in strange and almost sinister procession, the

Archbishop of Canterbury, John Stratford, died in August 1348, his appointed successor died in May 1349, and the next appointee three months later, all three within a year. Despite such weird vagaries, prelates in general managed to sustain a higher survival rate than the lesser clergy. Among bishops the deaths have been estimated at about one in twenty. The loss of priests, even if many avoided their fearful duty of attending the dying, was about the same as among the population as a whole.

26   Government officials, whose loss contributed to the general chaos, found, on the whole, no special shelter. In Siena four of the nine members of the governing oligarchy died, in France one third of the royal notaries, in Bristol 15 out of the 52 members of the Town Council or almost one third. Tax-collecting obviously suffered, with the result that Philip VI was unable to collect more than a fraction of the subsidy granted him by the Estates in the winter of 1347–48.

27   Lawlessness and debauchery accompanied the plague as they had during the great plague of Athens of 430 B.C., when according to Thucydides, men grew bold in the indulgence of pleasure: "For seeing how the rich died in a moment and those who had nothing immediately inherited their property, they reflected that life and riches were alike transitory and they resolved to enjoy themselves while they could." Human behavior is timeless. When St. John had his vision of plague in Revelation, he knew from some experience or race memory that those who survived "repented not of the work of their hands. . . . Neither repented they of their murders, nor of their sorceries, nor of their fornication, nor of their thefts."

COMPREHENSION

1. The title of this essay suggests a religious theme. Why did intellectuals and religious leaders associate the bubonic plague with biblical prophecy?
2. Does this essay have a thesis, or does it merely record in detail a period in European history? If it does have a thesis, is it implied or expressed directly? Explain your answer.
3. Does Tuchman suggest that Europe was "fated" to endure the tragic consequences of the plague owing to a higher power, or does she attribute the disaster to a confluence of history and chance? Explain your answer.

RHETORIC

1. Tuchman begins her essay by describing in detail the physical symptoms of the plague. What strategy lies behind this rhetorical decision?
2. Tuchman has a reputation as a historian whose goal was to bring "history to life." What methods does she use to realize this goal? Is she successful? Why or why not? What does the illustration on page 599 contribute?
3. Contemporary authors and filmmakers often select morbid themes for their sensational value or for financial gain, or both. For example, there is a plethora of "true-crime" stories, "re-creations" of natural disasters, and profiles of aberrant and

murderous personalities such as Jeffrey Dahmer, Ted Bundy, and the "Hillside Strangler." Is this Tuchman's purpose? Explain why or why not.

4. Note the particular parts of speech Tuchman uses to begin paragraphs 5–7, 9, 11, 12, 14, 16–18, 20, 22, and 23. All begin with either conjunctions or prepositions. How do these grammatical devices help maintain the flow of Tuchman's narrative?

5. Tuchman makes references to a vast number of historical figures and specific locations in 14th-century Europe. What is her assumption about the educational level of her intended audience? About the specialization of her readership? Is it necessary to know something about the people and places she cites to appreciate the essay? Or is Tuchman writing a book of general interest, with the implicit supposition that different readers will extract their own level of appreciation from her narrative? Explain.

6. Tuchman uses direct quotations from the observers and chroniclers of the times. Examine the use of such sources in paragraphs 10, 13, 15–20, and 23, among others. How does Tuchman weave their observations into her own narrative so that the essay maintains unity and coherence? How does her use of these citations affect the strength of her writing?

WRITING

1. Write a 300-word summary of Tuchman's essay.

2. For a research project, study Tuchman's philosophy regarding how history should be reported. Apply your research to her treatment of the Black Death.

3. **Writing an Argument:** Argue for or against the proposition that an epidemic as severe as the one that Tuchman describes could not possibly occur in the 21st century.

NETWORKING
Applying Digital and Multimedia Literacies

Using Visuals to Make Logical Appeals: In your response to question 3 under Writing, include at least one visual that supports your argument with hard data. If you use an existing chart or graph, be sure to document your source; and if you create a visual from data, be sure to cite the source that the data came from.

It's Spreading

Jill Lepore

Jill Lepore (b. 1966) is a prize-winning historian who teaches at Harvard University. She was born in Worcester, Massachusetts, and received degrees from Tufts University (BA, 1987), the University of Michigan (MA, 1990), and Yale University (1995) before embarking on her academic career. Among her several books are King Philip's War and the Origins of American Identity *(1998) and* New York Burning: Liberty and Slavery in an Eighteenth Century City *(2005). Lepore is also a staff writer at the* New Yorker, *in which the following essay on American epidemics appeared in 2009.*

1   On December 14, 1929, during a holiday shopping season darkened by the greatest stock-market crash in American history, Simon S. Martin bought a parrot for his wife, Lillian, at a pet shop on North Eutaw Street, in Baltimore. It was not, as it happened, a well parrot. Hoping to surprise his wife, Martin seems to have asked his daughter, Edith, and her husband, Lee Kalmey, the owner of an auto repair shop, to take care of the bird and bring it over to his house in Annapolis in ten days' time. By Christmas Eve, the parrot must have shown signs of illness: puffy eyes, a drooping head, and feathers as ruffled as if it had flown through a squall. Come Yuletide, the Martins had a dead parrot on their hands.

2   The pet-shop owner, who may have been wise to the fact that Simon Martin was secretary of the Annapolis Chamber of Commerce, at first offered a replacement, although by New Year's, when Lillian Martin and Edith and Lee Kalmey fell dangerously ill, he was backpedalling, denying that he had ever sold Martin a bird. Meanwhile, the Kalmeys were getting sicker and sicker, showing symptoms of both pneumonia and typhoid.

3   On January 6th, a local doctor examined the patients. He had just read a newspaper article about something called parrot fever: It had shown up in Argentina months earlier, when an actor playing a sailor had caught it from his stage parrot. The disease, also called psittacosis, had since spread through South America and Europe. No one seemed to know much about it except that it was deadly. The doctor sent a telegram to the U.S. Public Health Service, in Washington: "Can you place supply parrot fever serum our disposal immediately." Unfortunately, there was no serum, or any known treatment. The mayor alerted the governor. Within forty-eight hours, epidemiologists from the Baltimore City Health Department, the Maryland Department of Health, the United States Navy and Army, and the Public Health Service, including a team of men from the Hygienic Laboratory in Washington, arrived on the scene. Someone called the newspaper.

4   "'Parrot' Disease Baffles Experts" the Washington *Post* reported in an issue that went to press the night of January 8th, thrilling readers with a medical mystery that would capture the nation's attention with the prospect of a parrot-fever pandemic. Reports, cabled and wired and radioed across land and sea, were printed in the daily paper or broadcast, within minutes, on the radio: tallies, theories, postmortems, more to fear. Before it was over, an admiral in the U.S. Navy ordered sailors at sea to cast their pet parrots into the ocean. One city health commissioner urged everyone who owned a parrot to wring its neck. People abandoned their pet parrots on the streets. Every sneeze seemed a symptom. As the story grew, it took on certain familiar—and, as it turned out, durable—features, features that borrow as much from pulp fiction as from public health: super scientists fight super bugs in race to defeat foreign menace invading American homes, beneath the very Christmas tree.

Epidemics follow patterns because diseases follow patterns. Viruses spread; they 5 reproduce; they die. Epidemiologists study patterns in order to combat infection. Stories about epidemics follow patterns, too. Stories aren't often deadly but they can be virulent: spreading fast, weakening resistance, wreaking havoc. During the recent swine-flu panic, Joe Biden warned Americans not to ride the subway or fly on an airplane, and pharmacies ran out of surgical masks. Why was it so hard to tell, as the story was breaking, if a flu outbreak of pandemic proportions was under way? The world is a far better place for the work epidemiologists do. Maybe, though, we could do with a few more narratologists.

The stories about epidemics that are told in the American press—their plots 6 and tropes—date to the nineteen-twenties, when modern research science, science journalism, and science fiction were born. The germ theory of disease dates to the mid-eighteen-hundreds. Pasteur developed a rabies vaccine in 1885, launching a global battle against infectious illness. By the nineteen-twenties, scientists had developed a vaccine for diphtheria; other vaccines, like the one for polio, would take decades, but hopes ran high. In *The Conquest of Disease* (1927), Thurman B. Rice, a professor of sanitary science, predicted the eradication of sickness itself.

Meanwhile, ordinary people learned to blame germs, not God, for catastrophes 7 like the pandemic of 1918, when at least fifty million people, including nearly seven hundred thousand Americans, died of influenza. Germ theory, which secularized infectious disease, had a side effect: It sacralized epidemiology. The nineteen-twenties witnessed the inauguration of what the historian of medicine Nancy Tomes has called the "epidemic exposé," the hair-raising account of a disease that threatens to destroy the human race. The genre's master was a bacteriologist turned journalist named Paul de Kruif. He had taught at the University of Michigan and worked for the U.S. Sanitary Corps, studying the gangrene bacillus. After the war, he turned to writing. In 1925, his collaboration with Sinclair Lewis led to the publication of *Arrowsmith,* a novel about a young doctor fighting bubonic plague—an early medical thriller, for which de Kruif received twenty-five percent of the royalties. In 1926, de Kruif turned to nonfiction, publishing *Microbe Hunters,* a book of profiles of scientists, starting with Leeuwenhoek, who can see tiny things the rest of us can't, things that are trying to kill us.

Microbe Hunters, which inspired a generation of young readers to pursue 8 careers in science, appeared a month before the first issue of Hugo Gernsback's *Amazing Stories,* the first magazine of what is now called science fiction. Many of its stories concern the work of laboratory scientists; the issue of July, 1929, included "The Purple Death," the story of a young doctor who keeps a copy of *Microbe Hunters* on his desk.

The coming plague was Paul de Kruif's bread and butter. Three months be- 9 fore Simon Martin bought his wife a parrot for Christmas, de Kruif issued a warning in the lead article of *Ladies' Home Journal:* "In American milk today there lurks a terrible, wasting fever, that may keep you in bed for a couple of weeks, that may fasten itself on you for one, or for two, or even for seven years—that might culminate by killing you." What was this dread malady? Undulant fever. "At least

50,000 people are sick with it at this very moment," their ailment virtually unknown to "their baffled doctors." De Kruif's article, titled "Before You Drink a Glass of Milk," scared a lot of people and sold a lot of magazines. Boasting of its success, the editor of *Ladies' Home Journal* explained, "Nobody had ever heard of undulant fever before."

10   The experts who descended on Annapolis in early January, 1930, weren't half as baffled as the Washington *Post* made them out to be, but the reading public must have been at least twice as confused. Was parrot fever really something to worry about? Reading the newspaper, it was hard to say. "Not Contagious in Man," the *Times* announced. "Highly contagious," the Washington *Post* said. Who knew? Nobody had ever heard of it before. It lurked in American homes. It came from afar. It was invisible. It might kill you. It made a very good story. In the late hours of January 8th, editors at the Los Angeles *Times* decided to put it on the front page: "Two Women and Man in Annapolis Believed to Have 'Parrot Fever.'"

11   The next day, in Toledo, Mrs. Percy Q. Williams, whose husband had just returned from Cuba with two parrots, died in Mercy Hospital; in Baltimore, Mrs. Louise Schaeffer succumbed to what had at first appeared to be pneumonia. (Women, many of them widows, constituted the majority of the outbreak's victims. There were suggestions that lonely old women had got the disease by feeding their parrots mouth to mouth. Some called the disease "old maid's pneumonia.") Those deaths would normally have been unremarkable: two older women fading away in the cold of winter. Not this week. On learning that Schaeffer "had been in contact with a parrot several days before she became ill," physicians suspected parrot fever and ordered an autopsy, whereupon the Surgeon General, Dr. Hugh Smith Cumming (a eugenicist best known to history for launching the Tuskegee syphilis experiment, that same year), warned Americans to stay away from recently imported parrots. He insisted that he "did not fear an epidemic," but that, of course, only got people talking about one. Although the results of Schaeffer's autopsy were not yet available, "Baltimore Woman Dies" made it onto the front page of the Chicago *Daily Tribune* on January 11th and "Parrot Fever Kills 2 in this Country" appeared on page 3 of the *Times.* That paper also reported on efforts to trace deadly Argentine parrots that had come to the United States through what were called, as if they were criminals, "two suspected New York dealers."

12   Some people were worried about more than parrots. On January 11th, after several clerks in the poultry department of a Toledo store started coughing, the city's Health Department launched an investigation into "incipient cases" of psittacosis. Two days later, in a story that appeared on the front page of William Randolph Hearst's San Francisco *Examiner,* the Associated Press announced that the country's scientists had declared war: "The disease-fighting armament of the nation today was directed against a new and mysterious enemy." The microbe hunters had taken out their microscopes.

13   In the years following the First World War, a great many American scientists were looking for sources to fund their vital research. The nation's scientific organizations

hired publicity firms. In 1926, a coalition of scientists launched a campaign to raise "A National Fund for the Support of Research in Pure Science." Half the battle, though, had to do with winning over the public, and de Kruif's work made clear that stories were powerful ammunition. Before the First World War, journalists didn't generally report on science, and they certainly didn't profile scientists. After the war, scientists tried writing for newspapers and magazines, attempting to explain the value of their work, but, year by year, the number of scientists writing for a popular audience fell while the number of journalists specializing in science writing rose. Perhaps the era's most effective pro-science publicity machine was the Science Service, a wire service founded in 1920 and edited by a chemist named Edwin E. Slosson. Its purpose was to promote scientific research by feeding stories to newspapers. The service, Slosson said, would not "indulge in propaganda unless it be propaganda to urge the value of research and the usefulness of science." Financed by the newspaper publisher E. W. Scripps, and later by the American Association for the Advancement of Science and the National Research Council, the Science Service reached a fifth of the American reading public by the mid-nineteen-thirties.

What a microbe hunter needed to do to get funding was to hunt and kill a 14 microbe, preferably a lethal one that nobody had ever heard of before. On January 6, 1930, when that family doctor sent his telegram to the U.S. Public Health Service, the message was sent on to the Hygienic Laboratory, where Dr. Charles Armstrong, a forty-five-year-old pathologist, was charged with heading the investigation. Armstrong wanted to contain the outbreak, urgently; he also wanted to develop a serum, to save the lives of people already infected. Doing so would require experiments; those experiments required infected parrots and infected people. To gather subjects, Armstrong needed to spread the word about psittacosis. What Armstrong needed was a parrot-fever panic.

As Armstrong arrived in Annapolis, a team of public-health officials was sent 15 to that North Eutaw Street pet shop in Baltimore—where four employees were now sick—to track down the purchasers of all the recently imported parrots. Not all those parrots had stayed in town. Mrs. Hugh Lett bought a parrot in Baltimore on December 18th; the bird died on New Year's Eve; Mrs. Lett took sick on January 7th, by which time she was in Cambridge. Armstrong wired messages to public-health officials across the country, asking them to be on the lookout for psittacosis. In city after city, parrot dealers handed over to investigators sick parrots and lists of the people who had bought parrots for Christmas. Dead birds, some of which were exhumed, were shipped to Washington. Cases of suspected psittacosis cropped up in Providence and Chicago, New Haven and Los Angeles. The home of an Ohio family was quarantined after yet another Christmas parrot died. Inevitably, there were cases merely "simulating psittacosis," like the parents of fifteen-year-old Lillian Muller, of the Bronx, who had bought their daughter a parrot, imported from Argentina, at a pet shop in Harlem. The *Times* offered reassurance: "The Mullers' parrot has been eating regularly and has exhibited no signs of drooping." (One constabulary note: The A.P. reported from North

Adams, Massachusetts, on January 13th, "A parrot in a local family, whose name was not given out, recently died." Polly?)

16   By January 15th, the *Times* reported fifty cases nationwide, including eleven in New York City, and seven deaths, including one in Queens and one in Yonkers. Doctors insisted, in vain, that "there was no occasion for general alarm," and "stressed the fact that in none of the cases reported so far in New York has the diagnosis been definitely established as psittacosis." Later that day—after the *Times* went to press with the death count—authorities revealed that blood tests on the New York dead had all come out negative. The *Times,* whose coverage of parrot fever was, all things considered, a model of restraint and clarity, made a point of announcing those negative tests. Elsewhere, though, autopsies and blood cultures that came out negative for psittacosis didn't make it into the papers. By now, Lillian Martin and Edith and Lee Kalmey were fast improving; this was not widely reported, either. People who got better simply fell out of the news.

17 The nationwide sweep for psittacosis soon supplied Armstrong with enough samples—parrots, healthy, sick, and dead; the blood from infected humans; and even the scrapings from Lillian Martin's birdcage—to begin his work, which he conducted in two basement rooms in the Hygienic Laboratory, aided by his technician, Henry (Shorty) Anderson. "Those parrots were sure mean bastards," Armstrong said. Armstrong and Anderson wore rubber gloves, put trays filled with cresol in the doorways, and covered the birds' cages with disinfectant-soaked curtains. They were not, however, especially fastidious. "The only thing hygienic about the Hygienic Laboratory was its name," one researcher there said. Armstrong explained, "If we'd got too careful, we'd have spent all our time being careful and how could we have found out anything about it?"

18   This was yet another hallmark of the swashbuckling microbe hunter, who lacked the fussiness of the housewife. "Germ" became a household word in the nineteen-teens. By the twenties, Americans, and especially housewives, lived in fear of germs. Not only did newspapers and magazines run almost daily stories about newly discovered germs like undulant fever but their pages were filled with advertisements for hygiene products, like Listerine (first sold over the counter in 1914 and, in many ways, the granddaddy of Purell), Lysol (marketed, in 1918, as an anti-flu measure), Kotex ("feminine hygiene," the first menstrual pad, introduced in 1920, a postwar conversion of a surgical dressing developed by Kimberly-Clark), Cellophane (1923), and Kleenex (1924; another Kimberly-Clark product, sold as a towel for removing makeup until a consumer survey revealed that people were using it to blow their noses). Perhaps because kitchens and laboratories have much in common, journalists like de Kruif strove to underscore the manliness of the microbe hunter. Armstrong, de Kruif wrote, "was definitely not the kind of man who would even own a parrot, let alone kiss it."

19   Armstrong and Anderson and other government scientists worked night and day. On January 13th, the Chicago *Daily Tribune* reported a landmark success: "Parrot Fever Germ Isolated."

The parrot-fever story made the malady out to be virulent, mysterious, and exotic, 20 despite these facts: The disease was not baffling; it had been identified in the nineteenth century; it was known to infect members of the Psittacidae family, which includes parrots, parakeets, macaws, and cockatoos; in the nineteen-thirties, the only birds likely to be contagious were those brought to the United States during the last months of 1929; it is possible to catch the disease only from an infected bird (people can't spread it); it infected then, and continues to infect today, between one and two hundred Americans every year. There was a danger, to be sure. Psittacosis is now easily treated with antibiotics like doxycycline, but that wasn't the case in 1930, when one in five people infected with the disease died. Nevertheless, the only people who had much to worry about were people who had been in quite close contact with certain tropical birds very recently imported from South America.

Psittacosis incited, if briefly, a sizable panic among people who, by any rea- 21 sonable measure, had nothing to fear. That was dangerous. Even as the story unfolded, what to make of parrot fever and just how much responsibility the press or the scientific community bore for the panic proved matters of dispute. But what happened next seems nearly as dangerous as the panic itself: People suddenly started insisting that parrot fever didn't exist.

"U.S. Alarm Over Parrot Disease Not Warranted," the Chicago *Daily Tribune* 22 declared, on January 15th. Less than two weeks into the story, parrot fever looked, suddenly, silly. Parrot fever became a national joke. A Washington correspondent for the *Times* filed a story about a parrot owned by Secretary of State Henry Stimson. The parrot, named the Old Soak, had been locked in the basement of the Pan-American Building, "not because he has psittacosis" but because he had a habit of swearing. The *Wall Street Journal* ran this joke: What did the janitor say when the professor at the Polytechnic Institute asked him why he was cleaning the lab with carbolic acid? "'So none of de Poly students gets dis new parrot fever.'" Even the straight stories weren't taken seriously. "A parrot foundling made its appearance early yesterday morning when a green bird with a chipped beak was discovered in the vestibule of John Schreyer's home, 25–27 Humphreys Street, East Elmhurst, Queens," the *Times* reported, whereupon jailbirds at Sing Sing offered asylum for all unwanted parrots; the warden said, "The inmates here think this talk about parrot fever is nonsense."

A pro-parrot lobby formed. On January 17th, six of the country's leading 23 importers of winged pets, including the Odenwald Bird Company, the Imperial Pet Shop, and the Dahle Bird Company of Philadelphia, gathered at the Hotel Commodore in New York, where they founded the Bird Dealers' Association of America. Prussia and Bavaria, suffering from their own outbreaks, had already instituted parrot embargoes. The bird business was in a bad way. The Bird Dealers fought back by claiming that the disease did not exist, had never existed in human beings, "and that the scare over 'parrot fever' had been chiefly brought about by the active imagination of a Baltimore newspaper man."

Exaggeration breeds exaggeration. The counter-story spread as wildly as the 24 story had. And the Bird Dealers had a point about the imagination of newspapermen.

The first American doctor to believe he had seen psittacosis had read about it in the newspaper. The Martins' doctor probably read Hearst's Baltimore *American.* Every Sunday, Hearst produced for his papers a supplement called the *American Weekly.* Edited by Morrill Goddard, the *American Weekly* was something between *Parade* and the *National Enquirer.* Goddard knew how to sell a plague and knew, too, that selling plagues was good for his advertising accounts with hygiene-product manufacturers. In March, 1930, Goddard was interviewed by the staff of the J. Walter Thompson Company, one of the nation's most influential advertising agencies. "There is a lot of interest now in parrot fever," the interviewer observed, asking, "How far will the research on parrot fever have to go before you print something about it?" Goddard took umbrage at the suggestion that he had not already covered parrot fever—that he had not, in fact, *scooped* parrot fever. "We were the first newspaper to present it to the American public," he claimed, not quite accurately, "to warn them that parrots might be deadly in the home." As to how he had come by the story, Goddard explained that he spent his evenings reading obscure scientific journals, where he read about the outbreak in Buenos Aires:

> I sent down to our man there and he sent me a wretched story without details and I cabled him and he sent me a second story with further details and pictures and that story was printed about four or five weeks before the first case developed in New York. It gave all the details of what is known as "psittacosis." Now, it is a matter of dispute whether it is a germ or a virus but it is a matter of no consequence as far as making a feature out of it.

25 Goddard had no real interest in the science. He wanted to run a story about a danger lurking in American homes: "The fact that the parrot in the cage at your house may put you in the cemetery is enough for me."

26 On January 16th, just over one week after the Washington *Post* printed its first parrot-fever piece, the *Times* ran a story radioed in by a correspondent in Austria: A Viennese scientist believed that Americans were suffering from "mass suggestion." Dr. Julius Bauer said, "Psittacosis has been known to science since 1892. Now for some reason it has assumed in the public mind the dimensions of a plague." The next day, the Science Service, reporting on an article in the *Journal of the American Medical Association,* reminded Americans that "the possibility of unusual disorders must be ever present in the medical mind." Who knew what might infect us next? Parrot fever ought to serve as proof that "it is no longer possible for any person or any nation to live in isolation." The world, in short, was a dangerous place.

27 Or was it just a gullible one? "Every winter, America has to have a new malady, and this year it is Parrot Fever," a columnist for the *Post* wrote. "People are getting all worked up over this new 'parrot-fever,'" a writer for *Life* scoffed, "but Lord! it's been endemic at the Capitol since Polly was an egg." E. B. White figured that the country was suffering from nothing so much as a bad case of the heebie-jeebies, brought on by extended exposure to newspapers that were

forever issuing warnings about sharks infesting the beaches of New Jersey, anthrax spores contaminating unsterilized shaving brushes, and noxious gases escaping from iceboxes in the middle of the night. In an issue that went to press on January 20th, the *New Yorker's* Talk of the Town included a piece by White calling parrot fever merely "the latest and most amusing example of the national hypochondria":

> There have been hundreds of national menaces, keeping us all on tenterhooks, keeping the populace feeling the national pulse and applying the national stethoscope. Psittacosis is one of the best, because one of the most picturesque. What will probably happen will be that some reporter will invent a disease traceable to something that happens to everybody: "Otis heart" from riding in elevators, maybe, or "corn-flakes itch" from eating breakfast food, and we'll all die of autosuggestion.

That hasn't happened quite yet, but we still can't tell whether we are all about 28 to die or whether we are being sold a bill of goods. This condition is chronic.

On January 22, 1930, the *Post* reported that Lillian Martin and Edith and Lee 29 Kalmey had recovered. Herbert Hoover prepared to sign an executive order banning the importation of parrots. The story seemed more or less wrapped up. But then, terribly, scientists starting dying. On January 23rd, Dr. Daniel S. Hatfield, the chief of the bureau of communicable diseases of the Baltimore City Health Department, succumbed to psittacosis. Hatfield's colleague Dr. William Stokes died on February 10th. Shorty Anderson died on February 8th. That same day, Charles Armstrong was admitted to the U.S. Naval Hospital with a fever of 104 degrees.

The director of the Hygienic Laboratory, George McCoy, insisted on taking 30 over Armstrong's work himself. He took blood from a patient who had recovered from psittacosis and injected it into Armstrong's veins. Armstrong improved, and eventually recovered. Afterward, he wrote up his report, according to which there had been a total of a hundred and sixty-nine cases of psittacosis nationwide, and thirty-three fatalities. In his report, Armstrong credited the press, without which, he believed, "this outbreak would largely have escaped detection." Armstrong's work earned him a place in de Kruif's 1932 sequel to *Microbe Hunters,* a book titled *Men Against Death.*

In February and early March of 1930, while Armstrong was still recovering, 31 nine other people at the Hygienic Laboratory became sick. Psittacosis seemed to have contaminated the whole building. On March 15th, McCoy ordered the building evacuated. Alone, he walked down the stairs to Armstrong's basement laboratory. He killed, with chloroform, every parrot, mouse, pigeon, guinea pig, rat, and monkey that had been used in the psittacosis experiments. "He murdered and murdered and made a slick and clean job of it," de Kruif wrote. He burned the bodies in the building's incinerator. He sealed all the windows. The fumigation squad arrived at 2 P.M. and began spraying the building with cyanide. Sparrows flying fifty feet over the building froze, mid-flight, and fell to earth. The next day, the headline in the *Post* read, "Parrot Fever Panic Seizes Laboratory." Two months later, on May 26, 1930, Congress rewarded the Hygienic Laboratory by expanding it and granting it a new name: the National Institute of Health.

COMPREHENSION

1. Summarize the parrot fever epidemic that Lepore recounts. According to Lepore, what significance does this episode have for people today?
2. In paragraph 5, Lepore states, "Epidemics follow patterns because diseases follow patterns." What does she mean? What additional information in the essay supports this observation?
3. What does Lepore think about disease and epidemic "experts"? What is her opinion of media representatives who report on epidemics? Refer to the text to support your answer.

RHETORIC

1. How clearly does the essay's title express Lepore's thesis in this essay? How does she use the opening event in relation to her thesis? What sorts of materials does she use to develop her thesis?
2. Is Lepore's account objective or subjective? Explain your answer.
3. What primary organizational strategy does Lepore use to structure this essay? What other strategies are evident?
4. What transitional devices does Lepore use as she moves from section to section?
5. Explain the purpose of Lepore's concluding paragraph. What point is she trying to make?

WRITING

1. Select a current epidemic or pandemic, and write your own account of this disease.
2. Examine the proper role of the media in warning the public about epidemics.
3. **Writing an Argument:** Argue for or against the proposition that we are overly concerned about epidemics today.

NETWORKING
Applying Digital and Multimedia Literacies

Conducting a Multimedia Research Project: Respond to question 1 under Writing with a research project that incorporates multiple media to inform your audience about a current epidemic or pandemic. Consider approaching this as a documentary that includes visuals like graphs, maps, and photographs—or as a hyperlinked paper that includes links to interviews, newscasts, and so on. You could also do an oral presentation that incorporates audio, video, and even a print handout. Don't choose your project's components at random; figure out what genres and media would best suit your purpose: to educate your audience about this disease.

Synthesis: Classic and Contemporary Questions for Comparison

1. Discuss Tuchman's and Lepore's essays in terms of style, method, and tone. What level of language do they employ? What forms of authority do they bring to bear on their subject? What rhetorical strategies do they use? How does the fact that both writers are historians affect their approach to the subject? Does one argue and the other explain or do they both make similar assertions?
2. Compare Tuchman's view of the bubonic plague of the 14th century with Lepore's presentation of the parrot fever epidemic.
3. In groups of three or four, conduct research on epidemics throughout history not mentioned by either Tuchman or Lepore. How do these epidemics serve to reinforce the assertions that the two writers make?

Topic of Cancer

Christopher Hitchens

__Christopher Hitchens__ (1949–2011) was a controversial author, essayist, journalist, and public intellectual. He was born in Portsmouth, England, and received an undergraduate degree from Balliol College, Oxford in 1970. For decades, Hitchens was a columnist and literary critic in England and the United States. (He moved to the United States in 1970 and became a U.S. citizen in 2007.) Hitchens wrote for the Atlantic, Free Inquiry, Nation, Salon, Slate, *and* Vanity Fair, *among other publications. His articulate and combative debating style also made him a regular on talk shows. For years a stalwart defender of left-wing causes, Hitchens revised his thinking after the West's "tepid" response to the 1989 fatwa issued by Ayatollah Khomeini calling for the death of the writer's friend, Salman Rushdie. Renouncing socialism, Hitchens became a champion of the values of the Enlightenment. He also riled people by professing a "new atheism." His bestseller* God Is Not Great *(2007), followed by a memoir,* Hitch-22 *(2010), kept Hitchens in the limelight up to the time of his death from pneumonia brought on by esophageal cancer. In this harrowing essay on his medical condition, published in* Vanity Fair *in 2010, Hitchens enters into debate with a new adversary.*

I have more than once in my time woken up feeling like death. But nothing prepared me for the early morning last June when I came to consciousness feeling as if I were actually shackled to my own corpse. The whole cave of my chest and thorax seemed to have been hollowed out and then refilled with slow-drying cement. I could faintly hear myself breathe but could not manage to inflate my lungs. My heart was beating either much too much or much too little. Any movement, however slight, required forethought and planning. It took strenuous effort   1 for me to cross the room of my New York hotel and summon the emergency services. They arrived with great dispatch and behaved with immense courtesy and professionalism. I had the time to wonder why they needed so many boots and helmets and so much heavy backup equipment, but now that I view the scene in retrospect I see it as a very gentle and firm deportation, taking me from the country of the well across the stark frontier that marks off the land of malady. Within a few hours, having had to do quite a lot of emergency work on my heart and my lungs, the physicians at this sad border post had shown me a few other postcards from the interior and told me that my immediate next stop would have to be with an oncologist. Some kind of shadow was throwing itself across the negatives.

2   The previous evening, I had been launching my latest book at a successful event in New Haven. The night of the terrible morning, I was supposed to go on *The Daily Show* with Jon Stewart and then appear at a sold-out event at the 92nd Street Y, on the Upper East Side, in conversation with Salman Rushdie. My very short-lived campaign of denial took this form: I would not cancel these appearances or let down my friends or miss the chance of selling a stack of books. I managed to pull off both gigs without anyone noticing anything amiss, though I did vomit two times, with an extraordinary combination of accuracy, neatness, violence, and profusion, just before each show. This is what citizens of the sick country do while they are still hopelessly clinging to their old domicile.

3   The new land is quite welcoming in its way. Everybody smiles encouragingly and there appears to be absolutely no racism. A generally egalitarian spirit prevails, and those who run the place have obviously got where they are on merit and hard work. As against that, the humor is a touch feeble and repetitive, there seems to be almost no talk of sex, and the cuisine is the worst of any destination I have ever visited. The country has a language of its own, a lingua franca that manages to be both dull and difficult and that contains names like ondansetron, for anti-nausea medication, as well as some unsettling gestures that require a bit of getting used to. For example, an official met for the first time may abruptly sink his fingers into your neck. That's how I discovered that my cancer had spread to my lymph nodes, and that one of these deformed beauties, located on my right clavicle, or collarbone, was big enough to be seen and felt. It's not at all good when your cancer is palpable from the outside. Especially when, as at this stage, they didn't even know where the primary source was. Carcinoma works cunningly from the inside out. Detection and treatment often work more slowly and gropingly, from the outside in. Many needles were sunk into my clavicle area, *Tissue is the issue* being a hot slogan in the local Tumorville tongue, and I was told the biopsy results might take a week.

4   Working back from the cancer-ridden squamous cells that these first results disclosed, it took rather longer than that to discover the disagreeable truth. The word *metastasized* was the one in the report that first caught my eye, and ear. The alien had colonized a bit of my lung as well as quite a bit of my lymph node. And its original base of operations was located, had been located for quite some time, in my esophagus. My father had died, and very swiftly, too, of cancer of the esophagus. He was 79. I am 61. In whatever kind of a race life may be, I have very abruptly become a finalist.

The notorious stage theory of Elisabeth Kübler-Ross, whereby one pro- 5
gresses from denial to rage through bargaining to depression and the eventual
bliss of acceptance, hasn't so far had much application in my case. In one way, I
suppose, I have been in denial for some time, knowingly burning the candle at
both ends and finding that it often gives a lovely light. But for precisely that reason, I can't see myself smiting my brow with shock or hear myself whining about
how it's all so unfair: I have been taunting the Reaper into taking a free scythe in
my direction and have now succumbed to something so predictable and banal
that it bores even me. Rage would be beside the point for the same reason. Instead, I am badly oppressed by a gnawing sense of waste. I had real plans for my
next decade and felt I'd worked hard enough to earn it. Will I really not live to see
my children married? To watch the World Trade Center rise again? To read if not
indeed write the obituaries of elderly villains like Henry Kissinger and Joseph
Ratzinger? But I understand this sort of non-thinking for what it is: sentimentality
and self-pity. Of course my book hit the best-seller list on the day that I received
the grimmest of news bulletins, and for that matter the last flight I took as a
healthy-feeling person (to a fine, big audience at the Chicago Book Fair) was the
one that made me a million-miler on United Airlines, with a lifetime of free up-
grades to look forward to. But irony is my business and I just can't see any ironies
here: would it be less poignant to get cancer on the day that my memoirs were
remaindered as a box-office turkey, or that I was bounced from a coach-class
flight and left on the tarmac? To the dumb question Why me? the cosmos barely
bothers to return the reply: Why not?

The bargaining stage, though. Maybe there's a loophole here. The oncology 6
bargain is that, in return for at least the chance of a few more useful years, you
agree to submit to chemotherapy and then, if you are lucky with that, to radiation
or even surgery. So here's the wager: you stick around for a bit, but in return we
are going to need some things from you. These things may include your taste
buds, your ability to concentrate, your ability to digest, and the hair on your head.
This certainly appears to be a reasonable trade. Unfortunately, it also involves
confronting one of the most appealing clichés in our language. You've heard it all
right. People don't have cancer: they are reported to be battling cancer. No well-
wisher omits the combative image: You can beat this. It's even in obituaries for
cancer losers, as if one might reasonably say of someone that they died after a
long and brave struggle with mortality. You don't hear it about long-term sufferers
from heart disease or kidney failure.

Myself, I love the imagery of struggle. I sometimes wish I were suffering in a 7
good cause, or risking my life for the good of others, instead of just being a gravely
endangered patient. Allow me to inform you, though, that when you sit in a room
with a set of other finalists, and kindly people bring a huge transparent bag of
poison and plug it into your arm, and you either read or don't read a book while
the venom sack gradually empties itself into your system, the image of the ardent
soldier or revolutionary is the very last one that will occur to you. You feel
swamped with passivity and impotence: dissolving in powerlessness like a sugar
lump in water.

8   It's quite something, this chemo-poison. It has caused me to lose about 14 pounds, though without making me feel any lighter. It has cleared up a vicious rash on my shins that no doctor could ever name, let alone cure. (Some venom, to get rid of those furious red dots without a struggle.) Let it please be this mean and ruthless with the alien and its spreading dead-zone colonies. But as against that, the death-dealing stuff and life-preserving stuff have also made me strangely neuter. I was fairly reconciled to the loss of my hair, which began to come out in the shower in the first two weeks of treatment, and which I saved in a plastic bag so that it could help fill a floating dam in the Gulf of Mexico. But I wasn't quite prepared for the way that my razorblade would suddenly go slipping pointlessly down my face, meeting no stubble. Or for the way that my newly smooth upper lip would begin to look as if it had undergone electrolysis, causing me to look a bit too much like somebody's maiden auntie. (The chest hair that was once the toast of two continents hasn't yet wilted, but so much of it was shaved off for various hospital incisions that it's a rather patchy affair.) I feel upsettingly de-natured. If Penelope Cruz were one of my nurses, I wouldn't even notice. In the war against Thanatos, if we must term it a war, the immediate loss of Eros is a huge initial sacrifice.

9   These are my first raw reactions to being stricken. I am quietly resolved to resist bodily as best I can, even if only passively, and to seek the most advanced advice. My heart and blood pressure and many other registers are now strong again: indeed, it occurs to me that if I didn't have such a stout constitution I might have led a much healthier life thus far. Against me is the blind, emotionless alien, cheered on by some who have long wished me ill. But on the side of my continued life is a group of brilliant and selfless physicians plus an astonishing number of prayer groups. On both of these I hope to write next time if, as my father invariably said, I am spared.

COMPREHENSION

1. Summarize Hitchens's understanding of his condition. How does he confront his diagnosis?
2. What sense of himself does Hitchens present to his audience?
3. Explain in your own words the concept of the "new land" that Hitchens develops in his essay.

RHETORIC

1. Explain the voice and mood that Hitchens creates in the essay. How do these elements reinforce the thesis?
2. What is Hitchens's purpose in relying heavily on figurative language to compose his essay? What varieties of figurative language can you identify? What is the overall stylistic effect?
3. How does Hitchens use a pattern of cause and effect to organize elements in this essay? Where does he use process analysis?
4. Does Hitchens present an argument in this selection? Why or why not?
5. Where does the writer employ irony to illuminate his topic?

WRITING

1. Reflect on a time when you or someone you know confronted bad medical news.
2. Write an analytical essay in which you examine and evaluate the varieties of figurative language that make the selection by Hitchens so memorable.
3. **Writing an Argument:** Hitchens was an atheist who famously stated that if he ever returned to religion, it was the chemo talking. Argue for or against the proposition that someone who doesn't believe in God can face death with dignity.

NETWORKING
Applying Digital and Multimedia Literacies

Locate and review at least four online videos and/or podcasts of Hitchens's many speeches, debates, and interviews. How would you describe and define Hitchens's views? What about the tone he uses to express them? Do you find him more convincing in writing, or when you can hear and see him speak?

The Masked Marvel's Last Toehold

Richard Selzer

Richard Selzer (b. 1928) is a surgeon who started writing for several hours each night after he had already established a successful medical career. He was born in Troy, New York, and received degrees from Union College (BS, 1948) and Albany Medical College (MD, 1953). For more than two decades Selzer was on the faculty of the Yale School of Medicine. His first collection, Mortal Essays: Notes on the Art of Surgery *(1974), established Selzer as an essayist specializing in the world of medicine and surgery. Selzer employs an elegant prose style in describing the painful and often tragic world of medical procedures and patients. His essays have been collected in several books, among them* Confessions of a Knife *(1979),* Letters to a Young Doctor *(1982),* Taking the World in for Repairs *(1997), and* The Exact Location of the Soul *(2001). Selzer has also written for numerous magazines and has compiled a book of stories,* Imagine a Woman *(1997). The following essay demonstrates Selzer's experience as a surgeon as well as his ability to describe the world of medicine in poetic and haunting terms.*

Morning rounds.

On the fifth floor of the hospital, in the west wing, I know that a man is sitting up 1 in his bed, waiting for me. Elihu Koontz is seventy-five, and he is diabetic. It is two weeks since I amputated his left leg just below the knee. I walk down the corridor, but I do not go straight into his room. Instead, I pause in the doorway. He is not yet aware of my presence, but gazes down at the place in the bed where his leg used to be, and where now there is the collapsed leg of his pajamas. He is totally absorbed, like an athlete appraising the details of his body. What is he thinking, I wonder. Is he dreaming the outline of his toes? Does he see there his foot's incandescent ghost? Could he be angry? Feel that I have taken from him something for which he yearns now with all his heart? Has he forgotten so soon the pain? It was a pain so great as to set him apart from all other men, in a red-hot place where he had no kith or kin. What of those black gorilla toes and the soupy mess that was his heel? I watch him from the doorway. It is a kind of spying, I know.

2   Save for a white fringe open at the front, Elihu Koontz is bald. The hair has grown too long and is wilted. He wears it as one would wear a day-old laurel wreath. He is naked to the waist, so that I can see his breasts. They are the breasts of Buddha, inverted triangles from which the nipples swing, dark as garnets.

3   I have seen enough. I step into the room, and he sees that I am there.

4   "How did the night go, Elihu?"

5   He looks at me for a long moment. "Shut the door," he says.

6   I do, and move to the side of the bed. He takes my left hand in both of his, gazes at it, turns it over, then back, fondling, at last holding it up to his cheek. I do not withdraw from this loving. After a while he relinquishes my hand, and looks up at me.

7   "How is the pain?" I ask.

8   He does not answer, but continues to look at me in silence. I know at once that he has made a decision.

9   "Ever hear of The Masked Marvel?" He says this in a low voice, almost a whisper.

10   "What?"

11   "The Masked Marvel," he says. "You never heard of him?"

12   "No."

13   He clucks his tongue. He is exasperated.

14   All at once there is a recollection. It is dim, distant, but coming near.

15   "Do you mean the wrestler?"

16   Eagerly, he nods, and the breasts bob. How gnomish he looks, oval as the huge helpless egg of some outlandish lizard. He has very long arms, which, now and then, he unfurls to reach for things—a carafe of water, a get-well card. He gazes up at me, urging. He *wants* me to remember.

17   "Well . . . yes," I say. I am straining backward in time. "I saw him wrestle in Toronto long ago."

18   "Ha!" He smiles. "You saw *me.*" And his index finger, held rigid and upright, bounces in the air.

19   The man has said something shocking, unacceptable. It must be challenged.

20   "You?" I am trying to smile.

21   Again that jab of the finger. "You saw *me.*"

22   "No," I say. But even then, something about Elihu Koontz, those prolonged arms, the shape of his head, the sudden agility with which he leans from his bed

to get a large brown envelope from his nightstand, something is forcing me toward a memory. He rummages through his papers, old newspaper clippings, photographs, and I remember . . .

It is almost forty years ago. I am ten years old. I have been sent to Toronto to 23
spend the summer with relatives. Uncle Max has bought two tickets to the wrestling match. He is taking me that night.

"He isn't allowed," says Aunt Sarah to me. Uncle Max has angina.   24

"He gets too excited," she says.   25

"I wish you wouldn't go, Max," she says.   26

"You mind your own business," he says.   27

And we go. Out into the warm Canadian evening. I am not only abroad, I am 28
abroad in the *evening!* I have never been taken out in the evening. I am terribly excited. The trolleys, the lights, the horns. It is a bazaar. At the Maple Leaf Gardens, we sit high and near the center. The vast arena is dark except for the brilliance of the ring at the bottom.

It begins.   29

The wrestlers circle. They grapple. They are all haunch and paunch. I am 30
shocked by their ugliness, but I do not show it. Uncle Max is exhilarated. He leans forward, his eyes unblinking, on his face a look of enormous happiness. One after the other, a pair of wrestlers enter the ring. The two men join, twist, jerk, tug, bend, yank, and throw. Then they leave and are replaced by another pair. At last it is the main event. "The Angel vs. The Masked Marvel."

On the cover of the program notes, there is a picture of The Angel hanging from 31
the limb of a tree, a noose of thick rope around his neck. The Angel hangs just so for an hour every day, it is explained, to strengthen his neck. The Masked Marvel's trademark is a black stocking cap with holes for the eyes and mouth. He is never seen without it, states the program. No one knows who The Masked Marvel really is!

"Good," says Uncle Max. "Now you'll see something." He is fidgeting, waiting 32
for them to appear. They come down separate aisles, climb into the ring from opposite sides. I have never seen anything like them. It is The Angel's neck that first captures the eye. The shaved nape rises in twin columns to puff into the white hood of a sloped and bosselated skull that is too small. As though, strangled by the sinews of that neck, the skull had long since withered and shrunk. The thing about The Angel is the absence of any mystery in his body. It is simply *there.* A monosyllabic announcement. A grunt. One looks and knows everything at once, the fat thighs, the gigantic buttocks, the great spine from which hang knotted ropes and pale aprons of beef. And that prehistoric head. He is all of a single hideous piece, The Angel is. No detachables.

The Masked Marvel seems dwarfish. His fingers dangle kneeward. His short 33
legs are slightly bowed as if under the weight of the cask they are forced to heft about. He has breasts that swing when he moves! I have never seen such breasts on a man before.

There is a sudden ungraceful movement, and they close upon one another. The 34
Angel stoops and hugs The Marvel about the waist, locking his hands behind The

Marvel's back. Now he straightens and lifts The Marvel as though he were uprooting a tree. Thus he holds him, then stoops again, thrusts one hand through The Marvel's crotch, and with the other grabs him by the neck. He rears and . . . The Marvel is aloft! For a long moment, The Angel stands as though deciding where to make the toss. Then throws. Was that board or bone that splintered there? Again and again, The Angel hurls himself upon the body of The Masked Marvel.

35   Now The Angel rises over the fallen Marvel, picks up one foot in both of his hands, and twists the toes downward. It is far beyond the tensile strength of mere ligament, mere cartilage. The Masked Marvel does not hide his agony, but pounds and slaps the floor with his hand, now and then reaching up toward The Angel in an attitude of supplication. I have never seen such suffering. And all the while his black mask rolls from side to side, the mouth pulled to a tight slit through which issues an endless hiss that I can hear from where I sit. All at once, I hear a shouting close by.

36   "Break it off! Tear off a leg and throw it up here!"

37   It is Uncle Max. Even in the darkness I can see that he is gray. A band of sweat stands upon his upper lip. He is on his feet now, panting, one fist pressed at his chest, the other raised warlike toward the ring. For the first time I begin to think that something terrible might happen here. Aunt Sarah was right.

38   "Sit down, Uncle Max," I say. "Take a pill, please."

39   He reaches for the pillbox, gropes, and swallows without taking his gaze from the wrestlers. I wait for him to sit down.

40   "That's not fair," I say, "twisting his toes like that."

41   "It's the toehold," he explains.

42   "But it's not *fair*," I say again. The whole of the evil is laid open for me to perceive. I am trembling.

43   And now The Angel does something unspeakable. Holding the foot of The Marvel at full twist with one hand, he bends and grasps the mask where it clings to the back of The Marvel's head. And he pulls. He is going to strip it off! Lay bare an ultimate carnal mystery! Suddenly it is beyond mere physical violence. Now I am on my feet, shouting into the Maple Leaf Gardens.

44   "Watch out," I scream. "Stop him. Please, somebody, stop him."

45   Next to me, Uncle Max is chuckling.

46   Yet The Masked Marvel hears me, I know it. And rallies from his bed of pain. Thrusting with his free heel, he strikes The Angel at the back of the knee. The Angel falls. The Masked Marvel is on top of him pinning his shoulders to the mat. One! Two! Three! And it is over. Uncle Max is strangely still. I am gasping for breath. All this I remember as I stand at the bedside of Elihu Koontz.

47   Once again, I am in the operating room. It is two years since I amputated the left leg of Elihu Koontz. Now it is his right leg which is gangrenous. I have already scrubbed. I stand to one side wearing my gown and gloves. And . . . *I am masked.* Upon the table lies Elihu Koontz, pinned in a fierce white light. Spinal anesthesia has been administered. One of his arms is taped to a board placed at a right angle to his body. Into this arm, a needle has been placed. Fluid drips here from a bottle

overhead. With his other hand, Elihu Koontz beats feebly at the side of the operating table. His head rolls from side to side. His mouth is pulled into weeping. It seems to me that I have never seen such misery.

An orderly stands at the foot of the table, holding Elihu Koontz's leg aloft by 48 the toes so that the intern can scrub the limb with antiseptic solutions. The intern paints the foot, ankle, leg, and thigh, both front and back, three times. From a corner of the room where I wait, I look down as from an amphitheater. Then I think of Uncle Max yelling, "Tear off a leg. Throw it up here." And I think that forty years later I am making the catch.

"It's not fair," I say aloud. But no one hears me. I step forward to break The 49 Masked Marvel's last toehold.

COMPREHENSION

1. Who is (was) the Masked Marvel? What is Selzer's relation to this man? What are his personal feelings?
2. Is this essay strictly about an amputation? Why or why not?
3. Explain your understanding of the last bit of dialogue in this essay.

RHETORIC

1. Consider the importance of Selzer's title. What does it reveal about Selzer's purpose and thesis?
2. What aspects of narrative and descriptive technique stand out in this essay?
3. What stylistic shifts can you detect in this essay? For example, where does the writer use figurative language, and where does he use technical language? What is the effect?
4. Why does Selzer divide his essay into sections? How does each section function? Is this strategy effective? Justify your response.
5. Explain the atmosphere that Selzer evokes and the final tone of the piece.

WRITING

1. Analyze Selzer's essay as an example of effective narrative and descriptive technique.
2. Select a well-known athlete, and examine the ironies of a seemingly superbly conditioned individual whose career is compromised by injury, drug abuse, aging, or disease.
3. **Writing an Argument:** Argue for or against the proposition that a doctor should not let feelings interfere with his or her treatment of a patient.

NETWORKING
Applying Digital and Multimedia Literacies

Using Images to Enhance a Descriptive/Narrative Essay: Supplement Selzer's essay with images in a meaningful way that contributes to this story's use of narrative and description.

Between a Woman and Her Doctor

Martha Mendoza

Martha Mendoza *(b. 1969) was born and raised in Los Angeles and attended college at the University of California at Santa Cruz (BA, 1988). Based in San Jose, Mendoza is a national investigative reporter for the Associated Press. Her work has appeared in the* Los Angeles Times, Houston Chronicle, Newsday, *and elsewhere. Mendoza is also the co-author of* The Bridge at No Gun Ri: A Hidden Nightmare from the Korean War *(2001). In 2000, she won a Pulitzer Prize for investigative reporting. In this essay, which appeared in* Ms. *magazine in 2004, Mendoza tells of her abortion while at the same time exploring broader medical, social, and legal issues.*

1   I could see my baby's amazing and perfect spine, a precise, pebbled curl of vertebrae. His little round skull. The curve of his nose. I could even see his small leg floating slowly through my uterus.

2   My doctor came in a moment later, slid the ultrasound sensor around my growing, round belly and put her hand on my shoulder. "It's not alive," she said.

3   She turned her back to me and started taking notes. I looked at the wall, breathing deeply, trying not to cry.

4   I can make it through this, I thought. I can handle this.

5   I didn't know I was about to become a pariah.

6   I was 19 weeks pregnant, strong, fit and happy, imagining our fourth child, the newest member of our family. He would have dark hair and bright eyes. He'd be intelligent and strong—really strong, judging by his early kicks.

7   And now this. Not alive?

8   I didn't realize that pressures well beyond my uterus, beyond the too-bright, too-loud, too-small ultrasound room, extending all the way to boardrooms of hospitals, administrative sessions at medical schools and committee hearings in Congress, were going to deepen and expand my sorrow and pain.

9   On November 6, 2003, President Bush signed what he called a "partial birth abortion ban," prohibiting doctors from committing an "overt act" designed to kill a partially delivered fetus. The law, which faces vigorous challenges, is the most significant change to the nation's abortion laws since the U.S. Supreme Court ruled abortion legal in *Roe v. Wade* in 1973. One of the unintended consequences of this new law is that it put people in my position, with a fetus that is already dead, in a technical limbo.

10   Legally, a doctor can still surgically take a dead body out of a pregnant woman. But in reality, the years of angry debate that led to the law's passage, restrictive

state laws and the violence targeting physicians have reduced the number of hospitals and doctors willing to do dilations and evacuations (D&Es) and dilations and extractions (intact D&Es), which involve removing a larger fetus, sometimes in pieces, from the womb.

At the same time, fewer medical schools are training doctors to do these 11 procedures. After all, why spend time training for a surgery that's likely to be made illegal?

At this point, 74 percent of obstetrics and gynecology residency programs do 12 *not* train all residents in abortion procedures, according to reproductive health researchers at the National Abortion Federation. Those that do usually teach only the first trimester abortion procedures such as dilation and curettage—D&C, the 15-minute uterine scraping. Fewer than 7 percent of obstetricians are trained to do D&Es, the procedure used on fetuses from about 13 to 19 weeks. Almost all the doctors doing them are over 50 years old.

"Finding a doctor who will do a D&E is getting very tough," says Ron Fitzsim- 13 mons, executive director of the National Coalition of Abortion Providers.

My doctor turned around and faced me. She told me that because dilation and evacu- 14 ation is rarely offered in my community, I could opt instead to chemically induce labor over several days and then deliver the little body at my local maternity ward.

"It's up to you," she said.   15

I'd been through labor and delivery three times before, with great joy as well 16 as pain, and the notion of going through that profound experience only to deliver a dead fetus (whose skin was already starting to slough off, whose skull might be collapsing) was horrifying.

I also did some research, spoke with friends who were obstetricians and 17 gynecologists, and quickly learned this: Study after study shows D&Es are *safer* than labor and delivery. Women who had D&Es were far less likely to have bleeding requiring transfusion, infection requiring intravenous antibiotics, organ injuries requiring additional surgery or cervical laceration requiring repair and hospital readmission. A review of 300 second-trimester abortions published in 2002 in the *American Journal of Obstetrics & Gynecology* found that 29 percent of women who went through labor and delivery had complications, compared with just 4 percent of those who had D&Es.

The American Medical Association said D&Es, compared to labor and 18 delivery, "may minimize trauma to the woman's uterus, cervix and other vital organs."

There was this fact, too: The intact D&E surgery makes less use of "grasp- 19 ing instruments," which could damage the body of the fetus. If the body were intact, doctors might be able to more easily figure out why my baby died in the womb.

I'm a healthy person. I run, swim and bike. I'm 37 years old and optimistic. 20 Good things happen to me. I didn't want to rule out having more kids, but I did want to know what went wrong before I tried again.

21   We told our doctor we had chosen a dilation and evacuation.

22   "I can't do these myself," said my doctor. "I trained at a Catholic hospital."

23   My doctor recommended a specialist in a neighboring county, but when I called for an appointment, they said they couldn't see me for almost a week.

24   I could feel my baby's dead body inside of mine. This baby had thrilled me with kicks and flutters, those first soft tickles of life bringing a smile to my face and my hand to my rounding belly. Now this baby floated, limp and heavy, from one side to the other, as I rolled in my bed. And within a day, I started to bleed. My body, with or without a doctor's help, was starting to expel the fetus. Technically, I was threatening a spontaneous abortion, the least safe of the available options.

25   I did what any pregnant patient would do. I called my doctor. And she advised me to wait.

26   I lay in my bed, not sleeping day or night, trying not to lose this little baby's body that my own womb was working to expel. Wait, I told myself. Just hold on. Let a doctor take this out. I was scared. Was it going to fall out of my body when I rose, in the middle of the night, to check on my toddler? Would it come apart on its own and double me over, knock me to the floor, as I stood at the stove scrambling eggs for my boys?

27   On my fourth morning, with the bleeding and cramping increasing, I couldn't wait any more. I called my doctor and was told that since I wasn't hemorrhaging, I should not come in. Her partner, on call, pedantically explained that women can safely lose a lot of blood, even during a routine period.

28   I began calling labor and delivery units at the top five medical centers in my area. I told them I had been 19 weeks along. The baby is dead. I'm bleeding, I said. I'm scheduled for a D&E in a few days. If I come in right now, what could you do for me, I asked.

29   Don't come in, they told me again and again. "Go to your emergency room if you are hemorrhaging to avoid bleeding to death. No one here can do a D&E today, and unless you're really in active labor you're safer to wait."

30   More than 66,000 women each year in the U.S. undergo an abortion at some point between 13 and 20 weeks, according to the Centers for Disease Control and Prevention. The CDC doesn't specify the physical circumstances of the women or their fetuses. Other CDC data shows that 4,000 women miscarry in their second trimester. Again, the data doesn't clarify whether those 4,000 women have to go through surgery.

31   Here's what is clear: Most of those women face increasingly limited access to care. One survey showed that half of the women who got abortions after 15 weeks of gestation said they were delayed because of problems in affording, finding or getting to abortion services. No surprise there; abortion is not readily available in 86 percent of the counties in the U.S.

32   Although there are some new, early diagnostic tests available, the most common prenatal screening for neural tube defects or Down syndrome is done around the 16th week of pregnancy. When problems are found—sometimes

life-threatening problems—pregnant women face the same limited options that
I did.

At last I found one university teaching hospital that, at least over the telephone, 33
was willing to take me.

"We do have one doctor who can do a D&E," they said. "Come in to our emer- 34
gency room if you want."

But when I arrived at the university's emergency room, the source of the 35
tension was clear. After examining me and confirming I was bleeding but not
hemorrhaging, the attending obstetrician, obviously pregnant herself, defen-
sively explained that only one of their dozens of obstetricians and gynecologists
still does D&Es, and he was simply not available. Not today. Not tomorrow. Not
the next day. No, I couldn't have his name. She walked away from me and called
my doctor.

"You can't just dump these patients on us," she shouted into the phone, her 36
high-pitched voice floating through the heavy curtains surrounding my bed. "You
should be dealing with this yourself."

Shivering on the narrow, white exam table, I wondered what I had done 37
wrong. Then I pulled back on my loose maternity pants and stumbled into the
sunny parking lot, blinking back tears in the dazzling spring day, trying to understand the directions they sent me out with: Find a hotel within a few blocks from
a hospital. Rest, monitor the bleeding. Don't go home—the 45-minute drive might
be too far.

The next few days were a blur of lumpy motel beds, telephone calls to doctors, 38
cramps. The pre-examination for my D&E finally arrived. First, the hospital
required me to sign a legal form consenting to terminate the pregnancy. Then
they explained I could, at no cost, have the remains incinerated by the hospital
pathology department as medical waste, or for a fee have them taken to a funeral
home for burial or cremation.

They inserted sticks of seaweed into my cervix and told me to go home for 39
the night. A few hours later—when the contractions were regular, strong and
frequent—I knew we needed to get to the hospital.

"The patient appeared to be in active labor," say my charts, "and I explained 40
this to the patient and offered her pain medication for vaginal delivery."

According to the charts, I was "adamant" in demanding a D&E. I remember 41
that I definitely wanted the surgical procedure that was the safest option. One
hour later, just as an anesthesiologist was slipping me into unconsciousness,
I had the D&E and a little body, my little boy, slipped out. Around his neck,
three times and very tight, was the umbilical cord, source of his life, cause of
his death.

This past spring, as the wildflowers started blooming around the simple cross 42
we built for this baby, the Justice Department began trying to enforce the Bush
administration's ban and federal courts in three different cities heard arguments regarding the new law. Doctors explained that D&Es are the safest

procedure in many cases, and that the law is particularly cruel to mothers like me whose babies were already dead. In hopes of bolstering their case, prosecutors sent federal subpoenas to various medical centers, asking for records of D&Es. There's an attorney somewhere, someday, who may poke through the files of my loss.

43   I didn't watch the trial because I had another appointment to keep—another ultrasound. Lying on the crisp white paper, watching the monitor, I saw new life, the incredible spine, tiny fingers waving slowly across my uterus, a perfect thigh. Best of all, there it was, a strong, four-chamber heart, beating steady and solid. A soft quiver, baby rolling, rippled across my belly.

44   "Everything looks wonderful," said my doctor. "This baby is doing great."

COMPREHENSION

1. Explain the nature and extent of Mendoza's "sorrow and pain" (paragraph 8).
2. What is "D&E"? What is Mendoza's understanding of the procedure, and how does she react to it?
3. What elements of government policy does Mendoza discuss, and why?

RHETORIC

1. Mendoza's title might contain more than one level of meaning. Would you agree or disagree? Explain.
2. Why does Mendoza begin with personal narrative and then switch to exposition? How does she sustain this back-and-forth movement between narration and exposition?
3. Do you think that Mendoza develops an argument in this essay or attempts to persuade readers to adopt a certain position regarding abortion? Or is she merely investigating, as a journalist, a procedure that she and many other women experience? Elaborate on your response.
4. Mendoza's essay appeared in a feminist magazine. Why would the article and the position that Mendoza stakes out appeal to *Ms.* readers?
5. What elements of investigative reporting do you find in this essay?
6. What is your response to the conclusion? What is Mendoza's purpose in using an emotional appeal at this end point in the essay?

WRITING

1. Investigate "partial birth abortion," and write an essay analyzing the process.
2. Write a personal essay recounting an illness or painful medical procedure that you or someone close to you experienced.
3. **Writing an Argument:** Argue for or against the proposition that abortion should be strictly a matter "between a woman and her doctor."

NETWORKING
Applying Digital and Multimedia Literacies

Evaluating Web Sites about Abortion: Visit the listed sites about abortion and write a paragraph-long evaluation of each.

In your assessment, note (1) what organization sponsors this Web site, (2) what that organization's agenda or purpose is, (3) what position the site/organization takes on abortion, (4) what they hope visitors will come away with from the site, and (5) how various features on the site—its design, use of visuals, use of interactive features, and so on—contribute to its goals.

- Planned Parenthood
- Abortionfacts.com
- database of information and articles in the *New York Times*
- Friends in Adoption
- East Side Gynecology
- Balanced Politics
- Whole World in His Hands
- StandUpGirl
- Feminists for Life
- NARAL
- About.com
- AdoptionTV.com

Naked

Atul Gawande

Atul Gawande (b. 1965) is a prize-winning author, journalist, physician, and advocate for national and global health causes. He was born in Brooklyn, New York, to Indian immigrant parents who were doctors. Gawande grew up in Athens, Ohio. He received his BA from Stanford University in 1987, and attended Balliol College, Oxford as a Rhodes Scholar. Gawande received his medical degree from Harvard Medical School in 1994. Today he is an endocrine surgeon and associate director of the Center for Surgery and Public Health at Brigham and Women's Hospital in Boston. He is also an associate professor at the Harvard School of Public Health and associate professor of surgery at Harvard Medical School. Active in Democratic politics, Gawande served in the Clinton administration as one of the directors of the Clinton Health Care Task Force. Gawande has been a staff writer for the New Yorker *since 1998, contributing articles on medicine and public health.*

He writes for other magazines as well, including the online publication Slate. *Among his books are* Complications: A Surgeon's Notes on an Imperfect Science *(2002) and* The Checklist Manifesto: How to Get Things Right *(2009). In "Naked," which appeared in the August 18, 2005 issue of the* New England Journal of Medicine, *Gawande offers global insights into delicate procedures.*

1   There is an exquisite and fascinating scene in *Kandahar*, a movie set in Afghanistan under the Taliban regime, in which a male physician is asked to examine a female patient. They are separated by an opaque screen. Behind it, the woman is covered from head to toe by her burka. The two do not talk directly to each other. The patient's young son serves as the go-between. She has a stomachache, he says.

2   "Does she throw up her food?" the doctor asks.

3   "Do you throw up your food?" the boy asks.

4   "No," the woman says, perfectly audibly, but the doctor waits as if he has not heard.

5   "No," the boy tells him.

6   For the exam, the doctor has cut a two-inch circle in the screen. "Tell her to come closer," he says. The boy does. She brings her mouth to the opening, and through it he looks inside. "Have her bring her eye to the hole," he says. And so the exam goes. Such, apparently, can be the demands of decency.

7   When I started my surgical practice two years ago, I was not at all clear about what my own etiquette of examination should be. Expectations are murky; we have no clear standards in the United States; and the topic can be fraught with hazards. Physical examination is deeply intimate, and the way a doctor deals with the naked body—particularly when the doctor is male and the patient female—inevitably raises questions of propriety and trust.

8   No one anywhere seems to have discovered the ideal approach. A surgical colleague who practices in Iraq told me about the customs of physical examination there. He said he feels no hesitation about examining female patients completely when necessary, but because a doctor and a patient of opposite sex cannot be alone together without eyebrows being raised, a family member will always accompany them for the exam. Women do not remove their clothes or change into a gown for the exam, and only a small portion of the body is uncovered at any one time. A nurse, he said, is rarely asked to chaperone: if the doctor is female, it is not necessary, and if male, the family is there to ensure that nothing unseemly occurs.

9   In Caracas, according to a Venezuelan doctor I met, female patients virtually always have a chaperone for a breast or pelvic exam, whether the physician is male or female. "That way there are no mixed messages," the doctor said. The chaperone, however, must be a medical professional. So the family is sent out of the examination room, and a nurse brought in. If a chaperone is unavailable or has refused to participate, the exam is not done.

10   A Ukrainian internist told me that she has not heard of doctors in Kiev using a chaperone. If a family member is present, he or she will be asked to leave. Both patient and doctor wear their uniforms—the patient a white examining gown, the doctor a white coat. Last names are always used. There is no effort at informality

to muddy the occasion. This practice, she believes, is enough to solidify trust and preclude misinterpretation of the conduct of care.

A doctor, it appears, has a range of options.   11

In 2003, I set up my clinic hours, and soon people arrived to see me. I was, I 12 realized, for the first time genuinely alone with patients. No attending physician in the room or getting ready to come in; no bustle of emergency room personnel on the other side of a curtain. Just a patient and me. We'd sit down. We'd talk. I'd ask about whatever had occasioned the visit, about past medical problems, medications, the family and social history. Then the time would come to have a look.

There were, I will admit, some awkward moments. I had an instinctive aversion 13 to examination gowns. At our clinic they are made of either thin, ill-fitting cloth or thin, ill-fitting paper. They seem designed to leave patients exposed and cold. I decided to examine my patients while they were in their street clothes. If a patient with gallstones wore a shirt she could untuck for the abdominal exam, this worked fine. But then I'd encounter a patient in stockings and a dress, and the next thing I knew, I had her dress bunched up around her head, her tights around her knees, and both of us wondering what the hell was going on. An exam for a breast lump one could manage, in theory: the woman could unhook her brassiere and lift or unbutton her shirt. But in practice, it just seemed weird. Even checking pulses could be a problem. Pant legs could not be pushed up high enough. Try pulling them down over shoes, however, and . . . forget it. I finally began to have patients change into the damn gowns. (I haven't, however, asked men to do so nearly as often as women.)

As for having a chaperone present with female patients, I hadn't settled on a 14 firm policy. I found that I always asked a medical assistant to come in for pelvic exams and generally didn't for breast exams. I was completely inconsistent about rectal exams.

I surveyed my colleagues about what they do and received a variety of answers. 15 Many said they bring in a chaperone for all pelvic and rectal exams—"anything below the waist"—but only rarely for breast exams. Others have a chaperone for breast and pelvic exams but not for rectal exams. Some did not have a chaperone at all. Indeed, an obstetrician-gynecologist estimated that about half the male physicians in his department do not routinely use a chaperone. He himself detests the word "chaperone" because it implies that mistrust is warranted, but he offers to bring in an "assistant" for pelvic and breast exams. Few of his patients, however, find the presence of the assistant necessary after the first exam, he said. If the patient prefers to have her sister, boyfriend, or mother stay for the exam, he does not object—but he is under no illusion that a family chaperone offers protection against an accusation of misconduct. Instead, he relies on his reading of a patient to determine whether bringing in a nurse-witness would be wise.

One of our residents, who was trained partly in London, said he found the 16 selectivity here strange. "In Britain, I would never examine a woman's abdomen without a nurse present. But in the emergency room here, when I asked to have a nurse come in when I needed to do a rectal exam or check groin nodes on a woman, they thought I was crazy. 'Just go in there and do it!' they said." In England, he said, "if you need to do a breast or rectal exam or even check femoral pulses, especially on a young woman, you would be either foolish or stupid to do it without a chaperone. It doesn't take much—just one patient complaining, 'I came in with a foot pain and the doctor started diving around my groin,' and you could be suspended for a sexual-harassment investigation."

17   Britain's standards are stringent: the General Medical Council, the Royal College of Physicians, and the Royal College of Obstetricians and Gynaecologists specify that a chaperone must be offered to all patients who undergo an "intimate exam" (i.e., involving the breasts, genitalia, or rectum), irrespective of the sex of the patient or of the doctor.[1,2] A chaperone must be present when a male physician performs an intimate exam of a female patient. The chaperone should be a female member of the medical team, and her name should be recorded in the notes. If the patient refuses a chaperone and the examination is not urgent, it should be deferred until it can be performed by a female physician.

18   In the United States, we have no such guidelines. As a result, our patients have little idea of what to expect from us. To be sure, some minimal standards have been established. The Federation of State Medical Boards has spelled out that touching a patient's breasts or genitals for a purpose other than medical care is a disciplinable offense. So are oral contact with a patient, encouraging a patient to masturbate in one's presence, and providing services in exchange for sexual favors. Sexual impropriety which involves no touching but is no less proscribed includes asking a patient for a date, criticizing a patient's sexual orientation, making sexual comments about the patient's body or clothing, and initiating discussion of one's own sexual experiences or fantasies.[3] I can't say anyone taught me these boundaries in medical school, but I would like to think that no one needed to.

19   The difficulty for those of us who do not behave badly is that medical exams remain inherently ambiguous. Any patient can be led to wonder: Did the doctor really need to touch me there? Even when doctors simply inquire about patients' sexual history, can anyone be certain of the intent? The fact that all medical professionals have blushed or found their thoughts straying during a patient visit reveals the potential for impropriety in any encounter.

20   The tone of an office visit can turn on a single word, a joke, a comment about a tattoo in an unexpected place. One surgeon told me of a young patient who expressed concern about a lump in her "boob." But when he used the same word in response, she became extremely uncomfortable and later made a complaint. Another woman I know left her gynecologist after he made an off-hand, probably inadvertent, but admiring comment about her tan lines during a pelvic exam.

21   The examination itself—the how and where of the touching—is, of course, the most potentially dicey territory. If a patient even begins to doubt the propriety of what a doctor is doing, something is not right. So what then should our customs be?

---

[1]Intimate examinations. London: General Medical Council Standards Committee, December 2001.
[2]Gynaecological examinations: guidelines for specialist practice. London: Royal College of Obstetricians and Gynaecologists, July 2002.
[3]Ad Hoc Committee on Physician Impairment. Report on sexual boundary issues. Dallas: Federation of State Medical Boards of the United States, April,1996.

There are many reasons to consider setting tighter, more uniform profes- 22
sional standards. One is to protect patients from harm. About 4 percent of the
disciplinary orders that state medical boards issue against physicians are for
sex-related offenses. One of every 200 physicians is disciplined for sexual misconduct with patients sometime during his or her career.[4] Some of these cases
involve such outrageous acts as having intercourse with patients during pelvic
exams. The vast majority of cases involved male physicians and female patients,
and virtually all occurred without a chaperone present.[5] About one third of
cases studied in one state involved actual sexual intercourse with patients; two
thirds involved sexual impropriety or inappropriate touching short of sexual
contact. Another goal might be to reduce false accusations arising from misinterpretation.

Nonetheless, eliminating misconduct and accusations would be the wrong 23
aim to guide medical care. The trouble is not that such acts are rare (though the
statistics suggest they are), nor that total prevention—zero tolerance—is impossible. It is that, at some point, the measures required to achieve total prevention
will approach the Taliban-esque and harm care of patients.

Embracing more explicit standards for medical encounters, however, 24
might actually improve relationships with patients and that does stand as a
worthy goal. The new informality of medicine—with white coats disappearing,
and patient and doctor sometimes on a first-name basis—has blurred boundaries
that once guided us. If physicians are unsure about what is appropriate
behavior for themselves, is it any surprise that patients are, too? Or that misinterpretation can occur? We have jettisoned our old customs but have not bothered to replace them.

My father, a urologist, has thought carefully about how to avert such uncer- 25
tainties. From the start, he felt the fragility of his standing as an outsider, an
Indian immigrant practicing in a rural Ohio town. In the absence of guidelines
to reassure patients that what he does as a urologist is routine, he has made pains-
taking efforts to avoid question.

The process begins before the exam. He always arrives in a tie and white 26
coat. He is courtly. Although he often knows patients socially and doesn't hesitate
to speak with them about personal matters (the subjects can range from impotence to sexual affairs), he keeps his language strictly medical. If a female patient
must put on a gown, he steps out while she undresses. He makes a point of
explaining what he is going to do during the examination and why. If the patient
lies down and needs further unzipping or unbuttoning, he is careful not to help.
He wears gloves even for abdominal examinations. If the patient is female or
under 18 years of age, then he brings in a nurse as a chaperone, whether the
exam is "intimate" or not.

---

[4]Dehlendorf CE, Wolfe SM. Physicians disciplined for sex-related offenses. JAMA 1998; 279:1883-8.
[5]Enbom JA, Thomas CD. Evaluation of sexual misconduct complaints: the Oregon Board of Medical
Examiners, 1991 to 1995. Am J Obstet Gynecol 1997;176:1340-8.

27   His approach has succeeded. I grew up knowing many of his patients, and they trust him completely. I find, however, that some of his practices do not seem quite right for me. My patients are as likely to have problems above the waist as below, and having a chaperone present for a routine abdominal exam or a check of groin pulses feels to me absurd. I don't don gloves for nongenital exams. Nonetheless, I have tried to emulate the spirit of my father's visits—the decorum in language and attire, the respect for modesty, the precision of examination. As I think further about his example, it has also led me to make some changes: I now uniformly use an assistant not just for pelvic exams but also for rectal exams of female patients and as patients desire, for breast exams as well. For the comfort and reassurance of patients, these seem to be reasonable customs, even expectations, for more of us to accept.

28   A professor once told my medical school class that patients can tell when you've seen a thousand naked patients and when you haven't. I now know that's true. But I have also come to recognize that no patient has seen a thousand doctors. They therefore have little idea, coming to a doctor's office, of what is "normal" and what is not. This we can change.

COMPREHENSION

1. Circle, underline, or highlight the different approaches that physicians around the world take to the examination of their patients.
2. Summarize Gawande's findings about the role of "chaperones" during breast and pelvic examinations.
3. What is Gawande's own approach to conducting patient examinations? Where did he learn this procedure? What are its characteristics?

RHETORIC

1. What is Gawande's thesis? Does any single sentence state the main idea? Explain.
2. How do the title and introductory anecdote serve to establish the tone of the essay? Do you find a uniform tone in this piece or does the author vary it? Justify your response by referring to specific passages.
3. A professional journal places formal and stylistic demands on a writer. Where do you find these requirements or expectations operating in the essay?
4. Why does Gawande personalize the essay? What is the effect?
5. Identify the author's use of process analysis, classification, comparison and contrast, and causal analysis. Is he successful in mixing so many rhetorical patterns in one essay? Why or why not?

WRITING

1. Imagine that you are a physician. Describe the process you would use to examine a patient.
2. Compose a textual analysis of the various rhetorical strategies that Gawande relies on to develop his essay. Evaluate his relative success.
3. **Writing an Argument:** Argue for or against the proposition that the United States should have a uniform code of conduct and standards for conducting physical examinations.

| **NETWORKING** |
| *Applying Digital and Multimedia Literacies* |

Hyperlinking a Summary: Download the code of conduct for physicians conducting examinations in Great Britain. Provide a hyperlinked précis of your findings, providing readers with links that help clarify or expand on your summary.

The Terrifying Normalcy of AIDS

Stephen Jay Gould

Stephen Jay Gould *(1941–2002), an acclaimed contemporary science writer, taught biology, geology, and the history of science at Harvard University, where he was Alexander Agassiz Professor of Zoology. Born in New York City, he was educated at Antioch College (BA, 1963) and Columbia University (PhD, 1967). He wrote a monthly column, "This View of Life," for* Natural History *magazine and was the author of* Ever Since Darwin *(1977),* Ontogeny and Phylogeny *(1977),* The Panda's Thumb *(1980),* Wonderful Life *(1989),* Bully for Brontosaurus *(1991),* The Structure of Evolutionary Theory *(2002), and other books. In this 1987 essay, Gould explains in clear, precise language why AIDS is a "natural phenomenon" and warns against viewing it in moral terms.*

Disney's Epcot Center in Orlando, Fla., is a technological tour de force and a conceptual desert. In this permanent World's Fair, American industrial giants have built their versions of an unblemished future. These masterful entertainments convey but one message, brilliantly packaged and relentlessly expressed: Progress through technology is the solution to all human problems. G.E. proclaims from Horizons: "If we can dream it, we can do it." A.T.&T. speaks from on high within its giant golf ball: We are now "unbounded by space and time." United Technologies bubbles from the depths of Living Seas: "With the help of modern technology, we feel there's really no limit to what can be accomplished." 1

Yet several of these exhibits at the Experimental Prototype Community of Tomorrow, all predating last year's space disaster, belie their stated message from within by using the launch of the shuttle as a visual metaphor for technological triumph. The *Challenger* disaster may represent a general malaise, but it remains an incident. The AIDS pandemic, an issue that may rank with nuclear weaponry as the greatest danger of our era, provides a more striking proof that mind and technology are not omnipotent and that we have not canceled our bond to nature. 2

In 1984, John Platt, a biophysicist who taught at the University of Chicago for many years, wrote a short paper for private circulation. At a time when most of us 3 were either ignoring AIDS, or viewing it as a contained and peculiar affliction of homosexual men, Platt recognized that the limited data on the origin of AIDS and its spread in America suggested a more frightening prospect: We are all susceptible to AIDS, and the disease has been spreading in a simple exponential manner.

4   Exponential growth is a geometric increase. Remember the old kiddy problem: If you place a penny on square one of a checkerboard and double the number of coins on each subsequent square—2, 4, 8, 16, 32 . . .—how big is the stack by the sixty-fourth square? The answer: about as high as the universe is wide. Nothing in the external environment inhibits this increase, thus giving to exponential processes their relentless character. In the real, noninfinite world, of course, some limit will eventually arise, and the process slows down, reaches a steady state, or destroys the entire system: The stack of pennies falls over, the bacterial cells exhaust their supply of nutrients.

5   Platt noticed that data for the initial spread of AIDS fell right on an exponential curve. He then followed the simplest possible procedure of extrapolating the curve unabated into the 1990's. Most of us were incredulous, accusing Platt of the mathematical gamesmanship that scientists call "curve fitting." After all, aren't exponential models unrealistic? Surely we are not all susceptible to AIDS. Is it not spread only by odd practices to odd people? Will it not, therefore, quickly run its short course within a confined group?

6   Well, hello 1987—worldwide data still match Platt's extrapolated curve. This will not, of course, go on forever. AIDS has probably already saturated the African areas where it probably originated, and where the sex ratio of afflicted people is 1-to-1, male-female. But AIDS still has far to spread, and may be moving exponentially, through the rest of the world. We have learned enough about the cause of AIDS to slow its spread, if we can make rapid and fundamental changes in our handling of that most powerful part of human biology—our own sexuality. But medicine, as yet, has nothing to offer as a cure and precious little even for palliation.

7   This exponential spread of AIDS not only illuminates its, and our, biology, but also underscores the tragedy of our moralistic misperception. Exponential processes have a definite time and place of origin, an initial point of "inoculation"—in this case, Africa. We didn't notice the spread at first. In a population of billions, we pay little attention when one increases to two, or eight to sixteen, but when one million becomes two million, we panic, even though the *rate* of doubling has not increased.

8   The infection has to start somewhere, and its initial locus may be little more than an accident of circumstance. For a while, it remains confined to those in close contact with the primary source, but only by accident of proximity, not by intrinsic susceptibility. Eventually, given the power and lability of human sexuality, it spreads outside the initial group and into the general population. And now AIDS has begun its march through our own heterosexual community.

9   What a tragedy that our moral stupidity caused us to lose precious time, the greatest enemy in fighting an exponential spread, by down-playing the danger because we thought that AIDS was a disease of three irregular groups of

minorities: minorities of life style (needle users), of sexual preference (homosexuals) and of color (Haitians). If AIDS had first been imported from Africa into a Park Avenue apartment, we would not have dithered as the exponential march began.

The message of Orlando—the inevitability of technological solutions—is 10 wrong, and we need to understand why.

Our species has not won its independence from nature, and we cannot do all 11 that we can dream. Or at least we cannot do it at the rate required to avoid tragedy, for we are not unbounded from time. Viral diseases are preventable in principle, and I suspect that an AIDS vaccine will one day be produced. But how will this discovery avail us if it takes until the millennium, and by then AIDS has fully run its exponential course and saturated our population, killing a substantial percentage of the human race? A fight against an exponential enemy is primarily a race against time.

We must also grasp the perspective of ecology and evolutionary biology 12 and recognize, once we reinsert ourselves properly into nature, that AIDS represents the ordinary workings of biology, not an irrational or diabolical plague with a moral meaning. Disease, including epidemic spread, is a natural phenomenon, part of human history from the beginning. An entire subdiscipline of my profession, paleopathology, studies the evidence of ancient diseases preserved in the fossil remains of organisms. Human history has been marked by episodic plagues. More native peoples died of imported disease than ever fell before the gun during the era of colonial expansion. Our memories are short, and we have had a respite, really, only since the influenza pandemic at the end of World War I, but AIDS must be viewed as a virulent expression of an ordinary natural phenomenon.

I do not say this to foster either comfort or complacency. The evolutionary 13 perspective is correct, but utterly inappropriate for our human scale. Yes, AIDS is a natural phenomenon, one of a recurring class of pandemic diseases. Yes, AIDS may run through the entire population, and may carry off a quarter or more of us. Yes, it may make no *biological* difference to Homo sapiens in the long run: There will still be plenty of us left and we can start again. Evolution cares as little for its agents—organisms struggling for reproductive success—as physics cares for individual atoms of hydrogen in the sun. But we care. These atoms are our neighbors, our lovers, our children and ourselves. AIDS is both a natural phenomenon and, potentially, the greatest natural tragedy in human history.

The cardboard message of Epcot fosters the wrong attitudes: We must both re- 14 insert ourselves into nature and view AIDS as a natural phenomenon in order to fight properly. If we stand above nature and if technology is all-powerful, then AIDS is a horrifying anomaly that must be trying to tell us something. If so, we can adopt one of two attitudes, each potentially fatal. We can either become complacent, because we believe the message of Epcot and assume that medicine will soon generate a cure, or we can panic in confusion and seek a scapegoat for something so irregular that it must have been visited upon us to teach us a moral lesson.

15   But AIDS is not irregular. It is part of nature. So are we. This should galvanize us and give us hope, not prompt the worst of all responses: a kind of "new-age" negativism that equates natural with what we must accept and cannot, or even should not, change. When we view AIDS as natural, and when we recognize both the exponential property of its spread and the accidental character of its point of entry into America, we can break through our destructive tendencies to blame others and to free ourselves of concern.

16   If AIDS is natural, then there is no message in its spread. But by all that science has learned and all that rationality proclaims, AIDS works by a *mechanism*—and we can discover it. Victory is not ordained by any principle of progress, or any slogan of technology, so we shall have to fight like hell, and be watchful. There is no message, but there is a mechanism.

COMPREHENSION

1. What does Gould mean when he defines AIDS as a "natural phenomenon" (paragraph 12)? How does the title support this definition?
2. What does Gould mean by "our moral stupidity" in paragraph 9?
3. What connection does Gould make between our reaction to the AIDS crisis and our alienation from nature?

RHETORIC

1. What is Gould's main idea? Where in the essay is it stated?
2. What is the purpose of paragraphs 1 and 2? How do they contribute to Gould's argument? How do they help establish the tone of the essay? What is the tone? What is the importance of Epcot Center to Gould's thesis?
3. Gould uses scientific terminology in his essay. Define the words *exponential* (paragraph 3) and *pandemic* and *phenomenon* (paragraph 13). Is this essay intended for a specialized audience? Justify your response.
4. Trace the progression of ideas in paragraphs 2–5. What transitions does Gould employ?
5. Does Gould use rhetorical strategies besides argument in his essay? Cite evidence of this varied rhetorical approach.
6. Explain the final sentence in Gould's conclusion. What is its relation to the paragraph as a whole?

WRITING

1. Gould states that we must "reinsert ourselves into nature" (paragraph 14). What does he mean by this? How would this affect the way in which we deal with disease and death in our society? Explore this issue in a brief essay.
2. Write an extended definition of HIV/AIDS, attempting to avoid moralizing about the subject. Conduct research if necessary.
3. **Writing an Argument:** Write an essay in which you expand on Gould's belief that our moral stupidity has not only hindered society's recognition of the AIDS threat but continues to impede AIDS research and treatment.

NETWORKING	
Applying Digital and Multimedia Literacies	

Creating an Informational Web Page: After completing question 2 under Writing, write and design a single Web page that defines and provides important at-a-glance information about HIV/AIDS. Its purpose should be to inform the public by providing facts and dispelling harmful myths; it should *not* make an argument. Incorporate one image and provide a few select hyperlinks.

The Globalization of Eating Disorders

Susan Bordo

Susan Bordo (b. 1947) was born in Newark, New Jersey, and was educated at Carleton University (BA, 1972) and the State University of New York at Stony Brook (PhD, 1982). She is the Singletary Chair in the Humanities and a professor of English and women's studies at the University of Kentucky. A feminist philosopher and interdisciplinary scholar who focuses on Western culture's attitudes toward gender and the body, Bordo has written The Flight to Objectivity: Essays on Cartesianism and Culture *(1987),* Unbearable Weight: Feminism, Western Culture, and the Body *(1993, 2004),* Twilight Zones: The Hidden Life of Cultural Images from Plato to O.J. *(1997), and* The Male Body: A New Look at Men in Public and in Private *(1999). In this selection, Bordo offers an overview of a new kind of epidemic, fueled by Western media images, that is affecting cultures around the world.*

The young girl stands in front of the mirror. Never fat to begin with, she's been on a no-fat diet for a couple of weeks and has reached her goal weight: 115 lb., at 5′4″—exactly what she should weigh, according to her doctor's chart. But in her eyes she still looks dumpy. She can't shake her mind free of the "Lady Marmelade" video from Moulin Rouge. Christina Aguilera, Pink, L'il Kim, and Mya, each one perfect in her own way: every curve smooth and sleek, lean-sexy, nothing to spare. Self-hatred and shame start to burn in the girl, and envy tears at her stomach, enough to make her sick. She'll never look like them, no matter how much weight she loses. Look at that stomach of hers, see how it sticks out? Those thighs—they actually jiggle. Her butt is monstrous. She's fat, gross, a dough girl. 1

As you read the imaginary scenario above, whom did you picture standing in front of the mirror? If your images of girls with eating and body image problems have been shaped by *People* magazine and Lifetime movies, she's probably white, North American, and economically secure. A child whose parents have never had to worry about putting food on the family table. A girl with money to spare for 2 fashion magazines and trendy clothing, probably college-bound. If you're familiar with the classic psychological literature on eating disorders, you may also have read that she's an extreme "perfectionist" with a hyper-demanding mother, and that she suffers from "body-image distortion syndrome" and other severe perceptual and cognitive problems that "normal" girls don't share. You probably don't picture her as Black, Asian, or Latina.

3   Read the description again, but this time imagine twenty-something Tenisha Williamson standing in front of the mirror. Tenisha is black, suffers from anorexia, and feels like a traitor to her race. "From an African-American standpoint," she writes, "we as a people are encouraged to embrace our big, voluptuous bodies. This makes me feel terrible because I don't want a big, voluptuous body! I don't ever want to be fat—ever, and I don't ever want to gain weight. I would rather die from starvation than gain a single pound."[1] Tenisha is no longer an anomaly. Eating and body image problems are now not only crossing racial and class lines, but gender lines. They have also become a global phenomenon.

4   Fiji is a striking example. Because of their remote location, the Fiji islands did not have access to television until 1995, when a single station was introduced. It broadcasts programs from the United States, Great Britain, and Australia. Until that time, Fiji had no reported cases of eating disorders, and a study conducted by anthropologist Anne Becker showed that most Fijian girls and women, no matter how large, were comfortable with their bodies. In 1998, just three years after the station began broadcasting, 11 percent of girls reported vomiting to control weight, and 62 percent of the girls surveyed reported dieting during the previous months.[2]

5   Becker was surprised by the change; she had thought that Fijian cultural traditions, which celebrate eating and favor voluptuous bodies, would "withstand" the influence of media images. Becker hadn't yet understood that we live in an empire of images, and that there are no protective borders.

6   In Central Africa, for example, traditional cultures still celebrate voluptuous women. In some regions, brides are sent to fattening farms, to be plumped and massaged into shape for their wedding night. In a country plagued by AIDS, the skinny body has meant—as it used to among Italian, Jewish, and Black Americans— poverty, sickness, death. "An African girl must have hips," says dress designer Frank Osodi, "We have hips. We have bums. We like flesh in Africa." For years, Nigeria sent its local version of beautiful to the Miss World Competition. The contestants did very poorly. Then a savvy entrepreneur went against local ideals and entered Agbani Darego, a light-skinned, hyper-skinny beauty. (He got his inspiration from M-Net, the South African network seen across Africa on satellite television, which broadcasts mostly American movies and television shows.) Agbani Darego won the Miss World Pageant, the first Black African to do so. Now, Nigerian teenagers fast and exercise, trying to become "lepa"—a popular slang phrase for the thin "it" girls that are all the rage. Said one: "People have realized that slim is beautiful."[3]

---

[1]From the Colours of Ana website (http://coloursofana.com//ss8.asp).
[2]Reported in Nancy Snyderman, *The Girl in the Mirror* (New York: Hyperion, 2002), p. 84.
[3]Norimistsu Onishi, "Globalization of Beauty Makes Slimness Trendy," *The New York Times,* Oct. 3, 2002.

How can mere images be so powerful? For one thing, they are never "just   7
pictures," as the fashion magazines continually maintain (disingenuously) in their
own defense. They speak to young people not just about how to be beautiful but also
about how to become what the dominant culture admires, values, rewards. They tell
them how to be cool, "get it together," overcome their shame. To girls who have
been abused they may offer a fantasy of control and invulnerability, immunity from
pain and hurt. For racial and ethnic groups whose bodies have been deemed
"foreign," earthy, and primitive, and considered unattractive by Anglo-Saxon norms,
they may cast the lure of being accepted as "normal" by the dominant culture.

In today's world, it is through images—much more than parents, teachers, or   8
clergy—that we are taught how to be. And it is images, too, that teach us how to see,
that educate our vision in what's a defect and what is normal, that give us the models
against which our own bodies and the bodies of others are measured. Perceptual
pedagogy: "How to Interpret Your Body 101." It's become a global requirement.

I was intrigued, for example, when my articles on eating disorders began to be   9
translated, over the past few years, into Japanese and Chinese. Among the members
of audiences at my talks, Asian women had been among the most insistent that
eating and body image weren't problems for their people, and indeed, my initial
research showed that eating disorders were virtually unknown in Asia. But when,
this year, a Korean translation of *Unbearable Weight* was published, I felt I needed to
revisit the situation. I discovered multiple reports on dramatic increases in eating
disorders in China, South Korea, and Japan. "As many Asian countries become
Westernized and infused with the Western aesthetic of a tall, thin, lean body, a virtual
tsunami of eating disorders has swamped Asian countries," writes Eunice Park in
Asian Week magazine. Older people can still remember when it was very different. In
China, for example, where revolutionary ideals once condemned any focus on
appearance and there have been several disastrous famines, "little fatty" was a term
of endearment for children. Now, with fast food on every corner, childhood obesity
is on the rise, and the cultural meaning of fat and thin has changed. "When I was
young," says Li Xiaojing, who manages a fitness center in Beijing, "people admired
and were even jealous of fat people since they thought they had a better life. . . . But
now, most of us see a fat person and think 'He looks awful.' "[4]

Clearly, body insecurity can be exported, imported, and marketed—just like   10
any other profitable commodity. In this respect, what's happened with men and
boys is illustrative. Ten years ago men tended, if anything, to see themselves as
better looking than they (perhaps) actually were. And then (as I chronicle in detail in my book *The Male Body*) the menswear manufacturers, the diet industries,
and the plastic surgeons "discovered" the male body. And now, young guys are
looking in their mirrors, finding themselves soft and ill defined, no matter how
muscular they are. Now they are developing the eating and body image disorders that we once thought only girls had. Now they are abusing steroids, measuring their own muscularity against the oiled and perfected images of professional

[4]Reported in Elizabeth Rosenthal, "Beijing Journal: China's Chic Waistline: Convex to Concave,"
The New York Times, Dec. 9, 1999.

athletes, body-builders, and *Men's Health* models. Now the industries in body-enhancement—cosmetic surgeons, manufacturers of anti-aging creams, spas and salons—are making huge bucks off men, too.

11   What is to be done? I have no easy answers. But I do know that we need to acknowledge, finally and decisively, that we are dealing here with a cultural problem. If eating disorders were biochemical, as some claim, how can we account for their gradual "spread" across race, gender, and nationality? And with mass media culture increasingly providing the dominant "public education" in our children's lives—and those of children around the globe—how can we blame families? Families matter, of course, and so do racial and ethnic traditions. But families exist in cultural time and space—and so do racial groups. In the empire of images, no one lives in a bubble of self-generated "dysfunction" or permanent immunity. The sooner we recognize that—and start paying attention to the culture around us and what it is teaching our children—the sooner we can begin developing some strategies for change.

COMPREHENSION

1. How does Bordo define the "body-image distortion syndrome" (paragraph 2)?
2. Why have body image and weight problems become a global phenomenon? What is the main cause of this phenomenon?
3. How, according to the author, should we deal with the globalization of eating disorders?

RHETORIC

1. How does the author establish herself as an authority on her subject? Do you think that she succeeds? Why or why not?
2. What is the writer's claim? Where does she place it, and why?
3. Bordo begins with an imaginary situation. Does this strategy enhance or detract from the validity of her argument? Justify your response.
4. The writer uses several rhetorical strategies to advance her argument. Identify places where she employs description, illustration, comparison and contrast, and causal analysis.
5. The writer has been praised for her readable or accessible style. Do you think that this essay is well written and thought provoking? Explain.
6. How does Bordo develop this selection as a problem-solution essay? Where does the solution appear, and how effective is its placement within the essay?

WRITING

1. Write a causal essay analyzing young Americans' fascination with body image and the consequences of this preoccupation.
2. Why are women in the United States and around the world more susceptible to eating disorders than men? Answer this question in an analytical essay.
3. **Writing an Argument:** Write an essay titled "Body Images, Eating Disorders, and Cultural Imperialism." In this essay, argue for or against the proposition that American media are exporting potentially unhealthy images of the human body.

NETWORKING
Applying Digital and Multimedia Literacies

Critiquing a Web Site about Eating Disorders: Choose one of the following Web sites and write a careful critique of both its purpose and its effectiveness at achieving that purpose.

   Depending on the site you choose and your opinions, your critique might be favorable, mixed, or denunciatory. Whatever your position, it should be carefully illustrated with examples from the Web site, and your points of agreement or contention should be supported by other sources.

- Eating Disorder Research Center
- Women's Health
- Remuda Ranch
- Face the Issue
- Something Fishy
- Family Doctor
- Healthy Place
- ProAnaBlog
- National Eating Disorders Association

Synthesis: Connections for Critical Thinking

1. Research the current status of public health in the United States and what is being done to prevent major outbreaks of disease. Refer to at least three essays in this chapter to support your findings and thesis.
2. Compare approaches to women's health issues as discussed by several writers in this chapter, notably Gawande, Mendoza, and Bordo.
3. Compare and contrast the strategies that Gawande, Hitchens, and Bordo use to develop their arguments.
4. Referring to any three essays in this chapter, analyze some of the major moral, ethical, and religious issues raised by current medical research.
5. Compare and contrast the treatment of death in the essays by Tuchman, Lepore, and Selzer.
6. Compare and contrast the essays by Gawande and Bordo.
7. Research the subject of AIDS, and connect your findings to the essays by Tuchman and Gould.
8. Working with three other class members, develop a PowerPoint presentation informing your college about a health issue of campus concern.

NETWORKING
Applying Digital and Multimedia Literacies

1. Compare and contrast two Web sites devoted to some aspect of medicine and health—for example, stem-cell research, abortion, funeral practices, cosmetic surgery, or dieting.
2. Explore the World Health Organization Web site (*www.who.int/en*), and summarize what you find about global pandemics.

chapter 13

Nature and the Environment

How Do We Relate to the Natural World?

We are at a point in the history of civilization where consciousness of our fragile relationship with nature and the environment is high. Even as you spend an hour reading a few of the essays in this chapter, it is estimated that we are losing 3,000 acres of rain forest around the world and four species of plants or animals. From pollution, to the population explosion, to the depletion of the ozone layer, to global climate change, we seem to be confronted with ecological catastrophe. Nevertheless, as Rachel Carson reminds us, we have "an obligation to endure," to survive potential natural catastrophes by understanding and managing our relationship with the natural world.

Ecology, or the study of nature and the environment, as many of the essayists in this chapter attest, involves us in the conservation of the earth. It moves us to suppress our rapacious destruction of the planet. Clearly, the biological stability of the planet is increasingly precarious. More plants, insects, birds, and animals became extinct in the 20th century than in any era since the Cretaceous catastrophe more than 65 million years ago that led to the extinction of the dinosaurs. Within this ecological context, writers like Carson become our literary conscience, reminding us of how easily natural processes can break down unless we insist on a degree of ecological economy.

Of course, any modification of human behavior in an effort to conserve nature is a complex matter. To save the spotted owl in the Pacific Northwest, we must sacrifice the jobs of people in the timber industry. To reduce pollution, we must forsake gas and oil for alternate energy sources that are costly to develop. To reduce the waste stream, we must shift from a consumption to a conservation ethos. The ecological debate is complicated, but it is clear that the preservation of the myriad life cycles on earth is crucial, for we, too, could become an endangered species.

The language of nature is as enigmatic as the sounds of dolphins and whales communicating with their respective species. Writers like Barry Lopez and Rachel Carson and the vision expressed in the letter of Chief Seattle help us decipher the language of our environment. These writers encourage us to converse with nature, learn from it, and even revere it. All of us are guests on this planet; the natural world is our host. If we do not protect the earth, how can we guarantee the survival of civilization?

PREVIEWING THE CHAPTER

As you read the essays in this chapter and respond to them in discussion and writing, consider the following questions:

- According to the author, what should our relationship to the natural world be?
- What claims or arguments does the author make about the importance of nature? Do you agree or disagree with these claims and arguments?
- What specific ecological problem does the author investigate?
- How does the author think that nature influences human behavior?
- What cultural factors are involved in our approach to the environment?
- Is the writer optimistic, pessimistic, or neutral in the assessment of our ability to conserve nature?
- Do you find that the author is too idealistic or sentimental in the depiction of nature? Why?
- Based on the author's essay, how does he or she qualify as a nature writer?
- How have you been challenged or changed by the essays in this chapter?

Classic and Contemporary Images
ARE WE DESTROYING OUR NATURAL WORLD?

Using a Critical Perspective Imagine yourself to be part of each of the scenes depicted in these two illustrations. How do you feel, and why? Now examine the purpose of each image. What details do the artists emphasize to convey their feelings about our relationship to the natural world? What images does each artist create to capture your attention and direct your viewing and thinking toward a specific, dominant impression?

The painters of the Hudson River School such as John Frederick Kensett
(1816–1872) celebrated American landscapes in their art, painting
breathtaking scenes in meticulous detail. In *Along the Hudson* (1852),
the beauty of the river is unspoiled.

Vehicles travel on the 405 Freeway where it intersects with the 10 West Freeway in Los Angeles. California could take the lead in the international effort to reduce global warming after the state's Air Resources Board gave approval to a package of regulations that would cut vehicle emissions by as much as 25 percent.

Classic and Contemporary Essays
DO WE OWN NATURE?

The simple yet passionate reflections of Chief Seattle regarding the destruction of a world-view are complemented by the more scholarly and learned meditations, nearly a century and a half later, of the esteemed naturalist and writer Barry Lopez. Chief Seattle mourns the death of a way of life, a way of thinking, and a way of being as he accepts that the cultural world of his people is doomed to disappear with the encroachment of "civilization." The white man exploits nature, uses nature, and perhaps most radically of all, perceives himself as apart from nature. This is in profound contrast to the ways of Chief Seattle's people, who saw themselves as in harmony with nature or, more specifically, as inseparable from it—as inseparable perhaps as from a part of their own bodies. Chief Seattle's address is simple. And so perhaps is his message, although one should not confuse simplicity with lack of profundity. Barry Lopez has a similar message. Writing from the perspective of a 21st-century naturalist and teacher, Lopez speaks of "a sense of responsibility toward children." He urges adults to both teach and learn from children about the wonders of nature and how the natural world can inform us about our human condition. With a personal touch, Lopez recounts key encounters with children and nature, finding evidence of that union with nature that Chief Seattle spoke of so eloquently. Although Chief Seattle and Barry Lopez speak in different levels of discourse and from different perspectives, they share an awe of nature and a desire to inform their respective audiences of the sacredness of all life.

Letter to President Pierce, 1855

Chief Seattle

Chief Seattle *(1786–1866) was the leader of the Dewamish and other Pacific Northwest tribes. The city of Seattle, Washington, bears his name. In 1854, Chief Seattle reluctantly agreed to sell tribal lands to the U.S. government and move to the government-established reservations. The authenticity of the following speech has been challenged by many scholars. However, most specialists agree that it contains the substance and perspective of Chief Seattle's attitude toward nature and the white race.*

1 We know that the white man does not understand our ways. One portion of the land is the same to him as the next, for he is a stranger who comes in the night and takes from the land whatever he needs. The earth is not his brother, but his enemy, and

when he has conquered it, he moves on. He leaves his fathers' graves, and his children's birthright is forgotten. The sight of your cities pains the eyes of the red man. But perhaps it is because the red man is a savage and does not understand.

There is no quiet place in the white man's cities. No place to hear the leaves 2 of spring or the rustle of insect's wings. But perhaps because I am a savage and do not understand, the clatter only seems to insult the ears. The Indian prefers the soft sound of the wind darting over the face of the pond, the smell of the wind itself cleansed by a mid-day rain, or scented with the piñon pine. The air is precious to the red man. For all things share the same breath—the beasts, the trees, the man. Like a man dying for many days, he is numb to the stench.

What is man without the beasts? If all the beasts were gone, men would die from 3 great loneliness of spirit, for whatever happens to the beasts also happens to man. All things are connected. Whatever befalls the earth befalls the sons of the earth.

It matters little where we pass the rest of our days; they are not many. A few 4 more hours, a few more winters, and none of the children of the great tribes that once lived on this earth, or that roamed in small bands in the woods, will be left to mourn the graves of a people once as powerful and hopeful as yours.

The whites, too, shall pass—perhaps sooner than other tribes. Continue to 5 contaminate your bed, and you will one night suffocate in your own waste. When the buffalo are all slaughtered, the wild horses all tamed, the secret corners of the forest heavy with the scent of many men, and the view of the ripe hills blotted by talking wires, where is the thicket? Gone. Where is the eagle? Gone. And what is it to say goodbye to the swift and the hunt, the end of living and the beginning of survival? We might understand if we knew what it was that the white man dreams, what he describes to his children on the long winter nights, what visions he burns into their minds, so they will wish for tomorrow. But we are savages. The white man's dreams are hidden from us.

COMPREHENSION

1. What does Chief Seattle suggest is the major difference between the white man's relationship with nature and that of the red man?
2. Chief Seattle claims that perhaps the red man would understand the white man better if he understood better the "dreams" and "visions" of the white man. What does Chief Seattle suggest by these terms?
3. Chief Seattle refers to Native Americans as "savages." Why?

RHETORIC

1. The author uses a number of sensory details in describing both nature and the white man's crimes against nature. How does the eliciting of sensations help determine the relationship between writer, text, and reader?
2. The letter is written simply, with simply constructed paragraphs and sentences. What does this style suggest about the writer's voice?

3. There is a noted absence of transitional expressions in the writing, that is, such linking words as *in addition, furthermore, nevertheless,* and *moreover.* How does this absence contribute to the directness of the writing?

4. The author uses the convention of the series, as in the following examples: "For all things share the same breath—the beasts, the trees, the man" (paragraph 2) and "When the buffalo are all slaughtered, the wild horses all tamed, the secret corners of the forest heavy with the scent of many men, and the view of the ripe hills blotted by talking wires" (paragraph 5). What is the rhetorical effect of this device?

5. Note the opening and closing sentences of the letter. How do they frame the letter? What do they suggest about one of its major themes?

6. Some scholars dispute the authenticity of the letter, attributing it to a white man who was attempting to articulate the essence of Chief Seattle's oratory in an effort to champion Native American causes. What elements of the letter resemble the rhetorical elements of a speech?

WRITING

1. Write a 250-word summary in which you compare and contrast the major differences between the white man's and the red man's perception of and relationship to nature as conceived by Chief Seattle.

2. For a research project, trace the use of the word *savage* as it has been used to describe Native Americans.

3. **Writing an Argument:** Argue for or against the view that the charge by Chief Seattle that the white man is contemptuous of nature is still valid today. Use at least three points to support your thesis.

NETWORKING
Applying Digital and Multimedia Literacies

Writing a Radio PSA: Public service announcements, or PSAs, which you've likely heard on your campus radio station or NPR, are advertisements designed to raise awareness about issues, not sell products or services. Draft a PSA that informs or educates the public about an environmental issue.

Children in the Woods

Barry Lopez

Barry Lopez *(b. 1945) was born in New York City but grew up in southern California's San Fernando Valley, which at the time was still largely rural. He attended the University of Notre Dame (BA, 1966) and the University of Oregon (MA, 1968),* *and he pursued additional graduate work before starting a career as a full-time writer. Lopez's early essays in such periodicals as* National Geographic, Wilderness, Science, *and* Harper's *established him as an authoritative voice in the environmental movement. His first major nonfiction work,* Of Wolves and Men *(1978), brought him national acclaim, an American Book Award nomination, and the John Burroughs medal for nature writing. His venture into fiction with* River Notes: The Dance of Herons *(1979) and* Winter Count *(1980) were also well received. Among Lopez's other books are* Arctic Dreams: Imagination and Desire in a Northern Landscape *(1986),* Crossing Open Ground *(1988),* The Rediscovery of North America *(1991),* Crow and Weasel *(1999), the autobiography* About This Life *(1999), and a short-story collection,* Resistance *(2004). Lopez sees himself as a storyteller, someone who has the responsibility to create an atmosphere in which the wisdom of the work can reveal itself and, as he has written, "make the reader feel part of something." In this essay from his collection* Crossing Open Ground, *Lopez sets himself and other children in the natural world in order to discover their own part of something.*

When I was a child growing up in the San Fernando Valley in California, a trip into 1 Los Angeles was special. The sensation of movement from a rural area into an urban one was sharp. On one of these charged occasions, walking down a sidewalk with my mother, I stopped suddenly, caught by a pattern of sunlight trapped in a spiraling imperfection in a windowpane. A stranger, an elderly woman in a cloth coat and a dark hat, spoke out spontaneously, saying how remarkable it is that children notice these things.

I have never forgotten the texture of this incident. Whenever I recall it I am 2 moved not so much by any sense of my young self but by a sense of responsibility toward children, knowing how acutely I was affected in that moment by that woman's words. The effect, for all I know, has lasted a lifetime.

Now, years later, I live in a rain forest in western Oregon, on the banks of a 3 mountain river in relatively undisturbed country, surrounded by 150-foot-tall Douglas firs, delicate deer-head orchids, and clearings where wild berries grow. White-footed mice and mule deer, mink and coyote move through here. My wife and I do not have children, but children we know, or children whose parents we are close to, are often here. They always want to go into the woods. And I wonder what to tell them.

In the beginning, years ago, I think I said too much. I spoke with an encyclo- 4 pedic knowledge of the names of plants or the names of birds passing through in season. Gradually I came to say less. After a while the only words I spoke, beyond answering a question or calling attention quickly to the slight difference between a sprig of red cedar and a sprig of incense cedar, were to elucidate single objects.

I remember once finding a fragment of a raccoon's jaw in an alder thicket. I 5 sat down alongside the two children with me and encouraged them to find out who this was—with only the three teeth still intact in a piece of the animal's maxilla to guide them. The teeth told by their shape and placement what this animal ate. By a kind of visual extrapolation its size became clear. There were other clues, immediately present, which told, with what I could add of climate and terrain, how this animal lived, how its broken jaw came to be lying here. Raccoon, they surmised. And tiny tooth marks along the bone's broken edge told of a mouse's hunger for calcium.

6   We set the jaw back and went on.

7   If I had known more about raccoons, finer points of osteology, we might have guessed more: say, whether it was male or female. But what we deduced was all we needed. Hours later, the maxilla, lost behind us in the detritus of the forest floor, continued to effervesce. It was tied faintly to all else we spoke of that afternoon.

8   In speaking with children who might one day take a permanent interest in natural history—as writers, as scientists, as filmmakers, as anthropologists—I have sensed that an extrapolation from a single fragment of the whole is the most invigorating experience I can share with them. I think children know that nearly anyone can learn the names of things; the impression made on them at this level is fleeting. What takes a lifetime to learn, they comprehend, is the existence and substance of myriad relationships: It is these relationships, not the things themselves, that ultimately hold the human imagination.

9   The brightest children, it has often struck me, are fascinated by metaphor—with what is shown in the set of relationships bearing on the raccoon, for example, to lie quite beyond the raccoon. In the end, you are trying to make clear to them that everything found at the edge of one's senses—the high note of the winter wren, the thick perfume of propolis that drifts downwind from spring willows, the brightness of wood chips scattered by beaver—that all this fits together. The indestructibility of these associations conveys a sense of permanence that nurtures the heart, that cripples one of the most insidious of human anxieties, the one that says, you do not belong here, you are unnecessary.

10   Whenever I walk with a child, I think how much I have seen disappear in my own life. What will there be for this person when he is my age? If he senses something ineffable in the landscape, will I know enough to encourage it?—to somehow show him that, yes, when people talk about violent death, spiritual exhilaration, compassion, futility, final causes, they are drawing on forty thousand years of human meditation on *this*—as we embrace Douglas firs, or stand by a river across whose undulating back we skip stones, or dig out a camas bulb, biting down into a taste so much wilder than last night's potatoes.

11   The most moving look I ever saw from a child in the woods was on a mud bar by the footprints of a heron. We were on our knees, making handprints beside the footprints. You could feel the creek vibrating in the silt and sand. The sun beat down heavily on our hair. Our shoes were soaking wet. The look said: I did not know until now that I needed someone much older to confirm this, the feeling I have of life here. I can now grow older, knowing it need never be lost.

12   The quickest door to open in the woods for a child is the one that leads to the smallest room, by knowing the name each thing is called. The door that leads to the cathedral is marked by a hesitancy to speak at all, rather to encourage by example a sharpness of the senses. If one speaks it should only be to say, as well as one can, how wonderfully all this fits together, to indicate what a long, fierce peace can derive from this knowledge.

COMPREHENSION

1. What is Lopez's primary purpose in this essay? How does the title relate to the purpose?
2. Does Lopez assume his audience has the same value position as he does? Why or why not?
3. What, ultimately, does Lopez want children to learn about the natural world? How does he teach them?

RHETORIC

1. Does Lopez state his thesis or imply it? Justify your response.
2. Why does Lopez use a personal tone or voice at the start of this essay? How does his opening paragraph connect to the body of the essay?
3. Cite instances where Lopez moves from vivid description to response and reflection.
4. Where does Lopez employ the comparative method, and toward what objective?
5. What extended metaphor does Lopez establish in the final paragraph? Is this an appropriate and effective metaphor to end the essay? Why or why not?

WRITING

1. Write a narrative and descriptive essay in which you recount a childhood experience that taught you something about the natural world.
2. How would you speak to children if you were taking them on a nature walk? Write a reflective essay addressing this question.
3. **Writing an Argument:** Argue for or against the proposition that you can learn profound truths about yourself and the world by immersing yourself in nature.

NETWORKING
Applying Digital and Multimedia Literacies

Promoting the Natural World from the Virtual One: Create a blog or the home page of a Web site, the purpose of which is to get visitors excited about a natural space—a nearby national park, a reservoir, the Everglades—or an environmental issue—an endangered species, the effects of global climate change, ways to be more "green" around campus, and so on. Think of creative ways to use text, visuals, videos, sound, and even music to appeal to your readers.

Synthesis: Classic and Contemporary Questions for Comparison

1. Chief Seattle and Barry Lopez ponder the destruction of nature as a physical and spiritual presence. In what ways are their stakes in this destruction the same? In what ways are they different? Does either writer have the power to effect a transformation in our attitude toward nature? Explain.

2. It has often been said that intellectual knowledge changes one's relationship with the world environment. In what ways has Lopez's "book learning" and erudition made him a different person from Chief Seattle? Base your response on the style and tone of each author.

3. Chief Seattle is literally the leader and spokesperson of a defeated nation. How does he preserve his dignity in the face of being conquered? How does he indicate to the white man that his "victory" is temporary? Lopez, on the other hand, is a successful member of his society: esteemed naturalist, award-winning writer, popular lecturer. What is his relationship to society and to America? Explain by referring to the text.

Why I Hunt

Rick Bass

Rick Bass (b. 1958) was born in Fort Worth, Texas, and grew up in the Texas hill country where his grandfather taught him how to hunt. His collection of essays, The Deer Pasture *(1985), recounts his Texas years, the ethos of hunting, and the allure of the outdoors. Bass studied at Utah State University (BS, 1979) and worked as an oil and gas geologist in Mississippi for eight years. His time working in the oil fields of the deep South is documented in* Oil Notes *(1979). Bass has written more than a dozen works of nonfiction and fiction, many of them reflecting environmental issues and people's search for balance in the natural world. An environmental advocate and land conservationist, Bass lives in the remote Yaak Valley on the Montana– Canada border, a region depicted in books such as* Winter: Notes from Montana *(1991),* Brown Dog of the Yaak: Essays on Art and Activism *(1999), and* The Roadless Yaak: Reflections and Observations about One of Our Last Great Wild Places *(2002). His most recent book of fiction is* Why I Came West *(2008). Bass wrote this vivid and provocative essay on the allure of the hunt for* Sierra *magazine in 2001.*

1   I was a hunter before I came far up into northwest Montana, but not to the degree I am now. It astounds me sometimes to step back particularly at the end of autumn, the end of the hunting season, and take both mental and physical inventory of all that was hunted and all that was gathered from this life in the mountains. The woodshed groaning tight, full of firewood. The fruits and herbs and vegetables from the garden, canned or dried or frozen; the wild mushrooms, huckleberries, thimbleberries, and strawberries. And most precious of all, the flesh of the wild things that share with us these mountains and the plains to the east—the elk, the whitetail and mule deer; the ducks and geese, grouse and pheasant and Hungarian partridge and dove and chukar and wild turkey; the trout and whitefish. Each year the cumulative bounty seems unbelievable. What heaven is this into which we've fallen?

How my wife and I got to this valley—the Yaak—15 years ago is a mystery, a ₂ move that I've only recently come to accept as having been inevitable. We got in the truck one day feeling strangely restless in Mississippi, and we drove. What did I know? Only that I missed the West's terrain of space. Young and healthy, and not coincidentally new-in-love, we hit that huge and rugged landscape in full stride. We drove north until we ran out of country—until the road ended, and we reached Canada's thick blue woods—and then we turned west and traveled until we ran almost out of mountains: the backside of the Rockies, to the wet, west-slope rainforest.

We came over a little mountain pass—it was August and winter was already ₃ fast approaching—and looked down on the soft hills, the dense purples of the spruce and fir forests, the ivory crests of the ice-capped peaks, and the slender ribbons of gray thread rising from the chimneys of the few cabins nudged close to the winding river below, and we fell in love with the Yaak Valley and the hard-logged Kootenai National Forest—the way people in movies fall with each other, star and starlet, as if a trap door has been pulled out from beneath them: tumbling through the air, arms windmilling furiously, and suddenly no other world but each other, no other world but this one and eyes for no one, or no place, else.

Right from the beginning, I could see that there was extraordinary bounty in ₄ this low-elevation forest, resting as it does in a magical seam between the Pacific Northwest and the northern Rockies. Some landscapes these days have been reduced to nothing but dandelions and fire ants, knapweed and thistle, where the only remaining wildlife are sparrows, squirrels, and starlings. In the blessed Yaak, however, not a single mammal has gone extinct since the end of the Ice Age. This forest sustains more types of hunters—carnivores—than any valley in North America. It is a predator's showcase, home not just to wolves and grizzlies, but wolverines, lynx, bobcat, marten, fisher, black bear, mountain lion, golden eagle, bald eagle, coyote, fox, weasel. In the Yaak, everything is in motion, either seeking its quarry, or seeking to avoid becoming quarry.

The people who have chosen to live in this remote valley—few phones, very ₅ little electricity, and long, dark winters—possess a hardness and a dreaminess both. They—we—can live a life of deprivation, and yet are willing to enter the comfort of daydreams and imagination. There is something mysterious happening here between the landscape and the people, a thing that stimulates our imagination, and causes many of us to set off deep into the woods in search of the unknown, and sustenance—not just metaphorical or spiritual sustenance, but the real thing.

Only about 5 percent of the nation and 15 to 20 percent of Montanans are ₆ hunters. But in this one valley, almost everyone is a hunter. It is not the peer pressure of the local culture that recruits us into hunting, nor even necessarily the economic boon of a few hundred pounds of meat in a cash-poor society. Rather, it is the terrain itself, and one's gradual integration into it, that summons the hunter. Nearly everyone who has lived here for any length of time has ended up—sometimes almost against one's conscious wishes—becoming a hunter. This wild and powerful landscape sculpts us like clay. I don't find such sculpting

an affront to the human spirit, but instead, wonderful testimony to our pliability, our ability to adapt to a place.

7   I myself love to hunt the deer, the elk, and the grouse—to follow them into the mouth of the forest, to disappear in their pursuit—to get lost following their snowy tracks up one mountain and down the next. One sets out after one's quarry with senses fully engaged, wildly alert: entranced, nearly hypnotized. The tiniest of factors can possess the largest significance—the crack of a twig, the shift of a breeze, a single stray hair caught on a piece of bark, a fresh-bent blade of grass.

8   Each year during such pursuits, I am struck more and more by the conceit that people in a hunter-gatherer culture might have richer imaginations than those who dwell more fully in an agricultural or even post-agricultural environment. What else is the hunt but a stirring of the imagination, with the quarry, or goal, or treasure lying just around the corner or over the next rise? A hunter's imagination has no choice but to become deeply engaged, for it is never the hunter who is in control, but always the hunted, in that the prey directs the predator's movements.

9   The hunted shapes the hunter; the pursuit and evasion of predator and prey are but shadows of the same desire. The thrush wants to remain a thrush. The goshawk wants to consume the thrush and in doing so, partly become the thrush—to take its flesh into its flesh. They weave through the tangled branches of the forest, zigging and zagging, the goshawk right on the thrush's tail, like a shadow. Or perhaps it is the thrush that is the shadow thrown by the light of the goshawk's fiery desire.

10   Either way, the escape maneuvers of the thrush help carve and shape and direct the muscles of the goshawk. Even when you are walking through the woods seeing nothing but trees, you can feel the unseen passage of pursuits that might have occurred earlier that morning, precisely where you are standing— pursuits that will doubtless, after you are gone, sweep right back across that same spot again and again.

As does the goshawk, so too do human hunters imagine where their prey might be, or where it might go. They follow tracks hinting at not only distance and direction traveled, but also pace and gait and the general state of mind of the animal that is evading them. They plead to the mountain to deliver to them a deer, an elk. They imagine and hope that they are moving toward their goal of obtaining game. 11

When you plant a row of corn, there is not so much unknown. You can be fairly sure that, if the rains come, the corn is going to sprout. The corn is not seeking to elude you. But when you step into the woods, looking for a deer—well, there's nothing in your mind, or in your blood, or in the world, but imagination. 12

Most Americans neither hunt nor gather nor even grow their own food, nor make, with their own hands, any of their other necessities. In this post-agricultural society, too often we confuse anticipation with imagination. When we wander down the aisle of the supermarket searching for a chunk of frozen chicken, or cruise into Dillard's department store looking for a sweater, we can be fairly confident that grayish wad of chicken or that sweater is going to be there, thanks to the vigor and efficiency of a supply-and-demand marketplace. The imagination never quite hits second gear. Does the imagination atrophy, from such chronic inactivity? I suspect that it does. 13

All I know is that hunting—beyond being a thing I like to do—helps keep my imagination vital. I would hope never to be so blind as to offer it as prescription; I offer it only as testimony to my love of the landscape where I live—a place that is still, against all odds, its own place, quite unlike any other. I don't think I would be able to sustain myself as a dreamer in this strange landscape if I did not take off three months each year to wander the mountains in search of game; to hunt, stretching and exercising not just my imagination, but my spirit. And to wander the mountains, too, in all the other seasons. And to be nourished by the river of spirit that flows, shifting and winding, between me and the land. 14

COMPREHENSION

1. Why did Bass and his wife fall in love with the Yaak Valley? What does this fondness for wild places tell us about his character and interests?
2. Explain the relationship between the people residing in the Yaak Valley and their fondness for hunting.
3. Does Bass apologize for his fondness for hunting? Explain your response.

RHETORIC

1. Bass wrote this essay for the official magazine of the Sierra Club, of which he is an active member. Why would an organization whose goal is the preservation of wilderness and wildlife agree to publish an article expressing love for hunting? How does Bass anticipate objections to his argument?
2. What is Bass's claim and where does he state it? Does he rely on logical, ethical, or emotional appeal—or a combination—to advance his argument, and why?

3. What causal connection does Bass establish between landscape and human behavior? Where does he use comparison and contrast to distinguish this place and its people from other places and other Americans?
4. Cite examples of Bass's descriptive skills. How does description enhance the appeal of the writer's argument?
5. What is the dominant impression that Bass creates of the Yaak Valley region?
6. Evaluate Bass's conclusion. How does it serve as a writer's justification for hunting?

WRITING

1. Select a natural landscape that you know well and, including description as one rhetorical strategy, explain how this site affects the behavior of people and their ethical values.
2. **Writing an Argument:** What is the difference between killing the game that you consume and buying meat in a grocery store or supermarket? Is one act more ethical than the other? Compose an argumentative essay dealing with this issue.

NETWORKING
Applying Digital and Multimedia Literacies

Interpreting an Organization's Web Site: Go online and locate the Web site for the Sierra Club. Summarize the organization's goals, and then evaluate whether Bass's essay conforms to these objectives.

Parkinson's Alley

Joy Horowitz

Joy Horowitz, *a freelance journalist, was born in Cleveland, Ohio. She graduated from Harvard University in 1975 and worked as a copy girl, sports writer, and investigative reporter for the old* Los Angeles Herald-Examiner. *Subsequently she was a feature writer for the* Los Angeles Times *before attending Yale Law School, where she received a master's in Study of Law in 1982. Her writing has appeared in the* New York Times, *the* New Yorker, Los Angeles *magazine, and other national publications. Horowitz is the author of* Tessie and Pearlie: A Granddaughter's Story *(1996) and* Parts Per Million: The Poisoning of Beverly Hills High School *(2007). In this article, published in* Sierra *magazine in 2012, Horowitz investigates the impact of pesticides on some of the residents of California's Central Valley.*

Bruce McDermott tosses me the keys to his pickup, and I hoist his chrome   1
walker into the truck's bed. "You need to see this," he tells me as he angles his
torso and braced leg into the cab, then slams the door.

It's a rainy fall day in the Central Valley town of Visalia, California, and   2
McDermott wants to show me some of the houses of people here who've been
diagnosed with Parkinson's disease, the incurable neurodegenerative affliction
that, coupled with a recent car crash, has left him unable to drive. I've never been
at the wheel of such a behemoth truck before—or one with shotgun shells in the
door well, for that matter—but I know better than to argue. McDermott was once
the city's chief of police; when he makes suggestions, people tend to say, "Yes, sir."

A big, friendly bear of a man who likes to joke that his doctor calls him "fat   3
boy," McDermott wears khaki shorts, sandals, and a crisply pressed polo shirt.
Diagnosed with early-onset Parkinson's, he was forced to retire from the police
force in 1997, at age 46, after he tried to place his right hand on the Bible to swear
in a new officer but his arm shook so uncontrollably that people thought he was
waving hello.

As we near his boyhood home on Border Links Drive, McDermott points to   4
the house next door, where his godfather, a prominent attorney, died three years
ago from complications of Parkinson's. Nearby, he shows me a field where crop
dusters once landed their planes and routinely dumped their tanks. In a half-mile
stretch, McDermott points to four homes where residents have been diagnosed
with the disease.

Some neurologists dub the 300-mile-long string of Central Valley farm towns   5
between Bakersfield and Sacramento "Parkinson's Alley," and recently released
statistics back them up. A study published last year by researchers at the University of California, Los Angeles, found that Central Valley residents under age 60
who lived near fields where the pesticides paraquat and maneb had been used
between 1974 and 1999 had a Parkinson's rate nearly five times higher than other
residents in the region.

I steer McDermott's truck into the driveway of his friend Margaret Haworth,   6
a former tennis player and expert skier. Like McDermott, Haworth suffers from
early-onset Parkinson's; she was diagnosed 16 years ago, at age 49.

Our visit is a surprise, but Haworth welcomes McDermott as if he's family. As   7
he slowly makes his way up her front steps, she says of his walker, "I see you got
a new hot rod."

Haworth tells us her mother was also afflicted by Parkinson's but never spoke   8
of it. McDermott nods; it's a familiar story. "A lot of people in the valley won't tell
you they have Parkinson's disease if they do," he say. "I know doctors who would
lose their license if their insurance carriers knew they had it."

Research into the link between pesticides and Parkinson's in the Central Valley   9
dates back to 2000, when UCLA epidemiologist Beate Ritz began comparing mortality records with pesticide-application reports. She discovered that California
counties reporting the highest pesticide use also had the highest rates for
Parkinson's-related deaths. Examining agricultural records from 1989 to 1994,
Ritz found that when insecticides were applied to more than a third of a county's

acreage, the risk of its residents' dying from Parkinson's disease increased 2.5-fold. She also found studies that revealed that as many as 40 percent of the area's Parkinson's cases are never mentioned on death certificates, possibly because many migrant workers fail to report the disease, or move on before symptoms arise.

10   Ritz and her research team found that Central Valley residents who consumed private well water and lived within 500 feet of farmland with documented long-term pesticide use were almost twice as likely to get Parkinson's disease. Their 2009 report, produced under the auspices of the federally funded Parkinson's Environment and Genes Study, was the first to quantify residents' exposure to such chemicals by comparing land-use maps with state-mandated pesticide-application records. "We're seeing effects not just on people in their homes but also on farms and in workplaces," Ritz told me in Los Angeles before I traveled 200 miles north to meet with McDermott.

11   Visalia, a 160-year-old gold rush town, has grown by more than a third to about 120,000 people in the past decade. It's in the heart of the Central Valley—the vast farm belt west of the Sierra Nevada where about 7 percent of the nation's crops are grown, producing $20 billion in annual revenues. Growers here use about 115 million pounds of pesticides every year.

12   Some of those pesticides are finding their way into residential water supplies in accumulations that surpass government safety standards, according to a number of studies—including tests of private-well samples gathered exclusively for this article. More than 1 million people in the region have tap water that isn't safe to drink because of nitrate contamination from manure, fertilizers, and leaking septic tanks, according to a collaborative report by the Pacific Institute, Visalia's Community Water Center, the Clean Water Fund, and California Rural Legal Assistance Foundation. Most of those residents are from low-income and Spanish-speaking households.

13   More than half of Central Valley communities rely on water stored underground for their drinking supply, the Community Water Center reports. Recent groundwater sampling found that the water in 75 percent of the private domestic wells in Tulare County, of which Visalia is the seat, contains unsafe levels of nitrates.

14   "We pay twice for water each month," says Susana DeAnda, the center's co-executive director. "Once for contaminated well water and once for bottled water."

15   Nitrates can also be a sign of pesticide contamination, but testing for pesticides in drinking water is expensive and not mandated. Some testing is done, however, and last year the State Water Resources Control Board released the results of a domestic-well-water survey in Tulare County; pesticides turned up in 13 of 19 wells sampled.

16   By the time I park McDermott's truck in his driveway, the rain has stopped. Gripping his walker, he shuffles back inside his home. The walk leaves him breathless. A lifelong Republican who favors Fox News, McDermott says he had long assumed that, in America, if something was wrong, it would be fixed. Now he's not so sure.

17   "It's an ugly thing when you look at it and think maybe something could be done to prevent this," he says. "I'm convinced it's exposure to the environment. Something's going on here."

Currently, no federal or state water quality standards regulate domestic well wa- 18 ter in California, even though private wells are the primary source of drinking water for 1.6 million people in the state and more than 43 million, or 15 percent of the population, nationwide. The federal Safe Drinking Water Act covers public water supplies, but Congress never extended the law to include private wells, which can be more susceptible to contamination because they tend to draw from shallower aquifers and often are close to farms that use pesticides.

The federal Clean Water Act largely exempts normal agricultural activities from 19 regulation. California's Safe Drinking Water Act monitors water coming out of the tap but doesn't regulate the source. Although statutes are in place mandating the state to monitor and regulate agricultural pollution in drinking water, the program has yet to be implemented, according to Community Water Center cofounder Laurel Firestone. In California, the state Department of Pesticide Regulation conducts an annual survey of some domestic wells. Last year, for example, state regulators tested 136 wells and found pesticides in 103 of them. But the agency keeps the location of its testing confidential, citing concerns about terrorism.

"Nobody is testing domestic wells in any systematic way," says Robert J. 20 Gilliom, a hydrologist and the head of pesticide studies for the U.S. Geological Survey's water quality assessment program.

Since Ritz's UCLA research was based on historical data, I wanted to know 21 what pesticides are in the water now. But no one could tell me. So, I ordered some water-testing kits and set out to answer two simple questions: What pesticides are present in Central Valley well water and are any of them implicated for Parkinson's disease? The lab results revealed a potentially harmful mix of herbicides in tap water from 6 of the 10 private wells I tested. (See "Testing for Pesticides," below.)

Of course, not everyone wants to know what's in his or her water. When I 22 arrived at a walnut farm in Visalia to take water samples, I asked the grower— whose hand shook from Parkinson's—what pesticides he used on his property. He said, "Whatever the gestapo lets us use."

"I'm dying to know, but I also am afraid to find out," the widow of a Parkinson's 23 victim told me when I asked if I could test her drinking water. Her husband had worked for a program that advises farmers on how to use pesticides, and the couple had lived on a citrus ranch for more than 40 years. He sometimes came home "up to his elbows in the stuff." She told me I could take water samples on the ranch, but only if I didn't reveal her identity.

Off a country road outside Hanford, about 20 miles west of Visalia, I dropped 24 by the home of Peggy and Jim Greaser to take a water sample from their kitchen sink. Their living room window has a view of the cornfield next door. Both Peggy and Jim, a former Sears technician, complained that the "drift" from crop dusters often burns their eyes and has ruined the paint job on their car.

Jim, now a part-time DJ known as Jim Dee on K6RGZ, suffers from Parkinson's 25 disease. He drives a motorized cart from his front door to a nearby shack that houses his radio studio. Leather straps hang from shelves crammed with tape decks and vinyl records, so he has something to grasp.

26   "You start losing your walking ability," he said. "I've fallen so many times I've lost track."

27 Parkinson's, one of the most intractable of all neurological diseases, afflicts 500,000 to 1.5 million people in the United States. It's caused when nerve cells die in the area of the brain that produces dopamine, a neurotransmitter that's essential to everything from moving muscles to feeling pleasure. As dopamine levels decrease, messages that control motor function are blocked.

28   Although symptoms have been mentioned in texts dating back to biblical times, the disease was officially "discovered" in 1817, when British physician James Parkinson first described the "shaking palsy." But it wasn't until the mid-1980s that scientists stumbled on a link between pesticide exposure and Parkinson's disease, thanks to a bizarre outbreak among heroin addicts and an astute young San Francisco Bay Area neurologist named J. William Langston.

29   Langston, now scientific director at the Parkinson's Institute in Sunnyvale, California, had been asked to examine a cluster of young patients who looked like living statues; they could neither move nor speak and appeared to be in the advanced stages of Parkinson's disease. He learned that all of them had injected a new form of synthetic heroin. Alarmed, he called a press conference to alert the public to his "frozen addicts" and warn of bad drugs on the streets. When he prescribed levodopa, which is used to treat Parkinson's, the addicts, whose faces were so stiffened that they drooled uncontrollably, soon found that their symptoms abated.

30   The illicit drug they'd taken contained a compound known as MPTP, which has a similar chemical structure to that of paraquat—one of the most widely used herbicides in the world. Paraquat is of particular concern to Parkinson's researchers because of its synergistic effect, particularly when used with the fungicide maneb.

31   Taking their cues from Langston's earlier work, Ritz and her team discovered that long-term exposures to paraquat and maneb caused an eight-fold increase in the development of Parkinson's for people under age 60. Paraquat was banned by the European Union in 2007 but is still widely used in the United States; about 75,000 pounds of it are applied annually to alfalfa, grapes, and other crops in Tulare County. The EPA banned maneb for use on corn, grapes, and apples in 2005 but continues to allow its use on almonds, which are abundant in the Central Valley.

32   Another chemical of particular concern to Parkinson's researchers is the fungicide ziram. When the EPA proposed prohibiting ziram use on 35 crops in 2003, a plant pathologist with the U.S. Department of Agriculture insisted that the pesticide had a "clean bill of health" and said workers could protect themselves by wearing "long pants and long sleeves." But cell studies by the UCLA researchers and others have shown that ziram kills certain brain cells whose absence leads to Parkinson's, and the UCLA team found that people exposed to the fungicide for 25 years or longer have a three-times-greater chance of developing the disease.

33   In 2008, California regulators placed ziram on their risk-assessment "priority" list. Four years later, no one's followed up.

"We have no estimated date for the assessment," Lea Brooks, communica- 34 tions director with California's Department of Pesticide Regulation, told me. "Our work schedule is behind due to furloughs, retirements, and a hiring freeze. It's on the priority list for a risk assessment, but there is no timeline."

Once a month for the past 10 years, neurologist Jeff Bronstein has left his hillside 35 home in Los Angeles at four A.M. to drive more than 150 miles north to the Central Valley, where he meets with Parkinson's patients before they take their daily medications, which mask symptoms. As part of the UCLA Parkinson's research team, Bronstein, a professor of neurology and molecular toxicology at the university's David Geffen School of Medicine and director of its Movement Disorders Program, needs to make sure that patients enrolled in the Parkinson's Environment and Genes Study have been correctly diagnosed (since it's easy to mistake other neurological symptoms for those of Parkinson's disease) and to chart their progress.

Over the years, Bronstein has met with farmworkers, corporate executives, 36 police officers, college professors, and, of course, pesticide applicators. Although he lacks irrefutable evidence, he is convinced that pesticides are the culprit behind his patients' affliction.

"It's worth it," he told me of his five- to seven-hour round-trip commutes. 37 During one of them, he spoke to me on his car phone as a crop duster roared overhead. "How many years did it take to prove smoking causes lung cancer? That's where we are with pesticides. The onus is on us to prove this stuff is bad. And what's really goofy is that what's considered an 'acceptable' level is completely arbitrary. They come up with numbers based on acute toxicity. But it's years and years of low-level exposure that matter, not acute toxicity. You need to look at chronic exposure before any meaningful discussion can take place."

In 2007 the U.S. Department of Agriculture partnered with the EPA to begin 38 testing for pesticides at extremely low concentration levels in domestic well water. In 2009, the agencies took samples from 278 domestic, school, and farm wells in 16 states and detected pesticides in 152, or 45 percent, of them. "In the future, we'll see more and more pesticides in groundwater," said hydrologist Terry Councell, who runs the USDA's water monitoring program. "A lot of these pesticides haven't even hit the water table yet."

One morning I meet over coffee with Donna DeVries, former president of the Cen- 39 tral Valley Parkinson's Disease Support Group. DeVries, a 57-year-old dental office manager, tells me she spends the first Friday of every month at the local Methodist church, with the Visalia-based support group, which ranks second in the United States in fundraising. She spent years caring for her father and father-in-law, both of whom died after battling the disease.

"All of our doctors have told us, 'Move. Get out of the valley. It's not a healthy 40 place to be,'" she says. As she speaks, she sits on her right hand to control its shaking. She suspects she has Parkinson's too. "My doctor told me not to worry about it, but how can I not?"

Several dozen people attend the support group's Friday-morning meeting, 41 and the conversation ranges from sharing medication tips to dealing with the inevitable depression that accompanies the disease. "I told my wife, 'Put the guns in the safe,' " says a man in his 40s who has driven several hours to be here.

42   Not everyone is keen on such frank talk, though. Bruce McDermott, for one, swore off the group after he sat through a downer of a discussion about morticians. He likes to think of Visalia as a "roll-up-your-sleeves kind of town" where people who share his disease can live a normal life, and where he and others can change the future for the better by verifying—and publicizing—a link between pesticides and Parkinson's.

43   "If I can help one person," McDermott says, "I feel good."

TESTING FOR PESTICIDES

I don't profess to be a trained water quality researcher, but I wanted to know whether private water wells in California's farm belt are contaminated with pesticides. And since few public records of such tests exist, I decided to do it myself—with the help of a government scientist.

I took water samples from 10 wells, following procedures provided by an EPA-approved laboratory that specializes in analyzing chemicals in the parts-per-trillion range, an exacting and expensive testing process. My source inside the lab, which is connected to a government agency, offered to test the samples as long as I collected them myself and agreed not to identify the lab or the agency.

Using 10 specially equipped boxes, each containing ice packs to refrigerate the water for overnight delivery to the lab, I gathered my samples from garden hoses and kitchen sinks in the Central Valley. The toxicity tests revealed pesticide traces in 6 of 10 samples from private water wells. Five of the wells—in Visalia, Dinuba, and Orosi—contained three or more herbicides. A sample of tap water drawn from an Orosi home contained residues of five weed killers.

Four of the 10 samples came from households where a resident had been diagnosed with Parkinson's disease; 3 of those 4 showed signs of pesticide contamination.

Not surprisingly, half of the samples showed traces of the herbicides bromacil, diuron, and simazine—known groundwater contaminants in the area, according to California's Department of Pesticide Regulation. Despite the widespread presence of these weed killers in groundwater, there are no federal or state drinking water standards for bromacil or diuron in California.

The tests also detected metabolites, or breakdown products, of the weed killer atrazine, which was banned by the European Union in 2003 but is still one of the most widely used herbicides in the United States and one of the nation's most common herbicidal contaminants in groundwater. (Pesticide metabolites form when sunlight, high temperature, or microbial activity breaks down a parent chemical.) Two of the water samples contained atrazine metabolites at levels 20 times higher than what the EPA says is safe for atrazine in drinking water.

Atrazine's metabolites are a reliable sign of atrazine contamination and, according to the EPA, are nearly as toxic as the parent chemical. In 2007, researchers at the Centers for Disease Control and Prevention warned that by failing to include all of its metabolites in exposure assessments, public agencies are systematically underestimating Americans' exposure to atrazine.

COMPREHENSION

1. According to Horowitz, what is the impact of pesticides on people in Visalia, California?
2. Who are the people that Horowitz interviews and profiles? What are they like? What do they share in common? How do they differ in personalities and attitudes?
3. What would Horowitz have us learn from the lives of the people she portrays in her essay?

RHETORIC

1. How does Horowitz design her introductory section? Which rhetorical strategies does she blend in order to create a picture of people and landscape in Visalia and the Central Valley?
2. Horowitz is an investigative reporter. What stylistic and formal attributes of investigative reporting do you find in this essay? Should an investigative reporter be objective or subjective? Explain.
3. What is Horowitz's claim and how does she support it? What appeals to reason, emotion, and ethics does she make and where do they appear?
4. How many sections comprise this essay? What is the focus of each section? How do these sections interrelate and serve to advance the writer's argument?
5. Explain the relevance of the subsection "Testing for Pesticides" to the essay.

WRITING

1. Write a brief personal essay on your feelings about the water supply in your home town. Explain whether or not you drink tap water, and why.
2. Write a comparative essay linking Horowitz's article with the piece by Rachel Carson in this chapter.
3. **Writing an Argument:** Agree or disagree with the proposition that most tap water in the United States does not cause debilitating diseases, that our national water supply is safe.

NETWORKING
Applying Digital and Multimedia Literacies

Researching in a Group: Collaborating with other students, conduct online research into the relatively new method of oil extraction known as "fracking." Summarize the results of your research and offer a conclusion on whether you think that fracking is safe for the environment and especially for an area's water supply. If group members disagree, put forth several supported opinions.

The Environmental Issue from Hell

Bill McKibben

Bill McKibben (b. 1960) was born in Palo Alto, California. After receiving a BA from Harvard University (1982), McKibben became a staff writer for the New Yorker. *McKibben's chief concern is the impact of humans on the environment and the ways in which consumerism affects the global ecosystem. A prominent writer for the environmental movement, he has published several books, among them* The End of Nature *(1989),* The Age of Missing Information *(1992),* Long Distance: A Year of Living Strenuously *(2000),* Enough: Staying Human in an Engineered Age *(2003), and* The Bill McKibben Reader: Pieces from an Active Life *(2009). In the essay that follows, which was published in* These Times *in 2001, McKibben argues for a new approach to global warming.*

1 When global warming first emerged as a potential crisis in the late 1980s, one academic analyst called it "the public policy problem from hell." The years since have only proven him more astute: Fifteen years into our understanding of climate change, we have yet to figure out how we're going to tackle it. And environmentalists are just as clueless as anyone else: Do we need to work on lifestyle or on lobbying, on photovoltaics or on politics? And is there a difference? How well we handle global warming will determine what kind of century we inhabit—and indeed what kind of planet we leave behind. The issue cuts close to home and also floats off easily into the abstract. So far it has been the ultimate "can't get there from here" problem, but the time has come to draw a road map—one that may help us deal with the handful of other issues on the list of real, world-shattering problems.

2 Typically, when you're mounting a campaign, you look for self-interest, you scare people by saying what will happen to us if we don't do something: All the birds will die, the canyon will disappear beneath a reservoir, we will choke to death on smog. But in the case of global warming, that doesn't exactly do the trick, at least in the time frame we're discussing. In temperate latitudes, climate change will creep up on us. Severe storms already have grown more frequent and more damaging. The progression of seasons is less steady. Some agriculture is less reliable. But face it: Our economy is so enormous that it takes those changes in stride. Economists who work on this stuff talk about how it will shave a percentage or two off the GNP over the next few decades. And most of us live lives so divorced from the natural world that we hardly notice the changes anyway. Hotter? Turn up the air-conditioning. Stormier? Well, an enormous percentage of Americans commute from remote-controlled garage to office parking garage—it may have been some time since they got good and wet in a rainstorm. By the time the magnitude of the change is truly in our faces, it will be too late to do much

about it: There's such a lag time to increased levels of carbon dioxide in the atmosphere that we need to be making the switch to solar and wind and hydrogen power right now to prevent disaster decades away. Yesterday, in fact.

So maybe we should think of global warming in a different way—as the great 3 moral crisis of our time, the equivalent of the civil rights movement of the 1960s.

Why a moral question? In the first place, no one's ever figured out a more 4 effective way to screw the marginalized and poor of this planet than climate change. Having taken their dignity, their resources, and their freedom under a variety of other schemes, we now are taking the very physical stability on which their already difficult lives depend.

Our economy can absorb these changes for a while, but consider Bangladesh 5 for a moment. In 1998 the sea level in the Bay of Bengal was higher than normal, just the sort of thing we can expect to become more frequent and severe. The waters sweeping down the Ganges and the Brahmaputra rivers from the Himalayas could not drain easily into the ocean—they backed up across the country, forcing most of its inhabitants to spend three months in thigh-deep water. The fall rice crop didn't get planted. We've seen this same kind of disaster over the past few years in Mozambique and Honduras and Venezuela and other places.

And global warming is a moral crisis, too, if you place any value on the rest of 6 creation. Coral reef researchers indicate that these spectacularly intricate ecosystems are also spectacularly vulnerable. Rising water temperatures are likely to bleach them to extinction by mid-century. In the Arctic, polar bears are 20 percent scrawnier than they were a decade ago: As pack ice melts, so does the opportunity for hunting seals. All in all, the 21st century seems poised to see extinctions at a rate not observed since the last big asteroid slammed into the planet. But this time the asteroid is us.

It's a moral question, finally, if you think we owe any debt to the future. No 7 one ever has figured out a more thoroughgoing way to strip-mine the present and degrade what comes after—all the people who will ever be related to you. Ever. No generation yet to come will ever forget us—we are the ones present at the moment when the temperature starts to spike, and so far we have not reacted. If it had been done to us, we would loathe the generation that did it, precisely as we will one day be loathed.

But trying to launch a moral campaign is no easy task. In most moral crises, 8 there is a villain—some person or class or institution that must be overcome. Once the villain is identified, the battle can commence. But you can't really get angry at carbon dioxide, and the people responsible for its production are, well, us. So perhaps we need some symbols to get us started, some places to sharpen the debate and rally ourselves to action. There are plenty to choose from: our taste for ever bigger houses and the heating and cooling bills that come with them, our penchant for jumping on airplanes at the drop of a hat. But if you wanted one glaring example of our lack of balance, you could do worse than point the finger at sport utility vehicles.

SUVs are more than mere symbols. They are a major part of the problem—we 9 emit so much more carbon dioxide now than we did a decade ago in part because our fleet of cars and trucks actually has gotten steadily less fuel efficient for the past 10 years. If you switched today from the average American car to a big SUV, and drove it for just one year, the difference in carbon dioxide that you produced would be the equivalent of opening your refrigerator door and then forgetting to close it for six years. SUVs essentially are machines for burning fossil fuel that just happen to also move you and your stuff around.

10   But what makes them such a perfect symbol is the brute fact that they are simply unnecessary. Go to the parking lot of the nearest suburban supermarket and look around: The only conclusion you can draw is that to reach the grocery, people must drive through three or four raging rivers and up the side of a canyon. These are semi-military machines, armored trucks on a slight diet. While they do not keep their occupants appreciably safer, they do wreck whatever they plow into, making them the perfect metaphor for a heedless, supersized society.

11   That's why we need a much broader politics than the Washington lobbying that's occupied the big environmental groups for the past decade. We need to take all the brilliant and energetic strategies of local grassroots groups fighting dumps and cleaning up rivers and apply those tactics in the national and international arenas. That's why some pastors are starting to talk with their congregations about what cars to buy, and why some college seniors are passing around petitions pledging to stay away from the Ford Explorers and Excursions, and why some auto dealers have begun to notice informational picketers outside their showrooms on Saturday mornings urging customers to think about gas mileage when they look at cars.

12   The point is not that such actions by themselves—any individual actions—will make any real dent in the levels of carbon dioxide pouring into our atmosphere. Even if you got 10 percent of Americans really committed to changing their energy use, their solar homes wouldn't make much of a difference in our national totals. But 10 percent would be enough to change the politics around the issue, enough to pressure politicians to pass laws that would cause us all to shift our habits. And so we need to begin to take an issue that is now the province of technicians and turn it into a political issue, just as bus boycotts began to make public the issue of race, forcing the system to respond. That response is likely to be ugly—there are huge companies with a lot to lose, and many people so tied in to their current ways of life that advocating change smacks of subversion. But this has to become a political issue—and fast. The only way that may happen, short of a hideous drought or monster flood, is if it becomes a personal issue first.

COMPREHENSION

1. According to McKibben, what are the causes of global warming?
2. What instances of ecological disaster does the writer say will occur if we do not change our habits?
3. Why is a new approach to the problem of global warming needed? What approach does McKibben suggest?

RHETORIC

1. How does McKibben's title capture the tone of the essay? What is his purpose in writing the essay? Does he see his readers as hostile or sympathetic to his position? How do you know?
2. How does McKibben develop his introduction? Why does he pose questions? Where does he state his claim?
3. Does McKibben make his argument through appeals to reason, emotion, ethics—or a combination of these elements? Justify your response.
4. How does the writer contend with possible objections to his position on global warming?
5. Explain the pattern of cause and effect that McKibben uses to structure his essay.
6. What varieties of evidence does the writer present to support his claim? What extended illustration does he provide? How effective is it, and why?
7. In the concluding paragraph, McKibben issues a call to action. How does the body of the essay prepare the reader for this persuasive appeal?

WRITING

1. Write an essay in which you explain your own sense of the causes and effects of global warming.
2. Research your state's policy toward global warming. Present your findings in a summary essay.
3. **Writing an Argument:** McKibben argues that SUVs are a primary cause of wastefulness and global warming and that both moral persuasion and political activism are required to change consumers' habits. Do you agree or disagree with his assertions? Write an argumentative essay responding to this issue.

NETWORKING
Applying Digital and Multimedia Literacies

Delivering an Oral Presentation: Reshape your response to any of the three assignments under Writing to function as an oral presentation; incorporate visual aids (digital or hard copy) and one carefully designed and written handout for your listeners.

The Obligation to Endure

Rachel Carson

Rachel Carson (1907–1964) was a seminal figure in the environmental movement. Born in Pennsylvania, she awakened public consciousness to environmental issues through her writing. Her style was both literary and scientific as she described

nature's riches in such books as The Sea around Us *(1951) and* The Edge of the
Sea *(1954). Her last book,* Silent Spring *(1962), aroused controversy and concern
with its indictment of insecticides. In the following excerpt from that important book,
Carson provides compelling evidence of the damage caused by indiscriminate use of
insecticides and the danger of disturbing the earth's delicate balance.*

1   The history of life on earth has been a history of interaction between living things
and their surroundings. To a large extent, the physical form and the habits of the
earth's vegetation and its animal life have been molded by the environment.
Considering the whole span of earthly time, the opposite effect, in which life actually modifies its surroundings, has been relatively slight. Only within the moment
of time represented by the present century has one species—man—acquired
significant power to alter the nature of his world.

2   During the past quarter century this power has not only increased to one of
disturbing magnitude but it has changed in character. The most alarming of all
man's assaults upon the environment is the contamination of air, earth, rivers, and
sea with dangerous and even lethal materials. This pollution is for the most part
irrecoverable; the chain of evil it initiates not only in the world that must support
life but in living tissues is for the most part irreversible. In this now universal
contamination of the environment, chemicals are the sinister and little-recognized
partners of radiation in changing the very nature of the world—the very nature of
its life. Strontium 90, released through nuclear explosions into the air, comes to
earth in rain or drifts down as fallout, lodges in soil, enters into the grass or corn
or wheat grown there, and in time takes up its abode in the bones of a human
being, there to remain until his death. Similarly, chemicals sprayed on croplands
or forests or gardens lie long in soil, entering into living organisms, passing from
one to another in a chain of poisoning and death. Or they pass mysteriously by
underground streams until they emerge and, through the alchemy of air and
sunlight, combine into new forms that kill vegetation, sicken cattle, and work
unknown harm on those who drink from once pure wells. As Albert Schweitzer
has said, "Man can hardly even recognize the devils of his own creation."

3   It took hundreds of millions of years to produce the life that now inhabits the
earth—eons of time in which that developing and evolving and diversifying life
reached a state of adjustment and balance with its surroundings. The environment, rigorously shaping and directing the life it supported, contained elements
that were hostile as well as supporting. Certain rocks gave out dangerous radiation; even within the light of the sun, from which all life draws its energy, there
were shortwave radiations with power to injure. Given time—time not in years but
in millennia—life adjusts, and a balance has been reached. For time is the essential ingredient; but in the modern world there is no time.

4   The rapidity of change and the speed with which new situations are created
follow the impetuous and heedless pace of man rather than the deliberate pace of nature. Radiation is no longer merely the background radiation of rocks, the bombard-
ment of cosmic rays, the ultraviolet of the sun that have existed before there was any
life on earth; radiation is now the unnatural creation of man's tampering with the

atom. The chemicals to which life is asked to make its adjustment are no longer merely the calcium and silica and copper and all the rest of the minerals washed out of the rocks and carried in rivers to the sea; they are the synthetic creations of man's inventive mind, brewed in his laboratories, and having no counterparts in nature.

To adjust to these chemicals would require time on the scale that is nature's; it would require not merely the years of a man's life but the life of generations. And even this, were it by some miracle possible, would be futile, for the new chemicals come from our laboratories in an endless stream; almost five hundred annually find their way into actual use in the United States alone. The figure is staggering and its implications are not easily grasped—500 new chemicals to which the bodies of men and animals are required somehow to adapt each year, chemicals totally outside the limits of biologic experience.

Among them are many that are used in man's war against nature. Since the mid-1940s over 200 basic chemicals have been created for use in killing insects, weeds, rodents, and other organisms described in the modern vernacular as "pests"; and they are sold under several thousand different brand names.

These sprays, dusts, and aerosols are now applied almost universally to farms, gardens, forests, and homes—nonselective chemicals that have the power to kill every insect, the "good" and the "bad," to still the song of birds and the leaping of fish in the streams, to coat the leaves with a deadly film, and to linger on in soil— all this though the intended target may be only a few weeds or insects. Can anyone believe it is possible to lay down such a barrage of poisons on the surface of the earth without making it unfit for all life? They should not be called "insecticides," but "biocides."

The whole process of spraying seems caught up in an endless spiral. Since DDT was released for civilian use, a process of escalation has been going on in which ever more toxic materials must be found. This has happened because insects, in a triumphant vindication of Darwin's principle of the survival of the fittest, have evolved super races immune to the particular insecticide used, hence a deadlier one has always to be developed—and then a deadlier one than that. It has happened also because, for reasons to be described later, destructive insects often undergo a "flareback," or resurgence, after spraying in numbers greater than before. Thus the chemical war is never won, and all life is caught in its violent crossfire.

Along with the possibility of the extinction of mankind by nuclear war, the central problem of our age has therefore become the contamination of man's total environment with such substances of incredible potential for harm—substances that accumulate in the tissues of plants and animals and even penetrate the germ cells to shatter or alter the very material of heredity upon which the shape of the future depends.

Some would-be architects of our future look toward a time when it will be possible to alter the human germ plasm by design. But we may easily be doing so now by inadvertence, for many chemicals, like radiation, bring about gene mutations. It is ironic to think that man might determine his own future by something so seemingly trivial as the choice of an insect spray.

11   All this has been risked—for what? Future historians may well be amazed by our distorted sense of proportion. How could intelligent beings seek to control a few unwanted species by a method that contaminated the entire environment and brought the threat of disease and death even to their own kind? Yet this is precisely what we have done. We have done it, moreover, for reasons that collapse the moment we examine them. We are told that the enormous and expanding use of pesticides is necessary to maintain farm production. Yet is our real problem not one of *overproduction?* Our farms, despite measures to remove acreages from production and to pay farmers *not* to produce, have yielded such a staggering excess of crops that the American taxpayer in 1962 is paying out more than one billion dollars a year as the total carrying cost of the surplus-food storage program. And is the situation helped when one branch of the Agriculture Department tries to reduce production while another states, as it did in 1958, "It is believed generally that reduction of crop acreages under provisions of the Soil Bank will stimulate interest in use of chemicals to obtain maximum production on the land retained in crops."

12   All this is not to say there is no insect problem and no need of control. I am saying, rather, that control must be geared to realities, not to mythical situations, and that the methods employed must be such that they do not destroy us along with the insects.

13 The problem whose attempted solution has brought such a train of disaster in its wake is an accompaniment of our modern way of life. Long before the age of man, insects inhabited the earth—a group of extraordinarily varied and adaptable beings. Over the course of time since man's advent, a small percentage of the more than half a million species of insects have come into conflict with human welfare in two principal ways: as competitors for the food supply and as carriers of human disease.

14   Disease-carrying insects become important where human beings are crowded together, especially under conditions where sanitation is poor, as in times of natural disaster or war or in situations of extreme poverty and deprivation. Then control of some sort becomes necessary. It is a sobering fact, however, as we shall presently see, that the method of massive chemical control has had only limited success, and also threatens to worsen the very conditions it is intended to curb.

15   Under primitive agricultural conditions the farmer had few insect problems. These arose with the intensification of agriculture—the devotion of immense acreages to a single crop. Such a system set the stage for explosive increases in specific insect populations. Single-crop farming does not take advantage of the principles by which nature works; it is agriculture as an engineer might conceive it to be. Nature has introduced great variety into the landscape, but man has displayed a passion for simplifying it. Thus he undoes the built-in checks and balances by which nature holds the species within bounds. One important natural check is a limit on the amount of suitable habitat for each species. Obviously then, an insect that lives on wheat can build up its population to much higher levels on a farm devoted to wheat than on one in which wheat is intermingled with other crops to which the insect is not adapted.

The same thing happens in other situations. A generation or more ago, the 16
towns of large areas of the United States lined their streets with the noble elm
tree. Now the beauty they hopefully created is threatened with complete destruction as disease sweeps through the elms, carried by a beetle that would have only
limited chance to build up large populations and to spread from tree to tree if the
elms were only occasional trees in a richly diversified planting.

Another factor in the modern insect problem is one that must be viewed against 17
a background of geologic and human history: the spreading of thousands of different
kinds of organisms from their native homes to invade new territories. This worldwide
migration has been studied and graphically described by the British ecologist Charles
Elton in his recent book *The Ecology of Invasions.* During the Cretaceous Period,
some hundred million years ago, flooding seas cut many land bridges between continents and living things found themselves confined in what Elton calls "colossal sepa
rate nature reserves." There, isolated from others of their kind, they developed many
new species. When some of the land masses were joined again, about 15 million years
ago, these species began to move out into new territories—a movement that is not
only still in progress but is now receiving considerable assistance from man.

The importation of plants is the primary agent in the modern spread of 18
species, for animals have almost invariably gone along with the plants, quarantine
being a comparatively recent and not completely effective innovation. The United
States Office of Plant Introduction alone has introduced almost 200,000 species
and varieties of plants from all over the world. Nearly half of the 180 or so major
insect enemies of plants in the United States are accidental imports from abroad,
and most of them have come as hitchhikers on plants.

In new territory, out of reach of the restraining hand of the natural enemies 19
that kept down its numbers in its native land, an invading plant or animal is able to
become enormously abundant. Thus it is no accident that our most troublesome
insects are introduced species.

These invasions, both the naturally occurring and those dependent on human 20
assistance, are likely to continue indefinitely. Quarantine and massive chemical
campaigns are only extremely expensive ways of buying time. We are faced, according to Dr. Elton, "with a life-and-death need not just to find new technological means
of suppressing this plant or that animal"; instead we need the basic knowledge of
animal populations and their relations to their surroundings that will "promote an
even balance and damp down the explosive power of outbreaks and new invasions."

Much of the necessary knowledge is now available but we do not use it. We 21
train ecologists in our universities and even employ them in our governmental
agencies but we seldom take their advice. We allow the chemical death rain to fall
as though there were no alternative, whereas in fact there are many, and our ingenuity could soon discover many more if given opportunity.

Have we fallen into a mesmerized state that makes us accept as inevitable that 22
which is inferior or detrimental, as though having lost the will or the vision to
demand that which is good? Such thinking, in the words of the ecologist Paul
Shepard, "idealizes life with only its head out of water, inches above the limits of
toleration of the corruption of its own environment. . . . Why should we tolerate a

diet of weak poisons, a home in insipid surroundings, a circle of acquaintances who are not quite our enemies, the noise of motors with just enough relief to prevent insanity? Who would want to live in a world which is just not quite fatal?"

23   Yet such a world is pressed upon us. The crusade to create a chemically sterile, insect-free world seems to have engendered a fanatic zeal on the part of many specialists and most of the so-called control agencies. On every hand there is evidence that those engaged in spraying operations exercise a ruthless power. "The regulatory entomologists . . . function as prosecutor, judge and jury, tax assessor and collector and sheriff to enforce their own orders," said Connecticut entomologist Neely Turner. The most flagrant abuses go unchecked in both state and federal agencies.

24   It is not my contention that chemical insecticides must never be used. I do contend that we have put poisonous and biologically potent chemicals indiscriminately into the hands of persons largely or wholly ignorant of their potentials for harm. We have subjected enormous numbers of people to contact with these poisons, without their consent and often without their knowledge. If the Bill of Rights contains no guarantee that a citizen shall be secure against lethal poisons distributed either by private individuals or by public officials, it is surely only because our forefathers, despite their considerable wisdom and foresight, could conceive of no such problem.

25   I contend, furthermore, that we have allowed these chemicals to be used with little or no advance investigation of their effect on soil, water, wildlife, and man himself. Future generations are unlikely to condone our lack of prudent concern for the integrity of the natural world that supports all life.

26   There is still very limited awareness of the nature of the threat. This is an era of specialists, each of whom sees his own problem and is unaware of or intolerant of the larger frame into which it fits. It is also an era dominated by industry, in which the right to make a dollar at whatever cost is seldom challenged. When the public protests, confronted with some obvious evidence of damaging results of pesticide applications, it is fed little tranquilizing pills of half truth. We urgently need an end to these false assurances, to the sugar coating of unpalatable facts. It is the public that is being asked to assume the risks that the insect controllers calculate. The public must decide whether it wishes to continue on the present road, and it can do so only when in full possession of the facts. In the words of Jean Rostand, "The obligation to endure gives us the right to know."

COMPREHENSION

1. What does Carson mean by "the obligation to endure"?
2. What reasons does the author cite for the overpopulation of insects?
3. What remedies does Carson propose?

RHETORIC

1. What tone does Carson use in her essay? Does she seem to be a subjective or an objective writer? Give specific support for your response.

2. How does the use of words such as *dangerous, evil, irrevocable,* and *sinister* help shape the reader's reaction to the piece? What emotional and ethical appeals do such words indicate?
3. Examine the ordering of ideas in paragraph 4, and consider how such an order serves to reinforce Carson's argument.
4. Paragraph 9 consists of only one (long) sentence. What is its function in the essay's scheme?
5. Examine Carson's use of expert testimony. How does it help strengthen her thesis?
6. How effectively does the essay's conclusion help tie up Carson's points? What is the writer's intent in this final paragraph? How does she accomplish this aim?

WRITING

1. Write an essay in which you suggest solutions to the problems brought up in Carson's piece. You may want to suggest measures that the average citizen can take to eliminate the casual use of insecticides to control the insect population.
2. Write a biographical research paper on Carson that focuses on her involvement with nature and environmental issues.
3. **Writing an Argument:** Write an essay titled "Insects Are Not the Problem; Humanity Is." In this essay, argue that it is humanity's greed that has caused such an imbalance in nature as to threaten the planet's survival.

NETWORKING
Applying Digital and Multimedia Literacies

Composing an Interactive Argument Essay: Create question 1 or 3 under Writing as an electronic document, one that readers can interact with by clicking on links that take them to other essays and articles that both support *and* refute your position. Post the essay on a blog and enable comments so your classmates can actively engage with your topic. Respond to at least two comments, being sure to keep dialogue civil and arguments well supported. Make your Works Cited page interactive as well, documenting all sources and linking to any that are available online.

The Greenest Campuses: An Idiosyncratic Guide

Noel Perrin

Noel Perrin (1927–2004) was born in New York City and worked as an editor before starting a career as a college instructor at the University of North Carolina and then Dartmouth College, where he taught beginning in 1959. He was awarded two

Guggenheim Fellowships, contributed to numerous periodicals, and authored more than 10 books. His subject matter ranges from the scholarly, such as Dr. Bowdler's Legacy *(1969) and* Giving Up the Gun: Japan's Reversion to the Sword, 1543–1879 *(1979), to his experiences as a part-time farmer. Among the latter are* First Person Rural *(1978),* Second Person Rural *(1980),* Third Person Rural *(1983),* Last Person Rural *(1991), and* A Child's Delight *(1998). His concerns about the environment made him a popular speaker on ecological issues. In the following essay, first published in the* Chronicle of Higher Education *in April 2001, Perrin creates his own "best" college guide by ranking institutions of higher learning according to their environmental awareness.*

1   About 1,100 American colleges and universities run at least a token environmental-studies program, and many hundreds of those programs offer well-designed and useful courses. But only a drastically smaller number practice even a portion of what they teach. The one exception is recycling. Nearly every institution that has so much as one lonely environmental-studies course also does a little halfhearted recycling. Paper and glass, usually.

2   There are some glorious exceptions to those rather churlish observations, I'm glad to say. How many? Nobody knows. No one has yet done the necessary research (though the National Wildlife Federation's Campus Ecology program is planning a survey).

3   Certainly *U.S. News & World Report* hasn't. Look at the rankings in their annual college issue. The magazine uses a complex formula something like this: Institution's reputation, 25 percent; student-retention rate, 20 percent; faculty resources, 20 percent; and so on, down to alumni giving, 5 percent. The lead criterion may help explain why Harvard, Yale, and Princeton Universities so frequently do a little dance at the top of the list.

4   But *U.S. News* has nothing at all to say about the degree to which a college or university attempts to behave sustainably—that is, to manage its campus and activities in ways that promote the long-term health of the planet. The magazine is equally mum about which of the institutions it is ranking can serve as models to society in a threatened world.

5   And, of course, the world is threatened. When the Royal Society in London and the National Academy of Sciences in Washington issued their first-ever joint statement, it ended like this: "The future of our planet is in the balance. Sustainable development can be achieved, but only if irreversible degradation of the environment can be halted in time. The next 30 years may be crucial." They said that in 1992. If all those top scientists are right, we have a little more than 20 years left in which to make major changes in how we live.

6   All this affects colleges. I have one environmentalist friend who loves to point out to the deans and trustees she meets that if we don't make such changes, and if the irreversible degradation of earth does occur, Harvard's huge endowment and Yale's lofty reputation will count for nothing.

7   But though *U.S. News* has nothing to say, fortunately there is a fairly good grapevine in the green world. I have spent considerable time in the past two

years using it like an organic cell phone. By that means I have come up with a short, idiosyncratic list of green colleges, consisting of six that are a healthy green, two that are greener still, and three that I believe are the greenest in the United States.

Which approved surveying techniques have I used? None at all. Some of my 8 evidence is anecdotal, and some of my conclusions are affected by my personal beliefs, such as that electric and hybrid cars are not just a good idea, but instruments of salvation.

Obviously I did not examine, even casually, all 1,100 institutions. I'm sure I 9 have missed some outstanding performers. I hope I have missed a great many.

Now, here are the 11, starting with **Brown University.** 10

It is generally harder for a large urban university to move toward sustainable 11 behavior than it is for a small-town college with maybe a thousand students. But it's not impossible. Both Brown, in the heart of Providence, R.I., and Yale University (by no means an environmental leader in other respects), in the heart of New Haven, Conn., have found a country way of dealing with food waste. Pigs. Both rely on pigs.

For the past 10 years, Brown has been shipping nearly all of its food waste to 12 a Rhode Island piggery. Actually, not shipping it—just leaving it out at dawn each morning. The farmer comes to the campus and gets it. Not since Ralph Waldo Emerson took food scraps out to the family pig have these creatures enjoyed such a high intellectual connection.

But there is a big difference in scale. Where Emerson might have one pail of 13 slops now and then, Brown generates 700 tons of edible garbage each year. Haulage fee: $0. Tipping fee: $0. (That's the cost of dumping the garbage into huge cookers, where it is heated for the pigs.) Annual savings to Brown: about $50,000. Addition to the American food supply: many tons of ham and bacon each year.

Of course, Brown does far more than feed a balanced diet to a lot of pigs. 14 That's just the most exotic (for an urban institution) of its green actions. "Brown is Green" became the official motto of the university in August 1990. It was accurate then, and it remains accurate now.

Yale is the only other urban institution I'm aware of that supports a pig 15 population. Much of the credit goes to Cyril May, the university's environmental coordinator, just as much of the credit at Brown goes to its environmental coordinator, Kurt Teichert.

May has managed to locate two Connecticut piggeries. The one to which he 16 sends garbage presents problems. The farmer has demanded—and received—a collection fee. And he has developed an antagonistic relationship with some of Yale's food-service people. (There are a lot of them: The campus has 16 dining facilities.) May is working on an arrangement with the second piggery. But if it falls through, he says, "I may go back on semibended knee to the other."

Yale does not make the list as a green college, for reasons you will learn later 17 in this essay. But it might in a few more years

Carleton College is an interesting example of an institution turning green 18 almost overnight. No pig slops here; the dining halls are catered by Marriott. But change is coming fast.

19   In the summer of 1999, Carleton appointed its first-ever environmental coordinator, a brand-new graduate named Rachel Smit. The one-year appointment was
an experiment, with a cobbled-together salary and the humble title of "fifth-year
intern." The experiment worked beyond anyone's expectation.

20   Smit began publishing an environmental newsletter called *The Green Bean*
and organized a small committee of undergraduates to explore the feasibility of
composting the college's food waste, an effort that will soon begin. A surprised
Marriott has already found itself serving organic dinners on Earth Day.

21   Better yet, the college set up an environmental-advisory committee of three
administrators, three faculty members, and three students to review all campus
projects from a green perspective. Naturally, many of those projects will be buildings, and to evaluate them, Carleton is using the *Minnesota Sustainable Design
Guide,* itself cowritten by Richard Strong, director of facilities.

22   The position of fifth-year intern is now a permanent one-year position, and its
salary is a regular part of the budget.

23   What's next? If Carleton gets a grant it has applied for, there will be a massive
increase in environmental-studies courses and faculty seminars and, says the
dean of budgets, "a whole range of green campus projects under the rubric of
'participatory learning.'"

24   And if Carleton doesn't get the grant? Same plans, slower pace.

25   Twenty years ago, **Dartmouth College** would have been a contender for the
title of greenest college in America, had such a title existed. It's still fairly green.
It has a large and distinguished group of faculty members who teach environmental studies, good recycling, an organic farm that was used last summer in
six courses, years of experience with solar panels, and a fair number of midlevel
administrators (including three in the purchasing office) who are ardent believers
in sustainability.

26   But the college has lost ground. Most troubling is its new $50-million library,
which has an actual anti-environmental twist: A portion of the roof requires steam
from the power plant to melt snow off of it. The architect, Robert Venturi, may be
famous, but he's no environmentalist.

27   Dartmouth is a striking example of what I shall modestly call Perrin's Law:
No college or university can move far toward sustainability without the active
support of at least two senior administrators. Dartmouth has no such committed
senior administrators at all. It used to. James Hornig, a former dean of sciences,
and Frank Smallwood, a former provost, were instrumental in creating the
environmental-studies program, back in 1970. They are now emeriti. The current
senior administrators are not in the least hostile to sustainability; they just give a
very low priority to the college's practicing what it preaches.

28   **Emory University** is probably further into the use of nonpolluting and
low-polluting motor vehicles than any other college in the country. According to
Eric Gaither, senior associate vice president for business affairs, 60 percent of
Emory's fleet is powered by alternative fuels. The facilities-management office
has 40 electric carts, which maintenance workers use for getting around
campus. The community-service office (security and parking) has its own

electric carts and an electric patrol vehicle. There are five electric shuttle buses and 14 compressed–natural-gas buses on order, plus one natural-gas bus in service.

Bill Chace, Emory's president, has a battery-charging station for electric cars 29 in his garage, and until recently an electric car to charge. Georgia Power, which lent the car, has recalled it, but Chace hopes to get it back. Meanwhile, he rides his bike to work most of the time.

How has Emory made such giant strides? "It's easy to do," says Gaither, 30 "when your president wants you to."

If Carleton is a model of how a small college turns green, the **University of** 31 **Michigan at Ann Arbor** is a model of how a big university does. Carleton is changing pretty much as an entity, while Michigan is more like the Electoral College—50 separate entities. The School of Natural Resources casts its 6 votes for sustainability, the English department casts its 12 for humanistic studies, the recycling coordinator casts her 1, the electric-vehicle program casts its 2, and so on. An institution of Michigan's size changes in bits and pieces.

Some of the bits show true leadership. For example, the university is within 32 weeks of buying a modest amount of green power. It makes about half of its own electricity (at its heating plant) and buys the other half. Five percent of that other half soon will come from renewable sources: hydro (water power) and biomass (so-called fuel crops, which are grown specifically to be burned for power).

The supporters of sustainability at Michigan would like to see the university 33 adopt a version of what is known as the Kyoto Protocol. The agreement, which the United States so far has refused to sign, requires that by 2012 each nation reduce its emission of greenhouse gases to 7 percent below its 1990 figure. Michigan's version of the protocol, at present a pipe dream, would require the university to do what the government won't—accept that reduction as a goal.

The immediate goal of "sustainabilists" at Ann Arbor is the creation of a 34 universitywide environmental coordinator, who would work either in the president's or the provost's office.

Giants are slow, but they are also strong. 35

Tulane University has the usual programs, among green institutions, in recy- 36 cling, composting, and energy efficiency. But what sets it apart is the Tulane Environmental Law Clinic, which is staffed by third-year law students. The director is a faculty member, and there are three law "fellows," all lawyers, who work with the students. The clinic does legal work for environmental organizations across Louisiana and "most likely has had a greater environmental impact than all our other efforts combined," says Elizabeth Davey, Tulane's first-ever environmental coordinator.

At least two campuses of the **University of California** (Berkeley is not among 37 them) have taken a first and even a second step toward sustainable behavior. First step: symbolic action, like installing a few solar panels, to produce clean energy and to help educate students. With luck, one of those little solar arrays might produce as much as a 20th of a percent of the electricity the university uses. It's a start.

The two campuses are Davis and Santa Cruz, and I think Davis nudges 38 ahead of Santa Cruz. That is primarily because Davis the city and Davis the university have done something almost miraculous. They have brought car culture at least partially under control, greatly reducing air pollution as a result.

39   The city has a population of about 58,000, which includes 24,000 students. According to reliable estimates, there are something over 50,000 bikes in town or on the campus, all but a few hundred owned by their riders. Most of the bikes are used regularly on the city's 45 miles of bike paths (closed to cars) and the 47 miles of bike lanes (cars permitted in the other lanes). The university maintains an additional 14 miles of bike paths on its large campus.

40   What happens on rainy days? "A surprising number continue to bike," says David Takemoto-Weerts, coordinator of Davis's bicycle program.

41   If every American college in a suitable climate were to behave like Davis, we could close a medium-sized oil refinery. Maybe we could even get rid of one coal-fired power plant, and thus seriously improve air quality.

42   The **University of New Hampshire** is trying to jump straight from symbolic gestures, like installing a handful of solar panels, to the hardest task of all for an institution trying to become green—establishing a completely new mind-set among students, administrators, and faculty and staff members. It may well succeed.

43   Campuses that have managed to change attitudes are rare. Prescott College, in Prescott, Ariz., and Sterling College, in Craftsbury Common, Vt., are rumored to have done so, and there may be two or three others. They're not on my list—because they're so small, because their students tend to be bright green even before they arrive, and because I have limited space.

44   New Hampshire has several token green projects, including a tiny solar array, able to produce one kilowatt at noon on a good day. And last April it inaugurated the Yellow Bike Cooperative. It is much smaller than anything that happens at Davis, where a bike rack might be a hundred yards long. But it's also more original and more communitarian. Anyone in Durham—student, burger flipper, associate dean—can join the Yellow Bike program by paying a $5 fee.

45   What you get right away is a key that unlocks all 50 bikes owned by the cooperative. (They are repaired and painted by student volunteers.) Want to cross campus? Just go to the nearest bike rack, unlock a Yellow, and pedal off. The goal, says Julie Newman, of the Office of Sustainability Programs, is "to greatly decrease one-person car trips on campus."

46   But the main thrust at New Hampshire is consciousness-raising. When the subject of composting food waste came up, the university held a seminar for its food workers.

47   New Hampshire's striking vigor is partly the result of a special endowment—about $12.8 million—exclusively for the sustainability office. Tom Kelly, the director, refuses to equate sustainability with greenness. Being green, in the sense of avoiding pollution and promoting reuse, is just one aspect of living sustainably, which involves "the balancing of economic viability with ecological health and human well-being," he says.

Oberlin College is an exception to Perrin's Law. The college has gotten 48
deeply into environmental behavior without the active support of two or, indeed,
any senior administrators. As at Dartmouth, the top people are not hostile; they
just have other priorities.

Apparently, until this year, Oberlin's environmental-studies program was 49
housed in a dreary cellar. Now it's in the $8.2-million Adam Joseph Lewis Environ-
mental Studies Center, which is one of the most environmentally benign college
buildings in the world. The money for it was raised as a result of a deal that
the department chairman, David Orr, made with the administration: He could
raise money for his own program, provided that he approached only people and
foundations that had never shown the faintest interest in Oberlin.

It's too soon for a full report on the building. It is loaded with solar panels— 50
690 of them, covering the roof (for a diagram of the building, see www.oberlin.
edu/newserv/esc/escabout.html). In about a year, data will be available on how
much energy the panels have saved and whether, as Orr hopes, the center will not
only make all its own power, but even export some.

Northland College, in Wisconsin, also goes way beyond tokenism. Its 51
McLean Environmental Living and Learning Center, a two-year-old residence hall
for 114 students, is topped by a 120-foot wind tower that, with a good breeze coming off Lake Superior, can generate 20 kilowatts of electricity. The building also
includes three arrays of solar panels. They are only token-size, generating a total
of 3.2 kilowatts at most. But one array does heat most of the water for one wing of
McLean, while the other three form a test project.

One test array is fixed in place—it can't be aimed. Another is like that sun- 52
flower in Blake's poem—it countest the steps of the sun. Put more prosaically, it
tracks the sun across the sky each day. The third array does that and can also be
tilted to get the best angle for each season of the year.

Inside the dorm is a pair of composting toilets—an experiment, to see if stu- 53
dents will use them. Because no one is forced to try the new ones if they don't
want to—plenty of conventional toilets are close by—it means something when
James Miller, vice president and dean of student development and enrollment,
reports, "Students almost always choose the composting bathrooms."

From the start, the college's goal has been to have McLean operate so effi- 54
ciently that it consumes 40 percent less outside energy than would a conventional
dormitory of the same dimensions. The building didn't reach that goal in its first
year; energy use dropped only 34.2 percent. But anyone dealing with a new system knows to expect bugs at the beginning. There were some at Northland, including the wind generator's being down for three months. (As I write, it's turning
busily.) Dean Miller is confident that the building will meet or exceed the college's energy-efficiency goal.

There is no room here to talk about the octagonal classroom structure made 55
of bales of straw, built largely by students. Or about the fact that Northland's
grounds are pesticide- and herbicide-free.

If Oberlin is a flagrant exception to Perrin's Law, **Middlebury College** is a 56
strong confirmation. Middlebury is unique, as far as I know, in having not only

senior administrators who strongly back environmentalism, but one senior administrator right inside the program. What Michigan wants, Middlebury has.

57   Nan Jenks-Jay, director of environmental affairs, reports directly to the
provost. She is responsible for both the teaching side and the living-sustainably
side of environmentalism. Under her are an environmental coordinator, Amy Self,
and an academic-program coordinator, Janet Wiseman.

58   The program has powerful backers, including the president, John M. McCardell
Jr.; the provost and executive vice president, Ronald D. Liebowitz; and the executive
vice president for facilities planning, David W. Ginevan. But everyone I talked with at
Middlebury, except for the occasional student who didn't want to trouble his mind
with things like returnable bottles—to say nothing of acid rain—seemed at least
somewhat committed to sustainable living.

59   Middlebury has what I think is the oldest environmental-studies program in
the country; it began back in 1965. It has the best composting program I've ever
seen. And, like Northland, it is pesticide- and herbicide-free.

60 Let me end as I began, with Harvard, Yale, and Princeton. And with *U.S. News*'s
consistently ranking them in the top five, accompanied from time to time by the
California Institute of Technology, Stanford University, and the Massachusetts
Institute of Technology.

61   What if *U.S. News* did a green ranking? What if it based the listings on one of
the few bits of hard data that can be widely compared: the percentage of waste
that a college recycles?

62   Harvard would come out okay, though hardly at the top. The university recycled
24 percent of its waste last year, thanks in considerable part to the presence of Rob
Gogan, the waste manager. He hopes to achieve 28 percent this year. That's feeble compared with Brown's 35 percent, and downright puny against Middlebury's 64 percent.

63   But compared with Yale and Princeton, it's magnificent. Most of the information I could get from Princeton is sadly dated. It comes from the 1995 report of the
Princeton Environmental Reform Committee, whose primary recommendation
was that the university hire a full-time waste manager. The university has not yet
done so. And if any administrators on the campus know the current recycling
percentage, they're not telling.

64   And Yale—poor Yale! It does have a figure. Among the performances of the
20 or so other colleges and universities whose percentages I'm aware of, only
Carnegie Mellon's is worse. Yale: 19 percent. Carnegie Mellon: 11 percent.

65   What should universities—and society—be shooting for? How can you ask?
One-hundred-percent retrieval of everything retrievable, of course.

COMPREHENSION

1. Why does Perrin call his essay an "idiosyncratic guide" when environmentalism has
   become a major issue in most municipalities, regions, and countries?
2. Is Perrin's purpose to inform, argue, or both? Does he have a clear-cut thesis, or does
   he leave it up to the reader to infer the thesis? Explain.

3. What information is Perrin's informal guide providing that is not offered in more conventional college rankings? Is he suggesting that parents and students consider "green rankings" in choosing which college to apply to? Explain.

RHETORIC

1. What purpose might Perrin have for choosing to create a "green guide" for colleges when there are so many other institutions or items he could have selected for review, such as corporations, towns, cities, automobiles, and numerous household products? What makes colleges and universities a particularly apt target?
2. Usually, Ivy League colleges are at the top of college guide lists as most desirable. Where do they rank on Perrin's list? What ironic statement is Perrin making by providing their rankings on the "green scale"? What is he implying about American values, particularly as they pertain to education?
3. Colleges and universities often pride themselves on the renown of their faculties. Who are the people Perrin cites as models of academic worth? Why has he chosen them?
4. What is the ironic purpose behind the author mentioning "Perrin's Law" (paragraph 27)? Is it a true "law," like the law of gravity? What body of knowledge is the author satirizing by invoking such a law?
5. Perrin is not didactic, since he does not recommend that other colleges adopt the environmental measures his model colleges have chosen. Would more direct advocacy on his part have strengthened his argument or weakened it, or not have had any effect? Explain.
6. In Perrin's conclusion, he changes his purpose from providing a purely informational assessment to offering a strong reprimand and recommendation. Why does he wait until the concluding paragraph to do so?

WRITING

1. Describe an environmentally friendly practice conducted at your college or university. Is it truly helpful for the environment, or is it largely symbolic?
2. Compare and contrast the academically oriented courses and programs offered at your school with what your institution actually does in the way of helping the environment. Discuss which of the two priorities is more prominent, and why.
3. **Writing an Argument:** Argue for or against the proposition that a magazine such as *U.S. News & World Report* should include environmental awareness and practice in its formula for assessing the rankings of colleges.

NETWORKING
Applying Digital and Multimedia Literacies

Creating a Facebook Group for a Cause: With several of your classmates, create a Facebook group that calls for action or raises awareness about an environmental issue or natural space that is relevant to your campus or local community. Consider carefully what you'll call the group (names are important!), and in a mission statement, articulate what you hope to accomplish by organizing it.

The Last Americans: Environmental Collapse and the End of Civilization

Jared Diamond

Jared Diamond *(b. 1937), who was born in Boston, is a physiologist, ecologist, and prolific writer who has published hundreds of popular and scientific articles. He has a BA from Harvard University (1958) and a PhD from Cambridge University (1961). Currently a professor of geography at UCLA and formerly professor of physiology at UCLA's School of Medicine, Diamond has conducted research in ecology and evolutionary biology in New Guinea and other southwest Pacific islands. As a field researcher and director of the World Wildlife Fund, Diamond helped to establish New Guinea's national park system. He received the Pulitzer Prize for* Guns, Germs, and Steel: The Fates of Human Societies *(1997). Another well-received book of Diamonds's is* Collapse: How Societies Choose to Fail or Succeed *(2004). In the following essay, which appeared in the June 2003 issue of* Harper's, *Diamond examines the environmental crises and failures of previous societies and civilizations, and how we might be able to learn lessons from these lost worlds.*

I met a traveler from an antique land
Who said: Two vast and trunkless legs of stone
Stand in the desert. . . . Near them, on the sand,
Half sunk, a shattered visage lies, whose frown,
And wrinkled lip, and sneer of cold command,
Tell that its sculptor well those passions read
Which yet survive, stamped on these lifeless things,
The hand that mocked them, and the heart that fed:
And on the pedestal these words appear:
"My name is Ozymandias, king of kings:
Look on my works, ye Mighty, and despair!"
Nothing beside remains. Round the decay
Of that colossal wreck, boundless and bare
The lone and level sands stretch far away.

— *"Ozymandias," Percy Bysshe Shelley*

1   One of the disturbing facts of history is that so many civilizations collapse. Few people, however, least of all our politicians, realize that a primary cause of the collapse of those societies has been the destruction of the environmental resources on which they depended. Fewer still appreciate that many of those civilizations share a sharp curve of decline. Indeed, a society's demise may begin only a decade or two after it reaches its peak population, wealth, and power.

2   Recent archaeological discoveries have revealed similar courses of collapse in such otherwise dissimilar ancient societies as the Maya in the Yucatán, the

Anasazi in the American Southwest, the Cahokia mound builders outside St. Louis, the Greenland Norse, the statue builders of Easter Island, ancient Mesopotamia in the Fertile Crescent, Great Zimbabwe in Africa, and Angkor Wat in Cambodia. These civilizations, and many others, succumbed to various combinations of environmental degradation and climate change, aggression from enemies taking advantage of their resulting weakness, and declining trade with neighbors who faced their own environmental problems. Because peak population, wealth, resource consumption, and waste production are accompanied by peak environmental impact—approaching the limit at which impact outstrips resources—we can now understand why declines of societies tend to follow swiftly on their peaks.

These combinations of undermining factors were compounded by cultural 3 attitudes preventing those in power from perceiving or resolving the crisis. That's a familiar problem today. Some of us are inclined to dismiss the importance of a healthy environment, or at least to suggest that it's just one of many problems facing us—an "issue." That dismissal is based on three dangerous misconceptions.

Foremost among these misconceptions is that we must balance the environ- 4 ment against human needs. That reasoning is exactly upside-down. Human needs and a healthy environment are not opposing claims that must be balanced; instead, they are inexorably linked by chains of cause and effect. We need a healthy environment because we need clean water, clean air, wood, and food from the ocean, plus soil and sunlight to grow crops. We need functioning natural ecosystems, with their native species of earthworms, bees, plants, and microbes, to generate and aerate our soils, pollinate our crops, decompose our wastes, and produce our oxygen. We need to prevent toxic substances from accumulating in our water and air and soil. We need to prevent weeds, germs, and other pest species from becoming established in places where they aren't native and where they cause economic damage. Our strongest arguments for a healthy environment are selfish: We want it for ourselves, not for threatened species like snail darters, spotted owls, and Furbish louseworts.

Another popular misconception is that we can trust in technology to solve our 5 problems. Whatever environmental problem you name, you can also name some hoped-for technological solution under discussion. Some of us have faith that we shall solve our dependence on fossil fuels by developing new technologies for hydrogen engines, wind energy, or solar energy. Some of us have faith that we shall solve our food problems with new or soon-to-be-developed genetically modified crops. Some of us have faith that new technologies will succeed in cleaning up the toxic materials in our air, water, soil, and foods without the horrendous cleanup expenses that we now incur.

6   Those with such faith assume that the new technologies will ultimately succeed, but in fact some of them may succeed and others may not. They assume that the new technologies will succeed quickly enough to make a big difference soon, but all of these major technological changes will actually take five to thirty years to develop and implement—if they catch on at all. Most of all, those with faith assume that new technology won't cause any new problems. In fact, technology merely constitutes increased power, which produces changes that can be either for the better or for the worse. All of our current environmental problems are unanticipated harmful consequences of our existing technology. There is no basis for believing that technology will miraculously stop causing new and unanticipated problems while it is solving the problems that it previously produced.

7   The final misconception holds that environmentalists are fear-mongering, overreacting extremists whose predictions of impending disaster have been proved wrong before and will be proved wrong again. Behold, say the optimists: Water still flows from our faucets, the grass is still green, and the supermarkets are full of food. We are more prosperous than ever before, and that's the final proof that our system works.

8   Well, for a few billion of the world's people who are causing us increasing trouble, there isn't any clean water, there is less and less green grass, and there are no supermarkets full of food. To appreciate what the environmental problems of those billions of people mean for us Americans, compare the following two lists of countries. First ask some ivory-tower academic ecologist who knows a lot about the environment but never reads a newspaper and has no interest in politics to list the overseas countries facing some of the worst problems of environmental stress, overpopulation, or both. The ecologist would answer, "That's a no-brainer, it's obvious. Your list of environmentally stressed or overpopulated countries should surely include Afghanistan, Bangladesh, Burundi, Haiti, Indonesia, Iraq, Nepal, Pakistan, the Philippines, Rwanda, the Solomon Islands, and Somalia, plus others." Then ask a First World politician who knows nothing, and cares less, about the environment and population problems to list the world's worst trouble spots: countries where state government has already been overwhelmed and has collapsed, or is now at risk of collapsing, or has been wracked by recent civil wars; and countries that, as a result of their problems, are also creating problems for us rich First World countries, which may be deluged by illegal immigrants, or have to provide foreign aid to those countries, or may decide to provide them with military assistance to deal with rebellions and terrorists, or may even (God forbid) have to send in our own troops. The politician would answer, "That's a no-brainer, it's obvious. Your list of political trouble spots should surely include Afghanistan, Bangladesh,

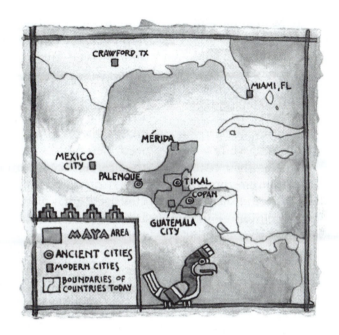

Burundi, Haiti, Indonesia, Iraq, Nepal, Pakistan, the Philippines, Rwanda, the Solomon Islands, and Somalia, plus others."

The connection between the two lists is transparent. Today, just as in the past, countries that are environmentally stressed, overpopulated or both are at risk of becoming politically stressed, and of seeing their governments collapse. When people are desperate and undernourished, they blame their government, which they see as responsible for failing to solve their problems. They try to emigrate at any cost. They start civil wars. They kill one another. They figure that they have nothing to lose, so they become terrorists, or they support or tolerate terrorism. The results are genocides such as the ones that already have exploded in Burundi, Indonesia, and Rwanda; civil wars, as in Afghanistan, Indonesia, Nepal, the Philippines, and the Solomon Islands; calls for the dispatch of First World troops, as to Afghanistan, Indonesia, Iraq, the Philippines, Rwanda, the Solomon Islands, and Somalia; the collapse of central government, as has already happened in Somalia; and overwhelming poverty, as in all of the countries on these lists.

But what about the United States? Some might argue that the environmental collapse of ancient societies is relevant to the modern decline of weak, far-off, overpopulated Rwanda and environmentally devastated Somalia, but isn't it ridiculous to suggest any possible relevance to the fate of our own society? After all, we might reason, those ancients didn't enjoy the wonders of modern environment-friendly technologies. Those ancients had the misfortune to suffer from the effects of climate change. They behaved stupidly and ruined their own environment by doing obviously dumb things, like cutting down their forests, watching their topsoil erode, and building cities in dry areas likely to run short of water. They had foolish leaders who didn't have books and so couldn't learn from history, and who embroiled them in destabilizing wars and didn't pay attention to problems at home. They were overwhelmed by desperate immigrants, as one society after another collapsed, sending floods of economic refugees to tax the resources of the societies that weren't collapsing. In all those respects, we modern Americans are fundamentally different from those primitive ancients, and there is nothing that we could learn from them.

11   Or so the argument goes. It's an argument so ingrained both in our subconscious and in public discourse that it has assumed the status of objective reality. We think we are different. In fact, of course, all of those powerful societies of the past thought that they too were unique, right up to the moment of their collapse. It's sobering to consider the swift decline of the ancient Maya, who 1,200 years ago were themselves the most advanced society in the Western Hemisphere, and who, like us now, were then at the apex of their own power and numbers. Two excellent recent books, David Webster's *The Fall of the Ancient Maya* and Richardson Gill's *The Great Maya Droughts,* help bring the trajectory of Maya civilization back to life for us. Their studies illustrate how even sophisticated societies like that of the Maya (and ours) can be undermined by details of rainfall, farming methods, and motives of leaders.

12 By now, millions of modern Americans have visited Maya ruins. To do so, one need only take a direct flight from the United States to the Yucatán capital of Mérida, jump into a rental car or minibus, and drive an hour on a paved highway. Most Maya ruins, with their great temples and monuments, lie surrounded by jungles (seasonal tropical forests), far from current human settlement. They are "pure" archaeological sites. That is, their locations became depopulated, so they were not covered up by later buildings as were so many other ancient cities, like the Aztec capital of Tenochtitlán—now buried under modern Mexico City—and Rome.

13   One of the reasons few people live there now is that the Maya homeland poses serious environmental challenges to would-be farmers. Although it has a somewhat unpredictable rainy season from May to October, it also has a dry season from January through April. Indeed, if one focuses on the dry months, one could describe the Yucatán as a "seasonal desert."

14   Complicating things, from a farmer's perspective, is that the part of the Yucatán with the most rain, the south, is also the part at the highest elevation above the water table. Most of the Yucatán consists of karst—a porous, spongelike, limestone terrain—and so rain runs straight into the ground, leaving little or no surface water. The Maya in the lower-elevation regions of the north were able to reach the water table by way of deep sinkholes called cenotes, and the Maya in low coastal areas without sinkholes could reach it by digging wells up to 75 feet deep. Most Maya, however, lived in the south. How did they deal with their resulting water problem?

Technology provided an answer. The Maya plugged up leaks on karst prom- 15
ontories by plastering the bottoms of depressions to create reservoirs, which collected rain and stored it for use in the dry season. The reservoirs at the Maya city
of Tikal, for example, held enough water to meet the needs of about 10,000 people
for eighteen months. If a drought lasted longer than that, though, the inhabitants
of Tikal were in deep trouble.

Maya farmers grew mostly corn, which constituted the astonishingly high 16
proportion of about 70 percent of their diet, as deduced from isotope analyses
of ancient Maya skeletons. They grew corn by means of a modified version of
swidden slash-and-burn agriculture, in which forest is cleared, crops are
grown in the resulting clearing for a few years until the soil is exhausted, and
then the field is abandoned for fifteen to twenty years until regrowth of wild
vegetation restores the soil's fertility. Because most of the land under a swidden
agricultural system is fallow at any given time, it can support only modest
population densities. Thus, it was a surprise for archaeologists to discover that
ancient Maya population densities, judging from numbers of stone foundations
of farmhouses, were often far higher than what unmodified swidden agriculture could support: often 250 to 750 people per square mile. The Maya probably achieved those high populations by such means as shortening the fallow
period and tilling the soil to restore soil fertility, or omitting the fallow period
entirely and growing crops every year, or, in especially moist areas, growing
two crops per year.

Socially stratified societies, ours included, consist of farmers who produce 17
food, plus nonfarmers such as bureaucrats and soldiers who do not produce
food and are in effect parasites on farmers. The farmers must grow enough food
to meet not only their own needs but also those of everybody else. The number
of nonproducing consumers who can be supported depends on the society's

agricultural productivity. In the United States today, with its highly efficient agriculture, farmers make up only 2 percent of our population, and each farmer can feed, on the average, 129 other people. Ancient Egyptian agriculture was efficient enough for an Egyptian peasant to produce five times the food required for himself and his family. But a Maya peasant could produce only twice the needs of himself and his family.

18   Fully 80 percent of Maya society consisted of peasants. Their inability to support many nonfarmers resulted from several limitations of their agriculture. It produced little protein, because corn has much lower protein content than wheat, and because the few edible domestic animals kept by the Maya (turkeys, ducks, and dogs) included no large animals like our cows and sheep. There was little use of terracing or irrigation to increase production. In the Maya area's humid climate, stored corn would rot or become infested after a year, so the Maya couldn't get through a longer drought by eating surplus corn accumulated in good years. And unlike Old World peoples with their horses, oxen, donkeys, and camels, the Maya had no animal-powered transport. Indeed, the Maya lacked not only pack animals and animal-drawn plows but also metal tools, wheels, and boats with sails. All of those great Maya temples were built by stone and wooden tools and human muscle power alone, and all overland transport went on the backs of human porters.

19   Those limitations on food supply and food transport may in part explain why Maya society remained politically organized in small kingdoms that were perpetually at war with one another and that never became unified into large empires like the Aztec empire of the Valley of Mexico (fed by highly productive agriculture) or the Inca empire of the Andes (fed by diverse crops carried on llamas). Maya armies were small and unable to mount lengthy campaigns over long distances. The typical Maya kingdom held a population of only up to 50,000 people, within a radius of two or three days' walk from the king's palace. From the top of the temple of some Maya kingdoms, one could see the tops of the temples of other kingdoms.

20   Presiding over the temple was the king himself, who functioned both as head priest and as political leader. It was his responsibility to pray to the gods, to perform astronomical and calendrical rituals, to ensure the timely arrival of the rains on which agriculture depended, and thereby to bring prosperity. The king claimed to have the supernatural power to deliver those good things because of his asserted family relationship to the gods. Of course, that exposed him to the risk that his subjects would become disillusioned if he couldn't fulfill his boast of being able to deliver rains and prosperity.

21   Those are the basic outlines of Classic Maya society, which for all its limitations lasted more than 500 years. Indeed, the Maya themselves believed that it had lasted for much longer. Their remarkable Long Count calendar had its starting date (analogous to January 1, A.D. 1 of our calendar) backdated into the remote preliterate past, at August 11, 3114 B.C. The first physical evidence of civilization within the Maya area, in the form of villagers and pottery, appeared around 1400 B.C., substantial buildings around 500 B.C., and writing around 400 B.C.

The so-called Classic period of Maya history arose around A.D. 250, when evidence for the first kings and dynasties emerged. From then, the Maya population increased almost exponentially, to reach peak numbers in the eighth century A.D. The largest monuments were erected toward the end of that century. All the indicators of a complex society declined throughout the ninth century, until the last date on any monument was A.D. 909. This decline of Maya population and architecture constitutes what is known as the Classic Maya collapse.

What happened? Let's consider in more detail a city whose ruins now lie in 22 western Honduras at the world-famous site of Copán. The most fertile ground in the Copán area consists of five pockets of flat land along a river valley with a total area of only one square mile; the largest of those five pockets, known as the Copán pocket, has an area of half a square mile. Much of the land around Copán consists of steep hills with poor soil. Today, corn yields from valley-bottom fields are two or three times those of fields on hill slopes, which suffer rapid erosion and lose most of their productivity within a decade of farming.

To judge by the number of house sites, population growth in the Copán valley 23 rose steeply from the fifth century up to a peak estimated at around 27,000 people between A.D. 750 and 900. Construction of royal monuments glorifying kings became especially massive from A.D. 650 onward. After A.D. 700, nobles other than kings got into the act and began erecting their own palaces, increasing the burden that the king and his own court already imposed on the peasants. The last big buildings at Copán were put up around A.D. 800; the last date on an incomplete altar possibly bearing a king's name is A.D. 822.

Archaeological surveys of different types of habitats in the Copán valley show 24 that they were occupied in a regular sequence. The first area farmed was the large Copán pocket of bottomland, followed by occupation of the other four bottomland pockets. During that time the human population was growing, but the hills remained uninhabited. Hence that increased population must have been accommodated by intensifying production in the bottomland pockets: probably some combination of shorter fallow periods and double-cropping. By A.D. 500, people had started to settle the hill slopes, but those sites were occupied only briefly. The percentage of Copán's total population that was in the hills, rather than in the valleys, peaked in the year 575 and then declined, as the population again became concentrated in the pockets.

What caused that pullback of population from the hills? From excavation of 25 building foundations on the valley floor we know that they became covered with sediment during the eighth century, meaning that the hill slopes were becoming eroded and probably also leached of nutrients. The acidic hill soils being carried down into the valley would have reduced agricultural yields. The reason for that erosion of the hillsides is clear: the forests that formerly covered them and protected their soil were being cut down. Dated pollen samples show that the pine forests originally covering the hilltops were eventually all cleared, to be burned for fuel. Besides causing sediment accumulation in the valleys and depriving valley inhabitants of wood supplies, that deforestation may have begun to cause a "man-made drought" in the valley bottom, because forests play a major role in water cycling, such that massive deforestation tends to result in lowered rainfall.

26   Hundreds of skeletons recovered from Copán archaeological sites have been studied for signs of disease and poor nutrition, such as porous bones and stress lines in the teeth. Those skeletal signs show that the health of Copán's inhabitants deteriorated from A.D. 650 to 850, among both the elite and commoners, though the health of commoners was worse.

27   Recall that Copán's population was growing rapidly while the hills were being occupied. The subsequent abandonment of all of those hill fields meant that the burden of feeding the extra population formerly dependent on the hills now fell increasingly on the valley floor, and that more and more people were competing for the food grown on that one square mile of bottomland. That would have led to fighting among the farmers themselves for the best land, or for any land, just as in modern Rwanda. Because the king was failing to deliver on his promises of rain and prosperity, he would have been the scapegoat for this agricultural failure, which explains why the last that we hear of any king is A.D. 822, and why the royal palace was burned around A.D. 850.

28   Datable pieces of obsidian, the sharp rock from which the Maya made their stone tools, suggest that Copán's total population decreased more gradually than did its signs of kings and nobles. The estimated population in the year A.D. 950 was still around 15,000, or 55 percent of the peak population of 27,000. That population continued to dwindle, until there are few signs of anyone in the Copán valley after around A.D. 1235. The reappearance of pollen from forest trees thereafter provides independent evidence that the valley became virtually empty of people.

29 The Maya history that I have just related, and Copán's history in particular, illustrate why we talk about "the Maya collapse." But the story grows more complicated, for at least five reasons. There was not only that enormous Classic collapse but also at least two smaller pre-Classic collapses, around A.D. 150 and 600, as well as some post-Classic collapses. The Classic collapse was obviously not complete, because hundreds of thousands of Maya survived, in areas with stable water supplies, to meet and fight the Spaniards. The collapse of population (as gauged by numbers of house sites and of obsidian tools) was in some cases much slower than the decline in numbers of Long Count dates. Many apparent collapses of cities were nothing more than "power cycling"; i.e., particular cities becoming more powerful at the expense of neighboring cities, then declining or getting conquered by neighbors, without changes in the whole population. Finally, cities in different parts of the Maya area rose and fell on different trajectories.

30   Some archaeologists focus on these complications and don't want to recognize a Classic Maya collapse at all. But this overlooks the obvious fact that cries out for explanation: the disappearance of between 90 and 99 percent of the Maya population after A.D. 800, and of the institution of the kingship, Long

Count calendars, and other complex political and cultural institutions. Before we can understand those disappearances, however, we need first to understand the roles of warfare and of drought.

Archaeologists for a long time believed the ancient Maya to be gentle and 31 peaceful people. We now know that Maya warfare was intense, chronic, and unresolvable, because limitations of food supply and transportation made it impossible for any Maya principality to unite the whole region in an empire. The archaeological record shows that wars became more intense and frequent toward the time of the Classic collapse. That evidence comes from discoveries of several types since the Second World War: archaeological excavations of massive fortifications surrounding many Maya sites; vivid depictions of warfare and captives on stone monuments and on the famous painted murals discovered in 1946 at Bonampak; and the decipherment of Maya writing, much of which proved to consist of royal inscriptions boasting of conquests. Maya kings fought to capture and torture one another; an unfortunate loser was a Copán king with the to us unforgettable name of King 18 Rabbit.

Maya warfare involved well-documented types of violence: wars among 32 separate kingdoms; attempts of cities within a kingdom to secede by revolting against the capital; and civil wars resulting from frequent violent attempts by would-be kings to usurp the throne. All of these events were described or depicted on monuments, because they involved kings and nobles. Not considered worthy of description, but probably even more frequent, were fights between commoners over land, as overpopulation became excessive and land became scarce.

The other phenomenon important to understanding all of these collapses is 33 the repeated occurrence of droughts, as inferred by climatologists from evidence of lake evaporation preserved in lake sediments, and as summarized by Gill in *The Great Maya Droughts.* The rise of Maya civilization may have been facilitated by a rainy period beginning around 250 B.C., until a temporary drought after A.D. 125 was associated with a pre-Classic collapse at some sites. That collapse was followed by the resumption of rainy conditions and the buildup of Classic Maya cities, briefly interrupted by another drought around 600 corresponding to a decline at Tikal and some other sites. Finally, around A.D. 750 there began the worst drought in the past 7,000 years, peaking around the year A.D. 800, and suspiciously associated with the Classic collapse.

The area most affected by the Classic collapse was the southern high- 34 lands, probably for the two reasons already mentioned: It was the area with the densest population, and it also had the most severe water problems because it lay too high above the water table for cenotes or wells to provide water. The southern highlands lost more than 99 percent of its population in the course of the Classic collapse. When Cortés and his Spanish army marched in 1524 and 1525 through an area formerly inhabited by millions of Maya, he nearly starved because he encountered so few villagers from whom to acquire corn. The Spaniards passed within only a few miles of the abandoned ruins of

the great Classic cities of Tikal and Palenque, but still they heard or saw nothing of them.

35 We can identify increasingly familiar strands in the Classic Maya collapse. One consisted of population growth outstripping available resources: the dilemma foreseen by Thomas Malthus in 1798. As Webster succinctly puts it in *The Fall of the Ancient Maya,* "Too many farmers grew too many crops on too much of the landscape." While population was increasing, the area of usable farmland paradoxically was decreasing from the effects of deforestation and hillside erosion.

36   The next strand consisted of increased fighting as more and more people fought over fewer resources. Maya warfare, already endemic, peaked just before the collapse. That is not surprising when one reflects that at least 5 million people, most of them farmers, were crammed into an area smaller than the state of Colorado. That's a high population by the standards of ancient farming societies, even if it wouldn't strike modern Manhattan-dwellers as crowded.

37   Bringing matters to a head was a drought that, although not the first one the Maya had been through, was the most severe. At the time of previous droughts, there were still uninhabited parts of the Maya landscape, and people in a drought area or dust bowl could save themselves by moving to another site. By the time of the Classic collapse, however, there was no useful unoccupied land in the vicinity on which to begin anew, and the whole population could not be accommodated in the few areas that continued to have reliable water supplies.

38   The final strand is political. Why did the kings and nobles not recognize and solve these problems? A major reason was that their attention was evidently focused on the short-term concerns of enriching themselves, waging wars, erecting monuments, competing with one another, and extracting enough food from the

peasants to support all those activities. Like most leaders throughout human history, the Maya kings and nobles did not have the leisure to focus on long-term problems, insofar as they perceived them.

What about those same strands today? The United States is also at the peak of 39 its power, and it is also suffering from many environmental problems. Most of us have become aware of more crowding and stress. Most of us living in large American cities are encountering increased commuting delays, because the number of people and hence of cars is increasing faster than the number of freeway lanes. I know plenty of people who in the abstract doubt that the world has a population problem, but almost all of those same people complain to me about crowding, space issues, and traffic experienced in their personal lives.

Many parts of the United States face locally severe problems of water re- 40 striction (especially southern California, Arizona, the Everglades, and, increasingly, the Northeast); forest fires resulting from logging and forest-management practices throughout the intermontane West; and losses of farmlands to salinization, drought, and climate change in the northern Great Plains. Many of us frequently experience problems of air quality, and some of us also experience problems of water quality and taste. We are losing economically valuable natural resources. We have already lost American chestnut trees, the Grand Banks cod fishery, and the Monterey sardine fishery; we are in the process of losing swordfish and tuna and Chesapeake Bay oysters and elm trees; and we are losing topsoil.

The list goes on: All of us are experiencing personal consequences of our 41 national dependence on imported energy, which affects us not only through higher gas prices but also through the current contraction of the national economy, itself the partial result of political problems associated with our oil dependence. We are saddled with expensive toxic cleanups at many locations, most notoriously near Montana mines, on the Hudson River, and in the Chesapeake Bay. We also face expensive eradication problems resulting from hundreds of introduced pest species—including zebra mussels, Mediterranean fruit flies, Asian longhorn beetles, water hyacinth, and spotted knapweed—that now affect our agriculture, forests, waterways, and pastures.

These particular environmental problems, and many others, are enor- 42 mously expensive in terms of resources lost, cleanup and restoration costs, and the cost of finding substitutes for lost resources: a billion dollars here, 10 billion there, in dozens and dozens of cases. Some of the problems, especially those of air quality and toxic substances, also exact health costs that are large, whether measured in dollars or in lost years or in quality of life. The cost of our home-grown environmental problems adds up to a large fraction of our gross national product, even without mentioning the costs that we incur from environmental problems overseas, such as the military operations that they inspire. Even the mildest of bad scenarios for our future include a gradual economic decline, as happened to the Roman and British empires. Actually, in case you didn't notice it, our economic decline is already well

under way. Just check the numbers for our national debt, yearly government budget deficit, unemployment statistics, and the value of your investment and pension funds.

43 The environmental problems of the United States are still modest compared with those of the rest of the world. But the problems of environmentally devastated, overpopulated, distant countries are now our problems as well. We are accustomed to thinking of globalization in terms of us rich, advanced First Worlders sending our good things, such as the Internet and Coca-Cola, to those poor backward Third Worlders. Globalization, however, means nothing more than improved worldwide communication and transportation, which can convey many things in either direction; it is not restricted to good things carried only from the First to the Third World. They in the Third World can now, intentionally or unintentionally, send us their bad things: terrorists; diseases such as AIDS, SARS, cholera, and West Nile fever, carried inadvertently by passengers on transcontinental airplanes; unstoppable numbers of immigrants, both legal and illegal, arriving by boat, truck, train, plane, and on foot; and other consequences of their Third World problems. We in the United States are no longer the isolated Fortress America to which some of us aspired in the 1930s; instead, we are tightly and irreversibly connected to overseas countries. The United States is the world's leading importer, and it is also the world's leading exporter. Our own society opted long ago to become interlocked with the rest of the world.

That's why political stability anywhere in the world now affects us, our trade 44
routes, and our overseas markets and suppliers. We are so dependent on the rest of
the world that if a decade ago you had asked a politician to name the countries most
geopolitically irrelevant to U.S. interests because of their being so remote, poor, and
weak, the list would have begun with Afghanistan and Somalia, yet these countries
were subsequently considered important enough to warrant our dispatching U.S.
troops. The Maya were "globalized" only within the Yucatán: the southern Yucatán
Maya affected the northern Yucatán Maya and may have had some effects on the
Valley of Mexico, but they had no contact with Somalia. That's because Maya transportation was slow, short-distance, on foot or else in canoes, and had low cargo
capacity. Our transport today is much more rapid and has much higher cargo
capacity. The Maya lived in a globalized Yucatán; we live in a globalized world.

If all of this reasoning seems straightforward when expressed so bluntly, one has 45
to wonder: Why don't those in power today get the message? Why didn't the leaders of the Maya, Anasazi, and those other societies also recognize and solve their
problems? What were the Maya thinking while they watched loggers clearing the
last pine forests on the hills above Copán? Here, the past really is a useful guide to
the present. It turns out that there are at least a dozen reasons why past societies
failed to *anticipate* some problems before they developed, or failed to *perceive*
problems that had already developed, or failed even to try to solve problems that
they did perceive. All of those dozen reasons still can be seen operating today. Let
me mention just three of them.

First, it's difficult to recognize a slow trend in some quantity that fluctuates widely 46
up and down anyway, such as seasonal temperature, annual rainfall, or economic indicators. That's surely why the Maya didn't recognize the oncoming drought until it was
too late, given that rainfall in the Yucatán varies several-fold from year to year. Natural
fluctuations also explain why it's only within the last few years that all climatologists
have become convinced of the reality of climate change, and why our president still
isn't convinced but thinks that we need more research to test for it.

Second, when a problem *is* recognized, those in power may not attempt to 47
solve it because of a clash between their short-term interests and the interests of
the rest of us. Pumping that oil, cutting down those trees, and catching those fish
may benefit the elite by bringing them money or prestige and yet be bad for society as a whole (including the children of the elite) in the long run. Maya kings
were consumed by immediate concerns for their prestige (requiring more and
bigger temples) and their success in the next war (requiring more followers),
rather than for the happiness of commoners or of the next generation. Those people with the greatest power to make decisions in our own society today regularly
make money from activities that may be bad for society as a whole and for their
own children; those decision-makers include Enron executives, many land developers, and advocates of tax cuts for the rich.

Finally, it's difficult for us to acknowledge the wisdom of policies that clash 48
with strongly held values. For example, a belief in individual freedom and a distrust of big government are deeply ingrained in Americans, and they make sense

under some circumstances and up to a certain point. But they also make it hard for us to accept big government's legitimate role in ensuring that each individual's freedom to maximize the value of his or her land holdings doesn't decrease the value of the collective land of all Americans.

49   Not all societies make fatal mistakes. There are parts of the world where societies have unfolded for thousands of years without any collapse, such as Java, Tonga, and (until 1945) Japan. Today, Germany and Japan are successfully managing their forests, which are even expanding in area rather than shrinking. The Alaskan salmon fishery and the Australian lobster fishery are being managed sustainably. The Dominican Republic, hardly a rich country, nevertheless has set aside a comprehensive system of protected areas encompassing most of the country's natural habitats.

50   Is there any secret to explain why some societies acquire good environmental sense while others don't? Naturally, part of the answer depends on accidents of individual leaders' wisdom (or lack thereof). But part also depends upon whether a society is organized so as to minimize built-in clashes of interest between its decision-making elites and its masses. Given how our society is organized, the executives of Enron, Tyco, and Adelphi correctly calculated that their own interests would be best promoted by looting the company coffers, and that they would probably get away with most of their loot. A good example of a society that minimizes such clashes of interest is the Netherlands, whose citizens have perhaps the world's highest level of environmental awareness and of membership in environmental organizations. I never understood why, until on a recent trip to the Netherlands I posed the question to three of my Dutch friends while driving through their countryside.

51   Just look around you, they said. All of this farmland that you see lies below sea level. One fifth of the total area of the Netherlands is below sea level, as much as 22 feet below, because it used to be shallow bays, and we reclaimed it from the sea by surrounding the bays with dikes and then gradually pumping out the water. We call these reclaimed lands "polders." We began draining our polders nearly a thousand years ago. Today, we still have to keep pumping out the water that gradually seeps in. That's what our windmills used to be for, to drive the pumps to pump out the polders. Now we use steam, diesel, and electric pumps instead. In each polder there are lines of them, starting with those farthest from the sea, pumping the water in sequence until the last pump finally deposits it into a river or the ocean. And all of us, rich or poor, live down in the polders. It's not the case that rich people live safely up on top of the dikes while poor people live in the polder bottoms below sea level. If the dikes and pumps fail, we'll all drown together.

52   Throughout human history, all peoples have been connected to some other peoples, living together in virtual polders. For the ancient Maya, their polder consisted of most of the Yucatán and neighboring areas. When the Classic Maya cities collapsed in the southern Yucatán, refugees may have

reached the northern Yucatán, but probably not the Valley of Mexico, and certainly not Florida. Today, our whole world has become one polder, such that events in even Afghanistan and Somalia affect Americans. We do indeed differ from the Maya, but not in ways we might like: We have a much larger population, we have more potent destructive technology, and we face the risk of a worldwide rather than a local decline. Fortunately, we also differ from the Maya in that we know their fate, and they did not. Perhaps we can learn.

COMPREHENSION

1. Explain the significance of Shelley's poem "Ozymandias" for Diamond's essay.
2. What are the "three dangerous misconceptions" (paragraph 3) about the environment that Diamond discusses?
3. List all the civilizations that Diamond mentions in this essay. Which civilization does he emphasize? According to Diamond, why did previous civilizations fail, and how do these collapses provide guides to the state of contemporary American civilization?

RHETORIC

1. State Diamond's argument or major proposition. Where does his claim appear most clearly? What minor propositions does he develop? How does he deal with opposing viewpoints?
2. What types of evidence does the writer provide to support his claim?
3. Why does Diamond divide his essay into so many sections? What relationships do you detect between and among these sections?
4. Where does Diamond use comparison and contrast and causal analysis to organize parts of his essay?
5. How does classification operate as a rhetorical element in this article?
6. Assess the relative effectiveness of Diamond's conclusion. How does the ending serve as a coda for the entire essay?

WRITING

1. Write an essay focusing on a local environmental problem. Analyze the ways in which this environmental problem affects the lives of nearby residents.
2. Select one civilization that Diamond mentions. Conduct research on this civilization, and then write a report on the environmental factors that led to the decline of that society.
3. **Writing an Argument:** Write a persuasive essay in which you warn readers about three environmental dangers confronting the United States today.

NETWORKING
Applying Digital and Multimedia Literacies

Analyzing the Use of Images: How do the illustrations in this essay interact with Diamond's written text? What is their rhetorical purpose, and how do they influence the text's tone?

Synthesis: Connections for Critical Thinking

1. Using support from the works of Lopez, Carson, Chief Seattle, and others, write a causal-analysis essay tracing our relationship to the land. To what extent have history, greed, and fear helped shape our attitude? Can this attitude be changed? How?

2. Consider the empathy and sensitivity Lopez has toward animals. How do his attitude and perceptions coincide with the views expressed by Bass and Chief Seattle concerning the natural world?

3. Write a letter to the op-ed page of a newspaper objecting to a governmental ruling harmful to the environment. State the nature of the policy, its possible dangers, and your reasons for opposing it. Use support from Horowitz, McKibben, Diamond, and any other writers in this chapter. Extra reading or research may be necessary.

4. Consider why we fear nature. Why do we consider it an enemy, an alien, something to be destroyed? How would Bass, Lopez, and Chief Seattle respond to this question? Do you agree or disagree with them?

5. Both Lopez and Diamond use narration and description to explore our relationship to the land. How do they approach their subject in terms of language, attitude, and style?

6. Choose an author in this chapter whose essay, in your opinion, romanticizes nature. Compare his or her attitude with that of a writer with a more pragmatic approach to the subject. Compare the two views, and specify the elements in their writing that contribute to the overall strength of their arguments.

7. Perrin uses enumeration and illustration to structure his essay. What are some of the strengths and weaknesses of employing traditional and orderly means of presenting one's thoughts?

8. Write an essay titled "Nature's Revenge" in which you examine the consequences of environmental abuse. Consider the short- as well as the long-term effects on the quality of life. Use support from any three writers in this chapter to defend your opinion.

9. Write specifically about our relationship to other living creatures on our planet. Is it one of exploitation, cooperation, or tyranny? How does this relationship influence how we treat each other? Explore the answers to these questions in an essay. Use the works of Lopez, Bass, and Chief Seattle to support your thesis.

NETWORKING
Applying Digital and Multimedia Literacies

Join an online newsgroup devoted to addressing a specific environmental issue—for example, atomic waste, overdevelopment, or environmental regulations and deregulations. Follow the conversation of the newsgroup for one month. Write an essay describing what the chief concerns of the newsgroup members are, how they address issues regarding the environment, and what specific actions they recommend or take over the course of your membership.

Chapter *14*

Science and Technology
What Can Science Teach Us?

Contrary to popular assumptions, contemporary science and technology are not dry subjects but rather are bodies of specialized knowledge concerned with the great how and why questions of our time. In fact, we are currently in the midst of a whole series of scientific revolutions that will radically transform our lives in the 21st century. The essential problem for humankind is to make sense of all this revolutionary scientific and technological knowledge, invest it with value, use it ethically, and make it serve our cultural and global needs.

As you will see in the essays in this chapter, human beings are always the ultimate subject of scientific investigation. Science and mathematics attempt to understand the physical, biological, and chemical events that shape our lives. Whenever we switch on a light or turn on a computer, take an aspirin or start the car, we see that science and technology have intervened effectively in our lives. Often the specialized knowledge of science forces us to make painful decisions, and the misuse of science can have disastrous results.

The technology that arises from science affects everyday decisions as well as the larger culture. Nowhere is the impact of science more apparent than in the field of biotechnology. As Dinesh D'Souza observes in his essay on the biotech revolution, science is intended to serve us, to help us with our common dilemmas. At the same time, biotechnology reminds us that despite advances, we are still mortals confronting ethical dilemmas. Even as knowledge flows from research laboratories, these mortal paradoxes tend to perplex and goad us as we seek scientific solutions to the complex problems of our era.

Science and technology as specialized bodies of knowledge can send contradictory messages because science and technology are socially constructed and reflect the contours of culture. How we manage the revolution in science—how we harness nuclear power or battle the ravages of AIDS—will determine the health of civilization in our century.

PREVIEWING THE CHAPTER

As you read the essays in this chapter and respond to them in discussion and writing, consider the following questions:

- Does the author take a personal or an objective approach to the subject? What is the effect?
- What area of scientific or technological inquiry does the writer focus on?
- What scientific conflicts arise in the course of the essay?
- Is the writer a specialist, a layperson, a journalist, or a commentator? How does the background of the writer affect the tone of the essay?
- What assumptions does the author make about his or her audience? How much specialized knowledge must you bring to the essay?
- How do social issues enter into the author's presentation?
- What gender issues are raised by the author?
- How have your perceptions of the author's topic been changed or enhanced? What new knowledge have you gained? Does the writer contradict any of your assumptions or beliefs?
- Is the writer optimistic or pessimistic about the state of technology or science? How do you know?

Classic and Contemporary Images
WHERE IS SCIENCE TAKING US?

Using a Critical Perspective   Make a series of observations about each of these images. Where does your eye rest in each one? How many objects and details do you see? What reasonable inferences can you draw about the relationship of the artist who created the 15th-century image to the culture and historical period? What purpose did the scientists who created and control the Hubble Space Telescope have? What purposes do the 15th-century artist and 20th-century scientist have in common? Argue for or against the proposition that art can actually capture the advances in science, technology, and humanity that we have experienced over time.

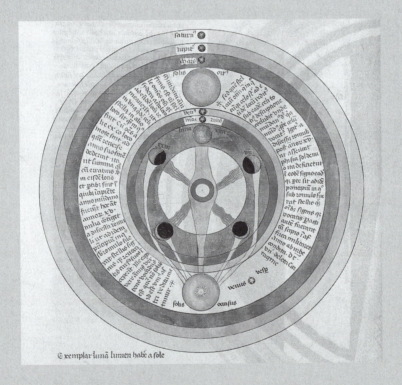

During the Renaissance in Europe, scientists such as Nicolaus Copernicus (1473–1543) and Galileo Galilei (1564–1642) revolutionized the way Europeans viewed the universe and their place in it by proving that the earth and the planets revolve around the sun, thus changing forever the worldview exemplified by the 15th-century Flemish depiction of the movements of the sun and moon shown here.

Galileo's primitive telescope was a distant forerunner of the powerful
Hubble Space Telescope, launched in 1990, which is able to take
photographs of extremely distant stars and other phenomena,
such as the gaseous pillars shown here, as it orbits the earth.

Classic and Contemporary Essays
HOW HAS NATURE EVOLVED?

Evolution seems to be more highly and hotly debated each year, insinuating itself into educational, political, scientific, and religious debates. Unfortunately, extreme positions on evolution tend to obscure what is valuable about the concept. The idea or theory of evolution is rooted in scientific creativity and the scientific method. Scientists are observers and collectors of information, and they use facts to build an explanation of the natural world and our place in it. Darwin looked carefully at nature and the physical world, as the following reading on natural selection illustrates. In his autobiography, Darwin observed that he "collected facts on a wholesale scale" before arriving at his theory of natural selection, and this inductive approach, at the heart of *On the Origin of Species* (1859), typifies his method of inquiry. But does evolutionary theory explain all the facts—all of humankind's problems? Does evolution mark the progress of human civilization, or are dimensions needed to explain our relationship to the world and the world's events? Verlyn Klinkenborg, who writes editorials and vignettes on science and nature for the *New York Times*, touches on these questions in an essay he composed celebrating the bicentennial of Darwin's birth. But Klinkenborg broadens his inquiry to touch on the scientific ideas of Mendel, the structure of DNA, and the broader issue of "our failure to come to terms with science and the teaching of science." Darwin's great idea, as Klinkenborg suggests, helps to explain our struggle for existence and meaning in the modern world.

Natural Selection

Charles Darwin

Charles Darwin *(1809–1882) was born in England and studied medicine at Edinburgh. He also studied for the ministry at Cambridge but soon turned his interest to natural history. Through his friendship with a well-known botanist, he was given the opportunity to take a five-year cruise around the world (1831–1836) aboard the H.M.S.* Beagle, *serving as a naturalist. This started Darwin on a career of accumulating and assimilating data that resulted in the formulation of his concept of evolution. He spent the remainder of his life carefully and methodically working over the information from his copious notes. He first published his findings in 1858 and a year later published his influential* On the Origin of Species. *This seminal work was supplemented and elaborated on in many later books, including* The Descent of Man *(1871). The following selection demonstrates the methodical and meticulous method Darwin used in developing his concepts.*

In order to make it clear how, as I believe, natural selection acts, I must beg permis- 1
sion to give one or two imaginary illustrations. Let us take the case of a wolf, which
preys on various animals, securing some by craft, some by strength, and some by
fleetness; and let us suppose that the fleetest prey, a deer for instance, had from any
change in the country increased in numbers, or that other prey had decreased in
numbers, during that season of the year when the wolf is hardest pressed for food.
I can under such circumstances see no reason to doubt that the swiftest and slim-
mest wolves would have the best chance of surviving, and so be preserved or
selected, provided always that they retained strength to master their prey at this or at
some other period of the year, when they might be compelled to prey on other animals. I can see no more reason to doubt this, than that man can improve the fleetness of his greyhounds by careful and methodical selection, or by that unconscious
selection which results from each man trying to keep the best dogs without any
thought of modifying the breed.

Even without any change in the proportional numbers of the animals on 2
which our wolf preyed, a cub might be born with an innate tendency to pursue
certain kinds of prey. Nor can this be thought very improbable; for we often
observe great differences in the natural tendencies of our domestic animals;
one cat, for instance, taking to catch rats, another mice; one cat, according
to Mr. St. John, bringing home winged game, another hares or rabbits, and
another hunting on marshy ground and almost nightly catching woodcocks or
snipes. The tendency to catch rats rather than mice is known to be inherited.
Now, if any slight innate change of habit or of structure benefited an individual
wolf, it would have the best chance of surviving and of leaving offspring. Some
of its young would probably inherit the same habits or structure, and by the
repetition of this process, a new variety might be formed which would either
supplant or coexist with the parent-form of wolf. Or, again, the wolves inhabiting
a mountainous district, and those frequenting the lowlands, would naturally be
forced to hunt different prey; and from the continued preservation of the individuals best fitted for the two sites, two varieties might slowly be formed. These
varieties would cross and blend where they met; but to this subject of inter-
crossing we shall soon have to return. I may add, that, according to Mr. Pierce,
there are two varieties of the wolf inhabiting the Catskill Mountains in the
United States, one with a light greyhound-like form, which pursues deer, and
the other more bulky, with shorter legs, which more frequently attacks the
shepherd's flocks.

Let us now take a more complex case. Certain plants excrete a sweet juice, 3
apparently for the sake of eliminating something injurious from their sap; this is
effected by glands at the base of the stipules in some Leguminosae, and at the
back of the leaf of the common laurel. This juice, though small in quantity, is
greedily sought by insects. Let us now suppose a little sweet juice or nectar to be
excreted by the inner bases of the petals of a flower. In this case insects in seeking
the nectar would get dusted with pollen, and would certainly often transport the
pollen from one flower to the stigma of another flower. The flowers of two distinct
individuals of the same species would thus get crossed; and the act of crossing,

we have good reason to believe (as will hereafter be more fully alluded to), would produce very vigorous seedlings, which consequently would have the best chance of flourishing and surviving. Some of these seedlings would probably inherit the nectar-excreting power. Those individual flowers which had the largest glands or nectaries, and which excreted most nectar, would be oftenest visited by insects, and would be oftenest crossed; and so in the long-run would gain the upper hand. Those flowers, also, which had their stamens and pistils placed, in relation to the size and habits of the particular insects which visited them, so as to favor in any degree the transportal of their pollen from flower to flower, would likewise be favored or selected. We might have taken the case of insects visiting flowers for the sake of collecting pollen instead of nectar; and as pollen is formed for the sole object of fertilization, its destruction appears a simple loss to the plant; yet if a little pollen were carried, at first occasionally and then habitually, by the pollen-devouring insects from flower to flower, and a cross thus effected, although nine-tenths of the pollen were destroyed, it might still be a great gain to the plant; and those individuals which produced more and more pollen, and had larger and larger anthers, would be selected.

4   When our plant, by this process of the continued preservation or natural selection of more and more attractive flowers, had been rendered highly attractive to insects, they would, unintentionally on their part, regularly carry pollen from flower to flower; and that they can most effectually do this, I could easily show by many striking instances. I will give only one—not as a very striking case, but as likewise illustrating one step in the separation of the sexes of plants, presently to be alluded to. Some holly-trees bear only male flowers, which have four stamens producing rather a small quantity of pollen, and a rudimentary pistil; other holly-trees bear only female flowers; these have a full-sized pistil, and four stamens with shriveled anthers, in which not a grain of pollen can be detected. Having found a female tree exactly sixty yards from a male tree, I put the stigmas of twenty flowers, taken from different branches, under the microscope, and on all, without exception, there were pollen-grains, and on some a profusion of pollen. As the wind had set for several days from the female to the male tree, the pollen could not thus have been carried. The weather had been cold and boisterous, and therefore not favorable to bees; nevertheless every female flower which I examined had been effectually fertilized by the bees, accidentally dusted with pollen, having flown from tree to tree in search of nectar. But to return to our imaginary case: As soon as the plant had been rendered so highly attractive to insects that pollen was regularly carried from flower to flower, another process might commence. No naturalist doubts the advantage of what has been called the "physiological division of labor"; hence we may believe that it would be advantageous to a plant to produce stamens alone in one flower or on one whole plant, and pistils alone in another flower or on another plant. In plants under culture and placed under new conditions of life, sometimes the male organs and sometimes the female organs become more or less impotent; now if we suppose this to occur in ever so slight a degree under nature, then as pollen is already carried regularly from flower to flower, and as a more complete

separation of the sexes of our plant would be advantageous on the principle of the division of labor, individuals with this tendency more and more increased, would be continually favored or selected, until at last a complete separation of the sexes would be effected.

Let us now turn to the nectar-feeding insects in our imaginary case: We may 5 suppose the plant of which we have been slowly increasing the nectar by continued selection, to be a common plant; and that certain insects depended in main part on its nectar for food. I could give many facts, showing how anxious bees are to save time; for instance, their habit of cutting holes and sucking the nectar at the bases of certain flowers, which they can, with a very little more trouble, enter by the mouth. Bearing such facts in mind, I can see no reason to doubt that an accidental deviation in the size and form of the body, or in the curvature and length of the proboscis, etc., far too slight to be appreciated by us, might profit a bee or other insect, so that an individual so characterized would be able to obtain its food more quickly, and so have a better chance of living and leaving descendants. Its descendants would probably inherit a tendency to a similar slight deviation of structure. The tubes of the corollas of the common red and incarnate clovers (Trifolium pratense and incarnatum) do not on a hasty glance appear to differ in length; yet the hive-bee can easily suck the nectar out of the incarnate clover, but not out of the common red clover, which is visited by humble-bees alone; so that the whole fields of the red clover offer in vain an abundant supply of precious nectar to the hive-bee. Thus it might be a great advantage to the hive-bee to have a slightly longer or differently constructed proboscis. On the other hand, I have found by experiment that the fertility of clover greatly depends on bees visiting and moving parts of the corolla, so as to push the pollen on to the stigmatic surface. Hence, again, if humble-bees were to become rare in any country, it might be a great advantage to the red clover to have a shorter or more deeply divided tube to its corolla, so that the hive-bee could visit its flowers. Thus I can understand how a flower and a bee might slowly become, either simultaneously or one after the other, modified and adapted in the most perfect manner to each other, by the continued preservation of individuals presenting mutual and slightly favorable deviations of structure.

I am well aware that this doctrine of natural selection, exemplified in the 6 above imaginary instances, is open to the same objections which were at first urged against Sir Charles Lyell's noble views on "the modern changes of the earth, as illustrative of geology"; but we now very seldom hear the action, for instance, of the coast-waves, called a trifling and insignificant cause, when applied to the excavation of gigantic valleys or to the formation of the longest lines of inland cliffs. Natural selection can act only by the preservation and accumulation of infinitesimally small inherited modifications, each profitable to the preserved being; and as modern geology has almost banished such views as the excavation of a great valley by a single diluvial wave, so will natural selection, if it be a true principle, banish the belief of the continued creation of new organic beings, or of any great and sudden modification in their structure.

COMPREHENSION

1. What does Darwin mean by the term *natural selection?*
2. What is Darwin attempting to refute by his concept of natural selection? Where in the essay is this refutation articulated?
3. Explain what Darwin means by the "physiological division of labor" (paragraph 4).
4. Define the following terms: *innate* (paragraph 2), *stamens* and *pistils* (paragraph 3), *rudimentary* (paragraph 4), *incarnate* (paragraph 5), and *doctrine* (paragraph 6).

RHETORIC

1. In the introduction, Darwin makes an analogy between the needs of humans and those of nature. What is this analogy, and why is it important in devising his argument?
2. What is the tone of the essay? Consider such phrases as "beg permission" (paragraph 1) and "Let us now" (paragraph 3).
3. Darwin uses two "imaginary illustrations" in an attempt to prove his point. What are they, and why are these hypothetical illustrations more effective than real-life ones for his purpose?
4. Darwin tends to use extremely long sentences when he wishes to illustrate a process. For example, the sentence in paragraph 3 that begins "We might have taken" is 101 words long. Deconstruct this sentence by paying special attention to its punctuation, its logical succession of clauses, and its effect on the reader of describing so many processes within its boundaries. What is the relationship between its rhetorical style and purpose?
5. Who is the implied audience for the essay? Cite specific aspects of the rhetoric that led you to your conclusion.
6. What gives Darwin his authority? Specifically, how is his authority linked to the specialized vocabulary of the essay and to the way Darwin uses language to articulate natural processes?
7. Darwin uses the argumentative technique of disarming potential critics in the final paragraph. What is the rhetorical function of this device? Does it strengthen or weaken his argument? Explain your view.

WRITING

1. Write a précis of the essay, focusing on the major points Darwin is trying to assert in his theory of natural selection.
2. **Writing an Argument:** In an essay, argue for or against the proposition that in order to agree with or refute Darwin's ideas of natural selection, one would have to have at least as much experience in observing nature as Darwin obviously had.
3. **Writing an Argument:** Argue for or against the view that Darwin's theory can have disastrous consequences for the human species if applied to politics, sociology, or economics.

NETWORKING
Applying Digital and Multimedia Literacies

Exploring a Museum's Online Exhibit: Locate online and visit the American Museum of Natural History's Web site and virtual exhibit about Charles Darwin, including an informational video. Which aspect of this exhibit do you find the most interesting, and why? How many types of media does the site make use of? What are your thoughts on the site's navigability? What about its design? How do all of these aspects contribute to its purpose?

Darwin at 200: The Ongoing Force of His Unconventional Idea

Verlyn Klinkenborg

Verlyn Klinkenborg (b. 1952) was born in Colorado and raised on an Iowa farm until he was 14, at which time his family moved to the San Francisco Bay Area. Klinkenborg studied at Pomona College (BA, 1974) and Princeton University (PhD, 1982); he has taught at Princeton, Pomona, Harvard University, Fordham University, Bard College, and elsewhere. His books include Making Hay *(1986),* The Last Fine Time *(1991),* The Rural Life *(2003), and* Timothy: Or, Notes on an Abject Reptile *(2006). Klinkenborg, who now lives on a farm in upstate New York, joined the editorial board of the* New York Times *in 1997, and his essays on rural life are a regular feature of the newspaper's editorial page. In this essay, published in the* Times *in 2009, Klinkenborg celebrates the bicentennial of Charles Darwin.*

I can't help wondering what Charles Darwin would think if he could survey the 1 state of his intellectual achievement today, 200 years after his birth and 150 years after the publication of *On the Origin of Species*, the book that changed everything. His central idea—evolution by means of natural selection—was in some sense the product of his time, as Darwin well knew. He was the grandson of Erasmus Darwin, who grasped that there was something wrong with the conventional notion of fixed species. And his theory was hastened into print and into joint presentation by the independent discoveries of Alfred Russel Wallace half a world away.

2   But Darwin's theory was the product of years of patient observation. We love to believe in science by epiphany, but the work of real scientists is to rigorously test their epiphanies after they have been boiled down to working hypotheses. Most of Darwin's life was devoted to gathering evidence for just such tests. He writes with an air of incompleteness because he was aware that it would take the work of many scientists to confirm his theory in detail.

3   I doubt that much in the subsequent history of Darwin's idea would have surprised him. The most important discoveries—Mendel's genetics and the structure of DNA—would almost certainly have gratified him because they reveal the physical basis for the variation underlying evolution. It would have gratified him to see his ideas so thoroughly tested and to see so many of them confirmed. He could hardly have expected to be right so often.

4   Perhaps one day we will not call evolution "Darwinism." After all, we do not call classical mechanics "Newtonism." But that raises the question of whether a biological Einstein is possible, someone who demonstrates that Darwin's theory is a limited case. What Darwin proposed was not a set of immutable mathematical formulas. It was a theory of biological history that was itself set in history. That the details have changed does not invalidate his accomplishment. If anything, it enhances it. His writings were not intended to be scriptural. They were meant to be tested.

5   As for the other fate of so-called Darwinism—the reductionist controversy fostered by religious conservatives—well, Darwin knew plenty about that, too. The cultural opposition to evolution was then, as now, scientifically irrelevant. Perhaps the persistence of opposition to evolution is a reminder that culture is not biological, or else we might have evolved past such a gnashing of sensibilities. In a way, our peculiarly American failure to come to terms with Darwin's theory and what it's become since 1859 is a sign of something broader: our failure to come to terms with science and the teaching of science.

6   Darwin does not fit our image of a scientist. From the 21st century, he seems at first to bear a closer resemblance to an amateur naturalist like Gilbert White in the 18th century. But that is an illusion. Darwin's funding was private, his habit was retiring and he lacked the kind of institutional support that we associate with science because it did not exist. But Darwin's extensive scientific correspondence makes it clear that he was not the least bit reclusive intellectually and that he understood the character of science as it was practiced in his day as well as anyone.

7   We expect these days that a boy or girl obsessed with beetles may eventually find a home in a university or a laboratory or a museum. But Darwin's life was his museum, and he was its curator. In June 1833, still early in the five-year voyage of the *Beagle,* he wrote about rounding Cape Horn: "It is a grand spectacle to see all nature thus raging; but Heaven knows every one in the *Beagle* has seen enough in this one summer to last them their natural lives." (In this same letter, he celebrates the parliamentary attack on slavery in England.)

8   The rest of Darwin's life did in fact revolve around that voyage. As you sift through the notes and letters and publications that stemmed from his years on the *Beagle,* you begin to understand how careful, how inquisitive and how various

his mind was. The voyage of the *Beagle*—and of a young naturalist who was 22 at its outset—is still one of the most compelling stories in science.

Darwin recedes, but his idea does not. It is absorbed, with adaptations, into the foundation of the biological sciences. In a very real sense, it is the cornerstone of what we know about life on earth. Darwin's version of that great idea was very much of its time, and yet the whole weight of his time was set against it. From one perspective, Darwin looks completely conventional—white, male, well born, leisured, patrician. But from another, he turned the fortune of his circumstances into the most unconventional idea of all: the one that showed humans their true ancestry in nature.

COMPREHENSION

1. According to Klinkenborg, why was Darwin's idea "unconventional"?
2. How does Darwin's theory reflect the scientific method?
3. What is Klinkenborg's opinion concerning "Darwinism" and "so-called Darwinism"? Would he be happy to see both terms disappear? Why or why not?

RHETORIC

1. Does Klinkenborg establish a claim in this essay, or does he simply want to celebrate the bicentennial of Darwin's birth? Justify your answer.
2. How does Klinkenborg use exemplification as a compositional strategy? What examples does he provide, and why?
3. Klinkenborg alludes to Erasmus Darwin, Alfred Russel Wallace, Mendel, Newton, and Gilbert White. Who were they, and what is the writer's purpose in referring to them?
4. Explain the way that definition serves to structure parts of this essay.
5. Do you find Klinkenborg's conclusion effective? Why or why not?

WRITING

1. Compose your own brief celebration of Charles Darwin.
2. Write an extended definition of evolutionary theory.
3. **Writing an Argument:** Argue for or against the proposition that "Darwinism" is no longer a useful term to describe evolutionary theory.

NETWORKING
Applying Digital and Multimedia Literacies

Creating a Hyperlinked Extended Definition: Format question 2 under Writing as an electronic text, using hyperlinks to clarify and expand on your definition of evolutionary theory.

**Synthesis: Classic and Contemporary
Questions for Comparison**

1. How do Darwin and Klinkenborg approach the subject of evolution? Do they have the same or different priorities, and why? Are they writing for the same audience? Use examples from both selections to support your response.
2. Analyze the language used in the two essays. What is similar or different about the style and diction of the two pieces? How does each use details? Is one essay more accessible to the modern reader? Why or why not?
3. How do both essays treat the scientific method? Is one selection more "scientific" in its approach than the other? Explain your response.

Planets in the Sky with Diamonds

Diane Ackerman

Diane Ackerman (b. 1948) is an American naturalist, essayist, poet, and children's book author. She was born in Waukegan, Illinois, where she lived for eight years before the family moved to Allentown, Pennsylvania. Ackerman attended Pennsylvania State University where she earned her BA. She received MA, MFA, and PhD degrees from Cornell University. She is best known for A Natural History of the Senses *(1990), which inspired a* Nova *miniseries; and her memoir,* The Zookeeper's Wife: A War Story *(2007), among more than a dozen nonfiction works. Ackerman has taught at several universities including Cornell and Columbia. In this essay from the October 2, 2011, issue of the* New York Times, *Ackerman scans the universe for signs of life.*

1   Goldilocks is alive in the constellation Vela. Her real name is HD 85512b, which may not roll off the tongue, but it's sheer poetry to the ears of sky watchers like me, who long for signs of an Earth-like planet that might harbor life.

2   This newly discovered planet orbits its sun in what's called the "Goldilocks," or habitable zone, at the right distance for liquid water to sparkle on the surface and life to bloom in the shallows. Life as we know it, anyway, with wings and dreams, if the planet has a rocky surface—and isn't too hot or too cold—as well as a tent of clouds for shade.

3   That's a lot of ifs, which is why other candidates have been scarce. This is our best hope, though she's 36 light-years away, beyond the reach of our spacecrafts or clear view of present telescopes, but well within the imagination. Her temperatures may range from 85 to 120 degrees, which conjures up images of equatorial Africa, or much of the hot, muggy United States this past July.

The past month has been a marvel in the planetary world. In addition to HD 4 85512b, astronomers spotted a planet that may be fashioned entirely of diamond, a brilliant diadem set in the black velvet of space. For all we know, it has baguette moons in tow. And a few weeks later, planet hunters confirmed the discovery of Kepler-16b, a planet that circles two suns in the constellation Cygnus.

In the *Star Wars* saga, Luke Skywalker hailed from such a world, Tatooine, 5 where he paused from work on his uncle's moisture farm to enjoy a smoldery suns-set. Until now a stable planet orbiting twin suns was science fiction, strictly hints and hunches. Wouldn't the quarreling gravity of two suns shear the planet apart, swallow it whole, or hurtle it off into space? Apparently not. Such solar systems, with winking suns that eclipse one another every few weeks, may be common throughout the universe. That's the best thing about discovery, how it widens the mind's eye, refines the scope of our inquiries.

However, we won't be glimpsing these worlds anytime soon, I'm afraid. If we 6 want to explore in fine detail, we'll need better eyes in the sky and faster robotic spaceships. I'm for both. Despite all the problems that beset us, we're on the threshold of a new era of exploration and discovery. Scientists are asking thrilling questions, like: what existed before the universe? How did we get from the Big Bang to the whole shebang? Can we design spaceships that fly faster than the speed of light? Do other planetarians haunt the wilderness of space, or are we alone? I hope we'll continue sending scouts around our solar system, and use the planets as stepping stones to the stars.

This is not a new goal, but one of humanity's oldest yearnings. Every society 7 has been tantalized by the great loom of the sky with its flowing quilt of stars. The Egyptian pyramids may have been arranged like the belt stars of Orion, pointing to Sirius, so that the pharaoh's soul would be launched into the heavens where he'd shimmer as a star. To the San people in the Kalahari, the Milky Way is the "backbone of night."

In the 20th century, we sent robot emissaries to explore the solar system and 8 voyage deep into space. With the cupped ears of radio telescopes, we began listening for voices from other worlds. We rode fierce winds to the Moon and looked back in wonder, amazed to see Earth whole. Viewed from space, Earth had no visible fences, military zones or national borders. But it did have the thinnest rind—an atmosphere embracing the sky, weather systems and all of human history. That image from an Apollo mission changed everything.

We're explorers by design, right down to our cells, and we thrive on quests. 9 Stars flare like distant campfires overhead, and we wonder if they're home to other worlds like our own. Or made of diamond. I'm hoping NASA will continue to find the boosters it needs, because our compass points to the stars.

COMPREHENSION

1. Does Ackerman support space exploration? Why or why not?
2. Why does Ackerman refer to *Star Wars*, ancient Egypt, and the San people of the Kalahari?

3. Why does Ackerman write in her concluding paragraph, "I'm hoping NASA will continue to find the boosters it needs"? What is the context here?

RHETORIC

1. Explain the allusion in Ackerman's title. How does this reference relate to the content of the essay?
2. How do the journalistic requirements of an op-ed newspaper piece dictate the style, organization, and content of Ackerman's essay?
3. What is the writer's tone? Is she objective or subjective? Explain.
4. What is Ackerman's claim? Where does she make appeals to reason and emotion?
5. Ackerman is the author of several books of poetry. What poetic elements do you find in this essay?

WRITING

1. Write an essay on the impact of science fiction films like *Star Wars* on the ways we think about the universe.
2. Ackerman's dissertation advisor at Cornell was the noted writer Carl Sagan, who has an essay in this chapter. Read Sagan's essay, and then write a comparative essay linking his piece to the article by Ackerman.
3. **Writing an Argument:** Do you think that life exists elsewhere in the universe? Respond in an argumentative essay.

NETWORKING
Applying Digital and Multimedia Literacies

Starting with an Author Web Site: Go to Ackerman's Web site. Explore the links that she provides, which will take you to interviews, talks, reviews, and other informational sites. Then compose a brief critical biography of the author.

Nutcracker.com

David Sedaris

David Sedaris (b. 1957), *who was born in Johnson City, New York, and grew up in Raleigh, North Carolina, is a well-known humorist, essayist, diarist, short-story writer, and radio commentator. After graduating from the Art Institute of Chicago in 1987, Sedaris held several temporary jobs, ranging from a cleaner of apartments to an elf in SantaLand at Macy's. His stint on National Public Radio's* Morning

Edition *established Sedaris as a popular if quirky humorist and led to his first collection of essays,* Barrel Fever *(2000). Termed by* Entertainment Weekly *"a crackpot in the best sense of the word," Sedaris has also written* Naked *(1997),* Me Talk Pretty One Day *(2000),* Dress Your Family in Corduroy and Denim *(2004),* When You're Engulfed in Flames *(2008), and other works. In this essay, Sedaris humorously explains why he is a technophobe.*

It was my father's dream that one day the people of the world would be connected 1 to one another through a network of blocky, refrigerator-size computers, much like those he was helping develop at IBM. He envisioned families of the future gathered around their mammoth terminals, ordering groceries and paying their taxes from the comfort of their own homes. A person could compose music, design a doghouse, and . . . something more, something even better. "A person could . . . he could . . . "

When predicting this utopia, he would eventually reach a point where words 2 failed him. His eyes would widen and sparkle at the thought of this indescribable something more. "I mean, my God," he'd say, "just think about it."

My sisters and I preferred not to. I didn't know about them, but I was hoping 3 the people of the world might be united by something more interesting, like drugs or an armed struggle against the undead. Unfortunately, my father's team won, so computers it is. My only regret is that this had to happen during my lifetime.

Somewhere in the back of my mind is a dim memory of standing in some line 4 holding a perforated card. I remember the cheap, slightly clinical feeling it gave me, and recall thinking that the computer would never advance much further than this. Call me naive, but I seem to have underestimated the universal desire to sit in a hard plastic chair and stare at a screen until your eyes cross. My father saw it coming, but this was a future that took me completely by surprise. There were no computers in my high school, and the first two times I attempted college, people were still counting on their fingers and removing their shoes when the numbers got above ten. I wasn't really aware of computers until the mid-1980s. For some reason, I seemed to know quite a few graphic designers whose homes and offices pleasantly stank of Spray Mount. Their floors were always collaged with stray bits of paper, and trapped flies waved for help from the gummy killing fields of their tabletops. I had always counted on these friends to loan me the adhesive of my choice, but then, seemingly overnight, their Scotch tape and rubber cement were gone, replaced with odorless computers and spongy mouse pads. They had nothing left that I wanted to borrow, and so I dropped them and fell in with a group of typesetters who ultimately betrayed me as well.

Thanks to my complete lack of office skills, I found it fairly easy to avoid 5 direct contact with the new technology. The indirect contact was disturbing enough. I was still living in Chicago when I began to receive creepy Christmas newsletters designed to look like tabloids and annual reports. Word processors made writing fun. They did not, however, make reading fun, a point made painfully evident by such publications as *The Herald Family Tribune* and *Wassup with the Wexlers!*

6   Friends who had previously expressed no interest in torture began sending letters composed to resemble Chinese take-out menus and the Dead Sea Scrolls. Everybody had a font, and I was told that I should get one, too. The authors of these letters shared an enthusiasm with the sort of people who now arrived at dinner parties hoisting expensive new video cameras and suggesting that, after dessert, we all sit down and replay the evening on TV. We, the regular people of the world, now had access to the means of production, but still I failed to see what all the fuss was about. A dopey letter is still a dopey letter, no matter how you dress it up; and there's a reason regular people don't appear on TV: We're boring.

7   By the early 1990s I was living in New York and working for a housecleaning company. My job taught me that regardless of their purported virtues, computers are a pain in the ass to keep clean. The pebbled surface is a magnet for grease and dirt, and you can pretty much forget about reaming out the gaps in the keyboard. More than once I accidentally pushed a button and recoiled in terror as the blank screen came to life with exotic tropical fish or swarms of flying toasters. Equally distressing was the way people used the slanted roofs of their terminals to display framed photographs and great populations of plush and plastic creatures, which would fall behind the desk the moment I began cleaning the screen. There was never any place to plug in the vacuum, as every outlet was occupied by some member of the computer family. Cords ran wild, and everyone seemed to own one of those ominous foot-long power strips with the blinking red light that sends the message YOU MUST LEAVE US ALONE. I was more than happy to comply, and the complaints came rolling in.

8   Due to my general aversion to machines and a few pronounced episodes of screaming, I was labeled a technophobe, a term that ranks fairly low on my scale of fightin' words. The word *phobic* has its place when properly used, but lately it's been declawed by the pompous insistence that most animosity is based upon fear rather than loathing. No credit is given for distinguishing between these two very different emotions. I fear snakes. I hate computers. My hatred is entrenched, and I nourish it daily. I'm comfortable with it, and no community outreach program will change my mind.

9   I hate computers for getting their own section in the *New York Times* and for lengthening commercials with the mention of a Web site address. Who really wants to find out more about Procter & Gamble? Just buy the toothpaste or laundry detergent, and get on with it. I hate them for creating the word *org* and I hate them for e-mail, which isn't real mail but a variation of the pointless notes people used to pass in class. I hate computers for replacing the card catalog in the New York Public Library and I hate the way they've invaded the movies. I'm not talking about their contribution to the world of special effects. I have nothing against a well-defined mutant or full-scale alien invasion—that's *good* technology. I'm talking about their actual presence *in* any given movie. They've become like horses in a western—they may not be the main focus, but everybody seems to have one. Each tiresome new thriller includes a scene in which the hero, trapped by some version of the enemy, runs for his desk in a desperate race against time. Music swells and droplets of sweat rain down onto the keyboard as he sits at his laptop,

frantically pawing for answers. It might be different if he were flagging down a passing car or trying to phone for help, but typing, in and of itself, is not an inherently dramatic activity.

I hate computers for any number of reasons, but I despise them most for what 10 they've done to my friend the typewriter. In a democratic country you'd think there would be room for both of them, but computers won't rest until I'm making my ribbons from torn shirts and brewing Wite-Out in my bathtub. Their goal is to place the IBM Selectric II beside the feather quill and chisel in the museum of antiquated writing implements. They're power hungry, and someone needs to stop them.

When told I'm like the guy still pining for his eight-track tapes, I say, "You 11 have eight-tracks? Where?" In reality I know nothing about them, yet I feel it's important to express some solidarity with others who have had the rug pulled out from beneath them. I don't care if it can count words or rearrange paragraphs at the push of a button, I don't want a computer. Unlike the faint scurry raised by fingers against a plastic computer keyboard, the smack and clatter of a typewriter suggests that you're actually building something. At the end of a miserable day, instead of grieving my virtual nothing, I can always look at my loaded wastepaper basket and tell myself that if I failed, at least I took a few trees down with me.

When forced to leave my house for an extended period of time, I take my 12 typewriter with me, and together we endure the wretchedness of passing through the X-ray scanner. The laptops roll merrily down the belt, while I'm instructed to stand aside and open my bag. To me it seems like a normal enough thing to be carrying, but the typewriter's declining popularity arouses suspicion and I wind up eliciting the sort of reaction one might expect when traveling with a cannon.

"It's a typewriter," I say. "You use it to write angry letters to airport authorities." 13

The keys are then slapped and pounded, and I'm forced to explain that if you 14 want the words to appear, you first have to plug it in and insert a sheet of paper.

The goons shake their heads and tell me I really should be using a computer. 15 That's their job, to stand around in an ill-fitting uniform and tell you how you should lead your life. I'm told the exact same thing later in the evening when the bellhop knocks on my hotel door. The people whose televisions I can hear have complained about my typing, and he has come to make me stop. To hear him talk, you'd think I'd been playing the kettledrum. In the great scheme of things, the typewriter is not nearly as loud as he makes it out to be, but there's no use arguing with him. "You know," he says, "you really should be using a computer."

You have to wonder where you've gone wrong when twice a day you're 16 offered writing advice from men in funny hats. The harder I'm pressured to use a computer, the harder I resist. One by one, all of my friends have deserted me and fled to the dark side. "How can I write you if you don't have an e-mail address?" they ask. They talk of their B-trees and Disk Doctors and then have the nerve to complain when I discuss bowel obstructions at the dinner table.

Who needs them? I think. I figured I'd always have my family and was devas- 17 tated when my sister Amy brought home a candy-colored laptop. "I only use it for e-mail," she said. Coming from her, these words made me physically ill. "It's fun," she said. "People send you things. Look at this." She pushed a button, and there, on the screen, was a naked man lying facedown on a carpet. His hair was graying and his hands were cuffed behind his doughy back. A woman entered the room. You couldn't see her face, just her legs and feet, which were big and mean-looking, forced into sharp-toed shoes with high, pencil-thin heels. The man on the carpet shifted position, and when his testicles came into view, the woman reacted as if she had seen an old balding mouse, one that she had been trying to kill for a long time. She stomped on the man's testicles with the toes of her shoes and then she turned around and stomped on them with the heels. She kicked them mercilessly and, just when I thought she'd finished, she got her second wind and started all over again.

18   I'd never realized that a computer could act so much like a TV set. No one had ever told me that the picture could be so clear, that the cries of pain could be heard so distinctly. This, I thought, was what my father had been envisioning all those years ago when words had failed him, not necessarily this scene, but something equally capable of provoking such wonder.

19   "Again?" Amy pushed a button and, our faces bathed in the glow of the screen, we watched the future a second time.

COMPREHENSION

1. What distinguishes the author from his father and his sister Amy?
2. Why does Sedaris hate computers? Does he actually enjoy being a "technophobe"? How do you know?
3. What sort of writer is Sedaris? Why doesn't he want to use computers to help him in the writing process?

RHETORIC

1. How do you interpret the title? How does the title prepare us for the tone of this selection?
2. Sedaris employs a personal voice in this essay. What does the "I" point of view contribute to the selection?
3. What comic strategies does the author develop? What details stand out? Does comedy serve to support or undercut his claim?
4. How does Sedaris argue his case? Does he actually have a case, or a cause, or is his purpose simply to amuse the reader? How do you know?
5. What principle of classification appears in the essay, and how does this rhetorical strategy serve the author's purpose?
6. How does the writer use comparison and contrast, narration, and description to develop the essay?
7. Explain the impact and significance of the concluding scene. How does the tone alter here? What is the final effect? What is the writer's parting message to his readers?

WRITING

1. In a personal essay employing narration and description as well as analysis, describe the impact of computers on your family life. Use a comic approach to the subject.
2. Write an analysis of the elements of humor that appear in Sedaris's essay. Why is comedy an appropriate strategy for dealing with the subject of computer technology?
3. **Writing an Argument:** Write an essay about why you love or hate computers. Use ironic humor to undercut your argument—to convince readers that your opinions are actually the opposite of what you proclaim.

NETWORKING
Applying Digital and Multimedia Literacies

Using Technology (and Humor) to Critique Technology: Make your response to question 3 under Writing even more humorous by employing specific aspects of technology just as you are declaring your dislike for or frustration with them. For instance, you might create a blog that complains about bloggers, or bemoan the lack of focus in hyperlinked texts in an essay that is rife with linkage. Have a little fun with this one.

How Computers Change
the Way We Think

Sherry Turkle

Sherry Turkle *(b. 1948), born and raised in New York City, attended Harvard University where she received her BA (1970), MA (1973), and PhD (1976). A professor in the Program in Science, Technology, and Society at the Massachusetts Institute of Technology, Turkle observes: "I study the sociology of sciences of mind, a study of the interactions among technical, literary, and popular discourses about the self as they develop in specific social contexts." The results of Turkle's research appear in* Psychoanalytic Politics: Freud's French Revolution *(1992),* The Second Self: Computers and the Human Spirit *(1984),* Life on the Screen: Identity in the Age of the Internet *(1995) and* Simulation and Its Discontents *(2009). "My work on computation," Turkle states, "begins with the premise that we live in a nascent computer culture that will exert an analogous influence on the way we think"—an idea she explores in the following essay, which appeared in a 2004 issue of the* Chronicle of Higher Education.

1   The tools we use to think change the ways in which we think. The invention of written language brought about a radical shift in how we process, organize, store, and transmit representations of the world. Although writing remains our primary information technology, today when we think about the impact of technology on our habits of mind, we think primarily of the computer.

2   My first encounters with how computers change the way we think came soon after I joined the faculty at the Massachusetts Institute of Technology in the late 1970s, at the end of the era of the slide rule and the beginning of the era of the personal computer. At a lunch for new faculty members, several senior professors in engineering complained that the transition from slide rules to calculators had affected their students' ability to deal with issues of scale. When students used slide rules, they had to insert decimal points themselves. The professors insisted that that required students to maintain a mental sense of scale, whereas those who relied on calculators made frequent errors in orders of magnitude. Additionally, the students with calculators had lost their ability to do "back of the envelope" calculations, and with that, an intuitive feel for the material.

3   That same semester, I taught a course in the history of psychology. There, I experienced the impact of computational objects on students' ideas about their emotional lives. My class had read Freud's essay on slips of the tongue, with its famous first example: The chairman of a parliamentary session opens a meeting by declaring it closed. The students discussed how Freud interpreted such errors as revealing a person's mixed emotions. A computer-science major disagreed with Freud's approach. The mind, she argued, is a computer. And in a computational dictionary—like we have in the human mind—"closed" and "open" are designated by the same symbol, separated by a sign for opposition. "Closed" equals "minus open." To substitute "closed" for "open" does not require the notion of ambivalence or conflict.

4   "When the chairman made that substitution," she declared, "a bit was dropped; a minus sign was lost. There was a power surge. No problem."

5   The young woman turned a Freudian slip into an information-processing error. An explanation in terms of meaning had become an explanation in terms of mechanism.

6   Such encounters turned me to the study of both the instrumental and the subjective sides of the nascent computer culture. As an ethnographer and psychologist, I began to study not only what the computer was doing for us, but what it was doing to us, including how it was changing the way we see ourselves, our sense of human identity.

7   In the 1980s, I surveyed the psychological effects of computational objects in everyday life—largely the unintended side effects of people's tendency to project thoughts and feelings onto their machines. In the 20 years since, computational objects have become more explicitly designed to have emotional and cognitive effects. And those "effects by design" will become even stronger in the decade to come. Machines are being designed to serve explicitly as companions, pets, and tutors. And they are introduced in school settings for the youngest children.

Today, starting in elementary school, students use e-mail, word processing, 8
computer simulations, virtual communities, and PowerPoint software. In the
process, they are absorbing more than the content of what appears on their
screens. They are learning new ways to think about what it means to know and
understand.

What follows is a short and certainly not comprehensive list of areas where 9
I see information technology encouraging changes in thinking. There can be
no simple way of cataloging whether any particular change is good or bad.
That is contested terrain. At every step we have to ask, as educators and citizens, whether current technology is leading us in directions that serve our
human purposes. Such questions are not technical; they are social, moral, and
political. For me, addressing that subjective side of computation is one of the
more significant challenges for the next decade of information technology in
higher education. Technology does not determine change, but it encourages
us to take certain directions. If we make those directions clear, we can more
easily exert human choice.

Thinking about privacy. Today's college students are habituated to a world 10
of online blogging, instant messaging, and Web browsing that leaves electronic
traces. Yet they have had little experience with the right to privacy. Unlike past
generations of Americans, who grew up with the notion that the privacy of their
mail was sacrosanct, our children are accustomed to electronic surveillance as
part of their daily lives.

I have colleagues who feel that the increased incursions on privacy have put 11
the topic more in the news, and that this is a positive change. But middle-school
and high-school students tend to be willing to provide personal information online
with no safeguards, and college students seem uninterested in violations of privacy and in increased governmental and commercial surveillance. Professors find
that students do not understand that in a democracy, privacy is a right, not merely
a privilege. In 10 years, ideas about the relationship of privacy and government
will require even more active pedagogy. (One might also hope that increased education about the kinds of silent surveillance that technology makes possible may
inspire more active political engagement with the issue.)

Avatars or a self? Chat rooms, role-playing games, and other technological 12
venues offer us many different contexts for presenting ourselves online. Those
possibilities are particularly important for adolescents because they offer what
Erik Erikson described as a moratorium, a time out or safe space for the personal
experimentation that is so crucial for adolescent development. Our dangerous
world—with crime, terrorism, drugs, and AIDS—offers little in the way of safe
spaces. Online worlds can provide valuable spaces for identity play.

But some people who gain fluency in expressing multiple aspects of self may 13
find it harder to develop authentic selves. Some children who write narratives for
their screen avatars may grow up with too little experience of how to share their
real feelings with other people. For those who are lonely yet afraid of intimacy,
information technology has made it possible to have the illusion of companionship without the demands of friendship.

14   **From powerful ideas to PowerPoint.** In the 1970s and early 1980s, some educators wanted to make programming part of the regular curriculum for K–12 education. They argued that because information technology carries ideas, it might as well carry the most powerful ideas that computer science has to offer. It is ironic that in most elementary schools today, the ideas being carried by information technology are not ideas from computer science like procedural thinking, but more likely to be those embedded in productivity tools like PowerPoint presentation software.

15   PowerPoint does more than provide a way of transmitting content. It carries its own way of thinking, its own aesthetic—which not surprisingly shows up in the aesthetic of college freshmen. In that aesthetic, presentation becomes its own powerful idea.

16   To be sure, the software cannot be blamed for lower intellectual standards. Misuse of the former is as much a symptom as a cause of the latter. Indeed, the culture in which our children are raised is increasingly a culture of presentation, a corporate culture in which appearance is often more important than reality. In contemporary political discourse, the bar has also been lowered. Use of rhetorical devices at the expense of cogent argument regularly goes without notice. But it is precisely because standards of intellectual rigor outside the educational sphere have fallen that educators must attend to how we use, and when we introduce, software that has been designed to simplify the organization and processing of information.

17   In *The Cognitive Style of PowerPoint* (Graphics Press, 2003), Edward R. Tufts suggests that PowerPoint equates bulleting with clear thinking. It does not teach students to begin a discussion or construct a narrative. It encourages presentation, not conversation. Of course, in the hands of a master teacher, a PowerPoint presentation with few words and powerful images can serve as the jumping-off point for a brilliant lecture. But in the hands of elementary-school students, often introduced to PowerPoint in the third grade, and often infatuated with its swooshing sounds, animated icons, and flashing text, a slide show is more likely to close down debate than open it up.

18   Developed to serve the needs of the corporate boardroom, the software is designed to convey absolute authority. Teachers used to tell students that clear exposition depended on clear outlining, but presentation software has fetishized the outline at the expense of the content.

19   Narrative, the exposition of content, takes time. PowerPoint, like so much in the computer culture, speeds up the pace.

20   **Word processing vs. thinking.** The catalog for the Vermont Country Store advertises a manual typewriter, which the advertising copy says "moves at a pace that allows time to compose your thoughts." As many of us know, it is possible to manipulate text on a computer screen and see how it looks faster than we can think about what the words mean.

21   Word processing has its own complex psychology. From a pedagogical point of view, it can make dedicated students into better writers because it allows them to revise text, rearrange paragraphs, and experiment with the tone and shape of

an essay. Few professional writers would part with their computers; some claim that they simply cannot think without their hands on the keyboard. Yet the ability to quickly fill the page, to see it before you can think it, can make bad writers even worse.

A seventh grader once told me that the typewriter she found in her mother's attic is "cool because you have to type each letter by itself. You have to know what you are doing in advance or it comes out a mess." The idea of thinking ahead has become exotic. 22

Taking things at interface value. We expect software to be easy to use, and we assume that we don't have to know how a computer works. In the early 1980s, most computer users who spoke of transparency meant that, as with any other machine, you could "open the hood" and poke around. But only a few years later, Macintosh users began to use the term when they talked about seeing their documents and programs represented by attractive and easy-to-interpret icons. They were referring to an ability to make things work without needing to go below the screen surface. Paradoxically, it was the screen's opacity that permitted that kind of transparency. Today, when people say that something is transparent, they mean that they can see how to make it work, not that they know how it works. In other words, transparency means epistemic opacity. 23

The people who built or bought the first generation of personal computers understood them down to the bits and bytes. The next generation of operating systems were more complex, but they still invited that old-time reductive understanding. Contemporary information technology encourages different habits of mind. Today's college students are already used to taking things at (inter) face value; their successors in 2014 will be even less accustomed to probing below the surface. 24

Simulation and its discontents. Some thinkers argue that the new opacity is empowering, enabling anyone to use the most sophisticated technological tools and to experiment with simulation in complex and creative ways. But it is also true that our tools carry the message that they are beyond our understanding. It is possible that in daily life, epistemic opacity can lead to passivity. 25

I first became aware of that possibility in the early 1990s, when the first generation of complex simulation games were introduced and immediately became popular for home as well as school use. SimLife teaches the principles of evolution by getting children involved in the development of complex ecosystems; in that sense it is an extraordinary learning tool. During one session in which I played SimLife with Tim, a 13-year-old, the screen before us flashed a message: "Your orgot is being eaten up." "What's an orgot?" I asked. Tim didn't know. "I just ignore that," he said confidently. "You don't need to know that kind of stuff to play." 26

For me, that story serves as a cautionary tale. Computer simulations enable their users to think about complex phenomena as dynamic, evolving systems. But they also accustom us to manipulating systems whose core assumptions we may not understand and that may not be true. 27

We live in a culture of simulation. Our games, our economic and political systems, and the ways architects design buildings, chemists envisage molecules, and 28 surgeons perform operations all use simulation technology. In 10 years the degree to which simulations are embedded in every area of life will have increased exponentially. We need to develop a new form of media literacy: readership for the culture of simulation.

29   We come to written text with habits of readership based on centuries of civilization. At the very least, we have learned to begin with the journalist's traditional questions: who, what, when, where, why, and how. Who wrote these words, what is their message, why were they written, and how are they situated in time and place, politically and socially? A central project for higher education during the next 10 years should be creating programs in information-technology literacy, with the goal of teaching students to interrogate simulations in much the same spirit, challenging their built-in assumptions.

30   Despite the ever-increasing complexity of software, most computer environments put users in worlds based on constrained choices. In other words, immersion in programmed worlds puts us in reassuring environments where the rules are clear. For example, when you play a video game, you often go through a series of frightening situations that you escape by mastering the rules—you experience life as a reassuring dichotomy of scary and safe. Children grow up in a culture of video games, action films, fantasy epics, and computer programs that all rely on that familiar scenario of almost losing but then regaining total mastery: There is danger. It is mastered. A still-more-powerful monster appears. It is subdued. Scary. Safe.

31   Yet in the real world, we have never had a greater need to work our way out of binary assumptions. In the decade ahead, we need to rebuild the culture around information technology. In that new sociotechnical culture, assumptions about the nature of mastery would be less absolute. The new culture would make it easier, not more difficult, to consider life in shades of gray, to see moral dilemmas in terms other than a battle between Good and Evil. For never has our world been more complex, hybridized, and global. Never have we so needed to have many contradictory thoughts and feelings at the same time. Our tools must help us accomplish that, not fight against us.

32   Information technology is identity technology. Embedding it in a culture that supports democracy, freedom of expression, tolerance, diversity, and complexity of opinion is one of the next decade's greatest challenges. We cannot afford to fail.

33   When I first began studying the computer culture, a small breed of highly trained technologists thought of themselves as "computer people." That is no longer the case. If we take the computer as a carrier of a way of knowing, a way of seeing the world and our place in it, we are all computer people now.

COMPREHENSION

1. According to Turkle, in what ways do computers change the ways we think?
2. What does Turkle mean by "the instrumental and subjective sides of nascent computer culture" (paragraph 6)? What examples of these two sides does she offer?
3. What are some of the challenges facing the "sociotechnical culture" Turkle says we are entering?

RHETORIC

1. Turkle published this essay in a weekly newspaper designed for people in higher education. What stylistic elements suggest that she gears her writing to this specialized audience? How does she make the article accessible to a broader, secondary audience?
2. What is Turkle's thesis, and where does she state it?
3. How does Turkle use classification to advance her thesis and organize the essay? Where does she employ process and causal analysis?
4. What comparative points does the writer draw between actual and virtual reality?
5. Turkle's paragraphs are relatively brief, some no more than two or three sentences. Why does she employ this method? Does this strategy ruin the coherence of the essay or weaken the emphasis on certain ideas? Why or why not?
6. In the final analysis, does Turkle prove the point made in the final paragraph, that "we are all computer people now"?

WRITING

1. Using Turkle's essay as a model, write a classification essay on the ways that computers are changing the way we think.
2. Select one area where information technology is changing our processes and habits of thought, and write an essay explaining this phenomenon.
3. **Writing an Argument:** Do you agree or disagree with Turkle's assertion that information technology can foster democracy? Write a persuasive essay that articulates your position on the issue.

NETWORKING
Applying Digital and Multimedia Literacies

Using Images to Strengthen a Classification Essay: Enhance question 1 under Writing by incorporating four or five images that help illustrate the classifications you put forth in the essay. Take care to use images purposefully, not merely for decoration.

Can We Know the Universe?
Reflections on a Grain of Salt

Carl Sagan

Carl Edward Sagan (1931–1996) received BA, BS, MA, and PhD degrees from the University of Chicago. Probably the most popular scientist in America in the 1970s and 1980s, he was the host of several television series on science and wrote a number

of best-selling books on science, including The Dragons of Eden *(1977) and* Broca's
Brain *(1979). The former earned him a Pulitzer Prize for general nonfiction in
1978. He also contributed hundreds of papers to scientific journals. Besides writing,
Sagan served as a full-time professor at Cornell University and a visiting professor at
dozens of other institutions of higher learning in the United States and abroad. He
was also an activist for many philanthropic causes and served as an advisor to
groups such as the Council for a Livable World Education Fund, the Children's
Health Fund, and the American Committee on U.S.–Soviet Relations. Despite controversies surrounding the speculative nature of his work, Carl Sagan was one of
modern science's most popular spokespersons. Sagan's philosophy may be summed
up in a statement he made in a* Time *interview: "We make our world significant by
the courage of our questions and by the depth of our answers."*

Nothing is rich but the inexhaustible wealth of nature. She shows us only surfaces,
but she is a million fathoms deep.

—Ralph Waldo Emerson

1   Science is a way of thinking much more than it is a body of knowledge. Its goal is
to find out how the world works, to seek what regularities there may be, to penetrate to the connections of things—from subnuclear particles, which may be the
constituents of all matter, to living organisms, the human social community, and
thence to the cosmos as a whole. Our intuition is by no means an infallible guide.
Our perceptions may be distorted by training and prejudice or merely because of
the limitations of our sense organs, which, of course, perceive directly but a small
fraction of the phenomena of the world. Even so straightforward a question as
whether in the absence of friction a pound of lead falls faster than a gram of fluff
was answered incorrectly by Aristotle and almost everyone else before the time
of Galileo. Science is based on experiment, on a willingness to challenge old
dogma, on an openness to see the universe as it really is. Accordingly, science
sometimes requires courage—at the very least the courage to question the conventional wisdom.

2   Beyond this the main trick of science is to *really* think of something: the
shape of clouds and their occasional sharp bottom edges at the same altitude
everywhere in the sky; the formation of a dewdrop on a leaf; the origin of a name
or a word—Shakespeare, say, or "philanthropic"; the reason for human social
customs—the incest taboo, for example; how it is that a lens in sunlight can make
paper burn; how a "walking stick" got to look so much like a twig; why the Moon
seems to follow us as we walk; what prevents us from digging a hole down to the
center of the Earth; what the definition is of "down" on a spherical Earth; how it is
possible for the body to convert yesterday's lunch into today's muscle and sinew;
or how far is up—does the universe go on forever, or if it does not, is there any
meaning to the question of what lies on the other side? Some of these questions
are pretty easy. Others, especially the last, are mysteries to which no one even
today knows the answer. They are natural questions to ask. Every culture has
posed such questions in one way or another. Almost always the proposed answers

are in the nature of "Just So Stories," attempted explanations divorced from experiment, or even from careful comparative observations.

But the scientific cast of mind examines the world critically as if many alter- 3 native worlds might exist, as if other things might be here which are not. Then we are forced to ask why what we see is present and not something else. Why are the Sun and the Moon and the planets spheres? Why not pyramids, or cubes, or dodecahedra? Why not irregular, jumbly shapes? Why so symmetrical worlds? If you spend any time spinning hypotheses, checking to see whether they make sense, whether they conform to what else we know, thinking of tests you can pose to substantiate or deflate your hypotheses, you will find yourself doing science. And as you come to practice this habit of thought more and more you will get better and better at it. To penetrate into the heart of the thing—even a little thing, a blade of grass, as Walt Whitman said —is to experience a kind of exhilaration that, it may be, only human beings of all the beings on this planet can feel. We are an intelligent species and the use of our intelligence quite properly gives us pleasure. In this respect the brain is like a muscle. When we think well, we feel good. Understanding is a kind of ecstasy.

But to what extent can we *really* know the universe around us? Sometimes 4 this question is posed by people who hope the answer will be in the negative, who are fearful of a universe in which everything might one day be known. And sometimes we hear pronouncements from scientists who confidently state that everything worth knowing will soon be known—or even is already known—and who paint pictures of a Dionysian or Polynesian age in which the zest for intellectual discovery has withered, to be replaced by a kind of subdued languor, the lotus eaters drinking fermented coconut milk or some other mild hallucinogen. In addition to maligning both the Polynesians, who were intrepid explorers (and whose brief respite in paradise is now sadly ending), as well as the inducements to intellectual discovery provided by some hallucinogens, this contention turns out to be trivially mistaken.

Let us approach a much more modest question: not whether we can know the 5 universe or the Milky Way Galaxy or a star or a world. Can we know, ultimately and in detail, a grain of salt? Consider one microgram of table salt, a speck just barely large enough for someone with keen eyesight to make out without a microscope. In that grain of salt there are about 10^{16} sodium and chlorine atoms. This is a 1 followed by 16 zeros, 10 million billion atoms. If we wish to know a grain of salt, we must know at least the three-dimensional positions of each of these atoms. (In fact, there is much more to be known—for example, the nature of the forces between the atoms—but we are making only a modest calculation.) Now, is this number more or less than the number of things which the brain can know?

How much *can* the brain know? There are perhaps 10^{11} neurons in the 6 brain, the circuit elements and switches that are responsible in their electrical and chemical activity for the functioning of our minds. A typical brain neuron has perhaps a thousand little wires, called dendrites, which connect it with its fellows. If, as seems likely, every bit of information in the brain corresponds to one of these connections, the total number of things knowable by the brain is no more than 10^{14}, one hundred trillion. But this number is only one percent of the number of atoms in our speck of salt.

7   So in this sense the universe is intractable, astonishingly immune to any human attempt at full knowledge. We cannot on this level understand a grain of salt, much less the universe.

8   But let us look a little more deeply at our microgram of salt. Salt happens to be a crystal in which, except for defects in the structure of the crystal lattice, the position of every sodium and chlorine atom is predetermined. If we could shrink ourselves into this crystalline world, we would see rank upon rank of atoms in an ordered array, a regularly alternating structure—sodium, chlorine, sodium, chlorine, specifying the sheet of atoms we are standing on and all the sheets above us and below us. An absolutely pure crystal of salt could have the position of every atom specified by something like 10 bits of information.[1] This would not strain the information-carrying capacity of the brain.

9   If the universe had natural laws that governed its behavior to the same degree of regularity that determines a crystal of salt, then, of course, the universe would be knowable. Even if there were many such laws, each of considerable complexity, human beings might have the capability to understand them all. Even if such knowledge exceeded the information-carrying capacity of the brain, we might store the additional information outside our bodies—in books, for example, or in computer memories—and still, in some sense, know the universe.

10   Human beings are, understandably, highly motivated to find regularities, natural laws. The search for rules, the only possible way to understand such a vast and complex universe, is called science. The universe forces those who live in it to understand it. Those creatures who find everyday experience a muddled jumble of events with no predictability, no regularity, are in grave peril. The universe belongs to those who, at least to some degree, have figured it out.

11   It is an astonishing fact that there *are* laws of nature, rules that summarize conveniently—not just qualitatively but quantitatively—how the world works. We might imagine a universe in which there are no such laws, in which the 10^{80} elementary particles that make up a universe like our own behave with utter and uncompromising abandon. To understand such a universe we would need a brain at least as massive as the universe. It seems unlikely that such a universe could have life and intelligence, because beings and brains require some degree of internal stability and order. But even if in a much more random universe there were such beings with an intelligence much greater than our own, there could not be much knowledge, passion or joy.

12   Fortunately for us, we live in a universe that has at least important parts that are knowable. Our common-sense experience and our evolutionary history have prepared us to understand something of the workaday world. When we go into

---

[1]Chlorine is a deadly poison gas employed on European battlefields in World War I. Sodium is a corrosive metal which burns upon contact with water. Together they make a placid and unpoisonous material, table salt. Why each of these substances has the properties it does is a subject called chemistry, which requires more than 10 bits of information to understand.

other realms, however, common sense and ordinary intuition turn out to be highly unreliable guides. It is stunning that as we go close to the speed of light our mass increases indefinitely, we shrink toward zero thickness in the direction of motion, and time for us comes as near to stopping as we would like. Many people think that this is silly, and every week or two I get a letter from someone who complains to me about it. But it is a virtually certain consequence not just of experiment but also of Albert Einstein's brilliant analysis of space and time called the Special Theory of Relativity. It does not matter that these effects seem unreasonable to us. We are not in the habit of traveling close to the speed of light. The testimony of our common sense is suspect at high velocities.

Or consider an isolated molecule composed of two atoms shaped something 13 like a dumbbell—a molecule of salt, it might be. Such a molecule rotates about an axis through the line connecting the two atoms. But in the world of quantum mechanics, the realm of the very small, not all orientations of our dumbbell molecule are possible. It might be that the molecule could be oriented in a horizontal position, say, or in a vertical position, but not at many angles in between. Some rotational positions are forbidden. Forbidden by what? By the laws of nature. The universe is built in such a way as to limit, or quantize, rotation. We do not experience this directly in everyday life; we would find it startling as well as awkward in sitting-up exercises, to find arms outstretched from the sides or pointed up to the skies permitted but many intermediate positions forbidden. We do not live in the world of the small, on the scale of 10^{-13} centimeters, in the realm where there are twelve zeros between the decimal place and the one. Our common-sense intuitions do not count. What does count is experiment—in this case observations from the far infrared spectra of molecules. They show molecular rotation to be quantized.

The idea that the world places restrictions on what humans might do is frus- 14 trating. Why *shouldn't* we be able to have intermediate rotational positions? Why *can't* we travel faster than the speed of light? But so far as we can tell, this is the way the universe is constructed. Such prohibitions not only press us toward a little humility; they also make the world more knowable. Every restriction corresponds to a law of nature, a regularization of the universe. The more restrictions there are on what matter and energy can do, the more knowledge human beings can attain. Whether in some sense the universe is ultimately knowable depends not only on how many natural laws there are that encompass widely divergent phenomena, but also on whether we have the openness and the intellectual capacity to understand such laws. Our formulations of the regularities of nature are surely dependent on how the brain is built, but also, and to a significant degree, on how the universe is built.

For myself, I like a universe that includes much that is unknown and, at the 15 same time, much that is knowable. A universe in which everything is known would be static and dull, as boring as the heaven of some weak-minded theologians. A universe that is unknowable is no fit place for a thinking being. The ideal universe for us is one very much like the universe we inhabit. And I would guess that this is not really much of a coincidence.

COMPREHENSION

1. What is the thesis of the essay? In what paragraph is this thesis most clearly expressed?
2. Why does Sagan say, in paragraph 12, that in many circumstances, "common sense and ordinary intuition turn out to be highly unreliable guides"?
3. Why does Sagan say, in his conclusion, that "the ideal universe for us is one very much like the universe we inhabit"?

RHETORIC

1. What is the function of the epigram by Emerson? How does it relate to the essay proper?
2. Many of the paragraphs in the essay begin with coordinating conjunctions (a structure frowned on by many high school English teachers). What is Sagan's rhetorical purpose in using them as connecting devices?
3. What specific clues are there in the essay that Sagan's tone is one of excitement and celebration regarding science?
4. Sagan refers often to what he calls "a law of nature." Where and how in the essay does he explain, describe, or define this term?
5. The essay begins abruptly with an explanation of the concept of science. What purpose is served by diving into the subject so dramatically?
6. What is the intended effect of combining the terms *universe* and *grain of salt* in the title and subtitle? How does the author exploit this juxtaposition in his essay?
7. Examine the italicized words in the essay. Why has Sagan chosen to italicize these words? Explain.

WRITING

1. Write a personal essay in which you describe how you felt when you suddenly understood a particular topic in school that had previously eluded you.
2. For a research paper, select one of the items Sagan enumerates in paragraph 2, such as "the formation of a dewdrop on a leaf," the origin of the name *Shakespeare* or the word *philanthropic,* "the incest taboo," or "how a 'walking stick' got to look so much like a twig." Write an expository essay on your topic.
3. **Writing an Argument:** Argue for or against the proposition that scientific knowledge takes the mystery out of life.

NETWORKING
Applying Digital and Multimedia Literacies

Using a Blog Entry as Prewriting for a Larger Assignment: Before you begin either question 1, 2, or 3 under Writing, get your thoughts (and maybe even some preliminary research) down by posting a blog entry that responds to the prompt. Depending on your work style, articulating your initial thoughts in a public forum might jump-start your essay even more than private prewriting would.

Staying Human

Dinesh D'Souza

Dinesh D'Souza, *a leading conservative thinker, was born in Bombay, India, and came to the United States for his high school education. He graduated from Dartmouth College (BA, 1983) and subsequently wrote for several magazines, notably the* National Review, *before becoming a policy analyst for the Reagan administration. His books include* Illiberal Education: The Politics of Race and Sex on Campus *(1991),* The End of Racism: Principles for a Multicultural Society *(1995),* The Virtue of Prosperity: Finding Values in an Age of Techno-Affluence *(2001),* What's So Great about America *(2002),* What's So Great about Christianity *(2007), and* The Enemy at Home: The Cultural Left and Its Responsibility for 9/11 *(2007). D'Souza has been a visiting scholar at the Hoover Institution and a research scholar at the American Enterprise Institute. In the following essay, written for the* National Review *in 2001, D'Souza offers a wide-ranging assessment of our emerging "techno-utopia."*

We are as gods, and we might as well get good at it.
—Kevin Kelly, author and techno-utopian

The most important technological advance of recent times is not the Internet, but rather the biotech revolution—which promises to give us unprecedented power to transform human nature. How should we use that power? A group of cutting-edge scientists, entrepreneurs, and intellectuals has a bold answer. This group—I call them the techno-utopians—argues that science will soon give us the means to straighten the crooked timber of humanity, and even to remake our species into something "post-human." 1

One of the leading techno-utopians is Lee Silver, who teaches molecular biology at Princeton University. Silver reports that biotechnology is moving beyond cloning to offer us a momentous possibility: designer children. He envisions that, in the not too distant future, couples who want to have a child will review a long list of traits on a computer screen, put together combinations of "virtual children," decide on the one they want, click on the appropriate selection, and thus—in effect—design their own offspring. "Parents are going to be able to give their children . . . genes that increase athletic ability, genes that increase musical talents . . . and ultimately genes that affect cognitive abilities." 2

But even this, the techno-utopians say, is a relatively small step: People living today can determine the genetic destiny of all future generations. Some writers, including physicist Stephen Hawking, have suggested that genetic engineering could be used to reduce human aggression, thus solving the crime problem and 3 making war less likely. James Watson, co-discoverer of the structure of DNA, argues that if biological interventions could be used to "cure what I feel is a very serious disease—that is, stupidity—it would be a great thing for people." Silver himself forecasts a general elevation of intellectual, athletic, temperamental, and artistic abilities so that we can over time create "a special group of mental beings" who will "trace their ancestry back to Homo sapiens," but who will be "as different from humans as humans are from the primitive worms with tiny brains that first crawled along the earth's surface."

4   These ideas might seem implausible, but they are taken very seriously by some of the best minds in the scientific community. The confidence of the techno-utopians is based on stunning advances that have made cloning and genetic engineering feasible. In theoretical terms, biotechnology crossed a major threshold with James Watson and Francis Crick's 1953 discovery of the structure of DNA, but practical applications were slow in coming. In 1997, an obscure animal-husbandry laboratory in Scotland cloned a sheep named Dolly; today, the knowledge and the means of cloning human beings already exist, and the only question is whether we are going to do it. And why stop there? As the scientific journal *Nature* editorialized shortly after the emergence of Dolly, "The growing power of molecular genetics confronts us with future prospects of being able to change the nature of our species."

5   In 1999, neurobiologist Joe Tsien boosted the intelligence of mice by inserting extra copies of a gene that enhances memory and learning; these mouse genes are virtually identical to those found in human beings. Gene therapy has already been successfully carried out in people, and now that the Human Genome Project has made possible a comprehensive understanding of the human genetic code, scientists will possess a new kind of power: the power to design our children, and even to redesign humanity itself.

The Hitler Scenario

6 The fact that these things are possible does not, of course, mean that they should be done. As one might expect, cloning and genetic engineering are attracting criticism. The techno-utopians have not yet made their products and services available to consumers; but one can reasonably expect that a society that is anxious about eating genetically modified tomatoes is going to be vastly more anxious about a scheme to engineer our offspring and our species.

7   A recent book communicating that sense of outrage is Jeremy Rifkin's *The Biotech Century*. Rifkin alleges that we are heading for a nightmarish future "where babies are genetically designed and customized in the womb, and where people are identified, stereotyped and discriminated against on the basis of their genotype." How can living beings be considered sacred, Rifkin asks, if they are treated as nothing more than "bundles of genetic information"? Biotechnology, he charges, is launching us into a new age of eugenics. In Rifkin's view, the Nazi idea of the superman is very much alive, but now in a different form: the illusion of the "perfect child."

Although Rifkin has a propensity for inflammatory rhetoric, he is raising   8
some important concerns: The new technology is unprecedented, so we should
be very cautious in developing it. It poses grave risks to human health. Cloning
and genetic engineering are unnatural; human beings have no right to do this to
nature and to ourselves.

These criticisms meet with derision on the part of the techno-utopians. Every   9
time a major new technology is developed, they say, there are people who forecast
the apocalypse. The techno-utopians point out that the new technology will deliver
amazing medical benefits, including cures for genetic diseases. How can it be
ethical, they ask, to withhold these technologies from people who need and want
them?

Lee Silver, the biologist, is annoyed at critics such as Rifkin who keep raising   10
the specter of Hitler and eugenics. "It is individuals and couples, not governments, who will seize control of these new technologies," Silver writes. The premise of the techno-utopians is that if the market produces a result, it is good. In this
view, what is wrong with the old eugenics is not that it sought to eliminate defec-
tive types and produce a superior kind of being, but that it sought to do so in a
coercive and collectivist way. The new advocates of biotechnology speak approv-
ingly of what they term "free-market eugenics."

The champions of biotechnology concede that cloning and genetic engineer-   11
ing should not be permitted in human beings until they are safe. But "safe," they
say, does not mean "error-free"; it means safe compared with existing forms of
reproduction. And they are confident that the new forms of reproduction will soon
be as safe as giving birth the natural way.

The techno-utopians are also not very concerned that the availability of   12
enhancement technologies will create two classes in society, the genetically advan-
taged and the genetically disadvantaged. They correctly point to the fact that two
such classes exist now, even in the absence of new therapies. Physicist Freeman
Dyson says that genetic enhancement might be costly at first, but won't remain
permanently expensive: "Most of our socially important technologies, such as
telephones, automobiles, television, and computers, began as expensive toys for
the rich and afterwards became cheap enough for ordinary people."

Dyson is right that time will make genetic enhancements more widely avail-   13
able, just as cars and TV sets are now. But the poor family still drives a secondhand Plymouth while the rich family can afford a new Porsche. This may not be
highly significant when it comes to cars, because both groups can still get around
fairly well. What about when it comes to genetic advantages conferred at birth?
Democratic societies can live with inequalities conferred by the lottery of nature,
but can they countenance the deliberate introduction of biological alterations that
give some citizens a better chance to succeed than others?

The techno-utopians have not, to my knowledge, addressed this concern.   14
They emphasize instead that it is well established in law, and widely recognized in
society, that parents have a right to determine what is best for their children.
"There are already plenty of ways in which we design our children," remarks
biologist Gregory Stock. "One of them is called piano lessons. Another is called

private school." Stock's point is that engineering their children's genes is simply one more way in which parents can make their children better people.

15   Some people might find it weird and unnatural to fix their child in the same way they fix their car—but, say the techno-utopians, this is purely a function of habit. We're not used to genetic engineering, so it seems "unnatural" to us. But think about how unnatural driving a car seemed for people who previously got around on horses and in carriages. "The smallpox virus was part of the natural order," Silver wryly observes, "until it was forced into extinction by human intervention." Diseases and death are natural; life-saving surgery is unnatural.

Not Sacred after All?

16 Nor are the techno-utopians worried about diminishing the sanctity of human life because, they say, it isn't intrinsically sacred. "This is not an ethical argument but a religious one," says Silver. "There is no logic to it." Biologist David Baltimore, a Nobel laureate, argues that "statements about morally and ethically unacceptable practices" have no place in the biotechnology debate "because those are subjective grounds and therefore provide no basis for discussion." Silver and Baltimore's shared assumption is that the moralists are talking about values while they, the hard scientists, are dealing in facts.

17   In this view, the subjective preferences of those who seek to mystify human life do not square with the truths about human biology taught by science. The cells of human beings, Silver points out, are not different in their chemical makeup from the cells of horses and bacteria. If there is such a thing as human dignity, Silver argues, it derives exclusively from consciousness, from our ability to perceive and apprehend our environment. "The human mind," Silver writes, "is much more than the genes that brought it into existence." Somehow the electrochemical reactions in our brain produce consciousness, and it is this consciousness, Silver contends, that is the source of man's autonomy and power. While genes fully control the activity of all life forms, Silver writes that in human beings "master and slave have switched positions." Consciousness enables man to complete his dominance over nature by prevailing over his human nature. Silver concludes that, in a bold assertion of will, we can defeat the program of our genes, we can take over the reins of evolution, we can choose the genetic code we want for our children, and we can collectively determine the future of our species.

18   This triumphant note is echoed by many techno-utopians. Biotech, writes journalist Ronald Bailey, "will liberate future generations from today's limitations and offer them a much wider scope of freedom." Physicist Gregory Benford is even more enthusiastic: "It is as though prodigious, bountiful Nature for billions of years has tossed off variations on its themes like a careless, prolific Picasso. Now Nature finds that one of its casual creations has come back with a piercing, searching vision, and its own pictures to paint."

19   These are ringing statements. But do they make sense? Clearly there are many problems with Silver's definition of human dignity as based in consciousness. Animals are conscious; do they deserve the same dignity as human beings?

Moreover, are human beings entitled to dignity only when they are conscious? Do we lose our right to be respected, and become legitimate subjects for discarding medical experiments, when we fall asleep, or into a coma? Surely Silver would disavow these conclusions. They do, however, flow directly from his definition, which is, in fact, just as heavily freighted with values as are the statements of his opponents.

There is, behind the proclamations of scientific neutrality, an ideology that 20 needs to be spelled out, a techno-Nietzschean doctrine that proclaims: We are molecules, but molecules that know how to rebel. Our values do not derive from nature or nature's God; rather, they arise from the arbitrary force of our wills. And now our wills can make the most momentous choice ever exercised on behalf of our species: the choice to reject our human nature. Why should we remain subject to the constraints of our mortality and destiny? Wealth and technology have given us the keys to unlimited, indeed godlike, power: the dawn of the post-human era.

What is one to make of all this? In many respects, we should celebrate the 21 advent of technologies that enable us to alleviate suffering and extend life. I have no problem with genetic therapy to cure disease; I am even willing to endorse therapy that not only cures illness in patients but also prevents it from being transmitted to the next generation. Under certain circumstances, I can see the benefits of cloning. The cloning of animals can provide organs for transplant as well as animals with medicinal properties ("drugstores on the hoof"). Even human cloning seems defensible when it offers the prospect of a biological child to married couples who might not otherwise be able to have one.

Creating the Perfect Child

But there is a seduction contained in these exercises in humanitarianism: They 22 urge us to keep going, to take the next step. And when we take that step, when we start designing our children, when we start remaking human beings, I think we will have crossed a perilous frontier. Even cloning does not cross this frontier, because it merely replicates an existing genetic palate. It is unconvincing to argue, as some techno-utopians do, that giving a child a heightened genetic capacity for music or athletics or intelligence is no different from giving a child piano, swimming, or math lessons. In fact, there is a big difference. It is one thing to take a person's given nature and given capacity, and seek to develop it, and quite another to shape that person's nature in accordance with one's will.

There is no reason to object to people's attempting brain implants and 23 somatic gene enhancements on themselves. Perhaps, in some cases, these will do some good; others may end up doing injury. But at least these people have, through their free choices, done it to themselves. The problem arises when people seek to use enhancement technologies to shape the destiny of others, and especially their children.

But, argues Lee Silver, we have the right to terminate pregnancy and control 24 our children's lives in every other way; why shouldn't parents be permitted to alter their child's genetic constitution? In the single instance of gene therapy to cure disease, I'd agree—because, in this one limited case, we can trust the parents to make a decision that there is every rational reason to believe their offspring would decide in the identical manner, were they in a position to make the choice. No child would say, "I can't believe my parents did that to me. I would have chosen to have Parkinson's disease."

25   But I would contend that in no other case do people have the right to bend the genetic constitution of their children—or anyone else—to their will. But they might, in good conscience, be tempted to do so; and this temptation must be resisted. Indeed, it must be outlawed—because what the techno-utopians want does, in fact, represent a fundamental attack on the value of human life, and the core principle of America.

Rescuing Humanity and the American Idea

26 The scientific-capitalist project at the heart of the American experiment was an attempted "conquest of nature." Never did the early philosophers of science, like Francis Bacon, or the American Founders conceive that this enterprise would eventually seek to conquer human nature. Their goal was to take human nature as a given, as something less elevated than the angels, and thus requiring a government characterized by separation of offices, checks and balances, limited power. At the same time, the Founders saw human nature as more elevated than that of other animals. They held that human beings have claims to dignity and rights that do not extend to animals: Human beings cannot be killed for sport or rightfully governed without their consent.

27   The principles of the Founders were extremely far-reaching. They called into question the legitimacy of every existing government, because at the time of the American founding, no government in the world was entirely based on the consent of the governed. The ideals of the Founders even called into question their own practices, such as slavery. It took the genius of Abraham Lincoln, and the tragedy of the Civil War, to compel the enforcement of the central principle of the Declaration of Independence: that we each have an inalienable right to life, liberty, and the pursuit of happiness, and that these rights shall not be abridged without our consent.

28   The attempt to enhance and redesign other human beings represents a flagrant denial of this principle that is the basis of our dignity and rights. Indeed, it is a restoration of the principle underlying slavery, and the argument between the defenders and critics of genetic enhancement is identical in principle, and very nearly in form, to the argument between Stephen Douglas and Abraham Lincoln on the issue of human enslavement.

29   In that tempestuous exchange, which laid the groundwork for the Civil War, Douglas argued for the pro-choice position. He wanted to let each new territory decide for itself whether it wanted slavery. He wanted the American people to agree to disagree on the issue. He advocated for each community a very high value: the right to self-determination.

Lincoln challenged him on the grounds that choice cannot be exercised with- 30 out reference to the content of the choice. How can it make sense to permit people to choose to enslave another human being? How can self-determination be invoked to deny others the same? A free people can disagree on many things, but it cannot disagree on the distinction between freedom and despotism. Lincoln summarized Douglas's argument as follows: "If any one man choose to enslave another, no third man shall be allowed to object."

Lincoln's argument was based on a simple premise: "As I would not be a 31 slave, so I would not be a master." Lincoln rejects in principle the subordination implied in the master-slave relationship. Those who want freedom for themselves, he insists, must also show themselves willing to extend it to others. At its deepest level, Lincoln's argument is that the legitimacy of popular consent is itself dependent on a doctrine of natural rights that arises out of a specific understanding of human nature and human dignity. "Slavery," he said, "is founded in the selfishness of man's nature-opposition to it, in his love of justice. These principles are in eternal antagonism; and when brought into collision so fiercely . . . convulsions must ceaselessly follow." What Lincoln is saying is that self-interest by itself is too base a foundation for the new experiment called America. Selfishness is part of our nature, but it is not the best part of our nature. It should be subordinated to a nobler ideal. Lincoln seeks to dedicate America to a higher proposition: the proposition that all men are created equal. It is the denial of this truth, Lincoln warns, that will bring on the cataclysm.

Let me restate Lincoln's position for our current context. We speak of "our 32 children," but they are not really ours; we do not own them. At most, we own ourselves. It is true that *Roe v. Wade* gives us the right to kill our unborn in the womb. The right to abortion has been defended, both by its advocates and by the Supreme Court, as the right of a woman to control her own body. This is not the same as saying the woman has ownership of the fetus, that the fetus is the woman's property. The Supreme Court has said that as long as the fetus is occupying her womb, she can treat it as an unwelcome intruder, and get rid of it. (Even here, technology is changing the shape of the debate by moving up the period when the fetus can survive outside the womb.) But once a woman decides to carry the pregnancy to term, she has already exercised her choice. She has chosen to give birth to the child, which is in the process of becoming an independent human being with its own dignity and rights.

No Place for Parental Tyranny

As parents, we have been entrusted with our children, and it is our privilege and 33 responsibility to raise them as best we can. Undoubtedly we will infuse them with our values and expectations, but even so, the good parent will respect the child's right to follow his own path. There is something perversely restrictive about parents who apply relentless pressure on their children to conform to their will—to follow the same professional paths that they did, or to become the "first doctor in the family." These efforts, however well intentioned, are a betrayal of the true meaning of parenthood. Indeed, American culture encourages a certain measure of adolescent rebellion against parental expectations, precisely so that young people making the transition to independence can "find themselves" and discover their own identity.

34   Consequently, parents have no right to treat their children as chattels; but this is precisely the enterprise that is being championed by the techno-utopians. Some of these people profess to be libertarians, but they are in fact totalitarians. They speak about freedom and choice, although what they advocate is despotism and human bondage. The power they seek to exercise is not over "nature" but over other human beings.

35   Parents who try to design their children are in some ways more tyrannical than slaveowners, who merely sought to steal the labor of their slaves. Undoubtedly some will protest that they only wish the best for their children, that they are only doing this for their own good. But the slaveowners made similar arguments, saying that they ruled the Negroes in the Negroes' own interest. The argument was as self-serving then as it is now. What makes us think that in designing our children it will be their objective good—rather than our desires and preferences—that will predominate?

36   The argument against slavery is that you may not tyrannize over the life and freedom of another person for any reason whatsoever. Even that individual's consent cannot overturn "inalienable" rights: One does not have the right to sell oneself into slavery. This is the clear meaning of the American proposition. The object of the American Revolution that is now spreading throughout the world has always been the affirmation, not the repudiation, of human nature. The Founders envisioned technology and capitalism as providing the framework and the tools for human beings to live richer, fuller lives. They would have scorned, as we should, the preposterous view that we are the servants of our technology. They would have strenuously opposed, as we should, the effort on the part of the techno-utopians to design their offspring; to alter, improve, and perfect human nature; or to relinquish our humanity in pursuit of some post-human ideal.

37   Mary Shelley's 1818 novel *Frankenstein* describes a monster that is the laboratory creation of a doctor who refuses to accept the natural limits of humanity. He wants to appropriate to himself the traditional prerogatives of the deity, such as control over human mortality. He even talks about making "a new species" with "me as its creator and source." In his rhetoric, Frankenstein sounds very much like today's techno-utopians. And, contrary to what most people think, the real monster in the novel isn't the lumbering, tragic creature; it is the doctor who creates him. This is the prophetic message of Shelley's work: In seeking to become gods, we are going to make monsters of ourselves.

COMPREHENSION

1. What is the meaning of D'Souza's title? According to the writer, what are the dangers we face in our effort to "stay human"? What must we do to retain our essential humanity?

2. What aspects of the biotech revolution does the author treat? What is his opinion of each?
3. What does the writer mean by the "Hitler Scenario" and the "American Idea"?

RHETORIC

1. What is D'Souza's purpose? What is his tone? Does he seem reasonable or unnecessarily argumentative? Objective or biased? How do you know? For what type of audience does he seem to be writing?
2. D'Souza begins his essay by introducing the ideas of such "leading techno-utopians" as Lee Silver, Stephen Hawking, James Watson and Francis Crick, and Joe Tsien. It this an effective opening strategy? Why or why not?
3. Explain the author's claim. What minor propositions does he provide? Where does he advance logical, ethical, and emotional appeals? Cite instances in which he employs refutation to advance his argument. What faults does he find with the techno-utopians?
4. Consider the essay's section headings. How do they serve to focus the content of each section? What characterizes the progression of ideas from section to section? How does the author's decision to divide the essay into sections help him to construct his argument?
5. Does D'Souza reveal any of his own biases in this essay? Explain.
6. In the concluding paragraph, D'Souza alludes to Mary Shelley's novel *Frankenstein*. Does this allusion flow naturally from the introduction and body? Why or why not?

WRITING

1. Write a 300-word summary of this essay, transcribing all of the main aspects of D'Souza's argument.
2. Write your own survey of the biotech revolution. Refer to some of the topics and ideas mentioned by D'Souza in his essay.
3. **Writing an Argument:** Select one aspect of the biotech revolution—for instance, cloning or stem-cell research—and write an argumentative essay supporting or opposing developments in the field.

NETWORKING
Applying Digital and Multimedia Literacies

Debating the Ethics behind Cloning: Work in groups of three to prepare for and engage in a debate about some aspect of cloning or stem-cell research. Two of you will be debaters, each doing research to inform your assigned position: one for and one against a proposed development. Come to the debate with notes and solid arguments and counterarguments prepared. The third person will serve as the moderator, who will come prepared with questions and possible follow-up questions, as well as with a one- or two-page informative, unbiased introduction to the issues. He or she will open the debate by reading this document. If possible, record the debate, and review it later. Discuss each of your strengths and weaknesses as public speakers/debaters, providing constructive criticism and praise.

Anybody Out There?

Oliver Sacks

Oliver Sacks (b. 1933), a well-known neurologist, was born in London and immigrated to the United States in 1960. He was educated at Queens College, Oxford, where he received a BA (1954) and subsequent degrees in chemistry and medicine. Sacks has practiced and taught medicine, surgery, and neurology at several institutions, including Albert Einstein College of Medicine, Bronx Psychiatric Hospital, and New York University Medical Center. An award-winning physician and science writer, Sacks has written numerous books, including Awakenings *(1973), which was made into a film starring Robin Williams and Robert De Niro;* The Man Who Mistook His Wife for a Hat, and Other Clinical Tales *(1985);* An Anthropologist on Mars *(1995);* Uncle Tungsten: Memories of a Chemical Boyhood *(2001);* Vintage Sacks *(2004), and* Musicophilia: Tales of Music and the Brain *(2007). In this essay, published in* Natural History *in 2002, Sacks speculates about the existence of life-forms in the universe.*

1 One of the first books I read as a boy was H. G. Wells's 1901 fable, *The First Men in the Moon.* The two men, Cavor and Bedford, land in a crater, apparently barren and lifeless, just before the lunar dawn; then, as the sun rises, they realize there is an atmosphere. They spot small pools and eddies of water, and then little round objects scattered on the ground. One of them, as it is warmed by the sun, bursts open and reveals a sliver of green. ("'A seed,' said Cavor . . . And then . . . very softly, 'Life!'") They light a piece of paper and throw it onto the surface of the Moon. It glows and sends up a thread of smoke, indicating that the atmosphere, though thin, is rich in oxygen and will support life as they know it.

2 Here, then, was how Wells conceived the prerequisites of life: water, sunlight (a source of energy), and oxygen. "A Lunar Morning," the eighth chapter in his book, was my first introduction to astrobiology.

3 It was apparent, even in Wells's day, that most of the planets in our solar system were not possible homes for life. The only reasonable surrogate for the Earth was Mars, which was known to be a solid planet of reasonable size, in stable orbit, not too distant from the sun, and so, it was thought, having a range of surface temperatures compatible with the presence of liquid water.

4 But free oxygen gas—how could that occur in a planet's atmosphere? What would keep it from being mopped up by ferrous iron and other oxygen-hungry chemicals on the surface unless, somehow, it was continuously pumped out in huge quantities, enough to oxidize all the surface minerals and keep the atmosphere charged as well?

5 It was the blue-green algae, or cyanobacteria, that infused the Earth's atmosphere with oxygen, a process that took between a billion and two billion years. The fossil

record shows that cyanobacteria go back three and a half billion years. Yet, amazingly, some of them still thrive today in odd corners of the world, forming strange, cushion-shaped colonies called stromatolites. It is an extraordinary experience to go to Shark Bay in western Australia, where stromatolites flourish in the hypersaline waters, to watch them slowly bubbling oxygen, and to reflect that, three billion years ago, this was how the Earth was transformed. The cyanobacteria invented photosynthesis: by capturing the energy of the sun, they were able to combine carbon dioxide (massively present in the Earth's early atmosphere) with water to create complex molecules—sugars, carbohydrates—which the bacteria could then store and tap for energy as needed. This process generated free oxygen as a byproduct—a waste product that was to determine the future course of evolution.

Although free oxygen in a planet's atmosphere would be an infallible marker 6
of life, and one that, if present, should be readily detected in the spectra of extrasolar planets, it is not a prerequisite for life. Planets, after all, get started without free oxygen, and may remain without it all their lives. Anaerobic organisms swarmed before oxygen was available, perfectly at home in the atmosphere of the early Earth, converting nitrogen to ammonia, sulfur to hydrogen sulfide, carbon dioxide to formaldehyde, and so forth. (From formaldehyde and ammonia the bacteria could make every organic compound they needed.)

There may be planets in our solar system and elsewhere that lack an atmo- 7
sphere of oxygen but are nonetheless teeming with anaerobes. And such anaerobes need not live on the surface of the planet; they could occur well below the surface, in boiling vents and sulfurous hot pots, as they do on Earth today, to say nothing of subterranean oceans and lakes. (There is thought to be such a subsurface ocean on Jupiter's moon Europa, locked beneath a shell of ice several miles thick, and its exploration is one of the astrobiological priorities of this century. Curiously, Wells, in *The First Men in the Moon,* imagines life originating in a central sea in the middle of the Moon and then spreading outward to its inhospitable periphery.)

It is not clear whether life has to "advance"—whether evolution must take place— 8
if there is a satisfactory status quo. Brachiopods—lampshells—for instance, have remained virtually unchanged since they first appeared in the Cambrian Period, more than 500 million years ago. But there does seem to be a drive for organisms to become more highly organized and more efficient in retaining energy, at least when environmental conditions are changing rapidly, as they were before the Cambrian. The evidence indicates that the first primitive anaerobes on Earth were prokaryotes: small, simple cells—just cytoplasm, usually bounded by a cell wall, but with little if any internal structure.

By degrees, however—and the process took place with glacial slowness— 9
prokaryotes became more complex, acquiring internal structure, nuclei, mitochondria, and so on. The microbiologist Lynn Margulis of the University of Massachusetts, Amherst, has convincingly suggested that these complex so-called eukaryotes arose when prokaryotes began incorporating other prokaryotes within their own cells. The incorporated organisms at first became symbiotic

and later came to function as essential organelles of their hosts, enabling the resultant organisms to use what was originally a noxious poison: oxygen.

10   Primitive as they are, prokaryotes are still highly sophisticated organisms with formidable genetic and metabolic machinery. Even the simplest ones manufacture more than five hundred proteins, and their DNA includes at least half a million base pairs. Hence it is certain that still more primitive life forms must have preceded the prokaryotes.

11   Perhaps, as the physicist Freeman Dyson of the Institute for Advanced Study in Princeton has suggested, there were "pro-genotes" capable of metabolizing, growing, and dividing but lacking any genetic mechanism for precise replication. And before them there must have been millions of years of purely chemical, pre-biotic evolution—the synthesis, over eons, of formaldehyde and cyanide, of amino acids and peptides, of proteins and self-replicating molecules. Perhaps that chemistry took place in the minute vesicles, or globules, that develop when fluids at very different temperatures meet, as may well have happened around the boiling midocean vents of the Archaean sea.

12   Life as we know it is not imaginable without proteins, and proteins are built from peptides, and ultimately from amino acids. It is easy to imagine that amino acids were abundant in the early Earth, either formed as a result of lightning discharges or brought to the planet by comets and meteors.

13   The real problem is to get from amino acids and other simple compounds to peptides, nucleotides, proteins, and so on. It is unlikely that such delicate chemical syntheses would occur in "some warm little pond," as Darwin imagined, or on the surface of a primordial sea. Instead, they would probably require unusual conditions of heat and concentration, as well as the presence of special catalysts and energy-rich compounds to make them proceed. The biochemist Christian de Duve of Rockefeller University suggests that complex organic sulfur compounds played a crucial role in providing chemical energy, and that these compounds may have formed spontaneously early in Earth's history, perhaps in the hot, acidic, sulfurous depths of the sea-floor vents (where, it is increasingly believed, life probably originated). De Duve imagines this purely chemical world as the precursor of an "RNA world," believed by many to represent the first form of self-replicating life. He thinks that the movement from one to the other was both inevitable and fast.

14   The two preeminent evolutionary changes in the early history of life on Earth—from prokaryote to eukaryote, from anaerobe to aerobe—took the better part of two billion years. And there then had to pass another 1,200 or 1,300 million years before life rose above the microscopic forms, and the first "higher," multicellular organisms appeared. So if the Earth's history is anything to go by, we should not expect to find any higher life on a planet that is still young. Even if extraterrestrial life has appeared, and all goes well, it could take billions of years for evolutionary processes to move it along to the multicellular stage.

15   Moreover, all those "stages" of evolution—including the evolution of intelligent, conscious beings from the first multicellular forms—may have happened against daunting odds. Stephen Jay Gould spoke of life as "a glorious accident";

Richard Dawkins of Oxford University likens evolution to "climbing Mount Improbable." And life, once started, is subject to vicissitudes of all kinds: from meteors and volcanic eruptions to global overheating and cooling; from dead ends in evolution to mysterious mass extinctions; and finally (if things get that far) the fateful proclivities of a species like ourselves.

We know there are microfossils in some of the Earth's most ancient rocks, 16 rocks more than three and a half billion years old. So life must have appeared within 100 or 200 million years after the Earth had cooled off sufficiently for water to become liquid. That astonishingly rapid transformation makes one think that life may develop readily, perhaps inevitably, as soon as the right physical and chemical conditions appear.

But can one argue from a single example? Can one speak confidently of 17 "earthlike" planets, or is the Earth physically, chemically, and geologically unique? And even if there are other "habitable" planets, what are the chances that life, with its thousands of physical and chemical coincidences and contingencies, will emerge? Life may be a one-off event.

Opinion here varies as widely as it can. The French biochemist Jacques 18 Monod regarded life as a fantastically improbable accident, unlikely to have arisen anywhere else in the universe. In his book *Chance and Necessity,* he writes, "The universe was not pregnant with life." De Duve takes issue with this, and sees the origin of life as determined by a large number of steps, most of which must have had a "high likelihood of taking place under the prevailing conditions." Indeed, de Duve believes that there is not merely unicellular life throughout the universe but complex, intelligent life, too, on trillions of planets. How are we to align ourselves between these utterly opposite but theoretically defensible positions?

What we need, what we must have, is hard evidence of life on another planet 19 or heavenly body. Mars is the obvious candidate: It was wet and warm there once, with lakes and hydrothermal vents and perhaps deposits of clay and iron ore. It is especially in such places that we should look, suggests Malcolm Walter, an expert on fossil bacteria that date from the Earth's earliest epochs. If the evidence shows that life once existed on Mars, we will then need to know, crucially, whether it originated there or was transported (as would have been readily possible) from the young, teeming, volcanic Earth. If we can determine that life originated independently on Mars (if Mars, for instance, once harbored DNA nucleotides different from our own), we will have made an incredible discovery—one that will alter our view of the universe and enable us to perceive it, in the words of the physicist Paul Davies, as a "biofriendly" one. It would help us to gauge the probability of finding life elsewhere instead of bombinating in a vacuum of data, caught between the poles of inevitability and uniqueness.

In just the past twenty years life has been discovered in previously unex- 20 pected places on our own planet, such as the life-rich black smokers of the ocean depths, where organisms thrive in conditions biologists would once have dismissed as utterly deadly. Life is much tougher, much more resilient, than we once thought. It now seems to me quite possible that microorganisms or their remains will be found on Mars and perhaps on some of the satellites of Jupiter and Saturn.

21 It seems far less likely, many orders of magnitude less likely, that we will find any evidence of higher-order, intelligent life forms, at least in our own solar system. But who knows? Given the vastness and age of the universe at large, the innumerable stars and planets it must contain, and our radical uncertainties about life's origin and evolution, the possibility cannot be ruled out. And though the rate of evolutionary and geochemical processes is incredibly slow, that of technological progress is incredibly fast. Who is to say (if humanity survives) what we may not be capable of, or discover, in the next thousand years?

22   For myself, since I cannot wait, I turn to science fiction on occasion—and, not least, back to my favorite Wells. Although it was written a hundred years ago, "A Lunar Morning" has the freshness of a new dawn, and it remains for me, as when I first read it, the most poetic evocation of how it may be when, finally, we encounter alien life.

COMPREHENSION

1. What is Sacks's answer to the question he poses in the title?
2. Explain the connection between the writer's boyhood reading and his interest in life elsewhere in the universe.
3. List and define some of the scientific evidence and scientific principles Sacks mentions in his essay.

RHETORIC

1. Why does Sacks begin with an anecdote about his boyhood? How might this strategy appeal to readers of *Natural History,* where the essay first appeared?
2. In what ways does Sacks demonstrate his expertise and authority as a scientist in this essay? What tone does he take in presenting this information?
3. What is Sacks's thesis? What types of evidence does he offer to support his main idea?
4. Identify the main sections in this essay and the transitions Sacks uses to link them.
5. Where does Sacks use definition, comparison and contrast, process analysis, and causal analysis? Does he mix patterns successfully? Why or why not?
6. Examine the conclusion. Why does Sacks ask questions, and why does he end on a provisional note?

WRITING

1. In an expository essay, examine the popularity of science fiction in literature and/or film. How does science fiction present the notion of life in the universe? Be certain to develop examples to support your thesis.
2. Conduct research on H. G. Wells, and then write an evaluative paper in which you highlight the ways in which he predicted the future.
3. **Writing an Argument:** Do you think that extraterrestrial life exists? Answer this question in an argumentative essay.

NETWORKING
Applying Digital and Multimedia Literacies

Creating an Online Literature Review: For question 1, 2, or 3 under Writing, compile a review of the literature you would use to research this topic and help write an essay about it. For each source, provide a Works Cited entry and a paragraph-long summary of the source and how it relates to your topic; for online sources, also provide a direct link to the source. If you work with question 1, be sure to include the science fiction novels you would like to discuss.

Synthesis: Connections for Critical Thinking

1. Using the essay of D'Souza, discuss the need for strict ethics among scientists in regard to their concern over the well-being of the general populace.
2. Imagine a conversation between Sedaris and Turkle. What would they say to each other?
3. Compare the process of natural selection as advanced by Darwin with the concept of evolution as defined by Sacks and Klinkenborg.
4. Rent the DVD version of the television series *Cosmos,* which was based on a novel by Carl Sagan. Compare the ideas set forth in the film with those in Sagan's essay "Can We Know the Universe? Reflections on a Grain of Salt."
5. Compare and contrast the expository methods Darwin uses to explain the process of natural selection and the narrative technique Sedaris uses to describe his technophobia.
6. Using Ackerman's and Sacks's essays, explore how science can be either a friend or a foe of humankind.

NETWORKING
Applying Digital and Multimedia Literacies

1. Search the Web for two sites: one promoting the idea of evolution, the other promoting the idea of creationism. Compare and contrast the approach of each site as well as responses by the visitors to each site.
2. Have your class create a private blog with user names that do not divulge the gender of the participants. Discuss the pros and cons of computers as described by Sedaris. Have a host tally the nature of the responses, reveal the gender of the students who participated, and discuss any differences between the responses of the male and female students.

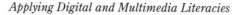

part 3

Research Writing
for a New Era

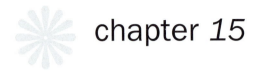

chapter *15*

Writing a Research Project

A research project is a report—often but not always an essay, or paper—in which you synthesize information on your topic, contributing your own analysis and evaluation to the subject. Research writing is a form of problem solving. You identify a problem, form a hypothesis (an unproven thesis, theory, or argument), gather and organize information from various sources, assess and interpret data, evaluate alternatives, reach conclusions, and provide documentation.

Research writing is both exciting and demanding. American essayist and novelist Joan Didion states, "The element of discovery takes place, in nonfiction, not during the writing but during the research." Nowhere is the interplay of the stages in the composing process more evident than in writing research papers. Prewriting is an especially important stage, for the bulk of your research and bibliographical spadework is done before you actually sit down to draft your report. Moreover, strategic critical thinking skills are required at every step of research writing. Here you sense the active, questioning, reflective activity of the mind as it considers a problem and sifts through the evidence to reach a solution, proof, or conclusion. Developing the ability to do research writing thus represents an integration of problem-solving and composing skills.

Research writing is a skill to be developed rather than a trial to be borne. Online library catalogs, electronic searches, and word processing have taken much of the drudgery out of writing research papers. And effective research writing goes beyond reporting information in a bland and boring recitation of facts.

Research actually means the careful investigation of a subject in order to discover or revise facts, theories, or applications. Your purpose is to demonstrate how other researchers approach a problem, how you synthesize their most useful ideas, and how you treat that problem yourself. A good research paper subtly blends your ideas and synthesizes the attitudes or findings of others. In research writing, you are dealing with ideas that are already in the public domain, but you are also contributing to knowledge.

RESEARCH WRITING: PRECONCEPTIONS AND PRACTICE

When your ideas—rather than the ideas of others—become the center of the research process, writing a research project becomes dynamic instead of static. The standard preconception about preparing a research paper is that the researcher simply finds a subject and then assembles information from sources found in a library. This strategy does teach

750

disciplined habits of work and thought, and it is a traditional way to conduct research for college courses. Yet, does this conventional preconception match the practices of professional researchers?

Consider the following tasks:

- Evaluating critical responses to a best-selling novel, a book of poetry, an album, or an award-winning film
- Analyzing the impact of voter turnout on presidential politics during a recent decade
- Investigating a literary, political, or scientific scandal of the previous century
- Assessing the effectiveness of urban, suburban, and rural schools, comparing specific measures of student success
- Defining a popular dietary or health-related term, examining how it influences consumer behavior when shopping for food
- Examining how media outlets use social networking Web sites to deliver content to audiences in target demographics

How would a professional researcher view these projects? First, the researcher sees a subject as a *problem* rather than a mere topic. Often this problem is authorized or assigned by a collaborator, an editor, or a supervisor in the researcher's workplace. The researcher has the task of developing or testing a hypothesis stemming from the particular problem—for example, whether a vegetarian diet effectively wards off cancer. *Hypothesis formation* is at the heart of professional research.

Second, the researcher often conducts primary as well as secondary research. *Primary research* relies on analysis and synthesis of texts, letters, manuscripts, and other materials, whether written, visual, or aural. *Secondary research* relies on sources that comment on the primary sources. For example, a critic's commentary on *Citizen Kane* or a historian's analysis of the 2012 presidential election would be secondary sources; the film itself or a speech delivered by Barack Obama in 2012 would be primary sources. Because primary sources are not necessarily more reliable than secondary sources, you must always evaluate the reliability of both types of material. Critics can misinterpret, and experts often disagree, forcing you to weigh evidence and reach your own conclusions.

Third, all researchers face deadlines. The solution to a research problem is required to take action, to reach a decision, to influence policy, or to determine a business plan. Confronted with deadlines, professional researchers learn to *telescope* their efforts in order to obtain information quickly. Common strategies include networking (using personal and professional contacts as well as guides to organizations), browsing or searching online, conducting bibliographical searches, and turning to online databases, annotated bibliographies (listing articles on the topic with commentaries on each item), and specialized indexes (focusing on a particular field or discipline). Other strategies include consulting review articles, which evaluate other resources, and browsing through current journals and periodicals (which may provide useful background as well as the most current thinking about the topic).

Finally, good researchers recognize that knowledge in this era tends increasingly toward interdisciplinary concerns and that they cannot confine their search for evidence to one subject area, such as history or physics. Much professional researching cuts across academic subjects and disciplines. The interdisciplinary nature of many research projects creates special problems for the researcher, especially in the use of bibliographical materials, which tend to be subject-oriented. Such research is not beyond your talents and abilities.

Learn not only how to use library and electronic sources selectively and efficiently, but also how to view the world outside your library and computer as a vast laboratory to be used fruitfully in order to solve your research problems.

NAVIGATING THE RESEARCH PROCESS

The research process involves thinking, searching, reading, writing, and rewriting. The final product—the research paper or project—is the result of your discoveries in and contributions to the realm of ideas about your topic. The process of researching and composing moves back and forth over a series of activities, and the actual act of writing remains unique to the individual researcher.

Writers with little experience in developing research papers do have to be more methodical than experienced researchers, who streamline and adjust the composing process to the scope and design of their projects. Regardless of a writer's experience or individual idiosyncrasies, he or she can benefit from thinking about the research process as a series of several interrelated phases.

Phases in the Research Process

Phase I: Defining Your Objective

1. Choose a *researchable* topic.
2. Identify a *problem* inherent in the topic that gives you the reason for writing about the topic.
3. Examine the *purpose* of or the *benefits* to be gained from conducting research on the topic.
4. Think about the assumptions, interests, and needs of your *audience*.
5. Decide how you are going to *limit* your topic.
6. Establish a working *hypothesis* to guide and control the scope and direction of your research.

Phase 2: Locating Your Sources

1. Decide on your *methodology*—the types or varieties of primary and secondary research you plan to conduct. Determine the method of collecting data.
2. Explore your library's online catalog (a utility that lets you search its holdings and databases to which it subscribes) to *determine the viability of your topic,* including how much secondary research has been done on your topic and whether your hypothesis is likely to stand up.

3. Develop a *tentative working bibliography,* a file listing sources that seem relevant to your topic.

4. Review your bibliography, and *reassess your topic and hypothesis.*

Phase 3: Gathering and Organizing Data

1. *Obtain your sources,* taking notes on all information related directly to your thesis.

2. Analyze and organize your information. Design a *preliminary outline* with a *tentative thesis* if your findings support your hypothesis.

3. *Revise your thesis* if your findings suggest alternative conclusions.

Phase 4: Writing and Submitting the Paper

1. Write a *rough draft* of the paper, concentrating on the flow of thoughts and integrating research findings into the text of the paper.

2. Write a *first revision* to tighten organization, improve style, and check on the placement of data. Prepare citations that identify the sources of your information. Assemble a list of the references you have cited in your paper.

3. *Prepare the manuscript* using the format called for by the course, the discipline, or the person authorizing the research paper.

Phase 1: Defining Your Objective

The first step in research writing is to select a topic that promises an adventure for you in the realm of ideas and that will interest, if not excite, your audience while meeting the expectations and requirements of your assignment.

You can maximize time and effort if you approach the research project as a problem to be investigated and solved, a controversy to take a position on, or a question to be answered. As a basis, you need a strong hypothesis or working thesis (which may be little more than a calculated guess). The point of your investigation is to identify, illustrate, explain, argue, or prove that thesis. Develop a hypothesis before you actually begin to conduct research; otherwise, you will discover that you are simply reading in or about a topic, instead of reading toward the objective of substantiating your thesis or proposition.

Of course, before you can formulate a hypothesis, you need to start with a general idea of what subject you want to explore, what your purpose is going to be, and how you plan to select and limit a topic from your larger subject area.

FORMULATING A HYPOTHESIS

A topic will lead to a researchable hypothesis if it does the following:

- Meets the demands of your assignment
- Strongly interests you
- Engages knowledge you already possess
- Raises questions that will require both primary and secondary research to answer
- Provokes you toward an opinion or argument

To help you find and limit a research topic, try the following strategies:

- *Reflect on the assignment.* If your professor gave you a specific written assignment—even if it doesn't include a specific topic—review the assignment with an eye toward keywords that indicate the purpose of your research work. Highlight or underline key verbs such as *solve, argue, find, discover,* or *present.* Write out questions for your professor, and either ask them in class or arrange for a conference with her or him.
- *Ask questions.* Ask yourself, in writing, a series of specific questions about your subject, combining related questions. Phrase questions in such a way as to pose problems that demand answers. Then try to determine which topic best fits the demands of the assignment.
- *Prewrite and brainstorm.* Idea generation strategies such as prewriting and brainstorming can help you to determine what you already know or believe about an assigned topic. If your assignment is to research gender roles in popular culture, you might begin by brainstorming on how male characters were depicted in the last three movies you saw. For more on prewriting strategies, see pages 68–70.
- *Do some background reading.* Your professor will probably assign a research topic that has something to do with the content of your class. Review the assigned readings for your course as well as your own notes. If your professor has suggested additional readings on the research topic or provided a bibliography, consult a few of those sources as well. Although the purpose of your background reading is to generate ideas, you should still use the note-taking strategies discussed in the following pages to ensure that you give proper credit later for any ideas you use from this preliminary reading.

Throughout, keep in mind that your purpose is to solve a *specific* problem, shed light on a *specific* topic, state an opinion on a *specific* controversy, or offer *specific* proofs or solutions. Your audience does not want a welter of general information, a bland summary of the known and the obvious, or free associations or meditations on an issue or problem. You know that your audience wants answers; consequently, a way to locate your ideal topic is to ask questions about it.

Phase 2: Locating Your Sources

Begin locating your sources as early as possible for a number of reasons. First, research takes time and patience. Second, you most likely will have to share sources with other students working on similar projects. Many sources are not available online, even through library databases, and some print sources only have one copy or are not in the library. Third, your library may not have access to every source you need; when this is the case, you will have to depend on interlibrary loan services (in which your library borrows the source temporarily or obtains photocopies or scans of it), which can take additional time.

If you have a sufficiently narrowed topic and a working hypothesis, you should know what type of information will be most useful for your report. Not all information on a topic is relevant, of course; with a hypothesis, you can distinguish between useful and irrelevant material.

To use your time efficiently, you have to *streamline* your method for collecting data. Most research writing for college courses relies heavily on secondary research material available in libraries or online. To develop a preliminary list of sources, go directly to general reference works or a list of sources or reserved readings provided by your professor. If you already have some knowledge about the subject, begin with resources that permit you to find a continuing series of articles and books on a single issue—specifically, periodical indexes, newspaper indexes, and online catalogs. Again, you should be moving as rapidly as possible from the general to the specific.

Should You Begin Your Research Online?   The immense capabilities of the Internet make it very tempting to begin your search for information online, via a commercial search engine such as Google. If your research topic demands very contemporary and localized knowledge (a current political campaign, a recent medical breakthrough, a trend in popular culture), beginning your search online can be optimal. This method can also be useful for background reading and idea generating. However, traditional research—both academic and professional—is generally more productive and efficient if begun via a library's online catalog. Commercial search engines usually generate very limited returns when research topics require you to provide deeper contexts and back-grounds, or when primary and secondary sources are restricted to academic journals and databases. Although we begin our discussion of locating sources with guidelines for searching online, only you can determine the most efficient and effective way of beginning your research.

Finding Online Materials   The Internet is composed of millions of Web pages, so knowing where to begin your search might seem like a daunting task. Your library, your college Web site, or your instructor's home page may list useful sites, organized by discipline or interest area. Online clearinghouses and print materials also identify especially useful sites for researchers. Depending on your topic, there are subject-specific online pages that link you to everything you could want, including both primary and secondary sources. *Findlaw* is a good example for law-related content; most of the sciences and many of the liberal arts have useful pages like this. The UC-Berkeley Library suggests also using subject directories (whose subject-specific contents are supplied by humans rather than computer programs), like *lii.org, academicinfo.net,* or *infomine.ucr.edu,* to look for academic resources. Once you have located a URL (universal resource locator) for a site on the Web, you can go directly to that location. The end of the address is one indication of the kind of location you will reach. Some of the most popular domain extensions include:

> .org = nonprofit organizations, including professional groups
>
> .edu = colleges, universities, and other educational institutions

.com = businesses and commercial enterprises

.gov = government branches and agencies

.mil = branches of the military

.net = major computer networks

.tv = video content

.museum = museums

.info = informational sites

.store = retail businesses

.web = sites about the World Wide Web

.coop = cooperative organizations

.int = international organizations

.pro = credentialed professionals

Domain extensions can also include the Web site's country of origin (like .au for Australia or .uk for United Kingdom). New domain extensions are created often to accommodate the ever-expanding volume of Web content. Keep in mind, though, that the domain extension is but the initial way to identify the content of a site. For example, some museums use the .museum extension, while others use .org; still others are part of universities and therefore use .edu. Some .com sites offer both commerce and information, just as some .org sites sell products or services. A careful evaluation of the contents and research about the organization responsible for the site's maintenance are called for before you rely on a source to help prove your hypothesis.

If you need to search the Internet for sources, try using a search engine like Google, using keywords. Given the enormous number of Web sites and their component pages, you need to select your search terms carefully so that you locate reasonable numbers of pertinent sources.

A Web page often supplies links to other useful sites, separately or as hyperlinked text. If you click on the link, usually distinguished from plain text by formatting or color, you can go directly to that related site. For example, the site *www.fedworld.gov*, sponsored by the federal government, includes links to federal databases and a keyword search that can lead to particular resources.

Following a chain of links requires critical thinking to assess whether each link seems reliable and current. This kind of research can take a great deal of time, especially if you explore each link and then follow it to the next. As you move from link to link, keep your hypothesis in mind so that you are not distracted from your central purpose.

Look beyond conventional online sources, too. Streaming media, like Webcasts (television and radio content) and podcasts (downloadable media files), can be gleaned for information, as can professional blogs (Web-based journals or commentaries written by content experts) and professional bulletin boards (sites where users can post and exchange content-specific information). Before using open source (wikis) and casual networking sites as sources for your paper, however, always ask your instructor for his/her policy. The content from such sites can be problematical because you cannot always verify its accuracy or the authority of the poster, and it is often not cited correctly (if at all).

EVALUATING ONLINE SOURCES

- Is the author identified? Is the site sponsored by a reputable business, agency, or organization? Does the site supply information so that you can contact the author or the sponsor?

- Does the site provide information comparable to that in other reputable sources, including print sources?

- Does the site seem accurate and authoritative or quirky and idiosyncratic?

- Does the site seem unbiased, or is it designed to promote a particular business, industry, organization, political position, or philosophy?

- Does the site supply appropriate, useful links? Do these links seem current and relevant? Do most of them work? Does the site document sources for the information it supplies directly?

- Has the site been updated or revised recently?

- Does the site seem carefully designed? Is it easy and logical to navigate? Are its graphics well integrated and related to the site's overall purpose or topic? Is the text carefully edited?

Using the Library's Online Catalog The library's catalog lists information by author, title, subject, and keyword. Of the four, the subject listings are the best place to look for sources, but they are not necessarily the place to start your research. Begin by determining what your library offers. For instance, the online catalog may include all library materials or only holdings acquired fairly recently. The catalog also may or may not supply up-to-date information because books may take several years to appear in print and some weeks to be cataloged. Thus you may need to turn to separate indexes of articles, primary documents, and online materials for the most current material. Remember also that when you search by subject, you are searching the subject fields that are assigned by the cataloger. This differs from a keyword search in which the researcher—you, the writer—selects key terms that describe the research situation and enters them into a search engine that will find these terms anywhere within the item record—whether they happen to be in the title, comments, notes, or subject fields.

On the other hand, if your library has a consolidated online system, you may have immediate access to materials available regionally and to extensive online databases. You may be able to use the same terminal to search for books shelved in your own library, materials available locally through the city or county library, and current periodicals listed in specialized databases. Such access can simplify and consolidate your search.

Subject indexing can be useful when you are researching a topic around which a considerable body of information and analysis has already developed. Identify as many keywords or relevant subject classifications as possible. Use these same terms as you continue your search for sources, and add additional terms identified in the entries you find. The accompanying example on page 758 illustrates a keyword search for materials on gender issues and advertising.

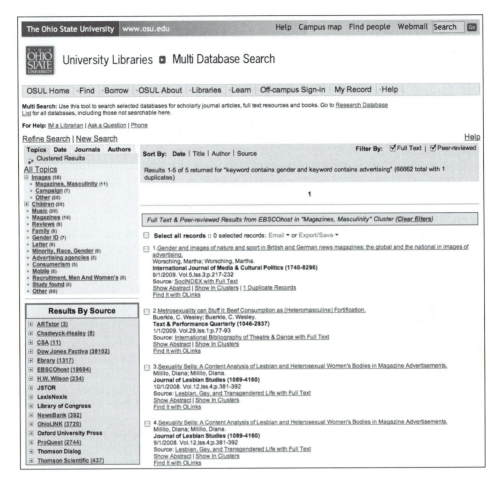

Results of an article search through the Ohio State University library's Web site. This search across subscription databases uses keywords and Boolean logic—"gender AND advertising." In this screen, the topic has been narrowed to EBSCOHost results and further limited to "Magazines, Masculinity." The researcher has also filtered results to include only peer-reviewed and full-text articles.

Clicking on the Extended Display option for an item supplies full bibliographic information as well as the location of the book in the library and its availability. On the facing page, you can see the wealth of information shown for the first item listed on the search screen above.

There are two ways to make this search of the keywords *gender* and *advertising* more complete. First, think of alternate terms that might come into play; for example, *sex* is an synonym for *gender,* and *advertising* is only one form of the verb *to advertise.* A searcher would probably want to include *advertise* or *advertisement.* Using the truncation symbol (in this case, *, but it varies in different library catalogs) would help to catch these

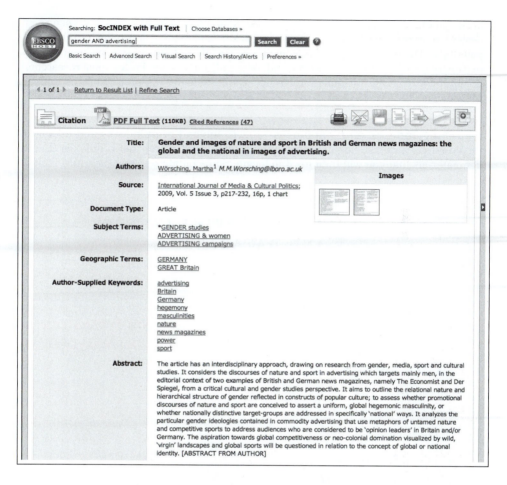

Detailed bibliographic entry in EBSCOHost for a potential source. Among other features, this page includes an abstract and a link to a PDF of the full-text article.

variations. The best course is to review the search tips that nearly always accompany any public catalog. Alternatively, select one of the titles you feel is most closely related to your subject, and pull up that record. For example, "Sex in advertising" and "Sex role in advertising" could yield fruitful links, directing you to other materials that have been assigned the same headings. This is a much more direct search than thumbing through the red Library of Congress Subject Headings volumes to find out what an appropriate subject heading might be, and it will catch those titles you might have missed when selecting your keywords.

Checking General Reference Sources   General reference sources include encyclopedias, dictionaries, handbooks, atlases, biographies, almanacs, yearbooks, abstracts, and annual reviews of scholarship within a field. Many of these sources are available both in print and online. Begin your search for these sources in your library's reference room. General reference sources can be useful for background reading and for an introduction to your topic. The bibliographies they contain (such as those that end articles in an encyclopedia) are generally limited, however, and frequently out-of-date. Professional researchers do not rely exclusively on general reference sources to solve research problems, and neither should you.

Searching Indexes and Databases   Electronic and print indexes and databases include up-to-date articles in journals, magazines, and newspapers. Indexes usually list materials that you will then need to locate. Some databases, however, may include

---

ELECTRONIC AND PRINT INDEXES AND DATABASES

General Resources

American Statistics Index

Congressional Information Service Index

Expanded Academic Index

FirstSearch Catalog

Magazine Index

National Newspaper Index

New York Times Index

Specialized Resources

Applied Science and Technology Index

Biological and Agricultural Index

Business Periodicals Index

Education Index

ERIC (Educational Resources Information Center)

General Business File

Humanities Index

Index Medicus or Medline

MLA (Modern Language Association) International Bibliography

PsychLit

Public Affairs Information Service (PAIS)

Social Sciences Index

complete texts of articles or even books. Ask a reference librarian how to access materials on microfiche, microfilm, CD-ROM, or online. If you need historical information or want to trace a topic back in time, however, you may need to use print indexes as well because electronic sources may cover only a certain number of years.

The indexes and databases listed here are just a few of the many resources that are widely available. Some are general; others are specialized by discipline or field.

Each index or database restricts the sources it lists in specific ways, based on the particular topics covered or the types of sources included. For example, the full title of the *MLA Bibliography* indicates that it lists "Books and Articles on the Modern Languages and Literatures." However, it also includes essays or chapters collected in a book, conference papers, films, recordings, and other similar sources, but it does not list summaries or encyclopedia articles. Its primary subjects include literary criticism, literary themes and genres, linguistics, and folklore. Thus you can search for an author's name, a title, a literary period, or subjects as varied as hoaxes, metaphysical poetry, and self-knowledge, all in relationship to studies in language and literature. This bibliography is available online and is updated regularly during the year. A search of the *MLA Bibliography* 1/91–8/12 for information on gender issues in advertising would turn up items such as the following:

TI: Towards a Critical Cognitive-Pragmatic Approach to Gender Metaphors in Advertising English
Au: Velasco-Sacristán, Marisol
SO: Journal of Pragmatics: An Interdisciplinary Journal of Language Studies, 2006 Nov; 38 (11): 1982–2002. (journal article)
ISSN: 0378-2166; *Sequence number:* 2006-3-6583 *Accession number:* 2006932266

TI: 'Discover the Power of Femininity!': Analyzing Global 'Power Femininity' in Local Advertising
AU: Lazar, Michelle M.
SO: Feminist Media Studies, 2006 Dec; 6 (4): 505–17. (journal article)
ISSN: 1468-0777; *Sequence number:* 2006-3-6342 *Accession number:* 2006444284

TI: 'Become the Man That Women Desire': Gender Identities and Dominant Discourses in Email Advertising Language
Au: Mullany, Louise
SO: Language and Literature: Journal of the Poetics and Linguistics Association, 2004 Nov; 13 (4): 291–305. (journal article)
ISSN: 0963-9470; 1461-7293 (electronic); *Sequence number:* 2004-3-6417 *Accession number:* 2004362398

TI: Post-Socialist Gender Trouble: Commercial Street Ephemera from Eastern Germany
AU: Morton, Joel
SO: German as a Foreign Language, 2005; 2: 49–80. (journal article)
ISSN: 1470-9570; *Sequence number:* 2007-4-8757 *Accession number:* 2007790888

TI: A Critical Cognitive-Pragmatic Approach to Advertising Gender Metaphors
AU: Velasco Sacristán, María Sol
SO: Intercultural Pragmatics, 2005; 2 (3): 219–52. (journal article)
ISSN: 1612-295X; 1613-365X (electronic); *Sequence number:* 2006-3-6582 *Accession number:* 2006931215

TI: Word, Truth and Gender Bending in Australia: The Drive to Amuse in Story or Report, Rather Than to Inform
AU: Ryan, J. S.
SO: Australian Folklore: A Yearly Journal of Folklore Studies, 2005 Nov; 20: 99–102. (journal article)
ISSN: 0819-0852; *Sequence number:* 2006-3-6414 *Accession number:* 2006971360

As your search progresses and your hypothesis evolves, you will find resources even more specifically focused on your interests.

EVALUATING PRINT SOURCES

- Is the author a credible authority? Does the book cover, preface, or byline indicate the author's background, education, or other publications? Do other writers refer to this source and accept it as reliable? Is the publisher or publication reputable?

- Does the source provide information comparable to that in other reputable sources?

- Does the source seem accurate and authoritative, or does it make claims that are not generally accepted?

- Does the source seem unbiased, or does it seem to promote a particular business, industry, organization, political position, or philosophy?

- Does the source supply notes, a bibliography, or other information to document its sources?

- If the source has been published recently, does it include current information? Are its sources current or dated?

- Does the source seem carefully edited and printed?

Using Nonprint Sources   In the library and online, you have access to potentially useful nonprint materials of all kinds—videos, slides, works of art, records of performances, microfiche, or other sources that might relate to your topic. You may find them in your library's main catalog or in a separate listing. In the catalog entry, be sure to note the location of the source and its access hours, especially if they are limited. If you need a projector or other equipment to use the material, ask the reference librarian.

Developing Field Resources   You may want to *interview* an expert, *survey* the opinions of other students, *observe* an event or situation, or examine it over a long period of time as a *case study.* Ask your instructor's advice as you design questions for an interview or a survey or procedures for a short- or long-term observation. Also be sure to find out whether you need permission to conduct this kind of research on campus or in the community.

The questions you ask will determine the nature and extent of the responses that you receive; as a result, your questions should be developed after you have established clear objectives for your field research. You also need to plan how you will analyze the answers before, not after, you administer the questionnaire or conduct the interview. Once you have drafted interview or survey questions, test them by asking your friends or classmates to respond. Use these preliminary results to revise any ambiguous questions and to test your method of analysis. If you are an observer, establish in advance what you will observe, how you will record your observations, and how you will analyze them. Get permission, if needed, from the site where you will conduct your observation. Your field sources can help you expand your knowledge of the topic, see its applications or discover real-world surprises, or locate more sources, whether print, electronic, or field.

Using Visuals in Your Paper   Some of the nonprint sources you consult in your research might be useful to include, rather than just cite or refer to, in your own final paper. Technology has made it very easy to cut and paste visuals from sources into your own work, as well as to create and incorporate your own visuals. Be sure that when you incorporate other visuals into your paper (or when you create a visual, such as a graph or chart, that draws on data from another source) you correctly and completely cite the source of the visual data. A caption that briefly describes the visual and gives its source information is not always sufficient; be sure to check what your professor or style guide (MLA, etc.) stipulates.

Using Nonprint Sources in Electronic or Online Versions of Your Paper   Working in some formats, you can enhance your paper's content, not only with visuals, but also with other media or resources. If you are submitting your project electronically or posting it online, you could create hyperlinks to electronic versions of primary and secondary sources. Hyperlinks are also useful when you need to link to electronic sources like audio or video files or when you want to make supplemental information on a topic or keyword available to be viewed by readers at their discretion. Occasionally you might also embed a feature like a YouTube clip in your project; however, be careful not to violate any copyright laws—especially if your work will appear on the open (not password-protected) Internet.

In order to gain expert information, you may wish to contact an informed individual directly by e-mail, following up on contact information supplied at a Web site or through other references. If your topic is of long-term interest to you and you have plenty of time to do your research, you may want to join a *listserv* or *e-mail conference,* a group of people interested in a particular topic, whose messages are sent automatically to all participants. Exchanges among those interested in a topic may also be posted on a *bulletin board server* or a *newsgroup,* where you can read both past and ongoing messages and exchanges. The information you receive from others may be very authoritative and reliable, but it may also represent the biased viewpoint of the individual. Assess it carefully by comparing it with information from other sources, print as well as electronic.

CONSIDERATIONS IN USING NONPRINT SOURCES IN YOUR RESEARCH

- Is a nonprint source the most effective and useful way to present data? For example, if your paper is researching the ways in which photojournalists depict presidential candidates, you will probably want to include sample photographs in your paper. If your topic is trends in voter turnout, you might consult charts and graphs in your research but describe in words the evidence from those visuals rather than reproduce them in your paper. The reverse can also be true: If a source contains great quantities of data, arranging it in an appropriate graph or chart can help readers understand a lot of complex information at a glance. Also, carefully constructed charts and graphs can help communicate across language and cultural barriers.

- Can the source be easily reproduced? What kinds of technology will you need to capture an image, import it into your text, and print it legibly (and, if necessary, in color)? What capabilities will your audience need to access a visual? For example, if you are submitting a paper electronically, remember that large visual files can take a long time to download. Also, your audience might need plug-ins, add-ins, or specific programs to view videos or listen to audio files.

- Have you gathered and noted all of the necessary source information, so that you can provide context (and, if necessary, a caption) for the visual as well as accurate bibliographical citation?

Preparing a Working Bibliography   The purpose of compiling a working bibliography is to keep track of possible sources, to determine the nature and extent of the information available, to provide a complete and accurate list of sources to be presented in the paper, and to make preparing the final bibliography much easier. Include in your working bibliography all sources that you have a hunch will be potentially useful. After all, you may not be able to obtain all the items listed, and some material will turn out to be useless, repetitious, or irrelevant to your topic. Such entries can easily be eliminated at a later stage when you prepare your final bibliography.

One way to simplify the task of preparing your final Works Cited section is to use a standard form for your working bibliography. The models given later in this chapter are based on one guide, abbreviated as MLA. The *MLA Handbook for Writers of Research Papers* (New York: Modern Language Association of America, 2009; 7th ed.) is generally followed in English, foreign languages, and other fields in the humanities. Instructors in other disciplines often favor a number of other style guides, including those of the American Psychological Association (APA), the *Chicago Manual of Style* (CMOS), and the Council of Science Editors (CSE). Because the preferred form of citation of sources varies considerably from field to field, check with your instructors to determine which format they prefer or if they recommend another style. Follow any specific directions from an instructor carefully.

INFORMATION FOR A WORKING BIBLIOGRAPHY

Record the following information for a book:

1. Name(s) of author(s)
2. Title of book, italicized
3. Place of publication
4. Publisher's name
5. Date of publication
6. Call number or location in library
7. URL or DOI and date of access online

Record the following information for an article in a periodical:

1. Name(s) of author(s)
2. Title of article, in quotation marks
3. Title of periodical, italicized
4. Volume number or issue number
5. Date of publication
6. Page numbers on which article appears
7. Call number or location in library
8. URL or DOI and date of access online

As you locate relevant sources, take down complete information on each item on a 3 × 5 note card or start a bibliographic file on your computer. Complete information, properly recorded, will save you the trouble of having to scurry back to the library or online for missing data when compiling your final bibliography. Be sure to list the source's call number and location in the library or its URL or DOI (digital object identifier); then you can easily find the material once you are ready to begin reading and relocate it if you need to refer to it again. When preparing bibliography cards for entries listed in annotated bibliographies, citation indexes, and abstracts, you might want to jot down notes from any pertinent summaries that are provided. Complete a separate card or file entry for each item that you think is promising.

Once you begin to build a bibliographic database, you can refer to your listings and supplement them each time you are assigned a paper.

Author	*Taranto, Gina*
Title of book	*Discourse Adjectives*
Place of publication	*New York*
Publisher Name	*Routledge*
Date of publication	*2006*
Call Number	*P273.T372006*

Author's first name: *Erin*
Author's last name: *Minear*
Title of article: *"Music and the Crisis of Meaning in Othello"*
Title of periodical: *Studies in English Literature 1500–1900*
Volume number: *49*
Issue number: *2*
Date of publication: *Spring 2009*
Page numbers of article: *355–70*
URL: *Wilson Web*
Date of access online: *15 August 2009*

Reassessing Your Topic   Once you have compiled your working bibliography, take the time to reassess the entire project before you get more deeply involved in it. Analyze your bibliography cards or files carefully to determine whether you should proceed to the next stage of information gathering.

Your working bibliography should send out signals that help you shape your thinking about the topic. The dominant signal should indicate that your topic is neither too narrow nor too broad. Generally, a bibliography of 10–15 promising entries for a 1,500-word paper indicates that your topic might be properly limited at this stage. A listing of only 3 or 4 entries signals that you must expand the topic or consider discarding it. Conversely, a listing of 100 entries warns that you might be working yourself into a research swamp.

Another signal from your working bibliography should help you decide whether your hypothesis is on target or could be easily recast to make it more precise. Entry titles, abstracts, and commentaries on articles are excellent sources of confirmation. If established scholarship does not support your hypothesis, it would be best to discard your hypothesis and begin again.

Finally, the working bibliography should provide signals about the categories or parts of your research. Again, titles, abstracts, and commentaries are useful. In other words, as you compile the entries, you can begin to think through the problem and to perceive contours of thought that will dictate the organization of the paper even before you begin to do detailed research. Your working bibliography should be filled with such signals.

Phase 3: Gathering and Organizing Data

If your working bibliography confirms the value, logic, and practicality of your research project, you can move to the next phase of the research process: taking notes and organizing information. Information shapes and refines your thinking; you move from an overview to a more precise understanding, analysis, and interpretation of the topic. By the end of this third phase, you should be able to transform your hypothesis into a thesis and your assembled notes into an outline.

Plagiarism and Intellectual Property　In this phase of the research process, it is especially critical that you maintain a clear distinction between ideas, opinions, information, words from other sources and your interpretation of that information. *Plagiarism,* or the illicit appropriation of content and ideas, can result from sloppy note taking or poor study habits. Taking care to summarize, paraphrase, and quote from sources with scrupulous care—as well as ensuring that you have given yourself enough time to consider your argument and write your paper—will go a long way toward avoiding plagiarism.

The temptation to plagiarize is especially keen in an age when essays can easily be purchased online and when primary and secondary source information can be cut and pasted at the click of a button into your work. Be aware that such behavior in the classroom may result in a failing grade, suspension, or worse. In the professional world, plagiarism can even result in the loss of a job, the destruction of a reputation, and criminal charges. Plagiarism is a kind of theft. What a plagiarist steals is called, in legal terms, *intellectual property*—the ideas, opinions, inventions, and discoveries in which another writer or researcher has invested considerable time and resources.

When you are unsure of whether or how to give credit to another source, *always* assume that you should give credit (and ask your professor or a writing center instructor for help with citation guidelines). If you are tempted to buy or "borrow" another person's work because of extenuating circumstances, remember that it is *always* better to ask for a deadline extension (and for additional help with your paper). Just as there is never any excuse for the theft of property, there is never any excuse for the theft of ideas.

Evaluating Sources　As you move into the third phase, begin by skimming your source material to sort out the valuable sources from the not-so-valuable ones. For a book, check the table of contents and index for information on your topic; then determine whether the information is relevant to your problem. For an article, see if the abstract or topic sentences in the body of the essay confirm your research interests. The guidelines below can help you determine if a source will be useful.

CRITERIA FOR ASSESSING THE VALUE OF A SOURCE FOR YOUR PROJECT

- Is it directly relevant to your topic?
- Does it discuss the topic extensively, uniquely, and authoritatively?
- Does it bear on your hypothesis, supporting, qualifying, or contradicting it?
- Does it present relatively current information, especially for research in the social and natural sciences?
- Does it meet the criteria for credibility discussed in "Evaluating Online Sources" (page 757) and "Evaluating Print Sources" (page 762)?

Taking Notes   Once you have a core of valuable material, you can begin to read these sources closely and take detailed notes. Skillful note taking—be it on your computer or mobile device, in a notebook, or on note cards—requires a subtle blend of critical thinking skills. It is not a matter of recording all the information available or simply copying long quotes. You want to select and summarize the general ideas that will form the outline of your paper, record specific evidence to support your ideas, and copy exact statements you plan to quote for evidence or interest. You also want to add your own ideas and evaluation of the material. All the notes you take must serve the specific purpose of your paper as stated in your hypothesis. It is essential that you record source information for *every* note that you take, whether that note is a summary, a paraphrase, or a direct quotation.

GUIDELINES FOR TAKING NOTES ABOUT YOUR TOPIC

1. Write the author's last name, the title of the source, and the page number at the top of each card or entry. (Complete information on the source should already be recorded on a card or in a file.)

2. Record only one idea or a group of closely related facts on each card or in each entry.

3. List a subtopic at the top of the card or entry. This will permit you to arrange your cards or entries from various sources into groups, and these groups can then serve as the basis of your outline.

4. List three types of information: (*a*) summaries of material, (*b*) paraphrases of material, in which you recast the exact words of the author, and (*c*) direct quotations, accurately transcribed.

5. Add your own ideas at the bottom of the card or following specific notes.

Summarizing, Paraphrasing, and Quoting   When you write a *summary* of a source, you focus on its main points and restate them in your own words. Summary notes can be especially helpful to remind you, as you draft, of sources that you might want to revisit and look at more closely. Summaries can also be introduced into the body of your essay, especially in an argument research paper, to provide additional information and support for your thesis. Here is an example of a primary source text and a student's summary:

Primary Source: Carl Elliott, "Humanity 2.0," The Wilson Quarterly, Autumn 2003
Even technologies that unambiguously provide enhancements will raise issues of social justice not unlike those we currently face with ordinary medical technologies (wealthy Americans, for example, get liver transplants, while children in the developing world die from diarrhea). We live comfortably with such inequities, in part because we have so enthusiastically embraced an individualistic ethic. But to an outsider, a country's expenditure of billions of dollars on liposuction, face-lifts, and Botox injections while many of its children go without basic health care might well seem obscene.

Student Summary

Topic label	*"Transhumanism" and bioethics*
Author of article	*Elliott*
Relevant pages/URL	*http://wwics.si.edu*
Summary	*Bioethicist and philosopher Carl Elliott defines "transhumanism" and describes a conference of "transhumanists" that he attended. As a bioethicist, Elliott argues that we need to pay attention to the ethical implications of the medical "enhancements" currently practiced or being developed that might contribute to the "transhumanist" goal of creating perfect human beings. In particular, our society's emphasis on developing medical technologies to make us more beautiful or intelligent at the expense of those less fortunate is especially disturbing.*

A *paraphrase* focuses on one specific point or piece of information in an article and restates it in your words. Writing a paraphrase of a source can help you to better understand it. When you paraphrase, follow the original writer's argument but do not mimic the writer's sentence structure or simply replace keywords with synonyms.

Student Paraphrase

Topic label	*"Transhumanism" and bioethics*
Author of article	*Elliott*
Relevant pages/URL	*http://wwics.si.edu*
Unacceptable paraphrase: The sentence structure of the original is imitated, and synonyms replace the original terms (*scandalous* for *obscene*).	*Even procedures designed for cosmetic purposes raise controversies over fairness (rich people get transplants while poor children die from basic diseases). Americans are fine with these inequalities because our culture values the individual. To non-Americans, the money we spend on plastic surgery even though many American children lack health insurance probably appears scandalous.*
Acceptable paraphrase: Key terms from the original source are directly quoted, and the source argument is rephrased in the student's terms.	*Elliott points out that our culture already seems to overlook the injustice of some individuals spending a great deal of money on cosmetic surgery (or "enhancements") while many lack access to basic health care. Elliott describes this as a uniquely American "individualist ethic" but points out that other cultures might see this inequality as "obscene." By extension, the willingness of the transhumanist movement to explore medical "enhancements" that will only benefit a very few wealthy people is also, ethically, "obscene."*

As these examples demonstrate, an acceptable paraphrase shows that the researcher is genuinely engaged with the source's *argument*—not just the words—and has thought about how this particular component of the argument supports the original author's thesis. The summary and paraphrase are introduced with signal phrases, which include the name of the source and an action verb (*says, suggest, acknowledge, maintain,* etc.). Signal phrases help your reader discern what comes from you and what comes from a source. They can also signal your tone, or attitude, toward the source.

When the language of source material is essential to understanding its argument, *quotation* is the most effective strategy. When you quote directly from a source, put quotation marks around the material that you are selecting.

Topic label	*"Transhumanism" and bioethics*
Author of article	*Elliott*
Relevant pages/URL	*http://wwics.si.edu*
Quotation	*"But to an outsider, a country's expenditure of billions of dollars on liposuction, face-lifts, and Botox injections while many of its children go without basic health care might well seem obscene."*

When you have completed all your research, organize your notes under the various subtopics or subheadings that you have established. Now, by reviewing your notes and assessing the data, you should be able to transform the calculated guess that was your hypothesis into a much firmer thesis. Focus on your thesis by stating it at the top of the page where you are working on your outline. If possible or desirable, try to combine some subtopics and eliminate others so that you have three to five major categories for analysis and development. You are now ready to develop an outline for the essay.

Designing an Outline   Because you must organize a lot of material in a clear way, an outline is especially valuable in a research essay. Spend as much time as is reasonable drafting an outline. Begin by creating a rough outline that simply lists your general subheadings and their supporting data. Next, work more systematically through your notes and fill in the rough outline with as much detail as possible, developing each point logically and in detail. If you are required to submit an outline with your research paper, you should begin to develop a full, formal outline at this stage. Such an outline would be structured like this:

I.
   A.
   B.
      1.
      2.
      3.
         a.
         b.
II.

Use roman numerals for your most important points, capital letters for the next most important points, arabic numbers for supporting points, and lowercase letters for pertinent details or minor points. If you are including visuals such as photographs or graphics, include them in the outline as well.

Phase 4: Writing and Submitting the Paper

As you enter the fourth and final phase of the research process, keep in mind that a research paper is a formal essay, not a rag-tag compilation of notes. You should be prepared to take your research effort through several increasingly polished versions, most likely at least a rough draft, a revised draft, and a final manuscript.

Writing the Rough Draft   For your rough draft, concentrate on filling in the gaps in your outline. Take the time to rearrange your notes in the topic order that your outline assumes. In this way, you will be able to integrate notes and writing more efficiently and effectively.

Even as you adhere to your formal outline in beginning the rough draft, you should be open to alternate possibilities and prospects for presenting ideas and information. Although your primary task in writing a first draft is to rough out the shape and content of your paper, the flow of your ideas will often be accompanied by self-adjusting operations of your mind, all aimed at making your research effort even better than you thought it could be at the outline stage.

Whether you incorporate quotations from your notes into the rough draft is a matter of preference. Some writers prefer to transcribe quotations and paraphrases at this point in order to save time at a later stage. Other writers copy and insert these materials directly from entries in a computer file for notes. Still others believe that their thought processes are interrupted by having to write out summarized, quoted, and paraphrased material and to design transitions between their own writing and the transcribed material. They simply write "insert" in the draft with a reference to the appropriate notes. Whatever your strategy, it is essential that you keep track of the sources of summarized, quoted, and paraphrased material so that you can properly cite the sources and avoid plagiarism.

The need to integrate material from several sources will test your reasoning ability during the writing of the rough draft. For any given subtopic in your outline, you will be drawing together information from a variety of sources. To an extent, your outline will tell you how to arrange some of this information. At the same time, you must contribute your own commentary, arrange details in an effective order, and sort out conflicting claims and interpretations. A great deal of thinking as well as writing goes into the design of your first draft. You are not involved in a dull transcription of material when writing the rough draft of a research paper. Instead, you are engaged in a demanding effort to think your way through a problem of considerable magnitude, working in a logical way from the introduction and the statement of your thesis, through the evidence, to the outcome or conclusion that supports everything that has come before.

Revising the Draft   In the rough draft, you thought and wrote your way through the problem. Now you must rethink and rewrite in order to give better form and expression to your ideas. Use the guidelines outlined below to approach your revision. Consider every aspect of your paper, from the most general to the most specific. Look again at the overall organization, key topics, paragraphs, and sentences; read through for clarity of expression and details of grammar, punctuation, and spelling. A comprehensive revision effort will result in a decidedly more polished version of your paper.

CRITERIA FOR REVISING
YOUR RESEARCH WRITING

- Does your title illuminate the topic of the essay and capture the reader's interest?
- Have you created the proper tone to meet the expectations of your audience?
- Does your opening paragraph hook the reader? Does it clearly establish and limit the topic? Is your thesis statement clear, limited, and interesting?
- Does the order of body paragraphs follow the order of your thesis? Do all the body paragraphs support your thesis? Is there a single topic and main idea for each paragraph? Do you achieve unity, coherence, and proper development? Is there sufficient evidence in each paragraph to support the main idea?
- Are there clear and effective transitions linking your ideas within and between paragraphs?
- Have you selected the best strategies to meet the demands of the assignment and the expectations of your audience?
- Are your assertions clearly stated, defined, and supported? Do you use sound logic and avoid faulty reasoning? Do you acknowledge other peoples' ideas properly? Do you use signal phrases to introduce your sources when summarizing, paraphrasing, and quoting? Are all of your summaries, paraphrases, and quotations appropriately cited?
- Is your conclusion strong and effective?
- Are your sentences grammatically correct? Have you avoided errors in the use of verbs, pronouns, adjectives, and prepositions? Have you corrected errors of agreement?
- Are your sentences complete? Have you corrected all fragments, comma splices, and fused sentences?
- Have you varied your sentences effectively? Have you employed clear coordination and subordination? Have you avoided awkward constructions?
- If you include visual information, do you provide adequate context? Is the placement of the visual logical? Is the visual clearly reproduced?
- For an electronic paper, if you include hyperlinks, are they clearly and appropriately placed in the text? Are the hyperlinks active? Do they connect to the correct files or pages?
- Are all words spelled correctly? Do your words mean what you think they mean? Are they specific? Are they concrete? Is your diction appropriate to college writing? Is your language free of clichés, slang, jargon, and euphemism? Do you avoid needless abstractions? Is your usage sound?
- Have you carefully attended to such mechanical matters as apostrophes, capitals, numbers, and word divisions?
- Does your manuscript conform to acceptable guidelines for submitting printed or online work?

Preparing the Final Manuscript   Leave time in your research effort to prepare a neat, clean, attractively designed manuscript. Store all of your files (notes, drafts, and final version) on a backup flash drive or external hard drive, and print or duplicate a copy of the paper. Submit a neat, clear version, and keep the copy. Consult your instructor for the desired format, and carefully follow the guidelines for manuscript preparation in your final version. Look also at the sample paper in Chapter 16, which illustrates how to present the final version of a paper in accordance with MLA style (see pages 805–825).

DOCUMENTING SOURCES

Documentation is an essential part of any research paper. Documenting your sources throughout the paper and in a Works Cited section tells your audience just how well you have conducted your research. It offers readers the opportunity to check on authorities, do further reading, and assess the originality of your contribution to an established body of opinion. Neglect of proper documentation can lead to charges of plagiarism (see page 767).

Quotations, paraphrases, and summaries obviously require credit, for they are the actual words or the theories or interpretations of others. Paraphrases and summaries also frequently offer statistics or data that are not well known, and this type of information requires documentation as well. Facts in a controversy (facts open to dispute or to varying interpretations) also fall within the realm of documentation. Visual information (maps, graphics, and photos) also require documentation, even if they show common knowledge (such as a map of Japan). Video and audio sources (like music files and podcasts), and even conversations, lectures, and e-mails require documentation.

MATERIALS THAT REQUIRE DOCUMENTATION

- Direct quotations
- Paraphrased material
- Summarized material
- Any key idea or opinion adapted and incorporated into your paper
- Specific data (whether quoted, paraphrased, or tabulated in graphs, charts, lists, or tables)
- Visual media like illustrations, maps, photographs, or screenshots
- Disputed facts

Parenthetical documentation—briefly identifying sources within parentheses in the text—is the most common method of indicating sources. The purpose of a parenthetical citation is to identify a source briefly yet clearly enough that it can be located in the list of references at the end of the paper. In MLA style, the author's last name and the page number in the source are included. Then complete information is listed, alphabetically by author or title (if a source has no specific author), in the Works Cited section following the text of the paper.

The bibliographic information you have collected should provide you with the details needed for the preparation of both parenthetical documentation and a list of sources.

GENERAL GUIDELINES FOR PARENTHETICAL DOCUMENTATION

1. Give enough information so that the reader can readily identify the source in the Works Cited (MLA) section of your paper.

2. Supply the citation information in parentheses placed where the material occurs in your text.

3. Give the specific information required by the documentation system you are using, especially when dealing with multivolume works, editions, newspapers, and legal documents.

4. Make certain that the sentence containing the parenthetical documentation is readable and grammatically correct.

With your parenthetical documentation prepared, turn your attention next to a final Works Cited section. To prepare this list of sources, simply transcribe those bibliography cards or entries that you actually used to write your paper, following the appropriate format.

GENERAL GUIDELINES FOR PREPARING A LIST OF SOURCES

1. Use the title Works Cited (MLA).

2. Include only works actually cited in the research paper unless directed otherwise by your instructor.

3. Arrange all works alphabetically according to author's last name or according to the title of a work if there is no author. Ignore *A, An,* or *The.*

4. Begin each entry at the left margin. Indent everything in an entry that comes after the first line by five spaces or ½ inch (MLA style) unless your instructor directs otherwise.

5. Double-space every line, both between and within sources.

6. Punctuate with periods after the three main divisions in most entries—author, title, and publishing information. Do not use a period after a URL, however.

In the following sections, you will find examples of MLA documentation forms. Use these examples to help you cite your sources efficiently and clearly.

MLA (MODERN LANGUAGE ASSOCIATION) DOCUMENTATION

Make it as clear as possible to your reader where a source begins (with a signal phrase) and ends (with a parenthetical citation) in your paper. When you cannot provide specific parenthetical information (such as when a source does not have page numbers), make it as easy as possible for your reader to find the citation on your Works Cited page by including key identification elements like the source's name within the sentence. The following examples illustrate how to cite some of the most common sources in the text and in the list of works cited at the end of a paper.

MLA Parenthetical Documentation

A basic MLA in-text citation includes the author's last name and the page number (for sources that use numbered pages), identifying exactly where the quotation or information is located. This in-text citation leads readers to an entry on the Works Cited page, which provides more complete information about the source.

Book

In the conclusion, he offers a gruesome description of the dying man's physical and

emotional struggles (Tolstoy 1252–3).

If the author's name is included in the text, it does not need to be repeated in the citation.

Garcia Marquez uses another particularly appealing passage as the opening of the

story (105).

If citing a quotation longer than four typed lines, set it off from the text of the paper and indented one inch from the left margin. Double-space the quote and move the period before the parenthetical citation.

It becomes apparent, however, that the narrator is describing horses rather than

children:

> Freedom, the freedom to run, freedom is to run. Freedom is galloping. What else
>
> can it be? Only other ways to run, imitations of galloping across great highlands
>
> with the wind. Oh, Philly, sweet Philly, my love! If Ev and Trigger couldn't keep up
>
> she'd slow down and come round in a while, after a while, over there, across the
>
> long, long field of grass, once she had learned this by heart and knew it forever, the
>
> purity, the pure joy. (LeGuin 852)

One Volume of a Multivolume Work (volume and page numbers)

A strong interest in this literature in the 1960s and 1970s inevitably led to "a significant

reassessment of the aesthetic and humanistic achievements of black writers"

(Inge, Duke, and Bryer 1: v).

Article in a Periodical   Use the periodical's page numbers.

Barlow's description of the family members includes "their most notable strengths

and weaknesses" (18).

For a newspaper article, include the section letter/number as well.

A report on achievement standards for high school courses found "significant variation

among schools" (Mallory B1).

Work without an Author   Use the full title of the work if it is brief; if the title is longer,
however, use a shortened version, beginning with the word you will use to alphabetize the
work on the Works Cited page.

Computerworld has developed a thoughtful editorial on the issue of government and

technology ("Uneasy Silence" 54).

Work by a Group or an Organization

The Commission on the Humanities has concluded that "the humanities are

inescapably bound to literacy" (69).

Work by Two or Three Authors   List the names in the same order as they appear on the
title page.

Studies show that online courses accommodate a variety of learning styles (Babb and

Mirabella 17–8).

Work by Four or More Authors

Lyndon Johnson's legacy "has been rehabilitated in the four decades since his

presidency, thanks in great part to his championing civil rights" (Freemont

et al. 23).

Several Works by One Author

In *The Coming Fury*, Catton identifies the "disquieting omens" that precede the Civil

War (6). As Catton concludes his history of the Civil War, he notes that "it began with

one act of madness and it ended with another" (*Never Call Retreat* 457).

If the author's name is not mentioned in the text, include it in the parenthetical citation,
followed by a comma, and include the title of the work and the page number.

The Civil War "began with one act of madness and it ended with another" (Catton,

Never Call Retreat 457).

Multiple Authors with the Same Last Name

It is possible that by the mid-21st century creating "designer babies" with specifically

desired physical traits will become not only viable but also affordable for many couples

who are starting a family (F. Jackson 44).

Work in an Anthology   Use the name of the author of the work, not the editor of the
anthology.

The narrator describes it as "a big, squarish frame house that had once been white,

decorated with cupolas and spires and scrolled balconies in the heavily lightsome

style of the seventies, set on what had once been our most select street"

(Faulkner 449).

One Work Quoted in Another

Samuel Johnson praises *She Stoops to Conquer* because Goldsmith's play achieves

"the great end of comedy—making an audience merry" (qtd. in Boswell 171).

More Than One Work in a Single Parenthetical Reference

Multiple studies conducted since 2000 indicate that educating children as young as six

about healthy eating and exercising habits reduces the incidents of childhood obesity

by 30 percent (Mickelson, par. 5; Waller and Jackson 45).

Common or Classical Literature   If an often-studied literary work exists in multiple editions, readers may need more information than just a page number if they have a different edition than the one you used. Including the chapter number helps them locate your source more easily.

> After Billy's violent death, Sonny feels "that he [is] the only person in town"
>
> (McMurtry 277; ch. 26).

Act, Scene, and Line Number(s) for a Play   Use Arabic numbers unless your instructor tells you to do otherwise.

> Shakespeare makes use of the classic anagnorisis, or recognition of one's tragic flaw,
>
> in the play when Hamlet tells Horatio he has learned to "Let be" (5.2.209).

Line Number(s) for Poem, or Song Lyrics   For the first quote, use the notation "line" or "lines" and the line number(s); afterward, use only the line number(s).

> Owen is particularly adept at using onomatopoeia to reinforce the persona's terror as
>
> he watches a fellow soldier's suffering: "In all my dreams, before my helpless
>
> sight, / He plunges at me, guttering, choking, drowning" (lines 15–16). Even the
>
> phrase "Gas! Gas!" imitates the insidious hissing sound of the mustard gas as it is
>
> released from the shell (9).

Citation for a Classroom Handout

> According to Professor Jane Smith, young children are often menaced in horror
>
> stories because innocence is attractive to evil ("Conventions of Horror Stories").

Citation for Historical, Legal, and Political Sources   The titles of legal cases are italicized in the text of your paper, whereas the titles of laws, acts, and historical or political documents are not.

> In *Miranda v. Arizona*, the US Supreme Court ruled in 1966 that police officers
>
> must inform criminal suspects in custody of their right to be represented by an
>
> attorney (US Const., amend. 6) and the right to avoid self-incrimination (US
>
> Const., amend. 5).

Citation for Visual Media (Map, Diagram, Graph, Chart, Photograph, Slide, Graphic, Cartoon, Screen Shot, etc.)   The label *Fig. 1* and caption of the medium should be placed below it, flush with the left margin. Figures should be numbered sequentially, and captions should be used to describe their contents; source information and any notations not discussed in the text should follow the figure.

According to the US Centers for Disease Control and Prevention (CDC), 350–500 million people contract malaria each year ("Malaria Facts"). Figure 1 illustrates the densest geographic distribution of the disease. The CDC reports that tropic and sub-tropic areas see the overwhelming majority of malaria cases, particularly Southern Africa ("Geographic Distribution and Epidemiology").

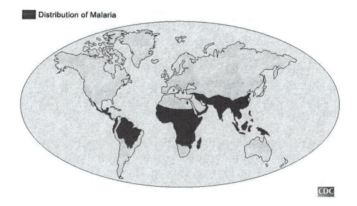

Fig. 1. Geographic Distribution of Malaria, United States, Centers for Disease Control and Prevention; "Malaria: Geographic Distribution." US CDC; 23 April 2004; Web; 1 August 2009.

Citation for a Live Performance, Speech, Lecture, or Interview   In the body of your paper, there is no need to provide specific information beyond the name/subject of the event. The Works Cited entry will provide details on the source.

During the speech, Professor Stephen Elliott explained the benefits of service learning projects in college courses. He emphasized that "the client must define what he or she needs, not leave it up to the volunteer."

Online Sources   Sometimes PDF files of articles and online versions of printed journals label the article's pages to correspond to the printed version, so use them if they are provided. Sometimes a source without page numbers will provide numbered screens, paragraphs, sections, chapters, or references, so use them to help your reader locate your sources. MLA parenthetical citation does not use a comma to separate the author's name from the page number (as does APA), but it does use commas to separate the author's name from the paragraph, section, or reference number.

(Markus, par. 15)   (Markus, sec. 3)

Most online sources, however, do not have page numbers for easy parenthetical citation. In that case, use the author's name or the title of the article or Web page.

Blackwelder observes that "Depp has [the central conflict of the movie] in his eyes in

every scene."

MLA List of Works Cited

Following your paper, list the references you have cited in alphabetical order on a separate page titled "Works Cited." See the Works Cited page of the sample paper (page 824) for an illustration of how you should prepare this page. Use the following sample entries to help you format your references in MLA style. Pay special attention to abbreviated names of publishers, full names of authors, details of punctuation, and other characteristic features of MLA citations, like noting the medium of access or publication. When publication information is not available, indicate the missing data by using *n.d.* (no date), *n.p.* (no place or no publisher), and the like.

Work by One Author   Note the punctuation and use of italics in the basic entry for a book.

Hannesberry, Karen Burroughs. *Femme Noir: Bad Girls of Film.* Jefferson:

McFarland, 2009. Print.

Reynolds, David S. *John Brown, Abolitionist.* New York: Knopf, 2005. Print.

Several Works by One Author   If you use several books or articles by one author, list the author's name in the initial entry. In the next entry or entries, replace the name with three hyphens. In the second entry, notice the hyphenated publisher—Pantheon is an imprint of Random House.

Said, Edward W. *Humanism and Democratic Criticism.* New York: Columbia UP, 2004.

Print.

- - -. *From Oslo to Iraq and the Road Map: Essays.* New York: Pantheon-Random, 2004.

Print.

Work with Two or Three Authors or Editors List the names of several authors in the sequence in which they appear in the book or article. Begin with the last name of the author listed first because it is used to determine the alphabetical order for entries. Then identify the other authors by first and last names.

Franceschi, Michel, and Ben Weider. *The Wars against Napoleon: Debunking the Myth*

of the Napoleonic Wars. New York: Savas, 2008. Print.

Work with More than Three Authors or Editors Name all those involved, or list only the first author or editor with et al., for "and others."

Clark, Virginia, Paul Eschholz, Alfred Rosa, and Beth Lee Simon, eds. *Language:*

Introductory Readings. 7th ed. Boston: Bedford, 2008. Print.

Clark, Virginia, et al., eds. *Language: Introductory Readings.* 7th ed. Boston: Bedford,

2008. Print.

Work with Group or an Organization as Author Alphabetize by the name of the group or organization.

Association for Library Service to Children. *The Newbery and Caldecott Awards: A*

Guide to the Medal of Honor Books. Chicago: American Library Association, 2006.

Print.

Work without an Author

Sir Gawain and the Green Knight. Trans. Bernard O'Donoghue. New York: Penguin,

2006. Print.

Work in a Collection of Pieces by the Same Author

Lasdun, James. "The Woman at the Window." *It's Beginning to Hurt: Stories.* New York:

Farrar, 2009. 113–20. Print.

Work or Chapter in an Edited Book or Anthology of Different Authors

Sher, Ira. "Nobody's Home." *Paraspheres: Extending beyond the Spheres of Literary and*

Genre Fiction. Eds. Rusty Morrison and Ken Keegan. Richmond: Omindawn,

2006. 303–10. Print.

Anthology Cited as a Whole

Morrison, Rusty, and Ken Kegan, eds. *Paraspheres: Extending beyond the Spheres of*

Literary and Genre Fiction. Richmond: Omindawn, 2006. Print.

Work in Several Volumes   If you use only one volume of a multiple-volume set, make note of that volume number; if you use two or more volumes, make note of the total number of volumes.

Smith, Andrew F., ed. *The Oxford Encyclopedia of Food and Drink in America.* 2 vols.

New York: Oxford UP, 2004. Print.

Work Translated from Another Language   The first entry below emphasizes the work of the original author by placing his name first. The next example shifts emphasis to the work of the translators by identifying them first.

Eco, Umberto. *On Literature.* Trans. Martin McLaughlin. New York: Harcourt, 2004.

Print.

Young, David, trans. *Du Fu: A Life In Poetry.* By Du Fu. New York: Knopf-Random,

2008. Print.

Work Appearing as Part of a Series

Oulton, Carolyn W. de la L. *Romantic Friendship in Victorian Literature.* Hampshire:

Ashgate, 2007. Print. The 19th Cen. Ser.

New Edition of an Older Book

Wharton, Edith. *The Custom of the Country.* 1913. Northridge: Aegypan, 2006.

Print.

Scholarly Edition of a Book

Stendhal. *The Red and the Black.* 1931. Trans. Robert M. Adams. Ed. Susanna Lee.

New York: Norton, 2007. Print.

Citation Entries for Online Sources

List the author, the title of the document/specific page (in quotes), and the title of the Web site (in italics), as well as any translator, editor, and entity responsible for the site's upkeep (if not available, use *n.p.*), and the date of the electronic publication or last update (if not available, use *n.d.*). Include the medium (Web) and conclude with the date on which you visited the electronic site where the source is located. MLA's newest guidelines stipulate that researchers should include a URL *only* if readers would have difficulty locating the source through a conventional Web or database search.

Book Accessed via an Electronic Database

Joseph, Jay. *The Missing Gene: Psychiatry, Heredity, and the Fruitless Search for Genes.*

New York: Algora, 2006. *NetLibrary.* Web. 27 Dec. 2008.

Online Book

Wollstonecraft, Mary. *A Vindication of the Rights of Women: With Strictures on Political*

and Moral Subjects. 1792. *Project Bartleby Archive.* Ed. Steven van Leeuwen,

Aug. 2008. Web. 27 Aug. 2008.

Entry from a Reference Volume   Treat less common reference books like other books, including place of publication, publisher, and date. For encyclopedias, dictionaries, and other familiar references, simply note the edition and its date. No page numbers are needed if the entries appear in alphabetical order in the reference volume. Add the definition or entry number to a dictionary citation if appropriate.

Everett, Deborah, and Elayne Zorn. "Eugene Alfred." *Encyclopedia of Native American*

Artists. Westport: Greenwood, 2008. Print. Artists of the Amer. Mosaic.

"Jazz." Def. 2. Merriam-Webster's Collegiate Dictionary. 11th ed. 2003. Print.

Entry from an Online Reference Volume   Include the date of access for Web-based references. This example is for an entry without an author.

"Franklin, Benjamin." *MSN Encarta Online.* Microsoft, 2008. Web. 28 Aug. 2008.

Article in a Scholarly Journal   Include the volume number (if available) and issue number (if available), followed by the year and the pages of the entire article.

Robson, Mark. "The Ethics of Anonymity." *Modern Language Review* 103.2 (2008):

350–63. Print.

Article from an Electronic Scholarly Journal

Pasztor, Tmara. "Celtic Warrior Trappings." *Chronicon: An Electronic History Journal.*

Vol. 3. Ed. Damian Bracken. History Dept. Univ. College [Cork, Ireland], 2007.

Web. 12 April 2008.

Journal Article Accessed via a Database

Nenon, Thomas J. "Some Differences between Kant's and Husserl's Conceptions of

Transcendental Philosophy." *Continental Philosophy Review* 41.4 (2008): 427–39.

Humanities Full Text. Web. 3 Jan. 2009.

Article in a Weekly or Biweekly Periodical   Include the day, month, year, and page numbers. If no author is listed, begin with the article's title.

Orlean, Susan. "The It Bird." *New Yorker* 28 Sept. 2009: 26–31. Print.

"Veiled Threat: What do the Iranian protests mean for the country's women?" *New*

Yorker 5 Oct. 2009: 38–43. Print.

Article in a Monthly or Bimonthly Periodical   If an article in a magazine or newspaper does not continue on consecutive pages, follow the page number on which it begins with a plus sign.

Barlett, Donald L., and James B. Steele. "Good Billions after Bad." *Vanity Fair*

Oct. 2009: 201+. Print.

Waters, Rob. "Medicating Aliah." *Mother Jones* May–June 2005: 50+. Print.

Article in a Print Magazine Available Online / Article in an Online Magazine

Rosen, Jeffrey. "Forced into a Gun Debate." *Time.com.* Time, Inc., 26 Apr. 2007.

Web. 2 May 2008.

Article in a Daily Newspaper—Print or Online

Skidmore, Sarah. "New Coupons Mean Users Clip Less." *Times* [Shreveport]

30 Aug. 2009: 11A+. Print.

Rice, Harvey. "In Galveston, Dead Trees See New Life as Art." *Chron.com*. Houston

Chronicle, 24 Aug. 2009. Web. 1 Sept. 2009.

Newspaper Article Accessed through an Online Database

Roberts, Shearon. "Activists See Chance to Cleanse Streams: State Review Spurs

Campaign." *Washington Post* 3 Aug. 2006, final ed.: T03. *LexisNexis Academic*. Web.

14 Oct. 2007.

News Story Broadcast Online

Heussner, Ki Mae. "Get Out of Jail Free: Monopoly's Hidden Maps." *ABCNews*.

American Broadcast Corp., 18 Sept. 2009. Web. 22 Sept. 2009.

Editorial in a Periodical / Letter to the Editor

Downes, Lawrence. "Remembering Sergeant Monti." Editorial. *New York Times*

18 Sept. 2009, New York ed.: A30. Print.

Posod, Melissa. Letter. *Ms.* Spring 2005: 6. Print.

Review—In Print or Online   If a review has a title, add it after the author's name.

Filkins, Dexter. "The Good Soldier." Rev. of *Where Men Win Glory*, by Jon Krakauer.

New York Times 13 Sept. 2009, New York ed.: BR11. Print.

Zinoman, Jason. "A Pair of New Witches, Still in Search of the Right Spell." Rev.

of *Wicked,* perf. Megan Hilty, Shoshana Bean, David Ayers, Rue

McClanahan, and Ben Vereen. *New York Times* 15 July 2005. Web.

2 Mar. 2008.

Interview—Published or Televised

Obama, Barack. "After the Great Recession." Interview by David Leonhardt.

New York Times 3 May 2009, New York ed.: MM36. Print.

Poehler, Amy. Interview by James Lipton. *Inside the Actor's Studio*. Bravo. 21 Sept.

2009. Television.

Entire Web Site

Crane, Gregory R., ed. *Perseus Digital Library.* Tufts Univ., 31 Mar. 2009. Web.

5 July 2009.

Document or Individual Page on a Web Site

"An Earful on Ethanol: Rising Food Prices, Inefficient Production and Other

Problems." *Knowledge@Wharton*. Wharton Sch., U of Penn., 28 May 2008. Web.

16 Nov. 2008.

Latham, Ernest. "Conducting Research at the National Archives into Art Looting,

Recovery, and Restitution." *The National Archives Library*. National Archives and

Records Administration, Sept. 2009. Web. 15 Sept. 2009.

Marvell, Andrew. "Last Instructions to a Painter." *Poets' Corner.* Ed. Bob Blair et al.

Poets' Corner Scripting, n.d. Web. 22 Sept. 2009.

Blog Post, or Comment on a Blog Post

Mehta, Seema. "Two Swine Flu Clinics Open Today for Uninsured and At-Risk L.A.

County Residents." Blog Entry. *L.A. Now.* Tribune, 23 Oct. 2009. Web. 28 Oct. 2009.

ccmom. "Two Swine Flu Clinics Open Today for Uninsured and At-Risk L.A. County

Residents." Comment. Seema Mehta. *L.A. Now*. Blog. Tribune, 23 Oct. 2009. Web.

28 Oct. 2009.

Electronic Posting to a Group, Bulletin Board, or Listserv

Khan, Badrul. "E-learning Excellence in the Middle East." *Distance Education Online

Symposium*. Adult Ed. Prog., Coll. of Ed., Penn State U, 5 Oct. 2007. Web.

31 Jan. 2008.

Computer Software

Dragon Naturally Speaking 10 Standard: Speech Recognition Software. Burlington:

Nuance, 2008. DVD-ROM.

CD, LP, MP3, or Other Sound Recording   What you want to emphasize determines how you will cite the source (e.g., a performer, a conductor, composer, etc.). Song titles are placed in quotation marks, while the entire compilation (album, in whatever format) is italicized. Remember to identify the format.

> Basie, Count. "Sunday at the Savoy." *88 Basie Street*. Rec. 11–12 May 1983. Pablo
>
> > Records, 1984. MP3.
>
> Strait, George. *Troubador*. MCA. 2008. CD.

Film, Slide, Videotape, Blu-Ray Disc, or DVD   Start with any actor, producer, director, or other person whose work you wish to emphasize. Otherwise, simply begin with the title of the film itself. Note the form cited—*DVD, Videocassette,* and so forth–or *Film* for the movie itself.

> von Donnersmarck, Florian Henckel, dir. *The Lives of Others*. Perf. Martina Gedeck,
>
> > Ulrich Muhe, and Sebastian Koch, 2006. Sony, 2007. DVD.
>
> *The Lovely Bones*. Prod. and dir. Peter Jackson. Perf. Saoirse Ronan, Mark Wahlberg,
>
> > and Rachel Weisz. Dreamworks, 2009. Film.

Programs on Radio or Television   You can cite the entire series (title in italics), a specific episode (title in quotation marks), and you can focus on a particular individual's performance or contribution.

> Hamm, John, perf. "Wee Small Hours." Dir. Scott Hornbacher. By Dahvi Waller and
>
> > Matthew Weiner. *The Wire*. AMC. 11 Oct. 2009. Television episode.
>
> "Pie-lette." *Pushing Daisies*. Dir. Barry Sonnenfeld. Perf. Lee Pace, Kristen Chenoweth,
>
> > Chi McBride, and Anna Friel. *The WB*. Warner Bros., *n.d.* Web. 2 May 2009.

Webcast or Web-based Video

> Gates, Bill. "2008 Microsoft CES Keynote." *Microsoft.com*. Microsoft, 6 Jan. 2008.
>
> > Web. 13 July 2008.
>
> "Herodotus and History." On Point with Tom Ashbrook. *NPR.org*. Natl. Public Radio,
>
> > 31 Jan. 2008. Web.
>
> "Nobody Knows the Trouble They've Seen: Close Combat in Iraq." By nickwalnut.
>
> > *YouTube*. Google, 18 June 2008. Web. 12 Dec. 2008.

Podcast or Streaming Audio

"Elizabethan Revenge." *In Our Time with Melvyn Bragg*. Perf. Melvyn Bragg, Jonathan

Bate, Julie Sanders, and Janet Clare. *BBC Radio 4*, British Broadcasting Corp.

Trust, 18 June 2009. Web. 27 July 2009. MP3 file.

PDF, MP3, or Other Digital Files Online / Offline

Commission on Teaching Credentialing. "California School Paraprofessional Teacher

Training Program." *Commission on Teaching Credentialing*. State of California,

8 Jan. 2009. Web. 2 June 2009. PDF file.

Files downloaded and stored independent of the Internet should be cited by title of the
file, and other pertinent information, including the medium.

Norman, Kimberley. "Drama during the English Renaissance." 2008. PDF file.

Richards, Charles. *Double Trees Church*. 2006. Photograph. JPEG file.

Live Performance   You can cite either the entire performance or an individual's
contribution.

Steel Magnolias. By Robert Harling. Dir. Jason Moore. Perf. Delta Burke, Christine

Ebersole, Rebecca Gayheart, Marsha Mason, Lily Rabe, and Frances Sternhagen.

Lyceum Theatre, New York. 31 July 2005. Performance.

Burke, Delta. perf. *Steel Magnolias*. By Robert Harling. Lyceum Theatre, New York. 31

July 2005. Performance.

Presentation at a Professional Meeting or Conference

Pogue, David. Utah Coalition for Educ. Tech. Taylorsville HS, Salt Lake City. 29 Feb.

2008. Address.

Table, Chart, Graph, Map, Cartoon, Photograph, or Other Visual Media

Official Highway Map of Louisiana. Map. Burlington: Meredith, 2007. Print.

"The Origins of Human Beings." Map. *Atlas of African-American History*. By James

Ciment. New York: Facts-Infobase, 2007. 2. Print.

Rose, John. "Snuffy Smith." Comic strip. *Dallas Morning News* 12 Sept. 2009: 3C. Print.

Artwork   Include the title of the work (in italics), the year of completion (*n.d.* if unknown), the medium, and the location of the artwork.

Rodin, Auguste. *Torso of a Young Woman*. 1910. Bronze. Musée Rodin, Paris.

Advertisement

Golden Double Stuf Oreo. Advertisement. *Entertainment Weekly* 11 Sept. 2009:

14–5. Print.

The Humane Society of the United States. Advertisement. WGN. 18 Sept. 2009.

Television.

Visual on a Web Site

Blackford, B. L. "Map of the Battlefield of Fredericksburg." *Civil War Preservation*

Trust. Civil War Preservation Trust, n.d. Web. 19 May 2009.

"Fredericksburg, Virginia." Map. *Yahoo! Local Maps.* Yahoo!, 20 Jan. 2007. Web.

20 Jan. 2007.

Work Issued by a Federal, State, or Other Government Agency   Depending on the emphasis you intend, you can start with either the writer or the government agency responsible for the publication. *GPO* stands for "Government Printing Office," the publisher of most federal documents.

Ashcroft, Bruce, and Joseph L. Mason. *Operation Dragon Comeback: Air Education and*

Training Command's Response to Hurricane Katrina. USAF History and Museums

Program. Washington: GPO, 2006. Print.

United States. USAF History and Museums Program. *Operation Dragon Comeback:*

Air Education and Training Command's Response to Hurricane Katrina. By Bruce

A. Ashcroft and Joseph L. Mason. Washington: GPO, 2006. Print.

United States. Cong. Senate. Committee on Commerce, Science, and Transportation.

The Minority Serving Institution Digital and Wireless Technology Opportunity Act of

2005: Report of the Committee on Commerce, Science and Transportation on S. 432.

109th Cong., 1st sess. S. Rep. 109-94. Washington: GPO, 2005. Print.

Reference to a Legal Document   When you discuss court cases in your paper, italicize their names. In your Works Cited entries, however, do not italicize them, or the names of laws, acts, or statutes. Consult *The Bluebook,* a legal style manual, for more examples (*www.legalbluebook.com*).

Aguilar v. Felton. 473 US 402. Supreme Court of the US. 1985. Print.

Nonperiodical Publication on DVD-ROM or CD-ROM

Bastarache, Michel. "The Experience of Canada in Dealing with the Adoption of

Legislation and the Administration of Justice in Two Official Languages at the

Federal Level." *The Legal Status of the Basque Language Today: One Language,*

Three Administrations, Seven Different Geographies and a Diaspora. Eds. Gloria

Totoricagüena and Iñigo Urrutia. Boise: Cenarrusa, 2008. 33–42. CD-ROM.

Published or Personal Letter

Lewis, C. S. "To Sarah Neylan." 1 Sept. 1950. *The Collected Letters of C. S. Lewis:*

Narnia, Cambridge, and Joy 1950–1963. Ed. Walter Hooper. Vol. 3. New York:

Harper, 2007. 4. Print.

Eastman, Martin. Letter to the author. 15 July 2007.

E-mail   Include the name of the writer, as well as the subject line, recipient, date, and medium.

Morris, Debbie. "Re: Cost of WiFi Air Card." Message to Barbara Jones. 5 March

2005. E-mail.

Personal Interview

Knight, Frank. Telephone interview. 18 June 2004.

Rowell, Wayne. Personal interview. 16 May 2008.

chapter *16*

A Research Project Casebook: Working with Sources Across Media

This chapter offers an in-depth look at how to conduct research and how to choose and integrate sources from various media into a research paper or project. You will see how one student develops an assignment, locates and evaluates appropriate sources, and correctly incorporates them into a research paper in order to prove her thesis.

PORTRAYALS OF MASCULINITY IN THE 1990S AND EARLY 21ST CENTURY

This casebook is intended to illustrate how to use sources correctly in a writing assignment. Highlighting sources from a number of media, it explores how a student, Clara Lee, developed an assignment, conducted pertinent research to find sources to strengthen her argument, evaluated and chose her sources, and incorporated her findings into her paper in order to prove her thesis.

Clara's instructor gave the class this assignment: *Analyze a film to explore how American cinema reflects a cultural or social change.* Clara was interested in how modern American films portray masculinity, but she realized her topic was too broad. After brainstorming, she narrowed her topic to how American films have portrayed masculinity in the latter part of the 1990s and early 21st century. She chose one film, *Donnie Brasco*, to analyze in depth because she believed it typifies an important shift in Hollywood's vision of American masculinity.

Clara began her research by watching *Donnie Brasco*. The first time she watched, she did so without taking notes, choosing simply to take in the story. The second time, she took notes on the performances, the camera shots, the interaction among the characters, and so on. Compared to other heroes she remembered from films made before the 1990s, Johnny Depp's character, Donnie Brasco, seemed to be more sensitive, more introspective, even more psychologically tortured. Clara thought this new kind of hero was more admirable because audiences could recognize his vulnerability and applaud him for his courage in spite of it.

FINDING SOURCES

Next, Clara searched for resources to help prove her thesis. She logged on to her university library's online catalog, and using keywords, she looked first for books on masculinity in American film. Then she moved on to the library's other databases, where she searched for scholarly articles, reviews of the film, and editorials about masculinity in late 20th- and early 21st-century America, in particular how it has been portrayed in American film. Finally, she used two commercial search engines, Google and Yahoo!, to look for nonprint sources about the movie.

EVALUATING SOURCES

Clara found a number of possible sources, but she realized she needed to evaluate those sources carefully to determine what was or was not useful. She remembered what her instructor told her about determining whether the source was trustworthy and scholarly, and whether it proved her thesis. Here is the list of sources Clara noted:

Even though this was an older source, Clara liked the in-depth discussion about masculinity in 1970s-era films, which she believed would help contrast the 1997 film under discussion.

Author's last name: Mellen

Author's first name: Joan

Book title: *Big Bad Wolves: Masculinity in American Film*

Publisher's location: New York

Publisher: Pantheon

Date published: 1977

Call number: PN 1995.9.M46

Notes: Looks at how masculinity in American film through the 1970s reflects competition; alpha-wolf?

Author's last name: Holmlund

Author's first name: Chris

Book title: *American Cinema of the 1990s: Themes and Variations*

Publisher's location: New Brunswick

Publisher: Rutgers

Date published: 2008

Call number: PN1993.5.U6

Notes: Collection of essays on 1990s films; Holmlund's essay, "1999: Movies and Millennial Masculinity," looks at "macho men in crisis" (229).

Clara discarded this source because it concentrated on detective fiction instead of looking at masculinity in general.

~~Author's last name: Gates~~

~~Author's first name: Philippa~~

~~Book title: *Detecting Men: Masculinity and the Hollywood Detective Film*~~

~~Publisher's location: Albany~~

~~Publisher: State University of NY Press~~

~~Date published: 2006~~

~~Call number: PN1995.9.D4~~

~~Notes: Looks at two kinds of detectives in film through the end of~~
~~the century; "musculinity"~~

~~Author's last name: Schleier~~

~~Author's first name: Merrill~~

~~Book title: *Skyscraper Cinema: Architecture and*~~
~~*Gender In American Film*~~

~~Publisher's location: Minneapolis~~

~~Publisher: University of Minnesota Press~~

~~Date published: 2009~~

~~Call number: PN1995.9.S.5535~~

~~Notes: Looks at how the skyscraper represents American values~~
~~and masculinity in films; mostly concentrates on films~~
~~before 1960~~

Clara also discarded this source because it was too narrowly focused (in this case pre-1960s films and the symbolic nature of the skyscraper).

Author's last name: Stallone

Author's first name: Sylvester

Article title: "Masculine Mystique"

Magazine title: *Esquire*

Issue: Dec. 1996

Pgs.: 89–96

Notes: Interview with Sylvester Stallone on how masculinity was changing in the latter part of the 20th century

~~Author's last name: Abele~~

~~Author's first name: Elizabeth~~

~~Article title: "Assuming a True Identity: Re/De-Constructing~~
~~Hollywood Heroes"~~

~~Journal title: Journal of American and Comparative Cultures~~

~~Issue: Vol. 25, Issue 3–4, pp. 447–54 (Fall/Winter 2002)~~

~~Notes: Discusses alter-egos created by technology and how that~~
~~affects masculinity in early 20th century movies~~

Clara discarded this source because its thesis depends on technological enhancements to the hero to create an alter-ego.

Author's last name: Schickel

Author's first name: Richard

Article title: "Depp Charge"

Magazine title: *Time*

Issue: 3 Mar. 1997

Web site: *Time.com*

Notes: A review of *Donnie Brasco* and Johnny Depp's performance

Author's last name: Blackwelder

Author's first name: Rob

Webpage: Review of *Donnie Brasco*

Web site: *SPLICEDwire.com*

Clara thought this source was important to her argument that men have become marginalized.

Author's last name: Garcia

Author's first name: Guy

Article title: "Men: The New Misfits"

Magazine title: *Fortune*

Issue: 13 Oct. 2008

Notes: Examines why men have become apathetic

Author's last name: Wloszczyna

Author's first name: Susan

Article title: "*Donnie Brasco:* A High Point for Lowlifes"

Newspaper title: *USA Today*

Issue: 28 Feb. 1997: 1D

Notes: Review of *Donnie Brasco*

This source helped Clara demonstrate how masculinity has been portrayed in movies since 9/11.

Author's last name: Cohen

Author's first name: Patricia

Article title: "Towers Fell, and Attitudes Were Rebuilt: An Interview with Susan Faludi"

Newspaper title: *New York Times*

Issue: 27 Sept. 2007, late edition: B10

Web site: *New York Times*

Notes: How movies changed right after 9/11

Author's last name: Goodwin

Author's first name: Christopher

Article title: "Enter the Flat Pack: The Sorry State of Masculinity in
American Movies"

Newspaper title: *Sunday Times* [London]

Issue: 27 Apr. 2008, Culture sec.: 8

Web site: *Times Online*

Date published: 27 Apr. 2008, Culture sec.: 8

Notes: Contends that current American films feature
less-than-masculine protagonists

Author's last name: Fern

Author's first name: Ong Sor

Article title: "There Will Be Masculinity: Two Oscar-Nominated Films
Look at What It Means to be a Man"

Newspaper: *The Straits Times* [Singapore]

Web site: *The Straits Times.com*

Date published: 14 Feb. 2008

Notes: Sees backlash in American films because of a lack of strong
masculine role models

Source: Mike Newell Interview on *Donnie Brasco*

Web site: YouTube video

Posted: 30 June 2007

Notes: Offers insight into script and directoral choices;
compares film to *Death of a Salesman*

WORKING WITH SOURCES

Printed Book

Clara needed to look for printed sources like books
that were scholarly and authoritative about her topic.
She chose *American Cinema of the 1990s* because a
chapter is devoted to "millennial masculinity" in film at
the end of the 20th century. By examining seven movies released in 1999, the author of the chapter, Chris
Holmlund, sets out to discover why and how the American ideal of traditional masculinity is under attack.

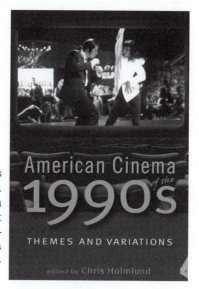

that Jeffrey Sconce labels "smart cinema," positioning themselves in opposition to mainstream cinema by using irony, experimenting with tone, and concentrating on dysfunction and identity in white, usually middle-class culture. Two new books, Susan Faludi's *Stiffed* and Susan Bordo's *The Male Body*, are pertinent here as popularizing takes on millennial masculinity. Faludi argued that the "hard bodies" of the Reagan eighties were being replaced by cheated men from the middle and working classes; Bordo maintained that cosmetic surgery and androgynous fashion were turning masculinity into a fluid, problematic category. Additionally, the largely university-educated directors and screenwriters who authored these seven films respond to vulgarized versions of the high theory practiced by Gilles Deleuze, Félix Guattari, Judith Butler, and Jean Baudrillard.[1]

Men on the Verge of a Nervous Breakdown

A number of the year's films showcase macho men in crisis. With substantial cult followings and domestic box office takes of $37 million and $171.5 million, *Fight Club* and *The Matrix* are two of the most controversial. Somewhat less successful at $22 million, *Magnolia* nonetheless netted an Oscar nomination for star Tom Cruise. Directed by David Fincher from Chuck Palahniuk's novel and even more violent screenplay, Twentieth Century Fox's $68 million *Fight Club* is a drama/black comedy that pairs a nerdy automobile recall insurance coordinator known solely as the Narrator (Edward Norton) with butch idol Tyler Durden (Brad Pitt). An operatic epic of nine interwoven Southern Californian lives, written and directed by Paul Thomas Anderson, New Line's $38 million *Magnolia* showcases Cruise as men's group guru Frank T. J. Mackey. *The Matrix*, which began as a comic book years earlier by the Wachowski brothers, became a $63 million science fiction/martial arts extravaganza from Warner Bros. The film capitalizes on Keanu Reeves's blankly kinetic portrayal of a superhero named Neo. All three movies are ambivalent about life in fin de siècle America, critiquing and promoting consumerism, fascinated by and yet fearful of digital potentialities. All are haunted by apocalyptic visions of millennial masculinity, proffering buff male bodies while recasting the robust masculinity they tender as, at heart, mere performance.

From the first tracking shots through the Narrator's brain out to his sweaty face as he swallows a gun held by another man, *Fight Club* centers on the Narrator's torment. In deadpan voiceover Norton says, "And suddenly I realize that all of this . . . has got something to do with a girl named Marla Singer." As Singer, Fincher cleverly casts Helena Bonham Carter

---

Holmlund reviews several theories about changing ideals of masculinity in America.

The author on three violent action films released in 1999: Violence is an acknowledgment that traditional masculinity is "mere performance."

In her discussion of this passage (below), Clara changed the original "men" to "man" for continuity and added brackets [ ] so the reader would know.

Clara needed to establish that what she observed in *Donnie Brasco* was part of a growing trend that continued, even into the next decade. She was careful to credit her source, Holmlund. Here is how she worked direct quotes and a short paraphrase into her paper:

By 1999, the sensitive, flawed hero was joined by what Chris

Holmlund calls the "macho [man] in crisis," who has to act out

his frustrations, in movies like *Fight Club* and *Magnolia* (229).

Holmlund echoes the argument of social critic Susan Bordo that things like "cosmetic surgery and androgynous fashion were turning masculinity into a fluid, problematic category" for American men at the cusp of the 21st century (229), and that violence seemed to be a natural antidote to the confusion. She notes, however, that such violence is used ironically by some filmmakers as an acknowledgment that traditional expressions of masculinity are "mere performance" (229).

> Clara used Holmlund's name in the sentence, so she did not need to repeat it in the parenthetical citation. She was also careful to acknowledge Susan Bordo's contribution to Holmlund's argument.

The Works Cited entry for this book should begin with the name of the author of the chapter:

Holmlund, Chris. "1999: Movies and Millennial Masculinity." *American Cinema of the*

1990s: Themes and Variations. Ed. Chris Holmlund. New Brunswick: Rutgers UP,

2008, 225–48. Print.

Scholarly Journal Article (Online Database)

Clara needed to find contemporary scholarship to bolster her thesis. She searched for peer-reviewed journal articles and chose one by David Buchbinder that argues modern portrayals of masculinity may be Hollywood's attempt to be more inclusive of an increasingly marginalized male audience. (*Note:* The full-text article can be accessed through Project Muse.)

> The representation of the inadequately or incompetently masculine male—the schlemiel figure—in film and television narratives may thus be understood as enacting *a resistance to or even a refusal of* the coercive pressure of the gender system. We may discern several ways in which that resistance or refusal take place. The first of . . .

Clara decided to paraphrase the source. She made certain to introduce the information with a signal phrase and to cite it parenthetically.

David Buchbinder also touches on traditional masculinity as "performance" and explores whether the schlemiel is popular because he is indicative of men who refuse to live by such artificial constraints (235) or because he makes them feel more capable when measured against him (236).

The Works Cited entry for this source:

Buchbinder, David. "Enter the Schlemiel: The Emergence of Inadequate or Incompe-

tent Masculinities in Recent Film and Television." *Canadian Review of American*

Studies 38.2 (2008): 227–45. *Project Muse*. Web. 22 Aug. 2009.

Web Images Videos Maps News Shopping Gmail more ▼   Web History | Search settings | Sign in

Google   time depp charge   Search   Advanced Search

Web   ⊞ Show options...   Results 1 - 10 of about 412,000 for time depp charge. (0.20 seconds)

DEPP CHARGE - TIME
A POWERHOUSE PERFORMANCE FINALLY PROPELS JOHNNY INTO THE
MAINSTREAM.
www.time.com/time/magazine/article/0,9171,986001,00.html

Depp Charge at GY&K: The Auditorium
While Depp won't be the primary resident of the house, it's safe to assume that the box office
star and 3-time Academy Award nominee will be visiting from ...
gykauditorium.com/?p=905 - Cached

Once Upon a Time in Mexico Movie Review - Antonio Banderas Johnny Depp
Review of the sequel to the movie Desperado, Once Upon a Time in Mexico, starring Antonio
Banderas, ... Rodriguez Releases a 'Depp' Charge in "Mexico" ...
movies.about.com/library/.../aaonceuponatimereview.htm - Cached - Similar

Johnny Depp : Johnny Depp News and Photos - South Florida Sun ...
There was a time when Trinidad South, one of the six themed .... Depp charge enlarge.
Johnny Depp's devilish goatee totally works, giving him. ...
www.sun-sentinel.com/.../johnny-depp-PECLB001381.topic - Cached - Similar

AltWeeklies.com | Salt Lake City Weekly | Depp Charge
Depp Charge Jack Sparrow returns for more giddy smiles in Pirates of the ... but they know
well enough not to mess too much with what worked the first time. ...
www.altweeklies.com/movies/depp_charge/Story?oid=166594 - Cached

Denver News - Depp Charge - page 2
Depp Charge. Continued from page 1 ... At the same time, we realized that getting to Depp
is an incredibly arduous task. Being filmmakers, we decided it had ...
www.westword.com/2005-03-03/news/depp-charge/2 - Cached

A Fan's Page for Johnny Depp - Time 1997
Time - March 3, 1997. DEPP CHARGE A POWERHOUSE PERFORMANCE FINALLY
PROPELS JOHNNY INTO THE MAINSTREAM. By Richard Schickel Photograph by Armando
Gallo ...
www.johnnydeppfan.com/interviews/time.htm - Cached - Similar

Google Brand Features are trademarks or distinctive brand features of Google, Inc.

Popular Magazine Article (Accessed Online)

Articles from popular but credible magazines or newspapers can sometimes be sources in an analytical paper. Credible sources strive for objectivity and accuracy. Clara needed to corroborate her theory that the film shows a more vulnerable hero than the more typically depicted rougher characters. She chose an article she found online at *Time.com*, reviewing Johnny Depp's performance in *Donnie Brasco*. The article had originally been published in *Time* magazine on 3 March 1997, and features a quote from the director, Mike Newell:

This is good strong stuff, not least because, as Newell says, Paul Attanasio's adaptation of Pistone's book offers "this absolutely novel point of view about the Mob," dealing as it does "with the lowest rung, the have-nots. I loved being at the bottom of the pond." So, obviously, did Depp. "He absorbs so much," says the wondering Pistone, with whom Depp hung out for weeks, perfecting all his mannerisms—right down to a nervous cough—that "he doesn't try. It just comes to him. And he remembers everything. He's like a sponge."

Clara incorporated Newell's quote and the writers' observations:

Mike Newell places special emphasis on Pistone's sensitive rela-

tionship with Lefty Ruggiero, his mentor in the mob, and on his imperiled relationship with his wife. Newell, a British director most famous for his vastly different romantic comedy *Four Weddings and a Funeral*, also boasted about Donnie Brasco's "'absolutely novel point of view about the Mob,'" focusing on "'the lowest rung, the have-nots'" (Schickel, Booth, and Harbison), rather than the rich and powerful men at the top so often depicted in mob movies. The film focuses on the soulful side of a male protagonist in a genre in which sensitivity is rare.

Since this was already in quotation marks in the original source, Clara had to acknowledge that with single quotation marks inside the double quotation marks.

The Works Cited entry for this source:

> Schickel, Richard, Cathy Booth, and Georgia Harbison. "Depp Charge." *Time.com*. Time, Inc., 3 Mar. 1997. Web. 10 Aug. 2009.

Article title in quotation marks

Web Site

Clara looked for a source that also recognized the director's choice to concentrate on Depp's eyes to show the character's torment. She found a review of *Donnie Brasco* on

A screenshot of the *Donnie Brasco* review at *SPLICEDwire.com*.

SPLICEDwire.com, professional film critic Rob Blackwelder's Web site. It is important to choose Web sources just as carefully as print sources. A professional film critic lends authority to Clara's assertion about the opening and closing scenes.

> Depp has this conflict in his eyes in every scene and his Joe Pistone seems ever in danger of succumbing to the Donnie Brasco identity he uses to infiltrate the infamous Bonanno family in the late 1970s.

Clara paired Blackwelder's quote with one similar:

Shot in wide-screen so that the eyes literally span the entire screen, the image is a black-and-white snapshot that appears during the opening credits and returns as a full-color close-up at the end of the movie. Depp's lustrous eyes are large and black and beautiful, and gazing at them up close gives the viewer a surprisingly intimate sensation. Even within the conventional narrative that makes up the body of the movie, they become notice-

Quotation from electronic source

ably important; Web-site critic Rob Blackwelder observes that "Depp has [the central conflict of the movie] in his eyes in every

Support from print source

scene," and Susan Wloszczyna of *USA Today* notes, "It's all in the eyes. Depp's intense orbs focus like surveillance cameras, taking in each crime and confrontation. He's sucked into the brutal, bullying lifestyle, and so are we" (28).

The Works Cited entry for the *SPLICEDwire* article:

Blackwelder, Rob. Rev. of *Donnie Brasco*, dir. Mike Newell, perf. Johnny Depp. *SPLICEDwire.com*. SPLICEDwire Film Rev. and Feature Content Svcs., n.d. Web. 12 Aug. 2009.

Visual Media: Film Still

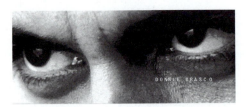

Close-up of Johnny Depp's eyes in *Donnie Brasco*.

A nonprint source, like a photograph, can help the writer demonstrate something more forcefully. The author must choose illustrations carefully, though, to make certain they enhance the narrative rather than just decorate the paper. Using screen capture software, Clara created a still shot that featured a close-up of Johnny Depp's eyes from the opening scene of the film. She made note of the actor's intensity in her opening paragraph and inserted the still shot to illustrate her point:

Mike Newell's 1997 film *Donnie Brasco* begins and ends with an extreme close-up of Johnny Depp's eyes. Shot in wide-screen so that the eyes literally span the entire screen, the image is a black-and-white snapshot that appears during the opening credits and returns as a full-color close-up at the end of the movie. Depp's lustrous eyes are large and black and beautiful, and gazing at them up close gives the viewer a surprisingly intimate sensation. Even within the conventional narrative that makes up the body of the movie, they become noticeably important.

Clara did not create a Works Cited entry for the screenshot since she already had an entry for the entire film. She did, however, create a caption for the still shot that acknowledged its origin.

Clara found a second nonprint source, a video of an interview given by director Mike Newell, in which he discusses several aspects of the film; it was located at *http://www. youtube.com/watch?v=neDvClbM5wY*. (*Note:* Although she found that she could access nearly the entire movie via shorter clips on YouTube, Clara hesitated to use these clips as sources in her paper because she knew the content was copyrighted and distributors could ask YouTube to remove it at any time.)

She incorporated part of Newell's comments into her discussion:

Mike Newell places special emphasis on Pistone's sensitive relationship with Lefty Ruggiero, his mentor in the mob, and on his imperiled relationship with his wife, turning *Donnie Brasco* into "a relationship movie . . . about conflict of loyalty" ("Interview").

The Works Cited entry for this source:

Newell, Mike. "Interview on *Donnie Brasco*." Interview. *YouTube*. Google. 30 June

2007. Web. 16 Aug. 2009.

REVISING

After reading the student's first draft, Clara's instructor pointed out that Clara needed to do more research. For example, she did not distinguish between gender and sex, nor did she identify the primary audience for the contemporary films she examined. Clara repeated her search for resources and also used the search directories *lii.org* and *academicinfo.net*. She found an article that explains the difference between gender and sex and discovered that gender is a learned behavior, or social construct, whereas sex is a biological fact. She also found that young men are the primary target audience of the inept, more comic heroes like those examined in Buchbinder's article. After a little more digging, Clara found an article that suggests that popular animated films like *Cars* and *Toy Story* feature kinder, gentler heroes and marginalize the more macho characters as comic relief.

Here is an excerpt from Clara's draft:

Relates to modern
cinema

Since 2007, writers and directors seem to have adopted a near-schizophrenic approach to capturing the changing idea of modern American masculinity on film. Romantic comedies have offered up a new kind of hero: the pasty, overweight underachiever; and with ticket sales soaring for such films, the less-than-heroic leading man is suddenly in vogue in virtually every film genre in Hollywood. More than ever, hapless men, incapable of or unwilling to assume the alpha-male stance, have come to symbolize masculinity in American films. Christopher Goodwin bemoans this "sorry state of masculinity in American movies today" and points out that even action heroes are "schlub[s] . . . pathetic, if well-meaning, losers [who] inevitably end up with the hottest chicks." He blames the trend, born in films like *Forgetting Sarah Marshall* and *Knocked Up,* in part on "wish fulfillment for most men, who can't imagine scoring so high" and on the acceptance of everyone's inner "nerd" (8). In looking at the proliferation of comedic "schlemiel" protagonists, David Buchbinder also touches on traditional masculinity as "performance" and explores whether

paraphrase

the schlemiel is popular because he is indicative of men who refuse to live by such artificial constraints (235) or because he makes them feel more capable when measured against him (236). This Hollywood portrayal of masculinity perhaps signals a paradigm shift in how women see men and, more important, how they see themselves.

Guy Garcia says that the American man's identity crisis is thanks to the emergent power of women. He claims that as women make strides in education and the business world, men are struggling with "the very definition of what it means to be a man" (185). Garcia believes that Americans enjoy "shows like *Ice Road Truckers* and *Deadliest Catch,* which glorify men who do dangerous, physically demanding jobs, [and which] have struck a nostalgic chord in the zeitgeist" (185). Perhaps to rage against this emotional paralysis, some filmmakers are introducing a new level of brutality in dramatic films and shifting the focus from the traditional hero onto a sinister figure, who would normally be identified as the antagonist. Ong Sor Fern cites two examples of films that concentrate on sadistic antiheroes, *There Will Be Blood* and *No Country for Old Men*. Fern muses, "It is tempting, even inevitable, to infer that this current obsession with strong male figures has something to do with the lack of [them] in America today." Buchbinder also sees films that promote traditional masculinity as Hollywood's "nostalgic" attempt to pacify "a certain hysteria, an anxiety on the part of at least some men that a familiar form of masculinity may be fading" (243). In the age of the metrosexual, the popularity of these testosterone-fueled escapades is an attempt to rehabilitate our definition of masculinity and reclaim a portion of the power white men felt during the days of *Dirty Harry*.

Here is how Clara revised this section to incorporate her new research. Her addition is in boldface.

Since 2007, writers and directors seem to have adopted a near-schizophrenic approach to capturing the changing idea of modern American masculinity on film. Romantic comedies have offered up a new kind of hero: the pasty, overweight underachiever; and with ticket sales soaring for such films, the less-than-heroic leading man is suddenly in vogue in virtually every film genre in Hollywood. More than ever, hapless men, incapable of or unwilling to assume the alpha-male stance, have come to symbolize masculinity in American films. Christopher Goodwin bemoans this "sorry state of masculinity in American movies today" and points out that even action heroes are "schlub[s] . . . pathetic, if well-meaning, losers [who] inevitably end up with the hottest chicks." He blames the trend, born in films like *Forgetting Sarah Marshall* and *Knocked Up,* in part on "wish fulfillment for most men, who can't imagine scoring so high" and on the acceptance of everyone's inner "nerd" (8). In looking at the proliferation of comedic "schlemiel" protagonists, David Buchbinder also touches on traditional masculinity as "performance" and explores whether the schlemiel is popular because he is indicative of men who refuse to live by such artificial constraints (235) or because he makes them feel more capable when measured against him (236).

This idea of traditional masculinity as a "performance" makes more sense when one realizes that, unlike one's sex (male), which is a product of biology, one's gender (masculine) is "socially constructed; it is learned" behavior that we adopt as a result of how we are reared, what we are exposed to, and how people react to us (Talbot 510). The indoctrination begins at birth (how our families interact with us, how our parents dress us, etc.) and continues through childhood (what toys we are given to play with, how our peers interact with and react to us, etc.). In fact, Hollywood influences the development of masculinity in childhood, according to Ken Gillam and Shannon R. Wooden. In "Post-Princess Models of Gender: The New Man in Disney/Pixar," Gillam and Wooden trace the villification of the traditional "alpha male" and the glorification of the kinder, gentler "beta male," who comes to realize that expressing his inner turmoil is admirable and praiseworthy (3). This Hollywood portrayal of masculinity perhaps signals a paradigm shift in how women see men and, more important, how they see themselves.

Guy Garcia says that the American man's identity crisis is thanks to the emergent power of women. He claims that as women make strides in education and the business world, men are struggling with "the very definition of what it means to be a man" (185). Garcia believes that Americans enjoy "shows like *Ice Road Truckers* and *Deadliest Catch,* which glorify men who do dangerous, physically demanding jobs, [and which] have struck a nostalgic chord in the zeitgeist" (185). Perhaps to rage against this emotional paralysis, some filmmakers are introducing a new level of brutality in dramatic films and shifting the focus from the traditional hero onto a sinister figure, who would normally be identified as the antagonist. Ong Sor Fern cites two examples of films that concentrate on sadistic antiheroes, *There Will Be Blood* and *No Country for Old Men.* Fern muses, "It is tempting, even inevitable, to infer that this current obsession with strong male figures has something to do with the lack of [them] in America today." Buchbinder also sees films that promote traditional masculinity as Hollywood's "nostalgic" attempt to pacify "a certain hysteria, an anxiety on the part of at least some men that a familiar form of masculinity may be fading" (243). In the age of the metrosexual, the popularity of these testosterone-fueled escapades is an attempt to rehabilitate our definition of masculinity and reclaim a portion of the power white men felt during the days of *Dirty Harry.*

The final draft of Clara's paper follows.

SAMPLE STUDENT PAPER
(MLA STYLE)

Lee 1

Clara Lee

Professor Paul Smith

Writing Workshop II

5 September 2009

The Courage of Intimacy:

Movie Masculinity in the 1990s and Early 21st Century

Mike Newell's 1997 film *Donnie Brasco* begins and ends with an extreme close-up of Johnny Depp's eyes. Shot in wide-screen so that the eyes literally span the entire screen, the image is a black-and-white snapshot that appears during the opening credits and returns as a full-color close-up at the end of the movie. Depp's lustrous eyes are large and black and beautiful, and gazing at them up close gives the viewer a surprisingly intimate sensation (See Fig. 1).

Even within the conventional narrative that makes up the body of the movie, they become noticeably important; Web-site critic Rob Blackwelder observes that "Depp has [the central conflict of the movie] in his eyes in every scene," and Susan Wloszczyna of *USA Today* notes, "It's all in the eyes. Depp's intense orbs focus like surveillance cameras, taking in each crime and confrontation. He's sucked into the brutal, bullying

---

Annotations (right margin):

Header:
Last name and page number ½ inch below top of page

Heading 1 inch below top of page

All lines double-spaced, including heading and title

Title centered
Title defines topic

Paragraph indented ½ inch or 5 spaces

1-inch side margins.

Opening interests reader with detail from film

Quotation from electronic source

Support from print source

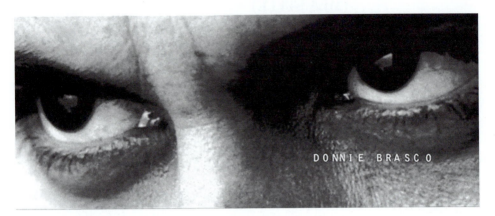

FIGURE 1. A close-up of Johnny Depp's eyes from the opening sequence of *Donnie Brasco,* Dir. Mike Newell, Sony, 1997.

lifestyle, and so are we" (28). The close-up image at the beginning and end is one of the few instances in which the film draws blatant attention to its own style, but the device calls attention to the film's central focus, its constant probing into the character at the center of the movie.

Somehow, without restricting the film to a first-person narration by Depp's undercover FBI agent, the audience comes to identify with him and understand the many pressures increasing inside his head simply by watching his eyes. They reflect his watchfulness, his uncertainty, his frustration, and his guilt—all without drawing too much attention to himself from his unsuspecting wiseguy companions. He is guarded with his words, Quotation from film   causing his closest Mafioso friend to remark, "You never say anything without thinking about it first." His quietness invites viewers to read his looks and expressions, to become intimately

Lee 3

acquainted with a character who constantly has to hide part of himself from the people around him, until they can virtually feel every twinge of fear or regret that the character feels. Seeing this man trapped in situations in which he faces crisis after crisis, unwillingly alienated from his family and eventually his employers, trying only to protect the people he loves, viewers can ultimately recognize him as a more sensitive, struggling, and courageous hero than those celebrated in the past.

Over the decades, Hollywood has glorified the gruff masculinity of actors from Humphrey Bogart to Sylvester Stallone. Joan Mellen notes in her 1977 book *Big Bad Wolves:*

1-inch margin at top
Heading ½ inch below top of page continues last name and page numbering

Thesis stated

Past contrasted with present

FIGURE 2. Johnny Depp in the title role of *Donnie Brasco,* Dir. Mike Newell, Sony, 1997.

Source identified in text

Masculinity in the American Film that in traditional Hollywood films, especially the stoic action films of the 1970s, "physical action unencumbered by effeminate introspection is what characterizes the real man" (5). In the 1990s, it seems that much changed; introspection became a central part of leading-male roles. We can see this clearly in the character-driven films of 1997 alone, which won accolades for such intimate roles as Robert Duvall's tormented evangelical preacher in *The Apostle,* Matt Damon's emotionally needy genius and Robin Williams's mourning therapist in *Good Will Hunting,* and the unemployed guys struggling over issues like impotence and child custody in *The Full Monty.* Thoughtfulness, vulnerability, and the ability to handle relationships became virtual requirements for the male "hero" in the 1990s. The old-fashioned masculinity of characters played by Clint Eastwood or John Wayne in the past has come to be regarded as emotionally repressed and overly macho.

Quotation from book with page number

Other examples noted

Background tied to thesis

The change is partly cyclical. Mellen cites the 1930s and 1950s as eras in film in which leading men were given greater depth. She says, "Despite the limitations imposed by a repressive society [in the fifties], film recovered for men an individual self with a distinctive identity and a flourishing ego" (191–92). Actors like Marlon Brando and James Dean, in particular, played insecure, emotionally torn rebels who express tenderness in their relationships with women and with other men.

Clarification added in brackets
Quotation with page numbers

Lee 5

FIGURE 3. John Wayne, the epitome of mid-20th century masculinity.

However, in the sixties, "as the Vietnam War progressed . . .

maleness itself appeared under siege and in need of defense,"

and "traumatic events of the sixties induced the Hollywood

hero to tighten up, reveal as little about himself as possible,

and to find comfort in his own recalcitrance" (248–49). Things

scarcely got better when "glorification of the vigilante male [be-

came] the dominant masculine myth of the seventies" (295)

with films like *Dirty Harry* and *Taxi Driver*. Mellen notes, "In the

Ellipses for words
omitted

Quotations and
summary from
source

seventies film, people are allowed no option: they must meet
force with force" (307). Following two decades of grim testos-
terone, there was a definite reaction in the bubble gum pop
culture of the eighties, with flashy cartoon violence starring
Sylvester Stallone or Arnold Schwarzenegger presenting highly
unrealistic images of masculinity, and lighter portrayals like
Marty McFly and Indiana Jones gaining in popularity. By the
nineties, American audiences were no longer taking tough guy
masculinity seriously, leading to a trend of ironic humor in action
films from *True Lies* to *Independence Day.* It is doubtful that Will
Smith would have been a favorite action hero before the 1990s.

Transition back to
present day

However, the crucial underlying shift in American culture is
the debilitation of the conventional white male hero in a country
he once monopolized. Trends in society within the past forty
years have led to greater freedom for women, minorities, and
homosexuals, and as pride and power among these groups increased, there has been a backlash against the white male. The
hero of the 1990s has to prove that he is sensitive and completely respectful of every group mentioned above in order to
remain sympathetic, forcing his previous role of unquestioned
dominance to change drastically. In addition, now that women
are going to work and less is expected of men in terms of being
the provider and protector of the family and society, more is
expected of them in their personal relationships. As noted in

1996 by Sylvester Stallone, a fitting symbol of the old macho

masculinity who tried to change his image to a more sensitive

one, "I think the leading man of the future will be one who is   Quotation from
                                                                   published interview
beleaguered by the need to constantly define on film the male-

female relationship." He also notes, "People want to nurture the

underdog. The day of the strongman is over" (94). The themes of

inefficacy in society, sensitivity in relationships, and a reaction to

the old strongman ideal show up clearly in *Donnie Brasco*.

    In the movie, FBI agent Joe Pistone, alias Donnie Brasco,   Analysis of film

goes undercover in the belief that he is on the side of law and

order, with the simple goal of booking some major criminals; in-

stead he finds a bunch of endearing but disturbingly violent men

who become his closest companions for several years. Particu-

larly perplexing is his relationship with Benjamin "Lefty" Rug-   Plot summary and
                                                                   interpretation
giero, the trod-upon hit man whose thirty years of faithful service

are rewarded with dirty-work assignments while younger wise-

guys are promoted over him. Lefty is the one who notices Donnie

and recruits him into the organization, and from the start his faith

in Donnie is clear; as Pistone smugly reports to a contact early in

the movie, "I got my hooks in this guy." However, Pistone's   Character analysis

smugness wears off as Lefty repeatedly invites him into his

home, confides in him with his complaints and his dreams, and

says unexpectedly one day waiting in the hospital where his own

son is in the E.R. for a drug overdose, "I love you, Donnie."

It is appropriate that the fictional Donnie Brasco is an orphan, because Lefty essentially becomes a surrogate father to him. Pistone, concerned for Lefty's fate, becomes more and more reluctant to "pull out" of his undercover assignment, revealing Donnie Brasco as a spy and leaving the blame (and death sentence) on Lefty. At one point he stops meeting his FBI contacts because they are pressuring him to pull out. Instead, he lets himself take on his mob alter ego more and more, tearing both his professional and personal lives apart.

In a way, the film is an interesting commentary on how ideals have changed, because it is set in the 1970s, the last decade of the full-fledged he-man hero, but made with a 1990s ideology. Because it is based on a book by the real agent Joe Pistone, who is currently living under the Witness Protection Program, one might think the portrayal would be strictly fact-based and would not be affected by the obsession with the sensitive male; but of course, one must never underestimate the power of filmmakers in any era to interpret their material with their own contemporary vision (note the portrayal of the Three Musketeers as aging and vulnerable in the 1998 screen adaptation of *The Man in the Iron Mask;* the seventies version of the same book depicted the Musketeers as brash and irreverent).

There is plenty of traditional macho posturing in the Mafia sequences of *Donnie Brasco,* but director Mike Newell places special emphasis on Pistone's sensitive relationship with Lefty Ruggiero, his mentor in the mob, and on his imperiled relationship with his wife, turning *Donnie Brasco* into "a relationship movie . . . about conflict of loyalty" ("Interview"). Newell, a British director most famous for his vastly different romantic comedy *Four Weddings and a Funeral,* also boasted about *Donnie Brasco's* "'absolutely novel point of view about the Mob,'" focusing on "'the lowest rung, the have-nots'" (Schickel, Booth, and Harbison), rather than the rich and powerful men at the top so often depicted in mob movies. The film focuses on the soulful side of a male protagonist in a genre in which sensitivity is rare.

Electronic source cited by authors' names only

In fact, *Donnie Brasco* has been recognized as an evolutionary step in the genre of gangster films. *Time* calls it a "neo-Scorsesian study of lowlife Mob life," and says that it "rises above the mire of its shopworn genre by showing the cracks in its characters' armor" (Schickel, Booth, and Harbison). Conventional gangster films usually depict the rise and fall of a charismatic criminal. The gangster movies of the thirties and forties featured fast-talking tough guys like James Cagney and Humphrey Bogart; Francis Ford Coppola's 1972 epic *The Godfather,* which revived the genre, depicted the same glamour, ruthlessness, and power of the Mafia, on an even greater romanticized scale. But after a spate of stylized mob movies in the previous thirty years, many reviewers of *Donnie Brasco* welcomed a new approach in a genre that was growing old and

Contrasts lead back to thesis

stale. Put another way, *Donnie Brasco* is the film that finally

brings its genre into the nineties by replacing its tough, glamor-

ous hero with a real guy who can't live up to the stereotypes.

Analysis of main character

Almost in direct response to the ideal of masculinity pre-

sented in the past, Newell shows that although at first Pistone

is doing everything right—fitting perfectly into his undercover

persona, doing top-rate work for the FBI, and sending checks

home regularly to his family—he cannot "be the man in the

f—kin' white hat" that he thought he could be, as he puts it late

in the movie. He knows how impossible it is to fulfill his male

responsibilities in all three of his very different worlds after he

has ditched the FBI, almost lost his marriage, and realized that

his undercover work, once revealed, will be the cause of Lefty's

death. He has failed his own expectations of himself to save the

day and make everything right. The contemporary audience

recognizes the realism of the situation. As Stallone states in his

interview, "The male is [only] the illusion of the protector and

guardian, . . . [b]ecause in this day and age, there is no security

he can offer" (94). By now the audience realizes that a hero

cannot always save the day in a conventional sense. In an odd

way, viewers even appreciate his failure because it has knocked

all of his arrogance out of him and left only an exposed, vulner-

able character.

Lee 11

A contemporary audience can especially relate to the issues of family breakdown, recognizing in Donnie's situation the roots of the culture of estrangement and divorce which is so widespread today. Violating the conventional lone male gangster/cop figure, Joe Pistone has not only a wife but three small daughters hidden away in suburbia, and he can't tell them anything about his job without putting them at risk. His visits home are less and less frequent, sometimes months apart, due to the consuming nature of his "job." Although viewers can see from the start the tenderness and love he has for his wife and daughters, his prolonged absences and broken promises (he misses his daughter's first Communion) lead to intensifying arguments between him and his wife. As she constantly reminds him, his job is tearing their home apart, and not knowing what he is doing makes it all the more unbearable. Pistone knows, as his identification with the Mafia grows deeper and deeper, that his involvement has serious consequences for his family, and this mounting pressure becomes impossible to resolve when weighed against the life of Lefty Ruggiero.

Analysis of relationships with other characters

Regarding the role of women in Mafia movies, Mellen points out that "well into the seventies the male protagonist of films from *The Godfather* (I or II) to *Serpico* uses women solely to discard them" (327). Wives in *The Godfather* are cheated on, lied to, and in one case, violently beaten. At a pivotal moment

Contrasting example

at the end of the movie, the wife of Michael Corleone tearfully asks him if he has ordered the death of his sister's husband, and he looks directly into her eyes and lies, saying he did not. She smiles and believes him. Her character is, in fact, constantly under the thumb of her husband who misleads her, ignores her, and coaxes her into marrying him after not contacting her for over a year. She and the other women in the movie are not once consulted or listened to, no matter how much their husbands' actions affect their lives.

Contrasting example related to film

Donnie Brasco could have been made in precisely the same way. Pistone's wife Maggie is, after all, left at home for months at a time while her husband is off doing his job for the FBI. However, Newell makes the relationship between them a pivotal storyline in the movie. Repeatedly in the course of the narrative, interrupting the Mafia sequences, the audience sees Pistone call or visit home, reinforcing his identity as a husband and father. Viewers also note the progression as his relation-

Incident from film substantiates interpretation

ship begins to sour. The lowest point comes when Pistone shows up at his home in the middle of the night to retrieve a bag containing $3 million in cash and confronts Maggie, who has found it and hidden it. When she tells him that he has become "like one of them," he strikes her, and both recoil in surprise, less shocked at the blow than at the realization of what their marriage has become. At this critical moment, he tries to

Lee 13

tell her the truth. He awkwardly explains the situation with Lefty

and his fear of being responsible for his death. He tells her that

he is not sure of what is right anymore. He tells her, "I'm not like   Quotation from film

them. I am them." It is evident that the troubles of Pistone's

marriage hurt himself as much as his wife, and in a sense, deal-

ing with them takes more courage than risking his life as an

undercover agent in the Mafia. The film treats this relationship

delicately, and the woman here is not merely discarded or lied

to, but confronted and confided in, with her concerns pre-

sented as clearly as his own.

What makes Pistone's situation so compelling is that he

starts out believing that he can be one of the traditional "soli-

tary heroes who solve all problems for themselves" (Mellen 23)   Source identified
                                                                      in citation
and instead comes up against situations that are too difficult to

handle. Joe Pistone slaps his wife, not to exert his male domi-

nance, but because he has lost control. When he tries to make

things right, he doesn't sweep her into his arms (and probably

have his way with her, in the true tradition of male heroes); he is

almost frightened to make a move and instead makes a   Detail from film
                                                            supports
gesture—kissing the back of her head—to try and reestablish   interpretation

the emotional (not sexual) intimacy between them. In his early

scenes with Lefty, Pistone is noticeably on his guard and de-

tached from the affection Lefty is developing for him; later,

when he has the opportunity to be promoted within the ranks of the mob and Lefty feels betrayed, Pistone tries to express his devotion by visiting him at the hospital where his son has overdosed. When Lefty orders him to leave, he refuses.

These gestures are some of Pistone's most heroic acts, at least as Newell presents it. Although he is given a medal and a check for $500 at the end of the movie for his undercover work (which is enough to secure scores of convictions), his feelings about it are clearly mixed; his loyalty to the FBI has been disintegrating as he has lost faith in their good guy/bad guy rhetoric, and his primary concern—Lefty's safety—is now uncertain. His success in infiltrating a group of depressed Brooklyn wiseguys is now a cause for guilt. Pistone's ambivalence and impotence are "like a version of *Death of a Salesman* . . . about a man at the end of his tether and at the end of his time, realizing that his whole life [has come] down to the point, really, of a cheap [reward], but set in mob terms" (Newell).

It is at this point at the end of the movie, as Pistone accepts his reward and his wife tells him it's all over, that Newell returns to the extreme close-up of Depp's eyes (see Fig. 1), and the audience sees how troubled they are. Viewers are left with that image, indicating that Newell intended for them to leave the theater asking themselves what it was all for— whether doing his job was really the right thing or not. True to life, there is no easy, happy ending, in which a man can die in

Return to detail used in first paragraph

Lee 15

battle or save the day and thus fulfill his "masculine" duties. What matters, however, as viewers return to that close-up, is that they have seen Joe Pistone/Donnie Brasco's vulnerability and his devotion within his relationships. If he feels confused or uncertain at the end, it is because he has faced these emotional issues, which are far more subtle than the challenges related to   `Return to thesis` his job. The audience has seen him show more courage in his private struggles than John Wayne ever did out on the frontier and can applaud him for that.

Like many films, *Donnie Brasco* is a cultural reflection of its makers and the audience, who were trying to come to grips with the changing view of the white male's place in society since the 1970s. By 1999, the sensitive, flawed hero was joined by what Chris Holmlund calls the "macho [man] in crisis," who acts out his frustrations in movies like *Fight Club* and *Magnolia* (229). Holmlund echoes the argument of social critic Susan Bordo that things like "cosmetic surgery and androgynous fashion were turning masculinity into a fluid, problematic category" for American men at the cusp of the 21st century (229), and that violence seemed to be a natural antidote to the confusion. She notes, however, that such violence has been used ironically by some filmmakers as an acknowledgment that traditional expressions of masculinity are "mere performance" (229).

Within a few years, however, a version of the straightforward hero of yore came roaring back in reaction to the anger and fear Americans felt after the terrorist attacks on 11 September 2001. In those first few years after 9/11, Susan Faludi observed "a powerful resurgence in traditional sex roles and a glorification of he-man virility as embodied by [John] Wayne, the ur-savior of virtuous but helpless damsels in distress." She points to Steven Spielberg's 2005 film *War of the Worlds* as an example of how American films tried to reshape and reclaim masculinity in the mid-2000s: "'It's some bizarre, weirdly out-of-proportion fixation, . . . an exaltation of American masculinity in an intergalactic crisis'" (qtd. in Cohen). The terror and anger the nation experienced as a result of 9/11 felt nearly that epic to most Americans for years, but with the diminishing sense of panic by the end of the decade, American films have turned an eye toward other kinds of masculinity.

Since 2007, writers and directors seem to have adopted a near-schizophrenic approach to capturing the changing idea of modern American masculinity on film. Romantic comedies have offered up a new kind of hero: the pasty, overweight underachiever; and with ticket sales soaring for such films, the less-than-heroic leading man is suddenly in vogue in virtually every film genre in Hollywood. More than ever, hapless men, incapable of or unwilling to assume the alpha-male stance,

Relates to modern cinema

have come to symbolize masculinity in American films. Christopher Goodwin bemoans this "sorry state of masculinity in
American movies today" and points out that even action heroes
are "schlub[s] . . . pathetic, if well-meaning, losers [who] inevitably end up with the hottest chicks." He blames the trend,
born in films like *Forgetting Sarah Marshall* and *Knocked Up,* in
part on "wish fulfillment for most men, who can't imagine scoring so high" and on the acceptance of everyone's inner "nerd"
(8). In looking at the proliferation of comedic "schlemiel" protagonists, David Buchbinder also touches on traditional masculinity as "performance" and explores whether the schlemiel is
popular because he is indicative of men who refuse to live by   Paraphrase
such artificial constraints (235) or because he makes them feel
more capable when measured against him (236).

This Hollywood portrayal of masculinity perhaps signals a
paradigm shift in how women see men and, more important,
how they see themselves. Guy Garcia says that the American
man's identity crisis is thanks to the emergent power of women.
He claims that as women make strides in education and the
business world, men are struggling with "the very definition of
what it means to be a man" (185). Garcia believes that Americans enjoy "shows like *Ice Road Truckers* and *Deadliest Catch,*
which glorify men who do dangerous, physically demanding
jobs, [and which] have struck a nostalgic chord in the zeitgeist"

(185). Perhaps to rage against this emotional paralysis, some filmmakers are introducing a new level of brutality in dramatic films and shifting the focus from the traditional hero onto a sinister figure, who would normally be identified as the antagonist. Ong Sor Fern cites two examples of films that concentrate on sadistic antiheroes, *There Will Be Blood* and *No Country for Old Men*. Fern muses, "It is tempting, even inevitable, to infer that this current obsession with strong male figures has something to do with the lack of [them] in America today." Buchbinder also sees films that promote traditional masculinity as Hollywood's "nostalgic" attempt to pacify "a certain hysteria, an anxiety on the part of at least some men that a familiar form of masculinity may be fading" (243). In the age of the metrosexual, the popularity of these testosterone-fueled escapades is an attempt to rehabilitate our definition of masculinity and reclaim a portion of the power white men felt during the days of *Dirty Harry*.

Given Mellen's assertion of the cyclical pattern of masculinity in American cinema, though, we can only hope that it won't be long before we see a renaissance of the enlightened hero, at his best when he is true-to-life, flawed so we can identify with him but not so flawed that we spend our time laughing at his ineptitude. We need the occasional stoic cowboy or renegade cop, but sometimes we really want a hero we can admire and emulate because he is able to triumph in the end despite his personal struggles. Such a depiction of masculinity would be a welcome alternative to the two extreme portraits that permeate American films today. Perhaps if we could agree on what masculinity means in 21st-century America, we wouldn't need to turn every good guy into one of Goodwin's "schlubs," nor would we need to bathe in the glorified violence of the antihero who rages against his social and cultural impotence. We could once again celebrate the personal triumphs of our Donnie Brascos, who can be both human and heroic.

Lee 20

Begins new page
Title 1 inch below
top of page and
centered

Works Cited

Blackwelder, Rob. Rev. of *Donnie Brasco*, dir. Mike Newell,

All lines double-
spaced, including
title and entries

perf. Johnny Depp. *SPLICEDwire.com.* SPLICEDwire Film

Rev. and Feature Content Svcs., n.d. Web. 12 Aug. 2009.

Entries in
alphabetical order

Buchbinder, David. "Enter the Schlemiel: The Emergence of

Inadequate or Incompetent Masculinities in Recent Film

and Television." *Canadian Review of American Studies* 38.2

(2008): 227–45. *Project Muse.* Web. 22 Aug. 2009.

First line at margin

Cohen, Patricia: "Towers Fell, and Attitudes Were Rebuilt: An

Next lines indented
½ inch or 5 spaces

Interview with Susan Faludi." *New York Times.* New York

Times, 27 Sept. 2007, late ed.: B10. Web. 19 Aug. 2009.

Donnie Brasco. Dir. Mike Newell. Perf. Johnny Depp. Tristar,

1997. Film.

Fern, Ong Sor. "There Will Be Masculinity: Two Oscar-

Nominated Films Look at What It Means to Be a Man in the

Context of American Society." *The Straits Times.com.* Sin-

gapore Press Holdings, 14 Feb. 2008. Web. 10 Aug. 2009.

Article title in
quotation marks

Garcia, Guy. "Men: The New Misfits." *Fortune* 13 Oct. 2008:

185–6. Print.

Goodwin, Christopher. "Enter the Flat Pack: The Sorry State of

Masculinity in American Movies." *Times Online* [London].

News International Group, 27 Apr. 2008, Culture sec.: 8.

Web. 9 Aug. 2009.

Holmlund, Chris. "1999: Movies and Millennial Masculinity."

  American Cinema of the 1990s: Themes and Variations.

  Ed. Chris Holmlund. New Brunswick: Rutgers UP, 2008,

  225–48. Print.

Mellen, Joan. *Big Bad Wolves: Masculinity in American Film.*   Book title italicized

  New York: Pantheon, 1977. Print.

Newell, Mike. "Interview on *Donnie Brasco.*" Interview. *YouTube.*   Movie title italicized

  Google. 30 June 2007. Web. 16 Aug. 2009.

Schickel, Richard, Cathy Booth, and Georgia Harbison. "Depp

  Charge." *Time.com.* Time, Inc., 3 Mar. 1997. Web. 10 Aug.

  2009.

Stallone, Sylvester. "The Masculine Mystique." Interview by

  Susan Faludi. *Esquire* Dec. 1996: 89–96. Print.

Wloszczyna, Susan. "*Donnie Brasco*: A High Point for Lowlifes."

  Rev. of *Donnie Brasco,* dir. Mike Newell, perf. Johnny

  Depp. *USA Today* 28 Feb. 1997: 1D. Print.

Glossary

Abstract/concrete   patterns of language reflect an author's word choice. Abstract words (for example, *wisdom, power,* and *beauty*) refer to general ideas, qualities, or conditions. Concrete words name material objects and items associated with the five senses—words like *rock, pizza,* and *basketball.* Both abstract and concrete language are useful in communicating ideas. Generally, you should not be too abstract in writing. It is best to employ concrete words, naming things that can be seen, touched, smelled, heard, or tasted in order to support generalizations, topic sentences, or more abstract ideas.

Acronym   is a word formed from the first or first few letters of several words, as in OPEC (Organization of Petroleum Exporting Countries).

Action   in narrative writing is the sequence of happenings or events. This movement of events may occupy just a few minutes or extend over a period of years or centuries.

Alliteration   is the repetition of initial consonant sounds in words placed closely next to each other, as in "what a *t*ale of *t*error now their *t*urbulency *t*ells." Prose that is highly rhythmical or "poetic" often makes use of this method.

Allusion   is a literary, biographical, or historical reference, whether real or imaginary. It is a "figure of speech" (a fresh, useful comparison) employed to illuminate an idea. A writer's prose style can be made richer through this economical method of evoking an idea or emotion, as in E. M. Forster's biblical allusion in this sentence: "Property produces men of weight, and it was a man of weight who failed to get into the Kingdom of Heaven."

Analogy   is a form of comparison that uses a clear illustration to explain a difficult idea or function. It is unlike a formal comparison in that its subjects of comparison are from different categories or areas. For example, an analogy likening "division of labor" to the activity of bees in a hive makes the first concept more concrete by showing it to the reader through the figurative comparison with the bees. Analogy in exposition can involve a few sentences, a paragraph or set of paragraphs, or an entire essay. Analogies can also be used in argumentation to heighten an appeal to emotion, but they cannot actually *prove* anything.

Analysis   is a method of exposition in which a subject is broken up into its parts to explain their nature, function, proportion, or relationship. Analysis thus explores connections and processes within the context of a given subject. (See *causal analysis* and *process analysis.*)

Anecdote   is a brief, engaging account of some happening, often historical, biographical, or personal. As a technique in writing, anecdote is especially effective in creating interesting essay introductions and also in illuminating abstract concepts in the body of the essay.

Antecedent   in grammar refers to the word, phrase, or clause to which a pronoun refers. In writing, antecedent also refers to any happening or thing that is prior to another or to anything that logically precedes a subject.

Antithesis   is the balancing of one idea or term against another for emphasis.

Antonym   is a word whose meaning is opposite to that of another word.

Aphorism   is a short, pointed statement expressing a general truism or an idea in an original or imaginative way. Marshall McLuhan's statement that "the medium is the message" is a well-known contemporary aphorism.

Archaic   language is vocabulary or usage that belongs to an earlier period and is old-fashioned today. The word *thee* for *you* is an archaism still in use in certain situations.

Archetypes   are special images or symbols that, according to Carl Jung, appeal to the total racial or cultural understanding of a people. Such images or symbols as the mother archetype, the cowboy in American film, a sacred mountain, or spring as a time of renewal tend to trigger the "collective unconscious" of the human race.

Argumentation   is a formal variety of writing that offers reasons for or against something. Its goal is to persuade or convince the reader through logical reasoning and carefully controlled emotional appeal. Argumentation as a formal mode of writing contains many properties that distinguish it from exposition. (See *assumption, deduction, evidence, induction, logic, persuasion, proposition,* and *refutation.*)

Assonance   is defined generally as likeness or rough similarity of sound. Its specific definition is a partial rhyme in which the stressed vowel sounds are alike but the consonant sounds are unlike, as in *late* and *make.* Although more common to poetry, assonance can also be detected in highly rhythmic prose.

Assumption   in argumentation is anything taken for granted or presumed to be accepted by the audience and therefore unstated. Assumptions in argumentative writing can be dangerous because the audience might not always accept the idea implicit in them. (See *begging the question.*)

Audience   is that readership toward which an author directs his or her essay. In composing essays, writers must acknowledge the nature of their expected readers—whether specialized or general, minimally educated or highly educated, sympathetic or unsympathetic toward the writer's opinions, and so forth. Failure to focus on the writer's true audience can lead to confusion in language and usage, presentation of inappropriate content, and failure to appeal to the expected reader.

Balance   in sentence structure refers to the assignment of equal treatment in the arrangement of coordinate ideas. It is often used to heighten a contrast of ideas.

Begging the question   is an error or a fallacy in reasoning and argumentation in which the writer assumes as a truth something for which evidence or proof is actually needed.

Causal analysis   is a form of writing that examines causes and effects of events or conditions as they relate to a specific subject. Writers can investigate the causes of a particular effect or the effects of a particular cause or combine both methods. Basically, however, causal analysis looks for connections between things and reasons behind them.

Characterization   is the creation of people involved in the action. It is used especially in narrative or descriptive writing. Authors use techniques of dialogue, description, reportage, and observation in attempting to present vivid and distinctive characters.

Chronology or chronological order   is the arrangement of events in the order in which they happened. Chronological order can be used in such diverse narrative situations as history, biography, scientific process, and personal account. Essays that are ordered by chronology move from one step or point to the next in time.

Cinematic technique   in narration, description, and occasionally exposition is the conscious application of film art to the development of the contemporary essay. Modern writers often are aware of such film techniques as montage (the process of cutting and arranging film so that short scenes are presented in rapid succession), zoom (intense enlargement of subject), and various forms of juxtaposition, and use these methods to enhance the quality of their essays.

Classification   is a form of exposition in which the writer divides a subject into categories and then groups elements in each of those categories according to their relationships with one another. Thus a writer using classification takes a topic, divides it into several major groups, and then often subdivides those groups, moving always from larger categories to smaller ones.

Cliché   is an expression that once was fresh and original but that has lost much of its vitality through overuse. Because expressions like "as quick as a wink" and "blew her stack" are trite or common today, they should be avoided in writing.

Climactic ordering   is the arrangement of a paragraph or essay so that the most important items are saved for last. The effect is to build slowly through a sequence of events or ideas to the most critical part of the composition.

Coherence   is a quality in effective writing that results from the careful ordering of each sentence in a paragraph and each paragraph in the essay. If an essay is coherent, each part will grow naturally and logically from those parts that come before it. Following careful chronological, logical, spatial, or sequential order is the most natural way to achieve coherence in writing. The main devices used in achieving coherence are transitions, which help connect one thought with another.

Colloquial language   is conversational language used in certain types of informal and narrative writing but rarely in essays, business writing, or research writing. Expressions like "cool," "pal," or "I can dig it" often have a place in conversational settings. However, they should be used sparingly in essay writing for special effects.

Comparison/contrast   as an essay pattern treats similarities and differences between two subjects. Any useful comparison involves two items from the same class. Moreover, there must be a clear reason for the comparison or contrast. Finally, there must be a balanced treatment of the various comparative or contrasting points between the two subjects.

Conclusions   are the endings of essays. Without a conclusion, an essay would be incomplete, leaving the reader with the feeling that something important has been left out. There are numerous strategies for conclusions available to writers: summarizing main points in the essay, restating the main idea, using an effective quotation, offering the reader the climax to a series of events, returning to the beginning and echoing it, offering a solution to a problem, emphasizing the topic's significance, or setting a new frame of reference by generalizing from the main thesis. A conclusion should end the essay in a clear, convincing, emphatic way.

Concrete   (See *abstract/concrete.*)

Conflict   in narrative writing is the clash or opposition of events, characters, or ideas that makes the resolution of action necessary.

Connotation/denotation   are terms specifying the way a word has meaning. Connotation refers to the "shades of meaning" that a word might have because of various emotional associations it calls up for writers and readers alike. Words like *patriotism, pig,* and *rose* have strong connotative overtones to them. Denotation refers to the "dictionary" definition of a word—its exact meaning. Good writers understand the connotative and denotative value of words and control the shades of meaning that many words possess.

Context   is the situation surrounding a word, group of words, or sentence. Often the elements coming before or after a certain confusing or difficult construction will provide insight into the meaning or importance of that item.

Coordination   in sentence structure refers to the grammatical arrangement of parts of the same order or equality in rank.

Declarative sentences   make a statement or assertion.

Deduction   is a form of logic that begins with a generally stated truth or principle and then offers details, examples, and reasoning to support the generalization. In other words, deduction is based on reasoning from a known principle to an unknown principle, from the general to the specific, or from a premise to a logical conclusion. (See *syllogism.*)

Definition   in exposition is the extension of a word's meaning through a paragraph or an entire essay. As an extended method of explaining a word, this type of definition relies on other rhetorical methods, including detail, illustration, comparison and contrast, and anecdote.

Denotation   (See *connotation/denotation.*)

Description   in the prose essay is a variety of writing that uses details of sight, sound, color, smell, taste, and touch to create a word picture and to explain or illustrate an idea.

Development   refers to the way a paragraph or an essay elaborates or builds upon a topic or theme. Typical development proceeds either from general illustrations to specific ones or from one generalization to another. (See *horizontal/vertical.*)

Dialogue   is the reproduction of speech or conversation between two or more persons in writing. Dialogue can add concreteness and vividness to an essay and can also help reveal character. A writer who reproduces dialogue in an essay must use it for a purpose and not simply as a decorative device.

Diction   is the manner of expression in words, choice of words, or wording. Writers must choose vocabulary carefully and precisely to communicate a message and also to address an intended audience effectively; this is good diction.

Digression   is a temporary departure from the main subject in writing. Any digression in the essay must serve a purpose or be intended for a specific effect.

Discourse (forms of)   relates conventionally to the main categories of writing—narration, description, exposition, and argumentation. In practice, these forms of discourse often blend or overlap. Essayists seek the ideal fusion of forms of discourse in the treatment of their subject.

Division   is that aspect of classification in which the writer divides some large subject into categories. Division helps writers split large and potentially complicated subjects into parts for orderly presentation and discussion.

Dominant impression   in description is the main impression or effect that writers attempt to create for their subject. It arises from an author's focus on a single subject and from the feelings the writer brings to that subject.

Editorializing   is to express personal opinions about the subject of the essay. An editorial tone can have a useful effect in writing, but at other times an author might want to reduce editorializing in favor of a better balanced or more objective tone.

Effect   is a term used in causal analysis to describe the outcome or expected result of a chain of happenings.

Emphasis   indicates the placement of the most important ideas in key positions in the essay. As a major principle, emphasis relates to phrases, sentences, and paragraphs— the construction of the entire essay. Emphasis can be achieved by repetition, subordination, careful positioning of thesis and topic sentences, climactic ordering, comparison and contrast, and a variety of other methods.

Episodic   relates to that variety of narrative writing that develops through a series of incidents or events.

Essay   is the name given to a short prose work on a limited topic. Essays take many forms, ranging from personal narratives to critical or argumentative treatments of a subject. Normally, an essay will convey the writer's personal ideas about the subject.

Etymology   is the origin and development of a word—tracing a word back as far as possible.

Evidence   is material offered to support an argument or a proposition. Typical forms of evidence are facts, details, and expert testimony.

Example   is a method of exposition in which the writer offers illustrations in order to explain a generalization or a whole thesis. (See *illustration*.)

Exclamatory sentences   in writing express surprise or strong emotion.

Expert testimony   as employed in argumentative essays and in expository essays is the use of statements by authorities to support a writer's position or idea. This method often requires careful quotation and acknowledgment of sources.

Exposition   is a major form of discourse that informs or explains. Exposition is the form of expression required in much college writing, for it provides facts and information, clarifies ideas, and establishes meaning. The primary methods of exposition are *illustration, comparison and contrast, analogy, definition, classification, causal analysis,* and *process analysis* (see entries).

Extended metaphor   is a figurative comparison that is used to structure a significant part of the composition or the whole essay. (See *figurative language* and *metaphor*.)

Fable   is a form of narrative containing a moral that normally appears clearly at the end.

Fallacy   in argumentation is an error in logic or in the reasoning process. Fallacies occur because of vague development of ideas, lack of awareness on the part of writers of the requirements of logical reasoning, or faulty assumptions about the proposition.

Figurative language   as opposed to literal language is a special approach to writing that departs from what is typically a concrete, straightforward style. It is the use of vivid, imaginative statements to illuminate or illustrate an idea. Figurative language adds freshness, meaning, and originality to a writer's style. Major figures of speech include *allusion, hyperbole, metaphor, personification,* and *simile* (see entries).

Flashback   is a narrative technique in which the writer begins at some point in the action and then moves into the past in order to provide crucial information about characters and events.

Foreshadow   is a technique that indicates beforehand what is to occur at a later point in the essay.

Frame   in narration and description is the use of a key object or pattern—typically at the start and end of the essay—that serves as a border or structure for the substance of the composition.

General/specific words   are the basis of writing, although it is wise in college composition to keep vocabulary as specific as possible. General words refer to broad categories and groups, whereas specific words capture with force and clarity the nature of the term. General words refer to large classes, concepts, groups, and emotions; specific words are more particular in providing meanings. The distinction between general and specific language is always a matter of degree.

Generalization   is a broad idea or statement. All generalizations require particulars and illustrations to support them.

Genre   is a type or form of literature—for example, short fiction, novel, poetry, or drama.

Grammatical structure   is a systematic description of language as it relates to the grammatical nature of a sentence.

Horizontal/vertical   paragraph and essay development refers to the basic way a writer moves either from one generalization to another in a carefully related series of generalizations (horizontal) or from a generalization to a series of specific supporting examples (vertical).

Hortatory style   is a variety of writing designed to encourage, give advice, or urge to good deeds.

Hyperbole   is a form of figurative language that uses exaggeration to overstate a position.

Hypothesis   is an unproven theory or proposition that is tentatively accepted to explain certain facts. A working hypothesis provides the basis for further investigation or argumentation.

Hypothetical examples   are illustrations in the form of assumptions that are based on the hypothesis. As such, they are conditional rather than absolute or certain facts.

Identification   as a method of exposition refers to focusing on the main subject of the essay. It involves the clear location of the subject within the context or situation of the composition.

Idiomatic language   is the language or dialect of a people, region, or class—the individual nature of a language.

Ignoring the question   in argumentation is a fallacy that involves the avoidance of the main issue by developing an entirely different one.

Illustration   is the use of one or more examples to support an idea. Illustration permits the writer to support a generalization through particulars or specifics.

Imagery   is clear, vivid description that appeals to the sense of sight, smell, touch, sound, or taste. Much imagery exists for its own sake, adding descriptive flavor to an essay. However, imagery (especially when it involves a larger pattern) can also add meaning to an essay.

Induction   is a method of logic consisting of the presentation of a series of facts, pieces of information, or instances in order to formulate or build a likely generalization. The key is to provide prior examples before reaching a logical conclusion. Consequently, as a pattern of organization in essay writing, the inductive method requires the careful presentation of relevant data and information before the conclusion is reached at the end of the paper.

Inference   involves arriving at a decision or opinion by reasoning from known facts or evidence.

Interrogative sentences   are sentences that ask or pose a question.

Introduction   is the beginning or opening of an essay. The introduction should alert the reader to the subject by identifying it, set the limits of the essay, and indicate what the thesis (or main idea) will be. Moreover, it should arouse the reader's interest in the subject. Among the devices available in the creation of good introductions are making a simple statement of thesis; giving a clear, vivid description of an important setting; posing a question or series of questions; referring to a relevant historical event; telling an anecdote; using comparison and contrast to frame the subject; using several examples to reinforce the statement of the subject; and presenting a personal attitude about a controversial issue.

Irony   is the use of language to suggest the opposite of what is stated. Writers use irony to reveal unpleasant or troublesome realities that exist in life or to poke fun at human weaknesses and foolish attitudes. In an essay there may be verbal irony, in which the result of a sequence of ideas or events is the opposite of what normally would be expected. A key to the identification of irony in an essay is our ability to detect where the author is stating the opposite of what he or she actually believes.

Issue   is the main question upon which an entire argument rests. It is the idea that the writer attempts to prove.

Jargon   is special words associated with a specific area of knowledge or a particular profession. Writers who employ jargon either assume that readers know specialized terms or take care to define terms for the benefit of the audience.

Juxtaposition   as a technique in writing or essay organization is the placing of elements—either similar or contrasting—close together, positioning them side by side in order to illuminate the subject.

Levels of language   refer to the kinds of language used in speaking and writing. Basically, there are three main levels of language—formal, informal, and colloquial. Formal English, used in writing or speech, is the type of English employed to address special groups and professional people. Informal English is the sort of writing found in newspapers, magazines, books, and essays. It is popular English for an educated audience but still more formal than colloquial (conversational) English. Colloquial English is spoken (and occasionally written) English used in conversations with friends, employees, and peer group members; it is characterized by the use of slang, idioms, ordinary language, and loose sentence structure.

Linear order in paragraph development means the clear line of movement from one point to another.

Listing is a simple technique of illustration in which facts or examples are used to support a topic or generalization.

Logic as applied to essay writing is correct reasoning based on induction or deduction. The logical basis of an essay must offer reasonable criteria or principles of thought, present these principles in an orderly manner, avoid faults in reasoning, and result in a complete and satisfactory outcome in the reasoning process.

Metaphor is a type of figurative language in which an item from one category is compared briefly and imaginatively with an item from another category. Writers use such implied comparisons to assign meaning in a fresh, vivid, and concrete way.

Metonymy is a figure of language in which a thing is not designated by its own name but by another associated with or suggested by it, as in "The Supreme Court has decided" (meaning the judges of the Supreme Court have decided).

Mood is the creation of atmosphere in descriptive writing.

Motif in an essay is any series of components that can be detected as a pattern. For example, a particular detail, idea, or image can be elaborated upon or designed to form a pattern or motif in the essay.

Myth in literature is a traditional story or series of events explaining some basic phenomenon of nature; the origin of humanity; or the customs, institutions, and religious rites of a people. Myth often relates to the exploits of gods, goddesses, and heroes.

Narration as a form of essay writing is the presentation of a story in order to illustrate an idea.

Non sequitur in argumentation is a conclusion or inference that does not follow from the premises or evidence on which it is based. The non sequitur thus is a type of logical fallacy.

Objective/subjective writing refers to the attitude that writers take toward their subject. When writers are objective, they try not to report their personal feelings about the subject; they attempt to be detached, impersonal, and unbiased. Conversely, subjective writing reveals an author's personal attitudes and emotions. For many varieties of college writing, such as business or laboratory reports, term papers, and literary analyses, it is best to be as objective as possible. But for many personal essays in composition courses, the subjective touch is fine. In the hands of skilled writers, the objective and subjective tones often blend.

Onomatopoeia is the formation of a word by imitating the natural sound associated with the object or action, as in *buzz* or *click*.

Order is the arrangement of information or materials in an essay. The most common ordering techniques are *chronological order* (time in sequence), *spatial order* (the arrangement of descriptive details), *process order* (a step-by-step approach to an activity), *deductive order* (a thesis followed by information to support it), and *inductive order* (evidence and examples first, followed by the thesis in the form of a conclusion). Some rhetorical patterns, such as comparison and contrast, classification, and argumentation, require other ordering methods. Writers should select those ordering principles that permit them to present materials clearly.

Overstatement is an extravagant or exaggerated claim or statement.

Paradox is a statement that seems to be contradictory but actually contains an element of truth.

Paragraph is a unit in an essay that serves to present and examine one aspect of a topic. Composed normally of a group of sentences (one-sentence paragraphs can be used for emphasis or special effect), the paragraph elaborates an idea within the larger framework of the essay and the thesis unifying it.

Parallelism is a variety of sentence structure in which there is balance or coordination in the presentation of elements. "I came, I saw, I conquered" is a standard example of parallelism, presenting both pronouns and verbs in a coordinated manner. Parallelism can appear in a sentence, a group of sentences, or an entire paragraph.

Paraphrase as a literary method is the process of rewording the thought or meaning expressed in something that has been said or written before.

Parenthetical refers to giving qualifying information or explanation. This information normally is marked off or placed within parentheses.

Parody is ridiculing the language or style of another writer or composer. In parody, a serious subject tends to be treated in a nonsensical manner.

Periphrasis is the use of many words where one or a few would do; it is a roundabout way of speaking or writing.

Persona is the role or characterization that writers occasionally create for themselves in a personal narrative.

Personification is giving an object, a thing, or an idea lifelike or human characteristics, as in the common reference to a car as "she." Like all forms of figurative language, personification adds freshness to description and makes ideas vivid by setting up striking comparisons.

Persuasion is the form of discourse, related to argumentation, that attempts to move a person to action or to influence an audience toward a particular belief.

Point of view is the angle from which a writer tells a story. Many personal and informal essays take the *first-person* (or "I") point of view, which is natural and fitting for essays in which the author wants to speak in a familiar way to the reader. On the other hand, the *third-person* point of view ("he," "she," "it," "they") distances the reader somewhat from the writer. The third-person point of view is useful in essays in which the writers are not talking exclusively about themselves, but about other people, ideas, and events.

Post hoc, ergo propter hoc in logic is the fallacy of thinking that a happening that follows another must be its result. It arises from a confusion about the logical causal relationship.

Process analysis is a pattern of writing that explains in a step-by-step way how something is done, how it is put together, how it works, or how it occurs. The subject can be a mechanical device, a product, an idea, a natural phenomenon, or a historical sequence. However, in all varieties of process analysis, the writer traces all important steps, from beginning to end.

Progression is the forward movement or succession of acts, events, or ideas presented in an essay.

Proportion refers to the relative emphasis and length given to an event, an idea, a time, or a topic within the whole essay. Basically, in terms of proportion, the writer gives more emphasis to a major element than to a minor one.

Proposition   is the main point of an argumentative essay—the statement to be defended, proved, or upheld. It is like a *thesis* (see entry) except that it presents an idea that is debatable or can be disputed. The *major proposition* is the main argumentative point; *minor propositions* are the reasons given to support or prove the issue.

Purpose   is what the writer wants to accomplish in an essay. Writers having a clear purpose will know the proper style, language, tone, and materials to utilize in designing an effective essay.

Refutation   in argumentation is a method by which writers recognize and deal effectively with the arguments of their opponents. Their own argument will be stronger if they refute—prove false or wrong—all opposing arguments.

Repetition   is a simple method of achieving emphasis by repeating a word, a phrase, or an idea.

Rhetoric   is the art of using words effectively in speaking or writing. It is also the art of literary composition, particularly in prose, including both figures of speech and such strategies as *comparison and contrast, definition,* and *analysis.*

Rhetorical question   is a question asked only to emphasize a point, introduce a topic, or provoke thought, but not to elicit an answer.

Rhythm   in prose writing is a regular recurrence of elements or features in sentences, creating a patterned emphasis, balance, or contrast.

Sarcasm   is a sneering or taunting attitude in writing, designed to hurt by evaluating or criticizing. Basically, sarcasm is a heavy-handed form of *irony* (see entry). Writers should try to avoid sarcastic writing and to use more acceptable varieties of irony and satire to criticize their subject.

Satire   is the humorous or critical treatment of a subject in order to expose the subject's vices, follics, stupidities, and so forth. The intention of such satire is to reform by exposing the subject to comedy or ridicule.

Sensory language   is language that appeals to any of the five senses—sight, sound, touch, taste, or smell.

Sentimentality   in prose writing is the excessive display of emotion, whether intended or unintended. Because sentimentality can distort the true nature of a situation or an idea, writers should use it cautiously, or not at all.

Series   as a technique in prose is the presentation of several items, often concrete details or similar parts of grammar such as verbs or adjectives, in rapid sequence.

Setting   in narrative and descriptive writing is the time, place, environment, background, or surroundings established by an author.

Simile   is a figurative comparison using *like* or *as.*

Slang   is a kind of language that uses racy or colorful expressions associated more often with speech than with writing. It is colloquial English and should be used in essay writing only to reproduce dialogue or to create a special effect.

Spatial order   in descriptive writing is the careful arrangement of details or materials in space—for example, from left to right, top to bottom, or near to far.

Specific words   (See *general/specific words.*)

Statistics are facts or data of a numerical kind, assembled and tabulated to present significant information about a given subject. As a technique of illustration, statistics can be useful in analysis and argumentation.

Style is the specific or characteristic manner of expression, execution, construction, or design of an author. As a manner or mode of expression in language, it is the unique way each writer handles ideas. There are numerous stylistic categories—such as literary, formal, argumentative, and satiric—but ultimately, no two writers have the same style.

Subjective (See *objective/subjective.*)

Subordination in sentence structure is the placing of a relatively less important idea in an inferior grammatical position to the main idea. It is the designation of a minor clause that is dependent upon a major clause.

Syllogism is an argument or form of reasoning in which two statements or premises are made and a logical conclusion is drawn from them. As such, it is a form of deductive logic—reasoning from the general to the particular. The *major premise* presents a quality of class ("All writers are mortal"). The *minor premise* states that a particular subject is a member of that class ("Ernest Hemingway was a writer"). The conclusion states that the qualities of the class and the member of the class are the same ("Hemingway was mortal").

Symbol is something—normally a concrete image—that exists in itself but also stands for something else or has greater meaning. As a variety of figurative language, the symbol can be a strong feature in an essay, operating to add depth of meaning and even to unify the composition.

Synonym is a word that means roughly the same as another word. In practice, few words are exactly alike in meaning. Careful writers use synonyms to vary word choice without ever moving too far from the shade of meaning intended.

Theme is the central idea in an essay; it is also termed the *thesis*. Everything in an essay should support the theme in one way or another.

Thesis is the main idea in an essay. The *thesis sentence,* appearing early in the essay (normally somewhere in the first paragraph) serves to convey the main idea to the reader in a clear and emphatic manner.

Tone is the writer's attitude toward his or her subject or material. An essay writer's tone may be objective, subjective, comic, ironic, nostalgic, critical, or a reflection of numerous other attitudes. Tone is the voice that writers give to an essay.

Topic sentence is the main idea that a paragraph develops. Not all paragraphs contain topic sentences; often the topic is implied.

Transition is the linking of ideas in sentences, paragraphs, and larger segments of an essay in order to achieve *coherence* (see entry). Among the most common techniques to achieve smooth transitions are (1) repeating a key word or phrase, (2) using a pronoun to refer to a key word or phrase, (3) relying on traditional connectives such as *thus, however, moreover, for example, therefore, finally,* or *in conclusion,* (4) using parallel structure (see *parallelism*), and (5) creating a sentence or paragraph that serves as a bridge from one part of an essay to another. Transition is best achieved when a writer presents ideas and details carefully and in logical order.

Understatement   is a method of making a weaker statement than is warranted by truth, accuracy, or importance.

Unity   is a feature in an essay whereby all material relates to a central concept and contributes to the meaning of the whole. To achieve a unified effect in an essay, the writer must design an effective introduction and conclusion, maintain consistent tone or point of view, develop middle paragraphs in a coherent manner, and above all stick to the subject, never permitting unimportant or irrelevant elements to enter.

Usage   is the way in which a word, phrase, or sentence is used to express a particular idea; it is the customary manner of using a given language in speaking or writing.

Vertical   (See *horizontal/vertical.*)

Voice   is the way you express your ideas to the reader, the tone you take in addressing your audience. Voice reflects your attitude toward both your subject and your readers. (See *tone.*)

Credits

Color Insert Photos

Page 1: © Mark J. Terrill/AP Photo; **p. 2:** Courtesy of The Advertising Archives; **p. 3 (bottom):** © AMC/Photofest; **p. 3 (top):** Courtesy of Photofest; **p. 4:** © AP Photo; **p. 5 (bottom):** © Tim Graham/Getty Images; **p. 5 (top):** © Kaveh Kazemi/Getty Images; **p. 8:** © Inwin Thompson/The Dallas Morning News/AP Photo.

Text and Illustrations

Ackerman, Diane. "Planets in the Sky with Diamonds." From *New York Times*, October 2, 2011. Copyright © 2011 The New York Times. All rights reserved. Used by permission and protected by the Copyright Laws of the United States. The printing, copying, redistribution, or retransmission of the Material without express written permission is prohibited.

Adler, Mortimer J. "How To Mark a Book." From *The Saturday Review of Literature*, July 6, 1941. Reprinted by permission of the author.

Alexie, Sherman. "Superman and Me." From *Los Angeles Times*, April 19, 1998. Copyright © 1998 by Sherman Alexie. All rights reserved. Reprinted by permission.

Armstrong, Karen. "What's God Got to Do with It?" From *The New Statesman*, April 10, 2006. Copyright © 2006. All rights reserved. Reprinted by permission of The New Statesman.

Baldwin, James. "Stranger in the Village." From *Notes of a Native Son*. Copyright © 1955, renewed 1983, by James Baldwin. Reprinted by permission of Beacon Press, Boston.

Barry, Dave. "Red, White, and Beer." From *Dave Barry's Greatest Hits* by Dave Barry. Copyright © 1988 by Dave Barry. Reprinted by permission of the author.

Bass, Rick. "Why I Hunt." First appeared in *Sierra*, July 2001. Copyright © 2001 by Rick Bass. Reprinted by permission of the author.

Bazelon, Emily. "The Next Kind of Integration." From *New York Times Magazine*, July 20, 2008. Copyright © 2008 The New York Times. All rights reserved. Used by permission and protected by the Copyright Laws of the United States. The printing, copying, redistribution, or retransmission of the Material without express written permission is prohibited.

Berger, John. "Hiroshima." From *The Sense of Sight*. Copyright © 1985 by John Berger. Reprinted by permission of Pantheon Books, a division of Random House, Inc. and the author. Any third party use of this material, outside of this publication, is prohibited. Interested parties must apply directly to Random House, Inc. for permission.

Bloom, Paul. "The Pleasures of Imagination." From *The Chronicle Review*, May 30, 2010. Copyright © 2010 by Paul Bloom. Reprinted by permission of the author.

Bordo, Susan. "The Globalization of Eating Disorders." Copyright © Susan Bordo, Otis A. Singletary Professor of the Humanities, University of Kentucky. Reprinted by permission of the author.

Carr, Nicholas. "Does the Internet Make You Smarter or Dumber?" From *Wall Street Journal,* June 5, 2010. Copyright © 2010 Dow Jones & Company, Inc, all rights reserved worldwide. Reprinted by permission of Wall Street Journal.

Carson, Clayborne. "Two Cheers for *Brown v. Board of Education*." From *Journal of American History*, June 2004: pp. 26–31. Copyright © Organization of American Historians. Reprinted by permission.

Carson, Rachel. "The Obligation to Endure." From *Silent Spring*. Copyright © 1962 by Rachel L. Carson, renewed 1990 by Roger Christie. Reprinted by permission of Houghton Mifflin Harcourt Publishing Company, Pollinger, Limited and the Estate of

Catton, Bruce. "Grant and Lee: A Study in Contrasts." From *The American Story*, edited by Earl Schenck Miers. Reprinted by permission of William Catton.
Chua, Amy. "The Right Road to America?" From *The Washington Post*, December 16, 2007. Copyright © 2007. Reprinted by permission of the author.
Clarke, Kevin. "Tweet Like an Egyptian." From *U.S. Catholic,* April 2011. Copyright © 2011 U.S. Catholic. Reproduced by permission of U.S. Catholic. For subscription information contact: 205 West Monroe, Chicago, IL 60606; call 1-800-328-6515; or visit http://www.uscatholic.org/.
Coles, Robert. "I Listen to My Parents and I Wonder What They Believe." Originally published in *Redbook* Magazine, February 1980. Reprinted by permission of the author.
Danticat, Edwidge. "Turning the Page on Disaster." From *Good Housekeeping*, January 2011, Vol. 52, Issue No. 1. Copyright © 2011. Reprinted by permission of the Hearst Corporation.
Diamond, Jared. "The Last Americans: Environmental Collapse and the End of Civilization." Copyright © 2003 by Harper's Magazine. All rights reserved. Reproduced from the June issue by special permission. Illustrations by Stan Fellows. Copyright © Stan Fellows. Reprinted by permission of the illustrator, c/o Joanie Bernstein, art rep.
Diaz, Junot. "The Money: Starting Out." From *The New Yorker*, June 13–20, 2011. Copyright © 2011. Reprinted by permission of Condé Nast Publications, Inc.
Didion, Joan. "In Sable and Dark Glasses." From *Vogue*, October 2011. Copyright © 2011. Reprinted by permission of Janklow & Nesbit Associates for the author.
Dillard, Annie. "An American Childhood." Excerpt from AN AMERICAN CHILDHOOD by ANNIE DILLARD, pp. 11–17. Copyright © 1987 by Annie Dillard. Reprinted by permission of HarperCollins Publishers and Lippincott Massie McQuilkin.
D'Souza, Dinesh. "Staying Human." From *National Review*, January 22, 2001. Reprinted by permission of the author.
Dyson, Esther. "Cyberspace: If You Don't Love It, Leave It." From *The New York Times*, July 16, 1995. Copyright © 1995 by Esther Dyson. Reprinted by permission.
Ehrenreich, Barbara. Excerpt from "Scrubbing in Maine." From *Nickel and Dimed: On (Not) Getting By in America* by Barbara Ehrenreich. Copyright © 2001 by Barbara Ehrenreich. Reprinted by arrangement with Henry Holt and Company, LLC.
Elbow, Peter. "Freewriting." From *Writing Without Teachers*, 2 ed., pp. 3–7. Copyright © 1973, 1998 by Oxford University Press, Inc. Reprinted by permission of Oxford University Press.
Ferguson, Niall. "America's Oh Sh*t Moment." From *Newsweek*, November 14, 2011. Copyright © 2011 by Niall Ferguson. Reprinted by permission of The Wylie Agency LLC.
Freeland, Chrystia. "The Rich are Different from You and Me." From *Atlantic Monthly*, July/August 2011. Copyright © 2011. All rights reserved. Reprinted by permission of *The Atlantic.*
Friedman, Thomas L. Excerpt from "Globalization the Super-Story." From LONGITUDES AND ATTITUDES by Thomas L. Friedman. Copyright © 2002 by Thomas L. Friedman. Reprinted by permission of Farrar, Straus and Giroux, LLC and International Creative Management, Inc.
Gates, David. "Finding Neverland." From *Newsweek*, July 13, 2009. Copyright © 2009 by David Gates. Reprinted by permission of the author.
Gates, Jr., Henry Louis. "Delusions of Grandeur." Originally published in *Sports Illustrated*, August 19, 1991. Copyright © 1991 by Henry Louis Gates Jr. Reprinted by permission of the author.

Tan, Amy. "Mother Tongue." Copyright © 1990 by Amy Tan. First appeared in *The Threepenny Review*. Reprinted by permission of the author and the Sandra Dijkstra Literary Agency.

Tannen, Deborah. "Sex, Lies and Conversation: Why Is It So Hard for Men and Women to Talk to Each Other?" From *The Washington Post,* June 24, 1990. Copyright © by Deborah Tannen. Permission granted by International Creative Management, Inc.

Thompson, Clive. "I'm So Totally, Digitally, Close to You." First published in *New York Times Magazine*, September 7, 2008. Copyright © 2008. Reprinted by permission of Featurewell.com and the author.

Tuchman, Barbara. "'This Is the End of the World': The Black Death." From *A Distant Mirror* by Barbara W. Tuchman. Text copyright © 1978 by Barbara W. Tuchman. Reprinted by permission of Alfred A. Knopf, a division of Random House, Inc. Any third party use of this material, outside of this publication, is prohibited. Interested parties must apply directly to Random House, Inc. for permission.

Turkle, Sherry. "How Computers Change the Way We Think." Originally appeared in *Chronicle of Higher Education*, January 30, 2004. Copyright © 2004 by Sherry Turkle. Reprinted by permission of the author.

Updike, John. "Moving Along." From JUST LOOKING by John Updike. Copyright © 1989 by John Updike. Reprinted by permission of Alfred A. Knopf, a division of Random House, Inc. and Penguin UK. Any third party use of this material, outside of this publication, is prohibited. Interested parties must apply directly to Random House, Inc. for permission.

Walker, Alice. "Saving the Life That Is Your Own: The Importance of Models in the Artist's Life." From *In Search of Our Mothers' Gardens: Womanist Prose*. Copyright 1976 by Alice Walker. Reprinted by permission of Houghton Mifflin Harcourt Publishing, the David Higham Agency, and The Wendy Weil Agency. All right reserved.

Warshow, Robert. "The Gangster as Tragic Hero." From *The Immediate Experience* by Robert Warshow. Copyright © 1962 by Robert Warshow. Reprinted by permission of the Estate of Robert Warshow.

Welty, Eudora. "One Writer's Beginnings" from ONE WRITER'S BEGINNINGS by Eudora Welty, pp. 5–12, Cambridge, Mass.: Harvard University Press. Copyright © 1983, 1984 by Eudora Welty. Reprinted by permission Harvard University Press and Russell & Volkening, as agents for the author's estate.

"Western Civilization's Killer Apps." From *Newsweek*, November 14, 2011. Reprinted by permission.

White, E.B. "Once More to the Lake." From *One Man's Meat*, by E.B. White. Text copyright © 1941 by E.B. White. Copyright renewed. Reprinted by permission of Tilbury House, Publishers, Gardiner, Maine and International Creative Management, Inc.

Woolf, Virginia. "Profession for Women." From *The Death of the Moth and Other Essays* by Virginia Woolf. Copyright 1942 by Houghton Mifflin Harcourt Publishing Company and renewed 1970 by Marjorie T. Parsons, Executrix.

Index